UNDERSTANDING COMPUTERS TODAY & TOMORROW

98 edition

CHARLES S. PARKER

THE DRYDEN PRESS
HARCOURT BRACE COLLEGE PUBLISHERS

FORT WORTH PHILADELPHIA SAN DIEGO NEW YORK AUSTIN ORLANDO SAN ANTONIO
TORONTO MONTREAL LONDON SYDNEY TOKYO

UNDERSTANDING
COMPUTERS
TODAY & TOMORROW
98
edition
CREATE
explore

Publisher	George Provol
Acquisitions Editor	Wesley Lawton
Product Manager	Federico Arrieta
Developmental Editor	Elizabeth Hayes
Project Editor	Kathryn Stewart
Production Manager	Carlyn Hauser
Art Director	Linda Wooton
Electronic Publishing Coordinators	Ellie Moore/Cathy Spitzenberger
Cover Image	Lamberto Alvarez

ISBN: 0-03-024481-1

Library of Congress Catalog Card Number: 97-69297

Portions of this work were published in previous editions.

Address for Orders
The Dryden Press, 6277 Sea Harbor Drive, Orlando, FL 32887
1-800-782-4479

Address for Editorial Correspondence
The Dryden Press, 301 Commerce Street, Suite 3700, Fort Worth, TX 76102

Web-site address
http://www.hbcollege.com

Printed in the United States of America

7 8 9 0 1 2 3 4 5 6 059 9 8 7 6 5 4 3 2 1

The Dryden Press
Harcourt Brace College Publishers

TO CHAMA

The Dryden Press Series in Information Systems

Fenrich
Practical Guidelines for Creating Instructional Multimedia Applications

Forcht
Management Information Systems: A Casebook

Gordon and Gordon
Information Systems: A Management Approach

Gray, King, McLean, and Watson
Management of Information Systems
Second Edition

Harrington
Database Management for Microcomputers: Design and Implementation
Second Edition

Harris
Systems Analysis and Design: A Project Approach
Second Edition

Head
An Introduction to Programming with QuickBASIC

Larsen
Using Microsoft Works 4.0 for Windows 95: An Introduction to Computing

Laudon and Laudon
Information Systems and the Internet: A Problem-Solving Approach
Fourth Edition

Laudon and Laudon
Information Systems: A Problem-Solving Approach
(A CD-ROM interactive version)

Lawlor
Computer Information Systems
Third Edition

Licker
Management Information Systems: A Strategic Leadership Approach

Lorents and Morgan
Database Systems: Concepts, Management, Applications

Martin
Discovering Microsoft Office 97

Martin/Parker
PC Concepts

Mason
Using Microsoft Access 97 in Business

Mason
Using Microsoft Excel 97 in Business

McKeown
Living with Computers
Fifth Edition

McKeown
Working with Computers
Second Edition

McKeown
Working with Computers with Software Tutorials
Second Edition

McLeod
Systems Analysis and Design: An Organizational Approach

Millspaugh
Business Programming in C for DOS-Based Systems

Morley
Getting Started with Computers

Parker
Understanding Computers: Today and Tomorrow
98 Edition

Parker
Understanding Networking and the Internet

Spear
Introduction to Computer Programming in Visual Basic 4.0

Spear
Visual Basic 3.0: A Brief Introduction
Visual Basic 4.0: A Brief Introduction

Sullivan
The New Computer User
Second Edition

Thommes and Carey
Introduction to CASE Using Visible Analyst Workbench v4.3 for DOS
CASE Tools: Using Visible Analyst Workbench for Windows

Martin and Parker
Mastering Today's Software Series

Texts available in any combination of the following:
Disk Operating System 5.0 (DOS 5.0)
Disk Operating System 6.0 (DOS 6.0)
Windows 3.1
Windows 95
Microsoft Office 97
Microsoft Office for Windows 95 Professional Edition
WordPerfect 5.1
WordPerfect 5.2 for Windows
WordPerfect 6.0 for DOS
WordPerfect 6.0 for Windows
WordPerfect 6.1 for Windows
Corel WordPerfect 7.0 for Windows 95
Word 6.0 for Windows
Word 7.0 for Windows 95
Word 97
Lotus 1-2-3 (2.2/2.3)
Lotus 1-2-3 (2.4)
Lotus 1-2-3 for Windows (4.01)
Lotus 1-2-3 for Windows (5.0)
Lotus 1-2-3 97
Excel 5.0 for Windows
Excel 7.0 for Windows 95
Excel 97
Quattro Pro 4.0
Quattro Pro 6.0 for Windows
dBASE III PLUS
dBASE IV (1.5/2.0)
dBASE 5 for Windows
Paradox 4.0
Paradox 5.0 for Windows
Access 2.0 for Windows
Access 7.0 for Windows 95
Access 97
PowerPoint 7.0 for Windows 95
PowerPoint 97
A Beginner's Guide to BASIC
A Beginner's Guide to QBASIC
Netscape Communicator

The Harcourt Brace College Outline Series

Kreitzberg
Introduction to BASIC

Kreitzberg
Introduction to Fortran

Pierson
Introduction to Business Information Systems

Veklerov and Pekelny
Computer Language C

Preface

We are living at a time when the key to success in virtually every profession depends on the skillful use of information. Whether one is a teacher, lawyer, doctor, politician, manager, or corporate president, the main ingredient in the work involved is information—knowing how to get it, how to use it, how to manage it, and how to disseminate it to others.

At the root of information-based work activities are computers and the systems that support them. There are millions of computer systems in the world today, and collectively, they are capable of doing thousands of different tasks. Some of the tasks that computer systems can now handle, such as creating virtual worlds and beating a reigning world chess champion at his own game, were thought impossible not too long ago. Few professions remain untouched by computers today or will remain so in tomorrow's world. No matter who you are or what you do for a living, it is highly likely that computers somehow impact both the way you work and your success at your work.

The importance of computers in virtually every profession brings us to the purpose of this book. *Understanding Computers: Today and Tomorrow,* 98 Edition, has been written with the user of computers in mind. This nontechnical, introductory text explains in straightforward terms the importance of learning about computers, types of computer systems and their components, principles by which computer systems work, practical applications of computers and related technologies, and ways in which the world is being changed by computers. The goal of the text is to provide students both with a solid knowledge of computer basics and with a framework for using this knowledge effectively in the workplace.

As the newest addition to Dryden's EXACT custom publishing program, *Understanding Computers: Today and Tomorrow,* 98 Edition, is available in a customized format that includes a choice of multichapter modules from the text as well as software applications and programming manuals. This textbook is but one component of a complete and flexible instructional package—one that can easily be adapted to virtually any teaching format. Supplementing the textbook is a comprehensive set of student and teacher support materials.

The Textbook

Understanding Computers: Today and Tomorrow, 98 Edition, is designed for students taking a first course in computers. The text meets the requirements proposed for the first course in computing by both the Data Processing Management Association (DPMA) and the Association for Computing Machinery (ACM). It provides a comprehensive introduction to the world of computers, with coverage given to both commercial and personal applications of computers and both large and small computer systems.

KEY FEATURES

Like previous editions, *Understanding Computers: Today and Tomorrow,* 98 Edition, offers a flexible teaching organization and a readable and engaging presentation. Learning tools in each chapter help students master important concepts. Sidebars on a variety of topics provide insight on current issues of interest. The thematic "Windows," each of which highlights a major aspect of information technology, bring the world of computers to life. A bottom-of-page running glossary and a glossary at the end of the book give concise definitions of important terms.

Flexible Organization In order to make the 98 edition as flexible as possible to meet a wide variety of classroom needs, the book is available in customized versions as well as the full 16-chapter text. As shown in the figure on page ix, the 16 chapters are grouped into the following seven modules:

Introduction (Chapter INT 1)
Hardware (Chapters HW 1, HW 2, and HW 3)
Software (Chapters SW 1 and SW 2)
Computer Networks (Chapters NET 1, NET 2, and NET 3)
Productivity Software (Chapters PS 1, PS 2, and PS 3)
Information Systems (Chapters IS 1 and IS 2)
Computers in Our Lives (Chapters LIV 1 and LIV 2)

Through the EXACT custom publishing program, instructors have the option of eliminating any module or modules—or rearranging modules—to tailor the text to meet the needs of any specific course. In addition, *Understanding Computers* can be bound with a variety of software manuals. Contact your local Dryden representative for further information concerning customization and the EXACT program.

Currency Perhaps more than textbooks in any other field, computer texts must reflect current technologies, trends, and classroom needs. The state-of-the-art content of this book and its support package reflects these considerations. Before the 98 edition was started, reviews were commissioned and meetings were held to identify key areas of change for the text and support package. Also, throughout the writing and production stages, enhancements and new developments were continually being made to ensure that the final product would be as state-of-the-art as possible throughout the life of the edition. A glance at the chapter outlines, sidebars, and Windows should illustrate why this text has been and will continue to remain a market leader.

Comprehensiveness and Depth In planning for the current edition of this book, the publisher conducted several extensive research studies to determine the selection of topics, degree of depth, and other features that instructors of introductory computer courses most want to see in their texts. As the manuscript evolved, instructors at a variety of schools around the country were asked for their comments. The resulting textbook accommodates a wide range of teaching preferences. It not only covers traditional topics comprehensively but also includes the facts every student should know about today's "hot" topics, such as the Internet, PCs, multimedia technology, wireless communications, electronic commerce, global computing issues, decision support and expert systems, data warehousing, object-oriented-language products, virtual reality, and user and programmer productivity tools.

Readability We remember more about a subject if it is presented in a straightforward way and made interesting and exciting. This book is written in a conversational, down-to-earth style—one designed to be accurate without being intimidating. Concepts are explained clearly and simply, without use of overly technical terminology. Where complex points are presented, they are made understandable with realistic examples from everyday life.

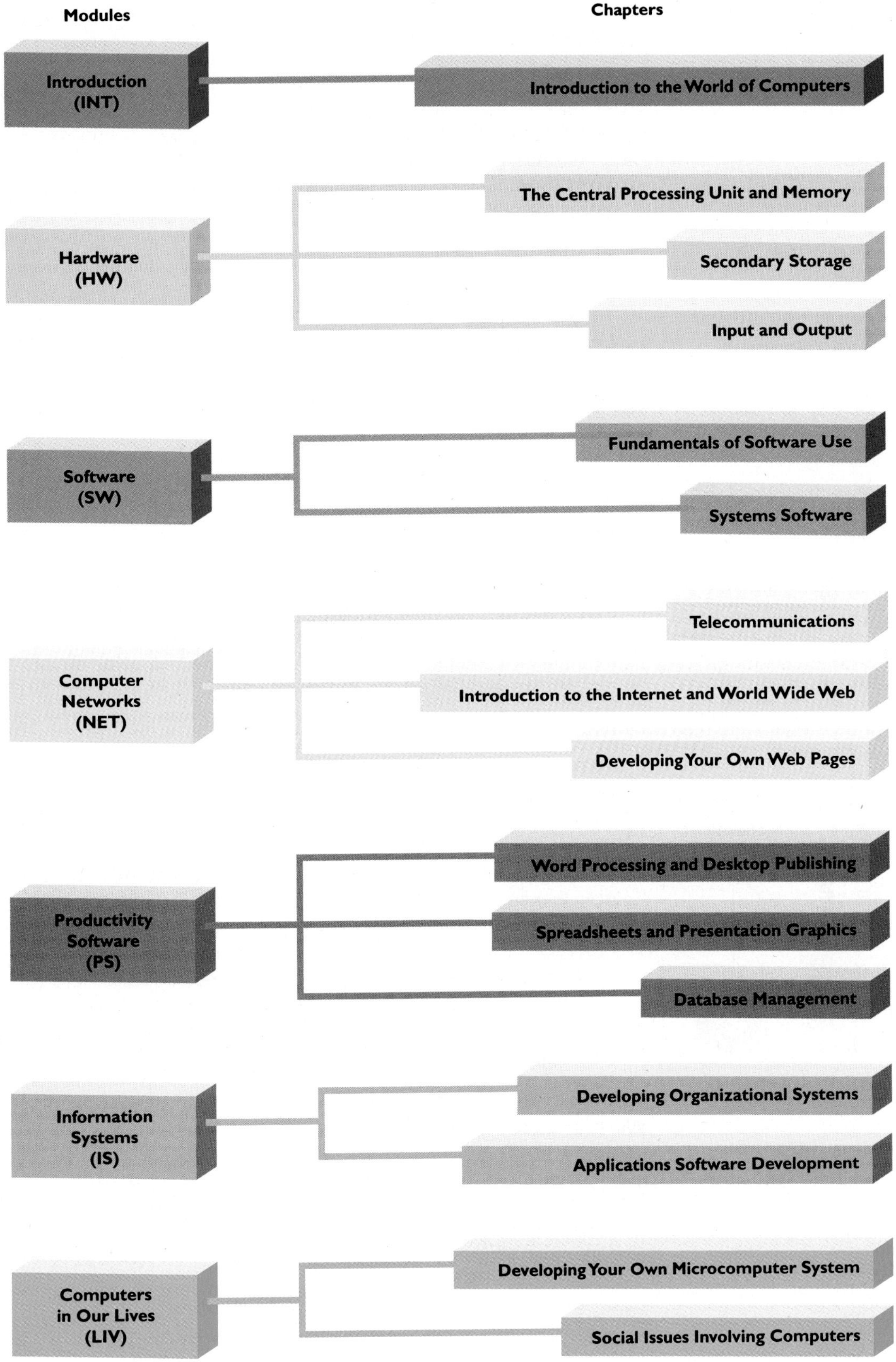

Modules	Chapters
Introduction (INT)	Introduction to the World of Computers
Hardware (HW)	The Central Processing Unit and Memory
	Secondary Storage
	Input and Output
Software (SW)	Fundamentals of Software Use
	Systems Software
Computer Networks (NET)	Telecommunications
	Introduction to the Internet and World Wide Web
	Developing Your Own Web Pages
Productivity Software (PS)	Word Processing and Desktop Publishing
	Spreadsheets and Presentation Graphics
	Database Management
Information Systems (IS)	Developing Organizational Systems
	Applications Software Development
Computers in Our Lives (LIV)	Developing Your Own Microcomputer System
	Social Issues Involving Computers

Custom publishing options. *Understanding Computers* can be ordered as a complete text of seven modules or as an abbreviated text with any combination of modules bound in any order you like.

Chapter Learning Tools Each chapter contains a number of learning tools to help students master the materials.

1. **Outline** An Outline of the headings in the chapter shows the major topics to be covered.
2. **Learning Objectives** A list of Learning Objectives is provided to serve as a guide while students read the chapter.
3. **Overview** Each chapter starts with an Overview that puts the subject matter of the chapter into perspective and lets students know what they will be reading about.
4. **Boldfaced Key Terms and Running Glossary** Important terms appear in boldface type as they are introduced in the chapter. These terms are also defined at the bottom of the page on which they appear and in the end-of-text Glossary.
5. **Tomorrow Boxes** These special elements, one in each chapter, provide students with a look at possible future developments in the world of computers and serve as a focus for class discussion.
6. **Feature Boxes** Each chapter contains one or more Feature boxes designed to stimulate interest and discussion about today's uses of technology.
7. **User Solution Boxes** User Solution boxes describe how technology is creatively being used to solve real-world problems. Each chapter contains at least one of these features.
8. **Inside the Industry Boxes** These boxes, one to each module, provide insight into some of the personalities and practices that have made the computer industry unique and fascinating.
9. **Illustrations and Photographs** Instructive, full-color figures and photographs appear throughout the book to help illustrate important concepts. Figures are annotated in a new, revised style to convey as much information as possible.
10. **Summary and Key Terms** This is a concise, section-by-section summary of the main points in the chapter. Every boldfaced key term in the chapter also appears in boldface type in the summary. Students will find the summary a valuable tool for study and review.
11. **Exercises** End-of-chapter Exercises allow students to test themselves on what they have just read. The exercises include matching, fill-in, discussion, and true-false questions as well as problems in a variety of other formats.
12. **Projects** End-of-chapter Projects require students to extend their knowledge by doing research beyond merely reading the book. Special icons (see left margin) denote projects that are recommended for groups, projects that should be done on the Internet, and projects that require hands-on computer skills with productivity software.

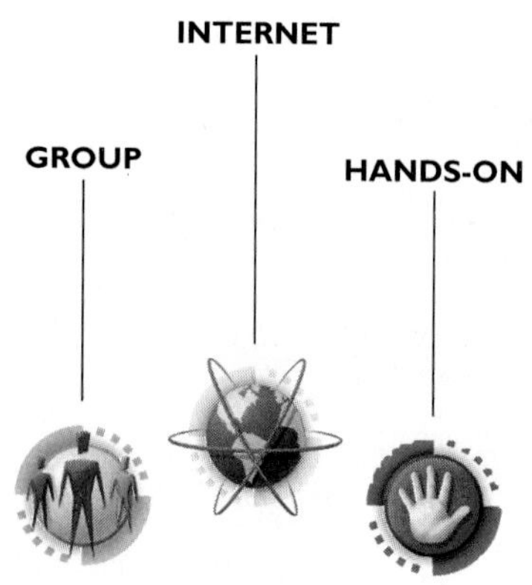

Windows The full, 16-chapter text contains four photoessays. Each of these "Windows" to the world of computers is organized around a major text theme and vividly illustrates interesting uses of computer technology.

End-of-Text Glossary The Glossary at the end of the book defines approximately 500 important computer terms mentioned in the text, including all boldfaced key terms. Each glossary item has a page reference indicating where it is boldfaced or where it first appears in the text.

CHANGES FROM THE PREVIOUS EDITION

Although previous editions of this text have been highly successful, the relentless pace of technology has regularly necessitated a number of key changes in each new edition in order to keep content fresh. Among the noteworthy differences between

Acknowledgments

I could never have completed a project of this scope alone. I owe a special word of thanks to the many people who reviewed the text—those whose extensive suggestions on past editions helped define the 98 edition, those whose comments on drafts of the 98 edition helped mold it into its final form, and those who reviewed the instructional package.

98 EDITION

Michael Atherton, *Mankato State University;* Jerry M. Chin, *Southwest Missouri State University;* Robert H. Dependahl Jr.; *Santa Barbara City College;* Jackie O. Duncan, *Hopkinsville Community College;* John W. Durham, *Fort Hays State University;* Ronald W. Fordonski, *College of Du Page;* Wade Graves, *Grayson County College;* John Groh, *San Joaquin Delta College;* Jim Johnson, *Valencia Community College;* Mary Louise Kelly, *Palm Beach Community College;* Mary Veronica Kolesar, *Utah State University;* Chang-Yang Lin, *Eastern Kentucky University;* Paul M. Lou, *Diablo Valley College;* Deborah R. Ludford, *Glendale Community College;* Donna Madsen, *Kirkwood Community College;* Vickie McCullough, *Palomar College;* James W. McGuffee, *Austin Community College;* William A. McMillan, *Madonna University;* John Melrose, *University of Wisconsin—Eau Claire;* William J. Moon, *Palm Beach Community College;* Marty Murray, *Portland Community College;* John F. Sanford, *Philadelphia College of Textiles and Science;* Tom Seymour, *Minot State University;* and Timothy M. Stanford, *City University.*

PREVIOUS EDITIONS

James Ambroise Jr., *Southern University, Louisiana;* Virginia Anderson, *University of North Dakota;* Robert Andree, *Indiana University Northwest;* Linda Armbruster, *Rancho Santiago College;* Gary E. Baker, *Marshalltown Community College;* Richard Batt, *Saint Louis Community College at Meremec;* Luverne Bierle, *Iowa Central Community College;* Jerry Booher, *Scottsdale Community College;* James Bradley, *University of Calgary;* Curtis Bring, *Moorhead State University;* Cathy Brotherton, *Riverside Community College;* James Buxton, *Tidewater Community College,* Virginia; Gena Casas, *Florida Community College, Jacksonville;* Thomas Case, *Georgia Southern University;* John E. Castek, *University of Wisconsin-La Crosse;* Mario E. Cecchetti, *Westmoreland County Community College;* Carl Clavadetscher, *California State Polytechnic University;* Vernon Clodfelter, *Rowan Technical College, North Carolina;* Laura Cooper, *College of the Mainland, Texas;* Cynthia Corritore, *University of Nebraska at Omaha;* Sandra Cunningham, *Ranger College;* Marvin Daugherty, *Indiana Vocational Technical College;* Donald L. Davis, *University of Mississippi;* Robert H. Dependahl Jr., *Santa Barbara College, California;* Donald Dershem, *Mountain View College;* John DiElsi, *Marcy College, New York;* Mark Dishaw, *Boston University;* Eugene T. Dolan, *University of the District of Columbia;* William Dorin, *Indiana University Northwest;* Hyun B. Eom, *Middle Tennessee State University;* Michael Feiler, *Merritt College;* J. Patrick Fenton, *West Valley Community College;* James H. Finger, *University of South Carolina at Columbia;* William C. Fink, *Lewis and Clark Community College, Illinois;* Connie Morris Fox, *West Virginia Institute of Technology;* Paula S. Funkhouser, *Truckee Meadows Community College;* Gene Garza, *University of Montevallo;* Timothy Gottleber, *North Lake College;* Kay H. Gray, *Jacksonville State University;* David W. Green, *Nashville State Technical Institute, Tennessee;* George P. Grill, *University of North Carolina, Greensboro;* Rosemary C. Gross, *Creighton University;* Dennis Guster, *Saint Louis Community College at Meremec;* Joe Hagarty, *Raritan Valley Community College;* Donald Hall, *Manatee Community College;* Sallyann Z. Hanson, *Mercer County Community College;* L. D. Harber, *Volunteer State Community College, Tennessee;* Hank Hartman, *Iowa State University;* Richard Hatch, *San Diego State University;* Mary Lou

A key indicating the chapter section from which each question was taken is also provided as part of the Test Bank. Keys are included with each questions, except for the matching questions. Also provided is a ten-question, ready-to-copy-and-distribute multiple-choice quiz for every chapter, which tests students on a representative sample of important topics.

COMPUTERS: AN INTERACTIVE LOOK, VERSION 2 CD-ROM

This CD-ROM supplement gives students the opportunity to explore computer concepts in an interactive format. *Computers: An Interactive Look* is made up of a series of interactive learning modules covering core topics such as hardware, software, the Internet, networking, and more. Within each learning module students will find extensive tutorials, exercises, and a self test for review purposes. The CD-ROM also inlcudes the text of *Understanding Computers,* the Electronic Transparencies, a ready-made PowerPoint presentation for each chapter, and a set of 800 text review questions. The CD-ROM may be bundled with the text or purchased separately by students.

THE PARKER WEB SITE

The Parker Web site located at

http://www.dryden.com/infosys/parker

provides constantly updated support for both instructors and students. In the Instructor's Only section, teachers can download Teaching Outlines, Teaching Tips, Lecture Anecdotes, answers to Exercises, suggestions for Projects, Electronic Transparencies, and other classroom resources. Students will find current links to all of the Web sites mentioned in the projects as well as additional exercises, projects, and sites of interest.

SOFTWARE MANUALS

Lab manuals, covering hands-on use of software packages, are available from Dryden Press for a number of widely used products. The packages supported include popular systems software such as Microsoft Windows 98, Windows 95, Windows 3.1, and MS-DOS, as well as the principal applications-software components of the market-leading software suites—Microsoft Office Professional, Corel Office Professional, and Lotus SmartSuite. Lab manuals are also available for such products Netscape Navigator, Microsoft Internet Explorer, dBASE, Harvard Graphics, Pagemaker, BASIC, and QBASIC. Applications-software manuals come in Windows 98, Windows 95, Windows 3.1, and MS-DOS versions. Using Dryden's custom-publishing option, you can have virtually any combination of components bound together for your classes. Check with your Dryden sales representative about the configuration options currently possible.

The Dryden Press will provide complimentary supplements or supplement packages to those adopters qualified under our adoption policy. Please contact your sales representative to learn how you may qualify. If as an adopter or potential user you receive supplements you do not need, please return them to your sales representative or send them to:

Attn: Returns Department
Troy Warehouse
465 South Lincoln Drive
Troy, MO 63379

Student and Teacher Support Materials

Understanding Computers: Today and Tomorrow is available with a complete package of support materials for instructors and students. Included in the package are an Instructor's Manual with transparency masters, a set of Electronic Transparencies, a Test Bank in hard-copy and computerized forms, a dedicated CD-ROM and Web site, a variety of software manuals to meet lab needs, and a number of additional items.

INSTRUCTOR'S MANUAL

In the Instructor's Manual I draw on my own teaching experience to provide instructors with practical suggestions for enhancing classroom presentations. The Instructor's Manual contains suggestions for adapting this textbook to various course schedules, including one-quarter, two-quarter, one-semester, two-semester, and night courses. For each of the 16 chapters of the text the Instructor's Manual provides:

1. A list of **Learning Objectives.**
2. A **Summary,** oriented to the instructor, with teaching suggestions.
3. A list of the **Key Terms** in the chapter and their definitions.
4. A **Teaching Outline** that gives a detailed breakdown of the chapter, with all major headings and subheadings, as well as points to cover under each. References to the Electronic Transparencies and Transparency Masters are keyed in to this outline.
5. **Teaching Tips,** with additional topics for class discussion, important points to cover in class, and book and Web-site recommendations.
6. **Lecture Anecdotes** providing additional stories, news items, projects, and information—specific to chapter content—to liven up lectures.
7. **Transparency Scripts** for each Electronic Transparency and Transparency Master in the instructional package.
8. **Answers to Exercises** that appear at the end of the chapter.
9. **Suggestions for Projects** that appear at the end of the chapter.
10. **Transparency Masters** covering the chapter outline, chapter learning objectives, and other key topics for classroom discussion.

ELECTRONIC TRANSPARENCIES

A set of over one hundred Electronic Transparencies for use in classroom presentations is available to help explain key points. The Electronic Transparencies cover key text figures as well as illustrations not found in the text. The Teaching Outlines in the Instructor's Manual indicate when to show each of the Electronic Transparencies and Transparency Masters, and the Transparency Scripts in the Instructor's Manual list points to make about each.

TEST BANK

The Test Bank contains over 3,200 test items in various formats, including true/false, multiple-choice, matching, fill-in, and short-answer questions. Answers are provided for all but the short-answer questions. The Test Bank is available in both hard-copy and computerized forms. The electronic versions—available for use with PC-compatible and Macintosh computers—allow instructors to preview, edit, and delete questions as well as to add their own questions, print scrambled forms of tests, and print answer keys.

the previous edition and the current edition of *Understanding Computers* are the following:

1. The book has been shortened from 17 to 16 chapters. Chapters IS 1 (Business Systems) and IS 2 (Systems Development) from the previous edition have been combined into a single chapter in this book, Chapter IS 1 (Developing Systems for Organizations). Also, to make room for the addition of two new chapters on the Internet—NET 2 (Introduction to the Internet and World Wide Web) and NET 3 (Developing Your Own Web Pages)—two chapters from the previous edition have been eliminated, their contents distributed elsewhere throughout this new book. These chapters are INT 2 (Computer Systems and Information Processing) and SOC 1 (Computers in Our Lives).
2. The TSW (Telecommunications and Software) module in the previous edition has been split into two separate modules—SW (Software) and NET (Computer Networks). This increases the number of modules from six to seven. The split was prompted by far more coverage on the Internet than in the previous edition. Materials on the Internet have also been woven into many other parts of the book.
3. The end-of-chapter Exercises and Projects are new to this edition. The Exercises—which require students to provide responses on what they have read in the chapter—replace the fill-in, matching, and discussion questions from the last edition. The Projects go beyond the chapter materials and ask students to do topical research, perform thought-provoking calculations, and take viewpoints on important issues involving computers and their uses.
4. The IS (Information Systems) and LIV (Computers in Our Lives) modules have been heavily reorganized from similar modules in the previous edition. You will notice that Chapter LIV 1 (Developing Your Own Microcomputer System) was moved from the IS module in the previous edition, where it was Chapter IS 4. Also, as mentioned earlier, chapters IS 1 and IS 2 of the previous edition have been combined into a single chapter.
5. The art program has been extensively revised. Each chapter includes dynamic, fully annotated illustrations integrated with the text material, as well as numerous color photos and screen shots that showcase the latest applications and programs. Many of the illustrations are rendered in a photorealistic style to show students the details of computer components close up.
6. The Inside the Industry boxes, also new to this edition, describe some of the colorful personalities and practices arising from microcomputers and related technologies. Features include how to find an "Easter egg" in a software program, how the Yahoo! Web-search site began, and computer-industry code names.
7. Continuing the trend from earlier editions, this book presents an increased emphasis on PC-based processing and communications. This shift reflects the trend in business applications as well as the social trend of more and more people getting involved with these facets of technology.
8. Several topics have emerged in importance since the text was last published and receive greater attention here. Among these topics are the Internet and the World Wide Web, organizational intranets and extranets, electronic commerce, plug-and-play computing, Windows 98, greater name recognition of important companies in the PC and telecommunications industry (such as Microsoft and Cisco Systems), color printers, software suites, client-server computing, mobile computing technologies, workgroup computing, DVD and new forms of secondary storage, multimedia applications and MMX-based processor chips, new forms of computer crime and cyberterrorism, virtual reality, RAID and parallel processing systems, object-oriented languages, and global and international issues.

Hawkins, *Del Mar College;* William Hightower, *Elon College, North Carolina;* Sharon A. Hill, *Prince George's Community College, Maryland;* Fred C. Homeyer, *Angelo State University;* Stanley P. Honacki, *Moraine Valley Community College;* L. Wayne Horn, *Pensacola Junior College;* J. William Howorth, *Seneca College, Ontario, Canada;* Peter L. Irwin, *Richland College, Texas;* Nicholas JohnRobak, *Saint Joseph's University;* Elizabeth Swoope Johnson, *Louisiana State University;* Robert T. Keim, *Arizona State University;* William R. Kenney, *San Diego Mesa College;* Richard Kerns, *East Carolina University, North Carolina;* Glenn Kersnick, *Sinclair Community College, Ohio;* Gordon C. Kimbell, *Everett Community College, Washington;* Robert Kirklin, *Los Angeles Harbor Community College;* Judith A. Knapp, *Indiana University Northwest;* James G. Kriz, *Cuyahoga Community College, Ohio;* Joan Krone, *Denison University;* Fran Kubicek, *Kalamazoo Valley Community College;* Rose M. Laird, *Northern Virginia Community College;* Robert Landrum, *Jones Junior College;* Shelly Langman, *Bellevue Community College;* James F. LaSalle, *The University of Arizona;* Linda J. Lindaman, *Black Hawk College;* Alden Lorents, *Northern Arizona University;* Barbara J. Maccarone, *North Shore Community College;* Wayne Madison, *Clemson University, South Carolina;* Donna L. Madsen, *Kirkwood Community College;* Richard W. Manthei, *Joliet Junior College;* Randy Marak, *Hill College;* Gary Marks, *Austin Community College, Texas;* Ed Martin, *Kingsborough Community College;* James McMahon, *Community College of Rhode Island;* William A. McMillan, *Madonna University;* Don B. Medley, *California State Polytechnic University;* Mary Meredith, *University of Southwestern Louisiana;* Marilyn Meyer, *Fresno City College;* Marilyn Moore, *Purdue University;* Don Nielsen, *Golden West College;* George Novotny, *Ferris State University;* Dennis J. Olsen, *Pikes Peak Community College;* Bob Palank, *Florissant Community College;* James Payne, *Kellogg Community College;* Robert Ralph, *Fayetteville Technical Institute, North Carolina;* Herbert F. Rebhun, *University of Houston-Downtown;* Arthur E. Rowland, *Shasta College;* Kenneth R. Ruhrup, *St. Petersburg Junior College;* Carol A. Schwab, *Webster University;* Larry Schwartzman, *Trident Technical College;* Benito R. Serenil, *South Seattle Community College;* John J. Shuler, *San Antonio College, Texas;* Harold Smith, *Brigham Young University;* Willard A. Smith, *Tennessee State University;* Alfred C. St. Onge, *Springfield Technical Community College, Massachusetts;* Michael L. Stratford, *Charles County Community College, Maryland;* Karen Studniarz, *Kishwaukee College;* Sandra Swanson, *Lewis &Clark Community College;* William H. Trueheart, *New Hampshire College;* Jane J. Thompson, *Solano Community College;* Sue Traynor, *Clarion University of Pennsylvania;* James D. Van Tassel, *MissionCollege;* James R. Walters, *Pikes Peak Community College;* Joyce V. Walton, *Seneca College, Ontario, Canada;* Diane B. Walz, *University of Texas at San Antonio;* Joseph Waters, *Santa Rosa Junior College, California;* Liang Chee Wee, *University of Arizona;* Fred J. Wilke, *Saint Louis Community College;* Charles M. Williams, *Georgia State University;* Roseanne Witkowski, *Orange County Community College;* James D. Woolever, *Cerritos College;* A. James Wynne, *Virginia Commonwealth University;* and Robert D. Yearout, *University of North Carolina at Asheville.*

I am indebted to scores of people at dozens of organizations for the images they provided for this text. I would especially like to thank Jessie O. Kempter at IBM, Carol Parcels of Hewlett-Packard, Nancy Beals of Microsoft, the many helpful people at Waggner Edstrom, Chuck Hixon of Bergmann Associates, Andy Amor at Cooper Carry & Associates, Annie Rhodes of R/Greenberg Associates, Corinne Whitaker of The Digital Giraffe, Dan Younger, and Steven Lyons.

At The Dryden Press, a special word of thanks to my publisher, George Provol, to my executive editors, Wesley Lawton and Scott Timian, to Elizabeth Hayes, senior developmental editor, and to Kathryn Stewart, project editor, for the suggestions and accommodations they made to produce a better manuscript. Also I would like to thank Linda Wooton, Ellie Moore, Cathy Spitzenberger, Federico Arrieta, Carlyn Hauser, Adele Krause, Shirley Webster, Annette Bratcher, and the many others who worked hard on behalf of this book.

Charles S. Parker

CONTENTS in Brief

Note: This contents in brief shows entries for all 16 chapters of the text. You may have a customized version of the text that does not contain all of the chapters indicated.

Contents

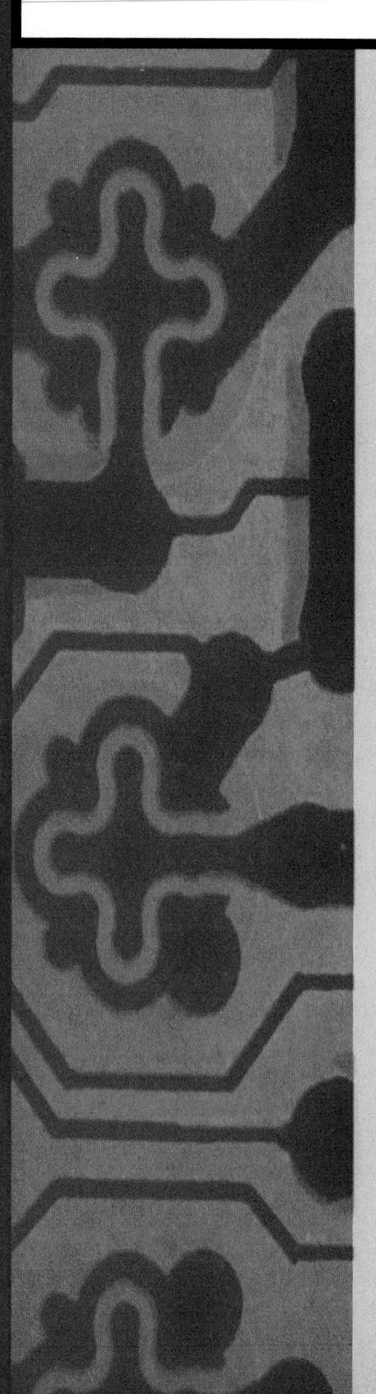

MODULE

INT

Introduction

We live in an age of computers. Businesses, government agencies, and other organizations use computers and related technologies to handle tedious paperwork, provide better service to customers, and assist managers in making good decisions, to name just a few things. As computers continue to offer growing benefits, and as the costs of technology continue to fall relative to the prices of everything else, computers will become even more widespread in our society. It is therefore essential to know something about them.

The chapter in this module introduces you to computers and some of their uses. It helps you understand what computer systems are, how they work, and how people use them. The chapter also presents some key terminology that you will encounter repeatedly throughout the text.

MODULE CONTENTS

Introduction

ISBN 0-03-024481-1

Introduction to the World of Computers

Outline

- Overview
- Computers in the Workplace
- What's a Computer and What Does It Do?
  - Computer Systems
  - Data, Information, and Programs
  - A Look at Computer Storage
  - Hardware and Software
  - Organizing Data and Programs
  - Users and the Experts
  - Computer Networks
- Computer Systems to Fit Every Need and Pocketbook
  - Microcomputers
  - Midrange Computers
  - Mainframes
  - Supercomputers
- Computers and Society

Learning Objectives

After completing this chapter, you will be able to:

1. Explain why it's especially important to learn about computers today.
2. Identify some of the major components in a computing environment, and detail their relationships to one another.
3. Describe several applications for computers in business and other areas of society where they play important roles.
4. Define several terms that arise in reading about or discussing computers.
5. Describe the social impact of computers.

Overview

Unless you plan to live as a recluse in the wilderness, computers and other forms of high technology will probably have a big impact on your life. Computer systems keep track of bank transactions and credit-card purchases. They are the cornerstones of the airlines' massive reservations systems. Computers perform the millions upon millions of computations needed to send equipment to distant places like Mars and to operate it once it's there. Computers also direct production in factories and provide business executives with up-to-date information that they need to make decisions. Computers are embedded in watches, television sets, phones, fax machines, kitchen appliances, and probably even the stationary workout bike at your local gym. They can even create the illusion of a real situation that does not exist (see User Solution INT 1-1, on page INT 14). In short, computers are used in virtually endless numbers of applications.

Fifty short years ago, computers were part of an obscure technology that interested only a handful of scientists. Today, they are part of almost everyone's daily life.

Computers share a characteristic with cars, in that you don't need to know everything about them to use them effectively. You can learn to drive a car without knowing much about internal combustion engines, and you can learn to use a computer without a complete understanding of technical details such as logic gates. Still, with both cars and computers, a little knowledge can give you a big advantage. Knowing something about cars can help you to make wise purchases and save money on repairs. Likewise, knowing something about computers can help you to use them for maximum benefit.

This book is a beginner's guide. If you're considering a career as a computer professional in business, it will give you a comprehensive introduction to the field. If not, it will give you the basic knowledge you need to understand and use computers in school and on the job. Today, many jobs depend heavily on computer-based information, and your success in the workplace is more likely to depend on your ability to use it.

This chapter will first examine what computers do and how they work. You'll learn about such concepts as input and output, memory, hardware and software, computer networks, and many others. A later section will look at the various sizes of computers that today's users encounter.

Computers in the Workplace

Prior to 1980, it was not critical for the average person to know how to use a computer in his or her job. Computers were large and expensive, and few people in the working world had access to them. Furthermore, the use of computers generally required a lot of technical knowledge. Most computers used in organizations were equipped to do little but carry out high-volume paperwork processing, such as issuing bills and keeping track of customer and product balances. Not only were most ordinary working people afraid of computers, but also there were few good reasons for getting familiar with them.

Then, suddenly, things began to change. Microcomputers—inexpensive personal computers (PCs) that you will read about later in this chapter—were created. Consequently, today there are thousands of times more computers and hundreds of times more people involved with computers than just a couple of decades or so ago. This transition has resulted in a flood of high-quality computer products in the marketplace. These products have changed the way many companies do business and the type of skills they seek in the people they hire.

Today we are living in the midst of a computer revolution, where most skill-based jobs heavily depend on the creation, collection, use, and dissemination of information. What's more, this revolution is showing no signs of slowing down; if anything, it's accelerating. Whether you become a teacher, lawyer, doctor, professional athlete, executive, or blue-collar worker, your performance will largely depend on information and your use of it. Because computer systems can process facts at dizzying speeds, their value to you is equivalent to having both a skilled researcher and an army of clerks at your disposal.

Figure INT 1-1 provides several examples of how computers are being used in the workplace to enhance personal productivity.

FIGURE INT 1-1

Computers shaping the workplace.

MULTIPURPOSE WORKSTATION
Most office workers today require their own desktop computer to prepare budgets and reports, exchange electronic mail, organize their work, and collect information from computer networks.

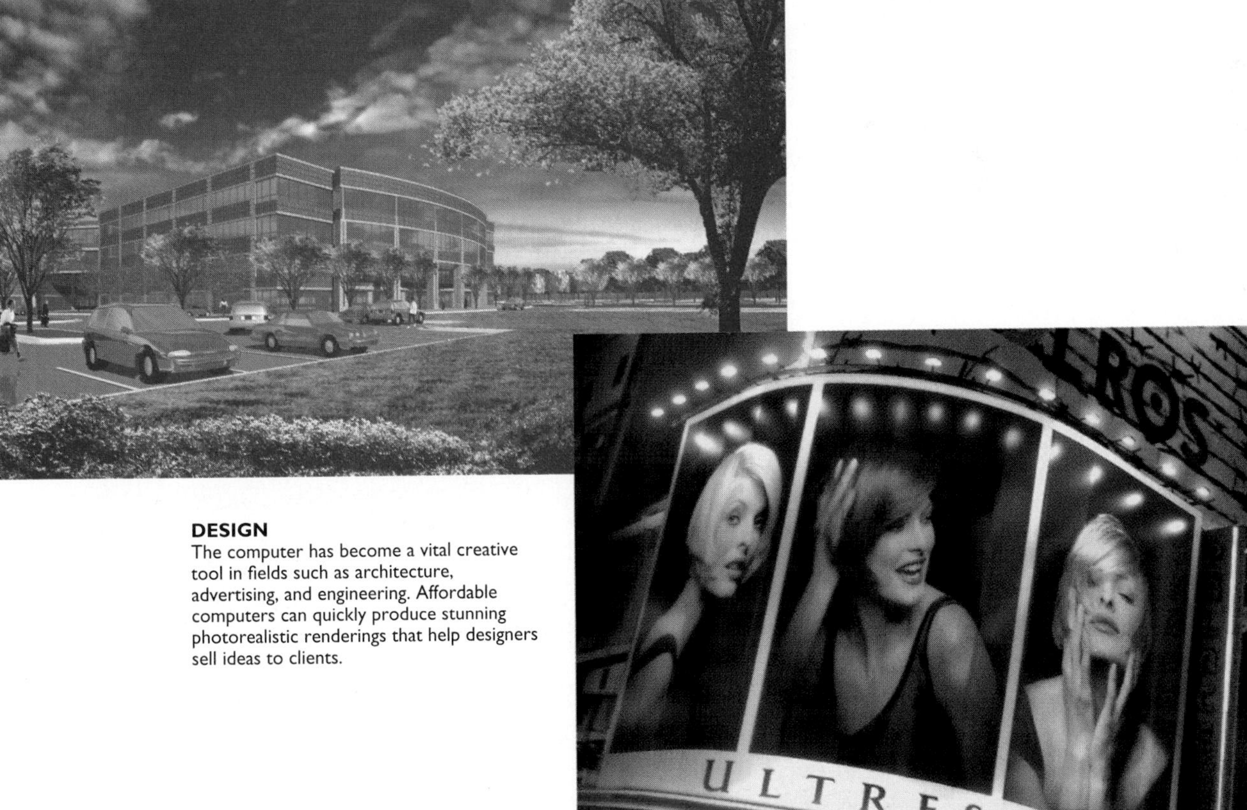

DESIGN
The computer has become a vital creative tool in fields such as architecture, advertising, and engineering. Affordable computers can quickly produce stunning photorealistic renderings that help designers sell ideas to clients.

continued

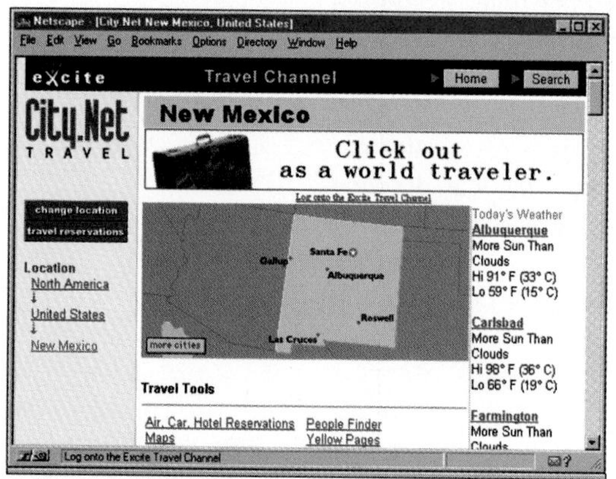

THE INTERNET
This vast collection of computer networks—which is redefining the workplace—enables people to get information on almost any imaginable topic, communicate with others around the globe, and conduct business electronically.

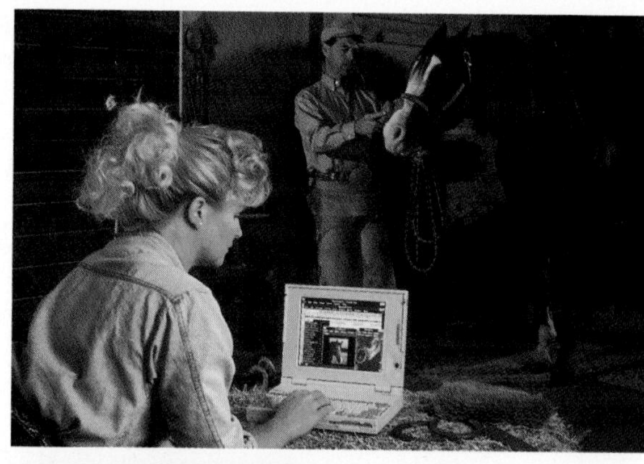

HOME-BASED BUSINESSES
Home-based businesspeople need computers in their work in the same way office workers do. Rural users often tap into the Internet to get up-to-date weather information and feed prices as well as to take classes at remote schools.

MUSIC
The computer has become an indispensible creative tool in the music world. Here, a music synthesizer makes it possible to produce and assemble artificial sounds that imitate those of real instruments.

WIRELESS COMMUNICATIONS
Computers supported with wireless technology help shippers communicate faster. Without computers linked at all levels in the manufacturing and distribution process, the rapid delivery of goods we've come to depend upon would be impossible.

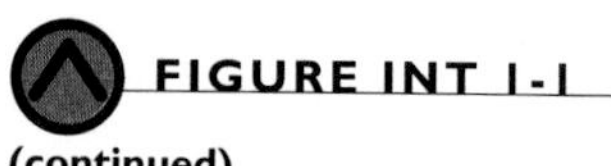

FIGURE INT 1-1
(continued)

What's a Computer and What Does It Do?

Four words sum up the operation of a computer system: **input, processing, output,** and **storage.** To see what these words mean, look at a comparable device you probably have in your own home—a stereo system.

A simple stereo system might consist of a compact disk (CD) player, an amplifier, and a pair of speakers. To use the system, you place a CD in the CD player and turn on power to the system. The player converts the patterns in the CD's tracks into

---

■ **Input.** What is supplied to a computer process. ■ **Processing.** The conversion of input to output. ■ **Output.** The results of a computer process. ■ **Storage.** An area that holds materials going to or coming from the computer.

electronic signals and transmits them to the amplifier. The amplifier receives the signals, strengthens them, and transmits them to the speakers, which play music. In computer terms, the CD player sends signals as *input* to the amplifier. The amplifier *processes* the signals and sends them to the speakers, which produce a musical *output.* The CD player is an **input device,** the amplifier is a processing unit, and the speakers are **output devices.** The amplifier is the heart of the system, whereas the CD player and speakers are examples of **peripheral equipment.**

Most stereo systems include a variety of other peripheral equipment. An antenna, for example, is another kind of input device. Headphones are output devices. A tape deck functions as both an input and an output device—you can use it to send signals to the amplifier or to receive signals from the amplifier. The tapes and CDs in your collection are, in computer terms, **storage media.** They *store* music in a **machine-readable form—**a form that the associated input device (tape deck or CD player) can recognize (that is, read) and convert into signals for the amplifier to process.

COMPUTER SYSTEMS

All of these elements in a stereo system have their counterparts in a computer system. At a minimum, a **computer system** consists of the computer itself and its peripheral equipment. It often includes collections of machine-readable instructions and facts that the computer processes, as well as operating manuals, procedures, and the people who use the computer. In other words, all of the components that contribute to the computer's functioning as a useful tool can be said to be parts of a computer system (see Figure INT 1-2).

At the heart of any computer system is the **computer** itself, or the **central processing unit (CPU).** The CPU in a computer system is the equivalent of the stereo system's amplifier. Like its counterpart, the CPU can't do anything useful without both peripheral equipment for input, output, and storage functions and storage media that hold the data it processes. Computer *input and output (I/O) devices* include, to name just a few, keyboards, display devices, and printers. *Storage devices* include the drives that hold disks and tapes—the storage media.

A computer system, of course, is not a stereo system, and a CPU is much more versatile than a stereo amplifier. For example, a computer system can perform an enormous variety of processing tasks and a stereo system only a few. Also, a computer can support a much greater variety of input and output devices than can a stereo amplifier.

Two of the things that give a computer its flexibility are its memory and its ability to be programmed. The computer's *memory,* or "workspace," is an electronic storage area that allows the computer to retain the inputs it receives and both the intermediate and final results it produces by processing these inputs. An ordinary home stereo system has no such memory; input from the compact disk player or tape recorder passes directly through the amplifier to the speakers. Because computers can hold materials in memory, they can rearrange or recombine *data* inputs in an amazing variety of ways under the direction of *program* inputs before sending them along as output.

■ **Input device.** Equipment that supplies materials to the computer. ■ **Output device.** Equipment that accepts materials from the computer. ■ **Peripheral equipment.** The devices that work with a computer. ■ **Storage media.** Objects that store computer-processed materials. ■ **Machine-readable form.** Any form that represents data so that computer equipment can read them. ■ **Computer system.** A collection of elements that includes the computer and components that contribute to making it a useful tool. ■ **Computer.** The piece of equipment, also known as the **central processing unit (CPU),** that interprets and executes program instructions and communicates with peripheral devices.

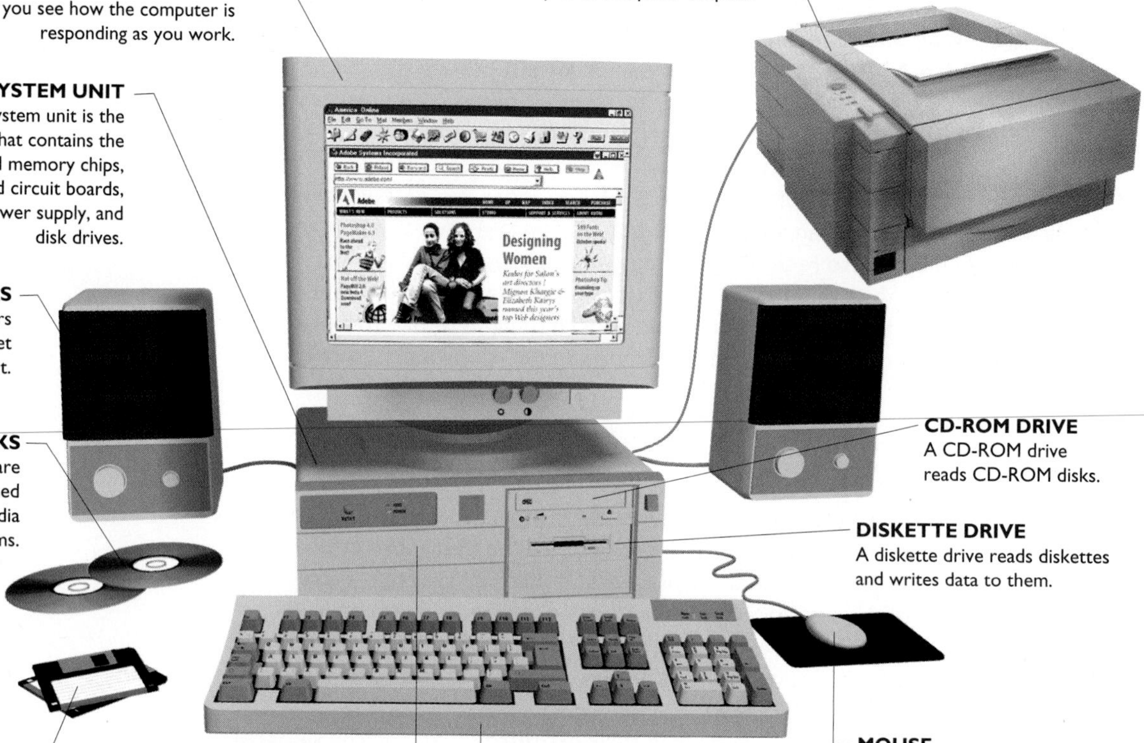

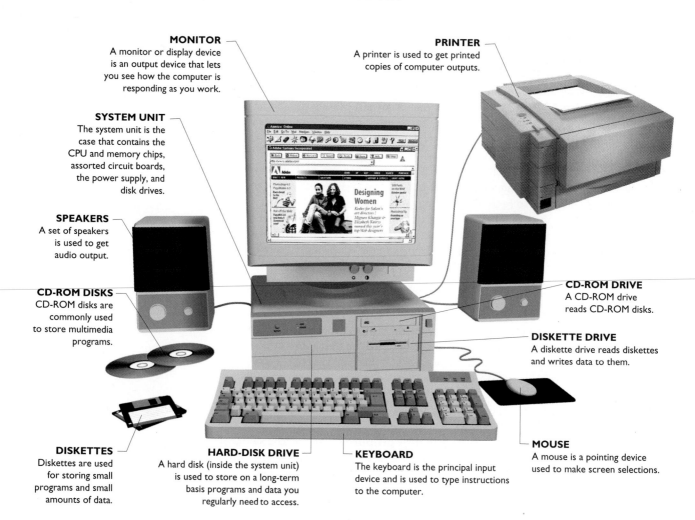

MONITOR
A monitor or display device is an output device that lets you see how the computer is responding as you work.

PRINTER
A printer is used to get printed copies of computer outputs.

SYSTEM UNIT
The system unit is the case that contains the CPU and memory chips, assorted circuit boards, the power supply, and disk drives.

SPEAKERS
A set of speakers is used to get audio output.

CD-ROM DISKS
CD-ROM disks are commonly used to store multimedia programs.

CD-ROM DRIVE
A CD-ROM drive reads CD-ROM disks.

DISKETTE DRIVE
A diskette drive reads diskettes and writes data to them.

DISKETTES
Diskettes are used for storing small programs and small amounts of data.

HARD-DISK DRIVE
A hard disk (inside the system unit) is used to store on a long-term basis programs and data you regularly need to access.

KEYBOARD
The keyboard is the principal input device and is used to type instructions to the computer.

MOUSE
A mouse is a pointing device used to make screen selections.

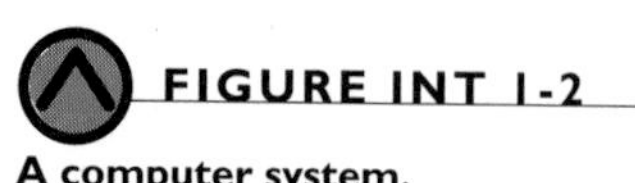

FIGURE INT 1-2

A computer system.

DATA, INFORMATION, AND PROGRAMS

As already suggested, to produce results, a computer uses two kinds of materials as input: *data* and *programs.* The result—or output—of the subsequent processing is information.

Data **Data** are essentially raw, unorganized facts. Almost any kind of fact or set of facts can become computer data: a letter to a friend, text and pictures for a 300-page book, a budget, a colorful graph, or a set of employee records.

Data can exist in many forms. Computer systems commonly handle four types of data: text, graphics, audio, and video data (see Figure INT 1-3).

Text data have been around the longest of all. These data usually consist of standard alphabetic, numeric, and special characters—that is, the type of data one normally sees in a simple word-processed letter, a budget, or a printed report.

Graphics data consist of still pictures such as drawings, graphs, photographs, and illustrations. Graphics data often require more sophisticated representations inside the computer than those for text, because graphics are naturally more complicated, often with multiple colors.

An example of *audio* data is an ordinary telephone conversation. Any type of sound—including music and voice—is considered audio data. Modern computers can store sounds in machine-readable form, just as they store any other type of data.

■ **Data.** A collection of raw, unorganized facts.

FIGURE INT 1-3

Data. The four types of data most commonly handled by computer systems are text, graphics, audio, and video data.

Video data consist of motion pictures, such as a movie clip, a feature-length film, or live pictures of a conference. Many computer systems sold today are capable of handling video data in one form or another.

Most of the computer systems sold today for use in the home are *multimedia computer systems.* That is, they can handle multiple types of data. Multimedia systems provide conventional text and graphics on a display screen, and they also play audio output over speakers and run video clips stored on CD-ROM disks.

Information When users input data into computer systems, they usually don't want to receive the same data back without changes. They want the system to process the data and give new, useful information. **Information,** in the language of computers, refers to data that have been processed into a meaningful form.

A computer user might want to know, for example, how many of a firm's employees earn more than $100,000, how many seats are available on a particular flight from Los Angeles to San Francisco, or what Cal Ripken's batting average was during last year's baseball season. The difference between data and information lies in the word *meaningful.* Cal Ripken's batting average may be meaningful to a baseball fan, because it could enhance the experience of watching baseball games. Someone who doesn't follow this sport, however, may regard Cal Ripken's batting average as completely meaningless—just ordinary data, not information. Thus, information is a *relative* term; it identifies something that has significance to a specific person in a specific situation. Like beauty, the difference between data and information is strictly in the eye of the beholder.

Of course, you don't need a computer system to process a set of facts and produce information. Anyone can go through an employee file and make a list of people

■ **Information.** Data that have been processed into a meaningful form.

earning a certain salary. By hand, however, this work would take a lot of time, especially for a company with thousands of employees. In contrast, their high speeds allow computers to perform such tasks almost instantly. Conversion of data into information is called by a variety of terms, one of which is *information processing.*

Information processing has become an especially important activity in recent years, as the success of many businesses depends heavily on the wise use of information. Because better information often improves decisions, many companies today regard information as among their most important assets and consider the creative use of information to be a key competitive strategy.

Programs **Programs** are sets of instructions that tell the computer how to process data to produce the results that you, the user, want. Like many other machines, the amplifier in your home stereo system is a *special-purpose* device. It is designed to support only a few specific tasks—interacting with a CD player, playing music through speakers or headphones, and so forth. These functions are built into its circuitry. To say the same thing another way, the amplifier is "hardwired" to perform a very limited number of specific tasks.

Most computers, in contrast, are *general-purpose* devices. They perform a large variety of tasks—for instance, preparing letters to clients, analyzing sales figures, and creating slide presentations, to name just a few. Because most computers must maintain flexible processing capabilities, they can't be hardwired to do all of these and hundreds of other tasks. Instead, they rely on programmed instructions for guidance. As a computer system processes each program, the user provides data for the program to "crunch" into a more useful form. The program and its data inputs then direct the circuits in the computer to open and close in the manner needed to do the desired task.

Computers cannot yet run programs written in ordinary English. Instead, specialists create programs in a **programming language—**a code that the computer system can read and translate into the electronic pulses that make it work. Programming languages come in many varieties—BASIC, Pascal, C, and Java are a few you may have heard about in the press. Millions of people now use computers without ever writing programs, leaving that task largely to computer professionals.

A LOOK AT COMPUTER STORAGE

So far, you've seen that you can get something done on a computer system only by supplying it with both facts (data) and instructions (a program) specifying how to process those facts. For example, if you want the system to write payroll checks, you must supply such data as employees' names, social security numbers, and salaries. The program instructions must indicate to the system how to compute taxes, how to take appropriate deductions, where and how to print checks, and so forth. Also, the computer relies on storage to retain all these details as it completes the work.

Actually, computer systems contain two types of storage. A **primary (internal) storage—**often called **memory—**temporarily holds the data and programs that the computer is currently processing. When the computer's memory captures data, it can rearrange or recombine them, as indicated by the instructions in the program. Memory is often on the floor of the system unit that houses the computer.

More often than not, the work that people create in a computer session needs to be used at a later time, say, tomorrow or next week. Because turning off the power to the computer destroys any data left in memory, another means of storage—called secondary storage—is needed for work to be saved, so it can be used multiple times.

■ **Program.** A set of instructions that causes the computer system to perform specific actions. ■ **Programming language.** A set of rules used to write computer programs. ■ **Primary (internal) storage.** Also known as **memory,** this section of the computer system temporarily holds data and program instructions awaiting processing, intermediate results, and processed output.

The most successful software products are revised every year or so to keep up with changes in technology, such as bigger disk drives, faster computer chips, larger memories, and the like. Each revision is commonly referred to as a *version* or *release* and assigned a number—for instance, Windows 98 or Office 97.

ORGANIZING DATA AND PROGRAMS

Data, as mentioned earlier, are essentially facts, and programs are the instructions that process these facts into meaningful information. Unfortunately, you can't just randomly input a collection of facts and instructions into a computer system and expect to get desired results. For a computer system to process them, data and programs must be organized in a systematic way (see Figure INT 1-7).

Documents and Folders One of the most fundamental ways that data and programs are organized is with documents and folders. For instance, when you are

Organizing data and programs.

DOCUMENTS AND FOLDERS
Documents and folders are handy for organizing such outputs as memos, letters, reports, budgets, and programs.

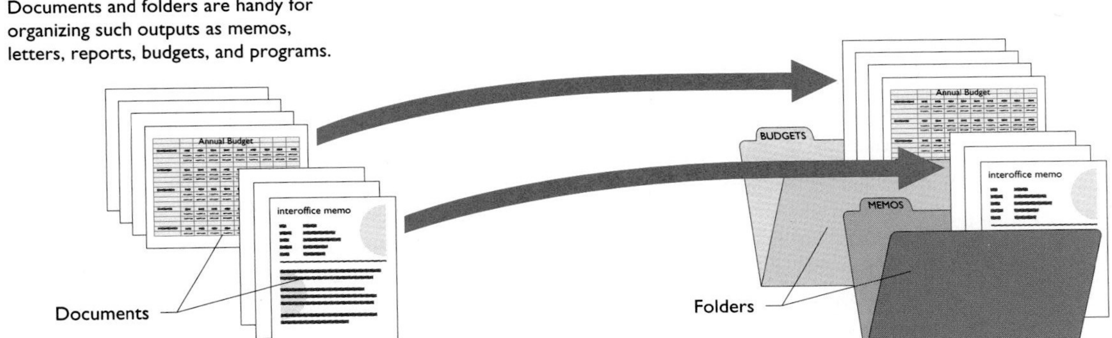

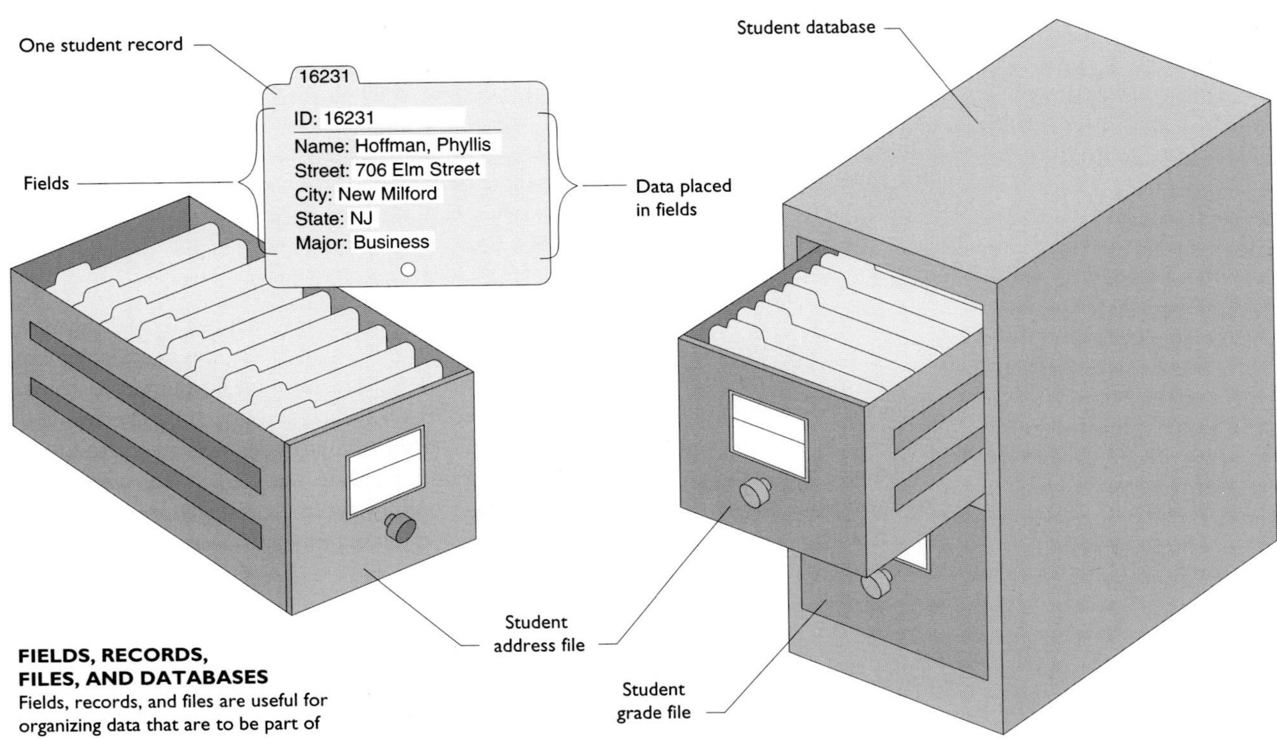

FIELDS, RECORDS, FILES, AND DATABASES
Fields, records, and files are useful for organizing data that are to be part of a database.

working with a word processing program, each memo, letter, or report that you create is stored as a separate **document.** Related documents are in turn stored in a **folder.** One folder, say, might contain memos to business associates while another holds a set of budgets for a specific project. Related programs are stored in their own folders, too. Organizing data into documents and folders is natural for most office workers, a number of whom were using file folders to organize paperwork well before computers became a fixture on desktops.

In the documents-folders method of organization used by computers, you can also create *subfolders* within each folder. Consequently, you might create a memos folder that contains a subfolder with memos sent to friends and a second subfolder with memos sent to potential employers. A folder can contain a mixture of subfolders and documents.

Fields, Records, Files, and Databases Another common procedure—which is most widely used with data but can apply to programs, as well—is to organize data into fields, records, files, and databases.

A **field** is a collection of characters (such as single digits, letters of the alphabet, or special symbols like a decimal point) that represents a single type of data. Two examples are a person's name and the price of a product. A **record** is a collection of related fields—say, the ID number, address, and phone number of John Q. Jones. A **file** is a collection of related records, and a **database** is a set of related files.

Your school, for example, probably has a *file,* stored on disk, of all students currently enrolled. The file contains a *record* for each student. Each record has several *fields* containing various types of data about a particular student: ID number, name, street, city and state of residence, major subject area, and the like. What's more, it probably even has a *database* that consists of several files—say, a student address file (such as the one in Figure INT 1-7), a student grade file (containing courses completed and grades earned by each student), and possibly other student-oriented files. Put another way, most of the information about students would be found in such a student database.

Entities such as documents, folders, fields, records, files, and databases usually have names or other unique ways of being identified. Both you and the computer system use such identifiers to find the entity when you wish to access, modify, or delete it.

Be aware that many of the terms you've learned about here can be used interchangeably or used in different contexts. For instance, a "word processed file" and a "word processed document" generally refer to the same thing—an output that a user creates with a word processing program and provides a name. Also, the term "file," traditionally used to mean "group of records," is commonly extended to programs. Thus, the term "program file" is in common usage and used interchangeably with "program." As you learn more about computers, you'll get to see that it's not unusual for several terms to mean the same thing or for one term to mean several things.

USERS AND THE EXPERTS

In the early days of computing, a clear distinction separated the people who made computers work from those who used the results that computers produced. This distinction remains, but as computers become more available and easier to use, it is breaking down.

Users, or *end users,* are the people who need output from computer systems. They include the accountant who needs a report on a client's taxes, the secretary who needs a word processing program to create a letter, the engineer who needs to know whether a bridge design will be structurally sound, the shop-floor supervisor who needs to know whether workers have met the day's quotas, and the company president who needs a report on the firm's profitability over the last ten years. Even people playing computer games or surfing the Internet are users.

■ **Document.** Any single piece of work that's created with software and, then, given a name by which it may be accessed. ■ **Folder.** A container for documents. ■ **Field.** A collection of related characters. ■ **Record.** A collection of related fields. ■ **File.** A collection of related records. ■ **Database.** A collection of related files. ■ **User.** A person who needs the results that a computer produces.

Programmers, on the other hand, are people who write the programs that produce such outputs. Creating computer programs is the primary job responsibility for people who are hired as programmers. Although some users may do modest amounts of programming to customize the software on their desktop computers, the distinction between an ordinary user and a professional programmer is based on the work that the person has been hired to do.

Along with programmers, organizations employ many other types of computer professionals. For instance, they pay *systems analysts* to design large computer systems within their companies. *Computer operations personnel,* in contrast, are responsible for the day-to-day operations of large computer systems. Few users know the programmers and other specialists who create the programs they use, because most programs today are written at software companies. However, programmers and analysts have begun to reveal their presence in other ways, such as by implementing Easter eggs in program code (see the Inside the Industry box on page INT 22).

COMPUTER NETWORKS

Users often need to share hardware, software, and data. They meet this need by tying computer systems together into networks (see Figure INT 1-8). You will find *computer networks* in many sizes and types. For instance, a small office network might link together five or six desktop PCs so that workers can share an expensive printer and a common

FIGURE INT 1-8

Computer networks. Computer systems meet users' need to share hardware, software, and data—as well as to communicate with each other—by tying devices together into networks.

ABOUT COMPUTER NETWORKS
Networks allow workers in an organization to communicate with each other, share expensive devices like printers, and send and receive materials to and from the outside world.

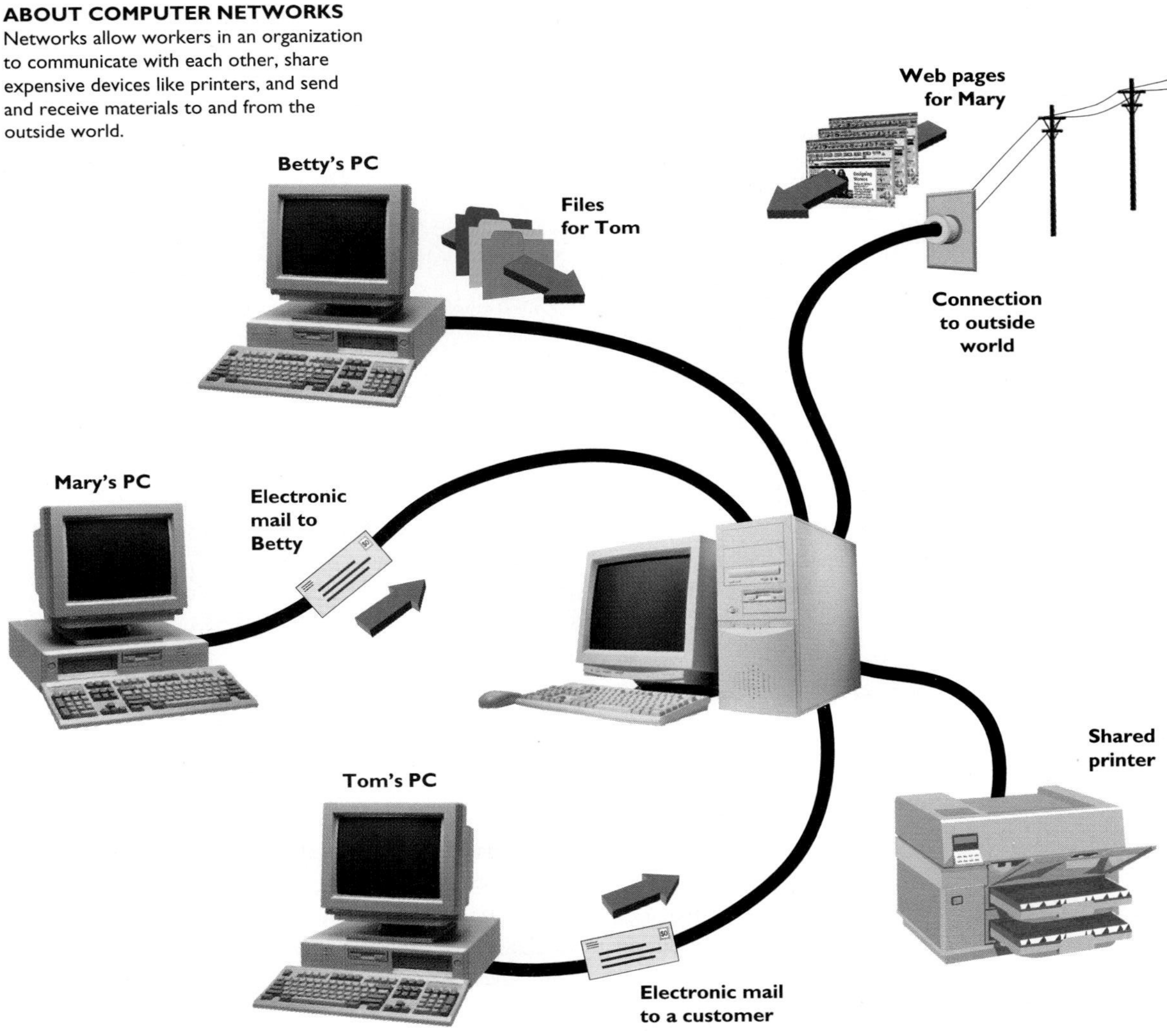

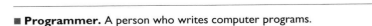

■ **Programmer.** A person who writes computer programs.

TOMORROW

Selling Tomorrow's Software

The Days of the Shrink-Wrapped Package Appear Numbered

Only a few years ago, virtually all software was sold in shrink-wrapped boxes. After stripping off the cellophane, you typically found inside the box one or more program disks, a printed reference manual, a printed or disk-based tutorial to help you get started, and a license to use the software forever. Piece by piece, that picture is starting to change, leading many people to wonder whether shrink-wrapped packages and anything like the familiar software-licensing agreements will survive into the twenty-first century.

A few short years ago, the revolution in CD-ROMs brought a major shift in software packaging. Not only did a single CD-ROM replace the 20 or 30 diskettes needed to install large software packages like Microsoft Office and CorelDRAW!, but also the vast storage space available on the CD-ROM allowed those disks to squeeze on reference manuals and tutorials. Electronic documentation is much cheaper to produce than the printed variety, so the printed manuals slowly began to disappear, and the remaining ones became much shorter. While electronic manuals do have certain advantages—such as allowing you to search quickly by keywords for topics—many critics still criticize them as poor substitutes for the hard-copy books they replaced.

The popularity of the Internet has marked another major shift in software distribution. Software publishers no longer have to mail out CD-ROMs; instead, buyers can connect their computers by phone lines to a publisher's Internet site and download needed software to their hard disks. This method of distribution brings several advantages. Users can try out software before buying it, and they can receive more frequent updates over the phone lines at their convenience. Three other advantages: (1) Publishers save money distributing software online, (2) users can get software updates about six months earlier than through disks and hard-copy manuals, which must first be manufactured and then distributed, and (3) patches and other small files that supplement the original program can be easily distributed. Many publishers still offer to send the original software-installation disk to you through the mail.

In addition to these changes in distribution, new methods of selling software are gaining popularity. For one, you can rent software online. With this method, you call up a company that has a product you want to use, and, as soon as you are connected, software is downloaded over the phone lines onto your hard disk. You can immediately begin working with it, paying for your usage by the hour or by some sort of flat per-use fee. In another variant, software metering, you pay for a certain number of hours to use the software; a built-in meter within the software disables it when your time expires. To prevent people from copying software without authorization, an embedded module may render it unusable if the communications link is broken.

The venerable software package. Not likely to disappear overnight.

Software by subscription is also spreading. In this system, you pay to use the software over a certain period of time—such as a year—just as you might pay to subscribe to a magazine over the same stretch. Status as a subscriber normally entitles you without any additional charge to any software updates and to online technical assistance. If you subscribe to a program such as a computer game, you may be able to buy it by the level at which you want to play, say $59 for advanced play and $49 for intermediate play. If you want to move from intermediate to advanced later on, you might pay an additional marginal fee of $15.

While several industry experts predict that most software will be sold online in the future, many of them hurry to point out that the shrink-wrapped package and CD are not likely to disappear soon. Far too many people are still locked into the traditional method of buying; they like to pick up boxes in a store and read them before making purchases. What's more, if the computer "crashes" for any reason and programs have to be reloaded onto the hard disk, it's comforting to know that you have CDs available with the exact versions of the programs you need.

bank of files on a very-high-capacity disk drive, both of which are also hooked up to the network. Far distant from such tiny networks on the size continuum is the *Internet*—a network that ties together thousands of other networks throughout the world. Millions of computers of all sizes, millions of people from all walks of life, and thousands of organizations worldwide are connected to the Internet.

Accessing Networks To access a computer network, you need at least two kinds of resources: a piece of hardware known as a *network adapter* and software that lets you connect to and use the facilities of the network. If you require the use of a network such as the Internet, you will also need an *access provider*—an organization that will enable you to access to the network as a user.

The most common type of adapter is a device called a *modem*. Through a modem, you can connect a computer system to virtually any public network—such as the Internet—that sends data over the phone lines.

The modem package usually includes the communications software you will need to connect to a network. If it doesn't, you can also acquire this software separately. To use network resources, you will also need other types of software from your access provider. Often, access providers supply most if not all of their customers' networking programs beyond the basic software that comes with a modem.

Most users gain access to networks like the Internet through their schools' or employers' computer systems or through other access providers. Providers commonly let users access, or *log on* to, the Internet via their systems after inputting secret identification numbers (IDs) and passwords.

Once you have an ID and a password and you set up your computer system to use a network, connecting is very simple. You might first use your keyboard or mouse to select the access provider's screen icon. At that point, the modem usually automatically dials a local access number for you. Next, a screen appears on your display asking you to enter your ID and password. After you give the right input, you're on the network. From there, you can select whatever type of application you want to run, just as you would with a regular software package.

Online and Offline Computer users often hear the terms *online* and *offline* with reference to computer networks and in various other contexts. Any computer in a condition that allows it to send data to or receive data from a computer network or other device is said to be **online** to the network or device. If a device isn't online, it's **offline.**

For instance, one large retail chain keeps member stores throughout North America online to the central computer system at all times during business hours so that headquarters-office managers can tightly control store prices. By keeping the stores online, the parent company also gains immediate access to the most recent sales information possible. Other companies may leave stores offline to headquarters computers most of the time, connecting to them only as needed to transmit and receive data.

Online and *offline* arise in a multitude of situations. For instance, when your printer is ready to receive signals from your computer system, it is online. Because computers have become so common in recent years, computer terms such as *online* and *offline* are slowly making their way into the public's vocabulary, as hinted in Feature INT 1-1 on page INT 26.

Computer Systems to Fit Every Need and Pocketbook

The computer market offers a great variety of systems to serve computer users' needs. This section will consider one important way in which computers differ from one another—size.

Computer systems are generally classified in one of four size categories: small, or microcomputers; medium-sized, or midrange computers; large, or mainframe computers; and superlarge, or supercomputers. In practice, the distinction among different sizes is not always clear-cut. Large midrange computers, for example, often are bigger than small mainframes.

■ **Online.** A state that allows a device to send data to or receive data from other devices. ■ **Offline.** A state that *does not* allow a device to send data to or receive data from other devices.

In general, larger computers have greater processing power. For example, big computers can usually process data faster than small computers. Big computers can also accommodate larger and more powerful peripheral devices. Naturally, larger computers and peripheral equipment also have higher prices. A computer system can cost anywhere from a few hundred dollars to several million.

MICROCOMPUTERS

A technological breakthrough in the early 1970s allowed circuitry for an entire CPU to fit on a single silicon chip smaller than a dime. These computers-on-a-chip, or *microprocessors,* could be mass produced at very low cost. Microprocessors were quickly integrated into all types of products, leading to powerful handheld calculators, digital watches, electronic toys, and sophisticated controls for household appliances such as microwave ovens and automatic coffeemakers.

Microprocessors also created the possibility of building inexpensive computer systems, such as those pictured in Figure INT 1-9, small enough to fit on a desktop or even in a shirt pocket. These small computer systems have informally come to be called **microcomputer systems** (or *microcomputers* or simply *micros*). Because they are inexpensive and small enough for one person to use at home or work for personal needs, they are also commonly called **personal computers (PCs).**

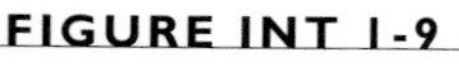

FIGURE INT 1-9

Microcomputers. (from left to right) Microcomputer with desktop-style system unit. Microcomputer with a tower-style system unit. Notebook computer. Palmtop computer.

Sizes of Microcomputer Systems As illustrated in Figure INT 1-9 and explained below, most microcomputer systems currently available to individuals for business and home use can be classified as desktop or portable units.

DESKTOP UNITS *Desktop computers* are most commonly found in schools, homes, and businesses. The names of these computer systems have become household words—IBM Aptiva, Apple Macintosh, Compaq DeskPro, and so on.

Desktop computers come in two models or styles. In the *desktop model* the system-unit case is designed specifically to rest on a desk. In the *tower model* the system-unit case stands upright on either a desktop or floor. Tower model cases have more room in which to mount secondary storage units, and they leave more work space on the

---

■ **Microcomputer system.** A computer system driven by a microprocessor chip. Also known as a **microcomputer**, or *micro.*
■ **Personal computer (PC).** A microcomputer system designed to be used by one person at a time. Also known as a *personal computer system.*

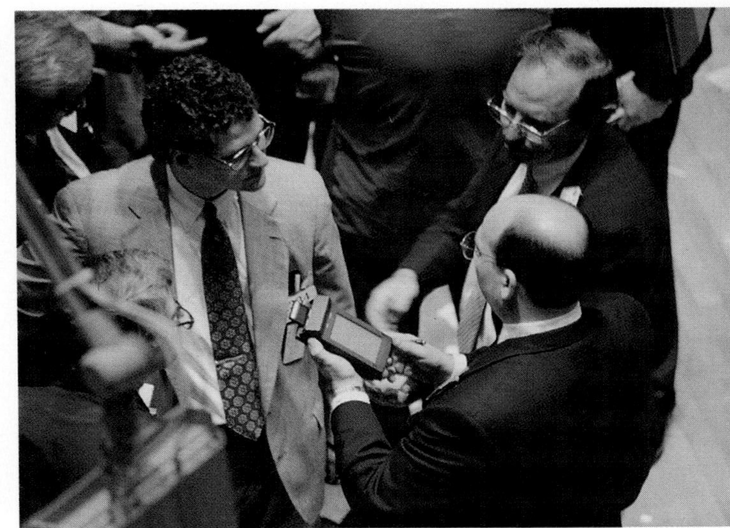

desktop. Because the cases often sit at a distance further from users, however, tower models may not provide as convenient a way to mount and dismount disks from drives.

PORTABLE UNITS *Portable PCs* come in a variety of sizes, including (from largest to smallest) laptop, notebook, subnotebook, and palmtop.

Laptop computers, commonly weighing anywhere from 8 to 15 pounds, were designed for users who needed access to their microcomputers at remote sites. Today, most people prefer to carry lighter *notebook computers* (6 to 8 pounds) or *subnotebook computers* (2 to 6 pounds). The lighter units also bring smaller physical dimensions, allowing them to fit conveniently into users' briefcases. Although many notebooks and subnotebooks provide just about the same power as their desktop cousins, they tend to cost more, have smaller screens, and have denser keyboard arrangements. Such disadvantages notwithstanding, sales of notebooks and subnotebooks are currently among the fastest-growing segments of the microcomputer industry.

Palmtop (or *handheld*) *computers* look and work a lot like standard pocket calculators. Most palmtop computers perform relatively narrow, specialized tasks—keeping track of golf or bowling scores, translating words into foreign languages, checking word spellings, and scanning or recognizing bar codes on packages. Palmtop devices called *personal digital assistants,* or *PDAs,* are specifically geared to help users carry out such office-oriented tasks as manipulating numbers, filling in forms, messaging, and other communications functions.

PC Compatible or Macintosh? Most users choose between two major computer **platforms** when they buy desktop, laptop, notebook, or subnotebook computers—

■ **Platform.** A foundation technology by which a computer system operates.

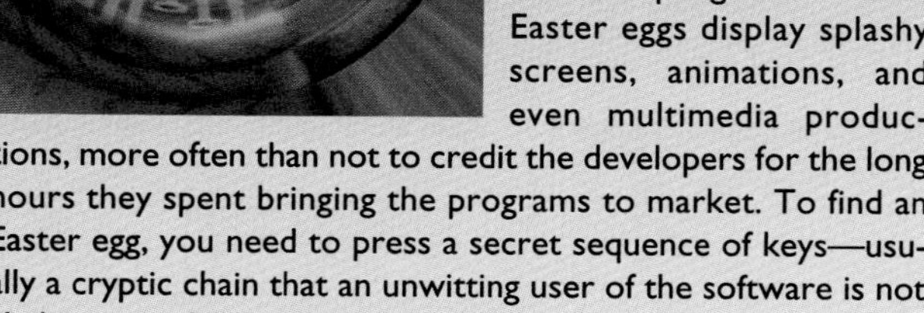

Easter Eggs

Programmers who develop some of the world's most popular software have increasingly placed their stamps on those products by implanting "Easter eggs" in the programs' code. Easter eggs display splashy screens, animations, and even multimedia productions, more often than not to credit the developers for the long hours they spent bringing the programs to market. To find an Easter egg, you need to press a secret sequence of keys—usually a cryptic chain that an unwitting user of the software is not likely to stumble upon when using the program.

One well-known Easter egg is contained in Microsoft's Excel spreadsheet program (Version 7 for Windows 95). To find it, you need to complete the following sequence:

1. Start Excel and begin a fresh worksheet.
2. Select the entire 95th row of the worksheet—say, by clicking the mouse button on the 95. When the row is highlighted, use the Tab key to move to Column B.
3. Select Help on the menu bar at the top of the screen, and then select About Microsoft Excel.
4. When the dialog box appears, click the mouse on the Tech Support button while holding down the Ctrl and Shift keys.

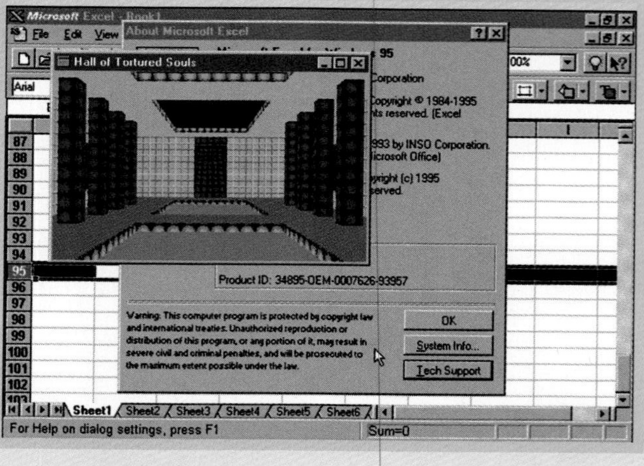

Excel Easter egg. Who said programmers have no fun?.

Excel will respond by displaying a window titled the Hall of Tortured Souls on your display (see accompanying screen). You can move around this dark and dreary world with the arrow keys. By moving forward and going up the glittering staircase, for instance—just keep pressing the up-arrow key—you can watch the names of people on the Excel development team scroll by. If you press the right-arrow or left-arrow keys as the names are scrolling, you can turn around the room. If you go to the blank wall at the far end of the room and type EXCELKFA, you will see a hidden passageway that you can explore further.

Project 8 on page INT 31 tells how to use the Internet to find other Easter Eggs.

PC compatibles and Macintosh compatibles. The drift toward the two major standards started over a decade ago, when the IBM PC and the original Apple Macintosh were the two front-running microcomputer systems.

Most vendors followed IBM's lead, building their systems around Intel microprocessor chips and (later) catering to Microsoft Windows applications. Such computer systems are known as **PC compatibles.** Close to 90 percent of computers made today are PC-compatible devices. Among the largest vendors of these machines are Compaq, IBM, Packard Bell, Dell, Hewlett-Packard, and Gateway.

Computers that instead follow Apple's design platform are known as *Macintosh compatibles.* Macintosh compatibles, because of their reputation for advanced graphics capabilities, are often the platform of choice for artists and designers. While PC-compatible computers have been around for over a decade, Macintosh-compatible computers are a comparatively recent development. The Macintosh line is still made by Apple; Macintosh-compatible vendors include Motorola, Umax, and Power Computing.

Network Computers Beginning in 1997, many computer manufacturers began producing *network computers (NCs).* These devices are essentially diskless desktop microcomputers with features optimized for use on the Internet and intracompany networks (see Figure INT 1-10). Many NCs sell for under $1,000. Companies consider

■ **PC compatible.** A personal computer based on Intel microprocessors or compatible chips.

LIV Module
Computers in Our Lives

Chapter IS 2
Applications Software Development IS 35

IS Module
Information Systems

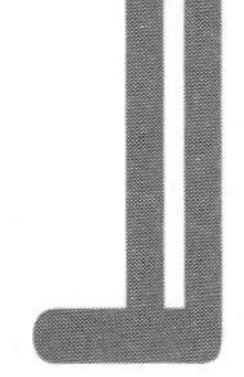

boxes

PS Module
Productivity Software

boxes

boxes

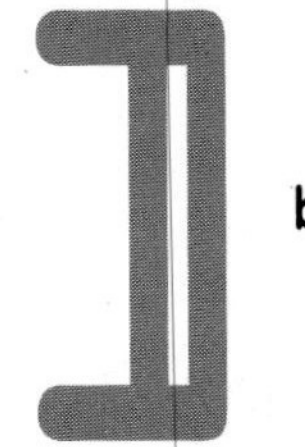

boxes

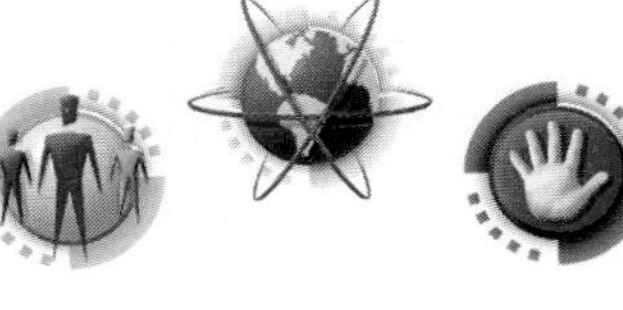

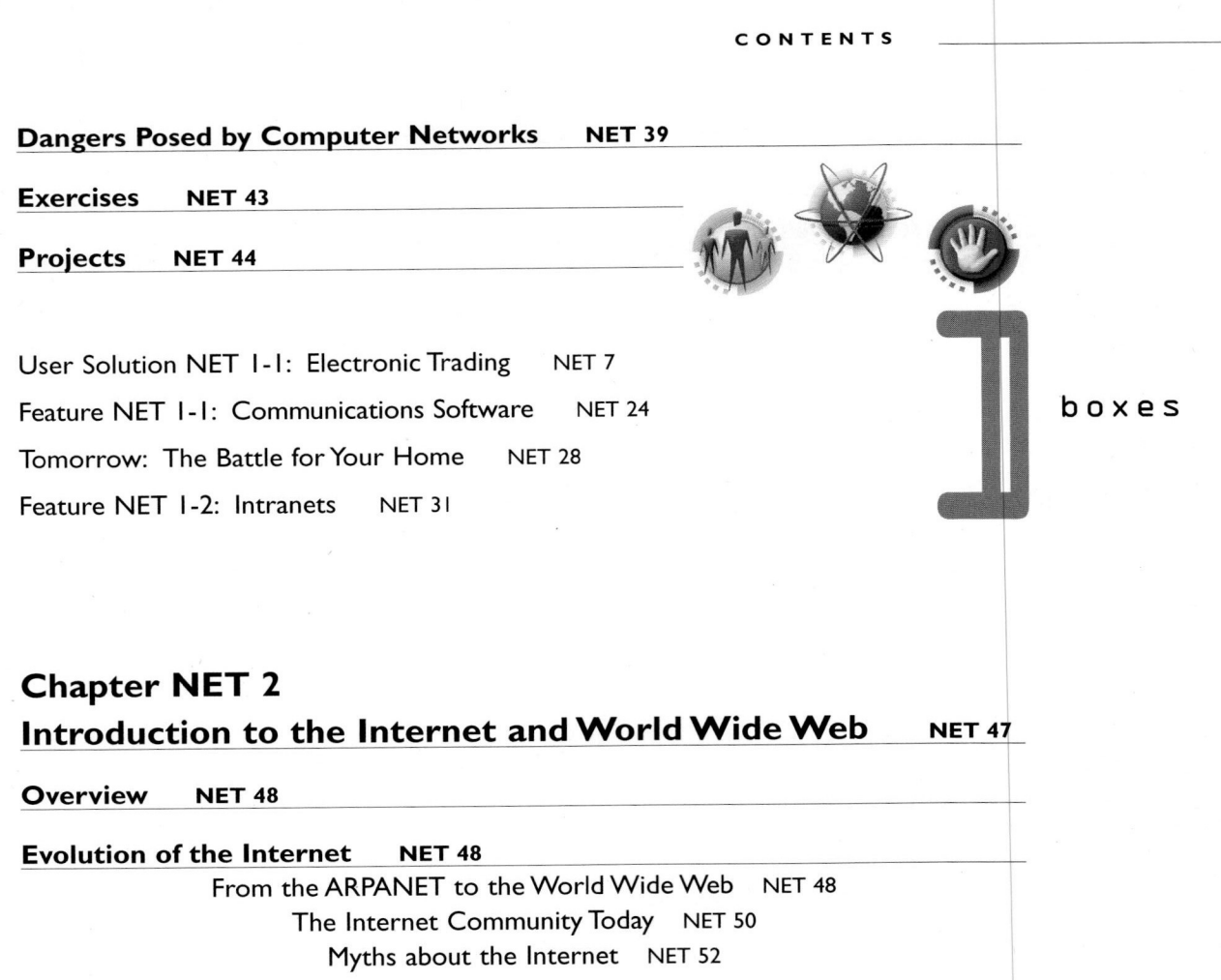

boxes

NET Module
Computer Networks

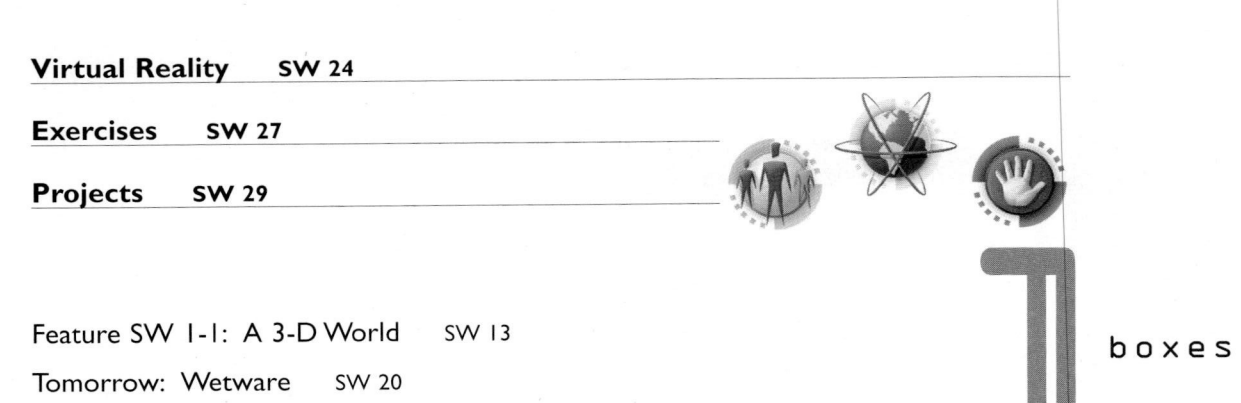

SW Module Software

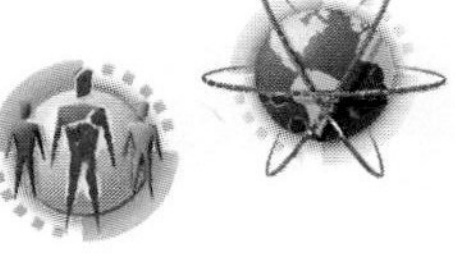

boxes

Chapter HW 2

INT Module Introduction

boxes

HW Module Hardware

Note: This table of contents shows entries for all 16 chapters of the text. You may have a customized version of the text that does not contain all of the chapters indicated.

Virtual Presence

A TV broadcasting company wants a famous newscaster to speak in a setting that catches the attention of viewers during a big event, but the event is only weeks away. The carpentry to construct the set would cost an outrageous amount, and the structure would never fit in the building. What to do? Build a 3-D virtual-reality set through computer images, and cut-and-paste a commentator inside it so that viewers think they see a person in a real setting. The technique is called *virtual presence.* CBS News developed one of its earliest uses outside the movie industry during the 1996 presidential elections (see image). Many industry observers predict that virtual presence will someday be widespread, and the newscaster who looks like he or she is reporting from a war-torn front will instead reach you from the cozy confines of New York's Rockefeller Plaza.

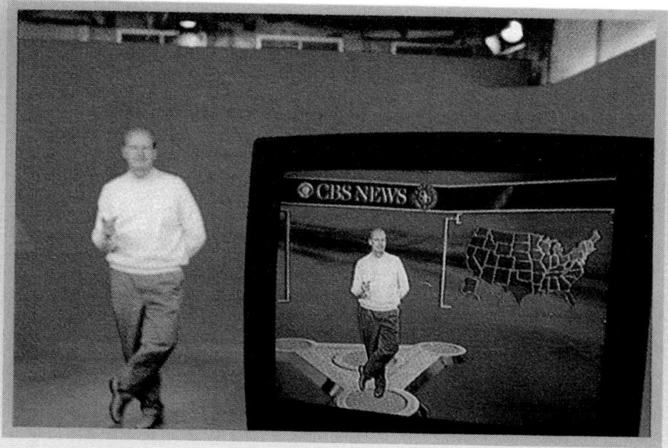

programs that supervise the computer system's work. Without the operating system, none of the other programs on your computer system can run.

When you buy software in a store or through the mail, you often receive it in some sort of a physical package (see Figure INT 1-6). Such a *software package* may consist of program disks, printed operating instructions and user manuals, instructional and help materials on disk, and a printed license to use the software, all or some of which are inside a shrink-wrapped box or plastic case. The programs on the disks have been written in some programming language. As a general rule, you will not have to learn a language to use the package. Increasingly, software is being sold and distributed over the Internet, and someday in the very near future, people may only rarely buy software in boxed packages (see the Tomorrow box on page INT 1-18).

FIGURE INT 1-6

Software package. A typical software package consists of one or more program disks, a printed user's guide, and a printed user's license inside a shrink-wrapped box.

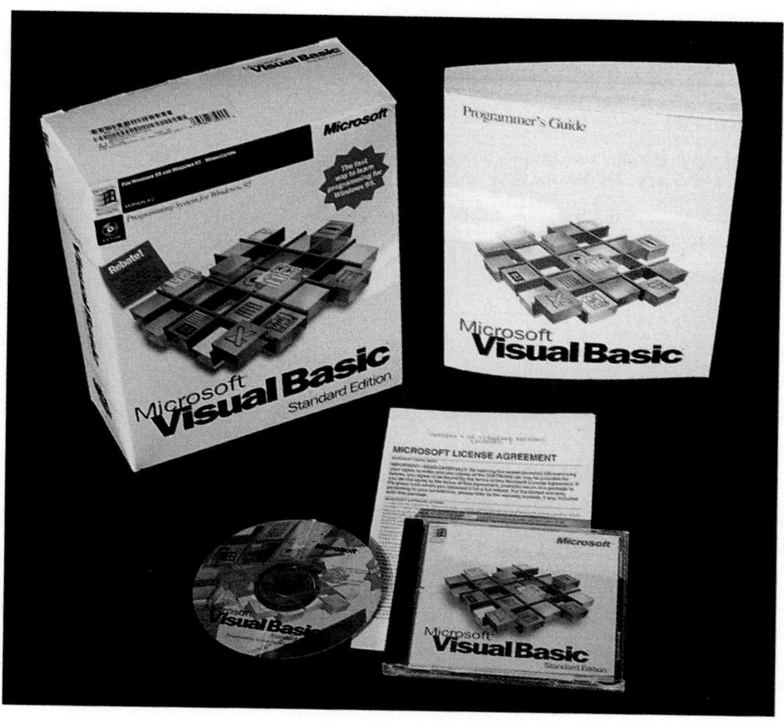

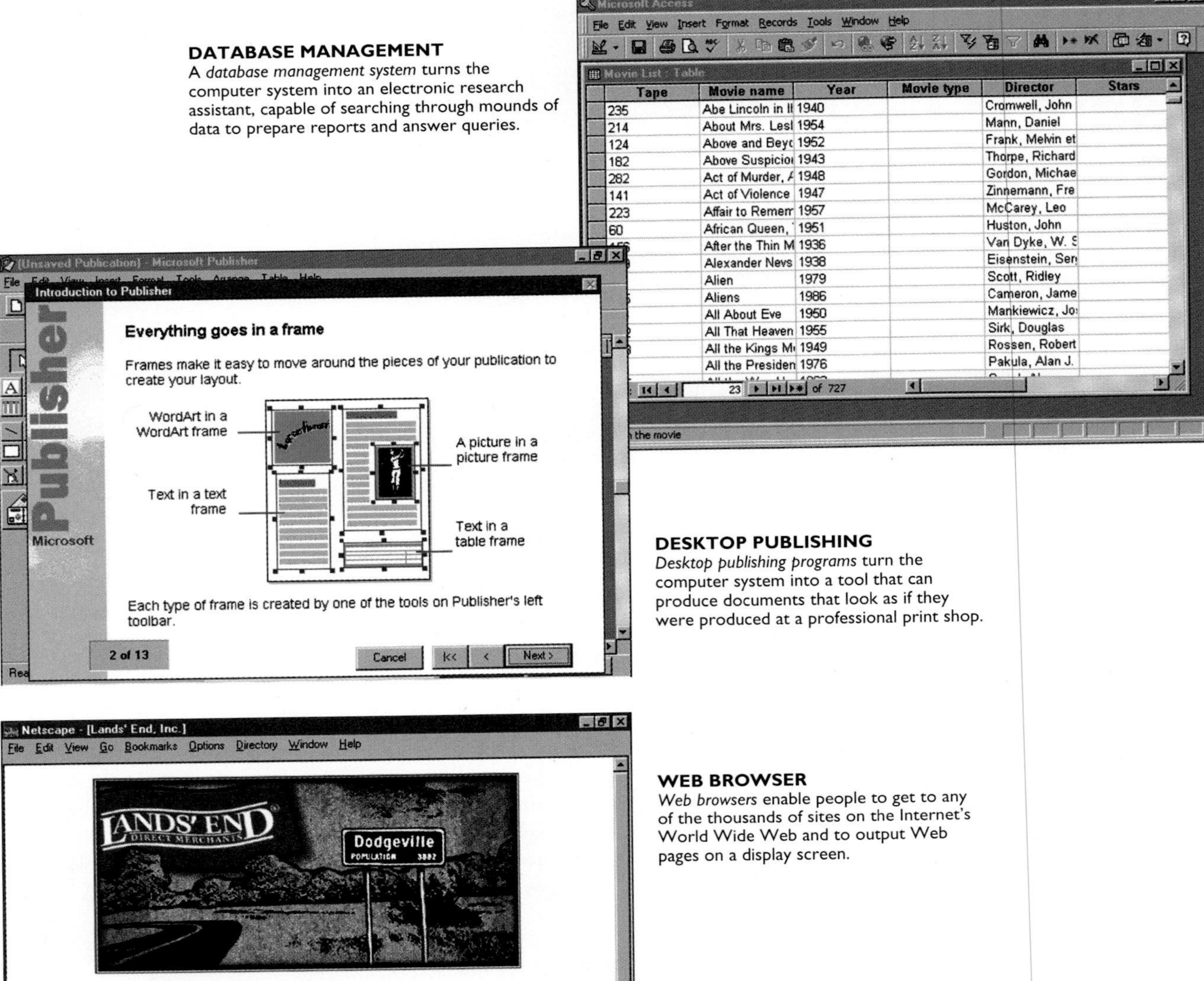

DATABASE MANAGEMENT
A *database management system* turns the computer system into an electronic research assistant, capable of searching through mounds of data to prepare reports and answer queries.

DESKTOP PUBLISHING
Desktop publishing programs turn the computer system into a tool that can produce documents that look as if they were produced at a professional print shop.

WEB BROWSER
Web browsers enable people to get to any of the thousands of sites on the Internet's World Wide Web and to output Web pages on a display screen.

analyzing budgets, managing files and databases, playing games, scheduling airline flights, and diagnosing hospital patients' illnesses. In other words, applications software makes possible the types of work that most people have in mind when they acquire computer systems. **Productivity software** is the class of applications software designed to make workers more productive at their jobs. Some important types of productivity software are described in Figure INT 1-5.

Systems software consists of programs operating in the background that enable applications software to run on a computer system's hardware devices. One of the most important pieces of systems software is the *operating system,* a set of control

■ **Productivity software.** Computer programs, such as word processors and spreadsheets, designed to make workers more productive in their jobs. ■ **Systems software.** Background programs, such as the operating system, that enable application programs to run on a computer system's hardware.

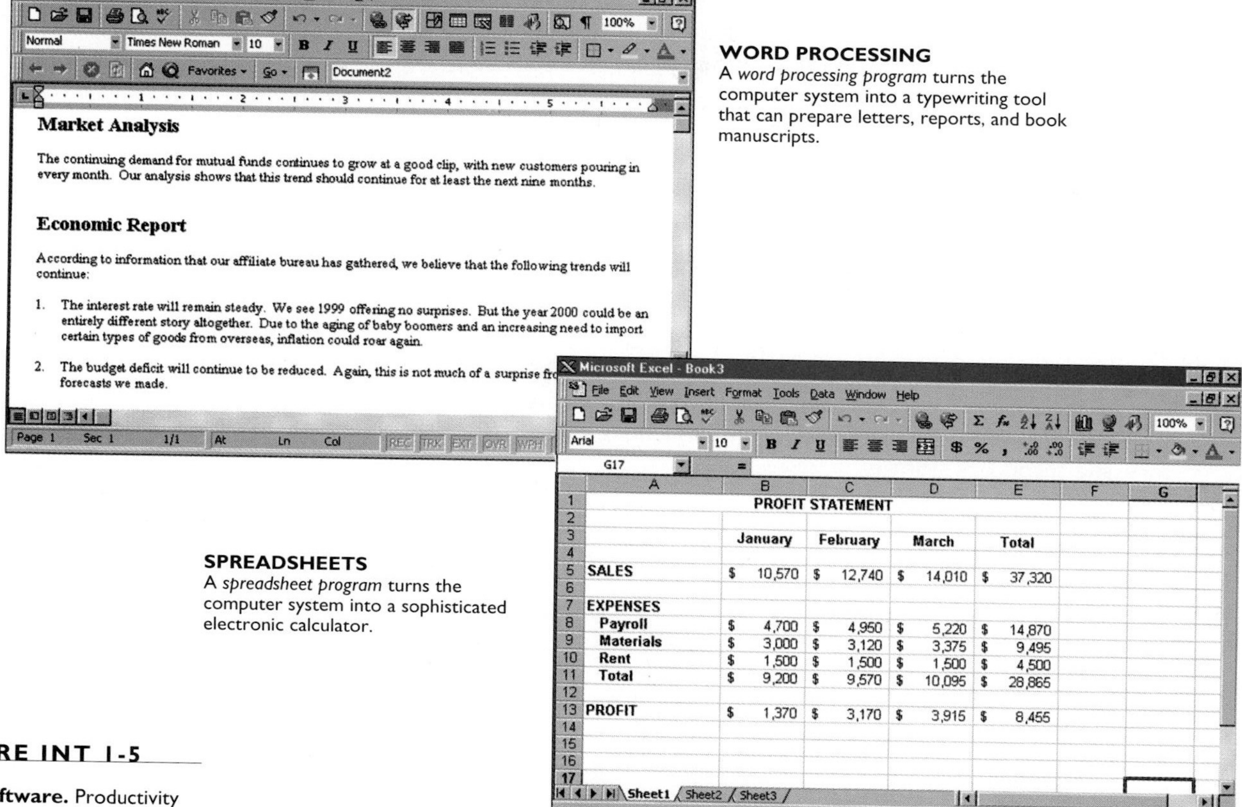

WORD PROCESSING
A *word processing program* turns the computer system into a typewriting tool that can prepare letters, reports, and book manuscripts.

SPREADSHEETS
A *spreadsheet program* turns the computer system into a sophisticated electronic calculator.

FIGURE INT 1-5

Productivity software. Productivity software is designed to help both ordinary users and computer professionals work more productively at their jobs.

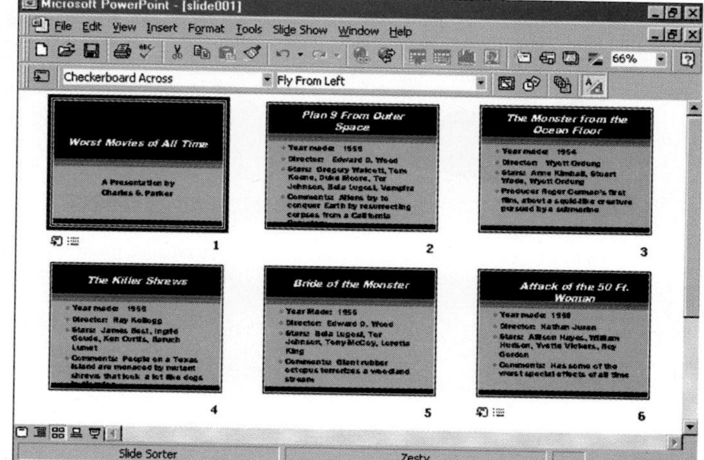

PRESENTATION GRAPHICS
Presentation graphics programs turn the computer system into a tool that can be used to prepare slides, overheads, and other presentation materials for meetings.

Software The word **software** refers to computer programs. As already mentioned, programs direct the computer system to do specific tasks, just as your thoughts direct your body to speak or move in certain ways. Computers use two basic varieties of software: applications software and systems software.

Applications software is designed to perform tasks such as computing bank-account interest, preparing bills, creating letters and book manuscripts, preparing and

■ **Software.** Computer programs. ■ **Applications software.** Programs that help with the type of work that people acquire computer systems to do.

The computer system stores data and programs that people need from session to session in **secondary (external) storage.** In large computer systems, equipment separate from the system unit provides secondary storage. Smaller computer systems usually provide secondary storage through equipment that is factory installed inside the system units. In either case, these pieces of equipment—usually disk and tape drives—are called *secondary storage devices.* They enable users to conveniently save large quantities of data and programs in machine-readable form, avoiding the need to rekey them into the system or reinstall them every time they're needed. Secondary storage devices can often store thousands of programs and billions of pieces of data.

When the CPU needs a certain program or set of data, it requests that input from a secondary storage device—much as you might request a particular song from a jukebox. It then reads the needed input into its memory for processing. Unlike the jukebox turntable, which puts the original record in play, the CPU puts only a copy of the original program or data into memory for use. The original version remains on the secondary-storage medium—usually disk—until you change it.

Figure INT 1-4 illustrates the relationships among input, processing, output, memory, and secondary storage.

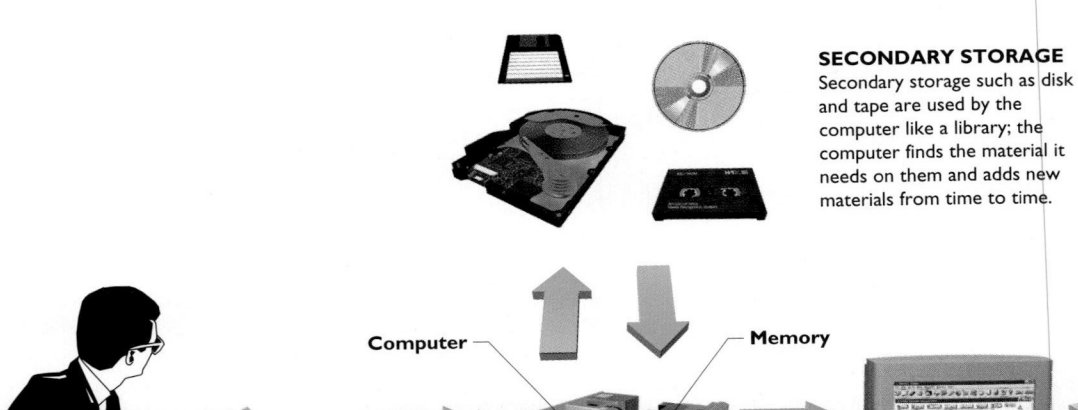

SECONDARY STORAGE
Secondary storage such as disk and tape are used by the computer like a library; the computer finds the material it needs on them and adds new materials from time to time.

INPUT
The user deploys a mouse and a keyboard to enter inputs to the computer.

PROCESSING
Every time the user inputs something, the computer must respond. For instance, when a program from secondary storage is requested, the computer must find it and load it into memory. Similarly, when a document is to be saved or output, the computer must transfer it from memory to secondary storage or to an output device.

OUTPUT
Output devices such as a monitor and a printer present computer results to the user.

FIGURE INT 1-4

Input, processing, output, and storage. These tasks require an interactive dialog between the user and computer.

HARDWARE AND SOFTWARE

In the world of computers, a distinction is made between hardware and software.

Hardware The word **hardware** refers to the actual machinery that makes up a computer system—for example, the CPU, input and output devices, and storage devices. A good portion of this chapter has already focused on the hardware parts of a computer system, many of which were featured in Figure INT 1-2, so this section won't dwell on them.

- **Secondary storage.** Storage on media such as disk and tape that supplements memory. Also called **external storage.**
- **Hardware.** Physical equipment in a computing environment, such as the computer and its peripheral devices.

buying such systems because they offer lower purchase and support costs as well as better control over employee computing activities. Since all software and data are stored on computer systems managing the network, central controls can prevent users from storing materials on their own that will wind up corrupting the main system. For home use, consumer-oriented NCs are targeted to television watchers with very little computer knowledge. These devices allow users to unleash the power of the Internet in their living rooms with the simple flick of a remote-control key.

FIGURE INT 1-10

Network computer. Network computers (NCs) are diskless microcomputers with features that optimize them for use on the Internet and intracompany networks.

Uses for Microcomputers Microcomputers are widely used in both small and large businesses. A small business might use its microcomputers for all of its computing tasks, including tracking merchandise, preparing correspondence, billing customers, and completing routine accounting chores. A large business might use microcomputers as productivity tools for secretaries and as analysis tools for decision makers, to name just two important applications. Also, portable computers are popular with salespeople who need to make presentations at client sites and with managers who need computing resources as they travel.

Microcomputers often connect to large communications systems to function as general-purpose workstations and *network servers*—computers that manage the storage devices that hold common banks of programs and data. Most microcomputers that function as network servers are based on the tower design, and they provide much more powerful capabilities than the "minitower" and desktop models that individuals buy for their own needs. Today, microcomputer networks—that is, computer networks in which microcomputer workstations and servers are prominent components—represent one of the hottest areas within the computer field.

MIDRANGE COMPUTERS

Midrange computers—sometimes called *minicomputers* or *minis*—are medium-sized computers (see Figure INT 1-11). Most of them fall between microcomputers and mainframes in processing power, although the very smallest midrange computers are virtually indistinguishable from the most powerful microcomputers, and the largest closely resemble small mainframes. Midrange computers usually cost far more than microcomputers, more than most individuals can afford.

Any of several factors might lead an organization to choose a midrange system over a micro or mainframe. A small or medium-sized company may simply find a microcomputer system too slow to handle its processing volume. Often, midrange buyers need computer systems that can interact with multiple users—perhaps hundreds—at the same time. Many microcomputer systems lack sufficient power to handle such complex applications. Mainframes, discussed in the next section of this chapter, can handle these applications with ease, but they are much larger and generally much more expensive than midrange computers.

■ **Midrange computer.** An intermediate-sized and medium-priced computer.

FIGURE INT 1-11

Midrange computers. Midrange computers are particularly useful where several people need to share a common system, such as in a small company or a department within a larger company.

MAINFRAMES

The **mainframe computer** (see Figure INT 1-12) is a standard choice for almost any large organization. It often operates 24 hours a day, serving thousands of users interacting through display devices during regular business hours and processing large jobs such as payroll and billing late at night. Many large organizations need several mainframes to complete their computing workloads. Typically these organizations own or lease a variety of computer types—mainframes, midrange computers, and micros—which collectively meet all of their processing needs. Increasingly, these organizations are linking together various sizes of computers into networks.

Most mainframes are assigned to handle high-volume processing of business transactions and routine paperwork. For a typical business, this workload includes tasks such as tracking customer purchases and payments, sending out bills and reminder notices, and paying employees. These operations were some of the earliest applications of computers in business and have been the responsibility of mainframes since the 1950s.

SUPERCOMPUTERS

Some organizations, such as large scientific and research laboratories, have extraordinary information processing needs. Applications such as sending astronauts into space, testing safety and aerodynamic features on cars and aircraft, and weather forecasting, for example, require extreme accuracy and extensive computations. To meet such needs, a few vendors offer very large, sophisticated machines called **supercomputers** (see Figure INT 1-13).

Supercomputers can cost several million dollars each. During the last few years, innovators have tried to build less-expensive supercomputers by linking together hundreds or thousands of microprocessor chips. The resulting class of supercomputers is often referred to as *massively parallel processors (MPPs)*.

■ **Mainframe computer.** A large computer that performs extensive business transaction processing. ■ **Supercomputer.** The fastest and most expensive type of computer.

FIGURE INT 1-12

IBS ES/9000 mainframe. The ES/9000 series sets the performance standard for today's mainframes. IBM makes close to 75 percent of all mainframes sold.

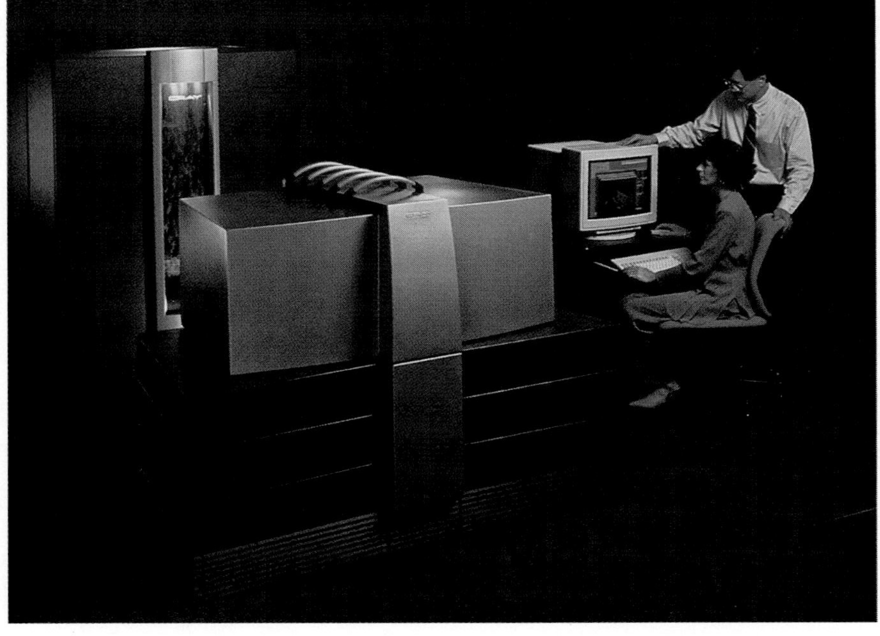

FIGURE INT 1-13

Cray supercomputer. Supercomputers process data much faster than conventional computers do. Cray produces most of the supercomputers sold worldwide.

A Technobabble Miniglossary

A Combat Guide to Talking Technology

Many years ago, computer jargon was spoken with confidence only at staff meetings of technical specialists. Now, however, computers have suddenly entered the mainstream, and everyone seems to want to belong to their growing subculture. One key to membership is *technobabble*—a dialect for digital conversations that are sometimes called *computerspeak*. Roughly explained, technobabble splices computer and networking terminology into everyday speech.

If you mingle with computer-savvy people, technobabble can save time and get your message across. If you're talking to an easily impressed person, technobabble might score you monster points toward an image as cerebral. But if you're at work and trying to gain the attention of busy people who can't differentiate computer terminology from Greek, spewing technobabble can easily get you branded as a computer snob and, possibly, someone who is unable to state a point in plain English.

With those warnings posted clearly, here's a smattering of technobabble terms to use or avoid at your pleasure:

Bandwidth Brain power. *Sample technobabble:* "She's a high-bandwidth woman."

Betazoid A person who lives to test prereleases, termed *beta copies,* of software. *Sample technobabble:* "The betazoids will be wild with delight when they see this new screen menu."

Big Iron Mainframe computer. *Sample technobabble:* "We replaced the big iron in the basement with a client-server network."

E To send someone electronic mail, or e-mail. *Sample technobabble:* "E me on that, would you?"

Flame Mail Electronic mail that is critical or abusive. *Sample technobabble:* "I got some flame mail from my supervisor this morning about my handling of that situation."

Granularity Fineness of detail. *Sample technobabble:* "I like your proposal, but it lacks granularity."

Internaut A user of the Internet. *Sample technobabble:* "Meet Joe and Jane; he's an Internaut and she's a betazoid."

Net Surfing Casually browsing a computer network to see what is there. *Sample technobabble:* "You won't believe what I found net surfing last night."

Newbie A new user to an online computer group. *Sample technobabble:*"Those know-nothing newbies are really slowing the system down today."

Technobabble 101. Don't leave home without your pocket computer dictionary.

Nonlinear Out of control. *Sample technobabble:* "My boss went nonlinear when I told her I was leaving the company."

Random Illogical or nutty. *Sample technobabble:* "His ideas on that subject are totally random."

Shovelware Extra, poorly integrated software or documentation that is hastily dumped by a software publisher onto a CD-ROM, to fill any space on the disk left over from the main application. *Sample technobabble:* "90 percent of this disk is pure shovelware."

Sneakernet A term used for transferring electronic information by manually carrying disks or tapes from one machine to another. *Sample technobabble:* "Not only does that company rely on snail mail (the Post Office), they're a sneakernet outfit, too."

Spammed Flooded with junk e-mail. *Sample technobabble:* "Don't go with that access provider unless you like getting spammed."

Speeds and Feeds The technical specifications of a product. *Sample technobabble:* "Give me the speeds and feeds of that new system, will ya?"

Taking It Offline Resolving an issue after a meeting. *Sample technobabble:* "I'll get back to you on that offline."

WADR In an online computer-chat session, a shorthand way of saying "with all due respect." *Sample technobabble:*"WADR and IMHO (in my humble opinion), I think you're not telling me the truth."

Zorch Raw power. *Sample technobabble:* "Does this machine have plenty of zorch, or what?"

Computers and Society

The ability of computers to sort through massive amounts of data and quickly produce useful information for almost any kind of user—from payroll clerk to president—makes them indispensable tools in our modern society. Without computers, businesses could never function at the level they do today. Banks would be overwhelmed by the job of tracking all the transactions they must process. Familiar airline and telephone services would be impossible. Moon exploration and the space shuttle would still belong to science fiction.

But along with these benefits, computers have brought some troubling problems to society ranging from health concerns to personal security and privacy to ethics. Workers often spend many hours in front of their display screens. Do the radiation and glare emanating from the screens impair health? Banks store data about customers' accounts on multiuser storage devices. Can they prevent clever criminals from using their own computer systems to tie into a banking network and steal from those accounts? The government maintains confidential information about every American taxpayer. Can it protect that information from unauthorized use? Because commercial software and a lot of data exist in electronic form, they can be easily copied or stolen. What restrictions should limit access to software and data?

These are serious issues, and this chapter can only cover them briefly. Subsequent parts of this book will explore further both the social benefits and problems created by computers.

Summary and Key Terms

Computers appear almost everywhere in today's world. They're embedded in consumer products, they help managers run businesses, and they direct production in factories, to name just a few applications.

Computers in the Workplace Computers abound in today's workplace largely because we are living in an era when most jobs heavily depend on the collection, use, creation, and dissemination of information.

What's a Computer and What Does It Do? Four words summarize the operation of a **computer system: input, processing, output,** and **storage.** The processing function is performed by the **computer** itself, which is sometimes called the **central processing unit,** or **CPU.**

The input and output functions are performed by **peripheral equipment,** such as **input devices** and **output devices.** Just as your stereo amplifier would play no music without speakers or headphones and turntable, tape deck, or CD player, the computer would be helpless without its peripheral devices.

Several of the peripheral equipment read from and write to **storage media.** Such media often store data and programs in **machine-readable form,** which the computer system can recognize and process.

A computer's input takes two forms: data and programs. **Data** are the raw, unorganized facts on which the computer carries out its processing; **programs** are sets of instructions that explain to the computer what to do with certain data. A program must be written in a **programming language** that the computer can understand. Data that the computer has processed into a useful form are called **information.**

Computer systems have two types of storage. **Primary storage** (sometimes called **memory** or **internal storage)** is usually built into the unit that houses the computer itself; memory holds the programs and data that the system is currently processing. **Secondary (external) storage** keeps programs and data indefinitely.

People who talk about computers commonly distinguish between hardware and software. **Hardware** refers to the actual machinery that makes up the computer system, such as the CPU, input and output devices, and secondary storage devices. **Software** refers to computer programs. Software comes in two basic forms: **applications software** and **systems software.** The class of applications software that helps people perform their jobs better is called **productivity software.**

One of the most fundamental ways that data and programs are organized is into **documents** and **folders.** Another common procedure is to organize into fields, records, files, and databases. A **field** is a collection of characters that represents a single type of data. A **record** is a collection of related fields. A **file** is a collection of related records. A **database** is a collection of related files.

Users are the people who need the output that computer systems produce. Within a computing environment, many types of experts help users to meet their computing needs; for example, **programmers** are responsible for writing computer programs.

To allow users to share hardware, software, and data, networks tie together computers and related devices. To access many computer networks, you need a piece of hardware known as a *network adapter,* appropriate software, and the services of an *access provider.* Any device in a condition that allows it to send data to or receive data from a computer network is said to be **online** to the network. If a device isn't online, it's **offline.**

Computer Systems to Fit Every Need and Pocketbook Small computers are often called **microcomputers (microcomputer systems)** or **personal computers (PCs,** *personal computer systems).* Most microcomputer systems today are either desktop or portable computers, and they fall within either the **PC-compatible** or *Macintosh-compatible* **platform.**

Medium-sized computers are called **midrange computers,** and large computers are called **mainframe computers.** The very largest computers, which run applications that demand the most speed and power, are called **supercomputers.**

While categories of computers based on size can provide helpful distinctions, in practice it is sometimes difficult to classify computers that fall on the borders of these categories.

Computers and Society Although computer systems have become indispensable tools for modern life, their growing use has created troubling problems, ranging from health concerns to personal security and privacy to ethics.

EXERCISES

1. Match each term with the description that fits best:
   a. Midrange computer
   b. Input device
   c. Mainframe
   d. Palmtop computer
   e. Supercomputer
   f. Hardware
   g. Microcomputer
   h. Network computer
   _____ The equipment that makes up a computer system
   _____ Another name for personal computer
   _____ A medium-sized computer
   _____ A large computer used to process business transactions in high volume
   _____ A diskless desktop computer
   _____ Any piece of equipment that supplies programs and data to a computer
   _____ The most powerful type of computer
   _____ The smallest type of computer
2. For the following list of computer hardware, write the *principal* function of each device in the space provided. Choices include input device, output device, storage device, and processing device.
   a. CPU __________
   b. Mouse __________
   c. Monitor __________
   d. CD-ROM drive __________
   e. Keyboard __________
   f. Diskette drive __________
   g. System unit __________
   h. Printer __________
   i. Subnotebook computer __________
3. Define the following terms:
   a. Hardware
   b. Peripheral equipment
   c. Online
   d. Secondary storage
   e. Systems software
4. What is the difference between data and information? Provide an example not discussed in the chapter.
5. Order the following list of computer systems by size from the least powerful to the most powerful.
   a. Notebook computer
   b. Mainframe computer
   c. MPP
   d. PDA
   e. Desktop computer
   f. Midrange computer
   g. Laptop computer
6. What is the difference between a file and a database? Provide an example of each.
7. How does memory differ from secondary storage? Name the secondary storage media covered in this chapter.
8. Match each term with the best description.
   a. Word processing program
   b. Operating system
   c. Presentation graphics package
   d. Spreadsheet program
   e. Database management system
   f. Web browser
   _____ Helps search through a large bank of facts, such as airline flight schedules
   _____ Supervises the running of all other programs on the computer
   _____ Helps prepare documents like letters and reports
   _____ Turns the computer into a sophisticated electronic calculator and analysis tool
   _____ Displays resources on the Internet
   _____ Helps prepare slides and graphs for meetings
9. Name the four types of data covered in the chapter and answer the following questions:
   a. How are these types of data related to the term *multimedia?*
   b. You type a letter to a friend and include with it a computerized picture of your dog. What types of data does the letter include?
10. Identify at least three social problems created by computer systems.
11. Fill in the blanks.
    a. Memory is sometimes called __________ storage, whereas tapes and disks are examples of __________ storage.
    b. Peripheral equipment fits in two categories: ________ devices, such as diskette and CD-ROM drives, and __________ devices, such as keyboards and printers.
    c. Another name for computer programs is ______.
    d. Programs are written using a programming __________.
    e. A desktop microcomputer without secondary storage is called a(n) __________ computer.
12. Each of the following definitions is not strictly true in some regard. In each definition, identify the flaw and correct it.
    a. Memory: Another name for computer storage
    b. Data: Information that has been processed into a meaningful form
    c. Computer: The CPU and all of the storage and input/output equipment that supports it
    d. Processing: The conversion of output to input
    e. Programmer: Anyone in an organization who writes computer programs

1. The Internet The Internet and World Wide Web are both handy tools that can help you to research topics covered in this textbook and to complete many of the projects. While a detailed explanation of the functions of the Internet and the Web is beyond the scope of this chapter—read Chapter NET 2 if you want to know more—it would be to your advantage to learn how to use these tools right from the outset. That's not a difficult task. It's just a matter of finding an Internet-enabled computer on your campus, logging on, typing in an address for a specific information site, and then choosing among onscreen selections.

a. Find a computer at your school that has access to the Internet, then follow the directions provided by your instructor or lab aide to log on to the Internet.
b. What is the name of the software package running on your computer that helps you browse through Internet information?
c. Access the home page of your school. What is the *Web address* of this page; that is, the string of characters that anyone at any location can type into a computer to locate your school? (Somewhere on the screen, a box should display a long string of characters that starts with *http://*; right after this set of characters—beginning with *www* and often ending with *edu*—is the address of your school's home page.)
d. What types of information did you find at your school's Web site? (To see information beyond the home page, select—with a mouse or keyboard—one of the highlighted pieces of text on the page. Each piece of highlighted text— distinguished by color, bold type, and underlining—is called a *hyperlink*. By selecting hyperlinks, you can move to other pages.
e. Access the home pages of at least two other schools. You can find them by accessing an Internet *search site* such as any of the four below (with Web addresses in parentheses). Such sites let you type in keywords to find information or, alternatively, let you use a comprehensive menu system.

   Yahoo! (http://www.yahoo.com)
   WebCrawler (http://www.webcrawler.com)
   Lycos (http://www.lycos.com)
   Alta Vista (http://www.altavista.com)

   When you reach the home page of the chosen search site, select the highlighted text that says *Colleges and Universities* or something like that. Then, keep on making selections on subsequent screens until you find the school you are seeking. What types of information or features did you find at these other college sites that were different from your own school's Web site?
f. What are the Web addresses of the two schools you looked up in part e?
g. Access the Parker Web site at

   http://www.dryden.com/infosys/parker/

   Here you will find updated information on the projects in this book as well as other items of interest. Make a preliminary exploration of the site by selecting hyperlinks.
h. Log off the Internet and shut off your computer.

2. Productivity Software Figure INT 1-5 lists several types of productivity software. For this project, find the names of two commercial programs that fit into each of the categories listed below. Also, identify the company that produces each of the programs you have chosen.

a. Word processing program
b. Spreadsheet program
c. Database management program
d. Presentation graphics program
e. Web browser

3. Computer Journals Go to your school library or a local bookstore and find five journals (magazines or newspapers) that focus on microcomputers. For each journal, list the following information:

a. The name
b. The frequency of publication (e.g., weekly, monthly, bimonthly)
c. The target audience (for instance, word processing users, users of Macintosh computers, people who use the Internet)
d. For each of the five journals you named in part a, determine if a Web site exists with an online edition of the journal. If it does, provide the Web address. (You do not need Internet access to get this information.)

4. Computer Advertisements Look in a computer journal—such as *PC Magazine* or *MacWorld*—for an advertisement featuring a microcomputer system for sale. What are the principal hardware components of this system and their functions? What systems and applications software does the ad offer as part of the purchase price and what—specifically—does each of these programs do? Does the hardware and software system provide complete capabilities for performing simple chores like creating letters and writing term reports, or do you have to purchase additional hardware or software?

5. Online Bookstores Online bookstores are appearing on the World Wide Web with increasing frequency. Two popular ones are the Amazon Bookstore

http://www.amazon.com

which offers one of the largest collections of book titles you'll find in a single place, and Computer Literacy Bookshops

http://www.clbooks.com/

which has one of the largest collections of computer books and magazines available anywhere.

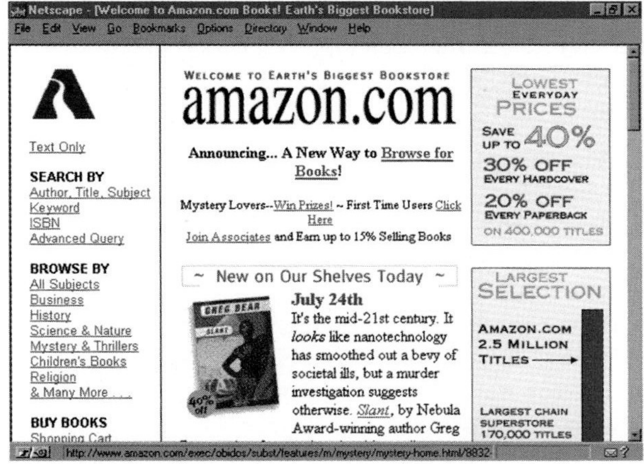

a. Get onto the Web and visit one of these bookstores (or perhaps another of your own choosing). Compare the online bookstore's prices on two computer books with prices at a conventional bookstore in your area. Are the online bookstore's prices higher or lower? (*Hint:* You can search for other online bookstores through a search site such as Yahoo! or WebCrawler. Type "online bookstores" into the space that offers the keyword search to see what is currently available.)

b. The software tools at many online bookstores let you search for books by typing in an author's name, a book's subject area, or a keyword from a book's title. Observe as many book-search tools as you can for at least one online bookstore and make a list of ways that you can locate books. Do you find the computer useful as a book-shopping tool?

c. The Amazon site currently lets visitors access book reviews and even write their own reviews for others to read. At the bookstore site you've chosen to visit, list as many features like this as you can—features that aren't typically available at conventional bookstores.

6. Palmtop Computers Hardware vendors today collectively sell a variety of palmtop computers, including personal digital assistants (PDAs). Choose a palmtop computer and report to your class about its features and price. Articles about palmtop computers appear regularly in computer journals such as *Computerworld* and *Infoworld;* check your campus library or perform a search on the Internet.

7. Online Shopping Figure INT 1-5 features, among other things, the Web site for Lands' End, a manufacturer and direct seller of apparel and related items. Visit the Lands' End Web site at

http://www.landsend.com

and report to the class about the contents of the site, how shoppers can electronically search for items of interest, how shoppers can select a certain size or color, and the choices available for payment.

8. Easter Eggs Revisited The Inside the Industry box covers Easter eggs—hidden blocks of code in a program that display splashy screens, animations, credits to developers, and the like, all of which have nothing to do with the operation of the program. For this project, find an Easter egg other than the one discussed in the box and report to the class how it works and what it produces. Articles on Easter eggs are frequently found in computer journals like *PC Magazine,* but probably the easiest way to find eggs is using a Web-based search engine such as Yahoo! or WebCrawler. To see what is currently available, type "Easter eggs" into the space that offers the keyword search.

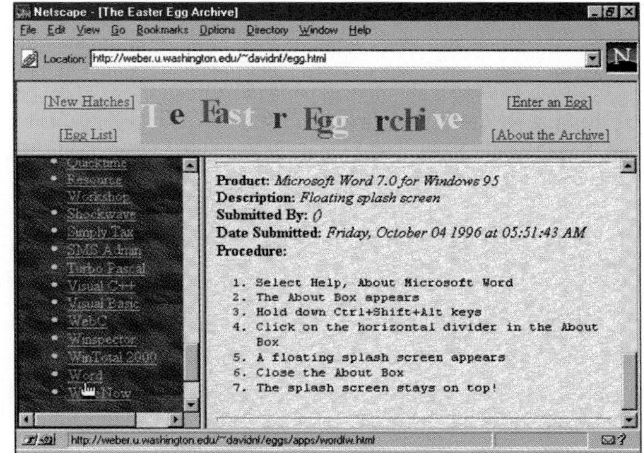

9. Computer Literacy The term *computer literacy*—knowing something about computers—is widely used today.

a. The table below lists some computer-oriented topics. For each one, declare whether or not you think it should be included among the basic skills that students should learn before they graduate from college. Give a short reason why you would or would not include each topic in the essential curriculum.

TOPIC	INCLUDE?	REASON
Using the Internet		
Programming in a specific computer language		
Understanding the technical details about how computers work		
Appreciating the dangers that computers pose to society		
Using a word processing package		
Learning the history of computers		
Understanding how businesses use computers		

b. A heated debate rages in many college computer departments over the emphasis placed on education versus training. *Training* prepares students to deal with situations they will likely encounter outside school, whereas *education* teaches students to deal with anything they might encounter. For instance, learning how to create reports with Microsoft Word is training; gaining an understanding of how to apply computers in the problem-solving process is education.

Many schools face a dilemma in this debate. Their mission is clearly education—they must teach students how to make tough decisions and to learn on their own. However, colleges also recognize a sad fact of life: Many companies won't hire graduates without a certain amount of training. Some people also argue that students need a certain amount of training to become educated; that is, you must complete several hands-on experiences with computers to become educated about them.

The list in part a addressed both matters that are related to training and matters that are related to education. Which matters relate to training? To education? To both education and training?

c. Prepare a statement one or two pages long that summarizes your beliefs about the types of computer skills that students should pick up in college.

10. Computer Case Study: Registering for Classes One of the ways computers have helped colleges and universities throughout the years is registering students for classes every semester.

a. On your own campus, how do computers help out in the registration process? Make a list of the individual tasks that computers perform that would otherwise be done manually.
b. News reports regularly feature stories about colleges using leading-edge technologies to help out in the registration process. For instance, some colleges let students register over the Internet or by Touch-Tone phone. Find one such story in a magazine or newspaper and report to your class about it.

11. Network Computers Computer users have heard a lot of talk over the last year or two about the so-called *network computer (NC)* as an inexpensive alternative to the standard desktop computer that people often acquire for home or business use at a cost of $2,000 or so. As the chapter notes, the diskless NC has both business and consumer benefits. For this project, locate a particular NC model and answer the following questions about it:

a. Who makes the NC and what is its name or model number?
b. How is the NC different from a standard desktop computer?
c. How much does the NC cost?
d. Is the chosen NC targeted for home or business use?
e. Finally, do you think that NCs will replace standard desktop computers in most homes and businesses in the near future? Support your answer with a well-reasoned argument.

12. Benefits Provided by Computers Organizations acquire computers for many reasons. Most of them first flocked to computers because these awesome devices could do certain types of jobs much faster than humans and with far fewer errors. Such capabilities enabled computers to displace humans in many types of work at a great savings in labor costs. Eventually, computers gained capabilities to do far more than just faster, more accurate, and cheaper work. For instance, they could also be deployed to provide better information to decision makers, improve customer service, and create products that few dreamed possible before the age of computers. For this project, provide at least one real-world example from a computer journal or from your personal experience that illustrates how computers can help an organization achieve one of these latter types of benefits.

MODULE

HW

Hardware

When most people think of computer systems, images of hardware fill their minds. Hardware comprises the exciting pieces of equipment that you unpack from their boxes when you buy a computer system. This module explores the rich variety of computer hardware available in today's marketplace. But as you'll see later in this book, hardware needs guidance from software to perform any useful function. Hardware without software is like a human who cannot reason and think.

This module divides coverage of hardware into three subject areas. Chapter HW 1 describes the functions of the CPU—the computer itself—and memory. Chapter HW 2 discusses the class of hardware that provides an indispensable library of resources for the CPU—secondary storage devices. Chapter HW 3 delves into input and output equipment.

MODULE CONTENTS

Hardware

ISBN 0-03-024481-1

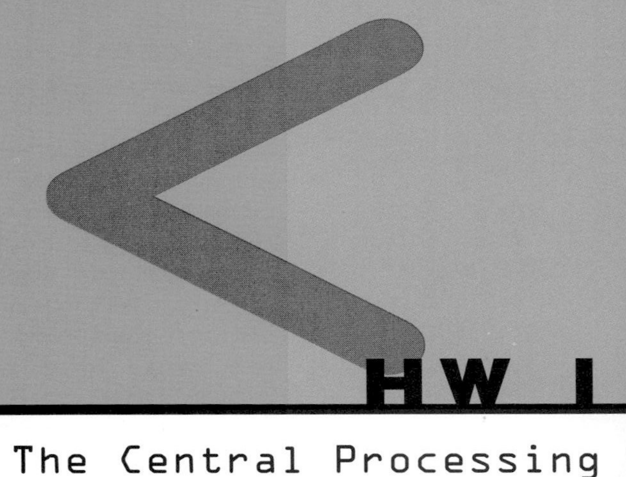

HW 1

The Central Processing Unit and Memory

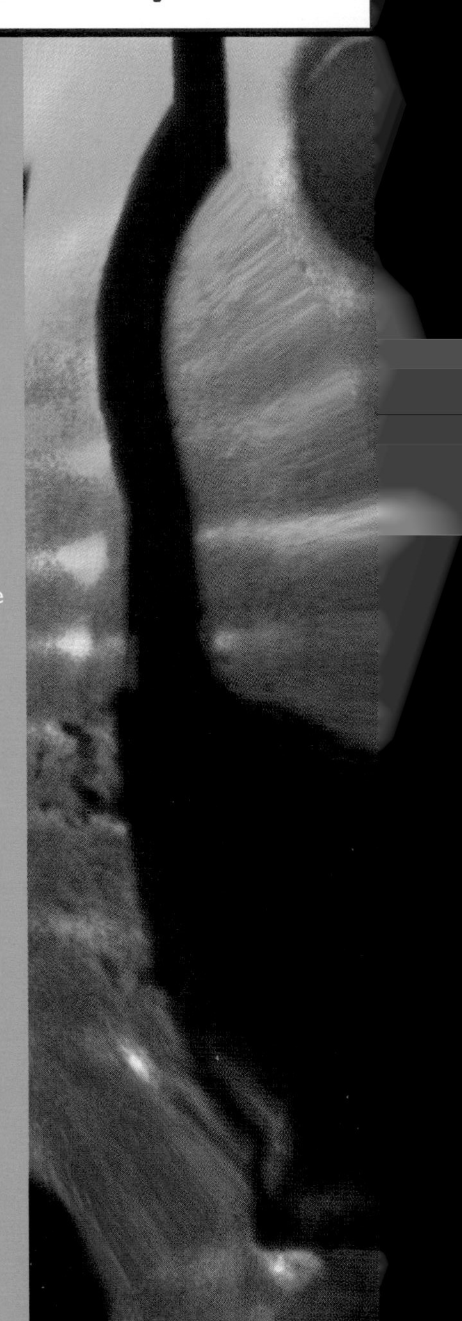

Outline

Learning Objectives

After completing this chapter, you will be able to:

1. Describe how the computer system's CPU and memory components process program instructions and data.
2. Identify several binary-based coding schemes used in computing environments.
3. Explain the functions of hardware components commonly found under the cover of a system unit.
4. Name several strategies for speeding the operations of computers.

Overview

So far, we've considered the system unit, which houses the CPU and memory, to be a mysterious "black box." In this chapter, we'll demystify that notion by flipping the lid off the box and closely examining the functions of the parts inside. In doing so, the chapter will try to give you a feel for how the CPU, memory, and other devices commonly found in the system unit work together.

To start, we'll examine how a CPU is organized and how it interacts with memory to carry out processing tasks. Next, we'll discuss how a computer system represents data and program instructions. Here we'll talk about the codes through which computers translate back and forth from symbols the CPU can manipulate to symbols in which people find meaning. These topics lead into a discussion of how the CPU and its memory are packaged with other computing and storage components inside the system unit. Finally, we look at strategies to speed up CPU operations.

How the CPU Works

Every computer's CPU is basically a collection of electronic circuits. Electronic impulses enter the CPU from an input device. Within the CPU, these impulses move under program control through circuits to create a series of new impulses. Eventually, a set of impulses leaves the CPU headed for an output device. What happens in those circuits? To begin to understand this process, you need to know first how the CPU is organized—what parts it includes—and then how electronic impulses move from one part to another to process data.

DIGITAL COMPUTERS

When we talk about computers today, most of us are referring to digital computers. **Digital computers** are devices that *count.* The types of microcomputers, midrange computers, mainframes, and supercomputers discussed in Chapter INT 1 are digital computers. As you will see in this chapter, digital computers do all of their counting by converting data and programs into strings of 0s and 1s, which they manipulate at lightning speed.

Analog computers are also widely found in practice. *Analog computers* are devices that *measure.* For example, a gasoline pump contains an analog computer that measures the amount of gas pumped and converts this reading into a gallon amount that appears on the pump's display. A car has an analog computer that measures rotation of a transmission shaft and converts this reading into speedometer output. Large systems call for analog computers, too; chemical processing companies use analog computers to measure such data as temperature and time so that automatic systems can open and close valves on tanks.

People began counting and measuring long before they developed computers. One can count entities such as pages of a book, dollars in a wallet or purse, and elk on a wildlife reserve—all of which exist naturally in indivisible units. When we estimate that a car's gas tank contains 10 gallons of fuel, however, we are measuring. The tank may contain 9.99999 gallons or 10.00001 or some other number. Concepts such as volume and weight are *continuous* variables that can only be approximated, whereas concepts such as number of dollars or elk are *discrete* variables that can in many circumstances be determined exactly.

Digital computers can work with analog concepts by using rounded estimates. Henceforth in this textbook, all discussions will pertain to digital computers.

■ **Digital computer.** A device that *counts.*

THE CPU AND MEMORY

The CPU works closely with memory to carry out processing inside the system unit. This relationship is described in the next few subsections.

The CPU The CPU has two principal sections: an arithmetic/logic unit and a control unit (see Figure HW 1-1). It also contains several registers and a bus, which later subsections will describe.

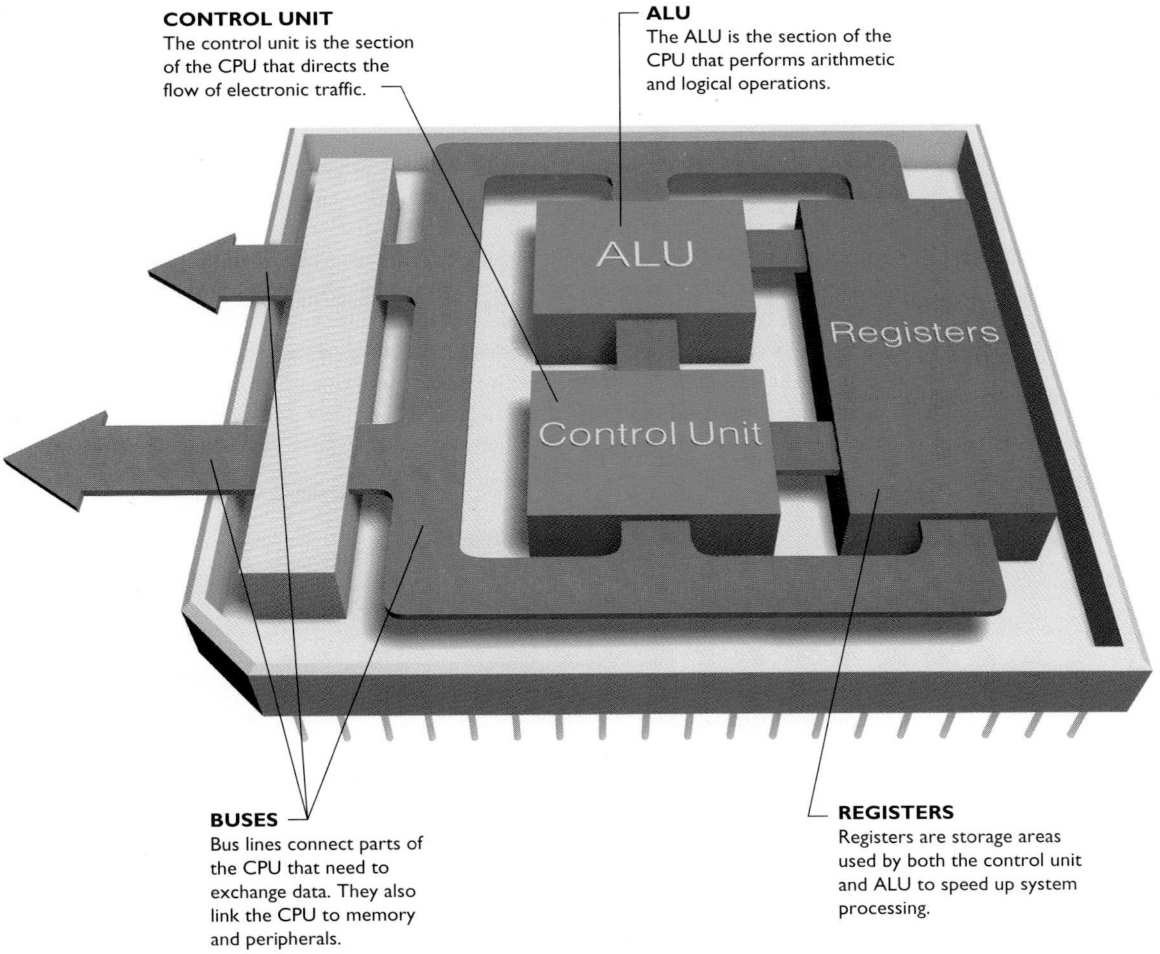

CONTROL UNIT
The control unit is the section of the CPU that directs the flow of electronic traffic.

ALU
The ALU is the section of the CPU that performs arithmetic and logical operations.

ALU

Registers

Control Unit

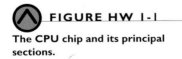

BUSES
Bus lines connect parts of the CPU that need to exchange data. They also link the CPU to memory and peripherals.

REGISTERS
Registers are storage areas used by both the control unit and ALU to speed up system processing.

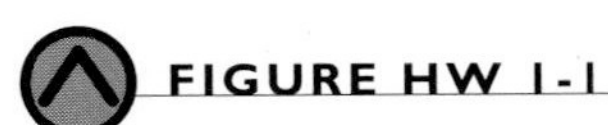

FIGURE HW 1-1

The CPU chip and its principal sections.

The **arithmetic/logic unit (ALU)** is the section of the CPU that performs arithmetic and logical operations on data. In other words, it's the part of the computer that computes. *Arithmetic* operations include addition, subtraction, multiplication, and division. *Logical* operations compare pairs of data items to determine whether they are equal and, if not, which is larger. As later discussions will show, all data coming into the CPU—including letters of the alphabet and nonnumeric data such as voice, graphics, and video—are coded in digital (numeric) form. The ALU can perform logical operations on any type of data.

The computer can perform only the basic arithmetic and logical operations just described. That might not seem very impressive. But when combined in various ways at great speeds, these operations enable the computer to perform immensely complex and data-intensive tasks.

■ **Arithmetic/logic unit (ALU).** The part of the CPU that contains circuitry to perform arithmetic and logical operations.

The **control unit** is the section of the CPU that directs the flow of electronic traffic between memory and the ALU and between the CPU and input and output devices. In other words, the control unit coordinates or manages the computer's operation.

Memory **Memory—**also called **primary (internal) storage—**holds:

- Programs and data passed to the computer system for processing
- Intermediate processing results
- Output ready for transmission to a secondary-storage or output device

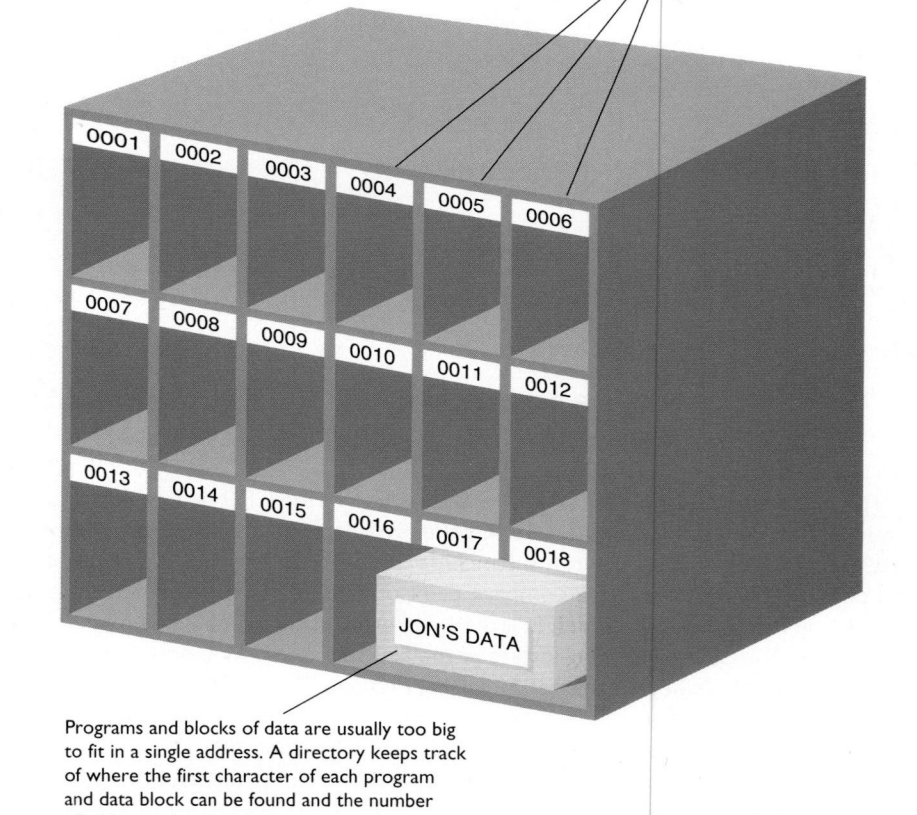

Once the CPU stores programs, data, intermediate results, and output in memory, it must be able to find them again. Thus, each location in memory has an *address*. Whenever a block of data, instruction, program, or result of a calculation is stored in memory, it is assigned an address so that the CPU can find it again as needed. Computer systems automatically set up and maintain tables that provide the addresses of the first character of all stored programs and data blocks.

Memory size varies among computer systems anywhere from a few million characters to several hundred billion. Because memory circuitry is relatively expensive, computer systems limit its size and use it only for temporary storage. Once the computer has finished processing one program and set of data, it writes another program and data set over the same storage space. Thus, the contents of each memory location constantly change. The address of each location, however, never changes. This process can be roughly compared with handling of the mailboxes in a post office: The number on each box remains the same, but the contents change as patrons remove their mail and new mail arrives (see Figure HW 1-2).

FIGURE HW 1-2

Memory.

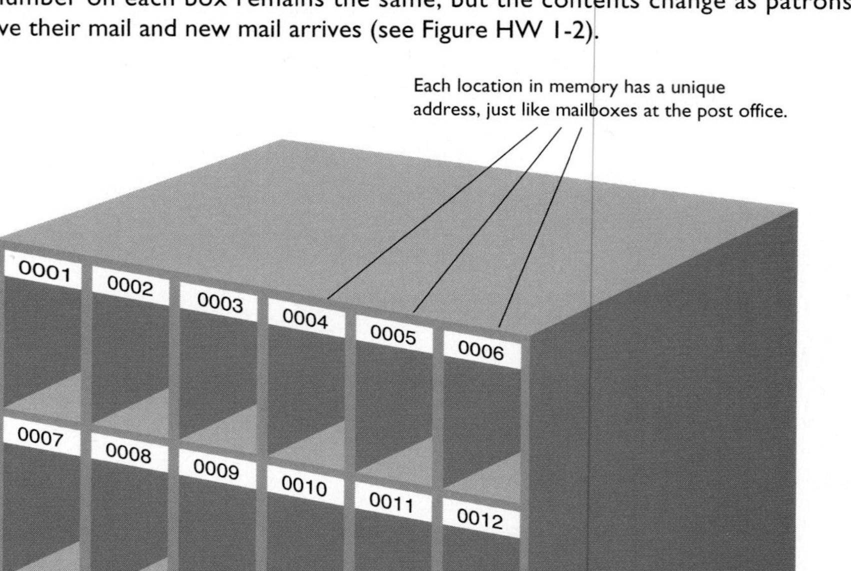

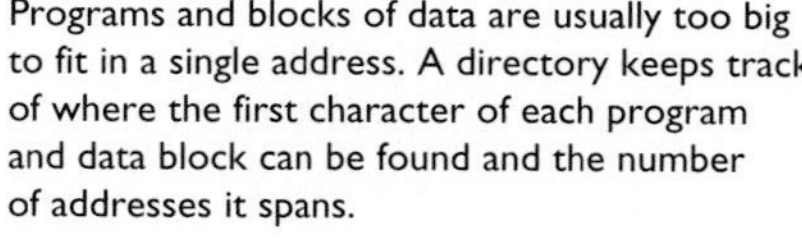

Programs and blocks of data are usually too big to fit in a single address. A directory keeps track of where the first character of each program and data block can be found and the number of addresses it spans.

■ **Control unit.** The part of the CPU that coordinates its operations. ■ **Memory.** The section of the computer system that holds data and program instructions awaiting processing, intermediate results, and processed output. Also called **primary (internal) storage.**

Sometimes the term *main memory* is used to distinguish conventional memory from storage products that have memory characteristics. These comparable products include *cache memory* and *read-only memory (ROM),* both covered later in the chapter.

Registers To enhance the computer's performance, the control unit and ALU access special storage locations that act as high-speed staging areas. These areas are called **registers.** Registers play a crucial role in achieving extremely high computer speeds. Because registers are actually a part of the CPU, the CPU can access their contents much more rapidly than it can access memory. Program instructions and data are normally loaded (that is, staged) into the registers from memory just before CPU processing.

MACHINE CYCLES

The descriptions of the CPU, memory, and registers lead to questions about how these elements work together to process an instruction. Every instruction that you issue to a computer, either by typing a command or pointing to an icon with a mouse and clicking, is broken down into several smaller, machine-level instructions called **microcode.** Each piece of microcode corresponds directly to a set of the computer's circuits.

The computer system's built-in **system clock** synchronizes its operations, just as a metronome can synchronize the activities of an orchestra. During each clock tick, the CPU can execute a single piece of microcode, a single piece of data can move from one part of the computer system to another, and so on. Microcode instructions are a form of *machine language,* covered briefly later in the chapter.

As the CPU processes a single, machine-level instruction, it completes a **machine cycle.** A machine cycle has two parts: an *instruction* cycle (I-cycle) and an *execution* cycle (E-cycle). During the **I-cycle,** the control unit fetches a program instruction from memory and prepares for subsequent processing. During the **E-cycle,** the CPU locates data and carries out the instruction. Let's see how this works in a little more detail, using simple addition as an example.

I-Cycle

1. The control unit *fetches* from memory the next command to be executed.
2. The control unit *decodes* the command into an instruction that the ALU can process. In one register, it stores the identity of the instruction, and in another, it stores information about the location in memory of any required data.

E-Cycle

3. The control unit retrieves the needed data from memory and commands the ALU to *execute* the required instruction; the ALU complies. Registers temporarily store the retrieved data and final result.
4. The control unit *stores* the result in memory.

Figure HW 1-3 depicts how the machine cycle works.

These steps may seem to define a tedious process, especially when a computer must go through thousands, millions, or even billions of machine cycles to complete a single program's processing. But computer hardware works at almost unimaginably high speeds. The slowest hardware performs an operation in **milliseconds** (thousandths of a second) or **microseconds** (millionths of a second). In the fastest

■ **Register.** A high-speed staging area within the CPU that temporarily stores data during processing. ■ **Microcode.** Instructions built into the CPU that control the operation of its circuitry. ■ **System clock.** The timing mechanism within the computer system that governs the transmission of instructions and data through the circuits. ■ **Machine cycle.** The series of operations involved in the execution of a single, machine-level instruction. ■ **I-cycle.** The part of the machine cycle in which the control unit fetches a program instruction from memory and prepares it for subsequent processing. ■ **E-cycle.** The part of the machine cycle in which the CPU locates data, carries out an instruction, and stores the results. ■ **Millisecond.** One one-thousandth of a second. ■ **Microsecond.** One one-millionth of a second.

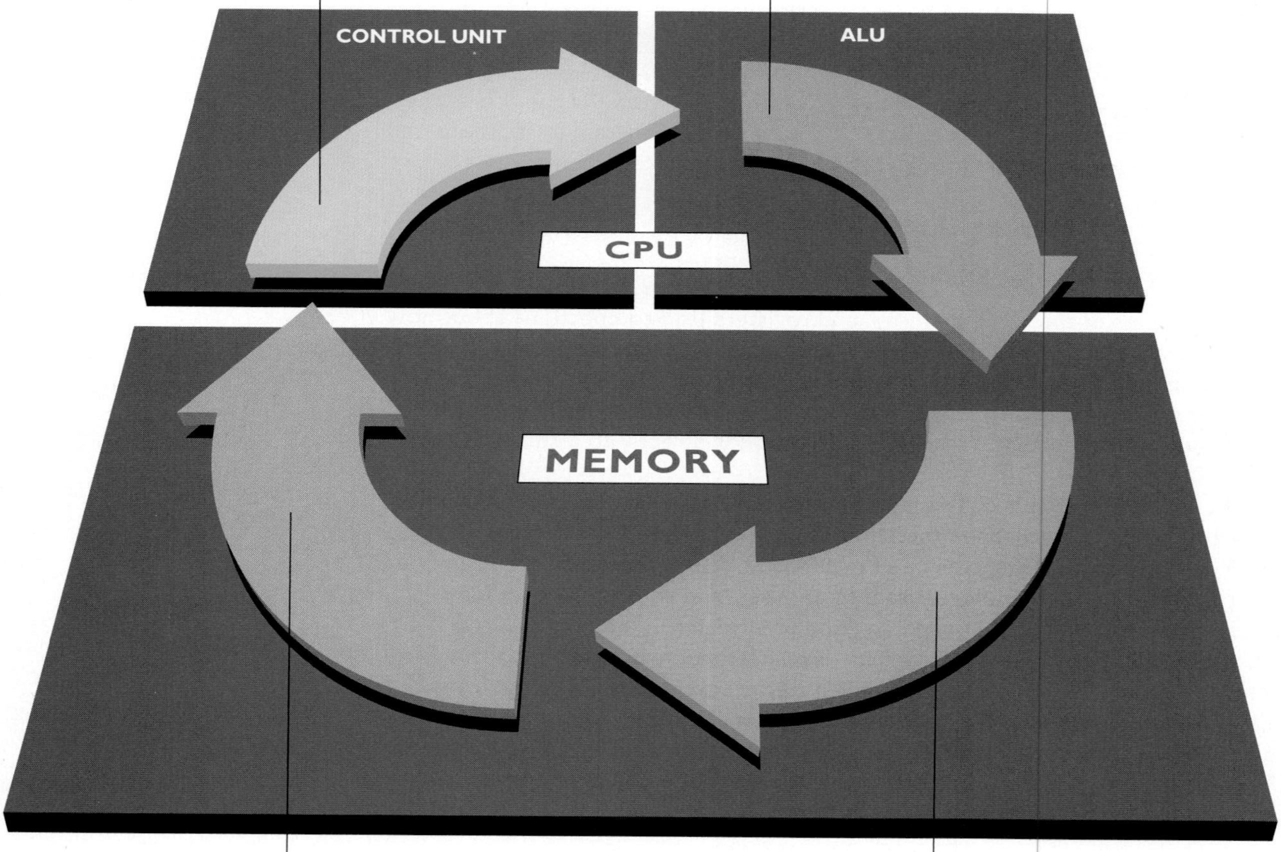

2. DECODE
The instruction is decoded into a form the ALU can process.

3. EXECUTE
The ALU executes the instruction.

CONTROL UNIT

ALU

CPU

MEMORY

1. FETCH
The next instruction is fetched from memory.

4. STORE
Results from the instruction execution are stored in memory.

FIGURE HW 1-3

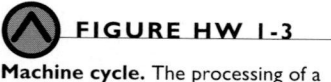

Machine cycle. The processing of a single machine-level instruction is accomplished in a four-step machine cycle.

hardware, speeds are measured in **nanoseconds** (billionths of a second) or **picoseconds** (trillionths of a second). One of the fastest computers in the world operates at 1.8 trillion operations per second; put another way, it can do in a second what a person can accomplish by completing one arithmetic calculation per second for 31,000 years without a break.

Different terms describe speeds in different types of computers. Microcomputer speeds are most commonly rated in *megahertz (MHz)*. Each 1 MHz represents 1 million clock ticks per second. While the original IBM PC of the early 1980s executed instructions at 4.77 MHz, many of today's desktop microcomputers run at 300 MHz or more. Mainframe speeds are often rated in *mips* (millions of instructions per second); for supercomputers, it's most often *mflops* (millions of floating-point operations per second). Many of these speed measures can apply to any CPU; for instance, today's microcomputers have become so fast that their speeds are often quoted in mips, and many mainframes handle some scientific work that calls for processing speeds measured in mflops.

■ **Nanosecond.** One one-billionth of a second. ■ **Picosecond.** One one-trillionth of a second.

Data and Program Representation

The electronic components of digital computer systems recognize two states. A circuit is either open or closed, a magnetic spot is either present or absent, and so on. This two-state, or **binary,** nature of electronic devices is illustrated in Figure HW 1-4. For convenience, think of these binary states as the *0-state* and the *1-state*. Computer people refer to such zeros and ones as **bits,** which is a contraction of the words

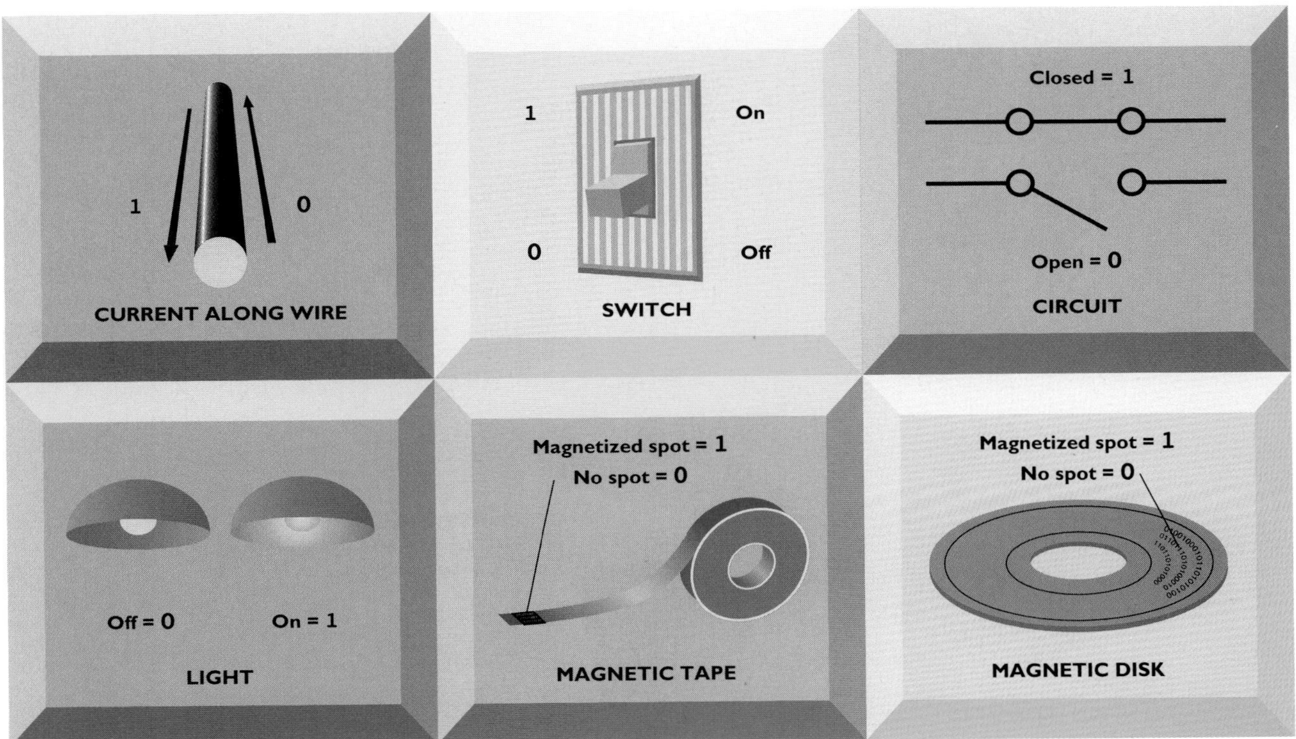

FIGURE HW 1-4

The binary nature of electronics. Circuits are either open or closed, a current runs one way or the opposite way, a charge is either present or absent, and so forth. The two possible states of an electronic component define *bits,* represented by computer systems as 0s and 1s.

*bi*nary dig*its*. With their electronic components, computers do all of their processing and communicating by representing programs and data in bit form. Binary, then, is the symbol set that forms the computer's "native tongue."

People, of course, don't speak binary language. You're not likely to go up to a friend and say,

0100100001001001

which translates in one binary coding system as "HI." People communicate with one another in *natural languages,* such as English, Chinese, and Spanish. Most people in your part of the world probably speak English. Also, they write with a 26-character alphabet and count with a number system that uses ten possible digits—0 through 9—rather than just two digits. Computers, however, understand only 0 and 1. So in order for us to interact with a computer, our messages to it must be translated into binary form and its messages to us must be translated from binary into a natural language.

The languages through which most people interact with computer systems consist of a wide variety of natural-language symbols. When we type a message, the computer system translates all the natural-language symbols in the message into 0s and 1s. After it completes processing, the computer system translates the 0s and 1s

■ **Binary.** The numbering system with two possible states. ■ **Bit.** A binary digit, such as 0 or 1.

that represent the program's results into natural language. This conversion process is illustrated in Figure HW 1-5.

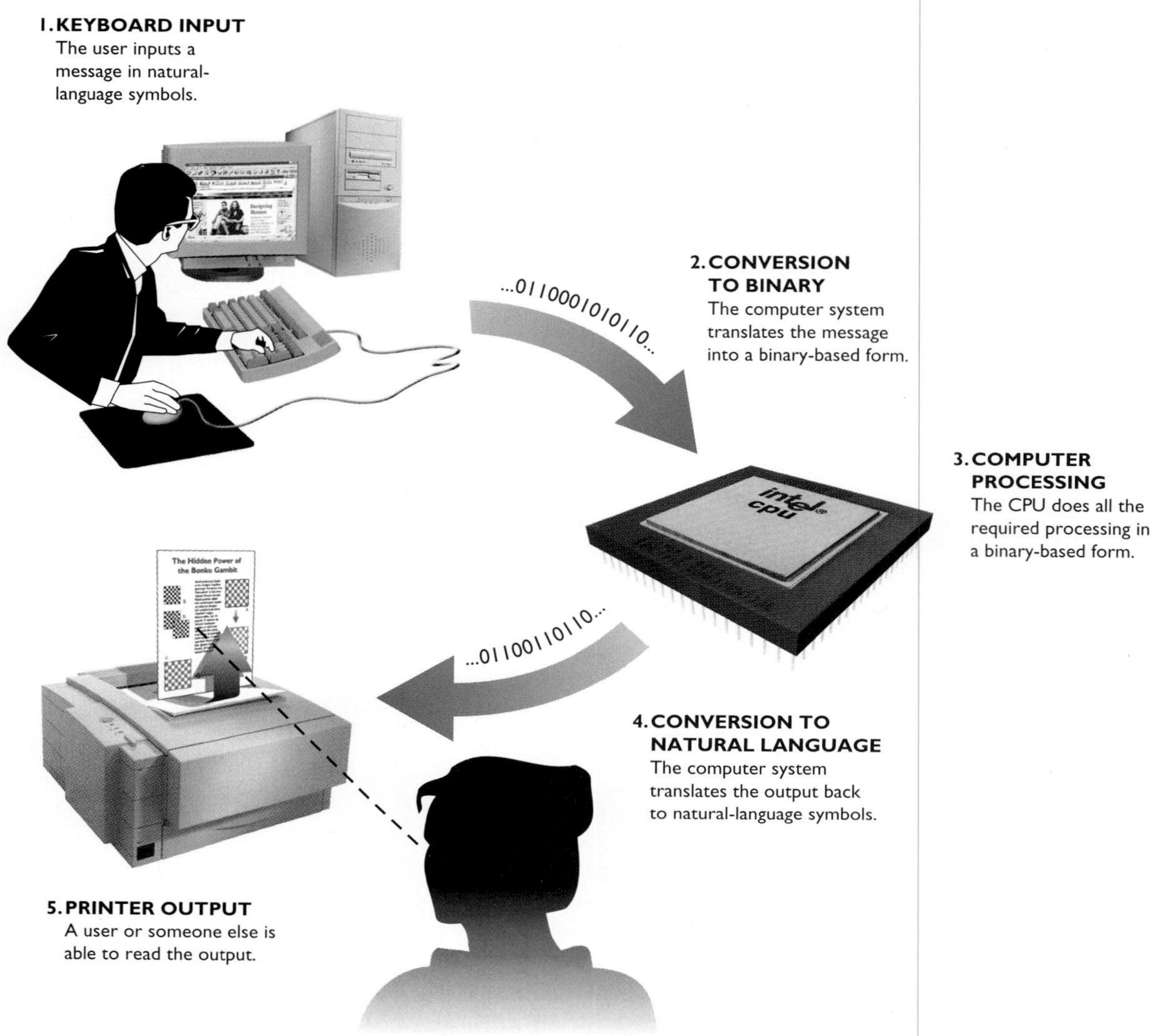

1. KEYBOARD INPUT
The user inputs a message in natural-language symbols.
...0110001010110...
2. CONVERSION TO BINARY
The computer system translates the message into a binary-based form.
3. COMPUTER PROCESSING
The CPU does all the required processing in a binary-based form.
intel cpu
...01100110110...
4. CONVERSION TO NATURAL LANGUAGE
The computer system translates the output back to natural-language symbols.
The Hidden Power of the Bonko Gambit
5. PRINTER OUTPUT
A user or someone else is able to read the output.

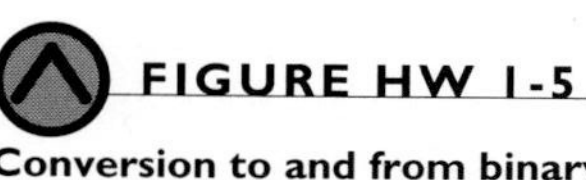

FIGURE HW 1-5

Conversion to and from binary form.

Computer systems represent programs and data through a variety of binary-based coding schemes. For example, when data and programs are sent to or from the CPU (steps 2 and 4 in Figure HW 1-5), a fixed-length, binary-based code such as ASCII or EBCDIC is often used to represent each character transmitted. The next subsection covers these two coding systems.

Once data and programs enter the CPU (step 3 of Figure HW 1-5), they are represented by other types of binary codes. For example, a program instruction about to be executed is represented by a code known as *machine language*. Data, in contrast, may be represented by several different types of binary codes during manipulation by the computer. One such code stores numbers in *true binary representation*. The appendix at the end of this chapter reviews this code, as well as some fundamentals of number systems, in more detail.

ASCII AND EBCDIC

As mentioned earlier, when data or programs are sent between the computer and its peripheral equipment, a *fixed-length*, binary-based code is commonly used. A fixed-length code allows communicating devices to tell where one character ends and another begins. Such codes represent *digits, alphabetic characters,* and *special characters* such as the dollar sign ($) and period (.).

Among the most widely used of these codes are **ASCII** (American Standard Code for Information Interchange) and **EBCDIC** (Extended Binary-Coded Decimal Interchange Code). Virtually all microcomputers employ ASCII, developed largely through the efforts of the American National Standards Institute (ANSI). ASCII is also widely adopted as the standard for data communications systems. EBCDIC, developed by IBM, is used primarily on IBM mainframes.

Both ASCII and EBCDIC represent each printable character as a unique combination of a fixed number of bits (see Figure HW 1-6). EBCDIC represents a character with 8 bits. A group of 8 bits allows 256 (2^8) different combinations; therefore, EBCDIC can represent up to 256 characters. This scheme leaves more than enough combinations to account for the 26 uppercase and 26 lowercase characters, the ten decimal digits, and several special characters.

HW

Character	ASCII Representation	EBCDIC Representation	Character	ASCII Representation	EBCDIC Representation
0	00110000	11110000	I	01001001	11001001
1	00110001	11110001	J	01001010	11010001
2	00110010	11110010	K	01001011	11010010
3	00110011	11110011	L	01001100	11010011
4	00110100	11110100	M	01001101	11010100
5	00110101	11110101	N	01001110	11010101
6	00110110	11110110	O	01001111	11010110
7	00110111	11110111	P	01010000	11010111
8	00111000	11111000	Q	01010001	11011000
9	00111001	11111001	R	01010010	11011001
A	01000001	11000001	S	01010011	11100010
B	01000010	11000010	T	01010100	11100011
C	01000011	11000011	U	01010101	11100100
D	01000100	11000100	V	01010110	11100101
E	01000101	11000101	W	01010111	11100110
F	01000110	11000110	X	01011000	11100111
G	01000111	11000111	Y	01011001	11101000
H	01001000	11001000	Z	01011010	11101001

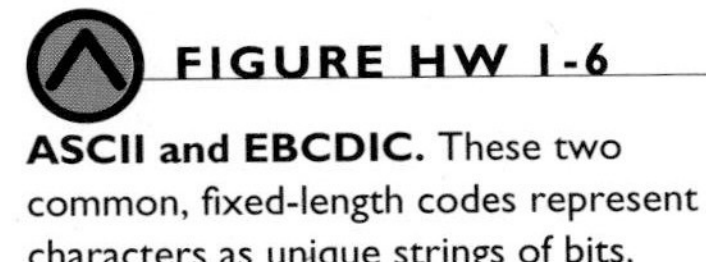

FIGURE HW 1-6

ASCII and EBCDIC. These two common, fixed-length codes represent characters as unique strings of bits.

ASCII originally was designed as a 7-bit code that could represent 128 (2^7) characters. Several 8-bit versions of ASCII have also been developed, because computers are designed to handle data in chunks of 8 bits. Many computer systems can accept data in either ASCII or EBCDIC and perform the necessary conversions to their native codes. The 8 bits that represent a character in ASCII or EBCDIC are collectively referred to as a *byte.*

A **byte** represents a single character of data. For this reason, many computer manufacturers define their machines' storage capacities in numbers of bytes. As you may have noticed, computer advertisements are filled with references to kilobytes, megabytes, gigabytes, and terabytes. In this terminology, 1 **kilobyte (KB)** equals a little over 1,000 bytes (1,024, to be precise); 1 **megabyte (MB** or *meg)* equals about

■ **ASCII.** A fixed-length, binary coding system widely used to represent data for computer processing and communications.
■ **EBCDIC.** A fixed-length, binary coding system widely used to represent data on IBM mainframes. ■ **Byte.** A configuration of 8 bits that represents a single character of data. ■ **Kilobyte (KB).** Approximately 1,000 bytes (1,024, to be exact). ■ **Megabyte (MB).** Approximately 1 million bytes.

1 million bytes; 1 **gigabyte (GB)** equals about 1 billion bytes; and 1 **terabyte (TB)** equals about 1 trillion bytes.

The typical desktop computer sold today has a memory of about 32 to 64 megabytes and a hard disk that can store a few gigabytes. For comparison, one of the fastest supercomputers in the world has a memory of 600 gigabytes and two terabytes of hard disk space. With computer storage capacities ever increasing, some vendors of software for large business and scientific applications have started to reach into the *petabyte (PB)* and *exabyte (EB)* ranges with their product offerings. A PB is about 1 quadrillion bytes; an EB about 1 quintillion.

Conversion from natural-language words and numbers to their ASCII (or EBCDIC) equivalents and back again usually takes place within an input or output device. When a user types a message, an encoder chip inside the keyboard usually translates this input into ASCII and sends it as a series of bytes to the CPU. The output that the CPU sends to the display screen or to some other output device is also coded in ASCII; the output device—with the aid of a decoder chip—translates this code into understandable words and numbers. Therefore, if the CPU were to send the ASCII message

0100100001001001

to your display device, the word *HI* would appear on your screen.

Computers usually handle data in byte multiples. For instance, a 16-bit computer is built to process data in chunks of 2 bytes; a (faster) 32-bit computer processes data in chunks of 4 bytes. These byte multiples are commonly called *words.* A later subsection of this chapter will look at words in more detail.

The Parity Bit Suppose you press the *B* key on your computer's keyboard. If the keyboard encoder supports ASCII coding, it will transmit the byte 01000010 to the CPU. Sometimes, however, something happens during transmission and the CPU receives a garbled message. Interference on the line, for example, might cause the 6th bit to change from 0 to 1 so that the CPU receives the message 01000110. Unless something indicated the mistake to the CPU, it would wrongly interpret this byte as the letter *F.*

To enable the CPU to detect such transmission errors, an additional bit position is often appended to EBCDIC and ASCII bytes. This bit, called the **parity bit,** is automatically set to either 0 or 1 to force the sum of the 1 bits in a byte to either an even or an odd number. Computer systems support either even or odd parity. In an *odd-parity system,* the parity bit forces the 1 bits in a byte to add up to an odd number. In an *even-parity system,* it makes them add up to an even number. Figure HW 1-7 shows how the parity bit works for the ASCII representation of the word "HELLO" on an even-parity system.

The parity bit is automatically generated by the keyboard's own circuitry. Thus, if you were to type the *B* character on an even-parity system, the keyboard would send 010000100 up the line to the CPU. If the message then became garbled so that the even-parity computer received 010001100 (an odd number of 1 bits), the CPU would immediately sense the error.

The parity check is not foolproof. For example, if 2 bits are incorrectly transmitted in a single byte, the errors will self-cancel. Such 2-bit errors rarely occur, though.

REPRESENTING NONTEXT DATA

So far, the discussion of data coding schemes has focused on *text* data, which consists of digits, letters, and special symbols such as the period and comma. Graphics, audio, and video data are also represented in binary form inside the computer system.

■ **Gigabyte (GB).** Approximately 1 billion bytes. ■ **Terabyte (TB).** Approximately 1 trillion bytes. ■ **Parity bit.** An extra bit added to the byte representations of characters to ensure there is always either an odd or even number of 1 bits transmitted with every character.

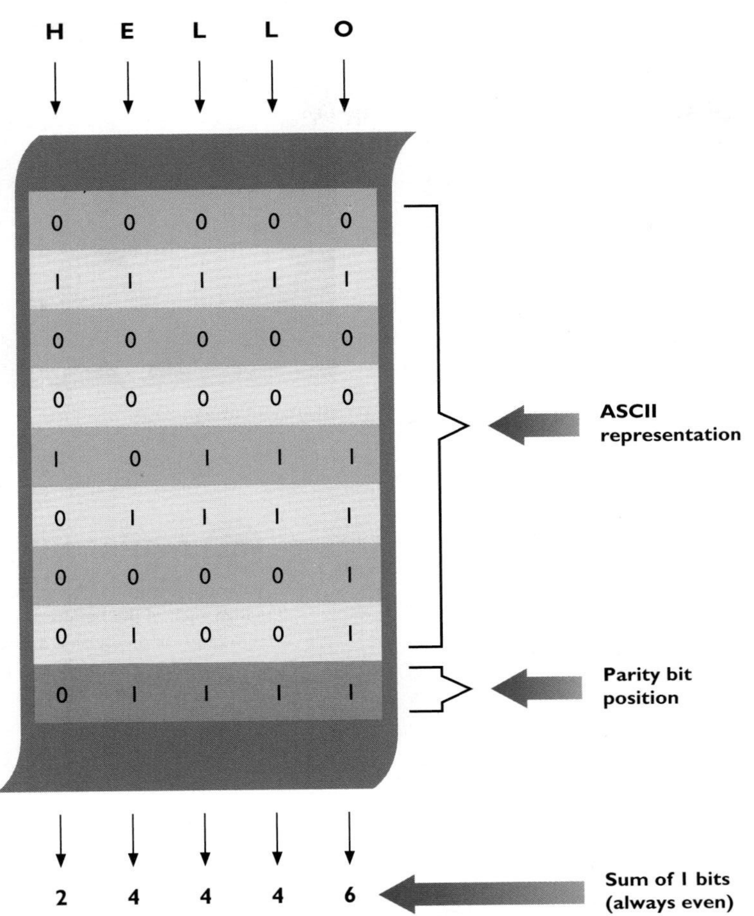

FIGURE HW 1-7

The parity bit. If a system supports even parity, as shown here, the number of 1 bits in every byte must always be an even number. The parity bit is set to either 0 or 1 in each byte to force an even number of 1 bits.

Graphics Data Graphics data consist of still pictures. One of the most common methods for storing graphics data is in the form of a bitmap. *Bitmap* graphics assign each of the hundreds of thousands of display-screen dots—called *pixels*—some combination of 0s and 1s that represents a unique shade or color.

The simplest type of bitmap, a *monochrome* graphic, must differentiate between only a foreground color and a background color. Suppose that these colors are black and white, and the 1 bit represents white, while the 0 bit represents black. The system can then translate any picture into a black-and-white electronic bitmap, as shown in the top part of Figure HW 1-8.

Above monochrome graphics on the scale of realism are *greyscale* images, in which each pixel can be not only pure black or pure white but also any of 254 shades of grey in between. Thus, each dot could appear in any of 256 possible states. You may remember from an earlier discussion that a single byte can represent any of 256 states. So, 11111111 could represent a pure white pixel, 00000000 a pure black one, and any byte in between—such as 11001000 and 00001010—some shade of grey (see the middle part of Figure HW 1-8).

Color coding works similar to greyscale graphics—that is, each pixel is represented by some number of bytes. Computers often handle graphics with 16 colors, 256 colors, or 16,777,216 colors. A 16-color image assigns only one-half byte to each pixel (e.g., 0000, 1111, or a combination in between); a 256-color image assigns 1 byte for each pixel; and a 16.78-million-color (photographic-quality) image requires 3 bytes per pixel (see the bottom part of Figure HW 1-8).

It's sometimes difficult for the eye to tell much of a quality difference between low-end and high-end color images. Sixteen-color images, such as those you see over

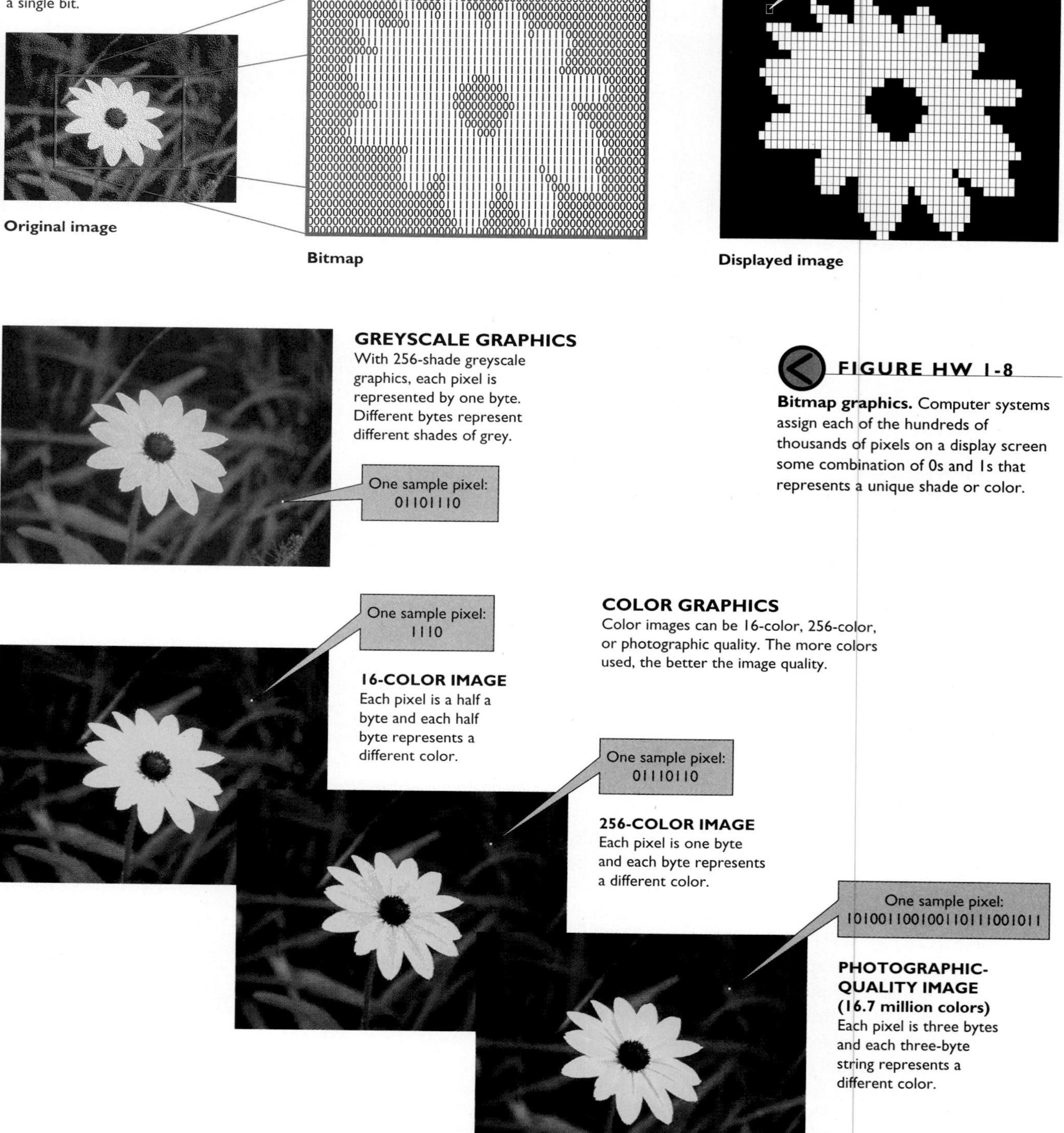

MONOCHROME GRAPHICS
With monochrome graphics, each pixel is represented by a single bit.
Original image
Bitmap
One sample pixel: 0
Displayed image
GREYSCALE GRAPHICS
With 256-shade greyscale graphics, each pixel is represented by one byte. Different bytes represent different shades of grey.
One sample pixel: 01101110
COLOR GRAPHICS
Color images can be 16-color, 256-color, or photographic quality. The more colors used, the better the image quality.
One sample pixel: 1110
16-COLOR IMAGE
Each pixel is a half a byte and each half byte represents a different color.
One sample pixel: 01110110
256-COLOR IMAGE
Each pixel is one byte and each byte represents a different color.
One sample pixel: 101001100100110111001011
PHOTOGRAPHIC-QUALITY IMAGE
(16.7 million colors)
Each pixel is three bytes and each three-byte string represents a different color.

FIGURE HW 1-8

Bitmap graphics. Computer systems assign each of the hundreds of thousands of pixels on a display screen some combination of 0s and 1s that represents a unique shade or color.

the Internet, can actually be quite respectable looking. To save time in transmitting large graphics files over the phone lines, computers often reduce 256-color images to 16 colors by a process called *dithering*. Dithering produces colors not on the limited palette by coloring neighboring pixels with 2 allowable colors that combine to make a new one. For instance, your eye will see a lime color on the screen when several yellow and green pixels are placed close together.

That the human eye cannot detect small alterations in some of a graphic image's pixels has led to a practice called *digital watermarking.* Digital watermarking protects digital images from theft or alteration (see User Solution HW 1-1 on page HW 18).

Audio Data Computers often process audio data—such as the sound of someone speaking or a symphony playing—after digital encoding by a method called *waveform audio.* Waveform audio captures several thousand digital snapshots, called *samples* of a real-life sound sequence every second. At the end of the sequence, the replayed collection of samples re-creates the voice or music.

Audio CDs sold in music stores, for instance, record sound sampled at a rate of 44,100 times per second. Each 2-byte sample corresponds to a unique sound. As you can imagine, when these sounds are played back at a rate of 44,100 per second, the human ear cannot distinguish them, and they collectively sound like real voice or music.

Video Data Films that you see at the movies or on TV are merely *moving* graphical data. Typically, films are projected at a rate of 30 frames per second; each frame is a still graphic. The amount of data involved in showing a 2-hour feature film can be quite substantial. For instance, just a single 256-color image shown on a 640-by-480-pixel display requires 307,200 bytes. When you multiply that figure by 30 times per second, 60 seconds per minute, and 120 minutes you get over 66 gigabytes of information. Chapter SW 2 will describe methods for compressing video data so that computers can more readily handle them. In the next chapter we'll look at DVD, a technology for storing feature-length films on CDs.

MACHINE LANGUAGE

So far, this section has covered schemes for representing *data* by 0 and 1 bits. Computer circuitry must also store and process *programs.*

Every program contains instructions. Instructions can be used to read the next record in a file, move a block of data from one place to another, summon a new window to the screen, and so on. Before your computer can execute any program instruction, it must convert it into a binary code known as **machine language.** An example of a typical machine-language instruction appears below:

```
01011000011100000000000100000010
```

A machine-language instruction may look like a meaningless string of 0s and 1s, but it actually organizes bits into groups that represent specific operations and storage locations. The 32-bit instruction shown here, for instance, moves data between two specific memory locations. Similar instructions transfer data from memory to a register and vice versa, add or subtract values in registers, divide and multiply values, and so on. The set of microcoded machine-language instructions available to a computer is known as that computer's *instruction set.*

The earliest computers, and the first microcomputers, required users to write all their own programs in machine language. Today, of course, hardly anyone uses machine language, and most users don't even write their own programs. Instead, programming specialists rely on *language translators*—special systems programs that automatically convert instructions such as "Read the next record" or "Move the value in location A to location B" into machine language. The translation is so transparent that most people aren't even aware that it is taking place.

Each computer platform has its own machine language. Machine-level code for an IBM microcomputer will be totally foreign to an Apple Macintosh. This fact explains why you must buy a program, such as a word processor or spreadsheet, in a form intended for your specific type of computer system.

■ **Machine language.** A binary-based programming language that the computer can execute directly.

The System Unit

Now that we've covered conceptually how the CPU and memory work, let's consider how they're realized in hardware and how they relate to other devices inside a system unit of a typical microcomputer system.

Almost all computers sold today follow a modular hardware design. For example, related circuitry is etched onto memory or processor chips, the chips are mounted onto carrier packages that are plugged into boards, and the boards are fitted into slots inside the system unit. The modules combine to make hardware components and define their capabilities.

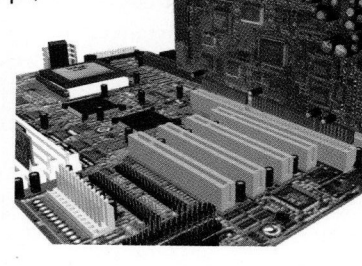

The port on an add-in board extends through the back of the system unit's case.

PORTS
Ports located at the back of the system unit enable you to plug in peripherals that work with the add-in boards.

The **system unit** often consists of at least one CPU chip, specialized processor chips, memory (RAM and ROM) chips, boards on which chips are mounted, ports that provide connections for external devices, a power supply, and internal circuitry to hook everything together (see Figure HW 1-9). Here we'll discuss these hardware elements. System units also often have built-in diskette, hard disk, and CD-ROM drives and sometimes even tape drives. Disks and tapes will be covered in detail in Chapter HW 2.

CPU CHIPS

Every microcomputer's system unit contains a specific microprocessor chip as its CPU (see Figure HW 1-10). This chip lies within a carrier package, and the carrier package is mounted onto a special board—called the **system board** or *motherboard*—inside the system unit. This board connects in one way or another to all other components of a microcomputer system and is usually located on the floor of the system unit, as shown in Figure HW 1-9.

Most microcomputer systems made today use CPU chips manufactured by either Intel or Motorola. Chips in the Intel line—such as the 80386, 80486, Pentium, Pentium Pro, and Pentium II—appear in microcomputer systems made by IBM as well as by Compaq, Dell, and scores of other makers of PC-compatible systems. Many of the older Intel chips are commonly known by the last three digits of their model numbers. For example, *486* refers to an 80486 chip. Many of the newer Pentium chips are MMX-enabled, meaning they are expressly configured for multimedia applications. In recent years, a number of *clone chips* have appeared on the market—made by companies such as Cyrix and Advanced Micro Devices—providing functionally compatible alternatives to Intel chips.

Chips in the Motorola line—including the 68000, 68020, 68030, and 68040—are found primarily in Apple Macintosh computers made before 1994. In recent years, Apple, Motorola, and IBM have teamed up to produce the PowerPC chip, which has become the standard CPU on Macintosh computers. The new chip employs the RISC-based architecture (explained later in the chapter) that underlies many powerful

■ **System unit.** The hardware unit that houses the CPU and memory, as well as a number of other devices. ■ **System board.** The main circuit board of the computer to which all computer-system components connect. Also called a *motherboard*.

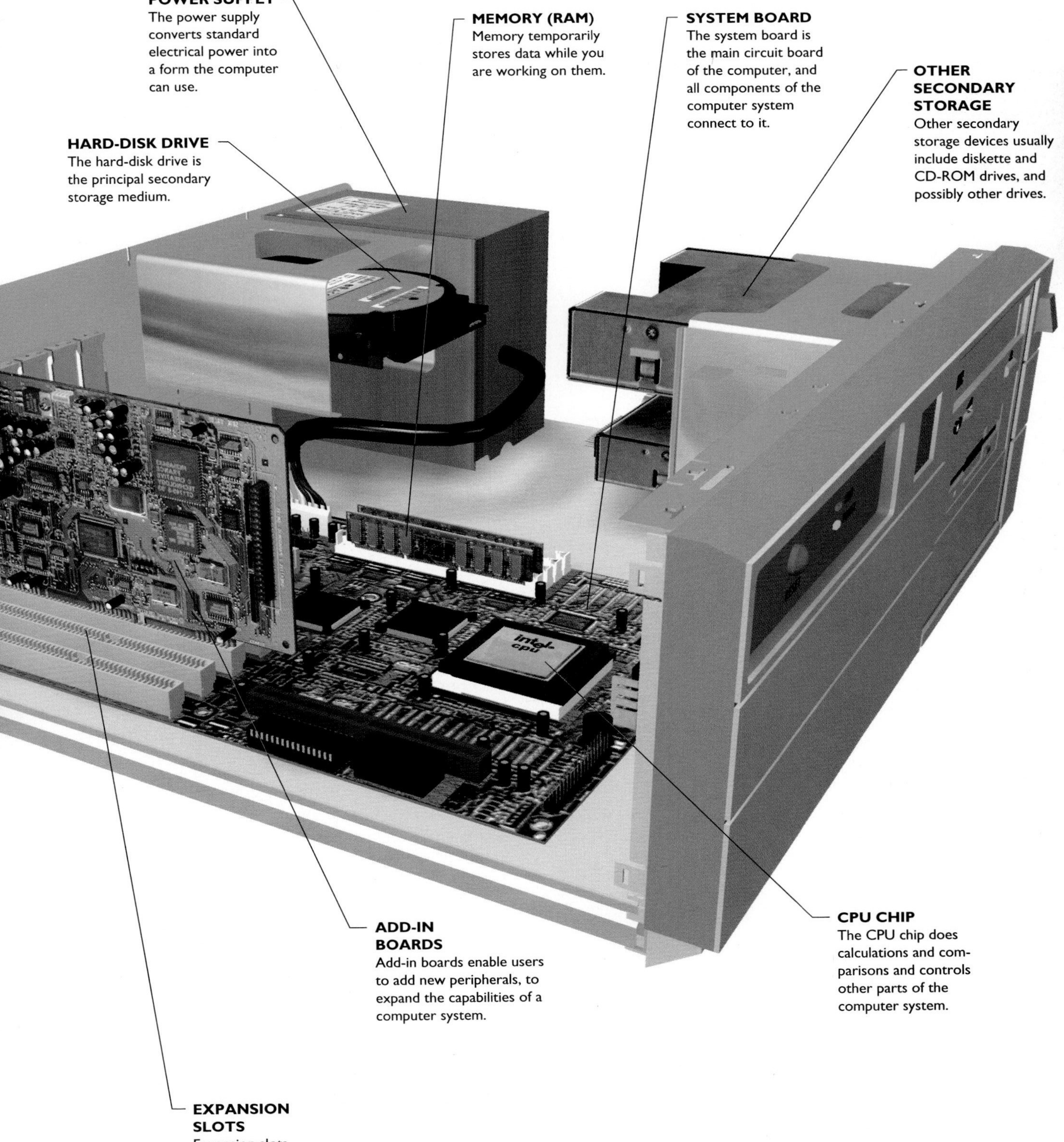
POWER SUPPLY
The power supply converts standard electrical power into a form the computer can use.
MEMORY (RAM)
Memory temporarily stores data while you are working on them.
SYSTEM BOARD
The system board is the main circuit board of the computer, and all components of the computer system connect to it.
OTHER SECONDARY STORAGE
Other secondary storage devices usually include diskette and CD-ROM drives, and possibly other drives.
HARD-DISK DRIVE
The hard-disk drive is the principal secondary storage medium.
ADD-IN BOARDS
Add-in boards enable users to add new peripherals, to expand the capabilities of a computer system.
CPU CHIP
The CPU chip does calculations and comparisons and controls other parts of the computer system.
EXPANSION SLOTS
Expansion slots exist so you can mount add-in boards in them.
intel cpu

FIGURE HW 1-9

Inside a system unit. With the cover of a system unit removed, you can see the parts inside.

Digital Watermarks

With the growth of computer networks, images such as copyrighted digital art have become ever more vulnerable to thieves who lurk online. Someone can relatively easily steal someone else's image, incorporate it into another work, and claim the finished product as their own. Digital watermarks have helped image creators demonstrate ownership of their work. The process randomly alters some pixel settings in an image ever so slightly. While the human eye cannot detect such changes, a computer prepared to read the underlying code can. The unique watermark pattern can identify the source of a stolen image.

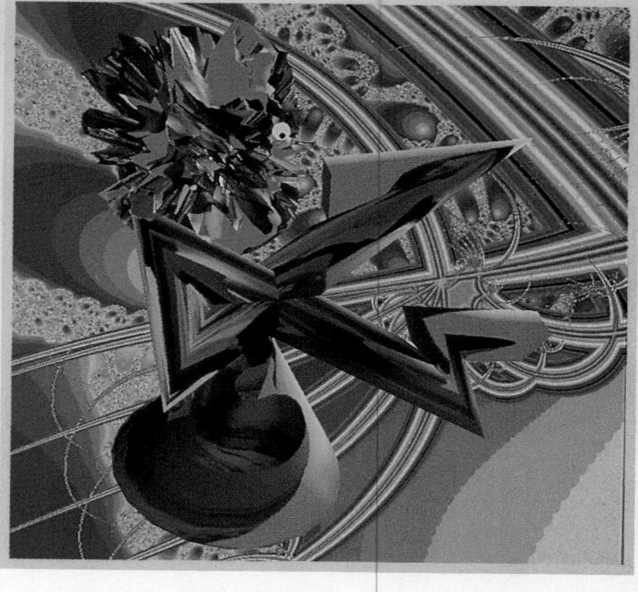

engineering workstations. The PowerPC chip is smaller in size and generally less expensive than comparable Intel microprocessors. Some models in the PowerPC line are the 601, 603, 604, and 620. Apple's Power Macintosh (or *Power Mac*) is one computer line based on PowerPC chips.

The type of CPU chip in a computer's system unit greatly affects what you can do with the system. Software is optimized to work on a specific chip or chip family, and a program that works on one chip may not function on another unless modified. For instance, software does not transfer easily between Intel and PowerPC chip families, as these families employ somewhat dissimilar design standards. Also, a program designed for a speedy Intel Pentium II chip may not work well, or even at all, on the earlier and far less-capable 80386 chip.

Feature HW 1-1 explains the growing problem of black-market chips undermining the efforts of computer chip makers.

Word Size CPU chips differ in many respects, one of the most important of which is word size. A computer **word** is a group of bits or bytes that a processor can manipulate as a unit. It is a critical concept, because the internal circuitry of virtually

FIGURE HW 1-10

CPU chip. CPU chips often vary in packaging design. Shown here are (left) an "Intel Pentium with MMX" chip in a conventional carrier package and (right) an Intel Pentium II chip in a cartridge that also contains cache memory components.

■ **Word.** A group of bits that a computer system treats as a single unit.

every computer system is designed around a certain word size. The Pentium Pro, for instance, has an *internal bus* designed for 64-bit words, which means that data move within the CPU chip's microcircuitry in 64-bit chunks. The Pentium Pro's *data bus,* or main bus, also accommodates 64-bit words, meaning that a 64-bit-wide data path leads from the CPU to memory. Usually, a larger word size allows faster processing in a computer system.

Figure HW 1-11 shows changes in processing power for several important CPU-chip families over the years.

PC-COMPATIBLE COMPUTERS (Intel x86 chip family)

Year	Chip	Speeds	Internal Bus	Data Bus
1978	8086	4.77 MHz	16 bits	16 bits
1979	8088	4.77 MHz	16 bits	8 bits
1982	80286	8-20 MHz	16 bits	16 bits
1985	80386	16-66 MHz	32 bits	16 bits
1989	80486	33-100 MHz	32 bits	32 bits
1993	Pentium	60-200 MHz	64 bits	64 bits
1995	Pentium Pro	133 MHz and higher	64 bits	64 bits
1997	Pentium II	233 MHz and higher	64 bits	64 bits

MACINTOSH COMPUTERS (Motorola 68x chip family and PowerPC chip family)

Year	Chip	Speeds	Internal Bus	Data Bus
1982	MC68000	8-12.5 MHz	32 bits	16 bits
1984	MC68020	16.7-33.3 MHz	32 bits	32 bits
1987	MC68030	20-50 MHz	32 bits	32 bits
1989	MC68040	25 MHz	32 bits	32 bits
1994	PowerPC 601	50-80 MHz	32 bits	64 bits
1994	PowerPC 603	66-80 MHz	32 bits	64 bits
1994	PowerPC 604	120-133 MHz and higher	32 bits	64 bits
1994	PowerPC 620	133 MHz and higher	64 bits	128 bits

FIGURE HW 1-11

CPU-chip families.

Specialized Processor Chips Working alongside the CPU chip in many system units are *specialized processor chips,* such as numeric and graphic coprocessors. These so-called *slave chips* are designed to perform specialized tasks for the CPU; by freeing it from certain processing burdens, they enhance overall system performance—often manyfold. A *numeric coprocessor* chip helps the CPU with arithmetic. A *graphics coprocessor* chip helps the CPU with the computationally intensive chore of creating complex screen displays.

RAM

RAM (random access memory)—the computer system's *main memory*—stores the programs and data on which the computer is currently working. Like the microprocessor, a microcomputer system's RAM consists of circuits etched onto silicon-backed chips. These chips are mounted in carrier packages, just as the CPU is, and the packages are arranged onto boards called *single in-line memory modules,* or *SIMMs.* These units plug into the system board.

Most desktop microcomputer systems sold today have enough RAM to store a few million to several million bytes of data. What's more, many computer systems

■ **Random access memory (RAM).** The computer system's main memory.

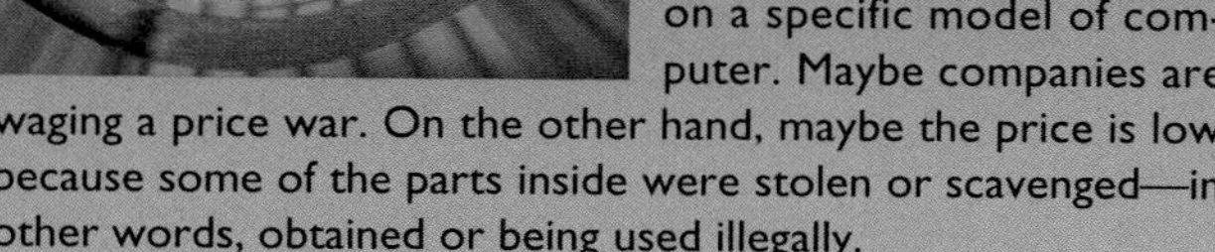

FEATURE HW 1-1

Black-Market Chips

Beware of Outrageously Inexpensive Computers

These days, computer shoppers often see prices that seem impossible to beat. Maybe the low price is due to a manufacturer's closeout on a specific model of computer. Maybe companies are waging a price war. On the other hand, maybe the price is low because some of the parts inside were stolen or scavenged—in other words, obtained or being used illegally.

Black-market chips—stolen computer and memory chips or used chips sold as new—have been a big problem for the computer industry. CPU and memory chips can be quite attractive to thieves; for instance, a single Pentium II chip can sell for several hundred dollars on the black market. Like the chop shops that dismantle stolen cars and resell their parts, some disreputable computer makers accept chips that are stolen or scavenged from computers that have been discarded and then assemble them into "new" computers.

By some estimates, an average of $1 million worth of equipment is stolen from high-tech companies in California's Silicon Valley each week. In some cases, employees smuggle chips out of plants; in others, thieves break into warehouses or delivery trucks. Some thieves even steal piles of discarded chips intended to be melted into scrap. The black-market problem goes well beyond Silicon Valley; it is a worldwide phenomenon.

When criminals steal computers or peripheral devices and extract these parts, they often remove and restamp original serial numbers. Thus, a 133 MHz Pentium chip can instantly gain a new identity as a 200 MHz chip.

Black-market chips. The 1990s answer to the hot watch.

The computer industry has been fighting back against this abuse. Plants have tightened security, the police have taken notice and clamped down, and legislators are trying to enact stiff, new penalties. Also, some computer manufacturers are now stamping hard-to-alter, machine-specific identification numbers on some components of the computer systems they produce. Others are building security codes into such components to limit access to legitimate users.

How can you tell if the equipment you're considering is a legitimate deal or a rip-off? Chances are, if you're buying a new or used machine from a reputable company, you will have no problem. In other cases, that too-good-to-be-true price should make you suspicious. All too often, it spells trouble.

allow memory expansion (within limits) to remedy insufficient amounts of RAM. RAM is *volatile,* meaning that the contents of memory are lost forever when the computer is shut off.

Ordinary RAM is often referred to as *DRAM* (for *d*ynamic *r*andom *a*ccess *m*emory) in the technical literature. This name refers to its need for regular recharging as processing takes place. During recharge, DRAM cannot be accessed by the CPU. A faster type of RAM—called *SRAM,* for *s*tatic *r*andom *a*ccess *m*emory—does not need recharging. However, SRAM chips also offer less capacity at higher cost than DRAM. Consequently, computer makers use it sparingly.

Cache Memory As you work at a desk, you naturally want to place the file folders or documents you need most within an arm's length. Other useful materials might rest in a nearby stack, somewhat farther away but still within easy reach.

The computer works in a similar way. Although it can access materials in main memory relatively quickly, it can work much faster if it places the most urgently needed materials into storage areas that allow even easier access. Such storage areas are known as **cache memory.** Every time the CPU requests data from RAM, it places a copy of them in cache memory. Thus, cache memory always contains the data

---

■ **Cache memory.** A storage area, faster than RAM, where the computer stores data it has most recently accessed.

most recently accessed by the CPU. Whenever the CPU needs data from RAM, it checks first to see if cache holds the needed input.

Two types of cache memory appear widely in computers. *Internal cache* is a form of cache memory that is built right into the CPU chip. *External (secondary) cache,* on the other hand, resides on SRAM chips located close to the CPU on the system board. Internal cache is the speedier of the two, but it also costs more than external cache and stores less data. As you might guess, the computer looks for data first in internal cache, then in external cache, and then in main memory. The relationship between cache memory and RAM is illustrated in Figure HW 1-12.

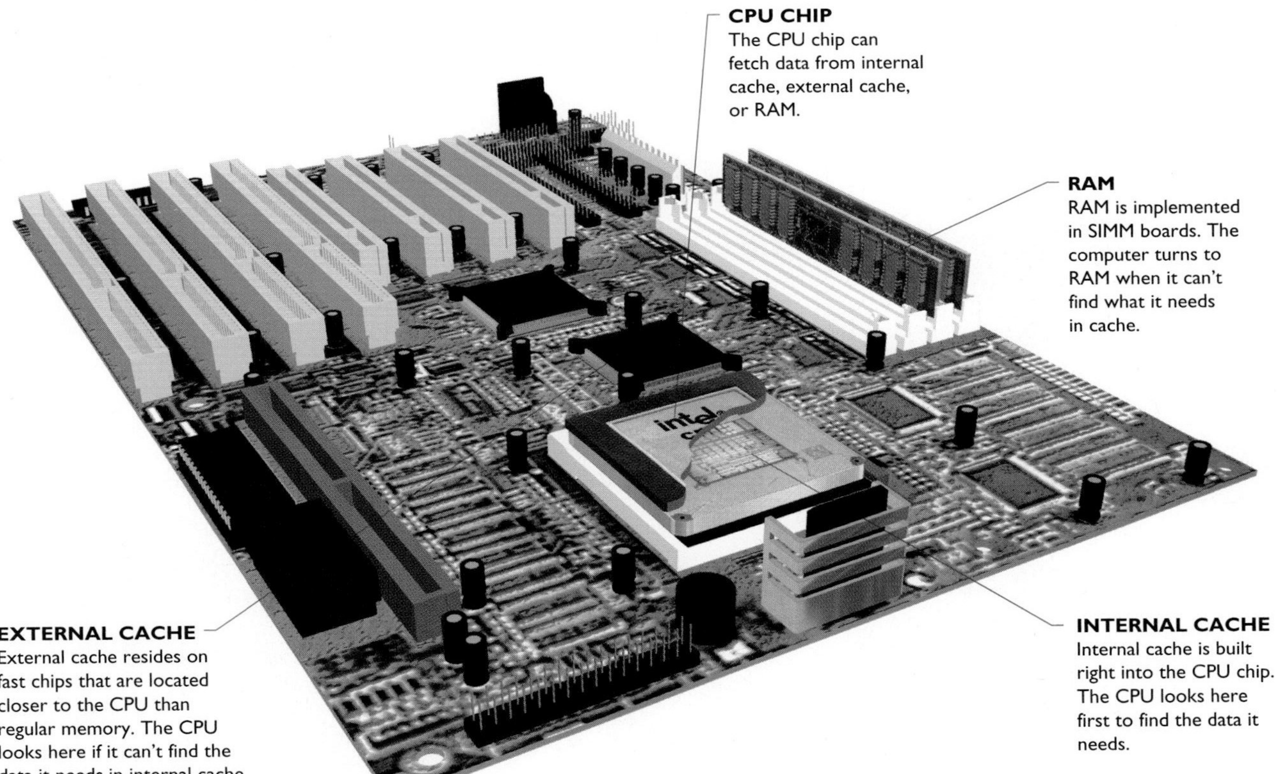
CPU CHIP
The CPU chip can fetch data from internal cache, external cache, or RAM.
RAM
RAM is implemented in SIMM boards. The computer turns to RAM when it can't find what it needs in cache.
EXTERNAL CACHE
External cache resides on fast chips that are located closer to the CPU than regular memory. The CPU looks here if it can't find the data it needs in internal cache.
INTERNAL CACHE
Internal cache is built right into the CPU chip. The CPU looks here first to find the data it needs.

FIGURE HW 1-12

Cache memory. Cache memory speeds processing by staging data in successive, fast-access storage areas.

ROM

Another kind of storage, **ROM** (for **read-only memory),** consists of nonerasable hardware modules that store program instructions. Like RAM, these software-in-hardware modules are mounted into carrier packages that, in turn, are plugged into one or more boards inside the system unit. You can neither write over these ROM programs (the reason they're called *read-only)* nor destroy their contents when you shut off the computer's power. (That is, they're *nonvolatile.)* The CPU can fetch a program from ROM more quickly than from disk, which is slower and located farther away.

Important pieces of systems software are often stored in ROM. For instance, one of the computer's first activities when you turn on the power is to perform a power-on self test (POST). The POST program is stored in ROM, and it produces the beeps you hear as your computer system begins operation, or "boots up." POST takes an inventory of system components, checks each component for proper functioning, and initializes system settings.

■ **Read-only memory (ROM).** A software-in-hardware module from which the computer can read data, but to which it cannot write data.

PORTS

Most system units feature built-in, exterior sockets that enable you to plug in external hardware devices. These sockets are known as **ports** (see Figure HW 1-13).

Serial ports can transmit data only a single bit at a time. However, they require very inexpensive cables, and they can reliably send data over long distances. In contrast, *parallel ports* can transmit data 1 byte at a time—making data transfers several times faster than those through serial ports—but they require more expensive cables and cannot reliably send data across distances over 50 feet. Parallel ports typically connect nearby printers and tape drives to a microcomputer system,

FIGURE HW 1-13

Ports.

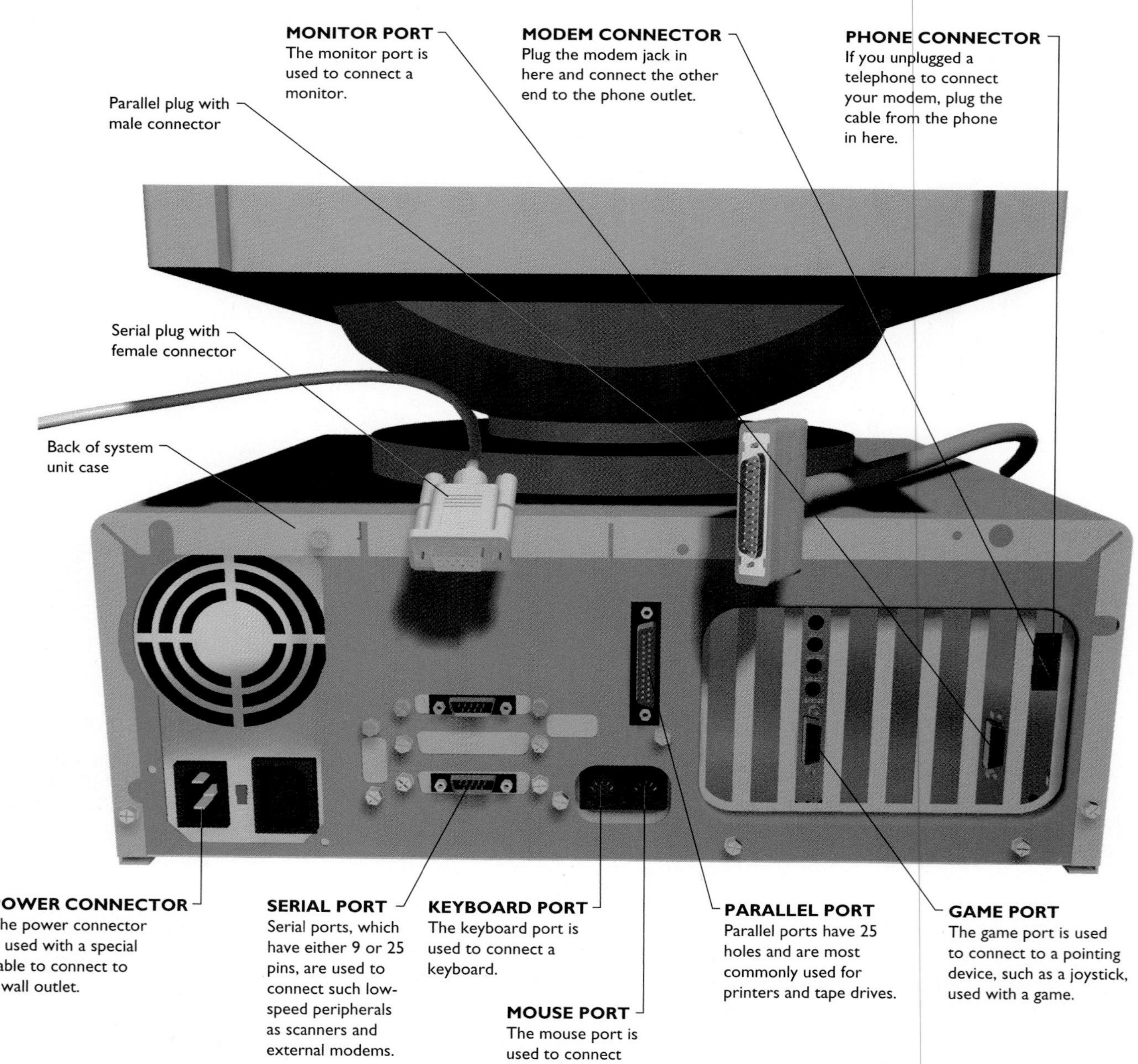

MONITOR PORT
The monitor port is used to connect a monitor.
MODEM CONNECTOR
Plug the modem jack in here and connect the other end to the phone outlet.
PHONE CONNECTOR
If you unplugged a telephone to connect your modem, plug the cable from the phone in here.
Parallel plug with male connector
Serial plug with female connector
Back of system unit case
POWER CONNECTOR
The power connector is used with a special cable to connect to a wall outlet.
SERIAL PORT
Serial ports, which have either 9 or 25 pins, are used to connect such low-speed peripherals as scanners and external modems.
KEYBOARD PORT
The keyboard port is used to connect a keyboard.
MOUSE PORT
The mouse port is used to connect a mouse.
PARALLEL PORT
Parallel ports have 25 holes and are most commonly used for printers and tape drives.
GAME PORT
The game port is used to connect to a pointing device, such as a joystick, used with a game.

■ **Port.** A socket on the back of a computer's system unit into which a peripheral device may be plugged.

whereas serial ports connect such devices as scanners and modems. Computers usually come with dedicated serial ports for keyboards and mice; they connect displays through dedicated parallel ports.

When you need to plug in an I/O device to a desktop system unit that has no built-in port for it, you normally must buy a special *add-in board* that has a port on it. When you install the board, the port extends through an opening in the back of the system unit so that you can plug the I/O device into it. For a notebook or handheld computer, a *PC card* provides add-in board functionality for external connections. The next section discusses add-in boards and PC cards in more detail.

SYSTEM EXPANSION

Not everyone wants the same type of computer system. One person may be satisfied with 16 MB of RAM, while others want 32 MB or 64 MB in the same model of computer. Similarly, while many people need only average sound capabilities from their computer systems, musicians and music buffs often desire top-of-the-line audio capabilities. To account for the wide variety of needs in the marketplace, most microcomputer-system vendors enable you to customize your system with either add-in boards or PC cards.

Add-In Boards **Add-in boards** expand the functions of desktop computers. These cardlike pieces of electronic circuitry plug into *expansion slots* within the computer's system unit (see Figure HW 1-14). Add-in boards enable users to add specific types of peripheral devices or otherwise expand the capabilities of their computer systems.

Computer systems accept many types of add-in boards. For example, displays usually connect to their own *video-adapter boards,* which both translate CPU instructions into a form the display can use and temporarily store information before it goes to the display screen. Similarly, your computer system can communicate with the Internet or with remote facsimile (fax) machines through a *fax/modem board.* To

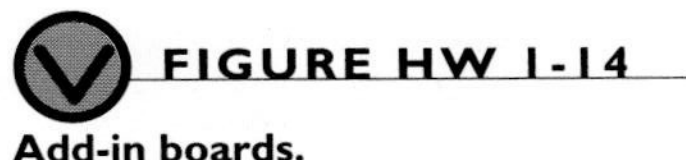

FIGURE HW 1-14
Add-in boards.

Types of Add-In Boards

Board Type	Purpose
Accelerator board	Uses specialized processor chips that speed up overall processing
Disk controller card	Enables a particular type of disk drive to interface with the microcomputer system
Video-adapter board	Enables a particular type of display to interface with the microcomputer system
Emulator board	Allows the microcomputer system to function as a communications terminal
Fax/modem board	Provides communications and facsimile capabilities
Graphics adapter board	Enables the computer system to conform to a particular graphics standard
Memory expansion board	Allows additional RAM to be put into the microcomputer system
Sound board	Enables users to attach speakers to a microcomputer system

■ **Add-in board.** A circuit board that may be inserted into a slot within a desktop computer's system unit to add one or more functions.

enhance your system's sound and graphics capabilities, you would respectively acquire a certain type of *sound board* and a certain type of *graphics board.* SIMMs are add-in boards, too. To add more memory to your system, you might plug in a SIMM with the extra storage you need—say 16 or 32 more megabytes.

You can customize your computer by adding the right boards when you purchase it or, as new needs evolve, add boards at a later time. Because adding boards to a functioning computer system can be time consuming—and because many users dislike the idea of removing the covers from their system units and poking around inside—many vendors have drifted toward a plug-and-play strategy to ease the difficulties of installing new devices.

Plug-and-play gives your computer system the ability to detect and automatically configure new hardware devices. Usage of the term sometimes optimistically implies that you can install new hardware simply by plugging a new device into the correct expansion slot or port and that, once the device is connected, the operating system will automatically recognize it the next time you turn on your computer. In reality, however, plug-and-play has not always worked as smoothly as vendors or users would like.

PC Cards For many years, users of laptop and notebook computers could not expand their machines very much. Most portable computers lack room inside their system units to accommodate either the standard desktop bus or its big internal boards. Then came PCMCIA. *PCMCIA*—which stands for *Personal Computer Memory Card International Association*—refers to a standard way to connect peripheral devices to notebook computers.

The mainstay of the PCMCIA standard is a credit-card-sized adapter card known as the *PCMCIA card,* or more commonly, the **PC card** (see Figure HW 1-15). PC cards typically plug into slots in the edge of a notebook computer's case. Cards come in three basic thicknesses. A Type I card, the thinnest of the lot, is often used to add memory. A Type II card typically adds networking capabilities or sound. Type III cards, the thickest type, often contain removable hard

FIGURE HW 1-15

PC cards. PC cards allow notebook users to enhance their computing environments.

NETWORKING
An Ethernet/modem card makes it possible to send data over an office network or the telephone lines.

STORAGE
A hard disk on a card can be used to supplement a computer's native storage.

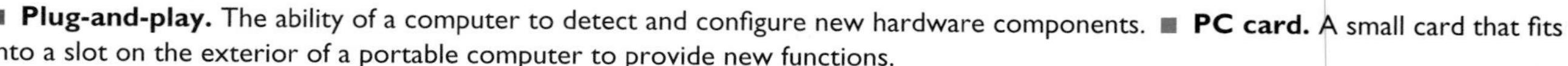

■ **Plug-and-play.** The ability of a computer to detect and configure new hardware components. ■ **PC card.** A small card that fits into a slot on the exterior of a portable computer to provide new functions.

drives. A notebook computer may provide a multipurpose slot that can accommodate two Type I cards, two Type II cards, or a single Type III card. Because the cards plug in externally to the computers, you can take them out as easily as unplugging a table lamp when you don't need them.

Hardware considerations impose a practical limit on the number of peripheral devices a CPU can handle. Generally, each new device interfaced through a port, an add-in board, or a PC card adds to the CPU's processing burden, possibly degrading system performance.

BUSES

A **bus** is an electronic path within a computer system along which bits are transmitted (see Figure HW 1-16). Earlier we touched on the *internal bus,* which moves data around the CPU chip. Here we'll cover buses that extend off of the CPU chip and show how the CPU connects to RAM as well as to peripheral devices.

FIGURE HW 1-16

Buses. Buses transport bits and bytes from one computer-system component to another.

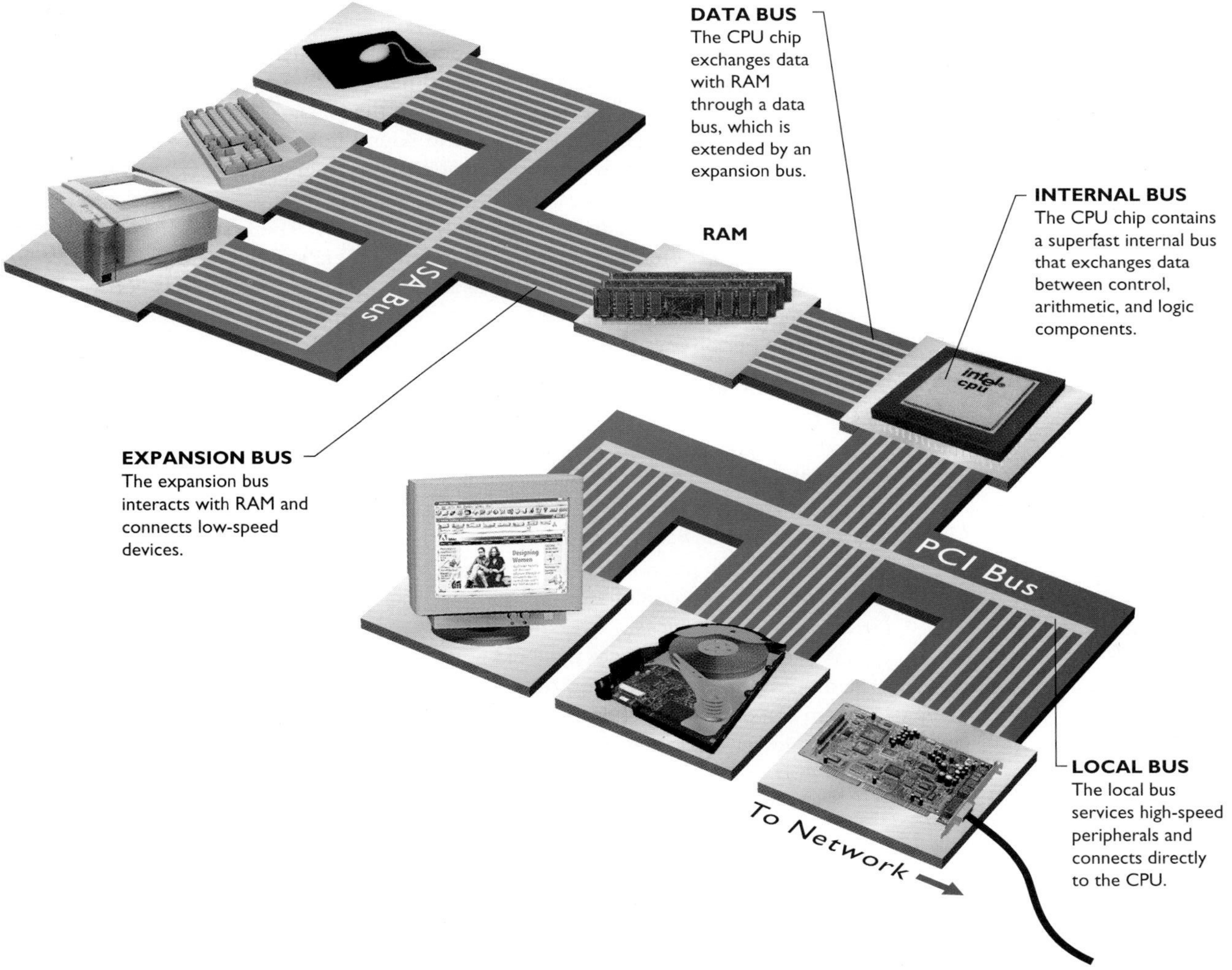

DATA BUS
The CPU chip exchanges data with RAM through a data bus, which is extended by an expansion bus.

RAM

INTERNAL BUS
The CPU chip contains a superfast internal bus that exchanges data between control, arithmetic, and logic components.

ISA Bus

EXPANSION BUS
The expansion bus interacts with RAM and connects low-speed devices.

PCI Bus

LOCAL BUS
The local bus services high-speed peripherals and connects directly to the CPU.

To Network

■ **Bus.** An electronic path within a computer system along which bits are transmitted.

Data and Expansion Buses A computer system's *data bus* links its CPU to RAM. From RAM, an *expansion bus* extends the data bus to establish links with peripherals. Today's computer systems implement a number of expansion bus standards. The most widely used, *ISA* (for *Industry Standard Architecture),* has been around since 1984. Three newer standards—*EISA,* for *Enhanced Industry Standard Architecture,* IBM's *Micro Channel Architecture,* and Apple's *NuBus*—define wider buses. Just a few years ago, many people in the computer industry figured that these newer bus designs would eclipse the ISA standard, but the large base of ISA boards in use and the recent popularity of local buses—which have diminished the demands placed on the standard expansion bus—have given ISA new life.

Local Buses Early microcomputers suffered from the drawback that a single expansion bus had to carry all of data and program traffic between RAM and peripheral devices. That arrangement created no problem in the days when monitors displayed text only, and data could creep along at a snail's pace. But times have changed. Graphical user interfaces (GUIs) have come to dominate computer software, and they demand fast speeds to generate their complex screens. Multimedia applications—with their video clips and other data-intensive needs—also require lightning quickness. Adding fuel to the fire, many more devices are around these days competing for expansion-bus space: mice, scanners, backup tape devices, sound boards, graphics boards—you name it.

To provide faster system response times, hardware producers have connected peripherals that need extremely fast response times—such as the display, disk drives, and boards connecting to high-speed local networks—to their own bus. This new device is called a *local bus,* and it links directly to the CPU. All other (slower) devices—such as the system's mouse, modem, and sound board—work off the traditional expansion bus. The local bus carries data in larger chunks and at faster clock speeds than the regular expansion bus.

Two local bus standards are commonly seen today. The first, *VESA* (which stands for *Video Electronic Standards Association),* is sometimes referred to as the *VL bus.* VESA is found mostly on 486 computers. The second and newer standard is *PCI,* for *Peripheral Component Interconnect.* PCI has made VESA almost extinct, because it can connect more peripherals and supports plug-and-play, which VESA does not.

The Universal Serial Bus (USB) The most recent advances in bus architectures have brought the *universal serial bus (USB).* USBs enable up to 64 devices—all of which use the same type of plug—to connect to a computer through a single port. You can link peripherals to a port by chaining them together—say, by plugging the printer into the port and then plugging a modem or a scanner into the printer, and so on.

USB makes devices *hot swappable.* This means that you can add or unplug devices with the system power on. Also, the computer system will immediately recognize the change, so you don't have to reboot in order to have the system acknowledge and work with new devices.

While users can connect their old peripheral devices to a USB-enabled computer, maximum performance requires USB-enabled peripherals. Ideally, a USB-enabled system can produce speeds about 100 times higher than those of systems with older buses. Newer operating systems, such as Windows 98, support the USB standard.

Making Computers Speedier

Over the years, computer designers have developed a number of strategies to achieve faster performance in their machines. This section discusses five of these methods.

Moving Circuits Close Together As complex as computers seem, all must follow one intuitive natural law: Shorter circuits require less time to move bits.

During the last several decades, computer-chip makers have packed circuitry progressively closer together. Today, they fit several million circuits on a single, fingernail-sized chip. This remarkable achievement doesn't mean that chip makers can continue to shrink circuitry without constraint. Unfortunately, when the circuits are in use, they generate heat; circuits placed too close together can become hot enough to melt the chip.

New Materials Most CPU chips today carry out processing through metallic circuitry etched onto a silicon backing. Silicon is used for a number of reasons. First, as the main ingredient in beach sand, it is one of the most plentiful elements known. Second, it is lightweight. Third, it is a natural *semiconductor.* It differs from copper, which conducts electricity, and wood, which doesn't; silicon falls somewhere in between. The significance of this is that its properties may be altered to let electricity pass or prevent it from passing. Silicon-backed chips have been in wide use since the 1970s, when manufacturing techniques for microminiature circuitry became widely available.

Today, because designers are quickly reaching limits on the number of circuits that they can pack onto a silicon chip without heat damage, several other alternative materials are attracting considerable attention (see the Tomorrow box).

Reduced Instruction Set Computing (RISC) An earlier chapter discussion mentioned that each computer has its own *instruction set.* Each instruction of this set corresponds to microcode.

Traditionally, computers have been built under a design principle called *complex instruction set computing (CISC).* A computer chip with CISC design contains a relatively rich and sophisticated set of instructions by which to process data. Such complexity comes at a cost, however—CISC computers often need several clock cycles to execute each instruction.

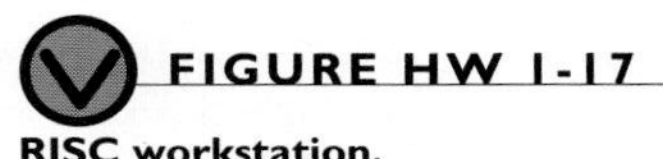

FIGURE HW 1-17

RISC workstation.

Starting in the mid-1970s, processors with limited instruction sets became available. These devices follow a principle called **reduced instruction set computing (RISC).** Experience has shown that computers with only a fraction of the traditional instructions actually process work faster. RISC processing is faster than CISC processing because most of the instructions that a computer processes are relatively simple operations. Thus, computers can maximize speed when they are designed to carry out this large body of simple instructions most rapidly. While RISC computers can execute simple instructions much faster than their CISC counterparts, they run more slowly when doing work that involves executing an usually large number of complex instructions. RISC chips must rely on software routines to break the latter into sequences of smaller instructions before processing can take place.

Today, RISC devices define performance standards in high-speed, graphically oriented environments—such as engineering and movie making (see Figure HW 1-17). RISC also represents the resident architecture of the PowerPC chip, and even Intel—a proponent of CISC architecture—is adding RISC components to many of its future CPU chips. One of the downsides to RISC-based computers is that conventional software needs modification to work on them. The Inside the Industry box on page HW 30 features one of the companies that specializes in RISC-based computing—Sun Microsystems.

Pipelining In older microcomputer systems, the CPU had to completely finish processing one microcoded instruction before starting another. Later computer systems,

---

■ **Reduced instruction set computing (RISC).** A processor design architecture that incorporates fewer instructions in CPU circuitry than conventional computer systems.

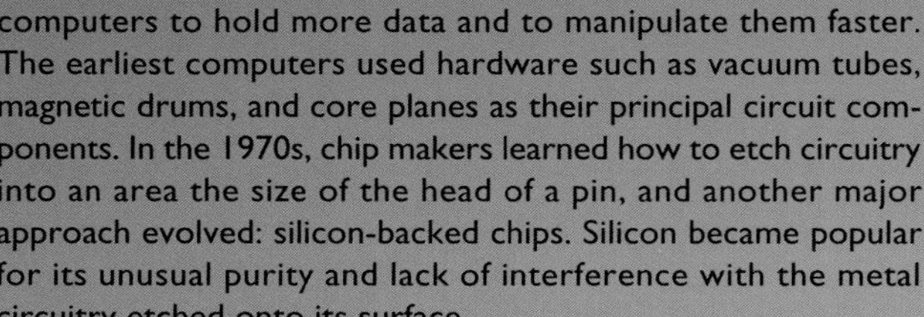

The Coming Chip Technologies

What Will Be the Next Major Challenger to Silicon?

Since the beginning of modern computing technology, researchers have searched constantly for new types of circuit technologies that would allow computers to hold more data and to manipulate them faster. The earliest computers used hardware such as vacuum tubes, magnetic drums, and core planes as their principal circuit components. In the 1970s, chip makers learned how to etch circuitry into an area the size of the head of a pin, and another major approach evolved: silicon-backed chips. Silicon became popular for its unusual purity and lack of interference with the metal circuitry etched onto its surface.

Today, even the ability to fit a few million microminiaturized circuit elements onto a silicon chip may not yield a high enough performance. Researchers are pressing forward with other approaches. Consider five of the leading challengers to silicon:

Gallium Arsenide One of the most promising new computer chip technologies involves gallium arsenide (GaAs). GaAs chips are superior to those made of silicon in several ways:

- They move electronic impulses around several times faster.
- They enable optical data transmissions, something silicon can't do.
- They can operate at much higher temperatures and emit less heat, creating the possibility of chip designs that pack circuits closer together.

Gallium arsenide products are already moving into the marketplace. Some of the more critical components of large computers now employ GaAs chips, and GaAs is rapidly taking hold in areas such as high-speed communications.

But gallium arsenide has some drawbacks. GaAs chips often cost several times more than those made of silicon. Also, today's early state of GaAs technology can currently fit far fewer circuits onto a single chip.

Superconductors One of the problems with conventional circuitry results from heat. When circuits get hot, their electrical resistance increases, impeding the flow of message-bearing electrons. If circuits are placed too close together, this heat can melt underlying materials. Superconductive materials, on the other hand, can transfer electrons without the worry of electrical resistance or heat buildup.

Every year, newly discovered materials more closely approach the ideal of superconductivity. While most of today's superconductors require external cooling systems in order to lose resistance and avoid meltdown, the search continues for materials that are superconductive at room temperature. If and when naturally superconductive materials emerge from the laboratories and reach successful implementation in products, they may result in circuitry that's 100 times faster than today's silicon-backed chips.

GaAs chip. Enough power to transmit 40 encyclopedia volumes every second.

Optical Processing Optical processing technology uses light waves to do the work of a silicon-backed chip's electrons. Optical chips currently available in the marketplace can move data several times faster than the speeds that silicon-backed chips can achieve. Theoretically, an optical processor would be capable of speeds hundreds of times faster than those of silicon—if surrounding components could input and receive data fast enough. Optical chips are surfacing today in such applications as collision-avoidance systems for cars, artificial vision systems for robots, and sensors for image processing.

Biotechnology Biotechnology offers yet another compelling alternative to today's silicon chip. Scientists have shown that they can grow and shape tiny molecules to act as electronic circuits. With such a technology, electrons pass from molecule to molecule. Some scientists believe that such a technology, if it is ever perfected, could result in circuits 500 times smaller than those on today's silicon chips.

Tubes on a Chip Just when everyone thought that it was dead and buried, vacuum tube electronic technology—popular in the 1940s and 1950s—is making a comeback. Scientists are now talking about the distinct possibility of arranging up to 10 billion microscopic tubes on a five-inch wafer. Why vacuum tubes? Electrons can travel much faster through a vacuum than through air. Unlike their predecessors, which needed heat to work, these new tubes implement an entirely different set of principles. Some researchers believe that tubes on a chip could pack 1,000 times the power of today's silicon chips.

however, practice a method called **pipelining,** which starts a new instruction as soon as the previous one reaches the next stage of the machine cycle. Figure

■ **Pipelining.** A CPU feature designed to begin processing a new instruction as soon as the previous instruction reaches the next stage of the machine cycle.

HW 1-18 illustrates this process. Note that by the time a pipelined CPU finishes processing the first instruction in a sequence, the second, third, and fourth instructions have entered the processing "pipeline" and are at various stages of completion. A nonpipelined CPU would not even have begun processing for any of these later instructions. CPUs are commonly built today with multiple pipelines.

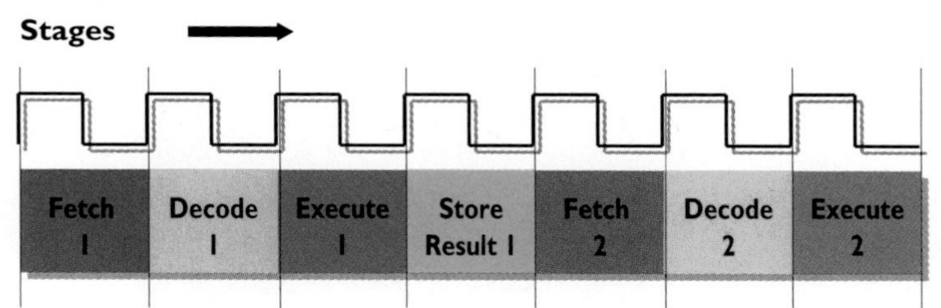

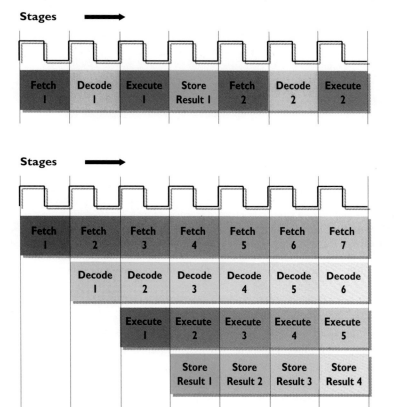

WITHOUT PIPELINING
Without pipelining, an instruction finishes an entire machine cycle before another instruction is started.

Stages

Fetch 1	Fetch 2	Fetch 3	Fetch 4	Fetch 5	Fetch 6	Fetch 7
	Decode 1	Decode 2	Decode 3	Decode 4	Decode 5	Decode 6
		Execute 1	Execute 2	Execute 3	Execute 4	Execute 5
			Store Result 1	Store Result 2	Store Result 3	Store Result 4

WITH PIPELINING
With pipelining, a new instruction is begun when the preceding instruction moves to the next stage of the machine cycle.

"1" means instruction 1, "2" means instruction 2, and so on.

FIGURE HW 1-18

Pipelining. Pipelining streamlines the machine cycle by staging instructions.

Parallel Processing Despite the astounding evolution of computer technology over the past half century, the vast majority of them are still driven by single CPUs. A single CPU executes instructions serially, or one at a time, whether it works exclusively on one program or juggles several concurrently.

In the race to develop tomorrow's ever-faster computer systems, scientists have developed ways for two or more sets of CPU and memory components to perform tasks in parallel. Instead of relying on one processor to perform a lengthy task, a computer system using **parallel processing** assigns portions of the problem to several CPUs operating simultaneously (see Figure HW 1-19).

The marketplace offers examples of two principal approaches to parallel-processing computer systems. One common approach that began several years ago is represented by the Cray-2, a supercomputer that carries a price tag of several million dollars. This computer's parallel design philosophy hooks up a small number of expensive, state-of-the-art CPUs. The Cray-2 uses four such processors, all of which carry out both parallel and serial processing.

The second method of parallel processing involves building computers from hundreds or thousands of relatively inexpensive, off-the-shelf microprocessors. Such

■ **Parallel processing.** A computing system in which two or more CPUs share work, simultaneously processing separate parts of it.

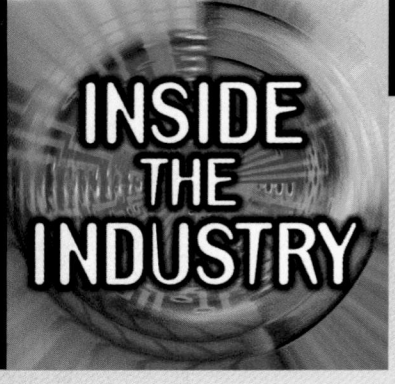

INSIDE THE INDUSTRY

The Mistake That Launched Sun Microsystems

One of the largest producers of workstations based on RISC microprocessors, and also the company that created the Java programming language, is Sun Microsystems. Like a few other billion-dollar giants in the computer industry, Sun got its start because of mistakes made by other companies.

Xerox made the first mistake. Several years ago, the Advanced Research Projects Agency (ARPA) of the U.S. Department of Defense wanted to buy a standard workstation for its employees. ARPA initially went to Xerox, but that company's price on its newly developed Alto workstation was too high even for the government. ARPA's search led next to nearby Stanford University, where it saw an attractive, generic workstation called *S.U.N.* (for *Stanford University Network).*

Stanford University is not a commercial enterprise, so the designer of the S.U.N., graduate student Andy Bechtolscheim, had to approach several private companies himself in order to get the product manufactured. For one reason or another, all of the firms he contacted turned down the offer. One was IBM.

Scott McNealy. The current Sun president was an original founder.

According to legend, Bechtolscheim, hearing about IBM's formal standards for dress and behavior, made his presentation wearing a tuxedo borrowed from Stanford's drama department along with white tennis shoes. When IBM balked at the deal, Bechtolscheim finally formed his own company, Sun Microsystems, in partnership with other graduate students. One of those graduate students was Scott McNealy, the company's current president.

computers are known as *massively parallel processors (MPPs)*. Today's trend emphasizes MPP and the possibilities it provides for *scalable* design; manufacturers can use the same chips in all sizes of computers and make any computer system more powerful at any time simply by adding more chips to it.

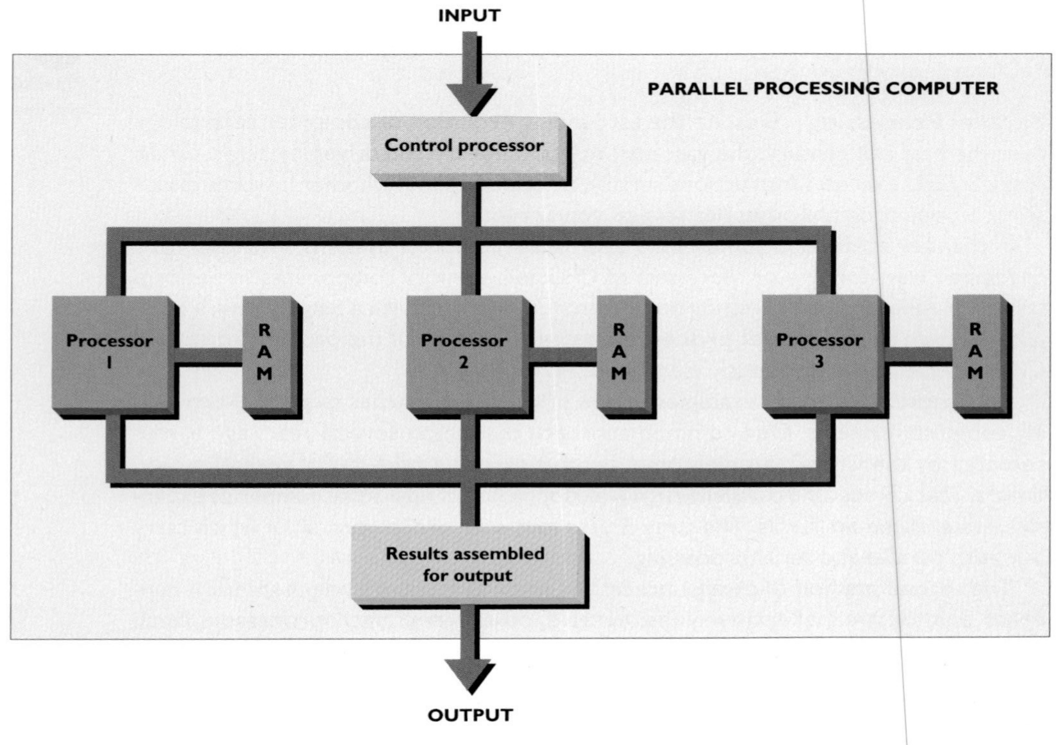

FIGURE HW 1-19

Parallel processing. A computer system using parallel processing divides up a computing problem and assigns portions of it to several processors operating simultaneously.

Summary and Key Terms

In Chapter HW 1 we flipped the lid off of a typical microcomputer's system unit and examined the functions of the parts inside.

How the CPU Works When we talk about computers today, most of us are referring to digital computers. **Digital computers** are devices that *count.*

A digital computer's CPU has two major sections. The **arithmetic/logic unit (ALU)** performs arithmetic and logical operations on data. The **control unit** directs the flow of electronic traffic between memory and the ALU and also between the CPU and input and output devices. Both of these units work closely with memory to carry out processing tasks inside the system unit.

Memory—also called **primary (internal) storage—**holds the programs and data that pass on to the CPU, the results of intermediate processing, and output ready for transmission to secondary storage or an output device. **Registers** are high-speed staging areas within the CPU that hold program instructions and data immediately before processing.

The CPU processes a single, machine-level instruction in a sequence called a **machine cycle.** Each machine-language instruction is broken down into subinstructions called **microcode,** and each piece of microcode corresponds directly to a set of the computer's processing circuits. The computer system has a built-in **system clock** that synchronizes the processing of microcode.

A machine cycle has two parts. During the **I-cycle** (instruction cycle), the control unit fetches and examines an instruction; during the **E-cycle** (execution cycle), the ALU executes the instruction under control-unit supervision. Processing times on computer hardware generally are measured in **milliseconds** (thousandths of a second), **microseconds** (millionths of a second), **nanoseconds** (billionths of a second), or **picoseconds** (trillionths of a second).

Data and Program Representation The electronic components of a digital computer work in a two-state, or **binary,** fashion. It is convenient to think of these binary states as the 0 state and the 1 state. Computer people refer to such 0s and 1s as **bits.**

Computers represent and process text data according to several binary-based codes. Two popular coding schemes are **ASCII** and **EBCDIC.** These systems assign fixed-length codes to represent single characters of data—a digit, alphabetic character, or special symbol—as strings of seven or eight bits. Each string of bits is called a **byte.** Computer systems allow for an additional bit position, called a **parity bit,** in each byte to reveal transmission errors.

The storage capacity of computers often is expressed in **kilobytes (KB),** or thousands of bytes; **megabytes (MB** or *meg),* millions of bytes; **gigabytes (GB),** billions of bytes; and **terabytes (TB),** trillions of bytes.

The binary system can represent not only text but also graphics, audio, and video data. **Machine language** is the binary-based code through which computers represent program instructions. A program must be translated into machine language before the computer can execute it.

The System Unit Almost all computer systems sold today combine modular hardware components to create functional units. For instance, related circuitry is etched onto processor chips or memory chips, and the chips are mounted onto carrier packages. These carriers are then fitted into boards, and the boards are positioned in slots inside the **system unit.**

Every microcomputer's system unit contains a specific microprocessor chip as its CPU. Within its carrier package, this chip is mounted onto a special board, called the **system board,** that fits inside the system unit. CPU chips differ in many respects; one difference is word size. A computer **word** is a group of bits or bytes that the processor can manipulate as a unit. A larger word size usually implies a more powerful processor.

Working alongside the CPU chip in many system units are specialized processor chips such as *numeric coprocessors* and *graphics coprocessors.*

The main memory chips on a microcomputer system are commonly referred to as **RAM,** for **random access memory.** Every time the CPU accesses data from RAM, it places a copy of them in a special place known as **cache memory,** from which it can retrieve them more quickly than from RAM. Memory chips that store nonerasable programs comprise the computer's **ROM,** for **read-only memory.**

Many system units have external input/output **ports** through which peripheral devices connect to the computer. Also, many desktop system units contain limited numbers of internal expansion slots, into which users can mount **add-in boards.** The **plug-and-play** standard provides a computer with the ability to detect and configure new hardware as a user adds it to the system. Owners of notebook computers normally expand their systems by adding **PC cards.**

The CPU connects to RAM, ROM, and peripherals over circuitry called a **bus.** The most widely used *expansion bus* architecture is ISA, and the most widely used *local bus* architecture is PCI.

Making Computers Speedier Over the years, computer designers have developed a number of strategies to make their machines work faster. The chapter text discussed five of these: packing circuits close together, building components out of new materials, **reduced instruction set computing (RISC), pipelining** instructions, and **parallel processing.**

EXERCISES

1. Match each term with the description that fits best.
   a. ALU
   b. binary
   c. bit
   d. EBCDIC
   e. ASCII
   f. word
   g. PC card
   h. parity bit

   _____ The numbering system that consists of 0s and 1s
   _____ The fixed-length code most often associated with IBM mainframes
   _____ A device that provides extra capability for a laptop computer
   _____ A fixed-length code developed by the American National Standards Institute
   _____ Used to check for transmission errors
   _____ The section of the CPU that performs computations
   _____ A group of bits or bytes that a processor can manipulate as a unit
   _____ A binary digit

2. What does each of the following acronyms stand for?
   a. RAM ______________________
   b. ROM ______________________
   c. USB ______________________
   d. RISC ______________________
   e. SIMM ______________________

3. Answer the following questions about byte representations of data:
   a. Given the following ASCII character representations and the specified parity settings, indicate whether a 0 or 1 should be added to the end of the character:

BYTE REPRESENTATION	PARITY	0 OR 1?
00110101	even	____
01011010	odd	____
01001001	odd	____
00110000	odd	____
01000001	even	____

   b. What five characters do the bytes in the table represent?
   c. You receive the following stream of bits in ASCII. Is odd or even parity in use? What does the message say?

   010101111010011111010101111

4. Calculate the following speeds and times:
   a. How many milliseconds are in a minute?
   b. How much faster is 5 microseconds than 200 milliseconds?

5. Fill in the blanks:
   a. A(n) __________ computer is one that counts.
   b. Most CPU chips today consist of metallic circuitry etched onto a(n) __________ backing.
   c. Through a method called __________, as soon as an instruction reaches the next stage of the machine cycle, the processor begins a new instruction.
   d. Processing shared by two or more computers working together is known as __________ processing.
   e. Two __________ bus standards are PCI and VESA.
   f. The term __________ refers to the ability of the computer system to automatically recognize and configure newly added hardware.
   g. __________ language is a binary-based dialect that the computer can execute directly.
   h. Another name for the system unit's motherboard is the __________.
   i. __________ memory is a storage area, faster than RAM, where the computer system stores data it has most recently accessed.
   j. A(n) __________ is a socket on the back of a computer's system unit into which a peripheral device may be plugged.

6. Define the following terms:
   a. PC card
   b. External cache memory
   c. POST
   d. Parallel processing
   e. Nonvolatile
   f. Expansion slots
   g. System clock

7. Identify each of the following statements as true or false:

   _____ Logical computer operations include such things as addition, subtraction, multiplication, and division.
   _____ A millisecond is one one-millionth of a second.
   _____ The computer's machine cycle consists of two parts: the I-cycle and the E-cycle.
   _____ "Megahertz" refers to a measure of a computer's speed.

_____ The 8 bits that represent a character in ASCII or EBCDIC are collectively referred to as a megabyte.

_____ CISC refers to a processor design architecture that incorporates fewer instructions in CPU circuitry than conventional computer systems.

_____ "MMX enabled" specifically refers to RAM chips that are especially configured for multimedia computing.

_____ A word is a group of bits that a computer system treats as a single unit.

_____ PC Cards are devices designed to be fit into expansion slots within a desktop PC's system unit.

_____ A computer's expansion bus extends its data bus.

8. Name at least eight devices located under the cover of a microcomputer's system unit. What functions do these devices perform?

9. What roles do the hardware units listed below play in a computer system?
   a. Control unit
   b. ROM
   c. Main memory
   d. Registers
   e. Internal cache memory

10. Match the PC component shown in each of the following pictures with the appropriate term.

_____ RAM SIMM board
_____ Plug for a parallel port
_____ PC card
_____ Plug for a serial port
_____ Add-in board

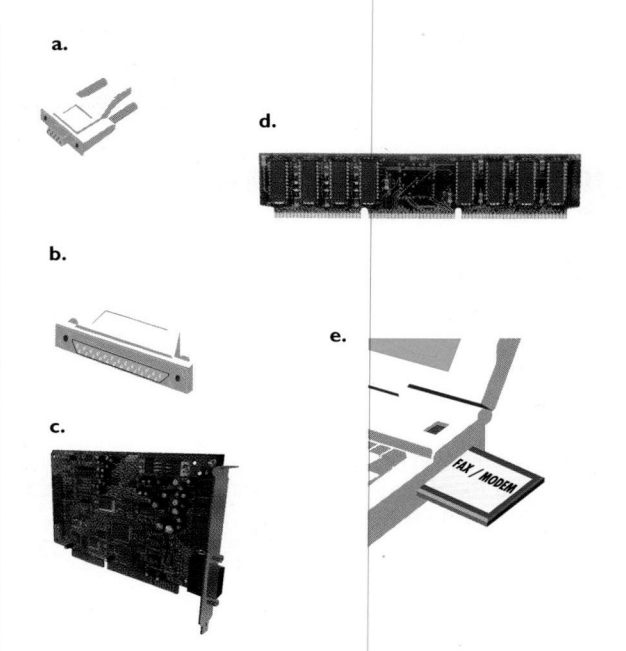

a.

d.

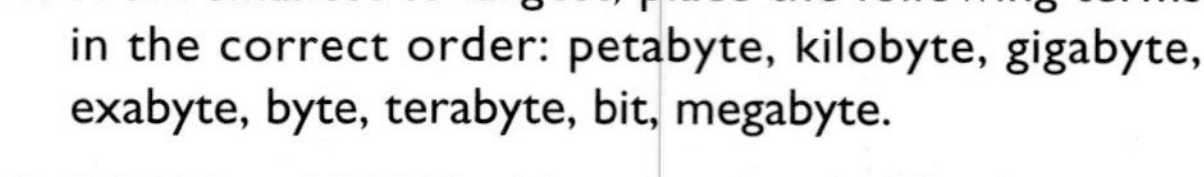

b.

e.

c.

11. From smallest to largest, place the following terms in the correct order: petabyte, kilobyte, gigabyte, exabyte, byte, terabyte, bit, megabyte.

12. DRAM and SRAM, although related, differ in a number of respects.
   a. What is the technical difference between the two?
   b. Which is used for external cache memory?
   c. Which gives faster access to data?
   d. Which is more expensive?
   e. Which provides more storage capacity?

PROJECTS

1. Intel Corp. Intel is the world's largest producer of CPU chips and also the leading chip vendor for PC-compatible computers. Consult either computer periodicals in a library available to you or Intel's Web site (http://www.intel.com), to answer the following questions:

a. What is the name of the fastest Intel CPU chip currently being sold with PCs?
b. At what speed does this chip run? State the answer in MHz.
c. What is the size of this chip's internal cache?
d. What products besides CPU chips does Intel produce?

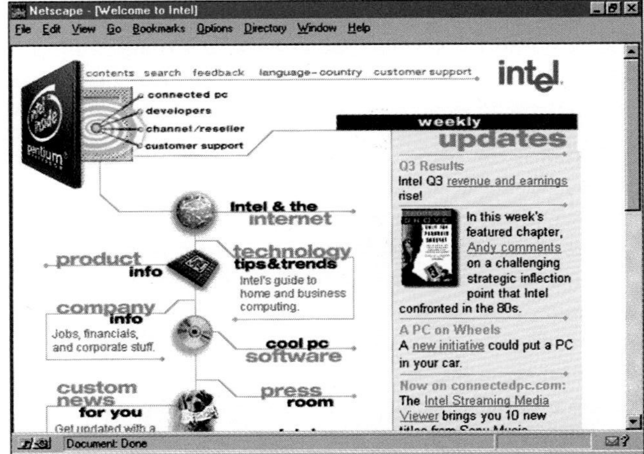

2. PC Makers Virtually all of the leading PC makers maintain Web sites and regularly run advertisements in computer journals. For any three of the PC makers listed below, answer the questions that follow. Feel free to do this project using either Web-based information or information found in computer journals. You can do the project in groups of three students each, if your instructor permits.

COMPANY	WEB SITE ADDRESS (HTTP://_____)
Acer	www.acer.com
Apple Computer	www.apple.com
AST	www.ast.com
Compaq	www.compaq.com
Dell	www.dell.com
Gateway 2000	www.gw2k.com
Hewlett-Packard	www.hp.com
IBM	www.ibm.com
Packard-Bell	www.packardbell.com

a. What is the model name or number of a current desktop computer sold by each vendor? A current notebook computer?
b. What top processing speeds do these computers achieve? Give your answer in MHz.
c. What type of CPU powers each of these computers—for instance, a Pentium II or PowerPC 620?
d. How many megabytes of RAM does each computer include as a maximum?
e. How large is the hard disk (measured in bytes)?

3. Desktop Mainframes The chapter mentions the continuing quest for faster computers. What difference might ordinary users experience if their microcomputers could match the power of today's supercomputers—processing, say, hundreds or thousands of times faster than current microcomputers? Write a small paper, not to exceed three pages, with your response.

4. New Key Terms A textbook chapter of this sort cannot possibly cover every important technology or term regarding the technical aspects of how computers work. Several important terms are listed below that are not covered in the chapter. Through library or Internet research, determine the meanings of any three of these terms, and write out a one-to-three sentence explanation describing each one in your own words.

a. VRAM
b. Flash memory
c. BIOS
d. CMOS RAM
e. Fault tolerance

(*Hint:* If you are going to research this topic through the Internet, you might want to consult some available online

HW

computer dictionaries and glossaries. For starters, access a search site such as Yahoo! or WebCrawler and select the hyperlink for reference materials. By making successive choices, you should easily access a computing dictionary.

5. Soapbox Department Comment on this statement: "Computers are now so easy to work with that it's no longer necessary for the average user to know any of the technical details about how they work." In making your comments, be sure to state how much technical knowledge about computers you think the average student needs.

6. Inspecting a System Unit Open up a system unit and look at the parts inside. Make one or two diagrams labeling components that you recognize. Be sure to include the following components: CPU chip, RAM SIMMs, expansion slots, add-in boards, hard-disk drive, diskette drive(s), CD-ROM drive (if present), power supply, and ports.

7. Microprocessor History Microprocessors improved dramatically between the 2,300-transistor Intel 4004 chip introduced in 1971 and the multimillion-transistor Pentium II that came out in 1997. For this project, determine the number of transistors, or circuit elements, in use on each of the eight Intel chips named in Figure HW 1-11.

8. Future Chips Companies such as Intel and Motorola often announce to the press plans for their future CPU chips well before these chips are available to the public. Using articles from such news-oriented computer periodicals as *Computerworld, PC Week, InfoWeek,* or *MacWeek,* write a paper (one or two pages) about a next-generation CPU chip—say, the one that either Intel or Motorola has on the drawing board to replace its current top-of-the-line model. Describe in the paper how much faster and more capable the newer chip is expected to be as compared to the current model.

9. Massively Parallel Processors Massively parallel processors (MPPs), which combine several microcomputer CPUs to work in concert with each other, have begun to appear on the market with increasing frequency in recent years. For this project, research a particular model of MPP and answer the following questions about it.

a. What is the name of the MPP?
b. How many microprocessors does the MPP use?
c. How fast (in MHz) is the MPP? How large (in bytes) are its memory and hard disk?
d. For what types of applications is the MPP used?

10. Extra Memory Virtually all desktop and notebook computers made today let you expand memory within certain limits. Pick out a desktop or notebook model and answer the following questions:

a. What is the name of the computer? How much memory does it come with?
b. How much would you have to spend to expand the base level of memory sold with the computer? Make sure that your answer includes the memory increments you could choose as well as the costs of those increments—for example, each 16 MB expansion often costs less than $100.
c. Up to what maximum can you expand the memory?

APPENDIX

Numbering Systems

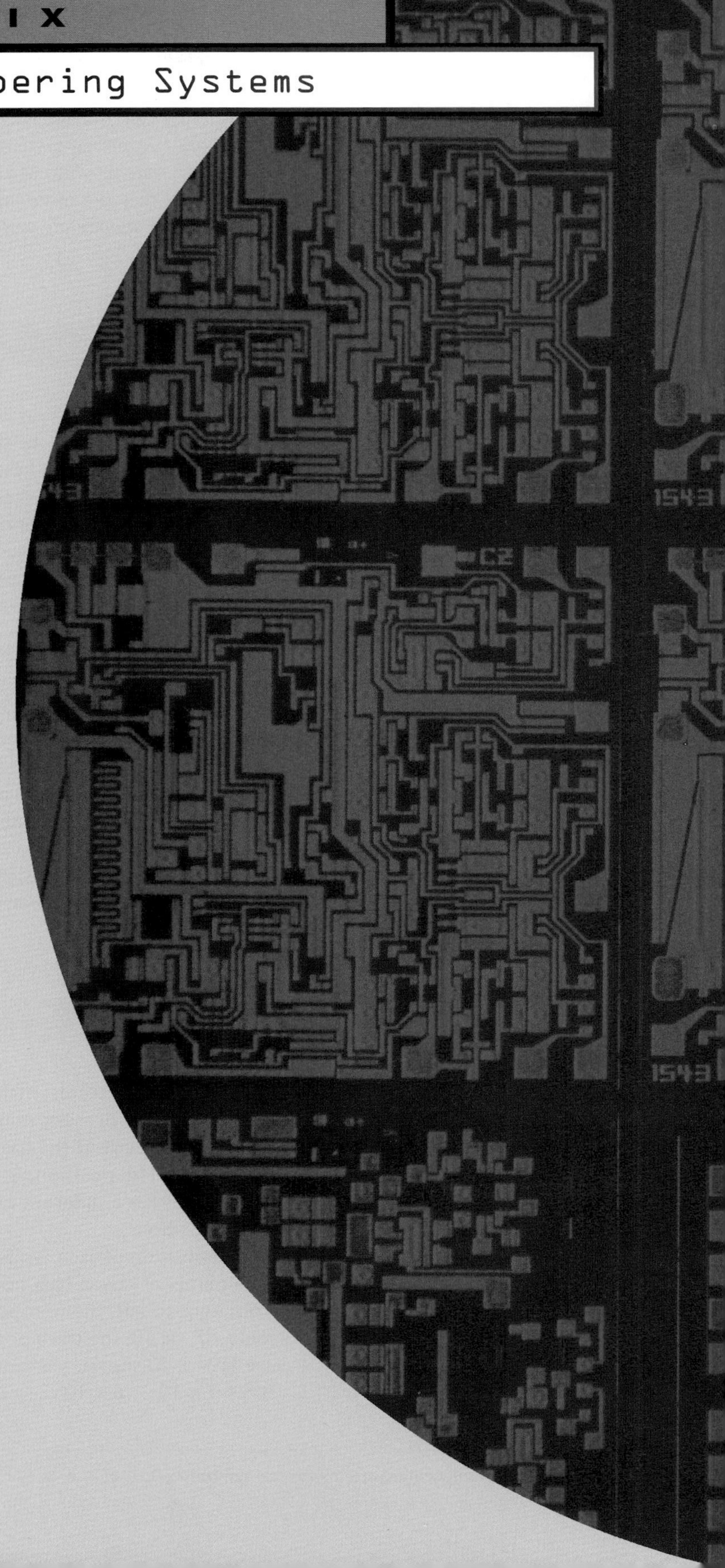

Outline

Overview
What Is a Numbering System?
The Decimal Numbering System
The Binary Numbering System
The Hexadecimal Numbering System
Computer Arithmetic

Learning Objectives

After completing this chapter you will be able to:

1. Describe how the decimal, binary, and hexadecimal numbering systems work.
2. Convert values from one numbering system to another.
3. Add and subtract within the binary and hexadecimal numbering systems.

In Chapter HW 1, you learned that fixed-length coding schemes such as ASCII and EBCDIC are often used to represent numbers, letters of the alphabet, and special characters. Although these codes are handy for storing data and transporting them around a computer system, the codes are not designed to do arithmetic operations. For this task, numbers must be stored in a true binary form that can be manipulated quickly by the computer.

This appendix covers several fundamental characteristics of numbering systems. The two primary systems discussed are the decimal numbering system (used by people) and the binary numbering system (used by computers). Also discussed is the hexadecimal numbering system, which is a shorthand way of representing long strings of binary numbers so that they are more understandable to people. The appendix also covers conversions between numbering systems and principles of computer arithmetic.

What Is a Numbering System?

A *numbering system* is a way of representing numbers. The system we most commonly use is called the *decimal,* or *base 10, system.* (The word *decimal* comes from the Latin word for *ten.*) It is called *base 10* because it uses ten symbols—the digits 0, 1, 2, 3, 4, 5, 6, 7, 8, and 9—to represent all possible numbers. Numbers greater than nine, such as 21 and 683, are represented by combinations of these symbols.

Because we are so familiar with the decimal system, it may never have occurred to most of us that we could represent numbers in any other way. However, nothing says that a numbering system has to have ten possible symbols. Many other numbers would do as a base.

We saw in Chapter HW 1 that the *binary,* or *base 2,* system is used extensively by computers to represent numbers and other characters. Computer systems can perform computations and transmit data thousands of times faster in binary form than they can using decimal representations. Thus, it's important for anyone studying computers to know how the binary system works. Anyone contemplating a professional career in computers should also understand the *hexadecimal* (base 16) system. Before we examine some of the numbering systems used in computing—and learn how to convert numbers from one system into another—let's look more closely at the decimal numbering system. Insight into how the decimal system works will help us understand more about the other numbering systems.

The Decimal Numbering System

All numbering systems, including the decimal system with which people work in everyday life, represent numbers as combinations of ordered symbols. As stated earlier, the **decimal** (or base 10) system has ten acceptable symbols—the digits 0, 1, 2, . . ., 9. The positioning of the symbols in a decimal number is important. For example, 891 is a different number than 918 (with the same symbols occupying different positions).

The position of each symbol in any decimal number represents the number 10 (the base number) raised to a power, or exponent, determined by that position. Going from right to left, the first position represents 10^0, or 1; the second position represents 10^1, or 10; the third position represents 10^2, or 100; and so forth. Thus, as Figure HW 1-20 shows, a decimal number such as 7,216 is understood as $7 \times 10^3 + 2 \times 10^2 + 1 \times 10^1 + 6 \times 10^0$.

■ **Decimal.** A numbering system with ten symbols—0, 1, 2, 3, 4, 5, 6, 7, 8, and 9.

Consider the decimal number

7216

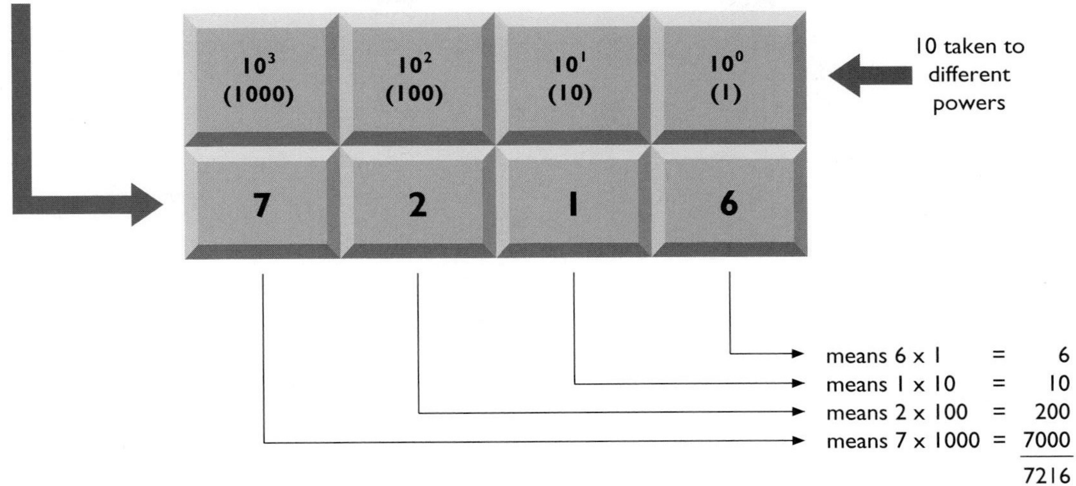

FIGURE HW 1-20

How the decimal (base 10) system works. Each digit in a decimal number represents 10 taken to a different power.

The Binary Numbering System

The **binary,** or base 2, system works in a manner similar to the decimal system. One major difference is that the binary system has only two symbols—0 and 1—instead of ten. A second major difference is that the position of each digit in a binary number represents the number 2 (the base number) raised to an exponent based on that position. Thus, the binary number 11100 represents

$$1 \times 2^4 + 1 \times 2^3 + 1 \times 2^2 + 0 \times 2^1 + 0 \times 2^0$$

which, translated into the decimal system, is 28. Another example of a binary–to–decimal conversion is provided in Figure HW 1-21.

FIGURE HW 1-21

Binary-to-decimal conversion. To convert any binary number to its decimal counterpart, take the right-most digit and multiply it by 2^0 (or 1), the next digit to the left and multiply it by 2^1 (or 2), and so on, as illustrated here. Then add up all the products so formed.

Consider the binary number

1011001

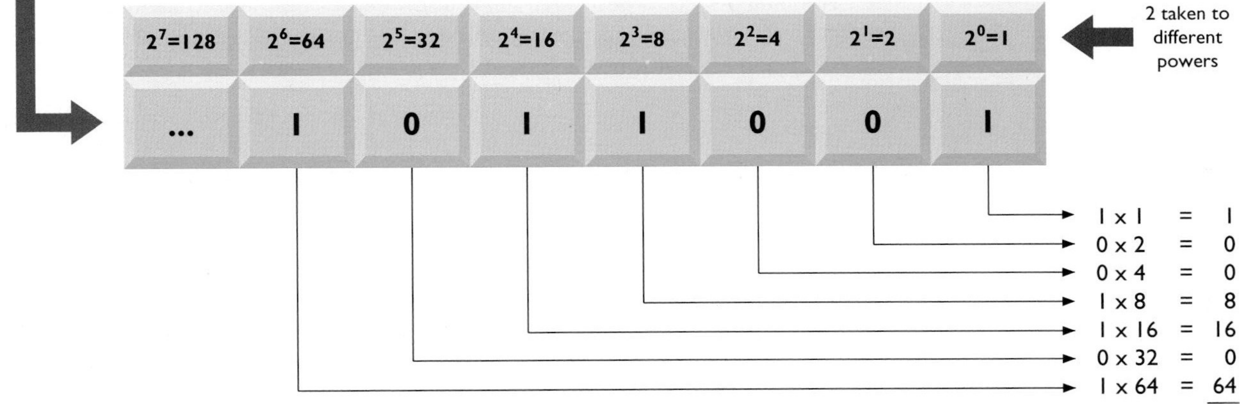

■ **Binary.** A numbering system with two possible states—0 and 1.

FIGURE HW 1-22

Decimal-to-binary conversion using the remainder method. This approach starts by using the decimal number to be converted (89) as the initial dividend. Each successive dividend is the quotient of the previous division. Keep dividing until you reach a zero quotient, whereupon the converted number is formed by the remainders taken in reverse order.

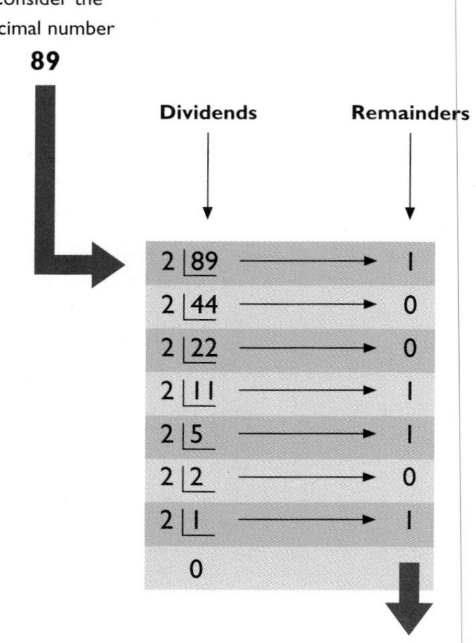

Consider the decimal number
89
Dividends
Remainders
2 | 89 → 1
2 | 44 → 0
2 | 22 → 0
2 | 11 → 1
2 | 5 → 1
2 | 2 → 0
2 | 1 → 1
0
Collecting the remainders backwards, we get the binary number 1011001.

Converting in the reverse direction—from decimal to binary—is also rather easy. A popular approach for doing this is the *remainder method.* This procedure employs successive divisions by the base number of the system to which we are converting. Use of the remainder method to convert a decimal to a binary number is illustrated in Figure HW 1-22.

To avoid confusion between different number bases, it is common to use the base as a subscript. So, referring to Figures HW 1-21 and HW 1-22, for example, we could write:

$$89_{10} = 1011001_2$$

In addition, when we are using numbering systems other than the decimal system, it is customary to pronounce each symbol individually. For example, 101_2 is pronounced "one-zero-one" rather than "one hundred one." This convention also applies to other nondecimal systems.

The binary system described here is sometimes referred to as *true-binary representation.* True-binary representation does not designate a fixed number of bits, as do ASCII and EBCDIC, nor is it used to represent letters or special characters.

The Hexadecimal Numbering System

Computers often output diagnostic and memory-management messages to programmers and technically oriented users in hexadecimal (or *hex*) notation. Hex is a shorthand method for representing the binary digits stored in the computer system. Because large binary numbers—for example, 1101010001001111101_2—can easily be misread by programmers, binary digits are grouped into units of four that, in turn, are represented by other symbols.

Hexadecimal means base 16, implying that there are 16 different symbols in this numbering system. With only 10 possible digits, hex uses letters instead of

■ **Hexadecimal.** Pertaining to the numbering system with 16 symbols: 0, 1, 2, 3, 4, 5, 6, 7, 8, 9, A, B, C, D, E, and F.

Hexadecimal Character	Decimal Equivalent	Binary Equivalent
0	0	0000
1	1	0001
2	2	0010
3	3	0011
4	4	0100
5	5	0101
6	6	0110
7	7	0111
8	8	1000
9	9	1001
A	10	1010
B	11	1011
C	12	1100
D	13	1101
E	14	1110
F	15	1111

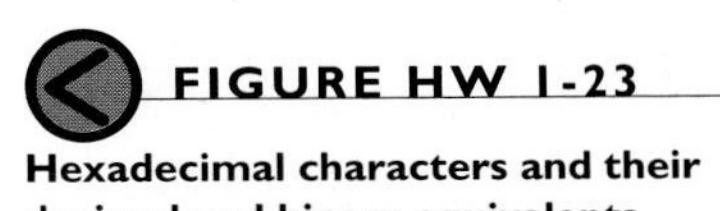

FIGURE HW 1-23

Hexadecimal characters and their decimal and binary equivalents.

numbers for the extra 6 symbols. The 16 hexadecimal symbols and their decimal and binary counterparts are shown in Figure HW 1-23.

Hexadecimal is not itself a code that the computer uses to perform computations or to communicate with other machines. This numbering system does, however, have a special relationship to the 8-bit bytes of ASCII and EBCDIC that makes it ideal for displaying messages quickly. As you can see in Figure HW 1-23, each hex character has a 4-binary-bit counterpart, so any combination of 8 bits can be represented by exactly 2 hexadecimal characters. Thus, the letter *A* (represented in EBCDIC by 11000001) has a hex representation of C1.

Let's look at an example to see how to convert from hex to decimal. Suppose you receive the following message on your display screen:

```
PROGRAM LOADED AT LOCATION 4F6A
```

This message tells you the precise location in memory of the first byte in your program. To determine the decimal equivalent of a hexadecimal number such as 4F6A, you can use a procedure similar to the binary-to-decimal conversion shown in Figure HW 1-21 (refer to Figure HW 1-24).

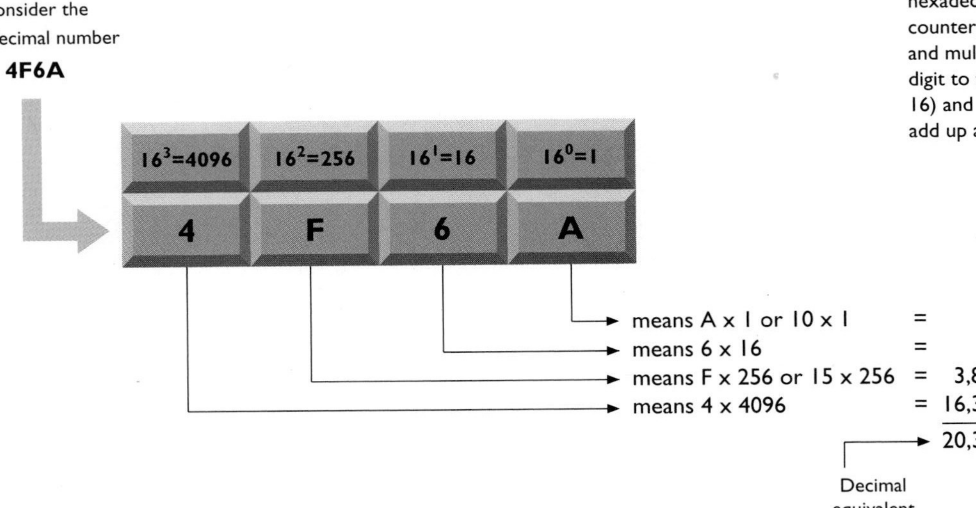

FIGURE HW 1-24

Hexadecimal-to-decimal conversion. To convert any hexadecimal number to its decimal counterpart, take the rightmost digit and multiply it by 16^0 (or 1), the next digit to the left and multiply it by 16^1 (or 16) and so on, as illustrated here. Then add up all the products so formed.

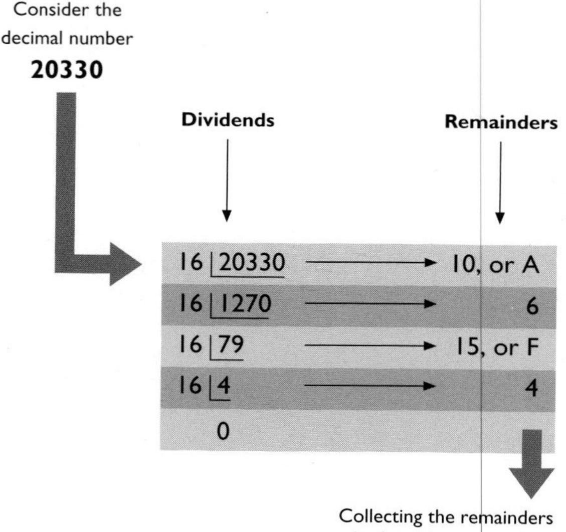
Consider the decimal number
20330
Dividends
Remainders
16 | 20330 → 10, or A
16 | 1270 → 6
16 | 79 → 15, or F
16 | 4 → 4
0
Collecting the remainders backwards, we get the hexadecimal number 4F6A.

FIGURE HW 1-25

Decimal-to-hexadecimal conversion using the remainder method. To convert $20{,}330_{10}$ to a hexadecimal number, start successive divisions by 16 using 20,330 as the initial dividend. Each successive dividend is the quotient of the previous division. As in Figure HW 1-22, divide until you reach a zero quotient and form the converted number by taking the remainders in reverse order.

To convert the other way—from decimal to hex—we again can use the remainder method, this time dividing by 16. A decimal-to-hex conversion using the remainder method is illustrated in Figure HW 1-25.

To convert from base 16 to base 2, we convert each hex digit separately to 4 binary digits (using the table in Figure HW 1-23). For example, to convert F6A9 to base 2, we get:

F	6	A	9
1111	0110	1010	1001

or 1111011010101001_2. To convert from base 2 to base 16, we go through the reverse process. If the number of digits in the binary number is not divisible by 4, we add leading zeros to the binary number to force an even division. For example, to convert 1101101010011_2 to base 16, we get:

0001	1011	0101	0011
1	B	5	3

or $1B53_{16}$. Note that three leading zeros were added to make this conversion. A table summarizing all of the conversions covered in this appendix is provided in Figure HW 1-26.

FIGURE HW 1-26

Summary of conversions.

	To Base		
From Base	2	10	16
2		Starting at right-most digit, multiply binary digits by 2^0, 2^1, 2^2, etc., respectively. Then add products.	Starting at right-most digit, convert each group of four binary digits to a hex digit.
10	Divide repeatedly by 2; then collect remainders in reverse order.		Divide repeatedly by 16; then collect remainders in reverse order.
16	Convert each hex digit to four binary digits.	Starting at rightmost digit, multiply hex digits by 16^0, 16^1, 16^2, etc., respectively. Then add products.	

Computer Arithmetic

To most people, decimal arithmetic is second nature. Addition and subtraction have been part of Western education since kindergarten or first grade. Addition and subtraction using binary and hexadecimal numbers are not much harder than the same operations with decimal numbers. Practically the only difference is in the number of symbols used in each system.

Figure HW 1-27 provides an example of addition and subtraction with decimal, binary, and hexadecimal numbers. Note that with binary and hexadecimal, as in decimal arithmetic, you carry to and borrow from adjacent positions as you move from right to left. Instead of carrying or borrowing 10, however—as you would in the decimal system—you carry or borrow 2 (binary) or 16 (hexadecimal).

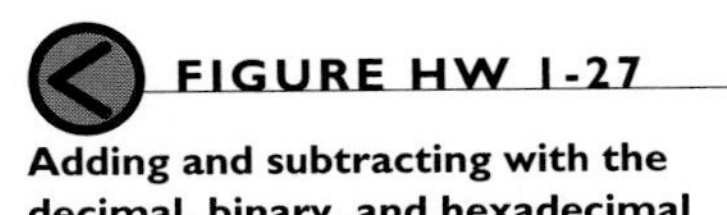

FIGURE HW 1-27

Adding and subtracting with the decimal, binary, and hexadecimal numbering systems.

	Decimal	Binary	Hexadecimal
Addition	142 +47 189	10001110 +101111 10111101	8E +2F BD
Subtraction	142 -47 95	10001110 -101111 1011111	8E -2F 5F

Summary and Key Terms

This appendix covers several fundamentals of numbering systems, including examples showing how numbering systems work, converting values between one numbering system and another, and performing simple types of computer arithmetic.

Numbering Systems A *numbering system* is a way of representing numbers.

The Decimal Numbering System The number system that people most commonly use is called the **decimal,** or base 10, system. It is called base 10 because it uses ten symbols—the digits 0, 1, 2, 3, 4, 5, 6, 7, 8, and 9—to represent all possible numbers. The position of each symbol in any decimal number represents the number 10 (the base number) raised to a power, or exponent, determined by that position.

Because we are so familiar with the decimal system, it may never have occurred to many of us that we could represent numbers in any other way. However, nothing says that a numbering system has to have ten possible symbols. Many other numbers would do as a base.

The Binary Numbering System The **binary,** or base 2, system works in a manner similar to the decimal system. One major difference is that the binary system has only two symbols—0 and 1—instead of ten. A second major difference is that the position of each digit in a binary number represents the number 2 (the base number) raised to an exponent determined by that position.

The binary system described in this appendix is sometimes referred to as *true-binary representation.* True-binary representation does not set a fixed number of bits, as do ASCII and EBCDIC, nor is it used to represent letters or special characters.

The Hexadecimal Numbering System Because large binary numbers can easily be misread by programmers, binary digits often are grouped and represented by other symbols. The **hexadecimal,** or base 16, system represents groups of four binary digits. With only ten possible digits, the letters A–F are used instead of numbers for the extra six symbols. The position of each digit in a hexadecimal number represents the number 16 raised to an exponent determined by that position.

Computer Arithmetic It is a relatively straightforward process to convert any value in one numbering system into a value in another system and to perform computer arithmetic on these values.

1. Convert the following binary numbers to decimal numbers:
   a. 1011_2
   b. 101110_2
   c. 1010011_2
2. Convert the following decimal numbers to binary numbers:
   a. 51_{10}
   b. 260_{10}
   c. 500_{10}
3. Convert the following binary numbers to hexadecimal numbers:
   a. 101_2
   b. 11010_2
   c. 111101000010_2
4. Convert the following hexadecimal numbers to binary numbers:
   a. $F2_{16}$
   b. $1A8_{16}$
   c. $39EB_{16}$
5. Convert the following hexadecimal numbers to decimal numbers:
   a. $B6_{16}$
   b. $5E9_{16}$
   c. $CAFF_{16}$
6. Drawing on techniques you've learned in this appendix, provide an expression to convert the base 6 (yes, six) number 451_6 to a decimal number.
7. Adding the binary numbers 11011001 and 1011101 yields __________.
8. Adding the hexadecimal numbers 8E and 5D yields __________.
9. Subtracting the binary number 1011 from 101110 yields __________.
10. Subtracting the hexadecimal number B6 from F2 yields __________.

Outline

HW 2

Secondary Storage

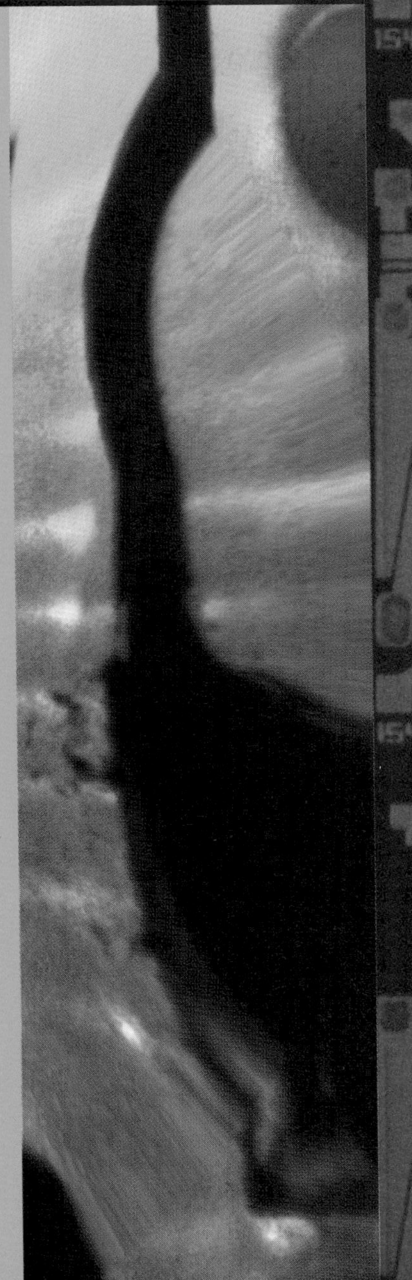

Learning Objectives

After completing this chapter, you will be able to:

1. Name several general properties of secondary storage systems.
2. Identify a number of storage systems based on magnetic disks and describe how they work and where they are particularly useful.
3. Detail the roles of optical-disk and magnetic-tape storage media and equipment.
4. Demonstrate the significance of several emerging secondary storage alternatives.
5. Name several types of data access and organization strategies and cite processing situations appropriate for each.

Overview

In Chapter HW 1, we discussed the role of memory. Memory circuitry is designed to provide immediate access to stored data and programs. It temporarily holds program instructions, input data, intermediate results, and output as the computer works on them. However, as soon as the computer finishes with programs and their data, it writes new ones over them. Thus, if programs, data, and processing results are to be preserved for repeated use, a computer system needs additional storage beyond memory. Secondary (external) storage fills this role. Although it provides slower access than memory can achieve, secondary storage is far more capacious and far less expensive.

We will begin this chapter with a discussion of certain common characteristics of secondary storage systems. Then we'll cover the most important kinds of secondary storage systems in use today—those based on magnetic disks. While this part of the chapter is mostly about diskettes and hard disks, we will also look at some emerging technologies, such as Zip and Jaz drives. From there we will study optical-disk and tape storage systems. Following this is a summary and comparison of the secondary storage devices we've covered in the chapter. Chapter HW 2 closes with a discussion of data organization strategies—methods of maintaining data in secondary storage for efficient access.

Properties of Secondary Storage Systems

Several important properties characterize secondary storage systems. Here, we will consider several of them, including the two physical parts of a secondary storage system, the nonvolatility property of secondary storage, the ability to remove storage media from a secondary storage device, and methods of accessing data.

Physical Parts Any secondary storage system involves two physical parts: a *peripheral device* and an *input/output medium.* A disk drive and a tape drive are examples of peripheral devices; diskettes and magnetic tape cartridges are types of media. The drives write data and programs onto and read them from the storage media. A medium must be situated on a peripheral device for the CPU to process its contents.

Peripheral storage devices can be internal or external. *Internal devices*—such as diskette, hard-disk, and optical-disk drives—typically come installed and configured within the system unit when you buy a computer system, whereas *external devices* are stand-alone pieces of hardware that connect via cables to ports on the system unit. Internal devices bring the advantage of requiring no additional desk space, but external devices can more easily be swapped between two or more computer systems.

The computer system keeps track of disk drives and other storage devices in an unambiguous way by assigning letters of the alphabet or names to each of them. Letter designations, which are common in the PC-compatible world, are illustrated in Figure HW 2-1. Thus, if you declare you want to save a document to the A drive, the computer system encounters no confusion about where you want the document to be stored.

In most secondary storage systems, media must pass by **read/write heads** in the peripheral devices for programs and data to be read from or written to the media. For instance, when you listen to music on a cassette or record it on your home stereo system, the tape passes by a head on the tape deck, which either plays or records music. Tapes and disks on computer systems work by similar principles.

■ **Read/write head.** The component of a disk access mechanism or tape drive that retrieves or inscribes data.

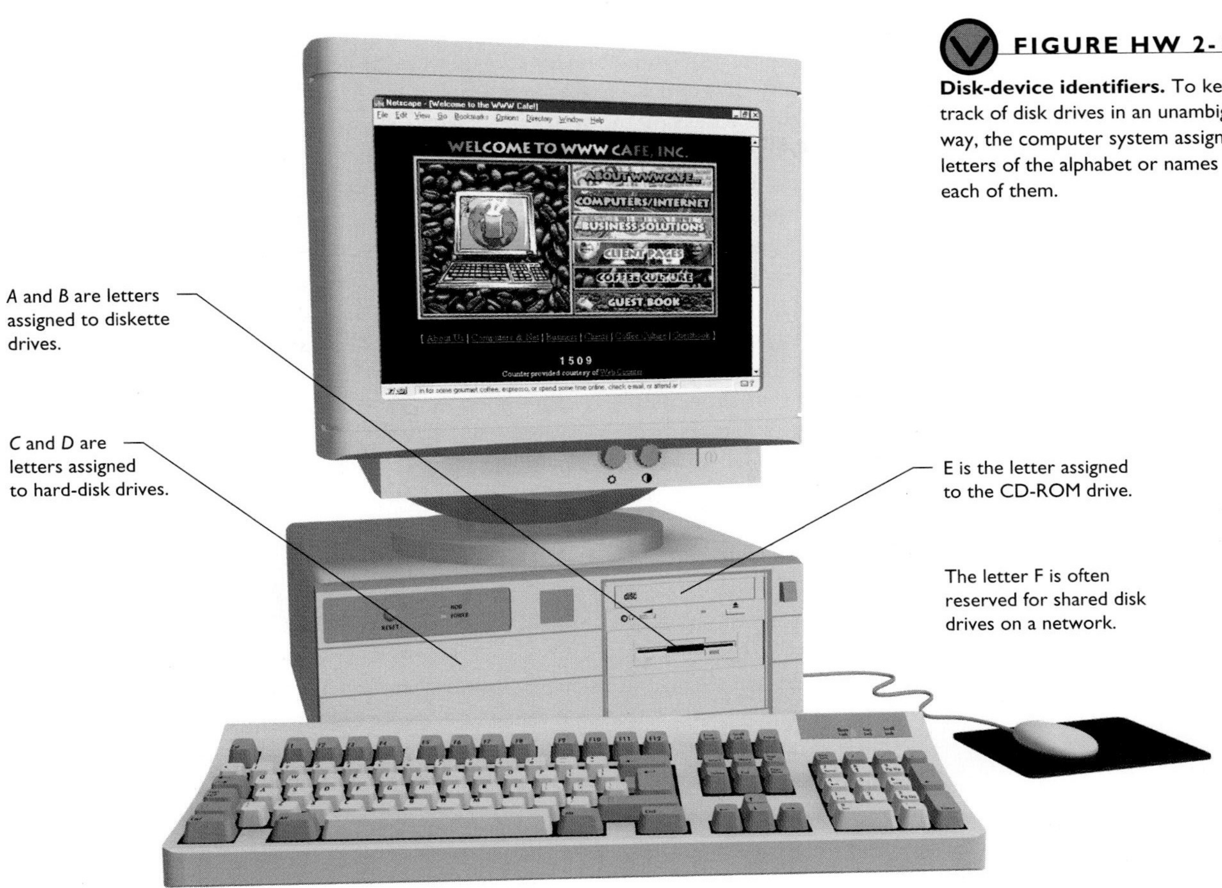
A and B are letters assigned to diskette drives.
C and D are letters assigned to hard-disk drives.
E is the letter assigned to the CD-ROM drive.
The letter F is often reserved for shared disk drives on a network.
WELCOME TO WWW CAFE, INC.

FIGURE HW 2-1

Disk-device identifiers. To keep track of disk drives in an unambiguous way, the computer system assigns letters of the alphabet or names to each of them.

Nonvolatility Property Secondary storage media are **nonvolatile.** This means that, when you shut off power to the peripheral device, the data stored on the medium remain there. This feature contrasts with many types of memory (including RAM), which are **volatile.** Data held in volatile storage disappear once you shut off the computer system's power.

Removable versus Nonremovable Media In many secondary storage systems, although the peripheral device is online to the computer, the associated medium must be loaded into the device before the computer can read from it or write to it. These are called *removable-media* secondary storage systems. Diskettes, CD-ROMs, and magnetic-tape cartridges are examples of removable media. On the other hand, *fixed-media* secondary storage systems, such as most hard-disk systems, encase the media in sealed units from which users cannot easily remove them.

Fixed-media devices generally provide higher speed and better reliability at lower cost than removable-media alternatives. Removability has its advantages, too, however, including the following:

- UNLIMITED STORAGE CAPACITY You can replace the medium on the storage device when it becomes full.
- TRANSPORTABILITY You can swap media between computers and people.
- BACKUP You can write a duplicate set of valuable data or programs onto the removable medium and store the copy offline, for use if the originals are destroyed.
- SECURITY Sensitive programs or data can be placed offline in a secured area.

Virtually all computer systems have both removable-media and fixed-media storage components.

■ **Nonvolatile storage.** Storage that retains its contents when power is shut off. ■ **Volatile storage.** Storage that loses its contents when power is shut off.

Accessing Data When the computer system receives an instruction pertaining to data or programs in secondary storage, it must first find the materials. The process of retrieving data and programs in storage is called *access.*

Two basic access methods are available: sequential and direct access. **Sequential access** means that you can retrieve the records in a file only in the same order in which they are physically stored on the medium. **Direct access,** also called **random access,** means that you can retrieve records in any order.

Computer systems' tape drives allow only sequential access to data. Computer tapes work like a cassette tapes on your stereo system—to get to some spot in the middle of the tape, you must pass through all of the preceding ones. Computer disks, in contrast, allow both sequential and direct access to data. They work like music CDs—you can play selections in sequence or get directly to a particular one.

Media that allow direct access—such as memory and disks—are *addressable.* This term means that the storage system can locate each stored data record or program at a unique *address,* which is automatically determined by the computer system. Tape systems, in contrast, are generally not addressable.

Magnetic Disk Systems

Speedy access to data and relatively low cost make **magnetic disks** the most widely used secondary storage media on today's computer systems. Without disk storage, many of the familiar computer applications we see around us would be impossible. In this section we cover the most common types of magnetic disks: hard disks and diskettes.

DISKETTES

Diskettes, or *floppy disks,* store data on small, round platters made of tough plastic (see Figure HW 2-2). Because they are removable and very inexpensive, diskettes are handy for such tasks as backing up small programs and small amounts of data, sending programs and data to others, storing rarely used files, and sharing data between two computers—such as a computer at home and one at school.

Uses for Diskettes

- Doing small amounts of backup
- Sending programs and files to others through the mail
- Storing rarely used files so they won't crowd your hard disk
- Sharing data among all of the computers you use

FIGURE HW 2-2

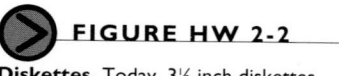

Diskettes. Today, 3½-inch diskettes have become the preferred standard on microcomputer systems.

■ **Sequential access.** Fetching stored records in the same order in which they are physically arranged on the medium. ■ **Direct access.** Reading or writing data in storage so that the access time is independent of the physical location of the data. Also known as **random access.** ■ **Magnetic disk.** A secondary storage medium that records data through magnetic spots on platters made of rigid metal or flexible plastic. ■ **Diskette.** A low-capacity, removable disk made of a tough, flexible plastic and coated with a magnetizable substance.

Diskette Sizes Most diskettes in use today measure 3½ inches in diameter. The actual, circular-shaped storage medium is contained in a square, rugged plastic case that can fit into a shirt pocket.

Despite its small dimensions, a 3½-inch diskette can store a respectable amount of data. Common capacities are 720 kilobytes and 1.44 megabytes. The 1.44-megabyte diskettes are often called *high-density* diskettes; the 720-kilobyte diskettes, *double-density* or *low-density* diskettes. Density, incidentally, refers to how tightly bits of data are packed onto the diskette. A diskette with a capacity of 1.44 megabytes has enough room to store the text of a book about 400 pages long.

Strange as it may seem, 3½-inch diskettes store more data than the 5¼-inch diskettes that were prevalent only a few years ago. Today, 5¼-inch diskettes have all but disappeared from the marketplace.

Physical Properties The physical properties of a diskette are illustrated in Figure HW 2-3. The plastic surfaces of a diskette's storage medium are coated with a magnetizable substance. The jacket is lined with a soft material that wipes the disk clean as it spins. The diskette's write-protect square can block writing operations, to prevent users from accidentally destroying data. To prevent the drive from writing to a diskette, slide the small piece of plastic to expose this square. Inside a drive, a diskette rotates when the drive mechanism engages its hub and begins to spin.

Diskette Addresses Each side of a diskette platter contains a specific number of concentric **tracks,** which the read/write head encodes with 0 and 1 bits when it writes data and programs to the diskette. In order to work on a particular computer

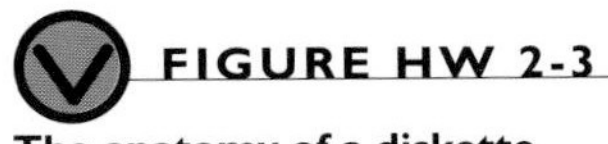

FIGURE HW 2-3

The anatomy of a diskette.

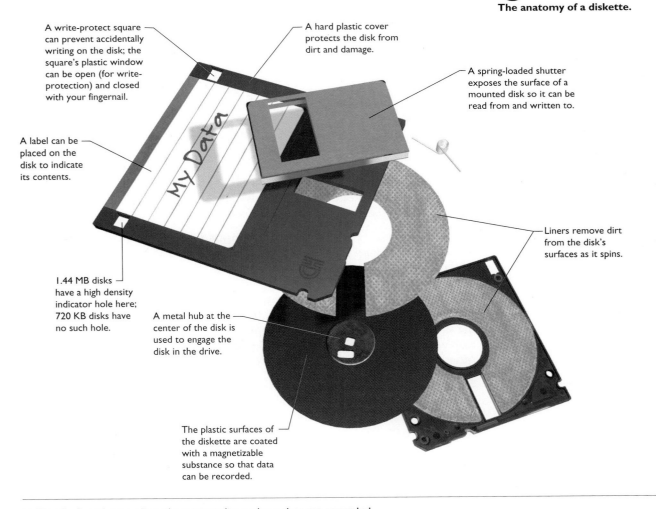

■ **Track.** A path on an input/output medium where data are recorded.

system, disks must be *formatted.* Formatting divides the disk surface into pie-shaped **sectors,** and thereby prepares it for use with a particular operating system. On many microcomputer systems, the part of any track crossed by a fixed number of contiguous sectors—anywhere from two to eight sectors is typical—forms a unit called a **cluster.** A cluster represents a single disk address (see Figure HW 2-4). You can buy preformatted diskettes, and you can also use your computer's operating system to format diskettes for you. A diskette cannot store data unless it has been formatted.

FIGURE HW 2-4

Diskette organization.

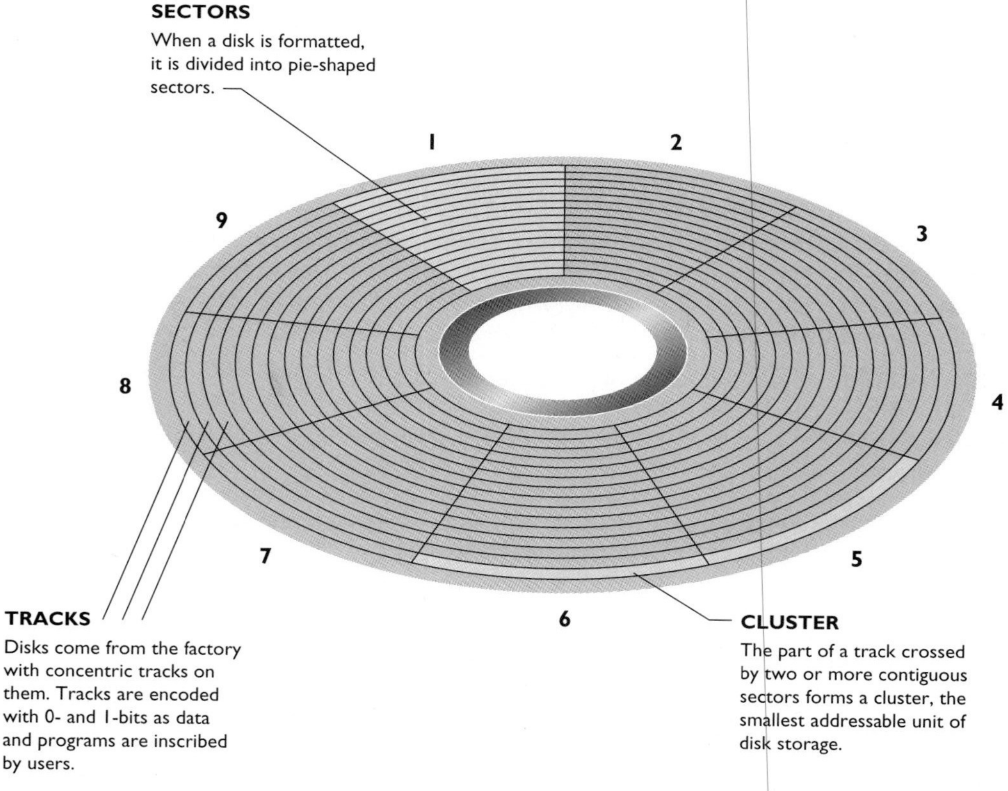

SECTORS
When a disk is formatted, it is divided into pie-shaped sectors.
1
2
3
4
5
6
7
8
9
TRACKS
Disks come from the factory with concentric tracks on them. Tracks are encoded with 0- and 1-bits as data and programs are inscribed by users.
CLUSTER
The part of a track crossed by two or more contiguous sectors forms a cluster, the smallest addressable unit of disk storage.

The computer system automatically maintains a diskette's **file directory,** which keeps track of the diskette's contents. This directory shows the name of each diskette file, its size, and the cluster at which it begins.

Using Diskettes To use a diskette, you insert it into a device called a **disk drive,** or *disk unit* (see Figure HW 2-5). There is only one correct way to insert the diskette into a drive—with the disk label facing up and the end with the metallic shutter mechanism going in first. Disk doors on 3½-inch drives automatically accept a disk that has been inserted properly—you'll hear a click when this happens.

While the diskette platter rotates, the read/write heads access tracks through the shutter's recording window. If the drive's *indicator light* is on, meaning that the read/write heads are accessing the tracks, you must not try to remove the diskette. After the light goes off, you generally press an *eject button* to remove the disk.

Superdiskettes A drawback to diskettes is their storage capacity. Not long ago, computer users considered 1.44 megabytes a reasonable amount of storage. Now, however, multimedia applications are rapidly increasing storage demands, and 1.44 MB is looking smaller and smaller with each passing year. Consequently, a number of

---

■ **Sector.** A pie-shaped area on a disk surface. ■ **Cluster.** An area formed where a fixed number of contiguous sectors intersect a track. ■ **File directory.** A listing on an input/output medium that provides data such as name, length, and starting address for each stored file. ■ **Disk drive.** A direct-access secondary storage device that uses a magnetic or optical disk as the principal medium.

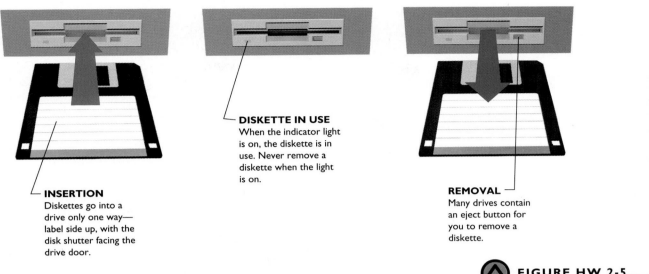

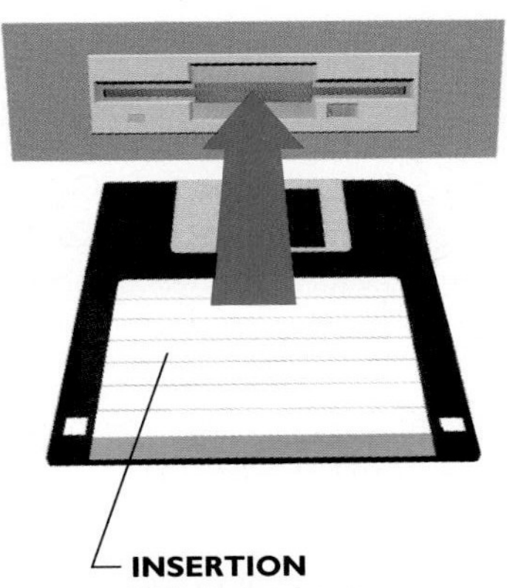

INSERTION
Diskettes go into a drive only one way—label side up, with the disk shutter facing the drive door.

DISKETTE IN USE
When the indicator light is on, the diskette is in use. Never remove a diskette when the light is on.

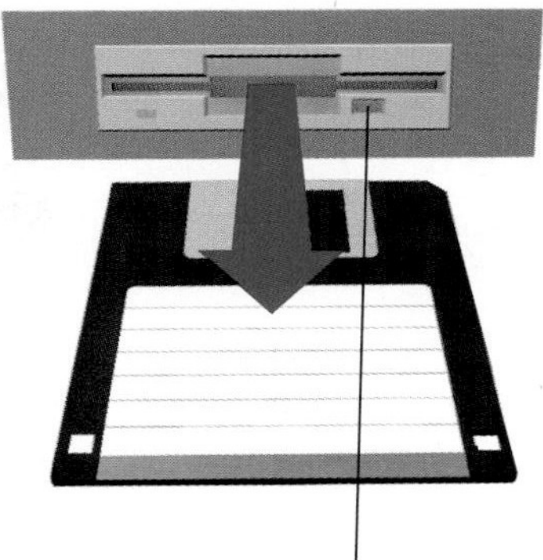

REMOVAL
Many drives contain an eject button for you to remove a diskette.

FIGURE HW 2-5

Inserting a diskette into a drive.

other storage products have emerged in recent years either as replacements for standard diskettes or as supplemental storage solutions (see Figure HW 2-6).

ZIP AND EZFLYER DRIVES Introduced by Iomega Corporation in 1995, *Zip drives* are magnetic-disk drives that accept removable 3½-inch disk cartridges with capacities of 100 or more megabytes. The drives and disks are incompatible with standard diskettes, but they provide a very affordable storage alternative. Drives typically run $200 or so and disks cost about $15 each. SyQuest Corporation makes a product similar to the Zip drive called the *EZFlyer drive.* Both Zip and EZFlyer drives are ideal for users who need to store large files offline or transfer large files between systems or other users.

External Zip drive

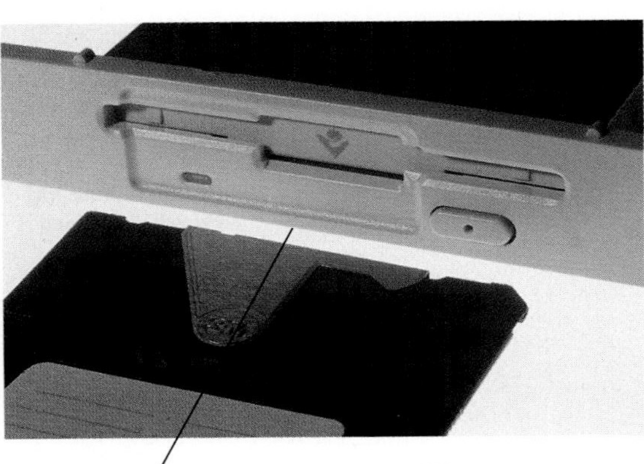

Internal LS-120 drive

FIGURE HW 2-6

Superdiskette drives with cartridges. Disk-cartridge products with capacities of 100 megabytes or more are commonly sold either as replacements for standard diskettes or as supplemental storage solutions.

LASER-SERVO DRIVES *Laser-servo (LS) drives* resemble Zip and EZFlyer drives in that they accept disk cartridges with capacities of 100 or more megabytes. While LS drives give slower access than Zip and EZFlyer drives, however, they can also read from and write to standard diskettes. LS drives work through a combination of magnetic and optical technology—storing data magnetically, but optically locating tracks and positioning read/write heads. Because optical positioning locates heads much more precisely than magnetic positioning, LS technology can place tracks closer together than conventional diskette drives can manage. In 1996, some computer makers began installing internal LS drives on some of their desktop computer systems.

HARD DISKS

Virtually every computer system today stores data and programs on some type of hard disk. A typical **hard disk** consists of one or more rigid metal platters mounted onto a shaft and sealed along with an access mechanism inside a case (see Figure HW 2-7). In PC systems, the terms *hard disk* and *hard-disk drive* commonly refer to the same thing—a single *pack* of disks as well as accompanying read/write heads, circuit board, and case.

FIGURE HW 2-7

A hard-disk drive. Hard-disk systems for microcomputers commonly have capacities in the gigabyte range. Featured here is an *internal* hard-disk system.

DISK CYLINDERS
On hard disks, the same relative track on each surface forms a disk cylinder. Cylinders are used in the formation of disk addresses.

MOUNTING SHAFT
The mounting shaft is always spinning at a speed of several thousand revolutions per minute while your computer is turned on.

The hard disk is hermetically sealed in a case to keep it free of air contamination.

ACCESS MECHANISM
The access mechanism moves the read/write heads in and out together between the disk surfaces to access required data.

CIRCUIT BOARD
Below the disks is a circuit board that contains the disk controller. This board makes sure the disk is rotating at a constant speed and tells the heads when to read and write.

READ/WRITE HEADS
There is a read/write head for each disk surface. On most systems, the heads move in and out together and will be positioned on the same cylinder.

Most microcomputer hard disks are hermetically sealed units. This precaution keeps the disk surfaces completely free of air contamination, enabling the disks to spin faster and limiting causes of operational problems. While a standard diskette spins at about 300 revolutions per minute (rpm), hard disks typically spin anywhere from 3,600 to 9,600 rpm.

Hard disks provide greater amounts of online storage and significantly faster access to programs and data than diskettes. New microcomputer hard disks most commonly offer capacities in the gigabyte range. Thus, if you have a 5-gigabyte hard disk, you have the online storage equivalent of over 3,400 3½-inch diskettes the minute you turn on the system's power. Also, you don't have to constantly shuffle diskettes into and out of drives. Speed improves, as well; hard disks can access data at least ten times faster than diskette drives. The difference results both from faster spinning and the fact that the hard disk is constantly rotating whenever your computer is turned on—eliminating the waiting time for the drive to come up to the correct speed. A diskette, in contrast, does not start spinning until you try to access it.

■ **Hard disk.** A system consisting of one or more rigid platters and an access mechanism.

Microcomputer systems can include internal or external hard disks (or both). An *internal* hard-disk system, such as the one in Figure HW 2-7, is by far the most common type. It is standard equipment on virtually all microcomputers sold. An *external* system is a detached device that can supplement the storage built into the computer system. External disks are often slightly slower and more expensive than their internal counterparts, but they provide flexibility by allowing two or more computers to share their contents.

While most hard disks are *fixed,* meaning that you cannot separate them from their drives, systems that use *removable* hard-disk cartridges are gaining in popularity (see Figure HW 2-8). One of the most widely used systems is Iomega's Jaz disk. A Jaz cartridge, which can store 1 gigabyte or more, takes slightly longer to access than a conventional, fixed hard disk. Jaz drives exist in both an internal and external version, each available for under $500.

FIGURE HW 2-8

Removable hard-disk cartridge. Iomega's Jaz drive works with removable, gigabyte-range cartridges to deliver performance close to a computer system's native fixed hard disk. The Jaz drive is available in external (pictured here) and internal models.

Like diskettes, hard disk surfaces are divided into tracks and sectors—but many more of both. A new hard disk is typically formatted for use at the factory before it is sold. On most desktop microcomputer systems and powerful network file servers, hard-disk platters measure 3½ inches in diameter; most notebook computers have 2½-inch hard disks.

Reading and Writing Data Most hard-disk systems have at least one read/write head for each recording surface. These heads are mounted on a device called an **access mechanism** (see Figure HW 2-7). The rotating mounting shaft spins at high speeds—thousands of revolutions per minute—and the access mechanism moves the heads in and out *together* between the disk surfaces to access the required data. Such a *movable access mechanism* as described here is by far the most popular type of access mechanism for hard disks.

A read/write head never touches the surface of a hard disk platter at any time, even during reading and writing. The heads approach the disk very closely, however—often within millionths of an inch above the recording surfaces. The presence of a human hair or even a smoke particle (about 2,500 and 100 millionths of an inch, respectively) on a hard-disk surface will damage the disks and heads—an event known as a *head crash.* As Figure HW 2-9 shows, the results are like placing a huge boulder on a road, and then trying to drive over it with your car.

Disk Cylinders An important principle for understanding disk storage and access strategies in hard-disk systems is the concept of **disk cylinders.** The two-disk pack in Figure HW 2-7 contains 4 possible recording surfaces. Suppose that each surface carries 800 tracks. You might envision the disk pack as a collection of 800 imaginary, concentric cylinders, each consisting of 4 vertically aligned tracks. For instance, one cylinder would represent Track 357 on Surface 1, Track 357 of Surface 2, and so on, all the way up to Track 357 of Surface 4. Outer cylinders fit over the inner ones like sleeves. Hard disks are commonly organized into anywhere from a few hundred to a couple of thousand cylinders.

Disk Access Time A hard disk with a movable access mechanism shifts the read/write heads in and out among the tracks in concert. It positions all the heads on the same cylinder when data are read from or written to any of the tracks on that cylinder. A disk system with a movable access mechanism must carry out three events in order to read or write data.

■ **Access mechanism.** A mechanical device in a disk drive that positions the read/write heads on the proper tracks. ■ **Disk cylinder.** On a disk pack, a collection of tracks that align vertically in the same relative position on different disk surfaces.

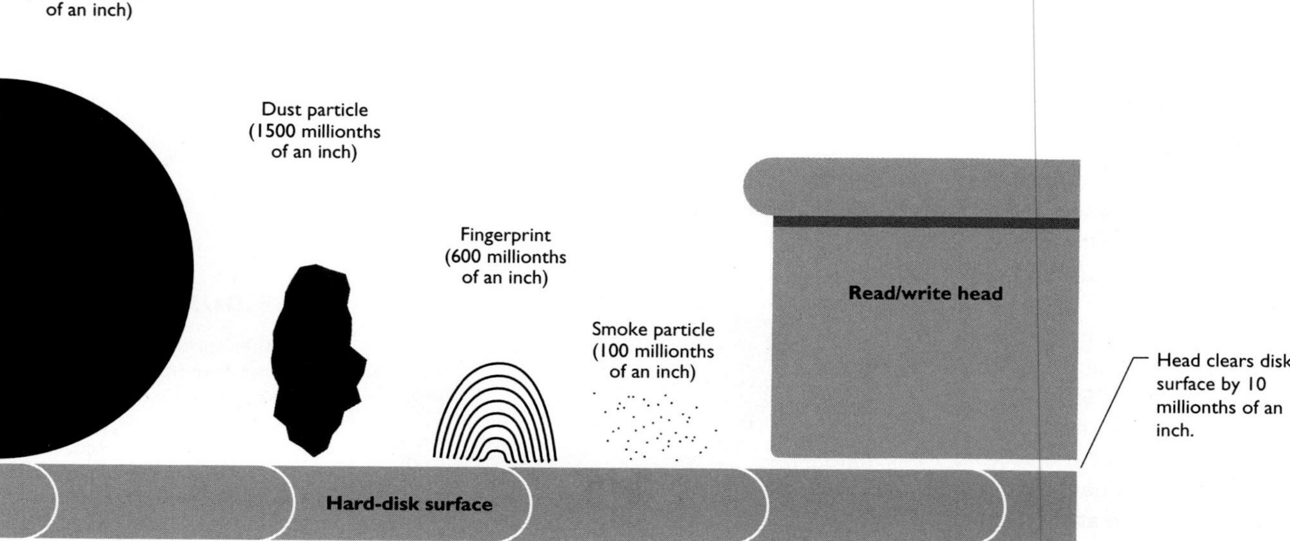

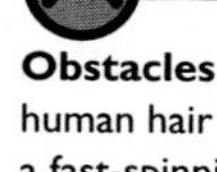

FIGURE HW 2-9

Obstacles on a hard-disk surface. A human hair or even a smoke particle on a fast-spinning hard-disk surface can damage both the surface and the read/write head.

First, the read/write heads must move to the cylinder that stores (or will store) the desired data. Suppose, for example, that the read/write head is on Cylinder 5, and it needs to retrieve data from Cylinder 36. To do this, the mechanism must move inward to Cylinder 36. The time required for this task is referred to as *seek time*.

When a read or write order is issued, the correct head is usually not aligned over the desired position on the track. Hence, some delay occurs while the mounting shaft rotates the disks into the proper position. (The disks are always spinning, whether or not reading or writing is taking place.) The time needed to complete this alignment is called *rotational delay*.

Third, once the access mechanism positions the read/write head over the correct data, the system must read the data from disk and transfer them to the RAM. (To write data, the reverse happens—the system must transfer them from RAM onto the moving disk.) This last step is known as *data movement time*. The sum of these three components—seek time, rotational delay, and data movement time—is known as **disk access time.**

Hard-disk access times often run from 10 to 20 milliseconds. To minimize disk access time on a system with a movable access mechanism such as the one depicted in Figure HW 2-7, drives store related data on the same cylinder. This strategy sharply reduces the seek-time component.

Disk Cache Disk caching refers to a strategy for speeding up system performance. Here's how it works: During any disk access, the computer system also fetches program or data contents in neighboring disk areas and transports them to a dedicated part of RAM known as a **disk cache** (see Figure HW 2-10). For instance, if a particular command calls for only a single data record, a disk-caching feature may direct the drive to read the entire track on which the record is located. The theory behind disk caching assumes that neighboring data will likely have to be read soon anyway, so the computer system can save disk accesses by bringing such data into RAM—an area from which they can be more quickly retrieved—early. When it's time for the next disk fetch, the computer system checks the disk-cache area first, to see if the

---

■ **Disk access time.** The time taken to locate and read (or position and write) data on a disk device. ■ **Disk cache.** A disk-management scheme that directs a drive to read more data than necessary for an immediate processing task during each disk fetch; a part of RAM stores the extra data to minimize the number of disk fetches.

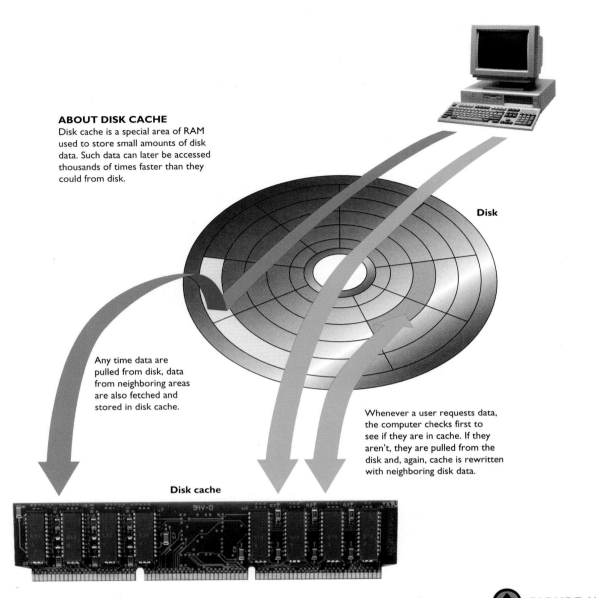

ABOUT DISK CACHE
Disk cache is a special area of RAM used to store small amounts of disk data. Such data can later be accessed thousands of times faster than they could from disk.

Disk

Any time data are pulled from disk, data from neighboring areas are also fetched and stored in disk cache.

Whenever a user requests data, the computer checks first to see if they are in cache. If they aren't, they are pulled from the disk and, again, cache is rewritten with neighboring disk data.

Disk cache

FIGURE HW 2-10

Disk cache.

data it needs are there. If they are, the data are transferred to main memory for processing; if they aren't, the computer makes another disk fetch.

Caching saves not only time but also wear and tear on the disk. In portable computers, it can also extend battery life. Disk caching is frequently implemented through circuitry on the disk controller board—the circuit board that manages the hard disk.

Disk Standards Buying a hard disk for a microcomputer system can lead to confusing chatter from vendors spiced with such acronyms as RLL, ESDI, IDE, EIDE, and SCSI. These acronyms generally refer to performance characteristics like the density with which data can be packed onto the disk, the speed of disk access, and the way the disk drive interfaces with other hardware.

Today, two standards dominate the market: *EIDE,* for enhanced *i*ntegrated *d*rive electronics, and *SCSI,* for small computer system Interface. EIDE is less expensive and often easier to configure, but SCSI provides faster access, enables you to connect more devices from a single board, and allows longer cable lengths. SCSI (pronounced "scuzzy") comes in several varieties, including SCSI-1, SCSI-2, SCSI-3, and UltraSCSI. In buying any new peripheral, it's important to check out which standards the device supports and to make sure your computer system is equipped to deal with them.

Partitioning Partitioning a hard disk enables you to divide its capacity into separate areas—or *partitions*. You can then treat each of the partitions as an independent disk drive, such as a C drive and a D drive. You can change the number and sizes of the partitions at any time, although this action will destroy any data in those partitions. Consequently, you should transfer any affected data onto another disk or tape first and then load the data back onto the repartitioned hard disk.

Partitioning a hard disk enables you to assign different operating systems—say, Windows 98 and UNIX—to parts of your disk. Each operating system has its own method of formatting and managing disk space. By assigning each operating system to a different partition, you gain a more flexible computer system while you avoid the problem of an operating system encountering data stored in a manner that is foreign to it.

DISK STORAGE FOR LARGE COMPUTER SYSTEMS

Hard-disk systems on large computers implement many of the same principles as microcomputer-based hard disks. Instead of finding a single disk pack sealed inside a case installed within a system unit, however, you are most likely to find several removable disk packs that are placed into a refrigerator-sized unit that is separate from the system unit (see Figure HW 2-11). Storage capacities on such disk systems can run from a few dozen gigabytes up into the terabyte range.

Not too long ago, disk systems on large computers stored data on very-large-diameter disks—say, 14 inches or so across. This design created several problems. Large disks cannot rotate at the high speeds that smaller ones can manage. What's more, larger disks require greater seek time. Also, as the diameter of a disk increases, so does the potential for wobble at its outer edge as it spins. Larger wobble forces the read/write heads to ride farther away from the disk surface to prevent a head crash. This also detracts from performance.

Today's large-system drives employ smaller disks. Even though they may need more platters to store the same amount of data, several smaller disks have even another critical advantage over a single, larger disk—they provide better support for parallel processing. For instance, if eight smaller disks replace a single, larger one, the system can read from all eight disk surfaces at the same time. Particularly in the computer-networking market, a small-disk storage procedure called RAID has been catching on fast.

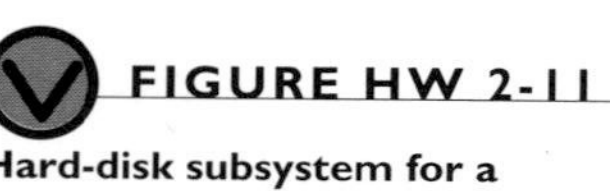

FIGURE HW 2-11

Hard-disk subsystem for a midrange computer. Hard-disk subsystems on larger computers often contain arrays of hard-disk packs, each array occupying its own drawer in a disk cabinet.

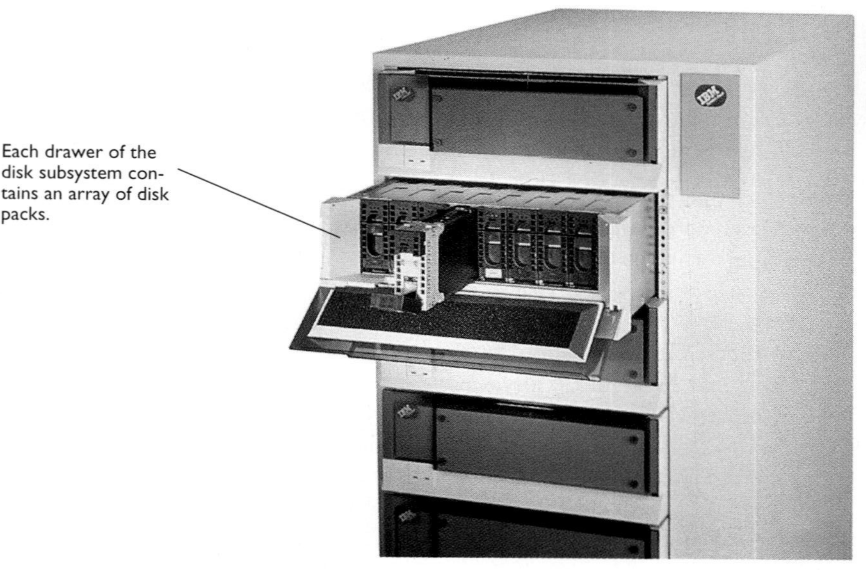

Each drawer of the disk subsystem contains an array of disk packs.

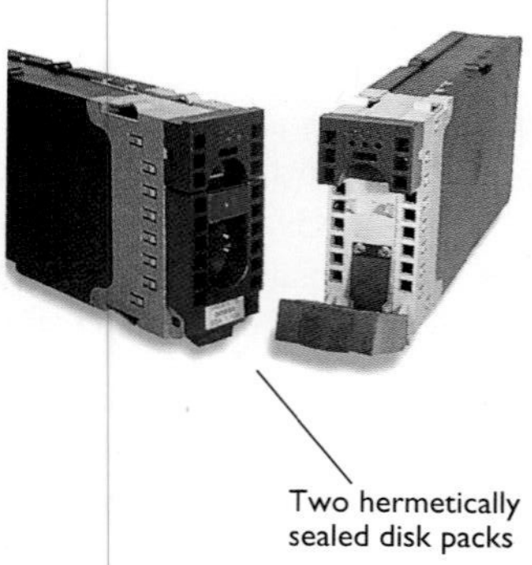

Two hermetically sealed disk packs

RAID **RAID** (for *r*edundant *a*rrays of *i*nexpensive *d*isks) hooks up several arrays of relatively small disks in parallel to do the job of a larger disk. The disks are separated from the system unit in a cabinet that, because it comprises a sophisticated system within the computer system, is often referred to as the *disk subsystem* (refer back to

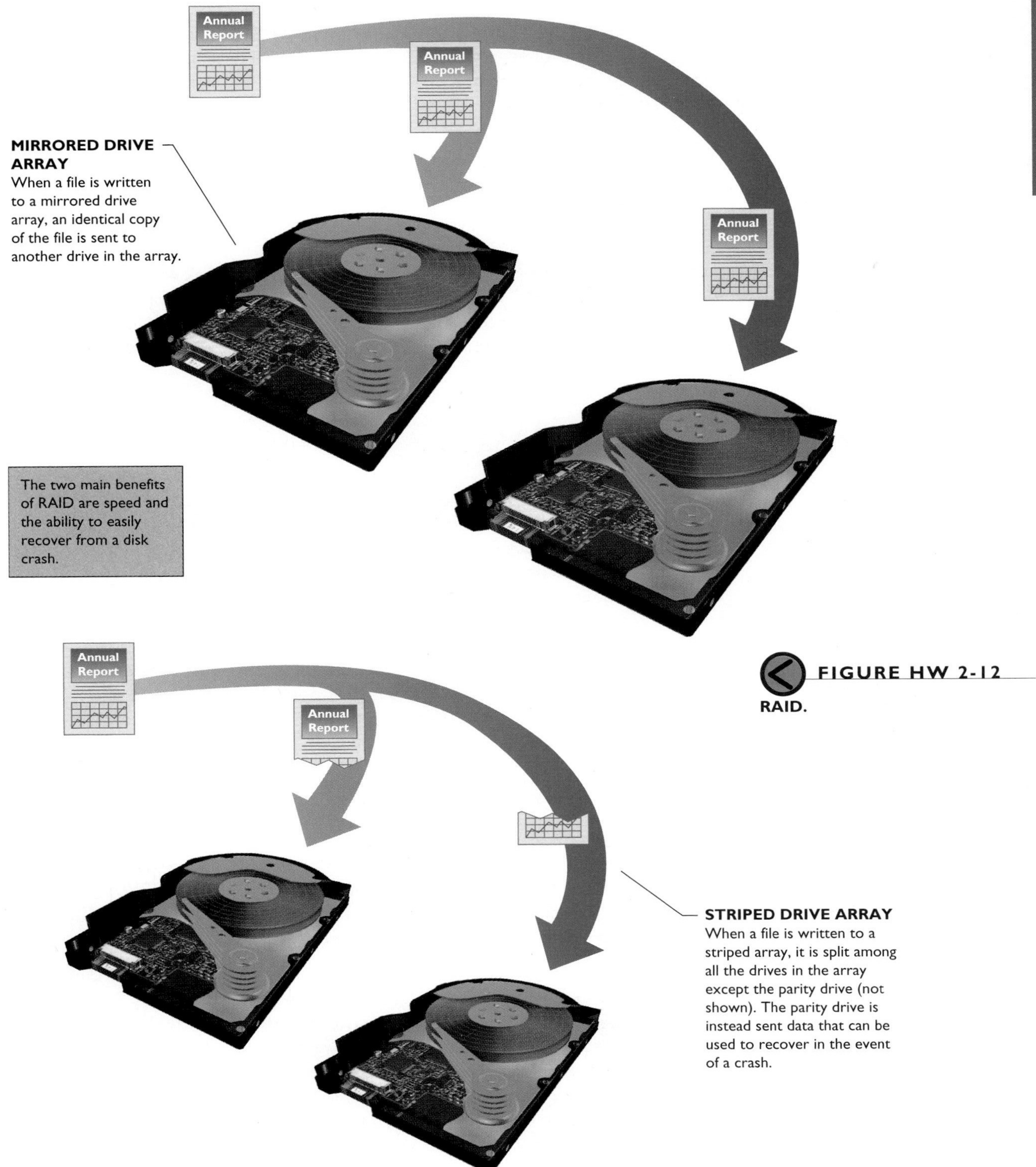

Annual Report
Annual Report
Annual Report
MIRRORED DRIVE ARRAY
When a file is written to a mirrored drive array, an identical copy of the file is sent to another drive in the array.
The two main benefits of RAID are speed and the ability to easily recover from a disk crash.
Annual Report
Annual Report
STRIPED DRIVE ARRAY
When a file is written to a striped array, it is split among all the drives in the array except the parity drive (not shown). The parity drive is instead sent data that can be used to recover in the event of a crash.

FIGURE HW 2-12
RAID.

■ **RAID.** A storage method that hooks up several small disks in parallel to do the job of a larger disk, but with better performance.

Figure HW 2-11). The subsystem is set up to record redundant copies of information so that, in the event of a system crash, the redundant data can be used to reconstruct the lost data.

Computer systems define several different *levels* of RAID. In the most expensive—known as RAID Level 1—a backup disk pack corresponds to each production disk pack (see the top part of Figure HW 2-12). If any production pack fails, its backup immediately takes over. Level-1 RAID is *hot swappable,* meaning that a defective pack can be taken offline for repair and replaced without even turning the power off. Duplicating the entire contents of a disk on another disk in this manner is sometimes described as *disk mirroring.*

When performance can be sacrificed to gain a cost advantage, a procedure called *striping* is often used (see the bottom part of Figure HW 2-12). All levels of RAID beyond Level 1 use some form of striping, which spreads files over several packs. These systems protect data by duplicating them on additional disk packs called *parity disks* or *check disks.* If the disk system crashes, any lost data can be reconstructed from the contents of the parity disks.

Major producers of mainframe RAID systems are StorageTek with its Iceberg, IBM with its Ramac, and EMC with its Symmetric disk subsystems. Compaq and Hewlett-Packard make highly praised RAID products that serve microcomputer networks. RAID subsystems targeted to midrange computers are also widely available.

Optical Disk Systems

An emerging technology has begun to produce a profound impact on storage strategies: the **optical disk,** often referred to as a *CD.* This technology employs laser beams to write and read data—which can consist of text, graphics, audio clips, or video images—at densities many times finer than those of a typical magnetic disk. Although hard disks offer faster access, CDs have caught on in a big way both in the business and consumer markets.

Today's optical disk can store anywhere from several hundred megabytes of data to several gigabytes on a single platter. So-called *optical jukeboxes* and *towers* are also available and offer online access to scores of optical disks. Like old phonograph-record jukeboxes, these optical data warehouses "play" selected platters from collections that can reach close to 2,000 online CDs.

TYPES OF OPTICAL DISKS

Optical-disk systems are used on computer systems of all sizes. The most common types of optical-disk systems are CD-ROMs, WORM CDs, and rewritable CDs (see Figure HW 2-13). Feature HW 2-1 introduces *digital versatile disk (DVD),* an emerging CD technology that many people expect to inherit the roles of both CD-ROM technology and videocassette recorders hooked to television sets.

CD-ROM By far, most optical disk-drives sold today are of the **CD-ROM** (compact disk, read-only memory) type. Specialized equipment stores data on CD-ROMs at the factory by burning tiny holes into the disks' surfaces with high-intensity laser beams. Then, your CD drive's lower-intensity laser beam reads the data so inscribed (see Figure HW 2-14). Because the storage process permanently etches the surface of the CD-ROM, you cannot write new data to the disk in any way.

■ **Optical disk.** A disk read by reflecting pulses of laser beams. ■ **CD-ROM.** An optical disk that allows a drive to read data but not write it.

Internal CD-ROM drives costing less than $300 are standard components of PCs today. CD-ROM functionality is generally acquired as part of a multimedia kit when buying a new PC. Such a kit often includes a CD-ROM drive, several CD-ROM disks, speakers, a sound board, and a video board.

Most CD-ROM disk drives available on the market today are touted as 8×, 12×, 16×, and so on. These labels convey the speeds of the drives. For instance, 8× indicates eight times the speed of the baseline unit that was originally manufactured.

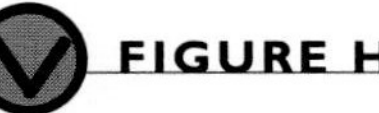

FIGURE HW 2-13

Optical-disk drives and their storage media.

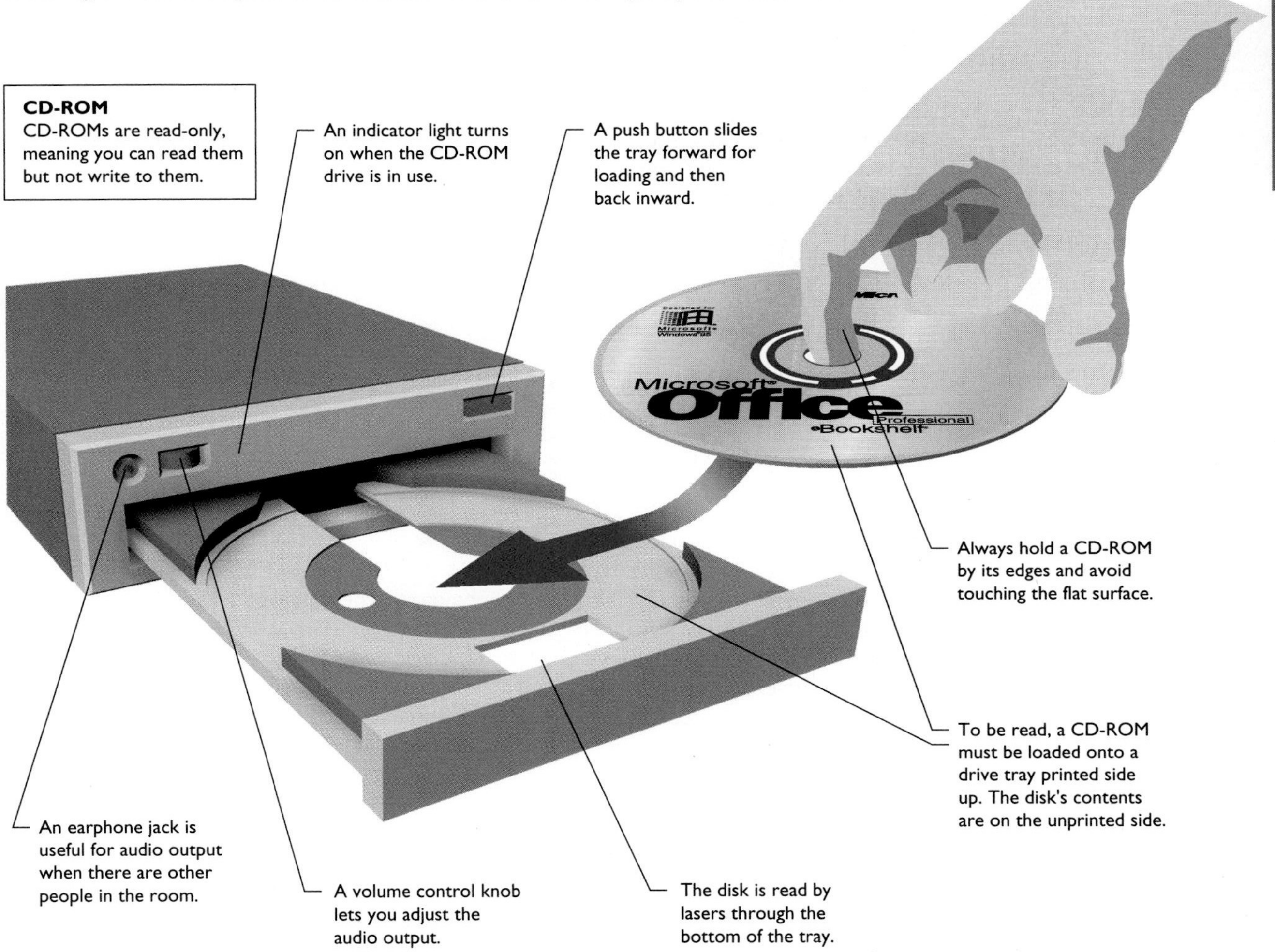

CD-ROM
CD-ROMs are read-only, meaning you can read them but not write to them.
An indicator light turns on when the CD-ROM drive is in use.
A push button slides the tray forward for loading and then back inward.
Microsoft Office Professional Bookshelf
Always hold a CD-ROM by its edges and avoid touching the flat surface.
To be read, a CD-ROM must be loaded onto a drive tray printed side up. The disk's contents are on the unprinted side.
An earphone jack is useful for audio output when there are other people in the room.
A volume control knob lets you adjust the audio output.
The disk is read by lasers through the bottom of the tray.

REWRITABLE CDS
Rewritable CDs, which can be written to if a special drive is used, often come in protective nonremovable plastic cases, or caddies.
3M
Rewritable Optical Disk Cartridge 512

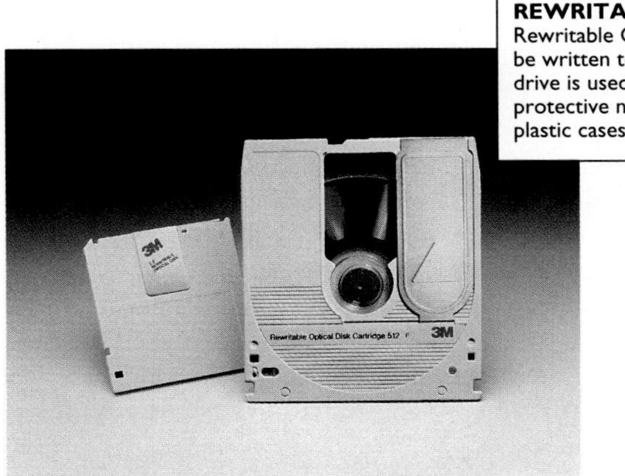

NETWORKED CDS
On networks, several CD-ROMs are often loaded into magazines and read by a CD player.
PIONEER
LaserMemory

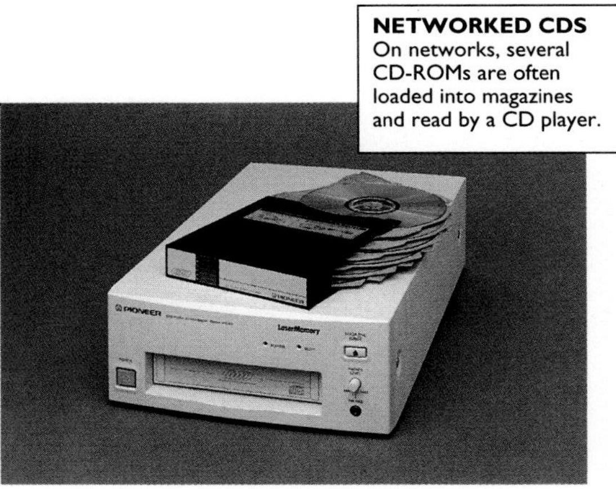

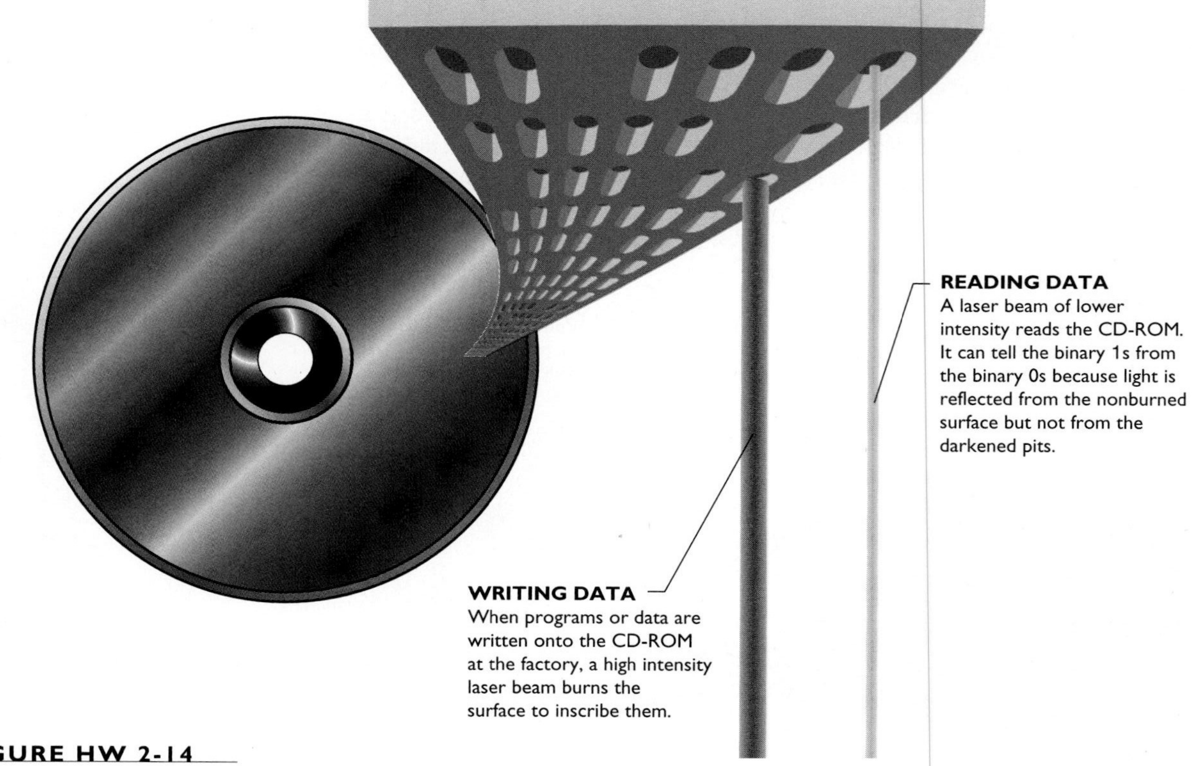

READING DATA
A laser beam of lower intensity reads the CD-ROM. It can tell the binary 1s from the binary 0s because light is reflected from the nonburned surface but not from the darkened pits.
WRITING DATA
When programs or data are written onto the CD-ROM at the factory, a high intensity laser beam burns the surface to inscribe them.

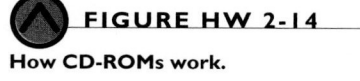

FIGURE HW 2-14
How CD-ROMs work.

Only one side of a CD-ROM contains data—the side opposite the printed label. When you mount a CD-ROM on a drive tray, you place it with the printed side up. Be careful not to get dirt—or anything else that might hinder light reflectivity—on the CD's surface.

Uses for CDs abound, as illustrated in the end-of-chapter window entitled "Multimedia Computing: The World of CD-ROMs." As mentioned in both the Window and in User Solution HW 2-1, another use has surfaced that few people would have imagined when CDs were first introduced—hybrid products that take advantage of the speed of a CD and the Internet's online interactions.

WORM Technology Some optical-disk systems let you write your own disks. Once written, however, you cannot erase the data and write over the same disk. These are called **WORM** (*w*rite *o*nce, *r*ead *m*any) systems. Because optical disks have very large storage capacities, most users can write to a single disk for a year or more before filling it (providing the WORM system has a *multisession* capability).

The most widely used WORM standard is *CD-R,* in which the *R* stands for *recordable.* CD-R lets users create their own CD-ROM master disks, which they can then duplicate to produce inexpensive CD-ROMs for distribution. At one time, CD-R was beyond the pocketbooks of most PC users, but prices for drives have come down to the $500 level, and master disks costing only about $8 apiece can be duplicated for as little as a couple of dollars per copy (in runs of about 1,000 disks). CD-R isn't for everybody. The software is generally targeted to sophisticated users. Also, if you're prone to make mistakes, CD-R can be expensive. Since it's a write-only technology, it's easy to "fry" master disks, thereby relegating them to frisbees.

While the recent increase in availability of rewritable optical disks has led many people to speculate that CD-R may go the way of the 5¼-inch diskette, CD-R does have some advantages. For one, CD-R drives are still cheaper than those for rewritable CDs. Perhaps the most noteworthy and most permanent advantage,

■ **WORM.** An optical disk that allows the user's drive to write data only once and then read it an unlimited number of times.

DVD Technology

Will It Become the Hit That Experts Predict?

The acronym *DVD* refers to a relatively new CD storage format—one with a higher capacity and a wider range of uses than such established formats as CD-ROM, WORM, and MO. DVD was developed primarily to store the full contents of a feature-length movie, consequently, the acronym once stood for *digital video disk*. However, proponents of the technology thought the *video* was too limiting—the disks can also store text, graphics, and audio data—so the longer name is now often dropped or the name *digital versatile disk* is substituted.

DVD technology is initially being targeted as the successor to music CDs, computer CD-ROMs, and prerecorded VHS videotapes that people buy or rent for home viewing. In other words, the first round of products (called DVD-ROM) serve the read-only market. If and when consumers begin to appreciate the extra value that DVD can offer, expect to see WORM and rewritable DVDs (the latter called DVD-RAM) coming into the market. In a few years, you may be able to record television shows at home on blank DVDs, just as you do today on blank VHS tapes.

Of course, each of these DVD applications needs its own peripheral device, so a whole new generation of hardware will appear as soon as each new technology is developed. DVD is designed to be backward compatible, so you can play your old CD-ROMs and music CDs on DVD peripheral devices.

Most DVDs hold about 4.7 GB of data—more than a dozen times what a conventional CD-ROM can carry—on a single side. They support a faster data-transfer rate than CD-ROMs, as well. Most importantly, a single DVD has enough capacity to hold a two-hour movie—one with a full-screen picture and digital-TV quality, not the grainy quarter-screen video you see with most CD-ROMs today. The DVD standard includes support for Dolby surround sound and multichannel digital sound, multiple language tracks, multiple subtitle channels, copy protection, and parental lockout capabilities.

Fans tout many advantages for DVD over conventional VHS tape: Images don't degrade over time, users need never wind or rewind, and DVDs cost far less than tapes to mass produce. However, consumers will certainly not throw away the $30 billion they've spent on VCRs and tapes overnight to get DVD. But *if* videotape-rental stores start renting DVDs and players inexpensively, and *if* people like what they see, and *if* reasonably priced DVDs and players start showing up in discount stores, then what happened to the vinyl record could happen to both the videotape and CD-ROM.

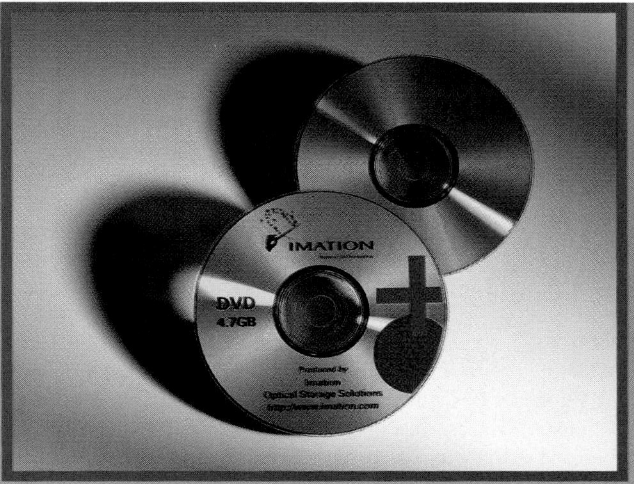

DVD. With enough storage to hold a two-hour movie, it is expected to replace both the CD-ROM and videocassette.

A double-sided, dual-layer disk currently under development allows a laser to read data at two levels on each surface, giving it a capacity of 17 GB. As layering technology progresses (see the chapter Tomorrow box on page HW 67), a single DVD may someday store an entire library of movies.

DVD technology has been ready to impact consumer markets for some time; originally, it was supposed to make a big splash in the 1996 Christmas season. However, introduction was held up by a lot of corporate and legal wrangling. For instance, DVD manufacturers needed to standardize on a single format to avoid a costly fight like the VHS-versus-Betamax battle during the early days of videocassettes. That particular hassle took some time to iron out, because each manufacturer wanted its own format chosen. In the end, VHS won out, but many consumers became wary of the risks involved in choosing the wrong way. Unfortunately, the DVD standards issue is still far from settled, and consumers have been holding back.

Hollywood has also seen DVD as a potential threat, holding up the wheels of progress even further. A movie released in U.S. theaters, say, could be replicated perfectly and sold in Europe well before its release in theaters there. To protect against piracy, many of the major studios have pressed to require design differences that prevent DVD players sold in one region of the world from loading DVDs produced in another region. The U.S. government has been in the middle of the brouhaha, too, through its restrictive policy on exports of scrambling—or encryption—technology.

though, comes from the fact that others can't write to the completed disk; you know that what you put there can't be erased or altered in any way.

Rewritable CDs Some optical-disk systems allow you to both write and erase data—theoretically, an unlimited number of times. Such **rewritable CDs** often use either magneto-optical (MO) or phase-change technology.

■ **Rewritable CD.** An optical disk that allows users to repeatedly read from and write to its surface.

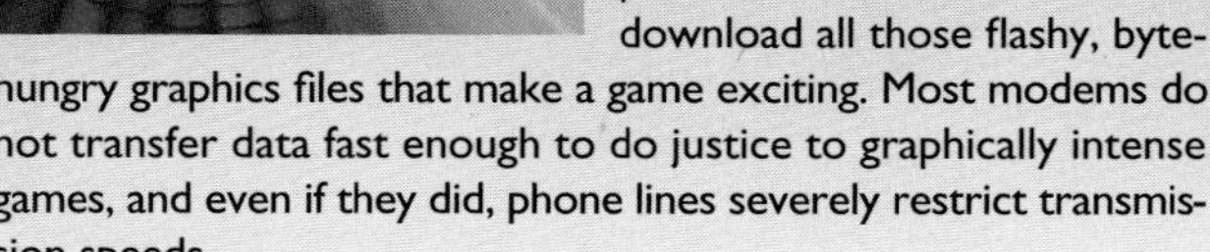

Extending CD-ROM through the Web

The Web offers two compelling advantages as a platform for computer games: its ability to keep content fresh and to enable people at different locations to interact with each other at the same time. However, a glaring disadvantage is the slow pace at which Web surfers can download all those flashy, byte-hungry graphics files that make a game exciting. Most modems do not transfer data fast enough to do justice to graphically intense games, and even if they did, phone lines severely restrict transmission speeds.

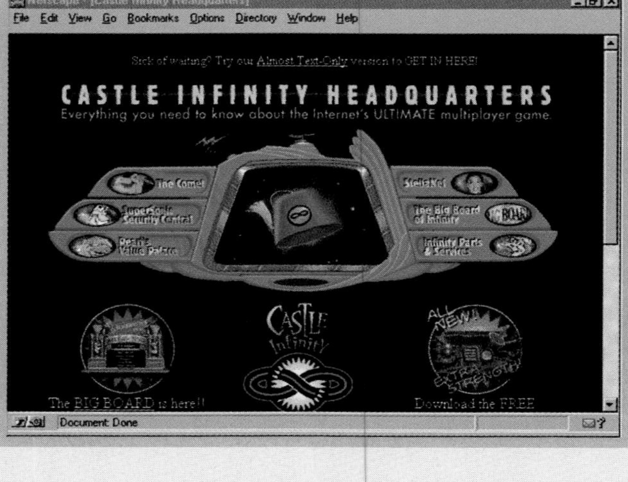

The solution for game developers? Put the byte-hungry graphics on a CD-ROM, where each user's computer system can retrieve them in a flash, and use the Web to distribute content that's easier to send over the phone lines. Starwave Corporation's Castle Infinity is one of several computer games that uses this hybrid approach.

MO SYSTEMS *Magneto-optical (MO)* disk systems combine magnetic and optical technology to read and write data. A laser beam heats a spot on a CD until it can be altered by a magnetic field. A read/write head similar to that of a magnetic disk then aligns the spot to create a digital representation of data. A weaker laser beam reads the data.

You can record on both sides of an MO disk, although you may have to manually flip the disk to access the other side. CD-ROM and MO systems are incompatible. MO drives are available for both desktop and notebook computers.

PHASE-CHANGE SYSTEMS *Phase-change* systems represent the newest rewritable CD technology covered here. As in an MO system, a laser beam heats spots on the disk to write data. However, no magnetic head makes a second pass; once the laser finishes writing data, another beam of lesser intensity can read it. This simplification makes phase-change drives generally faster than MO drives. Phase-change drives can also read conventional CD-ROMs—another big plus. On the negative side, the variety of MO drives on the marketplace are more compatible with one another, making it easier for users to exchange information.

CD PD (the *PD* is for *power drive)* and CD-RW (the *RW* is for *rewritable)* are two phase-change standards. You can theoretically write to a CD PD disk about 500,000 times before wearing it out; CD-RW disks, which are made of a different material, last for only about 1,000 rewrites. Consequently, CD PD is better suited to heavy-duty, random-access applications. Disks created on CD-RW drives, however, can also be read on CD-ROM and DVD devices.

Innovations such as CD-RW and DVD will not conclude the rapid development of optical disks. The near future should bring optical disks with even more capacity than today's models. For instance, new technology allows systems to layer several readable surfaces on the top or bottom of a CD (see the Tomorrow box on page HW 67).

Magnetic Tape Systems

Magnetic tape has provided a prominent secondary storage alternative for computer systems over several decades. It is far less popular than disk storage, because its

■ **Magnetic tape.** A plastic ribbon with a magnetizable surface that stores data as a series of magnetic spots.

sequential-access property makes it far slower. It does provide an extremely low cost per byte stored, however, so magnetic tape is still widely used both to back up the contents of other storage systems and to support low-speed, sequential-processing operations.

TYPES OF TAPE SYSTEMS

Virtually all magnetic-tape systems store data on either detachable-reel or cartridge tapes (see Figure HW 2-15). The tapes are made of plastic coated with a magnetizable substance that can be polarized to represent the bit patterns of digital data. Computer tapes differ in a number of respects, including the sizes of the reels or cartridges, tape width, and the formats and densities with which they record data.

FIGURE HW 2-15

Magnetic tape. Two tape cartridges rest on a detachable tape reel.

The device that reads magnetic tapes is called a **tape drive,** or *tape unit.* It may be an internal or external piece of hardware. The tape drives for microcomputers are small enough for a person to hold in one hand, while the refrigerator-sized drives connected to large mainframes often occupy several square feet of floor space. Whatever its size or type, every tape drive contains one or more read/write heads over which the tape passes to allow the drive to read or write data.

Tapes for Microcomputers **Cartridge tapes** are the predominant form of magnetic-tape storage medium for microcomputers (see Figure HW 2-16). Within its plastic casing, such a tape typically functions as a backup for the contents of a hard disk. You can copy onto a tape the entire contents of a hard disk—on many PCs, an hour or longer is not unusual for such a task—or just selected files. Because of their extremely long access times and other considerations, backup tapes do not normally directly support mainstream processing tasks. If you want a specific file on tape, you must transfer it first to hard disk.

Both internal and external tape drives are widely found in practice. While internal drives are faster, you can share an external drive between two or more computers. A drive may cost as little as $150; cartridges, $10–$20 apiece.

Cartridges for backing up desktop computers come in several sizes and formats. Today's systems commonly employ quarter-inch-wide *QIC-80* tapes and minicartridges that abide by one of the Travan formats, such as T-1 or T-4. A single tape can hold anywhere from a few hundred megabytes of data to a few gigabytes, and twice as much if you compress the data. The topic of data compression is covered in Chapter SW 2.

Microcomputer networks commonly include tape drives for higher-capacity, 4-millimeter-wide *DAT* (for *digital audio tape*). DAT can typically store several gigabytes of data each.

Tape Systems for Larger Computer Systems Larger computer systems—say, those powered by midrange or mainframe computers—often store data on either detachable-reel or cartridge tapes. The tape systems are always external devices, and they may perform either backup or processing duties.

Detachable-reel tapes, which commonly measure one-half inch wide, have been around the longest. When the tape drive is first actuated, a *supply reel* contains the data to be processed; an empty take-up reel winds tape with records that have finished processing. When processing is complete, the drive rewinds the tape back onto the supply reel. Such tape typically stores data at densities up to several thousand bits per inch (bpi). Because cartridges are easier to handle and provide far larger capacities than they offered only a few years ago, detachable-reel tape drives are losing popularity.

■ **Tape drive.** A secondary storage device that reads from and writes to mounted magnetic tapes. ■ **Cartridge tape.** Magnetic tape in which the supply and take-up reels are contained in a small plastic case. ■ **Detachable-reel tape.** Magnetic tape wound onto a single reel, which in turn is mounted next to an empty take-up reel onto a tape drive.

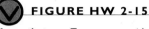

FIGURE HW 2-16

Microcomputer cartridge tape system. Microcomputer systems often back up the contents of hard disks on tape cartridges.

TAPE DRIVES
Cartridge tape drives are available as both internal and external devices.

CARTRIDGE TAPES
There are a very large number of tape formats in use—QIC-80, TR-1, DAT, and so on. When buying tapes, be sure that they conform to the format specified by the drive's manufacturer.

As a tape is being processed, it spools from one reel onto another and then back again.

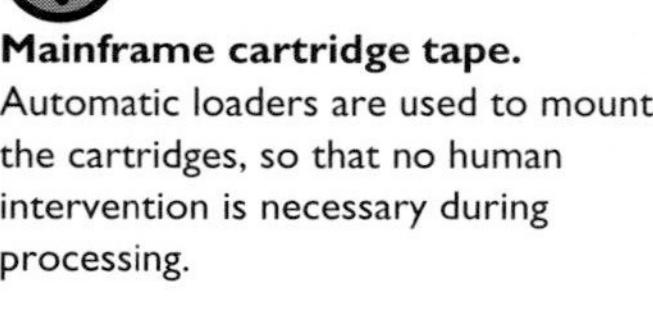

FIGURE HW 2-17

Mainframe cartridge tape. Automatic loaders are used to mount the cartridges, so that no human intervention is necessary during processing.

Many midrange and mainframe computers today store data on cartridge tape systems, such as the IBM 3590 tape storage system (see Figure HW 2-17). An automatic loader mounts the cartridges, eliminating the need for human intervention during processing. The tapes used in such systems have at least twice as many tracks as traditional, detachable-reel tapes, boosting their storage capacities into the gigabyte range. Storage densities can reach as high as 60,000 bpi.

USING TAPES

Figure HW 2-18 shows how data are often stored on tape. Some tape systems record data perpendicular to the edge of the tape, some (like QIC-80) parallel, and some (like DAT) at an angle. Data may be coded in 8-bit bytes of either the EBCDIC or ASCII systems. Magnetized (polarized) spots of iron oxide represent 1 bits; nonmagnetized (depolarized) areas represent 0s.

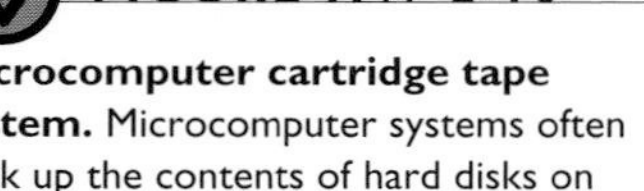

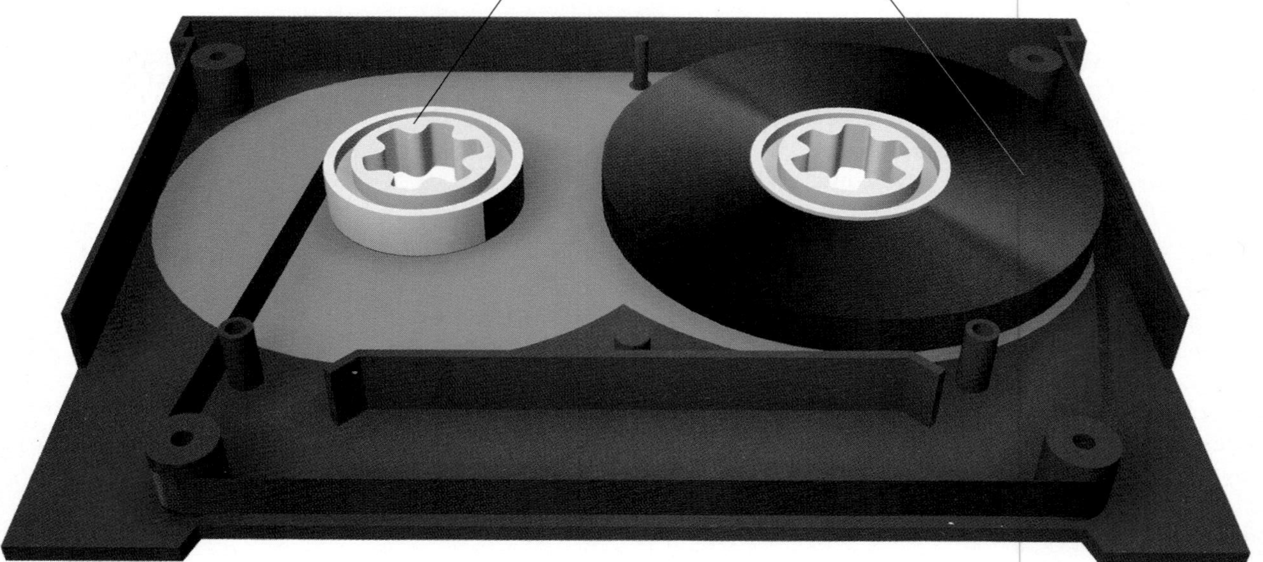

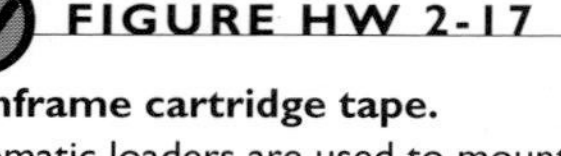

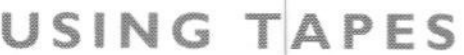

PARALLEL TRACKS
Tapes such as QIC-80 often use 20 or 32 parallel tracks. Each track organizes data into blocks of 512 or 1,024 bytes.

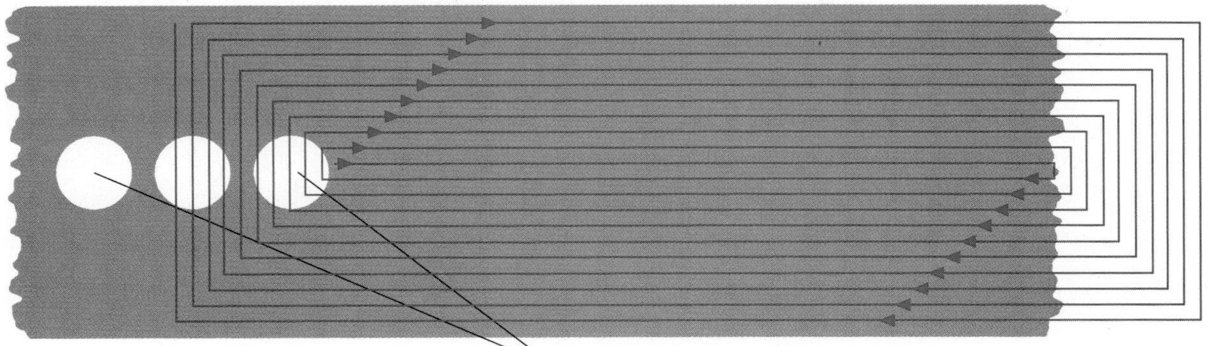

When the tape reaches either end of the spool, holes on the tape signal the drive to reverse direction, and the read/write head shifts up to the next outside track. The head loops through the tracks in the spiral fashion shown above.

DIAGONAL TRACKS
DATs store data diagonally to the edge of the tape. Fine storage densities can be achieved because data can be stored in crisscrossing tracks, each of which can be several times longer than the width of the tape. Data aren't misread, because the drive uses two sets of read/write heads, each of which reads or writes at a different polarity.

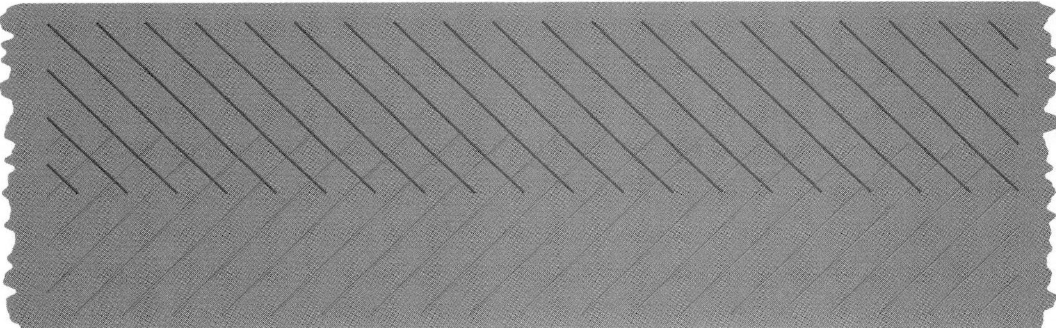

FIGURE HW 2-18

Storing data on magnetic tape. Data are stored either parallel or at an angle to the tape.

Comparing Secondary Storage Alternatives

Secondary storage alternatives are often compared by weighing a number of product characteristics and cost factors. Some of these product characteristics include internal versus external installation, access time (speed), types of access available, storage capacity, and ability to remove the storage media (see Figure HW 2-19).

Keep in mind that each storage alternative normally involves trade-offs. For instance, you usually must sacrifice access speed to gain the convenience of removability. Also, although virtually everyone wants the fastest possible secondary storage, higher speeds generally come at greater expense.

Today, most users need at least a fixed hard disk, a CD-ROM drive, and a diskette drive. Fixed hard disks have become the workhorses among secondary storage choices because they provide, at a reasonable cost, the fastest data access. CD-ROM optical disks are the most popular storage choices today for multimedia applications and for installing new software. Diskettes, on the other hand, are widely used for transferring small amounts of data between computer systems and for small backup jobs.

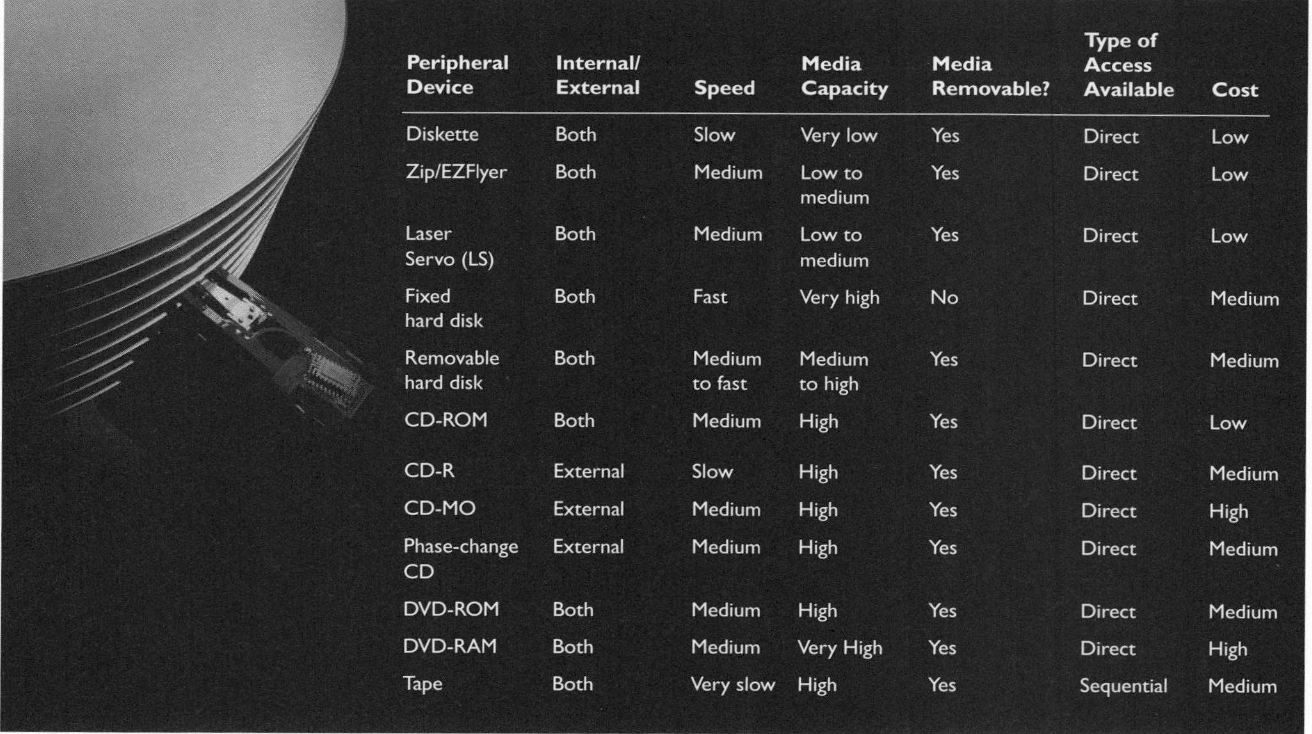

Peripheral Device	Internal/ External	Speed	Media Capacity	Media Removable?	Type of Access Available	Cost
Diskette	Both	Slow	Very low	Yes	Direct	Low
Zip/EZFlyer	Both	Medium	Low to medium	Yes	Direct	Low
Laser Servo (LS)	Both	Medium	Low to medium	Yes	Direct	Low
Fixed hard disk	Both	Fast	Very high	No	Direct	Medium
Removable hard disk	Both	Medium to fast	Medium to high	Yes	Direct	Medium
CD-ROM	Both	Medium	High	Yes	Direct	Low
CD-R	External	Slow	High	Yes	Direct	Medium
CD-MO	External	Medium	High	Yes	Direct	High
Phase-change CD	External	Medium	High	Yes	Direct	Medium
DVD-ROM	Both	Medium	High	Yes	Direct	Medium
DVD-RAM	Both	Medium	Very High	Yes	Direct	High
Tape	Both	Very slow	High	Yes	Sequential	Medium

FIGURE HW 2-19

Secondary storage alternatives compared.

To transfer data between systems or to back up greater amounts of data, users need to step up to either superdiskettes, WORM or rewritable optical disks, or magnetic tape. Recently, the Internet has begun to function in yet another role—as a backup alternative (see User Solution HW 2-2 on page HW 70).

Data Organization

When a computer system receives an instruction calling for data or programs from secondary storage, it must first find those materials. The process of retrieving data and programs in storage is called **data access.** Arranging data for efficient retrieval is called **data organization.**

Recall that a major difference between devices, say tape and disk, is that data on tape can be *accessed* only sequentially, whereas data on disk can be retrieved both sequentially and in a direct (random) fashion. With sequential access, the records in a file can be retrieved only in the same sequence in which they are physically stored. With direct, or random, access, the time needed to fetch a record is independent of its storage location.

The speed with which data must be retrieved necessarily dictates the choice of ways to *organize* data files. Consider a practical example. Most libraries organize their books in indexed systems ordered by title, author, and subject, so you can retrieve them directly from their places on the shelves. To locate a particular book, you simply look under the book's title in the index, find its call number, and go directly to the appropriate shelf. Books on the same subject matter are physically grouped together on the shelves because people often like to browse at titles once they've reached a particular subject area.

■ **Data access.** The process of fetching data either sequentially or directly from a storage device. ■ **Data organization.** The process of setting up data so that they may subsequently be accessed in some desired way.

Terabyte CDs

How Soon before Gigabyte CDs Are History?

Something new is shuffling in Buffalo, and it's not another recipe for chicken wings or a player acquisition by the football Bills. It's an advanced type of CD under development in the Photonics Research Laboratory at the State University of New York at Buffalo.

Whereas today's optical disks store anywhere from 640 megabytes up to a few gigabytes of data, one of these new disks—still largely in the pioneering stage—can currently store about a terabyte of data. That's 1,000 gigabytes, or 1 trillion characters. The key to the new technology is a dye-based system and a special infrared laser beam that can read these dyes.

Just as revolutions in manufacturing methods during the last several years have enabled chip makers to layer their CPUs with circuit patterns, one on top of another, these new CDs allow disk surfaces to be layered with dyes. A single surface can contain 100 or more layers, and each layer can store several gigabytes of data. In contrast, virtually every CD in wide use today records only a single layer of data in the form of pits on one or both of the disk's surfaces. By focusing the laser that reads the new disks at precise distances, this technology can fetch data at any layer within the disk.

As you might guess, since the new technology has barely moved out of the laboratory, it is still expensive. Don't expect to see multilayered CDs on store shelves anytime soon. While two-layer disks will appear shortly, products made up of scores of layers are still some distance away. What's more, CDs face stiff competition from online methods of information delivery, so by the time the new technology reaches a cost-effective level, you may have enough bandwidth on the cable or satellite dish going into your home to put the CD business out of business.

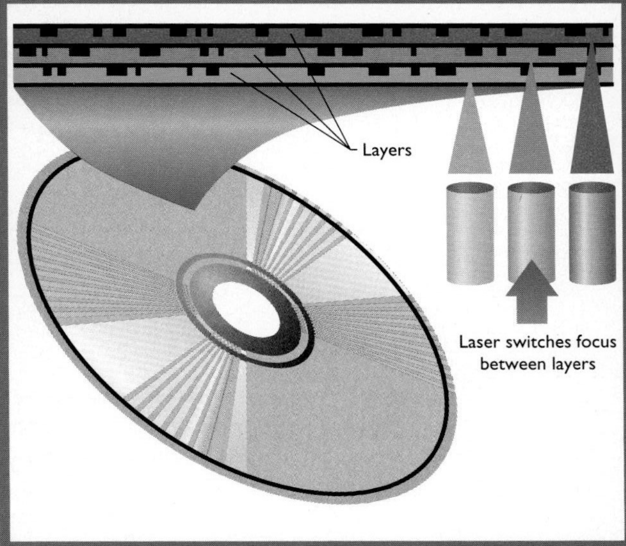

Multilayered CD. Precision focusing enables a laser beam to read data from any layer within the disk.

However, suppose that the librarians maintained no indexes and instead physically organized books alphabetically by title on shelves. With this sequential organization scheme, it would take you a long time to retrieve several books on a related subject—although you would get a lot of exercise.

People organize data on computers in a similar fashion. First, they decide on the type of access users need—direct, sequential, or both. Then they organize the data in a way that will minimize the time needed to retrieve them with the chosen access method.

Data may be organized in many ways. This section describes three: sequential, indexed, and direct organization. For any method of organization, typically one or more **key fields** must be declared so that records can be identified and processed. For instance, if the social-security-number field serves as a key field in an employee file, you can search employee records to find data about a unique employee or sort the entire file by social security numbers.

Sequential Organization In a file with **sequential organization,** records follow one another on the storage medium in a predetermined sequence. Sequentially organized files generally are ordered by the contents of some key field, such as an account number. Thus, if a four-digit account number serves as a file's key field, the record belonging to,

---

Key field. A field that helps identify a record. ■ **Sequential organization.** Arranging data on a physical medium in either ascending or descending order by the contents of some key field.

FIGURE HW 2-20

Sequential organization.

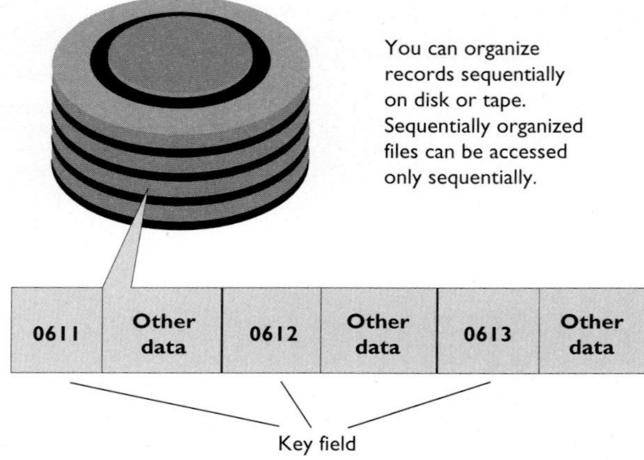
You can organize records sequentially on disk or tape. Sequentially organized files can be accessed only sequentially.
0611
Other data
0612
Other data
0613
Other data
Key field

say, Account 0612 will be stored after that for Account 0611 but before that for Account 0613 (see Figure HW 2-20).

Now that you have an idea of what sequential organization is, let's see how it might be used. Companies involved with billing often update customer balances at the end of each month. Such an activity is an example of **batch processing—** so named because transactions are batched together and processed on the computer all at one time. Processing often takes place at night, when computing demands are unlikely to disrupt other uses of the computer.

Two data files are often used in batch processing: a master file and a transaction file. The *master file* normally contains relatively permanent information such as a customer's account number, name, address, and phone number. For sake of example, let's say it also contains data about any outstanding balance the customer owes. The master file is often sorted by a key field like customer account number, and records are arranged in ascending sequence, from the lowest number to the highest. The *transaction file* contains data about all transactions during the month (or some other period) by old customers, whose records already appear in the master file, and by new customers, for whom the master file holds no current records. Transactions include purchases and payments. Like the master file, the transaction file can be ordered in ascending sequence by customer ID number.

A sequential batch updating operation processes the two files together in the manner shown in Figure HW 2-21. The update program reads a record from each file. If the key fields match, it performs the operation specified in the transaction file. Note from Figure HW 2-21 that the key fields of the first records in each file match. Thus, the program updates Record 101 to produce the new version of the customer master file. For example, if the transaction file shows that Customer 101 bought a toaster, the program adds the amount of this purchase to the outstanding balance in the master file.

Next, the program "rolls forward" both files to the next record. It observes that Customer 102 is not in the master file, because the next master file record after 101 is 103. Therefore, the record must relate to a new customer, and the program creates a new record for Customer 102 in the updated master file. At this point, it rolls forward only the transaction file, reaching a record for Customer 103. The program observes that this record matches the one to which it is currently pointing in the master file. However, the transaction file indicates that 103 is a new customer. The comparison appears to reveal an inconsistency, because the master file contains records only for old customers. The program makes no entry in the updated master file but sends information about this transaction to the error report. The processing continues in this manner until the program exhausts available records in both files.

Indeed Organization

Indexed Organization **Indexed organization** provides a way of arranging data for both sequential and direct access. This type of organization requires disk storage, because tapes cannot provide direct access. It orders records on the disk by key field. Also, several indexes indicate the locations of these records for later access. These indexes work similarly to the pages and columns of data in a phone

■ **Batch processing.** Processing transactions or other data in groups, at periodic intervals. ■ **Indexed organization.** A method of organizing data on a direct-access storage medium so that they can be accessed directly (through an index) or sequentially.

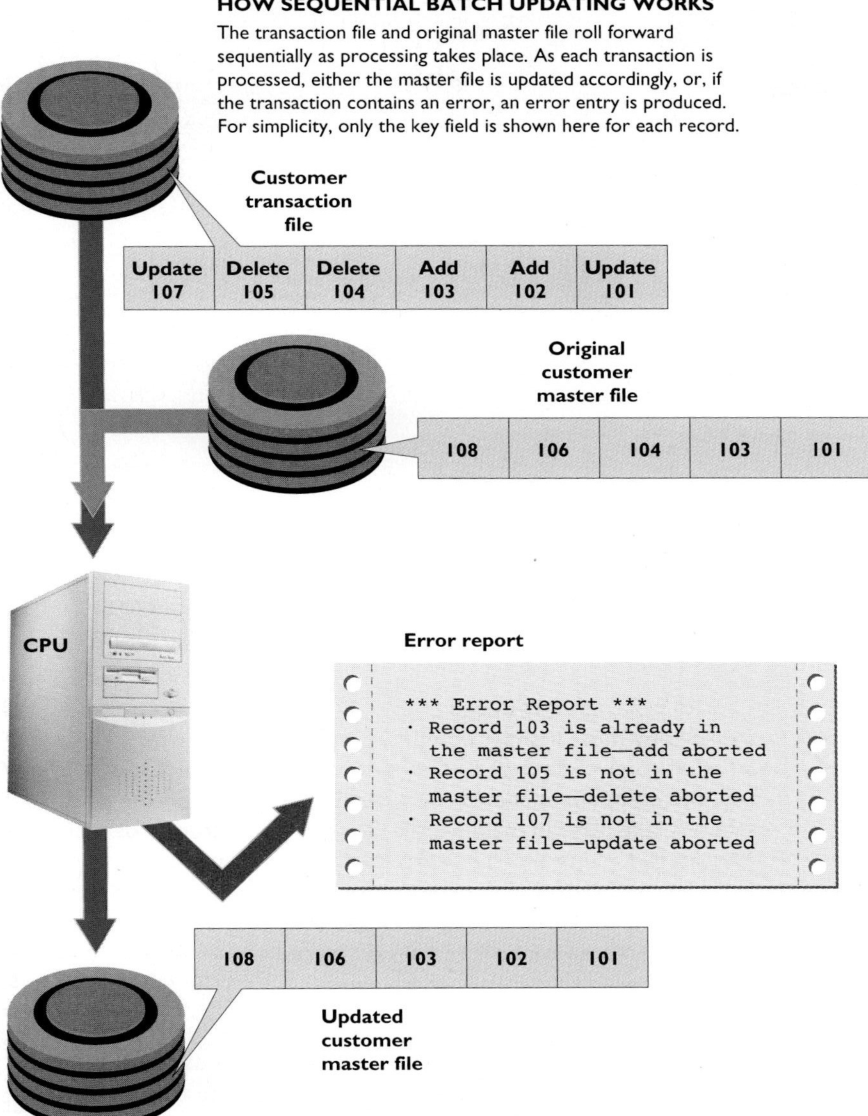
HOW SEQUENTIAL BATCH UPDATING WORKS
The transaction file and original master file roll forward sequentially as processing takes place. As each transaction is processed, either the master file is updated accordingly, or, if the transaction contains an error, an error entry is produced. For simplicity, only the key field is shown here for each record.
Customer transaction file
Update 107
Delete 105
Delete 104
Add 103
Add 102
Update 101
Original customer master file
108
106
104
103
101
CPU
Error report
*** Error Report ***
· Record 103 is already in the master file—add aborted
· Record 105 is not in the master file—delete aborted
· Record 107 is not in the master file—update aborted
108
106
103
102
101
Updated customer master file

FIGURE HW 2-21

A sequential batch update.

book. For example, if the top of a phone book page reads "Alexander–Ashton," you know to look for the phone number of Amazon Sewer Service on that page. When implemented on a computer, as Figure HW 2-22 shows, such indexes permit rapid access to records.

Both indexed and direct organization, covered in the next section, permit **transaction processing—**updating transaction data in random order. For instance, a teller in a bank's lobby may need to find out how much money is in Sandy Patz's checking account. Seconds later, a customer named Merlene Jones may call up someone working in a back room to find out her current balance. Then, a question comes up on Lee Shin's account. In each case, the computer must move back and forth randomly through the checking-account records to obtain information.

Processing of such transactions as bank withdrawals often takes place in realtime. **Realtime processing** implies that transactions are processed quickly enough so that

- **Transaction processing.** Processing transaction data in a random sequence, as the transactions normally occur in real life.
- **Realtime processing.** Processing that takes place quickly enough so that results can guide current and future actions.

Using the Internet as a Backup Device

Traditionally, most people have backed up their hard disks by storing data on additional hard disks, magnetic tape, or removable disk-cartridge units. Recently, another backup solution has presented itself: the Internet.

Two products offering such backup capability are McAfee's Personal Vault and Surefind Information's Surefind. (The second is available through the CompuServe information service.) Charges for backup storage normally run a few dollars a month or more, depending on storage needs.

Online backup brings important advantages, including the chance to avoid the cost of a backup device and media, as long as you have a modem. Also, such services store your files at different locations than the originals, preventing the possibility that both the original and backup files could be destroyed at the same time. For two disadvantages, it can take a long time to transmit files by conventional modem, and you have limited control over the storage site. Also, if your access provider's computers are having problems, you may not be able to get to your data.

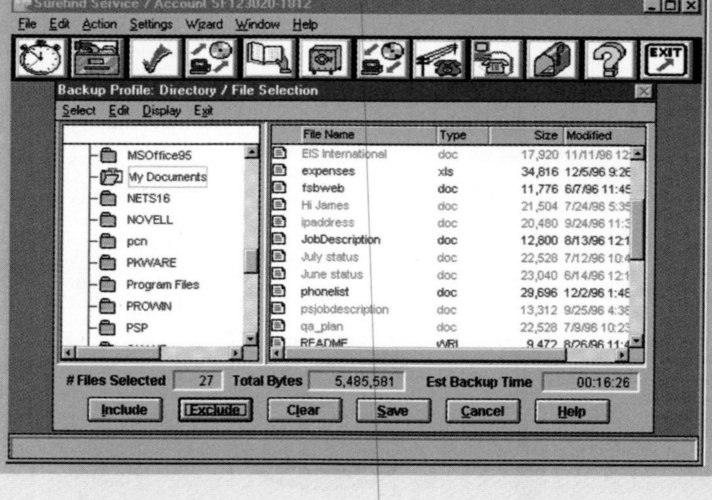

people can immediately act upon the results. For example, banks need to prevent overwithdrawals, so they must inspect computer records of balances in checking accounts as soon as customers attempt to take out money. If a withdrawal is subsequently permitted, the computer updates the customer's balance on the spot. Not all banking transactions take place in realtime; the recording of customer deposits, for instance, is usually batched and processed at day's end.

Systems software is available to help programmers set up indexes and index-organized files. As records are added to or deleted from a file, the software automatically updates the index. Because records remain organized sequentially on the disk, indexed files can be processed sequentially at any time.

Direct Organization Although indexed files are suitable for many applications, they demand a potentially time-consuming process of finding disk addresses through index searches. Direct-organization schemes have been developed to provide faster direct access.

Direct organization eliminates the need for an index by translating each record's key field directly into a disk address. The computer does this by applying mathematical formulas called *hashing algorithms.* Several hashing procedures have been developed. One of the simplest involves dividing the key field by the prime number closest to, but not greater than, the number of records to be stored. A prime number can be divided evenly by itself and 1 but not by any other number. The remainder of this division procedure (not the quotient) becomes the relative address at which the record will be stored.

Consider a reasonably straightforward example. Suppose that a company has 1,000 employees and therefore 1,000 active employee numbers. Suppose also that all employee identification numbers (the key field) are four digits long. Therefore, the possible range of ID numbers is from 0000 to 9999.

Assume that this company wants to store the record of Employee 8742 on disk. The hashing procedure defines a disk address as follows: The computer determines the prime number closest to 1,000, the number of records to be stored, to be 997.

■ **Direct organization.** A method of arranging data on a storage device so they can be accessed directly (randomly).

HOW INDEXED ORGANIZATION WORKS
Records are ordered on disk by key, and all record addresses are entered in an index. To process a request to find a record—say, record 200—the computer system first searches a cylinder index and then a track index for the record's address. In the cylinder index, it learns that the record is on cylinder 009. The computer system then consults the track index for cylinder 009, where it observes that the record is on track 2 of that cylinder. The access mechanism then proceeds to this track to locate the record.

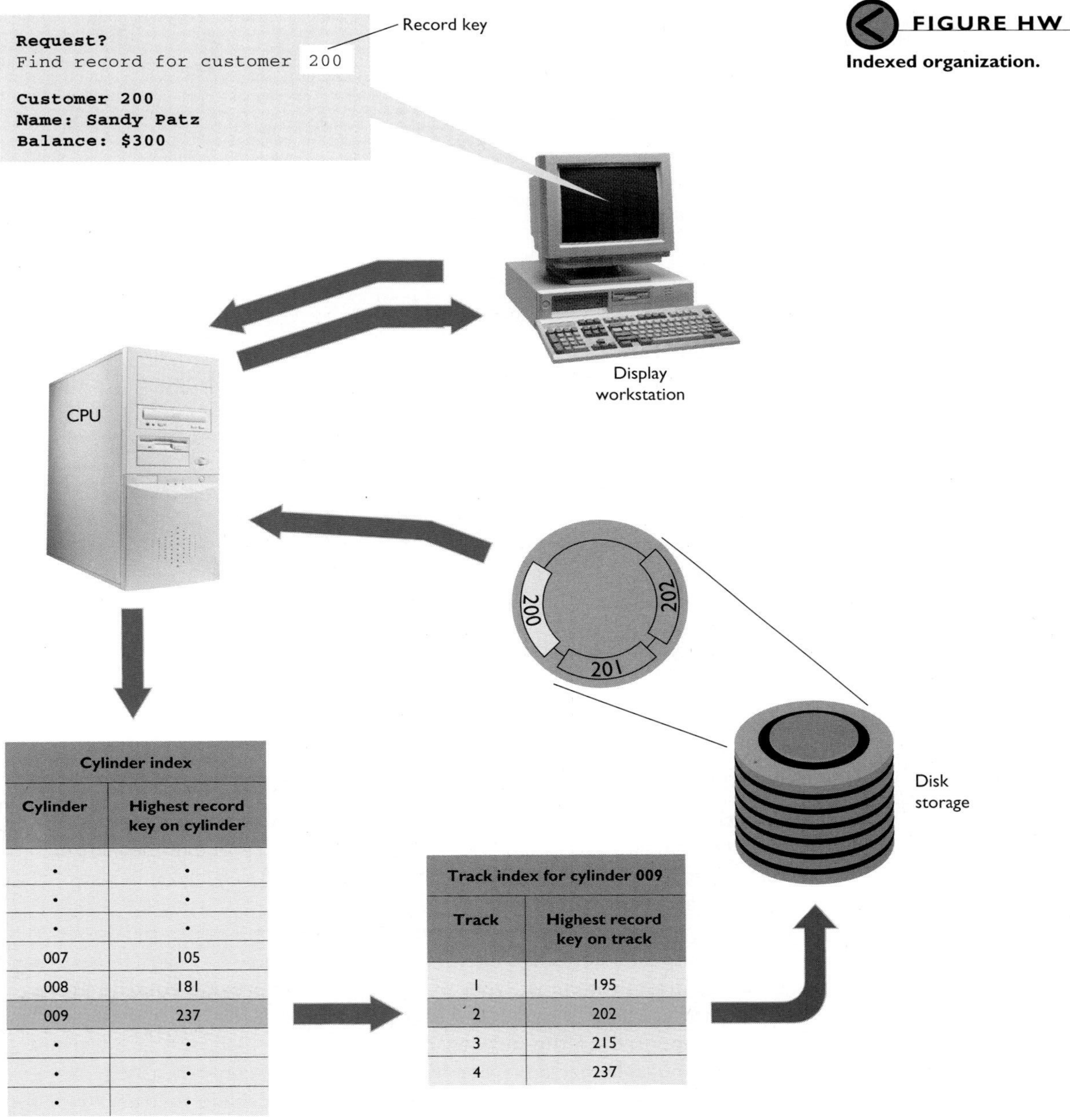

Cylinder index	
Cylinder	Highest record key on cylinder
•	•
•	•
•	•
007	105
008	181
009	237
•	•
•	•
•	•

Track index for cylinder 009	
Track	Highest record key on track
1	195
2	202
3	215
4	237

FIGURE HW 2-22

Indexed organization.

Figure HW 2-23 shows that the hashed disk address for Employee 8742's record computes to 766. After placing the record at an address corresponding to this number, the computer can retrieve it as needed by applying the hashing procedure to its key field again. The computer can usually calculate an address in this manner in much less time than it would take to search through one or more indexes.

Hashing procedures are difficult to develop, and they pose certain problems. For example, it is possible for two or more records to be hashed to the same relative

FIGURE HW 2-23

Direct organization.

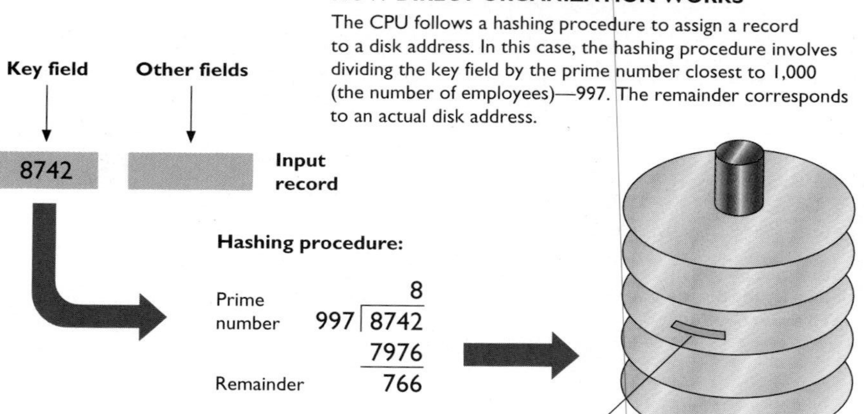
HOW DIRECT ORGANIZATION WORKS
The CPU follows a hashing procedure to assign a record to a disk address. In this case, the hashing procedure involves dividing the key field by the prime number closest to 1,000 (the number of employees)—997. The remainder corresponds to an actual disk address.
Key field
Other fields
8742
Input record
Hashing procedure:
Prime number
997
8742
8
7976
Remainder
766
Location of record on disk

disk location. This, of course, means they will "collide" at their common disk address. When this happens, one record is placed in the computed location and assigned a "pointer" that chains it to the other, which often goes in the closest-available location to the hashed address. Good hashing procedures result in few collisions.

While direct organization speeds access, it has another disadvantage. Because records are not stored in sequence on the medium, programs usually cannot practically process them sequentially.

Summary and Key Terms

Secondary storage technologies make it economically feasible to keep many programs and sets of data online to the CPU for repeated use. The most common types of secondary storage media are magnetic disk, optical disk, and magnetic tape.

Properties of Secondary Storage Systems Any secondary storage system involves two physical parts: a peripheral device and an input/output medium. In most systems, media must pass by **read/write heads** in the peripheral devices so the systems can access or record data.

Secondary storage media provide **nonvolatile storage—**when the power to an associated peripheral device is shut off, the data stored on its medium remain intact. This trait contrasts with most types of memory, which provide **volatile storage.** Secondary storage devices can record data on *removable media,* which provide access only when mounted on the devices, or *fixed media,* which remain permanently mounted. Removable media provide the advantages of unlimited storage capacity, transportability, safer backup capability, and security. Fixed media have the advantages of higher speed, lower cost, and greater reliability.

Two basic *access* methods characterize secondary storage systems: sequential and direct access. **Sequential access** allows a computer system to retrieve the records in a file only in the same order in which they are physically stored. **Direct access** (or **random access)** allows the system to retrieve records in any order. Disk systems provide flexible storage in that they allow both random and sequential access to data. Tape systems provide sequential access only.

Magnetic Disk Systems **Magnetic disk** storage is most widely available in the form of hard disks and diskettes.

Computer systems commonly store data on **diskettes** because they provide removable storage at low cost. Each side of a diskette holds data and programs in concentric **tracks** encoded with magnetized spots representing 0 and 1 bits. **Sector** boundaries divide a diskette surface into pie-shaped pieces. The part of a track crossed by a fixed number of contiguous sectors forms a **cluster.** The disk's **file directory,** which the computer system maintains automatically, keeps track of the contents at each disk address. To use a diskette, you insert it into a **disk drive,** or *disk unit.* A disk drive works only when the diskette is inserted correctly.

Today, diskettes are facing challenges from other removable media with much higher storage capacities. Products that can supplement or replace diskette drives include Zip drives, EZFlyer drives, and LS-120 drives.

Hard disks offer faster access than diskettes and greater data-carrying capacity. A hard-disk system encases one or more rigid disk platters in a permanently enclosed case along with an **access mechanism.** A separate read/write head corresponds to each recordable disk surface, and the access mechanism moves the heads in and out among the concentric tracks to fetch data. All tracks in the same position on the tiered platters of a disk pack form a **disk cylinder.**

Three events determine the time needed to read from or write to most disks. *Seek time* is the time required for the access mechanism to reach a particular track. The time needed for the disk to spin to a specific area of a track is known as *rotational delay.* Once the drive locates desired data, the time required to transfer them to or from the disk is known as *data movement time.* The sum of these three time components is called **disk access time.** A **disk cache** strategy increases speed by expanding the limits of any hard-disk access; the computer fetches program or data contents in neighboring disk areas and transports them to RAM.

Disk drives on larger computers implement many of the same principles as microcomputer-based hard disks. Instead of finding a single pack of hard disks inside a small box permanently installed within a system unit, however, a refrigerator-sized cabinet separate from the system unit often encloses several removable packs of disk platters. Recently, **RAID** technology (for *r*edundant *a*rrays of *i*nexpensive *d*isks) has infiltrated the disk market for larger computers.

Optical-Disk Systems **Optical disks,** which work with laser read/write devices, are a relatively recent secondary storage technology. Most optical-disk systems available today are **CD-ROM, WORM**, or **rewritable CD** systems. CD-ROM (*c*ompact *d*isk *r*ead-*o*nly *m*emory) systems enable an optical drive to read from a disk an unlimited number of times, but cannot write to these disks. A WORM (*w*rite *o*nce, *r*ead *m*any) system allows you to write only once to the disk, but you can read it an unlimited number of times. Rewritable systems, which allow repeated reading and writing, often rely on *MO* and *phase-change* technology.

Magnetic Tape Systems **Magnetic tape** stores data on a plastic strip coated with a magnetizable substance and wound onto a reel. A computer can access such a tape only if it is mounted on a hardware device called a **tape drive.** The drive spins the tape past a read/write head, which either reads from or writes to the tape.

Virtually all tape systems use either **cartridge tapes** or **detachable-reel tapes.** Computer tapes differ in a number of respects, including the sizes of the reels or cartridges, the width of the tape, and the format and density with which data are recorded.

Each character of data is represented in byte form across the tracks in the tape, either perpendicular, parallel, or at an angle to the edge of the tape. Often records are systematically organized on a tape by means of a key field, such as customer ID number.

Comparing Secondary Storage Alternatives Computer users often compare secondary storage alternatives by weighing a number of product characteristics relative to cost factors.

Data Organization The process of retrieving stored data and programs on disk or tape is called **data access.** Systematically arranging data for efficient retrieval is called **data organization.**

The three major methods of arranging files in secondary storage are sequential, indexed, and direct organization. **Sequential organization** often suits the data requirements of **batch processing** operations by ordering records with respect to a **key field. Indexed organization** also arranges records in order by key field on disk to facilitate sequential access; one or more indexes list storage addresses for specific records to permit direct access to them. **Direct organization** facilitates even faster direct access. Both indexed and direct organization support the data needs of **transaction processing** and **realtime processing** applications.

EXERCISES

1. Match each term with the description that fits best.
   a. diskette
   b. disk cache
   c. cartridge tape
   d. hard disk
   e. optical disk
   f. phase change

_____ A storage technology with media read by a laser beam
_____ A storage alternative, often under 2 megabytes in capacity, available in low-density and high-density formats
_____ A high-capacity storage alternative used on PCs mostly for backing up a hard disk
_____ A specialized CD technology
_____ The most indispensible of secondary-storage medium
_____ A method of accelerating storage access by fetching more data from disk on each read than the immediate processing task requires

2. Assume, for simplicity's sake, that a kilobyte is 1,000 bytes, a megabyte is 1,000 × 1,000 bytes, and a gigabyte is 1,000 × 1,000 × 1,000 bytes. You have a 2.5 gigabyte hard disk with the following usage characteristics:

APPLICATIONS	BYTES
Operating system	7,600,453
Other systems software	2,184,605
Office suite	83,701,460
Other software	479,842,809
Documents	27,904,668

What percentage of the hard disk is used up?

3. What term does each of the following acronyms stand for?
   a. SCSI ____________
   b. MO ____________
   c. RAID ____________
   d. WORM ____________
   e. DAT ____________

4. Define the following terms:
   a. Nonvolatile storage
   b. Random access
   c. Cluster
   d. Transaction processing
   e. RAID

5. Name a microcomputer-oriented storage medium discussed in the chapter that meets each of the following criteria:
   a. A sequentially organized medium with a low cost per byte of information stored
   b. A CD that allows both reading and one-time writing
   c. A medium that works like a standard diskette but provides 100 MB or more storage capacity instead of just 1.44 MB; you can use standard diskettes on the drive that reads this medium.

6. Match the PC component shown in each of the following pictures with the appropriate term.

_____ Removable hard disk and drive
_____ Cartridge tape
_____ Diskette
_____ CD-ROM
_____ RAID

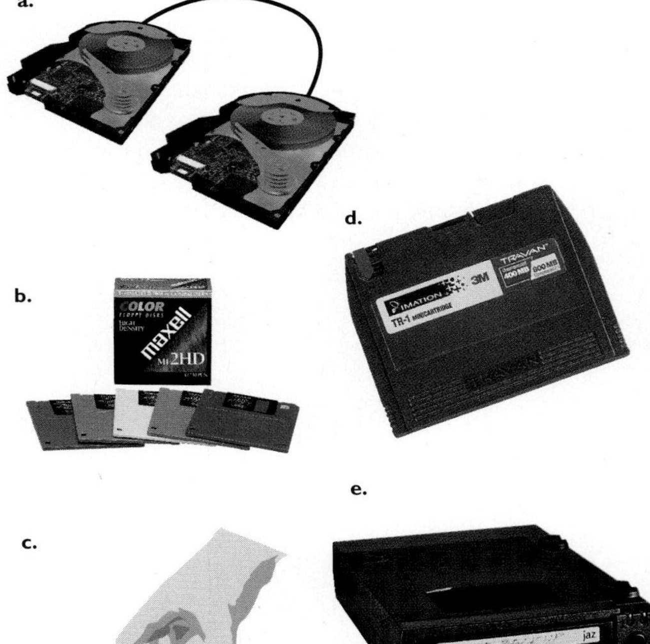

7. On PC-compatible storage systems, what type of storage device is normally assigned to the various letters?
   A: ____________
   B: ____________
   C: ____________
   D: ____________
   E: ____________
   F: ____________

8. Fill in the blanks:
   a. A storage medium is __________ if it loses its contents when the power is shut off.
   b. For rapid access, related data often are stored on the same __________, a collection of disk tracks that are in the same relative position on different surfaces of a disk pack.
   c. MO and CD-ROM refer to types of __________ disks.
   d. TR-1, QIC-80, and DAT are types of magnetic __________ storage.
   e. Iomega's __________ drive resembles a diskette drive, only it reads 100 MB cartridges.

9. What is the difference between sequential access and direct access?
   a. Which of the two would support faster processing of 25 records at random from a file of 100,000 records?
   b. Which of the two would be most appropriate in realtime applications?

10. Each of the following definitions is not strictly true in some regard. In each case, identify and correct the error.
   a. Realtime processing: Recording transactions on the computer as soon as they take place.
   b. Data movement time: The interval between the time a user types in a command to fetch disk data and the time the data appear on the display.
   c. Cluster: The intersection of a sector and a track on disk.
   d. Optical disk: A CD-ROM disk.
   e. Sequential organization: Arranging data in either ascending or descending order on a key field; used only with tape.

11. Identify each of the following statements as true or false.

_____ Superdiskette drives typically work with nonremovable media.
_____ 1.44 MB diskettes are called high-density.
_____ Exposing a diskette's write-protection square prevents writing anything to it.
_____ A disk cluster is typically larger than a disk track.
_____ Disk access time is greater than seek time.
_____ EIDE commonly refers to a tape format.
_____ A computer system with a C and D drive may have only one physical disk drive, which is partitioned.
_____ DVD refers to a hard-disk standard.
_____ You cannot write to a CD-RW disk an unlimited number of times.
_____ Even on a microcomputer system, it can take over an hour to back up a hard disk onto tape.

12. Compare and contrast the three types of data organization discussed in the chapter: sequential, indexed, and direct organization.

1. Secondary Storage Companies The table below lists the Web sites of several companies that make secondary storage devices. Choose any company on the list and determine the types of storage products it makes.

COMPANY	WEB SITE (HTTP://_____)
Seagate	www.seagate.com
Iomega	www.iomega.com
SyQuest	www.syquest.com
Quantum	www.quantum.com
Pinnacle Micro	www.pinaclemicro.com

(*Hint:* Many companies also have toll-free phone numbers, which you can get by dialing Directory Assistance. If you can't get the product information you need over the Internet, you may be able to get it though the mail or have it faxed to you.)

2. The Computer in Your Backyard Inspect the computer you regularly use in your lab, dorm room, or home and answer the following questions about it:

a. What devices are assigned to the drive letters A, B, C, D, and E? Does the system include other active drive letters or drive names? If so, what device is assigned to each of them?
b. What is the capacity of the hard disk?
c. What percentage of the hard disk is used up?
d. Is the hard disk on the system partitioned?

3. Magnetic Tape Tape systems are widely used on microcomputer systems for hard-disk backup. For this project, choose a particular tape drive and answer the following questions about it. Feel free to consult Internet resources in your research, as well as journal articles and product brochures.

a. What is the name of the drive and who makes it? Is it an internal or external device?
b. What is the approximate price of the drive?
c. What tape formats does the drive support—for instance, T-1, QIC-80, and so on?
d. What is the most capacious tape cartridge that the drive will accept? How much time will it take to back up a half-full 1 GB hard disk on such a tape?
e. What do tape cartridges cost?

4. Rewritable CD Choose a rewritable-CD storage device and answer the following questions. Feel free to consult Internet resources in your research, as well as journal articles and product brochures.

a. What is the name of the device? Who makes it?
b. Does the device use MO technology, phase-change technology, or something else?
c. What is the price of the device?
d. What storage capacities do the device's rewritable CDs provide? What are the unit prices of these CDs?
e. What is the device's average access time? How does this access time compare with that of a hard disk, which is also a read/write technology?
f. Can standard CD-ROMs be used in any way on the device?

5. CD Product Review Thousands of CD-ROM titles compete for attention in today's commercial marketplace. Some, such as *The 7th Guest* and *Myst* have become runaway bestsellers, while some others are arguably not worth the plastic needed to publish them. For this project, choose any CD-ROM title and write a short review about it, not exceeding three pages. In the review, cover both good and bad points that you see in the product. Also, make sure that your critique has a "bottom line;" in other words, after you weigh the pros and cons, would you recommend the CD to others or suggest that people stay away?

6. Diskette Prices Check a few stores in your area for an attractive price for 3½-inch diskettes in bulk (say, 20 or more diskettes). What is the price per diskette? Are the prices found any lower than those advertised in journals, computer-supply catalogs, or over the Internet? Microcomputer journals containing the information needed for this exercise may be available in your college or city library. Such journals are also carried by many bookstores and computer stores.

7. Photo CD A CD technology that has surfaced over the last few years to win a respectable following is Kodak's photo CD. Research this technology and answer the questions below. Feel free to consult Internet resources in your research as well as journal articles and product brochures.

a. For what types of applications would you recommend this technology?
b. How does a photo CD differ from a standard CD-ROM? Are the two technologies compatible?
c. Do photo CD applications require any special hardware, software, and I/O media? If so, name them.

8. Holographic Storage Holographic storage technology has received a lot of attention in the news lately as a possible replacement for conventional storage methods. As hard as it is to believe, the entire holdings of the Library of Congress could fit within a three-dimensional holographic cube smaller than the size of your PC's display device. Research this technology and answer these questions:

a. What is holographic storage?
b. What potential lies in holographic storage?
c. Is holographic storage targeted as a replacement for memory, hard disk, both memory and hard disk, or some other system component entirely?
d. How far advanced is holographic storage? In other words, how soon can people expect to use it on desktop PCs or in other applications?

9. "Dumb" Questions Project While the chapter mentions a number of useful facts about secondary storage technologies, it does not always provide reasons why certain things work the way they do. In some cases, the answers are self-evident; in others, the underlying reasons are more complicated and will demand a little research on your part. With that background, answer the following questions:

a. Why do hard disks continue to spin while the computer is turned on, even when you do not access them?
b. Since RAM is so much faster than hard disks and costs less than a hundred dollars for every 16 megabytes, why not just put more RAM into every computer and completely eliminate the hard disk?

10. Removable Hard Disks Scan the Internet, journal articles, or product brochures to find a state-of-the-art removable hard-disk system for a microcomputer. Answer the following questions about it.

a. Who makes the hard-disk drive? What is the name of the drive?
b. What is the capacity of the cartridges the drive can accept?
c. What is the speed of the drive relative to a conventional, fixed hard disk?
d. How much does the drive cost? How much do cartridges cost?

window

Multimedia Computing

A PICTURE ESSAY OF THE WORLD OF CD-ROMS

Multimedia computing—in which text, graphics, audio, and video data intermingle—is one of the applications that CD-ROMs serve best. In this window, we look at a few of the areas in which CD-ROMs sparkle, including computer games and products that specialize in reference, education, and history.

1. Could the Babe handle Koufax's smoke? Stormfront Studio's *Old Time Baseball* is a game that can answer such questions, by pitting legendary sluggers against hurlers of another era, in stadiums from baseball's golden age. The game uses mathematical routines to statistically "level the playing field," thereby making possible fair contests among the 12,000 players in baseball's 110 years.

cinemania

Microsoft's *Cinemania* is a CD-ROM product that provides text information about movies and movie stars, audio and video clips from many films, recommendations on picking films, and more.

2 • Guided tours delve into the work of film celebrities. Here, AMC's Bob Dorian discusses the films of legendary director Alfred Hitchcock.

3–4 • As you start to type a star's name into a text box at the northwest corner of image 3, the contents window underneath changes. When you then highlight and select the name in the window, a page pops up (image 4). From there, you can pull up clips, biographical and film information, and a list of awards.

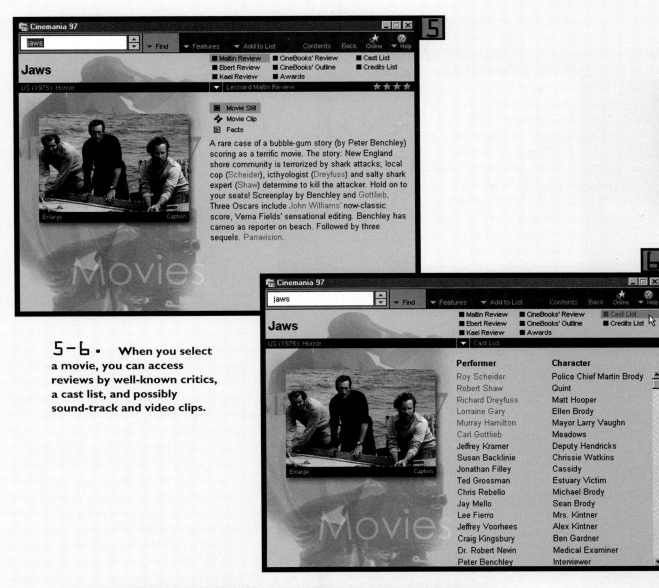

5–6 • **When you select a movie, you can access reviews by well-known critics, a cast list, and possibly sound-track and video clips.**

7 • **A suggestions feature in the package enables you to cull movies that conform to a certain mood or category.**

Like many new CD-ROM products today, Cinemania is extended with World Wide Web support.

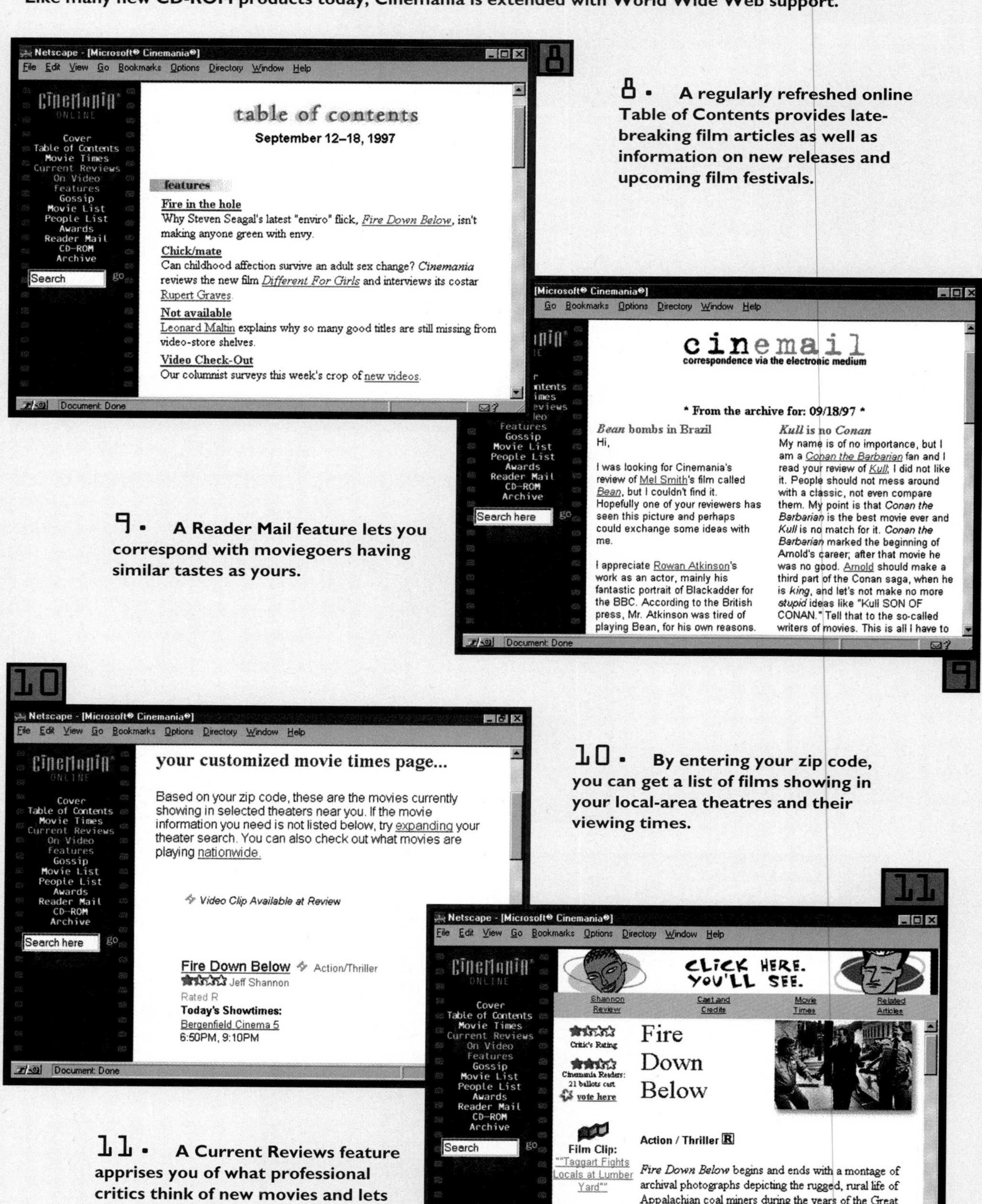

8 • A regularly refreshed online Table of Contents provides late-breaking film articles as well as information on new releases and upcoming film festivals.

9 • A Reader Mail feature lets you correspond with moviegoers having similar tastes as yours.

10 • By entering your zip code, you can get a list of films showing in your local-area theatres and their viewing times.

11 • A Current Reviews feature apprises you of what professional critics think of new movies and lets you observe film clips.

home cooking with master chefs

Hosted by famed chef Julia Child, *Home Cooking with Master Chefs* provides those who like to hang around the kitchen with both a standard cookbook and a variety of information about food preparation.

12. The contents menu is a colorful imagemap showing you what's on the CD-ROM.

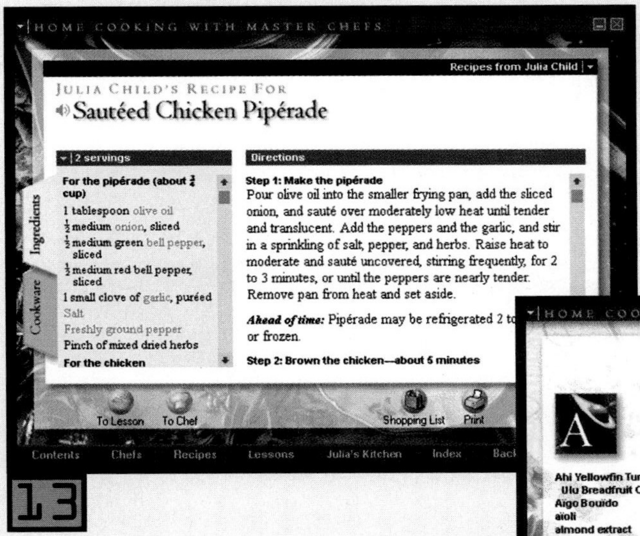

13-14. Gourmet recipes and an index are familiar items to anyone who reads cookbooks. You can print out the recipes so as not to get your keyboard gooey while cooking.

15. The food-preparation lessons come with audio and video clips. You can also hyperlink to recipe information or facts about the recipe's creator (see images 18 and 19).

16
HOME COOKING WITH MASTER CHEFS
Julia's Kitchen
KNIVES & UTENSILS
WINES
THE PANTRY
PLATES & PLATTERS
COOKWARE
Contents Chefs Recipes Lessons Julia's Kitchen Index Back Options

16–17. In the Julia's Kitchen section of the CD-ROM, you can learn about such things as cookware and wine. By clicking on any of the wine selections in image 17, information about the wine displays.

HOME COOKING WITH MASTER CHEFS
WINES TOUR
Six Wines From Julia's Cellar
Contents Chefs Recipes Lessons Julia's Kitchen Index Back Options
17

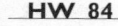

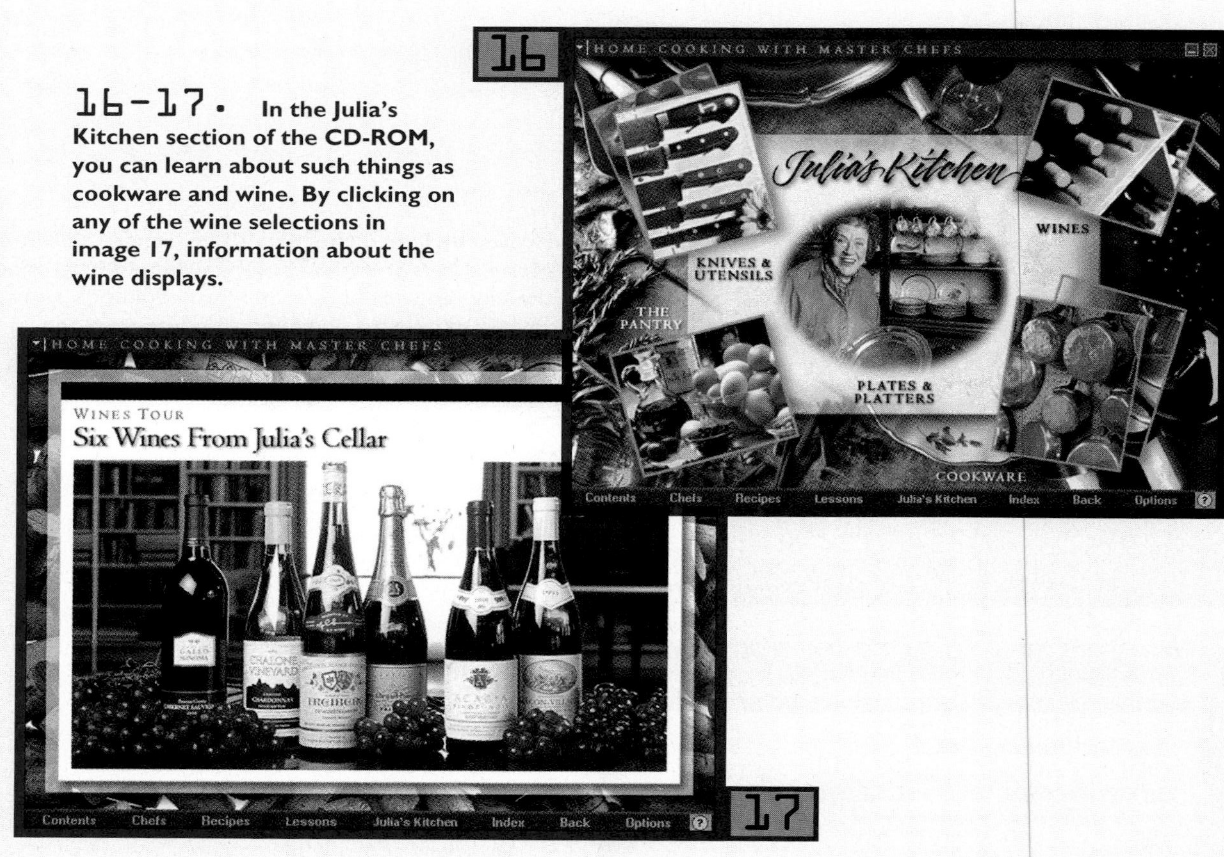

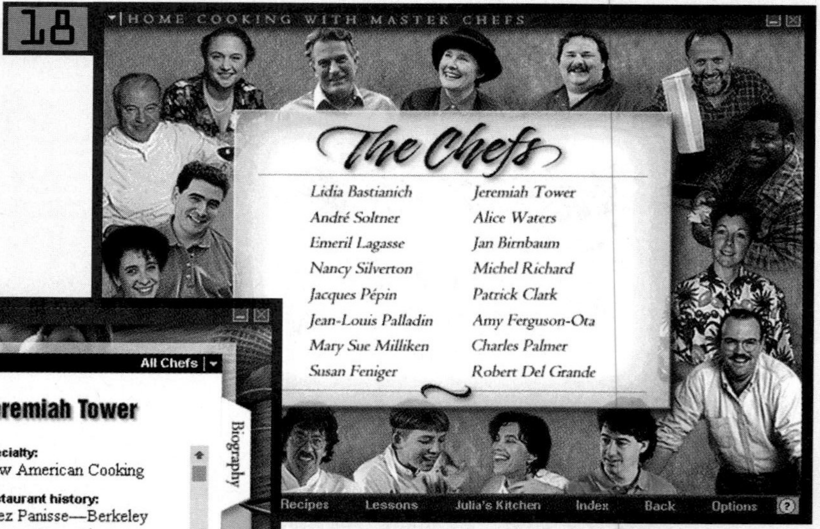

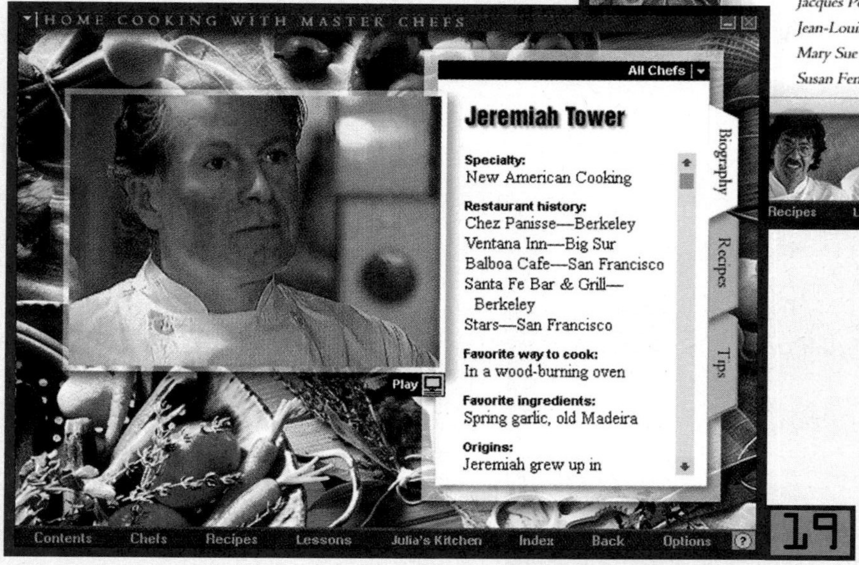

18
HOME COOKING WITH MASTER CHEFS
The Chefs
Lidia Bastianich
André Soltner
Emeril Lagasse
Nancy Silverton
Jacques Pépin
Jean-Louis Palladin
Mary Sue Milliken
Susan Feniger
Jeremiah Tower
Alice Waters
Jan Birnbaum
Michel Richard
Patrick Clark
Amy Ferguson-Ota
Charles Palmer
Robert Del Grande
Recipes Lessons Julia's Kitchen Index Back Options

18–19. In the Chefs section of the CD-ROM, you can access recipes and tips from some of the world's leading authorities on cooking.

HOME COOKING WITH MASTER CHEFS
All Chefs
Jeremiah Tower
Specialty:
New American Cooking
Restaurant history:
Chez Panisse—Berkeley
Ventana Inn—Big Sur
Balboa Cafe—San Francisco
Santa Fe Bar & Grill—Berkeley
Stars—San Francisco
Favorite way to cook:
In a wood-burning oven
Favorite ingredients:
Spring garlic, old Madeira
Origins:
Jeremiah grew up in
Biography
Recipes
Tips
Play
Contents Chefs Recipes Lessons Julia's Kitchen Index Back Options
19

Titanic: adventure out of time

Both an educational tour and suspense-adventure game, *Titanic: Adventure Out of Time* centers around an historical event that has spawned over eight decades of books, films, and documentaries—and, most recently, about 100 Web sites.

20. The opening screen provides access to the product's features

21. A 1912 newspaper reports the sinking of the world's most elegant ship on its maiden voyage. Many had claimed the *Titanic* to be unsinkable.

22-23. A lip-synchronized waiter can be summoned to tell you about certain people on the ship—such as J. Bruce Ismay, owner of the *Titanic* and one of the survivors of the disaster.

24

25

26

24–28 • In both the tour and the game, you get to inspect various parts of the ship. You can press the arrow keys to see around a room and click on items to inspect them further.

27

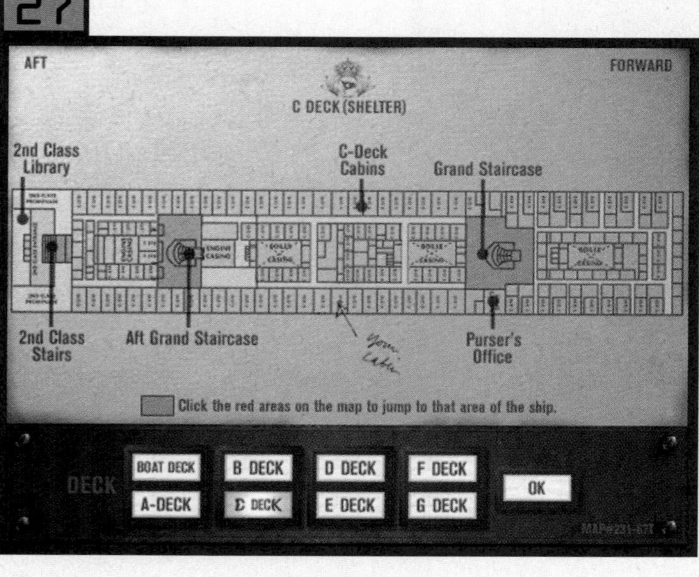

28

In the game, you get to play a secret agent who was aboard the ship on its fateful journey. Although you can't prevent the sinking, you do have time to complete a mission that would prevent the outbreak of World War I.

Input and Output

Outline

- Overview
- Input and Output
- Keyboards
- Pointing Devices
- Source Data Automation
  - Optical Character Recognition (OCR)
  - Image Scanners
  - Digital Cameras
  - Other Technologies
- Display Devices
  - Resolution
  - Color Displays
  - CRT and Flat-Panel Display Devices
  - Graphics Standards
- Printers
  - Types of Printers
  - Printers for Small Computer Systems
  - Printers for Large Computer Systems
- Other Output Equipment

Learning Objectives

After completing this chapter, you will be able to:

1. Identify several types of input and output devices and explain their functions.
2. Describe the characteristics of input equipment that most users encounter regularly—namely, keyboards and pointing devices.
3. Explain what source data automation means and discuss several ways to accomplish it.
4. Describe the characteristics of output equipment that most users encounter regularly—namely, display devices and printers.
5. Discuss several other types of output equipment.

Overview

In Chapter HW 2, we covered secondary storage devices. Although those devices perform both input and output operations for the computer, storage is their main function. In this chapter, we turn to equipment designed primarily for inputting programs and data into a form the computer can use, outputting results to users, or both. Many of these devices possess limited amounts of storage capacity, as well.

We'll begin the chapter with a look at input. First up are keyboards and then pointing devices such as mice and trackballs. Most users at home and in offices require these types of devices to enter commands, programs, or data into their computer systems.

From there, we'll cover hardware designed for source data automation. This equipment provides fast, relatively error-free input for certain kinds of applications.

Then we'll explore output, starting with display devices. Here, we'll highlight some of the qualities that distinguish one display device from another.

Next, we will turn to printers. In this section, you will learn about the wide variety of devices that place computer output on paper.

The chapter then discusses other types of output equipment. Included among these devices are speakers, machines that record computer output onto microfilm, voice-output hardware, plotters, and film recorders.

Keep in mind that this chapter describes only a small sample of the input/output equipment available today. In fact, the marketplace offers thousands of hardware products, and they can work together in so many ways that you can create a computer system to fit almost any conceivable need.

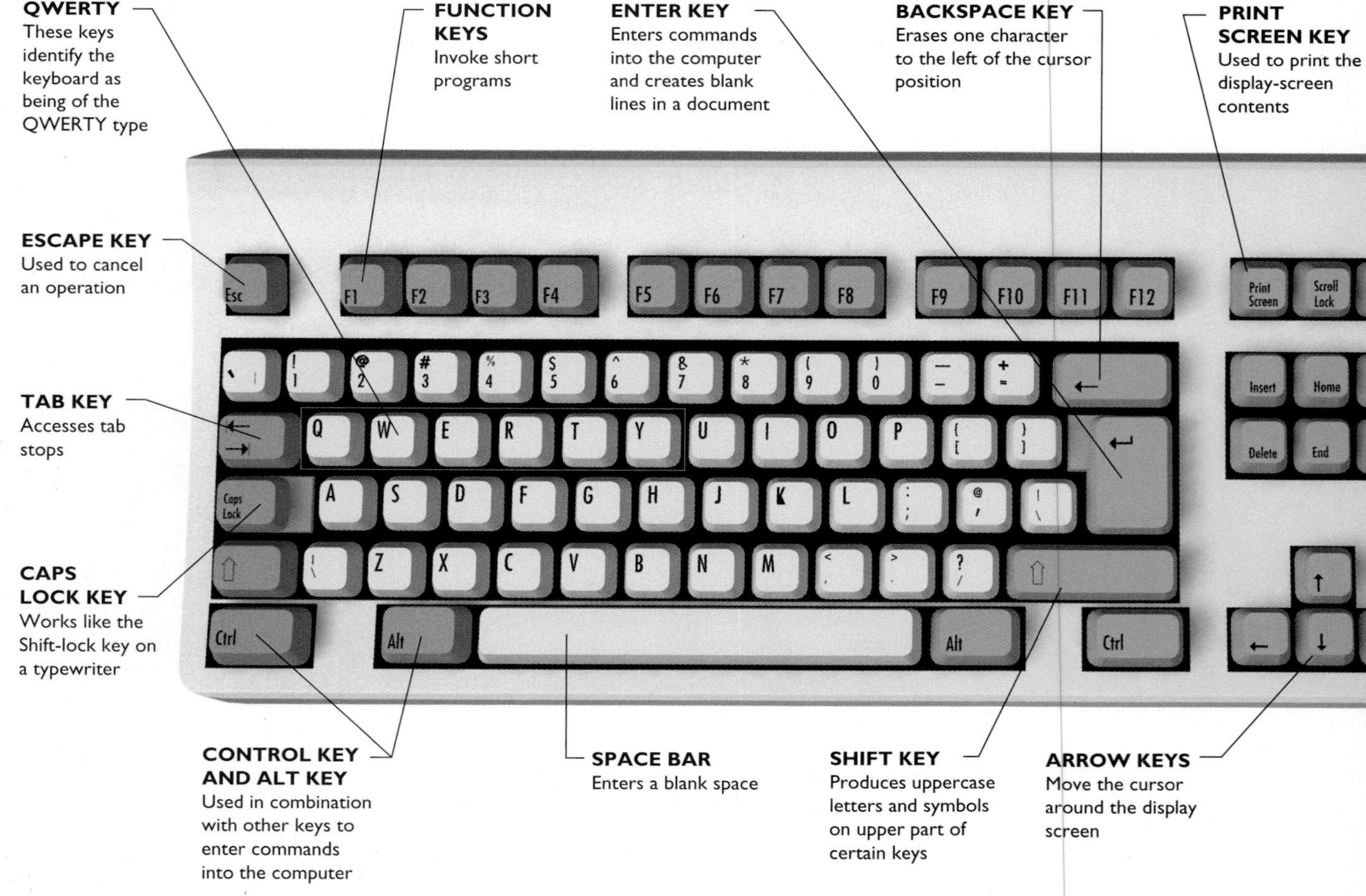

QWERTY These keys identify the keyboard as being of the QWERTY type
FUNCTION KEYS Invoke short programs
ENTER KEY Enters commands into the computer and creates blank lines in a document
BACKSPACE KEY Erases one character to the left of the cursor position
PRINT SCREEN KEY Used to print the display-screen contents
ESCAPE KEY Used to cancel an operation
TAB KEY Accesses tab stops
CAPS LOCK KEY Works like the Shift-lock key on a typewriter
CONTROL KEY AND ALT KEY Used in combination with other keys to enter commands into the computer
SPACE BAR Enters a blank space
SHIFT KEY Produces uppercase letters and symbols on upper part of certain keys
ARROW KEYS Move the cursor around the display screen

FIGURE HW 3-1

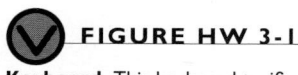

Keyboard. This keyboard typifies those sold with many microcomputers. For operator convenience, the keyboard features duplicates of many keys.

Input and Output

Input and output equipment allow people to communicate with computers. An **input device** converts data and programs that humans can understand into a form the computer can process. Such a device translates the letters, numbers, and other natural-language symbols that humans conventionally use in reading and writing into the configurations of 0 and 1 bits that the computer processes. **Output devices,** on the other hand, convert strings of computer bits back into natural-language form to make them understandable to humans. These devices present output on screen displays, on paper or film, and in other forms.

Much of a computer system's peripheral equipment performs input or output functions. Keyboards and optical character recognition devices are designed primarily for input. Printers and monitors specialize in output. Output devices produce results in either hard-copy or soft-copy form. The term **hard copy** generally refers to output permanently recorded onto an easily portable medium such as paper or film. Printed reports and output put into slide or transparency form are common examples. The term **soft copy** generally refers to display output—output that appears temporarily in a form with limited portability.

Keyboards

Most computers would be useless without **keyboards** (see Figure HW 3-1). Keyboards are the main devices through which computers receive user input. The large majority of keyboards follow a standard arrangement for letter keys called *QWERTY* (named for the first six letter keys at the top-left of most typewriter keyboards).

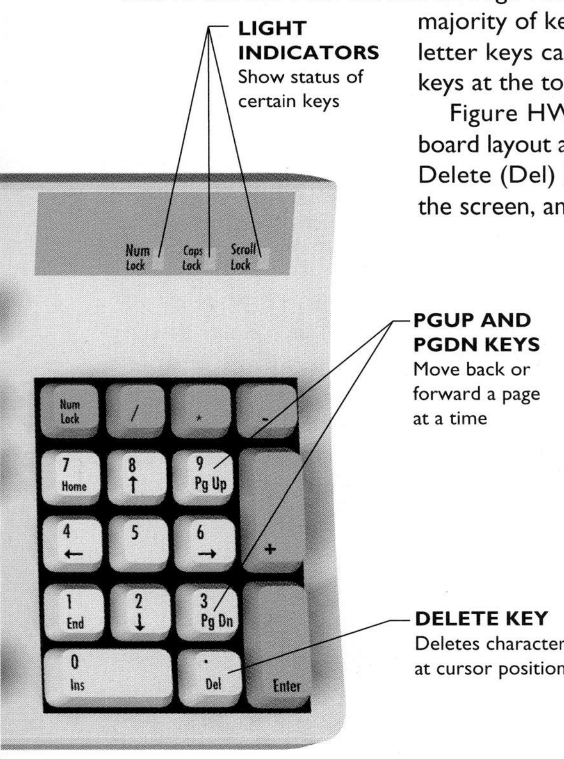

Figure HW 3-1 shows a typical microcomputer keyboard layout and describes the purposes of several keys. A Delete (Del) key, for example, removes characters from the screen, and an Insert (Ins) key enables the user to add characters between those on the current display. Keyboards also feature several *function keys,* which are labeled F1, F2, F3, and so on (see the top of Figure HW 3-1). When the user taps one of these keys, the keystroke initiates a special command or even an entire computer program. Each software package defines the actions of function keys in its own way. For example, tapping the F2 key in your word processing program may enable you to block-indent text, but the same keystroke would let you edit cells in your spreadsheet program. Most keyboards also have a *numeric keypad*; activate it by pressing the NumLock key, and you can easily and quickly enter numbers.

■ **Input device.** Equipment that supplies data and programs to the computer. ■ **Output device.** Equipment that accepts data and programs from the computer. ■ **Hard copy.** A permanent form of computer system output—for example, information printed on paper or film. ■ **Soft copy.** A nonpermanent form of computer system output—for example, a screen display. ■ **Keyboard.** An input device composed of numerous keys, arranged in a configuration similar to that of a typewriter, that generate letters, numbers, and other symbols when depressed.

The number of special keys, as well as their capabilities and placement, varies among manufacturers. When buying a computer system, look carefully at the keyboard's key selection and the placement of keys. Also, when buying a portable computer, pay special attention to spacing between the keys, and make sure that the keyboard allows comfortable typing.

Pointing Devices

Pointing devices refer to input hardware that moves an onscreen pointer such as an arrow, cursor, or insertion point. As the pointing device is moved along a surface or, alternatively, as it remains stationary while a finger or hand operates it, the pointing device determines position, distance, or speed and repositions the onscreen pointer accordingly.

Seven common types of pointing devices are the mouse, light pen, touch screen, joystick, trackball, crosshair cursor, and graphics tablet.

Mouse Many people supplement keyboard input with a **mouse** (see Figure HW 3-2). When you move the mouse along a flat surface, the onscreen pointer—often referred to as a *mouse pointer*—moves correspondingly. Mice provide capabilities to move rapidly from one location to another on a display screen, to make screen selections, to move and resize screen images, and to draw on the screen. A mouse often accomplishes such tasks much faster or far more effectively than you could complete them by pressing combinations of keys on the keyboard.

Mice are especially handy tools for working with *icons* on the screen—small graphics symbols that represent commands or program options. When you use the mouse to *select* an icon, you point to it on the screen and press—or click—the left mouse button once or twice. To *move* an icon from one part of the screen to another, you position the mouse pointer on the icon, hold down the button while moving the mouse to drag the icon to its new position, and release the mouse button. This operation is commonly known as *dragging and dropping.*

While most mice sold with computer systems connect via serial cables to a computer's system unit, cordless mice are also available. These mice, powered by batteries, send wireless signals to which the computer responds.

Light Pen A **light pen** senses marks or other indicators through a light-sensitive cell in its tip. When the tip of the pen is placed close to the screen, the display device can identify its position (see Figure HW 3-3). Some pens are equipped with buttons that users press to flip stored pages forward or backward on the screen, and many come with their own command sets. Potential users of portable computers equipped with light pens include inspectors, factory workers, sales representatives, real-estate agents, police officers, doctors and nurses, insurance adjusters, store clerks, and truck drivers—in other words, anybody that regularly carries around a clipboard and has forms to fill out.

Touch Screen Some display devices are designed to allow a finger rather than a light pen to activate onscreen commands. They are commonly called **touch screen displays** (see Figure HW 3-4). Touch screens are widely employed today in information *kiosks,* which are often used by people who are not computer literate. These input devices are also useful for factory applications and field work, where users wear gloves or cannot operate input devices for other reasons.

■ **Pointing device.** A piece of input hardware that moves an onscreen pointer such as an arrow, cursor, or insertion point. ■ **Mouse.** A common pointing device that you slide along a flat surface to move a pointer around a display screen and make selections. ■ **Light pen.** An electrical device, resembling an ordinary pen, used to enter computer input. ■ **Touch-screen display.** A display device that generates input when you touch a finger to the screen.

Joystick A **joystick** (see Figure HW 3-5) provides input through a grip that looks like a car's gearshift. This input device often supports computer games and computer-aided design (CAD) work. The speed at which the joystick is manipulated and the distance it travels determine the screen pointer's movement. Today, some electronic games replace joysticks with gloves containing built-in sensors, enabling the computer to detect hand movements directly.

Trackball A **trackball** (see Figure HW 3-5) consists of a sphere with its top exposed through a case. The onscreen pointer travels in the same direction as the operator spins the sphere. In fact, a trackball is merely a mouse turned upside down. Recently, a number of devices have come on the market to compete with the traditional trackball and mouse. The *pointing stick,* which appears on the keyboard of many notebook computers, is ideal when trackball-like functionality is needed and it's inconvenient to carry around or use a conventional trackball (see Figure HW 3-5). A *touchpad* uses another pointing strategy—it follows your finger's motion across a small surface to move the pointer around the screen (see Figure HW 3-5).

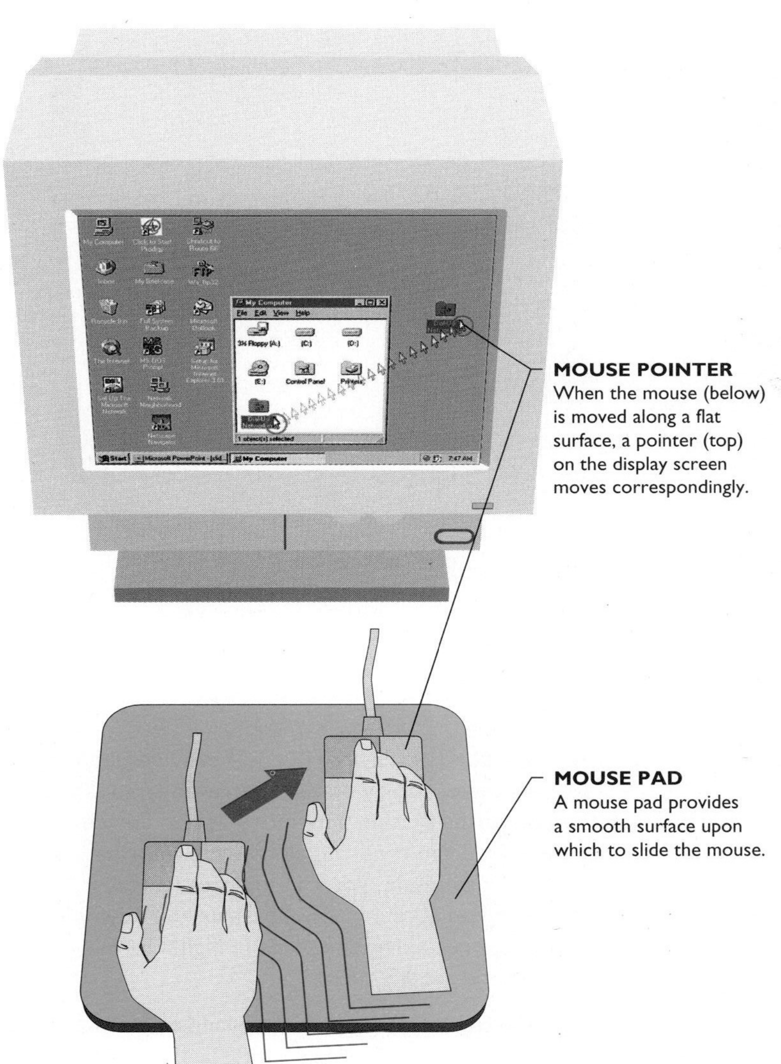

MOUSE POINTER
When the mouse (below) is moved along a flat surface, a pointer (top) on the display screen moves correspondingly.
MOUSE PAD
A mouse pad provides a smooth surface upon which to slide the mouse.

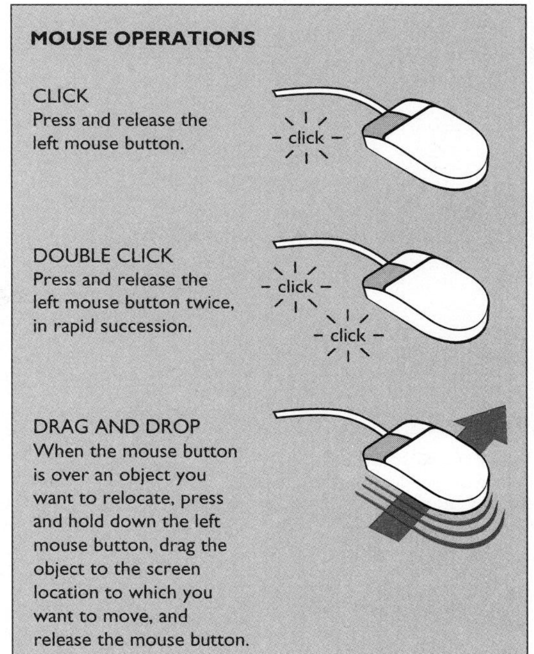

MOUSE OPERATIONS
CLICK
Press and release the left mouse button.
click
DOUBLE CLICK
Press and release the left mouse button twice, in rapid succession.
click
click
DRAG AND DROP
When the mouse button is over an object you want to relocate, press and hold down the left mouse button, drag the object to the screen location to which you want to move, and release the mouse button.

FIGURE HW 3-2

Using a mouse.

■ **Joystick.** An input device that resembles a car's gear shift. ■ **Trackball.** An input device that exposes the top of a sphere, which the user moves to control an onscreen pointer.

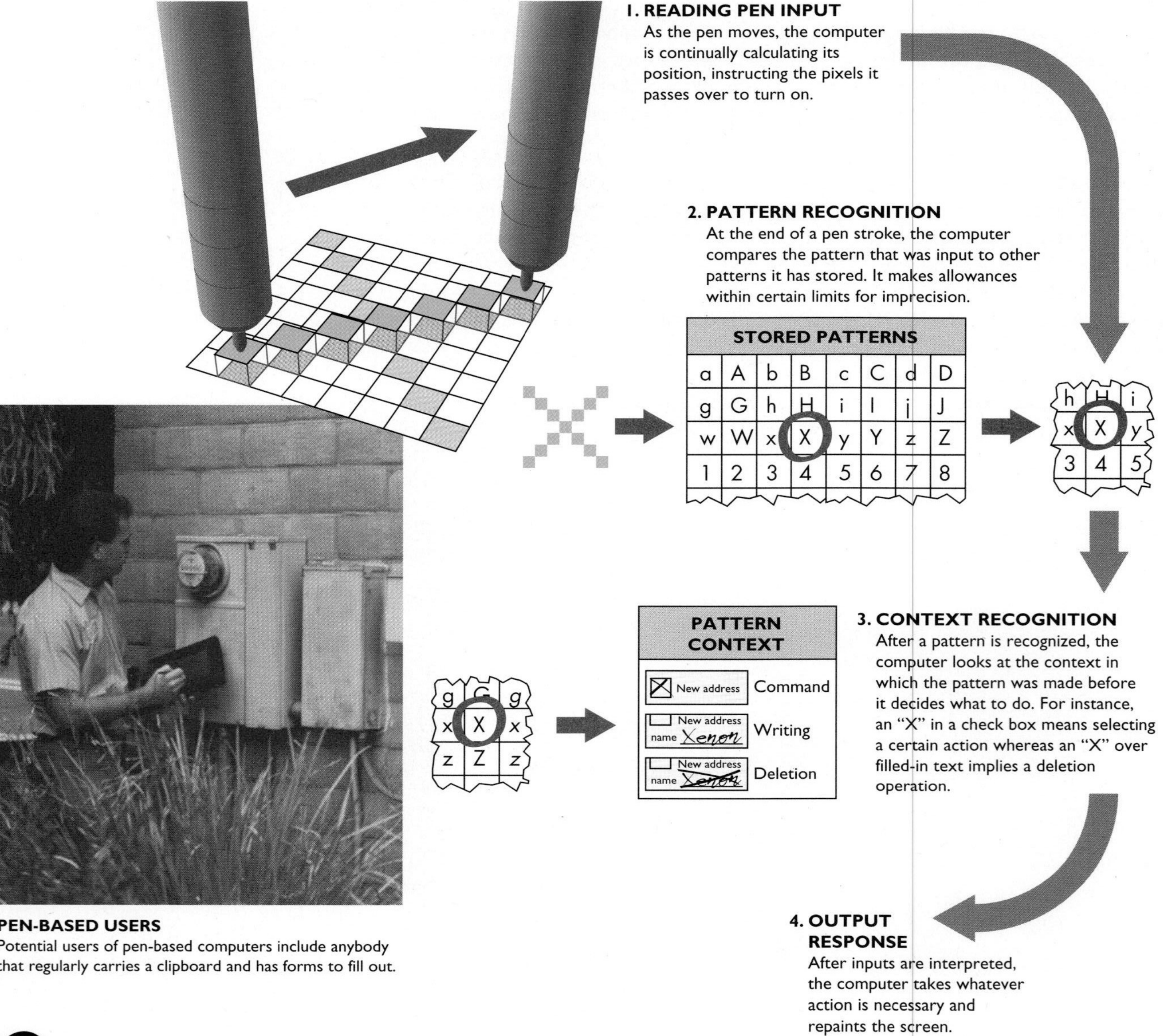

PEN-BASED USERS
Potential users of pen-based computers include anybody that regularly carries a clipboard and has forms to fill out.

FIGURE HW 3-3
Pen-based computing.

Crosshair Cursor A **crosshair cursor** (see Figure HW 3-5) provides input when you place it over hard-copy images of maps, survey photos, and even large drawings. The image is recorded into the computer system's memory as the device passes over it. Using a keypad on the device, you can enter supplementary information into the memory. While scanning maps, for example, you can indicate features such as rivers, roads, and buildings by carefully positioning the crosshair and keying in any identifying labels from the keypad. After recording the maps in digital form, you can call them up for display on the screen and modify them.

Graphics Tablet A **graphics tablet,** or *digitizing tablet,* usually employs either a crosshair cursor or a penlike stylus (see Figure HW 3-5). Using one or the other, you can trace over a drawing placed on the flat, touch-sensitive tablet. You can think of the tablet as a matrix of thousands of tiny dots, each with its own machine address.

■ **Crosshair cursor.** An input device that you move over hard-copy images of maps and drawings to enter them into computer storage. ■ **Graphics tablet.** An input device that consists of a flat board and a pointing mechanism that traces over it, storing the traced pattern in computer memory.

KIOSKS
Touch screens are ideal for information kiosks, where people can't be assumed to be computer literate.

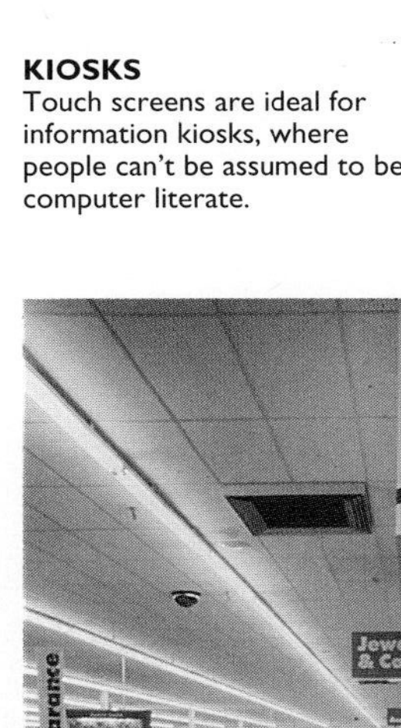

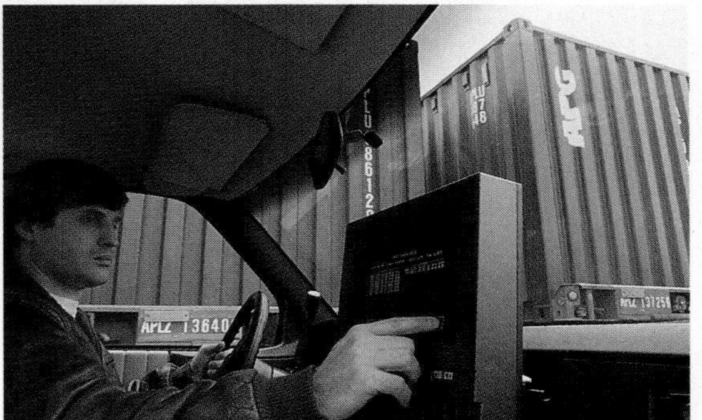

FIELD WORK
Field workers often use touch screens because a keyboard or mouse is impractical for input.

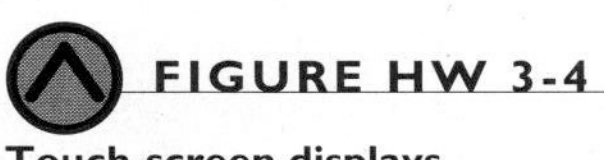
FIGURE HW 3-4
Touch-screen displays.

When you trace a line on the tablet, the stylus or cursor passes over some of the dots, causing their status in computer memory to change from a 0 state to a 1 state. When the drawing is complete, it is stored in digital form as a large matrix of 0s and 1s; you can then recall it at any time.

Source Data Automation

Applications often require translation of handwritten data into digital form that allows electronic processing. This procedure sometimes consumes thousands of hours of wasteful, duplicated effort, and it can result in many mistakes and delays. Data originally recorded by hand onto source documents or forms must then be keyed into digital form on some input device, verified, and read into the computer. Usually, several people must cooperate in such a process, complicating matters further.

Source data automation eliminates much of this duplicated effort, delay, extra handling, and potential for error by initially collecting data in digital form. The people who collect ready-to-process transaction data are those who know most about the events that the data represent. Thus, such people can instantly check for accuracy

■ **Source data automation.** The process of collecting data at their point of origin in digital form.

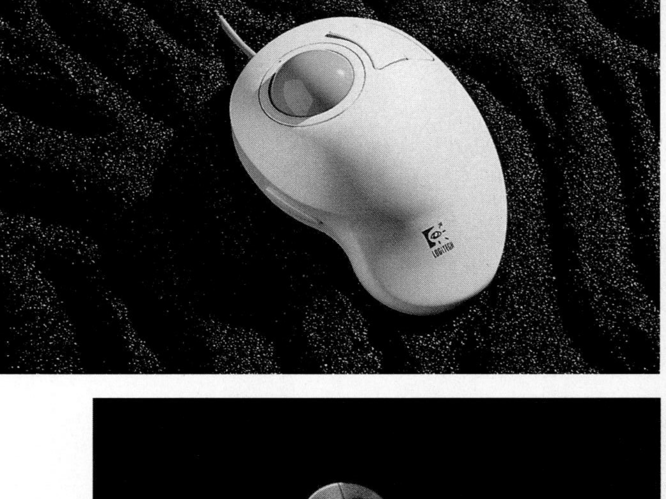

TRACKBALL
A trackball consists of a sphere in a case, with only the top of the sphere exposed. A trackball requires less desk space to use than a mouse.

POINTING STICK
Many notebook computers have a small keyboard stick that you push in different directions to move the onscreen pointer.

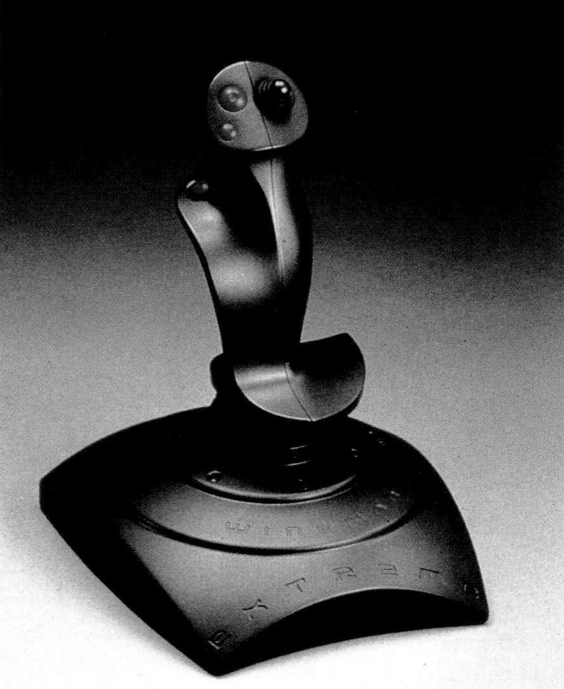

JOYSTICK
A joystick looks like a car's stick shift and is most often used for computer games.

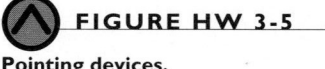

FIGURE HW 3-5
Pointing devices.

during the data entry process. Its many benefits have made source data automation a compelling choice for many types of commercial data entry today.

Source data automation has transformed a number of information-handling tasks. For example, workers who take orders over the phone today usually enter needed input directly at display workstations, so they don't have to record the same data twice. Source data automation also speeds up checkout lines and inventory taking at supermarkets, quality control operations in factories, and check processing by banks. This section discusses several technologies and devices that contribute to source data automation.

OPTICAL CHARACTER RECOGNITION (OCR)

Optical character recognition (OCR) technology encompasses a wide range of optical-scanning procedures and equipment designed for machine recognition of marks, characters, and codes. OCR devices transform symbols into digital data for storage in the computer.

■ **Optical character recognition (OCR).** The use of reflected light to input marks, characters, or codes.

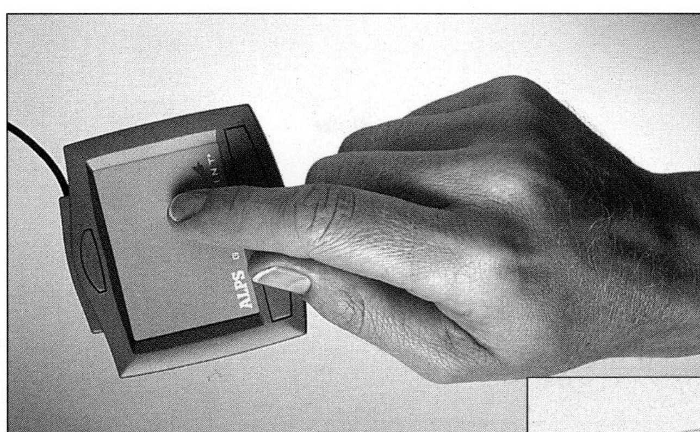

TOUCHPAD
To move the onscreen pointer, a touchpad requires you to move your finger about its surface, which is pressure and motion sensitive.

GRAPHICS TABLET
A graphics tablet is used to draw or trace on and thereby create data the computer can read.

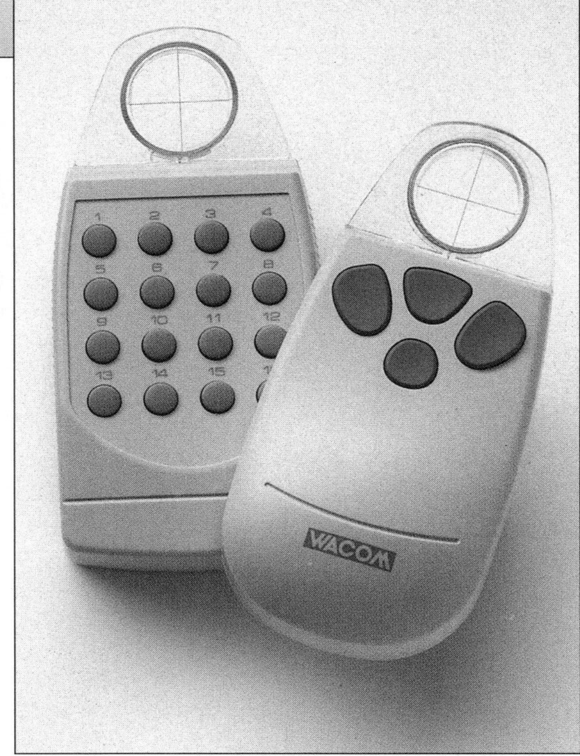

CROSSHAIR CURSOR
Crosshair cursors are moved over hard-copy images of maps, survey photos, and drawings in order to digitize them for computer use.

Optical Marks One of the oldest applications of OCR focuses on processing tests and questionnaires completed on special forms using *optical marks.* For example, a student darkens the bubbles on an answer sheet to indicate the answers to multiple-choice test questions. A hardware device called an optical document reader scans the answer sheets offline by passing a light beam across the spaces corresponding to the sets of possible responses to the questions. Filled-in responses reflect the light, and the machine tallies that choice. Results can be compiled on a disk or tape cartridge, or uploaded to a network, for processing by a computer system.

Optical Characters *Optical characters* are characters specially designed to be identifiable by humans as well as by some type of OCR reader. Optical characters conform to a certain font design, such as the one shown in Figure HW 3-6. The optical reader shines light on the characters and converts the reflections into electronic patterns for machine recognition. The reader can identify a character only if it is familiar with the font standard used. Today, most machines are designed to read several standard OCR fonts, even when these fonts are mixed in a single document.

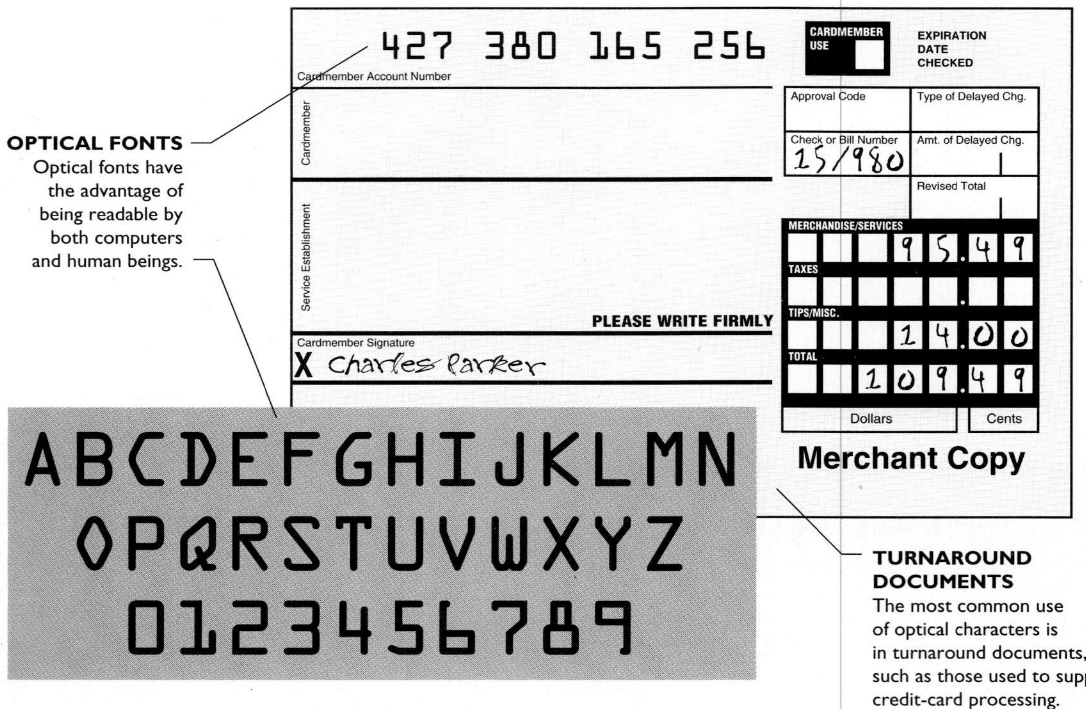

FIGURE HW 3-6

Optical characters.

Optical characters are widely used in processing *turnaround documents,* such as the credit-card slips used for customer transactions in stores and restaurants. They also speed processing of the monthly bills that are typically sent by credit-card, utility, and cable-TV companies to their customers. Such documents are imprinted in certain places with optical characters that aid processing when consumers send them back with payment—or "turn them around." Sometimes, as in the case of the restaurant bill in Figure HW 3-6, it's easy to spot the optical characters (see the top row of numbers). Today, however, many OCR fonts look so much like normal text that it's hard for an ordinary person to tell what parts the digital systems can read.

Optical Codes The most widely used type of *optical code* is the **bar code,** which records data by arranging several vertical bars of varying widths. The code supplies data on a product or transaction when the system reads it, either by the operator passing a scanning *wand* or *gun* over the coded label or moving the item past a *fixed scanning station* (see Figure HW 3-7).

The most familiar bar code is the *universal product code (UPC)* commonly found on packaged goods in supermarkets and in use since the early 1970s. Each code describes a product and identifies its manufacturer. The checkout system's bar-code reader gathers data that allows computers to identify the item, look up the latest price, and print the information on a receipt. While many customers are still suspicious of the accuracy of bar-coded-pricing systems, a 1996 study by the Federal Trade Commission reported that such systems are far more accurate than manual data entry and that customers are more likely to be undercharged than overcharged.

While supermarket packaging probably represents the most common use of bar codes, codes similar to the UPC support a variety of other applications. For instance, shippers such as Federal Express and United Parcel Service use their own bar codes to mark and track packages, hospitals use bar codes to identify patient samples, and the police use bar codes to mark evidence.

■ **Bar code.** A machine-readable code that stores data as sets of bars of varying widths.

BAR-CODE READERS
Most bar-code readers employ either a gun, wand, or scanning station.

GUN
A gun is used with cash-register terminals in many types of retailing environments.

WAND
A wand is lightweight and particularly handy when the operator has to do scanning while on the move.

BAR CODE
The most widely known bar code is the universal product code (UPC), used on supermarket products. The numbers below the bars identify the manufacturer and product.

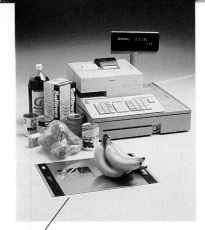

SCANNING STATION
A scanning station is the type of reader found most in supermarkets.

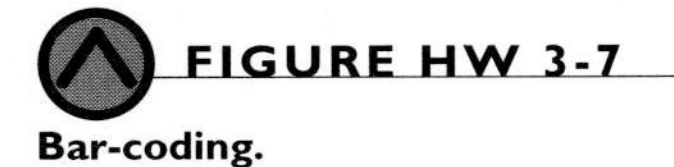

FIGURE HW 3-7
Bar-coding.

Retail-based bar-coding systems that use special terminals to verify customer credit, compute sales taxes on transactions, and record transaction data—such as product descriptions and sales amounts—are examples of **point-of-sale (POS) systems.** The scanning gun shown in Figure HW 3-7, for instance, is part of a POS system. When the store clerk reads the label attached to each purchased item with a hand scanner connected to the sales register, a computer within the register performs all of the necessary arithmetic, prepares a customer receipt, and accumulates input for subsequent management analysis. Not all POS systems use bar codes; for example, those at restaurants and hotels often work exclusively with the magnetic strips on credit-cards, supplemented with keyboard input.

IMAGE SCANNERS

Image scanners convert flat images such as photographs, drawings, and documents into digital data. After storing the images in the computer system, you can manipulate them as you like and then drop them into slides, a desktop-published document, or another type of output.

Scanners work in a variety of ways (see Figure HW 3-8). A *flatbed scanner* inputs a page at a time and works a lot like a photocopier. Many models scan color documents, and some even have attachments for capturing image data from 35 mm slides. A *drum scanner* functions in ways similar to a flatbed scanner, with a few important differences. For instance, it accepts source materials differently; a roller mechanism grasps and carries inputs fed through a narrow slot. This design cuts the scanner's cost, the amount of desk space required, and makes sheet feeding easy. However, the feature also generally prevents the device from scanning bound-book pages. *Handheld scanners* are useful for inputting small amounts of data and cost less than other types of scanners, but they also provide the most limited capabilities.

Many image scanners that work with PCs scan at resolution rates of 300 or 600 dpi (dots per inch). As you might expect, a higher number of dots generates better resolution when the image is finally output. Keep in mind that image resolution is ultimately determined by an output device, however, so it may not make sense to buy a 600 dpi scanner if your printer can't produce hard copy sharper than 300 dpi.

Image scanners labeled "dumb" devices can't recognize any of the text they read. So-called "intelligent" image scanners, on the other hand, are accompanied by optical character recognition (OCR) software, which enables them to recognize as well as read most standard text characters. Thus, an OCR-capable image scanner can produce text that can later be edited through a standard word processing program.

Scanners can cost anywhere from a hundred to a few thousand dollars, and professional-level models can cost tens of thousands of dollars.

DIGITAL CAMERAS

Digital cameras are much like regular cameras, but instead of recording images on print or slide film they record onto removable memory cards like those used in notebook computers. As snapshots are taken, the cards are loaded with the digital data that forms the picture image.

Digital cameras targeted for consumers use storage media that hold from 16 to 100 or more images. The number held depends both on the capacity of the medium and the image resolution you select. Many cameras will let you preview an image after

---

■ **Point-of-sale (POS) system.** A computer system, commonly found in department stores and supermarkets, that uses electronic cash register terminals to collect, process, and store data about sales transactions. ■ **Image scanner.** A device that can read into computer memory a hard-copy image such as a text page, photograph, map, or drawing. ■ **Digital camera.** A camera that records pictures as digital data instead of as film images.

FLATBED SCANNER
A flatbed scanner looks and works a lot like a photocopier, except that it produces a computer file instead of paper output.

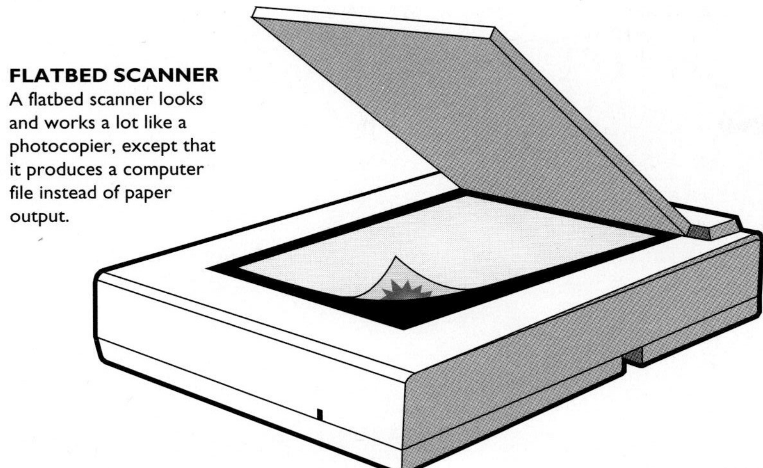

RESOLUTION
Many scanners let you specify the resolution (in dpi) at which you wish to scan. High-resolution images look sharper but take more time to input and require more bytes to store.

DRUM SCANNER
Drum scanners use a roller as opposed to a flatbed mechanism to input images.

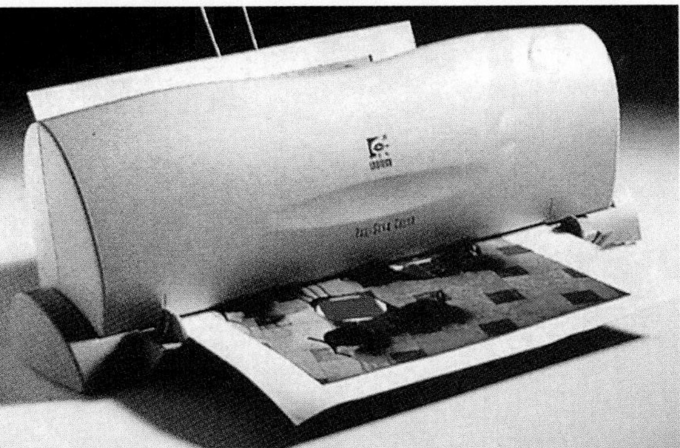

HANDHELD SCANNER
Handheld scanners are useful for inputting small amounts of information and work by sliding over images.

FIGURE HW 3-8

Image scanning.

you take it so that you can immediately erase it if it's not suitable. Once the card is full, you often connect the camera via a special cable to a port on your PC. The software that comes with the camera then allows you to transfer images to the PC's RAM. The software also clears the card's memory so that you can take more pictures at a later time. After storing the images on your PC's hard disk, you can retouch them with image-enhancement software, adjusting contrast, brightness, color, and focus—or adding special effects such as sepia tones or psychedelic colors.

Digital cameras for consumer use often cost anywhere from $500 to $1,000 or so, and professional-level digital cameras can cost well over $10,000. Despite their hefty sticker prices, even professional digital cameras cannot match the quality of images produced by a conventional, 35 mm film camera that sells for several hundred dollars. Conventional film forms an image by arranging millions of grains of silver, so even a few hundred thousand pixels produce far-less-sharp pictures.

Disadvantages notwithstanding, digital cameras can produce respectable images that make them useful for most types of business and recreational applications. For instance, an insurance adjuster may need a no-fuss picture of accident damage that can be quickly inserted into an electronic database. A home or business user may require a simple snapshot for a newsletter or presentation. A news photographer often needs to capture an image immediately and send it over phone wires to an anxious editor. Two compelling advantages to digital cameras are that you need not develop film and you don't need a scanner to get images into the computer.

Figure HW 3-9 illustrates some of the tools of digital photography.

DIGITAL CAMERA
Digital cameras look a lot like regular cameras, but instead of recording images on print or slide film they store picture images on electronic cards.

CAMERA SOFTWARE
Digital cameras often come with image-enhancement software that lets you adjust on your PC such elements as focus, brightness, and color.

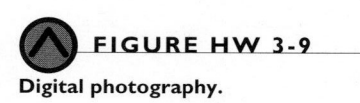

FIGURE HW 3-9
Digital photography.

OTHER TECHNOLOGIES

Many other technologies in addition to the ones we've already covered exist for source data automation. Four we'll briefly cover here are voice-input devices, handwriting-recognition devices, smart cards, and magnetic ink character recognition (MICR).

Voice-Input Devices Pieces of hardware that can convert spoken words into digital data are known as **voice-input devices.** If you stop to think about the complex work that humans do in interpreting speech, you can appreciate the challenge of designing a device to do the same thing. Two people may pronounce the same word differently because of accents, personal styles of speech, and the unique quality of each person's voice. A single person may even pronounce words differently at various times—when eating, say, or when suffering from a cold. Moreover, in listening to others, humans not only ignore background noises but also decode sentence fragments.

Equipment designers have tried a number of tricks to overcome the obstacles for which humans naturally compensate. Many voice-input devices are designed to screen out background noises and to accept "training" from users, who repeat words until the machines recognize the patterns in their voices. Unfortunately, most voice-input devices can recognize only limited numbers of isolated words and often not whole sentences composed of continuous speech. Thus, they can respond to messages of

■ **Voice-input device.** A device capable of recognizing the human voice.

only limited complexity. Still, the possible applications of this technology and its current price and performance levels are exciting. Today, you can buy a system that can recognize 60,000 words for under $400.

A computer system that both accepts voice input and generates spoken output is described in User Solution HW 3-1.

Handwriting Recognition Devices **Handwriting recognition devices** often collect data through a flat-screen display tablet and a penlike stylus. In theory, as users write words and numbers on the tablet, the devices recognize this input. In practice, however, handwriting recognition is still in the pioneering stage, and most systems available today can recognize only hand-printed characters. That computer systems have difficulty recognizing characters should not strike you as surprising. After all, if humans have difficulty reading each others' handwriting, how can computers be programmed to fare much better?

Smart Cards A **smart card** is a credit-card-sized piece of plastic that contains, at a minimum, a microprocessor chip and memory circuits (see Figure HW 3-10). The memory capacity may be as small as a few thousand characters or as large as a few million. Smart cards serve most often as electronic payment systems for retail purchases and to transfer funds between bank accounts,

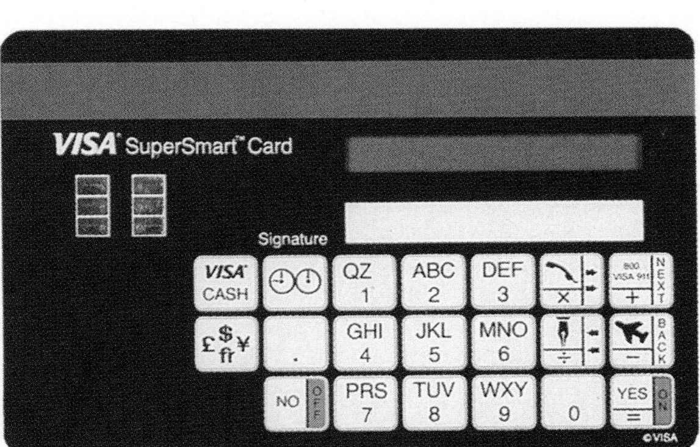

FIGURE HW 3-10

Smart card. The VISA SuperSmart Card shown here contains a keyboard and tiny display to complement its CPU and memory.

Although they remain largely in the pioneering stage, uses for smart cards abound. A university might issue such cards to allow students access to their own grade or financial data. Smart cards also could be useful for making phone calls; a cardholder would have an electronic record of all phone calls made—useful for tax and billing purposes—right on the card. In security applications, such a card could carry a digitized version of a fingerprint or voice and serve as an electronic passkey, allowing an authorized user access to restricted areas or a sensitive computer network. A new twist on the smart-card concept, the *smart purse,* is examined in Feature HW 3-1 on page HW 105.

■ **Handwriting recognition device.** A device that can identify handwritten characters. ■ **Smart card.** A credit-card-sized piece of plastic with storage and microprocessor.

Voice I/O for Securities Price Quotes

Discount broker Charles Schwab & Co. has recently found a new way to save money. Its newly installed VoiceBroker system enables customers to speak into a phone to request quotes on stock and mutual fund prices in conversational English. A computer understanding voice input provides a voice response back within seconds. With the new system—not yet available in all states—customers no longer have to wade through a series of menus on a touch-tone phone, as many systems for automated quotes require.

One of the biggest challenges in developing the new system was programming the computer to recognize not only different speech patterns but also the scores of ways in which clients might request information. Schwab designed its system so that you can refer to IBM as "IBM," "International Business Machines," or "Big Blue," and the computer will still be able to figure out what you mean.

Magnetic Ink Character Recognition (MICR) **Magnetic ink character recognition (MICR)** is a technology confined almost exclusively to the banking industry, where it supports high-volume processing of checks. Figure HW 3-11 illustrates a check encoded with MICR characters and a reader/sorter that processes such checks. The standard font adopted by the industry contains only 14 characters—the

FIGURE HW 3-11

MICR.

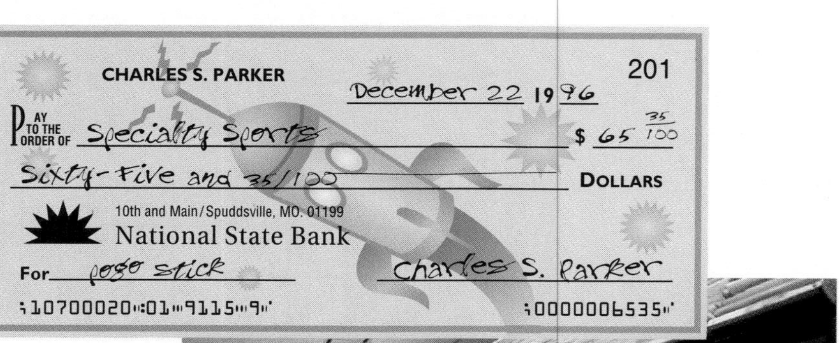

MICR-ENCODED CHECK
MICR characters on the bottom of the check respectively identify bank, account number, and check amount. The first two (left bottom) are put on when checks are preprinted; the latter (right bottom) is added when a check is cashed.

MICR READER/SORTER
The high-speed IBM device shown here is capable of processing 2,400 checks a minute.

■ **Magnetic ink character recognition (MICR).** A banking-industry technology that processes checks by sensing special characters inscribed in a magnetic ink.

ten decimal digits (0 through 9) and four special symbols. MICR characters are inscribed on checks with a magnetic ink by a special machine. As people write and cash checks, the recipients deposit them in the banking system. At banks, reader/sorter machines magnetically sense and identify MICR-encoded characters. Such a system sorts and records checks so that they can be routed to the proper banks for payment.

Display Devices

A **display device** presents computer system output on some kind of viewing screen, often resembling a television set. Most display devices fall into one of two categories: monitors and display terminals. A **monitor,** which is the type of display most people have on their PCs, is an output device limited to a viewing screen. The keyboard is a separate device, with its own port on the system unit. A *display terminal*—which is found on many large business networks—is a communications workstation that includes a screen (for output) and an attached keyboard (for input).

On all display devices, as each key on a keyboard is tapped, the corresponding character representation of the key appears on a display screen at the *cursor* position. The cursor—or *insertion point* as it is called in some contexts—is a highlighted symbol on the screen that indicates where the operator input will be placed. Alternatively, the cursor may point to an option that the user can select.

Display devices are handy when the user requires only small amounts of output and has to see what is being sent as input to the computer system. A student word processing a paper for a class, an airline clerk making inquiries to a flight information database, a stockbroker analyzing a security, and a bank teller checking the status of a customer account would each employ a display device. However, displays are useful only up to a point. If, for example, the student writing the paper wanted to take a copy of it home, he or she would have to direct the output to a printer.

Most monitors sold for desktop computers come with screens of 14 or 15 inches, 17 inches, or 20 or 21 inches—measured diagonally along the screen surface. Many features other than screen size differentiate the hundreds of display devices currently in the market. The following sections discuss some noteworthy features.

RESOLUTION

A key characteristic of any display device is its *resolution,* or sharpness of the screen image. Most displays form images by lighting up tiny dots on their screens called **pixels** (a contraction of the phrase "picture elements"). Resolution is measured by the density of these pixels, or dot pitch. A display's *dot pitch* indicates the distance between pixels in millimeters. Many displays in use today have a dot pitch of .26 or .28. A smaller dot pitch produces better resolution—that is, a crisper picture.

Resolution is often also specified as a matrix of pixels. A display resolution of, say, 640 by 480 means that the screen consists of 640 columns by 480 rows of pixels—that is, 640 × 480, or 307,200 pixels. In order to get the maximum resolution and the maximum number of colors a specific display allows, the video-adapter board used with the display must allow them as well.

Display devices form text characters and graphics and video images alike by lighting appropriate configurations of pixels (see Figure HW 3-12). Because pixels are so finely packed, when viewed from a distance they appear to blend together to form continuous images.

■ **Display device.** An output device that contains a viewing screen. ■ **Monitor.** A display device without a keyboard. ■ **Pixel.** A single dot on a display screen.

FIGURE HW 3-12

Pixels.

Each pixel on a screen is individually assigned a color to form the screen image. The higher the pixel density, or resolution, the crisper the screen image.

A typical desktop display electronically manipulates and refreshes pixels at lightning-fast speeds by firing an electron gun. Pixels on the screen are refreshed—that is, redrawn with the gun so they will remain bright—at a typical rate of 60 times each second.

COLOR DISPLAYS

By far, most monitors sold with desktop PCs today produce *color* output and are of the *red-green-blue (RGB)* type (see Figure HW 3-13). An RGB monitor forms all colors available on the screen by mixing combinations of only these three colors. Three colors may not sound like much of a base, but when a monitor blends red, green, and blue light of varying intensities—for each of the hundreds of thousands of pixels on the screen—it can produce an enormous spectrum of colors.

FIGURE HW 3-13

Color display on an RGB monitor.

ONE COLOR PIXEL
Each pixel on the screen is made up of some combination of red, green, and blue light. When red, green, and blue light of varying intensities are blended, a very wide range of colors is possible.

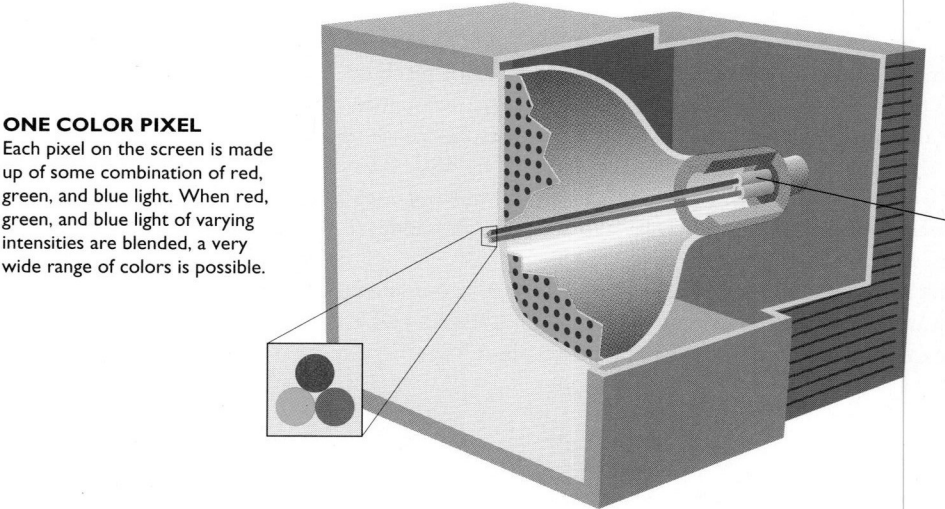

Pixels on a typical desktop display screen are refreshed—that is, recharged with built-in electron guns so they will remain bright—at a rate of 60 times each second.

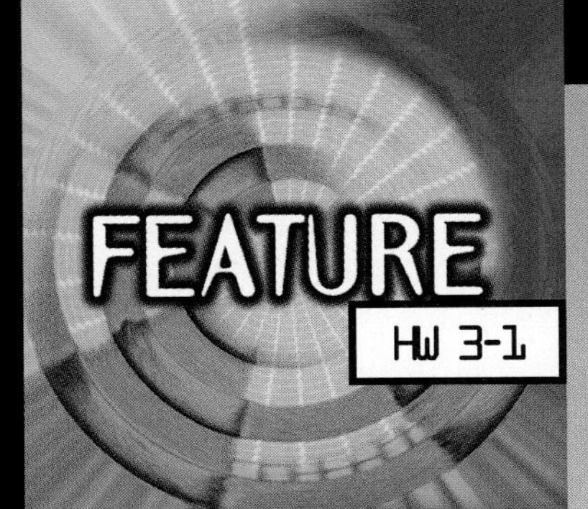

Smart Purses

A New Use for Smart Cards

It doesn't look like real money, but it has the same effect. It's called a *smart purse* or *virtual wallet*. It's a smart card that has a specific amount of money loaded onto it.

For the most part, smart purses are still in the testing stage. One way they can work is as follows. You go into your local bank with your preissued smart purse and stick it into a vending machine or an automatic teller machine (ATM). After you type in a password and the amount you would like to withdraw, the amount is written onto the card. When you go to a store to buy goods, the amount of your purchase is automatically deducted from the smart purse.

Smart purses have several advantages. You don't have to carry lots of money around—just the card. Because you load only a fixed amount of money on the card, it minimizes losses due to theft. A virtual variation of such cards could also be a major solution to problems with electronic commerce over the Internet's World Wide Web. The "card" would exist in electronic form as a file on your computer or your bank's computer, and it would contain just enough money so that you could make routine purchases. Separate accounts would hold the greater bulk of your savings in more secure systems.

Smart purses also have several limitations. Today, less than 1 percent of ATMs can read smart cards, and many stores accept only cash or credit cards. A more formidable obstacle is consumer expectations. People used to the combination of credit cards and cash may resist smart purses. Some industry analysts also express skepticism whether another card product can muscle its way into general usage.

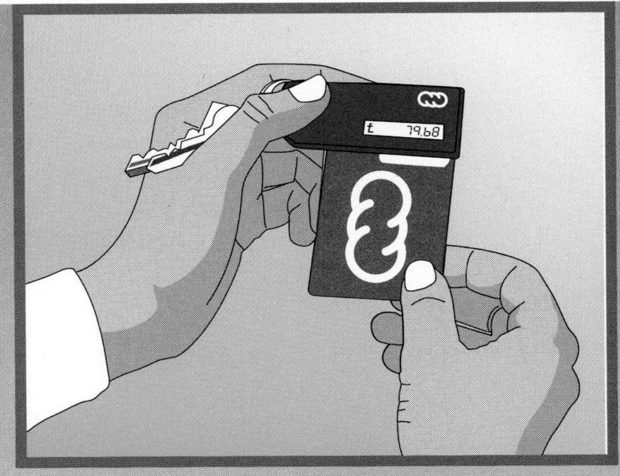

Smart purses. A high-tech cure for fishing for exact change.

The most likely scenario for smart purses is use in limited applications. For instance, governments might issue them as an alternative to food stamps for welfare recipients, and insurance companies might base distribution of medical payments on similar cards. Recently, the city of West Hollywood, California has struck on a similar idea. They've installed parking meters that can accept computer-chip-embedded keys that are, in effect, smart purses. Buy a key for $10 or $100, and you can shop virtually all day without worrying about getting ticketed. The city also expects that the keys will thwart meter thieves and save on coin-collection time.

Most monitors sold today with desktop PCs produce *noninterlaced* images (see Figure HW 3-14). This term means that a monitor draws every screen line on each screen refresh in order to provide a stable image. *Interlaced displays*—including most television sets—instead redraw every other line of the image on each pass and fill in alternate lines on the next pass. While interlaced monitors cost less than noninterlaced

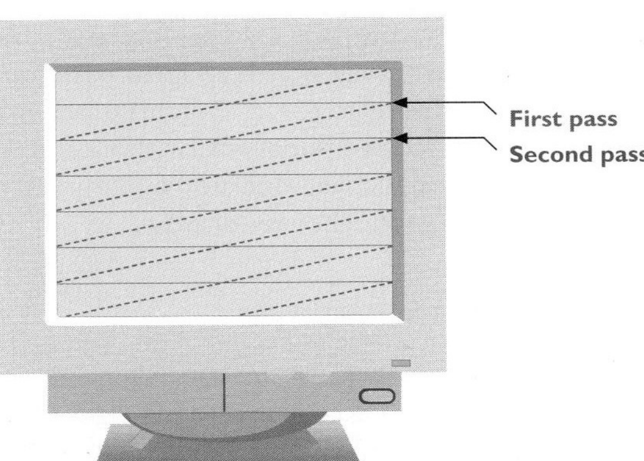

INTERLACED MONITOR
Every other line of the image is drawn on a refresh and alternate lines are filled in on the next pass.

NONINTERLACED MONITOR
Every screen line is redrawn on each screen refresh.

FIGURE HW 3-14

Interlaced and noninterlaced monitors.

ones, they can produce some screen flicker. Recently, the television industry is attempting to support both screen-refreshing standards, moving television and Internet technology closer together (see the Tomorrow box).

Most monitors for desktop PCs present images with a **landscape** orientation, which means that their screens are more wide than high. Some monitors reverse these measurements to provide a **portrait** orientation. Portrait screens are more high than wide. Figure HW 3-15 shows a monitor that can tilt to change between the portrait and landscape modes.

FIGURE HW 3-15

Portrait and landscape modes.

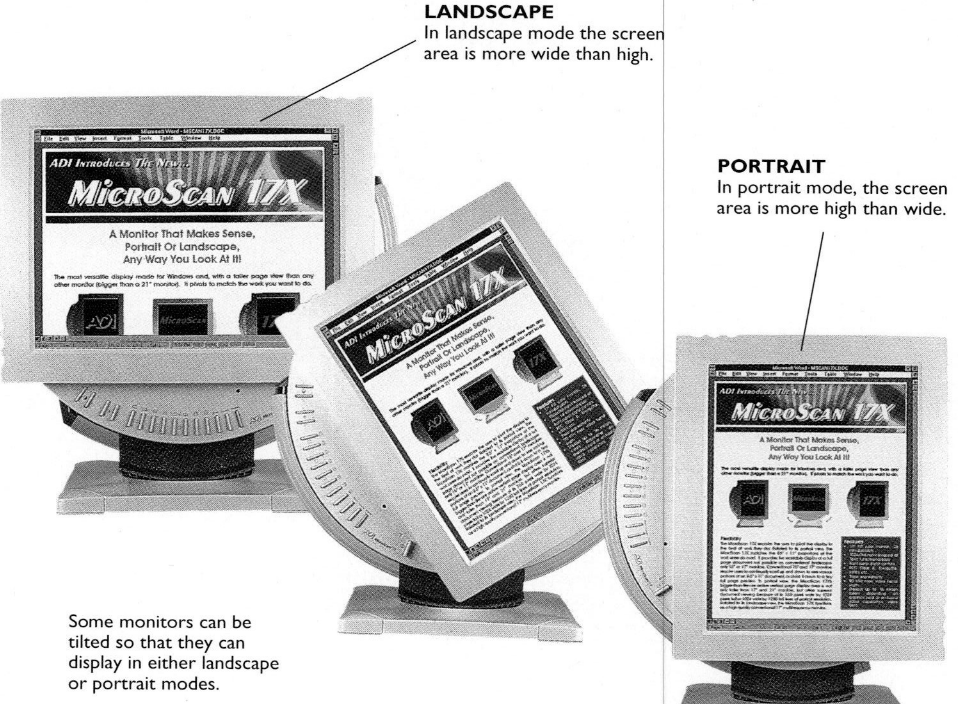

LANDSCAPE
In landscape mode the screen area is more wide than high.
PORTRAIT
In portrait mode, the screen area is more high than wide.
Some monitors can be tilted so that they can display in either landscape or portrait modes.
ADI Introduces The New...
MicroScan 17X
A Monitor That Makes Sense,
Portrait Or Landscape,
Any Way You Look At It!

Many color monitors can also produce greyscale and monochrome output. *Greyscale* output resembles the pictures on old black-and-white television sets. These images include not only black and white, but also many shades of grey in between. A *monochrome* image, on the other hand, features a single foreground color and single background color; the contrast reveals images on the screen.

Displays that produce only monochrome output are also widely available. Because they cost slightly less than color displays, they often perform basic output tasks in factories and field work that do not require color. Organizations may settle on these simple displays when they must acquire hundreds or thousands of devices at a time, creating very price-sensitive purchase decisions. Many mainframe, midrange, and palmtop computers utilize monochrome displays.

CRT AND FLAT-PANEL DISPLAY DEVICES

Monitors for most desktop systems project images on large picture-tube elements similar to those inside standard TV sets. This type of monitor (illustrated in Figure HW 3-13) is commonly called a **CRT (cathode-ray tube)** display. CRT technology is

■ **Landscape.** An output mode with images more wide than high. ■ **Portrait.** An output mode with images more high than wide.
■ **Cathode-ray tube (CRT).** A display device that projects images on a long-necked display tube similar to that in a television set.

GRAPHICS STANDARDS

The earliest display devices were strictly *character addressable;* that is, they could display only certain text characters in limited sizes as output. As demand grew for devices with graphics capabilities, manufacturers developed displays capable of more complex output.

Almost all monitors sold with PCs today generate screen images through a technique called **bit mapping.** Bit mapping allows software to control each pixel on the screen as an individual element. Thus, the computer can create virtually any type of image on the screen. Monitors sold today can output text in a variety of sizes, complex graphics images, and moving video sequences.

Computer graphics standards specify several modes in which a display device can operate. For example, a VGA display (for video graphics array)—the standard for many 386 and 486 computers with 14-inch and 15-inch displays—uses a resolution of 640 by 480 pixels. VGA allows a screen to display at most 256 colors.

The SVGA standard (for super VGA) took over when Pentium computers and 17-inch monitors became popular. It allows even larger pixel matrices. SVGA monitors often display at resolutions of either 800 by 600 pixels or 1,024 by 768 pixels and feature up to 16,777,216 colors (see Figure HW 3-17). An SVGA monitor can display 2½ times as much information as a VGA monitor of the same size. A major drawback to displaying at fine resolutions is that characters are minimally readable on a 14- or 15-inch display and often unreadable on a laptop screen. Two other drawbacks are speed—because there is more information to paint on a high-resolution screen, the screen takes longer to rewrite every time it is changed—and the greater memory required.

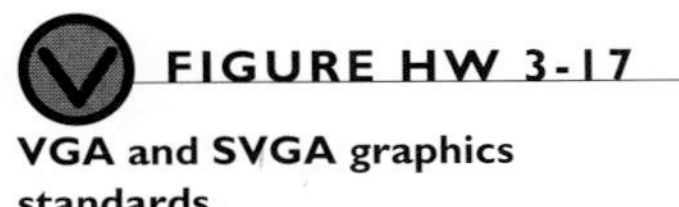

VGA and SVGA graphics standards.

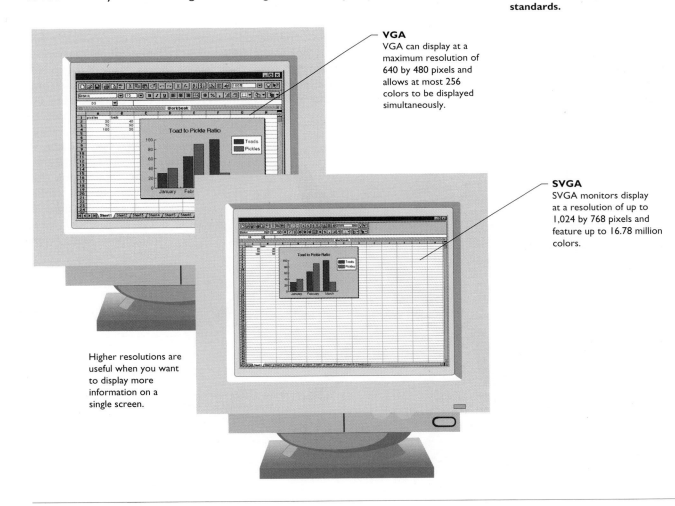

VGA
VGA can display at a maximum resolution of 640 by 480 pixels and allows at most 256 colors to be displayed simultaneously.

SVGA
SVGA monitors display at a resolution of up to 1,024 by 768 pixels and feature up to 16.78 million colors.

Higher resolutions are useful when you want to display more information on a single screen.

■ **Bit mapping.** A graphical output technique in which software individually controls each pixel in a screen image.

In response to the large number of currently active graphics standards and display modes—VGA and SVGA are only two of well over a dozen standards widely seen in practice—many manufacturers have developed *multisync* monitors. These devices accommodate a wide variety of graphics standards and—supported by matching video-adapter boards—they can display images at various resolutions. Software controls a multisync monitor's screen resolution. By making the appropriate screen-menu choice, for instance, you can operate an SVGA monitor in VGA mode.

Printers

Displays have two major limitations as output devices: (1) Only a small amount of data can appear on the screen at one time, and (2) their soft-copy output lacks portability. To obtain portable output, you must either take notes or direct the output to a device that captures it on paper. **Printers** overcome these limitations by producing hard copy—a permanent record of computer system output.

TYPES OF PRINTERS

Printers differ in a number of important respects. One involves the technology through which they output images. Another is size; you can hold some computer printers in your hand, while others—like those that serve high-speed mainframe systems—can fill your living room. Here, we consider such differences.

Dot-Matrix Characters Most printing technologies today form characters as matrices of dots. In contrast, if you look at the printing mechanism of an old typewriter, you'll notice a selection of embossed, solid characters on spokes. Many of the earliest computer printers used similar print heads to stamp output onto paper—and some printers still do. However, most of today's printers form not only characters but also graphics images, too, by placing dots on paper in some way. Resolution from *dot-matrix printers* has become so good in recent years that the characters on paper look like smooth, continuous strokes rather than collections of dots—even under close inspection (see Figure HW 3-18).

FIGURE HW 3-18
Dot-matrix printing.

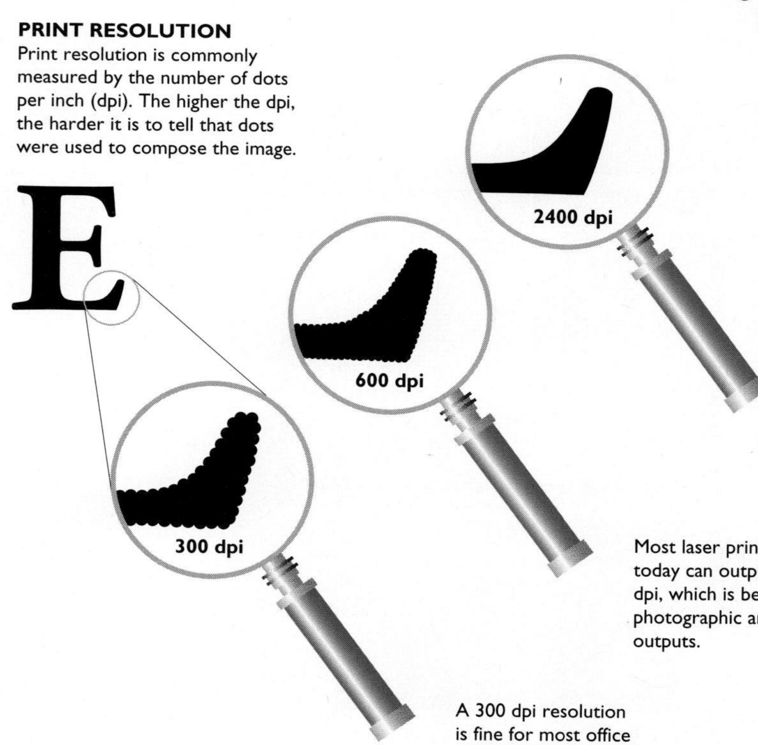

PRINT RESOLUTION
Print resolution is commonly measured by the number of dots per inch (dpi). The higher the dpi, the harder it is to tell that dots were used to compose the image.
E
2400 dpi
600 dpi
300 dpi
High-print-quality magazines are produced on typesetting equipment that works at over 1000 dpi.
Most laser printers sold today can output at 600 dpi, which is better for photographic and artistic outputs.
A 300 dpi resolution is fine for most office documents.

■ **Printer.** A device that records computer output on paper.

Impact versus Nonimpact Printing Printers produce images through either impact or nonimpact technologies. **Impact printing** is the older method of the two, mimicking the operation of typewriters, which were invented over a century ago. A typewriter key activates a metal hammer embossed with a character, which strikes a print ribbon and presses the character's image onto paper.

An **impact dot-matrix printer** for a desktop computer system works in a similar fashion—a print head produces characters by repeatedly activating one or more vertical columns of pins, as illustrated in Figure HW 3-19. The pins press into a ribbon and force it to strike the paper. Before 1995, most computer printers sold for personal use employed impact dot-matrix technology. In recent years, however, the popularity of these printers has been eclipsed by sales of ink-jet and laser printers. Ink-jet and laser printers often sell at slightly higher prices than impact dot-matrix printers but operate more quietly and produce better-looking output. Today, impact dot-matrix printers, with many models selling for under $200, are favored mostly for producing multipart forms like those for invoices and credit-card receipts.

Nonimpact printing does not depend on the impact of a print head on paper. In fact, the printing mechanism makes no physical contact at all with the paper. This, of

Impact dot-matrix printing.

IMPACT DOT MATRIX PRINTING
Because of the force of the print head on paper, impact dot-matrix printers are ideal for printing multipart forms. Many impact dot-matrix printers cost less than $200 and cost about a penny a page to operate.

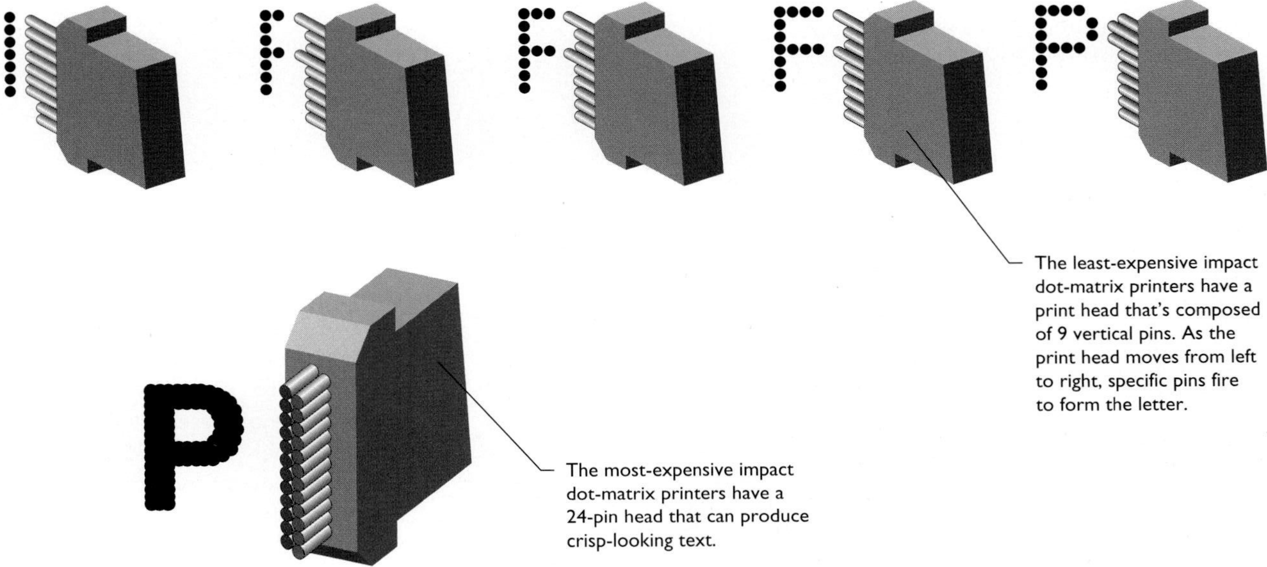

The least-expensive impact dot-matrix printers have a print head that's composed of 9 vertical pins. As the print head moves from left to right, specific pins fire to form the letter.
The most-expensive impact dot-matrix printers have a 24-pin head that can produce crisp-looking text.

■ **Impact printing.** A technology that forms characters by striking a pin or hammer against an inked ribbon, which presses the desired shape onto paper. ■ **Impact dot-matrix printer.** A device with a print head holding multiple pins, which strike an inked ribbon in various combinations to form characters on paper.

course, makes for quiet operation. Also, because nonimpact printers contain fewer moving parts than impact-based alternatives, they generally work much faster and more reliably with fewer breakdowns. They are cost competitive, too. Today, the printer market is inclined clearly toward nonimpact printers, and the large majority of the printers sold today are nonimpact machines.

PRINTERS FOR SMALL COMPUTER SYSTEMS

Most printers found in small computer systems today are of the desktop variety and are geared to either personal use or to shared, specialized needs (such as those of a team of artists or compositors). These printers create images through either laser, ink-jet, thermal-transfer, solid-ink, or electrothermal technology, all of which are nonimpact methods. Here, we'll discuss each of these technologies in turn.

FIGURE HW 3-20

Laser printing. Most laser printers sold today produce only monochrome and greyscale outputs.

Laser printers operate on a principle similar to that of copying machines. A laser beam charges a rotating drum where images are to appear, and toner from a cartridge adheres to the charged places. A heating unit then fuses the toner to the paper.

Heating unit

Toner cartridge

HELLO

HELLO

Charged drum

Rotating mirror

HELLO

Laser

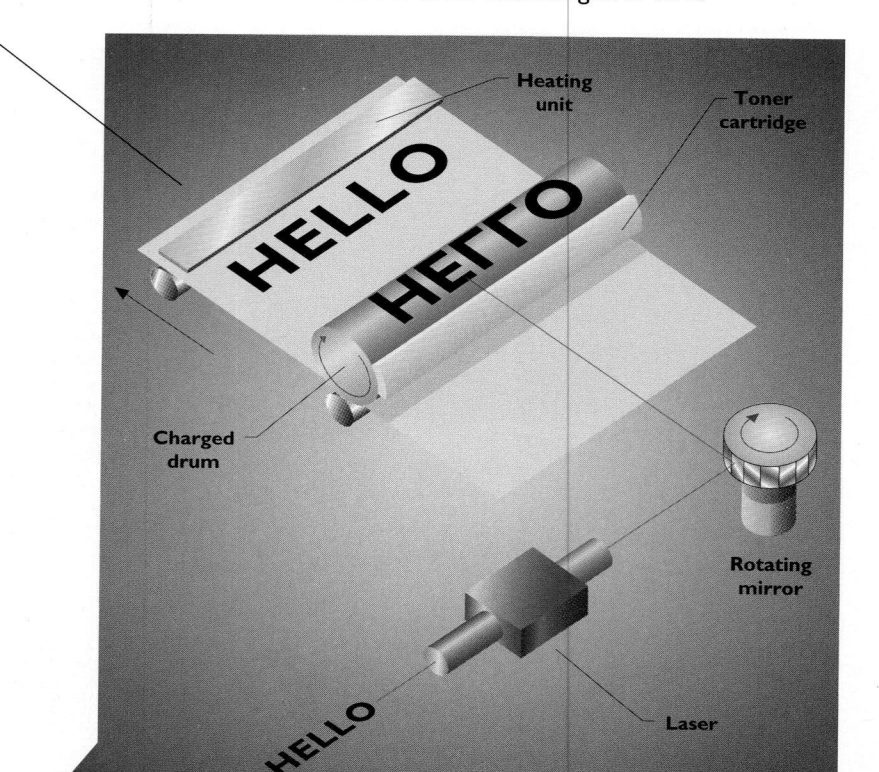

ABOUT LASER PRINTERS

Because of their speed and output quality, laser printers are by far the most popular type of printer for business applications.

Common speeds for personal laser printers are 4, 6, 8, and 12 pages per minute (ppm).

Many personal printers come with 1 MB RAM. While this is fine for text, 4 MB is better for intensive graphics work.

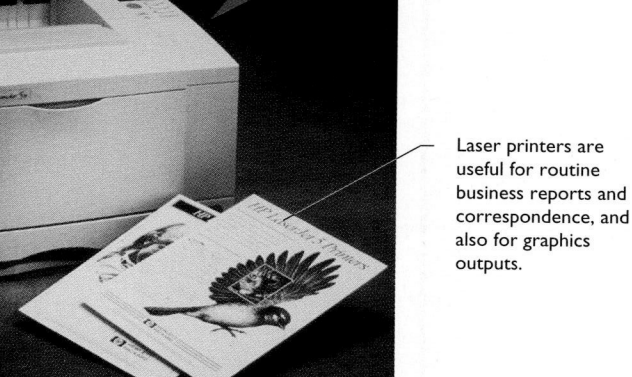

Laser printers are useful for routine business reports and correspondence, and also for graphics outputs.

Laser Printers Many microcomputer systems rely on relatively inexpensive personal **laser printers** costing between $450 and $1,500 and printing 4 to 12 pages per minute (ppm). Many of these generate resolutions of either 300 or 600 dpi. At 600 dpi, every square inch of the output image is broken down into a 600-by-600 matrix of dots. That's 360,000 dots packed into every square inch. Laser devices are especially popular

■ **Nonimpact printing.** A technology that forms characters and other images on a surface by means of heat, lasers, photography, or ink jets. ■ **Laser printer.** A printer that works on a principle similar to that of a photocopier.

in business, in fact, they are the most common type of printer sold to that market segment.

Laser printers form images much as photocopying machines do—by charging thousands of dots on a drum with a very-high-intensity laser beam. The charged positions attract oppositely charged particles of toner from a cartridge. When paper contacts the drum, it picks up the toner that forms an image. A heating unit fuses the image permanently onto the paper (see Figure HW 3-20).

While most laser printers—like the one featured in Figure HW 3-20—produce only monochrome and greyscale outputs, some color laser printer models now cost only a few thousand dollars (see Figure HW 3-21). While they do not generate output of photographic quality, color laser printers work faster than many other types of color printers, and the output quality is quite acceptable for a rather simple page image. For magazine-quality images, these printers often produce pages sharp enough to accommodate proofing purposes.

FIGURE HW 3-21

Color laser printer. Models costing only a few thousand dollars have recently become available.

Ink-Jet Printers **Ink-jet printers** produce images by spraying thousands of droplets of electrically charged ink onto a page (see Figure HW 3-22). For the last several years, ink-jet printing has been the technology of choice for home users who want to produce affordable, hard-copy color output from their personal desktop systems. Most ink-jet printers sold today can produce black-and-white, greyscale, and color outputs.

The principal advantage to ink-jet printing is its low cost. While some commercial-level ink-jet printers cost thousands of dollars, you can buy a respectable color ink-jet printer for your desktop PC for as little as $250. Color printers using other technologies generally carry higher prices on low-end models. Ink-jet printers bring some disadvantages, too. They often take longer to output text than laser printers require, and the hard copy may not look as crisp. What's more, ink-jet printers draw ink from replaceable color cartridges, and the cost of new cartridges can mount up over time if you print documents with a lot of color.

Thermal-Transfer Printers Thermal-transfer printers place color images on paper by heating ink from a wax-based ribbon or by heating dye. Users buy these types of printers almost exclusively for their color-printing capabilities, although they can produce crisp-looking text output, as well.

Thermal-wax-transfer printers often cost $2,000 or more. They produce output that's similar in quality to comparatively priced, high-end ink-jet printers. Thermal-wax-transfer printers achieve their best performance producing color transparencies and proofs of complex color images. If you want color images with a magazine-cover look, you'll have to step up to a thermal-dye-transfer printer.

Thermal-dye-transfer printers, often called *dye-sublimation printers,* yield photographic-quality color output (see Figure HW 3-23). The printers themselves are expensive—$3,000 to $5,000 is a typical price range for a commercial-level device—and you can spend about $4.50 per page in color ink and other consumable supplies to operate one of them. New to the consumer market in 1997 are *snapshot printers*—small dye-sublimation printers costing about $500 that are targeted to photographers.

Solid-Ink Printers *Solid-ink printers*—also known as *solid-wax, phase-change,* and *wax-jet printers*—apply color supplied by wax sticks. A heating device in the printer melts the differently colored sticks before printing starts, and a print head sprays the color out of small nozzles. However, instead of shooting the colors directly

■ **Ink-jet printer.** A printer that forms images by spraying droplets of charged ink onto a page.

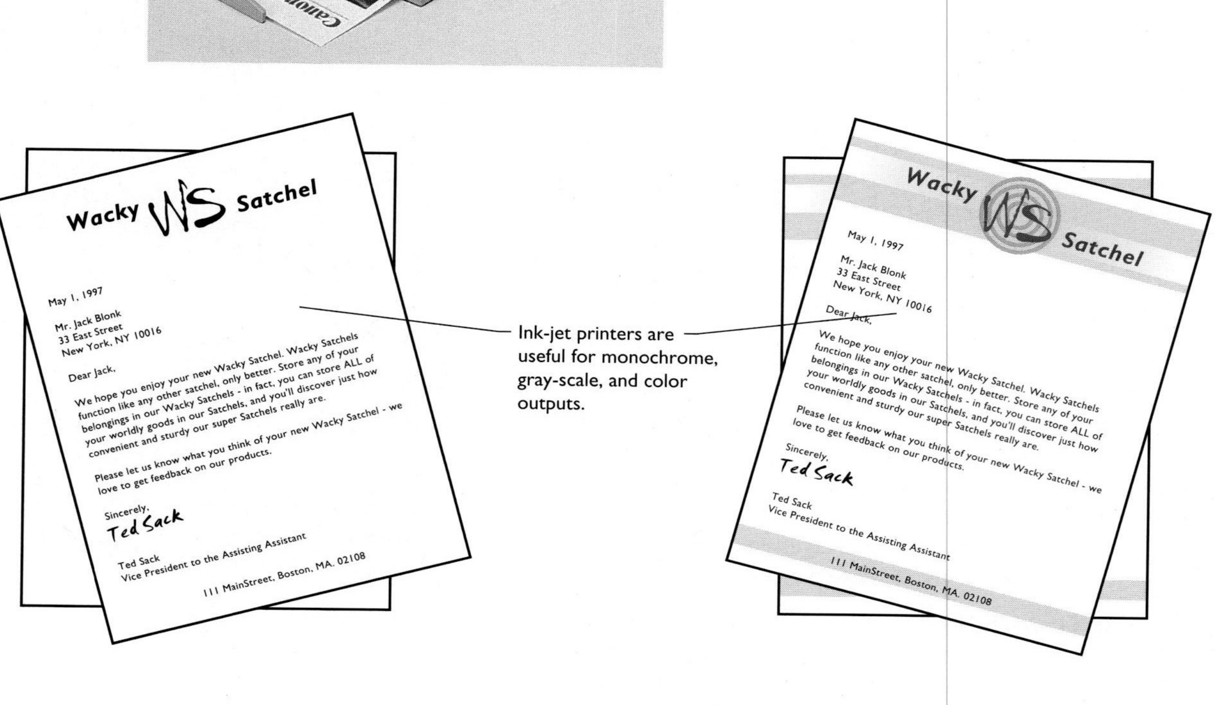

FIGURE HW 3-22
Ink-jet printing.

onto paper as an ink-jet printer does, the nozzles apply the droplets to a rapidly rotating drum. Then, as in laser and offset printing, the drum transfers the color image to paper. An advantage over ink-jet printing is that the ink dries faster.

Compared to color laser printers, solid-ink printers are less picky about the type of paper or transparency film they handle. Solid-ink printers also work at faster speeds for color output and often cost less per page of output produced. On the downside, output is not as crisp.

Electrothermal Printers In *electrothermal printing,* a device burns characters onto a special paper by heating rods on a print head. Electrothermal printers carry low price tags, but they often suffer from serious disadvantages: poor output quality, a need for special paper (which may feel slippery), and inability to produce color output. Electrothermal printing is most commonly found in low-end fax machines and portable printers.

Figure HW 3-24 highlights many of the characteristics of the printers covered in this subsection. Many of these printer types correspond to high-end models used in large computer systems.

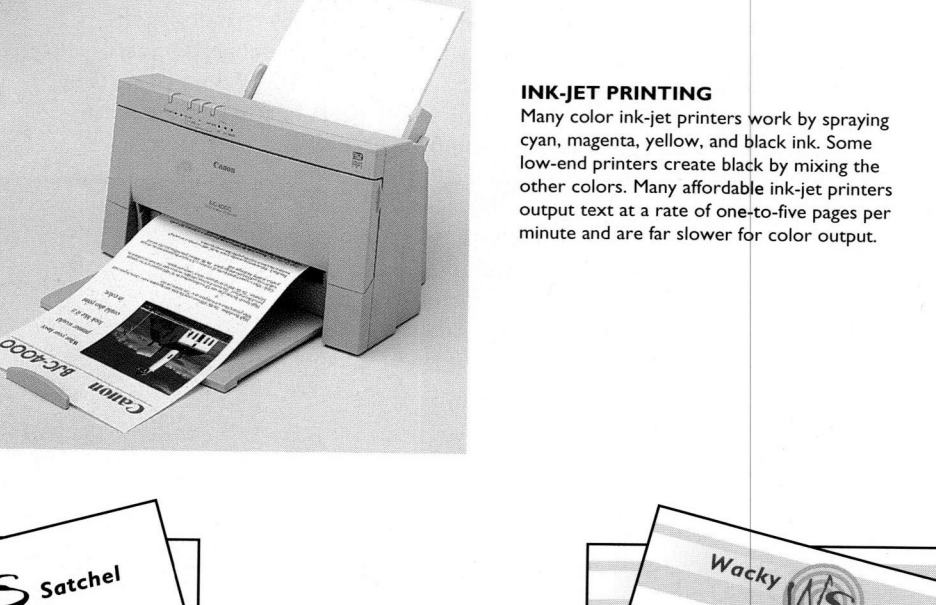

 **FIGURE HW 3-23**

Thermal-transfer printing. Thermal-transfer printers that use a dye-sublimation technology are capable of producing photographic-quality outputs, like the images you see on slick magazine covers.

PRINTERS FOR LARGE COMPUTER SYSTEMS

In a networked computer system, a printer is often shared by several people. The people may be located in the same office, floor, building, or site. High-end printers targeted to shared usage generally are too big to fit on a desktop. They begin their speed ranges where those of printers meant for personal use top out. High-end printers may work from twice as fast to 100 or more times as fast as their personal-system counterparts and cost anywhere from a few thousand dollars to more than $100,000.

Line Printers **Line printers** get their name because they print a line of text at a time. Not long ago, virtually all printers in midrange and mainframe computer systems were line printers, but now such devices are less common than those using other technologies. In one of their common uses today, line printers function as shared devices on office networks (see Figure HW 3-25).

 **FIGURE HW 3-24**

Comparison of printing technologies.

	Printer Type					
Criterion	**Impact Dot Matrix**	**Laser**	**Ink Jet**	**Thermal Transfer**	**Solid Ink**	**Electrostatic**
Type	Impact	Nonimpact	Nonimpact	Nonimpact	Nonimpact	Nonimpact
Speed	Slow to medium	Medium to very fast	Medium to fast	Medium to fast	Medium to fast	Slow to fast
Text quality	Fair to good	Excellent	Good to excellent	Excellent	Excellent	Fair to good
Cost	Low	Medium to high	Low to high	Medium to high	Medium to high	Low to high
Graphics capabilities	Limited	Good to excellent	Good to excellent	Good to excellent	Good to excellent	Fair to good
Color	Fair if you buy a color kit	Good in color laser printers	Good	Good to Superior	Good	Fair to good, if available

■ **Line printer.** A high-speed printer that produces output a line at a time.

Most line printers produce images through impact printing. *Band printers,* which form lines of text by impact of character-embossed metal print ribbons, are currently the most common type of line printer. Speeds typically range from a few hundred to a few thousand lines per minute (lpm).

Page Printers As the name suggests, a **page printer** produces a full page of output at a time. On office networks, the most common type of page printer is the *network laser printer.* Typically, these printers are bigger versions of personal laser printers, with several additional paper trays (see Figure HW 3-26). Network laser printers work much faster than their personal counterparts, producing output at a rate of anywhere from 12 to 40 ppm. Many of the high-end models can collate and staple, as well. A typical 24-ppm office printer is designed to handle workloads of up to 100,000 pages of output per month.

FIGURE HW 3-25

Line printers. These devices can produce hard-copy output at speeds ranging from a few hundred to a few thousand lines per minute.

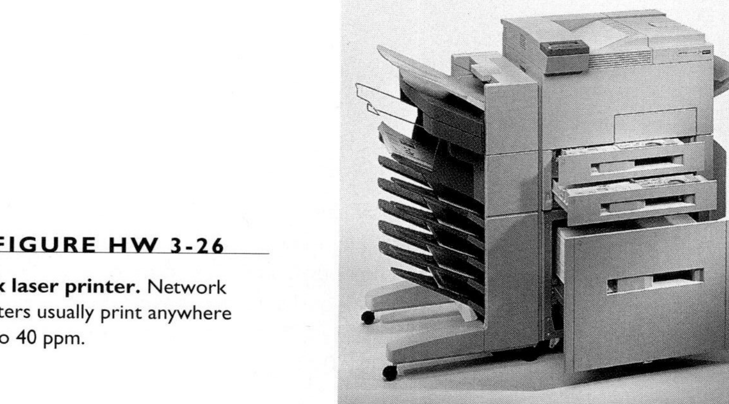

FIGURE HW 3-26

Network laser printer. Network laser printers usually print anywhere from 12 to 40 ppm.

Network lasers let you keep a variety of paper sizes loaded in different trays. With software, you can even mix paper from different trays into a single print job.

Page printers for midrange and mainframe computer systems can print up to a few hundred pages of output per minute (see Figure HW 3-27). Such printers may cost $100,000 or even more. An organization that produces several hundred thousand or more pages of output per month may find one of these machines an extremely cost-effective alternative.

Page printers offer an advantage over line printers in their ability to output digital images of forms and letterheads. They can even print on both sides of the paper. Thus, page printers can offer considerable savings over line printers, which require human intervention to switch paper and printing elements when a change in output dictates a new form or format.

Other Output Equipment

In addition to display devices and printers, computer systems often need hardware to generate several other kinds of output. In this section, we will consider speakers,

■ **Page printer.** A high-speed printer that generates a full page of output at a time.

FIGURE HW 3-27

Page printer. Operating at peak capacity over a weekend, some page printers can produce well over 1 million pages of output.

plotters, voice-output devices, film recorders, and computer-output microfilm (COM)—all of which are output devices appropriate for specialized uses.

Speakers Most computer systems sold today, especially for home use, come with a set of **speakers.** Speakers provide audio output for such consumer-oriented multimedia applications as playing computer games, listening to background music on CD, and watching television in an onscreen window. Common business applications include video demonstrations and presentations as well as videoconferencing. As more and more computer systems include sound capabilities, increasing numbers of applications are integrating sound components.

Computer speaker systems resemble their stereo-system counterparts. You can pay well under $100 for a set, or you can spend over a thousand dollars. While an inexpensive speaker outputs the full frequency range through a single cone, a costlier model might include a special bass unit and separate output cones for different sound frequencies; collectively, these components may even provide near-theater-quality audio. Cases on speakers are often shielded to prevent magnetic interference with nearby storage devices. Also, speakers may come with brackets, stands, or other mounting devices to provide you flexibility in arranging them on your desk or wall.

Just as important as the purchase of the speaker system itself is the selection of a sound card. A *sound card* is an add-in board that fits in an expansion slot inside a desktop system unit. It lets your computer system play sound through speakers or headphones. On the input side, the sound card also supports recording through a microphone or music keyboard. Many of the sound cards sold today provide audio compatible with the Sound Blaster standard. Sound Blaster was one of the first computer sound boards to win a large following among users and computer-game makers. Notebook computers can gain sound-card capabilities through added PC cards.

Plotters A **plotter** is an output device that is designed primarily to produce charts, drawings, maps, three-dimensional illustrations, and other forms of hard copy. Plotters work by a variety of technologies. The two most common types of plotters in use today are ink-jet plotters and electrostatic plotters (see Figure HW 3-28).

■ **Speakers.** Output devices that produce sound. ■ **Plotter.** An output device that prints graphs and diagrams.

INK-JET PLOTTER
Ink-jet plotters are useful for wide-format graphics that are too big for a standard ink-jet printer.

ELECTROSTATIC PLOTTER
Electrostatic plotters are usually faster and more expensive than ink-jet plotters. They work with a toner bed similar to that of a copying machine.

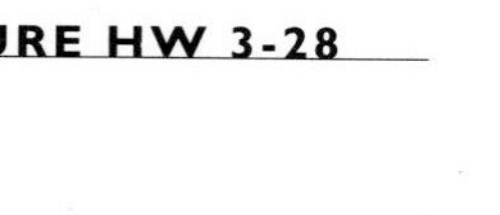

FIGURE HW 3-28

Plotters.

At the low-cost and relatively slow end of the plotter market are *ink-jet plotters.* Ink-jet technology has dropped dramatically in price in recent years, and the popularity of these plotters has surged as a result. Many of them roll out paper over a space-saving drumlike mechanism, while others use cut sheets stored in a feeder tray. While virtually all ink-jet printers can also double as plotters, users with specialized graphics needs—say, an engineer who produces oversized drawings—may want to consider ink-jet devices targeted principally to commercial plotting rather than general-purpose desktop applications.

Electrostatic plotters define the faster and more expensive end of the plotter market. These widely used devices create images with a toner bed similar to that of a photocopying machine, but instead of light pulses, they use a matrix of tiny wires to charge the paper with electricity. When the charged paper passes over the toner bed, the toner adheres to it and produces an image.

Voice-Output Devices For a number of years, computers have been able to communicate with users, after a fashion, by imitating human speech. How often have you dialed a phone number only to hear, "We're sorry, the number you are trying to reach, 555-0202, is no longer in service," or "The time is 6:15. . . . The downtown temperature is 75 degrees?" **Voice-output devices,** the machines responsible for such messages, convert stored digital data into spoken messages.

Computerized voice output systems operate extensively at airline terminals to broadcast information about flight departures and arrivals. In the securities business, they quote the prices of stocks and bonds; in supermarkets, they announce descriptions and prices of items that pass over the scanner; in electronic-mail systems, they greet users and tell them about any waiting electronic mail. In business, voice output has great potential in any company with employees who do little other than, say, verbally provide account balances, prices, and status reports. This technology also

■ **Voice-output device.** A piece of hardware that plays back or imitates human speech.

adds value to applications—such as electronic mail—that have not until recently had voice components.

There are two types of voice-output systems. The first type digitizes voice messages, stores them electronically, and then converts them back to voice messages when the user triggers a playback command—sort of the digital version of the traditional tape recorder. Probably the most common examples of this type of voice output are the phone-menu-message systems that answer calls at many businesses. The second type of system produces synthetic speech by storing digital patterns of word sounds and then creating sentences extemporaneously. Many of the systems that rely on synthetic speech have vocabularies of about several hundred words and limited abilities to combine words dynamically to form intelligible sentences. As a result, these devices perform best in creating short messages—a telephone number, stock price, and so on.

Film Recorders **Film recorders** convert high-resolution, computer-generated images directly into slides, transparencies, and other film media. Just a few years ago film recorders served only large computer systems, through such applications as art, medical imaging, and scientific work. Today, they connect to PCs and are used for such applications as making slides for meetings and client presentations. Today, computer-generated slides account for a large percentage of all business slides made.

Film recorders, like cameras, are "dumb" devices that do not recognize images in order to record them. Film recorders can transfer onto film virtually any image that can be captured on a display screen.

Computer Output Microfilm A **computer output microfilm (COM)** system places computer output on microfilm media, typically either a *microfilm reel* or *microfiche card.* Microfilming can result in tremendous savings in paper costs, storage space, mailing, and handling. A four-by-six-inch microfiche card can store the equivalent of 270 printed pages. COM technology is useful for organizations that must keep massive files of information that they need not update. It's also useful for organizations that need to manipulate large amounts of data but find online access to a computer system impractical or too costly. In recent years, as optical disks have gained in popularity, COM systems have faced serious challenges to the near monopoly they once held on archival document storage and retrieval.

Summary and Key Terms

Today's computer marketplace offers a wide and expanding variety of input and output devices.

Input and Output Input and output devices enable people and computers to communicate. **Input devices** convert data and program instructions into a form that the CPU can process. **Output devices** convert computer-processed information into a form that people comprehend.

Output devices produce results in either hard copy or soft copy form. The term **hard copy** generally refers to output that has been recorded in a *permanent* form onto a medium such as paper or microfilm. The term **soft copy,** in contrast, generally refers to display output, which appears only *temporarily.* Hard-copy output is the more portable of the two, but it costs more to produce and creates waste.

Keyboards Most people could not interact with a computer system without a **keyboard,** which is often the main source of system input. The large majority of keyboards lay out keys in the QWERTY arrangement.

■ **Film recorder.** A device that converts computer output to film. ■ **Computer output microfilm (COM).** A system for reducing computer output to microscopic form and storing it on photosensitive film.

Pointing Devices **Pointing devices** include input hardware that moves an onscreen pointer. The most widely used pointing device is the **mouse.** Some other common pointing devices are the **light pen, joystick, trackball, crosshair cursor,** and **graphics tablet.** Display devices that are designed to allow a finger rather than a light pen to activate onscreen commands are called **touch-screen displays.**

Source Data Automation **Source data automation** deploys technologies to collect digital data at their point of origin. Many input technologies fall within this description.

Optical character recognition (OCR) refers to a wide range of optical-scanning procedures and equipment designed for machine recognition of marks, characters, and codes—such as **bar codes.** Among the best-known uses of OCR are the **point-of-sale (POS) systems** installed at checkout counters in stores.

An **image scanner** allows users to input such images as photographs, drawings, and documents into a computer system. Many scanners are of the *flatbed, drum,* or *handheld* type. Scanners are often accompanied by OCR software that enables computer systems to recognize scanned text characters.

Digital cameras work much like regular cameras, but instead of capturing images on print or slide film, they record digital data onto memory cards like those found in notebook computers. When you take a snapshot, the camera loads its memory card with digital data that enable a desktop PC to later process the image.

Voice-input devices enable computer systems to recognize spoken words. Voice-input technologies offer tremendous work-saving potential, but they are only slowly reaching market acceptance.

Practical **handwriting recognition devices** are still in the pioneering stage, and virtually all systems commercially available today can recognize only hand-printed characters.

Smart cards are credit-card-sized pieces of plastic that contain microprocessor chips and memory circuitry. They, too, remain largely in the pioneering stage.

Magnetic ink character recognition (MICR) is an input technology confined almost exclusively to the banking industry; it enables automated systems to rapidly sort, process, and route checks to the proper banks.

Display Devices **Display devices** are peripheral hardware that contain television-like viewing screens. Most display devices fall into one of two categories: **monitors** and display terminals. A key characteristic of any display is its *resolution,* or the sharpness of its screen image. On many displays, users measure resolution by the number of dots, or **pixels,** that make up the screen.

By far the largest number of displays sold with computer systems today produce color output and are *noninterlaced.* Most also present images with a **landscape** orientation; that is, more width than height. Some displays reverse this arrangement for a **portrait** orientation.

Most desktop displays on the market today project images on large, picture-tube elements similar to those found inside standard TV sets. These devices are called **CRTs (cathode-ray tubes).** Slim-profile devices called **flat-panel displays** also are in wide use, especially on portable computers. Most flat-panel devices use *LCD (liquid crystal display)* technology.

Bit mapping allows software to control the placement of each pixel on the screen. Most displays implement either the VGA or SVGA graphics standard.

Printers **Printers** produce hard-copy output through either impact or nonimpact printing technology. In **impact printing,** the older of the two, metal pins or embossed characters strike paper or ribbons to form characters. The most common type of impact printer is the **impact dot-matrix printer. Nonimpact printing,** which is quieter and more reliable, is by far the most prevalent type of printing technology today. Nonimpact printing creates printed images through any of a wide variety of techniques.

The most popular printers today for microcomputer systems are **laser printers** and **ink-jet printers.** Both employ nonimpact methods. Other relatively common nonimpact devices are thermal-transfer, solid-ink, and electrothermal printers.

Most of the printing done on large computer systems is accomplished by line or page printers. **Line printers** produce a line of output at a time, and **page printers** produce a full page of output at a time.

Other Output Equipment A large number of other output devices accommodate a variety of applications. Among these are speakers, plotters, voice-output devices, film recorders, and computer output microfilm (COM) equipment.

Most computer systems sold today come with **speakers** for audio output. Just as important as the speaker system itself is the selection of a *sound card.*

A **plotter** is an output device designed primarily to produce graphics output such as charts, maps, and engineering drawings. *Ink-jet plotters* squirt jets of ink on the paper surface, and *electrostatic plotters* create images by adhering toner to electrostatic charges.

Voice-output devices enable computer systems to play back or compose spoken messages from digitally stored words, phrases, and sounds. One of the main shortcomings of this technology is the limited number of messages that the computer can extemporaneously create.

Film recorders convert computer-generated images to 35 mm slides, transparencies, and other film media. They can output onto film virtually any image that can be captured on a display screen.

Computer output microfilm (COM) systems place computer output on microscopically read media such as microfilm reels or microfiche cards. COM can cut document costs for paper, storage space, mailing, and handling.

EXERCISES

1. Fill in the blanks:
   a. The term __________ generally refers to output that has been recorded onto a medium such as paper or film.
   b. Resolution on a display screen is measured by the number of dots, or __________.
   c. A display device that outputs images in a single foreground color is known as a(n) __________ display.
   d. A(n) __________ printer heats ink from a dye-based or wax-based ribbon and deposits it onto paper.
   e. A(n) __________ is a device that converts computer-generated images directly onto 35 mm slides.
   f. __________ is a term that refers to the process of collecting data, at their point of origin, in digital form.
   g. A(n) __________ is a device that provides computer input when you place it over hard-copy images of maps, survey photos, and even large drawings.
   h. A(n) __________ is an electrical device, resembling an ordinary pen, used to enter computer data.
   i. A display device that generates input when you touch a finger to the screen is called a(n) __________ device.
   j. A(n) __________ system, commonly found in department stores and supermarkets, uses electronic cash register terminals to collect, process, and store data.

2. Match each term with the description that fits best.
   a. memory card
   b. OCR
   c. noninterlaced
   d. UPC
   e. LCD
   f. SVGA
   g. plotter
   h. trackball

_____ Used to make flat-panel display devices but not CRTs
_____ A graphics standard for displays
_____ A collection of different technologies devoted to optical recognition of marks, characters, and codes
_____ A code that appears prominently on the packaging of most supermarket goods
_____ A type of output device designed especially to produce graphics images on paper
_____ A device that stores images within a digital camera
_____ A device that moves a pointer rapidly around the display screen
_____ A characteristic of some CRTs that controls how they refresh screen images

3. Review the list of input and output devices that follows, and state whether each device provides input to the computer, provides output to the user, or both.
   a. Electrostatic plotter
   b. Joystick
   c. Graphics tablet
   d. Image scanner
   e. Digital camera
   f. Film recorder
   g. Handwriting recognition device
   h. Trackball
   i. Light pen
   j. Crosshair cursor

4. Identify each of the following statements as true or false.

_____ Digital cameras are known as film recorders.
_____ The human finger can serve as a pointer-movement device in some computer systems.
_____ QWERTY refers to the way some keyboards are arranged.
_____ Many voice-output devices need to be trained before they are put into operation.
_____ Interlaced monitors are superior to noninterlaced ones.
_____ Relative to such input devices as image scanners, handwriting recognition devices are still in the pioneering stage.
_____ Pages that are output in a portrait mode are output in a wider format than if they had been specified as landscape.
_____ Touch screens are widely employed today in factory applications and field work, where users wear gloves.
_____ Many notebook computers employ a pointing stick that the user can push in different directions to move an onscreen pointer.
_____ The most widely known bar code is POS.

5. Describe the following characteristics of display devices:
   a. Active-matrix
   b. LCD
   c. Noninterlaced
   d. VGA
   e. Multisync
   f. CRT
   g. RGB
   h. Resolution

6. Identify at least six pointing devices designed for entering data into the computer system.

7. What type of microcomputer printer would you prefer for each of the following applications?
   a. To get very inexpensive color outputs
   b. To get photographic-quality color output
   c. To generate both daily business correspondence and weekly drafts of a book you are writing in your spare time
   d. To generate multipart forms

8. Answer the following questions about source data automation.
   a. What is source data automation and what are its benefits?
   b. Name as many technologies as you can that can fall under the heading of source data automation.
   c. Why isn't voice output considered part of source data automation?

9. Match the pictures with the terms. Note that each term can match one or two pictures or none at all.

a.

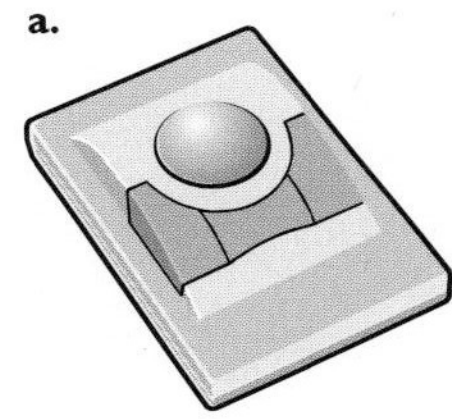

d.

b.

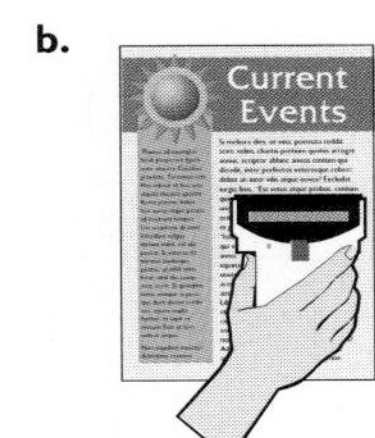

e.

c.

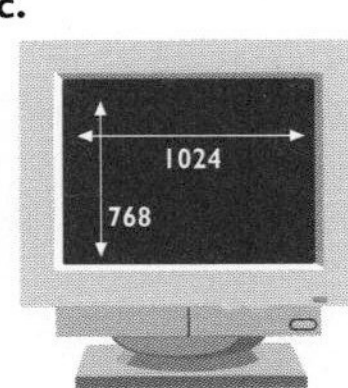

_____ VGA
_____ MICR
_____ SVGA
_____ Joystick
_____ Image scanner
_____ POS
_____ Thermal-wax printer
_____ Digital camera
_____ Trackball
_____ Crosshair cursor

10. Define the following terms:
   a. Soft copy
   b. Solid-ink printer
   c. Bar code
   d. Nonimpact printing
   e. Smart card
   f. Dot pitch
   g. Point-of-sale system
   h. Universal product code

11. Digital cameras have become increasingly popular with both business and home users in recent years.
   a. How does a digital camera take pictures?
   b. How do you transfer the pictures the camera takes into a desktop computer's storage?
   c. What can you do if the pictures you take turn out too light?
   d. For what types of applications is a digital camera suitable and unsuitable?

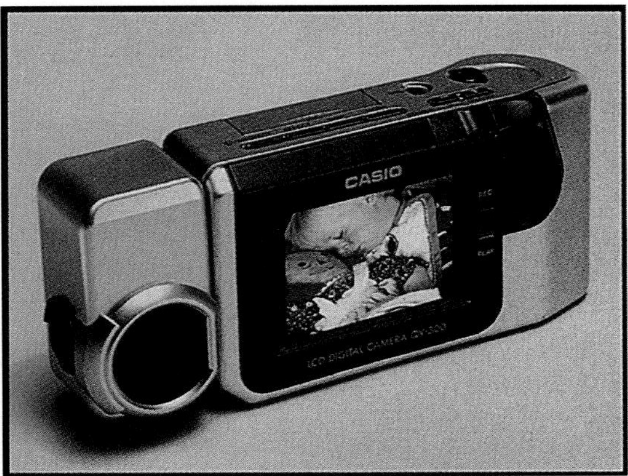

12. For each of the following units of measure, describe both what it measures and a hardware device to which the measurement applies.
   a. dpi
   b. ppm
   c. lpm

13. What are the purposes of the following keyboard keys?
   a. Escape key
   b. Function keys
   c. Ctrl key
   d. Backspace key
   e. Arrow keys
   f. Del key
   g. Numeric keypad keys

14. Each of the following definitions is not strictly true in some regard. In each case, identify and correct the error.

a. Dot pitch (dpi): The amount of space, measured in millimeters, between pixels on a display screen.
b. Monochrome monitor: A monitor that can output in only a single color.
c. Voice-output device: A device designed to create sentences extemporaneously from digitally stored words.
d. Display device: Peripheral equipment that outputs computer-processed results on a screen; also known as a *display terminal.*
e. Dot-matrix printer: A printer that uses hammers to produce output onto paper as configurations of dots.

15. Match each term with the description that fits best.
   a. pixel
   b. MICR
   c. nonimpact
   d. bit mapping
   e. COM
   f. light indicator
   g. landscape
   h. thermal transfer

_____ A term that refers to the placement of output on microfilm.
_____ A banking-industry technology that processes checks by sensing special characters inscribed in a magnetic ink.
_____ A technology that places color images on paper by heating ink from a wax-based ribbon or by heating dye.
_____ Found on most keyboards, it can tell the user whether or not the Caps Lock is activated.
_____ Resolution on a display screen is specified by the density of these.
_____ An output mode with images more wide than high.
_____ A graphical output technique in which software individually controls each pixel in a screen image.
_____ A technology, used in printing, that forms characters by striking a pin or hammer against an inked ribbon.

PROJECTS

1. Keyboards One interesting story claims that the QWERTY keyboard, which became a typewriter standard more than a century ago, was actually created to slow down typists, so that they wouldn't get their fingers stuck between the keys. Despite the QWERTY keyboard's somewhat controversial design, it has managed to survive through the years, becoming the standard keyboard arrangement for computer systems, as well. For this project, answer the questions below. Feel free to consult Internet resources in your research as well as journal articles and books.

a. Why has QWERTY prevailed over other, more highly praised keyboard designs?
b. Many people prefer the Dvorak keyboard over QWERTY. How does the Dvorak keyboard differ, and why do many people prefer it?
c. What is the least-expensive way to implement a Dvorak keyboard?

2. I/O Products Find a currently available product within each of the technologies listed below. For each product, identify the manufacturer, model name, and model number. Additionally, write a short paragraph on each product telling of its capabilities, such as its speed or resolution. Feel free to consult Internet resources in your research as well as journal articles and product brochures.

a. Laser printer
b. Ink-jet printer
c. Thermal-dye-transfer printer
d. SVGA monitor
e. Color flatbed scanner

3. Bit-Picking Project A page of text typed and saved with a word processing program takes up a different amount of storage than a copy of that same page read by a scanner. Why do you think this is so? Which would take up more space? Support your argument by presenting some calculations.

4. Ink-Jet Printers Ink-jet printers have become very popular in recent years. Three important characteristics have contributed to their acceptance: low cost, low noise level, and color capabilities. For this project, choose a vendor of ink-jet printers and answer the following questions about the products in its current line. Feel free to consult Internet resources in your research, as well as journal articles and product brochures.

a. What are the names and/or model numbers of the ink-jet printers produced by the manufacturer you have chosen?
b. Provide as many of the following statistics as you can about each of these printers: list or street price, rated speed for text pages, rated speed for color pages, number of ink cartridges used, colors of ink cartridges used, and maximum resolution possible.

Hint: Three of the biggest makers of ink-jet printers are Canon, Epson, and Hewlett-Packard. These companies provide product information at the following Web addresses:

COMPANY	WEB SITE (HTTP://_____)
Canon	www.canon.com
Epson	www.epson.com
Hewlett-Packard	www.hp.com

Also note that *PC* magazine publishes an annual printer issue, usually in November, that contains a lot of useful information for this project.

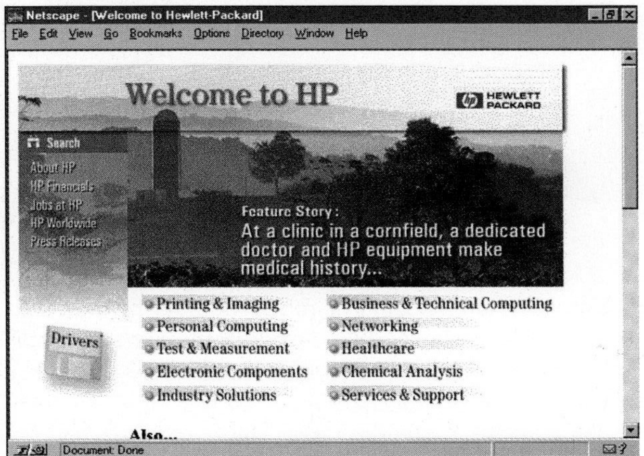

5. Laser Printers Laser printers that produce black-and-white and greyscale outputs define today's standard for business use. For this project, choose a vendor of such laser printers and answer the following questions about the products in its current line. Feel free to consult Internet resources in your research as well as journal articles and product brochures.

a. What are the names and/or model numbers of the laser printers produced by the manufacturer you have chosen?
b. Provide as many of the following statistics as you can about each of these printers: list or street price, maximum speed, and maximum text resolution.
c. Which of these printers qualify as *personal* laser printers? Which are *network* laser printers?

Hint: Two of the biggest makers of laser printers are Hewlett-Packard and NEC. These companies provide product information at the following Web addresses:

COMPANY	WEB SITE (HTTP://_____)
Hewlett-Packard	www.hp.com
NEC	www.nec.com

Also note that *PC* magazine publishes an annual printer issue, usually in November, that contains a lot of useful information for this project.

6. Color Scanners Color scanners have become very popular peripheral devices in recent years for home and office use. Scanners convert flat images—such as a page of text or a photograph—into digital files that you can manipulate on your computer. For this project, choose a recent color personal scanner model, and answer the following questions about it. Feel free to consult Internet resources in your research as well as journal articles and product brochures.

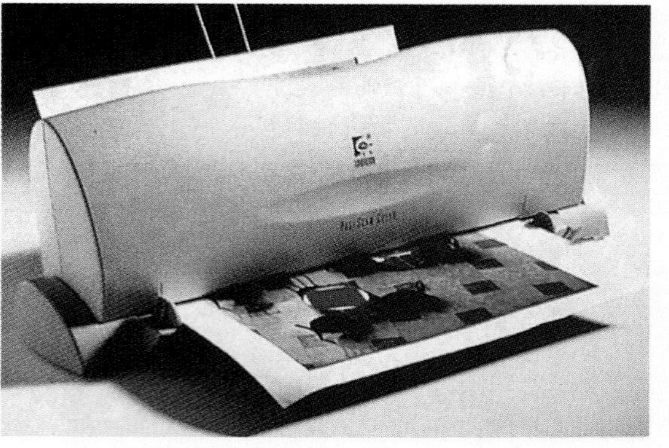

a. What is the name and/or model number of the scanner you have chosen? Who manufactures the product?
b. How does the scanner handle documents—through a flatbed or drum mechanism, or by moving a handheld unit over the documents, or in some other way?
c. Does any software come with the scanner? If it does, describe the types of capabilities the software provides.
d. At what color depths does the scanner work—16-bit color, 24-bit, or something else?
e. At what maximum resolution (stated in dpi) does the scanner accept inputs?
f. What is the list or street price of the scanner?

7. Should We Trash Electronic Cash? A scathing editorial recently appeared in a well-known computer periodical blasting the notion of the widespread use of smart purses (see Feature HW 3-1) to replace cash. The author suggested that electronic-cash equivalents will never fully replace paper money and pointed out a number of reasons why:

- You sacrifice privacy; the government, for instance, can find out how, when, and where you're spending every cent.
- People just don't trust computers enough with their money.
- You can't you tell when you're about to go broke.
- You can't complete simple exchanges like tipping the valet at a parking lot.

Do you feel that any of these objections cite problems serious enough to prevent the spread of electronic money as cash replacements, or will advances in technology eventually make the smart purse just as universal as cash and credit cards? Write a three-page paper stating your position on this issue. If you have a version of the book that contains the IS module, read the Tomorrow box in Chapter IS 1 for more information on this topic.

8. WebTV The chapter's Tomorrow box covers the recently begun marriage of television and Internet technologies, a joining many industry observers expect will eventually result in blockbuster entertainment products. As mentioned in the box, there are many ways that the two technologies can be combined. One such way is currently implemented in a product called WebTV. WebTV enables a standard television set to be equipped so that it can accept certain types of information from the Internet. With such an arrangement, a viewer can see both regular television programming and Internet information while watching the set.

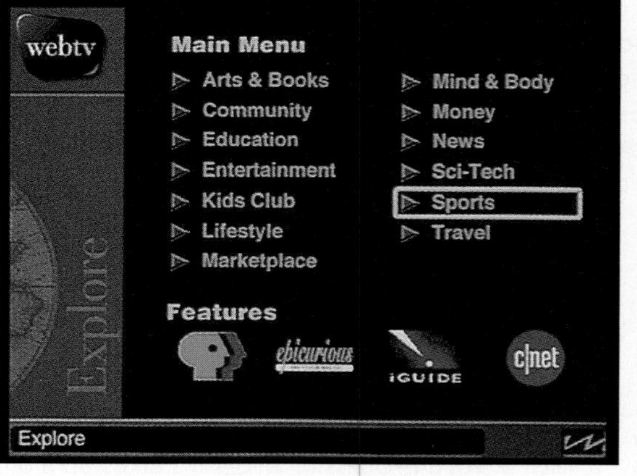

a. How much does WebTV cost?
b. Where can you buy WebTV?
c. What do you have to do with your television set to install WebTV on it?
d. What are the benefits and limitations to WebTV?
e. What types of alternatives to WebTV are currently available that make your TV set more Internet-like?

9. Digital Cameras Digital cameras are beginning to appear more often for various types of applications. For this project, choose a digital camera that costs less than $1,000 and answer the following questions about it. Feel free to consult Internet resources in your research as well as journal articles and product brochures.

a. What is the name and/or model number of the camera you have chosen? Who manufactures the product?

b. Describe the storage medium the camera substitutes for conventional film.
c. At what maximum resolution can the camera take pictures? At what minimum resolution? Also determine the number of pictures that can be taken at each resolution.
d. What is the street or list price of the camera?
e. Some people classify the digital camera as a type of scanner. In what ways are the two devices similar?

Hint: Among the companies currently making digital cameras are Kodak, Sony, Epson, Canon, and Casio. Each of these companies maintains Web sites, any of which you can easily get to by typing the company name in between the "www." and ".com" in the Web address (for instance, www.kodak.com). Most of these companies also maintain toll-free phone numbers for product information, which you can obtain for free from Directory Assistance.

10. Computer Math SVGA displays can produce up to 16,777,216 colors.

a. How do manufacturers arrive at such a number?
b. How many bits would the computer need to color a pixel in any of 16,777,216 colors?

11. Flat-Panel Screens Flat-panel displays have become extremely popular during the last several years for a variety of applications. Several uses are illustrated in Figure HW 3-16 in the chapter and another is shown below. Can you come up with five others?

12. Bar Codes As Figure HW 3-7 in the chapter and the image below illustrate, bar codes are useful in such applications as identifying products in grocery and retail stores, meter reading, and airline-baggage ticketing. Can you name five other applications for bar codes that you've either seen or read about?

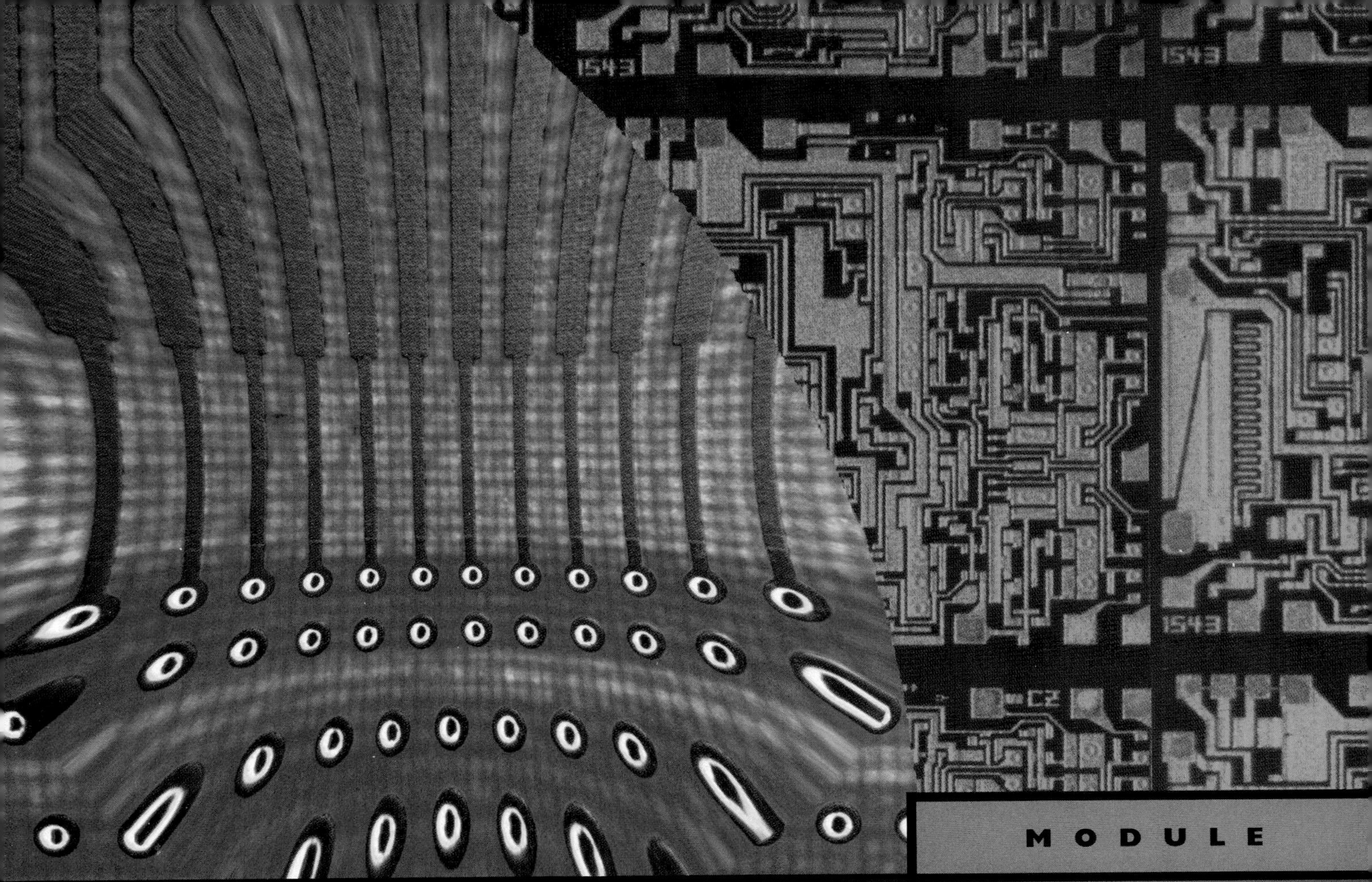

MODULE

Software

SW

In this module, we look at the software concepts that you should be familiar with in order to get up and running on a computer system. The module serves as a springboard for working with applications programs—the reason you acquire a computer system.

Chapter SW 1 offers an overall introduction to the world of software. Here, you will learn about the principal categories of software as well as many of the graphical tools that make today's software products easy to use.

Systems software, the subject of Chapter SW 2, encompasses the programs that enable hardware devices to run applications software. Every computer user must in some way interact with systems software.

MODULE CONTENTS

Software

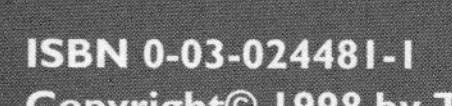

ISBN 0-03-024481-1

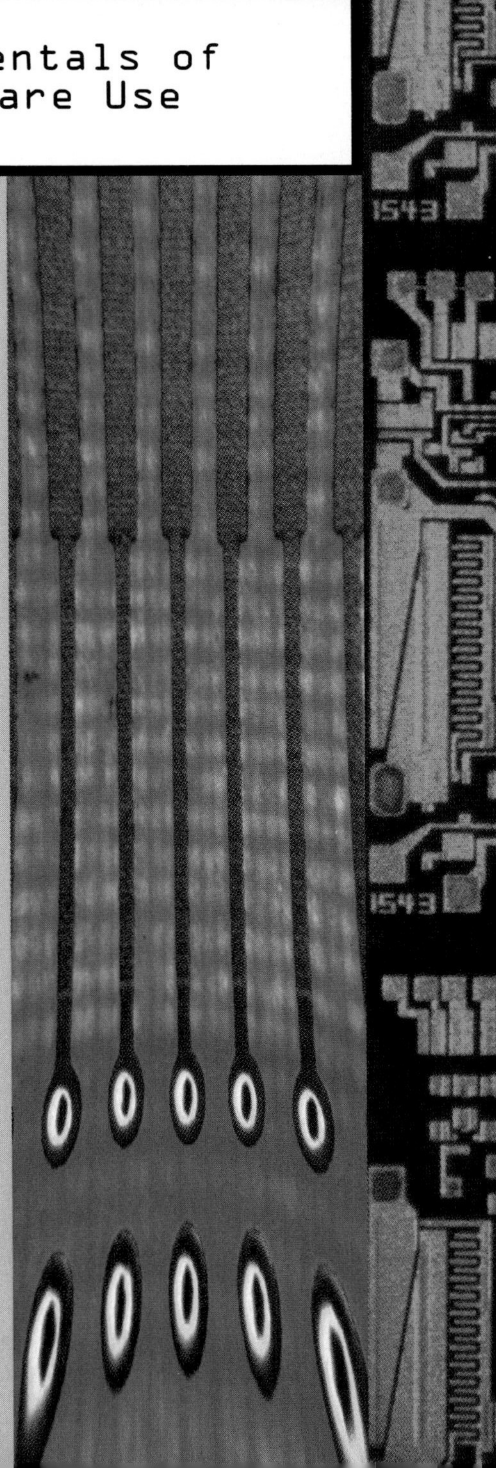

SW 1

Fundamentals of Software Use

Outline

Learning Objectives

After completing this chapter, you will be able to:

1. Describe the major classes of software available in the marketplace.
2. Demonstrate how users gain access to software and the restrictions that sometimes limit their activities.
3. Explain the differences among user interfaces.
4. Identify common elements of a graphical user interface (GUI) and their functions.
5. List the types of online help available.
6. Describe what virtual reality is and discuss its applications.

Overview

Today's computer users choose among thousands of different software products that perform a wide range of different tasks. Users can buy software to write and produce books, keep track of their finances, send mail and schedule meetings, learn foreign languages, entertain themselves, create music and movies, manage entire businesses, monitor RAM functions, and compress files; the complete list of uses is far too long to enumerate. Despite many differences, software products share some striking similarities. These similarities—which include the tools that most users require to perform basic types of work—are the subject of this chapter.

To begin, we will review the difference between systems software and applications software. We will also explore the benefits of software suites and document-centered computing and consider such topics as proprietary software, shareware, and freeware.

Next, we turn to the user interface. Not long ago, most computer users had to write their own applications in programming languages to get computers to perform needed work. This situation has radically changed over the past decade or two. Desktop systems with sophisticated graphics capabilities and *graphical user interfaces* have emerged to set the standard for computers, making it easy for even novice users to take advantage of technology.

Chapter SW 1 deals chiefly with the components of graphical user interfaces. It covers the wide variety of menus, windows, and icons you are likely to encounter, and it indicates where to turn when you need online help. The chapter also looks briefly at trends that will lead toward the interfaces of the future—including social and virtual-reality interfaces that are beginning to pop up in software packages.

About Software

In this section we'll address a variety of general topics related to software, including systems software and applications software, software suites, software ownership, and software updates.

SYSTEMS SOFTWARE AND APPLICATIONS SOFTWARE

Computers run two general classes of software: systems software and applications software (see Figure SW 1-1).

Systems Software **Systems software** consists of "background" programs that enable applications software to work with a computer system's hardware devices. This class of software enables you to perform important jobs like transferring files from one storage medium to another, configuring your computer system to work with a specific brand of printer or display device, managing files on your hard disk, and protecting your computer system from unauthorized use.

Three types of systems software are the operating system, language translators, and utility programs. The next chapter will cover these types of programs.

Applications Software **Applications software** provides tools to carry out the types of computer work for which users buy computer systems. When you write a letter within a word processing program or when your bank uses a program to produce your monthly checking account statement, applications software performs the job. Applications programs are often referred to as *applications.*

■ **Systems software.** Computer programs, such as the operating system, that enable applications programs to work with a computer system's hardware. ■ **Applications software.** Programs that provide tools for performing the type of work that people buy computer systems to do; commonly called *applications programs,* or simply, applications.

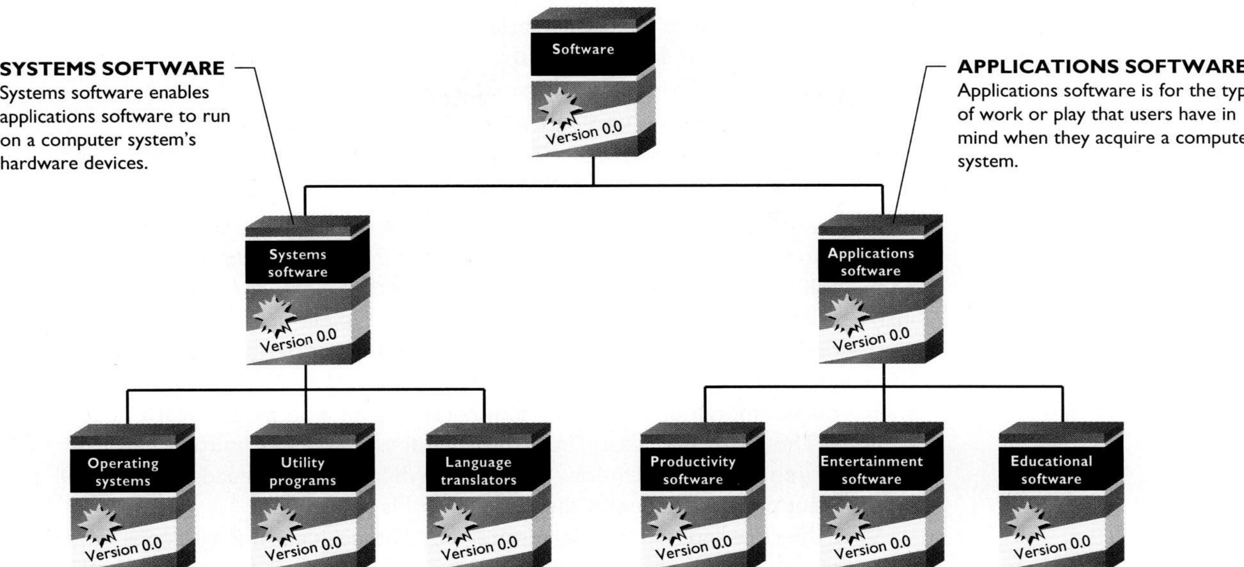
SYSTEMS SOFTWARE
Systems software enables applications software to run on a computer system's hardware devices.
APPLICATIONS SOFTWARE
Applications software is for the types of work or play that users have in mind when they acquire a computer system.
Software
Version 0.0
Systems software
Applications software
Operating systems
Utility programs
Language translators
Productivity software
Entertainment software
Educational software

FIGURE SW 1-1

Systems and applications software.

The largest body of applications software is *productivity software,* which is designed to improve workers' job performance. The principal types of productivity software—word processing programs, spreadsheet programs, presentation graphics programs, and database managers—are covered in depth in versions of this book that contain a PS module. Other types of applications software include computer games, educational software, software geared to scientific research, and programs to make gadgets such as exercise bikes and television sets work better.

The difference between systems and applications software is not always so clear-cut in practice. Systems programs often contain applications-software components. For example, Microsoft's Windows operating system contains such productivity-software enhancements as a calendar and notepad. A program's classification as systems or applications software usually depends on the principal task the program does.

SOFTWARE SUITES AND DOCUMENT-CENTERED COMPUTING

Only just a few years ago, most computer users who wanted to write letters bought stand-alone word-processing programs. Those who wanted to create business worksheets and charts acquired separate spreadsheet programs. All of that has now changed.

Software Suites Today, most office-oriented programs such as word processors and spreadsheets are sold bundled together with other related applications software in **software suites.** The dominant leader in suite sales for office applications is Microsoft Office. The Professional Edition of this package bundles Word (for word processing), Excel (for spreadsheet work), PowerPoint (for presentation graphics), and Access (for database management) together with several other features. You can also buy suites that are targeted to other applications—such as desktop illustration and Web-site development—as well as *minisuites* that bundle together fewer programs. Minisuites, as you might guess, cost less than full software suites.

Closely related to suites are *integrated software programs*—such as Microsoft Works and Corel's PerfectWorks—which compress suite functionality. Thus, instead of a full-featured word processor or spreadsheet, an integrated software package

■ **Software suite.** A collection of software products bundled together into a single package and sold at a price that is less than the sum of the prices of the individual components.

incorporates watered-down versions of each, providing only their main features in a single package. Users in the home market usually do not miss the omitted capabilities; most people who buy full-featured software for their own use wind up using only a tiny fraction of the features, anyway. Companies prefer full suites, however, which allow them to satisfy with a single package the needs of a large numbers of users. The purchase price of integrated software is less than suite software and requires less storage and fewer other system resources to run.

Document-Centered Computing A software suite handles its core applications—word processing and spreadsheets, for instance—through shell programs. Each shell contains all of the needed code used to perform its work except for instructions to do tasks that are common to other shells in the suite. Shells request instructions from a shared *task library* for this latter set of duties. Thus, if you want to create a diagram in a document you are writing within your word processing shell, you summon a drawing program by clicking an icon on the word processor's toolbar. The word processor in turn calls for an art-tools routine from the task library. If you later want to draw something while in your spreadsheeting shell, the spreadsheet program requests the same art-tools routine.

Since the core applications of the suite need not include redundant code for shared functions, the task library both lowers storage requirements for the user and simplifies the development of new programs for the software maker. What's more, a suite presents users with a single interface for handling tasks.

Suites also allow users to easily nest applications and to jump back and forth between applications. For instance, let's say you are writing a letter in your word processing program, and you want to insert a spreadsheet table. You can *launch* (start or open) your spreadsheet program, locate the particular table you want in a stored worksheet, and then copy and paste the table back into your letter—all without ever leaving the word processing program.

Software suites and their nesting capabilities have moved computer users toward a work routine called **document-centered computing.** The term implies that a user can call on a variety of applications programs at any time as needed to help create a document. Such phrases as "word processing application" and "spreadsheet application" are of limited use in the context of document-centered computing; they are certainly not as pivotal as the document itself.

WHO OWNS SOFTWARE?

Knotty questions sometimes arise about ownership and user rights regarding software products. Typically, a software maker or publisher develops a program, secures a copyright on it, and then retains ownership of all rights to it. The publisher then dictates who can use, copy, or distribute the program. Below, we discuss various classes of ownership and use.

Proprietary Software The large majority of the systems and applications software used today is **proprietary software.** This means that someone owns the rights to the program, and the owner expects users to buy their own copies.

Microsoft Office is a typical example. If you want to acquire this software to write letters or produce graphs, you must purchase a registered copy in a store, through a mail-order house, or over the Internet. In buying the software, you pay not to own it, but to acquire a *license* that makes you an authorized user (see Figure SW 1-2). Organizations such as businesses and schools, which may need software for use by several people, generally acquire **site licenses** that allow access by multiple users.

■ **Document-centered computing.** A view of computing in which the document itself is more central than the applications program or programs in which the document was created. ■ **Proprietary software.** A software product to which someone owns the rights. ■ **Site license.** An agreement that allows access by several people in an organization to a proprietary software product.

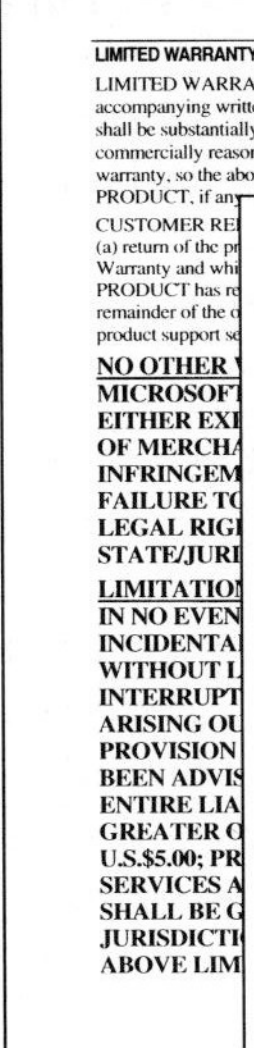

MICROSOFT OFFICE 97
PROFESSIONAL EDITION
WITH BOOKSHELF BASICS
LICENSES: 1

END-USER LICENSE AGREEMENT FOR MICROSOFT SOFTWARE

IMPORTANT—READ CAREFULLY: This Microsoft End-User License Agreement ("EULA") is a legal agreement between you (either an individual or a single entity) and Microsoft Corporation for the Microsoft software product identified above, which includes computer software and may include associated media, printed materials, and "online" or electronic documentation ("SOFTWARE PRODUCT"). By installing, copying, or otherwise using the SOFTWARE PRODUCT, you agree to be bound by the terms of this EULA. If you do not agree to the terms of this EULA, do not install or use the SOFTWARE PRODUCT; you may, however, return it to your place of purchase for a full refund.

SOFTWARE PRODUCT LICENSE

The SOFTWARE PRODUCT is protected by copyright laws and international copyright treaties, as well as other intellectual property laws and treaties. The SOFTWARE PRODUCT is licensed, not sold.

1. GRANT OF LICENSE. This EULA grants you the following rights:
   - **Applications Software.** You may install and use one copy of the SOFTWARE PRODUCT, or any prior version for the same operating system, on a single computer. The primary user of the computer on which the SOFTWARE PRODUCT is installed may make a second copy for his or her exclusive use on a portable computer.
   - **Storage/Network Use.** You may also store or install a copy of the SOFTWARE PRODUCT on a storage device, such as a network server, used only to install or run the SOFTWARE PRODUCT on your other computers over an internal network; however, you must acquire and dedicate a license for each separate computer on which the SOFTWARE PRODUCT is installed or run from the storage device. A license for the SOFTWARE PRODUCT may not be shared or used concurrently on different computers.
   - **License Pak.** If you have acquired this EULA in a Microsoft License Pak, you may make the number of additional copies of the computer software portion of the SOFTWARE PRODUCT authorized on the printed copy of this EULA, and you may use each copy in the manner specified above. You are also entitled to make a corresponding number of secondary copies for portable computer use as specified above.
2. DESCRIPTION OF OTHER RIGHTS AND LIMITATIONS.
   - **Academic Edition Software.** If the SOFTWARE PRODUCT is identified as "Academic Edition" or "AE," you must be a "Qualified Educational User" to use the SOFTWARE PRODUCT. If you are not a Qualified Educational User, you have no rights under this EULA. To determine whether you are a Qualified Educational User, please contact the Microsoft Sales Information Center/One Microsoft Way/Redmond, WA 98052-6399 or the Microsoft subsidiary serving your country.
   - **Not for Resale Software.** If the SOFTWARE PRODUCT is labeled "Not for Resale" or "NFR," then, notwithstanding other sections of this EULA, you may not resell, or otherwise transfer for value, the SOFTWARE PRODUCT.
   - **Limitations on Reverse Engineering, Decompilation, and Disassembly.** You may not reverse engineer, decompile, or disassemble the SOFTWARE PRODUCT, except and only to the extent that such activity is expressly permitted by applicable law notwithstanding this limitation.
   - **Separation of Components.** The SOFTWARE PRODUCT is licensed as a single product. Its component parts may not be separated for use on more than one computer.

(Continued)

Microsoft

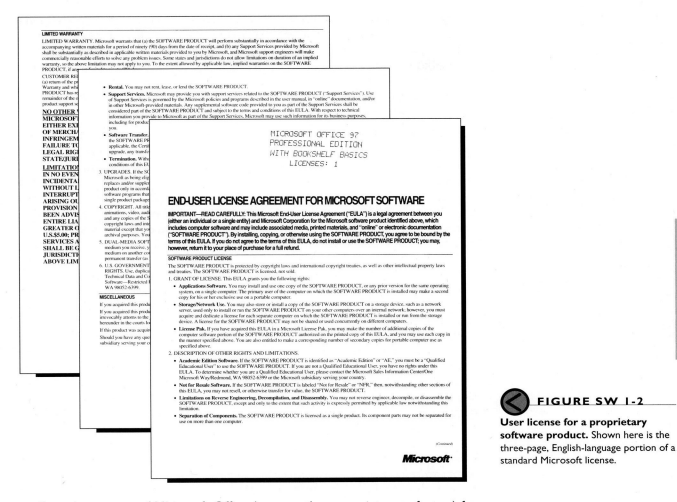

FIGURE SW 1-2

User license for a proprietary software product. Shown here is the three-page, English-language portion of a standard Microsoft license.

If you buy a copy of Microsoft Office (or any other proprietary software) for your own use, you cannot legally make copies of it for your friends, nor can you reproduce parts of the package's code to build your own suite program. You cannot even rent or lease the software to others. You have bought only the right for yourself to operate the software for its intended use—creating documents. Part of the price that you pay for the program becomes profit for the software publisher—Microsoft Corporation—for its efforts in bringing the product to the marketplace.

Along with its restrictions, proprietary software generally brings many benefits, including quality, ongoing product support, and a large base of users. If, for instance, you buy a product from a well-known software maker such as Microsoft, Corel, or Lotus Development, you generally know that millions of dollars supported its creation, that the product will likely remain in use for several years, and that many sources will be available to offer help.

Shareware Some software is available as **shareware.** While you don't have to pay to use shareware, you must pay for support of any type. The software publisher expects you to pay a nominal contribution or "registration fee" to receive written or online documentation, software updates, and/or technical help and advice. The amount charged typically ranges anywhere from $5 to $75. Many shareware creators also ask that you register their software if you continue to use it for a certain period of time—say, a month or longer.

The shareware creator normally doesn't mind if you make copies of the program for your friends. That's because even though you may want to acquire the program

■ **Shareware.** Software that people can copy and use in exchange for a nominal fee.

"on the cheap," your friends may love it more than you do and decide, later on, to pay the creator for support items. After all, support is how this type of software publisher makes money, so the more exposure its programs get, the better.

Keep in mind that many shareware products are copyrighted, so someone owns their rights. Thus, you cannot copy code from such a program to make your own competing program. Internet sites provide access to many shareware and freeware programs (see Figure SW 1-3).

Freeware **Freeware,** or *public-domain software,* refers to programs that you can use free of charge, with no strings attached. One very popular piece of freeware is Mosaic, a browsing program that enables you to navigate the Internet and its World Wide Web. Mosaic was created at the University of Illinois, and you can download it for free through one of that school's Web sites. Not all versions of Mosaic, incidentally, are gratis. Recognizing that many commercial users prefer to pay for fully documented and supported software for mission-critical activities—so someone is accountable for any problems that may crop up—many software publishers develop and sell enhanced versions of Mosaic.

Who, you may ask, would want to give away software and not make so much as a dime off of it? Plenty of people, it so happens. College and university professors, and also graduate students, are motivated to develop freeware because they are doing something academic institutions promote—advancing the state of the art of computer science and making new breakthroughs available as soon as possible to the public. Others may want to develop freeware just because it can be fun or because it provides excellent practice in honing one's programming skills. Still others may want to encourage as many people as possible to test their software's marketability. If the freeware turns out to be popular, the developer may polish it up a bit and include documentation and support—and then turn around and sell the program for profit.

One caution about freeware—because it is free, the chance is reasonable that the software may contain major errors, even plenty of them. After all, you often get what you pay for—and freeware is, after all, a giveaway. Proprietary software and shareware will often have gone through much more rigorous testing than freeware. Because the creators of proprietary-software and shareware products charge you to use them in some way, they are more vulnerable to legal problems if the programs turn out rife with errors. The potential limitations of freeware notwithstanding, many of these programs provide top-quality capabilities and serve large bases of users.

FIGURE SW 1-3

Shareware and freeware. Shareware and freeware sites are common on the Internet.

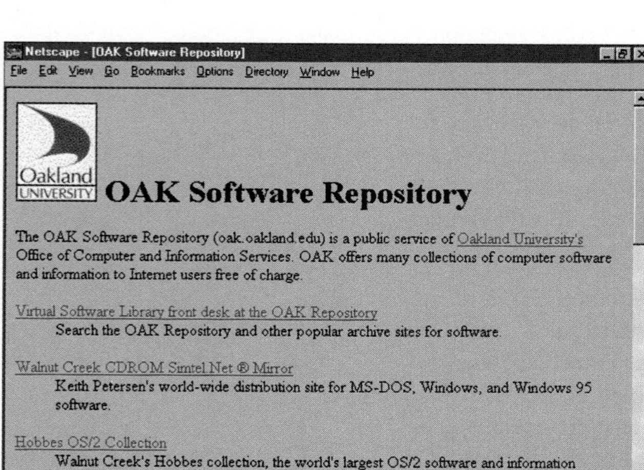

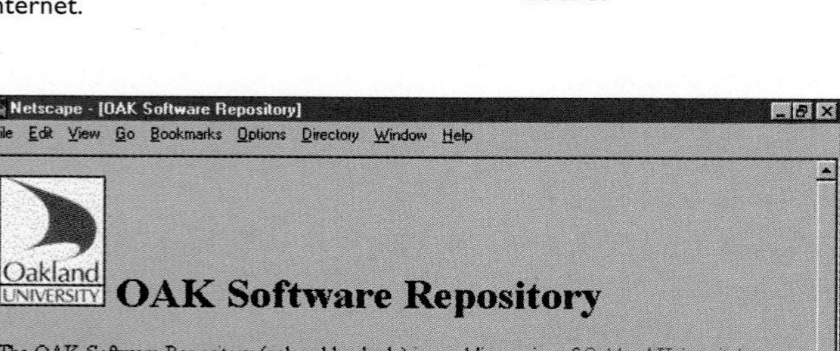

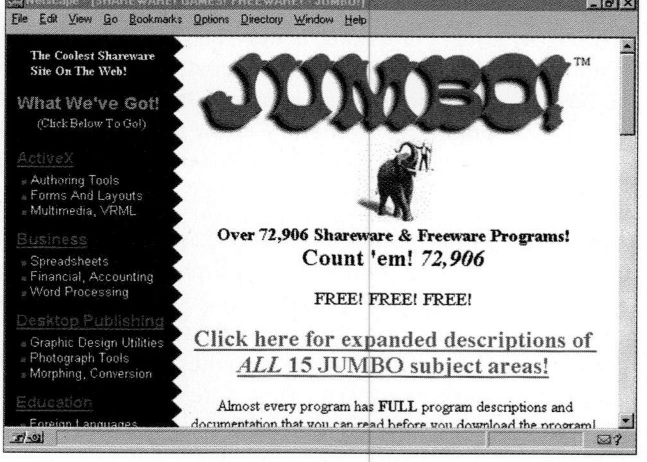

■ **Freeware.** Software offered for use without charge.

The User Interface

Users interact with software in a variety of ways. Those whose computers run Microsoft's MS-DOS operating system, for instance, often perform work by typing DOS-language commands at a prompting character. Users of Microsoft's Windows, on the other hand, choose options from menus and point and click icons with mice to perform similar operations. The manner in which a program makes its resources available to users is known as its **user interface.** In this section, we will look at elements commonly found in user interfaces.

The backbone of most software packages is their command set. It is by issuing commands that you get a package to perform any desired action. Commands are often invoked either by typing in statements that conform to a command syntax, by using shortcut keystrokes, or by making selections from a graphical user interface (GUI) with a mouse or keyboard.

SW

COMMAND SYNTAX

Early user interfaces required users to type precise instructions indicating exactly what the computers should do. Until the 1980s, this command-line interface was pretty much the only way to work with computers. At some type of system **prompt,** the user typed a command that conformed to a strict command syntax. **Syntax** refers to the grammatical rules that govern the structure and content of statements in a particular computer language.

For instance, the MS-DOS operating system accepts typed commands at the operating-system prompt. If you are pointed to the DOS directory on the C drive and want to erase a file named FRED from the A drive, then at the prompt:

```
C:\DOS>
```

you must type:

```
ERASE A:FRED
```

If you were to type:

```
ERASE FRED FROM A
```

an error message would display on the screen, indicating that the command does not conform to the official syntax of the MS-DOS language.

Unfortunately, using a command syntax effectively is often beyond the patience and capabilities of most users. Syntax can impose exacting demands, and the average person tends to treat such formal rules rather casually and to make typing mistakes. For instance, imagine having to regularly create DOS statements such as:

```
DEVICE=C:\DOS\DRIVER.SYS /D:0 /F:1
```

Not only do you have to be very careful in making sure each of the characters in the statement is correct—including blank spaces appearing where they should be—but also, if you can't remember the syntax, you have to look it up.

To make software available to the widest audience possible, software publishers have added features such as shortcut keystrokes and GUIs to simplify the work of entering commands. However, such developments have not completely eliminated command syntax. Although shortcut keystrokes and graphical user interfaces have certainly helped more people than ever to interact easily with computers, many applications still require painstakingly typing in commands. Examples include creating one's

■ **User interface.** The manner in which a computer program makes its resources available to users. ■ **Prompt.** Displayed text or symbols indicating the computer system's readiness to receive user input. ■ **Syntax.** The grammatical rules that govern a language.

own computer programs and customizing software packages to work in nonstandard ways. Also, many users still prefer working with command syntax, because it frees the computer from the processing necessary to handle graphical screens. Therefore, it requires fewer system resources than GUIs, speeding the computer's work.

SHORTCUT KEYSTROKES

Shortcut keystrokes enable you to invoke commands with a minimal number of keystrokes. For instance, when you want to indent text with many versions of WordPerfect, you strike the F4 function key. Next, you type the text you want indented. To turn off the indent, you tap the Enter key. To perform the same type of task with a command syntax—something people had to do during the early days of word processing—would take much greater effort (see Figure SW 1-4).

In some versions of WordPerfect, you can change from single- to double-spacing in a document just as easily. Hold down the Shift key while tapping the F8 function key, then strike the 1 key, the 3 key, and the 2 key in succession. Written down, this process might look like:

Shortcut keystrokes save a great deal of time when compared to conventional command syntax. However, they can also tax the user's memory. Someone who can't remember the shortcut keystrokes for seldom-used commands will have to spend time looking them up in a printed manual.

GRAPHICAL USER INTERFACES (GUIs)

Graphical user interfaces (GUIs) have become popular in recent years with the availability of high-resolution display screens, faster CPUs, and more capacious RAM

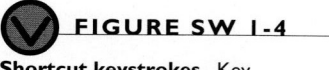

FIGURE SW 1-4

Shortcut keystrokes. Key combinations help users issue commands such as indenting a paragraph with minimal input from the keyboard.

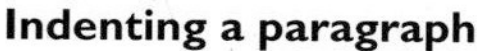

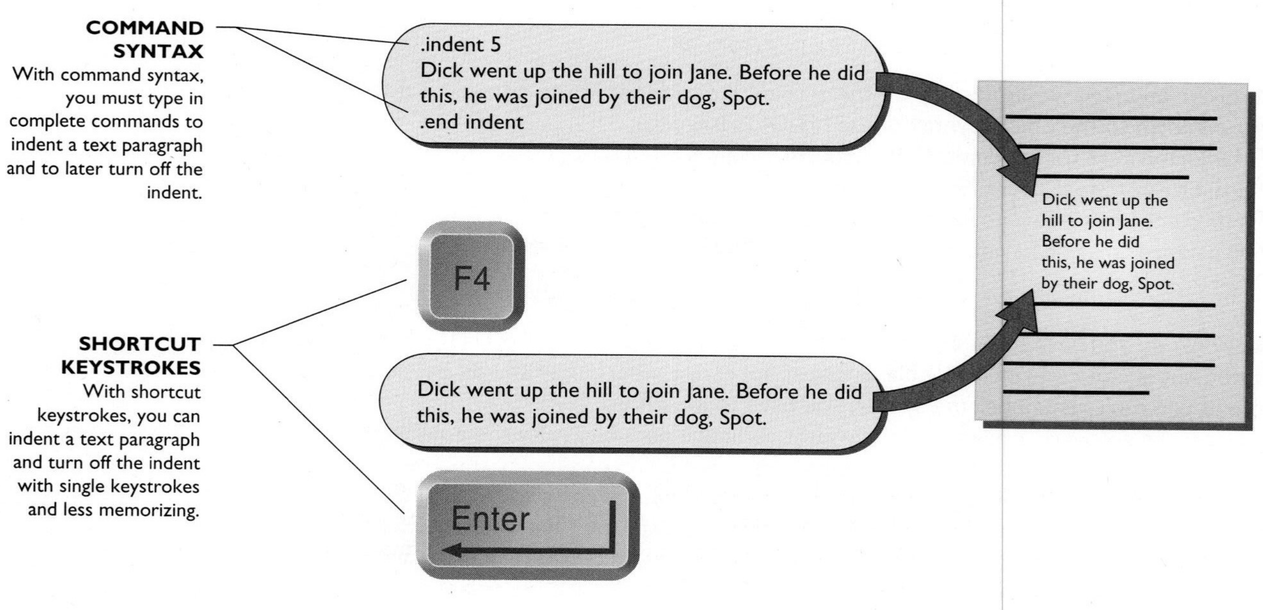

COMMAND SYNTAX
With command syntax, you must type in complete commands to indent a text paragraph and to later turn off the indent.
.indent 5
Dick went up the hill to join Jane. Before he did this, he was joined by their dog, Spot.
.end indent
Dick went up the hill to join Jane. Before he did this, he was joined by their dog, Spot.
F4
SHORTCUT KEYSTROKES
With shortcut keystrokes, you can indent a text paragraph and turn off the indent with single keystrokes and less memorizing.
Dick went up the hill to join Jane. Before he did this, he was joined by their dog, Spot.
Enter

■ **Shortcut keystrokes.** Keystrokes that make it possible for commands to be entered with minimal keystroking. ■ **Graphical user interface (GUI).** A term that refers to the graphics screens that make it easier for users to interact with software.

and hard disks. Before these types of hardware improvements, computer designers could not practically implement GUIs. The systems of the day could adequately deliver neither graphical icons and windows nor *WYSIWYG* displays (for *what you see is what you get*) showing screen images that resemble printed documents. Early graphics monitors displayed output that looked too crude. And later, when screen outputs started to look attractive, the systems just took too long to generate the graphics on the computer.

GUIs employ such devices as pull-down menus, windows and icons, and toolbars to make it easier than ever for users to navigate successfully through their favorite software packages (see Figure SW 1-5). Instead of having to remember a complicated command syntax or shortcut-keystroke sequence, all the user has to do is look for the command on a menu, point to it using a mouse or keyboard, and select it. A variety of online tools are available to assist users who cannot recall instantly the specific command necessary to perform a specific operation.

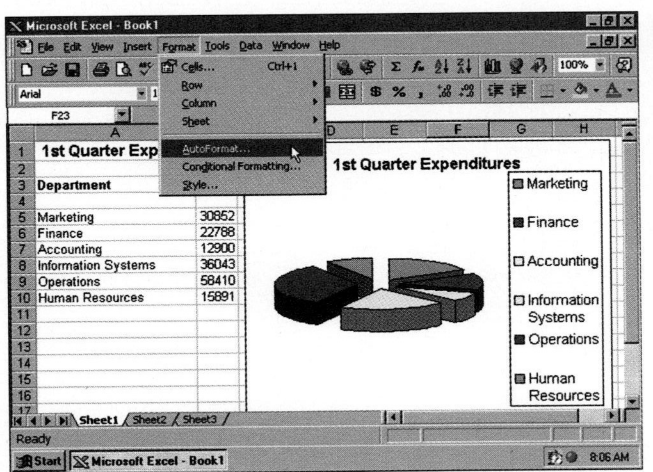

FIGURE SW 1-5

Graphical user interfaces. GUIs, which contain menu choices that you can select with a mouse pointer, became the standard desktop user interface as graphics displays evolved.

GUIs also provide a means of customizing screens to suit each user's personal work style. Menus can often be personalized with favorite commands and then moved anywhere on the screen. Also, screens can be altered in a variety of different ways to suit individual tastes. For instance, with a couple of mouse actions, users can temporarily get rid of the bottom-of-screen *taskbar* (containing the Start button and time) and other screen clutter to make more room for documents.

Despite the usefulness of GUIs, some users may not want to rely exclusively on them. For example, longtime users of a particular product complete tasks faster by typing familiar shortcut keystrokes than by selecting comparable commands from menus. Also, longtime users of MS-DOS often prefer to copy files using its command syntax rather than performing the same operation through a sequence of selections from Windows menus. GUIs are particularly helpful, however, in jogging your memory when you need to issue seldom-used commands. Today, most software packages combine command syntax, shortcut keystrokes, and GUIs, enabling users to switch among these alternatives.

GUIs do not represent the only software breakthrough brought on by powerful graphics hardware. As the window starting on page SW 31 hints, the new equipment has brought with it a revolution in the world of art.

OTHER INTERFACES

Although using a keyboard or a mouse with a standard GUI is by far the most common way for people to interact with computer systems today, several other methods are in wide use. Among these are pen-based user interfaces, touch screens, and voice input and output—all of which were covered in Chapter HW 3. A more recent development that is rapidly gaining favor is the social interface.

Social Interfaces *Social interfaces* borrow techniques from 3-D graphics to immerse users into environments that simulate those in real life (see Figure SW 1-6).

FIGURE SW 1-6

Social interfaces. Social interfaces immerse users into environments that simulate real life.

Net2Phone's dialing interface looks just like a real phone.

A ticket counter makes visitors to airlines Web sites immediately familiar about where to go for specific information.

Computer Associates' *Simply Village* interface uses a village square. Buildings, some of which have elevators, contain software and information.

The interest in social interfaces is spurred by the realization that today's familiar GUIs take time to master and, also, by advances in techniques to create three-dimensional desktop graphics (see Feature SW 1-1). Users of the Windows and Macintosh GUIs often take months to get reasonably comfortable with the icons, folders, and shortcut keystrokes involved. What's more, users often limit themselves to working with only a small percentage of the features in these massive programs—they don't bother to learn the rest. A more intuitive social interface could not only cut learning time dramatically but also make it simple for users to find useful features they would not otherwise know about. Later in the chapter we will look at *virtual reality,* a hardware-and-software technology that extends the social-interface concept with sensory phenomena such as sound, movement, and feeling. The Tomorrow box on page SW 20 features *Wetware,* a frontier technology in the area of social interfaces.

Elements of a Graphical User Interface

Most software packages today interact with users through graphical user interfaces of some type. Consequently, virtually everyone learning about computers should know how GUIs work.

MENUS

A **menu** is a set of options from which the user can choose to take a desired action in a program. Several types of menus are used, including those that follow.

■ **Menu.** A set of options from which the user chooses to take a desired action.

A 3-D World

Today's Hot Interface Will Likely Power Tomorrow's Standard GUI

Discussions of three-dimensional (3-D) images on flat surfaces often conjure up memories of the funny glasses that people used to wear in the 1950s to watch grade-B movies. Expensive graphics workstations have offered 3-D graphics for many years. Now, with costs decreasing and technology improving, 3-D is gaining a place in mainstream PC products.

In the world of computers, a 3-D object is one that is modeled along three axes. Like a real-life object, you can rotate it and view it from different angles. If you look at it close up rather than from afar, you may see changes in contour and reflections. Also, lighting routines in the software change the illumination of objects as viewing angles change.

Among the principal markets today for 3-D displays are movies and computer games. Also, such fields as architecture and engineering employ three-dimensional visualization software to allow clients to experience the look and feel of a structure before it is actually built. Medical applications of 3-D images help to generate realistic models of the human body, and the military implements 3-D in flight-simulation training.

3-D graphics seem likely to form part of virtually every hardware and software product in the not-too-distant future. The reasons seem apparent: Computer systems are becoming ever more powerful and 3-D offers a natural way for people to view information. After all, we look at a 3-D world in everyday life. To get an impressive 3-D effect on your current computer screen, you need special hardware and software. Tomorrow's systems will likely include such hardware and software as standard-issue components.

One of the major changes brought by 3-D will be in desktop operating systems. Current operating systems, such as Windows, can squeeze only so many icons onto a single flat screen. A 3-D screen can arrange choices on cubes or globes that rotate—individually or all at once—revealing vast amounts of information much more quickly than you could possibly achieve or even assimilate in the present hunt-and-peck 2-D world. What's more, as social and virtual-reality interfaces improve, it is likely that they, too, will be incorporated into the operating systems of the future.

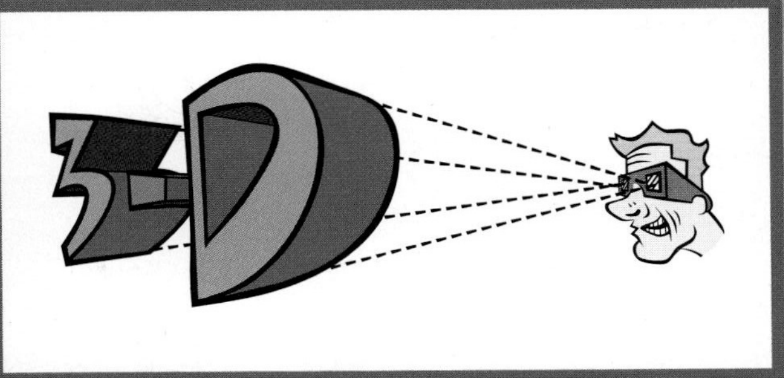

3-D software. You can see the illusion of 3-D on your computer screen without the funny glasses.

SW

Menu Bars At the top of many GUI screens or windows is a **menu bar** showing the governing command set (see Figure SW 1-7). Generally, commands can be selected with a mouse or by some simple shortcut-keystroke procedure. For instance, to select the View command off the menu bar in Figure SW 1-7, you can either click on it with a mouse or depress, say, the Alt key while tapping the *V* key on the keyboard. Generally, the key that is to be struck in combination with the Alt key (or another control key) is underlined or highlighted on the menu, thereby putting less of a strain on your memory. Such special keys are called *access keys.*

Pull-Down Menus **Pull-down menus** (or *drop-down menus)* display on the screen when the user makes a choice on a menu bar. Subcommand options on pull-down menus prompt the user for finer levels of detail. Pull-down menus typically conform to certain conventions:

ACTIVE AND DEFAULT CHOICES The active and default commands are respectively highlighted on the menu bar and pull-down menu. The *active* command (View, in Figure SW 1-7, which is highlighted by having a depressed appearance) is the command that you have already selected, while the *default* command (Header and Footer, in Figure SW 1-7) is a command that can be activated merely by striking the Enter key or by clicking the mouse button.

■ **Menu bar.** A horizontal list of choices that appears on a highlighted line, usually below the window title. Often called the *main menu.* ■ **Pull-down menu.** A menu of subcommands that drops down vertically from a horizontal menu bar or appears alongside another pull-down menu. Also called a *drop-down menu.*

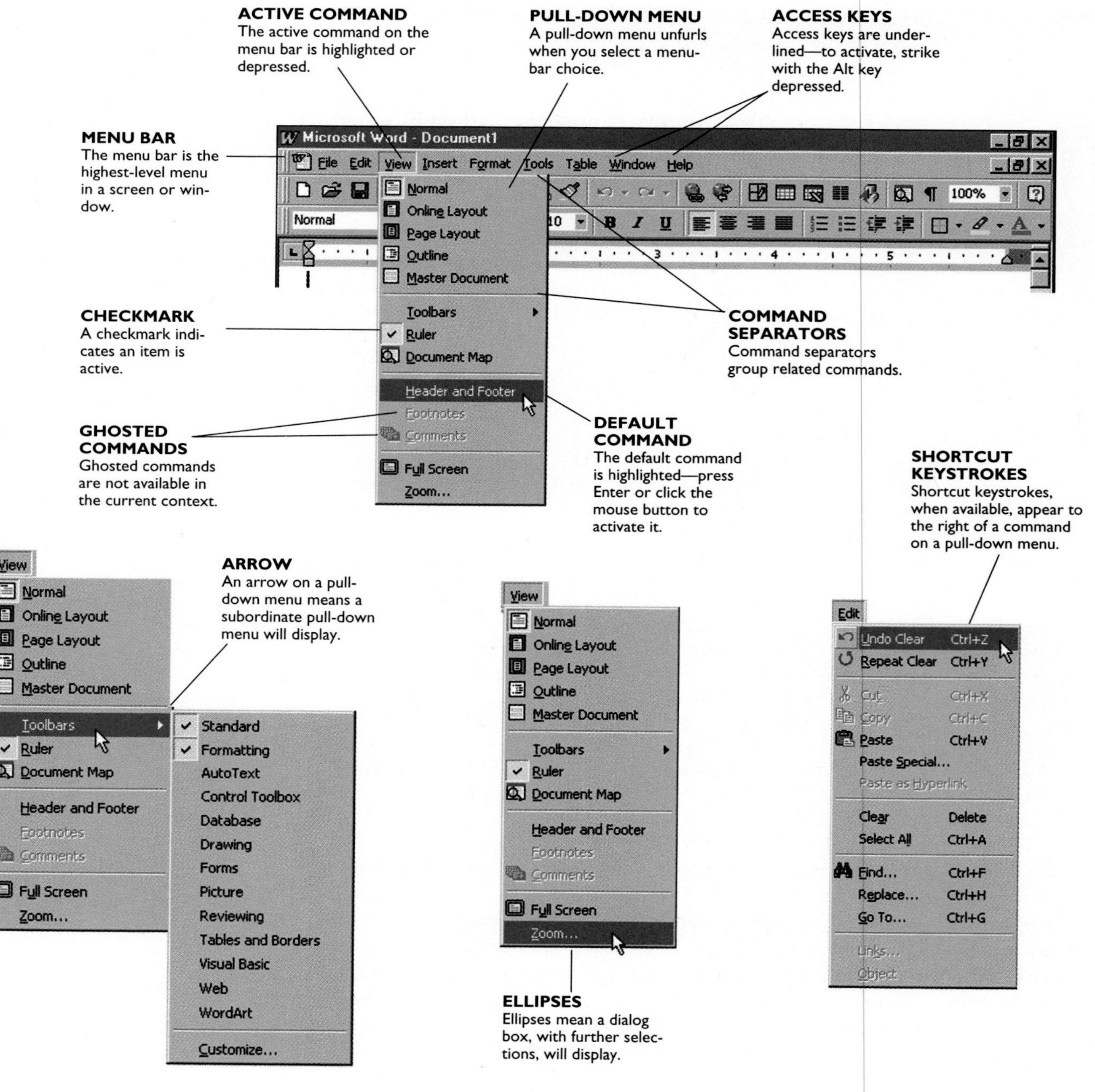
ACTIVE COMMAND
The active command on the menu bar is highlighted or depressed.
PULL-DOWN MENU
A pull-down menu unfurls when you select a menu-bar choice.
ACCESS KEYS
Access keys are underlined—to activate, strike with the Alt key depressed.
MENU BAR
The menu bar is the highest-level menu in a screen or window.
Microsoft Word - Document1
File Edit View Insert Format Tools Table Window Help
Normal
Online Layout
Page Layout
Outline
Master Document
Toolbars
Ruler
Document Map
Header and Footer
Footnotes
Comments
Full Screen
Zoom...
CHECKMARK
A checkmark indicates an item is active.
COMMAND SEPARATORS
Command separators group related commands.
GHOSTED COMMANDS
Ghosted commands are not available in the current context.
DEFAULT COMMAND
The default command is highlighted—press Enter or click the mouse button to activate it.
SHORTCUT KEYSTROKES
Shortcut keystrokes, when available, appear to the right of a command on a pull-down menu.
ARROW
An arrow on a pull-down menu means a subordinate pull-down menu will display.
Standard
Formatting
AutoText
Control Toolbox
Database
Drawing
Forms
Picture
Reviewing
Tables and Borders
Visual Basic
Web
WordArt
Customize...
Edit
Undo Clear Ctrl+Z
Repeat Clear Ctrl+Y
Cut Ctrl+X
Copy Ctrl+C
Paste Ctrl+V
Paste Special...
Paste as Hyperlink
Clear Delete
Select All Ctrl+A
Find... Ctrl+F
Replace... Ctrl+H
Go To... Ctrl+G
Links...
Object
ELLIPSES
Ellipses mean a dialog box, with further selections, will display.

FIGURE SW 1-7

Menu-bar and pull-down menu elements.

You can often escape from an active command by striking the Escape key or merely by pointing to another command on the menu bar. As you slide the mouse sideways, you'll see other pull-down menus unfurl as the *mouse pointer* passes over corresponding menu-bar commands. There are several ways to select a choice other than a default—you can position the mouse pointer on it and click the mouse button, invoke its access key, or move to it with the appropriate arrow key on the keyboard and then strike the Enter key.

GHOSTED TYPE On the View pull-down menu of Figure SW 1-7, the Footnotes and Comments subcommands are shown in *ghosted* or faded type. This means that these particular choices are unavailable in the context of what you're currently doing. For instance, if you haven't created any footnotes in a document, viewing any is impossible. Ghosted type extends beyond pull-down menus to other GUI elements, such as menu tabs and command buttons.

CHECKMARKS An item with a *checkmark* to the left of it means that the associated option is "active" or "selected." For instance, the check by Ruler in Figure SW 1-7 means that this element will appear on the screen display. Software packages also have ways of letting you deselect checkmarked options. One widely used procedure is allowing you to point to the option and then selecting it again with a mouse or by striking the Enter key. So, for instance, by selecting Ruler after it had already been checked, both the onscreen ruler and its checkmark on the pull-down menu would disappear.

COMMAND SEPARATORS A command separator is used to group related commands. In Figure SW 1-7, Normal, Online Layout, Page Layout, Outline, and Master Document all pertain to ways to view an onscreen document. Normal view is used for everyday typing and editing, for instance, whereas Page Layout shows how elements such as graphics will be put on a page.

ARROWS An *arrow* to the right of a pull-down menu option (►)—such as Toolbars in Figure SW 1-7—means that the choice leads to another, subordinate pull-down menu. When you position the mouse pointer over the Toolbars choice, the pull-down menu showing the available toolbars automatically appears.

ELLIPSES On pull-down menus, *ellipses* (...) often display to the right of a command—such as Zoom in Figure SW 1-7. Ellipses mean that by selecting the command, you will call up a dialog box (discussed shortly). The box contains further available selections.

SHORTCUT KEYSTROKES Many GUI menus show shortcut keystrokes next to command options, such as Ctrl + Z for Undo Clear and Ctrl + Y for Repeat Clear in Figure SW 1-7. You can execute such command options with the mouse button, the appropriate access keys (the *U* key for Undo Clear), or the corresponding shortcut-keystroke sequence (holding down the Ctrl key while tapping the *Z* key).

Icon Menus Often, menus are in the form of a set of **icons.** An icon can represent a computer program or a group of computer programs, a command or a group of commands, a document—such as a letter or fax transmission—or a group of documents, and the like. As you can see, virtually anything that can go into a computer file or a collection of files can be represented onscreen as an icon. When you select an icon from the displayed arrangement, software takes the corresponding action.

Figure SW 1-8 shows a variety of icon menus. Several types of elements found in icon menus are described below.

PROGRAMS AND APPLICATIONS Program components or applications are commonly represented as icons. If such icons are not built into a software package you wish to use, no problem. Many packages allow you to prepare a set of commands to perform a job you frequently want done and, then, enable you to create a customized icon to represent the job. The icon can be placed either in a conventional icon menu like the one at the top of Figure SW 1-8 or turned into a toolbar button like those you see in the middle part of the same figure.

TOOLBARS A **toolbar** is an icon menu composed of small graphics called *toolbar buttons* that stretches either horizontally or vertically across the screen. Each button has a name, which displays if you point to the button (see Figure SW 1-9). In a software suite, toolbar buttons often store tasks that are common across applications—for instance, saving documents, printing documents, changing and sizing typefaces, and so on.

IMAGEMAPS *Imagemaps* are pictures with embedded links or icons that can take you to other programs or features. When you click on any of the links, you are launched somewhere else—such as to a new Web page or to a particular feature in the program you are using.

■ **Icon.** A graphical image on a display screen that invokes some action when selected. ■ **Toolbar.** An icon menu composed of small graphics called *buttons* that stretches either horizontally or vertically across the screen.

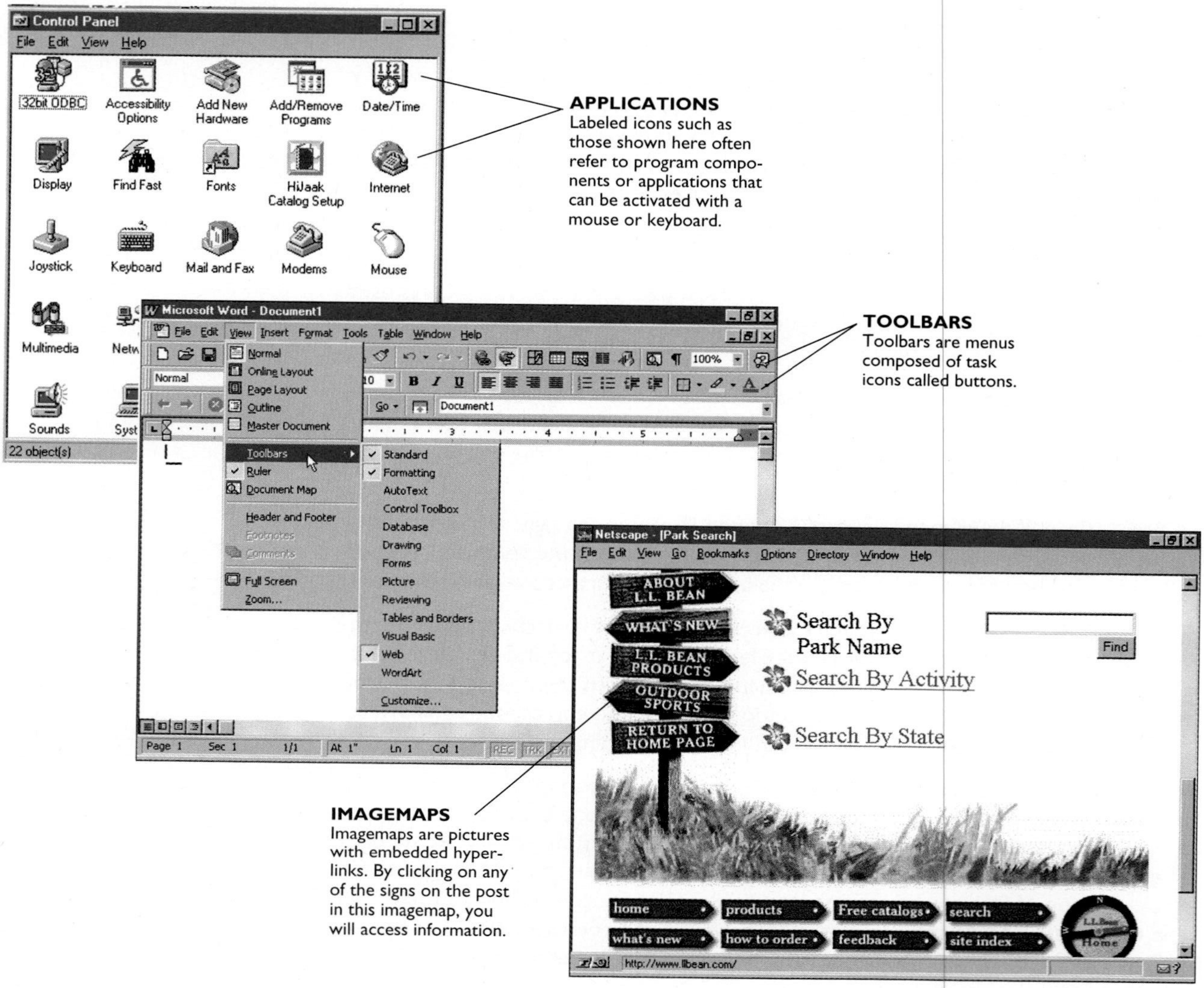

APPLICATIONS
Labeled icons such as those shown here often refer to program components or applications that can be activated with a mouse or keyboard.

TOOLBARS
Toolbars are menus composed of task icons called buttons.

IMAGEMAPS
Imagemaps are pictures with embedded hyperlinks. By clicking on any of the signs on the post in this imagemap, you will access information.

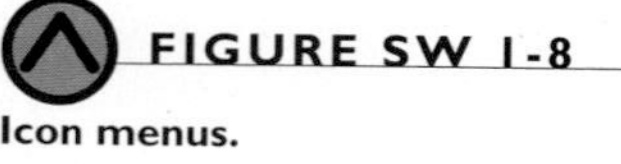

FIGURE SW 1-8

Icon menus.

COMMAND BUTTONS A *command button* is an icon that represents a simple program command (see Figure SW 1-10). For instance, command buttons labeled *OK* and *Cancel* allow users to approve or abort program actions. A ghosted command button represents an action that is unavailable for current operation.

You can often customize icon menus to meet your application needs. For instance, you may be able to choose the icons that are to appear on a menu, sequence the icons in any desired order, and move the icon menu to the most convenient place on the screen—say, to the top or right. As already hinted, you can usually also create your own icons to place on menus.

What Does the Scissors Button Do?

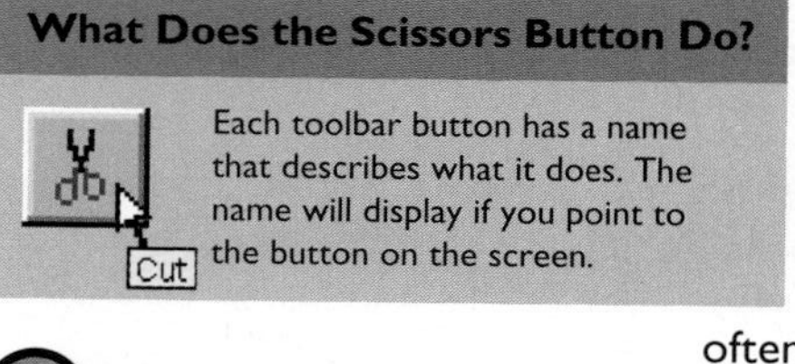

Each toolbar button has a name that describes what it does. The name will display if you point to the button on the screen.

FIGURE SW 1-9

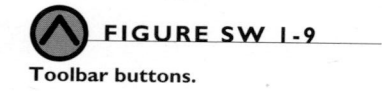

Toolbar buttons.

Hypertext Menus Textual **hyperlinks—**referred to as *hypertext*—add another common control option in GUIs, especially on the Internet's World Wide Web (see Figure SW 1-11). Hypertext is commonly boldfaced and underlined to make it stand out and is often in a different color than regular text. When you move the mouse pointer over hypertext, the pointer's shape often changes to a pointing finger. Clicking then selects the link, generally retrieving a new Web page to your screen. Sometimes, in the context of the Internet, the term *hypermedia* is used to include not only hypertext but also other items such as feature-launching graphical icons and imagemaps.

■ **Hyperlink.** An icon or specially marked text that represents a link to a new file or application.

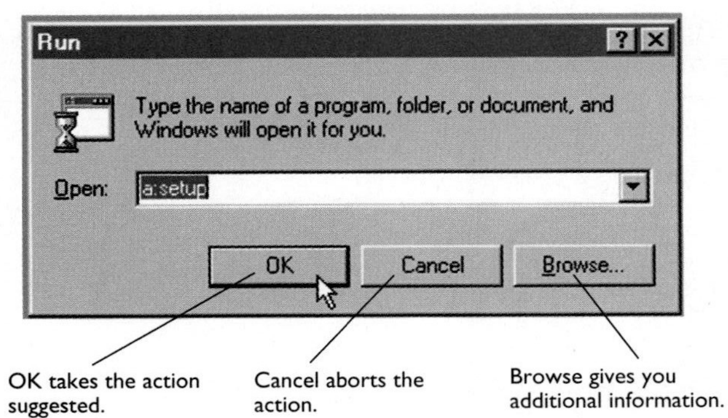

FIGURE SW 1-10

Command buttons.

Palettes A **palette** is a menu that enables you to choose among colors, textures, and other art-oriented items. Generally, the palette is arranged in an array—as in Figure SW 1-12—and you choose a selection either by clicking with the mouse or by tapping the arrow keys to highlight it and striking the Enter key.

Tab Menus A common fixture in GUIs is the *tab menu,* such as the one shown in Figure SW 1-13. Tab menus organize a screen into natural-looking file-folder tabs. By clicking on any of the tabs, the information inside can be accessed. Tab menus are functionally equivalent to the more conventional bar and pull-down menus.

Dialog Boxes Menu items also often appear in *dialog boxes* that pop onto the screen. These items—which include radio buttons, check boxes, and list boxes—will be discussed shortly.

WINDOWS

The staple of the GUI is the window. A **window** is a box of information that is overlaid on the display screen. A window can contain facts about software use, menu items, instructions, and a variety of other types of data.

Customizing Windows Often, windows can be tailored to meet your application's needs. Several of the ways this can be done are described below.

CASCADING VERSUS TILING WINDOWS As shown in Figure SW 1-14, a user can neatly arrange windows onscreen in either of two ways: by *cascading* them one on top of another (left part of Figure SW 1-14) or by *tiling* them side by side (right part of Figure SW 1-14). Tiling enables you to see information in several windows at the same time, while cascading lets you see as much information as possible in the foreground window but only the titles of the windows underneath.

Whatever arrangement you choose for your windows, only one window can be

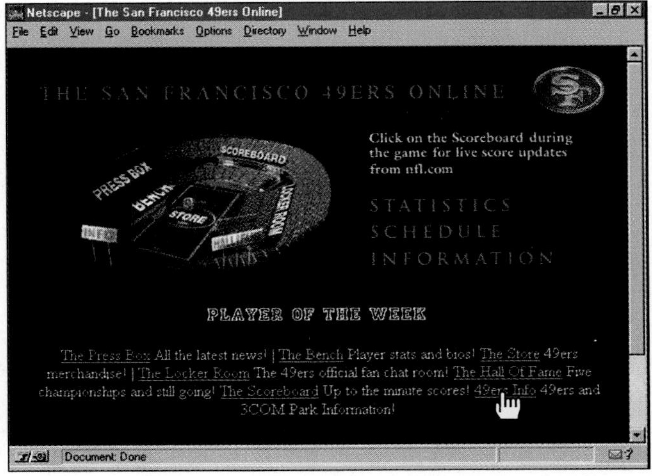

FIGURE SW 1-11

Hypertext. Hypertext changes the mouse pointer to a pointing finger when the pointer passes over it. By selecting hypertext, you are launched to a new screen, feature, or application.

■ **Palette.** A menu that enables users to choose such attributes as colors and textures. ■ **Window.** A box of related information that appears overlaid on a display screen.

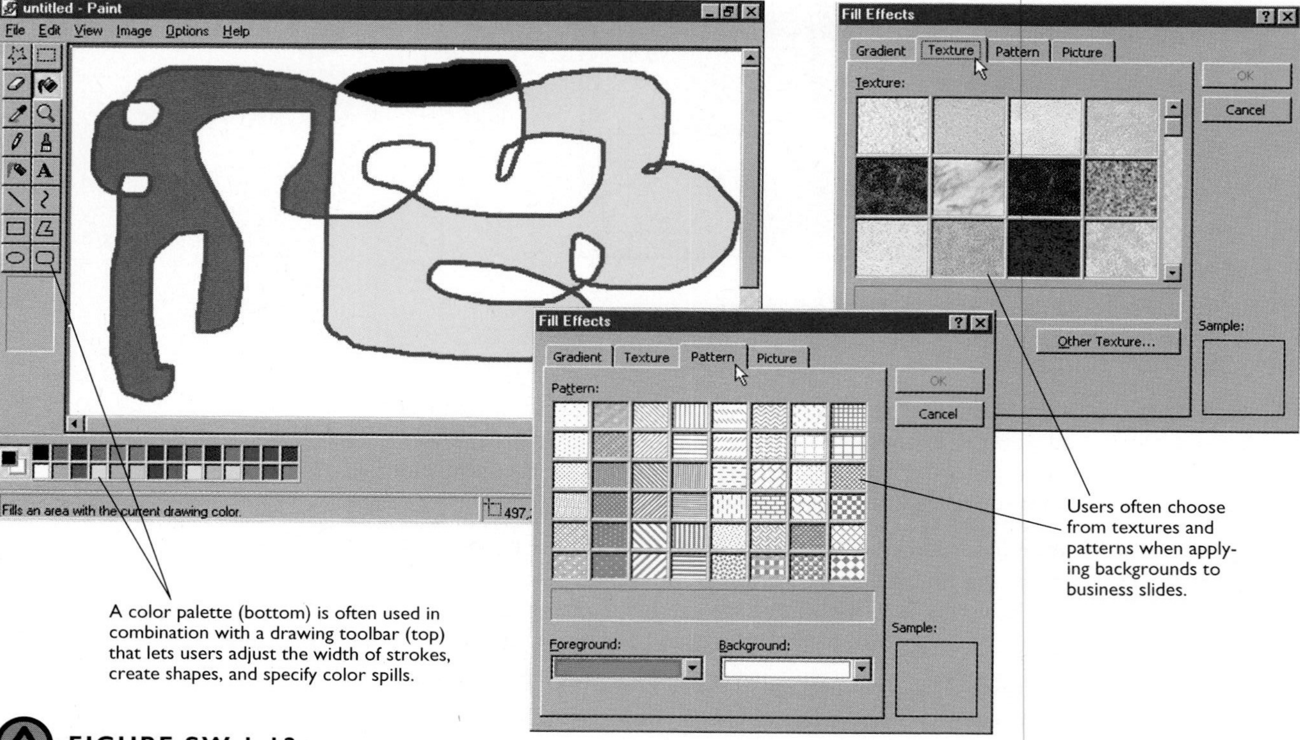

A color palette (bottom) is often used in combination with a drawing toolbar (top) that lets users adjust the width of strokes, create shapes, and specify color spills.

Users often choose from textures and patterns when applying backgrounds to business slides.

FIGURE SW 1-12

Palettes. A palette is a menu that allows users to specify colors, textures, fills, and other attributes for art-oriented output.

active at a time. To make any onscreen window active, click the mouse with the pointer inside it. When you are cascading, the foreground window is active; when you are tiling, a darkened title bar indicates the active window. (The *title bar* shows the name of the file displayed in the window.)

RESIZING AND MOVING WINDOWS Resizing windows, making them larger or smaller, allows more detailed control of a screen display. Many software products let you resize the active window by selecting a window border, the frame enclosing the window, with a mouse. When the mouse pointer is moved over a window border, it looks like a double-pointed arrow. You can make the window wider or taller by moving the pointer inward or outward with the mouse button depressed. Alternatively,

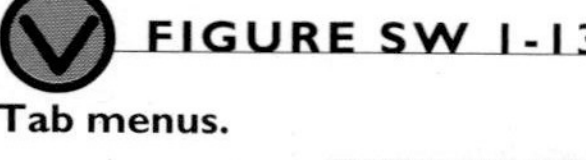

FIGURE SW 1-13

Tab menus.

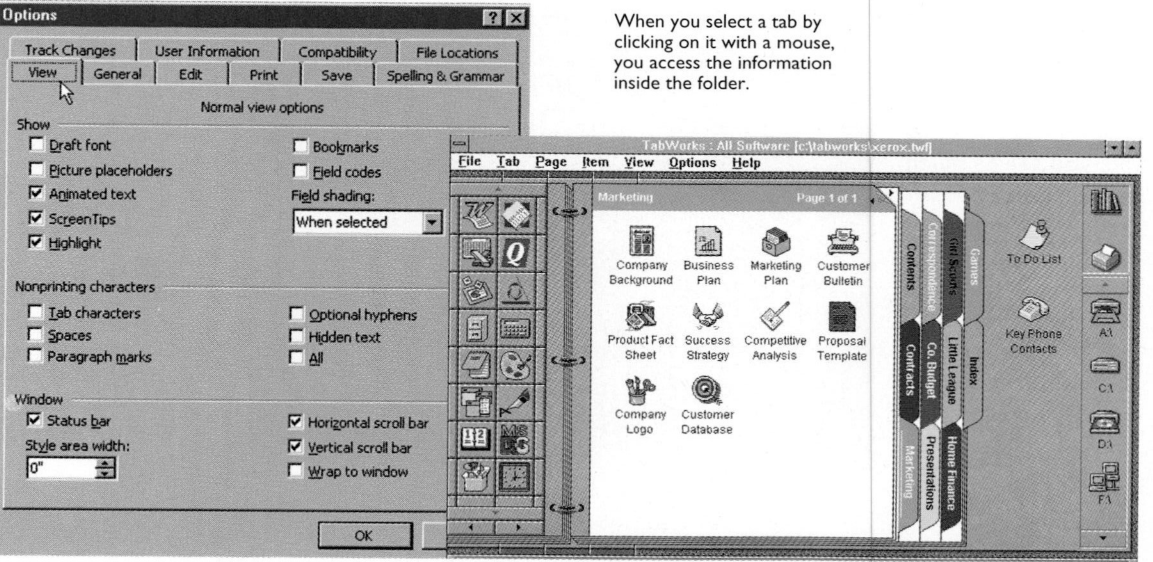

When you select a tab by clicking on it with a mouse, you access the information inside the folder.

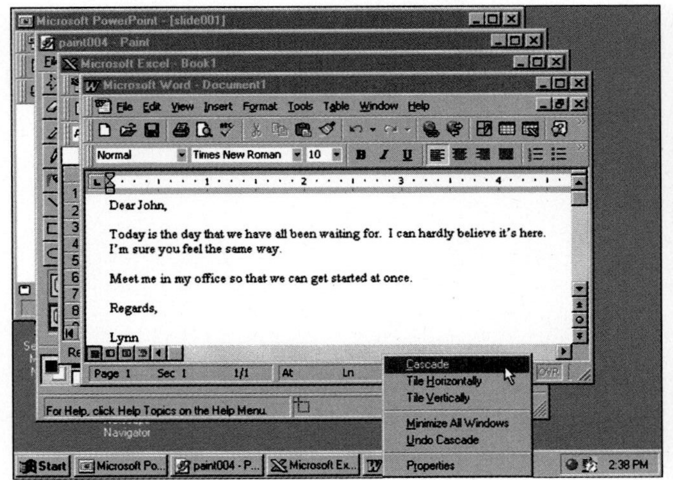

CASCADED WINDOWS
Cascading overlaps windows. It lets you see as much information as possible in the foreground window but only the titles of the windows underneath.

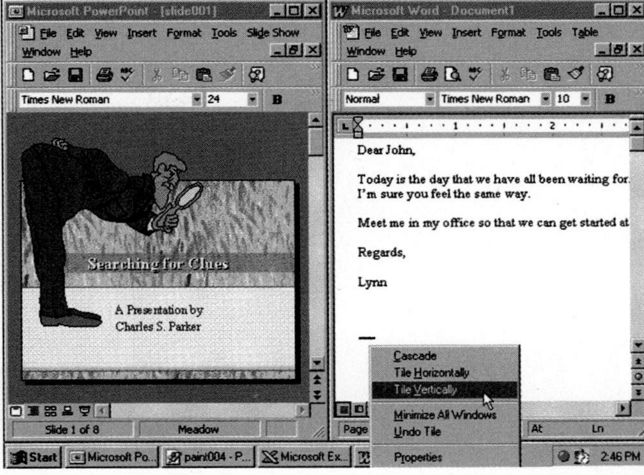

TILED WINDOWS
Tiling places windows side by side and enables you to see information in two or more windows at the same time.

FIGURE SW 1-14

Cascaded and tiled windows.

to adjust the window width and height at the same time, point the mouse at a *sizing handle* at the window's corner; then, hold down the button and drag the mouse. Each of these methods are illustrated in Figure SW 1-15.

You can often customize your display further by moving any window from one part of the screen to another. Typically, this requires you to select the window's title bar with a mouse, hold down the mouse button, and then drag the window to the desired location and release the mouse to drop it there.

MINIMIZING VERSUS MAXIMIZING WINDOWS Windows can be minimized to icon size or maximized to fill the entire screen. In the Windows 95 and 98 environments, buttons to do either of these tasks are at the top right of most applications windows (such as those in Figure SW 1-15). By clicking on the *minimize button* (▁), the window is reduced to an icon on the taskbar. A program that has been minimized is still actively running in the background and you can pull it up on the screen again by selecting it. By clicking on the *maximize button* (□), the window fills the screen. To close a window and thereby leave the application for good, you must click on the *close button* (✕) at the far upper-right corner of the window. In some cases, in the space where you would normally see a maximize button, a *restore button* (🗗) will appear. Restore simply reduces a maximized window to its previous size.

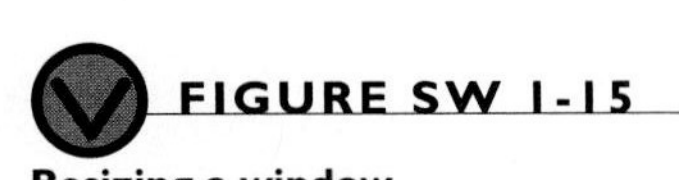

FIGURE SW 1-15

Resizing a window.

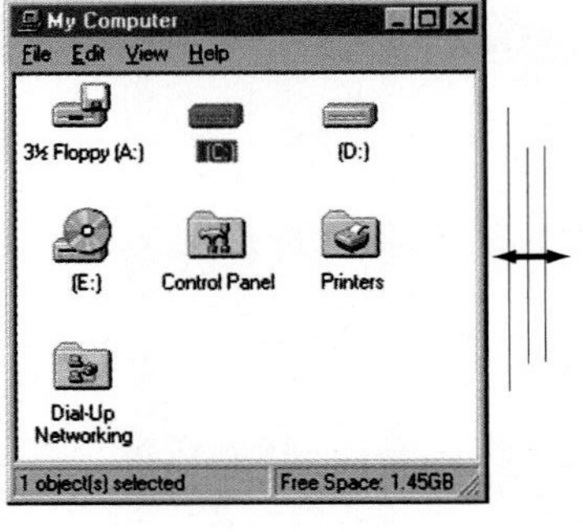

WIDTH
You change the width of a window by dragging its left or right border edge.

HEIGHT
You change the height of a window by dragging its top or bottom border edge.

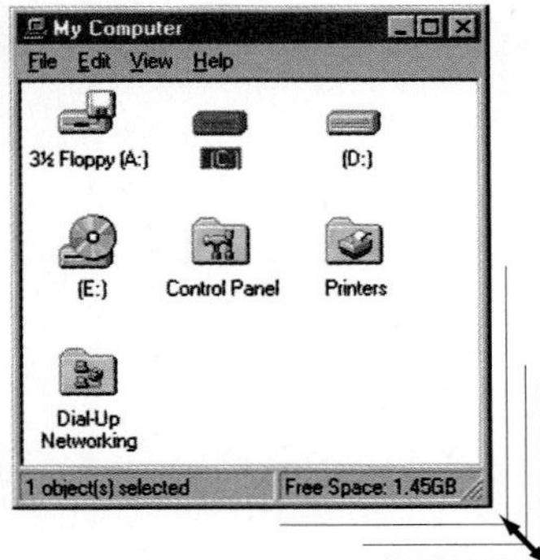

WIDTH AND HEIGHT
You change both width and height together by dragging a corner sizing handle.

TOMORROW

Wetware

The Ultimate User Interface

You've had a bad day at the office, and you come home feeling completely stressed. Within picoseconds of your arrival, a computer in your house senses your presence and goes to work. It automatically adjusts the lights in your living room to a comfortable level and commands your stereo system to play subliminally soothing music—just the type that you realize you wanted, in fact, when you came through the door.

This system is *wetware*—a software-and-hardware user interface that can read your mind and act appropriately on the information it gets. It's nothing less than a telepathic computer system.

Although this scenario sounds like the part and parcel of science fiction—and much of it is—many companies are working on computer systems that can interpret brain waves, with the ultimate possibility of reading human thoughts. Want to phone your main squeeze and tell her or him about your long day? No problem when true wetware is available—without so much as a keystroke, the number will be looked up for you. When you pick up the phone, the system automatically dials. Want to write a business letter? Just think for a second or two about what you would like to say and the mood you'd like to convey. Touch your computer, and your word processor will automatically boot up with the letter on the screen.

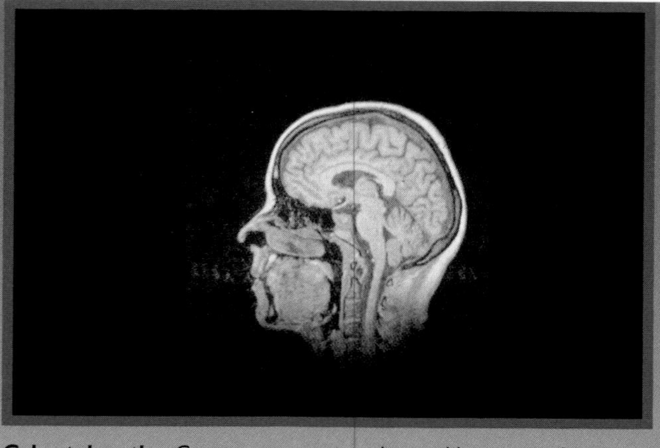

Cybertelepathy. Computers may someday read human minds.

Don't expect true fully functional wetware to reach your local computer store next week, or even next year. In fact, no one can say whether anything close to it will become available during your lifetime—if ever. The human mind is amazingly complex, and, relatively speaking, very little is known about how we perceive, store, access, and act upon data.

Today's most advanced wetware systems are thoroughly primitive in comparison with their potential, and virtually all of them can best be described as research in progress. But who knows? Maybe an unexpected breakthrough will bring telepathic computers within a generation or two.

As you perform work within screen windows, the mouse pointer often visibly changes in a **context-sensitive** way. In other words, the shape of the pointer is automatically altered with respect to the operation you are performing. Figure SW 1-16 shows some of the shapes that you may see on the screen. For instance, when you are resizing a window (refer back to Figure SW 1-15), the pointer will often resemble a double-pointed arrow. Also, as discussed earlier, when you are moving the pointer over hypertext, the pointer often changes to a hand with a pointed finger.

FIGURE SW 1-16

Context-sensitive pointer shapes. Many software packages cause the mouse pointer to be context sensitive, changing its shape with respect to the operation the user is performing.

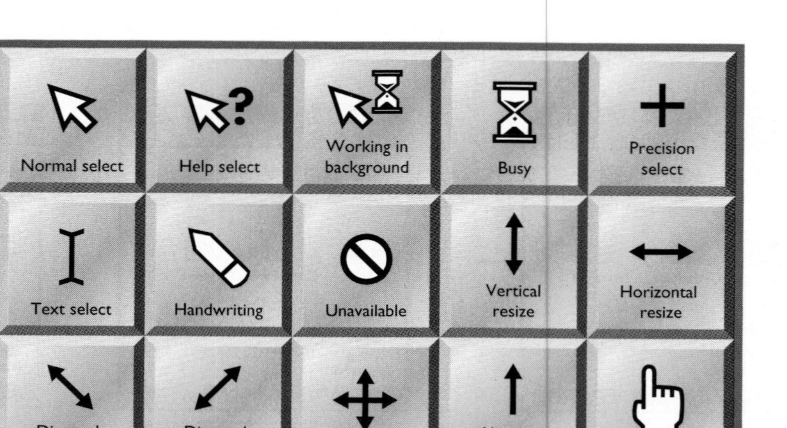

■ **Context sensitive.** A characteristic of a user interface that adjusts program actions to accommodate the type of operation the user is currently performing.

Scroll Bars Often, a screen window is not big enough to display all of the information required for a particular file. When this happens, **scroll bars** appear at the bottom and/or right edge of the window (see Figure SW 1-17). By manipulating elements in these bars, you can display the rest of the information.

Scrolling moves information up, down, and even sideways through the window or screen. When you are scrolling down, for example, as lines successfully disappear from the top of the window or screen, new ones appear at the bottom.

By activating a *scroll arrow* on any scroll bar, you move the window a small amount, in the direction of the arrow, to see offscreen information. The principle resembles slowly moving a magnifying glass (the window) over a map (the information).

Between its two scroll arrows, each scroll bar contains a scroll box. By clicking and dragging with the mouse, you can move this box up or down (or left to right) in the direction of the desired information. For instance, if you move the scroll box from the top of the scroll bar to the middle, the display will immediately move halfway through the information. By clicking before or after a scroll box, you move the screen one page at a time.

In Windows 3.1, scroll boxes are always square; in Windows 95 and 98, they are sized in proportion to the percentage of information currently displayed. Instead of the scroll bars, you can often use the keyboard's cursor-movement keys—such as PgUp, PgDn, and Tab—to scroll up, down, left, or right.

SW

DIALOG BOXES

Dialog boxes are special windows that prompt the GUI user to provide further information. Such information can be supplied by a variety of means, several of which are covered in the following subsections and illustrated in Figure SW 1-18.

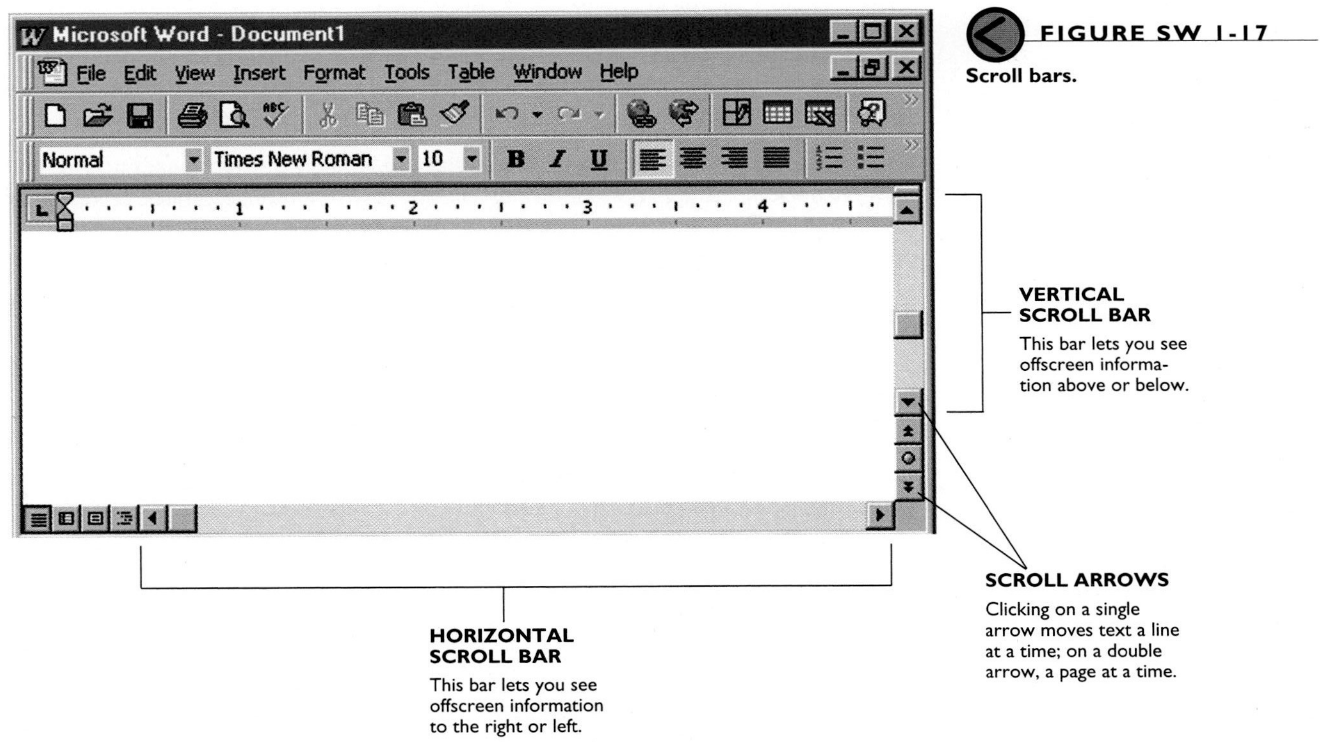
Microsoft Word - Document1
File Edit View Insert Format Tools Table Window Help
Normal
Times New Roman
10
VERTICAL SCROLL BAR
This bar lets you see offscreen information above or below.
SCROLL ARROWS
Clicking on a single arrow moves text a line at a time; on a double arrow, a page at a time.
HORIZONTAL SCROLL BAR
This bar lets you see offscreen information to the right or left.

FIGURE SW 1-17

Scroll bars.

■ **Scroll bar.** A horizontal or vertical bar along an edge of a window that allows the user to view information that will not fit within the window. ■ **Dialog box.** A box that requires the user to supply information to the computer system about the task being performed.

RADIO BUTTONS

Radio buttons work like the push buttons on old radios in that only one button in a panel can be active at one time.

SIMPLE LIST BOXES

In a list box, you make a choice by clicking on it with a mouse or by reaching it through the arrow keys and striking Enter. A vertical scroll bar lets you access choices not currently onscreen.

CHECK BOXES

When a check is placed in a check box, the associated action is selected. Several, none, or all boxes in a check-box panel can be active at one time.

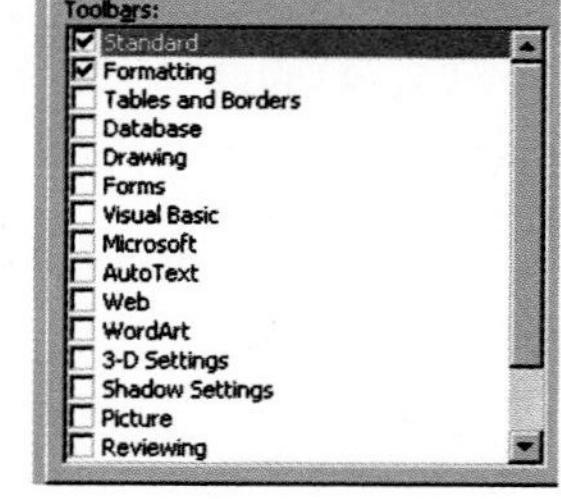

DROP-DOWN LIST BOXES

A drop-down list box has a down-facing arrow to the right of the first choice in the list. When you click on the arrow, other choices appear.

SPIN BOXES

A spin box controls a fixed set of values. You click on an up or down arrow to the right of a value to make the value higher or lower.

TEXT BOXES

Text boxes require you to type information into the computer—such as a page number.

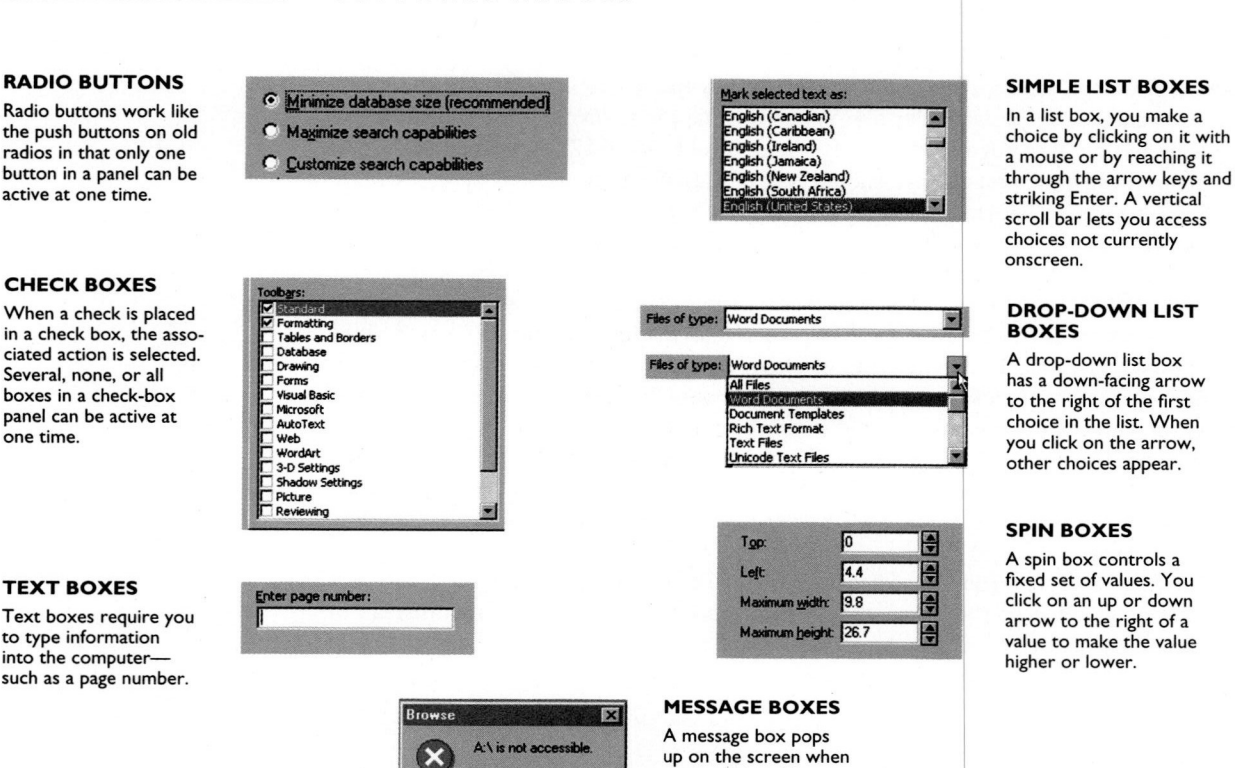

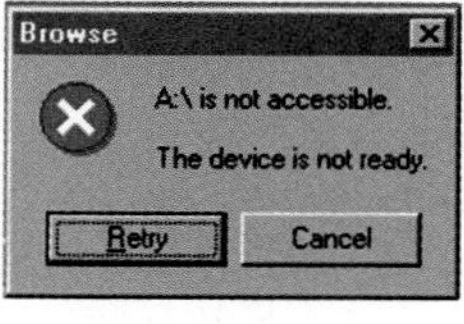

MESSAGE BOXES

A message box pops up on the screen when a potential problem is unfolding.

FIGURE SW 1-18

Dialog-box elements.

Radio Buttons *Radio buttons,* also known as *option buttons,* are rounded buttons that work like the push buttons on old radios—only one choice in the panel can be active at any one time. You activate or deactivate buttons by clicking on them.

Check Boxes To make any of the choices in a panel of *check boxes* active, you place a check in the appropriate box by clicking it with a mouse. Check boxes differ from radio buttons in that you can activate more than one option in the panel or no options at all. To deactivate any check box, click on its check mark.

Text Boxes *Text boxes* provide spaces where you can type information into the computer—such as a percentage, an absolute amount, or the name of a particular document or folder. After you type the information into the text box, striking the Tab key generally moves the cursor forward to the next section of the dialog box.

List Boxes Several kinds of list boxes appear in Figure SW 1-18. Like a pull-down menu, a *simple list box* presents a list of options, allowing you to choose any one. Often, the list exceeds the size of its window, and a vertical scroll bar or similar mechanism allows you to see parts of the list currently off the screen.

To save even more space, a dialog box sometimes includes a *drop-down list box,* which displays only one selection initially, allowing you to see the others by activating the drop-down arrow to the right. A *spin box* lets you tweak a value up or down by clicking on an up-arrow or down-arrow icon.

Message Boxes A *message box* pops on the screen when the program needs to provide status information or when a potential problem is unfolding. You may see such a message when you attempt to execute an improper command or try to take an action for which a mistake could have grave consequences. In any type of message box, the user must acknowledge the message by choosing one of the supplied command buttons—Retry or Cancel in Figure SW 1-18—before proceeding further.

ONLINE HELP

Most people run into problems or think of questions as they work with a software package. To provide help without forcing you to leave your computer screen, many GUIs have an *online help feature.* Programs employ a variety of tools to provide online assistance, as Figure SW 1-19 and the following paragraphs explain.

Help Table of Contents A highly useful online support tool is a help table of contents (TOC), which works similar to the TOCs found in many books. The TOC shown in Figure SW 1-19 features a selection of book icons related to help files on some general topics. Selecting a book opens the associated information to reveal either another set of books or a set of question marks. The question marks represent the specific information that you ultimately want; they link you to screenfuls of facts about topics. Some such screens contain hyperlinks to further levels of support information. An online help TOC is useful when browsing through a list of topics to trigger insights.

Indexing Many help routines sport an *indexing feature* that lets you choose from a lengthy list of help topics. The topics are displayed in a list box, and you can scroll to

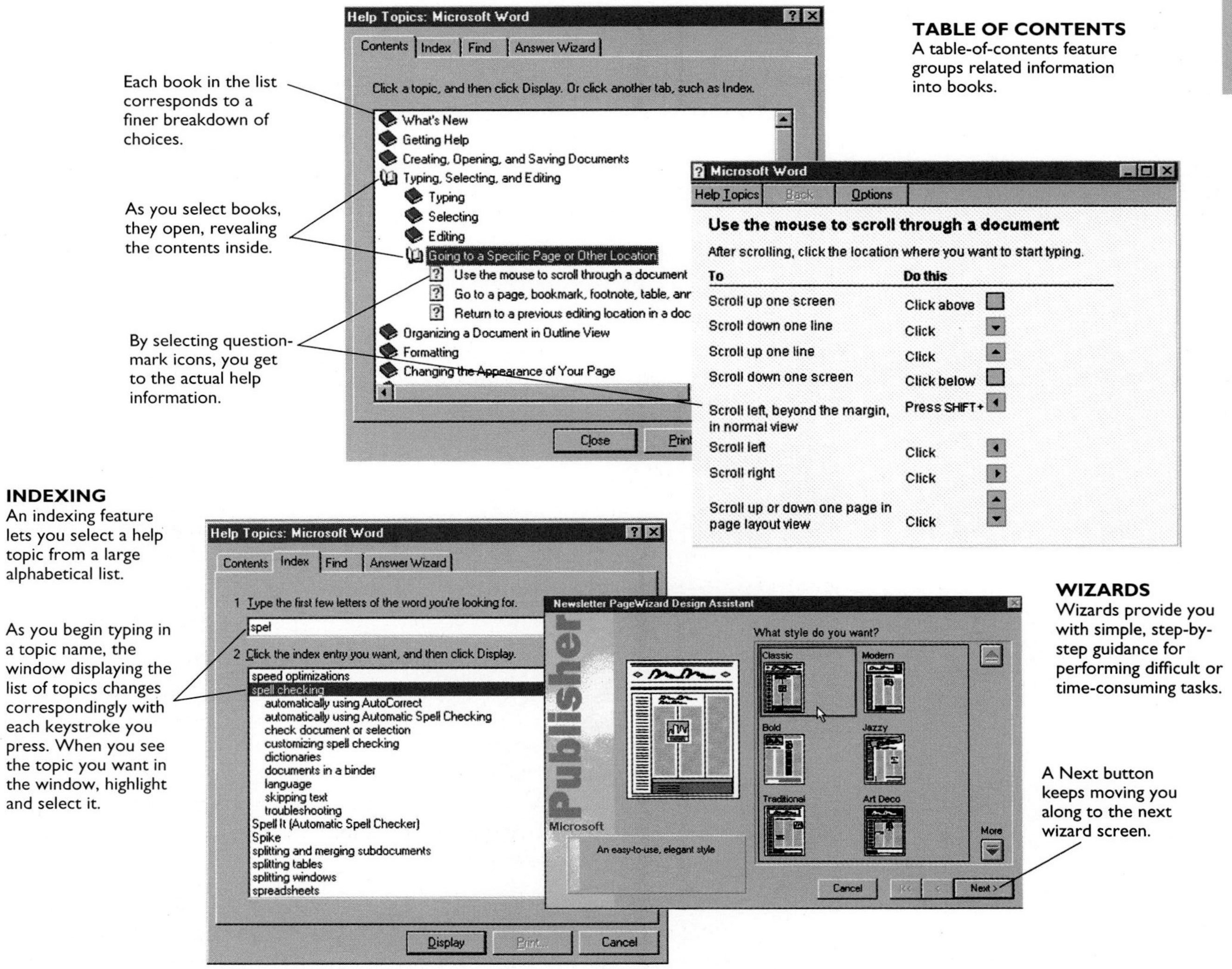

TABLE OF CONTENTS
A table-of-contents feature groups related information into books.

Each book in the list corresponds to a finer breakdown of choices.

As you select books, they open, revealing the contents inside.

By selecting question-mark icons, you get to the actual help information.

INDEXING
An indexing feature lets you select a help topic from a large alphabetical list.

As you begin typing in a topic name, the window displaying the list of topics changes correspondingly with each keystroke you press. When you see the topic you want in the window, highlight and select it.

WIZARDS
Wizards provide you with simple, step-by-step guidance for performing difficult or time-consuming tasks.

A Next button keeps moving you along to the next wizard screen.

FIGURE SW 1-19
Online help.

the topic you wish to find in the standard fashion. The topic list may be huge, however, and there is a way that lets you search even faster. As illustrated in Figure SW 1-19, you can position the screen cursor in a typing area, and then begin to type in the word you want to look up in the index. As you key in each letter, the list-box display changes accordingly. As soon as the topic you want to look up appears in the display window, you can point to it with the mouse or keyboard and select it.

Wizards Many programs provide automated tools to assist users by quickly performing repetitive or complicated tasks. Different software publishers call these tools **wizards,** *coaches, assistants, tutors, experts, advisors,* or similar names. By any name, such a tool guides you through a step-by-step procedure for completing standard tasks, such as preparing letters, invoices, reports, and the like. They do this either by providing directed tutorials or by performing the difficult phases of a task automatically. Figure SW 1-19 shows how a wizard might help you to prepare a newsletter.

Natural-Language Help Many programs today supply a limited form of *natural-language help* to users—that is, help in which you type in a question and the software package tries to recognize the topic on which assistance is required. For instance, in Microsoft Office 97, clicking on the question-mark icon that's located on the standard toolbar makes a text box pop up for you to type in a query. Office 97 then looks for keywords in the sentence you've entered and tries to provide help on what it believes to be the suggested topic.

Online Tutorials With CDs and the Web, and with hard-disk capacity for the average PC user now in the gigabyte range, many software publishers provide online tutorials with their software packages. These tutorials enable you to do such things as learn how to use the package as well as observe examples and demonstrations.

Virtual Reality

Virtual reality, or *VR,* is a hardware-and-software technology that refers to using computer systems to create illusion (see Figure SW 1-20). Here's an example of

FIGURE SW 1-20

Virtual reality. Such a hardware-and-software technology applies computer power to simulate real events and sensations.

■ **Wizard.** A program feature that assists users in completing tasks. ■ **Virtual reality.** A hardware-and-software technology that allows computer systems to create illusions of real-life experiences.

Interfaces with Feeling

If you think that 3-D user interfaces go about as far as computers can reach to simulate reality, guess again. The latest computer-game and medical-visualization software allows you to actually *feel* the effects of computer-generated events.

Take medical visualization. First-generation computerized virtual reality models enabled medical students to view a human body in three dimensions and practice operating on it with software tools rather than real scalpels. These days, to make such experiences even more realistic, a hypodermic-needle device teaches students to give injections using feedback that approximates the sensation of skin popping back as the needle pierces it. Another example: As a student practices removing a liver, a software-hardware interface can detect and feed back to the student the collision of scalpel with organ.

Many computer games now feature similar interfaces. A special joystick lets users feel the bumps in simulated roads, the recoils of a piston, or the jar of a crash landing.

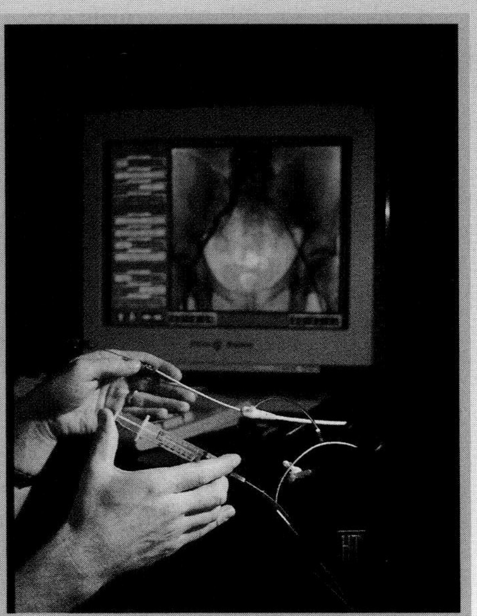

how it works: A VR user with special goggles for viewing an artificial, comic-book world makes a movement with a special glove. As the movement is made, the display in the goggles changes instantly to reflect new information that is presented from the user's point of view.

Although we are still far from the virtual reality that science fiction writers tell us about, many industry experts believe that standard user-and-computer interfaces will someday seem like real-life experiences. Several VR applications are highly visible in the world of today, and new applications are regularly being reported by the press. Below is a small sample.

Architecture Through VR, it is possible to take "tours" of buildings whose foundations are yet to be poured. A computer model of the building is first made in three dimensions. Later, a client taking a computer "tour" on a desktop can move from room to room in the order in which he or she chooses, inspecting the premises close up or far away and from different views. Routines are also available that can show how natural light falls in the building on a sunny or rainy day and how artificial light changes a room. Does the client hate the look and size of the lounge? No problem. With a remodeling software package, it can be reshaped, repainted, relighted, refurnished, and ready for reinspection—in seconds.

Entertainment VR applications have arrived at full force in the entertainment industry, where illusion is the principal product. In many cities, amusement arcades feature virtual reality games in which players can battle demons on realistic computer-generated landscapes. In many cases, the VR participant must don special goggles, which project computer-generated images directly toward the eye, and wear gloves with built-in sensors, which change the goggle images when the hands are moved. Feature-length movies and computer-game software are also increasingly employing virtual-reality technology.

Investments Investment analysts apply VR techniques to the study of securities. One of the problems inherent in conventional analysis is the complexities of tracking a group of securities relative to changes in the market as a whole. A virtual reality system can color-code stocks belonging to a certain group—say, technology stocks. A 3-D animation of general stock movements over time can help the analyst to clearly visualize how a particular group behaves within the overall market.

Other Applications In addition to the applications already mentioned, press reports regularly highlight a variety of other VR applications. For instance, medical students use VR techniques to simulate injections and medical operations before needles or scalpels ever touch patients (see User Solution SW 1-1). In sports, researchers using VR techniques can model subtle body movements in order to figure out what makes certain athletes fantastically successful.

Summary and Key Terms

In Chapter SW 1 we explore several fundamental properties of computer software.

About Software The computer world generally divides software into two distinct classes: **systems software** and **applications software.** Within each of these classes are several subdivisions.

Software publishers often bundle together programs such as word processors and spreadsheets along with other software into **software suites.** An *integrated software program* compresses the functionality of a suite into a smaller package. The success of bundling has supported **document-centered computing.**

Many of the applications and systems software products on the market today are examples of **proprietary software.** Individual users purchase licenses authorizing them to use such software, while businesses often seek **site licenses.** Some software is also available as **shareware.**The shareware creator normally does not charge for use of the software, but you will have to pay for any support. Still another class of software is **freeware—**programs that are available without charges of any sort.

The User Interface The manner in which a program makes its resources available to users is known as its **user interface.**

The three most widely used user interfaces are command syntax, shortcut keystrokes, and graphical user interfaces. Command **syntax** relies on users typing in, at some sort of software **prompt,** statements that conform to strict grammatical rules and structure. **Shortcut keystrokes,** which represent commands, are designed to be both easier and faster than using a command syntax. **Graphical user interfaces (GUIs)** employ such screen-oriented recall devices as pull-down menus, windows, and icons to make it easy for users to execute commands.

Elements of a Graphical User Interface Most users today work with programs that have graphical user interfaces.

Menus are often one of several principal types. At the top of many GUI screens or windows is a **menu bar** showing the governing command set. **Pull-down menus** unfurl on the screen when the user makes a choice from a menu bar or another pull-down menu. Menus also exist in the form of a set of **icons;** names such as **toolbars,** command buttons, and **hyperlinks** refer to *icon menus.* Additionally, tab menus, **palettes,** and dialog boxes are other types of menus.

The staple of the GUI is the **window—**a box of related information that is overlaid on the display screen. A *title bar* at the top of a window normally names the document or program displayed inside. Windows can be customized onscreen to meet applications needs in a variety of ways. The mouse pointer is **context sensitive** and changes with respect to the operation the user is performing onscreen. When the information available to a window cannot fit on the screen at one time, **scroll bars** can be used to get to other parts of it.

Dialog boxes are special windows that prompt the user for further information. They employ a variety of tools, including radio buttons, check boxes, text boxes, list boxes, message boxes, and the like.

Many GUIs have an *online help* feature to make it easy for users to get help when they are sitting at their display screens. Some examples of online help are a table-of-contents feature, an indexing feature, **wizards,** a natural-language help feature, and tutorials.

Virtual Reality **Virtual reality,** or *VR,* is a hardware-and-software technology through which computer systems create illusions of real-life experiences.

1. Fill in the blanks:
   a. Software that doesn't cost anything—either to use or for support—is referred to as __________.
   b. A group of related, fully featured programs bundled together for sale is called a(n) __________.
   c. Software that you must purchase a license to use is known as __________.
   d. The manner in which a program package makes its resources available to the user is known as its __________.
   e. The grammatical rules that govern a computer language are called the language's __________.
   f. A(n)__________ lets you control the computer by entering keystrokes such as Alt + F1 or Del instead of typing in a command.
   g. GUI is an acronym for __________.
   h. A command __________ is a horizontal line that groups related commands.
2. Describe the purpose of each of the following GUI elements:
   a. Ghosted type
   b. Imagemap
   c. Command buttons
   d. Ellipses
   e. Spin box
   f. Checkmark
3. In your own words, define the following terms:
   a. Hypertext
   b. Context sensitive
   c. Toolbar
   d. Palette
   e. Site license
   f. Virtual reality
4. Match each term with the description that fits best.
   a. Menu bar
   b. Pull-down menu
   c. Cascading
   d. Tiling
   e. Toolbar
   f. Scroll bar
   g. Radio button
   h. Text box

   _____ A method of arranging windows side by side
   _____ A dialog-box feature that provides a set of options preceded by round symbols, only one of which can be darkened
   _____ A dialog box that requires you type some input
   _____ A horizontally arranged menu that appears at the top of the screen
   _____ A method of arranging windows so that they overlap
   _____ A feature that lets you move offscreen information into a window
   _____ A type of icon menu
   _____ A menu that drops vertically below a choice made on a menu bar
5. Describe and compare the three basic ways in which software designers enable users to enter commands into computers.
6. In your own words, define the following terms and describe their similarities and differences:
   a. Software suite
   b. Software minisuite
   c. Integrated software package
   d. Document-centered computing

7. Describe in a sentence each of the following types of online help:
   a. Table of contents
   b. Indexes
   c. Wizards
   d. Natural-language help
   e. Tutorials
8. Match the terms with the pictured dialog-box elements.

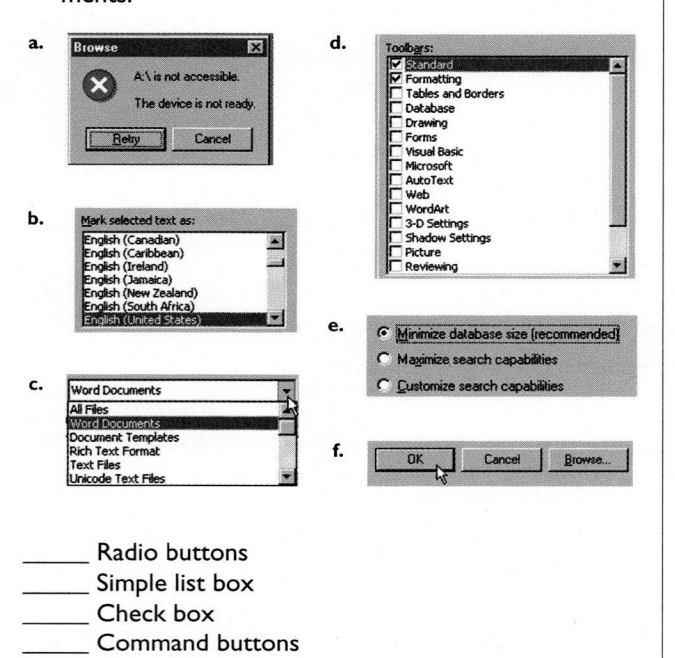

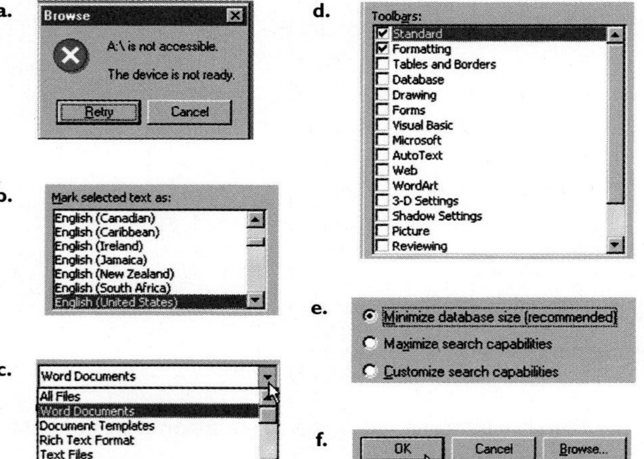

_____ Radio buttons
_____ Simple list box
_____ Check box
_____ Command buttons
_____ Message box
_____ Drop-down list box

9. Match the phrases with the pictured GUI elements.

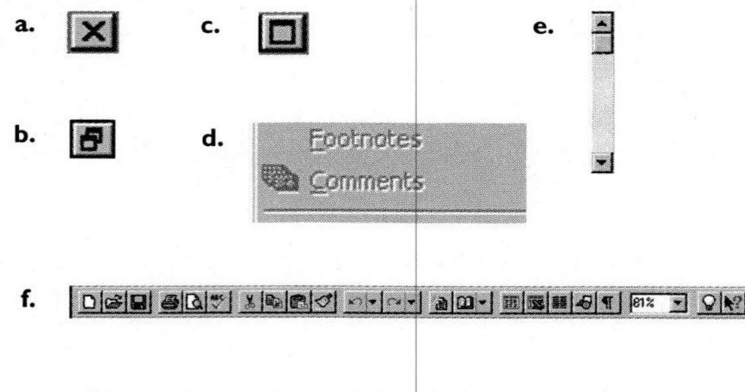

_____ Options aren't available in the current context
_____ A toolbar
_____ Restores the previous screen size
_____ Closes an application
_____ Lets you see offscreen information
_____ Expands an application to fill the entire screen

10. Explain the differences, if any, between the following pairs:
    a. Shareware and freeware
    b. Pull-down menu and menu bar
    c. Radio button and option button
    d. Maximizing and minimizing a window
    e. Scroll arrow and scroll box
    f. Simple list box and drop-down list box
    g. Ellipses and arrow (on a pull-down menu)
    h. Access key and shortcut keystroke

PROJECTS

1. Microsoft Office Microsoft Office is by far the best-selling software suite, with over an 80 percent share of the office-suite market. For the version of Microsoft Office at your school, answer the following questions:

a. What version number does your school run?
b. What are the names and functions of the main-component programs in the suite?
c. How many toolbars can you summon through the Toolbars command? What are the names and purposes of these toolbars? Where, exactly, is the Toolbars command located? How do you get rid of one toolbar and summon another?
d. Identify the name and purpose of each toolbar button pictured below. Also, identify the toolbar on which each button appears.

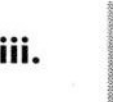
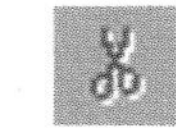

2. Office-Suite Comparison The three major fully featured office-software suites in the marketplace are Microsoft Office Professional, Lotus SmartSuite, and Corel Office Professional.

a. Pick any one of these suites. Identify the main program components in the suite and the principal function of each component.
b. The three products identified in this project may also exist in *standard editions,* or minisuites. Does a standard edition exist for the fully featured product, or *professional edition,* that you have chosen? If it does, state how it differs from the professional edition of the same program.

3. Software Licenses Virtually every proprietary software package that you buy in a store includes a usage license tucked inside the shrink-wrapped box. For this project, your instructor might decide to distribute a typical license to everyone in the class or ask you to find a license on your own. In either case, answer the following questions about the sample license:

a. How does the license state the passage that prohibits you from copying the software and distributing it to others?
b. How does the license state the passage that prohibits you from renting the software?
c. Does the license allow you to copy the software onto both a desktop computer and a portable computer? If so, where does it say so?
d. Suppose that you don't like the software and want to sell it for half price to a friend (removing it from your own computer in the process). Does the license prohibit such a sale?

4. Shareware and Freeware Find the names of at least five products that are either shareware or freeware. For each product, write down the following:

a. The name of the product and the publisher
b. The program's intended application
c. For shareware, the suggested registration fee

(Hint: For this project, you may wish to search the Internet for any of the many sites that offer shareware and freeware for downloading. If you are using a search engine, type "Shareware" or "Freeware" into the text box provided for the search string.)

5. Online Help Choose any current applications program—such as a word processor or a spreadsheet—and research its online help feature. For the package you have chosen, report the following characteristics to your class:

a. The types of online help available within the program
b. How you would access each of the types of help described in part a
c. The names and descriptions of the wizards available within the program

6. Online Documentation Increasingly, software publishers are putting the documentation telling how their products work—documentation such as tutorials and reference manuals—on the installation CD-ROMs that come with those products. When you install the programs, you can then reference this documentation online. While this practice saves the cost of printing hard-copy documentation and supports online searches, many users have objected. Some feel that online help cannot effectively replace a well-written manual for learning about and using a software package.

For this project, list the advantages and disadvantages of online documentation relative to hard-copy documentation from your own perspective as a user. What kind of documentation is likely to provide the most valuable help to you in learning or using a software package?

7. Command Syntax Many long-time computer professionals who have become familiar with command syntax complain that GUIs interfere with their work and slow down the computer. Do you feel any sympathy for this position, or do you feel that these people just don't like change? Defend your position in a paragraph or two.

8. Properties of Good User Interfaces Effective user interfaces should be transparent, attractive, forgiving, unburdensome, and customizable. *Transparent* interfaces make software function in a way that seems natural to users. *Attractive* interfaces inspire more use than ugly ones. *Forgiving* interfaces help users to recover easily from mistakes. *Unburdensome* interfaces make the software accommodate users rather than users compensating for the program's quirks. *Customizable* interfaces allow users to tweak settings to fit personal work habits. For this project, choose a suite product—such as Microsoft Office Professional or Lotus SmartSuite—and provide one example of a well-designed feature for each of the five properties.

9. Social Interfaces Much research has focused on creating social interfaces within the past few years. The interest in social interfaces is spurred by the realization that even today's popular GUIs can take a long time to master and by the recent emergence of techniques for three-dimensional desktop graphics. For this project, choose a program with a social interface and write a paper two or three pages long about it. Make sure you cover the following points:

a. The name of the interface and/or the environment in which it operates
b. The name of the company owning the interface
c. The principal tactic for simulating something from everyday life

(Hint: Many World Wide Web sites employ social interfaces. You many wish to base this project on one of those sites.)

10. Virtual Reality Virtual reality elements are becoming increasingly common in applications environments. The chapter text mentioned several such environments—architecture, entertainment, investments, medicine, and sports. For this project, find a specific application of virtual reality and report to the class about it. In addition to naming the product and the company that created it, explain what type of virtual world or space the product creates, who makes up the audience for the product, how users gain access to the product, and whether or not the product requires any special hardware.

window

The Electronic Canvas

A PEEK AT THE LEADING EDGE IN COMPUTER ART

Probably no field exemplifies the rapid advances made in computer output over the years more vividly than the field of computer art. Early computer artists were scientists who worked on supercomputers. As demand grew for computer-generated art in such fields as advertising, publishing, and movie-making, specialized software for non-computer professionals working on PCs began to emerge. The field of computer art is relatively young, and one can only guess what the leading edge will look like ten years from now.

1 • **Judy York—whose *Renascence* appears here—was a traditional illustrator and oil painter before discovering the computer.**

2 • Greg Hermanovic of Side Effects Software uses a lens flare as the central element in *Forest*.

3 • Bruce Drachmeister, a Denver-area draftsman by profession, is entirely self-taught on the computer and learned mostly by trial and error and reading computer books.

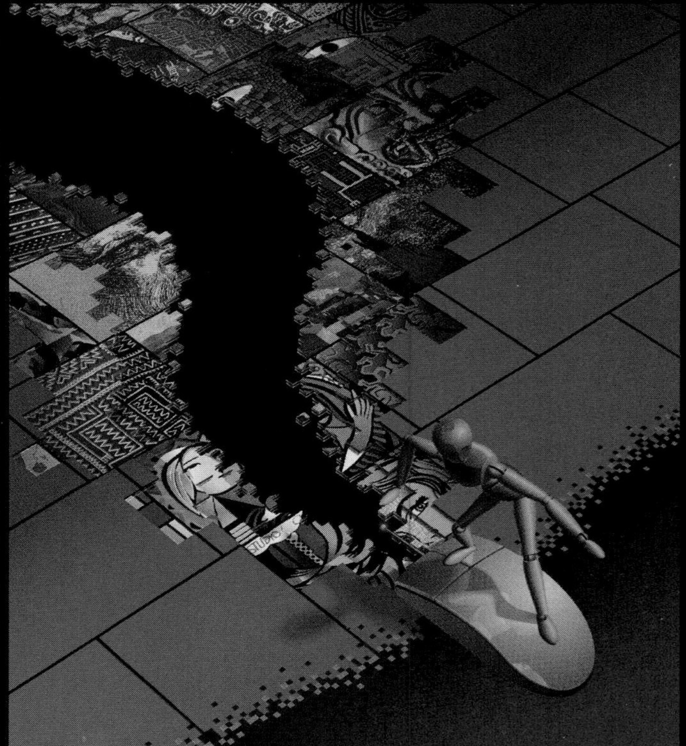

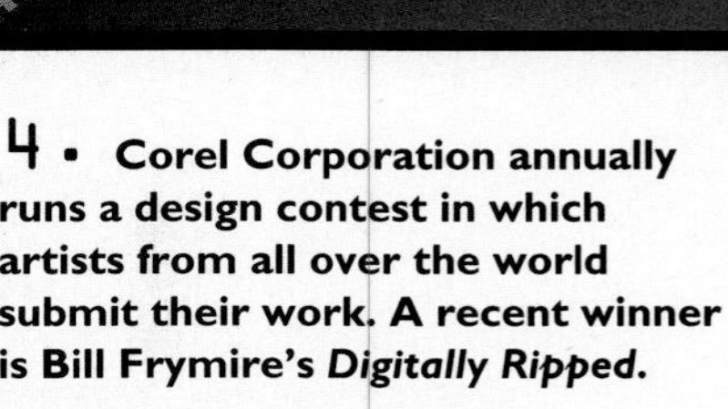

4 • Corel Corporation annually runs a design contest in which artists from all over the world submit their work. A recent winner is Bill Frymire's *Digitally Ripped*.

5–6 • The images of Dan Younger, an assistant professor of art at the University of Missouri–St. Louis, evoke thoughts of the 1950s and the sci-fi craze. Represented here are *Look There* and *Overflight*.

5

6

7–8 • Steven Lyons, a California-based artist, creates distinctive images, many of which are commissioned by high-tech companies. Among his client list are such computer-industry hevayweights as Motorola and Adobe.

7

8

9 • Corinne Whitaker—who began working with computers after a successful career as a photographer—has achieved national acclaim for her abstract art.

10 • Charles Homuth's *Impending Disaster,* a first-place winner in a recent Intergraph art contest, features two wedding bands around a glass.

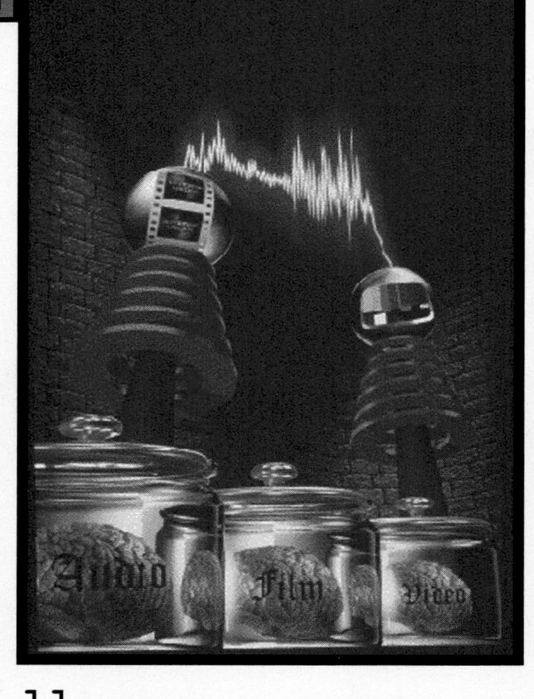

11 • This image by Christopher Thomas, produced on a Silicon Graphics workstation, evokes a Frankensteinian aura.

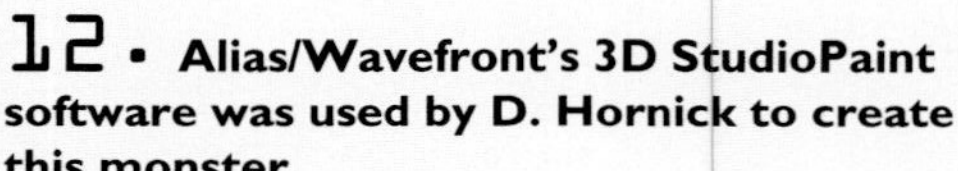

12 • Alias/Wavefront's 3D StudioPaint software was used by D. Hornick to create this monster.

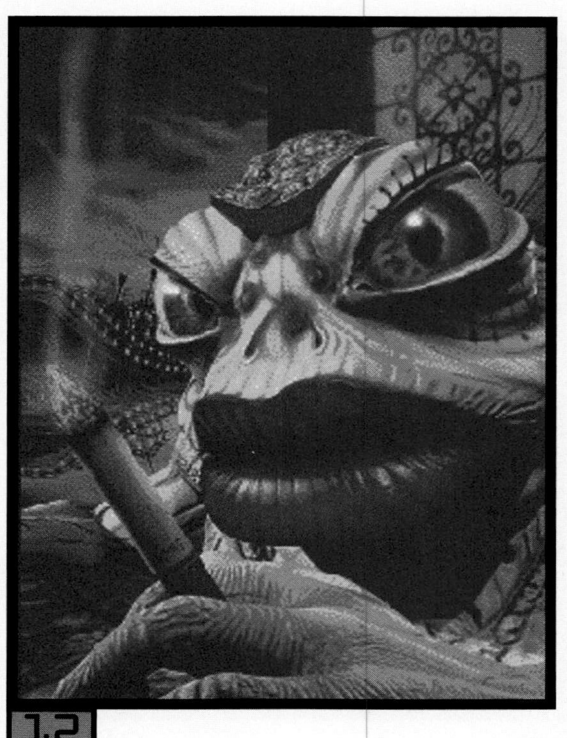

SW 2

Systems Software

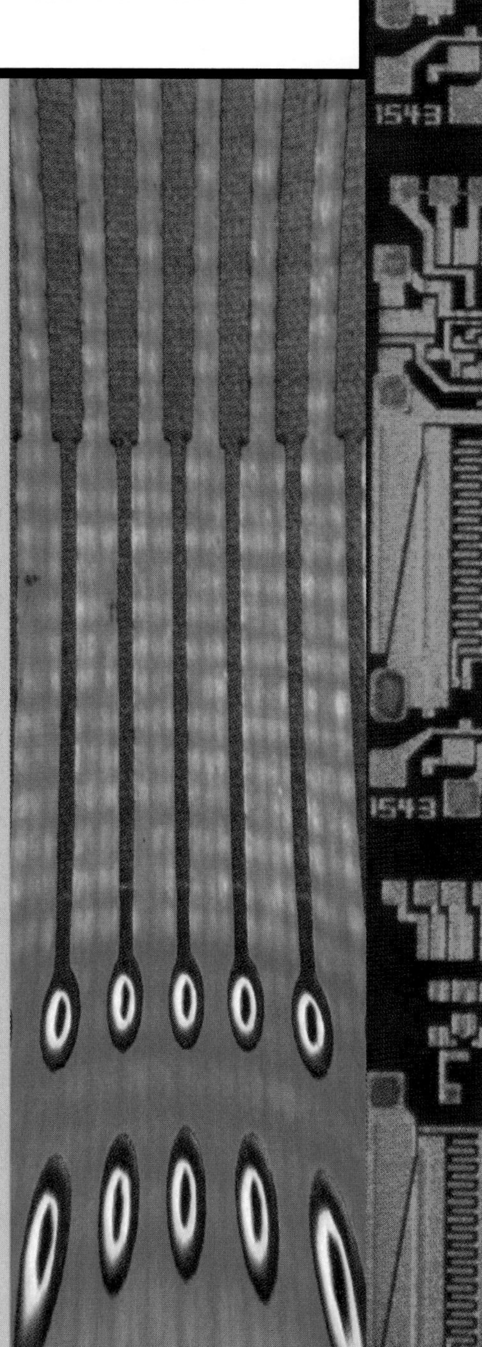

Outline

Learning Objectives

After completing this chapter, you will be able to:

1. Describe the types of systems software.
2. Explain the activities of an operating system and cite some similarities and differences between operating systems.
3. List several ways in which computer systems interleave operations to enhance processing efficiency.
4. Name today's most widely used operating systems and highlight the strengths and weaknesses of each.
5. Detail the role of a utility program and outline several duties that these programs perform.
6. Explain the role of a language translator and describe several types of language translators.

Overview

Systems software consists of programs that coordinate the various parts of the computer system to make it run efficiently. These programs perform such tasks as translating your commands into a form that the computer can understand, managing your program and data files, and getting your applications software and hardware to work together, among many other things.

Most users aren't aware of all the tasks that systems software is doing for them. On a microcomputer system, for example, issuing a Save command to store a document on disk requires that systems software looks for adequate space on the disk, writes the document onto this space, and updates the disk's directory so both you and the computer system can find the document again. As users run their systems to communicate with databases on remote mainframes, they may not realize that systems software busily checks the validity of their ID numbers or passwords and translates their database commands into machine language.

Systems software is available in three basic types: operating systems, utility programs, and language translators. In this chapter, we'll first look closely at the *operating system,* which is the main piece of systems software. Here we'll discuss what operating systems do and examine various similarities and differences among them. Next, we will cover *utility programs,* or utilities. Utilities typically perform support functions for the operating system, or less-critical types of functions, such as allowing you to install new types of hardware or to recover inadvertently erased disk files. Finally, we look at *language translators.* Such programs translate sets of instructions coded in BASIC, COBOL, or any other programming language into machine language.

The Operating System

A computer's **operating system** is the main collection of programs that manage its activities. The primary chores of an operating system are management and control. The operating system ensures that all actions requested by a user are valid and processed in an orderly fashion. It also manages the computer system's resources to perform those operations with efficiency and consistency.

Most tasks that you do on the computer involve some work by the operating system. For example, when you want to finish the letter you started typing yesterday, the operating system fetches the appropriate word processing program and document from disk and loads them into memory. It also prepares the CPU and printer. As the word processor carries out its processing tasks, the operating system acts as a watchdog, monitoring every step of the application to make sure it doesn't perform illegal operations that would corrupt other computer-system resources. Typically, the operating system does all of these things and much more as you issue commands. When you finish, it saves your updated document onto disk and, often, logs you off the computer system, too.

In effect, the operating system is the go-between that meshes you and your applications needs with the computer's hardware (see Figure SW 2-1). Because of its central role in coordinating all of the computer's work, many consider the operating system to be the most critical piece of software in the computer system. Without an operating system, no other program can run.

■ **Systems software.** Computer programs that enable application programs to run on a given set of hardware. ■ **Operating system.** The main collection of systems software that enables the computer system to manage the resources under its control.

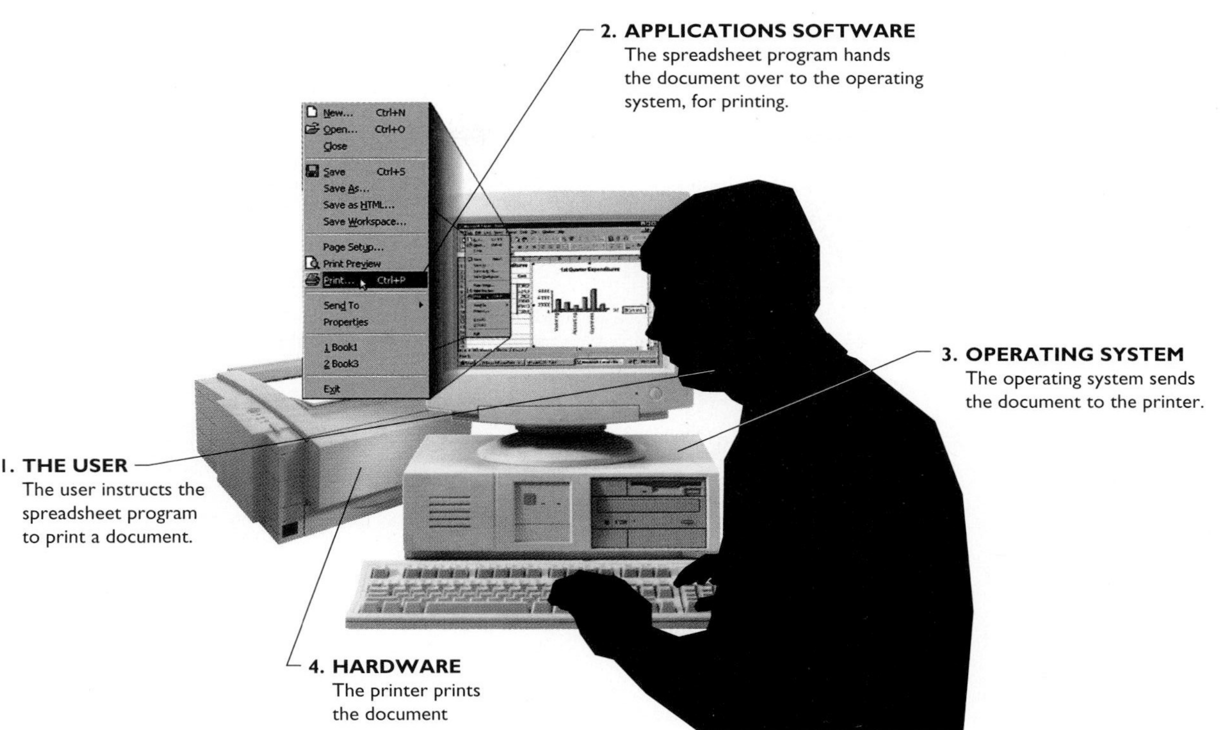

2. APPLICATIONS SOFTWARE
The spreadsheet program hands the document over to the operating system, for printing.
3. OPERATING SYSTEM
The operating system sends the document to the printer.
1. THE USER
The user instructs the spreadsheet program to print a document.
4. HARDWARE
The printer prints the document

The gateway role of the operating system. The operating system is the gateway between user applications and the computer system's hardware.

DIFFERENCES AMONG OPERATING SYSTEMS

The marketplace offers a wide selection of operating systems (see Figure SW 2-2). Because the needs of people differ, there are often major differences among operating systems. As figure SW 2-2 hints, less clear-cut differences also distinguish these products.

A major distinction between operating systems is whether they meet personal or network-administration needs. About a decade or so ago, when PCs were far less powerful than today's machines, most operating systems accommodated either single users or multiple users, not both. Single-user products such as MS-DOS served people working alone on their PCs in their homes or on company desks. Multiple-user products such as Unix and IBM's MVS—now known as OS/390—served those working on larger computer systems, who needed links to shared resources and other users. This product distinction still persists, but it is breaking down around the edges. Many operating systems designed principally for single users can also control small networks, and some versions of operating systems intended mainly for network applications can also meet needs at the desktop (workstation) level.

FUNCTIONS OF AN OPERATING SYSTEM

Now that you have a general idea of what operating systems do and what some of the differences among them are, we can discuss their properties in greater detail. As we examine these properties, keep in mind that not all of them will apply to the operating system on your own computer.

Interacting with Users One of the principal roles of *every* operating system, as Figure SW 2-1 suggests, is to translate user intentions into a form the computer understands. In the other direction, it translates any feedback from the hardware—such as a signal that the printer has run out of paper or the CPU is busy with a processing task—into a form the user understands. In the last chapter we saw that there were several ways that users can command a computer to take an action. Two of these—*typing* instructions that conform to a command syntax and *selecting* instructions from

FIGURE SW 2-2

Some popular operating systems. Operating systems can differ substantially with respect to ease of use, speed, features, portability, and cost. Each operating system is targeted to one or more specific types of computers.

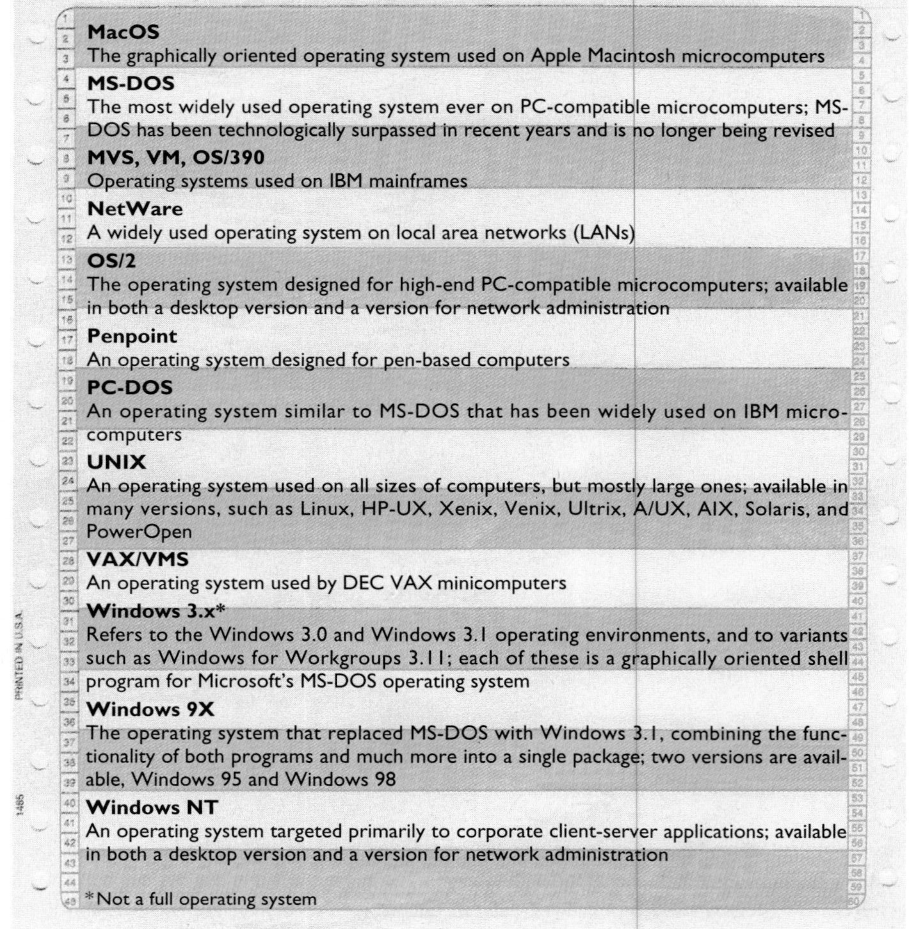

MacOS
The graphically oriented operating system used on Apple Macintosh microcomputers

MS-DOS
The most widely used operating system ever on PC-compatible microcomputers; MS-DOS has been technologically surpassed in recent years and is no longer being revised

MVS, VM, OS/390
Operating systems used on IBM mainframes

NetWare
A widely used operating system on local area networks (LANs)

OS/2
The operating system designed for high-end PC-compatible microcomputers; available in both a desktop version and a version for network administration

Penpoint
An operating system designed for pen-based computers

PC-DOS
An operating system similar to MS-DOS that has been widely used on IBM microcomputers

UNIX
An operating system used on all sizes of computers, but mostly large ones; available in many versions, such as Linux, HP-UX, Xenix, Venix, Ultrix, A/UX, AIX, Solaris, and PowerOpen

VAX/VMS
An operating system used by DEC VAX minicomputers

Windows 3.x*
Refers to the Windows 3.0 and Windows 3.1 operating environments, and to variants such as Windows for Workgroups 3.11; each of these is a graphically oriented shell program for Microsoft's MS-DOS operating system

Windows 9X
The operating system that replaced MS-DOS with Windows 3.1, combining the functionality of both programs and much more into a single package; two versions are available, Windows 95 and Windows 98

Windows NT
An operating system targeted primarily to corporate client-server applications; available in both a desktop version and a version for network administration

*Not a full operating system

a graphical user interface—are the ways that most people will interact with operating systems.

As soon as the user enters keystrokes or clicks a mouse, the operating system summons a translator to convert what the user wants done into machine language. It then passes these digitally coded instructions to the CPU for processing. In the absence of instructions from the user, the operating system makes some standard assumptions about appropriate activities. Such assumptions are called **defaults,** and you can often override any of them if you wish. For instance, you can change the standard default of one printed copy of a document by asking for two, or you can change the way characters and graphics appear on the screen by asking for a higher or lower resolution.

To work effectively with your operating system, you must observe certain conventions. For instance, every operating system sets rules for naming files (or documents) and the directories (or folders) that group them together. Also, many operating systems supplement filenames with sets of characters called **file extensions** that carry special meanings. Usually, a file extension identifies the type of file in use, say, a Word document or a specific type of graphics file. Figure SW 2-3 shows how filenames and extensions work on many PC-compatible systems.

A systematic naming of files and extensions is useful when working with computers. For instance, by naming the 25 chapters of a book on your hard disk Chap01, Chap02, and so on, to Chap25, a single command such as

---

■ **Default.** The assumption that a computer program makes when the user indicates no specific choice. ■ **File extension.** A group of characters appended to the main part of a filename to qualify it or to identify a specific type of file.

ABOUT FILENAMES
Every operating system has its own rules for naming files and adding extensions.

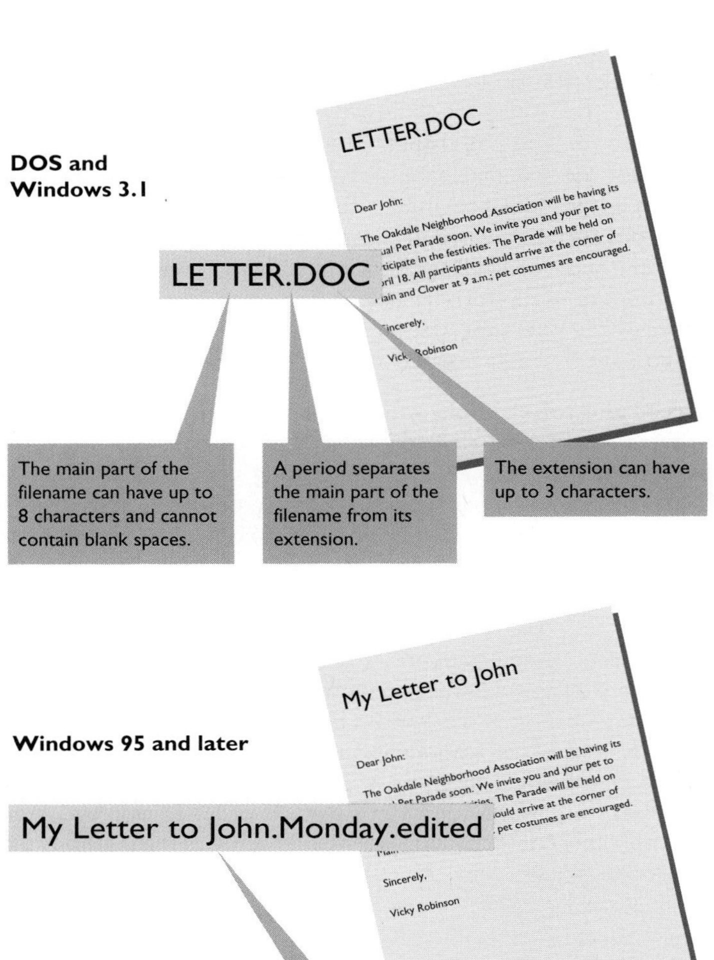
DOS and Windows 3.1
LETTER.DOC
LETTER.DOC
Dear John:
Sincerely,
The main part of the filename can have up to 8 characters and cannot contain blank spaces.
A period separates the main part of the filename from its extension.
The extension can have up to 3 characters.
Windows 95 and later
My Letter to John
My Letter to John.Monday.edited
Dear John:
Sincerely,
Vicky Robinson
Filenames can have up to 255 characters, including blank spaces and multiple extensions.

WIDELY USED EXTENSIONS			
DOCUMENTS			
.doc	.txt	.htm	.html
PROGRAMS			
.bat	.com	.exe	
GRAPHICS			
.bmp	.pict	.jpg	.eps
.gif	.png	.cdr	.pcx
AUDIO			
.wav	.au		
VIDEO			
.mpg	.mov	.avi	
COMPRESSED FILES			
.arc	.arj	.bin	.zip
.lhz	.pak	.seq	.sit

FIGURE SW 2-3
Filenames and extensions.

```
COPY Chap* A:
```

would allow you to transfer the entire book manuscript from hard disk to diskette. Similarly, a command such as

```
COPY *.DOC A:
```

would transfer between the same two disks all files with DOC extensions. Many operating systems allow you to specify **wildcard characters** like the asterisk (*) in the two examples to signify that a command should apply to filenames with any characters in the same space.

Making Resources Available When you first turn on power to the computer system, the operating system **boots** up or is *bootstrapped.*

During the booting procedure, parts of the operating system are loaded into memory. Before control is passed to the user, the operating system determines what hardware devices are online, makes sure that its own files tell it how to deal with those devices, and reads an opening batch of directives. These directives—which the user

■ **Wildcard character.** A character that substitutes for other characters in a filename. ■ **Boot.** The process of loading the operating system into the computer system's RAM.

can customize to his or her tastes—assign chores for the operating system to carry out before the current user session begins; for instance, checking for computer viruses.

As a session begins and you start to request programs and data, the operating system retrieves them from disk and loads them into RAM as needed. Once the operating system activates an applications program, it relinquishes some control to that program. While a program such as a word processor or spreadsheet might accept keystrokes from users or conduct a spelling check on its own, however, it generally leaves the operating system to ensure proper use of storage and availability of hardware. In managing storage, the operating system protects memory so that an error in a program will not corrupt vital data created in other programs.

Scheduling Resources and Jobs Along with assigning system resources to user jobs, the operating system performs a closely related process: scheduling those resources and jobs. Scheduling routines in the operating system determine the order in which jobs are processed on hardware devices. An operating system serving multiple users does not necessarily assign jobs on a first-come, first-served basis. Some users may have higher priority than others, the devices needed to process the next job in line may not be free, or other factors may affect the processing sequence.

The operating system also schedules operations throughout the computer system so that different parts work on different portions of the same jobs at the same time. Because input and output devices work much more slowly than the CPU itself, the CPU may complete billions of calculations for several programs while the contents of a single program are being printed or displayed. Using a number of techniques, the operating system juggles the computer's work in order to employ system devices as efficiently as possible. A later section will discuss some of the methods that allow a computer to process a number of jobs at more or less the same time. These procedures—such as multitasking and multiprogramming—are known collectively as *interleaved processing techniques.*

Monitoring Activities Another major function of operating systems is overseeing activities while processing is under way. For instance, the operating system terminates programs that contain errors or exceed their maximum storage allocations. In doing so, it sends an appropriate message to the user or system operator. Similarly, the operating system informs the user of any equipment abnormalities that arise.

Besides apprising users when problems occur, many operating systems also monitor routine computer system performance and report on its status. Users and system administrators need to know information like how much hard-disk space is used up, how fast the hard disk accesses data, and how response time changes as more and more users try to access the same resources. Programs called *performance monitors* keep track of such activities.

Housekeeping One of the most important tasks of the operating system is housekeeping, and one of the most important housekeeping tasks is organizing the hard disk and making users aware of its contents.

To simplify access to hard disks, operating systems commonly organize files hierarchically into **directories.** As Figure SW 2-4 shows, at the top of the hierarchy is a "master" directory called the *root directory.* The root directory contains, among other elements, several lower-level directories, or *subdirectories.* You can organize your operating-system files in one directory, your applications programs in several other directories, and the files you create with those applications programs in still others. As shown in Figure SW 2-4, for instance, you can organize your word-processed files by putting letters and course papers into their own directories. In many

■ **Directory.** A collection of files grouped under a name of its own. Also commonly called a *folder.*

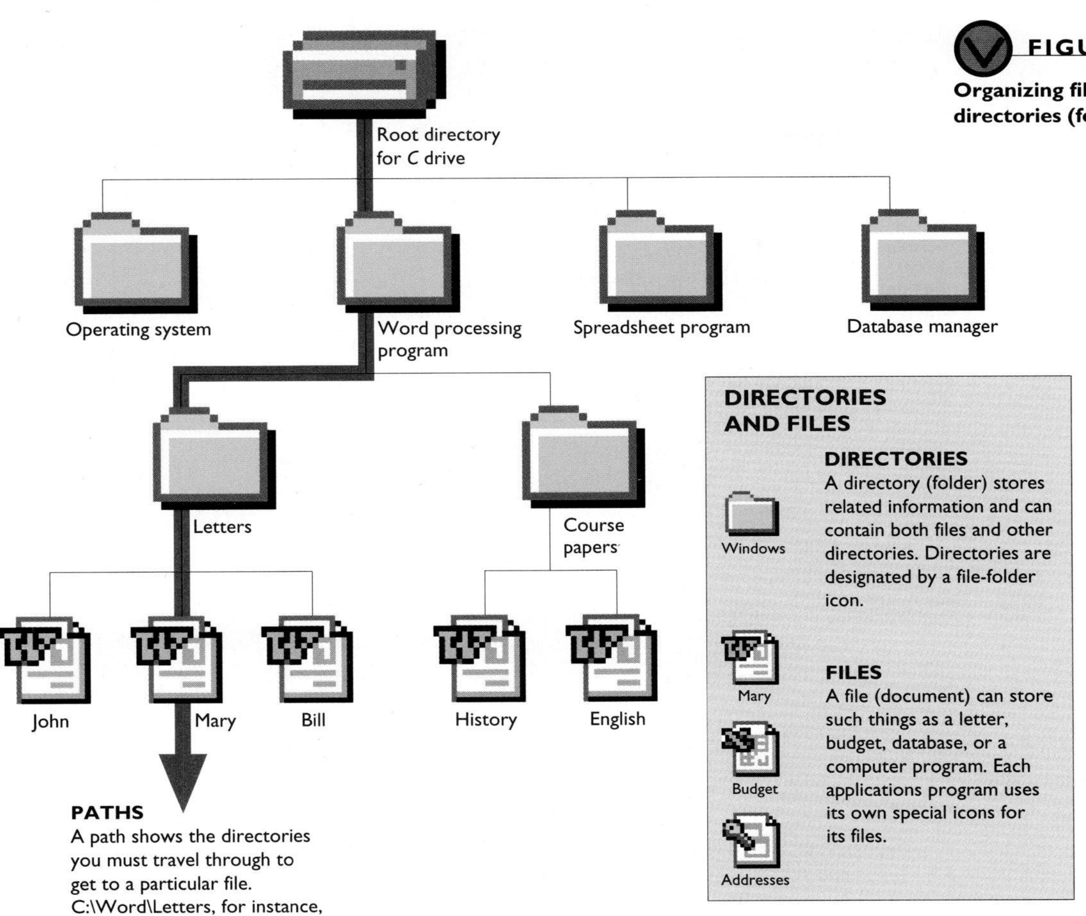
Root directory
for C drive
Operating system
Word processing
program
Spreadsheet program
Database manager
Letters
Course
papers
John
Mary
Bill
History
English
PATHS
A path shows the directories
you must travel through to
get to a particular file.
C:\Word\Letters, for instance,
is the path to Mary's letter.
DIRECTORIES
AND FILES
DIRECTORIES
A directory (folder) stores
related information and can
contain both files and other
directories. Directories are
designated by a file-folder
icon.
Windows
FILES
A file (document) can store
such things as a letter,
budget, database, or a
computer program. Each
applications program uses
its own special icons for
its files.
Mary
Budget
Addresses

FIGURE SW 2-4

Organizing files (documents) into directories (folders).

S W

GUI-oriented operating systems, files and directories are respectively referred to as *documents* and *folders*.

When you want to access a file in any directory, you must specify the **path** through the directories to reach it. For example, as Figure SW 2-4 shows, the path

```
C:\Word\Letters
```

leads through the C, Word, and Letters directories to a file named Mary. The same path can also be used to access the files John and Bill.

Most operating systems with graphical user interfaces provide special programs to display the contents of hard disks and other storage devices (see Figure SW 2-5). Such programs can also provide screen listings that detail the sizes of files and directories, in bytes, along with the dates and times that the files and directories were last accessed—and by whom.

The housekeeping functions of the operating system extend well beyond file and directory status. Many operating systems compile records of user log-on and log-off times, programs' running times, programs that each user has run, and other useful information. In some environments, such records enable organizations to bill users. They also assist with security.

While most operating systems today lay out data in two-dimensional interfaces made up of files and directories, future operating systems will likely present 3-D, virtual-reality organization schemes (see User Solution SW 2-1).

■ **Path.** An ordered list of directories that lead to a particular file or directory.

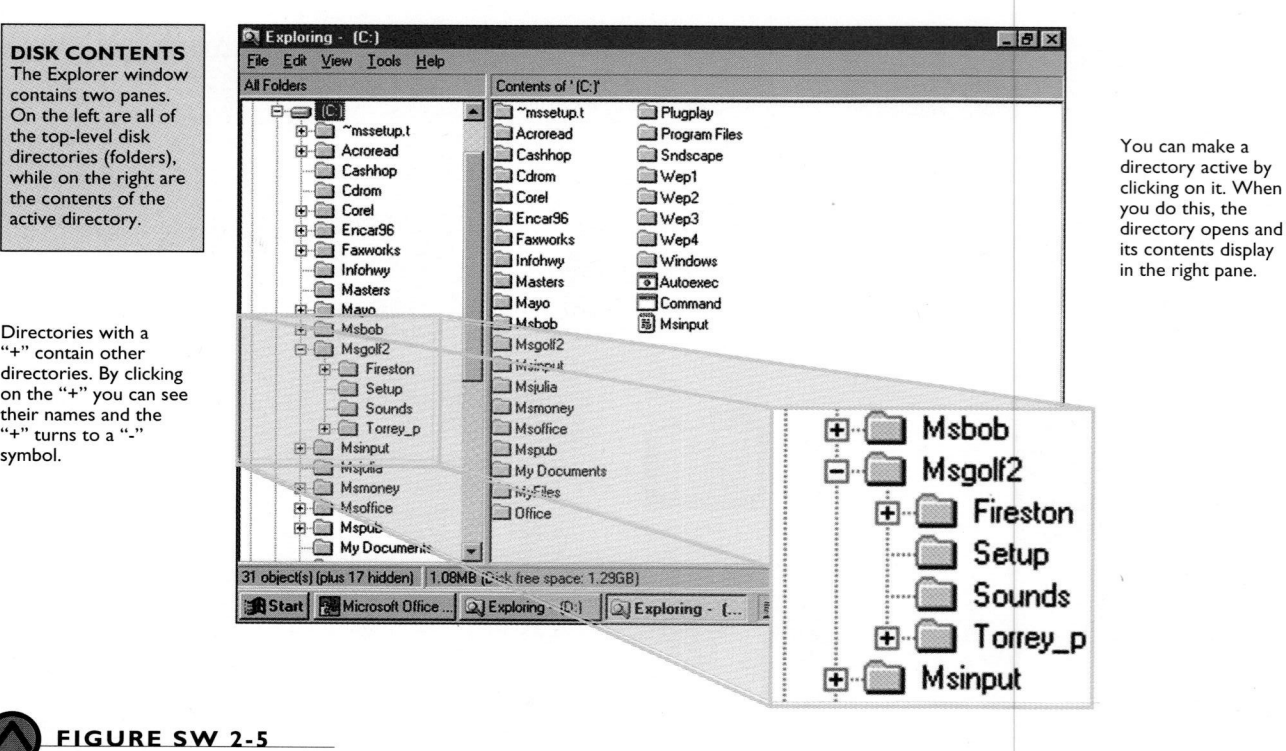

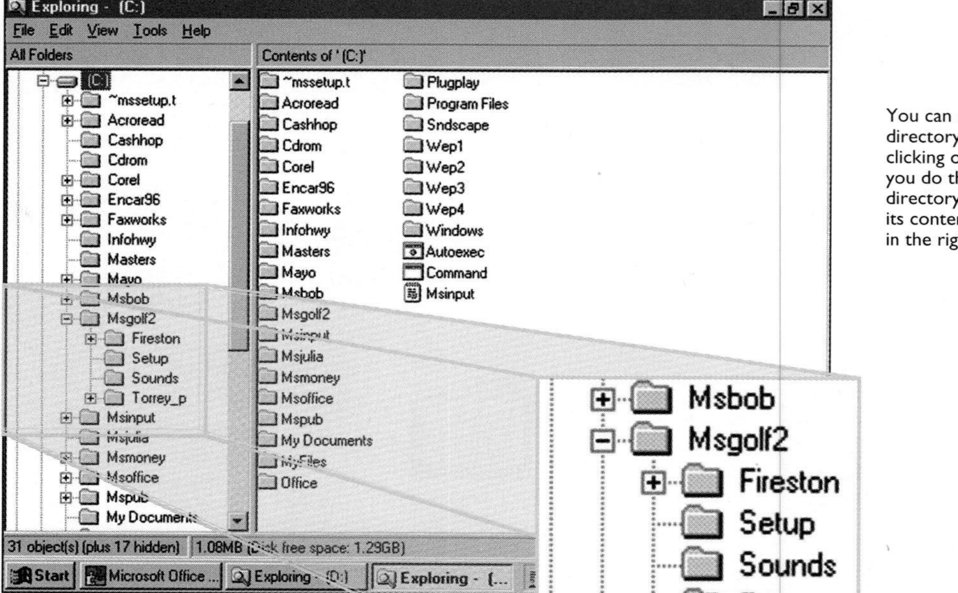

DISK CONTENTS The Explorer window contains two panes. On the left are all of the top-level disk directories (folders), while on the right are the contents of the active directory.

You can make a directory active by clicking on it. When you do this, the directory opens and its contents display in the right pane.

Directories with a "+" contain other directories. By clicking on the "+" you can see their names and the "+" turns to a "-" symbol.

FIGURE SW 2-5

Using Windows Explorer to view disk contents.

Security A computer's operating system can protect it against unauthorized access by collecting system-usage statistics for those in charge of the computer system and by reporting any attempts to breach system security. To further ensure the security of computer systems, many operating systems contain *password* procedures to prevent outsiders from accessing system resources not open to them. Many also provide *encryption* procedures that disguise valuable programs and data. The subject of security is a lenghty one, and we will be considering it at depth in a later chapter.

Other Tasks The tasks already described in this section should give you a pretty good idea of the types of work that operating systems do. In addition, each operating system usually has a variety of standard utility programs available to it that perform such chores as formatting disks, copying files from one medium onto another, sorting records, and so on. A number of third-party, or aftermarket, vendors produce software that performs additional utility functions or improves on the standard functions of an operating system. A later section of this chapter covers utility programs.

INTERLEAVED PROCESSING TECHNIQUES

Computers often take advantage of *interleaved processing techniques* to operate more efficiently. These techniques enable computers to process many programs at almost the same time, so, consequently, they increase system throughput—the number of jobs the computer system can handle in any given period.

Multiprogramming **Multiprogramming,** a term that typically refers to multiuser operating systems, is somewhat similar to the operation of a busy dentist's office. The dentist *concurrently* attends to several patients in different rooms within a given time period. The dentist may pull a tooth in Room 1, move to Room 2 to prepare a cavity for filling, move back to Room 1 to treat the hole left by the pulled

■ **Multiprogramming.** Concurrent execution of two or more programs on a single, multiuser computer.

3-D Comes to System Software

The not-too-distant future should bring 3-D operating system displays to most people's computer screens. While users aren't likely to discard Windows to start at the bottom of a new learning curve anytime soon, natural-looking, 3-D interfaces are already slowly creeping into other areas of systems software.

Take network management. Computer Associates' Unicenter TNG enables computer managers to "fly" in and out of buildings—anywhere in the world—and to zero in on the computers or systems that are giving them problems (see image). IBM offers a similar product, Global Enterprise Manager. With the attention to 3-D among some industry heavyweights, might a 3-D version of Windows show up before long?

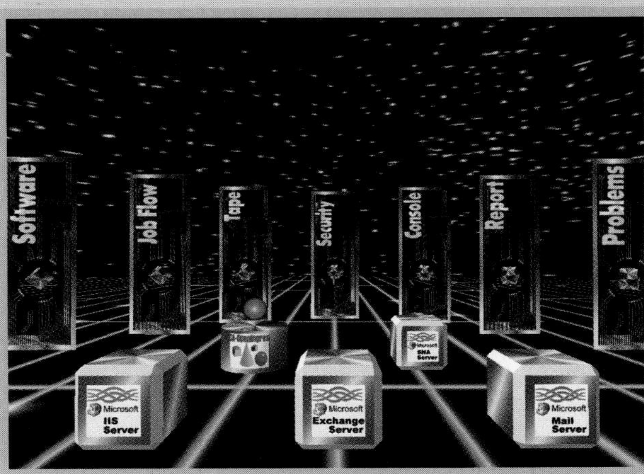

tooth, and so forth. As the dentist moves from patient to patient, assistants carry out minor tasks.

A computer operating system with multiprogramming capabilities can manipulate several applications programs stored in memory at the same time. The CPU, like the dentist, works on only one program at a time. When it reaches a point at which peripheral devices or other elements of the computer system can take over some of the work, the CPU interrupts processing to move on to another program, returning to the first one when the situation allows further processing. While the computer waits for a disk drive to read data on one program, for example, it can perform calculations for another program. The systems software for the disk unit, like a dental assistant, does background work; in this case, it retrieves the data stored on disk.

Multiprogramming speeds processing because computers can perform thousands of computations in the time a disk drive can load a single piece of data. Such disk I/O operations run much more slowly than computations because the computer must interact with an external device to obtain needed data. Also, secondary storage speeds cannot keep pace with CPU speeds.

Multitasking **Multitasking** most commonly refers to a multiprogramming capability on a single-user operating system. It's the ability of an operating system to enable two or more programs or program tasks, from a single user, to execute concurrently on one computer. This feature allows a user to perform such work as editing a file for one program while the computer performs calculations in another program or printing a document while editing it at the same time. Remember, one processor, like one dentist, can attend to only one task at a time. But today's CPUs work so fast that users often perceive two things happening at once.

Users can fully appreciate multitasking when they need continuing access to their computers while performing operations that require exceptionally long processing times. For example, suppose that you want to search through a large employee file for all people between the ages of 25 and 35 with six years of service and some experience with computers. On a relatively small computer with an extremely large employee file, such a search may take several minutes; multitasking allows you to use your computer to perform another task, on the same or a different program, while the search continues in the background.

■ **Multitasking.** A capability of an operating system to execute for a single user two or more programs or program tasks concurrently.

Several types of multitasking are found in practice. *Preemptive multitasking,* or *true multitasking,* works without annoying delays; for instance, you need not wait to type text for a document because another program is being output by the printer. By contrast, *cooperative multitasking* is fraught with delays; one task (say, typing) may have to yield to another task (say, printing) when the two tasks are concurrently active. Preemptive multitasking also allows the operating system to seize control of the computer system to serve the user if an application causes conflicts. This results in fewer system crashes. In cooperative multitasking, one task may freeze the computer system, and the user can regain control only by turning the system off.

The difference between the two types of multitasking described here is a process called *multithreading.* A thread is a set of processing activities smaller than a task; that is, many threads make up a single task. Preemptive multitasking schedules operations thread by thread, making the computer more responsive to the user, whereas cooperative multitasking completes operations only in full tasks.

Time-Sharing **Time-sharing** is an interleaved processing technique that allows a single computer system—usually a mainframe—to support numerous users at separate display terminals. The operating system cycles through all the active programs in the system that need processing and gives each one a small time slice during each cycle.

For example, say that users have loaded 20 programs into the system, which allocates a time slice of 1 second for each one. (Time-sharing systems usually slice processing time in pieces much smaller than this, and all pieces are not necessarily equal.) The computer works on Program 1 for 1 second, then on Program 2 for 1 second, and so forth. When it finishes working on Program 20 for 1 second, it returns to Program 1 for another second, Program 2 for another second, and so on. Thus, if 20 programs run concurrently on the system, each program will get a total of 3 seconds of processing during each minute of actual clock time, or 1 second in every 20-second period. As you can see, in a time-sharing system it is difficult for a single program to dominate the CPU's attention, thereby holding up the processing of shorter programs.

Both time-sharing and multiprogramming work on many programs concurrently by allotting short, uninterrupted time periods to each. They differ in the way they allot time, however. A time-sharing computer spends a fixed amount of time on each program and then goes on to another. A multiprogramming computer works on a program until it encounters a logical stopping point, such as a need to read more data, before going on to another program. Many computers today combine time-sharing and multiprogramming techniques to expedite processing.

Virtual Memory In the early days of computing, users faced numerous problems loading large programs into memory. Often, they had to split programs into pieces so that only small portions of them resided in the limited memory at any one time. In the early 1970s, operating systems responded to this problem by offering a virtual-memory feature. This development permitted users to write extremely long programs, leaving the operating systems to automatically split up and manage them. Today, even personal operating systems like Windows 95 and Windows 98 use virtual memory.

Virtual memory uses disk storage to extend conventional memory, or RAM. It usually works in a sequence like this: The operating system delivers programs for processing to the virtual-memory area on disk. Here the programs generally are divided into either fixed-length pages or variable-length segments. Whether the programs are subdivided into pages or segments depends on the operating system's capabilities.

■ **Time-sharing.** An interleaved processing technique for a multiuser environment in which the computer handles users' jobs in repeated cycles. ■ **Virtual memory.** An area on disk where the operating system stores programs divided into manageable pieces for processing.

Who Will Be the Next Challenger to Microsoft?

Today's Most Talked About Prospects

Microsoft Corporation is the most powerful PC-software company in the world and arguably the most talked about. It has sometimes drawn criticism by competitors and in press reports for its dominance in desktop software. Company critics say that Microsoft sometimes engages in ruthless competitive practices and that its dominant position in systems software gives it an unfair advantage in applications software. Company defenders point out that nobody is forced to buy Microsoft products, that Microsoft's leadership role in setting software standards has stabilized the industry, and that consumers have ultimately benefited from the "price wars" in which the company is sometimes engaged.

Such arguments will likely continue far into the future, and many of them will likely never be resolved. Future events will, however, resolve the question whether or not Microsoft will continue to lead the pack. Wall Street is currently betting that it will, but other scenarios are possible.

One possibility is that competitive alliances between a few strong companies in the industry could lead to the emergence of compelling alternative platforms to compete with Windows and Office. Such a prospect, while possible, is fraught with several difficulties. Windows and Office are so well entrenched that many users and businesses would certainly resist switching. Also, the products and approaches of several vendors would have to dovetail together into a working whole for an alliance to work. History has shown time and again that companies seldom agree so completely. What's more, the increasing turmoil in technology is driving businesses toward simplicity and manageability in product choices—another trend that favors Microsoft.

Another possibility is that the U.S. Justice Department—which has looked closely into practices at Microsoft at the urging of its competitors—intervenes and comes up with a ruling that severely inhibits the company's ability to compete. Those old enough to remember, however, observe that the Justice Department did very little to diminish IBM's competitive position back when Big Blue had a lock on most of the computer industry. The natural forces of competition, not government intervention, eventually brought IBM within reach of its competitors. Some business scholars also wonder if the Justice Department might shoot the U.S. software industry in the foot and leave it vulnerable to foreign competitors if it were to severely impede one of the country's shining stars.

Microsoft. The undisputed leader in software.

Of course, it is always possible that Microsoft could suffer the same type of malaise that hit IBM starting in the 1980s. According to many industry observers, IBM relied too much on its own strength in mainframes and underestimated the importance of PCs. Over time, it wound up ceding leadership in PCs to other companies—Intel, Microsoft, and Compaq being the most visible examples. Microsoft has so far kept swimming skillfully with the tide, often leading price cuts and creating new growth areas, some of which—like the Internet—could eventually cannibalize its current base of users.

Then what can possibly put the brakes on Microsoft? Perhaps no foreseeable development seems likely to hobble this industry giant—not competitors, not the Web, not government. Microsoft's competitors might envision a hopeful scenario in which legendary leader Bill Gates (see the Feature on page SW 55) decides to pursue a new challenge with his billions and retire early.

A virtual-memory system based on paging might break a program 40 kilobytes long into ten pages of 4 kilobytes each. As the computer works on the program, it stores only a few pages at a time in RAM. As it requires other pages during program execution, it selects them from virtual memory and writes over the pages in RAM that it no longer needs. All the original pages, or modified ones, remain intact in virtual memory as the computer processes the program. If the computer again needs a page previously in RAM but now written over, it can readily fetch the needed instructions. This process continues until the program finishes executing.

Segmentation works somewhat like paging except that the lengths of segments vary. Each segment normally consists of a contiguous block of logically interrelated program instructions. Some systems combine segmentation and paging.

Not all operating systems offer virtual memory. Although this technique permits a computer system to get by with limited RAM, it can chew up a lot of processing time swapping pages or segments in and out of RAM.

Multiprocessing **Multiprocessing** links together two or more computers to perform work at the same time. Of course, the operating system must acknowledge multiple processors and assign processing tasks to them as efficiently as possible. In contrast with multiprogramming, in which a single computer processes several programs or tasks *concurrently* (taking turns during the same time interval), multiprocessing carries out multiple programs or tasks *simultaneously* (at precisely the same instant) on separate processors. Computer systems often implement multiprocessing through either coprocessing or parallel processing.

Coprocessing, mentioned briefly in Chapter HW 1, coordinates the functions of a native central processor (CPU) with those of "slave" processors that perform specialized chores, such as high-speed calculations for screen graphics. At any point in time, two or more processors may be performing work simultaneously, but the single CPU still largely determines the time taken to perform an entire job.

In *parallel processing,* the most sophisticated and fastest method of multiprocessing, there are several processors, each of which constitutes a full-fledged general-purpose CPU that operates at roughly the same level as the others. These tightly integrated computers work together on a job at the same time by sharing memory. This concept may sound simple, but many practical problems complicate its implementation, and parallel processing often requires special software. *Symmetric multiprocessing* is a form of parallel processing that appears commonly in today's networks. Symmetric multiprocessing splits up tasks so that multiple processors can work simultaneously on separate threads; however, the processors must all run the same operating system.

Symmetric multiprocessing is closely related to *fault-tolerant computing,* in which a computer system includes duplicates of important circuitry. The duplicate components may or may not function together. In one example of fault-tolerant computing, if one critical component fails, its identical backup component can take over. In another example, both components may be working side-by-side on the same task, comparing results at check points.

Spooling Software Some input and output devices work at extremely low speeds. Tape drives and printers, for example, work at a snail's pace compared to the CPU. If the CPU had to wait for these slower devices to finish their work, the computer system would face a horrendous bottleneck. For example, suppose that the computer has just completed a five-second job that generated 100 pages of hard copy for the printer. A printer might output 8 pages per minute, requiring over 12 minutes to finish the job. If the CPU had to deal directly with the printer, memory would be tied up waiting for the printer to complete the job. As a result, other programs would have to sit unattended while this output was sent from memory to paper.

To avoid such a delay, many computer systems set up *output spooling areas* in disk storage to store output destined for the printer (see Figure SW 2-6). When the computer receives a Print command, a **spooling program** rapidly transfers, or spools, the output from memory to the disk spooling area. The computer is then free to process another program in this memory area, leaving it to the spooling program to transfer the output of the first program from disk to printer.

As Figure SW 2-6 shows, spooling can also be used to hold, or stage, input on its way to the computer. As programs enter the computer system, they are stored in an *input spooling area,* or *queue.* When the operating system is ready to deliver the next program to the CPU, it checks the queue to see which one to process next. On many computer systems, priorities can be assigned to programs. If this is possible, the computer will attend to high-priority jobs before it processes jobs that may have been waiting longer but have a lower priority.

■ **Multiprocessing.** A technique for simultaneous execution of two or more program sequences by multiple processors operating under common control. ■ **Spooling program.** A program that manages input or output by temporarily holding it in secondary storage to expedite processing.

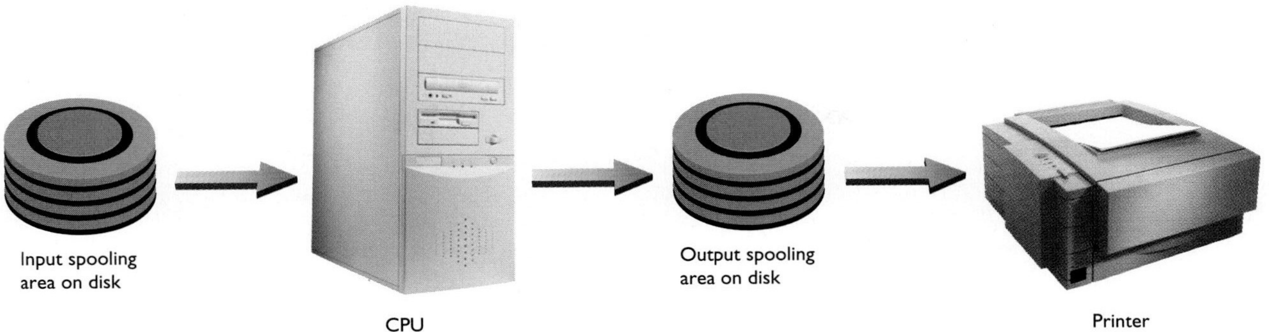

FIGURE SW 2-6

Spooling. On busy computer systems, input is spooled before it is processed and output is spooled before it is sent to the printer.

SW

Personal Operating Systems

Here, we briefly cover several of the most widely used operating systems employed by individuals for *personal use* on their own desktops, including MS-DOS and PC-DOS, Windows 95 and Windows 98, Mac OS, and OS/2. We will also cover the Windows 3.1 operating environment. The Microsoft programs discussed in this section are covered from oldest to newest, since the historical sequencing of these products makes them easier to appreciate.

MS-DOS AND PC-DOS

During the 1980s and early 1990s, DOS* (for Disk Operating System) was the dominant operating system for microcomputers. Millions of copies of DOS have been sold to date, making it one of the most widely used software packages ever developed. Even though it has been made technologically obsolete by newer products, many of today's microcomputer users still work with DOS.

DOS is available in two forms: PC-DOS and MS-DOS. Both were originally developed by Microsoft Corporation of Redmond, Washington (discussed in Feature SW 2-1 on page SW 55 and the Tomorrow box on page SW 45). Only minor differences separate these virtually identical operating systems. **PC-DOS** was created originally for IBM microcomputers, whereas **MS-DOS** was devised to operate on PC-compatibles. PC-DOS is now owned by IBM. Microsoft still owns MS-DOS, but the firm no longer updates the program.

Both the MS-DOS and PC-DOS operating systems have passed through many revisions since they were first developed. All versions starting with the number 1 (such as 1.0 and 1.1) were designed for the original IBM PC and other early PCs, which used only floppy disks and cassette tapes for secondary storage. Some of today's computers run DOS Versions 6 and 7 with capabilities for managing hard disks, networks, and the latest Intel microprocessors. Yet its original design based on 16-bit CPU chips—which supported only 1 megabyte of RAM—prevents DOS from taking full advantage of the power of newer chips.

A sample of DOS commands is provided in Figure SW 2-7.

* For simplicity, this text limits the acronym *DOS* to MS-DOS and PC-DOS. DOS is not a proprietary name, however, and many less well-known operating systems also include the acronym in their names.

■ **PC-DOS.** The operating system designed for and widely used on early IBM microcomputers. ■ **MS-DOS.** An operating system widely used on early PC-compatible microcomputer systems.

Command	Description	Example	Explanation
`COPY`	Copies individual files	`COPY BOSS A:WORKER`	Makes a copy of BOSS and stores it, on the A drive, in WORKER
`DIR`	Displays the names of files on a disk	`DIR A:`	Displays names of files on the A drive
`ERASE (DEL)`	Erases individual files	`ERASE A:DOLLAR`	Erases DOLLAR from the A drive
`REN`	Renames individual files	`REN SAM BILL`	Renames SAM to BILL
`DISKCOPY`	Copies the contents of one disk to another disk	`DISKCOPY A: B:`	Copies the contents of the disk in drive A to the disk in drive B
`FORMAT`	Prepares a disk for use, erasing what was there before	`FORMAT A:`	Formats the disk in the A drive

DOS. Even though DOS has become technologically obsolete, many PCs still use it. This table lists some of the most common DOS commands.

DOS WITH WINDOWS 3.x

Microsoft created **Windows 3.x** in an effort to meet the needs of users frustrated by issuing DOS commands. Windows 3.x—the *x* stands for the version number of the software—is an interconnected series of programs that supplies a graphical user interface for microcomputer systems that use DOS. By replacing the DOS command line with a system of menus, windows, and icons, Windows 3.x eliminates the need to remember a command syntax.

All versions of Windows 3.x—such as 3.1 (for single-user environments) and 3.11 (for small-network environments)—are not fully fledged operating systems. Instead, they merely define *operating environments* that form a graphical shell around DOS, allowing users to point and click the mouse instead of typing long command strings—thereby making DOS easier to use. Windows 3.x allows DOS to address more than 1 megabyte of RAM, perform cooperative multitasking, and run several built-in utility applications—such as a card file, calendar, and paint program. Still, the shortcomings of DOS limits the effectiveness of Windows 3.x.

The basic elements of a Windows 3.1 desktop are shown in Figure SW 2-8.

WINDOWS 9X

Although Windows 3.1 and 3.11 continue in wide use, they are only graphical shells and not entire operating systems. In 1994, Microsoft announced that all soon-to-be-released versions of Windows after 3.11 would bundle language commands (including those in DOS) and a graphical user interface into a single product. It also announced a new numbering system. Instead of calling the next upgrade Windows 4.0—as many had anticipated about the new operating system that Microsoft had been code-naming "Chicago" (see the Inside the Industry box on page 57)—it would number new versions of Windows with respect to the year of release. So, for instance, Windows 95 refers to the 1995 version of Windows and Windows 98 refers to the 1998 version. Collectively, the versions are often referred to as **Windows 9X**.

Windows 9X employs a similar but easier-to-learn-and-use GUI than the one in Windows 3.x (see Figure SW 2-9). Along with this improved interface and faster system response—the latter owing to it being a predominantly 32-bit operating system—Windows 9X permits preemptive multitasking, longer filenames than Windows 3.x, and plug-and-play support. Windows 98 differs from Windows 95 in that it adds new Web-browsing capabilities (see Project 10 on page SW 64), more options for customizing the desktop user interface, the ability to turn a computer on and off automatically in order to perform tasks while the user is away, improved support for large

■ **Windows 3.x.** A graphical operating environment created by Microsoft Corporation to run in conjunction with DOS. Two widely used versions are Windows 3.1 and Windows 3.11. ■ **Windows 9X.** The operating system that succeeded the combination of DOS with Windows. Two versions are Windows 95 and Windows 98.

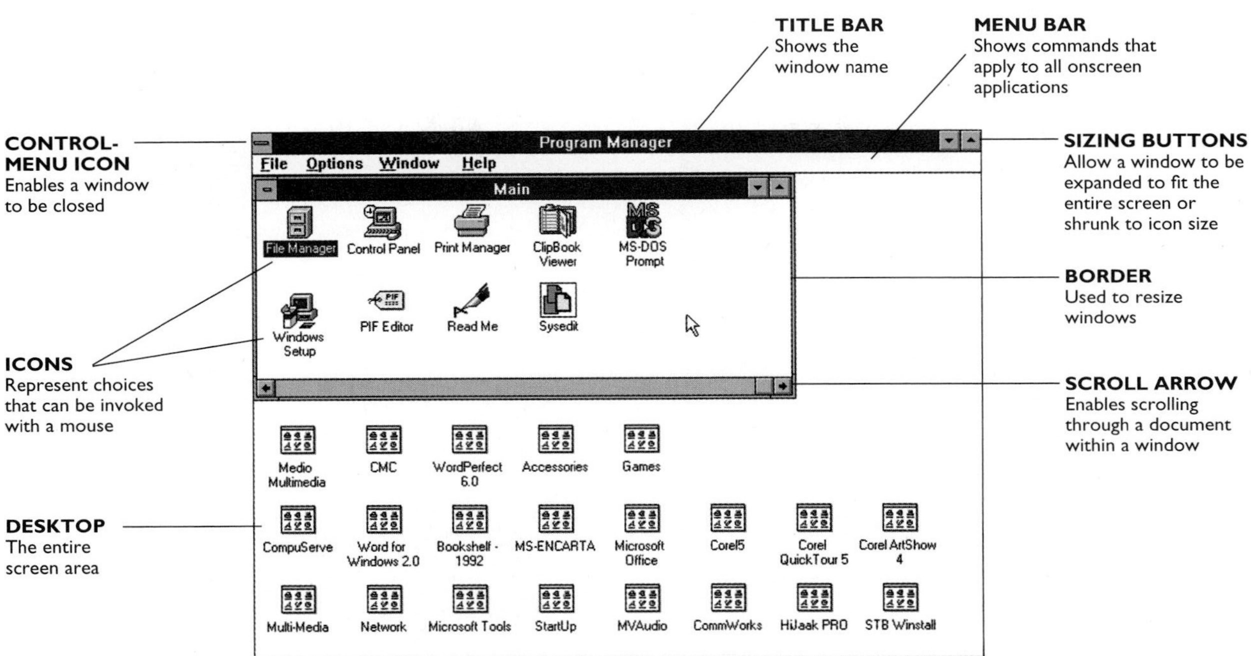

FIGURE SW 2-8

Microsoft Windows 3.1. Microsoft Windows 3.1 provides computers running DOS with a graphical user interface. Annotated in the figure are some of the principal elements of the Windows 3.1 electronic desktop.

hard disks, and support for the digital versatile disk (DVD) and the universal serial bus (USB) standards.

MAC OS

Mac OS—until recently called *Macintosh Operating System*—is the proprietary icon-oriented operating system for Apple's Macintosh line of computers. The Apple Macintosh, introduced in 1984, set the standard for graphical user interfaces. Many of today's new operating systems follow the trend that the Mac started.

Mac OS has grown with the times, keeping pace with increases in power brought by each new CPU chip and Macintosh model. The latest version of the operating system is Version 8.

Mac OS works almost exclusively on Macintosh-compatible computers. An example of its graphical user interface appears in Figure SW 2-10. Macintosh computers that help manage networks often run Unix.

OS/2

OS/2 is a full 32-bit operating system with capabilities for preemptive multitasking and multiuser support. It runs on most PC-compatible computers sold today. OS/2 performs duties comparable to those of Mac OS and Windows 9X. Its graphical user interface also roughly resembles those competing programs.

Users run two principal versions of OS/2. One of these, OS/2 Warp, is intended for personal use. The latest version of Warp accepts voice-actuated commands, recognizing a vocabulary of around 20,000 words. The other version, OS/2 Warp Server, provides an operating system similar to Windows NT. Both OS/2 Warp Server and Windows NT handle system management tasks for computer networks.

■ **Mac OS.** The operating system for Apple's Macintosh line of computer systems. ■ **OS/2.** An operating system designed for both desktop PC-compatible computers and office networks.

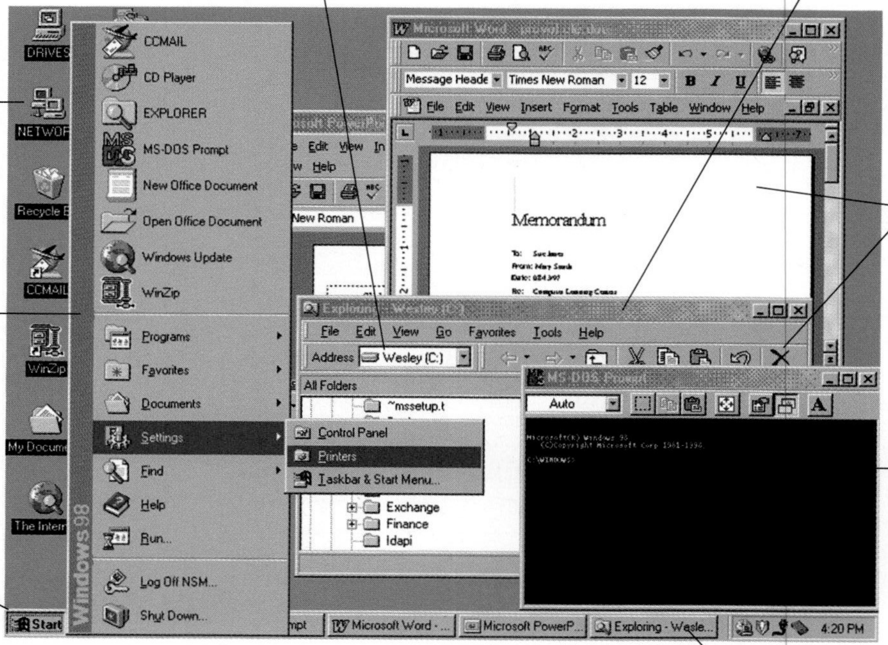

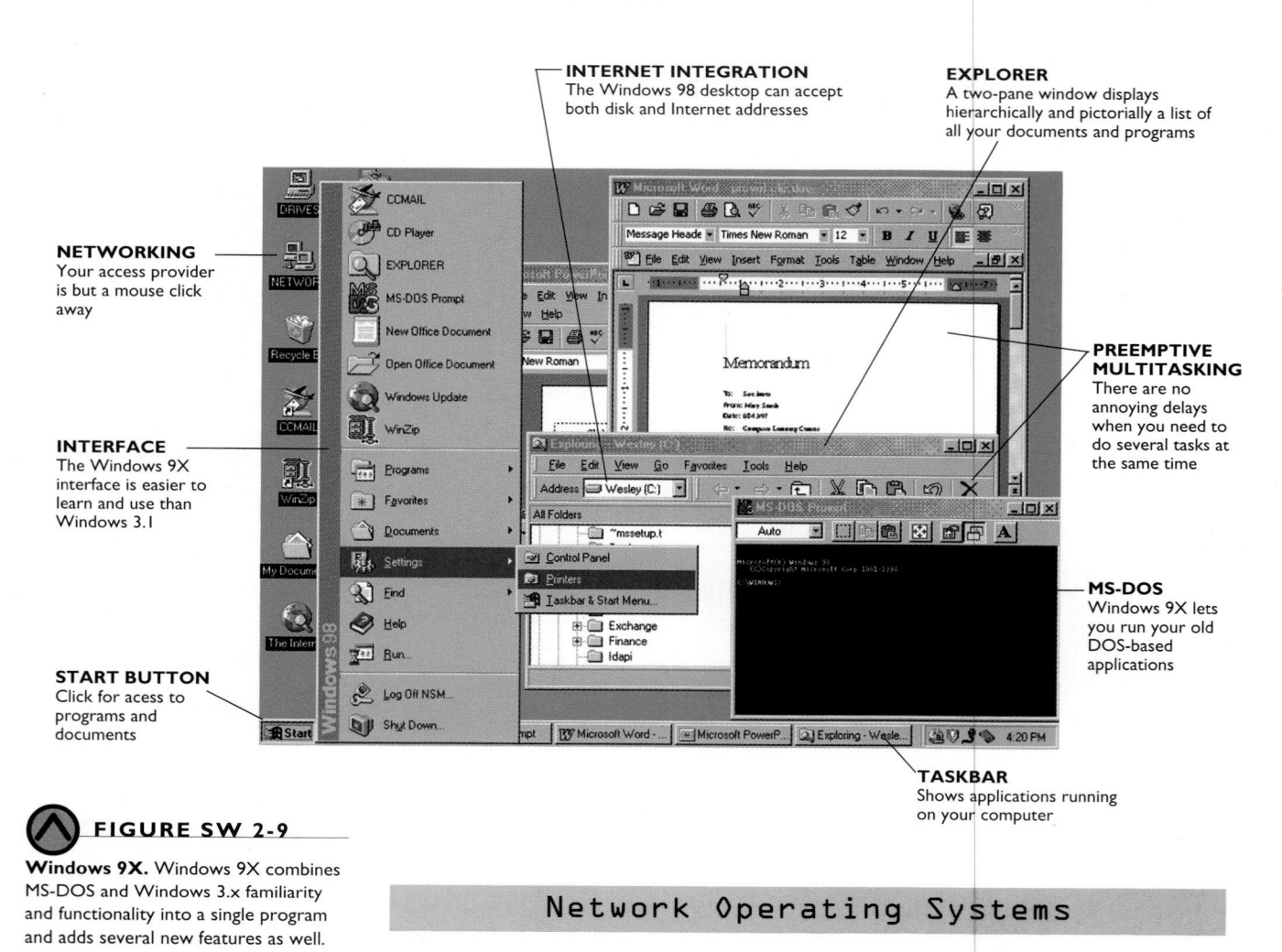

INTERNET INTEGRATION
The Windows 98 desktop can accept both disk and Internet addresses

EXPLORER
A two-pane window displays hierarchically and pictorially a list of all your documents and programs

NETWORKING
Your access provider is but a mouse click away

PREEMPTIVE MULTITASKING
There are no annoying delays when you need to do several tasks at the same time

INTERFACE
The Windows 9X interface is easier to learn and use than Windows 3.1

MS-DOS
Windows 9X lets you run your old DOS-based applications

START BUTTON
Click for acess to programs and documents

TASKBAR
Shows applications running on your computer

FIGURE SW 2-9

Windows 9X. Windows 9X combines MS-DOS and Windows 3.x familiarity and functionality into a single program and adds several new features as well. Pictured here is Windows 98.

Network Operating Systems

The latest version of OS/2 illustrates the increasing difficulty of slotting operating systems as either single-user or multiuser programs. Many new operating systems offer two versions—one that can help network administrators run networks, often called a *network operating system (NOS),* and a second version that can serve the applications needs of ordinary desktop users. This section will cover three widely used NOSs found in PC-network environments: Unix, NetWare, and Windows NT. All except NetWare come also in desktop, or personal, versions.

UNIX

Unix was originally developed more than two decades ago at Bell Laboratories as an operating system for midrange computers. Many properties of Unix make it a compelling choice for high-end 32-bit PCs and graphics workstations, as well.

First, Unix has established a long and relatively successful track record as a multiuser, multitasking operating system. During the quarter-century since its introduction, Unix has attracted a large and loyal following. Today, Unix is the most frequent choice on server computers that store information carried over the Internet.

Second, Unix is flexibly built, so it can be used on a wide variety of machines. Unlike other operating systems—such as Windows 9X and OS/2, which are based on Intel chips, or Mac OS, which is based on Motorola and PowerPC chips—Unix is not built around a single family of processors. Computer systems from micros to

■ **Unix.** A long-standing operating system for midrange computers, microcomputer networks, graphics workstations, and the Internet.

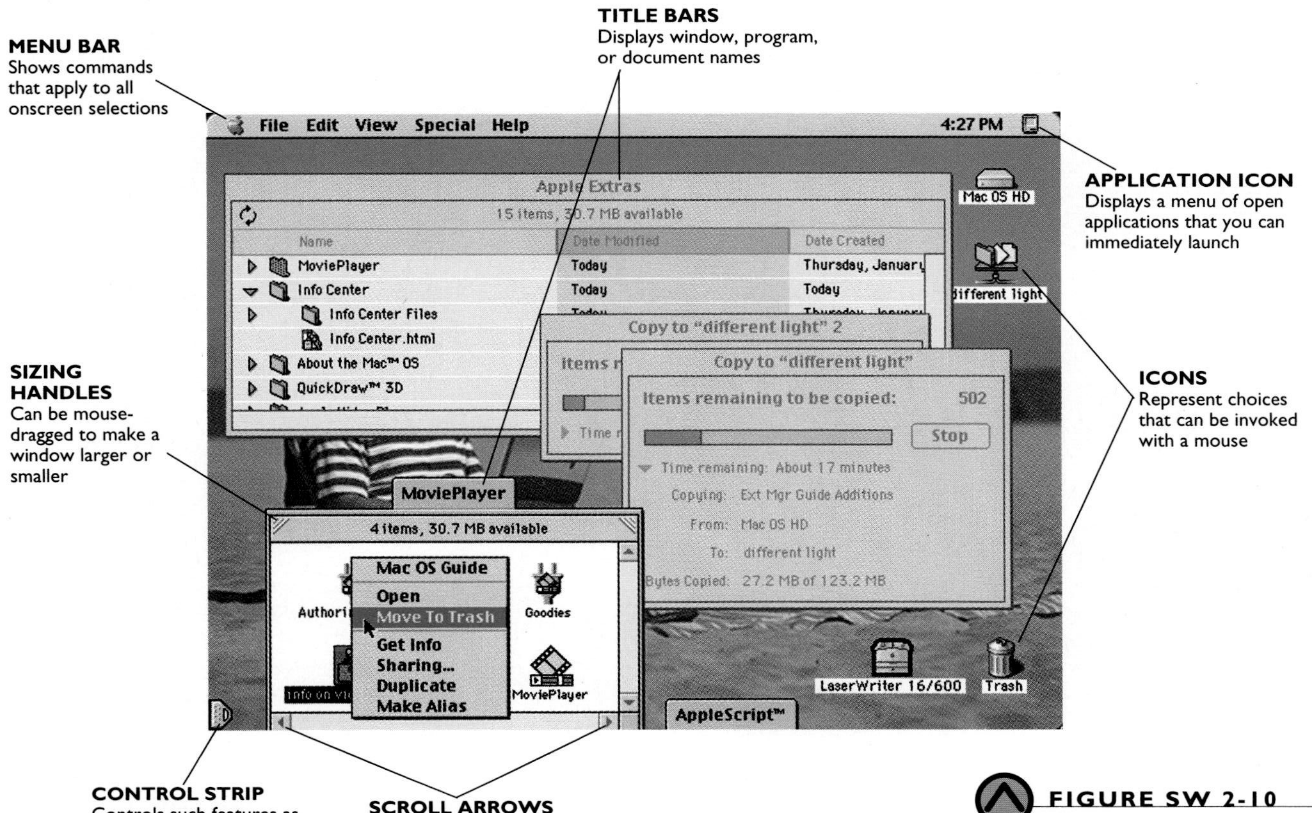

FIGURE SW 2-10

Mac OS 8. Mac OS remains very popular many years after emerging as the first commercially successful operating system with a graphical user interface.

mainframes can run Unix, and it can easily integrate a variety of devices from different manufacturers through network connections. This flexibility gives Unix a big advantage over competing operating systems for many types of applications.

But certain disadvantages also plague Unix. Many people complain that it isn't very easy to use. What's more, the same features that give Unix its flexibility make it run more slowly than operating systems tailored around a particular family of microprocessors. This characteristic limits the benefits of applying Unix in an environment dominated by, say, Intel CPUs. Perhaps the greatest disadvantage of Unix is that several "brands" of it are now available, many of them incompatible with each other.

NETWARE

NetWare—developed by Novell, Inc., during the mid-1980s—is today the most widely used operating system on microcomputer-based local area networks (LANs). Most users of NetWare interact with it when they log on to a network or when they deal with a network print server or a file server. NetWare provides a shell around your personal, desktop operating system through which you can retrieve files from or save them on a shared hard disk and also print them on a shared printer (see Figure SW 2-11). The shell routine enables you to communicate with NetWare, which is located on the shared disk.

Here's how a typical NetWare session might unfold on a PC network: When you turn on a connected workstation, the network sends a prompt—such as F>— to your display. At this point, you can decide to work on or off the network. If you

■ **NetWare.** The most widely used operating system on local area networks (LANs).

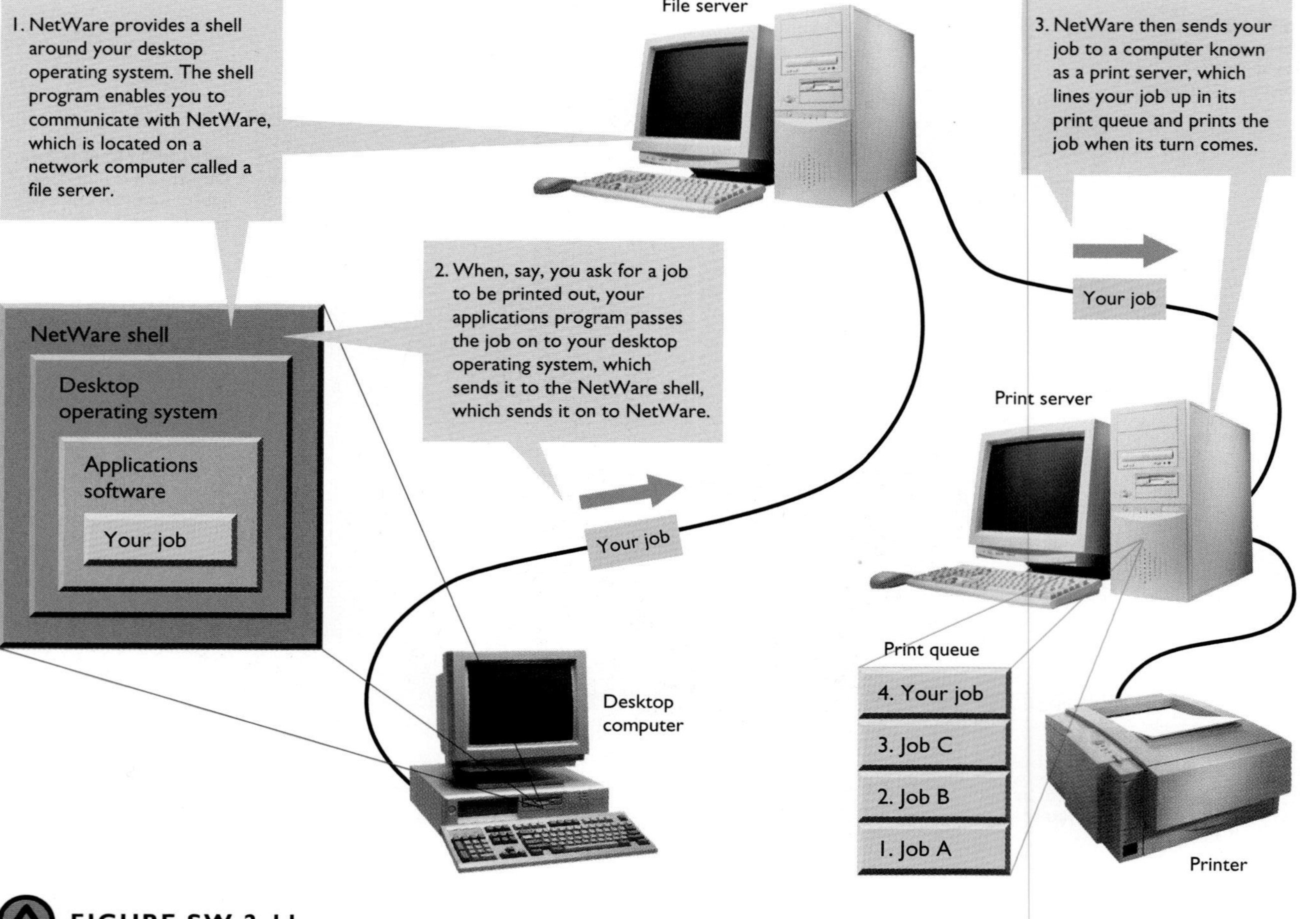

1. NetWare provides a shell around your desktop operating system. The shell program enables you to communicate with NetWare, which is located on a network computer called a file server.
File server
3. NetWare then sends your job to a computer known as a print server, which lines your job up in its print queue and prints the job when its turn comes.
2. When, say, you ask for a job to be printed out, your applications program passes the job on to your desktop operating system, which sends it to the NetWare shell, which sends it on to NetWare.
Your job
NetWare shell
Desktop operating system
Applications software
Your job
Print server
Your job
Print queue
4. Your job
3. Job C
2. Job B
1. Job A
Desktop computer
Printer

FIGURE SW 2-11

Working with a NOS. The diagram shows how you would interact with a NetWare-controlled computer network. Many other network operating systems work in similar ways.

wish to work on the network, you type a log-on message. For instance, if the network recognizes you as KJOHNSON, you might have to type in KJOHNSON.

When the operating system accepts your input, it gives you *access rights* to the network, and you are free to do any network operation within those assigned access rights. They include such operations as reading or writing to files, executing programs, and creating or deleting files. When you are working at the F> prompt, which typically corresponds to the shared hard disk on the network, you generally treat it simply as another disk drive on your own computer system.

If you choose not to work on the network, you simply type A, B, C, D, or E at the F> prompt. This input points your computer to local diskette drives (A or B), local hard disks (C or D), or your CD-ROM drive (E). You then work just as you would on an independent computer system. Keep in mind, however, you can gain access to a program on the shared hard disk, save a program to the shared hard disk, or output to a shared printer only after you reestablish network access. Many other NOSs work similarly to NetWare as regards basic operations.

WINDOWS NT

Windows NT (for *New Technology)* is a full 32-bit operating system developed by Microsoft Corporation for organizational computer systems. Called *NT* for short, users encounter two principal forms of this package. The *workstation* edition is targeted to ordinary users working at powerful desktop computers, while a *server* edition is aimed at network administrators and advanced network-management tasks (see Figure SW 2-12).

■ **Windows NT.** An operating system designed by Microsoft Corporation for both workstation and network applications within organizations.

The Internet and TV

A Marriage Awaiting a "Killer" Application

As the Internet's World Wide Web became popular over the last few years, many people began speculating about what would happen as soon as the Web and television got together. The two technologies seem destined for marriage, a phenomenon called digital convergence. After all, television is the premier entertainment medium in the home, and the Web is perhaps the ultimate computer application for delivering even richer content than traditional television broadcasts provide.

To date, only a handful of products combine television and the Web, and these pioneering efforts fall far short of the ideal that many futurists have imagined. Today you can surf the Web on your living-room TV if you buy a special set-top box for it. Alternatively, with proper software and hardware on your office computer system, you can receive TV signals. And coming soon: high-definition television (HDTV) that will provide even more capabilities to showcase the converging technologies.

What's still missing, however, is a so-called *killer application*—a must-have entertainment product that *tightly* interrelates the Web and TV. Except in a few small instances, you can't click on a screen button while in TV mode to search through supplemental Web information that is designed to enhance a particular TV program's viewing. Alternatively, while playing around on the Web, you can't yet access crisp-looking, large-output-format video at the sites you visit. A lot of essential technology is available today, but precious little content is available that gets rave reviews.

The lack of products so far and their limitations have not resulted from lack of imagination. Integrating two massive communications systems like the Internet and television is an enormous undertaking. Home bandwidth needs dramatic upgrade. Satellite and cable systems need redesign. Participating organizations must agree upon standards so that the efforts of hundreds of companies dovetail into a system that works across scores of equipment platforms. Furthermore, the Web is still considered largely a technical product and still has a long way to go to become as easy to use as television—an important condition to move the technology into the average living room. The bottom line: Many billions of dollars need to be spent.

Digital convergence. Its success depends on greater bandwidth to the home and compelling content.

Of all the uncertainties, probably the heaviest is that nobody really knows for sure that the marriage of the Web and television will even produce a killer application—or what such an application will look like. Will it be on-demand television? The answer depends on how much of a premium people will pay when they can already get over a hundred channels. Will a drive for better information propel development? The answer depends on whether most people watching television will make proactive demands for more information, or whether they will remain content as passive "couch potatoes."

Consider another interesting wrinkle that could spark demand: As the Web interface and greater bandwidth open up the distribution pipeline for new products, virtually everyone with a good home PC will be able to produce their own television channels. Affordable technology will allow people to create broadcast-quality content on their PCs and then use the power of the Web to bring that content into any Internet-enabled residence. What's more, no one needs approval to get messages "on the air." Looking 50 years down the road, virtually every kid may want his or her own TV channel—and have the means to make it happen.

The future of the Web and TV looks interesting, to say the least, as both are exploring a frontier that straddles the multi-billion-dollar computing and entertainment industries.

relatively mature, and over the years, CRTs have become very inexpensive and have gained capabilities for excellent color output. These features notwithstanding, CRTs are bulky and fragile, and they consume a great deal of power.

Another class of display devices form images by manipulating charged chemicals or gases sandwiched between panes of glass instead of firing a bulky electron gun. These much slimmer alternatives to CRTs are called **flat-panel displays.** Flat-panel displays are compact, lightweight, and require little power. Because of these features, they are commonly found on notebook and pen-based computers and in a variety of other products (see Figure HW 3-16).

■ **Flat-panel display.** A slim-profile display device.

FIGURE HW 3-16

Flat-panel displays. These compact, lightweight displays suit a wide range of applications.

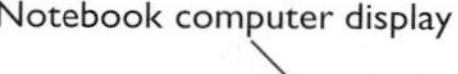

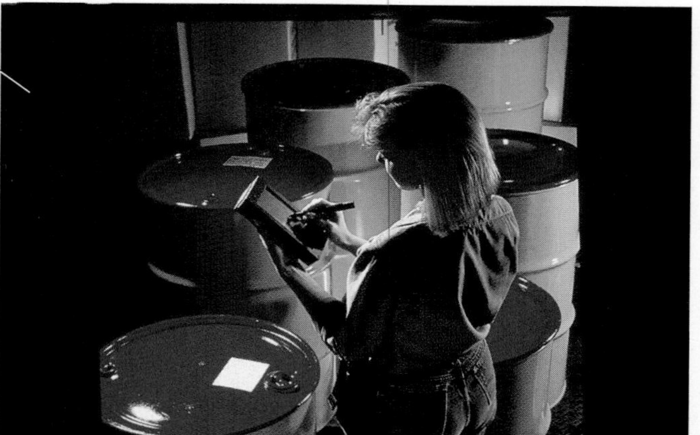

Electronic clipboard for mobile worker

Notebook computer display

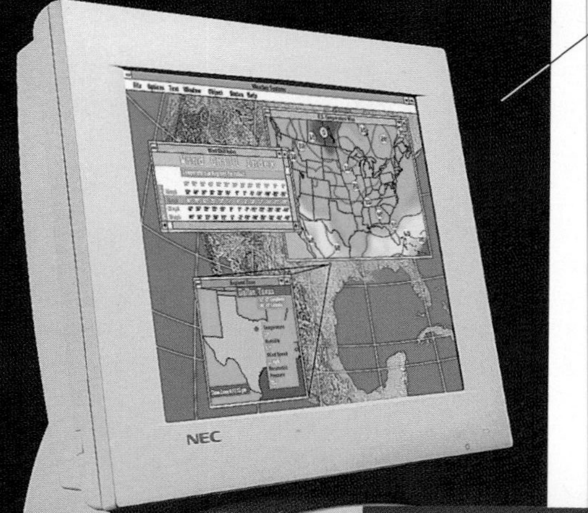

Desktop computer display

Entertainment/business panels for air travelers

Large-screen presentation monitor

Flat-panel displays on portable computers often use *liquid crystal display (LCD)* technology. LCD displays light up charged liquid crystals, and special color filters manipulate this light to paint the screen. LCD is the most common type of flat-panel-display technology in use. The major advantages of LCDs over CRTs are low power consumption, portability, and compact size. LCDs also do not emit any electromagnetic radiation. However, LCDs also cost more than CRTs; what's more, their screens may provide less contrast with more glare and poorer resolution.

Many notebook computers use either *active-matrix* or *passive-matrix* color-display technology. Active-matrix displays provide much sharper screen images than passive-matrix screens, but they provide this benefit at a higher cost.

Both versions present the same graphical user interface employed in Windows 9X. An important feature of Windows NT is its ability to be run on a variety of computer systems, not just those using conventional Intel chips. Thus, applications written for Windows NT can be developed on a desktop microcomputer system that uses a Pentium chip and run on a workstation that uses an RISC chip such as the PowerPC. Another key feature of NT is its two principal versions. This flexibility gives it an advantage in some environments over NetWare, which offers no personal version.

Although Windows NT has had a later start than both Unix and NetWare, many industry experts consider it to be the front-running NOS in the race to capture the lead in corporate networking. One of the major disadvantages of Windows NT relative to Windows 9X as a personal operating system is its large storage requirements.

FIGURE SW 2-12

Windows NT. Windows NT comes in both a workstation edition, for ordinary users, and a server edition, for network administrators.

Utility Programs

Computer users must perform some tasks repeatedly in the course of routine processing, including sorting records, checking spelling and grammar, and copying programs from one medium to another. Programmers prefer to avoid the extremely inefficient practice of including code for these tasks in every program. General-purpose software tools called **utility programs** help to eliminate this waste by performing standard processing routines for all applications that require them. Computer systems normally include large libraries of utility programs to perform common functions.

Utility programs are packaged in a variety of ways. Some are bundled into operating systems. For instance, standard utilities for copying disk files accompany the Windows 9X operating system. In other cases, utilities are independent programs that can be acquired from third-party vendors and made to run with a given operating system. This latter class of programs can do chores your operating system is incapable of doing as well as do some types of operating-system tasks better.

Two widely used types of utility programs that we will cover in depth here are disk utilities and device drivers. Figure SW 2-13 briefly describes these and other types of utilities.

DISK UTILITIES

A **disk utility** is a program that performs useful operations for controlling a hard disk. Four types of disk utilities are disk toolkits, data compression programs, disk optimizers, and backup utilities.

Disk Toolkits *Disk toolkits* help users to recover from accidental data destruction. Such a program allows you to recover damaged or erased files, repair damaged format markings and directories, and recover from a disk crash (a crippling failure of the disk itself). At one time, virtually all disk toolkits came from third-party vendors, but operating systems are increasingly including very adequate disk toolkits. Still, vendors of disk toolkits seem to supply a continuing stream of useful disk-management routines beyond those of operating-system software.

Data Compression Programs **Data compression** programs enable files to be stored in a smaller space. This helps to free up disk space and to speed transmissions of files over networks. Sending compressed files over a network requires the receiver to run the proper decompression program. Data compression is also commonly a space-saving strategy in file backup.

- **Utility program.** A general-purpose program that performs some frequently encountered operations in a computer system.
- **Disk utility.** A program that assists users with such disk-related tasks as backup, data compression, space allocation, and the like.
- **Data compression.** A utility function that squeezes data into a smaller storage space than it would normally require.

FIGURE SW 2-13

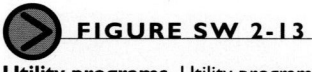

Utility programs. Utility programs extend the capabilities of a computer's systems software.

Control Panel

Antivirus programs
Protect your system from virus attack

Backup utilities
Quickly and easily back up the contents of a hard disk

Data compression utilities
Enable files to be compressed

Desktop enhancers
Let you customize your graphical user interface—say, by changing the way in which menus are presented

Device drivers
Enable applications software to work on a specific configuration of hardware

Diagnostic software
Enables problems to be more easily rooted out of your computer system

Disk optimizers
Better utilize space on disk; for instance, disk defragmenters rearrange files for faster access

Disk toolkits
Recover and repair damaged or lost files

Document managers
Enable you to find a lost file on your system by typing in part of its name or by typing in short strings of text known to be contained in the file

Extenders
Let you add new fonts, commands, or programs to your system

File viewers
Make it easy to view files without opening the applications in which they were created

Internet utilities
Enable you to more easily locate and keep track of resources on the Internet, censor downloaded content, keep track of connect time, and so forth

Keyboard utilities
Let you construct keyboard macros (small programs that execute when you press a certain key) or let you reconfigure your keyboard

Memory managers
Enable you to increase available memory and/or speed up system performance

Performance monitors
Tell you how efficiently your computer system is performing its work

Screen-capture programs
Enable you to download any screen image onto a storage or output device, as well as to edit and view images

Screen savers
Show random patterns on the display to prevent the phosphor coating on the screen from burning

Uninstallers
Remove applications programs, including all files and directories and any references to them

22 object(s)

Data compression has become a relatively hot topic in recent years, largely because of two trends: the spread of multimedia applications and the ever-increasing popularity of the Internet. Color graphics, sound, and video all consume a great deal of storage space. Even text sent in volume over the telephone lines can cause bottlenecks unless it is compressed. Feature SW 2-2 explains how data compression works.

Disk Optimizers *Disk optimizers* enable programs on disk to be accessed faster. They perform such tasks as allocating certain files to outer disk cylinders (where the read/write heads can reach them quickly), consolidating fragmented files (that is, rewriting related blocks of programs and data in contiguous sectors on the disk surface for fast access), and sorting file-folder names for fast access.

Disk fragmentation has certainly become a major problem as multimedia resources and large applications programs have imposed growing demands. A file becomes fragmented when it's too large to be stored in contiguous locations (clusters) on disk. When this happens, the file is split and stored in noncontiguous locations. A *defragmentation utility* speeds disk access by rearranging files and free space on your disk, so files are stored in contiguous locations and free space is consolidated into a single block. Figure SW 2-14 shows how such a utility consolidates fragmented files. Many operating systems have their own defragmentation utilities.

Bill Gates

The First and Most Famous High-Tech Billionaire

In the late 1970s, few people would have predicted that a systems-software programmer—a "techie"—would become the richest person in the United States. But that's exactly what happened.

Today, William H. Gates III has a net worth of over $35 billion. As founder and chairman of the board of Microsoft Corporation, the largest microcomputer-software company in the world, Gates became the first American ever to reach billionaire status—and he's not even 50 years old! Bill Gates has made scores of other people rich, too. Had you bought $1,000 worth of Microsoft stock when the company went public in 1986, those shares would be worth well over $100,000 today.

Before he graduated from high school, Bill Gates was already an accomplished computer programmer. He wrote a class-scheduling program for his high school and a traffic-logging program for the city of Bellevue, Washington. What's more, he also worked as a programmer for TRW, a large computer-services firm—reportedly the only time he has ever worked for someone else.

Bill Gates. The first $35 billion man in U.S. history.

After high school, Gates continued on to Harvard. He never finished, dropping out instead in the mid-1970s to work on a BASIC language translator for the Altair 8800 computer, the world's first microcomputer system. The Altair was a commercial flop. (Available only in kit form, it would only work if a diligent and talented buyer assembled it correctly.) Despite this market failure, the microcomputer industry continued to grow, and Gates started creating language translators for others.

His biggest break came around 1980, when IBM was looking for a company to deliver an operating system for the IBM PC, its first foray into microcomputers. At that time, Microsoft employed only 50 people writing mostly BASIC, COBOL, and FORTRAN language translators. IBM first contacted a California company called Digital Research, which produced CP/M, then the most widely used operating system for personal computers. According to industry legend, however, Digital Research founder Gary Kildall, who was already rich beyond most people's wildest dreams, was off flying his plane in the Santa Cruz mountains when the IBM people came calling. Put off, the IBMers left for the state of Washington to meet with Bill Gates.

The rest, as they say, is history. Microsoft is now the largest software company in the world. It employs more than 20,000 people, over 3,000 of whom are reported to have become millionaires.

Backup Utilities *Backup utilities* are programs designed to back up a hard-disk's contents (see Figure SW 2-15). You can back up an entire disk or merely selected directories and files. Most serious backup systems store copies on magnetic tape, rewritable optical disk, or some other such high-capacity medium. Many users rely on the backup utilities supplied by their disk- or tape-drive makers.

DEVICE DRIVERS

When a computer system's hardware must communicate with input or output hardware such as a display device, printer, or scanner, the operating system commonly works through a utility program known as a *device driver.* **Device drivers** make it possible for specific hardware devices to function with software.

■ **Device driver.** A utility program that enables an operating system to communicate with a specific hardware device.

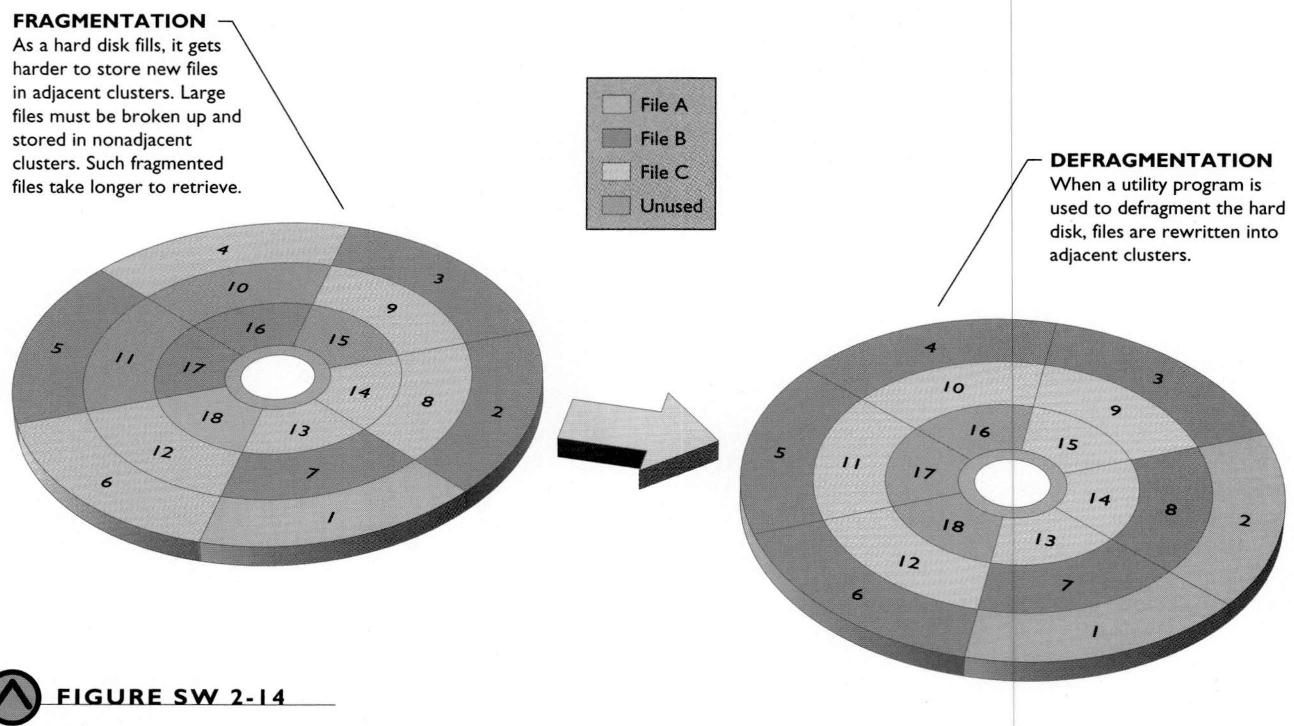

FRAGMENTATION
As a hard disk fills, it gets harder to store new files in adjacent clusters. Large files must be broken up and stored in nonadjacent clusters. Such fragmented files take longer to retrieve.
File A
File B
File C
Unused
DEFRAGMENTATION
When a utility program is used to defragment the hard disk, files are rewritten into adjacent clusters.

FIGURE SW 2-14

Defragmenting a hard disk.

Most hardware you buy will include one or two diskettes with device drivers that enable the equipment to be installed on your specific type of computer system. You can tell when you buy the hardware which types of drivers are included; for instance, if the outside package says "for Windows 98" or "for Mac OS 8," then you know that drivers for those systems are inside. Generally, the major PC hardware vendors create drivers to support a large variety of computer systems.

Driver installation requires some relatively easy steps. Typically, you mount the diskette in the computer's A drive and run the programs on it, following the instructions printed on the disk label and on the screen. After all the questions are satisfactorily answered, the necessary driver files will be stored on your hard disk, and the equipment will be ready to use.

FIGURE SW 2-15

Backing up a hard disk on tape. Most tape backup utilities, like the Colorado Backup program shown here, allow you to back up either the full or partial contents of a hard disk.

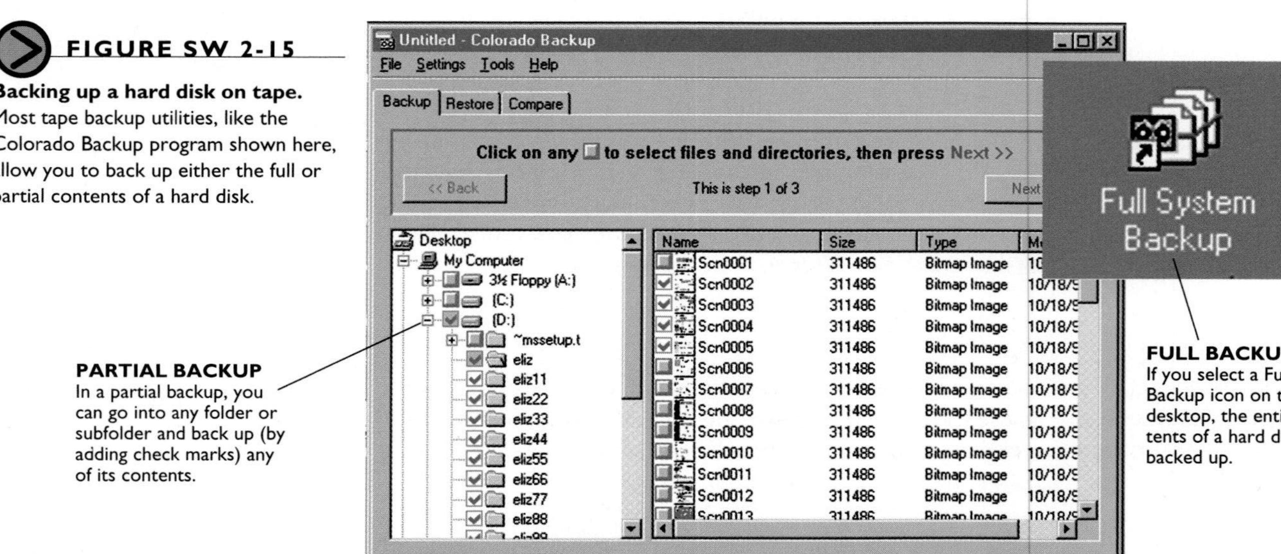

Project Code Names

KLAMATH MEMPHIS Copeland Cairo
Nashville Pandora ROAD PIZZA Harpo
Bladerunner Tsunami Rolling Rock
Kitty Hawk Jaws Zappa Calimari
Wombat Ali Baba Snow White
Sweet Pea KRYPTONITE ROSEBUD
Zone V Expresso Visine Dr. Pepper

When computer companies are developing new hardware and software products, they typically assign internal code names to the projects. For instance, Microsoft assigned the code names Chicago and Memphis, respectively, to the prerelease versions of Windows 95 and Windows 98. Less well-known code names for Windows products are Champaign (Windows NT 3.5), Cairo (Windows NT 4.0), Sparta (Windows for Workgroups), and Cleveland (Windows 4, which was never released).

Often, companies stick with standard themes for code names on related products. For Windows, Microsoft has gone with midwestern city names. Development of IBM's OS/2 operating system featured project names with a Star Trek theme, such as Warp, Borg, Q, and Ferengi. Other popular themes include beer, sushi, boats, Shakespeare, celebrities, animals, and mythical gods. Some code names stick; for instance, Macintosh and OS/2 Warp.

Some of the most interesting code names are Road Pizza (Apple's QuickTime software), Bladerunner (Borland's dBASE for Windows), Rolling Rock (Go Corporation's PenPoint for Hobbit), Shamu (the GUI for CompuServe), CyberDog (Apple browser), Dr. Pepper (an AppleTalk protocol), Mothra (Borland's Paradox for DOS 4.0), Big Foot (Borland's 32-bit DOS extender), and Bogart (Apple's Applesearch). One of the least interesting code names is P5 (Intel's Pentium chip).

Language Translators

As mentioned earlier, computers can execute programs only in the form of instructions stated in machine language. Programmers write instructions in other, easier-to-code languages, however, so something must translate programmers' statements into machine language. A **language translator** is a systems software program that converts an applications program into machine language.

If you create a program in the BASIC or COBOL programming languages, you cannot run it on the computer until you summon a translator to restate your commands in machine language. A translator also goes to work when you issue commands in your database management system or spreadsheet package. A translator is behind the scenes even when you type commands at an operating-system prompt or select commands from a graphical-user-interface display.

Three common types of language translators are compilers, interpreters, and assemblers. Each one performs translations in its own way.

Compilers A **compiler** translates an entire program into machine language before executing it. Every compiler-oriented language requires its own special compiler. For instance, a COBOL program needs a COBOL compiler; it cannot run on a BASIC compiler.

The collection of program statements that you write and enter in the computer is called a *source module*. The compiler then produces a machine-level equivalent of your program called an *object module*.

Normally, before the object module actually begins execution, it combines with other object modules that the CPU may need in order to process the program. For example, most computers can't compute square roots directly. To do so, they rely on

■ **Language translator.** Systems software that converts applications programs into machine language. ■ **Compiler.** A language translator that converts an entire program into machine language before executing it.

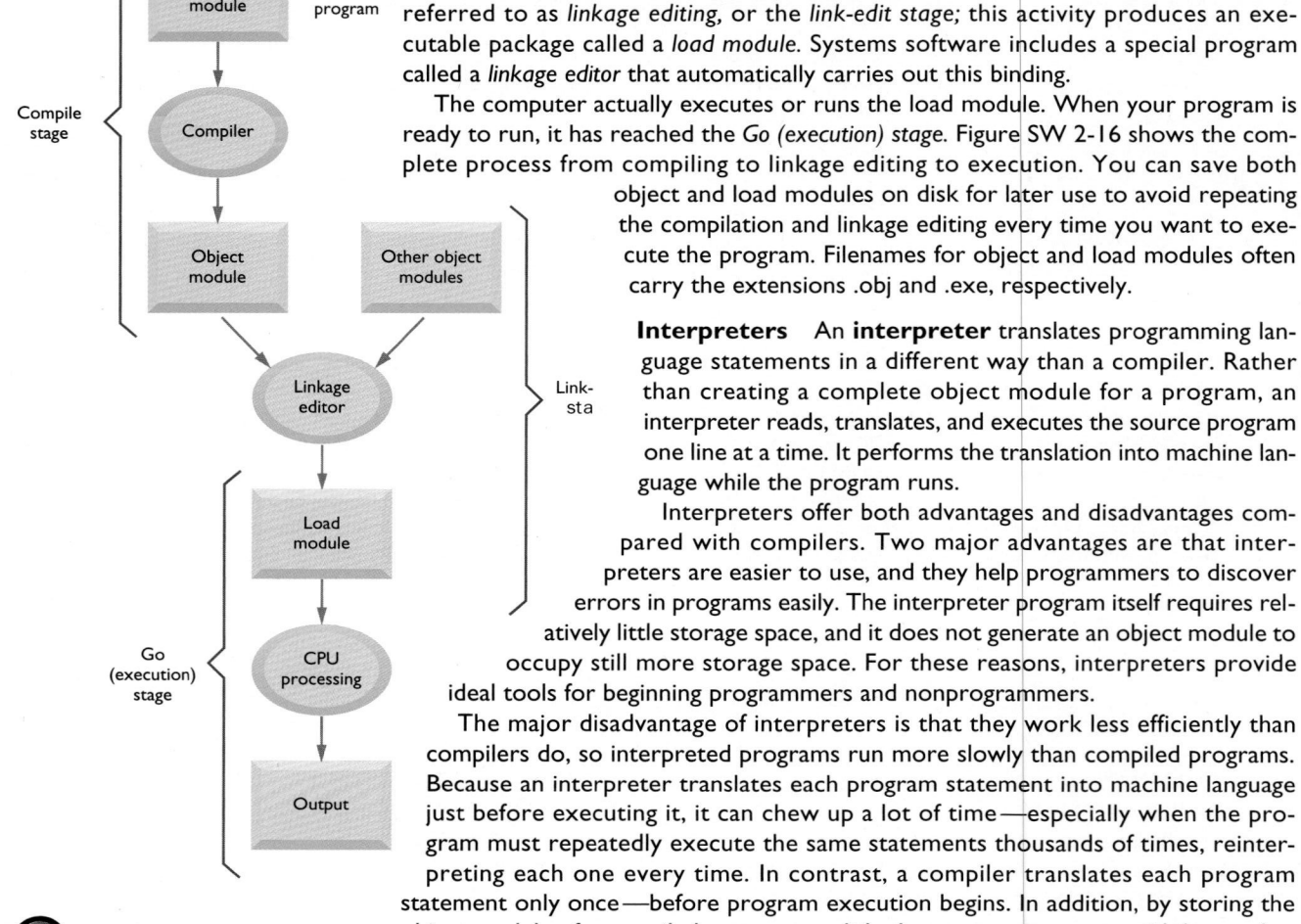

small object modules held in secondary storage. If your program calls for a square root calculation, the operating system temporarily binds the object module of your program together with a copy of the square root routine. The binding process is referred to as *linkage editing,* or the *link-edit stage;* this activity produces an executable package called a *load module.* Systems software includes a special program called a *linkage editor* that automatically carries out this binding.

The computer actually executes or runs the load module. When your program is ready to run, it has reached the *Go (execution) stage.* Figure SW 2-16 shows the complete process from compiling to linkage editing to execution. You can save both object and load modules on disk for later use to avoid repeating the compilation and linkage editing every time you want to execute the program. Filenames for object and load modules often carry the extensions .obj and .exe, respectively.

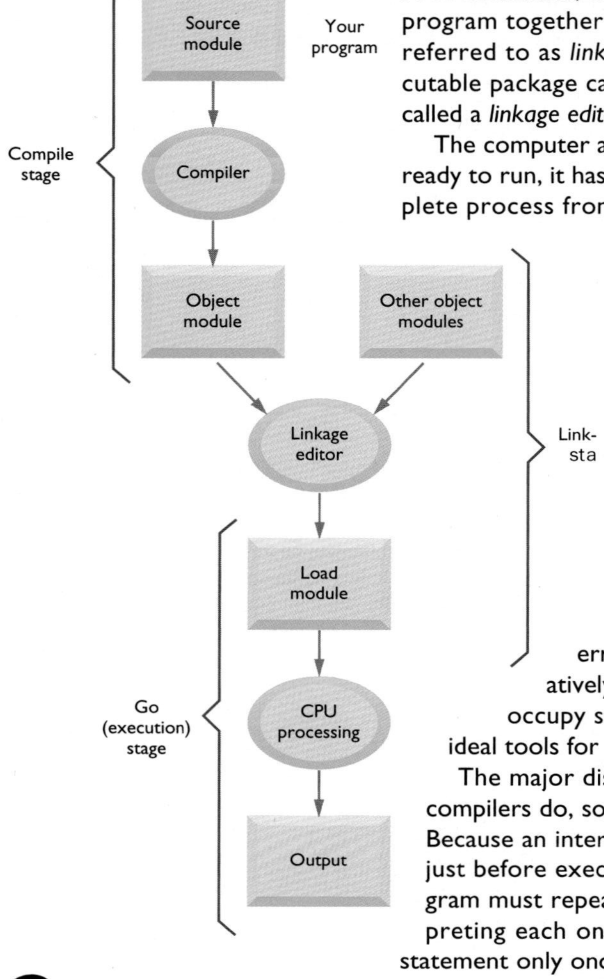

FIGURE SW 2-16

Compile, link edit, go. A compiler and linkage editor convert a source module into a load module for processing by the CPU.

Interpreters An **interpreter** translates programming language statements in a different way than a compiler. Rather than creating a complete object module for a program, an interpreter reads, translates, and executes the source program one line at a time. It performs the translation into machine language while the program runs.

Interpreters offer both advantages and disadvantages compared with compilers. Two major advantages are that interpreters are easier to use, and they help programmers to discover errors in programs easily. The interpreter program itself requires relatively little storage space, and it does not generate an object module to occupy still more storage space. For these reasons, interpreters provide ideal tools for beginning programmers and nonprogrammers.

The major disadvantage of interpreters is that they work less efficiently than compilers do, so interpreted programs run more slowly than compiled programs. Because an interpreter translates each program statement into machine language just before executing it, it can chew up a lot of time—especially when the program must repeatedly execute the same statements thousands of times, reinterpreting each one every time. In contrast, a compiler translates each program statement only once—before program execution begins. In addition, by storing the object module of a compiled program on disk, the programmer can avoid the need to retranslate the source program every time the program runs.

Some programming-language packages include both interpreter and compiler software, giving the programmer the best of both worlds. He or she can work with the interpreter to root out program errors and then compile the error-free program, saving and running it in object-module form.

Assemblers The third type of language translator, an **assembler,** converts only assembly language statements into machine language. *Assembly languages* are used almost exclusively by professional programmers to write efficient programming code. An assembler works like a compiler, producing a stored object module. A computer system typically operates only one assembly language; thus, only one assembler is required.

Users of any language-translator program should recognize the difference between it and the programming language it translates. A programming language is a set of rules for coding program commands, whereas a language translator is a systems software program that translates code written under the rules into the bits and bytes that the computer understands.

■ **Interpreter.** A language translator that converts program statements line by line into machine language, immediately executing each one. ■ **Assembler.** A language translator that converts assembly language instructions into machine language.

Data Compression

How to Squeeze More Data into Less Space

Even though storage capacities of ordinary desktop systems now approach the multigigabyte range—an unimaginable threshold until very recently—software developers continue to feel pinched by limitations on storage space. Some might even say that user expectations have increased so much that the space problem has actually intensified.

Blame the increasing demand for photographic-quality screen displays and full-motion desktop video, both of which put acute strains on storage. A modest photographic-quality image that you see in a book can easily consume 20 megabytes or so. That's the capacity of about 14 high-density diskettes. Now think of simultaneously storing several such images on your hard disk and running full-motion video at about 30 frames per second, and you can see why software developers are crying the blues.

Developers have found one way out of the storage crunch by compressing data. The following paragraphs discuss a few of many compression methods.

Stacking Algorithms Some software packages apply stacking algorithms, or formulas, to perform modest data compression. The stacker program included with most tape drives, for instance, enables you to double the space on your tape. Similar stacker programs let you double hard-disk space.

When you turn on the stacker, it compresses anything written to the storage medium or, alternatively, decompresses data as you read it. You generally have the option of choosing which applications you want compressed. Compression and decompression eat up time, so that decision requires some thought.

Zipping Files *Zip* refers to a particular method of compressing files onto a diskette or hard disk, say, by using PKZIP—a shareware utility program. Compressing data is known as *zipping* a file and decompressing is known as *unzipping.* PKZIP can perform only modest amounts of file compression—say, somewhere around 70 or 80 percent of the original file size—and it works best for text and Windows BMP files.

JPEG and MPEG The JPEG and MPEG standards define compression routines in the world of computer graphics. JPEG (named for the Joint Photographic Experts Group that developed it) implements an algorithm to compress still images. It can reduce the size of a picture file to take up 100 times less space than the original version (referred to as a 100:1 compression ratio). JPEG works by looking for redundant information in a picture. For instance, an image half filled with blue sky has a lot of redundancy. The JPEG algorithm reproduces this image by describing the color blue to the computer and telling the computer how many adjacent pixels to paint that shade of blue.

WinZip (Unregistered) - elizxx.zip

File Actions Options Help

New Open Add Extract View CheckOut

Name	Date	Time	Size	Ratio	Packed	Path
S0060.bmp	10/19/96	13:12	311,486	95%	16,346	
Scn0049.bmp	10/19/96	11:36	311,486	96%	12,406	
Scn0048.bmp	10/19/96	11:35	311,486	89%	35,159	
Scn0047.bmp	10/19/96	11:33	311,486	89%	32,821	
Scn0046.bmp	10/19/96	11:30	311,486	86%	44,859	
Scn0045.bmp	10/19/96	11:28	311,486	89%	34,763	
Scn0044.bmp	10/19/96	11:18	311,486	75%	79,097	
Scn0043.bmp	10/19/96	11:16	311,486	97%	8,567	
Scn0042.bmp	10/19/96	11:03	311,486	97%	8,112	
Scn0041.bmp	10/19/96	10:49	311,486	89%	34,752	
Scn0040.bmp	10/19/96	10:39	311,486	97%	9,970	
Scn0039.bmp	10/19/96	10:36	311,486	82%	55,517	
Scn0038.bmp	10/19/96	10:27	311,486	90%	29,748	
Scn0037.bmp	10/19/96	10:25	311,486	93%	20,818	

Selected 0 files, 0 bytes | Total 131 files, 40,443KB

Zipped files. Zipping is a common practice for compressing BMP files.

MPEG (named for the Moving Pictures Expert Group) defines a standard for compressing video data that works a lot like JPEG, except that it also removes redundancy from image to image. Adjacent frames on a piece of film look very similar; the illusion of movement comes from small differences between them. MPEG attempts to remove the redundant information in such a sequence of images, producing a 200:1 or greater compression ratio. MPEG also cheats a bit, removing some information that is never restored on decompression. It does this because humans cannot process 30 frames per second and still perceive every detail.

Fractals Some of the highest compression ratios result from fractal algorithms. Fractal algorithms generate random numbers and formulas to produce patterns "on the fly," leaving hardly any data to store. For instance, a program sequence might describe to a computer what a single leaf of a tree looks like and how the leaf can vary in texture, shape, and color. The computer can then generate a realistic-looking tree with thousands of leaves in almost no time, using hardly any stored data. Fractal algorithms have also successfully produced images of erosion patterns on mountains.

Data compression utilities provide valuable benefits beyond conserving disk or tape space. Compression of many data transmissions sent over the Internet, for instance, saves line capacity.

Summary and Key Terms

Systems software consists of programs that coordinate the activities in various parts of the computer system to promote rapid and efficient operation. The basic role of systems software is to act as a mediator between applications programs and the computer system's hardware.

The Operating System A computer's **operating system** is the main collection of systems-software programs that manage the computer system's resources. The functions of the operating system include communicating with the user, making computer-system resources available for use, scheduling jobs for processing, monitoring activities, housekeeping, and security.

As soon as the user enters keystrokes or clicks a mouse, the operating system summons a translator to convert this input into machine-language commands. In the absence of instructions from the user, the operating system implements assumptions called **defaults.**

To interact effectively with your operating system, you must recognize certain conventions. Every operating system maintains its own rules for naming files, adding **file extensions,** and grouping files into directories or folders, among other things. Systematic naming of filenames and extensions help computer users to keep track of a file's contents. **Wildcard characters** help users to perform copying, moving, and deleting operations.

When you turn on power to the computer, the operating system **boots** up. During the boot procedure, the operating system checks for hardware devices online, verifies the presence of files that tell it how to deal with those hardware devices, and does a number of other setup chores before the user begins the current session.

To manage the enormous collection of files on a hard disk, the operating system commonly allows the user to organize files hierarchically into **directories.**To access a file in any directory, the user must specify the **path** that leads through intervening directories to the file. In many desktop operating systems, *files* and *directories* are respectively referred to as *documents* and *folders.*

Computers often enhance efficiency by implementing interleaved processing techniques. **Multiprogramming** allows a multiuser computer system to work concurrently on several programs from several users. **Multitasking** allows concurrent execution of two or more programs from any single user as well as concurrent execution of two or more tasks performed by a single program. **Time-sharing** is a technique in which the operating system cycles through all active programs currently running in the system that need processing, giving a small slice of time on each cycle to each one. **Virtual memory** employs disk storage to extend conventional memory. **Multiprocessing** links together two or more computers to perform work at the same time. **Spooling programs** free the CPU from time-consuming interaction with I/O devices such as printers.

Personal Operating Systems Some of today's most widely used personal operating systems include MS-DOS and PC-DOS (with or without Windows 3.x), Windows 95 and Windows 98, Mac OS, and OS/2.

MS-DOS and **PC-DOS** are commonly found on older PC-compatible microcomputers and similar devices. DOS—the abbreviated name for these operating systems—is one of the most widely used software packages ever developed. Today, many DOS users prefer the Windows user interface. Rather than a separate operating system, **Windows 3.x** adds a GUI shell to DOS that replaces its command line with a system of menus, icons, and screen boxes called *windows.* **Windows 9X**, the successor to Windows 3.x, is a 32-bit operating system that frees the user from the limitations of working with DOS.

Mac OS is the operating system native to the Apple Macintosh line of computers. **OS/2** is an operating system that works with today's PC-compatible microcomputer systems, largely as an alternative to Windows.

Network Operating Systems Network operating systems (NOSs) are so named because their main purpose is serving several users working over a computer network. **Unix** is a flexible, general-purpose operating system that works on mainframes, midrange computers, PCs that act as network servers, graphics workstations, and even the desktop PCs of ordinary users. **NetWare** is an operating system specifically designed to manage the activities of server computers on local area networks (LANs). **Windows NT** is a general-purpose operating system. It runs mostly on server and desktop computers in local area networks.

Utility Programs A **utility program** is a type of systems software program written to perform repetitive processing tasks. There are many types of utility programs. **Disk utility** routines extend the operating system's disk-management capabilities, enabling users to recover erased files, perform **data compression,** reorganize disk data for fast access, and back up data, among other things. **Device drivers** act as interfaces between operating systems and specific hardware devices.

Language Translators A **language translator** is a systems software program that converts into machine language an applications program written in a higher-level language. There are three common types of language translators: compilers, interpreters, and assemblers.

A **compiler** translates a program entirely into machine language before preparing it for execution. An **interpreter** reads, translates, and executes source programs one line at a time. The translation into machine language occurs while the program runs. The third type of translator, an **assembler,** works like a compiler, but it converts only assembly language programs.

EXERCISES

1. Fill in the blanks:
   a. In a multiuser computer system with __________, the computer works on several users' programs concurrently, leaving one idle at some logical stopping point to begin work on another.
   b. __________ is a technique with cooperative and preemptive varieties.
   c. A(n)__________ is an assumption that a computer program makes when the user has indicated no specific choice.
   d. __________ programs are systems software written to perform standard processing tasks, such as sorting and copying data.
   e. Loading the operating system into RAM is known as __________ up the operating system.
2. Define the following terms in your own words:
   a. Data compression
   b. Multitasking
   c. Time-sharing
   d. Virtual memory
   e. Multiprocessing
3. Identify the operating system or operating environment, covered in the chapter, that is described in each sentence.
   a. Windows 3.x provides a graphical user interface for it.
   b. Microsoft designed it to run in organizations, on both office-desktop machines and the network administrator's workstation.
   c. It was originally developed at Bell Labs over 20 years ago.
   d. This product by Novell is designed to manage local area networks (LANs).
   e. While this Microsoft product cannot provide multithreading, it does allow cooperative multitasking.
4. Define the following terms in your own words.
   a. Path
   b. Directory
   c. File extension
   d. Fault-tolerant computing
   e. Wildcard character
5. Match each term with the description that fits best.
   a. Device driver
   b. Compiler
   c. Disk utility
   d. Spooling software
   e. Interpreter
   f. Operating system

   _____ A language translator that reads, translates, and executes source programs a line at a time
   _____ A program that temporarily saves output on disk and then sends it on to the printer as needed
   _____ A program that enables an operating system to work with a specific hardware device
   _____ A data-compression program is an example
   _____ A collection of systems software without which a computer cannot function
   _____ A language translator that creates an object module
6. Describe, in your own words, the differences between the following terms.
   a. Multiprogramming and multiprocessing
   b. Cooperative multitasking and preemptive multitasking
   c. Compiler and interpreter
   d. Segmentation and paging
   e. Coprocessing and parallel processing
7. Explain what happens to a disk when it becomes fragmented. Also, describe what happens when a fragmented disk is defragmented.
8. In what ways do Windows 95 and Windows 98 improve on Windows 3.1?
9. Which of these files would be copied from one disk to another in response to a COPY command with each set of wildcard characters?

MARY	CH01	CH05	FILE3
MAX	CH02	WAV	MMX
MARTY	CH03	TAXES	X23.WAV

   a. MA* c. AX.* e. CH* g. *.WAV
   b. M* d. *.* f. *3 h. *X
10. Fill in the blanks:
   a. __________ is a simplified form of parallel processing that splits up tasks on multiple processors running the same operating system.
   b. Windows NT comes in two versions: a(n) __________ edition, for ordinary users, and a(n) __________ edition, for network administrators.
   c. An input spooling area is sometimes called a(n) __________.
   d. IBM's most advanced microcomputer operating system is called __________.
   e. In network operating systems, a user's __________ specify the types of tasks that the user is authorized to carry out.

1. Windows Two up-to-date forms of Windows enjoy large user bases today: Windows 98 and Windows NT 5.0, Workstation Edition. Research these two operating systems and answer the following questions:

a. In what major ways are these two operating systems alike? In what major ways are they different?
b. What is the street or list price of Windows 98? Windows NT?
c. How much RAM does a microcomputer need to run Windows 98? Windows NT?

2. The Operating System at Your School Gather the following information about the operating system that runs your school's PC lab:

a. Find out the name of the operating system, the name of the company that makes it, and the version your class uses. You should be able to find out the version number from the operating system itself by clicking on a menu choice or typing a command.
b. Which of the following capabilities does the operating system support?

   Multithreading
   Symmetric multiprocessing
   Virtual memory
   Spooling
   Preemptive multitasking
   Multiple users

c. How much disk storage does the operating system use up?

3. Using an Operating System Using the operating system on your own computer or the computers in your school's PC lab, complete any ten of the following tasks:

a. Open a file.
b. Close a file.
c. Format a diskette.
d. Copy a file from the hard disk to a diskette.
e. Make a duplicate copy of a diskette.
f. Rename a file.
g. Create a new folder.
h. Delete a document.
i. Restore a deleted document.
j. View the contents of the hard disk.
k. Access the online help feature.
l. Find all files with a certain extension.

4. Compression Problems Answer the following questions about compression ratios, which were covered in Feature SW 2-2. For simplicity, assume that a megabyte is exactly 1,000 KB.

a. A software package offers a compression ratio of 150:1. How much space will a 50 MB file consume after compression?
b. If a 10 MB file compresses to 100 KB, what's the compression ratio?
c. A software package offers compression ratios that range from 10:1 to 200:1. What's the smallest compressed size of a 5 MB file?

5. Utility Software Look through computer journals or consult the Internet to identify at least one independent software product in each of the listed categories. Besides giving the name of each product, also name the company that sells it, and state its list or street price. In addition, write a sentence or two describing the capabilities of the product.

a. Desktop enhancer
b. Uninstaller
c. Antivirus
d. File viewer
e. Memory manager

6. Backup Many operating systems include built-in routines for backing up hard disks. For any one of the following—DOS, Windows 3.1, Windows 95, Windows 98, Windows NT, Mac OS, or OS/2—answer the following questions:

a. How can you access the backup feature?
b. How does the backup feature work?
c. On what types of storage media can you store backup copies? Does the operating system impose any limitations on the amount of hard-disk storage you can back up?
d. Identify at least one utility software product sold by a third-party vendor with backup capabilities comparable to or better than those of your operating system. Provide the name of the product's vendor and the product's approximate street price.

7. New Key Terms A textbook of this sort can't cover every important development or feature in systems software technology. Several important terms are listed below that are not covered in the chapter. Through library-journal or Internet research, look up any three of these terms, and write out an explanation one-to-three-sentences long describing each one in your own words.

a. The Solaris operating system
b. The Windows 9X Registry

SW

c. The Windows CE operating system
d. AUTOEXEC.BAT file
e. QuickTime
f. Middleware

Hint: If you use the Internet, you might want to consult some of the online computer dictionaries and glossaries that are available. For starters, try any of those available at search sites such as Yahoo! and WebCrawler by doing a category search on such words as "reference," "dictionary," or "computer."

8. Microsoft Corporation Microsoft Corporation—like IBM and many other prominent companies in the history of business—has stirred strong opinions among many people about its practices. Write position statements a paragraph or two in length on each of the following questions.

a. Some observers have suggested that Microsoft can determine the future direction of desktop PC software better than any other company, because it easily leads the market in sales of both desktop and systems PC software. Comment on this statement.
b. Some people have criticized Microsoft's dominance in systems software as an unfair advantage in the market for applications software. Comment on this statement from three separate viewpoints: as a competitor to Microsoft, as a consumer and user of desktop software, and as a representative of the federal government charged with protecting the public interest. As you take the government's viewpoint, be sure to define your vision of the public interest.

9. Researching an Operating System Information about major operating systems is widely available on the Internet and can be collected by visiting the sites of software publishers, user groups, and people who have an interest in this type of systems software. You easily can find such sites if you know the name of an operating system's publisher or if you type the name of the operating system into a Web-based search engine like Yahoo!, WebCrawler, or Alta Vista. For this project, choose an operating system—say, one from the list in Figure SW 2-2. Then, prepare a short report (not exceeding 5 pages) describing such important matters as the operating system's origin or history, user base, main features, hardware requirements, future direction, and the like. Your report should go well beyond the coverage of the operating system in the chapter. Be sure to state the sources of your information and be sure to double-check any facts coming from sources that you think may be unreliable.

10. Windows 98 and the Internet Tools for using the Internet are integrated tightly into the Windows 98 operating system (see figure). This improvement to the Windows user interface enables the Windows 98 electronic desktop—called the *Active Desktop*—to look more like a Web browser, and vice versa, at the user's option. Three examples of this integration:

- Standard office documents and folders can be organized and viewed like Web pages
- The Active Desktop can contain not only standard icons but also entire Web pages and such Java components as a stock ticker or a weather map with temperatures that periodically change
- A history *browser bar* enables you to see in the left third of your screen places you've been to and things you've done—both on and off the Web

For this project, make a reasonably thorough list of Internet features that are integrated into Windows 98 and report your findings to the class. Where possible, describe each feature.

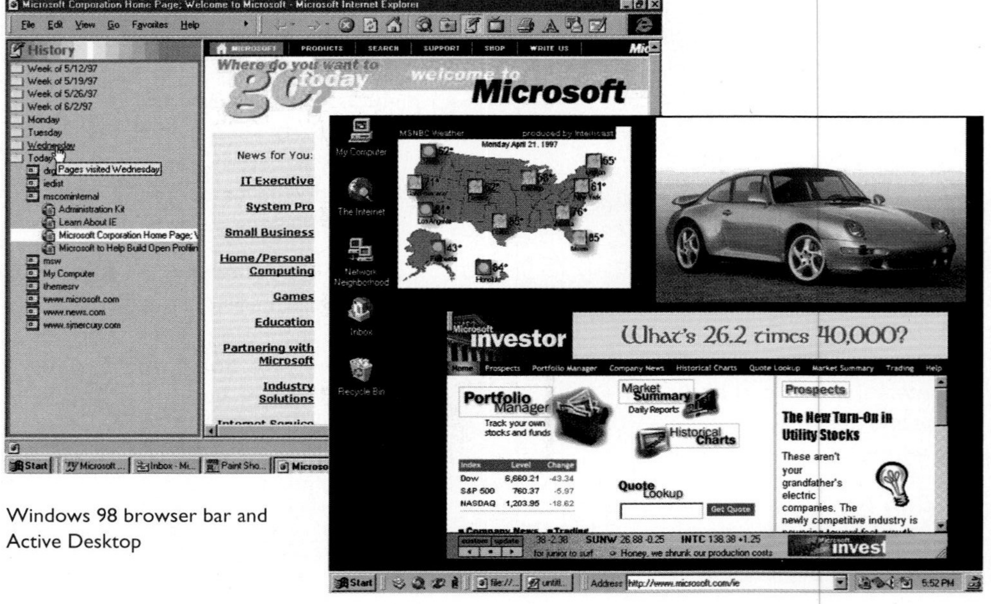

Windows 98 browser bar and Active Desktop

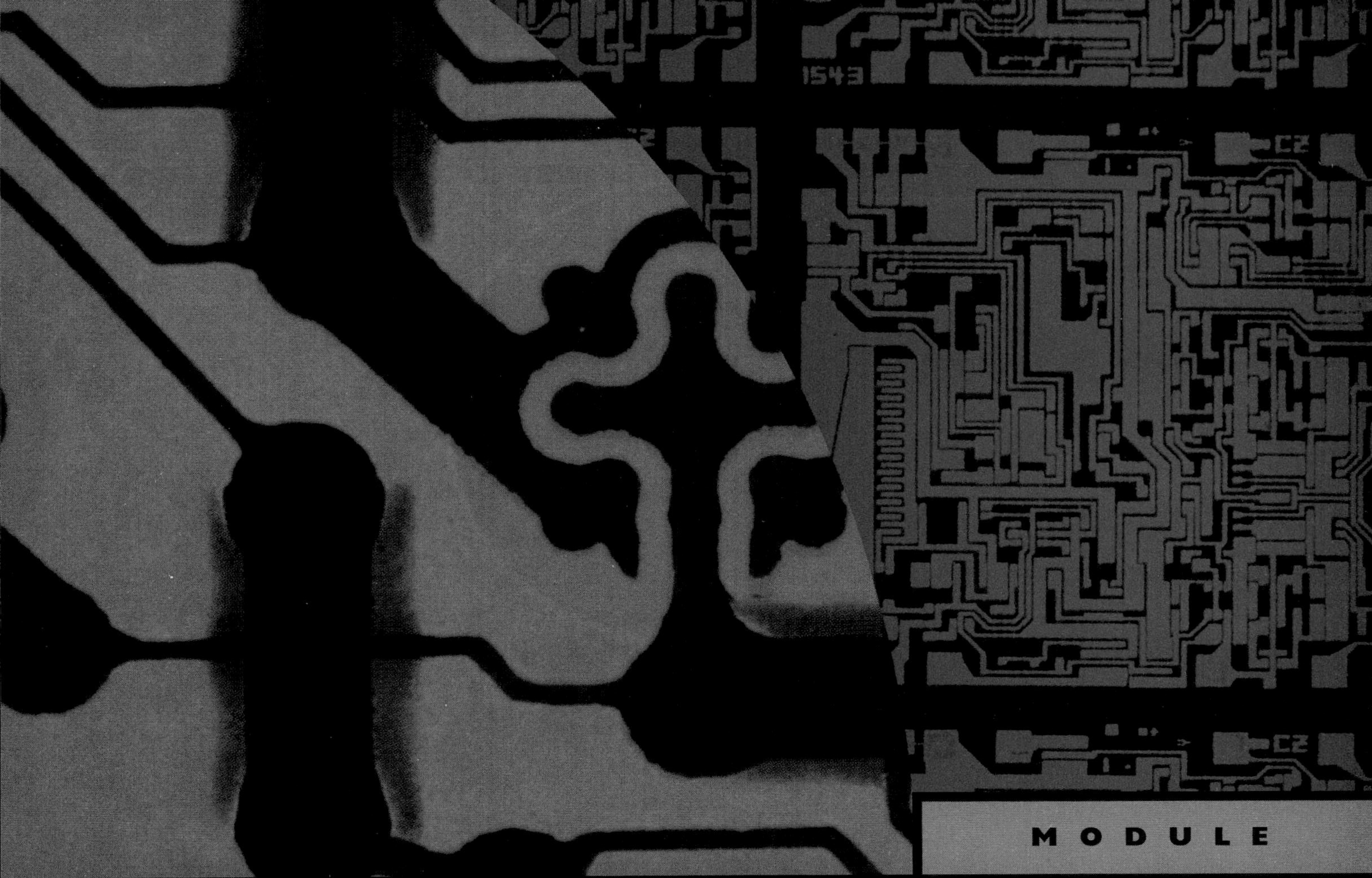

MODULE

Computer Networks NET

Computer networks play a critical role in society and business today. Without computer networks, it would be impossible for us to enjoy many of the modern conveniences upon which we have come to depend or for most businesses to compete effectively.

Chapter NET 1 introduces principles of telecommunications. Here you will learn about many of the hardware, software, and communications-media products used to build networks as well as common types of networks and transmission methods.

The Internet and its World Wide Web are covered in Chapter NET 2. We will look in turn at the components that comprise the Internet, how addresses on the Internet work, Web browsers and their support tools, and choosing among the alternatives available for getting online.

In Chapter NET 3 you will be introduced to some of the principles behind creating Web pages. Advances in software are making it easier and easier for ordinary people to develop their own presence on the Internet. It is conceivable that some day in the not-too-distant future creating a personal Web site will be a task expected of most business professionals.

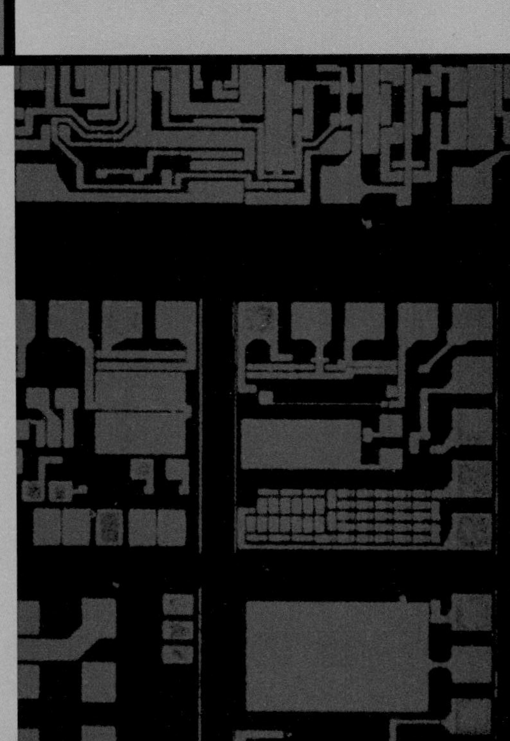

MODULE CONTENTS

Computer Networks

ISBN 0-03-024578-8

NET 1

Telecommunications

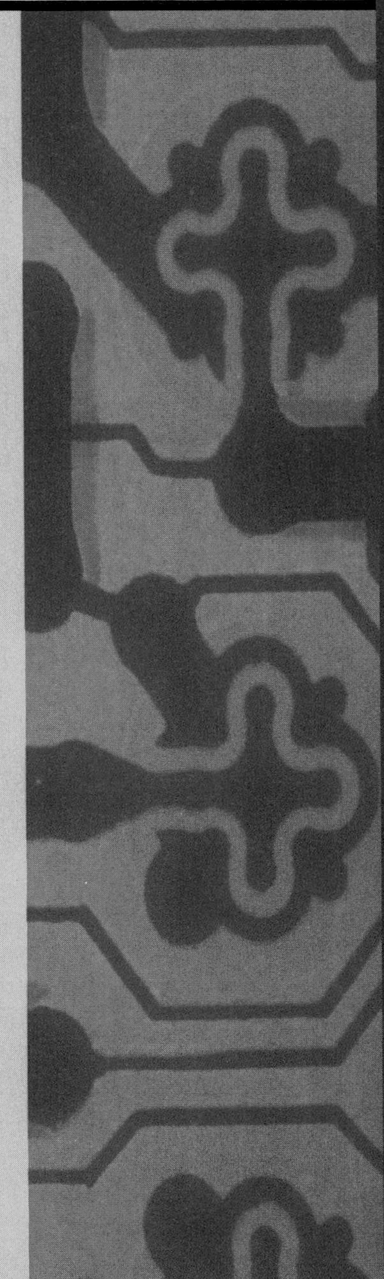

Outline

- Overview
- Telecommunications Applications
  - Electronic Mail and Messaging
  - Information Retrieval
  - Workgroup Computing
  - Transaction Processing
- The Telecommunications Industry
  - The Major Players
  - Government Legislation
- Telecommunications Media
  - Wire Media
  - Wireless Media
- Adapting Computers to Telecommunications Media
  - Sending Data over Media
  - Network Interface Cards and Modems
  - ISDN and Beyond
- Network Topologies
- Local Networks
  - Local Area Networks (LANs)
  - Other Types of Local Networks
- Wide Area Networks (WANs)
  - Handling WAN Traffic
- Communications Protocols
- Dangers Posed by Computer Networks

Learning Objectives

After completing this chapter, you will be able to:

1. Describe several uses of telecommunications technology.
2. Appreciate the changing nature of the telecommunications industry and the effects of government legislation.
3. Name various types of communications media and explain how they carry messages.
4. Identify the hardware, software, and procedural components that link telecommunications systems.
5. Describe several types of local networks and how they work.
6. Explain how users transmit data over wide area networks.
7. Identify some of the dangers posed by computer networks.

Overview

Telecommunications, or *telecom,* refers to communications over a distance—over long-distance phone lines, privately owned cables, or satellites, for instance. Telecommunications has both extended the usefulness of the computer in the workplace and boosted its popularity as a fixture in the home.

In business, telecommunications has become an integral part of operations through the years. Businesspeople throughout the world regularly use electronic mail and messaging systems to communicate with fellow employees and distant associates. Documents that companies once maintained in dog-eared file folders and hand delivered from person to person now zip along at electronic speeds from one desktop computer to another at the press of a button. Ordering and shipping systems depend on computers that regularly touch base with other computers miles away, thereby ensuring on-time deliveries and keeping customers informed. The list of applications is virtually endless.

In the home, the biggest telecom happening in recent years has been the whirlwind popularity of the Internet and World Wide Web. Almost overnight and in a big way, the desktop computer has evolved into a vehicle through which people communicate with faraway friends and surf to exciting online sites. Information on virtually any topic, stored on computers located almost anywhere on the globe, can be retrieved within seconds or minutes (see User Solution NET 1-1). With telecom companies scrambling to bring faster transmissions into the home and with the Internet evolving to deliver new forms of entertainment, many industry experts predict that the best is yet to come.

In Chapter NET 1, we look first at several critical business applications of telecommunications. Next, we profile the telecommunications industry and discuss how government legislation has shaped its growth. Then, we touch on a number of technical issues, including the various ways in which computers transmit data and how networked devices connect to one another. From there, we proceed to the two major types of networks, local networks and wide area networks. The chapter closes with coverage of some of the dangers posed by computer networks. The Internet is treated in depth in Chapters NET 2 and NET 3.

Telecommunications Applications

Today, a wide variety of important business applications involve telecommunications, and the roster of uses is growing rapidly.

ELECTRONIC MAIL AND MESSAGING

One of the biggest applications for telecommunications today is electronic mail and messaging. Several technologies play key roles.

Electronic Mail **Electronic mail,** or **e-mail,** is an application in which users employ software known as *e-mail programs* to exchange electronic messages. The user often composes a message within such a program at a desktop PC workstation and then sends it over long-distance wires or interoffice cable by clicking a Send button. The software deposits the message in an electronic mailbox maintained by the

■ **Telecommunications.** Transmission of data over a distance. ■ **Electronic mail.** The computer-to-computer counterpart for interoffice mail or the postal service. Also called **e-mail.**

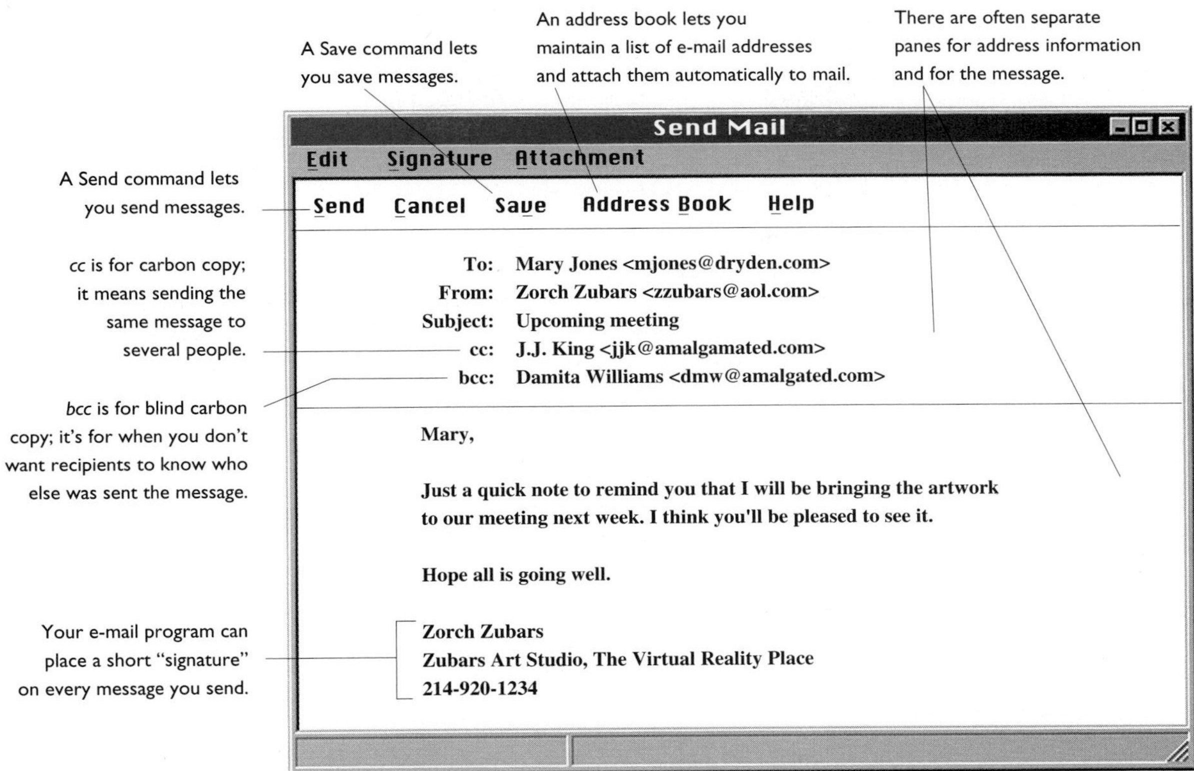
A Save command lets you save messages.
An address book lets you maintain a list of e-mail addresses and attach them automatically to mail.
There are often separate panes for address information and for the message.
Send Mail
Edit Signature Attachment
A Send command lets you send messages.
Send Cancel Save Address Book Help
cc is for carbon copy; it means sending the same message to several people.
bcc is for blind carbon copy; it's for when you don't want recipients to know who else was sent the message.
To: Mary Jones <mjones@dryden.com>
From: Zorch Zubars <zzubars@aol.com>
Subject: Upcoming meeting
cc: J.J. King <jjk@amalgamated.com>
bcc: Damita Williams <dmw@amalgated.com>
Mary,
Just a quick note to remind you that I will be bringing the artwork to our meeting next week. I think you'll be pleased to see it.
Hope all is going well.
Your e-mail program can place a short "signature" on every message you send.
Zorch Zubars
Zubars Art Studio, The Virtual Reality Place
214-920-1234

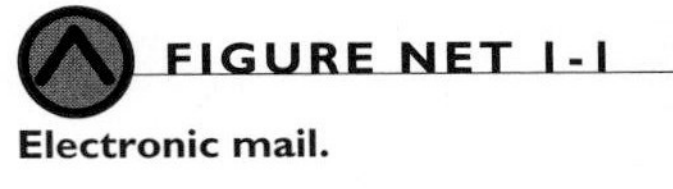
FIGURE NET 1-1
Electronic mail.

receiver, where it can be read at a convenient time. **Electronic mailboxes** are the computer equivalents of traditional mailboxes. They represent space on some computer's hard disk set aside to store e-mail messages. Figure NET 1-1 shows how using e-mail software works.

Voice Mail **Voice mail** is a telecommunications technology that takes electronic mailboxes one step further. A voice-mail system digitizes the sender's spoken message and stores it in bit form on an answering device at the receiver's location. When the receiver presses a Listen key, the digitized message is reconverted to voice data.

Bulletin Boards Unlike an electronic mailbox, which restricts access to an area on disk to only a single individual, an electronic **bulletin board system (BBS)** sets up an area to which several people have access. Functionally, BBSs work like the bulletin boards at supermarkets or health-foods stores—people broadcast notices that may interest others, any of whom may respond. Typically, a single computer bulletin board focuses on a particular interest area. For instance, a company may set up a bulletin board for employees to post computer-related questions, while another bulletin board set up by a college professor may encourage members of a class to share ideas about projects or assignments.

- **Electronic mailbox.** A storage area on a hard disk that holds messages, memos, and other documents for the receiver.
- **Voice mail.** An electronic mail system that digitally records spoken phone messages and stores them in an electronic mailbox.
- **Bulletin board system (BBS).** A computer file shared by several people that enables them to post or broadcast messages.

Facsimile **Facsimile,** or **fax,** technology resembles e-mail, except it employs different methods and it can be more convenient or less convenient for certain types of uses (see Figure NET 1-2).

Facsimile (fax) machines allow users to send images of hard-copy documents from one location to another over ordinary phone lines. For example, a secretary in Seattle may place a short document containing both text and pictures into a fax machine like the one in Figure NET 1-2. The fax machine digitizes the page images and transmits the resulting data over the phone lines to Chicago and Boston. In Chicago, another fax machine receives the electronic page images and reproduces them in hard-copy form. In Boston, a PC's hard disk picks up the fax image in soft-copy form for later viewing on a display screen. All of this data exchange may take place in less than a minute.

PCs need *fax modems* and *fax software* to communicate with both fax machines and other computers with faxing capabilities (return to Figure NET 1-2). Computer-to-computer faxing brings certain advantages, including saving paper, preventing time lost waiting in line for the office fax machine, and allowing recipients to electronically save and modify faxed documents and to route them elsewhere.

FIGURE NET 1-2

Facsimile.

FAX MACHINES
Facsimile (fax) machines make it possible for hard-copy images of documents to be sent from one location to another over ordinary phone lines.

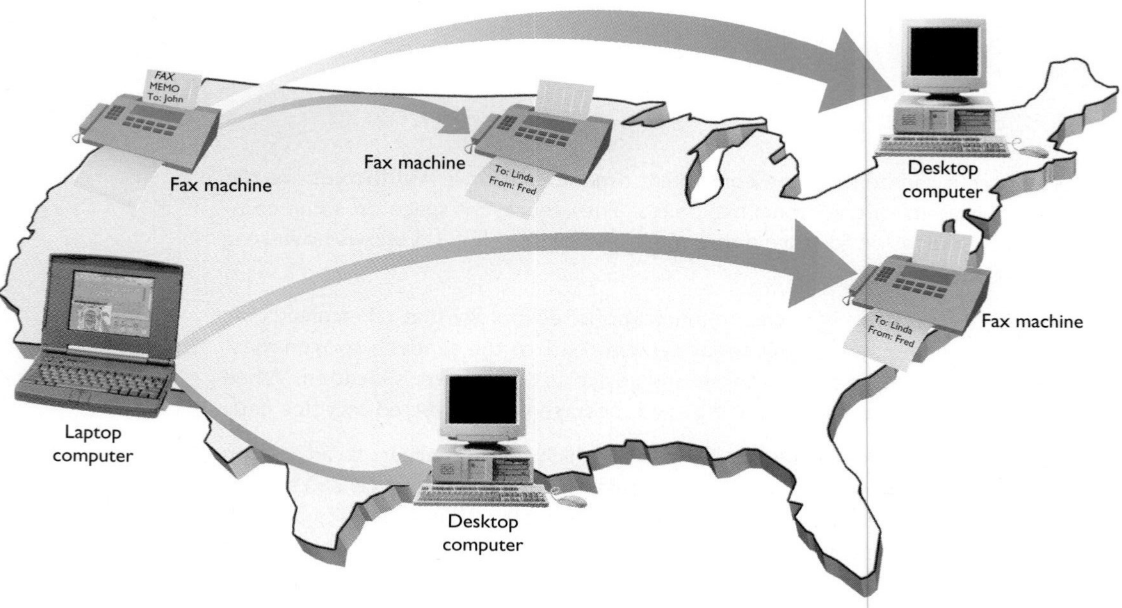

FAX MODEMS
Fax modems and fax software make it possible for PCs to communicate with both fax machines and other PCs with faxing capabilities.

■ **Facsimile.** A method for transmitting text documents, pictures, maps, diagrams, and the like over the phone lines. Abbreviated as **fax.**

Electronic Trading

The rise in computer networks and the Internet have benefited both stock brokerages and small investors. Investors can use their computers to automatically keep track of their stocks, analyze their portfolios, buy and sell stocks and other types of securities, access research materials and reports, and form online communities with other small investors. The brokerage firms like online investing, too. They save on personnel costs when their customers can interact directly with their mainframes. What's more, the investor assumes the responsibility of entering correct trade data. To show their appreciation, most brokerages charge smaller commissions to online traders.

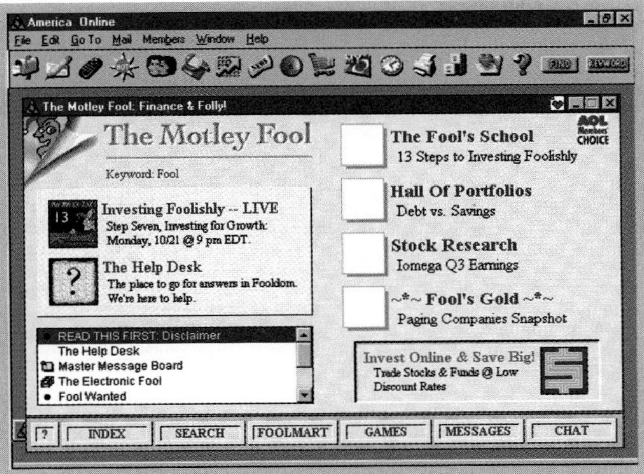

NET

Faxing capabilities are often integrated with other mail and messaging technologies. For instance, e-mail-to-fax software lets users turn their e-mail messages into faxes.

Paging Through a pocket-sized, wireless device called a *pager,* someone can send short messages to another person who is on the move, even across the world (see Figure NET 1-3). Pagers provide either send-only or send-and-receive capabilities, and they often communicate over special wireless networks. Some newer pagers will also let users exchange e-mail messages with anyone having an e-mail connection—including other pager users. More than 35 million people use pagers in the United States alone, and that number is growing annually at double-digit rates.

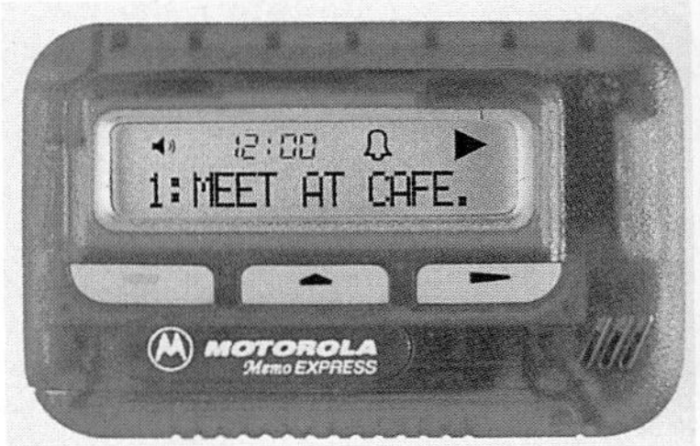

FIGURE NET 1-3

Paging. Pagers are carried by people on the move. More than 35 million people use pagers in the United States alone.

INFORMATION RETRIEVAL

The assortment of information you can get over the phone lines today is, in a word, amazing. Thousands of public and private databases are currently available for online *information retrieval.* Database services catering to the public specialize in the needs of recreational users, shoppers, businesses, researchers, travelers, and others with particular information needs.

Subscription Services Many people get their online information by paying a particular *commercial online service* to supply it. In the strictest sense, the term *commercial online service* applies rather broadly to include any dial-up entity providing an online service, such as any of the thousands of local bulletin board services with tiny audiences. However, we will follow common practice and use the term to refer to the big, nationally promoted services that provide a wide range of information to paying subscribers.

America Online, CompuServe, Prodigy, and the Microsoft Network are four of the biggest commercial online services. These companies work much like cable television providers, which buy rights to broadcast certain television channels, bundle the channels into several attractive packages, and resell the packages to consumers. When you subscribe to a package—or plan—from a commercial online service, you gain access to the information databases to which it, in turn, subscribes. Such services

AMERICA ONLINE
From AOL's newsstand can be accessed dozens of online versions of popular magazines.

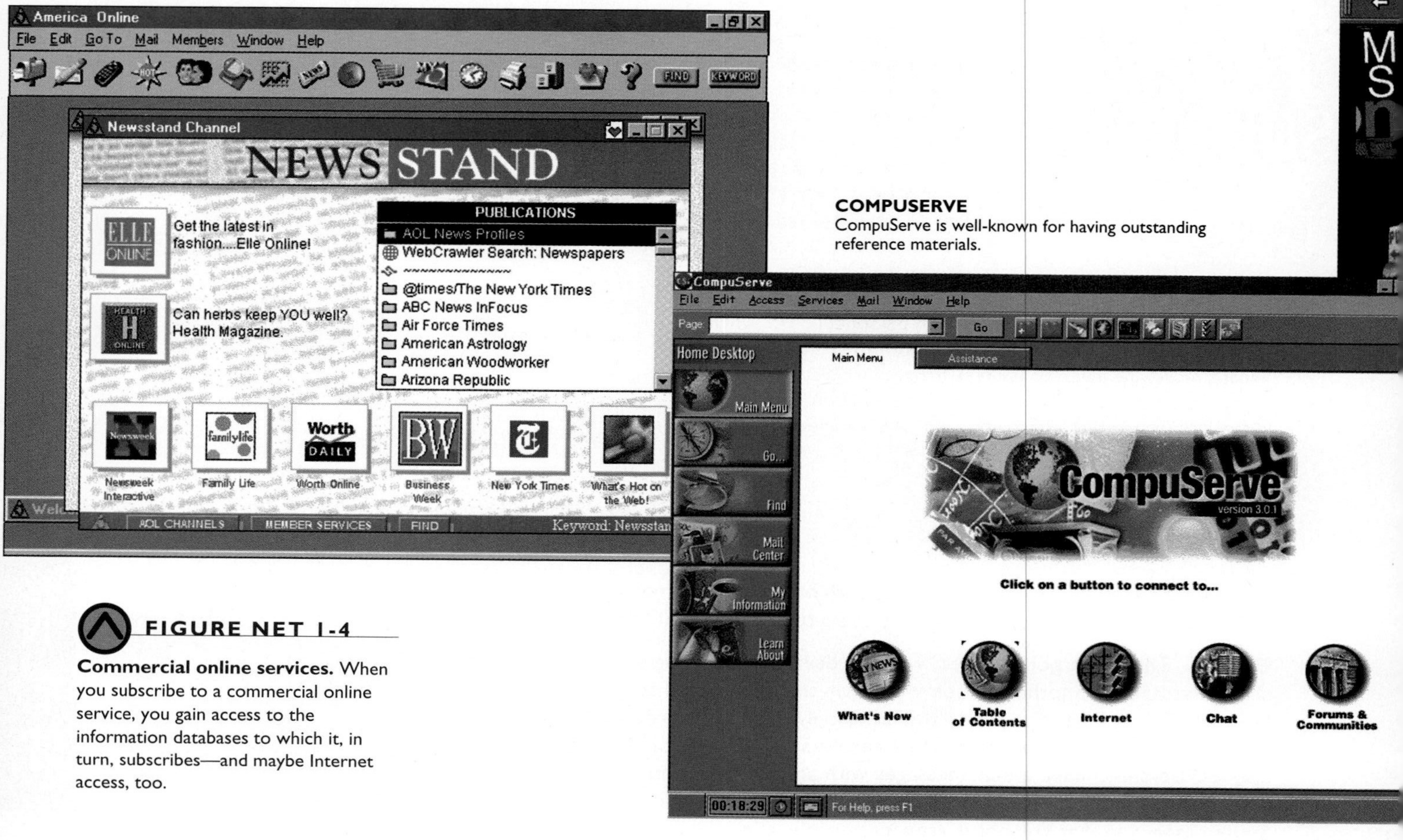

COMPUSERVE
CompuServe is well-known for having outstanding reference materials.

FIGURE NET 1-4

Commercial online services. When you subscribe to a commercial online service, you gain access to the information databases to which it, in turn, subscribes—and maybe Internet access, too.

provide information useful to the average person, such as news and weather, personal investing and money management, travel, entertainment, and shopping (see Figure NET 1-4). They also provide access to the Internet.

Most commercial online services charge a monthly fee and, depending on the plan to which a user subscribes, possibly an hourly hookup charge, as well. Additional charges are levied for some types of services—such as faster transmission speeds and access to magazines, newspapers, and special reports. Most commercial online services also provide e-mail, their own bulletin boards, and a variety of other information-related services.

The Internet The **Internet** (named as a contraction of the two words *inter*connected *net*works) is a global web linking tens of thousands of networks and millions of individual users, businesses, schools, government agencies, and other organizations. It is a favorite source of information today because its resources include a vast storehouse of facts with which people can easily play or work. The Internet is widely used

■ **The Internet.** A global network linking tens of thousands of networks and millions of individual users, schools, businesses, and government agencies.

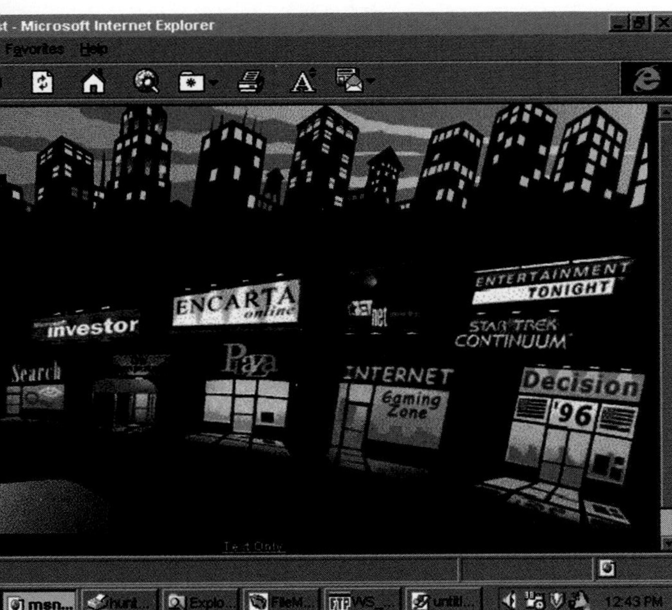

THE MICROSOFT NETWORK
MSN has its own news bureau and a lot of unique content that is highly entertaining.

PRODIGY
Prodigy has scores of resources that can be enjoyed by both children and adults.

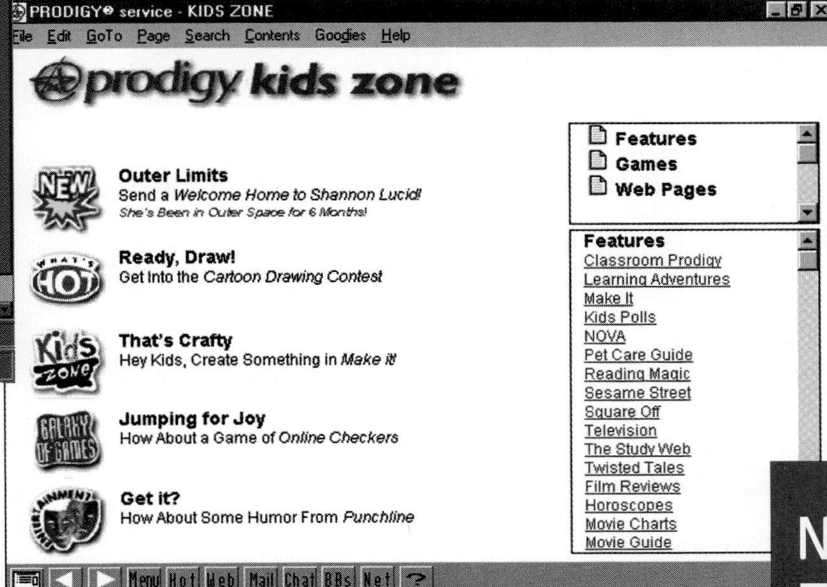

for information retrieval and e-mail along with a variety of other applications (see Figure NET 1-5).

Many individuals are able to access the Internet virtually without charge through their schools, companies, or local libraries. Why would anyone want to pay for information through a commercial online service when they could get it free on the Internet, you ask? The commercial online services are generally easier to use, they shield people from the chaos that sometimes prevails on the Internet, and they package information better. Also, if you want to use the Internet for personal purposes when you leave school, you will probably have to pay for access, anyway—either through a commercial online service or some other type of Internet service provider.

Many computer-industry experts believe that the Internet will become the engine for the so-called *information superhighway* through which businesses and homes will be able to tap into an even more dazzling array of computerized services than is available today. We will be covering the Internet in depth in Chapters NET 2 and NET 3.

WORKGROUP COMPUTING

A telecom application that has become very popular in recent years is workgroup computing. **Workgroup computing** allows several people to use their desktop workstations to collaborate in their job tasks.

■ **Workgroup computing.** Several people using desktop workstations to collaborate in their job tasks.

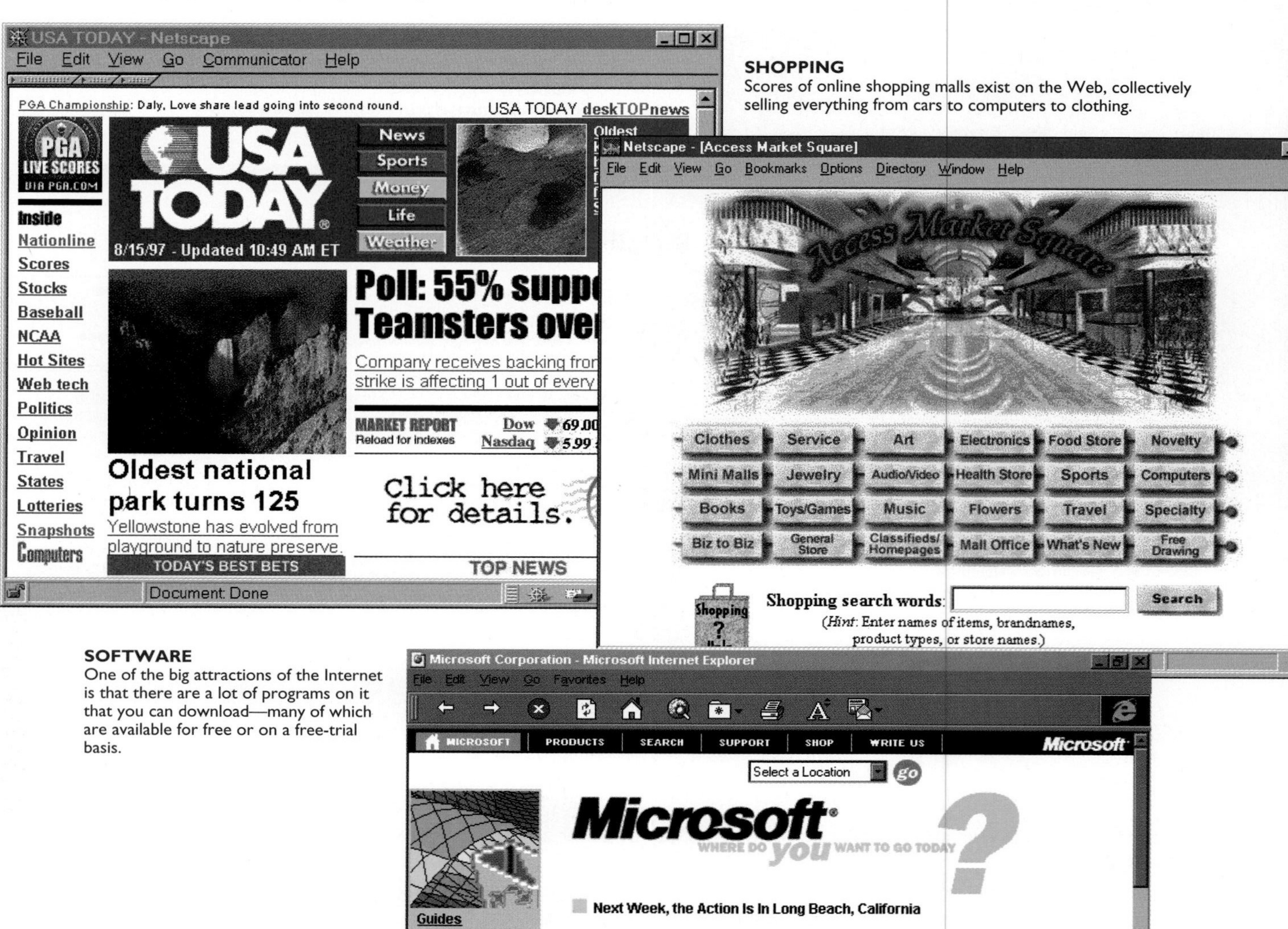

FIGURE NET 1-5

The Internet's World Wide Web. One of the most popular features of the Internet is the World Wide Web, which brings virtually any sort of information anyone could imagine to a computer's display screen in the form of easy-to-read pages.

The insurance industry provides a good example. Years ago, clerks would have processed an accident claim by filling out forms by hand and manually walking file folders around from desk to desk for approvals and signatures. Today, such claims are processed electronically with special *workgroup-computing software*, or *groupware* as it is more commonly known. The software generates electronic forms and displays them as necessary so workers can fill them in with data, review their work, and approve payment at desktop computer workstations. The software can automatically route and monitor the progress of forms, as well. Consequently, insurers can process claims more rapidly and reliably and with far fewer errors than they could before groupware was available. Better service is often provided, too, since an adjuster can give claimants progress reports after pressing only a few keystrokes. Alternatively, claimants can get reports themselves over the Internet.

Groupware is getting attention wherever people need to collaborate on their jobs. Engineers and architects commonly use groupware to collaborate on designs, newspapers use it to circulate pieces among writers and editors, professionals use it to take part in online conferences, and so on.

TRANSACTION PROCESSING

Transaction-processing operations such as entering orders and handling accounts receivable are the lifeblood of most companies. Pull the plug on the computers doing these tasks, and the companies go out of business.

At one time, transaction-processing operations were totally centralized. As communications systems allowed firms to distribute workloads to multiple sites, many organizations modified their transaction-processing systems accordingly.

The airlines' passenger reservation systems offer a noteworthy example; thousands of ticketing agents located across the globe use display workstations to tap into distant computerized databases full of flight, hotel, and rental-car information. While a computer in, say, Chicago is gathering flight information for an agent in Cerritos, California, that same agent may be completing local processing of a ticket for another client. Credit-card systems, such as the one for VISA illustrated in Figure NET 1-6, are also good examples of distributed transaction processing. Once a store clerk inserts a credit card into a verification terminal, computers hundreds or thousands of miles away approve or deny the purchase.

FIGURE NET 1-6

Distributed processing: trailing a VISA transaction. In a routine transaction, the response retraces the same path as the query back to the originating store. Total elapsed time for a typical transaction is approximately 15 seconds.

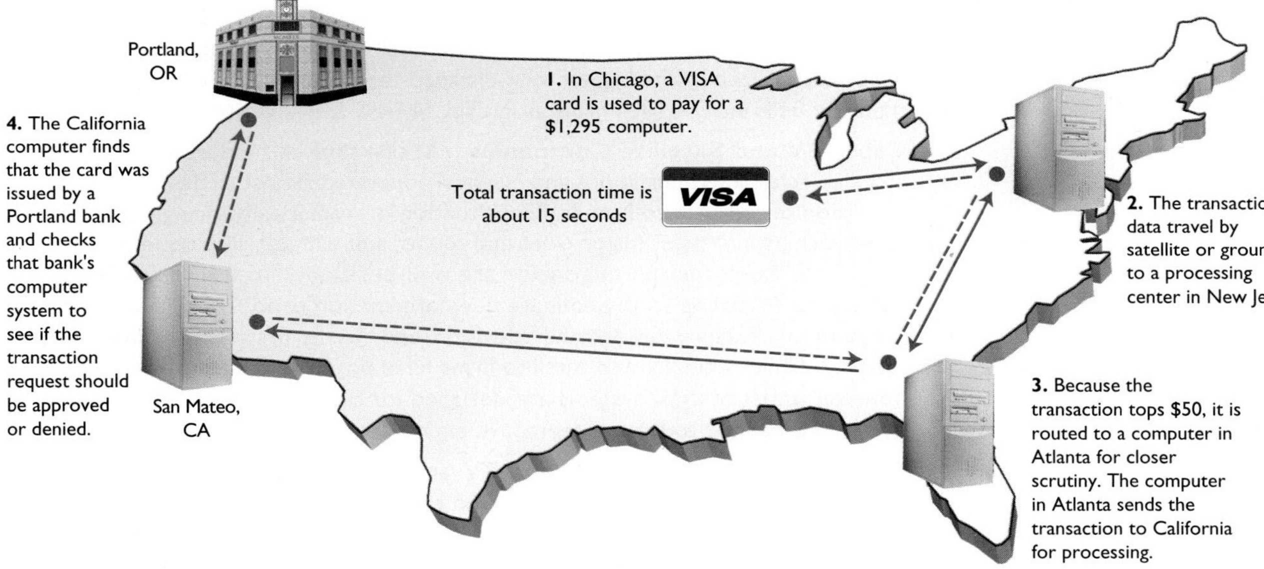
Portland, OR
1. In Chicago, a VISA card is used to pay for a $1,295 computer.
4. The California computer finds that the card was issued by a Portland bank and checks that bank's computer system to see if the transaction request should be approved or denied.
Total transaction time is about 15 seconds
VISA
2. The transaction data travel by satellite or ground to a processing center in New Jersey.
San Mateo, CA
3. Because the transaction tops $50, it is routed to a computer in Atlanta for closer scrutiny. The computer in Atlanta sends the transaction to California for processing.

Virtually every large organization today maintains several types of distributed transaction-processing systems. For instance, chain stores often collect and process data locally, and then transmit these data to headquarters sites for timely analysis. Mail-order firms frequently process orders at central sites and then transmit transaction data to warehouse sites to initiate packing and delivery. The applications are countless.

Interorganizational Systems Recently, many companies have extended their distributed transaction-processing systems a step further by creating *interorganizational systems (IOSs),* which strategically link their computers to the computers of key customers and/or suppliers. For instance, many of the major automakers constantly monitor their suppliers' computer systems via internal computers to ensure proper inventory levels for critical parts. They also use the IOSs to shop electronically for the best prices.

Another common type of interorganizational system, **electronic data interchange (EDI),** facilitates the exchange of standard business documents—such as purchase orders and invoices—from one company's computer system to the system of another company. What's more, the company doing the purchasing often uses EDI to electronically track its order's progress on the seller's computer system. Many large companies today order sizable percentages of their supplies or raw materials through EDI.

Some firms use modern communications technology to take EDI a step further. At such giant companies as General Motors and DuPont, large suppliers of key items no longer even have to wait for purchase orders. When the suppliers see low stocks of materials on General Motors's or DuPont's computers, they automatically ship the goods and send electronic invoices.

The Telecommunications Industry

Here, we look at the types of firms that make up the telecommunications industry. We also consider the role government plays in shaping that industry's future.

THE MAJOR PLAYERS

At one time, the telecommunications industry was synonymous with the phone company. While phone companies are still a major part of the telecommunications scene, these days many more players participate, as well.

Phone Companies The phone companies own the mammoth telephone network that can connect virtually any two points on the globe. These companies not only provide regular phone service, but they also transmit data between businesses and handle most of the traffic on the Internet. Phone companies are of two types—long-distance carriers and regional Bell operating companies (RBOCs) or "Baby Bells." Two of the biggest long-distance service providers are AT&T and MCI; the Baby Bells include such firms as PacTel, Nynex, and Ameritech.

Cable-TV and Satellite Companies At one time this industry sector—which includes Tele-Communications and Hughes—operated almost exclusively to transmit television broadcasts to homes. The situation is dramatically changing. With cable now reaching into most major cities and towns, and with satellite dishes serving outlying areas, companies in this sector are well-positioned to use their communications infrastructures to disseminate new information products such as electronic shopping and banking, on-demand television, and twenty-first-century Internet applications. While cable-TV and satellite firms have powerful transmission capabilities, however, most of their systems are designed for one-way broadcasting, and major overhaul is needed to handle interactive exchanges.

Content Providers Phone, cable-TV, and satellite companies own and operate the infrastructure over which information travels. By contrast, content providers—such as Disney and America Online—create or package the information products that the infrastructure carries. Although content providers know what types of products turn people on, they often have relatively little experience with the technical details of telecommunications. Thus, they must rely on infrastructure companies to reach into homes and businesses.

Other Companies This group includes software companies—like Microsoft, IBM, and Oracle—whose main strength centers on building the necessary computer capabilities into the information products of the future. Will people use a Windows-like interface to control the television sets of tomorrow? Some people think so. Also included in this industry-support group are firms like Cisco Systems and Bay Networks, both of which have expertise in the area of supplying communications hardware to the marketplace.

■ **Electronic data interchange (EDI).** A computer procedure that enables firms to electronically exchange standard business documents such as purchase orders and invoices.

Throughout the entire telecom industry, the current wave of mergers and acquisitions, partnering arrangements, and shakeouts will determine within the next few years who will win and who will lose. Firms that have traditionally operated in one sector are quickly expanding into other sectors to position themselves for success. For instance, a communications infrastructure needs content to deliver, and a content provider needs infrastructure to carry its product. Furthermore, all of this activity requires the development of new software and the construction of new networks. In order to deliver the information products of the future, companies will have to think beyond their traditional markets and boundaries. Microsoft is one familiar company that's seriously taken a plunge into this uncertain future, for instance, rapidly transforming itself from strictly a software company to a provider of both software and content.

GOVERNMENT LEGISLATION

Before 1968, AT&T was "the" phone company in the United States. It owned essentially all of the phone lines and, also, all of the phones on its lines. The federal government believed that the survival of the phone system depended on protecting the interests of a single provider. The government also tightly regulated both AT&T and practices within its industry.

The wheels of change began to turn in 1968, when the Federal Communications Commission (FCC) produced the *Carterfone Decision,* allowing a small company to connect its own two-way radios to the phone lines. This ruling opened the doors for anyone to buy a non-AT&T phone and hook it up to the AT&T system. Later federal-government rulings forced AT&T to divest its regional phone services—today's Baby Bells—and enabled companies like MCI and Sprint to compete with AT&T for long-distance phone business.

Despite the injection of competition, however, industry regulation was still relatively tight at the end of the 1980s. A license to operate in one sector of the industry often prohibited a company from entering another. Critics of government policy argued that this regulatory model would not serve the public well in the upcoming age of fast-paced technological change. They felt that if government were to tear down barriers to competition, so that companies were free to operate wherever they wanted, consumers would ultimately get better products at lower prices.

The Telecommunications Act of 1996 essentially deregulated the entire telecommunications industry. Consequently, telephone companies, cable-TV and satellite operators, and firms in other segments of the industry are now free to enter each other's markets. If telephone companies can compete unrestricted with cable-TV operators, so the thinking goes, then perhaps the final result will be better television programming and service at lower prices. Similarly unconstrained cable-TV operators might also be able to produce better results with phone service.

Conventional wisdom may or may not prove correct, and you should expect turbulence in the future regulatory environment of the telecommunications industry. Of course, it is not out of the realm of possibility that the government could reverse itself back into a regulatory mode. A change in policy would be most likely if deregulation served to produce monopolistic giants who kept prices high while thwarting industry progress.

Telecommunications Media

Figure NET 1-7 shows a simple telecommunications system, in which two distant hardware units transfer messages over some type of **communications medium.**

■ **Communications medium.** The intervening link, such as a telephone wire or cable, that connects two physically distant hardware devices.

FIGURE NET 1-7

A simple telecommunications system.

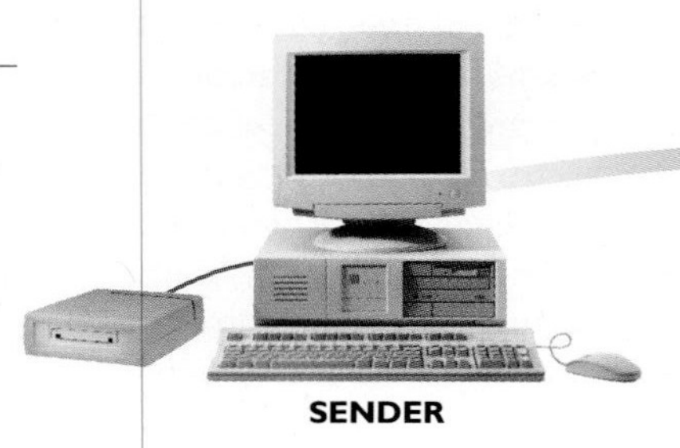

The hardware units may be two desktop computers, a desktop computer and a mainframe, or some other combination of two devices. The medium may be a privately operated set of cables or it may consist of the public phone lines, microwaves, or some other alternative. When a message is transmitted, one of the hardware units is designated as the *sender* and the other as the *receiver.* The message may be sent over the medium in several ways, as this section will demonstrate.

Communications media fall into one of two classes: wire and wireless media.

WIRE MEDIA

Telecommunications systems commonly carry messages over three types of wiring: twisted-pair wires, coaxial cable, and fiber optic cable (see Figure NET 1-8).

TWISTED-PAIR WIRES

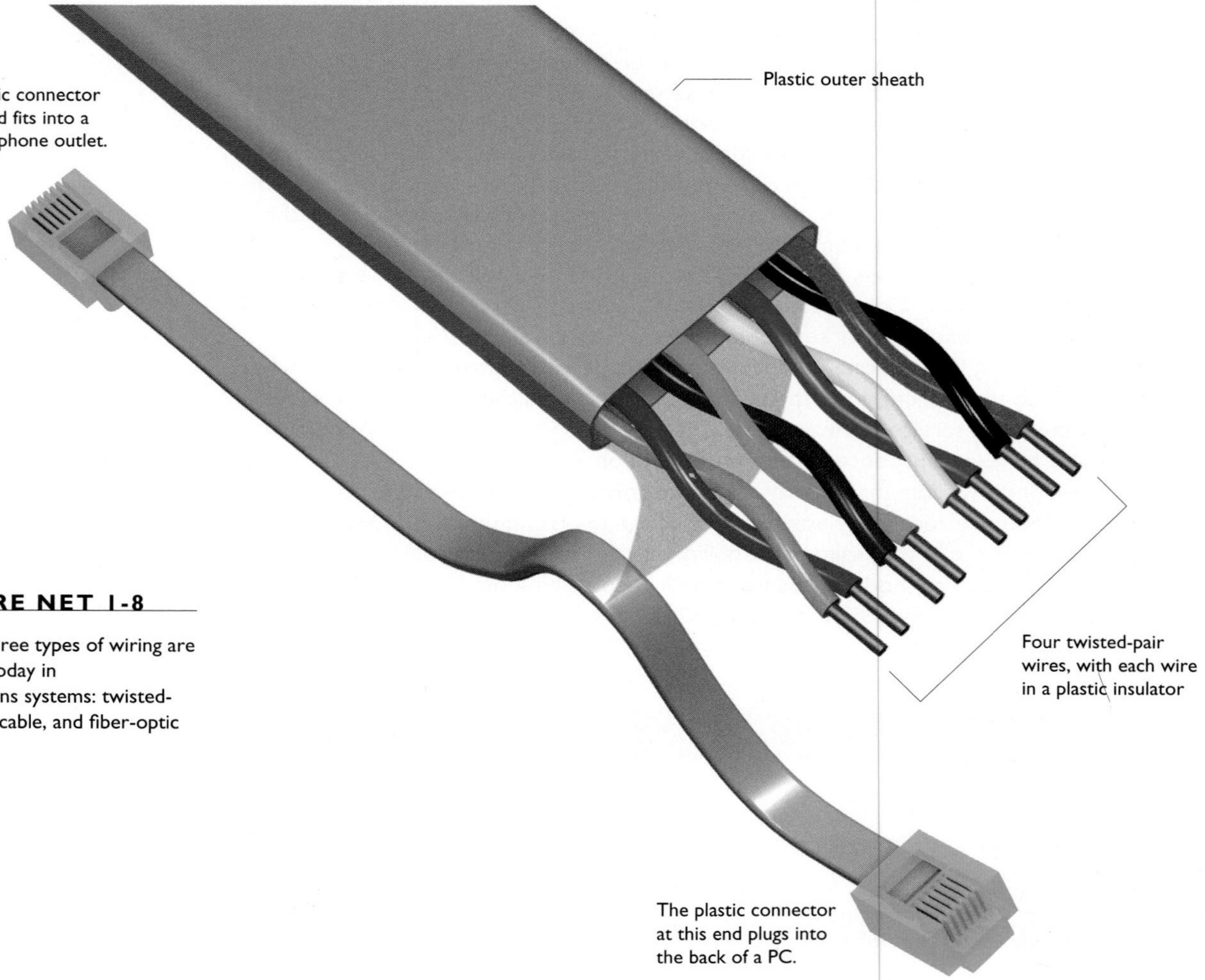

Plastic outer sheath

The plastic connector at this end fits into a standard phone outlet.

Four twisted-pair wires, with each wire in a plastic insulator

The plastic connector at this end plugs into the back of a PC.

FIGURE NET 1-8

Wire media. Three types of wiring are commonly used today in telecommunications systems: twisted-pair wire, coaxial cable, and fiber-optic cable.

Twisted-Pair Wires **Twisted-pair wires,** in which thin strands of wire are twisted together in sets of two, is the communications medium that has been in use the longest. The telephone system still carries most of the data transmitted in this country and abroad primarily over inexpensive twisted-pair wires. In some cases, several thousand pairs may be bound together into single cables to connect switching stations within a city. By contrast, only a few pairs are needed to connect a home phone to the closest telephone pole.

Coaxial Cable **Coaxial cable,** the medium pioneered by the cable television industry, was originally developed to carry high-speed, interference-free video transmissions. Coaxial cable is now also widely used in other types of communication applications, such as linking computers in office networks. Additionally, phone companies rely heavily on coaxial cable.

MESSAGE

As complicated as telecommunications systems may seem, at their simplest level they allow one device to communicate effectively with another.

COAXIAL CABLE

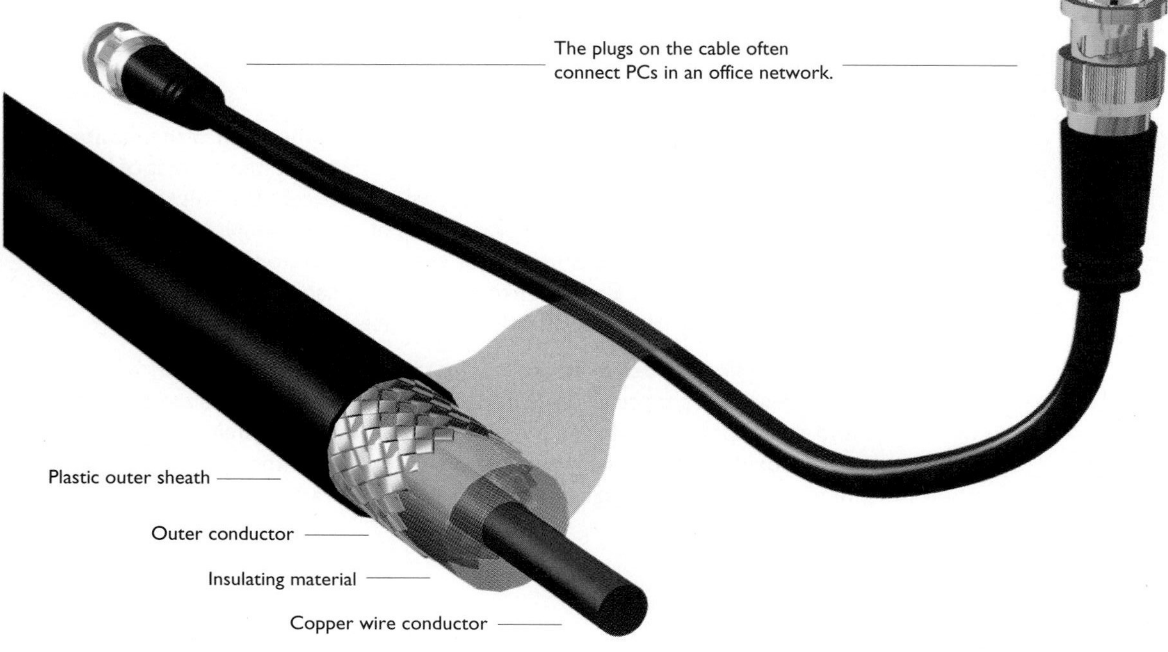

continued

NET

■ **Twisted-pair wire.** A communications medium consisting of wire strands twisted in sets of two and bound into a cable.
■ **Coaxial cable.** A transmission medium, consisting of a center wire inside a grounded, cylindrical shield, capable of sending data at high speeds.

FIBER-OPTIC CABLE

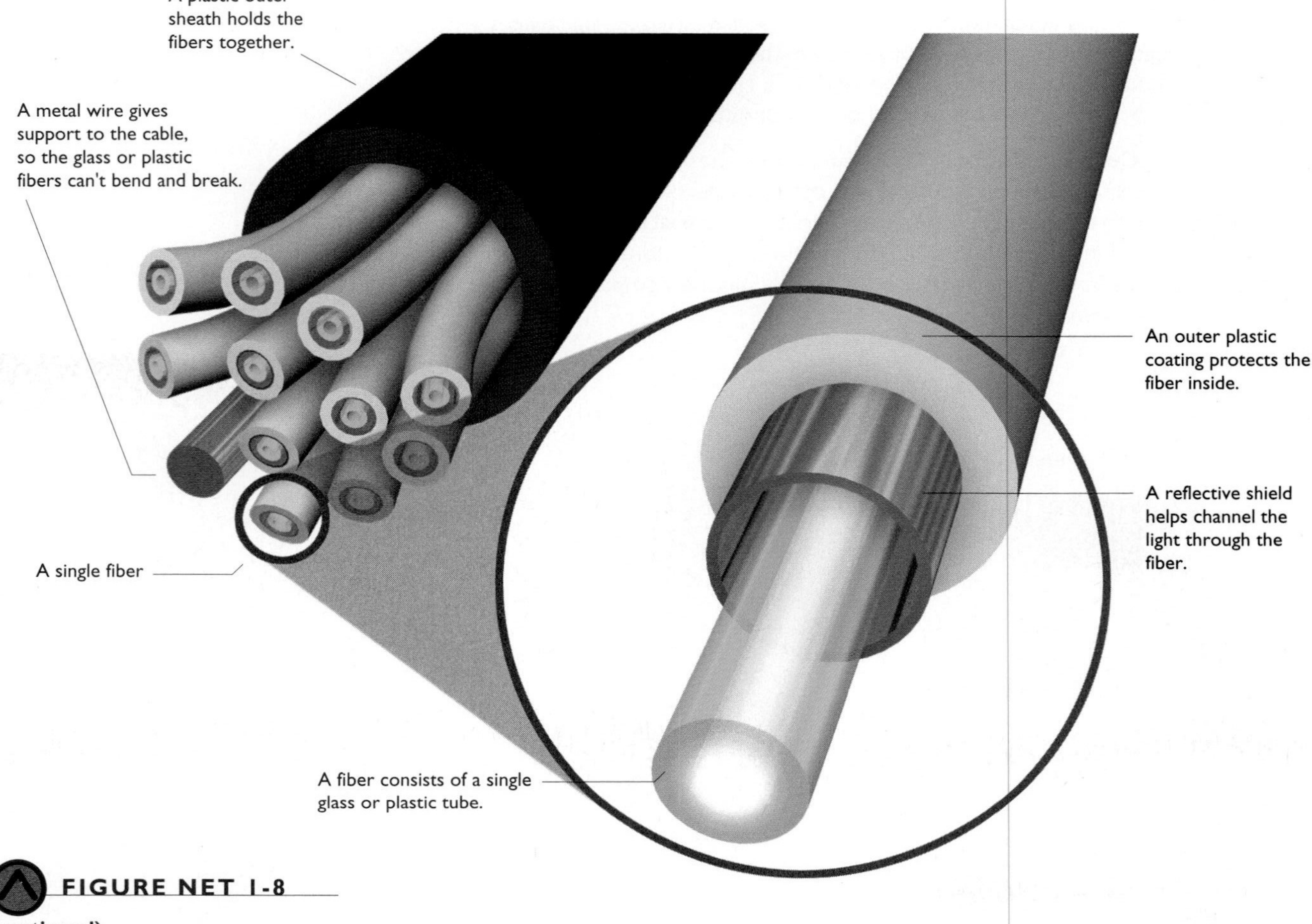

A plastic outer sheath holds the fibers together.
A metal wire gives support to the cable, so the glass or plastic fibers can't bend and break.
A single fiber
An outer plastic coating protects the fiber inside.
A reflective shield helps channel the light through the fiber.
A fiber consists of a single glass or plastic tube.

FIGURE NET 1-8
(continued)

Fiber-Optic Cable One of the most successful developments in transmission media in recent years has been fiber optics. **Fiber-optic cables** often consist of hundreds of clear glass or plastic fiber strands, each approximately the thickness of a human hair. Transmission requires the transformation of data into light beams, which are sent through the cable by a laser device at speeds on the order of billions or even trillions of bits per second. Each hairlike fiber has the capacity to carry data for several television stations or thousands of two-way voice conversations.

The advantages of fiber optics over other wire media include speed, size, weight, security, and longevity. In particular, enormous speed differences separate conventional wire and fiber-optic cable. In the six seconds it takes to transmit a single page of Webster's unabridged dictionary over conventional wire, more than a dozen copies of the entire 2,000-plus pages of the work can be transmitted over a single fiber-optic strand.

WIRELESS MEDIA

Wireless transmission media have become especially popular in recent years. They support communications in situations in which physical wiring is impractical. What's

■ **Fiber-optic cable.** A transmission medium composed of hundreds of hair-thin, transparent fibers along which lasers carry data as light waves.

more, the lack of wiring can serve to make devices highly portable. Three widely used media for wireless communications are microwave technology, cellular technology, and infrared technology.

Microwave Technology **Microwaves** are high-frequency radio signals. Text, graphics, audio, and video data can all be converted to microwave impulses and transmitted through the air. Microwave signals can be sent in two ways: via terrestrial stations or by way of satellites (see Figure NET 1-9). Both can transmit data in large quantities and at high speeds.

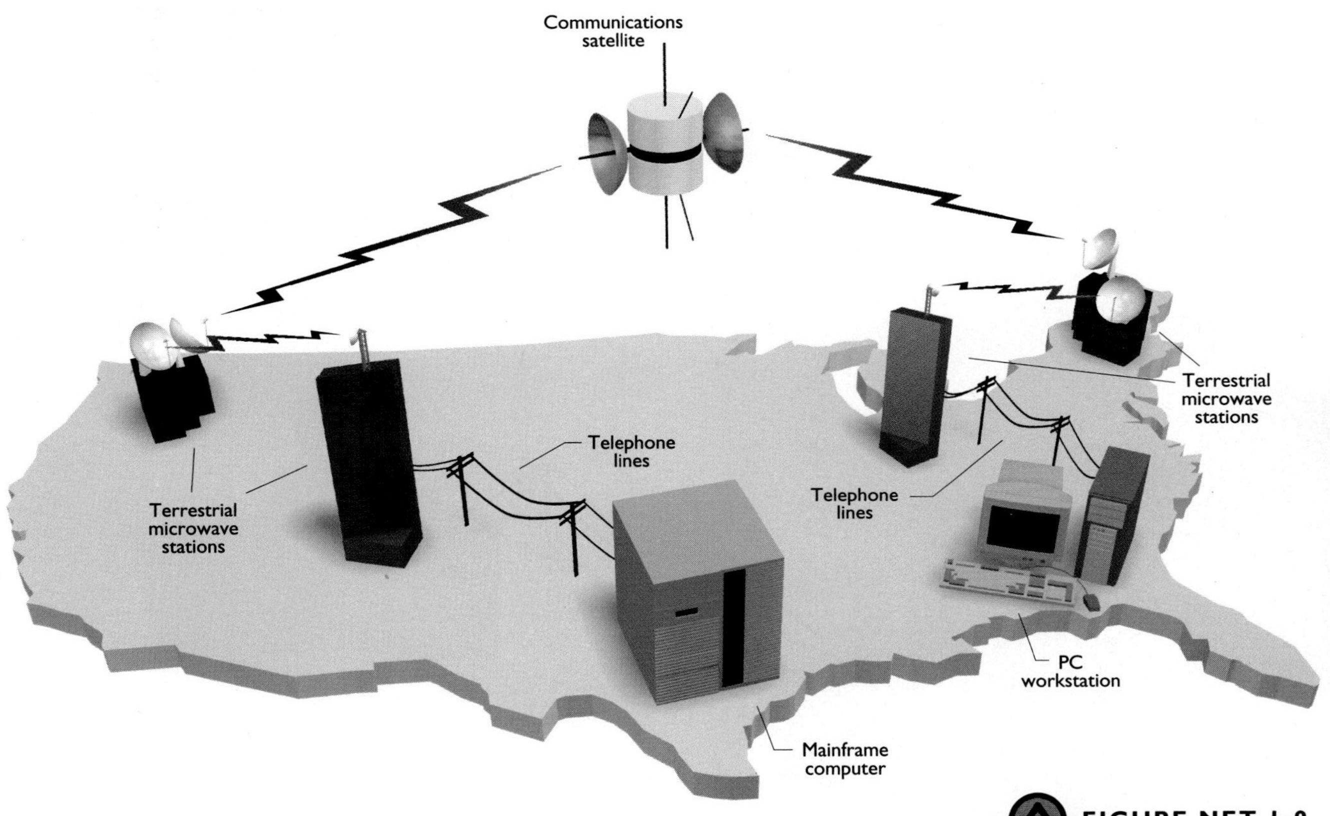

FIGURE NET 1-9

Microwave transmission. Microwave signals can move in two ways: via terrestrial stations or by way of satellites.

Terrestrial microwave stations can communicate with each other directly over distances of no more than 25 to 30 miles. The stations need not be within actual sight of each other; however, they should have a clear path along which to communicate. To avoid obstacles like mountains and the curvature of the earth, the stations often are placed on tall buildings and mountaintops. When one station receives a message from another, it amplifies it and passes it on to the next station.

Communications satellites were developed to reduce the cost of long-distance transmission via terrestrial microwave repeater stations and to provide a cheaper and better overseas communications medium than undersea cable. Communications satellites maintain *geosynchronous orbits* thousands of miles above the earth. "Geosynchronous" means that, because the satellites travel at the same speed as the earth's rotation, they appear to remain stationary over a given spot on the globe.

■ **Microwave.** An electromagnetic wave in the high-frequency range. ■ **Terrestrial microwave station.** A ground station that receives microwave signals, amplifies them, and passes them on to another station. ■ **Communications satellite.** An earth-orbiting device that relays communications signals over long distances.

Both communications satellites and terrestrial microwave stations work best when they transmit large amounts of data one way at a time. Thus, they are ideal for applications such as television and radio broadcasting.

Cellular Technology **Cellular phones** are mobile telephones that do not need hookups to standard phone outlets in order to work. They can put two people into communication with each other almost anywhere, even if the parties are in motion.

Cellular phones, which use radio waves, operate by keeping in contact with cellular antennae (see Figure NET 1-10). These antennae, which resemble tall, metal telephone poles, are strategically placed throughout a calling area. Calling areas are divided into zones measuring 10 miles wide or so, called *cells,* each with its own antenna. The antennae perform two essential functions: (1) They enable a moving cellular phone to transmit and receive uninterrupted by passing signals off to antennae in contiguous cells into which the phones are moving, and (2) they provide an interface with the regular public phone network via a switching office.

FIGURE NET 1-10

Cellular phones.

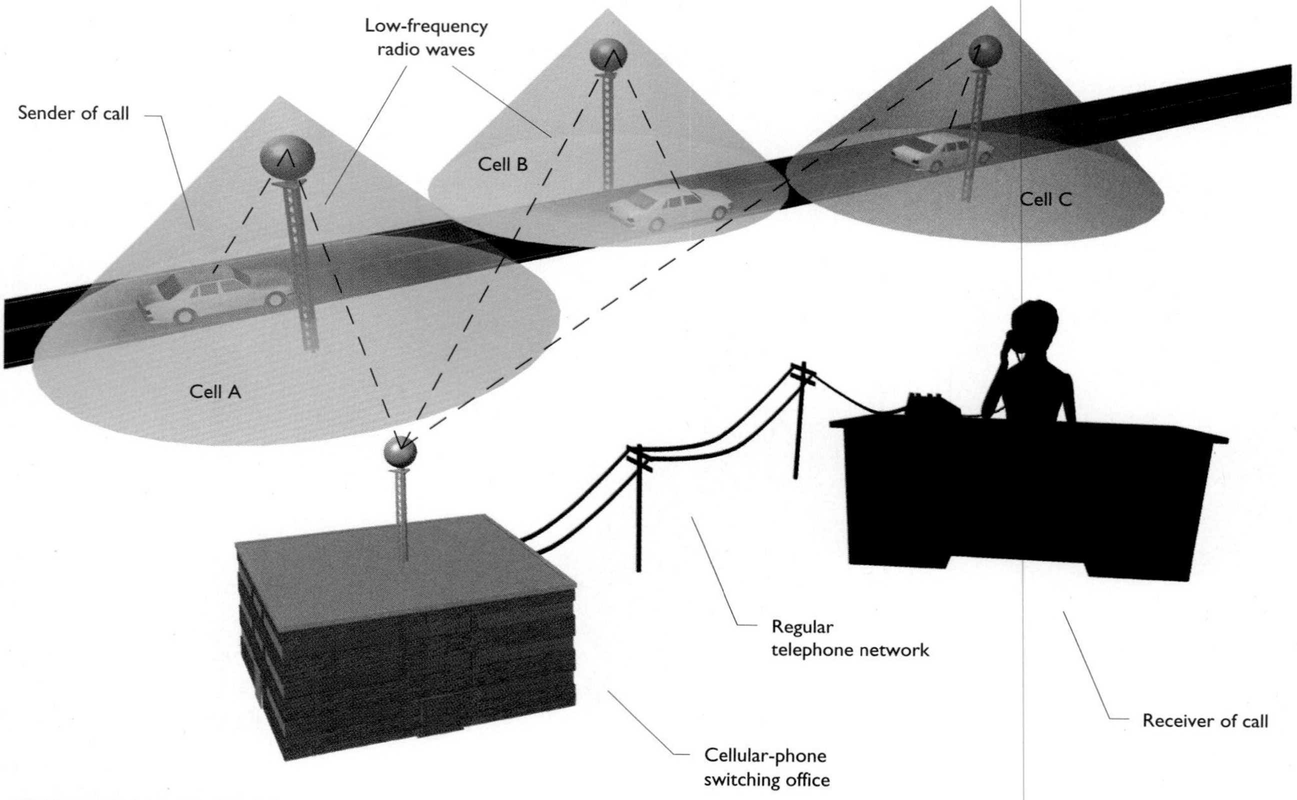

ABOUT CELLULAR CALLS

When you make a cellular call from your car, it is picked up by the antenna in the cell from which you are calling. As you move from one cell to another, the call is switched seamlessly to the new cell's antenna—which broadcasts at a different frequency.

Currently, those who most benefit from the cellular phone boom are people who need to maintain constant contact with the office or clients but must be on the move, as well—such as a busy executive, salesperson, truck driver, or real-estate agent. Farmers, refinery workers, and others who work outdoors are reaping the benefits

---

■ **Cellular phone.** A mobile phone that transmits calls through special ground stations that cover areas called *cells* to communicate with the regular phone system.

of cellular technology to stay in contact with others when they cannot afford the time it would take to get to a regular phone.

The transmission networks that support cellular phones are also useful for sending business data. Through a laptop computer with a cellular modem, you can gain access to huge databases of information while you are far from an office or a regular phone. Cellular networks are a hit internationally, too, especially in less-developed countries such as Poland and China. In places like these, communication systems are crude by North American standards, and it is much easier to build new cellular networks than to fix current facilities or to install wired systems.

Infrared Technology *Infrared technology* has gained popularity in recent years as a way to set up wireless links between office microcomputers. As opposed to microwave and cellular technologies, which use *radio* waves, infrared technology sends data as *light* rays. One system, for instance, places a device on each computer through which it can send and receive messages via a transmitter located on the office ceiling. This setup provides an unobstructed, line-of-sight path to and from the computers. Recently, a beaming device has become available that hooks up with a PC card and cable to a laptop's infrared (IRDA) port. The device relays print commands to a desktop computer's display screen, which wires the message to its attached laser printer (see Figure NET 1-11).

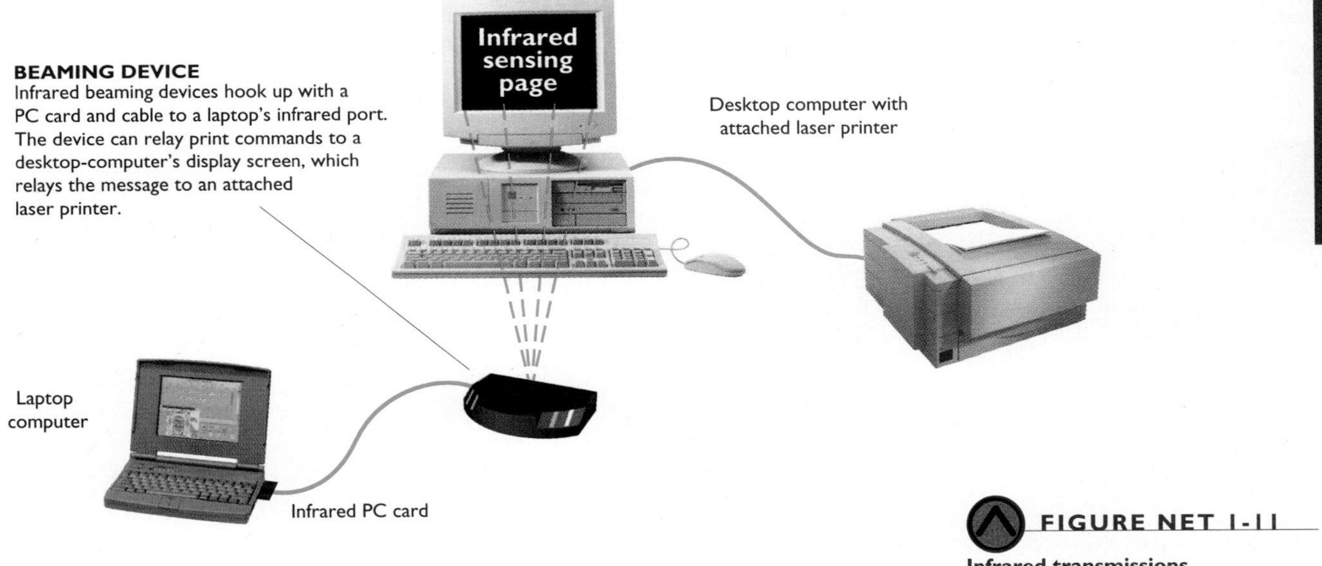

FIGURE NET 1-11

Infrared transmissions.

NET

Adapting Computers to Telecommunications Media

A computer needs special equipment to send messages over a communications medium. The type of equipment depends on such factors as the medium itself and how data are sent over it.

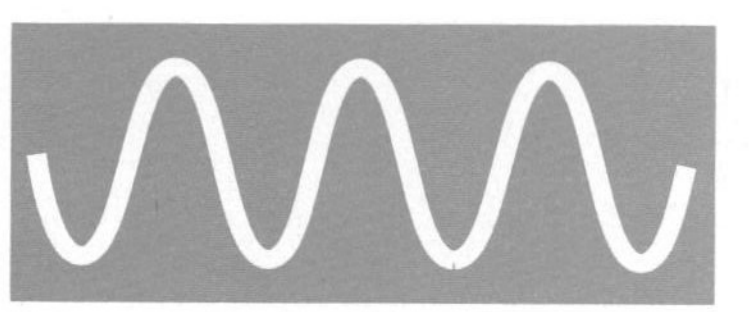

Analog mode

Digital mode

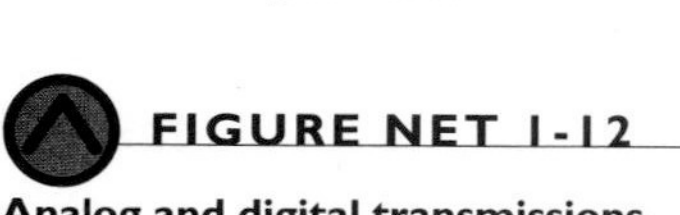

FIGURE NET 1-12

Analog and digital transmissions.

FIGURE NET 1-13

Speed. A wider bandwidth allows a medium to carry more data per unit of time and to support more powerful communications applications.

SENDING DATA OVER MEDIA

Data travel over communications media in various ways. The following paragraphs describe several of them.

Analog or Digital? One of the most fundamental distinctions in data communications is the difference between analog and digital transmissions (see Figure NET 1-12).

The phone system, established many years ago to handle voice traffic, carries **analog** signals—that is, *continuous* waves over a certain frequency range. Changes in the continuous wave reflect the myriad variations in the pitch of the human voice. Transmissions for cable TV and large satellite dishes also use analog signals, as do most cellular networks.

Most business computing equipment, in contrast, transmits **digital** signals, which handle data coded in two *discrete* states: 0 and 1 bits. Your desktop computer is a digital device; so, too, are midrange and mainframe computers. Also, within office buildings, networks often carry digitally encoded data transmissions. Whenever communications require an interface between digital computers and analog networks, an adaptive device called a *modem* (covered in more detail shortly) is needed to translate between the two.

Bandwidth and Speed Over an analog medium, data travel at various frequencies. The difference between the highest and lowest frequencies available on such a medium is known as the medium's **bandwidth.** For example, many telephone lines have a bandwidth of 3,000 hertz (Hz), which is the difference between the highest (3,300 Hz) and lowest (300 Hz) frequencies at which it can send data. Transmissions of text data require the least amount of bandwidth and video data need the most.

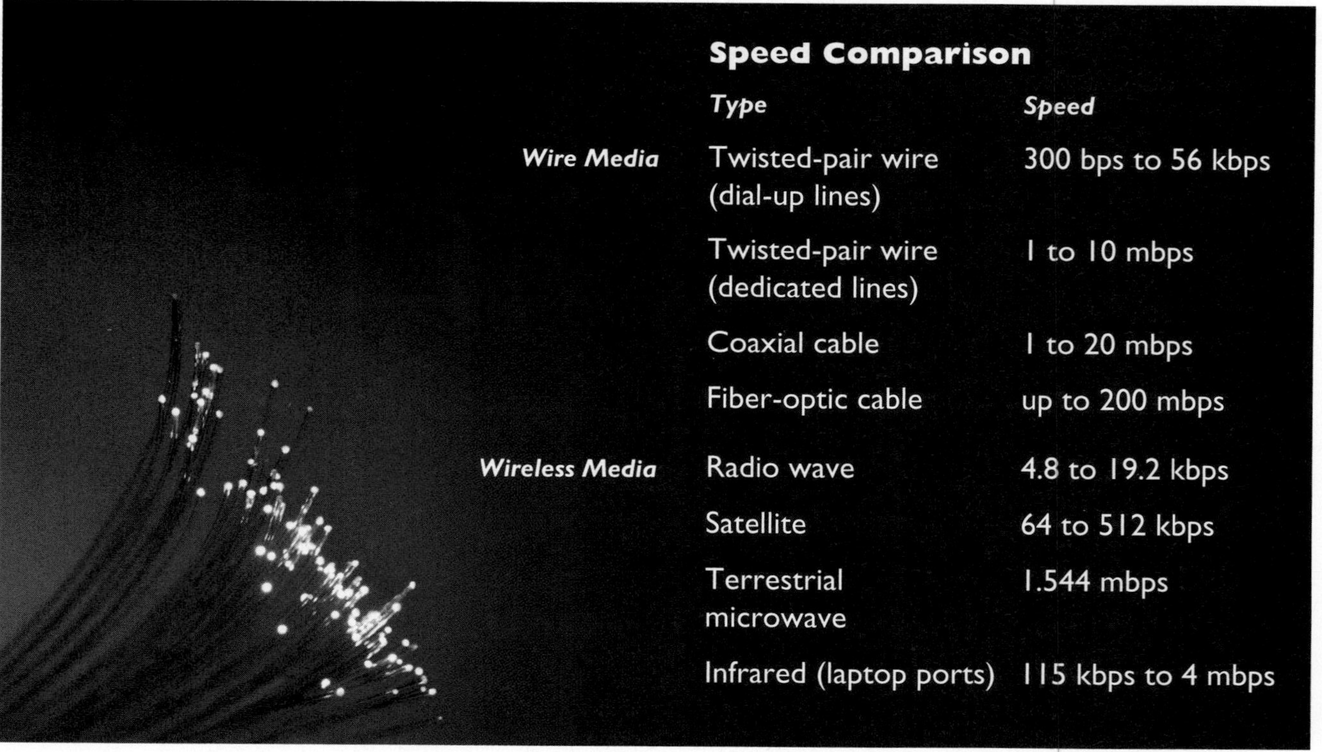

Speed Comparison

	Type	*Speed*
Wire Media	Twisted-pair wire (dial-up lines)	300 bps to 56 kbps
	Twisted-pair wire (dedicated lines)	1 to 10 mbps
	Coaxial cable	1 to 20 mbps
	Fiber-optic cable	up to 200 mbps
Wireless Media	Radio wave	4.8 to 19.2 kbps
	Satellite	64 to 512 kbps
	Terrestrial microwave	1.544 mbps
	Infrared (laptop ports)	115 kbps to 4 mbps

■ **Analog.** Transmission of data as continuous-wave patterns. ■ **Digital.** Transmission of data as 0 and 1 bits. ■ **Bandwidth.** The difference between the highest and lowest frequencies that a transmission medium can accommodate.

Just as a wide firehose permits more water to pass through it per unit of time than a narrow garden hose, a medium with great bandwidth allows more data to pass through it per unit of time than a medium of small bandwidth. Put another way, greater bandwidth allows data to travel at higher speeds. The speed at which data travel over both analog and digital media is often given in **bits per second (bps),** kbps (thousands of bits per second), or mbps (millions of bits per second).

Figure NET 1-13 compares the speeds of several media. As the figure shows, twisted-pair wire has the lowest speed, with increasingly better rates for coaxial cable, radio waves, and fiber-optic cable. Twisted-pair wire is often called a "low-bandwidth" medium; fiber-optic cable, a "high-bandwidth" medium.

Parallel versus Serial Transmission In most communications networks, and especially where long distances are involved, data travel serially. In **serial transmission,** all of the bits in a message are sent one after another along a single path. On the other hand, **parallel transmission** sends each set of 8 bits needed to convey each

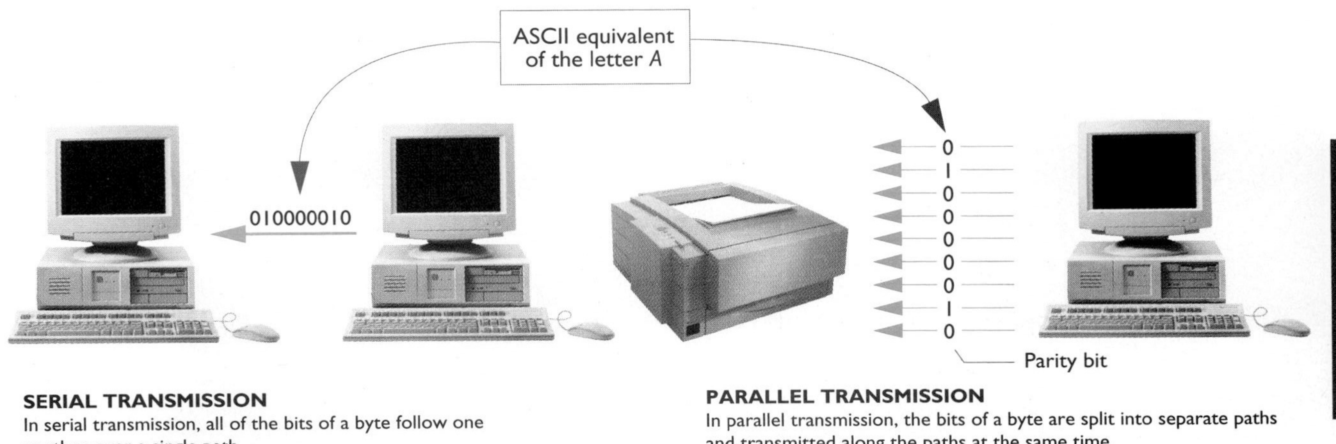

SERIAL TRANSMISSION
In serial transmission, all of the bits of a byte follow one another over a single path.

PARALLEL TRANSMISSION
In parallel transmission, the bits of a byte are split into separate paths and transmitted along the paths at the same time.

FIGURE NET 1-14

Serial and parallel transmissions. The figure illustrates a transmission of the ASCII representation of the letter *A*.

byte in a message at one time over eight separate paths. Figure NET 1-14 illustrates the difference between the two.

As the figure suggests, parallel transmission is much faster than serial transmission. However, because it requires a cable with eight tracks rather than one, it is also much more expensive. Thus, parallel transmission usually is limited to short distances, such as computer-to-printer communications.

NETWORK INTERFACE CARDS AND MODEMS

Workstations such as PCs and display terminals are usually connected to a network with either a network interface card or a modem. The type of connection required often depends on whether the workstation accesses the network through a *dedicated line* that is set up for private use (which plugs into a network interface card) or through a conventional *dial-up line* (which plugs into a modem).

■ **Bits per second (bps).** A measure of a transmission medium's speed. ■ **Serial transmission.** Data transmission in which every bit in a byte must travel down the same path in succession. ■ **Parallel transmission.** Data transmission in which each bit in a byte follows its own path simultaneously with all other bits.

Dial-up lines—the type of telephone connections found in most homes and businesses—let you call anywhere in the world. They are sometimes called "switched lines" because switching stations within the phone network route your call to the desired destination. A dedicated line, on the other hand, provides a permanent connection between two points. Although dial-up lines are cheaper, they are slower, and busy signals often prevent connections.

Network Interface Cards A **network interface card (NIC)** is an add-in board that plugs into an expansion slot within the system unit (see Figure NET 1-15). These cards often connect to coaxial cables between the workstations in *local networks,* which span small areas like an office building or college campus. NICs pass on to the network any outgoing data from workstations, and they also collect incoming data to the workstations.

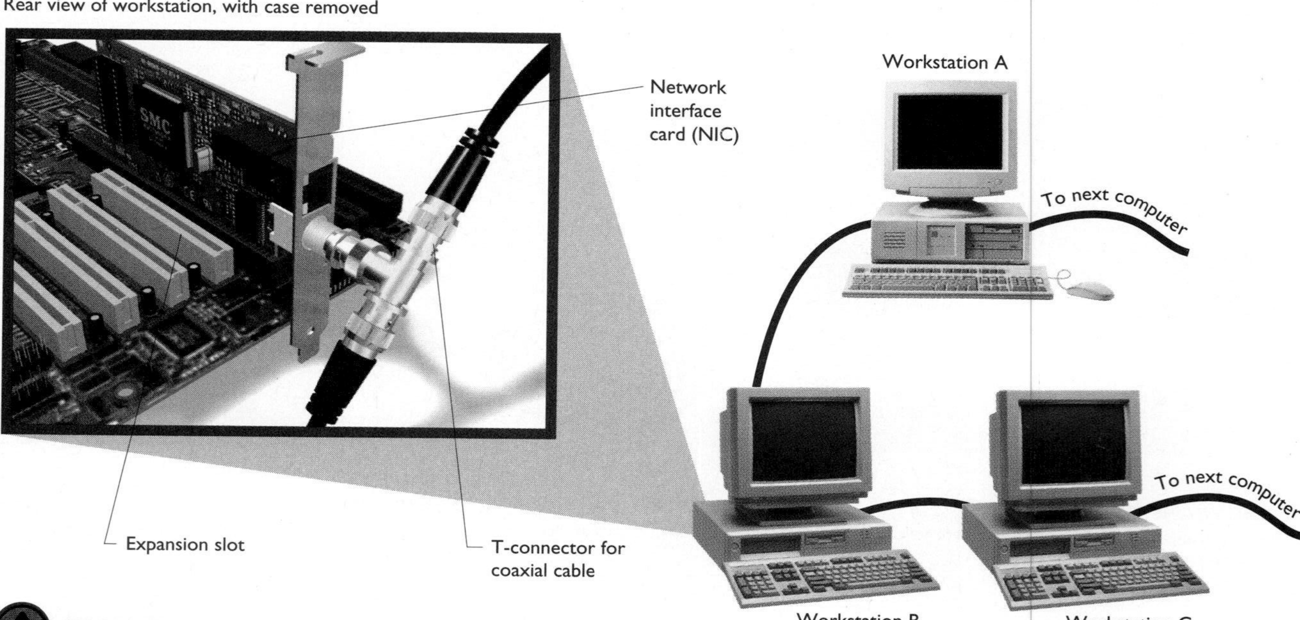

FIGURE NET 1-15

Network interface cards (NICs). NICs are often used to connect workstations via coaxial cable to networks that span small areas, like office buildings or college campuses.

Modems Because digital impulses—such as those sent by desktop workstations—cannot be transmitted over analog phone lines, communications require some means of translating each kind of signal into the other. Conversion of signals from digital to continuous-wave form is called *modulation,* and translation from continuous waves back to digital impulses is termed *demodulation.* A **modem** (coined from *mo*dulation and *dem*odulation) takes care of both operations.

Modems are most often used to connect desktop computers to *wide area networks,* such as the Internet. Wide area networks join devices spread much farther apart than just a few miles. As Figure NET 1-16 shows, when a workstation sends a message to a remote CPU over an analog line, a modem at the sending end converts from digital to analog, and another at the receiving end converts from analog to digital.

Modems are available as add-in boards, which are designed to be inserted into an expansion slot within a desktop computer's system unit, and as stand-alone hardware devices (see Figure NET 1-17). The former type, called *internal modems,* are

■ **Network interface card (NIC).** An add-in board through which a workstation connects to a local network. ■ **Modem.** A communications device that enables digital computers and their support devices to communicate over analog media.

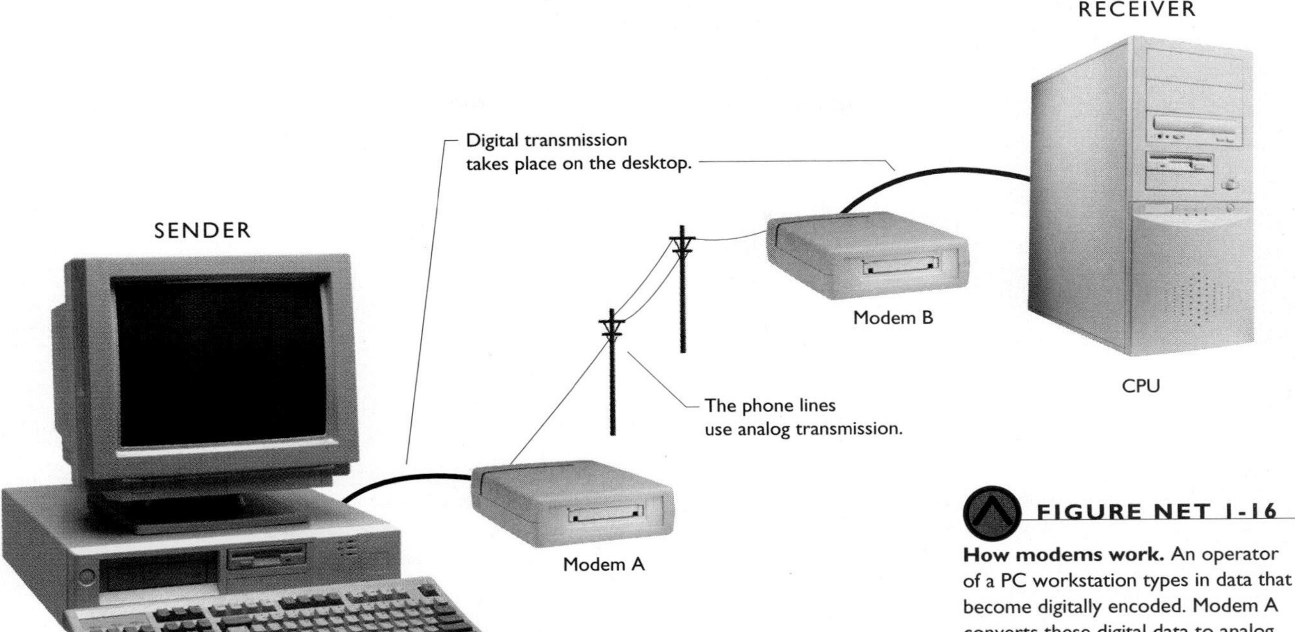

FIGURE NET 1-16

How modems work. An operator of a PC workstation types in data that become digitally encoded. Modem A converts these digital data to analog form and sends them over the phone lines to Modem B. Modem B reconverts the data to digital form and delivers them to the receiving CPU. This latter CPU transmits back to the workstation by reversing these steps.

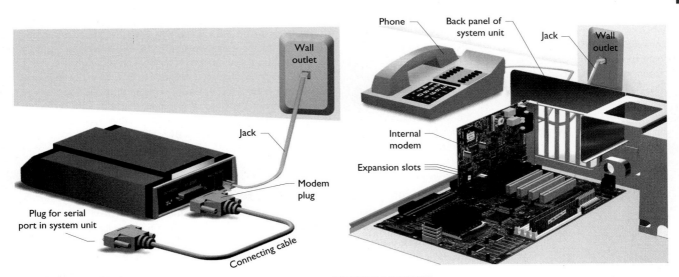

Wall outlet

Jack

Modem plug

Plug for serial port in system unit

Connecting cable

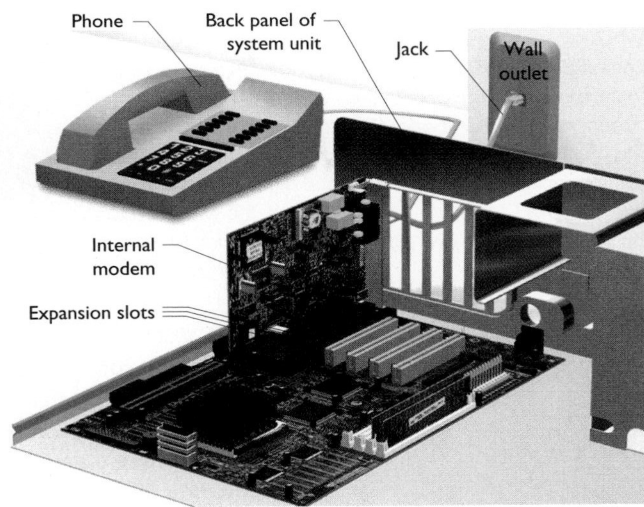

EXTERNAL MODEM
External modems are detached from the system unit and can be moved from computer to computer.

INTERNAL MODEM
Internal modems are boards that fit in an expansion slot within the system unit and are the type of modem recommended for most personal uses.

FIGURE NET 1-17

Modems. Modems are either external or internal.

Communications Software

Programs That Control Modems

Modems are hardware devices that require software to work. Specialized programs work with modems to enable your PC to communicate with the Internet and remote databases; these programs are commonly referred to in the microcomputing world as *communications software.* When you buy a new computer with a modem, you will usually get communications software as part of the bundle.

Although products in the communications-software marketplace provide different features, most of them let you:

- Access information services such as America Online and the Microsoft Network as well as the Internet
- Receive and send electronic mail and faxes
- Exchange files with other computers
- Access other computers all over the globe

In addition, most software packages will automatically place and answer calls for you, interface with voice machines, provide security for your files, and simplify a number of routine, phone-related tasks (such as accessing phone directories and keying in IDs and passwords to online service providers or bulletin boards). The accompanying image shows some information you may typically have to supply when setting up applications within communications software. When you buy a PC with a modem and communications software preloaded, most of this information will already be entered for you. You may need to specify whether you are using pulse or tone dialing—most people use tone dialing—and the name of the communications port that you want to use—most people pick COM2.

As you build a phone directory, you may want to set up a file of calling parameters for each phone number you want the communications software to dial. For instance, if you regularly call America Online, you could create a file with its phone number, your account number, and other pertinent calling data (see figure). Then, later, upon selecting the screen icon associated with America Online and declaring your password, the software would put your call through automatically. If you've specified Y for the auto redial prompt, the modem will periodically keep redialing the phone number if it receives a busy signal.

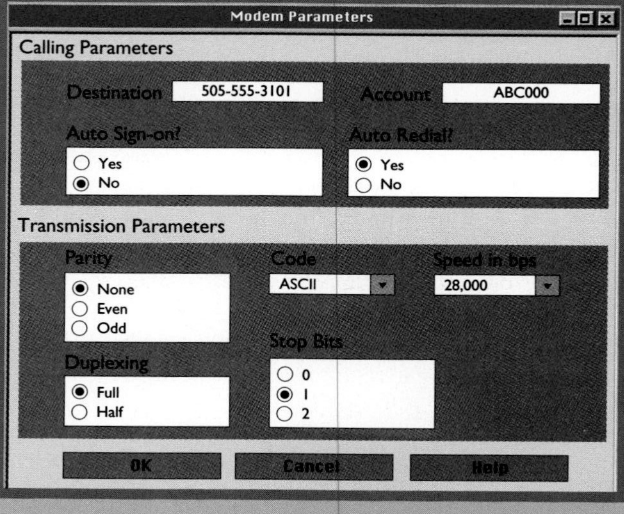

Communications software. When you buy a new computer with a modem, the purchase usually includes communications software.

Transmission parameters such as the parity and duplexing settings, communications speed, code used, and number of stop bits ensure that your modem sends data in the form the receiver expects. Generally, when you subscribe to a service provider like America Online, you receive information about acceptable settings for these parameters. In many cases today, the service provider's software can communicate directly with your communications software—turning the modem on and off for you, automatically setting most of the transmission parameters, and dialing in unassisted—as soon as you select the provider's screen icon and enter your password. Most products will let you edit parameter files if you need to change settings.

The screen shown in the figure is one of many that may appear in a communications software session. As soon as you dial up a service provider, the software of that utility controls your computer system. Each of them has its own set of menu screens and retrieval procedures.

much more common because they don't take up extra desk space and are generally cheaper. Some prefer the latter type, called *external modems,* because they can be moved from one computer to another and because they have display panels that provide useful diagnostics. PC-card modems for laptop computers are also available. Common transmission rates found on modems are 1.2, 2.4, 4.8, 9.6, 14.4, 28.8, 33.6, and 56 kbps. Modems capable of higher speeds are designed to function at the lower rates, as well.

A few words of caution about modems: Your commercial online service or Internet service provider may not support your calling area with the highest possible speeds, even though your modem is capable of them. Also, your phone company may not be able to deliver data at your modem's top speed because of line loads. What's more, data compression can slow down considerably the rate at which information is handled.

Modems can now deliver data as fast as the present phone system can carry it. To achieve more speed, you need either an ISDN line or some other faster alternative.

Feature NET 1-1 explains in more detail how modems work.

ISDN AND BEYOND

If you need more speed than you can squeeze out of a modem, your best bet is an ISDN line or something even faster.

ISDN (for *Integrated Services Digital Network)* is a digital phone service that operates over ordinary dial-up phone lines or over dedicated lines leased for private use. ISDN gives access to one or two 64 kbps channels. With two channels, you can use each separately—say, one to talk to a friend about a homework assignment while you watch as a Web page downloads from the Internet over the other. You can also combine the two lines into one for a full 128 kbps of bandwidth. To use ISDN, a special *ISDN adapter*—the ISDN counterpart of a modem—must be connected to your computer. The adapter allows you to communicate with other ISDN devices, such as the ISDN adapter owned by your Internet service provider.

ISDN is more expensive than modem transmission. An adapter can easily run over $300, and the installation charge on an ISDN line—if you don't live too far out in the country—can run another couple of hundred dollars or so. Also, you must often pay a per-minute connect charge for your time on the line, even for a local call.

Other alternatives offer more speed than ISDN, but—no surprise—they also bring higher prices. With a *T1 dedicated line* or a *frame-relay service,* for instance, you can get speeds up to a few mbps over coaxial cable. Companies often lease these lines and then split the bandwidth among several users. Less expensive than but not as fast as T1 and frame relay is *DirecPC,* which works with a small satellite dish that is similar to the one used with digital television's DirecTV service. DirecPC can provide up to 400 kbps speeds when data are downloaded but only modem-fast speeds when data are sent the other way, up to the satellite. Fortunately, most applications require far more data sent down than up.

If you need far more speed than the alternatives already mentioned, *T3 fiber optic dedicated lines* can reach 45 mbps and upward. Also, lines that follow the *asynchronous transfer mode (ATM)* standard can deliver speeds of 155 mbps over fiber optic lines—and perhaps over 600 mbps in the near future. T3 and ATM are most often used for network *backbones*—those parts of a network that carry the most traffic.

The Tomorrow box covers two promising alternatives for the future of mass communication in the home—cable modems and ASDL. These two technologies are the ones most mentioned with regard to the coming of Internet-enabled television.

Network Topologies

Telecommunications networks can be classified in terms of their *topologies,* or patterns (see Figure NET 1-18). Three common topologies are the star, bus, and ring.

Star Networks The **star network**—the oldest topology for computer networks—often consists of a large computer hierarchically connected to several workstations through point-to-point links. Star networks are common in traditional mainframe environments. The mainframe serves as the *host computer,* and it hooks up to several microcomputer workstations or to several display terminals. The display terminals are sometimes referred to as *dumb terminals* because they are workstations that can do little more than send and receive data; the mainframe does virtually everything else.

■ **ISDN.** A digital phone service that offers high-speed transmissions over ordinary phone lines. ■ **Star network.** A telecommunications network consisting of a host device connected directly to several other devices.

BASIC TOPOLOGIES

Most network topologies follow a simple star, bus, or ring pattern.

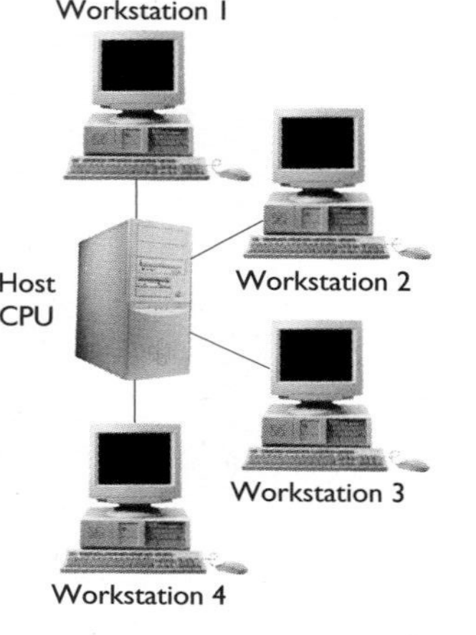

STAR NETWORK
A star network often consists of a mainframe host that's connected to several workstations in a point-to-point fashion.

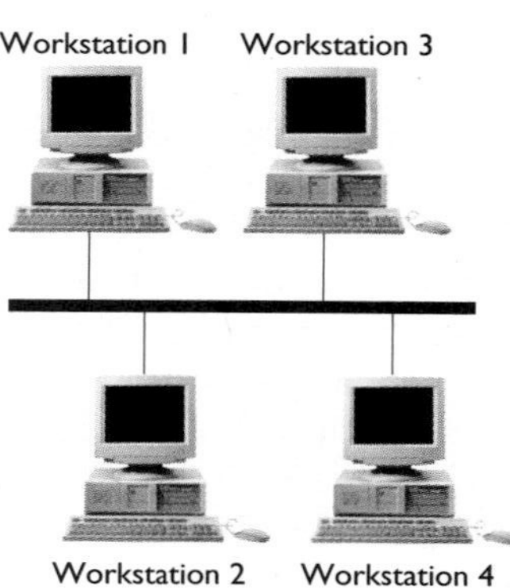

BUS NETWORK
A bus network uses a high-speed cable that workstations tap into—in the manner shown—to pick up and drop off messages.

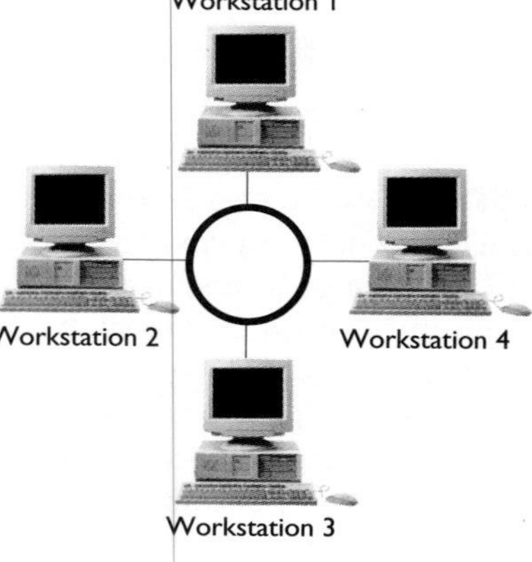

RING NETWORK
In a ring network, computers and other devices are connected in a loop.

COMBINATION TOPOLOGIES

Many networks are formed by combining topologies—such as the bus and star.

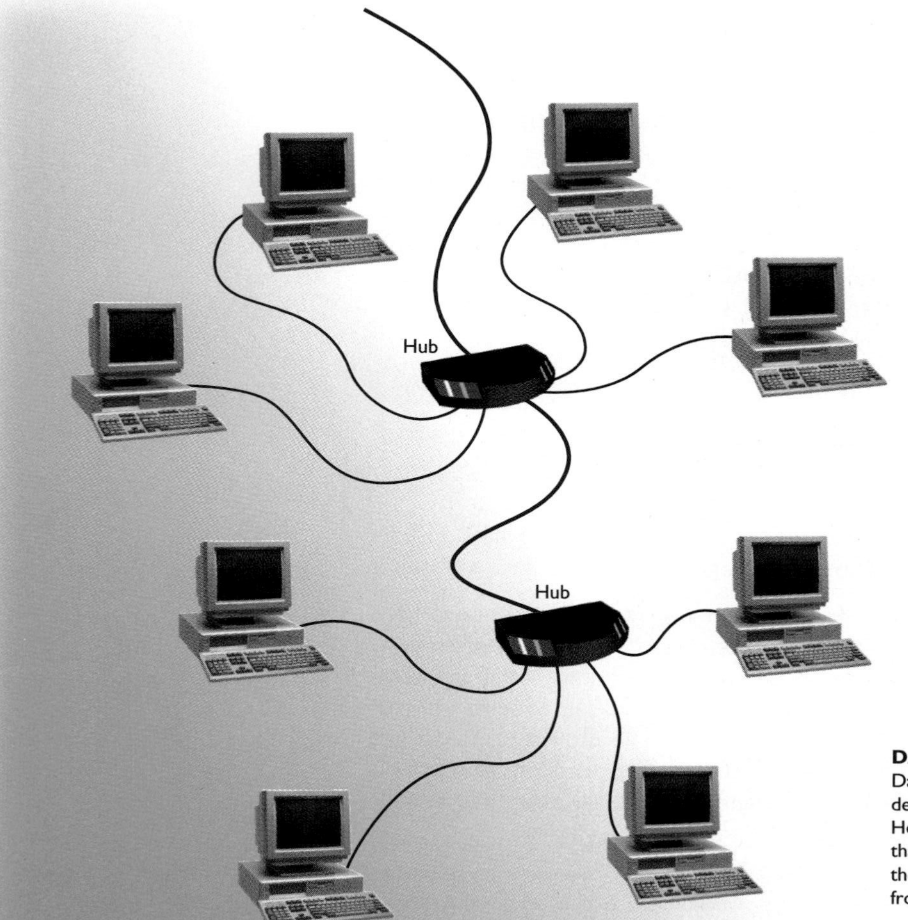

DAISY CHAINING
Daisy chaining refers to connecting devices serially with a bus line. Here, two hubs (cluster stations that manage workstations) coordinate the sending and receiving of messages from two star networks.

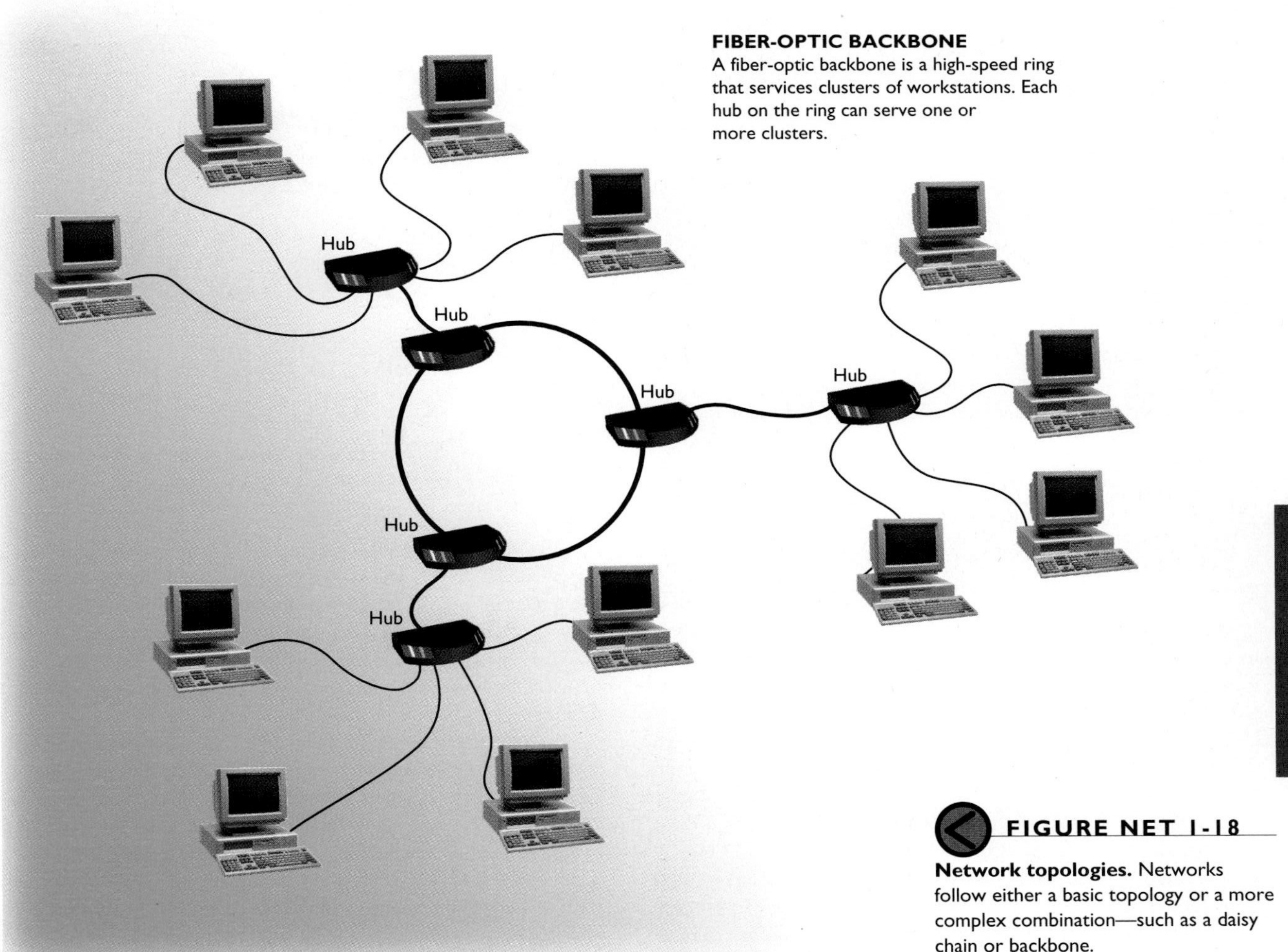

FIBER-OPTIC BACKBONE
A fiber-optic backbone is a high-speed ring that services clusters of workstations. Each hub on the ring can serve one or more clusters.
Hub
Hub
Hub
Hub
Hub
Hub

NET

FIGURE NET 1-18

Network topologies. Networks follow either a basic topology or a more complex combination—such as a daisy chain or backbone.

Bus Networks A **bus network** operates a lot like ordinary city buses in a ground transportation system. The hardware devices are like bus stops, and the data move like passengers. For example, the bus network labeled in Figure NET 1-18, at the top of page NET 26, contains four workstations (bus stops) at which the system picks up or lets off data (passengers). The bus line commonly consists of a high-speed cable with inexpensive twisted-pair wires dropped off each workstation. A bus network contains no host computer.

Ring Networks A less common and more expensive alternative to the star and bus is the **ring network,** which lacks any host computer; instead, a number of computers or other devices are connected by a loop. A ring network is also shown in Figure NET 1-18, at the top of page NET 26.

■ **Bus network.** A telecommunications network consisting of a transmission line with lines dropped off for several devices. ■ **Ring network.** A telecommunications network that connects machines serially in a closed loop.

TOMORROW

The Battle for Your Home

Who Will Win the Race to Deliver High-Bandwidth Products?

Companies in the telecommunications industry are struggling to solve a huge problem. They know that twenty-first-century, consumer-oriented multimedia products are ready for prime time, and interactive TV and Web TV are waiting in the wings. They see vast promise, but how can they get such products to work over computer networks when most homes connect only through ordinary telephone lines, which transmit at comparatively snail-paced speeds?

The answer, many feel, is to build a new communications infrastructure. Unfortunately, conventional modems have pretty much peaked and cannot support further large speed increases, so observers see little likelihood of big advancements on that front. What's more, today's television infrastructure is mostly geared for one-way broadcasting—a huge limitation for a system that will incorporate computers.

A technology that many industry analysts see as a front-runner to become the medium of choice in the early twenty-first-century home is two-way cable. Two-way cable—a hybrid system based on coaxial and fiber-optic cables—would replace or augment the one-way cable that currently serves most of today's cable-TV customers. It would connect devices through an interfacing device called a *cable modem.*

How fast is two-way cable? It can reach 10 and maybe up to 30 mbps, say the cable companies—hundreds of times faster than today's top-of-the-line conventional modems. Put another way, it would take 46 minutes to transmit a 10 MB file by 28.8 kbps modem and only 8 seconds by 10 mbps cable modem.

The upgrade of existing cable networks is expected to cost the cable companies billions of dollars, and the investment will probably pay off only over a long time. The small number of businesses that are now using two-way cable pay a few hundred dollars per month for the privilege, far above what the average consumer will likely want to spend. By 2000, only about 6 million U.S. homes are expected to be using the new cable service.

The principal rival to two-way cable—a technology called *ADSL* (for Asymmetric Digital Subscriber Line)—is being served up by the phone companies. ADSL, the successor to ISDN, uses a digital-filtering method to turn twisted-pair copper wires into digital lines with megabit-per-second speeds. ADSL lines now in the test stage provide speeds of about 6 mbps for transmissions downstream (from the service provider to the user) and 640 kbps upstream (from the user to the provider). This rate is more than adequate to provide high-speed television and Internet service, as well as phone service.

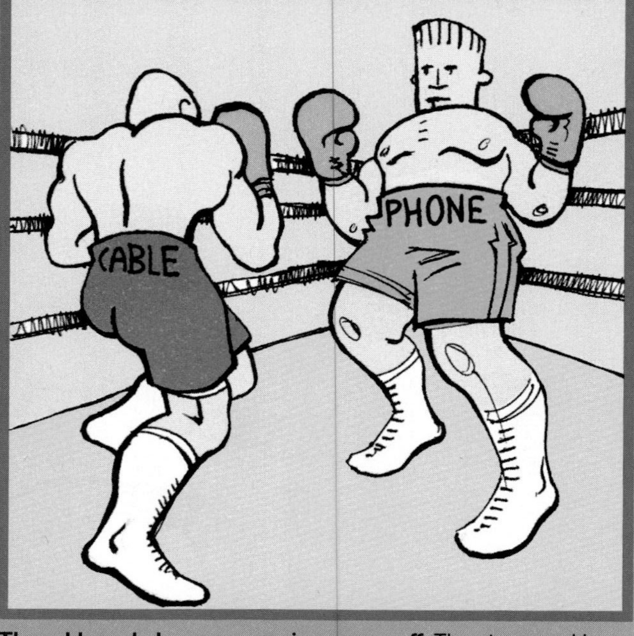

The cable and phone companies square off. The winner could wind up providing TV, Internet, and phone service to most homes.

The likely winner of the upcoming battle between the cable and phone companies is at this point in time anyone's guess. Cable modems are closer to mass delivery than ADSL, but they cost far more to implement. What's more, the cash-strapped cable companies are fending off assaults on their mainstream business—cable television service—by digital satellite services such as DirecTV and digital wireless cable. Both cable modem and ASDL put the cable and phone companies on a collision course, since it will be possible to get phone service over cable modem and TV service over ASDL.

The battle to network your home has enormous stakes. Most consumers prefer to receive all of their communications—TV, Internet, and telephone service—from a single company. Consequently, firms that bet on the right technology may wind up winning the lion's share of the communications business.

Networks often combine topologies, in effect aggregating smaller networks into larger ones. Figure NET 1-18 shows two star networks *daisy chained* together with a bus. In the figure, cluster stations—or *hubs*—coordinate the traffic of sent and received messages on workstations that are hooked up to them. Figure NET 1-18 also shows three star networks linked together in a ring by a high-speed *fiber-optic backbone.* Additionally, network topologies can contain redundant links, as the Internet does, so that they conform to no well-known, geometric pattern.

Workstations send and receive messages according to some predefined method or *protocol.* The topic of protocols is discussed later in the chapter.

Local Networks

Organizations need communications facilities that connect geographically close resources, say, microcomputers located in the same college campus or dormitory or, perhaps, workstations located in the same office. Such networks are known as **local networks.** Three common types of local networks are host-independent local area networks (LANs), hierarchical local networks, and private branch exchanges (PBXs).

LOCAL AREA NETWORKS (LANs)

The term **local area networks (LANs)** typically refers to local networks without any host computer as such. Instead, most LANs use either a bus or ring topology, and computers within the network itself manage workstations' demands for shared facilities. LANs are available principally in the client-server and peer-to-peer varieties.

Client-Server LANs **Client-server LANs** are so named because each workstation that receives network service is called a **client,** while the computers that manage the requests for facilities within the network are called **servers** (see Figure NET 1-19). For example, a *file server* might manage disk-storage activities, enabling workstation users to access any of several available operating systems, applications

FIGURE NET 1-19

Client-server LAN. In a client-server LAN, each workstation that receives network service is called a *client,* while the computers that manage requests for network services are called *servers.*

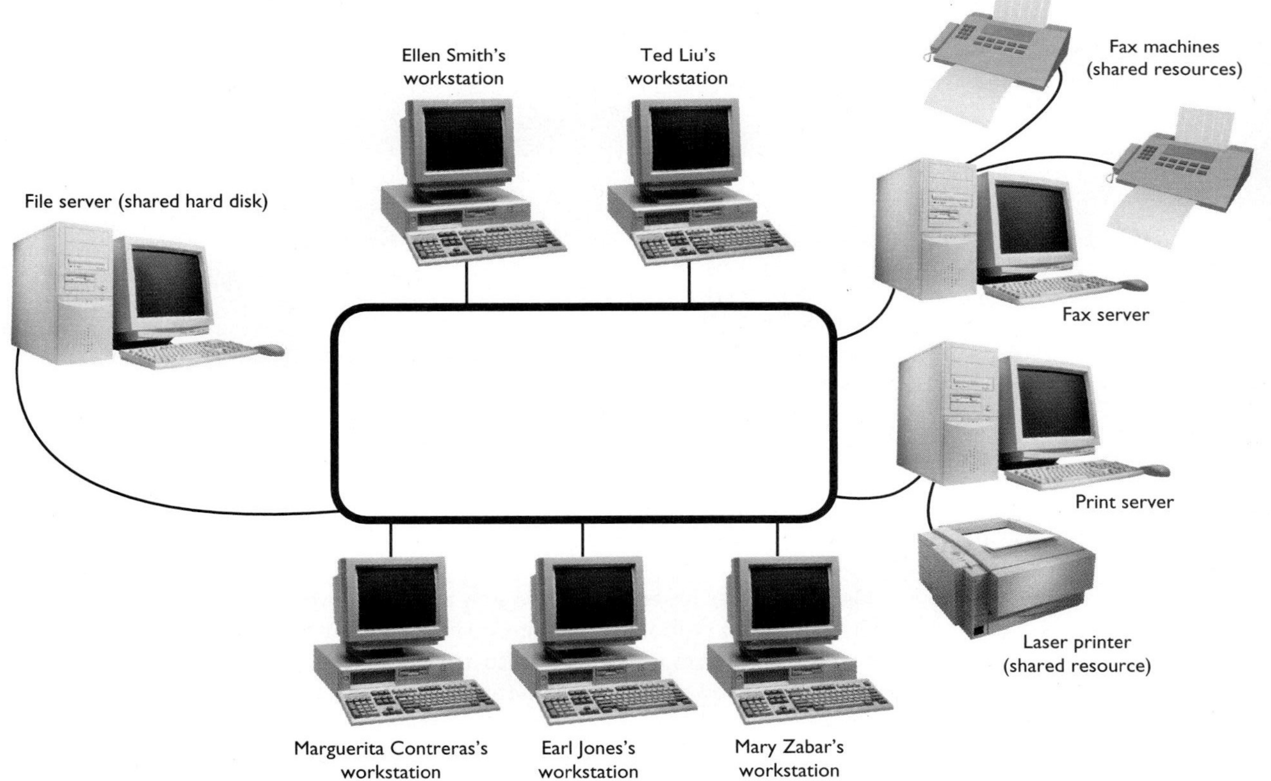

NET

■ **Local network.** A privately run communications network of several machines located within a few miles or so of one another. ■ **Local area network (LAN).** A local network without a host computer, usually composed of microcomputer workstations and shared peripherals. ■ **Client-server LAN.** A LAN composed of *client* devices, which receive network services, and *server* devices, which provide the services. ■ **Client.** A device designed to receive service in a client-server network. ■ **Server.** A computer that manages shared devices, such as laser printers or high-capacity hard disks, on a client-server network.

programs, or data files. Similarly, a *print server* handles printing-related activities, such as managing user outputs on a high-quality network printer. LANs also incorporate such devices as *mail servers* and *fax servers,* which are dedicated to managing electronic mail and facsimile transmissions, respectively.

Because servers often manage large databases, perform certain types of processing chores for clients, and interact with several other computers, LANs often include powerful microcomputers like those based on the latest Intel and PowerPC processor chips to perform server duties. In very large LANs, midrange and mainframe computers often function as servers.

Peer-to-Peer LANs Applications that require small networks often use **peer-to-peer LANs.** These LANs do not predesignate computers as clients and servers per se. Instead, all of the user workstations and shared peripherals work on the same level, and users have direct access to each other's workstations and shared peripherals. Peer-to-peer LANs were designed as a way to bring networking to small groups without the complexity and expense that normally accompany client-server systems. Peer-to-peer capabilities are built into many desktop operating systems.

LANs are used for a variety of applications, the simplest of which involve just sharing expensive hard disks and laser printers. LAN technology has evolved beyond these initial applications to include numerous other uses (see Figure NET 1-20). One of the newest functions is the so-called *intranet.* An **intranet** is a private LAN—set up by a company for its employees—that implements the infrastructure and standards of the Internet and its World Wide Web. Feature NET 1-2 explores this concept further.

Uses for LANs

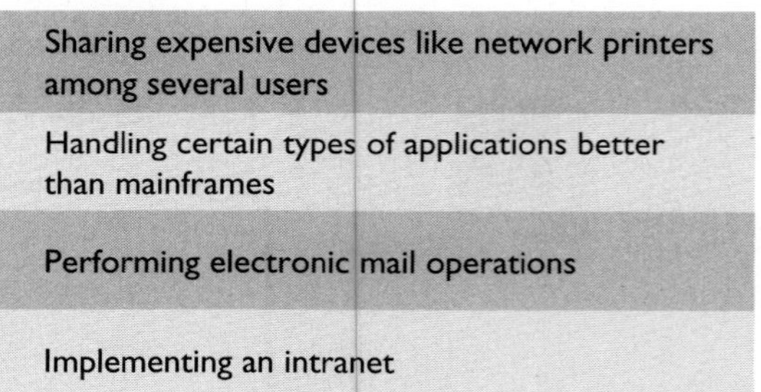

Sharing expensive devices like network printers among several users
Handling certain types of applications better than mainframes
Performing electronic mail operations
Implementing an intranet

Uses for LANs.

Microcomputer-based LANs have a big advantage over host-based hierarchical systems, which we'll be looking at next: Organizations can inexpensively add small increments of extra computing power to their LANs as needs grow. For instance, companies can add extra workstations or more servers at any time. Also, expandable machines called *scalable superserver computers,* which cater to LANs, have designs expressly intended for easy additions of processing power and memory. On the disadvantage side, security on LANs still lags behind that on mainframe-based host systems, and LANs often run up higher costs for development and support.

- **Peer-to-peer LAN.** A LAN in which all of the user workstations and shared peripheral devices operate on the same level.
- **Intranet.** A private network—often one set up by a company for employees—that implements the infrastructure and standards of the Internet and World Wide Web.

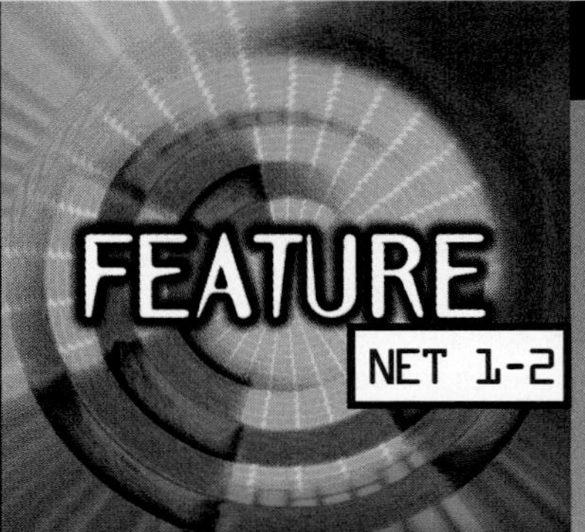

Intranets

"Local Area Internets"

Over the last couple of years, one of the hottest new technology concepts to hit the corporate scene has been the intranet. An *intranet* is a company network—complete with e-mail, Web pages, and multimedia—that has the look and feel of the public-access Internet used by millions of people. The principal difference is that intranets are designed for internal use only; the general public has no access.

Intranets today serve a variety of purposes, such as making company phone books and procedure manuals available to employees, disseminating forms, and enabling employees to work together on projects (see accompanying figure). Because many company sites are fitted with high-bandwidth cable media, intranets make possible much richer multimedia displays than the Internet at large, which is constrained by the speeds available through dial-up modems and ordinary phone lines.

It has been estimated that over 90 percent of the world's largest companies now operate intranets of some type. In many ways, intranets provide the logical framework with which to build a company LAN. Many employees are already familiar with the Internet and its World Wide Web, so the similar-looking intranets minimize training requirements. Also, Internet technology can function on almost any computer platform, and many companies have diverse mixtures of computers that need to communicate with one another. What's more, development costs are relatively small—no proprietary system has to be designed, and companies can get intranets up and running simply by following the current standards and guidelines of the Internet and World Wide Web.

In many companies, both intranets and independent, internal Web sites have taken off like wildfire. For instance, Silicon Graphics—one of the leading manufacturers of graphics workstations—hosted 800 internal Web sites comprising close to 150,000 pages at the beginning of 1996. The company has only a little over 7,000 employees.

Most intranets are protected from outside penetration by security devices known as *firewalls*. While outsiders can't get in, employees can saunter from their intranets out onto the Internet or World Wide Web if they choose.

- ☑ Facilitating electronic mail
- ☑ Maintaining internal phone books
- ☑ Storing procedure manuals
- ☑ Posting training materials
- ☑ Disseminating employee forms
- ☑ Posting internal job listings
- ☑ Providing electronic catalogs for ordering supplies
- ☑ Facilitating workgroup computing
- ☑ Scheduling meetings & appointments
- ☑ Making available critical expertise
- ☑ Disseminating newsletters
- ☑ Posting reports & other types of information

Applications for intranets. Any or all of these applications can become part of a company intranet.

NET

OTHER TYPES OF LOCAL NETWORKS

Two other common types of local networks are hierarchical local networks and PBXs.

Hierarchical Local Networks **Hierarchical local networks** are the oldest type of local computer network. They follow a star topology. At the top of the hierarchy is a host computer such as a mainframe or midrange computer that controls virtually all of the processing. At the bottom are display workstations. Between the top and bottom, devices such as communications controllers manage exchanges between the host and workstations.

Workstations in hierarchical local networks can either download files from the host or upload files to it. **Downloading** means that copies of existing files move from

■ **Hierarchical local network.** A local network in which a relatively powerful host CPU at the top of the hierarchy interacts with workstations at the bottom. ■ **Downloading.** The process of transferring a file from a remote computer to a requesting computer over a network.

the host to the microcomputer workstations. **Uploading** means that new data created at the microcomputer workstations move to the host system.

Both downloading and uploading usually require stringent organizational control. Downloading presents the danger of unauthorized access to data, whereas uploading entails the risk of garbage data corrupting other applications. Uploading and downloading are also common operations in client-server LANs, where clients download files off of a server or upload files to it.

A major difference between a hierarchical local network and a host-independent client-server LAN is *where* the processing takes place. In the client-server LAN, a lot of the processing can be done at the client or desktop level. Except for database retrievals, possibly very little other processing is done at the server end. In the hierarchical local network, by contrast, the processing is typically concentrated at the host or "server" level. In many such systems, the "client" is a dumb terminal that has very little processing capability beyond sending and receiving data.

Private Branch Exchanges (PBXs) The telephone system consists of numerous switching stations that essentially are public branch exchanges. When a company leases or purchases a switching station for its own use, such a facility becomes a **private branch exchange (PBX).** Most PBXs are commonly referred to as "company switchboards"—you call a company's number and a private operator routes you to the proper extension. A PBX is essentially a hierarchical local network dedicated to intracompany phoning.

In today's world of computers and Touch-Tone phones, modern PBXs minimize the workloads on human operators by putting technology to work for most incoming calls. Callers hear a voice recording of menu options and make selections from their Touch-Tone phones. Host computers control the PBXs, routing machine-to-machine calls automatically and letting the human operator deal with interpersonal communications as exceptions. Sometimes, these computer-based private branch exchanges are referred to as *CBXs (computerized branch exchanges)* or *PABXs (private automatic branch exchanges).*

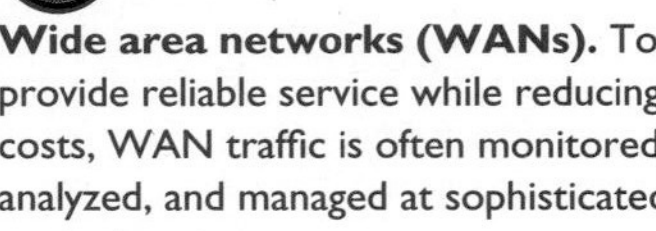

FIGURE NET 1-21

Wide area networks (WANs). To provide reliable service while reducing costs, WAN traffic is often monitored, analyzed, and managed at sophisticated control centers.

Wide Area Networks (WANs)

Wide area networks (WANs) are communications networks that encompass relatively wide geographical areas. Many WANs link together geographically dispersed LANs or LAN clusters. The mix also often includes hundreds or thousands—in the case of the Internet, millions—of independent workstations that connect from remote locations. WANs may be publicly accessible, like the Internet, or privately owned and operated.

HANDLING WAN TRAFFIC

Two big issues with WANs are interconnectivity and network management (see Figure NET 1-21). Because these networks tie together so many devices across such

■ **Uploading.** The process of transferring a file from a local computer to a remote computer over a network. ■ **Private branch exchange (PBX).** A call-switching station dedicated to a single organization. ■ **Wide area network (WAN).** A network that spans a large geographic area.

long distances, they need a number of special pieces of equipment. These devices will be discussed in the paragraphs that follow.

Repeaters *Repeaters* are devices that amplify signals along a network. WANs need them because signals often have to travel farther than the wires or cables that carry them are designed to support. Repeaters are also commonly used on LANs, when longer distances are involved.

Routers **Routers** work in large switched networks—like the Internet—to pass messages along to their destinations. Each router along the path to the destination passes any message it receives along to the next router, and the routers work together to share information about the network. If one part of the network is congested or out of service, a router can choose to send a message by an alternate route. Routers are to networks like the Internet what switching stations are to the phone system, with one important exception: The phone network predetermines the message path whereas routers on the Internet make their own decisions and one never knows ahead of time the path a message will take.

Gateways and Bridges Local networks often must communicate with outside resources, such as those on wide area networks and other local networks. Messages sent between two distinct networks reach their destinations via gateways and bridges.

A **gateway** is a collection of hardware and software resources that enables devices on one network to communicate with those on another, *dissimilar* network. Workstations on a LAN, for instance, require a gateway to access the Internet. Suppose an executive working at an office workstation on a LAN wishes to access the Internet through America Online; a gateway is necessary to link the two kinds of networks.

To link two networks based on similar technology—such as a LAN in one city and a LAN in another—they communicate via a device called a bridge. A **bridge** is a collection of hardware and software resources that enables devices on one network to communicate with devices on another, *similar* network. Bridges can also partition a large network into two smaller ones and connect two LANs that are nearby each other.

Multiplexers Communications lines almost always have far greater capacity than a single workstation can use. Because communications lines are expensive, networks can run efficiently if several low-speed devices share the same line. A special device called a **multiplexer** makes this possible by interleaving the messages of several low-speed devices and sending them along a single high-speed path.

Concentrators A **concentrator** is a multiplexer with a store-and-forward capability. Messages from slow devices accumulate at the concentrator until it collects enough characters to make a message worth forwarding to another device. In airline reservation systems, for instance, concentrators placed at such key sites as New York and Los Angeles allow travel agents to share communications lines economically. Messages initiated by agents are sent to the concentrator, stored, multiplexed with messages from other agents, and transmitted at very high speeds over long-distance lines to central processing sites. In the world of LANs, concentrators are known as *hubs*.

■ **Router.** A device used on WANs to decide the paths along which to send messages. ■ **Gateway.** An interface that enables two dissimilar networks to communicate. ■ **Bridge.** An interface that enables two similar networks to communicate. ■ **Multiplexer.** A communications device that interleaves the messages of several low-speed devices and sends them along a single, high-speed path. ■ **Concentrator.** A communications device that combines control and multiplexing functions.

Communications Protocols

Because manufacturers have long produced devices that use a variety of transmission techniques, the telecommunications industry has adopted standards called *protocols* to rectify the problem of conflicting procedures.

The term *protocol* comes from the areas of diplomacy and etiquette. For instance, at a dinner party in the elegant home of a family on the Social Register, the protocol in effect may be formal attire, impeccable table manners, and remaining at the table until beckoned to the parlor by the host or hostess. At a backwoods country barbecue, a different protocol will probably exist. In the communications field, protocols have comparable roles.

A communications **protocol** is a collection of procedures to establish, maintain, and terminate transmissions between devices. Protocols specify how devices will physically connect to a network, how data will be packaged for transmission, how receiver devices will acknowledge signals from sender devices (a process called *handshaking),* how errors will be handled, and so on. Just as people need an agreed-upon set of rules to communicate effectively, machines also need a common set of rules to help them get along with one another.

Protocols are found in all types of networks. How many protocols are there? Thousands. The following paragraphs discuss a few of the most common ones. As you will shortly see, each protocol addresses a highly specific type of situation.

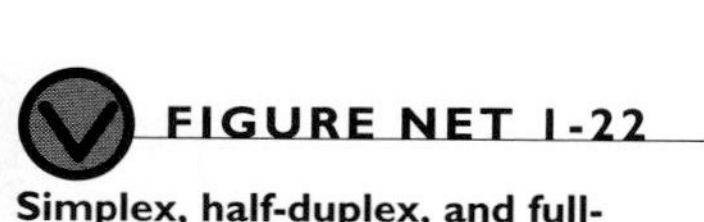

FIGURE NET 1-22

Simplex, half-duplex, and full-

Simplex, Half Duplex, or Full Duplex? One level of protocol found in virtually all types of telecommunications addresses the direction in which transmitted data move (see Figure NET 1-22).

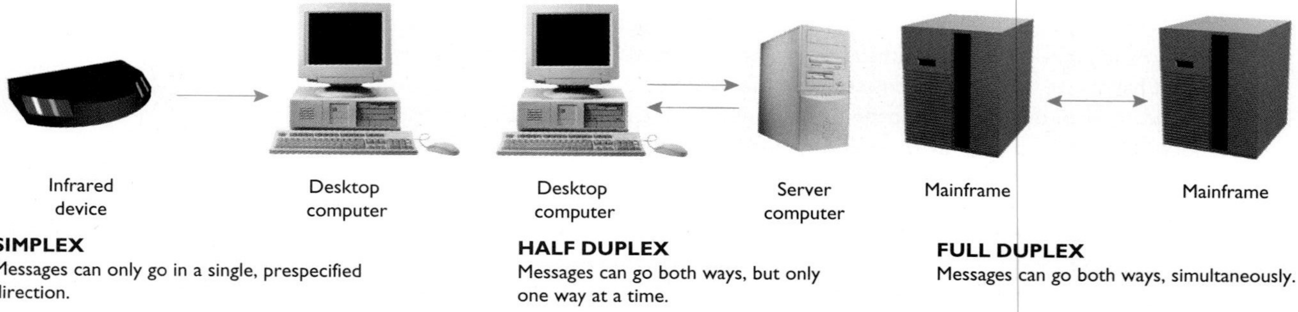
Infrared
device
Desktop
computer
Desktop
computer
Server
computer
Mainframe
Mainframe
SIMPLEX
Messages can only go in a single, prespecified direction.
HALF DUPLEX
Messages can go both ways, but only one way at a time.
FULL DUPLEX
Messages can go both ways, simultaneously.

Simplex transmission allows data to travel only in a single, prespecified direction. An example from everyday life is a doorbell—the signal can go only from the button to the chime. Two other examples are television and radio broadcasting. The simplex standard is relatively uncommon for most types of computer-based telecommunications applications; even devices that are designed primarily to receive information, such as printers, must be able to communicate acknowledgment signals back to the sender devices.

In **half-duplex transmission,** messages can move in either direction, but only one way at a time. The press-to-talk radio phones used in police cars employ the half-duplex standard; only one person can talk at a time. Often the line between a desktop workstation and a remote CPU conforms to the half-duplex pattern, as well. If another computer is transmitting to a workstation, the operator cannot send new messages until the other computer finishes its message or pauses to acknowledge an interruption.

■ **Protocol.** A set of conventions by which machines establish communication with one another in a telecommunications environment. ■ **Simplex transmission.** Any type of transmission in which a message can move along a path in only a single, prespecified direction. ■ **Half-duplex transmission.** Any type of transmission in which messages may move in two directions—but only one way at a time—along a communications path.

Full-duplex transmission works like traffic on a busy two-way street—the flow moves in two directions at the same time. Full-duplexing is ideal for hardware units that need to pass large amounts of data between each other, as in mainframe-to-mainframe communications.

Asynchronous versus Synchronous Transmission Another level of protocol commonly encountered by PC owners addresses packaging of data for serial transmission. As mentioned earlier, most data are transmitted serially in communications networks.

In **asynchronous transmission,** one character at a time is sent over a line. When the operator strikes a key on a keyboard, the character's byte representation moves up the line to the computer. Striking a second key sends the byte for a second character, and so forth. But because even the fastest typist can generate only a very small amount of data relative to what the line can accept, the line sits idle a lot of the time. Furthermore, each character sent must be packaged with a "start bit" and "stop bit," resulting in substantial transmission overhead.

When large blocks of data have to be sent, asynchronous transmission is too slow. **Synchronous transmission** increases speed on a line by dispatching data in blocks of characters rather than one at a time. Each block can consist of thousands of characters. The blocks are timed so that the receiving device knows that it will be getting them at regular intervals. Because no idle time occurs between transmission of individual characters in the block—and because less transmission overhead is required—this method allows more efficient utilization of the line. Synchronous transmission is made possible by a *buffer* at the workstation, a storage area large enough to hold a block of characters. As soon as the buffer is filled, all the characters in it are sent up the line to the destination computer.

Figure NET 1-23 shows the difference between asynchronous and synchronous transmission. Synchronous transmission is available on most high-speed modems.

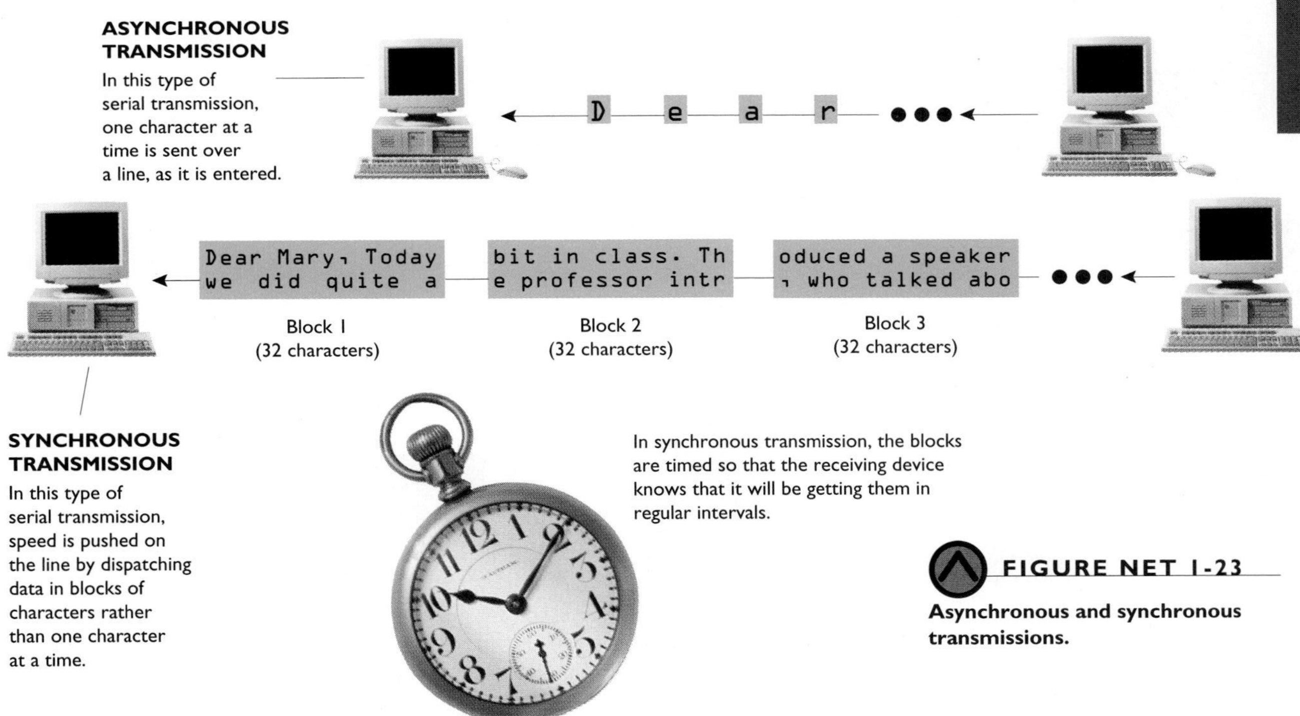

ASYNCHRONOUS TRANSMISSION
In this type of serial transmission, one character at a time is sent over a line, as it is entered.
D e a r
Dear Mary, Today we did quite a
bit in class. The professor intr
oduced a speaker, who talked abo
Block 1 (32 characters)
Block 2 (32 characters)
Block 3 (32 characters)
SYNCHRONOUS TRANSMISSION
In this type of serial transmission, speed is pushed on the line by dispatching data in blocks of characters rather than one character at a time.
In synchronous transmission, the blocks are timed so that the receiving device knows that it will be getting them in regular intervals.

FIGURE NET 1-23

Asynchronous and synchronous transmissions.

■ **Full-duplex transmission.** A type of transmission in which messages may travel in two directions simultaneously along a communications path. ■ **Asynchronous transmission.** The transmission of data over a line one character at a time, with variable time intervals between characters. ■ **Synchronous transmission.** The timed transmission of data over a line one block of characters at a time.

LAN Protocols In the LAN world, the protocols in effect depend on the particular type of network architecture used. *Network architecture* refers to both the particular topology the network follows—say, bus or ring—as well as scores of little details, only a few of which we'll talk about here. By far, the two most common LAN architectures are Ethernet and token ring.

ETHERNET **Ethernet** refers to a collection of protocols that specify a standard way of setting up a LAN in a bus network. It specifies the types and lengths of cables, how the cables connect, how devices communicate data, how the system detects and corrects problems, and so on.

Data communications and problem checking in an Ethernet network require a set of procedures collectively called *CSMA/CD,* which stands for *carrier sense multiple access with collision detection* (see Figure NET 1-24). *Carrier sense* means that, when a workstation has to send a message, it first "listens" for other messages on the line. If it senses no messages, it sends one. *Multiple access* means that two workstations

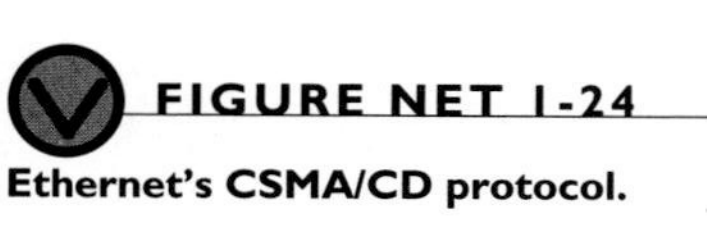

FIGURE NET 1-24

Ethernet's CSMA/CD protocol.

That message is addressed to me.
I'm sending a message to A.
That message is NOT addressed to me.
A
B
C
Bus line
To A
SENDING MESSAGES
Workstation B checks to see if the network is free and sends a message if it thinks it is. The message is broadcast across the network to all workstations, but only the one it is addressed to, A, can pick it up.
I'm sending a message to C.
I'm sending a message to C.
Ooops! The messages collided. Chances are they won't on the next try.
A
B
C
Bus line
To C
To C
COLLISIONS
Collisions occur when two workstations send messages at precisely the same time, both thinking the network is free. When a collision occurs, the workstations can sense it, and each waits a random fraction of a second before transmitting its message again.

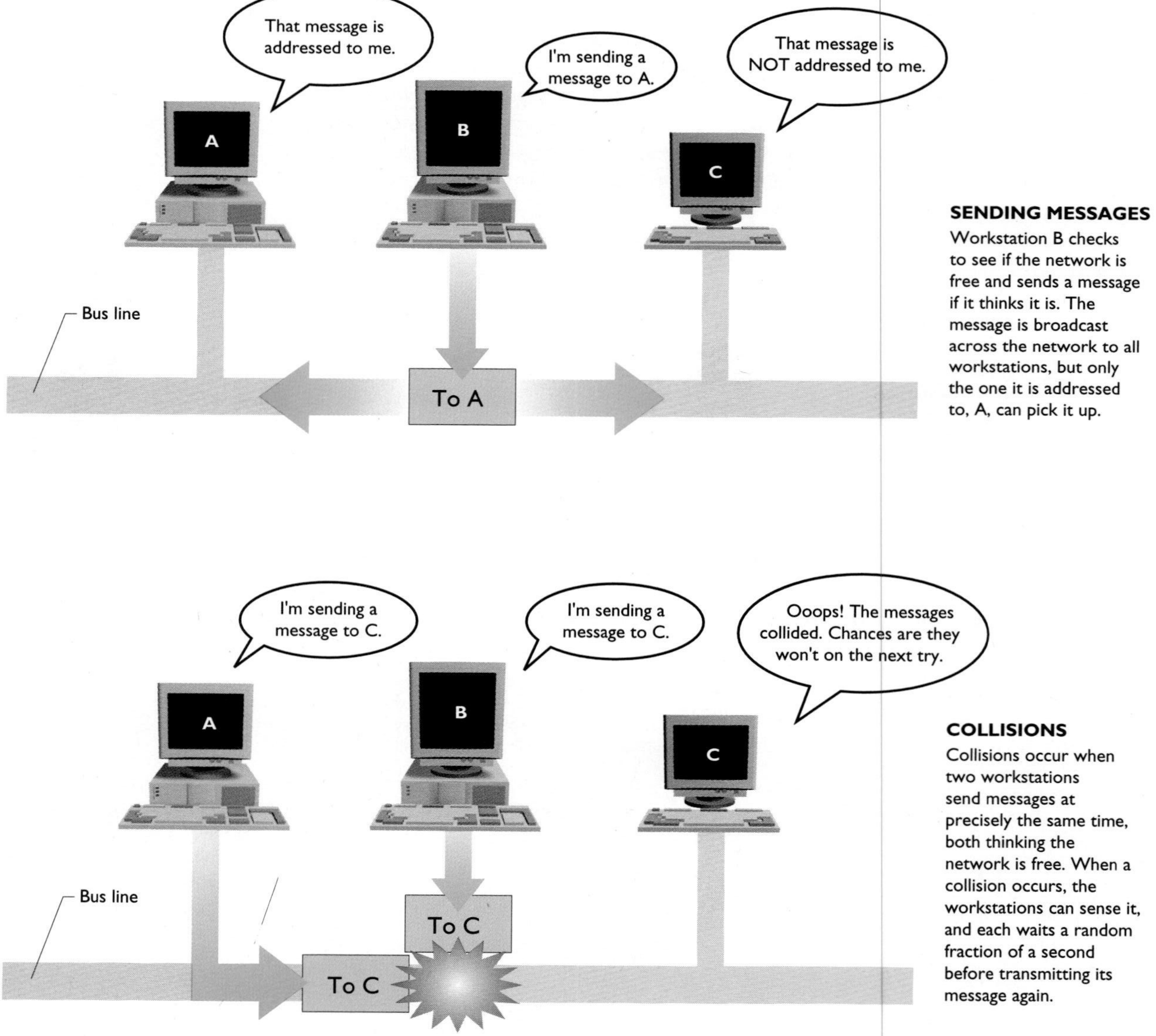

■ **Ethernet.** A collection of protocols that specify a standard way of setting up a bus-based LAN.

might want to send a message at the same time. *Collision detection* means that when a workstation initiates a message, it listens to see if the message might have collided with one from another workstation.

A collision takes place when two messages are sent at exactly the same time, so they temporarily jam the network. When they suspect a collision, the two sending workstations wait for short, random periods of time and send their messages again. The chance of the messages colliding a second time is extremely small.

A standard Ethernet system can send data at a rate of up to 10 mbps, and newer versions can transmit even faster. *Fast Ethernet,* for instance, runs at 100 mbps and *gigabit Ethernet* is even faster.

TOKEN RING Like Ethernet, **token ring** is a network architecture. It is used with a ring network topology and employs a *token-passing* protocol.

Here's how a token-ring network works (see also Figure NET 1-25): A small packet called a *token*—which has room for messages and addresses—is sent around the ring. As the token circulates, workstations either check to see if the token is addressed

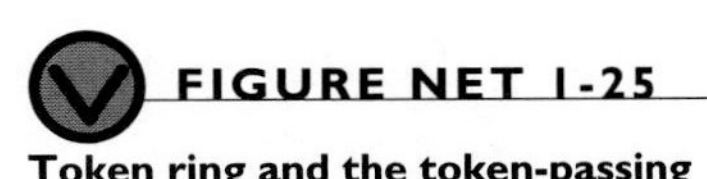

Token ring and the token-passing protocol.

1. A carrier called a token circulates around the ring. The token is "free" if a message is not attached to it; "busy," otherwise.

2. A workstation wanting to send a message checks the token when it passes by to see if it is free. If it is, the message is attached to the token, and the token's status is changed from "free" to "busy."

3. Each workstation checks busy tokens that pass by to see if they are carrying messages addressed to them. If messages are addressed elsewhere, the tokens move on to the next workstation along the ring.

4. When a workstation finds a token carrying a message addressed to it, it reads the message and changes the status of the token from "busy" to "free."

Free Token

Busy Token

To C

A

B

C

NET

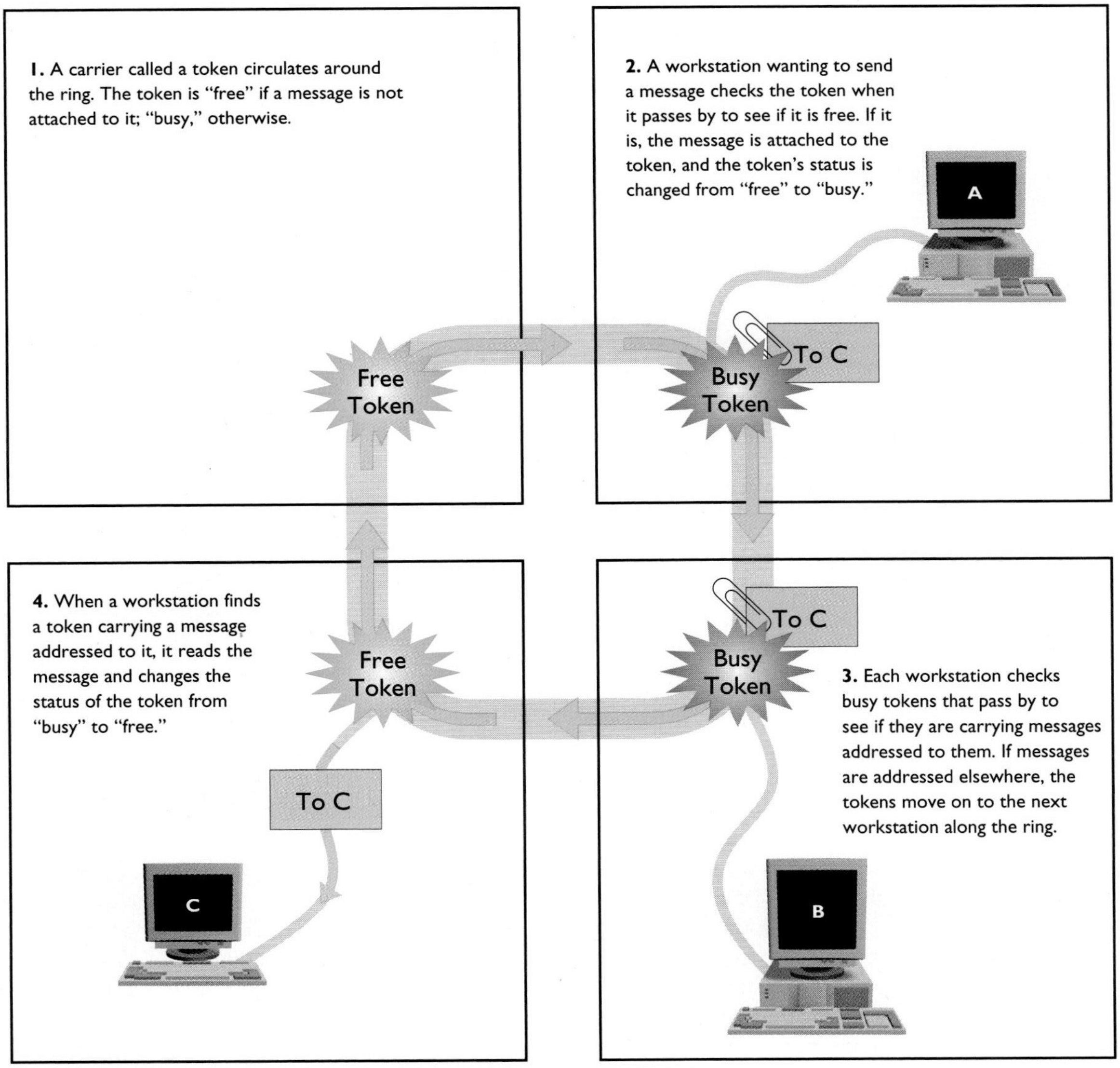

■ **Token ring.** A ring-based LAN that uses token passing to control transmission of messages.

1. Each message is split into packets.

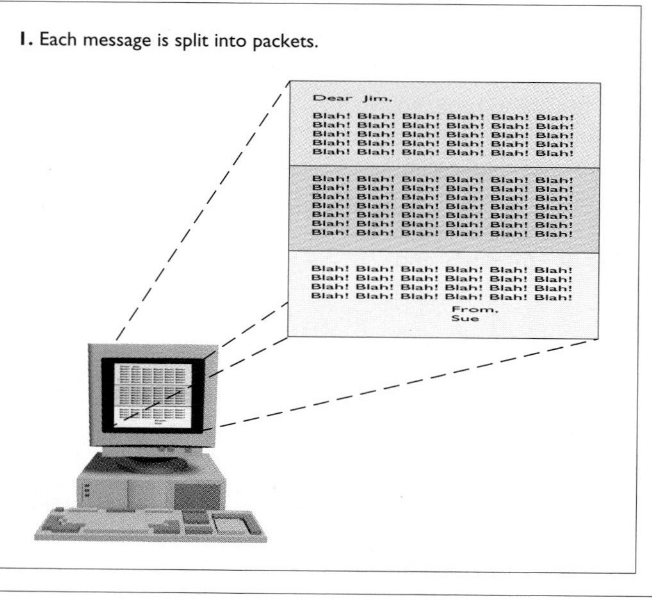

2. The packets are addressed to the same destination.

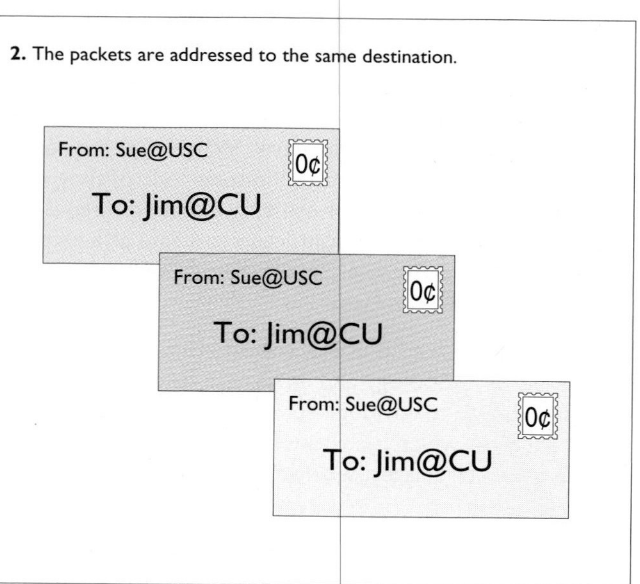

3. The packets may travel the same or different routes to the destination.

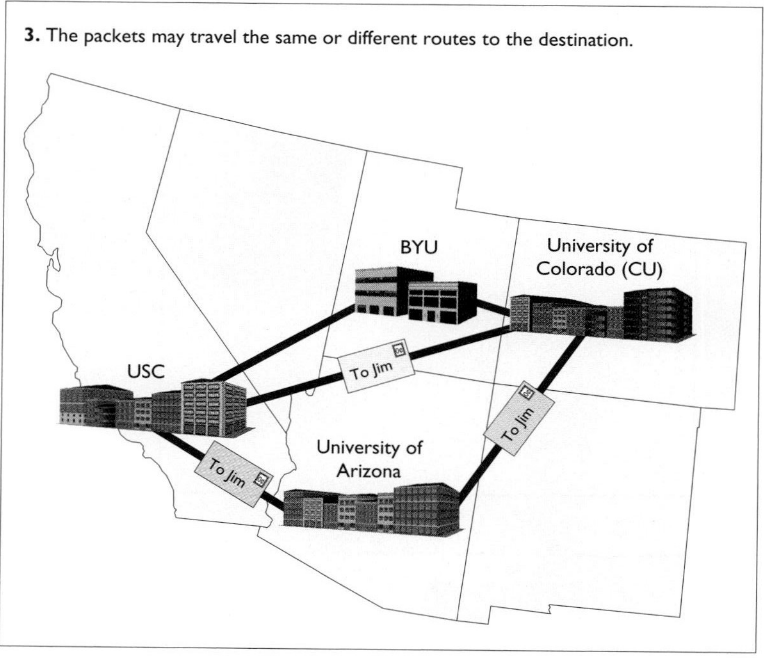

4. The packets are reassembled into the message at the destination.

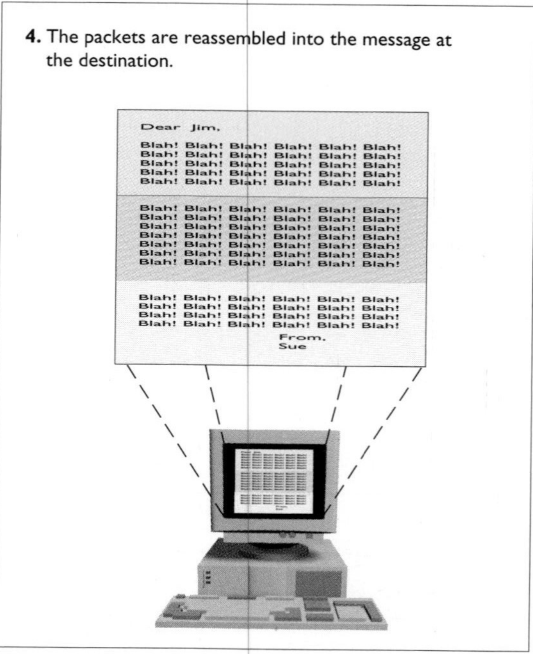

FIGURE NET 1-26
Packet switching.

to them or try to seize it so that they can assign messages to it. A token contains a control area, which specifies whether the token is free or carries a message. When a sender device captures a free token, it changes the status of the token from free to busy, adds an addressed message, and releases the token. The message then travels around the ring to the receiver location. The receiver copies the message and changes the status of the token back to free.

Although the token ring architecture maintains more order than Ethernet in that it allows no collisions, sometimes a computer with a defective NIC will swallow a token. If the token is gone for too long, the LAN assumes it's vanished and generates another. Several versions of the token ring architecture exist, the newer ones being faster and allowing more than a single token. Typical speeds run from a few mbps to several.

WAN Protocols Like LANs, WANs also conform to particular network architectures. One rather common architecture, *Systems Network Architecture (SNA),* has operated for years in the IBM mainframe world. SNA is most commonly used for private networks—such as airlines' reservation systems and large banking networks—that have tens of thousands of workstations. Instead of CSMA/CD or token passing, SNA often runs a *polling* protocol to transmit data. With polling, devices are asked—one by one and over and over again—if they have messages to send.

Another widely used architecture, *Fiber Distributed Data Interface (FDDI),* is commonly used to set up the fiber-optic backbones that connect dispersed campus LANs at large universities. These backbones use a ring topology and a token-passing protocol similar to token-ring networks to span over a hundred miles or more and run at speeds of over 100 mbps (refer back to Figure NET 1-18).

The Internet, too, relies on many protocols. One, called *transmission control protocol/Internet protocol (TCP/IP),* specifies how to package and send messages for the hundreds of different types of computers that hook up to the Internet. TCP/IP relies on a procedure known as packet switching to do this. **Packet switching** (see Figure NET 1-26) divides messages into smaller units called *packets.* Packets may travel along the Internet to their destination by the shortest path, but sometimes links along this path are heavily congested or broken due to the weather or an accident. Consequently, packets can be routed through any feasible link to reach their destination, and they are reassembled when they arrive. A typical router can handle about 10,000 packets per second, and some routers are rated at 200,000 or more packets per second.

Note that just because a network divides data into packets, it does not necessarily mean that packet switching is in effect. Strictly speaking, any block of data—from a single asynchronous bit to several thousand bytes—can be referred to as a packet.

Dangers Posed by Computer Networks

So far in this chapter we've looked at the opportunities that computer networks have made possible. Unfortunately, there is also a dark side to this rosy picture. Because computers and networks are so pervasive today—and the social controls needed to harness them have lagged well behind the torrid pace set by technological change—there is unprecedented opportunity for criminals and other individuals to commit acts that are not in the public interest. Such acts run the gamut from stealing money to intentionally destroying corporate data to stalking children over the Internet.

Figure NET 1-27 lists many of the dangers that computer networks pose to society. Some of these dangers—such as those associated with the risk of using credit cards over the Internet—are explored in Chapter NET 3. In versions of this textbook that contain the LIV module, we cover in greater detail many of the problems created by technology in general.

■ **Packet switching.** A transmission technique that breaks messages into smaller units that travel to a destination along possibly different paths.

DANGERS POSED BY COMPUTER NETWORKS
Stealing and/or distributing information that individuals or organizations consider confidential or private, such as corporate secrets, credit-card numbers, tastes and habits, and the like
Stealing money, software, phone time, and other assets
Intentionally destroying or corrupting the data and programs of others, say, by implanting computer viruses on their computer systems or by altering materials in storage
Distributing pornographical materials, hate literature, and other objectionable items
Distributing, without express permission, materials that are owned and merchandised by someone else
Sending nuisance electronic mail, or "spam"
Snooping around computer systems that are considered off limits
Stalking people through the Internet
Using communications technology to misrepresent a situation, for purposes of committing a crime

FIGURE NET 1-27

Dangers posed by computer networks.

Summary and Key Terms

Telecommunications, or *telecom,* refers to communications over a distance—over long-distance phone lines, via privately owned cables, or by satellite, for instance.

Telecommunications Applications A wide variety of important business applications involve telecommunications. Among these are **electronic mail** or **e-mail** (exchanging messages through **electronic mailboxes), voice mail, bulletin board systems (BBSs), facsimile** or **fax,** paging, information retrieval (including **Internet** access), **workgroup computing,** transaction processing, and interorganizational systems such as **electronic data interchange (EDI).**

The Telecommunications Industry The key players in the telecommunications industry include phone companies, cable-TV and satellite companies, content providers, and a wide variety of supporting hardware and software companies. Current deregulation is creating a telecom industry characterized by mergers and acquisitions, partnering arrangements, and shakeouts that will determine the winners and losers in the early part of the twenty-first century.

Telecommunications Media Messages sent in a telecommunications system are transmitted over some type of **communications medium.** Wiring, such as **twisted-pair wires, coaxial cable,** and **fiber-optic cable,** constitutes one major class of media. Messages also are commonly sent through the air in the form of **microwave** signals or over cellular or infrared networks. **Terrestrial microwave stations** accommodate microwave transmissions when either the sender or the receiver is on the ground. **Communications satellites** reduce the cost of long-distance transmissions via terrestrial microwave stations and provide overseas communications. **Cellular phones** use special ground stations that cover areas called *cells* to enable users to communicate with others. *Infrared technology* relies on infrared light beams to transmit data.

Adapting Computers to Communications Media Signals sent along a phone line travel in an **analog** fashion—that is, as continuous waves. Computers and their support equipment, however, are **digital** devices that handle data coded into 0s and 1s.

The difference between the highest and lowest frequencies on an analog medium is known as the medium's **bandwidth.** A higher bandwidth allows a medium to support more powerful communications applications. Media speed is often measured in **bits per second (bps),** kbps (thousands of bits per second), or mbps (millions of bits per second).

Messages move between machines either in **parallel transmissions,** in which each bit of a byte follows a different path, or in **serial transmissions,** in which bits of a byte follow one another in series along a single path.

Workstations are usually connected to a network through either a **network interface card (NIC)** or a **modem.** Typically, NICs connect workstations to local networks with dedicated lines, whereas modems connect workstations to wide-area networks with dial-up lines. If you need more bandwidth than you can squeeze out of a modem, your best bet is an **ISDN** line or something beyond.

Network Topologies Telecommunications networks can be classified in terms of their *topologies,* or geometrical patterns. Three common topologies are the **star network,** the **bus network,** and the **ring network.** Network topologies are often combined to aggregate smaller networks into larger ones.

Local Networks Many organizations build their own **local networks,** which connect devices in a single building or at a single site. Three common types of local networks are local area networks, hierarchical networks, and private branch exchanges.

Local area networks (LANs) fall into two categories. The first, **client-server LANs,** consist of **server** devices that provide network services to **client** workstations. Services often include access to expensive printers and vast secondary storage, database access, and computing power. In the second type of LANs, **peer-to-peer LANs,** the user workstations and shared peripherals in the network operate at the same level. The term **intranet** refers to a private LAN that implements the infrastructure and standards of the Internet and World Wide Web.

A **hierarchical local network** consists of a powerful *host* CPU at the top level of the hierarchy and microcomputer workstations or display terminals at lower levels. The workstations or terminals can either **download** data from the host or **upload** data to it.

A **private branch exchange (PBX)** consists of a central, private switchboard that links internal devices to switched lines.

Wide Area Networks **Wide area networks (WANs)** are communications networks that span relatively wide geographical areas. Because they tie together so many devices over such long distances, they require a number of special pieces of equipment.

Repeaters amplify signals along a network. **Routers** work in large switched networks like the Internet to pass messages along to their destinations. Devices on two dissimilar networks can communicate with each other if the networks are connected by a **gateway.** Devices on two similar networks can communicate with each other if they are connected by a bridge. A **multiplexer** enables two or more low-speed devices to share a high-speed line. A **concentrator** is a multiplexer with a store-and-forward capability.

Protocols A communications **protocol** is a collection of procedures to establish, maintain, and terminate transmissions between devices. Because devices transmit data in so many ways, they collectively employ scores of different protocols.

One type of protocol classifies transmissions in the **simplex, half-duplex,** or **full-duplex** modes.

Serially transmitted data are packaged either **asynchronously** (one byte to a package) or **synchronously** (several bytes to a package). Synchronous transmissions use a timing mechanism to coordinate exchanges of data packets between senders and receivers.

Two major LAN architectures are **Ethernet** and **token ring.** Each of these architectures is specified in a detailed set of protocols. Ethernet LANs commonly use a protocol called *CSMA/CD* to exchange messages, whereas token ring LANs use a protocol called *token passing.*

Like LANs, WANs also conform to particular network architectures. Three such architectures are *SNA, FDDI,* and *TCP/IP*. TCP/IP relies on a procedure known as **packet switching.**

Dangers Posed by Computer Networks Because computers and networks are so widespread, there is unprecedented opportunity for criminals and other individuals to commit acts that are not in the public interest. Such acts run the gamut from stealing money to intentionally destroying corporate data to stalking children over the Internet.

EXERCISES

1. Define the following terms and answer the questions that follow.
   a. E-mail
   b. Voice mail
   c. Fax
   d. Paging

   Which of the four would most effectively transmit a 15-page business report that has several handwritten comments by the boss? Which of the four would most effectively remind a person walking in a park of an important phone call that must be made this afternoon?

2. Fill in the blanks:
   a. Two types of modems are _________ modems and _________ modems.
   b. _________ is the process of transferring a file from a host or server computer to a requesting workstation over a network.
   c. A(n) _________ is a private LAN that uses the standards of the Internet and World Wide Web.
   d. All the bits in a byte follow each other in succession over a single path in _________ transmission.
   e. In _________-duplex transmission, messages may travel in two directions simultaneously.

3. Name at least one company in each of the following segments of the telecommunications industry.
   a. Phone company
   b. Cable-TV company
   c. Content provider
   d. Computer-software company
   e. Communications-hardware company

   Why is it getting increasingly difficult to put many large companies into any one segment?

4. List the types of telecommunications media covered in the chapter. Which is the most appropriate for each of the following situations?
   a. Getting output from a hard disk on a laptop computer onto a nearby desktop printer without the use of wire
   b. Transmitting data as quickly as possible, regardless of the cost
   c. Establishing contact between two people on the move
   d. Connecting a modem to a wall in the cheapest way possible
   e. Connecting workstations in a LAN

5. Many types of communications software will tell you how long you will spend downloading a particular file. Answer the questions below, assuming that a 10-page document occupies about 35 kilobytes (35,000 bytes) of storage space. Assume also 8 bits in a byte, and each byte is transmitted with an extra parity bit for error checking—in other words, a byte actually takes up 9 bits.
   a. How long will a 28.8 kbps modem take to download 100 pages of information? A 14.4 kbps modem?
   b. How much faster could you complete the transfer in part *a* over an ISDN line that runs at 128 kbps? Over a 1.54 mbps T1 connection? Over a fiber-optic backbone that runs at 100 mbps?
   c. All of the calculations you have made so far reflect maximum speeds. What real-world conditions would slow the rate of transfer?

6. Identify the three most basic network topologies and answer the following questions.
   a. Which is most appropriate to link a host mainframe computer with dumb terminals?
   b. Which most commonly uses a token-passing protocol?
   c. On which does Ethernet most commonly run?

7. What terms do the following acronyms represent?
   a. bps
   b. LAN
   c. PBX
   d. EDI
   e. NIC

8. Describe in your own words the functions of each of the following types of equipment.
   a. Router
   b. Repeater
   c. Gateway
   d. Bridge
   e. Concentrator

9. How does CSMA/CD work? How does it differ from token passing?

10. Identify several dangers posed by computer networks.

11. Determine whether the following statements are true or false.
    a. Most modems plug into dedicated lines.
    b. Infrared transmission is a wireless transmission technique that works with radio waves.
    c. A ring network connects devices serially in a closed loop.
    d. An intranet is a private LAN.
    e. A bridge is an interface that enables two dissimilar networks to communicate.

f. "Internet" is a contraction of two words: "internal" and "network."
g. The "Baby Bells" include such firms as America Online and CompuServe.
h. Coaxial cable consists of a center wire inside a grounded, cylindrical shield.
I. Microwaves are radio signals.
j. Peer-to-peer LANs are often smaller networks than client-server LANs.

12. Match each term with the description that fits best.
   a. NIC
   b. Analog
   c. Token passing
   d. Bps
   e. ISDN
   f. Uploading

   _____ A protocol used in a type of LAN.
   _____ The process of transferring a file from a local computer to a remote computer over a network.
   _____ A digital phone service that offers high-speed transmission over ordinary phone lines.
   _____ An add-in board through which a workstation connects to a local network.
   _____ A measure of a transmission medium's speed.
   _____ The transmission of data as continuous wave patterns.

PROJECTS

1. The Telecommunications Industry The telecommunications industry has evolved in the last quarter of a century to encompass many organizations, not just a single phone company. Among today's key players are companies that provide the infrastructure over which communications services are offered, content providers, communications-hardware companies, and communications-software companies. For this project, write a small report not to exceed ten pages that discusses some aspect of the telecommunications industry. You can choose any of the topics that follow or choose one of your own. Your report should go well beyond the information presented in the text.

- A History of AT&T
- The Baby Bells: Products and Services
- Cisco Systems: A Closer Look at One of the Internet's Most Successful Hardware Providers
- The Evolution of Satellite Products: What's Around the Corner?
- How the Need for Bandwidth Is Shaping the Telecommunications Industry
- Blockbuster Communications Products for the Twenty-First Century: Some Predictions

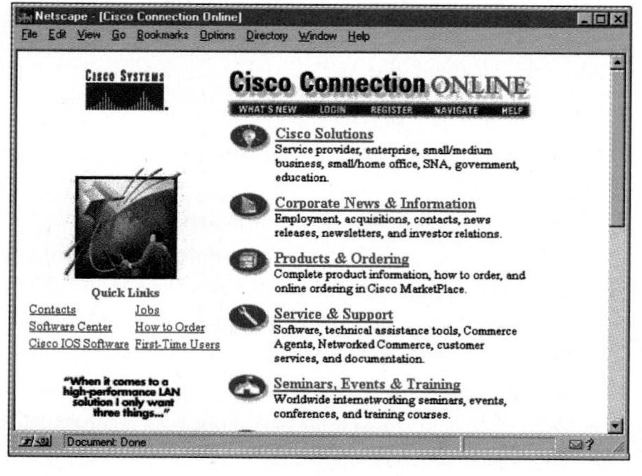

Use the Internet or local library resources to help you with your research. If your report is on a particular company, note that all of the major players in the telecommunications industry maintain Web sites containing useful information about their products and services (see accompanying figure). You can easily reach any of these sites by typing the company's name into the search box of any widely used, Web-based search engine. A list of search engines and information on how to reach them is given in Project 7 on page NET 89.

2. Fun and Games on the Internet A variety of sites exist on the Internet that can provide users with both a fun and rewarding time. Some such sites that you may want to check out are:

- THE INTERNET MOVIE DATABASE A must-see for movie buffs, this site is located at
  http://us.imdb.com/
  and is one of the most comprehensive free sources of movie information to be found anywhere.
- L.L. BEAN At the site
  http://www.llbean.com/
  you'll find L.L. Bean's online outdoor catalog as well as information about hiking, the outdoors, cross-country skiing, and national parks.
- THE GOOD HEALTH CLUB If you want to find health-related information, the site
  http://www.social.com/health/
  is a great place to start.
- THE ACCESS MARKET SQUARE SHOPPING MALL If you've never visited a cybermall before, the site
  http://www.icw.com/ams.html
  is an interesting one to see.

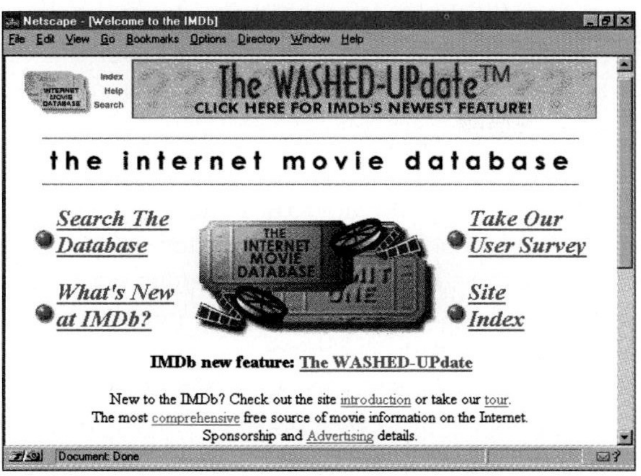

- E-ZINES Want an electronic magazine or newspaper to read? Scores of links to electronic publications, many of them available for free, can be found at the following sites
  www.ecola.com/news/
  www.enews.com
- BIOGRAPHIES You can find facts about over 15,000 famous people at the Web site run by the A&E channel's Biography program at
  www.biography.com
- FINDING PEOPLE Phone numbers and e-mail addresses are available for free on the Web at several different Web sites. Three sites that you may want to try can be found at the following locations
  www.bigfoot.com
  www.bigbook.com
  www.bigyellow.com

Visit each of these sites—or alternate ones suggested by your instructor or listed at the Parker site—and summarize each of their contents in a single paragraph.

3. Research on the Internet The Internet contains lots of information on communications-related topics. Use the Internet and a search site such as Yahoo! or WebCrawler to find information about any three of the following topics.

ISDN
Ethernet
Fiber-optic cable
Client-server LANs
Intranets
The World Wide Web
Satellites

Report to the class about the sites you visited and the contents of each one.

4. Digital Satellites You can do this project—and any others marked with the Group icon—in groups of two or more people.

Some exciting new digital satellite services are being pioneered by companies such as DirecTV (18-inch rooftop dishes that can accept as many as 175 television channels with sharp resolution) and DirecPC (digital information downloads from satellite to your PC). What potential do you foresee for these relatively new telecommunications technologies, as television and computing technologies merge together? Can you buy one system that will cater to both TV and PC needs?

5. If You Think PBXs Can Be Obnoxious, Please Raise Your Hand Here's a project in human engineering. Many people dislike dealing with PBX phone-menu systems because they often involve long waits as recorded voices rattle off choices. Also, you can often spend a couple of minutes making choices on early menus and then wind up at a final menu without a suitable choice. As your project, look into a PBX-menu system of your choice or your instructor's choice and evaluate its good points and weak points. A number of such menus can be reached by local dialing or toll-free numbers (with 800 and 888 area codes), so you won't get stuck paying long-distance charges.

6. Wireless LANs LANs often use cellular and other types of wireless technologies to link stations. Name three types of applications that work best through wireless LANs and identify in each case the benefits that result.

7. Becoming a High Roller Online A rapidly growing application on the Internet is personal investing. Users can look up stock prices by computer, maintain lists of their favorite stocks or mutual funds for automatic price quotes, buy and sell stocks and mutual funds online, communicate with other investors about specific companies, access research reports and filings at the Securities and Exchange Commission (SEC), and so on. For this exercise:

a. Find at least one online site that caters to investors. For this site, name the types of services offered.
b. What, in your opinion, are the three biggest advantages of the Internet for the small investor?

8. LANs Evaluate a client-server LAN on your campus or at a local business and answer the following questions.

a. Does the LAN use Ethernet, token ring, or some other LAN architecture?
b. How many workstations are connected to the LAN?
c. Identify the servers on the network and tell what each one does.
d. How fast can data travel through the LAN?

9. Research Revisited A textbook of this sort cannot possibly cover every emerging communications technology. The following list identifies several technologies that have received a lot of attention in the computer press in recent years. For any three of these, explain what the technologies do and their significance.

a. PCS (personal communciations services)
b. GPS (global positioning system)
c. ARCnet
d. Thin clients
e. Baud rate
f. Http (hypertext transfer protocol)

10. ISDN Many telecommunications-industry experts think that ISDN is the next step for residential customers who need more speed than a conventional modem can give them. All of the Baby Bells offer ISDN service, and so do many commercial online services and Internet service providers. Contact your local phone company and find out the price to install an ISDN line in your home. Be sure to check the following items:

a. Installation charge for 128 kpbs service
b. Monthly flat rate to maintain the line
c. Per-minute or per-call charges

Also figure in the cost of an ISDN adapter. Do the installation and monthly maintenance charges cover this cost? Can you buy and install your own to save money?

11. Extranets Feature NET 1-2 covers *intranets,* private networks that companies set up for their employees that implement the infrastructure and standards of the Internet and World Wide Web. Much newer to the scene are *extranets,* extensions of intranets out onto the Internet itself. Extranets provide such people as mobile workers and selected customers and suppliers access to a company's internal data and applications via the Web. For this project, find an example of an extranet reported in a magazine or newspaper and report to the class about it. Be sure to cover such details as the name of the company that runs the extranet, the types of users and applications involved, and the method by which unauthorized users are blocked out.

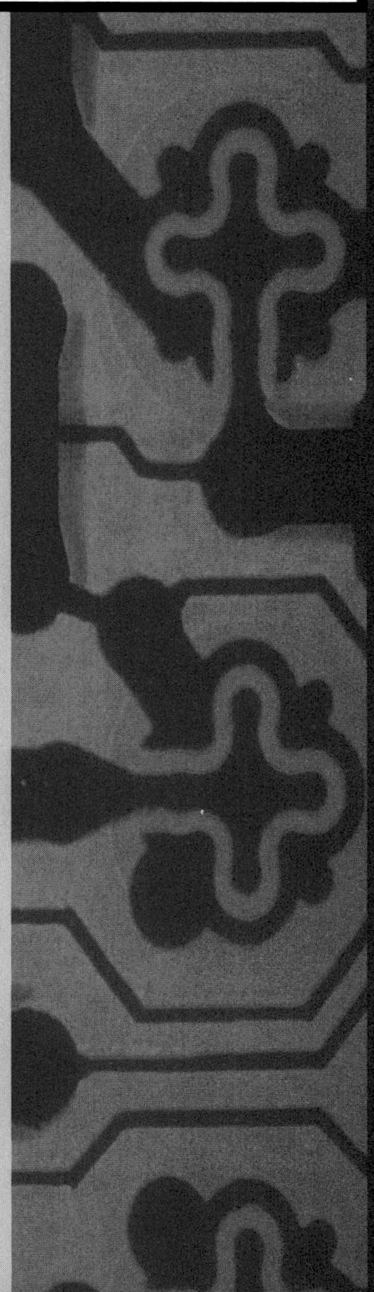

NET 2

Introduction to the Internet and World Wide Web

Outline

Learning Objectives

After completing this chapter, you will be able to:

1. Discuss how the Internet has evolved to become what it is today.
2. Identify the resources available on the Internet and explain the particular prominence of the World Wide Web.
3. Explain how the Internet benefits individuals and businesses.
4. Name a variety of tools available for working on the Internet.
5. List and evaluate the available options for connecting to the Internet.

Overview

It's hard to believe that, before 1990, few people outside of the computer industry and academia had ever heard of the Internet. It's really a small wonder, though. Hardware, software, and communications tools were not available back then to unleash the power of this tool and to make it a viable resource for almost everyone, as it is today.

What a difference a few years make. Today, "Internet" is a household word, and, in many ways, it has redefined how people think about computers and communications. Not since the early 1980s, when microcomputers swept into homes and businesses, has the general public been so excited about a new technology.

Despite the popularity of the Internet, however, many users cannot answer some important, basic questions about it. What makes up the Internet? Is it the same thing as the World Wide Web? Does the term "Internet" mean the same thing as the term "information superhighway?" How did the Internet begin, and where is it heading? What types of tools are available to help people make optimum use of the Internet? This chapter and the next address such questions.

Chapter NET 2 begins with a discussion of the evolution of the Internet, from the late 1960s up to the present time. Then it looks into the many resources that the Internet offers—such as e-mail and the World Wide Web—and how individuals and businesses are using the Internet in their work and leisure time. Next, so you can appreciate how the Internet's content arrives at your desktop, the chapter covers how Internet addresses work. Then, it's on to the software and hardware resources required for access. The final section of the chapter covers connecting to the Internet. Here you will learn about types of organizations available to assist you with making an Internet link and how to select among them.

Evolution of the Internet

The **Internet** is a worldwide collection of networks that supports personal and commercial communications and information exchange. It consists of tens of thousands of separate networks that are interconnected and accessed daily by millions of people. Just as the shipping industry has simplified transportation by providing standard containers for carrying all sorts of merchandise via air, rail, highway, and sea, in the same way the Internet furnishes a standard way of sending messages across many types of computer platforms and transmission media. While "Internet" has become a household word during the last few years, it has actually operated in one form or another for decades.

FROM THE ARPANET TO THE WORLD WIDE WEB

The Internet began in 1969 as an experimental project. The U.S. Department of Defense (DOD) wanted to develop a network that could withstand outages, such as those caused by nuclear attack. A principal goal was creating a system that could send messages along alternate paths in the event part of the network was disabled. With this purpose in mind, the DOD enlisted researchers in colleges and universities to assist with the development of protocols and message-packeting systems to standardize routing information.

■ **The Internet.** A global network linking tens of thousands of networks and millions of individual users, schools, businesses, and government agencies.

ARPANET At its start and throughout most of its history, the Internet was called **ARPANET** (pronounced *ar-pan-ette*). ARPANET was named for the group that sponsored its development, the Advanced Research Projects Agency of the DOD. During its first few years, ARPANET enabled researchers at a few dozen academic institutions to communicate with each other and with government agencies on topics of mutual interest.

However, the DOD got much more than it bargained for. With the highly controversial Vietnam War in full swing, ARPANET's e-mail facility began to handle not only legitimate research discussions but also heated debates about U.S. involvement in Southeast Asia. As students began to access ARPANET, computer games such as Space War gradually found their way into the roster of applications along with online messaging methods to share game strategies. Such unintended uses led to the development of bulletin boards and discussion groups devoted to other special interests.

As the experiment grew during the next decade, hundreds of colleges and universities tapped into ARPANET. By the 1980s, advances in communications technology enabled many of these institutions to develop their own local networks, as well. These local networks collectively served a mixture of Windows-based computers, Apple Macintoshes, UNIX-speaking workstations, and so on. Over the years, ARPANET became a connecting thread of protocols that tied together such disparate networks. Throw in the government networks also under development during that time—and add to that the decision to let friendly foreign countries participate—and you can see how ARPANET turned into a massive network of networks.

By the end of the 1980s, the Internet—renamed from ARPANET—could perhaps best be described as a vehicle for thousands of technically oriented people throughout the world to communicate electronically about anything from their work to sports to their love lives.

The 1990s and the World Wide Web Despite its popularity in academia, the Internet went virtually unnoticed by the general public and the business community for over two decades. Why? For two reasons—it was hard to use and slow. Users had to know cryptic programming commands, since attractive graphical user interfaces (GUIs) were still largely unknown.

As always, however, technology improved and new applications quickly evolved. First, communications hardware improved and computers gained speed and better graphics capabilities. Then, in 1989, a researcher named Tim Berners-Lee, working at a physics laboratory called CERN in Europe, proposed the idea of a *World Wide Web.* The Web concept would organize Internet information into pages linked together through selectable graphics on a display screen.

Matters really got rolling with the arrival of Microsoft Windows 3.0 (and later versions) and its widely used graphical user interface. As sales of Windows soared, friendly Web *browsers* sporting the Windows GUI became available to make surfing the World Wide Web both easy and fun (see Figure NET 2-1). The Web is only part of the Internet—not all of the Internet is organized like the Web into easy-to-read pages—but it is by far the most popular and fastest-growing part today.

As the World Wide Web was catching on in significance, government and business groups in the United States started talking seriously about building a national *information superhighway (Iway)* to link homes, businesses, schools, libraries, hospitals—you name it—with high-speed data paths. Such paths would give people easy access to electronic books, magazines, and research materials from all over the country and the world. Eventually, it may give people the ability to click a few buttons on a keypad and instantly watch virtually any movie or TV show ever made.

When government and business groups began considering the design of a software vehicle to deliver all of the new electronic "products" that an Iway would conceivably

■ **ARPANET.** The forerunner to the Internet, named after the Advanced Research Projects Agency (ARPA), which sponsored its development.

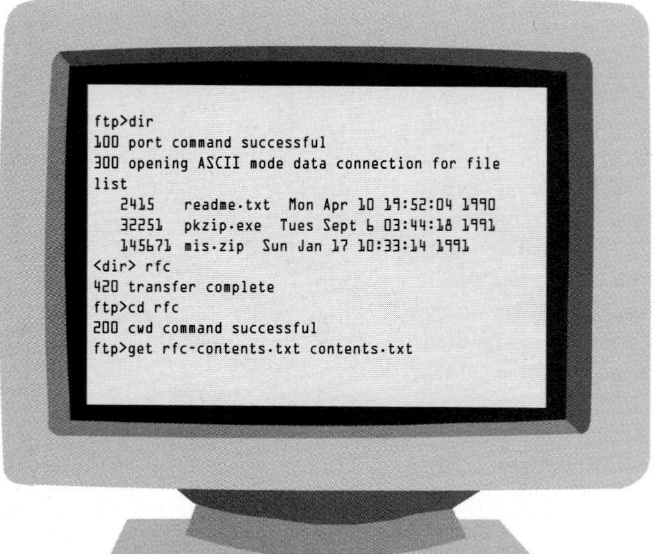

EARLY 1990s
Even at the beginning of the 1990s, using the Internet for most people meant learning how to work with a cryptic sequence of commands.

TODAY
Today's Internet features the World Wide Web, which organizes much of the Internet's content into easy-to-read pages and replaces the cryptic command sequences with linkages that you can activate with a mouse click.

FIGURE NET 2-1

Using the Internet: Back in the "old days" versus now.

make possible, they identified two primary possibilities—building a delivery vehicle from scratch or improving upon an already existing vehicle. Because the Internet had a proven track record of reaching large numbers of people over diverse computer platforms—and because businesses couldn't afford to wait—by default, it became the front-running choice. As interest in the Internet snowballed, scores of companies began looking for ways to make it more accessible to people, to make the user interface even more dazzling, and to make more services available over it.

To show you how fast the Internet and Web have grown, consider that in the middle of 1993, only about 100 computers—called *Web servers*—distributed Web pages throughout the Internet. Talk about rapid change: Today that count is in the hundreds of thousands! While the Internet itself has been doubling in size almost every year in recent times, the Web has been doubling every few months.

THE INTERNET COMMUNITY TODAY

The Internet community of today is populated by individuals working for their own purposes, companies, and a variety of other organizations located both at home and throughout the world (see Figure NET 2-2). Virtually anyone with a computer that has communications capabilities can be part of the Internet, either as a user or as a supplier of information or services. Most members of the Internet community fall into one or more of the following groups.

Users *Users* are people who avail themselves of the information content of the Internet in their work or play. The user base still shows a decided tilt toward the United States, although Europeans widely use the Internet, and access is available in almost 200 countries. While users are both young and old and come from a variety of backgrounds, recent studies have shown that users are typically college educated, white, male, and above average in affluence. This profile is expected to change con-

SERVICE PROVIDERS
Service providers connect individual users and user organizations to the Internet.

USERS
These are the people who work on or play with the Internet.

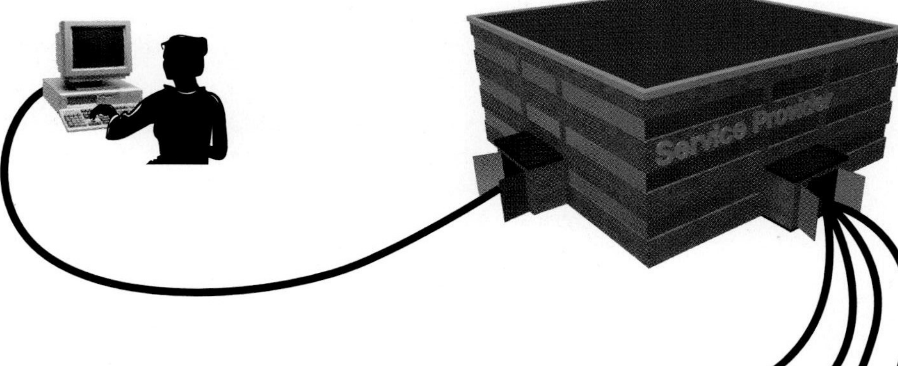

CONTENT PROVIDERS
These consist of the organizations and individuals that create or distribute information on the Internet.

COMPANIES

COLLEGES AND UNIVERSITIES

GOVERNMENT

INDIVIDUALS

GUIDE ORGANIZATIONS
Several groups act as watchdogs on the Internet, make up the rules that govern it, and help manage sections of it.

SOFTWARE AND HARDWARE COMPANIES
These companies make Internet-related programs and equipment.

FIGURE NET 2-2

The Internet community. Today's Internet community is composed of users, service and content providers, government and academia, and several other types of organizations.

siderably in the years ahead, as the Internet becomes easier to use and begins to approach the popularity of the phone and personal computer. Recent surveys have shown that the user base is gravitating toward numbers that are closer in line with population averages—a sure sign that the Internet is achieving mass-market appeal.

Service Providers **Service providers**—often called *access providers*—are organizations that supply Internet connections to others. They operate very much like a cross between the cable-television and phone companies in that they provide a window for you to see what's out there in the wider world and to interact with it.

Service providers usually charge each subscriber a monthly fee to access the Internet, and some charge setup fees to open accounts. They also furnish e-mail addresses, which work like phone numbers. Additionally, many providers offer to post Web pages for subscribers. A later section of the chapter will cover service providers in more detail.

Content Providers **Content providers** are the parties that furnish the information available on the Internet. If service providers work like the phone companies, content providers resemble the people you talk to when you dial phone numbers. Here are some examples of content providers:

- A photographer creates electronic copies of some of her best work and places them—along with her e-mail address and phone number—on the Internet.
- A political-action group sponsors an online forum for discussions between people who share its opinions.
- A software company maintains an Internet address that users can dial up to both get information and download trial copies of software.

Software and Hardware Companies In addition to service and content providers, a wide variety of software and hardware companies make and distribute Internet-related products. The firms that supply browser and e-mail software fall into this category. So, too, do the companies that make routers, server computers, server software, and Web-page publishing tools.

Other Organizations Many other organizations influence the Internet and its uses. Governments have among the most visible impact; their laws limit both information content and access in the Internet community. A voluntary group called the *Internet Society* is another key organization. It proposes guidelines for the direction and technical development of the Internet, and it also decides which protocols to support and how Internet addresses should work. Also playing an important support role is an organization called *InterNIC* (for Internet Networking Information Center). Created by the National Science Foundation, InterNIC controls the registration of Internet addresses to ensure that no two are the same. Last but not least, many colleges and universities support Internet research and manage large blocks of the Internet's resources.

MYTHS ABOUT THE INTERNET

Because the Internet is so unique in the history of the world—and still a relatively new phenomenon—several widespread myths about it have surfaced.

Myth 1: The Internet Is Free This falsehood has been perpetuated largely by the fact that people can freely engage in long-distance e-mail or chat exchanges without paying extra. It is true that the Internet's design never anticipated distance billing, and it is certainly also a fact that many people, such as students and employees, pay nothing to use the Internet. Yet it should also be obvious that someone, somewhere has to be forking out money to keep the Internet up and running.

Businesses, schools and public libraries, self-employed individuals working from home, and content providers often pay service providers at flat rates to link to the Internet. The service providers—along with the phone companies—pay to keep the physical links of the network running smoothly. Providers also pay software and hardware companies for the resources they need to support users.

■ **Service provider.** An organization that sells online access to remote information. ■ **Content provider.** An organization or individual providing information for distribution over the Internet.

Some industry observers feel that, in some not-too-distant day, market forces will determine much about who has access to what on the Internet. As more and more demands for bandwidth clog the Internet—including memory-hungry multimedia Web pages, phone calls, video and videoconferencing applications, and software robots that cruise Web sites for information—customers who need speed and reliability will be forced to pay for it.

Myth 2: Someone Controls the Internet The popularity of conspiracy theories in recent years has contributed to the spread of this myth. In fact, no one group or organization controls the Internet, although many would undoubtedly like to do so. Governments in each country have the power to regulate content and use of the Internet within their borders. However, legislators often face serious obstacles getting acts passed into law—let alone getting them enforced. Making governmental control even harder is the bombproof design of the Internet itself. If a country tries to block access to or from another country, users can establish links between the two countries through a third one.

Guidelines of watchdog groups such as the Internet Society have sometimes even given way before the tidal wave of people and organizations that have flocked to the Internet. For instance, the policy that discouraged commercial use has fallen by the wayside in recent years. In the middle of 1994, only about 14 percent of Web sites were deemed to be commercial; today, that number is close to 90 percent.

Myth 3: The Internet and World Wide Web Are Identical Since you can use Web browser software to get virtually anywhere on the Internet today, many people think the Internet and the Web are the same thing. They're not, as you will see in the next section, which describes parts of the Internet. While the Web is the fastest-growing component of the Internet, it's not even the largest one. More people, in fact, use the Internet's e-mail facility than the Web.

What Does the Internet Have to Offer?

Since the Internet evolves so rapidly, the features offered over it also change constantly. This section describes some of the more popular features. Figure NET 2-3 covers many commercial and leisure opportunities that these features have made possible.

E-MAIL

Electronic mail, or **e-mail,** was one of the first applications to appear on the Internet, and it remains the most widely used one. If you are connected to the Internet, you can send an e-mail message to anyone with an Internet e-mail address, just as you can reach anyone with a phone number through the phone system.

You can create an e-mail message either on your word processor or—as most people do—with e-mail software. When you finish composing the message, you then send it via the e-mail program to the electronic mailbox of another person (or the mailboxes of several people). Most service providers furnish easy-to-use e-mail facilities as part of their monthly service fees. Such a facility typically lets users edit, sort, and copy into folders any incoming mail; in addition, they can create and edit outgoing mail messages. Many e-mail programs also enable users to attach documents, voice clips, and graphics to outgoing messages and to receive messages enhanced in this way.

Users can send and receive e-mail over private networks, the Internet, or some combination of the two. Corporate LANs, which often use network protocols other

■ **Electronic mail.** The computer-to-computer counterpart for interoffice mail or the postal service. Also called **e-mail.**

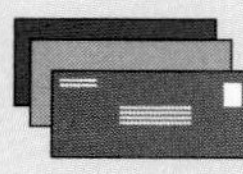

Electronic mail. Internet mail service now links people in almost 200 countries. Futurists predict a universal electronic mail network similar to the phone system.

Information retrieval. Virtually any type of information can be found on the Internet—tutorials on various subjects, hobby information, legal and medical advice—you name it.

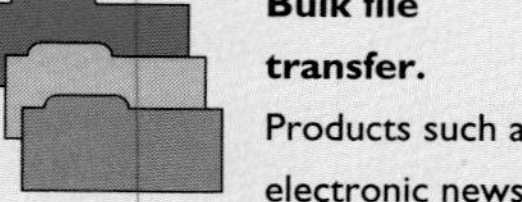

Bulk file transfer. Products such as electronic newspapers and magazines—as well as software and music—are distributed over the Internet, saving the cost of print media, disks, and mailing.

Discussion groups and forums. You can take part in worldwide discussions and forums on matters of personal interest—simply browse the network to find topics you wish to discuss.

On-demand movies and television. Someday it will be possible to order virtually any movie and television show by computer, choosing your own viewing times.

Social video gaming. Games in which several people participate are now available over the Internet. As video and communications capabilities improve, expect participation in TV game shows via Internet links.

Shopping procurement. It is now possible to search through scores of electronic malls for products. "Intelligent agent" programs will help you find what you want.

Customer support. Many companies assist customers over the Internet. The Internet is also widely used to distribute advertising literature about products and to update software.

News and weather. Information about news events and weather happening all over the globe are updated regularly on the Internet. You can even access satellite data.

Education. You can find learning materials on virtually every topic imaginable on the Internet. Eventually, you will be able to access millions of books online instead of having to go to your local library to find them.

Access to remote computing. If your own computer isn't powerful enough to perform certain types of tasks, you can access larger computers located elsewhere—and their software, too.

Conferencing. Futurists predict that a picture phone—a phoning device that enables people to see each other as they speak—will someday be a standard feature on the Internet.

FIGURE NET 2-3

Commercial and leisure opportunities made possible by the Internet.

than TCP/IP (the Internet standard), have traditionally used proprietary e-mail programs such as Microsoft Mail and Lotus cc:Mail. The growth of the Internet and corporate intranets, and the resulting spread of standards based on TCP/IP, have led to a variety of less-expensive e-mail options, including shareware programs.

Figure NET 2-4 illustrates how the Internet distributes e-mail. Also, refer back to Figure NET 1-1, which illustrates the components of a typical e-mail message.

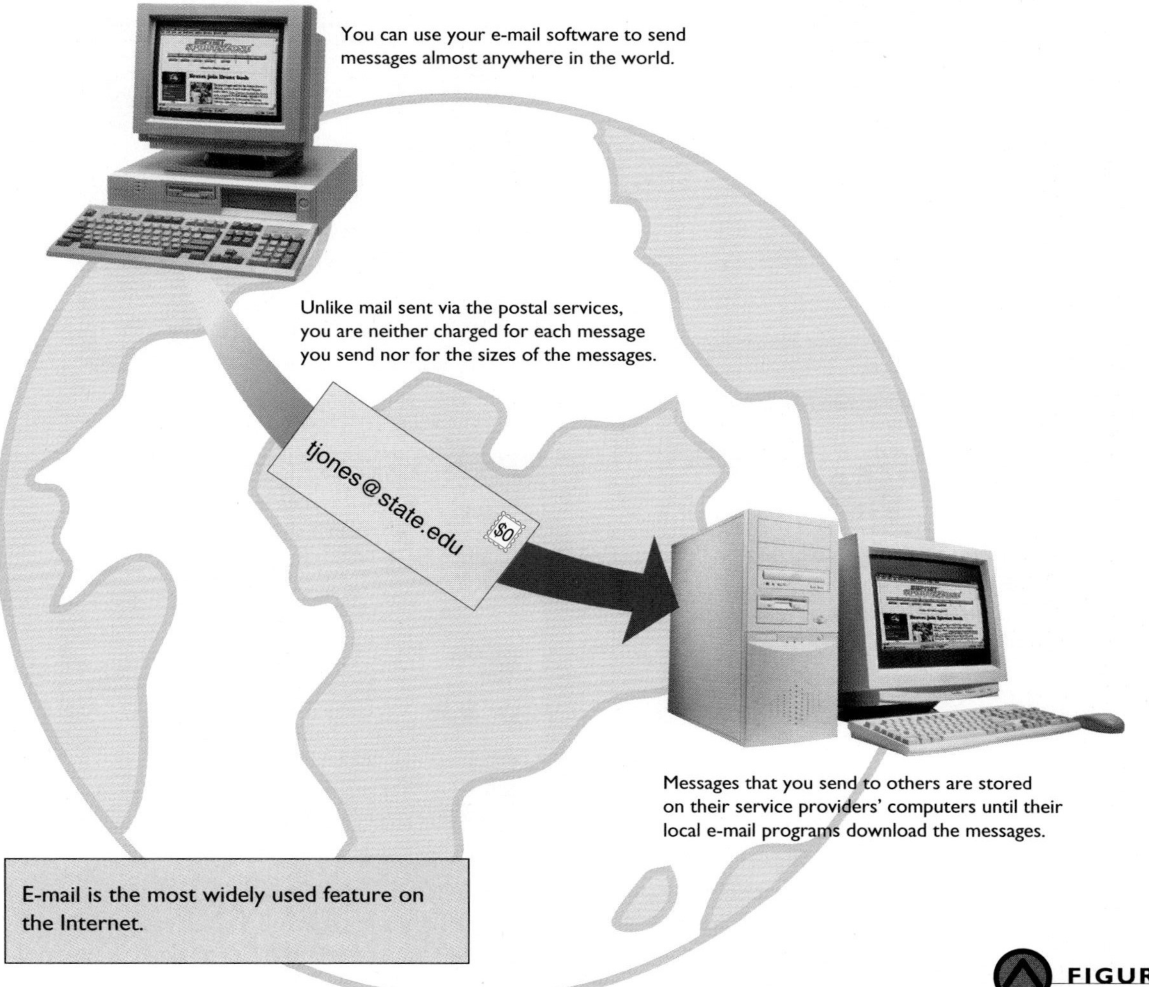

You can use your e-mail software to send messages almost anywhere in the world.
Unlike mail sent via the postal services, you are neither charged for each message you send nor for the sizes of the messages.
tjones@state.edu
$0
Messages that you send to others are stored on their service providers' computers until their local e-mail programs download the messages.
E-mail is the most widely used feature on the Internet.

FIGURE NET 2-4

E-mail over the Internet.

INFORMATION RETRIEVAL AND THE WORLD WIDE WEB

One of the most popular uses of the Internet today is information retrieval. While the World Wide Web is by far the most popular way for people to access information on the Internet—and the method to which this and the next chapter will devote a great deal of attention—it is not the only one.

The World Wide Web The **World Wide Web (WWW),** or *Web,* is a retrieval system based on technology that organizes information into pages. The pages are called *Web pages,* or "documents." Web pages are connected by **hyperlinks,** which are often referred to as **hypermedia.** Hyperlinks often appear onscreen as

- **World Wide Web (WWW).** A network within the Internet consisting of data organized as page images with hyperlinks to other data.
- **Hyperlink.** Boldfaced and underlined text or a graphic icon within a World Wide Web page that summons new information to the screen when the user selects it. Often also called **hypermedia.**

NET

Hyperlinks commonly appear as boldfaced and underlined text, or icons, that—when you click on them—take you to other pages on the Web.

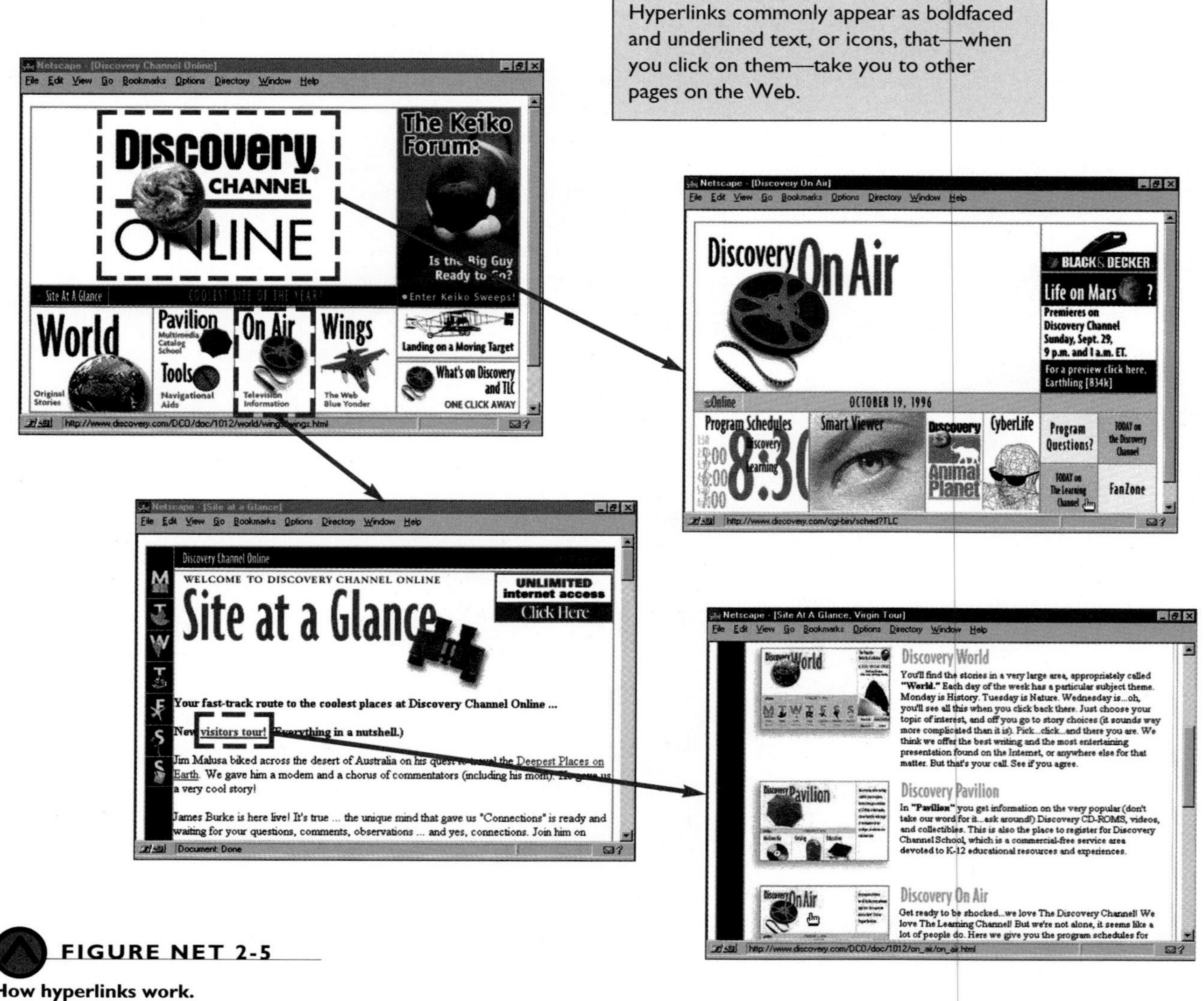

FIGURE NET 2-5

How hyperlinks work.

boldfaced and underlined text or as selectable icons. When you select a hyperlink by clicking on it with a mouse, the current page on your screen is refreshed with new information—such as a new Web page, another part of the same Web page, a sound, or a movie clip. Web pages and hyperlinks are illustrated in Figure NET 2-5. A hyperlink that takes you to another part of the same Web page is called a *jump*.

When a content provider makes available one or more Web pages that relate to a specific topic or business, the result is called a **Web site.** Today, most medium-sized to large companies in the United States maintain one or more Web sites, and thousands of individuals have them, too. A computer that hosts one or more Web sites is called a **Web server.** Servers run specialized software for each type of Internet application, including the Web, e-mail, UseNet news, and so on.

A Web site can contain anywhere from one to hundreds or thousands of pages. Your visit to a Web site often begins at the site's **home page.** A home page at a large multipage site usually presents a table of contents with hyperlinks to other pages. The Web lets you freely navigate among such pages and others by selecting any of the hyperlinks, in any order you wish.

You need a piece of software called a *Web browser* to see pages on the Web and to navigate between Web sites (called *Web surfing,* when the navigation is done in a

■ **Web site.** A collection of related Web pages belonging to an individual or organization. ■ **Web server.** A computer that stores and distributes Web pages upon request. ■ **Home page.** The first page you encounter on most Web-site visits.

casual manner). In the vernacular of the client-server Internet environment, desktop browsers are often called *Web clients*. Web clients display desired information by putting in requests for pages at Web servers. Often today the processing work on the Web is shared between client and server. With servers bending under ever-larger page-request burdens as the Web grows, clients are taking over a lot more of the computing work—from displaying pages to running small interactive elements called "applets" that make pages more exciting.

A later section of the chapter will cover Web browsers in much greater detail. Suffice it to say for now that these programs are evolving into one-stop solutions for users to link up not only to Web pages but also to virtually all other resources of the Internet, including e-mail, Gopher, FTP, and so on. In the future, say some observers, the Web's page concept will fade into the background and most people will be tuning into Web "channels" to get their information (see the Tomorrow box on page NET 62).

Gopher **Gopher,** developed at the University of Minnesota, is another information-retrieval feature within the Internet. Gopher generates hierarchical, text-intensive menus that allow the user to access resources by making successive menu selections with an onscreen pointer (see Figure NET 2-6).

FIGURE NET 2-6

Gopher.

THE GOPHER SYSTEM

Gopher generates hierarchical, text-intensive menus that allow users of the Internet to access resources by making successive hyperlink selections.

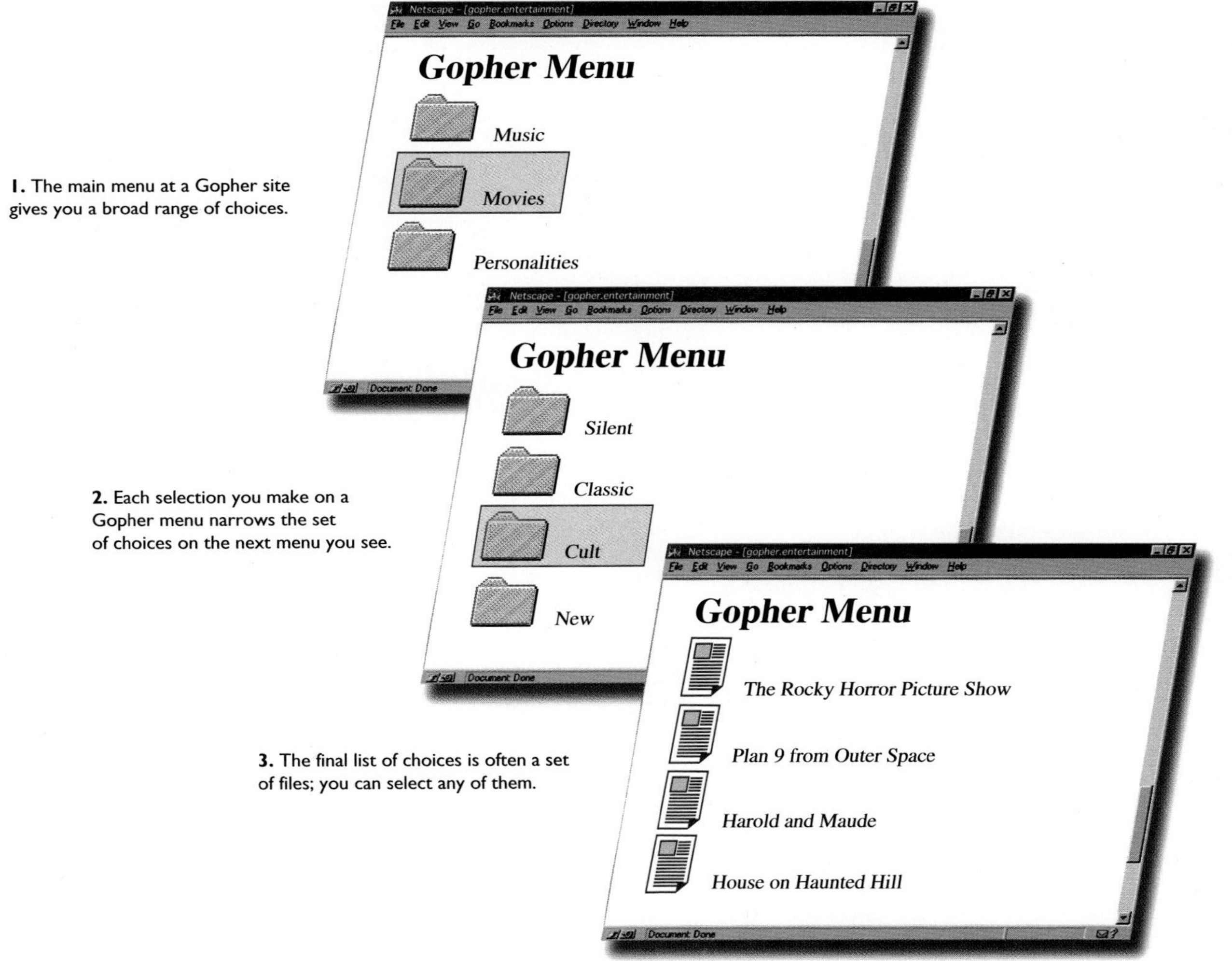

1. The main menu at a Gopher site gives you a broad range of choices.
Gopher Menu
Music
Movies
Personalities
2. Each selection you make on a Gopher menu narrows the set of choices on the next menu you see.
Gopher Menu
Silent
Classic
Cult
New
3. The final list of choices is often a set of files; you can select any of them.
Gopher Menu
The Rocky Horror Picture Show
Plan 9 from Outer Space
Harold and Maude
House on Haunted Hill

■ **Gopher.** An information-retrieval tool for the Internet that generates hierarchical, text-intensive menus; successive topic choices narrow a search to a particular resource.

NET

Gopher is almost as easy to use as the Web. In fact, before the Web came along with its flashy, tantalizing graphics, Gopher was the rave of the Internet. While you will find far fewer Gopher sites than Web sites today, and the growth of Gopher has slowed, thousands of sites still offer valuable content. What's more, a lot of information is available on the Gopher system that has not yet been put on the Web. Many academic institutions, companies, and government agencies maintain Gopher sites in addition to their Web sites.

Gopher is organized similarly to the Web. People who want to distribute information in this way set up Gopher sites on Gopher servers, and people who want to download from such sites must have Gopher "client" software built into their browsers. Web pages often contain links to Gopher sites and vice versa.

File Transfer Protocol (FTP) FTP sites preceded both Web and Gopher sites in the evolution of the Internet, and they remain good places to visit to get copies of programs and files. **FTP** stands for **file transfer protocol,** the communications protocol that facilitates the transfer of files between an FTP server and a user's computer. FTP sites allow you to download files by selecting them from menus that list file and folder names (see Figure NET 2-7). Selecting a file name often initiates an immediate

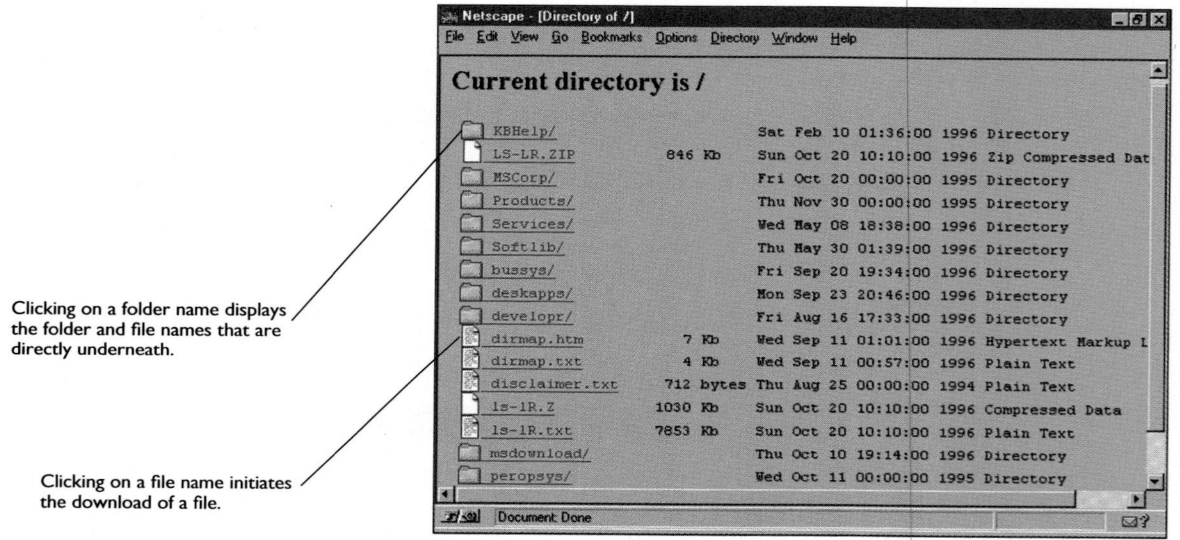

FIGURE NET 2-7

File transfer protocol (FTP). FTP sites allow you to download files directly by making successive selections from menus of folders and files at those sites.

file download to your computer. By selecting a folder name instead, you get to see the names of the files and subfolders inside it.

Most people who access FTP sites extensively do so through an FTP program. For instance, this textbook was developed largely through FTP software, with the author uploading and downloading text and graphics files at the publisher's FTP site. The Web also allows you to visit FTP sites and to download files from them.

While such reputable companies as Microsoft and Corel distribute free utility software through secure FTP sites, you cannot always count on bug-free software from less-reliable FTP sources. Consequently, it's a good idea to run a virus scan through any downloaded program files from unknown sources before running the software.

At most FTP sites, you must log on before you can access files. If you don't have an account at the site—and most people won't—you must log in as an *anonymous* FTP user, or guest. Many FTP sites limit access by anonymous users to certain files, and many do not allow anonymous log-ins at all. You can find sites that allow anonymous users listed in such directories as *The Internet Yellow Pages* or through a special online Internet service called Archie. **Archie** client software included with many Web

■ **File transfer protocol (FTP).** A communications protocol that facilitates the transfer of files between a host computer and a user's computer. ■ **Archie.** A software tool that enables Internet users to search through public servers to find the locations of downloadable files on particular subjects.

browsers enables you to search through FTP computers to find the locations of downloadable files on particular subjects.

Telnet In today's networking environment, desktop clients often download software from remote network servers and run it themselves. Powerful desktop personal computers have made this arrangement possible. However, in earlier days, servers—or *hosts,* as they have been traditionally called—had to do virtually all of the processing. The remote workstations hooked up to them were dumb terminals that could do little more than send and receive data. Users typed commands at their terminals, which sent them to the host; the host ran the programs and delivered the results back to the terminals. To accommodate such simple transmissions, Telnet was developed. **Telnet** is a communications protocol that lets a workstation behave like a dumb terminal when interacting with remote servers.

Many applications—even modern ones—still require the host to run the application and treat your fancy desktop computer as a dumb terminal. In a popular application, people often play games over networks with others, and Telnet hosts run the games for all players. Many bulletin-board systems are also set up on Telnet computers throughout the world.

Telnet is another feature built into many Web browsers. You can access Telnet sites using a Web browser just as easily as you can reach Gopher and FTP sites.

MAILING LISTS

In addition to e-mail and information retrieval, people often use the Internet to distribute information through mailing lists. A **mailing list** is a topical discussion group that communicates through shared e-mail messages. Hundreds of mailing lists provide messages about all sorts of topics on the Internet.

Mailing-list participants typically focus their discussions on specific subjects, for instance, the Grateful Dead or classic movies or diabetes. Generally, anyone can send messages to a mailing list, but you must subscribe to receive any e-mail from it. To handle mailing-list applications, a server computer must run a mailing-list-manager program. When mailing-list subscribers send e-mail messages to the program, it makes copies and sends one to each of the subscribers on the list. Some mailing lists are completely automated, whereas others involve some human intervention.

The individual or company that controls the mailing list, called the *mailing-list administrator,* may or may not charge subscribers. In order to subscribe to a mailing list, you must generally send an e-mail request directly to the administrator's mailbox. Mailing lists are sometimes *moderated,* meaning that someone screens messages for appropriateness before distributing them.

Mailing lists often evolve into online communities. Even though subscribers may never physically meet, they often develop close personal relationships.

NEWSGROUPS

Like mailing lists, Internet newsgroups are targeted to specific topics, such as a particular television show or hobby. Participants often receive messages by subscribing, and they post messages by sending e-mail to a central site. What's more, newsgroups can be moderated or unmoderated. Unlike mailing lists, however, **newsgroups** function like electronic newspapers. E-mail messages are grouped together and organized before users see them.

Newsgroups have their own vernacular and set of tools (see Figure NET 2-8). For instance, messages sent to a newsgroup are called *articles,* and replies tacked to

■ **Telnet.** A communications protocol that lets workstations serve as terminals to a remote server computer. ■ **Mailing lists.** A service through which discussion groups communicate via shared e-mail messages. ■ **Newsgroup.** A service that works like an electronic newspaper, carrying *articles* posted by subscribers and responses to them (called *threads).*

NEWSGROUPS
Each newsgroup is formed around a different topic or category. E-mail sent to a particular newsgroup is organized and grouped together before it is sent on to subscribers.

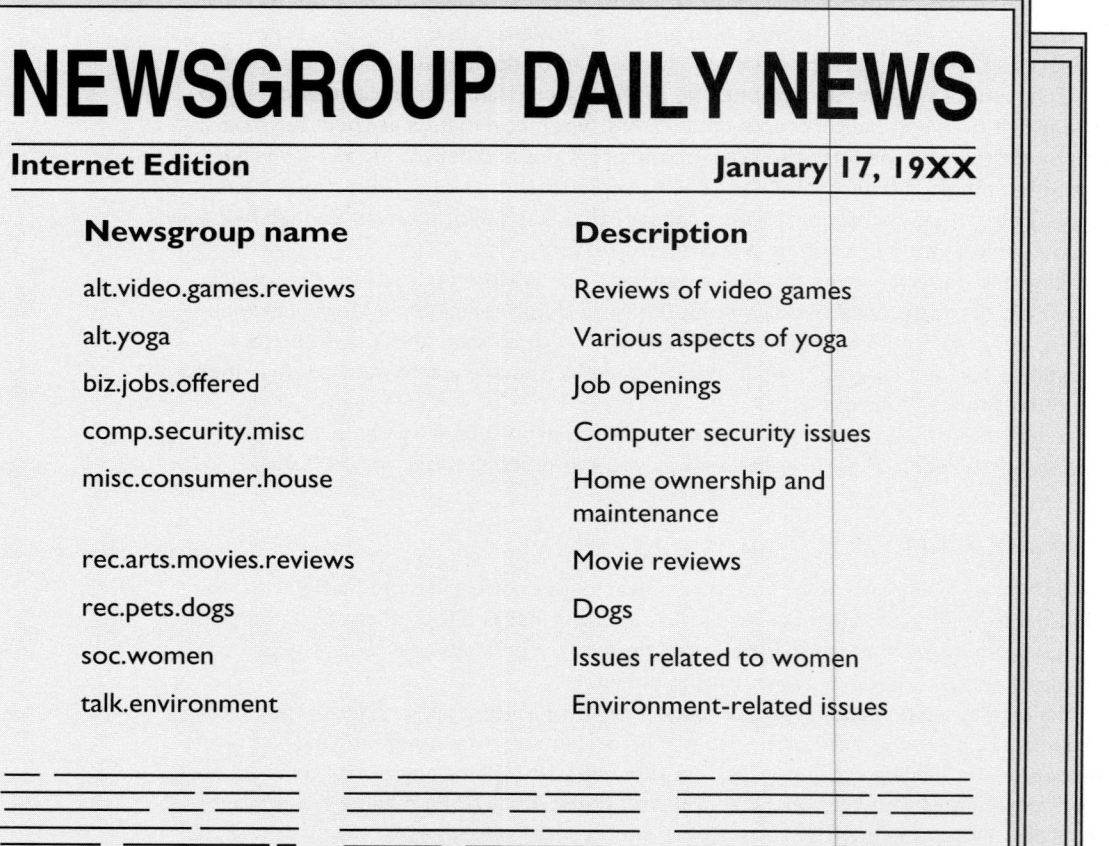

NEWSGROUP DAILY NEWS

Internet Edition **January 17, 19XX**

Newsgroup name	Description
alt.video.games.reviews	Reviews of video games
alt.yoga	Various aspects of yoga
biz.jobs.offered	Job openings
comp.security.misc	Computer security issues
misc.consumer.house	Home ownership and maintenance
rec.arts.movies.reviews	Movie reviews
rec.pets.dogs	Dogs
soc.women	Issues related to women
talk.environment	Environment-related issues

ARTICLES AND THREADS
Messages consist of articles and threads.

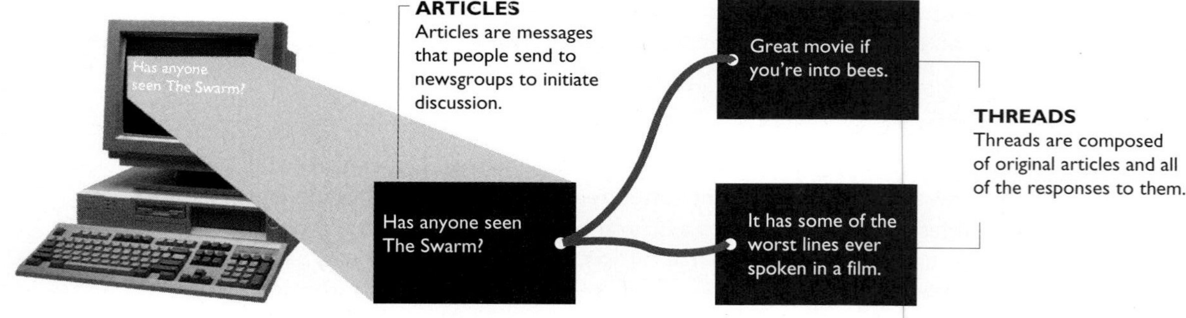

ARTICLES
Articles are messages that people send to newsgroups to initiate discussion.
Has anyone seen The Swarm?
Has anyone seen The Swarm?
Great movie if you're into bees.
It has some of the worst lines ever spoken in a film.
THREADS
Threads are composed of original articles and all of the responses to them.

FIGURE NET 2-8
Newsgroups.

articles are known as *threads*. Most Web browsers interface with a *newsreader*—software that displays articles and threads in an attractive way.

You can often determine the type of information addressed by the newsgroup by the newsgroup's name—for instance, rec.arts.tv or sci.military.moderated. The first three or four letters tell you the category of the topic being discussed, and each of the abbreviations that follow narrow the topic area.

CATEGORIES

Page 002

Internet Edition January 17, 19XX

Newsgroup categories	Description
alt	alternative
biz	business
comp	computer
k12	education
misc	miscellaneous
rec	recreation
sci	science
soc	social
talk	controversial

NEWSGROUP NAMES
A newsgroup is named by the type of topic it discusses. Names consist of two or more words separated by periods.

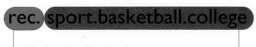

rec. sport.basketball.college

The first identifier describes the main category area (example: **rec** for recreation).

Each subsequent identifier further narrows the category.

UseNet is the protocol that determines how newsgroup messages are handled between computers. UseNet servers are computers that host newsgroup sites.

A special etiquette—referred to as **netiquette—**has evolved on the Internet to guide communications via newsgroups and other forms of electronic mail (see

■ **UseNet.** A protocol that defines how server computers handle newsgroup messages. ■ **Netiquette.** Proper etiquette for exchanges on the Internet.

Web Channels

Is the Web Headed for a Mass-Customization Delivery System?

If you've spent any amount of time casually surfing around the Web, you've probably realized that finding the information you want can involve a lot of time typing in complex addresses and waiting for pages to load. Some people have come up with what they think is a better idea: the Web channel.

The notion of Web channels borrows from the channel concept in the radio and television industries. On radio and TV, many if not most channels follow particular themes—talk, movies, sports, country music, and so on. Thus, when you tune in to a particular channel, you know more or less what general type of content to expect.

"Webcasting" works in a similar way, with "webcasters" that are like cable-TV companies. When you turn on a news-service channel, for instance, the host webcaster continuously scrolls and refreshes Web pages with news content on your screen. You may be able to indicate to the webcaster at the beginning of the session the precise type of information you want—say, only news about Microsoft and Netscape or about the American League pennant race. The special skills of the webcaster in packaging items shields you from the chaos of nuisance Web pages, and saves you the trouble of consulting several sources to get what you want.

Webcasting can be implemented in many interesting ways. Let's say you are driving to or from work. An audio webcast that you've customized to your needs provides the latest traffic information right in your car; in addition, it supplies weather reports for both your area and the mountain location where you are planning to spend the weekend, goings on at your favorite local restaurants, and news and sports events of special interest to you. When you arrive at your destination and turn on your computer to the webcaster's channel, the screen presents multimedia-rich pages with the same types of information.

Today, webcasting is just in its beginning stages. Users often complain that webcasters do not effectively select the material they really want. But some industry analysts—as well as Marc Andreesen, the president of Netscape—feel that webcasting is the way many if not most people will eventually want to use the

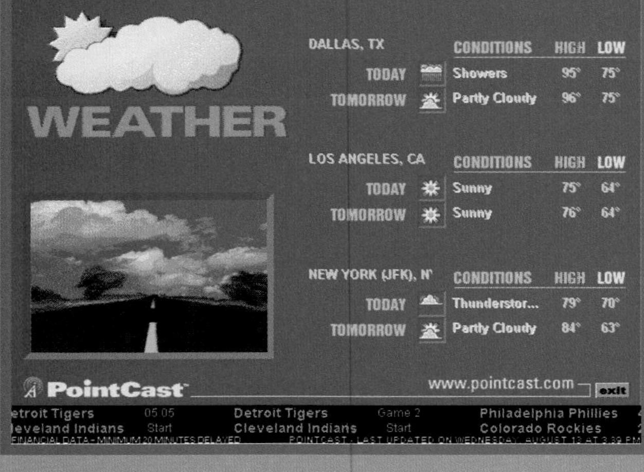

Channeling. The push to make the Web seem more like television is gaining momentum.

Web. It's certainly easier than self-navigation, and it has the potential to provide greater information content within a shorter period of time. Some people believe that the Web channel may replace the Web page as the WWW's paradigm.

Who pays for the webcast? The answer depends how the webcaster sets up its service. A system called PointCast has become a runaway hit already; advertisers flash messages on the screen from time to time, and their payments largely foot the bill for the service. Users can click on an ad to get more information or place orders. Commercial online services such as the Microsoft Network and America Online have also dabbled in the channel concept in their subscription packages. Expect some type of evolution as webcasting catches people's interest. Just as cable TV proved that people would pay for television, it is possible that many people will pay for commercial-free webcasts of high quality.

Webcasting brings drawbacks as well as benefits. One of the major issues for the future is privacy. Information about your personal tastes can be sold to marketers, who may then clog your electronic and physical mailboxes with junk mail. Another drawback is lack of spontaneity. One of the things that printed magazines and television do extremely well is regularly surprise you with news items that you wouldn't normally have requested but that prove extremely valuable to your knowledge about the world. Unlike surfing for pages, where you must actively *pull* specific information to your screen, webcasts are designed to *push* information to it while you passively sit by.

Figure NET 2-9). Newcomers to a newsgroup—called "newbies"—are advised to read the newsgroup's posted **FAQs,** or **frequently asked questions.** FAQ files enable you to learn many of the accepted ground rules about communicating with the newsgroup, so that your interactions with it do not disrupt those of more informed members or waste their time.

■ **Frequently asked questions (FAQs).** Typical questions asked by newcomers to Internet newsgroups, mailing lists, and chat rooms, accompanied by the answers to those questions.

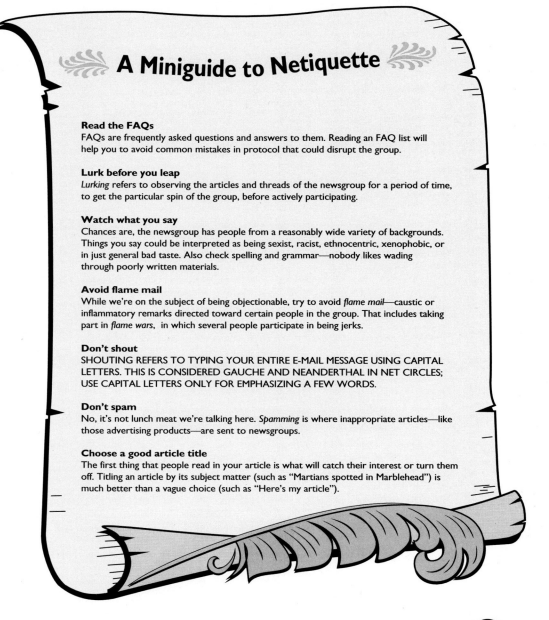

A Miniguide to Netiquette

Read the FAQs
FAQs are frequently asked questions and answers to them. Reading an FAQ list will help you to avoid common mistakes in protocol that could disrupt the group.

Lurk before you leap
Lurking refers to observing the articles and threads of the newsgroup for a period of time, to get the particular spin of the group, before actively participating.

Watch what you say
Chances are, the newsgroup has people from a reasonably wide variety of backgrounds. Things you say could be interpreted as being sexist, racist, ethnocentric, xenophobic, or in just general bad taste. Also check spelling and grammar—nobody likes wading through poorly written materials.

Avoid flame mail
While we're on the subject of being objectionable, try to avoid *flame mail*—caustic or inflammatory remarks directed toward certain people in the group. That includes taking part in *flame wars*, in which several people participate in being jerks.

Don't shout
SHOUTING REFERS TO TYPING YOUR ENTIRE E-MAIL MESSAGE USING CAPITAL LETTERS. THIS IS CONSIDERED GAUCHE AND NEANDERTHAL IN NET CIRCLES; USE CAPITAL LETTERS ONLY FOR EMPHASIZING A FEW WORDS.

Don't spam
No, it's not lunch meat we're talking here. *Spamming* is where inappropriate articles—like those advertising products—are sent to newsgroups.

Choose a good article title
The first thing that people read in your article is what will catch their interest or turn them off. Titling an article by its subject matter (such as "Martians spotted in Marblehead") is much better than a vague choice (such as "Here's my article").

FIGURE NET 2-9

Netiquette.

CHAT

Chat refers to a facility that enables people to engage in interactive conversations over the Internet. Two common types of chat are Internet relay chat and voice chat (see Figure NET 2-10).

Internet Relay Chat *Internet relay chat (IRC)* allows people to type messages to others and to get responses in real time. Thus, IRC works like a regular phone call, except you're typing instead of talking. Two people or several can participate in IRC. Multiperson chats are usually organized around specific topics, and participants often adopt nicknames to maintain anonymity. To participate in IRC, you need a client program that enables you to connect to an IRC server.

Voice Chat *Voice chat* takes IRC a step further. If you and the person with whom you are interacting have the proper software and hardware, you can actually *speak*

■ **Chat.** An Internet feature that supports interactive discussion groups on selected topics.

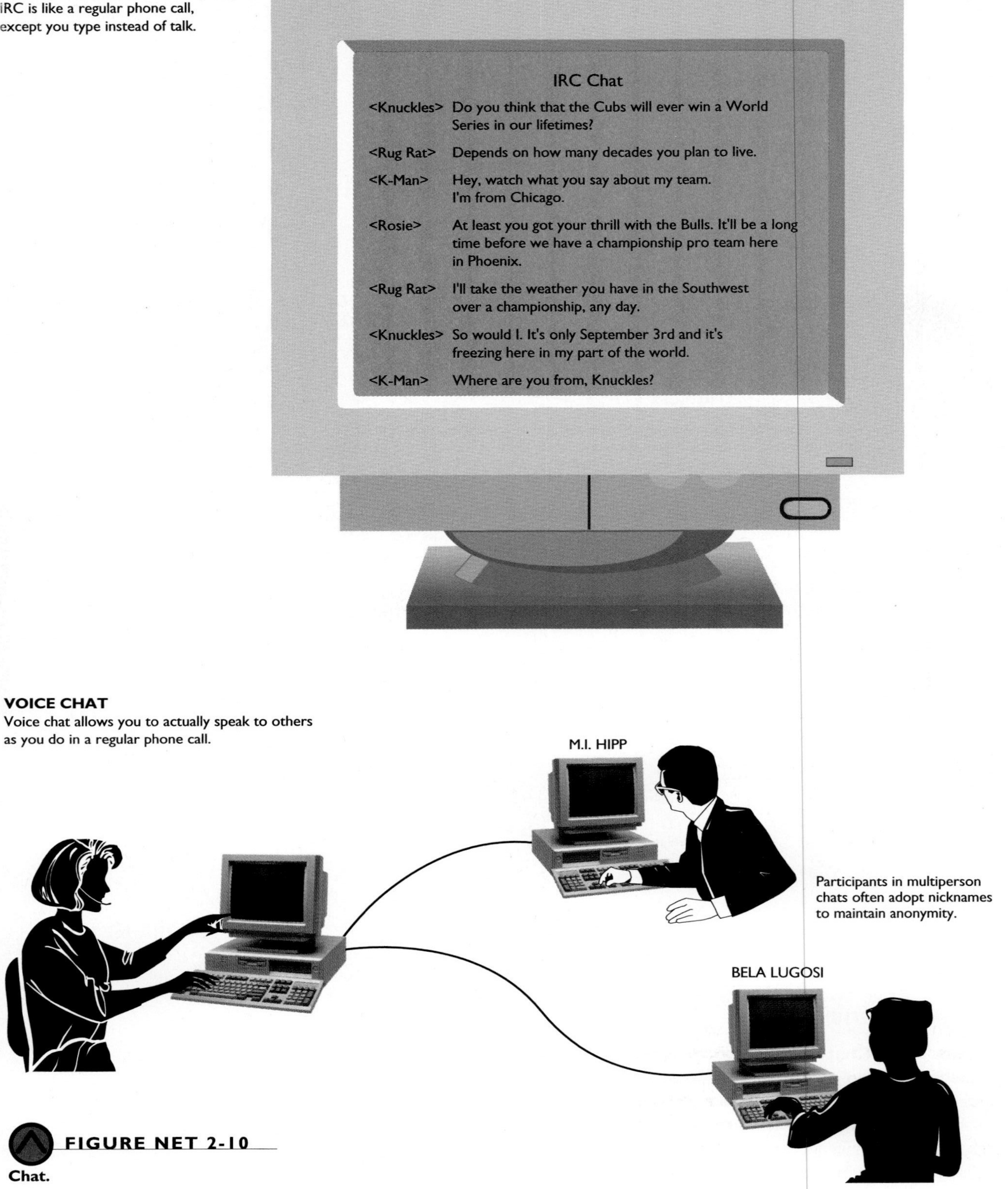

INTERNET RELAY CHAT (IRC)
IRC is like a regular phone call, except you type instead of talk.
IRC Chat
<Knuckles> Do you think that the Cubs will ever win a World Series in our lifetimes?
<Rug Rat> Depends on how many decades you plan to live.
<K-Man> Hey, watch what you say about my team. I'm from Chicago.
<Rosie> At least you got your thrill with the Bulls. It'll be a long time before we have a championship pro team here in Phoenix.
<Rug Rat> I'll take the weather you have in the Southwest over a championship, any day.
<Knuckles> So would I. It's only September 3rd and it's freezing here in my part of the world.
<K-Man> Where are you from, Knuckles?
VOICE CHAT
Voice chat allows you to actually speak to others as you do in a regular phone call.
M.I. HIPP
Participants in multiperson chats often adopt nicknames to maintain anonymity.
BELA LUGOSI

FIGURE NET 2-10

Chat.

to each other via the Internet as you would in a regular phone call. Older voice-chat packages implement half-duplex transmission techniques, allowing only one person to speak at a time; more recent ones use full-duplex sound cards and let you interrupt

Intelligent Agents

Benevolent Servants and Potential Social Problems

Imagine arriving at work each morning to find your PC booting up as soon as you walk in your office building. On the screen, you see today's agenda, a list of phone calls and e-mailings that came in since you left your desk, and a file of news items culled from the morning paper and neatly organized in a folder. These events show software agents have been busily at work, saving you time and attention that you can devote to more useful tasks.

Software agents are small pieces of program code that carry out specific, repetitive, and useful tasks for a computer user. Put another way, software agents are digital servants. The concept of software agents is not new; it originated in the 1950s with the evolution of the field of artificial intelligence (AI). What's more, you are probably using agent code today without even knowing it. Software agents are often built into communications software, operating systems, e-mail programs, and a variety of other products. Today's use notwithstanding, the golden age of software agents lies in the future—especially programmable agents that can be customized by users and agents that can search the contents of multiple databases.

Potential uses for agents abound. You could request them to throw out junk e-mail and arrange all other messages in decreasing order of importance; they could search for stocks that meet certain buying criteria that you specify or browse through scores of online e-malls to find the best price on a Pentium Pro computer with 64 MB RAM and at least 5 gigabytes of hard-disk space (see the accompanying figure).

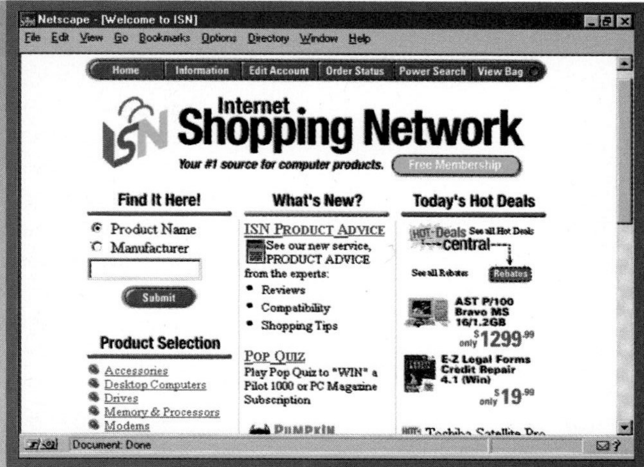

Okay, but where can I find . . . ? Agents attempt to search among the millions of products online to find exactly what you want.

Agents perform a variety of useful services for businesses, too. Internet search engines like Yahoo! use them to travel across the World Wide Web and pick up information about new sites, such as keywords with which to classify those sites. Companies in the telecommunications industry use agents to monitor network transmissions and report traffic problems.

The use of agents leads to some very important social concerns. Will companies regularly rely on software agents to monitor the performance of employees? What types of workers might intelligent agents eventually replace? Should agents be allowed to automatically carry out tasks like supplying intravenous medicine to hospital patients? Can sensitive databases protect their contents from hostile agents? Questions like these are sure to merit serious debate as the twenty-first century unfolds.

the other person as you would in a regular phone call. If you want to participate in voice chat, make sure you have a microphone, a sound card and speakers, a fast modem, and voice-chat software that's compatible with the packages of the people with whom you want to talk.

Like other Internet services, both IRC and voice chat promote interactions without incurring separate long-distance phone charges. Full-duplex phone chat has become a particular concern of phone companies lately because it allows people who have the proper software and hardware to make calls worth thousands of dollars a month without paying anything extra. Some studies have shown that as much as 15 percent of voice traffic could move via the Internet by the year 2000.

ONLINE SHOPPING

In a growing use of the Internet, people have begun to shop online. You can buy products directly from large companies—like L. L. Bean, Dell Computer, and Microsoft—at their Web sites, or you can shop at the Web sites of electronic malls (called *e-malls*), where thousands of smaller companies collectively display their wares.

Electronic catalogs on the Web show you color graphics of products. Search tools and *intelligent agents* may help you to locate the product you desire without excessive browsing (see Feature NET 2-1). If you want to buy a computer, you may be able to configure your system online so it precisely meets your needs. If you want software, there's a good chance that you'll be able to download a trial copy of it.

While many businesses have engaged in electronic commerce for years, online shopping by consumers is a relatively new phenomenon. According to some industry experts, it's also about to take off in a big way. Online shopping and purchasing benefits both businesses and consumers, since businesses don't need salespeople to sell online and some of the savings in labor costs can be passed on to consumers.

One of the major obstacles to electronic commerce so far is consumer concern for *security.* Many customers feel uncomfortable paying by credit card over the Internet, where cyberthieves lurk. (The Tomorrow box in the next chapter addresses this topic.) Another concern is *privacy*—consumers would rather browse the Web without letting merchants know who they are, but merchants feel that they could do a much better and more pleasant job of selling if they knew the identities and tastes of their customers.

Internet Addresses

An **Internet address** performs the same function as a residential or business address in everyday life. It tells where to locate something on the Internet—a particular person, Web site, or Web page. Addresses on the Internet are unique; each one is assigned to one and only one person or resource.

Mailbox Addresses People are most often located on the Internet through their e-mail addresses. An individual's e-mail address usually consists of a username (a set of characters, unique to accounts on that person's mail server, assigned to the individual's mailbox) followed by the @ symbol, followed by the mail server's **domain name.** For instance,

```
mjordan@dryden.com
tarzan@dryden.com
```

are the e-mail addresses of two hypothetical mailboxes at The Dryden Press, the publisher of this textbook, respectively assigned to mjordan and tarzan. The characters "dryden.com" state the name of Dryden's server computer. People with e-mail addresses can be reached via private networks or over the Internet.

Note that domain names—and the server computers they represent—function like apartment buildings in everyday life. Each apartment building's address is unique to the mail system, but several individuals may have mailboxes at the building address.

The set of three letters that generally appears as the rightmost part of a domain name is called the *root domain.* Root domains—such as *com* (for *commercial), edu* (for *education), gov* (for *government),* and *mil* (for *military)*—indicate the type of Internet account. Two symbols occasionally follow the root domain to indicate the country of origin. For instance, the domain name:

```
jsc.nasa.gov.us
```

suggests a government computer in the United States—the one at NASA's Johnson Space Center.

Addresses for World Wide Web Pages Web pages and links to information at Gopher, FTP, and other sites are most commonly located on the Internet through **uniform resource locators,** or **URLs** (see Figure NET 2-11). Every Web page

■ **Internet address.** A unique identifier assigned to a specific location on the Internet, such as a host computer, Web site, or user mailbox. ■ **Domain name.** An ordered group of symbols, separated by periods, that identifies an Internet server. ■ **Uniform resource locator (URL).** A unique identifier representing the location of a specific Web page on the Internet.

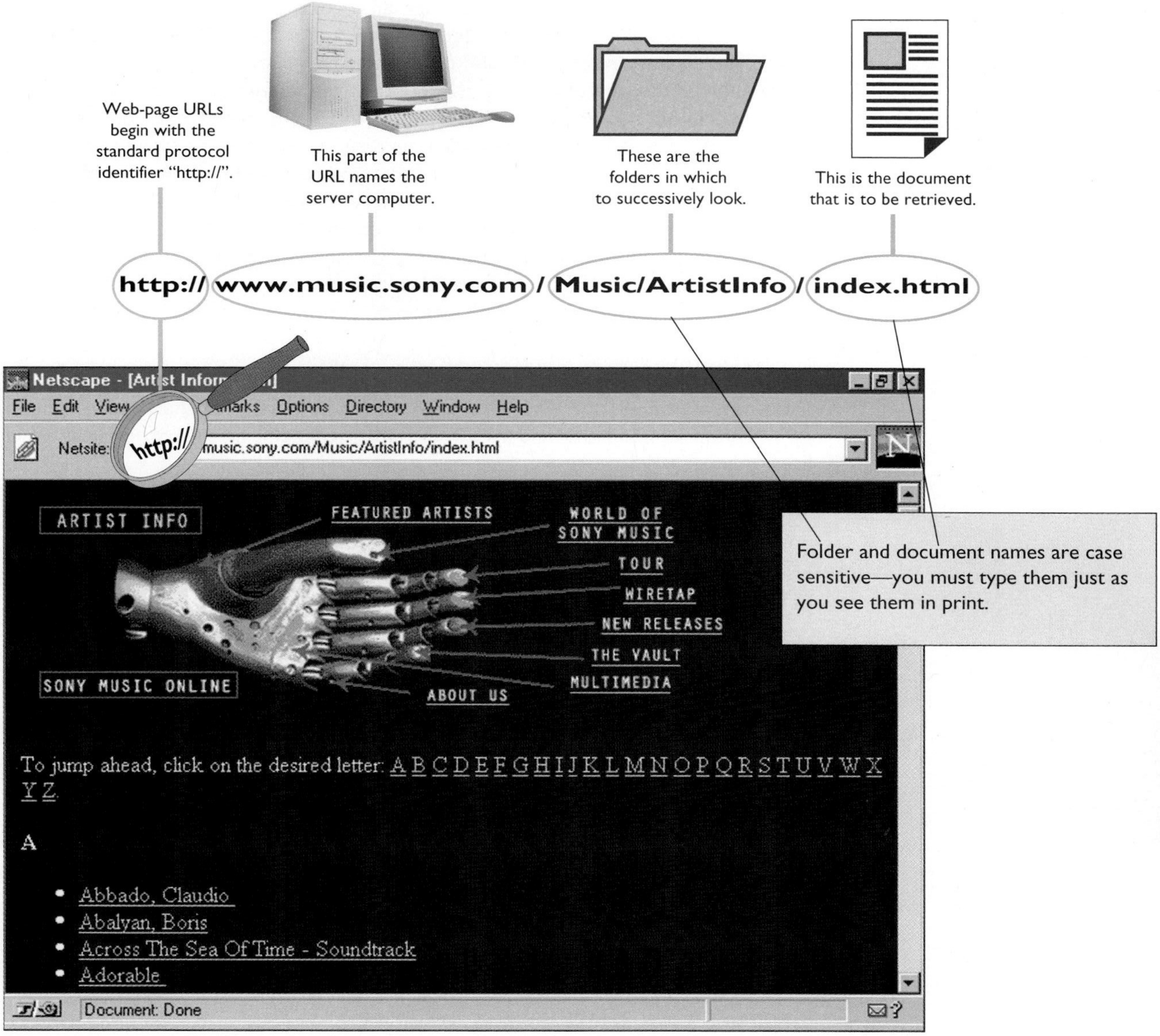

Web-page URLs begin with the standard protocol identifier "http://".

This part of the URL names the server computer.

These are the folders in which to successively look.

This is the document that is to be retrieved.

http:// www.music.sony.com / Music/ArtistInfo / index.html

Folder and document names are case sensitive—you must type them just as you see them in print.

has its own URL (pronounced "earl"). If you know a page's URL, type it in the specified area of your Web browser's screen and the page will display.

Web-site URLs usually contain the three letters *www* preceded by the *protocol identifier* http:// (for *hypertext transfer protocol).* For instance, the Web home page for Microsoft Corporation, the University of Virginia, and the Yahoo! search site, respectively, have the following URLs:

```
http://www.microsoft.com
http://www.virginia.edu
http://www.yahoo.com
```

The set of symbols after the double slashes—for instance, "www.microsoft.com"—designates a server computer's domain name.

Often, URLs contain more specific types of information. For instance, the URL

```
http://www.music.sony.com/Music/ArtistInfo/index.html
```

identifies the music section of Sony Corporation's Web site. To the right of the domain name (www.music.sony.com), the URL identifies a sequence of two *folders*

FIGURE NET 2-11

How URLs work.

(Music/ArtistInfo) that you must open in order to find a specific *document* (index.html). In many contexts, folders are referred to as *directories,* a set of folders is referred to as a *directory path,* and documents are referred to as *files.*

Sometimes the part of the URL that contains the folder names and the document name is called the *request.* In the Sony example, note that the request—Music/ArtistInfo/index.html—contains a mixture of uppercase and lowercase letters. Requests are *case sensitive,* which means that you must type in this part of the URL in uppercase or lowercase letters, just as you see them. The domain name, by contrast, is not case sensitive; capitalization makes no difference.

As you have probably already noticed, URLs can become lengthy and take time to type. Fortunately, you often don't need to type them to reach desired Web pages. URLs also correspond to hyperlink elements; you can simply point and click hyperlinks to see the documents to which they refer.

Addresses for Pages on Other Servers When you are retrieving information from, say, a Gopher or FTP site through a Web browser, the characters *gopher* or *ftp* will often replace *http://* and *www* in the URL, depending on the particular interface. For instance,

```
gopher://gopher.micro.umn.edu
ftp://ftp.microsoft.com
```

are URLs you would type into your browser to access, respectively, the University of Minnesota Gopher site and Microsoft's FTP site.

Desktop Tools for Accessing the Internet

This section covers the software and hardware you need to become a user of the Internet. Most people can accomplish what they want with a good Web browser and e-mail package, a few search tools, and reasonably current computer hardware. If you need a capability that your browser doesn't have, you can usually find it in a plug-in or helper package.

BROWSERS AND PLUG-IN PACKAGES

As mentioned earlier, the Internet was not always so easy and so much fun to use. The first text-intensive Web browsers were not much to rave about. It was not until 1993, when a browsing program called NCSA **Mosaic** became available, that the world began to notice the Web. Mosaic presented an easy-to-use graphical user interface, and you could download it for free. Today, most commercial browsers improve upon and extend the interface popularized by the original Mosaic.

What, Exactly, Is a Browser? A **browser,** or *Web browser,* is a software package that enables you to display Web pages as well as navigate the Web and other parts of the Internet. The concept of a browser is evolving rapidly. Originally, most browsers were stand-alone products; today, browser functionality is woven into many other types of software packages, enabling you to tap immediately into the Web from wherever you are on your computer. For instance, if you are writing to a friend who has never seen New York, you can hop from your word processor into the Web and extract a map of New York to insert in your letter.

■ **Mosaic.** A freeware tool that was the first GUI Web browser to gain wide acceptance; most commercial browsers today are enhanced forms of Mosaic. ■ **Browser.** A software tool that makes it easy for users to find and display Web pages.

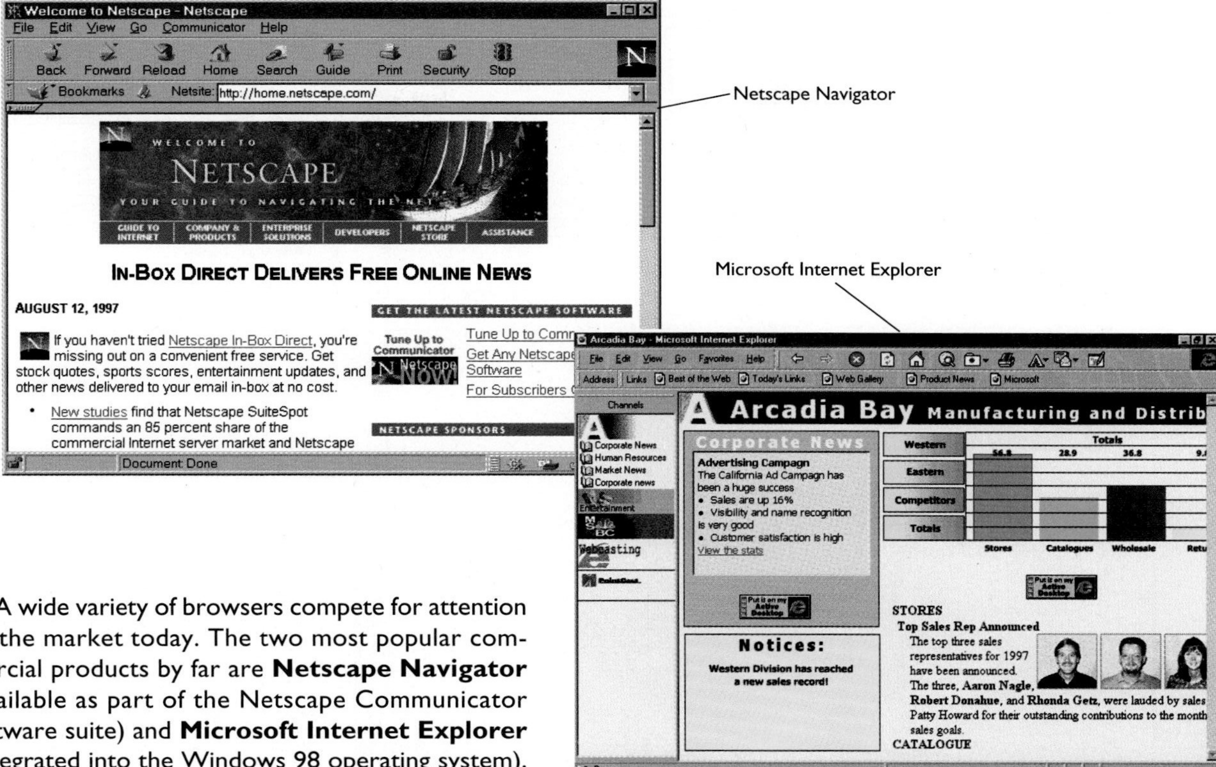

A wide variety of browsers compete for attention on the market today. The two most popular commercial products by far are **Netscape Navigator** (available as part of the Netscape Communicator software suite) and **Microsoft Internet Explorer** (integrated into the Windows 98 operating system). Other familiar products include Spyglass Mosaic and Sun's HotJava, as well as the proprietary browsers offered by such commercial online services as America Online, CompuServe, and Prodigy. Some browsers, like the latest version of NCSA Mosaic, are still available as freeware over the Internet.

FIGURE NET 2-12

Browsers. Netscape Navigator and Microsoft Internet Explorer have emerged as the two most widely used browsers. Both employ similar graphical user interfaces and menu commands.

Properties of Browsers The rapid evolution of browsers brings with it product updates every several months—the fastest rate in the computer industry—with each new version incorporating more and more features. When selecting a particular browser for your own use, you should look for several important properties:

- FUNCTIONALITY What basic functions does the browser perform? While many of the earliest browsers were designed mostly to help users navigate the Web, increasingly they are evolving into multipurpose Internet tools that accommodate additional functions like e-mail, chat, Gopher, FTP, Telnet, and mailing-list and newsreading applications. Because most users would strongly prefer to learn a single software product rather than mastering several, Web browsers are becoming "one-stop shopping" solutions.
- NAVIGATIONAL TOOLS Virtually all browsers offer easy-to-use navigational tools such as a menu bar, toolbars, and special navigation buttons (see Figure NET 2-12). These tools enable you to retrieve, display, find, save, and print Web pages along with a variety of other operations.

  Browsing through Web pages is like reading a book; often you would like to return to earlier pages. To help you locate those pages painlessly, a full-featured browser should incorporate such features as a *history list* (to record pages you've visited during the current session or previous ones), *bookmarks* and *hotlists* (to let you name and save the addresses of your favorite sites in a folder), and *special toolbar buttons* (to help you easily reach a few chosen

■ **Netscape Navigator.** A widely used browsing program. ■ **Microsoft Internet Explorer.** A widely used browsing program.

BOOKMARKS
A bookmarking feature lets you save the locations of your favorite Web sites so that you can easily return to them.

ADDING BOOKMARKS
If you are currently viewing a page for which you want to add a bookmark, select Add Bookmark from the Bookmarks pull-down menu. If you then select Go to Bookmarks from the same menu, you will see the new entry added to your bookmark list.

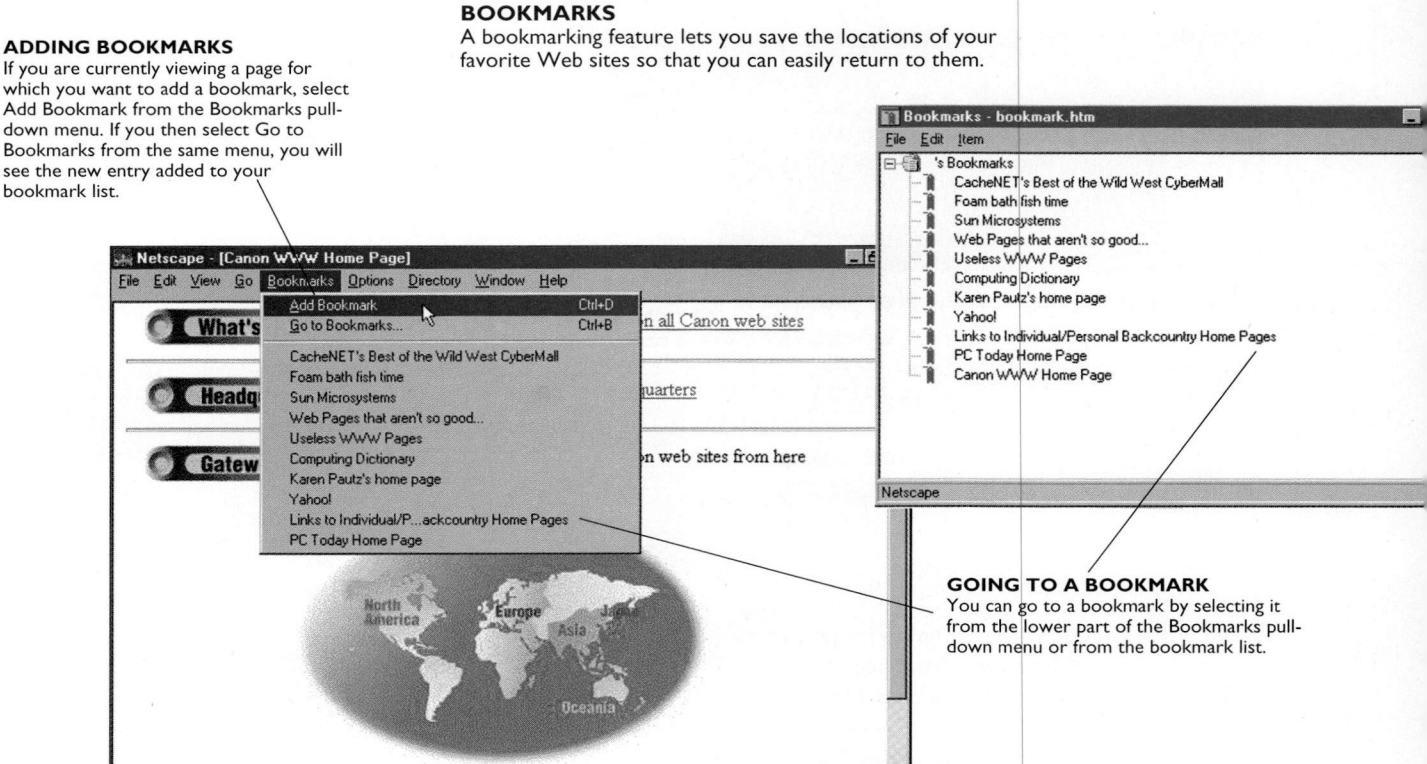

GOING TO A BOOKMARK
You can go to a bookmark by selecting it from the lower part of the Bookmarks pull-down menu or from the bookmark list.

FIGURE NET 2-13

Using bookmarks and a history list. The figure shows how to use the bookmarking and history-list features of Netscape Navigator. In Internet Explorer, bookmarks are called "favorites."

Web sites). Figure NET 2-13 illustrates the usefulness of history lists and bookmarks.

Browsers differ in their implementation of navigational tools. For instance, some browsers may let you organize bookmarks into multiple lists and arrange and edit bookmarks in many ways. Others provide less-flexible options.

- SPEED Web browsers often incorporate a variety of techniques to speed applications. For instance, a *progressive graphics display* capability (see Figure NET 2-14) lets you see some text and a low-resolution version of images almost immediately while your computer downloads more data and sharpens the images in front of you. Through an interlacing process, the software draws alternate lines of each image on a page, so you get the flavor of it while waiting for the rest of it to display. If you don't like what you see as the image is displaying, you can abandon the Web page for another.

  Browsers running on Windows 95 and similar operating systems also support *multitasking*. This capability enables you to perform several searches and other functions in parallel. For instance, you could have your computer downloading software from an FTP site while you are browsing for other information.

  To display Web pages extremely quickly, most graphical browsers allow you to toggle off their graphics features. While pages with graphics may look more exciting than those composed entirely of text, they take far longer to display and can slow information retrieval down to a crawl on a slower computer system. Incidentally, while most browsers today support graphics, not all do. Users with older equipment or with text-only workstations rely on *text browsers* such as Lynx to get their Internet information.

- FRAMING A *frame* is an independent area, or window, on a screen page. A browser's *framing capability* allows a screen to be partitioned into separate frames, with different Web pages (each with its own set of scroll bars)

HISTORY LIST
A history-list feature displays the names and descriptions of sites you've most recently visited.

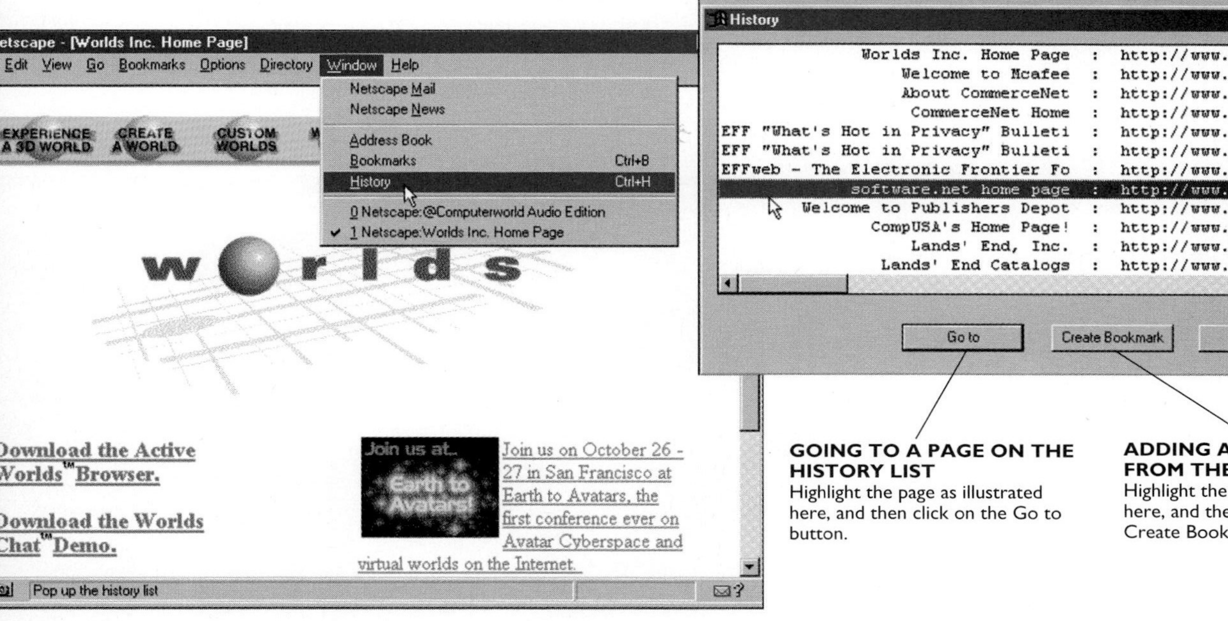

GOING TO A PAGE ON THE HISTORY LIST
Highlight the page as illustrated here, and then click on the Go to button.

ADDING A BOOKMARK FROM THE HISTORY LIST
Highlight the page as illustrated here, and then click on the Create Bookmark button.

NET

FIGURE NET 2-14

Progressive graphics display.
This feature lets you see a low-resolution version of an image while your computer downloads all of the data needed to display the image at full resolution.

Some text usually appears onscreen within a few seconds, so you can begin reading parts of the page right away. Low-resolution versions of graphics images also appear so that you can quickly get an idea what's in store.

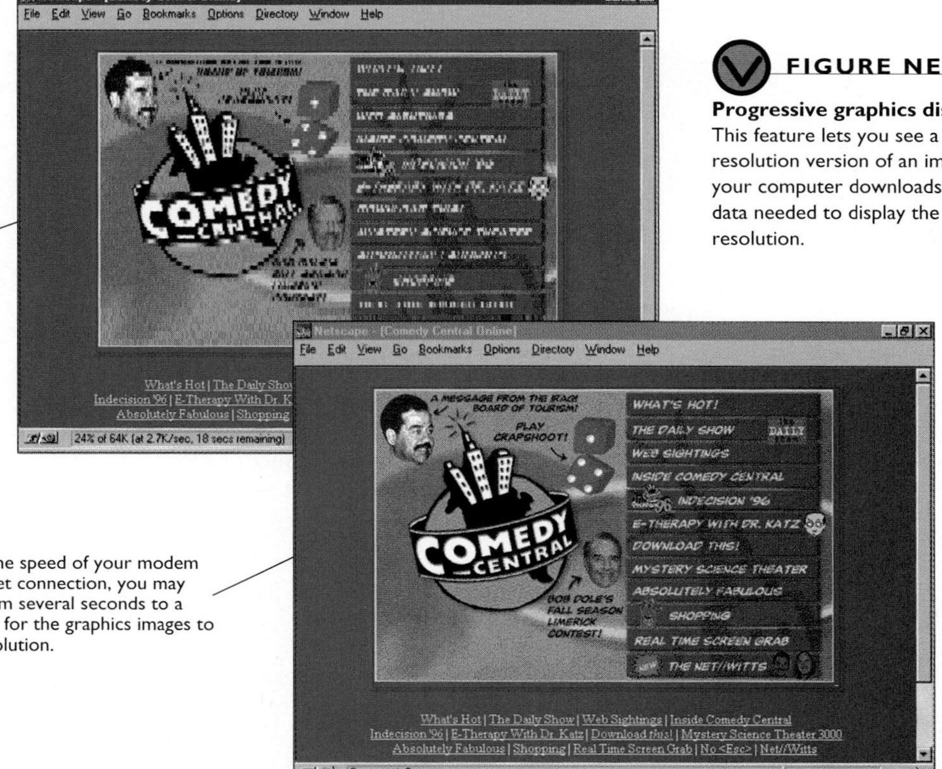

Depending on the speed of your modem and your Internet connection, you may have to wait from several seconds to a minute or more for the graphics images to show at full resolution.

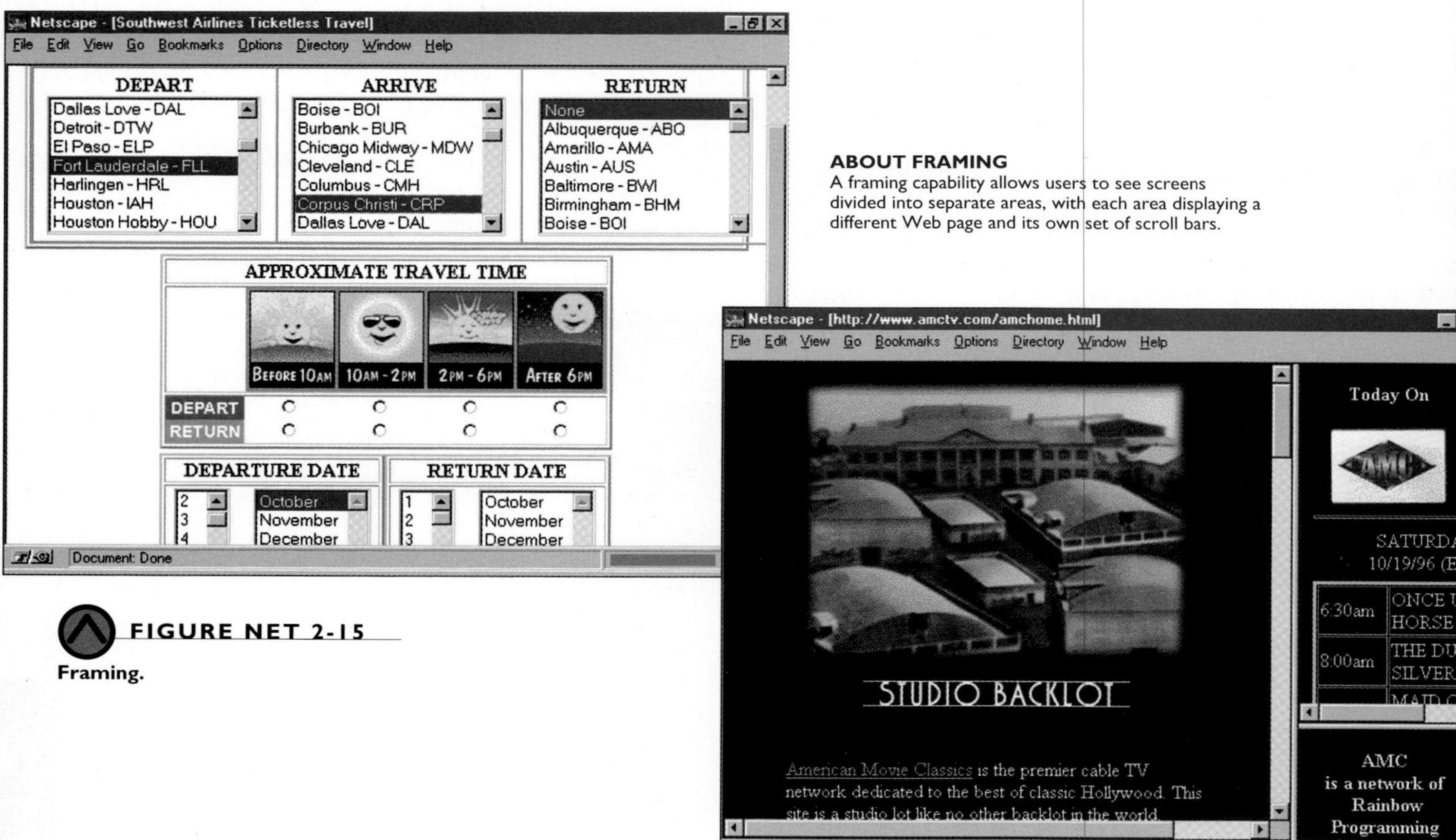

ABOUT FRAMING
A framing capability allows users to see screens divided into separate areas, with each area displaying a different Web page and its own set of scroll bars.

FIGURE NET 2-15

Framing.

displaying in each of the frames (see Figure NET 2-15). The framing technique is also catching on in the television world, allowing viewers to divide the viewing screen into several areas and watch a different channel in each one.

- JAVA AND ACTIVEX SUPPORT *Java* is a programming language developed at Sun Microsystems. A browser with a built-in Java translator can accept small programs called Java *applets* off of the Web and run them on a Web page. Such a feature has the potential to add tremendously exciting interactive functions to a Web page. A person shopping on the Web for a car or home loan, for instance, can download a calculator applet from a Web page and figure out monthly payments on the spot.

  ActiveX is a set of controls developed at Microsoft Corporation. It does for Web pages what OLE (object linking and embedding) does for office applications; that is, it provides a containering method whereby one application can be launched within another. Thus, ActiveX allows you to do things like edit a Word or WordPerfect document while in your browser or, conversely, edit a Web page within your word processor. Likewise, you can use ActiveX controls to embed animations into Web pages—just as you might do with a Java applet.

  Java and ActiveX will be discussed in more detail in Chapter NET 3 together with other similar products.

- WORKGROUP COMPUTING Among their newest features, the latest browsers have incorporated support for workgroup computing—allowing two or more people to collaborate on common projects. This feature is especially beneficial for users on corporate intranets and to users who need to share ideas with people in other organizations.

- SUPPORT FOR COMPLEX APPLICATIONS Among the hottest browser applications today are multimedia, realtime processing, and virtual reality.

  Most browsers support a number of forms of *multimedia*—for instance, several types of compressed sound and video files. Unfortunately, your desktop hardware and the phone line going into your home may not handle data fast enough for you to run high-end multimedia applications. Live digital video is currently the toughest frontier; it requires 100 times the bandwidth of audio. To optimize audio and video applications on client PCs, many software publishers use a *streaming* approach, whereby sounds or video images start outputting on your computer before the associated files are fully downloaded.

  A *realtime processing* capability enables two or more users to interact on projects as if they were working side by side in the same room. Realtime capabilities can run from the simple—such as voice chat—to the complex—such as videoconferencing applications in which people can both see and hear each other. In between are a variety of other applications—such as workgroup software in which changes made to documents on one desktop system are reflected immediately throughout the organization via the Internet. As with multimedia applications, special hardware and transmission facilities—and even special software—may be needed to supplement a browser's capabilities.

  A *virtual reality* feature allows users to explore three-dimensional environments on the Web, observing them from any number of views. If the interior of a house were modeled in virtual reality, you could walk through rooms, observe the objects in it closer or further away or from different angles, and so on. To explore virtual worlds, you need either a 3-D browser program that supports virtual-reality modeling language (VRML) or a plug-in 3-D package that works with your regular browser. Three popular 3-D programs are WebSpace, WebFX, and WorldView. The biggest problem today with viewing VRML sites on the Web is that virtual-reality applications require a lot of graphics, which in turn require a lot of bandwidth.
- WEB-PUBLISHING CAPABILITIES Increasingly, people are rushing to the Web to post their own home pages. Many browsers have built-in publishing capabilities that will let you create Web pages of your own. In addition, you can test your pages in a simulated Web environment. Web publishing has become a particular hot area of late because of the popularity of corporate intranets and the arrival of tools that enable office documents to be automatically converted to Web pages. Chapter NET 3 is all about Web publishing, so this subsection won't dwell on it.
- SECURITY Browsing software can protect the confidentiality of the data you are sending—such as your credit-card number—and it can tell you about security safeguards at sites to which you send data. Some even come with a *digital signature* feature, which downloads only pages with a special code from sources that you preapprove; at the other end of the line, this feature can identify you to a commercial site. Java's ability to supplement desktop browsers with applets downloaded from remote servers has raised a whole new security issue: Will browsers be able to keep applets from implanting viruses on your computer system?

Plug-In Packages The rapid evolution of the Internet has created a large market for *browser plug-ins*—programs that update your browser with features that it currently lacks.

One widely used plug-in package, Adobe Acrobat, enables your browser to view pages that have been formatted as Adobe PDF files (see Figure NET 2-16). PDF files display documents more or less exactly the way they appear in print. Precision can be critical in some applications; a misplaced digit in a financial statement or an altered angle in a technical drawing can result in a major legal problem. Acrobat also helps Web-page authors to control the way their pages display on other computer systems that support PDF.

Acrobat enables your browser to display a document in a format very similar to the way it appears in print.

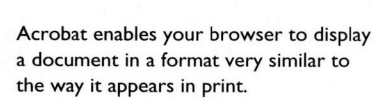

FIGURE NET 2-16
Adobe Acrobat.

Other popular types of plug-in packages include those that offer full-duplex phoning and videoconferencing capabilities, those that offer improved support for multimedia and virtual-reality applications, and those that enable you to easily create your own Web pages without having to code them from scratch. A listing of some widely used browser plug-ins appears in Figure NET 2-17.

FIGURE NET 2-17
Browser plug-ins.

Package	Vendor	Description
Acrobat	Adobe Systems	Displays documents similar to the way they appear in print
Broadway	Data Translation	Lets you view MPEG videos from your browser
Carbon Copy	Software Publishing	Lets you direct Internet outputs to a computer other than your own
Coolfusion	Iterated Systems	Lets you view AVI videos from your browser without having to wait for a complete download
Live3D	Netscape	Lets you enjoy virtual-reality worlds
NetMeeting	Microsoft	Adds Internet/intranet telephony, a whiteboard and shared clipboard, a chat area, and the ability to share Microsoft Office applications in a conference
Pronto96	CommTouch Software	Lets you handle voice messages as e-mail attachments
Quicktime	Apple	Lets you view Quicktime videos from your browser
RealAudio	Progressive Networks	Provides realtime audio and FM-quality sound to your browser
Shockwave	Macromedia	Lets you interact with Director, Macromedia's multimedia program
Sizzler	Totally Hip	Enhances your browsing experience with animation
VR Scout	Chaco Communications	Lets you enjoy virtual-reality worlds

How Dave and Jerry's Guide to the Web Became Yahoo!

Yahoo!—the Web's first search engine—started in 1994 as the hobby of a couple of graduate students, Dave Filo and Jerry Yang. According to Yang in a recent interview in *Internet World,* the two were "wasting" a lot of time on the Web in late 1993. They began collecting URLs for sites they found because "David was sick of me asking him where was that link we saw yesterday." As their collection of sites grew, other people wanted access to it, and soon they had the makings of a thriving business.

Filo and Yang thought that the original name of their search engine—Dave and Jerry's Guide to the Web—sounded stupid, so one night they resolved to lock themselves in the office to change it. They decided they wanted an acronym for a name and that the full name should start with the words *Yet Another.* At that point, they consulted a dictionary and found the word *yahoo.* It was catchy, and they liked thinking of themselves as a couple of yahoos.

What does *Yahoo!* stand for? Yet Another Hierarchical Officious Oracle. Good thing they wanted an acronym.

Yahoo! founders. Search engine began as a hobby.

In addition to the large number of plug-ins, other *helper packages* are available that work alongside (as opposed to inside) your regular browser to enhance your Internet experience. One such product, the so-called *offline browser,* lets you capture pages of information and entire Web sites onto your hard disk so you can surf the sites at your leisure. Once the pages are stored locally on your hard disk, you can view them more rapidly than you could see them online, even if you had a T1 line connecting your home to the Internet.

If history is a good indicator of the future, expect the next generation of browsers to incorporate many of the best features from the current crop of plug-in and helper programs. What's more, operating systems and software suites are rapidly gaining browser features themselves. The latter trend has led many people to predict that browsers as we know them today may become extinct in a few years, their functions absorbed into other software packages.

SEARCH ENGINES

While casual surfing is a popular Web pastime, people often turn to the Internet to find specific types of information, as well. When you know generally what you want but don't know at which URL to find it, one of your best options is a search engine. A **search engine** is a software facility that resembles both a table of contents and an index, with the full power of a computer behind them to electronically locate possibilities and automatically retrieve Web pages.

Using a Web-Resident Engine You can use many of the best search engines—such as **Yahoo!** (profiled in the Inside the Industry feature), WebCrawler, Lycos, and Alta Vista—free of charge by accessing their Web sites. Once you locate and enter a site (see Project 7 for several addresses), you can perform two types of search operations: (1) selecting successive hyperlinks from categories displayed on the screen or (2) typing in a search string that represents a relevant keyword before you begin selecting hyperlinks (see Figure NET 2-18).

■ **Search engine.** A software tool used to look for specific information over the Internet. ■ **Yahoo!.** A widely used search engine.

DOING A CATEGORY SEARCH

As each menu comes up, you make a selection from it. As you do this, the search progressively narrows until, eventually, you access a specific Web site.

FIGURE NET 2-18

Using a search engine. Most search engines—such as Yahoo! and WebCrawler—enable you to search either by selecting from menus of categories (left page) or by typing search strings (right page).

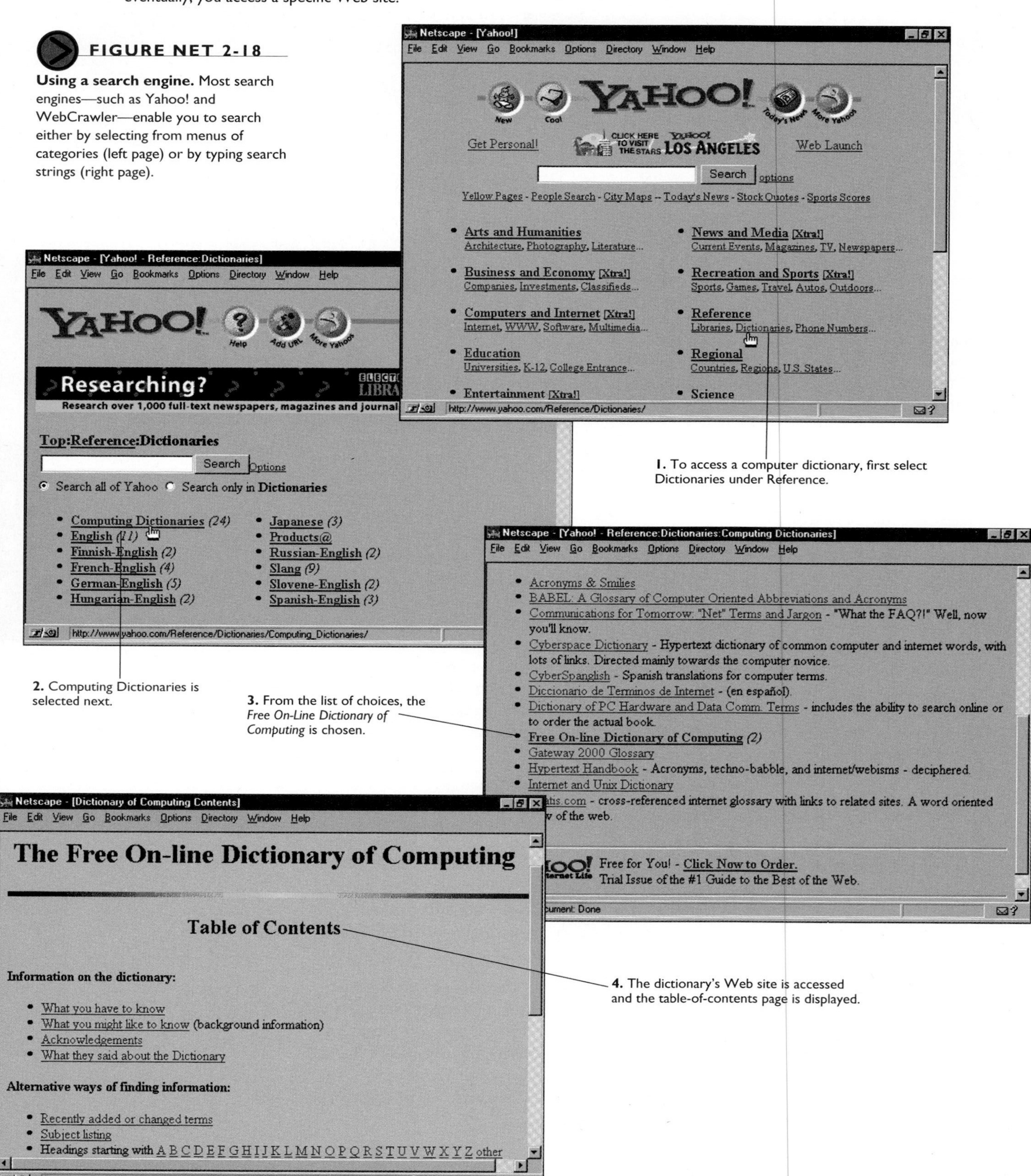

1. To access a computer dictionary, first select Dictionaries under Reference.

2. Computing Dictionaries is selected next.

3. From the list of choices, the *Free On-Line Dictionary of Computing* is chosen.

4. The dictionary's Web site is accessed and the table-of-contents page is displayed.

DOING A STRING SEARCH

A string search lets you type in a keyword or phrase that relates to the topic on which you desire information.

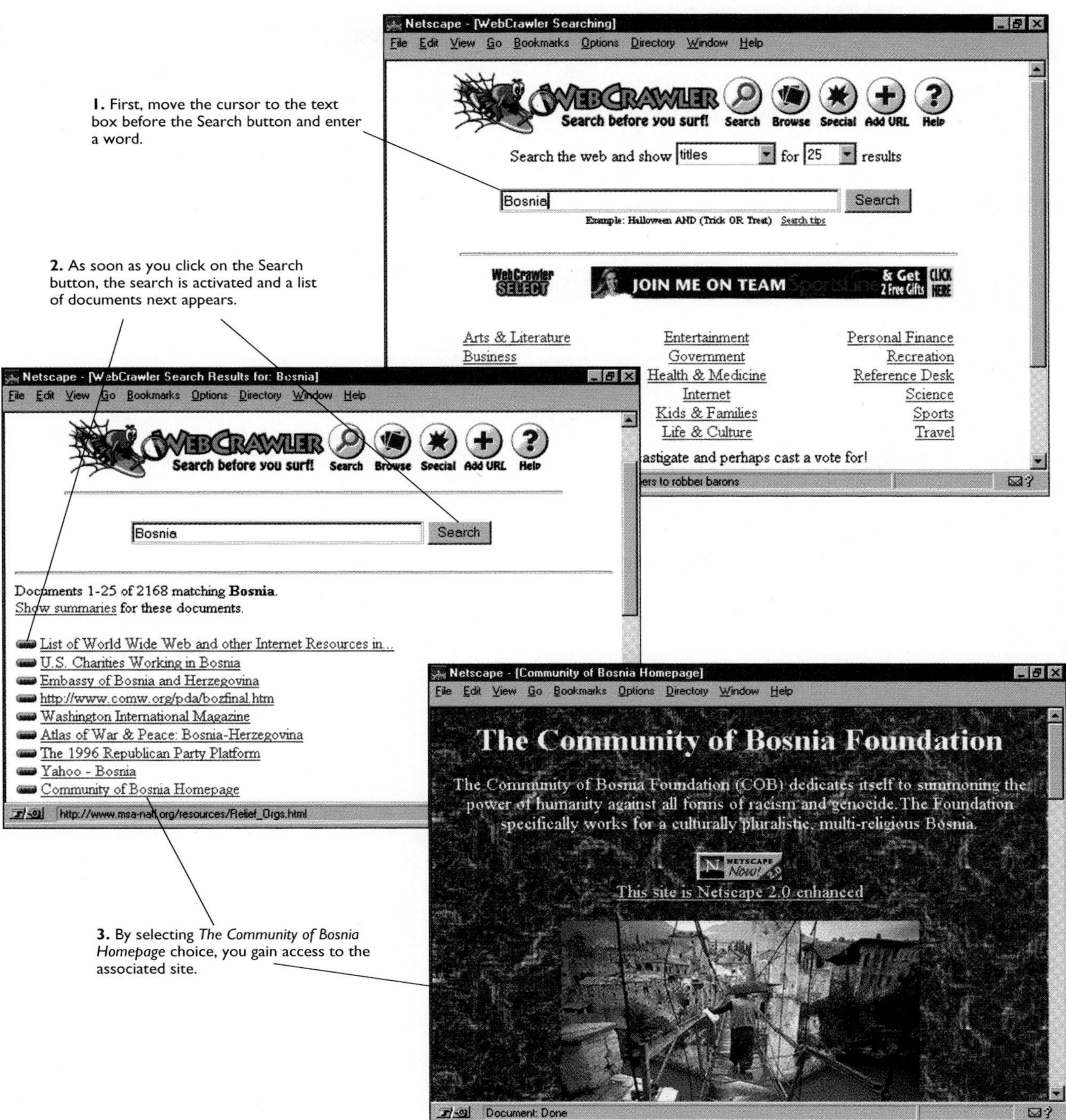

In the first type of search operation, doing a category search, you will first be presented with several categories on the screen. Then, after you select a hyperlink, you will next see a screen showing a finer breakdown of choices. Eventually, after making choice after choice on a sequence of such screens, you will arrive at someone's home page.

To understand the second type of search, inputting a search string, let's say you want information on Bosnia and you do not see an associated link on the screen

Search Engines

How They Try to Find What You Want

Search engines use a variety of techniques to help users locate information. While a comprehensive discussion of these methods is beyond the scope of this book, several bear mention

Relevance Ranking

When you search for a keyword, the search engine typically responds with a list of document names. Such a list can be extensive, and many search engines try to help you wade through it by presenting the documents in order of decreasing importance. They do this through a technique called *relevance ranking.* Relevance ranks are usually based on a single criterion or on a formula that weighs several criteria. Some of the criteria used in relevance ranking include:

- FREQUENCY The document receives a higher rating as your search word(s) appear more frequently in its description within the search engine's database. For instance, suppose you asked a search engine a question such as "Where can I find information about dog training?" The engine would first extract the two keywords in the sentence—"dog" and "training"—and then rank documents according to how many times they included these two words. You could also specify that the search should return only documents that included both words.
- LOCATION The placement of the words in the document description can also matter. For instance, documents with the words "dog" and "training" in their titles would get higher ranks than if the same words appeared in the general description of the document that was filed when the site was cataloged. (This is an important fact to remember if you ever create your own Web pages.)
- WEIGHT Words that appear more frequently in the search engine's database are given less weight. For instance, if "training" appears less often than "dog" in all of the search engine's document descriptions, it assumes that the less common word defines more closely what people want, and it will assign higher ranks to documents that include that word. Of course, common words like "where" and "about" receive virtually zero weight.

Recently, some companies have sparked a controversy by paying search-engine vendors to achieve higher rankings. For instance, a hotel chain could pay to have its pages listed first any time a traveler requested general information about *hotels.*

Stemming

Most search engines on the Web permit *stemming*—in other words, counting derivatives of the originally entered words. For instance, a word like *trainer* would count just as much as *training* in ranking documents, as it probably should.

Concept-Based Searching

This type of search attempts to determine what you mean. Not every search engine supports this relatively advanced form of probing. For instance, back to the dog-training example, a concept-based engine would realize that "teaching" and "disciplining" a dog can mean roughly the same as "training" the dog.

Phrase Searches

Many words that make sense in a phrase do not make sense when you break the phrase apart. Take "1996 World Series," for instance. If it were to break this phrase into its component pieces, the search engine would have serious trouble finding what you wanted. Many search engines let you put key phrases in quotes as an alert to their importance.

Case Insensitivity

Many search engines treat queries using lowercased letters as case-insensitive keywords, but when you type uppercase letters, the engines look for exact matches. Thus, if you typed "NBC," you might find matches only to the NBC television and radio stations. By typing "nbc," instead, you would match NBC sites as well as that for msnbc, the news-reporting joint venture between Microsoft and NBC.

menu. You would type *Bosnia* into the area of the screen that's specifically provided to enter search strings. Clicking the Search button will retrieve screens on Bosnia with further choices; by making ever narrower selections, you will eventually wind up on some sort of Bosnia home page.

Specifying strings enables you to do *boolean searches*—that is, searching on multiple keywords using the operators AND, OR, and NOT. For instance, if you wanted a search engine to find all documents that covered *both* Dennis Rodman and Madonna, you might specify your request to an engine supporting boolean searches as *Dennis Rodman AND Madonna.* If, instead, you wanted documents that discussed *either* (or both) of these celebrities, the request *Dennis Rodman OR Madonna* would be your entry. On the other hand, if you wanted Dennis Rodman documents that are cataloged with no mention of Madonna, *Dennis Rodman NOT Madonna* is what you would type in the search text box. Every search engine has its own way of letting you do a boolean search, so you should check out the preferred style before conducting one.

Search Databases At the core of a search engine is a database that resembles a huge index. Typically, the database contains millions of pieces of information about Internet sites throughout the world. When you select a hyperlink or type in a search string, the search engine consults its index to find all URLs with descriptions that match up to that word. It then provides results of the search within seconds (see also Feature NET 2-2).

Search engines differ in their comprehensiveness. Some, such as Alta Vista, search deeper than others and will produce matches even to obscure references. This result can be good or bad, depending on how long a list of matches the search returns—it can run into the thousands of documents—and how much time you want to spend manually looking through the list for something interesting enough to pursue further. Once you find a match, generally you can simply point and click to retrieve the underlying information.

Many search engines are *metaengines*—that is, they consult multiple databases, including those of other search engines. Most of the Web-based search engines, for instance, query not only their own databases but also those at a few other sites. Some of the more sophisticated metaengines can query more than a dozen other sites simultaneously and then provide you with a listing in which duplicate entries are eliminated. To trim the listing further, some will even let you search on a second string.

Search engines commonly employ intelligent software called *spiders, crawlers,* or *robots* to gather information. These programs visit Web sites daily to collect vital data, such as URLs, descriptive information, and hyperlinks. Spiders can be tremendously fast, visiting in excess of 1 million sites per day. Search engines also collect information by having people who create Web sites e-mail vital data to them.

Browsers That Search Twists on the search-engine concept are occurring regularly. Recently, browsers themselves have begun to incorporate searching capabilities with Web-resident engines. For instance, Microsoft's Internet Explorer contains an auto-search capability that lets users carry out string searches on the Web directly from Explorer's URL address field. Through an alliance between Microsoft and Yahoo!, the typed-in word automatically activates a Yahoo! search. In another recent innovation, a search product loads promising documents onto your hard disk as it searches, so it can inspect the actual text of the documents themselves. When it completes the search, it leaves the best dozen or so pages—you specify how many—on the disk for your perusal.

Auxiliary Search Software While a number of high-quality search engines are available for free use on the Web, they face some limitations. Since you temporarily borrow the program during a Web session, many Web-based search engines cannot remember from one session to the next what they did for you. Also, you cannot customize many Web-resident engines—Excite is one exception—to do such housekeeping tasks as organizing information for you and collecting new information about your favorite subjects as it becomes available over the Internet. To meet such additional needs, a number of auxiliary search-software products are available—for a fee. Netscape's SmartMarks, Quarterdeck's WebCompass, and Forefront's WebSeeker are three examples.

HARDWARE CONSIDERATIONS

As earlier sections of this chapter and book have hinted, a more powerful computer system is more likely to give you access to the advanced features of the Internet. A 28.8 kbps (or faster) modem, an SVGA monitor, and a good sound system will equip you pretty well to handle the complexity of most Web pages today. Increasingly, computer systems are being made with the Internet in mind. For instance, diskless *network computers (NCs)* have made Internet and intranet access available for under $1,000. Also, many computers made today are being advertised as "Internet ready," implying you will find such resources as a browser, sound and graphics capabilities, and provider software factory installed. Remember, however, that the Internet was set up to run on virtually any type of computer platform. Thus, you can access the text portions of it from most any type of computer system.

Connecting to the Internet

Connecting to the Internet usually involves two steps. The first is selecting a service provider. The second is using startup software to get the Internet programs supplied by the service provider up and running on your system.

TYPES OF SERVICE PROVIDERS

Among the many ways to connect to the Internet, by far the most common involve an account with one of the so-called *commercial online services* or access through an *Internet service provider.* This section discusses each of these alternatives as well as criteria for making a choice.

Commercial Online Services The "big four" **commercial online services** are **America Online (AOL), CompuServe, Prodigy,** and the **Microsoft Network** (see Figure NET 2-19). As mentioned in the previous chapter, these big nationally promoted services provide a broad range of information to paying subscribers. Commercial online services extend the Internet with their own proprietary content—such as business information, reference materials, exposure to celebrities, and free mailing lists and newsgroups—and they also simplify its use.

Basically, the commercial online services pursue a common strategy: Find the hottest and most desirable online infor-

FIGURE NET 2-19

Accessing the Web with America Online (AOL).

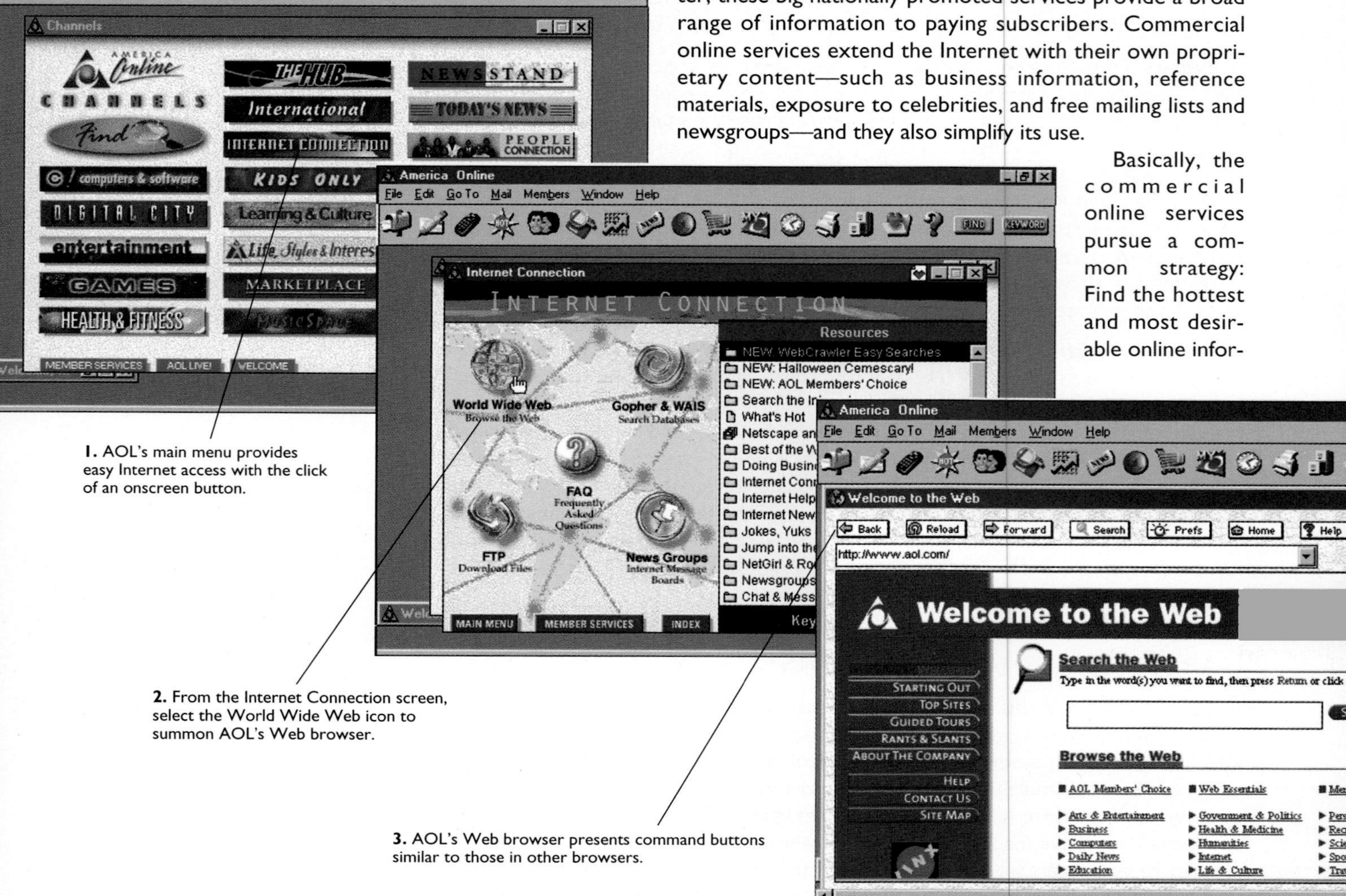

mation products (including Internet access), package them in a way that makes them easy to use and reliable, and make them available through a single service to paying subscribers. While the Internet duplicates much of what the commercial online services have to offer, these companies hope that many users will pay a premium for easier access and protection from some of the chaos of the Internet.

In general, the commercial online services tend to charge slightly higher prices than people pay for Internet access alone from the basic Internet-only service providers. What's more, you may not get full access to the Internet when you subscribe to one of the commercial package offerings. For instance, many services block Internet content deemed obscene or objectionable. Also, some services do not support such features as Telnet and chat, e-mail attachments, third-party plug-in packages, and Java. Such disadvantages notwithstanding, you will usually get more help from the commercial online services to make your Internet experience easy and free of frustration.

The commercial online services usually have their own proprietary browsers, modeled after such industry leaders as Netscape Navigator and Microsoft Internet Explorer. You may also be able to install another browser to work with these services.

Internet Service Providers If you are willing to forgo some of the "hand holding" you get with the commercial online services—and you desire Internet-only access—then a basic **Internet service provider (ISP)** is probably for you. Most ISPs are local organizations, and you can find them in your area's *Yellow Pages,* listed under such headings as *Computers* or *Internet.* An increasing number of ISPs—such as Netcom, GNN, and Earthlink—are national companies. Many of the commercial online services have also entered the ISP business—for instance, Prodigy with its Prodigy Internet service.

Basic Internet access is being increasingly provided by many deregulated companies in the telephone and television industries. Telephone companies like AT&T (via Worldnet) and television-service providers like DirecTV (via DirecPC) are now players in the ISP arena. Based on the recent success of AT&T's Worldnet, many industry observers are predicting that large national telecommunications companies will come to dominate the ISP business within the next few years.

Many of the larger ISPs have built their own backbone networks to handle their parts of the Internet. Many smaller ISPs are resellers that purchase Internet connectivity from larger ISPs and then turn around and sell services to users.

Two popular ways of connecting with an ISP—and also with a commercial online service—are with SLIP and PPP accounts. A **SLIP** connection (for *serial line Internet protocol)* is the oldest and least expensive method. However, SLIP does not check to see that information arrives to you error free. **PPP** service (for *point-to-point protocol)* checks for errors and also provides better security. Both SLIP and PPP are versions of the **TCP/IP** protocol, a collection of communications protocols that allow PCs accessing the Internet to understand each other and exchange data.

Other Providers Besides the sources already named, you can connect to the Internet in several other ways. For instance, many colleges and universities—and also thousands of companies—are plugged in. Consequently, if you are a student or an employee affiliated with one of these organizations, you may be able to hook up to the Internet through that connection for free. Many libraries also offer free access to the Internet. An additional option is a visit to a cybercafé (see User Solution NET 2-1).

■ **Commercial online service.** An information service such as America Online or CompuServe that provides proprietary content along with Internet access. ■ **America Online (AOL).** A commercial online service headquartered in Vienna, Virginia. ■ **CompuServe.** A commercial online service headquartered in Columbus, Ohio. ■ **Prodigy.** A commercial online service headquartered in White Plains, New York. ■ **Microsoft Network.** A commercial online service run by Microsoft Corporation. ■ **Internet service provider (ISP).** An organization that provides basic access to the Internet. ■ **SLIP.** A version of TCP/IP that enables individuals and organizations to connect to the Internet over ordinary phone lines ■ **PPP.** A protocol that resembles SLIP but allows more reliable and secure communications. ■ **TCP/IP.** A collection of communications protocols through which PCs accessing the Internet can understand each other and exchange data.

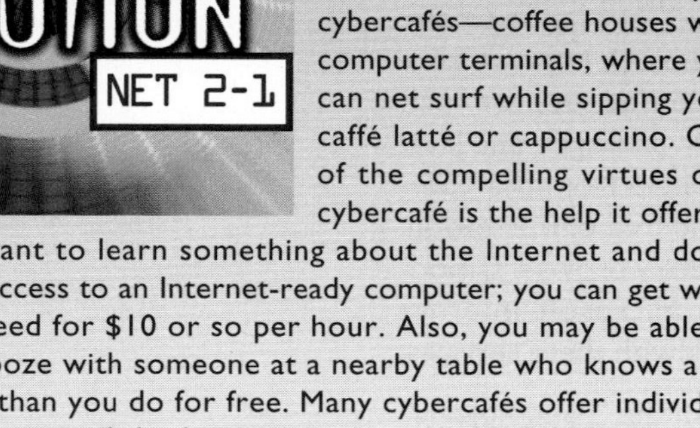

Surfing and Sipping

What do Urbis Orbit, Discovery Incubator, Cybersmith, and the Icon Byte Bar and Grille all have in common? They're cybercafés—coffee houses with computer terminals, where you can net surf while sipping your caffé latté or cappuccino. One of the compelling virtues of a cybercafé is the help it offers if you want to learn something about the Internet and don't have access to an Internet-ready computer; you can get what you need for $10 or so per hour. Also, you may be able to schmooze with someone at a nearby table who knows a lot more than you do for free. Many cybercafés offer individual instruction and also let patrons play with CD-ROM games. For a list of cybercafés both in the United states and abroad, check out http://www.easynet.co.uk/pages/cafe/ccafe.htm on the Web, or consult a search engine or the *Yellow Pages* of your phone book.

SELECTING A PROVIDER

Many people evaluate service providers with respect to a number of criteria—including those listed here—before making their selections.

Information Access The information you receive depends upon your provider's offerings and the type of plan you select. The commercial online services generally let you see less of the Internet than the ISPs. Yet, they may offer other information that you will find useful—for instance, a better stock-market feature than you can find on the Internet. Also keep in mind that you must carefully judge the accuracy and reliability of the information you find online, unless it comes from a reputable source.

Cost The commercial online services typically sell a variety of plans, each with a different level of service and price. A standard plan might involve a flat monthly charge for a certain number of hours of **connect time**—the amount of time during which your computer has online access. The fee often includes a limited number of hours of Internet usage. If you exceed the service's standard connect time or if you use more Internet hours than your chosen plan calls for, you usually pay per-hour charges for any overage. A typical plan might cost $10 per month for five hours of access to either proprietary content or the Internet. Or, if your online needs are more substantial, you may pay $20 per month for anywhere from 20 to unlimited hours of access. Expect a $1- to $3-per-hour surcharge for every hour above the basic amount.

ISPs commonly charge flat monthly fees for Internet service, as well as additional fees to get connected. ISPs, too, offer several pricing options. You might pay about $25 to connect and about $20 per month for unlimited Internet access by today's pricing standards.

You should also consider in your cost evaluation the price of long-distance calls. Even a provider located outside your city or town probably has a local number there

■ **Connect time.** The amount of time you spend online with a service provider's computers.

that you can dial up. Dialing a local number, of course, means that you pay no long-distance charges. But beware—the free local line you are dialing into from a small town may run at a slower speed than the line in the provider's home city.

Most providers will let you switch from plan to plan as your usage pattern changes. What's more, some will let you use the Internet for free during off-peak hours. Currently, a price war among providers will probably send prices falling. Beware if the price of an Internet connection looks too good to be true; it might be a sign that the provider is struggling and about to go out of business. Paying a provider on a month-to-month basis limits such a risk.

Speed An important consideration centers on how fast the service works. While the speed of your Internet application depends in part on the speed of your modem, it also depends on how fast the provider's line moves data to you. A provider offering 28.8 kbps lines speeds data along to you twice as quickly as a provider offering only 14.4 kbps lines. If you are connecting from a town or from a business site, you may be able to take advantage of an ISDN or a high-speed T1 line.

Service and Support One of the most important service-related criteria is reaching a help line when you need it. Try calling at 3 P.M. on a Saturday or at 11 P.M. on a weekday. Does anyone answer? Some service providers have earned unsavory reputations for letting users linger on the line half an hour or more because of chronic understaffing. The quality of support help is important, too. You want to talk to people who can solve your problems.

Establishing a connection through your provider can also be troublesome at times. Before signing up, ask the provider about the average number of people it has assigned to each modem or line. If that ratio exceeds 15:1 you may wind up too often getting a busy signal when you're trying to connect. A ratio of 10:1 is optimal. On a related note, look into how often and for how long the provider has had to cut users off from its system due to technical difficulties.

Many people connecting to the Internet as users will eventually want to develop Web pages of their own. If you think that you may become a Web author some day, ask providers what types of support they offer in this area and the cost of such support. Many providers will furnish Web-authoring tools and advice. They will also run a home page for you—and possibly several other pages—for free or for a nominal cost.

Ease of Use At the least, the service you select should be easy enough to use so that you aren't spending too much time seeking technical assistance. The browser and other packages the service provides should have friendly interfaces and possess features that make sense for your needs.

SETTING UP YOUR SYSTEM

The specific steps that you must follow to connect to the Internet depend on the service provider you choose. Many will supply you with a *startup kit* with installation software stored on a CD-ROM or diskette. All you generally have to do is follow the directions on the disk to begin running the startup program. After the program takes over, it will supply screens that tell you at each step of the way what to do next. In some cases, you won't have to ask for a startup disk at all. Your operating system's opening screens may already display a *setup icon* for your provider. If this is the case, select the icon and follow the instructions on the screen.

Figure NET 2-20 shows how getting set up with a service provider is done, by illustrating some of the steps you will actually take to connect to America Online (AOL). You would follow very similar setup procedures for the other commercial online services. For any of them, you would need to supply identifying information about yourself, select a plan and choose a method of payment, and provide such connect data as your modem speed and home phone number if your computer system can't figure such information out. Connecting to an ISP usually involves more steps and complexity, requiring you to select specific protocols and server settings.

FIGURE NET 2-20

Getting connected to a commercial online service. You can get connected to most commercial online services in a few minutes by supplying information on a series of simple screens.

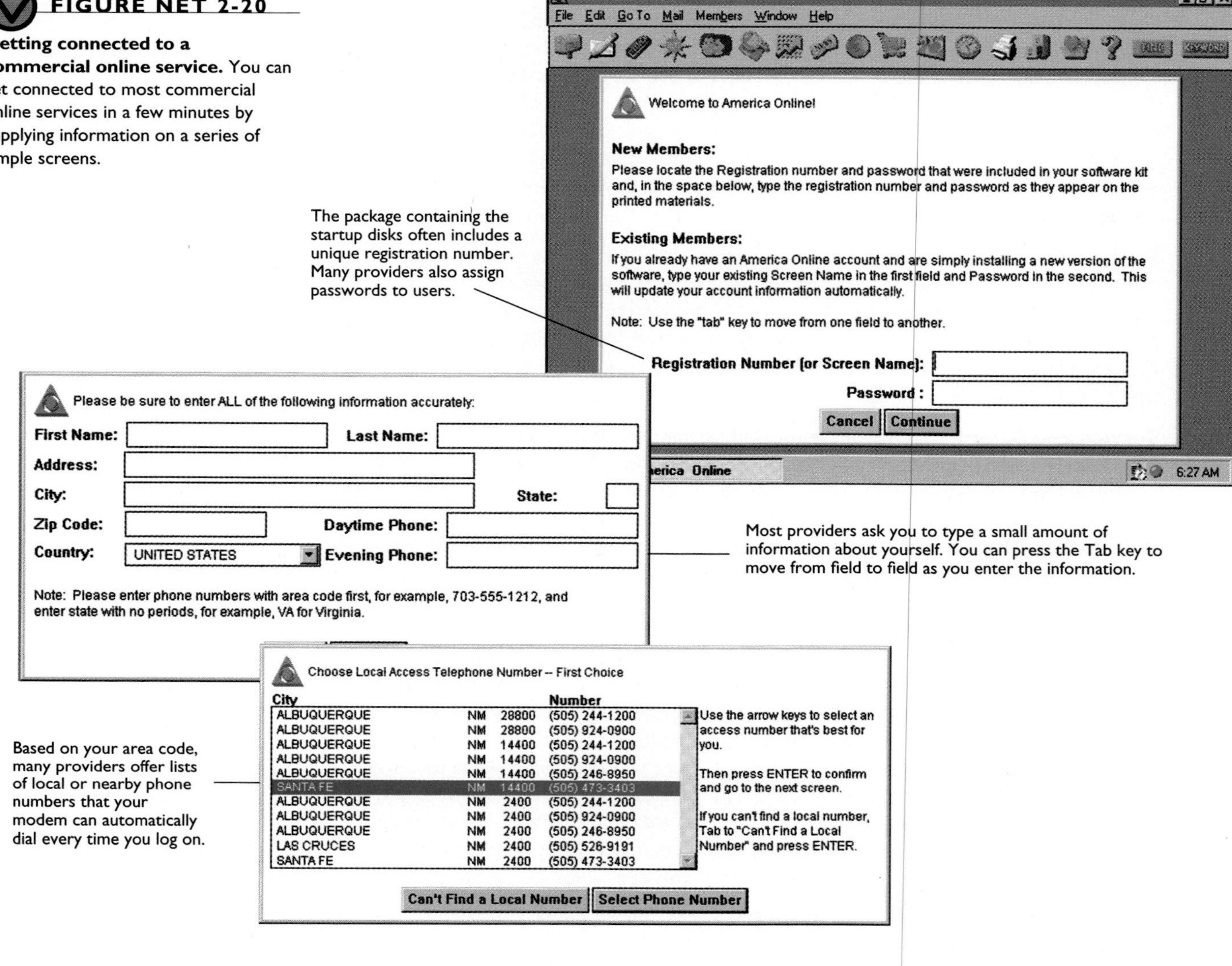

After you set up your connection to the provider, you are ready to go. During the setup process, an *access icon* will be placed on one of your operating system's opening screens. Every time you turn on your computer system, you can connect to the provider simply by selecting the access icon and logging on.

Summary and Key Terms

Internet has become a household word. In many ways, the Internet has redefined how people think about computers and communications.

Evolution of the Internet The **Internet**—a worldwide phenomenon that consists of tens of thousands of linked networks that are accessed by millions of people daily—dates back to the late 1960s. At its start and throughout most of its history, the Internet was called the **ARPANET.** It was not until the development of graphical user interfaces and the World Wide Web that public interest in the Internet began to soar.

The Internet community is made up of individuals, companies such as **service providers** and **content providers,** and many other types of organizations. Virtually anyone with a computer that can communicate can be part of the Internet, either as a user or supplier of information or services.

Because the Internet is so unique in the history of the world—and it remains a relatively new phenomenon—several widespread myths about it have surfaced. Three such myths are that the Internet is free, that it is controlled by some central force, and that it is equivalent to the World Wide Web.

What Does the Internet Have to Offer? The Internet is home to many features.

Electronic mail, or **e-mail,** was one of the first applications to appear on the Internet, and it is still the most widely used feature.

The **World Wide Web (WWW),** or *Web,* is the feature most people talk about; it is used for *information retrieval.* Information is organized into chunks called *Web pages,* which are connected by **hyperlinks** (or **hypermedia)**—indicated onscreen by boldfaced and underlined text or by selectable icons. When a content provider creates one or more Web pages that relate to a specific topic or business, the result is called a **Web site.** A Web site contains anywhere from one to hundreds or thousands of pages, with the first page the user sees called a **home page.** Web sites are hosted at computers called **Web servers.**

The Web is one of many information-retrieval tools on the Internet. **Gopher** is another; it generates hierarchical, text-intensive menus that allow users to access resources by making successive selections with an onscreen pointer. FTP sites are good places to visit to get free copies of programs and files. **FTP** stands for **file transfer protocol,** the procedure that facilitates transfers of files between an FTP server and users' computers. **Archie** is a tool that enables you to search through FTP servers to find particular downloadable files. **Telnet** is a protocol that lets a desktop workstation behave like a dumb terminal to a remote server.

A **mailing list** is a discussion group that uses e-mail to communicate. Hundreds of mailing lists on the Internet cover a variety of subjects.

Members of **newsgroups** also share e-mail messages, but with a format somewhat like an electronic newspaper. **UseNet** is the protocol that describes how newsgroup messages are handled between computers. A special etiquette—referred to as **netiquette**—has evolved on the Internet for those who communicate via newsgroups and other forms of electronic mail. Newcomers to newsgroups should read through those groups' **FAQs,** or lists of **frequently asked questions.**

Chat refers to a facility that enables people to engage in interactive conversations over the Internet. Two common types of chat are Internet relay chat and voice chat.

In a growing use of the Internet, many people now shop online.

Internet Addresses An **Internet address** indicates where something on the Internet can be located. Internet addresses are unique; each one is assigned to one and only one resource or person.

People are most commonly reached on the Internet through their *e-mail addresses.* The part of the address before the @ symbol is the person's username; the part following that symbol is the mail server's **domain name.** Web pages and links to information at Gopher, FTP, and other sites are accessed through **uniform resource locators,** or **URLs.**

Desktop Tools for Accessing the Internet A **browser,** or *Web browser,* is a software package that enables you to navigate the World Wide Web as well as other parts of the Internet. The first successful browser was and still is called **Mosaic.** Among a variety of browsers on the market today, the most popular commercial products are **Netscape Navigator** and **Microsoft Internet Explorer.**

Browser software is constantly evolving. Some properties that you may want to consider in a browser include functionality, navigational tools, speed, framing capabilities, a workgroup-computing facility, support for complex applications, Java and ActiveX support, publishing capabilities, and security. A large market has developed for *plug-in packages* and *helper packages,* both of which enable you to add features and functions to your current browsing environment.

When you know generally what you want, but you don't know at which URL to find it, one of your best options is a **search engine.** One of the most popular search engines is Yahoo!, which can be found on the Web and used for free. You can also purchase auxiliary search software to meet additional searching needs.

A more powerful computer system will more likely give you access to the advanced features of the Internet.

Connecting to the Internet Many types of service providers furnish Internet connections, but by far the most common are the **commercial online services** and the **Internet service providers (ISPs).** The "big four" commercial online services are **America Online (AOL), CompuServe, Prodigy,** and the **Microsoft Network.** Often, you will connect to an ISP through a **SLIP** or **PPP** account, both of which are variations of the **TCP/IP** protocol.

People often select service providers by considering several criteria. Among their priorities are the information a service provides and other features including price, speed, service and support, and ease of use. Fees usually include set monthly amounts and extra charges for **connect time** in excess of the standard amount.

How you connect to the Internet depends on the provider you have chosen.

EXERCISES

1. Define the following terms.
   a. Home page
   b. The Internet
   c. Domain name
   d. Content provider
2. Describe the purposes of the following Internet services.
   a. World Wide Web
   b. Chat
   c. Newsgroups
   d. FTP
   e. E-mail
   f. Telnet
3. Newsgroups are organized by topic, as indicated by their names; for instance, *rec* stands for *recreation* and *sci* for *science*. Name as many other newsgroup classifications as you can as well as their associated three- or four-letter abbreviations.
4. Participants in such Internet services as newsgroups and mailing lists should follow proper netiquette. Identify at least five rules of netiquette.
5. For each of the following situations, name the Internet service you would probably be using. Choose from e-mail, newsgroups, mailing lists, the World Wide Web, Gopher, FTP, Telnet, and chat.
   a. You need to find information on virtual reality, in the easiest way possible, for a term paper.
   b. You want to send a letter to a friend at Northern Arizona University.
   c. You would like to visit the Internet Underground Music Archive at http://www.iuma.com/.
   d. You want to initiate with other people a series of articles and threads on flying saucers and other extraterrestrial objects.
   e. You want to communicate interactively with a friend in real time, with each of you in turn typing something into your computer.
   f. You want to download free software.
   g. You are communicating with a computer in a foreign country, and it treats your fancy new computer like a dumb terminal.
   h. You want to search through government computers to find the locations of downloadable files on Watergate.
6. You are talking with a friend who has some definite misconceptions about the Internet. What can you tell your friend to set him or her straight on the following misconceptions?
   a. The Internet is free.
   b. The Internet is controlled by the FBI.
   c. The World Wide Web is really the same thing as the Internet; purists just like to say they're different.
7. Describe in your own words the difference between the following terms: *Web client, Web site,* and *Web server.* Into which of those three categories—if any of them—would you place the following?
   a. A computer that stores thousands of Web pages
   b. The home page for television's Discovery Channel
   c. The area on a mainframe computer that stores e-mail going to students
   d. The browser on your PC
8. A large selection of plug-in and helper programs can enhance browsing environments such as those provided with Internet Explorer and Netscape Navigator. Supply at least five examples of such packages and describe what each one does.
9. Name at least three Web-resident search engines. What uses and limitations do such search engines have?
10. Identify several criteria by which people often choose among service providers. Also, describe what type of action you should take in each of the following situations.
    a. You've absolutely decided to open an account with a certain provider, but a friend tells you she read that the provider is having financial problems.
    b. A provider says its help line is available 24 hours a day, 7 days a week, and service availability is a top concern of yours.
    c. You've just read about a great deal in the newspaper: For a $50 connect fee, you can get unlimited Internet access at a price of $5 a month from an ISP for as long as you live.

PROJECTS

1. Commercial Online Services Select two commercial online services—such as America Online and CompuServe—and compare them with respect to the list of criteria below. Note that each service probably offers several monthly plans, so pick a similar plan within each service to ensure a good basis of comparison.

a. Monthly base cost
b. Local line availability: Do you have to dial long distance, or is a local line available?
c. Number of connect hours included (possibly unlimited) in the base cost
d. Number of Internet hours included in the base cost
e. Surcharge per extra hour over allotted hours
f. Number of e-mail messages included in base cost: Does this number include messages sent or received or the total of the two? Also, what do you have to pay for e-mail messages that run over the maximum allowed?
g. Fastest modem speeds available in your area.
h. Cost of an ISDN line
h. Proprietary content or extras: Does the commercial online service offer any benefits that would be worth paying a premium price over the cost of an ISP?

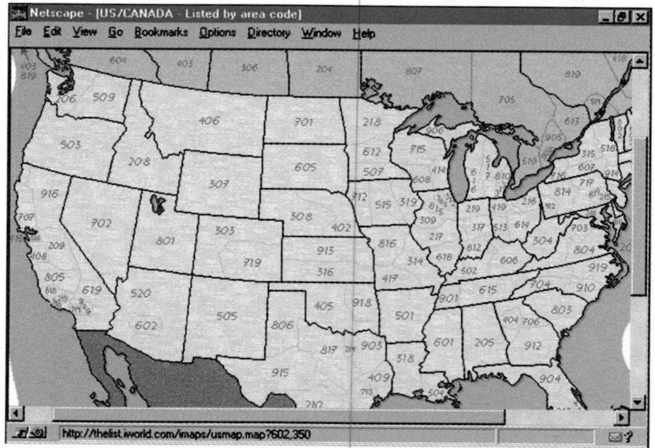

A site called *The List* (http://www.thelist.com) offers a clickable map and directory of about 4,500 ISPs worldwide.

2. Internet Service Providers ISPs often give you deeper access into the Internet than the commercial online services provide. Also, a heavy user of the Internet would probably run up lower monthly costs through an ISP. As your project, find an ISP in your local area or nationally and compare it to one of the commercial online services with respect to the following criteria:

a. Monthly cost: Assume for comparison that you will need 5 hours of Internet access a week. Then, redo the comparison assuming 15 hours.
b. E-mail costs: Let's assume that you are going to be sending or receiving more than 50 e-mail messages a month and that you need at least 5 megabytes of memory in your mailbox.
c. Setup costs, if any
d. Browsers available: What browsers are available, and how do they stack up in comparison?
e. Ease of connecting to the Internet: Compare the procedures involved with both providers.
f. Your "window" to the Internet: To what parts of the Internet do any of the providers deny access?
g. Technical support available: Must you pay any charges for answers to phoned questions? During what hours and what days of the week is support available?

3. E-Mail As mentioned in the chapter text, the most widely used feature of the Internet is electronic mail, or e-mail. For this project, research a stand alone e-mail package of your own choice and report to the class about it. Two popular Internet e-mail packages that run on both the Windows and Macintosh platforms are Qualcomm's Eudora Pro and NetManage's Z-Mail Pro. Make sure you answer the following questions in your report:

a. What is the name of the chosen package? Who is the package's publisher? How much does the package cost?
b. What are the product's main features?

4. Online Catalogs Online catalogs have become increasingly popular features of the Web and corporate intranets. Many people have speculated that this trend may bring the end of the printed catalog. Answer the following questions, limiting your comments to two pages or less:

a. What compelling advantages do online catalogs have over their printed counterparts?
b. Do you see any advantages of printed catalogs over their online counterparts? If so, name them.
c. How do you feel about the predicted demise of the printed catalog?

5. Navigating the Web Browsers vary in the way that their *history-list* and *bookmark* features are implemented. For the browser you are using, answer the following questions:

a. How would you return most quickly to the Web page that was on your screen immediately before the one that is there now?
b. How does the history-list feature work?
c. How do you add a bookmark?
d. How do you jump to a bookmark?
e. How many bookmarks can you store in a bookmark list?
f. How many separate bookmark lists can you create?
g. How can you remove bookmarks when you don't need them anymore?

6. Web Browser Features Web browsers come with many exotic features in addition to the standard ones. For the browser you are using in your lab—or, if your lab is not Internet ready, for any browser of your choice (that you can research in a computer journal)—answer the following questions:

a. Is a framing capability available?
b. Are there any workgroup-computing capabilities?
c. Does the browser provide built-in Java support?
d. Can you create your own Web pages with the browser, or do you need some type of plug-in or helper program to do this?
e. What types of security features does the browser provide?

7. Search Engines You can access several free search engines on the Web, including Yahoo!, WebCrawler, Lycos, and Alta Vista. The URLs of these and other engines can be found in the accompanying table.

For this project, choose any two search engines and compare them with respect to how easy they locate information for you. Base your comparisons on any two of the following search tasks.

a. Finding the home page of the University of New Mexico
b. Getting information about the town of Moscow, Idaho (Assume you will be visiting there next week and want a variety of visitor-related information.)
c. Finding information that will help in the hobby of collecting stamps
d. Getting information about Bill Gates, the founder and chief executive officer of Microsoft Corporation (Assume you are doing a paper on his life and need historical information and interesting stories about him.)
e. Getting a list of Internet service providers (ISPs) in the Los Angeles area

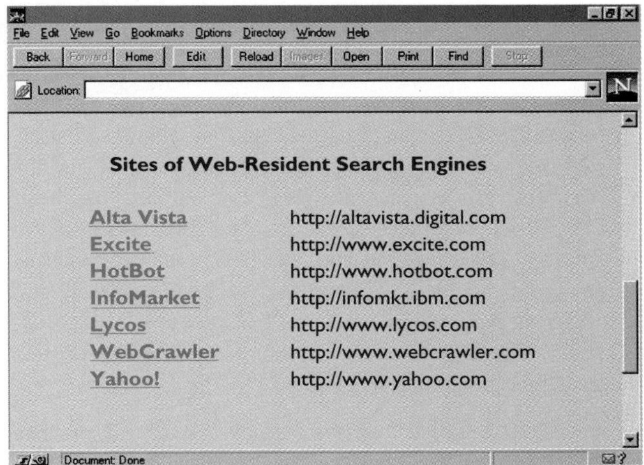

Sites of Web-Resident Search Engines

Alta Vista	http://altavista.digital.com
Excite	http://www.excite.com
HotBot	http://www.hotbot.com
InfoMarket	http://infomkt.ibm.com
Lycos	http://www.lycos.com
WebCrawler	http://www.webcrawler.com
Yahoo!	http://www.yahoo.com

8. Commercial Use of the Internet Not too long ago, very few companies were represented on the Internet. Recently, all of that has changed and commercial accounts—those with a *com* root domain—are far and away the most prevalent type of account. This change in composition of the Internet community has both good and bad aspects. Name as many of each as you can, and use your list to write a 3- to 5-page position paper on the following question: Is commercial use of the Internet a good or bad thing?

9. Get a Job In recent years, the Internet has become a great place to look for jobs. As your project, find at least one source that posts job announcements in your career area. Describe the source, telling approximately how many jobs are listed and what types of online tools are available to help with job searches. For instance, some sites offer search tools

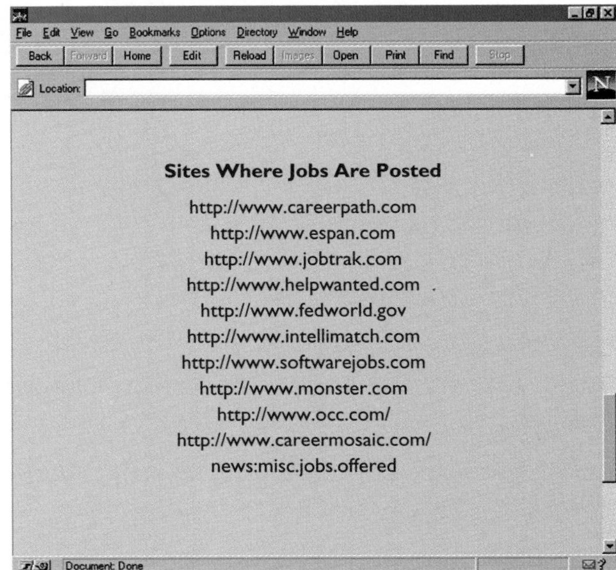

Sites Where Jobs Are Posted

http://www.careerpath.com
http://www.espan.com
http://www.jobtrak.com
http://www.helpwanted.com
http://www.fedworld.gov
http://www.intellimatch.com
http://www.softwarejobs.com
http://www.monster.com
http://www.occ.com/
http://www.careermosaic.com/
news:misc.jobs.offered

to help you find particular jobs, information about job and salary trends, and calculators that show how much you will need to make in particular geographic areas to maintain your current standard of living. Note that the Internet lists both national and regional job-search sites.

To help you to get started, feel free to check out any of the sites in the accompanying table. Also think about using search engines—click on the "Business and the Economy" category—to find more. You may additionally want to look at the "Computer Careers" section that appears in every weekly issue of *Computerworld;* this publication often lists Web sites useful for computer professionals who are hunting for jobs.

10. Internet Yellow Pages A terrific printed reference for locations on the Internet where you can find information on a variety of topics is the *Internet Yellow Pages*. It's organized in A-to-Z fashion like the phone company's *Yellow Pages*—you look up the topic on which you want information to find both descriptions of sites and their URLs. As your project, use the *Internet Yellow Pages* or some other similar reference or search tool to locate on the Internet information on any of the following topics:

a. Baseball (or some other sport)
b. Hiking (or some other hobby)
c. Dogs (or some other pet)

What types of information did you find? (In other words, if you are a dog owner, just what types of things can you find on the Internet about dogs?) Report your findings to the class.

11. Internet Research If you want to do research on some aspect of the Internet, you'll find no shortage of information available. You can go online and retrieve information off the Internet itself or run into a conventional bookstore and probably find several relevant books. As your project, find at least one book and/or one Web site, as indicated, devoted to each of the Internet topics listed below. Write a short description of each book or site, giving any identifying information and telling about the subject of the book or site.

a. A complete description of the Internet and its various parts (Find both a book and Web site.)
b. Cool places on the Web (Find a Web site only.)
c. How to develop your own home page (Find both a book and a Web site.)
d. How to use Netscape Navigator (Find either a book or a Web site.)
e. How to program in Java (Find either a book or a Web site.)

12. Cybercafés Locate a cybercafé reasonably near your home or school and pay a visit. Then, answer the following questions:

a. What is the name of the cybercafé? What is its postal address? Its Web and/or e-mail address?
b. What types of hardware does the cybercafé use—fully equipped PCs with diskette drives or dumb terminals that work through a larger computer?
c. What types of browsers are available? What plug-ins or other helper software is available to enhance your Internet experience?
d. How much do you have to pay per hour to use the computers?
e. Does the cybercafé offer classes or individual instruction? If so, what's the cost?

13. Paying for the Internet The chapter mentions the expectation of some industry analysts that pay-per-use Internet access is rapidly approaching. Some have suggested that users should pay charges for the Internet just as they would if they used a toll road—say, paying fees that are proportional to the load they create for Internet resources. Others feel that charges for the Internet by usage are both unnecessary and likely to discourage people from learning to use a critical educational resource. They propose that the Internet's cost could be subsidized by advertisers or by a method similar to the way that many states offer residents free roads—by increasing general taxes slightly or by adding taxes to hardware and/or software purchases.

How do you think the Internet should be supported?

14. Electronic Commerce Book Report A number of good books on the subject of electronic commerce are available. Five such books are listed below:

- *The Digital Economy,* by Don Tapscott (ISBN 0-07-062200-0)
- *Digital Money, The New Era of Internet Commerce,* by Daniel C. Lynch (ISBN 0-471-14178-X)
- *Presenting Digital Cash,* by Seth Godin (ISBN 1-57521-062-2)
- *Digital Cash, Commerce on the Net,* by Peter Wayner (ISBN 0-12-738763-3)
- *Frontiers of Electronic Commerce,* by Ravi Kalakota and Andrew B. Whinston (ISBN 0-201-84520-2)

For this project, read any one of these books—or a similar one—and write a 5- to 8-page paper about it. Summarize the author's findings and provide a critical review of either the author's conclusions or the methodology for reaching them.

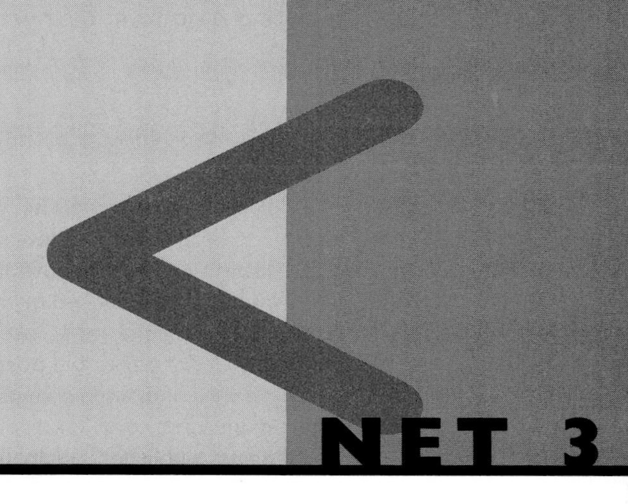

NET 3

Developing Your Own Web Pages

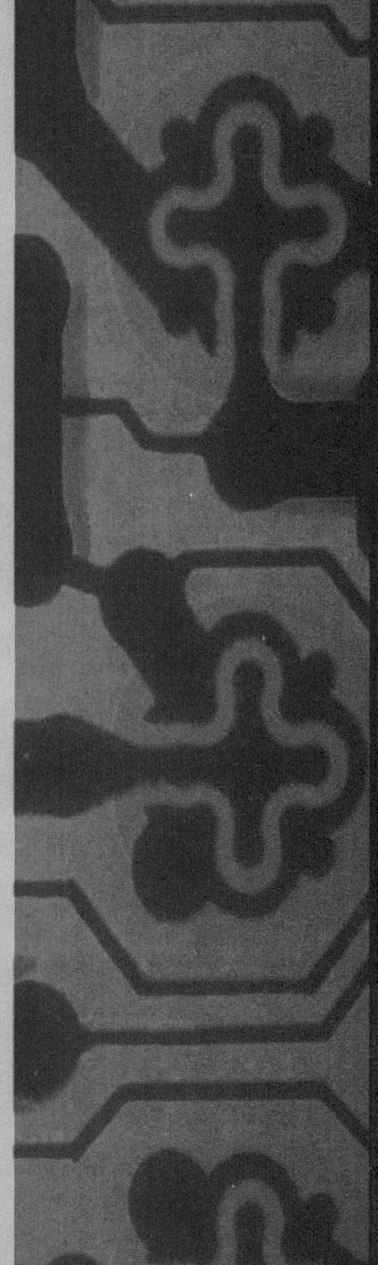

Outline

- Overview
- The Web as a Publishing Medium
  - Advantages of Web Publishing
  - Disadvantages of Web Publishing
- Why Publish on the Web?
- Developing a Publishing Plan
- Designing Your Site
  - Principles of Web Design
  - Tips on Making Pages Sizzle
  - Flowcharts and Storyboards
- Tools for Creating Web Pages
  - Hypertext Markup Language (HTML)
  - Java, ActiveX, and Scripting Languages
  - Web-Authoring Programs
- Testing Your Pages
- Promoting and Maintaining Your Web Site
- Publishing-Related Issues
  - Copyrights
  - Censorship
  - Security

Learning Objectives

After completing this chapter, you will be able to:

1. Define the many evolving opportunities available in Web publishing.
2. Name the various steps required in developing Web pages for the Internet.
3. Describe the types of tools that authors use to create Web pages.
4. Identify social issues that relate to Web publishing.

Overview

Almost overnight, the World Wide Web grew from the dream of a handful of researchers to the format of choice for presenting information over the Internet. How many people use the Web? Nobody knows for sure; by the last count, the number has reached many millions, and it's doubling every several months.

One of the most interesting aspects of the Web is the ability to develop your own Web pages and post them on the Internet—an opportunity that's unique in the history of mass communications. If you write an article for a magazine—or a book manuscript, movie screenplay, or television script—you have to sell your idea to an agent, publisher, or producer before you can reach an audience. Not so with Web publishing. You can whip up your own Web pages, pay someone with a Web server to host them, and—bingo—you're in business and immediately reaching out to millions of people throughout the world.

One of the main challenges of Web publishing is that it's a relatively new application for computers, one with unbounded potential. In many ways, the state of the art in Web publishing today is like the film industry in the early days of Hollywood or the television industry in the early 1950s. It's a landscape for pioneers, and nobody knows what its killer application—the one that brings mass-market acceptance—will be. The final rule book is still to be written. Anyone can play, and play in his or her own style.

Chapter NET 3 opens with a general discussion of Web publishing. From there, it goes into the steps you will need to follow to create your own Web pages. These steps are pretty much the same ones you would follow in developing any type of computer program or commercial project. The chapter also covers some important side issues that concern Web publishers, such as copyrights, security, and censorship.

The Web as a Publishing Medium

The Web is unlike traditional publishing media such as books, newspapers and magazines, and movies and television. In fact, it is quite unlike any publishing medium ever known.

Web publishing is defined as developing pages for the Web; in other words, creating your own **Web site** or *Web presence.* Depending on how ambitiously you plan, the site can range in size and scale from a single page featuring your favorite chili recipe to a multipage electronic catalog from which people can order goods. You can start up your own Web site without owning or operating server computers and a fleet of modems to distribute your pages to remote users. Most Web authors store the needed files on their service providers' computers.

ADVANTAGES OF WEB PUBLISHING

The Web offers several advantages over traditional publishing media.

Anyone Can Play One of the big differences from other media that distinguishes Web publishing is that anyone can participate. If you have a great idea, you can immediately get it published and, what's more, published in your preferred style. You don't have to get clearance from anyone else. Furthermore, you can often work on your own timetable.

■ **Web publishing.** The process of developing pages for the Web. ■ **Web site.** A collection of related Web pages belonging to an individual or organization.

People writing for traditional media regularly feel frustrated when editors say they want submissions that are *different* and then reject works that are *too* different because they are perceived as too risky for one reason or another. As your own Web publisher, you are more or less free to do your own thing. Web surfers encounter increasing clutter from look-alike products, so an unusual appearance is an attractive site-design goal. This statement does not mean that you will never feel any restraints on page design. If you are a company employee developing a Web site, or you are in the business of developing sites for clients, you will probably have to adhere to some guidelines.

The Online Nature of Web Products Traditional media are distributed through static printed pages, broadcasts, or filmings. These media are essentially *serial* in nature—that is, they are laid out in specific chapter-by-chapter or scene-by-scene order so that their audiences must more or less accept the author's intended method of experiencing the products.

Web pages, by contrast, have hyperlinks that encourage readers to jump around and thereby experience the products in their own personalized ways. In this sense, Web *users*—those who read the pages produced by Web publishers—take on the role of authors; they dynamically create what they read seconds later.

Consider a couple of other, related advantages to online publishing: Web publishers can update pages with fresh materials whenever they want to, and they can include a wide variety of *interactive* elements—such as selectable sound and video clips—that traditional media can't use.

Low Cost Relative to other media, publishing on the Web is cheap. Take content. As a Web publisher, you don't even have to create all of your content or pay for it. For instance, you can download thousands of free art and audio clips from the Web for use at your own site. Also, you can provide hyperlinks on your home page to any of the millions of Web pages that have been created by others, incorporating other sites as part of your own presentation.

You don't have to spend very much—if anything at all—to publish and distribute your page, either. Many colleges and universities let students, faculty, and staff publish materials on the Internet for free. If you've signed up with a commercial provider, once you pay to get your pages hosted on its server, you face no printing and mailing costs. Many commercial providers let regular users of their services run single home pages for free or for very nominal fees, with modest charges for any additional pages. This fact does not imply that you can expect no hidden costs. Many commercial providers charge you to update pages, and some bill extra if your site creates a lot of traffic.

Keep in mind that, theoretically speaking, all Web pages are equally accessible. Someone can visit your home page about as easily as they can find the Microsoft or Disney home page. If your pages are interesting and exciting, strong word-of-mouth advertising will inform people about them. Also, some places on the Web help you to promote your site for free.

DISADVANTAGES OF WEB PUBLISHING

As a prospective Web publisher, be advised that the medium also suffers from certain disadvantages and limitations. For one, developing Web pages takes certain skills. Are you willing to invest the time to pick them up? Also, you have to decide whether you want to commit to keeping your pages constantly updated with fresh material. That process can require a lot of work, too, but people generally will not return to your site unless they are constantly rewarded with new, useful information.

Another knotty problem emerges as you try to ensure that your document presents a consistent look over a wide variety of computer platforms. As a later section will discuss, you can count on no absolute guarantee that the beautiful pages you develop on your computer system will look the same on someone else's. Some extra effort on your part, however, will minimize the chances of surprises later on.

Why Publish on the Web?

The first question every prospective Web publisher needs to answer is both simple and complex: Why am I doing this? It's the same question you should ask before writing a book or a movie script. The answer defines your *goal,* or purpose.

Goals People work toward all types of goals when they create Web pages. Many develop their own Web presences to share knowledge or some burning passion: Making pasta, raising horses, collecting stamps—you name it. If you love, say, raising horses, your home page can contain links to other Web hotspots in the horse world—online horse publications, Web pages of other horse lovers, Web pages of guest ranches, and so on.

Others establish Web presences to post their employment résumés (see Feature NET 3-1 on page NET 106) or just to announce to the world at large what great people they are or where they fall in the political spectrum. If you're single, your home page can help you to meet the love of your life. Of course, your Web site can also have profit as a motive. Many businesses set up Web pages to establish organizational presences or images, to generate sales leads by getting users to fill out informational forms, and to close sales on the spot by getting purchase commitments. Figure NET 3-1 illustrates several purposes for developing a Web presence.

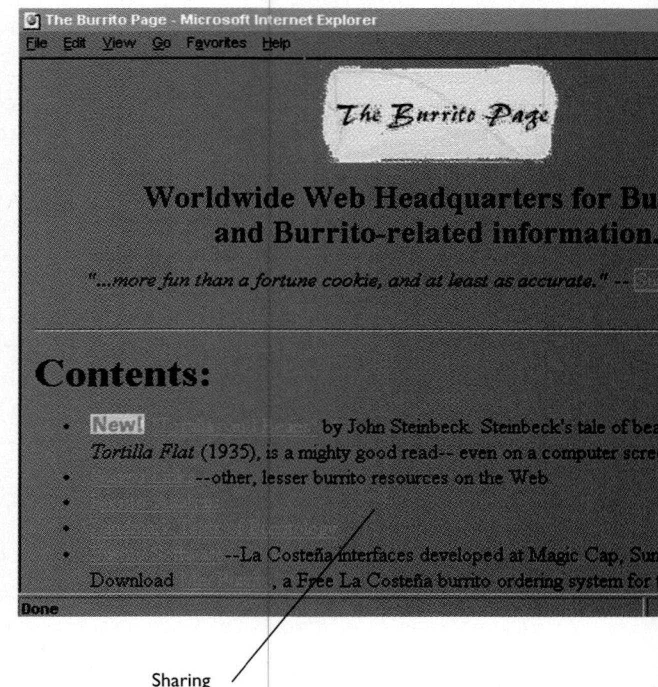

Knowing precisely why you want to publish on the Web leads to the next critical question: Who is your audience—your target market?

Audience Most people who establish their own sites on the Web have something they want to say. The big question is Do others out there on the Web want to listen? If you feel that an audience wants to see your Web message or product, define who these people are and determine what will turn them on. What is their age range? Is the audience mostly male or female? Who does your audience admire? You should also ask yourself whether the Web is the best way of reaching these people. Maybe an ad in your local paper would be both easier and far more effective.

Competition Even if you anticipate finding an audience for your Web idea, a competing Web site already on the Internet may duplicate your intentions. You should spend time with search engines like Yahoo! or WebCrawler to see what existing sites resemble your planned site. Keep in mind that getting a message or product to market first gives you an advantage, but it doesn't guarantee you'll wind up the

FIGURE NET 3-1

Some goals for developing a Web presence.

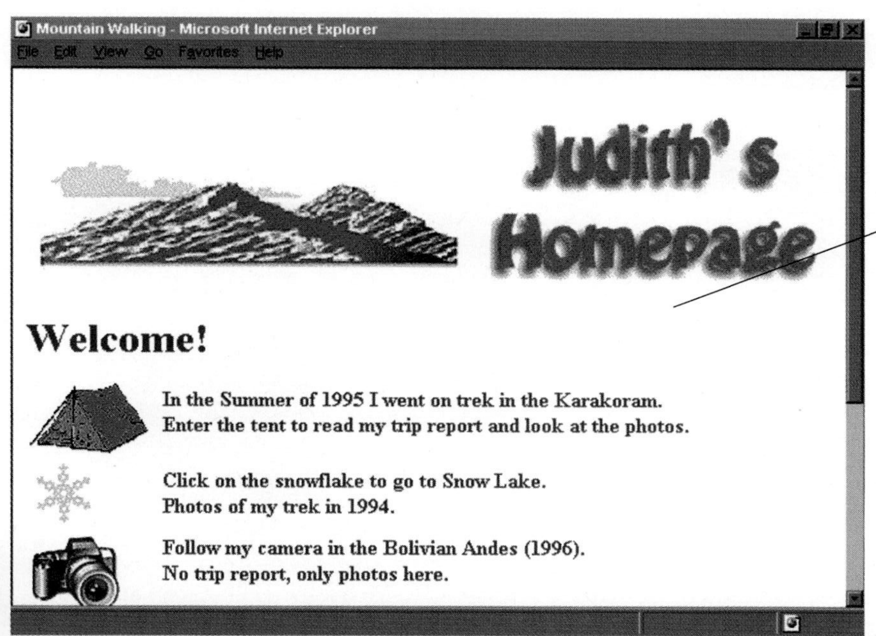

Creating a personal home page

Delivering a political message

continued

eventual winner. The history of personal computers proves this point rather conclusively; such first-to-market companies as Apple (computers), WordStar (word processing), VisiCalc (spreadsheets), and dBASE (databases) have been eclipsed in the marketplace by more nimble competitors.

You can also use competitors' sites to your advantage. By developing links at your site to information at other sites, you might use them to complement what you're doing.

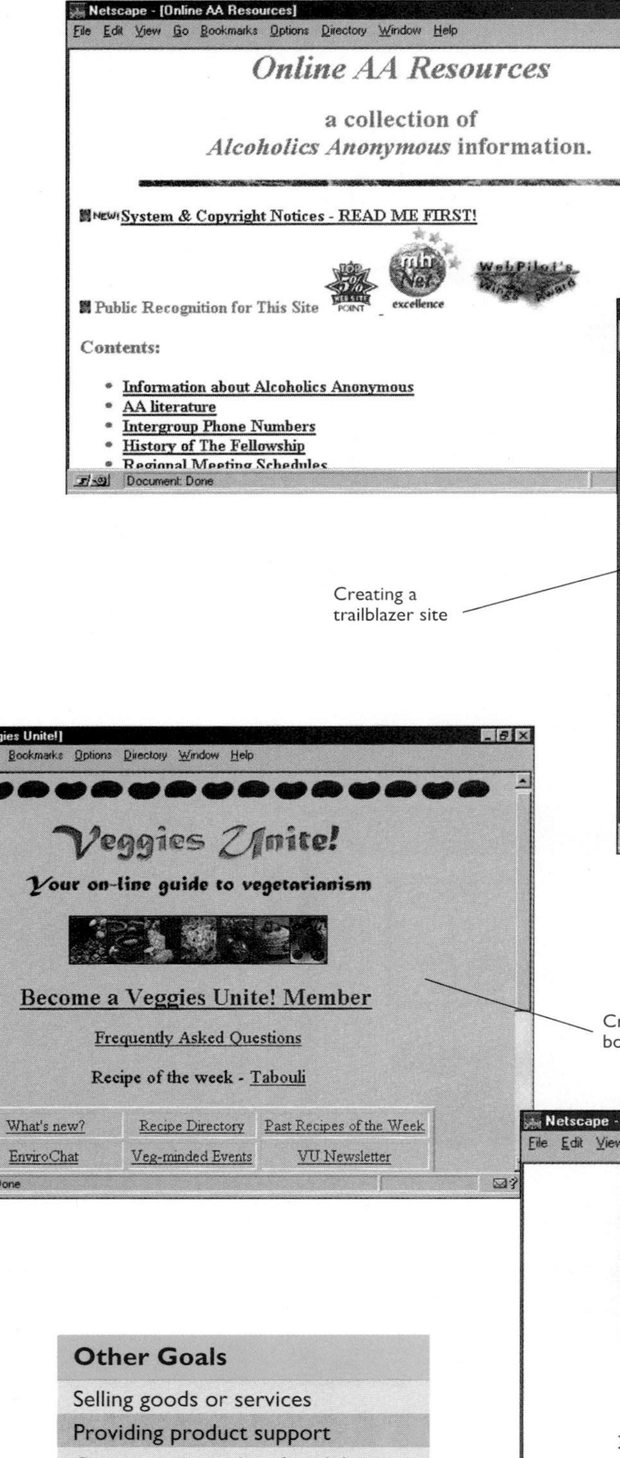

Providing support to others

Creating a trailblazer site

Creating an online book or magazine

Promoting communities

Other Goals
Selling goods or services
Providing product support
Organizing an online fan club

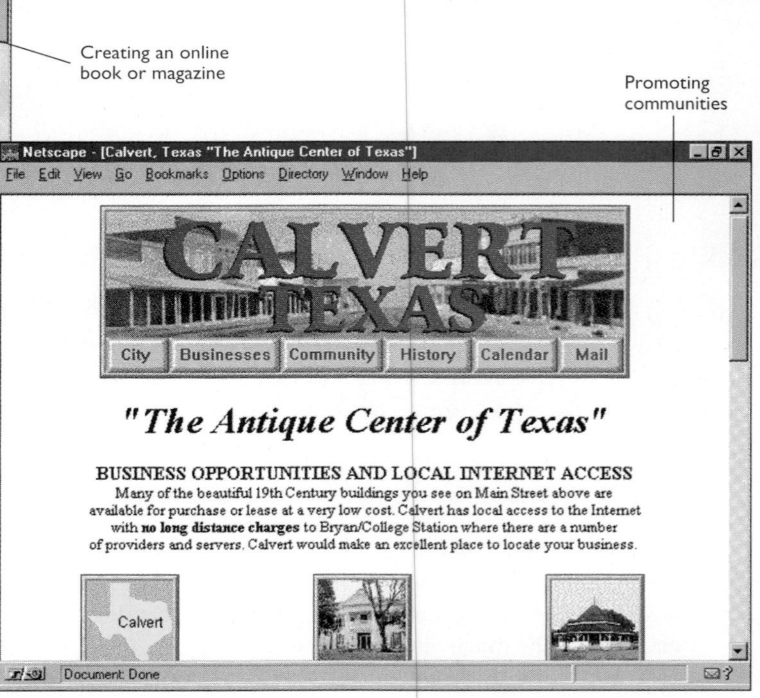

Netscape - [Calvert, Texas "The Antique Center of Texas"]
CALVERT TEXAS
City
Businesses
Community
History
Calendar
Mail
"The Antique Center of Texas"
BUSINESS OPPORTUNITIES AND LOCAL INTERNET ACCESS
Many of the beautiful 19th Century buildings you see on Main Street above are available for purchase or lease at a very low cost. Calvert has local access to the Internet with no long distance charges to Bryan/College Station where there are a number of providers and servers. Calvert would make an excellent place to locate your business.
Calvert

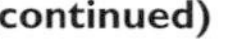

FIGURE NET 3-1
(continued)

Developing a Publishing Plan

You need to spend time thinking about such matters as your purpose, your audience, and the competition as part of developing a *plan* for publishing on the Web. In this planning stage, you size up a prospective Web project before beginning. In other words, you lay out the step-by-step process through which you will develop your own Web pages, as well as the project's benefits and costs. A thoughtful plan will reduce the chance that an unexpected event will disrupt your Web-site development experience.

Figure NET 3-2 shows some of the issues you should resolve during the planning stage of Web-page development. As part of this planning, you should check out prospective **Internet presence providers (IPPs)—**the organizations whose servers host Web pages. Determine how they set their prices, what types of services they offer to help you create pages, how they would list your site on the Web, and what types of performance statistics they would provide to help you judge traffic at your site. Most providers of Internet services—such as the commercial online services and Internet service providers (ISPs) discussed in Chapter NET 2—also act as IPPs.

As part of your project analysis, you should weigh doing a single home page versus a more substantial presentation of several pages. A single page is easier and less expensive than a larger site to produce—you may even be able to post it for free—but its limited space may not effectively convey your message.

NET

FIGURE NET 3-2

Issues to consider during the planning stage.

Goals

- What is my goal? — If you don't know, neither will your audience.
- Is the Web the best place for achieving my goal?
- What is my timetable for getting my site online?

Reaching Others

- Who is my target audience? — Ask yourself if people are going to want your message or product.
- What other Web products currently exist that interest my audience?
- Can other Web products support mine?

Site Design

- How many pages should my site run? — Don't get too carried away.
- How do other Web pages entice users?
- What is considered good design? Bad design? — Simple and uncluttered go a long way.
- What can I do to make my site different? — It's going the extra mile that can make a site exceptional.

continued

■ **Internet presence provider (IPP).** An organization whose servers host Web pages.

(continued)

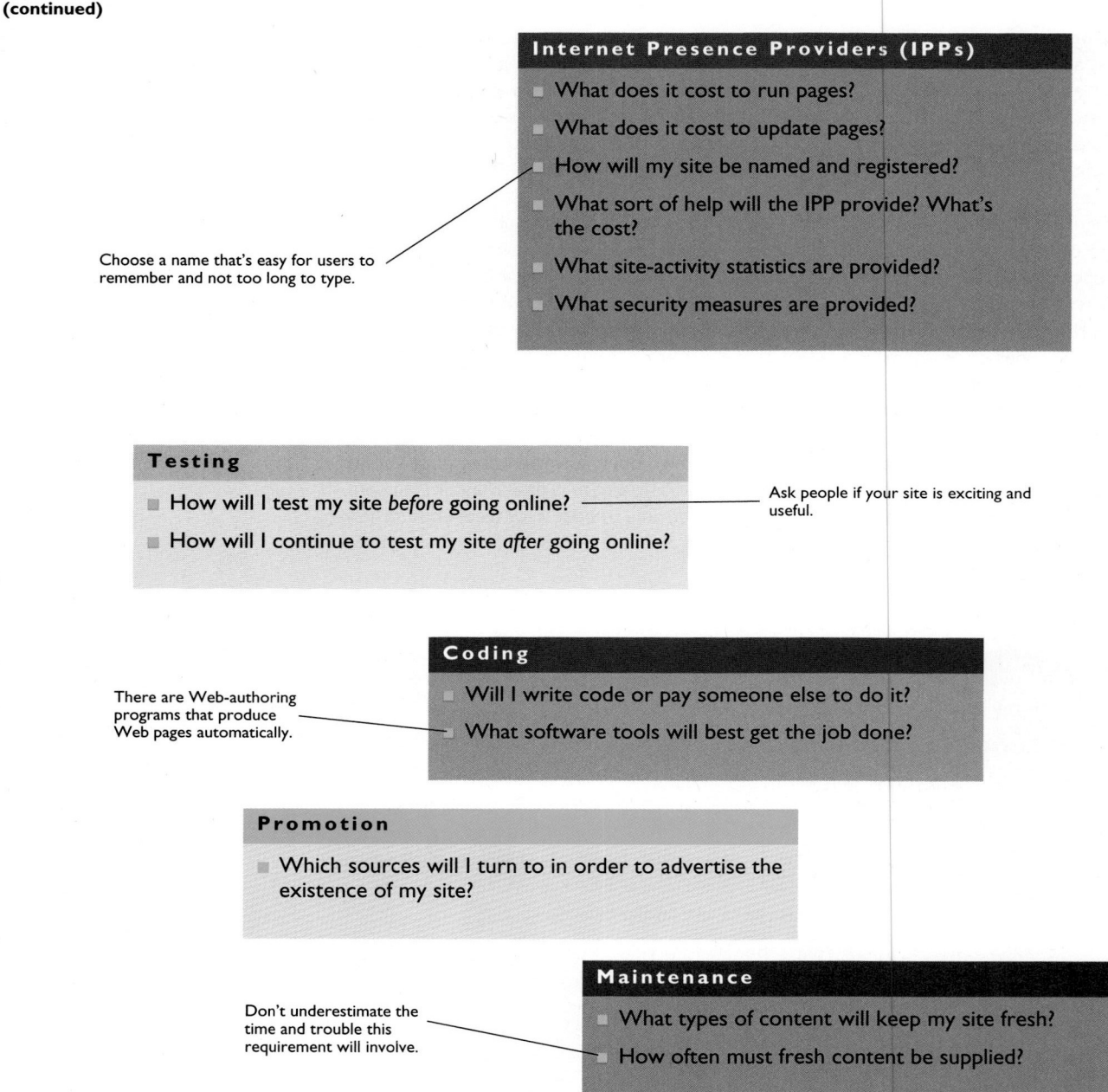

Internet Presence Providers (IPPs)

- What does it cost to run pages?
- What does it cost to update pages?
- How will my site be named and registered?
- What sort of help will the IPP provide? What's the cost?
- What site-activity statistics are provided?
- What security measures are provided?

Choose a name that's easy for users to remember and not too long to type.

Testing

- How will I test my site *before* going online?
- How will I continue to test my site *after* going online?

Ask people if your site is exciting and useful.

Coding

- Will I write code or pay someone else to do it?
- What software tools will best get the job done?

There are Web-authoring programs that produce Web pages automatically.

Promotion

- Which sources will I turn to in order to advertise the existence of my site?

Maintenance

- What types of content will keep my site fresh?
- How often must fresh content be supplied?

Don't underestimate the time and trouble this requirement will involve.

Other

- Do I have permission to use materials I don't own?
- Will my site in any way offend others?
- Am I asking for information over the Web that would better be collected by phone or in writing?
- Will the benefits accruing from the site exceed the costs?

This is the ultimate question to ask: What's the "bottom line?"

Designing Your Site

Design refers to the process of planning what your Web site will look like and how it will work. Again, remember the catchphase "look before you leap." You don't have to be a professional designer to create Web pages that are both attractive and effective. However, you must invest some time to discover differences that separate good design from bad design.

PRINCIPLES OF WEB DESIGN

Every professional Web-page designer would probably agree with the following two statements: (1) Users like interesting, exciting, and intuitive sites; (2) to hold an audience, you must keep refreshing your site content with new information.

A site is *interesting* if it provides information with value to its target audience; visitors find it *exciting* if it rewards them with a stimulating experience. Unfortunately, interest and excitement wear off over time. If visitors see the same old information at your site day after day or week after week, boredom will set in and they will stop coming.

Intuitive means that pages are easy to use and that the site presents information in a way that makes sense. For instance, users understand more intuitively what to do with a noun-specific hyperlink such as this:

Would you like us to send a **brochure?**

as opposed to an ambiguous reference like this:

Click **here** to get a copy of our brochure.

Web surfers generally don't have much patience; if they have a hard time figuring out what your page is all about and how to get around your site, they'll probably just say *hasta la vista,* baby—forever.

One other interesting point affects site design: Web surfers like freebies. You might not be able to offer much, but if you can point users to places where they can get free literature or see other potentially valuable information, or win a coffee cup or a contest that gets their names posted at your next update, your URL is more likely to become a regular destination.

TIPS ON MAKING PAGES SIZZLE

One of the first steps you should take in designing your site is to jump on the Web and surf around it for ideas—page layouts, graphics, backgrounds and colors, navigation buttons, freebies, fill-out forms, and so on. As you learn more about what thrills you about certain Web sites, you gain insight for designing your own.

Some of the most creative sites are those maintained by companies in the entertainment and design businesses. Also, look for the sites of firms with pockets deep enough to commission the best professional designers. Many places both on and off the Web regularly publish the URLs of cool Web sites; stop there on your tour for ideas (see Figure NET 3-3). If you can, use a screen-capture utility program to download onto your hard disk any pages that you wish to study further.

Novice designers may have difficulty identifying some design guidelines just by looking at a few sample pages. One such guideline is the so-called *rule of three.* Professionals who have studied Web users have discovered that most won't find content if it is buried more than three links away from the user's starting screen. Another important rule is to avoid overloading a page with hyperlinks; ten per page is plenty.

■ **Design.** The process that defines the look of a product and how it will work.

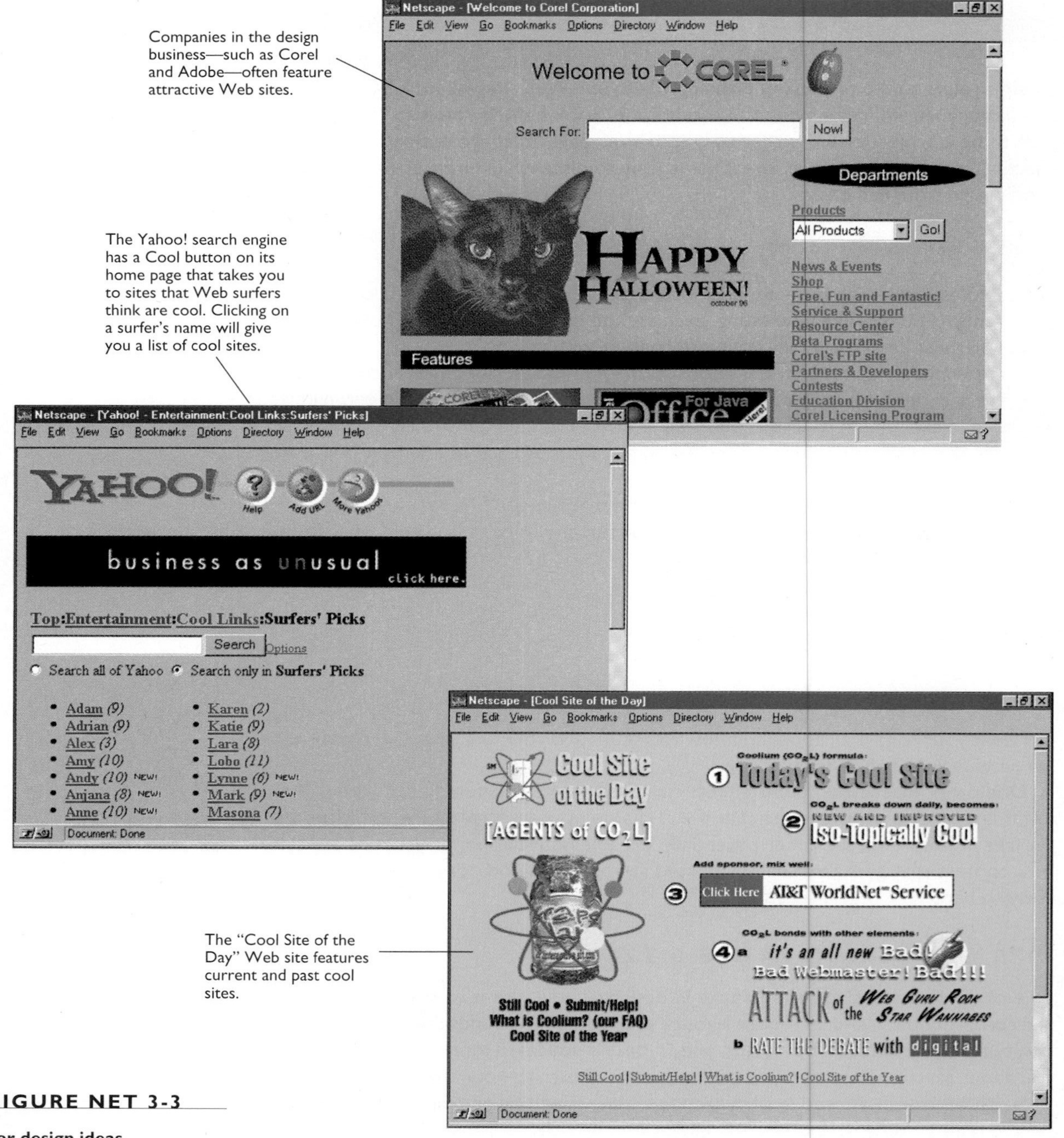

FIGURE NET 3-3

Surfing for design ideas.
Two good sources of ideas are the Web sites of companies in the design business and those that identify "cool Web sites."

Be aware that some of your target audience—maybe even most of it—will not be as smart, sophisticated, or energetic as you are. Not all Web users know how to use a scroll bar, for instance, and those who do often won't bother with it. If you have something critical to provide—like your site URL, e-mail address, and phone number—it's a good idea to place them where users will see them almost as soon as they arrive at your page. Many designers try to avoid scrolling almost entirely by creating *landscape* pages that fit nicely on most desktop displays rather than *portrait* pages that are deeper than their widths, creating a need to scroll.

Keep in mind also that your audience will display your page on any of several different computer platforms. Will most people in your audience have systems that can

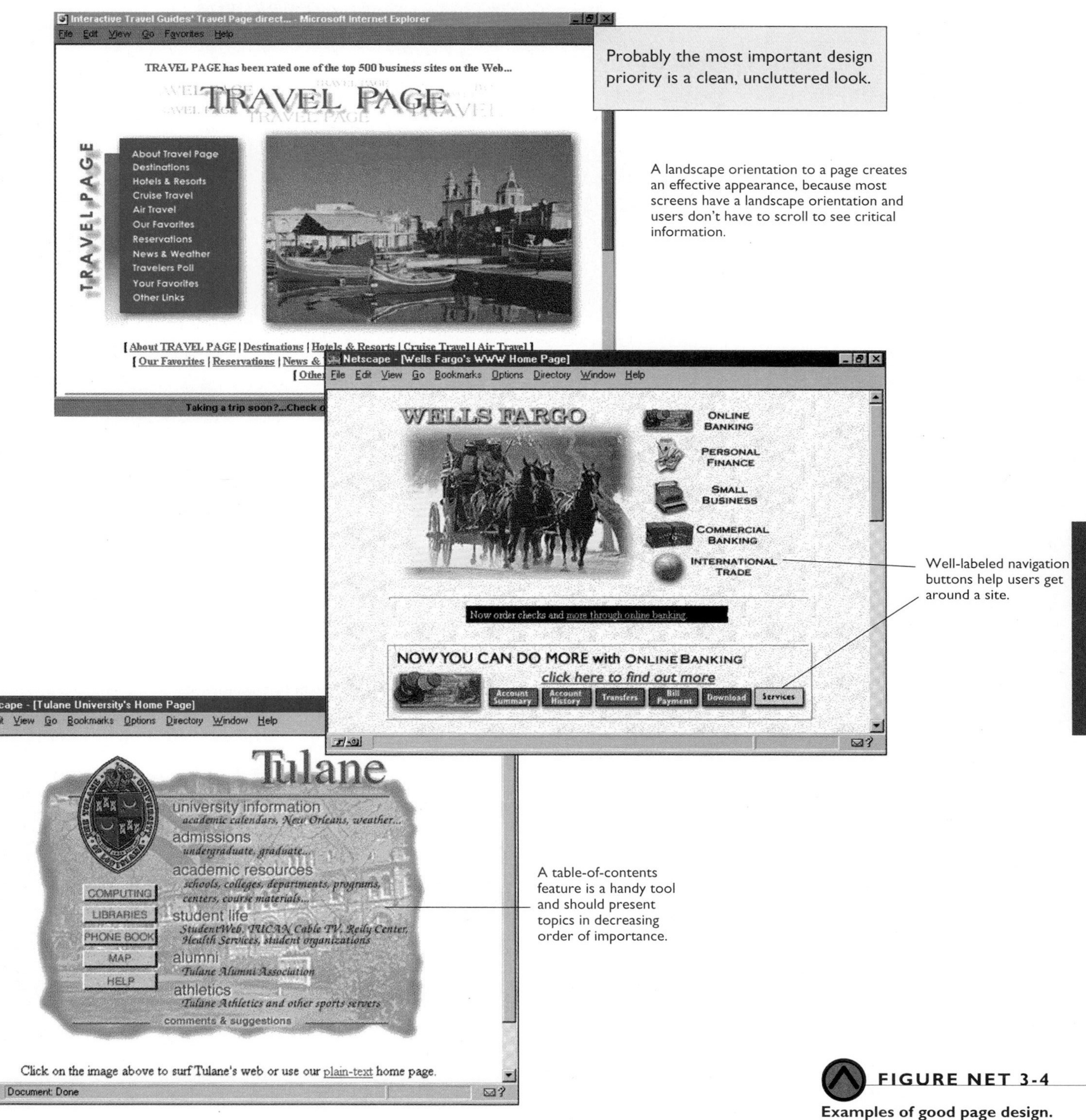

FIGURE NET 3-4

Examples of good page design.

handle MPEG video clips, or should you limit your design to still images, which far more systems can handle? Consider also the patience factor; studies have shown that users do not like to wait any longer than 30 seconds or so for a page to display. In sum, omit exotic screens that only a small fraction of your audience can appreciate.

Figure NET 3-4 shows several attractive pages and highlights some of their design qualities. Figure NET 3-5 provides some examples of practices to avoid.

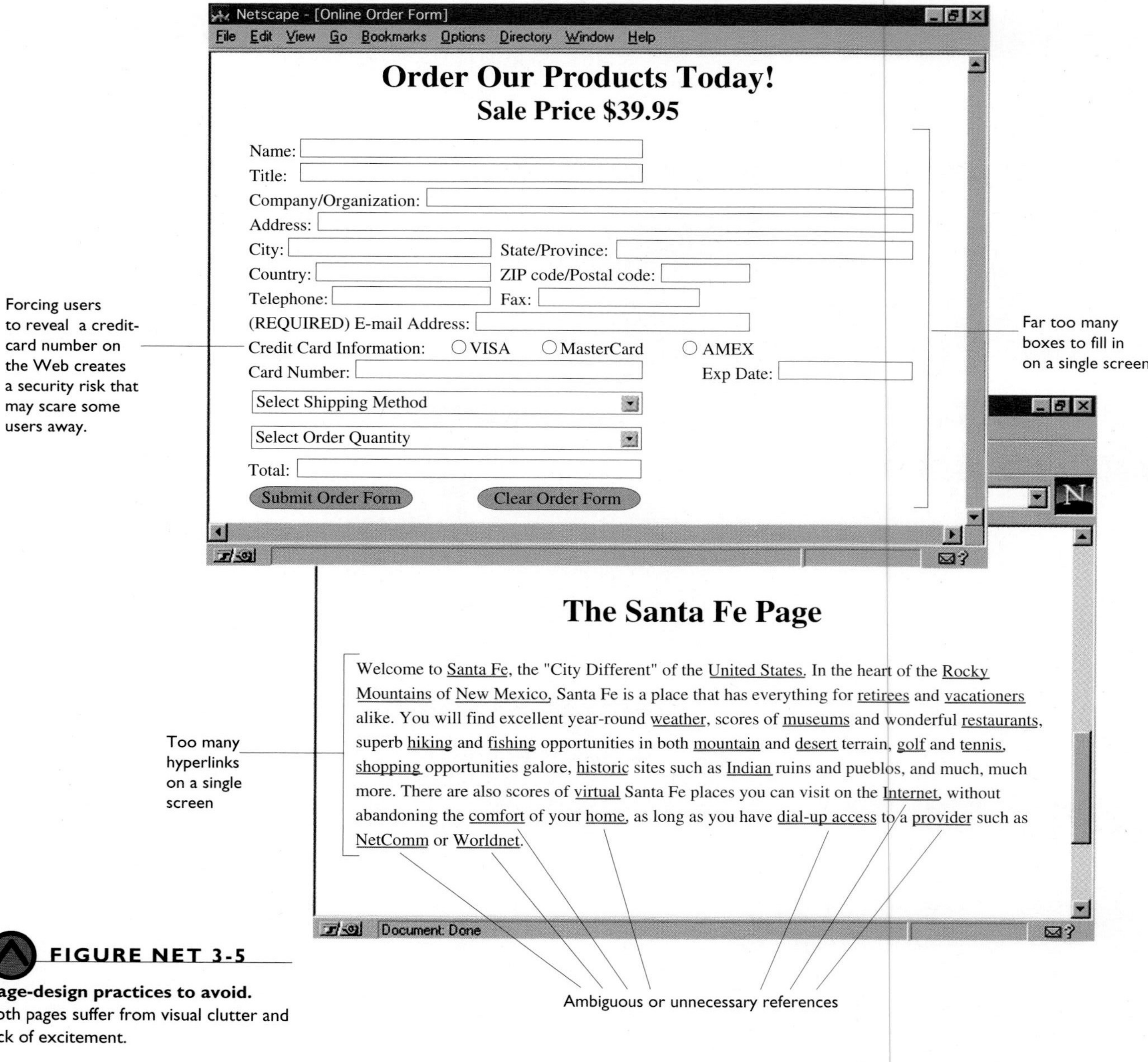

FIGURE NET 3-5

Page-design practices to avoid. Both pages suffer from visual clutter and lack of excitement.

FLOWCHARTS AND STORYBOARDS

If you are developing a substantial Web presentation rather than just a single home page, tools such as flowcharts and storyboards can assist with the design process.

A Web **flowchart** describes how Web pages relate to one another. The top part of Figure NET 3-6 shows a flowchart for a restaurant's Web presentation. Note that each box in the flowchart represents a separate Web page, and the lines between boxes show which pages logically relate to others. Remember that you can hyperlink pages in any way you like; the lines between the flowchart boxes need not represent hyperlinks.

A Web **storyboard** is an ordered series of sketches—done by hand or with the help of software—that show what each page in a Web presentation should look like (see the bottom part of Figure NET 3-6). The storyboard also shows the hyperlinks

■ **Flowchart.** A series of boxes or other symbols, connected by lines, that shows how ideas fit together. ■ **Storyboard.** An ordered series of sketches that show what each page in a presentation should look like.

FLOWCHARTS
A Web flowchart describes how Web pages relate to one another. Each box represents a separate Web page, and the lines between them show which pages logically link.

Flowcharts and storyboards provide useful tools for creating multipage Web sites.

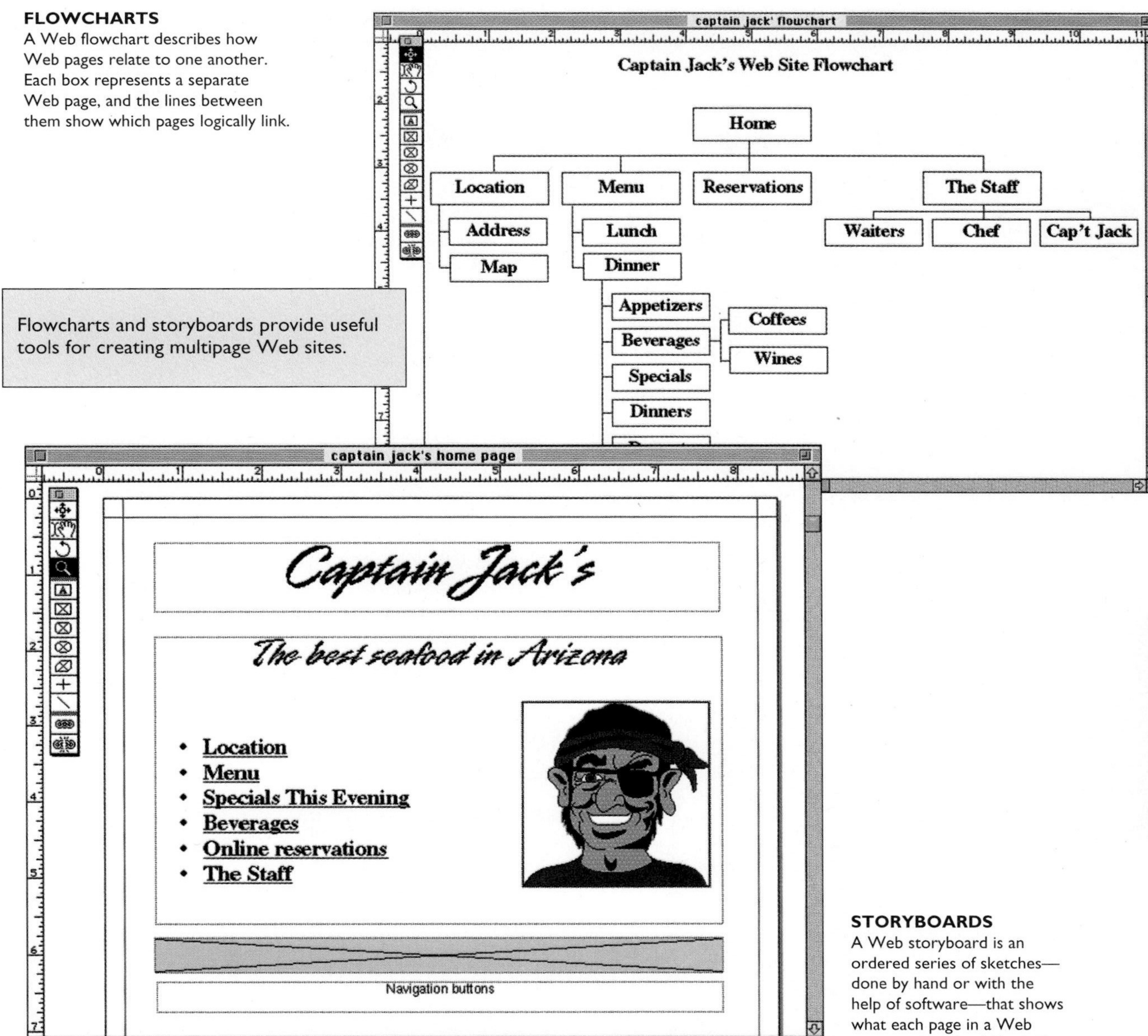

STORYBOARDS
A Web storyboard is an ordered series of sketches—done by hand or with the help of software—that shows what each page in a Web presentation should look like.

FIGURE NET 3-6

A flowchart and storyboard for a restaurant's prospective Web site.

on each page. If you use a software package to set up a storyboard, there's a good chance you can load it into a code-generator program that can create much of the Web-page programming you would otherwise later have to produce.

Tools for Creating Web Pages

After you complete the design of your Web presence, the next step is specifying it in computer code. Several programming languages are available for this task, including HTML and Java. This section looks at such coding tools and at page-authoring alternatives that will enable you to develop Web pages without a single peek at programming-language syntax (or with only a quick glance).

FEATURE NET 3-1

Creating an Exciting Online Résumé

How to Promote Yourself with Web Authoring Skills

Jon Rush—whose story is true, although names are disguised here to protect anonymity—wanted to live the good life. So did Linda, his wife. So the two of them and their two young daughters left the congested California city in which they were living and moved to a small Montana town.

They had one big problem. Neither Jon nor Linda had jobs. But Jon had an outdated computer and modem from his college days and began using it to learn how to surf the Internet. He became intrigued by seemingly ordinary people from all walks of life who could create their own Web pages. He began using the View command on his browser to study the code behind the Web pages appearing on his screen, and he tested pieces of code by simple trial and error. He gained enough knowledge in this way to create an attractive-looking résumé—complete with clever graphics and hyperlinks—and then he posted it on the Web.

Within a week, Jon got a call from someone in a company that provided online educational services. A colleague of the caller had stumbled across Jon's résumé while surfing, and it intrigued her greatly. The company flew Jon out for an interview and hired him on the spot. Montana? No problem—he could work there and upload his output to headquarters by modem. His salary far exceeded what local work would have paid.

This story is likely to be played out in increasing frequency over the next several years. Several factors under your control determine your success in an online job search. They include why you post, where you post, and how you post.

The most important *why* question you must answer is what job objective you want to pursue. You should state it clearly, in specific terms. However, you normally don't want to be too specific. When professionals read résumés, they like to think that the person they may hire is eager to learn, willing to take on new roles as business conditions change, and prepared to do whatever it takes to get the job done.

Most of the people currently hired over the Web get jobs in high-tech fields like the computer industry—although that picture is beginning to change. With more and more people becoming Web literate and the Web becoming more important in everyday business, employers are also reaching across the Web to fill sales, marketing, secretarial, and administrative-assistant positions. While technical people are likely to be dazzled by sophisticated Web-page features, keep in mind that such pages may take a long time to download; impatient types won't wait. Also remember that any sound or video elements will be lost when the résumé is printed out for later inspection. An enduring quality in a résumé is simplicity.

To determine *where* you should post your résumé on the Web, consider your own site or the hundreds of sites maintained by online employment agencies. Such an agency makes a sensible stop for an employer looking to hire—and many of them won't charge you. Some agencies will create a Web page for you for $50 or less, so you don't even need Web access.

How you post your résumé also matters. For instance, make sure to set up your résumé as a separate file that you or someone else can e-mail. Also, include your e-mail address and any URL where others can reach you. If you don't have an e-mail address, your online agency might be able to create a mailbox for you for a nominal fee. Also, make sure your page has a set of clearly labeled jumps, like the one in the accompanying diagram, to save potential employers from having to scroll around to find information.

Employers may wade through résumés with some type of search tool, so flag yours with interest-inducing keywords in the title or description—include nouns of high-demand skills like *Java* and *client-server* computing if they are appropriate. Finally, make sure your agency can provide you with activity statistics on your résumé, such as the number of hits it generated and how much time people spend looking at your résumé.

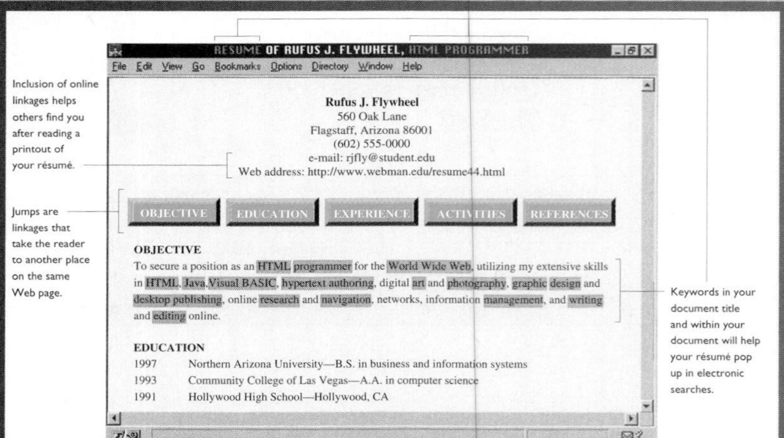

Web résumé. If you're looking for a computer-related job, it's a good first start for demonstrating your skills.

HYPERTEXT MARKUP LANGUAGE (HTML)

Most Web pages today are coded in **hypertext markup language (HTML).** This and other **markup languages** were created to make it possible to rapidly transmit documents over a network using minimal line capacity.

■ **Hypertext markup language (HTML).** The most widely used language for developing Web pages. ■ **Markup language.** A language made up of tags or symbols that describe what document elements should look like when displayed.

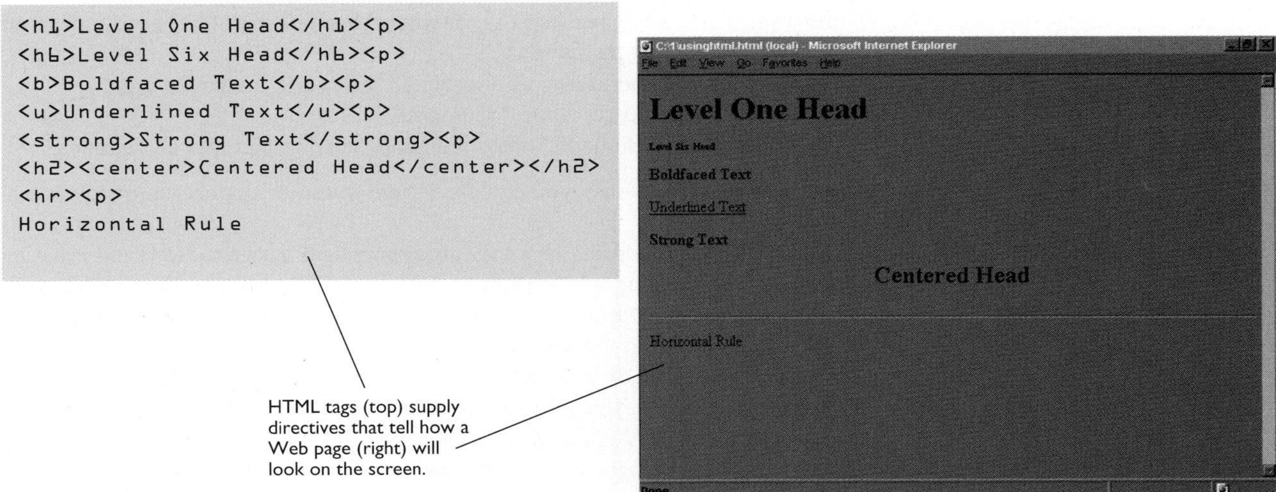

HTML tags (top) supply directives that tell how a Web page (right) will look on the screen.

Sample HTML Tags

HTML tag	Purpose
<html>	Starts and ends an HTML program
<title>	Provides a page title
<h#> (# a digit from 1-6)	Formats a heading in a type size larger or smaller than that used in the main body of text
<p>	Marks the end of a paragraph
<img>	Designates an imported picture file
<a>	Creates a hypertext link
<b>	Boldfaces text
<i>	Italicizes text
<u>	Underlines text
<strong>	Makes letters more intense
<center>	Centers text and graphics
<hr>	Puts a horizontal rule across the page

Some HTML tags begin with backslashes (/) to toggle off certain features. For instance, </b> turns off boldfacing.

NET

FIGURE NET 3-7

HTML tags. People who have learned HTML say it is one of the easiest languages to pick up.

For instance, consider a server computer sending the banner headline "Martians Invade the Earth" in 18-point boldfaced Goudy type over the telephone lines to a desktop-client computer. Large fonts such as this require lots of storage, and all of those extra bytes take transmission time. Markup languages address this transmission problem by sending the Martian-invasion headline over the wires in regular type *marked* as a "title" (i.e., text to appear in very large type). The client workstation's browser then determines the particular display font and figures out how large "very large" type should be.

The strength of markup languages is also their main weakness. Because they simplify pages to send them rapidly, they also can produce some unexpected surprises. For instance, small type that might just barely be discernible on your screen might look like an unreadable mess on another. Web browsers do offer ways, however, to control the look of a screen document. They typically achieve this goal with browser plug-in programs such as Adobe Acrobat, as discussed in the previous chapter.

An example of an HTML program, the Web page it produces, and some sample HTML commands are shown in Figure NET 3-7. Note that HTML command instructions, or **tags,** are contained within angled brackets (<>), while the actual text that will appear on the page lies outside the brackets. Tags perform such tasks as:

■ **Tag.** An HTML code that sends a document-formatting instruction to a browser.

- Declaring titles for pages
- Identifying the sizes of headings (e.g., first-level head, second-level head, and so on)
- Marking the ends of paragraphs
- Establishing such text styling as underlined, italic, and boldfaced type
- Setting up hyperlinks to other documents
- Inserting complex elements into documents, such as pictures and sounds

Tags are *not* case sensitive; you can type them in either uppercase or lowercase letters.

HTML is widely considered a very easy programming language to learn and use. One of the principal ways that people learn to program in HTML is by identifying Web pages they find attractive and studying the HTML code that produced the pages. You can usually find the HTML program for any of the Web documents appearing on your browser through a View command on your browser's main menu (see Figure NET 3-8).

The version of HTML that works on your browser supports a specific HTML *standard* (such as HTML Version 3.0). It probably also contains several useful *HTML extensions,* tags that perform operations beyond those of the standard. You should

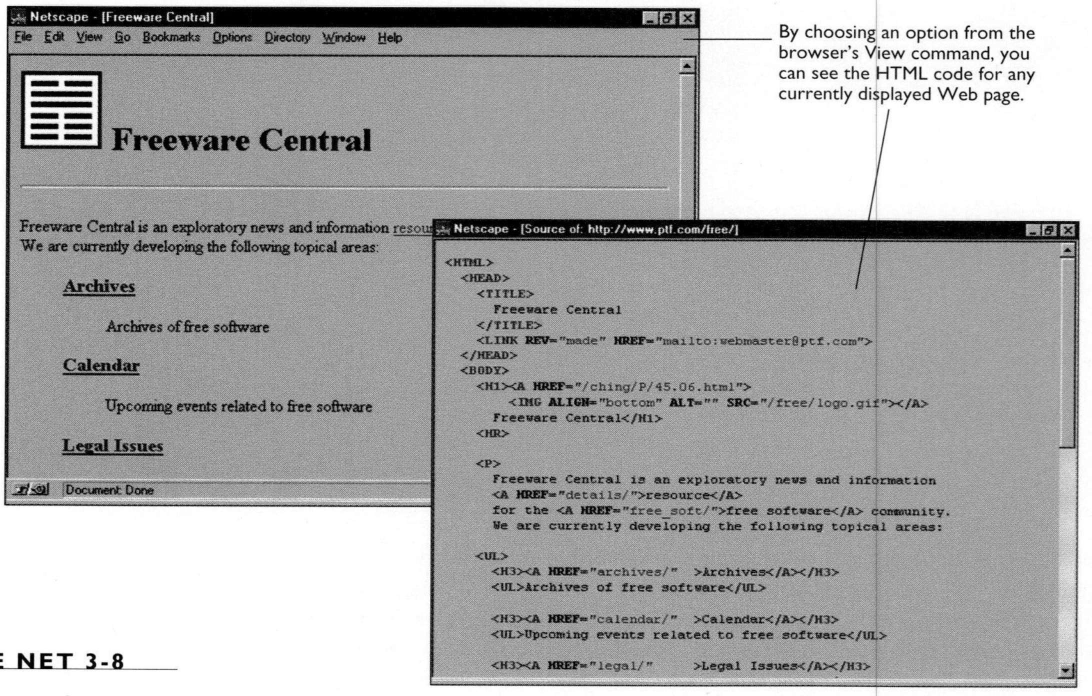

FIGURE NET 3-8

Browser View command.

be wary of relying on a browser's extensions; while they may produce stunning pages with that particular browser configuration, other systems without the extensions will consequently ignore them when processing HTML documents. Web sites often display warnings such as "This site optimized for Netscape Navigator 4.0." This statement means that the site was created using HTML extensions that only a Netscape Navigator 4.0 browser understands.

You can create HTML programs using a *text editor* such as Windows 95's Notepad, a Web browser, or a word-processing program such as Word or WordPerfect. Increasingly, productivity software packages of all types include such tools for Web-page development as *HTML editors,* which this chapter covers shortly. These tools enable you to produce HTML pages without programming in HTML.

A detailed treatise on HTML is beyond the scope of this chapter. If you are interested in learning this language, bookstores carry several good books on the subject—

ranging from ones that promise to get you coding in HTML in 10 days or less to more exhaustive treatments. Several guides for learning HTML are also located on the World Wide Web itself (see Project 7 at the end of the chapter).

JAVA, ACTIVEX, AND SCRIPTING LANGUAGES

Markup languages such as HTML are principally designed for laying out Web pages, much as a desktop-publishing program is designed for laying out printed pages. Thus, HTML has minimal programming tools to create Web pages that change as the user looks at them or to enable users to interact with Web pages on their screens. HTML will let users link to other Web pages via hyperlinks and help launch plug-in or helper programs, but that's about the extent of its nonlayout capabilities. If you want to develop pages with dynamic instead of static content, you'll have to go to tools such as Java, ActiveX, or a scripting language.

Java **Java,** a language developed at Sun Microsystems, was created to add dynamic content to Web pages. It does this by enabling a Web-page developer to code small programs, called **applets,** that supplement the contents of HTML pages. Java applets can be read and executed by any Java-enabled desktop browser (see Feature NET 3-2).

Here's a simple example that shows how a language such as Java can provide dynamic content to Web pages: A user calls up the home-loan Web page of a mortgage company. The page contains a form to fill in various pieces of data about requirements for a mortgage loan. It also comes with an applet that computes for the user monthly payments and other useful loan information based on this input data. When the user finishes filling in the form, he or she selects a Calculate Mortgage Payment button. The button activates the applet, which inputs numbers to a Java-written calculator that figures the payments on the spot.

The applet is originally downloaded from the server with the Web page, so calculations employ the processing capacity of the user's workstation, eliminating delays for access to a remote computer. Wonder what the monthly payment will be with a different down payment and interest rate? Just enter new figures into the form and recalculate. Later, when the Web page disappears from the user's computer, so does the applet.

Applets provide all sorts of interesting possibilities for Web applications—for instance, adding animated cartoons to a page. When such a page is summoned to the user's screen, the program runs and the cartoon moves. A variation on this is the flashing message that changes every couple of seconds (see Figure NET 3-9). A real-time news ticker is another example—an applet scrolls the latest headlines, sports scores, and weather forecasts through a small screen window.

You can liven up your own Web pages with applets by choosing among several options. One is learning how to write program code in a language such as Java or one of its main competitors in the marketplace. Another is downloading free generic applets from the Web. If you do this, make sure you scan the applet code with virus-vaccination software before using it to make sure it doesn't contain anything that will make your system crash.

ActiveX **ActiveX,** developed by Microsoft Corporation, is a set of controls that provides an alternative to Java for creating interactivity on a Web page. In a nutshell, ActiveX extends object linking and embedding (OLE)—also developed by Microsoft and adopted widely as a standard by the software industry—to work on the Web. OLE permits you to take such actions as launching a spreadsheet from your word processor and vice versa. It also lets you copy and paste spreadsheet *objects* such as

NET

■ **Java.** A programming language, created at Sun Microsystems, that adds interactive or dynamic features to Web pages. ■ **Applet.** A small program that provides a dynamic or interactive quality to a Web page. ■ **ActiveX.** A set of controls that enables programs or content of virtually any type to be embedded within a Web page.

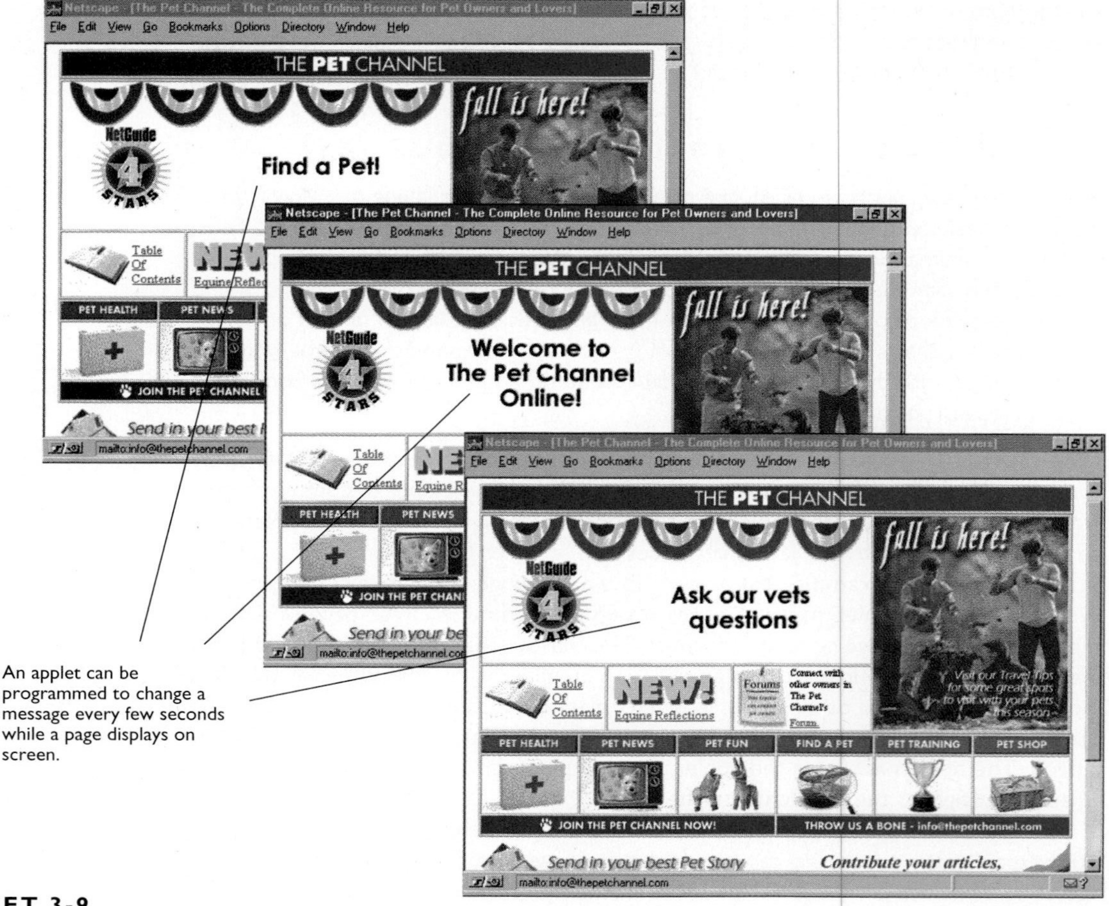

FIGURE NET 3-9

An applet at work. One of the most common uses of applets today is to flash changing messages across an area of the screen while a page is being viewed.

charts and tables into your word-processed document. Put in a more general way, OLE is a containering method that lets you nest any OLE-supported applications inside of each other as you are preparing a document. ActiveX, in extending OLE to the Web, allows you to do such things as launch your word processor or spreadsheet from your Web browser and share objects among applications.

An ActiveX component can be virtually any type of object—a Java applet, a C++ program, an animation, a PowerPoint presentation, and so on. Software that supports ActiveX sets up any such object as an interactive component on the Web page; thus, ActiveX forms the "glue" that holds the page elements together. What ActiveX in effect allows Web publishers to do is grab files from their hard disks that are suitable for the Web and drop them directly into HTML documents. Such a capability is especially useful for office intranets, where a lot of potential Web-page content already exists in office documents.

Scripting Languages A third way that Web-page developers can supply interactivity to a page is through a **scripting language.** Such languages enable you to build programs, or *scripts,* directly into HTML page code. Scripts handle actions like checking the accuracy of information a user has entered into the page—say, a name, address, and credit-card number. Also, if your Web pages are going to use free-standing applets that are independent of your HTML pages, scripts can form the threads that connect the pages to the applets.

■ **Scripting language.** A programming language that assists with supplying interactive or dynamic content to HTML documents.

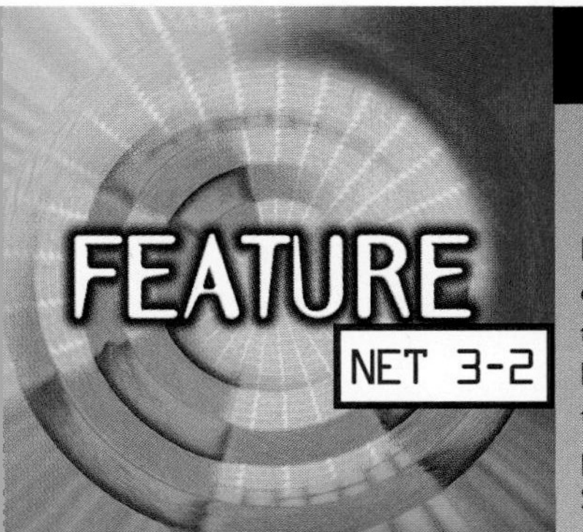

Java

Will It Fulfill Expectations?

Every few years or so, a hardware or software product comes along that sets the computer world buzzing with excitement. One of the latest such products is Java, a programming language created at Sun Microsystems.

Java was designed to enable programs written in it to run on many different computer platforms, without special accommodation. Such a feat is widely considered to be a big deal in computer programming—generally, programs need modification to port them (translate their code to accommodate system differences) from one computer to another. On the Internet, where countless different equipment configurations mingle, a *machine-independent language* is an especially big plus.

Java is a comprehensive language that can be used to create either Java applets or Java applications. *Java applets* are short programs that are embedded into HTML-coded Web pages to give them interactive features. Applets are designed to be downloaded from a server computer onto a Java-enabled Web browser—such as Netscape Navigator or Microsoft Internet Explorer—running on a PC workstation. Applets reside on servers in a machine-independent "bytecode format." This enables the Java interpreters within the browsers to translate the applets into the machine-language code native to the resident workstation for execution. Typically, a Java-enabled browser identifies a Java applet because its code is preceded by the HTML tag <applet>.

Java applications are more substantial programs that can run in either Internet or non-Internet network environments. For instance, a company's programmers could use the language to write programs that might otherwise be written in a language such as C++ or Visual BASIC. Java is based on C++, but it excludes seldom-used features of that language and adds its own system for security—a principal concern for people working on networks.

Java's security features remain to be fully worked out to make it 100 percent safe. Ideally, once a Java applet is downloaded to your computer system, it should not be able to perform such potentially damaging activities as write to your hard disk, directly address memory, or call your operating system or other programs on its own. When such antipenetration measures become strictly enforceable, they will make it difficult if not impossible for a Java applet to implant a virus on your computer system.

Java and ActiveX. The two are the major contenders in the Web-applet battle.

Some people have said that, just as the Web turned the Internet into a giant disk drive, a language such as Java has the potential to turn the Web into a giant computer—one with a never-ending supply of software applications. Others claim that this change will take a long time, because Java applets run much slower on PCs than do native applications. As people begin to create Web documents that contain their own Java or Javalike processors, the difference between applications and applications software may eventually blur.

Java isn't the only alternative for creating applets for the Web. For instance, by using ActiveX controls, users can embed objects from virtually any ActiveX-supported application within an ActiveX-enabled Web page. To date, ActiveX is more machine dependent than Java, working best in a Windows-oriented environment. Also, ActiveX uses a different approach to security than Java, for instance, enabling you to store downloaded code on your hard disk as long as it comes from a preapproved source.

Two of the major scripting languages in use today are Microsoft's VBScript (which is part of the Visual BASIC development environment) and Netscape's JavaScript (which, oddly enough, bears little resemblance to Java).

WEB-AUTHORING PROGRAMS

The coding required in any type of computer programming—HTML, Java, VBScript, and so on—can create a tedious burden that exceeds the capabilities of many would-be

Web-page developers. A variety of Web-authoring programs—commonly called *HTML editors*—are available to ease considerably the job of creating Web pages. An **HTML editor** is a program that simplifies the writing of Web pages by automatically generating HTML statements to accomplish user-specified tasks. Some widely used HTML editors are listed in Figure NET 3-10 along with features they provide.

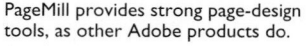

HTML EDITORS	
EDITOR	**PUBLISHER**
FrontPage	Microsoft
Home Page	Claris
HotMetal Pro	SoftQuad International
InContext Spider	InContext
Navigator Gold	Netscape
PageMill	Adobe Systems
SiteMill	Adobe Systems
WebAuthor	Quarterdeck
Web.Designer	Corel

Web authors use editors in many forms, including standard features of browsers or applications software, plug-ins, and stand-alone helper programs.

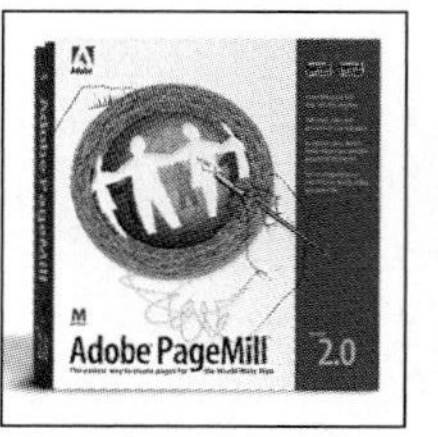

PageMill provides strong page-design tools, as other Adobe products do.

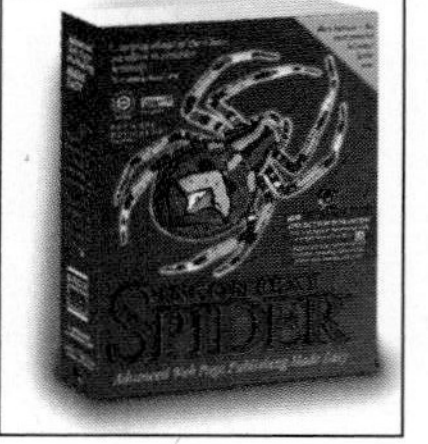
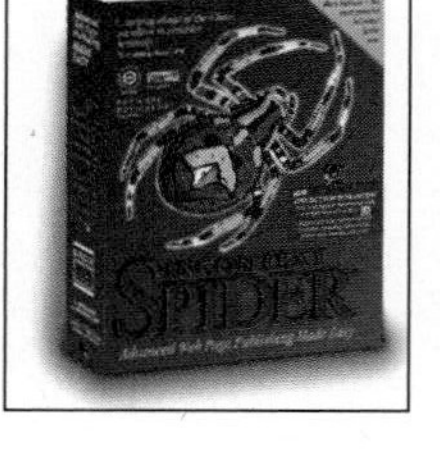

InContext Spider has a feature that helps users understand how HTML pages work.

HotMetal Pro recognizes a wide range of document formats and is popular with advanced users.

COMPONENTS OF HTML EDITORS*
Wizards and templates that make it easy to create Web pages through onscreen selections
Utilities that convert ordinary text documents into Web pages and vice versa
Libraries of frequently used HTML code and graphics
Clip art, backgrounds, and audio clips
Stylesheet features to apply a particular page design to pages
Drag-and-drop tools that let you pull text and graphics stored in other documents on your computer into your HTML documents
Tools for creating such sophisticated Web graphics as imagemaps
Form-filling routines that enable you to create and process interactive forms
Menus for selecting HTML tags, if you want to do HTML coding
Facilities for testing your document
Integration with suite software
*Not all editors include the same components.

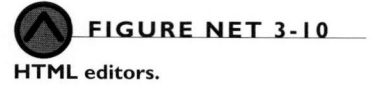

FIGURE NET 3-10

HTML editors.

HTML editors use a variety of strategies to help users create pages. Two principal tools are wizards and converters.

Wizards An *HTML wizard* is a program that automatically generates an HTML document from screen selections made by the user. A wizard offers one of the easiest

■ **HTML editor.** A program that simplifies the creation of Web pages by automatically generating HTML code.

ways to create Web pages, and many IPPs provide wizard software as part of their basic user services. Users of America Online, for instance, have access to a wizard called Personal Publisher (see Figure NET 3-11). Generally, you begin by selecting a template that suggests a basic page design. Then, you successively answer questions

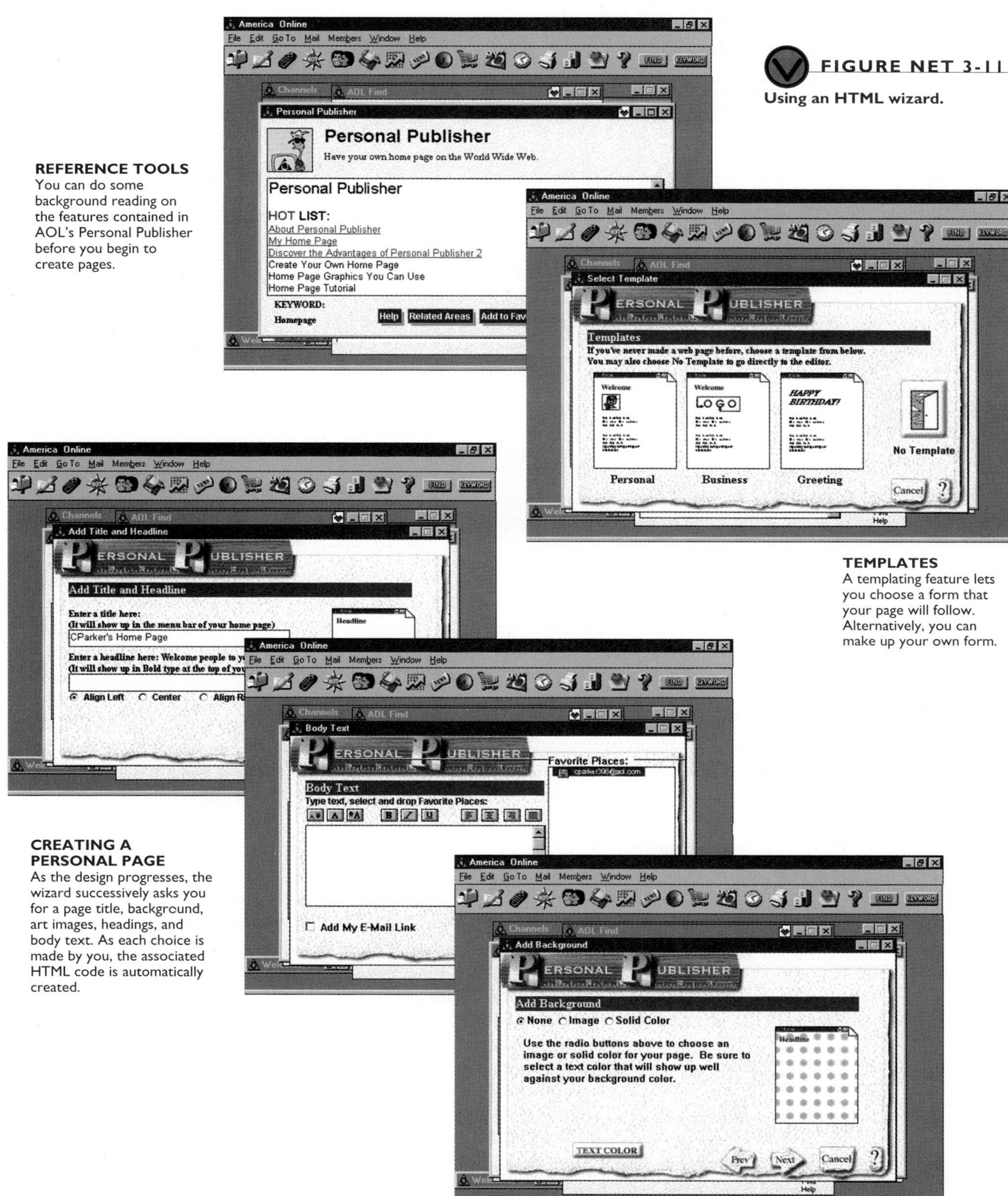

FIGURE NET 3-11
Using an HTML wizard.

REFERENCE TOOLS
You can do some background reading on the features contained in AOL's Personal Publisher before you begin to create pages.

TEMPLATES
A templating feature lets you choose a form that your page will follow. Alternatively, you can make up your own form.

CREATING A PERSONAL PAGE
As the design progresses, the wizard successively asks you for a page title, background, art images, headings, and body text. As each choice is made by you, the associated HTML code is automatically created.

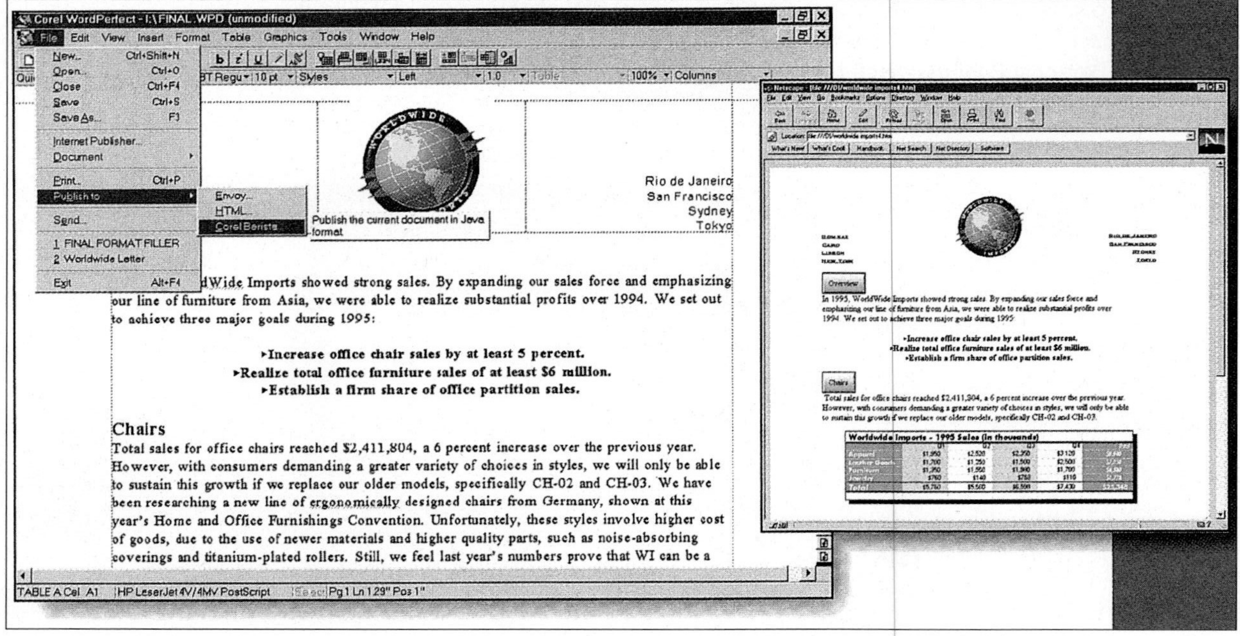

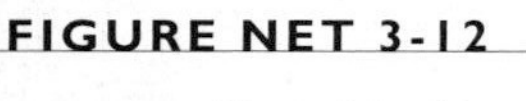

FIGURE NET 3-12

HTML converter. Most of the latest versions of office suites—such as Corel Professional Office—can automatically convert files to and from HTML within core applications.

about your Web-page text and select from libraries of royalty-free clip art and backgrounds. Based on your selections, the wizard generates HTML code for your Web page. Typically, if you don't like what you see on your page, you can edit it either through the wizard or by adding your own HTML directives to the code the wizard has produced.

Converters *HTML converters* work in a different way than wizards. Typically, they are plug-in programs that are designed to produce HTML code from documents already created in other formats. For instance, if your word processor has an HTML converter built into it—and most of the latest ones do—you can turn virtually any word-processed document into an HTML-coded Web page (see Figure NET 3-12). What's more, your browser may contain a similar routine that converts a Web page into text that you can edit with your word processor. Today, not only word processing software but also productivity software of all types—desktop publishing programs, database management systems, you name it—come equipped with HTML converters. In fact, it is becoming increasingly common to find both HTML-wizard and HTML-converter software within the same software packages.

HTML editors will spare you a lot of the tedium of writing HTML code, applets, or scripting components—and they will also ensure that your Web pages work within one or more specific browsing environments. Still, these tools do not substitute completely for knowledge of programming for Web pages. By becoming proficient enough to write your own code, you gain flexibility to create pages that conform to your precise specifications. For instance, if you don't like the page backgrounds a wizard offers or you want blinking lights on a Christmas tree in the corner of your page, you can do your own thing if you know HTML or Java.

While novice developers often find HTML editors sufficient to meet ordinary page-creation needs, professional developers frequently resort to some combination of editors, HTML, Java, ActiveX components, and scripting languages to create Web pages. The editors can provide the basic code for pages quickly, while HTML and interactive supplements can fine-tune the pages to meet more specific needs.

HTML editors on the market provide widely varying functionality, ease of use, and cost. For instance, as already hinted, some are plug-ins or helper programs that are designed to work with specific browsers, while others are stand-alone programs that work independently. One trend is clear—with more and more people wanting to create their own Web sites, you can expect HTML editors to become easier and easier to use.

Testing Your Pages

You must perform a certain amount of testing as you create Web pages. The HTML development tools covered in the previous section will enable you to write code for Web pages from scratch or generate the code, test it in a simulated Web environment to ensure that it produces the results you want, and modify it as a result of the tests.

Now, let's say you've finished creating your Web page, and it looks good on your screen. At this point, you should conduct some further tests.

Recall that different browsers implement different versions of HTML. You may also remember reading that people worldwide have access to Web pages over a wide variety of different computer platforms. Thus, you will need to check out what happens to your page when it appears on systems other than your own. You can't test every browser in the world, but you can certainly test your page on some of the more common ones—such as Netscape Navigator and Microsoft Internet Explorer. Consider also evaluating your page's support for text-based browsers such as Lynx, if only because a lot of people in the world approach the Web from nongraphical platforms. What's more, some people using graphical browsers turn off the graphics features to speed downloading.

Some programs let you test a page at a variety of common screen resolutions—such as 480 by 640 pixels, 800 by 600 pixels, and so on. What's more, some programs will indicate how quickly your pages will download over certain types of Internet connections, such as a 28.8 kbps modem or T1 line. Most important, think about your target audience and the computing environments in which they are likely to be working.

In another testing step, you should seek feedback from friends and/or associates. What do they think of the colors you picked? Did they find any grammatical or spelling errors? The graphics aren't tacky, are they? In addition to getting comments about details, be sure to ask what people think of your site overall. In the end, the most important question may not be how beautiful the screen display looks but whether or not the site works.

Remember that friends often say one thing when their body language suggests another, so observe them working with your site. Do they seem to know what your home page is all about? Are they confused with the navigational buttons or layout?

Testing Web pages is an ongoing activity. One common mistake among page developers results from failure to check from time to time the validity of hyperlinks that reach out from their pages to other parts of the Web. Sites often disappear or change addresses. One of the most frustrating experiences of Web users is pointing and clicking on *dead links* that lead only to error messages.

Promoting and Maintaining Your Web Site

If you've reached this point, you're close to seeing the first results from your efforts. Assuming that you've interacted with your IPP already, getting your Web pages online should be almost as easy as pulling a switch. Your IPP will likely offer software that will easily upload your pages to its own server from your desktop computer. You will also

Selling Art Online

What happens when a professional photographer decides that the Web is a great place to open an art gallery? He develops his own—where he and several artist clients can showcase and sell their work—and then uses the experience to become a multiple-award-winning Website designer and consultant. Ed LaBane of Santa Fe, New Mexico, confesses that he knew very little about computers before he began to get involved with the Web back in 1995. Neither did many other people, so Ed had to get more involved than he had intended in order to get precisely the type of site he wanted—one that exhibited photographs and paintings in an unusually attractive setting. The site also had to ensure that no one could "steal" art by downloading it in print form, had to maintain security for credit-card transactions, and had to provide useful IPP site statistics as marketing feedback to clients.

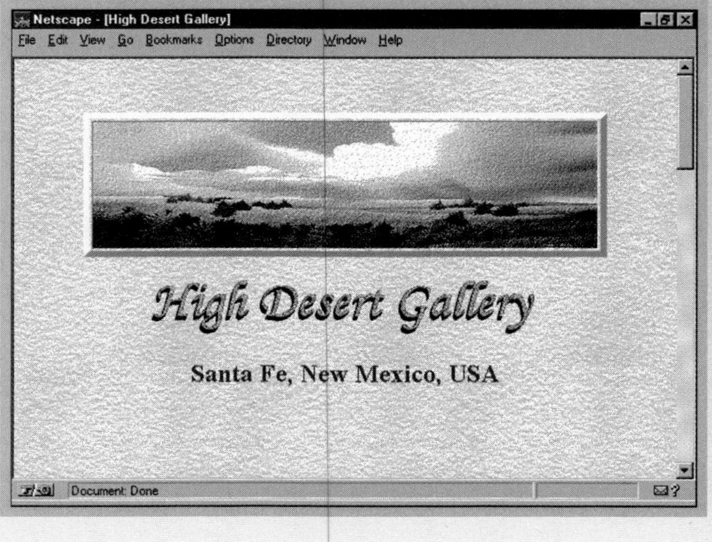

need to set up a permanent address on your IPP's server so people can reach you on the Web. This process differs from the one for setting up a *user* account, which does not receive a permanent Web address. You should arrange to set up a permanent address through your IPP during the planning stage or at least well before you are ready to go online with your Web site.

Promoting Your Site *Promotion* of your site—that is, advertising its whereabouts—provides a critical connection to people you want to find you. One of the best ways to promote your site is a listing with a search engine—as many as you can—such as Yahoo!, WebCrawler, Lycos, and so on. The organizations that produce search engines typically let you fill out online forms on which you describe your site to them. In your description, you should provide keywords—mostly nouns—that you expect people to enter when looking for a site like yours as well as the URLs that link to those keywords. If you've developed a Web site for a fishing-tackle-and-outfitter business in Boise, Idaho, for instance, you want to make sure that people can find it through such informative words as fishing, trout, hobby, outfitter, outdoor, recreation, Boise, and Idaho.

As another useful form of promotion, you might pursue listings on any *trailblazer pages* that deal with the subject of your site. A trailblazer page is a "metaindex" that provides a comprehensive list of Web resources on a given subject (refer back to Figure NET 3-1). Returning to the fishing-tackle-and-outfitter business example, you would want to locate as many trailblazer sites as you could devoted to fishing, trout, and related subjects. E-mail the administrators of those sites about adding your URL to their lists. The easiest way to locate trailblazer sites is through a Web search engine or by looking for possible matches to your subject area in a comprehensive book like the *Internet Yellow Pages.*

You may want to consider several other promotional options. You might arrange for a storefront in a cybermall, post messages to newsgroups and mailing lists that touch on your subject matter, and print your site URL and e-mail address on your business cards and letterheads.

Maintaining Your Site Visitors will come back to your Web site regularly if you constantly refresh it with interesting or exciting information. This is another planning issue that requires careful attention during an early stage of development. What type of information needs refreshing? How often? What will your IPP charge for site updates? Be warned that maintenance can take considerable time.

Your IPP should willingly supply activity statistics showing how much interest your Web site is generating. One such statistic is the number of **hits** your page receives, or the number of file accesses each page generates when it appears on someone's screen. Judge this potentially misleading statistic with care. A *hit counter,* which records the number of hits, usually will not tell you directly how many visitors came to your site. For example, a visit to a page with four graphics files on it will typically generate five hits—one for the page and one each for the graphics files that the server had to download along with it. A hit counter also cannot tell you how long visitors hung around at your site, whether visitors just passed through on their way elsewhere, or whether visitors represent new or repeat customers. Several new software tools attempt to deduce from hit data more useful statistics, such as the number of visitors per period and the number of times each Web page is visited during a period.

Many IPPs will also provide a summary showing the number of times each *link* at your site was accessed as well as a log that chronicles when each such access was recorded. From such information, you can determine just how far down into your site—and where—users are going. The log showing the precise time each hit took place can help you determine whether those graphics that seem to take forever to download are working as you had hoped or users are bypassing them. Also, if your site has several pages, you may be able to calculate the time a visitor lingers on a page or have your IPP tell you the average time spent on each page visit and average number of pages viewed per visit.

Some IPPs will also give you analysis of accesses by region or by country. Two other useful pieces of information an IPP can provide is the URL of the page a visitor was viewing prior to coming to your site and the type of browser and operating system the visitor was using. When you're trying to attract people, it helps to know how they are finding out about you. Knowing the types of platforms they are most likely to be using is useful because you always have the option of optimizing viewing for certain platforms.

It's a good idea to check with an IPP about the types of statistics it provides for free and which others it offers for a fee; again, well before you begin to design your pages or sign up for service. If you are developing sites for clients, you can turn information on how people are reacting to their presence into a valuable marketing tool (see User Solution NET 3-1).

As part of your maintenance routine, you may want to include some type of form that users can fill out to give you their opinions (see Figure NET 3-13). Information supplied on such forms can give you an excellent profile of your users. Most users like to be rewarded for extra work, so you may want to consider an offer to entice them to fill out the form—say, free literature or a small prize. Forms are interactive components that require scripting commands; however, many HTML editors have this detail covered with built-in routines that will enable you to handle forms without having to do any programming.

FIGURE NET 3-13

A form to solicit information from users. Informational forms should never ask too many questions. Also, they should provide escapes within each question for users who may not want to supply certain types of facts (such as a credit-card number or phone number).

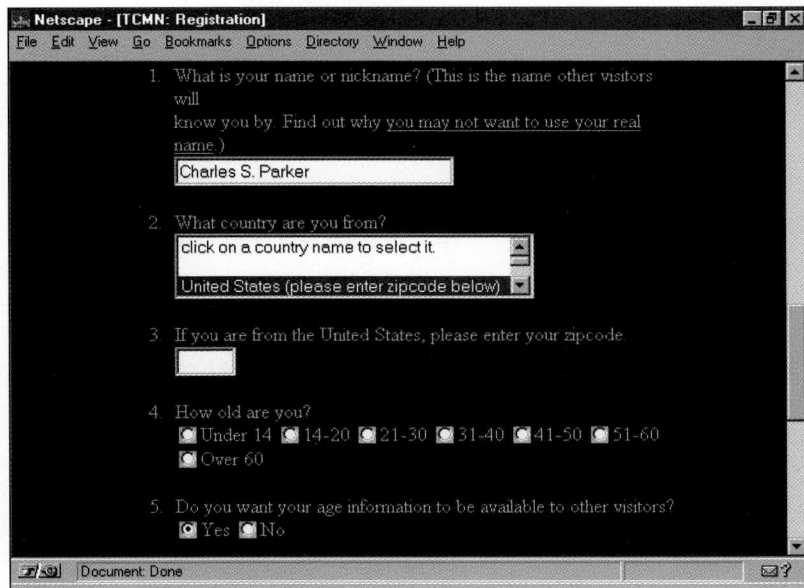

NET

■ **Hit.** One request for access to a page or a graphics file made to a server computer.

Publishing-Related Issues

As you develop your Web site, you should consider many publishing-related issues. Three of the most important are copyrights, censorship, and security.

COPYRIGHTS

Rights to control intellectual property such as books and movies are protected in the United States by copyright laws. Most of these laws were enacted well before the age of computers. Consequently, confusion prevails in legal circles about how these laws apply to materials on the Internet.

Here's an example: U.S. copyright law forbids anyone from copying books or movies and then selling the copies for a profit without the permission of the owners. Bookstores can't print their own copies of this textbook and sell them. They have to pay the publisher of this book for copies; the publisher, in turn, compensates the author. A provision in copyright law does allow *fair use,* in which someone may copy small portions of this book or any other protected work for such noncommercial purposes as teaching, news, parody, or criticism. Fair use has also been successfully extended in recent years to people making videotaped copies of television programs for viewing later at a more convenient time.

Publishers of all types dread the possibility that the Internet will allow people to set up Web sites to distribute books, movies, and music that the publishers own and want to sell elsewhere. Publishers claim that even if such unauthorized sites didn't take money in return for such services, they could have a devastating effect on sales. Historically, copyright laws have supported this viewpoint. Outside of fair use, when you use the creative work of another in a way that impairs the owner's profits, you are taking a big risk.

On the other side of the fence are people who want the Web clear of government interference. They claim that many copyright fears are overhyped and that the legal community, with its conflicting priorities, could wind up destroying the very fabric of the Web itself. For instance, the law might interpret even looking at a copy of a copyright-protected work over the Internet as a criminal act; this creates the possibility that even a person who casually surfs onto such a work may be guilty of a crime, since downloading can be construed as copying.

Expect the legal battle regarding copyrights to continue for some time. Members of the online community have proposed solutions to the copyright problem including self-policing and setting up arbitration agencies to deal with disputes. To be on the safe side as a Web publisher, you should ask permission to use any materials that are not your own—except those that are specifically designated in writing as royalty-free resources.

One final point: While copyright laws forbid copying the protected work of someone else and selling it for profit, they don't extend to copying an *idea* here and there. This protection has allowed companies to refine product features introduced elsewhere, as when Microsoft developed its Windows software. Many critics have claimed Windows is a knockoff of the graphical user interface pioneered by the Apple Macintosh—and much earlier by Xerox. Consequently, you can copy ideas from other Web pages. But beware—while copyright laws let you copy ideas here and there, they expressly forbid you to copy a sophisticated sequence of ideas.

CENSORSHIP

The First Amendment to the U.S. Constitution guarantees a citizen's right to free speech. This protection allows people to say or show things to others without fear of arrest. People must observe some limits to free speech, of course, such as prohibitions of obscenity over the public airwaves and dealing in child pornography.

But how should the law react to alleged patently offensive or indecent materials on the Internet, where they can be observed by surfing children and the public at large? The courts recently struck down the Communications Decency Act, which proposed making such actions illegal. The courts have so far had difficulty defining just what is "patently offensive" and "indecent." What's more, they have concluded that numerous self-policing mechanisms now available at the *client* level reduce the need for new laws that restrict content made available at the *server* level. For instance, a large selection of **blocking software** on the market allows users to block from view materials on the Internet that are objectionable to them or to family members.

Blocking-software packages work in a variety of ways. Many commercial online services automatically censor portions of the Internet with their own software. Some also provide tools that let each user do his or her own blocking. Users can also acquire blocking software on their own, independently of their provider. The software may suggest a list of subjects or keywords that will automatically prevent access to a site; typically, you can trim or add to this list. For instance, parents could block their home computer from displaying information on sex, drugs, bomb making, or hate literature if any of those topics were not already censored by their service provider. Many of the latest browsers also allow users to block access in one way or another.

Despite the failure so far of the Communications Decency Act, the censorship battle surrounding the Internet continues to rage. Arguments against censorship point out that policing the Internet effectively would require prohibitively expensive and difficult effort. Arguments for censorship claim that blocking software assumes computer-literate parents, and many do not and never will meet this standard. In all likelihood, say many industry experts, the Internet will wind up policing itself, as the movie industry does, at least in the short term. (If the situation doesn't improve, harsher measures may follow.)

Momentum is building within the Internet community to create an identification and rating system for Web sites. For instance, a site might voluntarily rate its content on a scale of 0 to 4 on each of several dimensions—such as language, nudity, sex, and violence. Users could automatically assign noncomplying sites 4 ratings on all scales. Enabled desktop software, such as a browser, would let users establish the maximum number on each dimension that they would tolerate, placing these controls in password-protected files, out of the reach of children. When anyone navigated the Internet from the user's account, the software would read a site's rating and block access if the rating exceeded the allowable rating.

As a prospective Web publisher, you should be aware that—law or no law—what you say on the Internet is subject to scrutiny and may come back to haunt you. Even if your site inadvertently uses a word that has an offbeat connotation, you could get blocked from a portion of your target audience. Not too long ago, for instance, a well-known service provider blocked access to sites that included the keyword "breast," unintentionally severing earnest users from information about breast cancer. Remember also that many people are turned off by bad taste, so even though you reach them, you may not hold their attention for long. Worse yet, they may complain to your IPP, who may curtly inform you to change or leave.

SECURITY

One of your concerns as a prospective Web publisher should center on securing your Web pages—and any transactions that occur over those pages—from transmission errors and unauthorized uses. You can secure pages in several ways; if you have a sensitive application, you should check with your IPP to determine what types of protections are available. The Tomorrow box discusses several security methods now in use.

NET

■ **Blocking software.** A program that blocks access to certain parts of the Internet deemed objectionable based on predetermined criteria.

TOMORROW

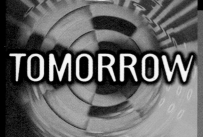

Electronic Commerce

The Quest for Security's Magic Bullet

In the early 1980s, when the first PCs began appearing in large numbers on desktops, many bankers and merchants felt a new heyday of electronic commerce with consumers just around the corner. They were disappointed. While companies have used capabilities for banking and purchasing over networks for a long time, consumers have greeted new methods with wariness. Their big reservation focuses on security. TV reports and the newspapers overflow with horror stories of criminals breaking into systems and walking off with money and secret information.

With the popularity of the Internet and World Wide Web at an all-time high over the last couple of years, businesses are making a new push to get consumers—and their money—online. It will probably be some time before most people are comfortable about having their checking or savings account information available online through a public network. However, many consumers are venturing out on the Web to make purchases of goods as companies lower the risks and increase the incentives of doing business there.

Today, you can buy online using any of several payment plans. The plan you use depends on where you shop. Some of the alternatives now being used are listed here:

- CREDIT CARD You can pay for online purchases with a credit card just as you can over the phone. You simply select the goods you want to buy, type in your credit-card number, and the sale is either approved or rejected on the spot. In recent years, VISA and MasterCard have jointly developed the Secure Electronic Transaction (SET) protocol for encrypting credit-card-transaction data (disguising them with secret codes) for safe passage over networks. A *digital signature* method has also been developed to authenticate the identities of buyers and sellers. Credit cards provide a relatively safe payment method for consumers, because credit-card companies are often required by law to limit consumer liability on bogus transactions.
- PAYMENT SERVICES This method is a twist on the credit-card payment system. For it to work, you need a valid credit card, such as VISA or MasterCard, and an e-mail address. At a company called First Virtual, for instance, you set up an account for a small processing fee—such as $2—and get a personal identification number (PIN). When you buy an item from a participating merchant, you supply your encrypted PIN, and the merchant forwards it with the transaction data to First Virtual. First Virtual then e-mails you to confirm the purchase. Upon your approval, your credit card is automatically billed.

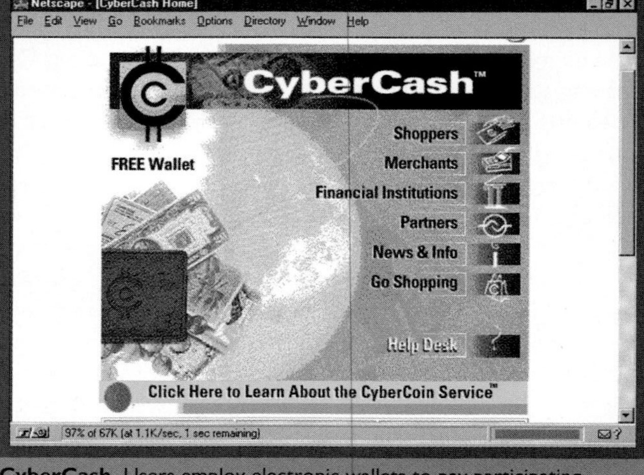

CyberCash. Users employ electronic wallets to pay participating merchants for goods.

- ELECTRONIC WALLETS Various online services set up small accounts for consumers, which are debited for each purchase. One of these, DigiCash's ecash system, loads your PC's memory with virtual money as soon as you sign on. To use the system, you establish an ecash account with any of several participating banks. The ecash is then stored as data on your PC and transferred in secure form to a merchant, who accepts it as payment when you make a purchase. The banks are responsible for certifying the authenticity of the ecash. A similar system is used at CyberCash (see image).
- CONVENTIONAL PAYMENT Many online merchants realize that consumers are wary of conducting business over the Internet. They allow buyers to pay by conventional means. As you make a purchase onscreen, you can check a box to have a person phone you about paying by check or credit card. While merchants usually welcome business of any sort, their costs rise when they have to hire staff to close business in this fashion. As more and more people feel comfortable using all-electronic commerce, you can expect merchants to provide incentives for consumers to transact business that way.

A high-stakes race continues to develop systems that make consumers both want to shop online and feel comfortable about paying. How can stores that require human workers to transact business ever compete on a cost basis with staffless electronic stores? Can online shopping catalogs become so alluring that they threaten the survival of hard-copy-catalog companies? What changes will the age of 3-D, virtual-reality shopping bring? Nobody knows for sure the answers to such questions, but fortunes are expected to be made and lost by companies as they scramble to court the online consumer.

Fasten your seat belts for a wild and interesting ride.

The topic of security requires lengthy discussion that extends well beyond the Web. If your version of this textbook contains the LIV module, refer to Chapter LIV 2 for an in-depth discussion.

Summary and Key Terms

Among the most interesting aspects to Web publishing is its unique contribution to the history of mass communications.

The Web as a Publishing Medium **Web publishing** is defined as developing pages for the Web; in other words, creating a **Web site** or Web presence. Web publishing brings certain advantages: Anyone can do it, people can create their own looks for messages and products, and costs are relatively low. It also creates disadvantages: Most people doing it will be required to develop new types of skills, and Web sites often need constantly refreshed content.

Why Publish on the Web? One of the first issues faced by a prospective Web publisher is his or her reasons, or *goals,* for creating a presence on the Web. Sites serve many types of goals—from having a personal home page to selling and advertising products. Web publishers are well-advised to carefully define their target audiences and competitors before starting site development in earnest.

Developing a Publishing Plan The first step in evaluating a prospective Web-site project is to thoroughly size up its requirements before taking the plunge. Consider both the step-by-step site-development process you will need to complete as well as benefits and costs. During this step, check out possible **Internet presence providers (IPPs)**—the organizations whose servers host Web pages.

Designing Your Site **Design** refers to the process of figuring out what your Web site will look like and how it will work. You don't have to be a professional designer to create attractive, effective Web pages, but you should invest some time to discover differences that separate good design from bad design. Two tools that can assist in the design process are Web **flowcharts** and **storyboards.**

Tools for Creating Web Pages Computer code for most Web pages today is written in **hypertext markup language (HTML). Markup languages** reduce the bandwidth requirements for transmitting documents over a network. HTML instructions called **tags** contained within angled brackets (<>) provide formatting instructions, while the actual text of the displayed Web page lies outside those brackets.

Java, a language developed at Sun Microsystems, allows you to add dynamic or interactive content to your Web pages. It does this by creating small programs or objects, called **applets,** which can be placed within the code for the page. An alternative to Java, **ActiveX** controls, can embed within a Web page objects that are applications created in virtually any supported software package. You can supply interactivity to a page in a third way through a **scripting language.**

Because writing HTML and Java code and page scripts can be tedious, a variety of software alternatives help to simplify the job of creating Web pages. An **HTML editor** is a program that automatically generates Web-page code and spares you from some or all of the programming involved.

Editors come in a number of forms, two of which are wizards and converters. An *HTML wizard* is a program that creates an HTML document from your onscreen selections. An *HTML converter* produces HTML code from an existing document in another format.

Testing Your Pages Web authors test pages at many levels. You will carry out a certain amount of testing as you create Web pages. After you finish your pages, you will need to check out what they look like on browsers and computer systems other than yours. Also, you should solicit feedback from friends and/or associates. Testing Web pages is an ongoing activity.

Promoting and Maintaining Your Web Site *Promotion* of your site—that is, advertising its whereabouts—provides critical guidance for people you want to find you. Be sure to get your site listed in as many places as is feasible. A major part of *maintenance* involves keeping your site updated with fresh information. Carefully evaluate the site statistics provided by your IPP, such as the number of **hits** generated by elements at your site.

Publishing-Related Issues You may encounter several publishing-related issues in developing a Web site. Three of the most important concern copyrights, censorship (including **blocking software**), and security.

EXERCISES

1. How is Web publishing different from publishing in a hard-copy magazine or book?
2. Name at least eight different reasons—or goals—for creating a Web presence.
3. For each of the Web-publishing tasks listed in the following table, state whether it forms part of the planning, design, coding, testing, promotion, or maintenance phases of Web-site creation. In other words, fill in each blank with one of those six choices.

ACTIVITY	PHASE
Making a Web flowchart	________
Choosing a presentation goal	________
Estimating the cost and time required for site development	________
Having friends evaluate your site and suggest improvements	________
Using an HTML wizard to create pages	________
Developing a Java applet	________
Getting a search engine to list your site	________
Adding fresh content weekly to a site	________
Developing a storyboard	________
Sizing up your competitors	________

4. Someone at school offers the following suggestions for designing a Web presence for a small mail-order business. Identify whether each suggestion is a good or bad idea.

SUGGESTION	GOOD OR BAD?
Include at least 30 hyperlinks per page	________
Use the most sophisticated graphics possible	________
Insert your own navigation buttons	________
List the business's e-mail address on the home page	________
Run hyperlinks at least five levels deep	________

5. Define the following terms.
   a. Applet
   b. Trailblazer page
   c. Internet presence provider
   d. Blocking software
   e. Java
   f. ActiveX
6. What is the purpose of each of the following HTML tags?

TAG	PURPOSE
<b>	________
<p>	________
<html>	________
<h2>	________
<img>	________

7. Answer the following questions about markup languages.
   a. Why is the concept of a markup language so important to Web publishing?
   b. What is the main limitation of a markup language?
   c. What is the difference between HTML and Java?
8. The text described an identification and rating system to blocking certain content on the Internet from view.
   a. Explain briefly how such a system might work.
   b. What part of the system has been proposed to work on a voluntary basis?
   c. What part of the system is controlled by the user?
   d. How can parents keep their children from seeing materials they deem objectionable?
9. Answer the following questions about Web-site performance.
   a. What is a *hit* to a Web site?
   b. How can a hit counter provide misleading results?
   c. What types of statistics can an IPP provide that show how a Web site is being used?
10. Explain, in your own words, how the Internet has posed dangers to companies and individuals who own copyrighted materials.

1. Market Research One of the first and most important steps in developing a home page is knowing what types of people use the World Wide Web and the Internet at large. A variety of surveys are available online that provide interesting Internet statistics and demographics.

One of your best bets to get the freshest possible survey information is to use a search engine such as Yahoo!, WebCrawler, Lycos, Excite, or Alta Vista. In Yahoo!, for instance, you can do a category search on the selection "Computers and the Internet," and successively choose such topics as "Internet," "World Wide Web," and "Statistics and Demographics" to get links to survey data. Entering the search string "User survey" will also produce useful links.

After reading the results of at least one such survey, report to your classmates about the underlying user profile. Several questions might interest your classmates: What percentage of users are male and female? What percentages fit in various minority groups? How educated is the average user? What type of salary does the average user make? What professional groups are more likely to use the Web or service than others?

For updated information on Internet survey data, refer to the Parker Web site.

2. Goals For at least three of the goals listed in the first column of the table that follows, visit a Web site that conforms to the goal. In the Site URL column, provide the Web address of the site. In the Description column, describe the site—for instance, "maintains a list of Web sites for stamp collectors" or "tells the world what a great governor __________ will make." In the Comments column, list what you feel the site did right or wrong to communicate the stated goal.

GOAL	SITE URL	DESCRIPTION	COMMENTS
Sharing professional knowledge	______	______	______
Communicating a political message	______	______	______
Selling goods or services	______	______	______
Providing product support	______	______	______
Creating a trailblazer page	______	______	______

3. The Good, the Bad, and the Ugly Find two or three examples each of well-designed and poorly designed Web pages. If you have access to the Internet, download the pages on a printer or diskette. If you don't have Internet access, photocopy them from a book or magazine. In any case, bring your pages into class and be prepared to defend your selections by saying why each one succeeds or fails in implementing standards of good design.

4. Developing a Polished Web Presence If you want to see Web pages that really sizzle before you start designing yours, among the best places to go are sites maintained by some of the world's leading corporations. These organizations hire professionals to design their pages, so you can expect a polished look that reflects state-of-the-art design ideas. As your project, check at least five such sites and report your findings to the class. You can find home-page URLs in magazine advertisements, on television, or through a search engine—just type in the name of the company. The accompanying table provides 20 home-page URLs to help get you started.

Which was your favorite site of the five you checked out? What feature did you like the most at this site? Of the sites you looked at, what was the goal of each one—to establish a corporate image, to sell online, to gather sales leads, to provide product support, or something else?

5. Have Résumé, Will Travel: A Design Exercise Many students will look for jobs after they graduate by

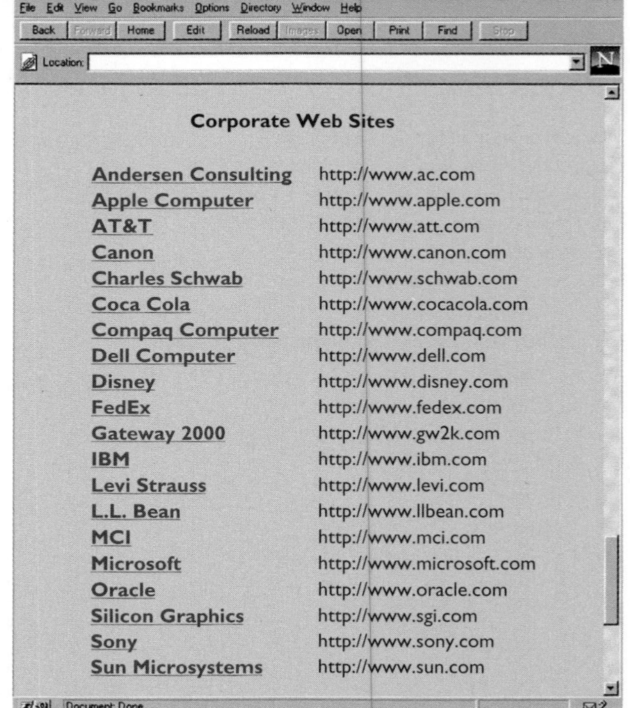

Corporate Web Sites

Andersen Consulting	http://www.ac.com
Apple Computer	http://www.apple.com
AT&T	http://www.att.com
Canon	http://www.canon.com
Charles Schwab	http://www.schwab.com
Coca Cola	http://www.cocacola.com
Compaq Computer	http://www.compaq.com
Dell Computer	http://www.dell.com
Disney	http://www.disney.com
FedEx	http://www.fedex.com
Gateway 2000	http://www.gw2k.com
IBM	http://www.ibm.com
Levi Strauss	http://www.levi.com
L.L. Bean	http://www.llbean.com
MCI	http://www.mci.com
Microsoft	http://www.microsoft.com
Oracle	http://www.oracle.com
Silicon Graphics	http://www.sgi.com
Sony	http://www.sony.com
Sun Microsystems	http://www.sun.com

posting home pages containing their résumés on the Web. Use your word processor to design a single-page résumé, setting the words you intend as textual hyperlinks in boldfaced and underlined type. Feel free to hand sketch any graphical hyperlinks on the page, if you can't border text with your word processor. Also, describe on a separate piece of paper any graphical information to which each of the hyperlinks will lead—such as, a scanned-in picture of yourself.

Before designing your presentation, you might want to check out a few other professional résumés on the Web to see how others have approached this task. The two sites listed below include résumés that you can inspect:

- http://www.resumenet.com
- http://tbrnet.com

Scores of résumés can also be found through using a search engine. In Yahoo!, for instance, you can do a category search on the menu selection "Business and the Economy," and successively choose "Employment," "Résumés," and "Individual Résumés" to get links to over a thousand résumés of individuals. You might additionally consult some excellent written sources on finding jobs on the Web. Two you might wish to check out are *Electronic Job Search Revolution* and *Electronic Resume Revolution*. Both are paperbacks, written by Joyce Lain Kennedy and published by John Wiley & Sons (see below).

6. Web Flowcharts Think of a small business you might be interested in starting, other than a conventional restaurant, an example of which appears in the chapter. Develop a Web flowchart of a Web site you might create for this business. Each box on the flowchart should represent a single Web page. Show with lines how lower-level boxes relate logically to higher-level ones, and be sure that the flowchart extends no deeper than three levels (counting the home page). If you don't have any ideas for a small business of your own, here are a few suggestions upon which to base your flowchart:

- Health-food store
- Bookstore
- Videotape rental store
- Music store
- Travel agency
- Automobile dealership

7. HTML Resources Both the Internet and your local bookstore are good places to look for information about HTML programming.

a. Several HTML works are published on the Web. Locate two sites containing tutorials on HTML and write a few sentences about each one that describe what's there. Use a search engine such as Yahoo!, WebCrawler, or Lycos to locate the sites, or follow any of the URLs in the accompanying table to locate materials. In Yahoo!, use the string "HTML tutorials" to get links to promising sites.

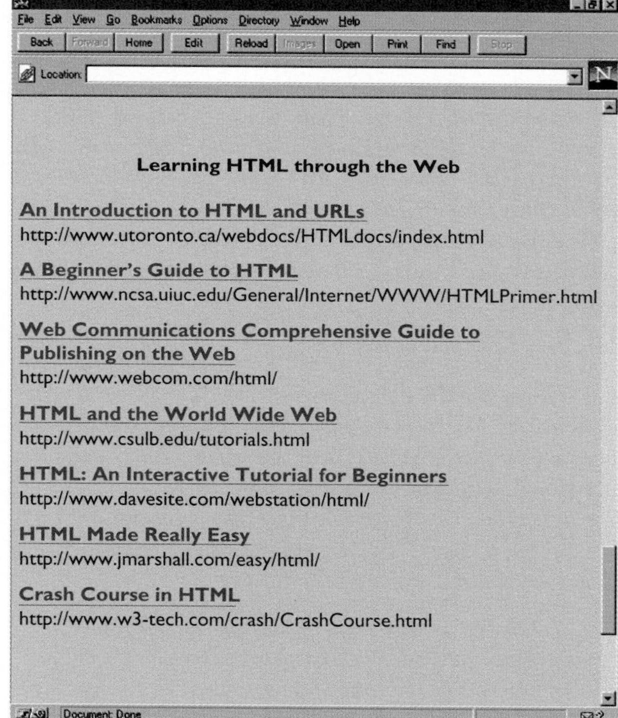

b. Shop for HTML books on the Web. Two Web bookstores you should check out are the Amazon Bookstore (http://www.amazon.com) and Computer Literacy Bookshops (http://www.clbooks.com/). Use the tools available at these sites to complete title searches on the string *HTML*. How many HTML book titles did you find at each site?

c. At a local bookstore, find a good book on HTML that's on your level. Does the book you have chosen also contain a section on HTML editors?

8. Freebie Corner Prospective Web authors can find a lot of freebies online. Countless background graphics for Web pages, clip art, and audio files are readily available and cost only the time it takes to download them. Search through the Web and locate at least one free source of downloadable information in each of the categories in the following table. In completing the table, provide the Internet address of the site in the Source URL column; in the Description column, describe what you've found at the site—for instance, "ten audio files of animal sounds."

CATEGORY	SOURCE URL	DESCRIPTION
Web-page backgrounds	________	________________
Clip art	________	________________
Audio files	________	________________

9. Internet Presence Providers Internet presence providers (IPPs) supply resources that help users to develop their own Web sites. Many also act as Internet service providers (ISPs). Find an IPP and answer the following questions about its operations:

a. How does it charge for running a single home page—by the month and/or by the activity it generates? Would the IPP charge less if it were also your ISP?
b. Web pages need to be regularly updated with fresh information to keep users returning. How does the IPP charge for updates?
c. How would the page charges in steps *b* and *c* change if you wanted to run 12 pages instead of just 1? How about 100 pages?
d. What types of Web-page development services does the IPP offer, and how will you pay for them? For instance, will the IPP code your HTML pages and write Java code for you? At what cost? Will the IPP provide you with an HTML editor through which you can develop applications on your own?
e. What types of site-activity statistics will the IPP provide? How often? What statistics does it give for free, and what does it charge for others?

Hint: Yahoo! provides a list of companies that sell Web-site-development services to prospective Web publishers. To see lists of national and regional IPPs and get links to any of the IPPs on the lists, use the search string "Internet presence providers." Consider also doing a string search in other search engines to complete this exercise.

10. Placing Your Own Home Page on the Web Develop an idea for your own home page and create it using HTML, an HTML editor, or any other Web-page-authoring tool. Your instructor will tell you how to get your home page up and running on your campus network.

As you complete this exercise, fill in the following blanks:

a. The goal of my home page is __________.
b. The audience for my home page is __________.
c. My home page is well designed because __________.
d. People will know about my home page through __________.
e. I will find out how much activity my home page generates by __________.

11. HTML Editors Several HTML editors—such as Adobe PageMill and Claris' Home Page—are listed in Figure NET 3-10. Choose any package from the list in this figure, or any other HTML editor, and report to the class about it. Be sure to cover the following details in your report.

a. The name of the product and the company that makes it
b. The cost of the product
c. How the product works with other computer-system resources; in other words, is it a browser plug-in, stand-alone product that works independently of a browser, or something else?
d. The principal features of the product

12. Blocking Software As mentioned in the chapter text, blocking software can prevent access to objectionable materials. For this project, find a software product that blocks Internet content and write a paper (3 to 5 pages) about it. Your paper should cover the following issues:

a. The name of the product and the company that makes it
b. The cost of the product
c. How the product works with other computer-system resources; in other words, is it a browser plug-in, a stand-alone product that works independently of a browser, or something else?
d. The method by which the product blocks parts of the Internet that the user deems objectionable

13. Free Speech and Censorship Controversy has swirled around the issue of what types of materials are appropriate or inappropriate for display on the Internet. For this project, prepare a paper (3 to 5 pages) stating your views about online censorship. Be sure to cover the following issues:

a. Does the phrase "anything goes" sum up your attitude, or do you feel that some types of materials should never be posted on the Internet?
b. How do you feel about settling the censorship issue at the individual-workstation level, where each user can choose for himself or herself whether to view a site or not?
c. How do you feel about the system of voluntary policing discussed in the chapter? Do you feel it can work as is, or do you foresee some implementation problems that will render the entire system useless?

14. Security Check out the security procedures followed at any commercial Web site—or, alternatively, at the location of any service provider or access provider that will share information about this topic. For two suggestions, you might ask at your school or a local company. Report to the class what you find. Make sure that, at a minimum, you check out how the organizations handle the following problems:

a. Keeping bogus information or transactions to a minimum
b. Protecting the system from computer viruses
c. Maintaining the confidentiality of individual users, if that's an issue
d. Minimizing the impact of disruptive individuals, if that's an issue

MODULE

PS

Productivity Software

Over the past decade or so, computers have completely transformed the workplace. Look at the desktop of a manager, analyst, designer, engineer, secretary, and even company president today, and you will usually see a computer system. At the heart of this workplace transformation is productivity software.

Productivity software refers to applications-software packages that help users to perform their jobs. These packages save time, reduce costs, and perform work that people couldn't possibly complete without the aid of a computer system.

This module opens, in Chapter PS 1, with a look at word processors and desktop publishing systems, both of which help people to develop documents. Chapter PS 2 covers spreadsheets and presentation graphics. Spreadsheets aid in analysis of numbers, while presentation graphics packages help users to prepare graphs and charts showing information in many pictorial formats. Chapter PS 3 closes the module with a discussion of database management systems, which specialize in providing rapid access to electronically stored collections of facts.

MODULE CONTENTS

Productivity Software

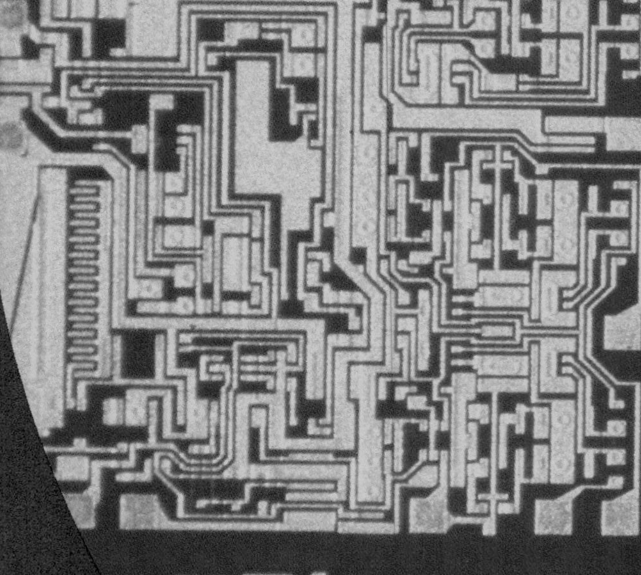

ISBN 0-03-024481-1

PS 1

Word Processing and Desktop Publishing

Outline

Learning Objectives

After completing this chapter, you will be able to:

1. Describe word processing.
2. Identify the operations that you must master to use word processing software effectively.
3. Explain the features common to many word processing programs.
4. Identify the software and hardware components found in many desktop publishing systems.

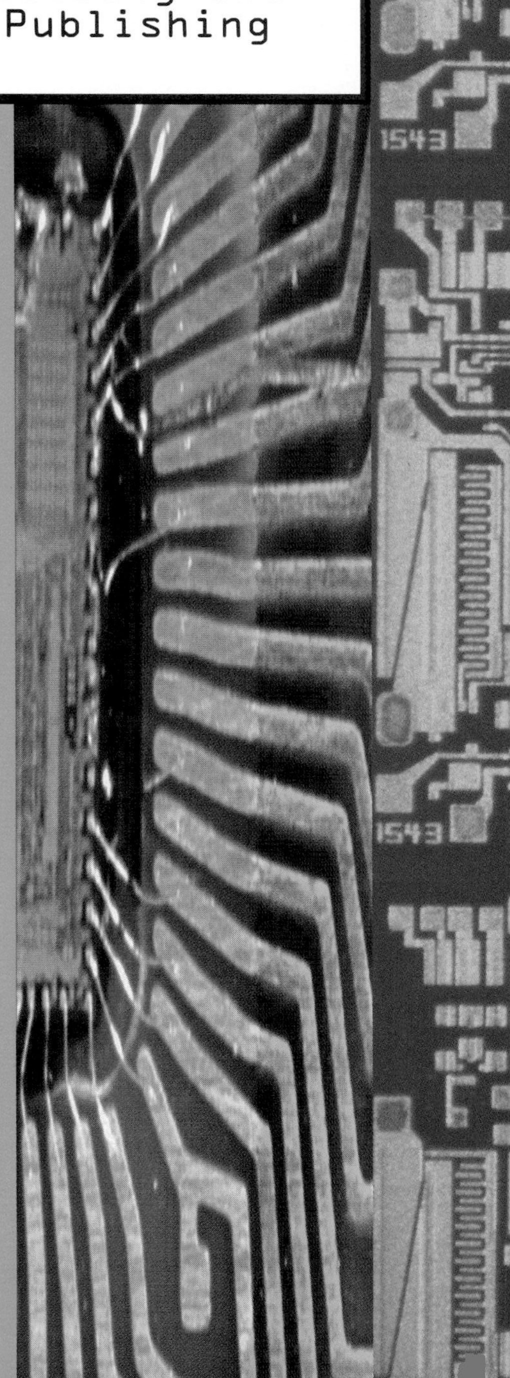

Overview

Word processing and desktop publishing are technologies that deal with the manipulation of words. *Word processing* enables a computer system to serve as a powerful writing tool. It organizes computer resources to help you quickly create, edit, and print documents and manage them in ways no ordinary typewriter can match. *Desktop publishing,* available only since high-powered microcomputers entered the marketplace, carries word processing a step further. With desktop publishing hardware and software, one can more fully create and develop documents that look as though they were prepared by a professional print shop.

In this chapter, we'll first discuss word processing. We'll explore in detail what word processing entails and cover many of the features currently found in programs now in use. Then we'll turn to desktop publishing and the hardware and software found on high-end desktop publishing systems.

Word Processing Software

When you use your computer to do the kinds of work that people have performed on typewriters throughout most of this century, you're doing word processing. **Word processing** applies computer technology to create, manipulate, and print text materials such as letters, legal contracts, manuscripts, and other documents. Word processing saves so much time and work and offers so many more capabilities than the ordinary typewriter, in fact, that relatively few people use typewriters anymore.

Virtually all formal writing today employs a word processing program. Most such programs are *general purpose;* that is, they are designed to suit the needs of a variety of users—from heavy users such as secretaries and authors to average microcomputer users who may just need to type letters now and then. Among today's best-selling word processing programs are Microsoft's Word, Corel's WordPerfect, and Lotus's Word-Pro. All three form components of software suites, and many users buy them in these packages rather than as stand-alone products (see the Tomorrow box). Special-purpose word processing programs, such as those designed to serve the needs of scriptwriters for television and movies, are also comercially available.

Most word processing programs offer hundreds of features, but only a handful of them account for 90 percent or more of what most people will do during the course of word-processing a typical document. This basic set of word processing operations can be divided into three main groups: *document-handling operations, entering and editing operations,* and *print-formatting operations.*

DOCUMENT-HANDLING OPERATIONS

To use virtually any type of productivity software program—say, a word processor or spreadsheet—you need to know how to carry out a number of general document-handling tasks. These tasks, such as opening documents for use and printing them, are illustrated in Figure PS 1-1. They correspond to such activities as starting and braking when driving a car. Because almost everyone needs fast access to document-handling commands, all of these operations are usually located on easy-to-reach menus that are but a mouse click or two away. The trend today in software suites is a document-centered graphical user interface (including a menu bar, pull-down menus, and toolbars) that is similar from program to program. This arrangement makes it easy to learn a new program once you have mastered one or two others.

■ **Word processing.** The use of computer technology to create, manipulate, and print text materials such as letters, legal contracts, and manuscripts.

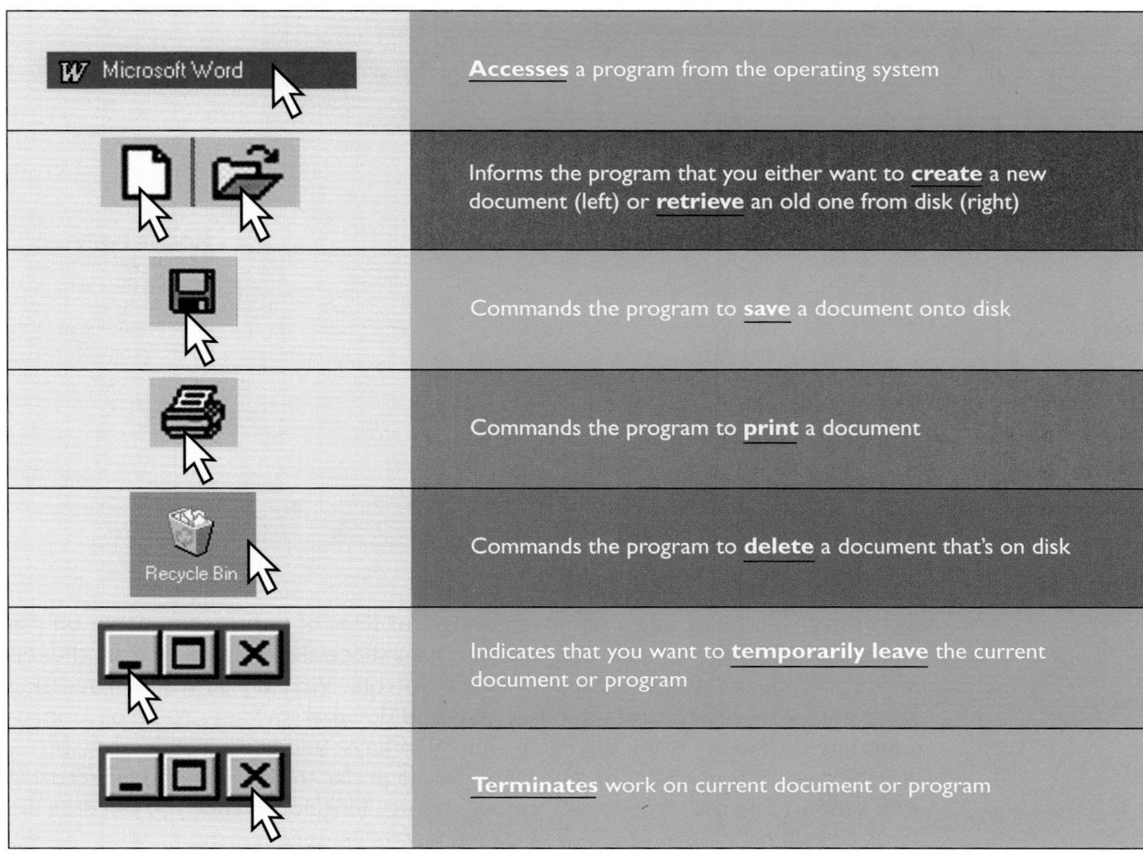

Microsoft Word
Accesses a program from the operating system
Informs the program that you either want to create a new document (left) or retrieve an old one from disk (right)
Commands the program to save a document onto disk
Commands the program to print a document
Recycle Bin
Commands the program to delete a document that's on disk
Indicates that you want to temporarily leave the current document or program
Terminates work on current document or program

FIGURE PS 1-1

General operations needed for using productivity software.

ENTERING AND EDITING OPERATIONS

Every word processor contains an assortment of entering and editing operations. These capabilities accept both text keyed in by the user and the insertion of computer graphics into documents and they allow the user to manipulate both text and graphics on the screen.

Moving the Insertion Point Virtually all word processors show a blinking cursor character on the screen called an **insertion point** to designate where a newly entered character will appear (see Figure PS 1-2). The insertion point moves to the right as you type new characters into your document. You can also move the insertion point to other positions within your document by rolling the mouse along a flat surface and then clicking the left mouse button, by tapping any of several cursor-movement keys, or by entering a short directive from a menu or dialog box. As the insertion point changes position, the *status bar* at the bottom of the screen changes correspondingly. The status bar always shows where you are in the document by displaying information such as the current page number and the place on the page where the insertion point is positioned.

There are usually dozens of ways to move the insertion point throughout a document. You can move it a character, a word, a line, or a screen at a time, as well as to the beginning or the end of a document. You can also move to a specific page number or to a *bookmark* you've set up to mark a special place.

The insertion point is also used for selecting the place in a document to insert text and computer graphics coming from other programs.

P S

■ **Insertion point.** A cursor character that shows where the next key pressed will appear onscreen.

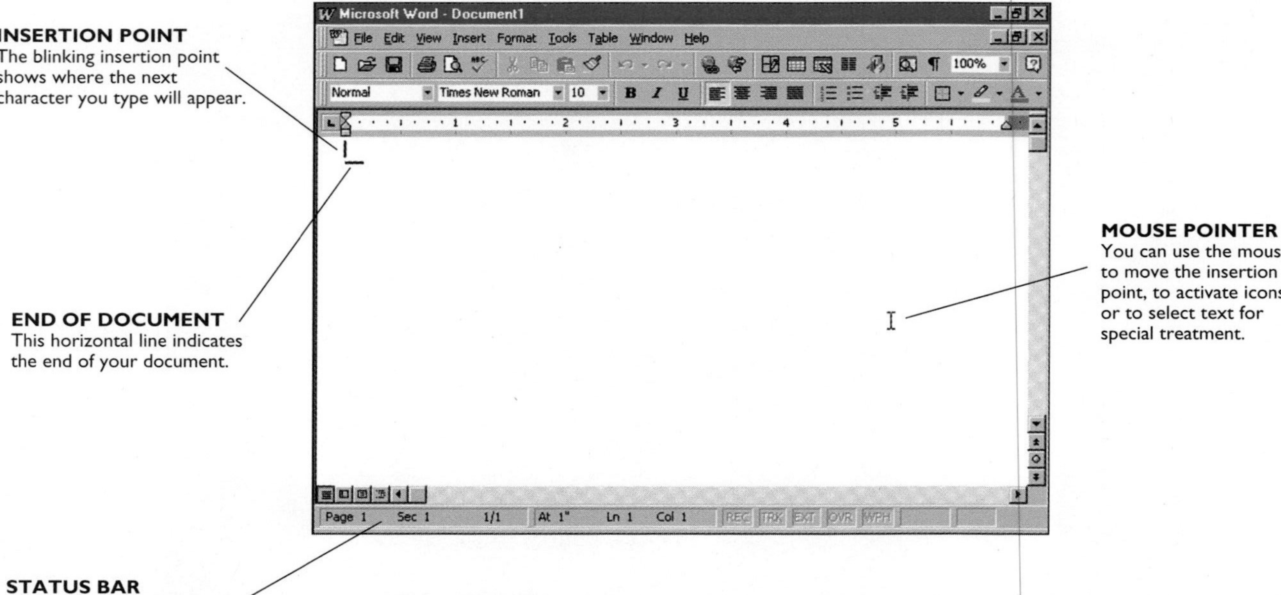
INSERTION POINT
The blinking insertion point shows where the next character you type will appear.
END OF DOCUMENT
This horizontal line indicates the end of your document.
MOUSE POINTER
You can use the mouse to move the insertion point, to activate icons, or to select text for special treatment.
STATUS BAR
The status bar shows details about the document on which you're working.
Microsoft Word - Document1
File Edit View Insert Format Tools Table Window Help
Normal
Times New Roman
10
100%
Page 1 Sec 1 1/1 At 1" Ln 1 Col 1 REC TRK EXT OVR WPH

FIGURE PS 1-2

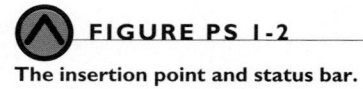

The insertion point and status bar.

Scrolling Scrolling lets you move contiguous lines of text up and down on the screen. When you scroll down, for example, lines successively disappear from the top of the screen, and new ones appear at the bottom. Virtually all word processing programs allow you to press the up-arrow and down-arrow keys to scroll a document line by line. By using the PgUp and PgDn keys, you can scroll even faster—page by page instead of line by line. Many people prefer to do most of their scrolling with a mouse and the scroll bars. To move through long documents, you can drag the scroll box with a mouse to achieve maximum scrolling speeds.

Making a Line Return Typing on a conventional typewriter generally requires you to press the Return key to define the end of every line. Not so with a word processor. Word processors provide an automatic line return when the insertion point reaches a certain column position at the right-hand side of the screen. This return is called a **soft return,** and the built-in feature that provides soft returns is called a **wordwrap** feature.

A word processor does also allow you to key in a **hard return** at any point by tapping the Enter key. A hard return automatically advances the insertion point to the beginning of the next line. Normally, you will use hard returns to mark the end of paragraphs or to create space on the page after typing in titles or headings. You should not tap the Enter key after you have reached the right margin on each line; it will deny you any chance of reformatting paragraphs later on as you make changes to them.

Inserting and Deleting Inserting and deleting text are two of the most basic editing operations. Virtually all word processors default to an *insert mode* that lets you insert characters at the insertion-point position on the screen. As each character is added to the screen, all characters to the right of the insertion point slide over one column position. You can switch out of the insert mode at any time to an *overtype mode* by tapping the Insert key on the keyboard. As new characters are added at the insertion-point position in the overtype mode, they replace characters to the right.

Word processors generally allow you to delete a character, word, sentence, or block of characters at a time. Deleting one character at a time is normally done by tapping either the Delete or Backspace key, once you have the insertion point

■ **Soft return.** An automatic line return carried out by word processing software. ■ **Wordwrap.** The feature of a word processor that automatically places soft returns. ■ **Hard return.** A line break inserted when the user presses the Enter key to control line spacing in a document.

Is Bloatware Clogging Your Computer's Arteries?

The End May Not Be in Sight

One of the problems that often frustrates users is that they have too much software on their hard disks, most of which they'll never use. What's more, they're "forced" to pay for this burden, and it often gets in the way of doing work.

One of the main culprits is the software suite. Only a few years ago, for instance, users were ecstatic just to have a word processor that could prepare letters with proportionally spaced typefaces—and maybe a fancy font or two for headings. Today, they have word processors that are virtually fully featured desktop publishing and illustration programs—not to mention complete office systems that can handle spreadsheets, presentation graphics, and databases, as well, whether they're needed or not. Oops, did we forget to mention Web surfing?

This enrichment in software capability has led to the term *bloatware*—software that contains "everything but the kitchen sink." While such software can provide some users with useful capabilities that they wouldn't otherwise have, many users actually wind up worse off. Not only does bloatware cost more than software that provides only the basics, but also it gobbles up hard disk space like it's going out of style. Bloatware can get in the way of creating applications, too, because screens are clogged with toolbars and icons and rulers and tip wizards and Internet add-ons and ... Oops, did we forget to mention that applications carrying all of this overhead take longer to run?

New network products such as Java and ActiveX are hailed by many as relief for the bloatware burden. These products support programming to create small *applets,* sections of code that wait in network storage for users to download and execute on their own desktops. The applets are built into documents themselves, giving those documents their own native computing capabilities. Thus, when you call for a document over a network, the document can have its own viewer for you to communicate with it, its own audio and video drivers for you to hear sound and see film clips, its own calculator to perform arithmetic, and so on. When you finish your work on the document, all of the software that you used with it return to the network. No need to burden your hard disk. Who even needs a hard disk, anyway?

Unfortunately, compelling as the argument may seem for applets taking over chores done by conventional desktop-installed software, it breaks down in a lot of places. For instance, throughout the history of computing, users have shown that they like control over their own environments. Software stored on networks results in having far less control. Phone lines can be hit with power outages or be clogged with traffic, servers can crash, and software can be changed without your approval. Control was one of the big reasons why people switched from mainframe display terminals to PCs in the first place, and it is one of the reasons people like their hard disks packed with software they can trust—with installation CDs tucked safely nearby.

There are other reasons to think that bloatware will not disappear so easily. It costs software publishers very little extra to produce over a stand-alone program—that is, if you're a big company like Microsoft, IBM, or Corel. Why not give users extra functionality—at a bargain price—if you have it laying around in other programs that you also produce? Even if users feel they don't need the functionality today, the nagging fear that they may need it tomorrow and that it's available at a give-away price may be enough to get an edge on a competitive product.

Bloatware is also a strategic weapon for a software publisher in that it raises the barrier to competition and makes user exit-costs higher. For instance, it's harder than ever today for a new company to come out of the blue and develop a superior word processor—unless it has a whole suite of office applications it can peddle with it, too. What's more, users who go through torture learning a bloatware program are not quick to abandon it when a new product comes along, no matter how good it appears to be.

So, when you read all of those articles in the press that say bloatware is going away, do so with that proverbial grain of salt.

Bloatware. Byte-hungry software has become the norm on the average desktop.

properly positioned. Deleting one word or sentence or block of text at a time is done by first *selecting* the word, sentence, or block to be deleted and then tapping either the Delete or Backspace keys. **Selecting text—**which refers to highlighting the text on the screen—is illustrated in Figure PS 1-3 and is also necessary when you want to move, copy, or format text in a certain way.

■ **Selecting text.** The process of highlighting text on the screen in order to move or copy it, delete it, or apply a special formatting treatment to it.

ABOUT SELECTING TEXT
You can select text with a mouse or keyboard. Selected text is highlighted onscreen. Once text is selected, you can delete, move, copy, or format it in a certain way.

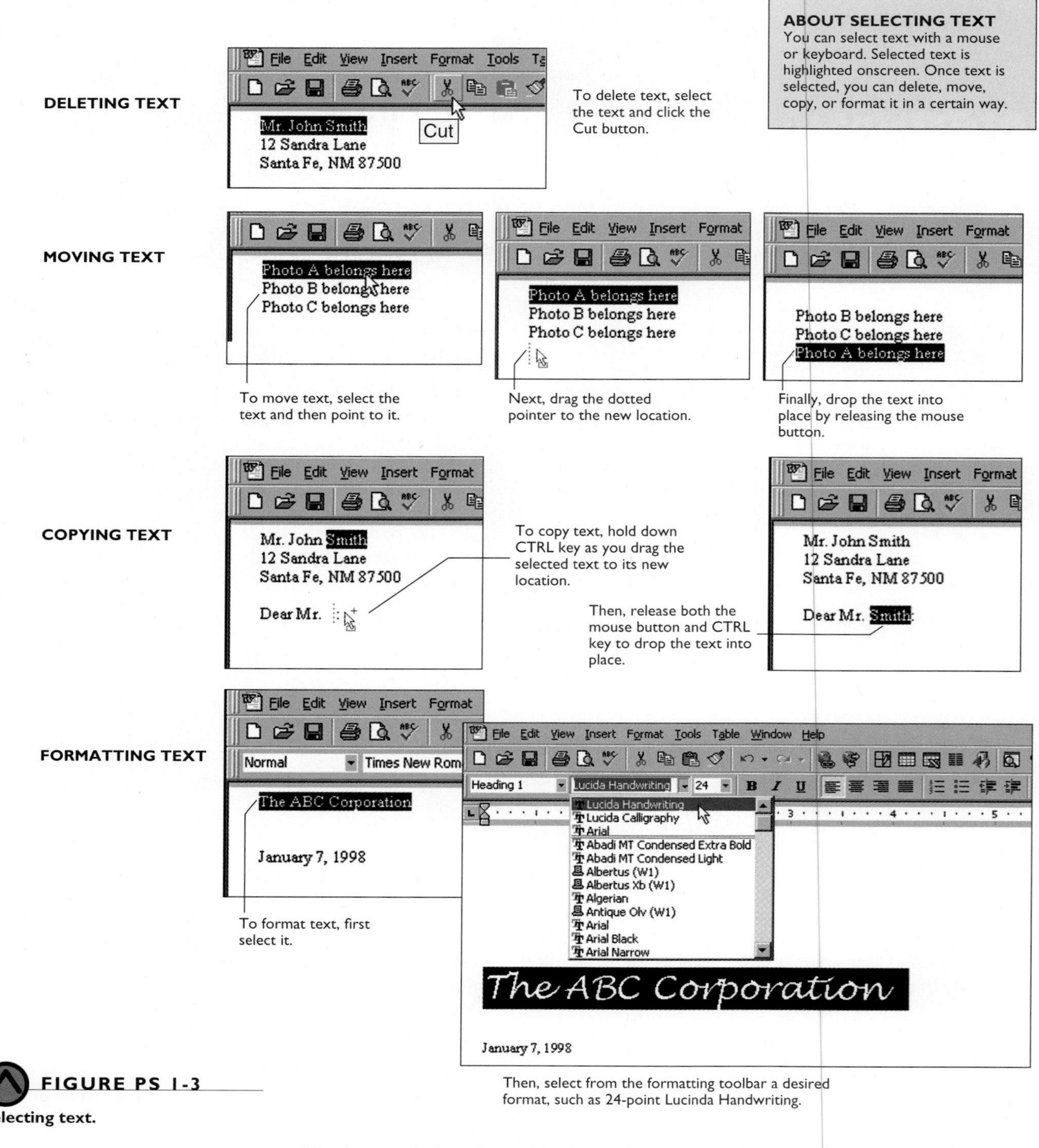

FIGURE PS 1-3
Selecting text.

Moving and Copying Moving and copying operations allow you to relocate or replicate text within a document. *Moving* means identifying a specific block of text and physically putting it in a new place in the document. *Copying* is similar to moving except that a copy of the block remains in the original place as well.

Moving and copying can often be done through pull-down menu selections, by copy and paste buttons on the word processor's toolbar, and by dragging and dropping with the mouse. For instance, to copy a block of text, you can select it and then choose the *Copy* button from the main toolbar. Copying moves the text temporarily onto the operating system's clipboard. Then, after you place the insertion point where you want the copy of the text to appear, you use the *Paste* button to relocate it. As Figure PS 1-3 suggests, you can also use the mouse to copy text by first selecting it and then dragging and dropping the text into its new position. Using the mouse in this way is commonly called *drag-and-drop editing.*

Finding and Replacing Finding and replacing are extremely useful features of word processing software. The *find operation* lets you search automatically for all occurrences of a particular word or phrase. The *replace operation* gives you the option of changing the word or phrase to something else.

For example, let's say you've typed out a long document that should repeatedly refer to a person named Snider. If you've misspelled this name as Schneider, you can instruct the word processor to look up all occurrences of *Schneider* and change them to *Snider.* Some people take dangerous shortcuts when finding and replacing. For example, suppose you ask the word processor to change all occurrences of *chne* to *n.* This will change all *Schneider* occurrences to *Snider,* but it will also change a name such as *Schneymann* to *Snymann,* which you probably did not intend to do.

Figure PS 1-4 shows a document before and after a simple finding and replacing operation.

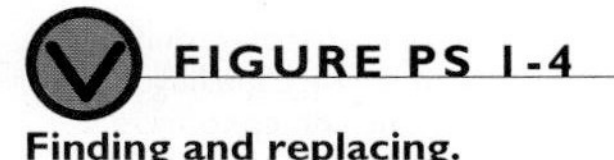

FIGURE PS 1-4

Finding and replacing.

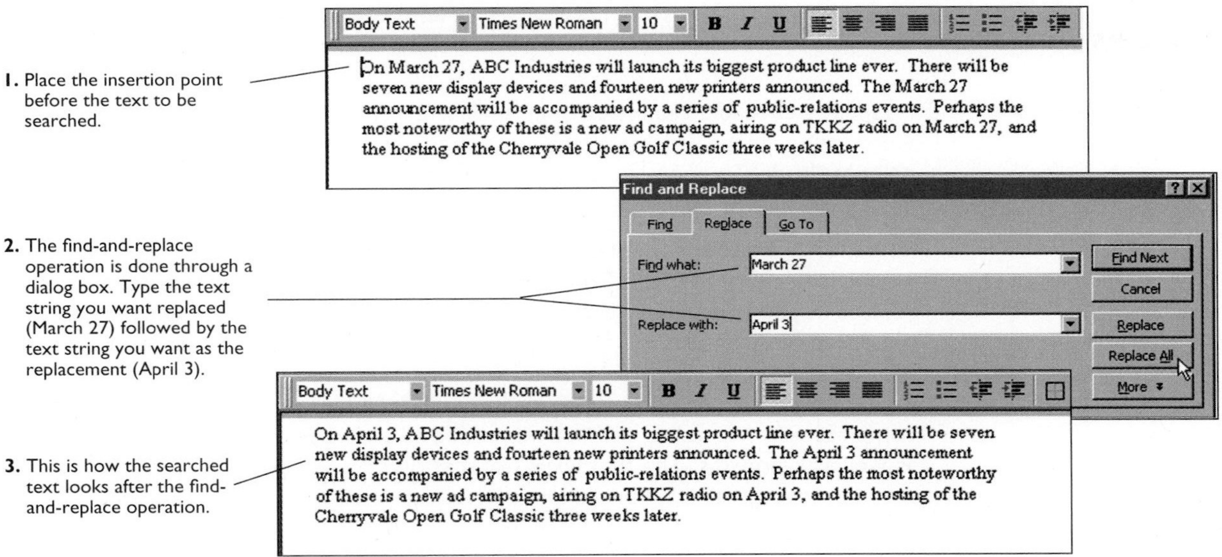

Spell-Checking Virtually every word processing program today includes a routine that searches a document for misspelled words. This routine and its accompanying dictionary are collectively known as a **spelling checker.**

The capabilities of spelling checkers can vary dramatically. Many spelling checkers designed for ordinary word processors have dictionaries that contain over 100,000 words, whereas professional-level spelling checkers used by newspapers and magazines may have a million or more. A particularly important feature is the ability to place additional words into a dictionary. A writer of a computer text or medical article, for example, uses very specialized terms, most of which aren't in the dictionaries of standard spelling checkers. Specialized dictionaries are also available from aftermarket (third-party) vendors.

Spelling checkers allow you to check for misspellings either *after* you finish typing text for a document or *while* you type. If you choose the latter option, the word processor monitors input as you type and alerts you whenever you key in a word that doesn't appear in spelling checker's dictionary. A spelling checker is illustrated in Figure PS 1-5.

PS

■ **Spelling checker.** A program or routine that checks for misspelled words.

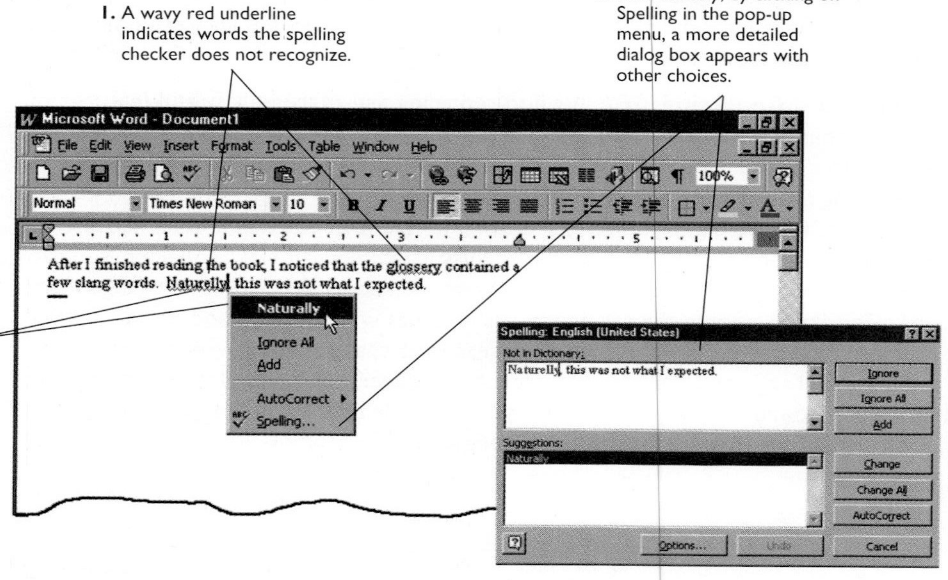

1. A wavy red underline indicates words the spelling checker does not recognize.

2. By moving the insertion on a marked word and pressing the right mouse button, a pop-up menu appears with what the spelling checker thinks is the correct spelling. Click on the choice to have it inserted automatically.

3. Alternatively, by clicking on Spelling in the pop-up menu, a more detailed dialog box appears with other choices.

FIGURE PS 1-5

Using a spelling checker. Many spelling checkers highlight words that they don't recognize.

Spelling checkers cannot catch all spelling errors. For instance, if you misspell the word *their* as *there,* which is also a word in the English language, the spelling checker will not flag it. To root out errors of this sort, you need a grammar checker (discussed later in the chapter).

Thesaurus Feature A **thesaurus feature** allows you to identify possible synonyms for selected words. To use a thesaurus, you first select a word you wish to replace in your document. If the thesaurus feature recognizes the word, it displays suggested replacements in a format resembling that of a hard-copy thesaurus (see Figure PS 1-6). In many programs, when you see a word you like, you can simply click a Replace button to perform the replacement. Many thesaurus routines allow you to complete word searches within other word searches, and many provide antonyms as well as synonyms. The thesaurus features that accompany the leading word processors typically contain less than 100,000 words. Electronic thesauruses used by companies in the publishing industry have far more.

Displaying Text Different word processors use a variety of methods for displaying text on the screen. Older products that are built around monitors with minimal graphics capabilities rely exclusively on *embedded formatting codes* to apprise users what's going on. Boldface, italic, and underlined characters generally do not display conveniently onscreen even though they can be output as such on printed documents. So, the user must place codes for such special formats before and after a word or phrase that is to be output in a special way. A code placed before a word or phrase alerts the printer to turn on a formatting feature; the code following the word or phrase alerts it to turn off the feature. For instance, [BOLD] and [bold] might respectively be used to turn boldfacing on and off.

Now that powerful graphical user interfaces are widely available, most word processors use a **WYSIWYG** display, in which text shows onscreen more or less the way it will appear in print. WYSIWYG—which is pronounced "wizzy-wig"—is an acronym for *what you see is what you get.* With WYSIWYG, the user can make toolbar-button choices onscreen to format text in a certain way, leaving it up to the computer to automatically handle any embedded codes.

■ **Thesaurus feature.** A program or routine that enables electronic lookup of word synonyms. ■ **WYSIWYG.** An acronym for the phrase *what you see is what you get,* indicating a display screen image identical or very close to the look of the eventual printed output.

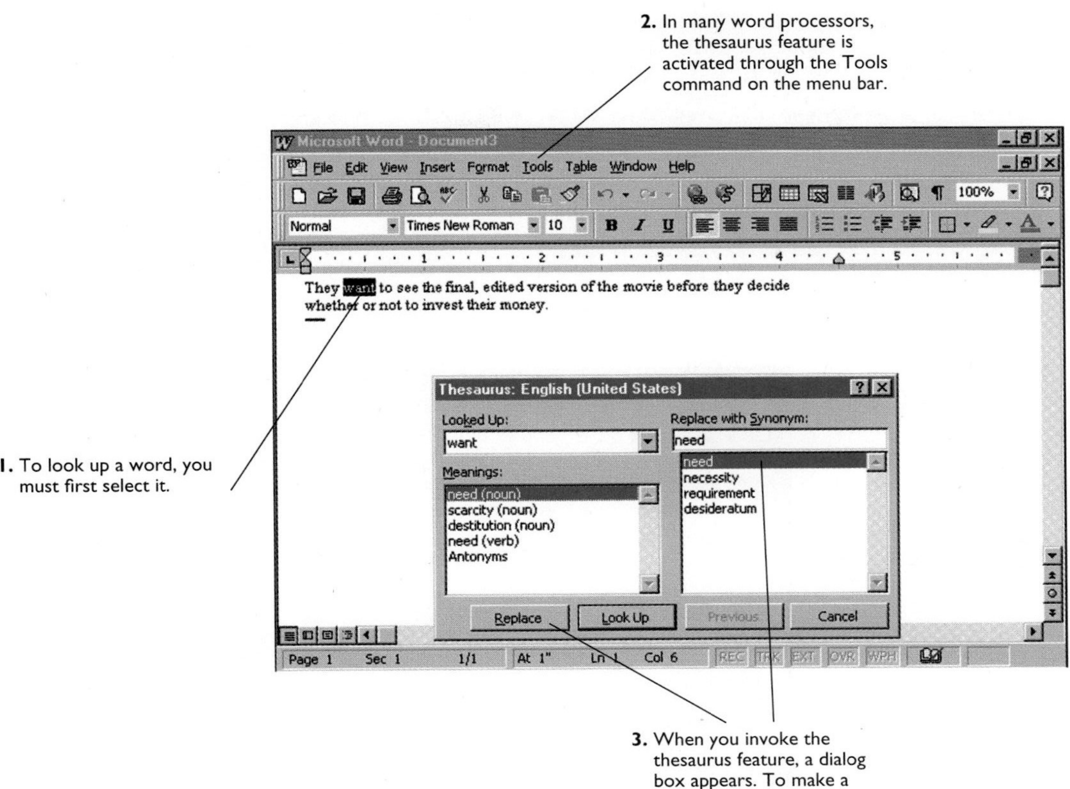

FIGURE PS 1-6

Using a word processor's thesaurus.

Typically, users have a choice of WYSIWYG modes in which to enter and edit their documents. A *normal mode* reveals the basic look of the document; users spend most their time working in normal mode. A *page-layout mode* supplements the document display with elements such as graphics, page numbers, footnotes, and columns that the user has specified. While the latter mode is "more WYSIWYG" than the former, it is slower to work with and better suited to fine-tuning a document that's almost ready to print.

Besides giving you a choice of WYSIWYG modes in which to operate, most word processors have a **zoom feature** that will let you magnify text or graphic elements on a page (see Figure PS 1-7).

PRINT-FORMATTING OPERATIONS

Print-formatting operations tell the printer how to output text onto paper. Several of these operations are discussed below.

Adjusting Line Spacing Adjusting line spacing is an important word processing operation. Suppose that you've single-spaced a paper, for instance, but your English 101 instructor wants all the essays you hand in to be double spaced. Virtually any word processor would enable you to adjust the line spacing of the existing text to double-space the paper in a few seconds. Many programs also permit you to place fractional blank lines between text lines, add space before and after paragraphs, and choose several other line-spacing options.

■ **Zoom feature.** A feature that lets you magnify text or graphics images onscreen.

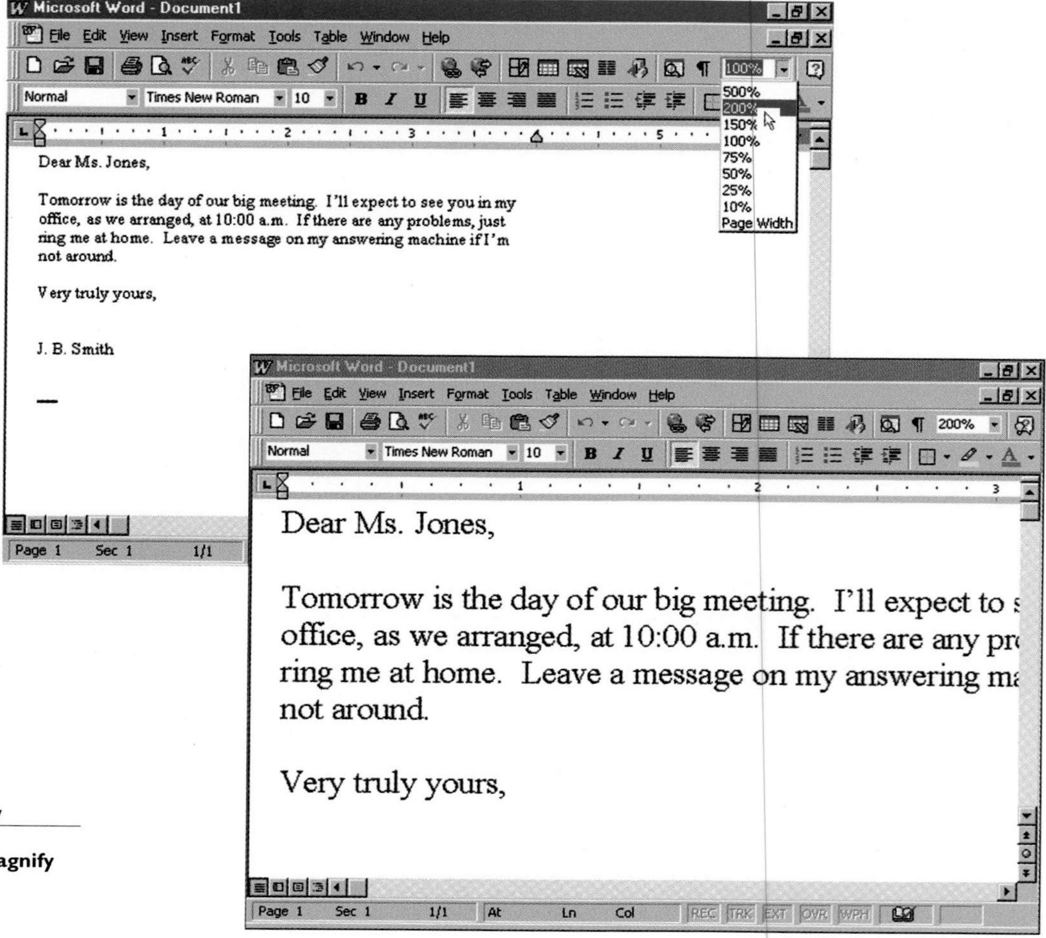

FIGURE PS 1-7

Using a zoom feature to magnify text on the screen.

The Ruler Line Most users will occasionally have a need to adjust margins, to set tab stops, and to set off certain paragraphs or quotes for emphasis. Many word processors have a **ruler line** that enables you to reset margins back and forth as you are typing (see Figure PS 1-8). Using the ruler, you can indicate indents from the left

FIGURE PS 1-8

Using a ruler line.

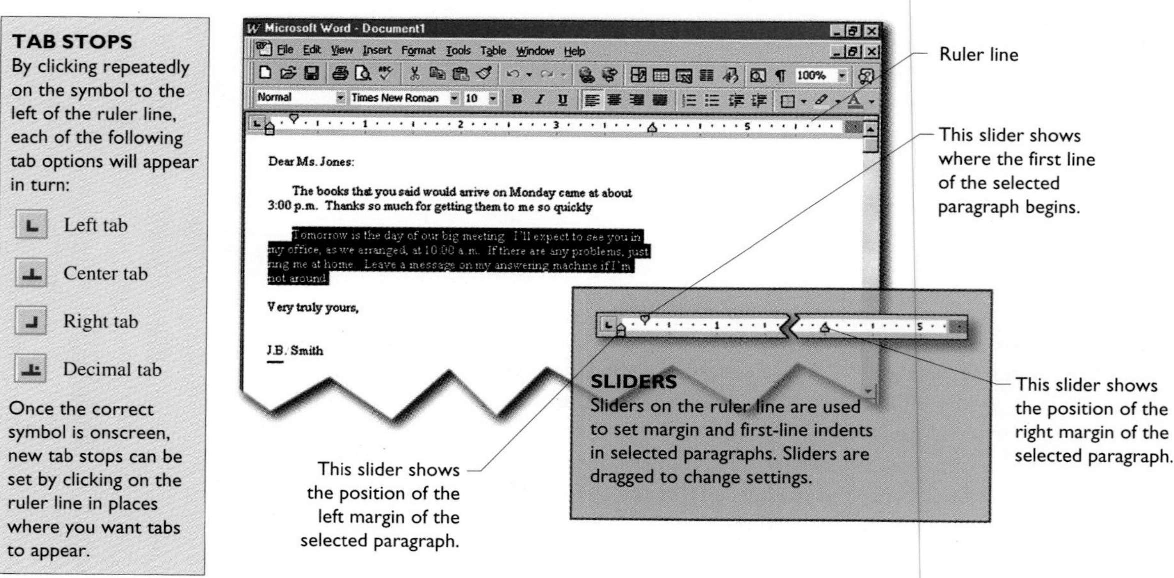

TAB STOPS
By clicking repeatedly on the symbol to the left of the ruler line, each of the following tab options will appear in turn:
Left tab
Center tab
Right tab
Decimal tab
Once the correct symbol is onscreen, new tab stops can be set by clicking on the ruler line in places where you want tabs to appear.
Microsoft Word - Document1
Dear Ms. Jones:
The books that you said would arrive on Monday came at about 3:00 p.m. Thanks so much for getting them to me so quickly
Very truly yours,
J.B. Smith
Ruler line
This slider shows where the first line of the selected paragraph begins.
SLIDERS
Sliders on the ruler line are used to set margin and first-line indents in selected paragraphs. Sliders are dragged to change settings.
This slider shows the position of the left margin of the selected paragraph.
This slider shows the position of the right margin of the selected paragraph.

■ **Ruler line.** An onscreen element, resembling a physical ruler, that enables you to set line widths, tab settings, indents, and the like.

or right margins (or both) or indent only the first line of a paragraph. You can usually also specify indents and set margins through pull-down menus and dialog boxes.

Like typewriters, word processors let you set tab stops. They also enable you to set several types of tabs—for instance, the popular left tab, where text is left aligned at the tab stop, as well as center, right, and decimal tabs, where text is respectively centered, right aligned, or aligned on a decimal point. The tab-stop positions on the screen are reached through the Tab key. You press Tab to go forward a Tab stop and Shift + Tab to go backward a tab stop. Default tabs are usually preset every five spaces; you can use the ruler line to set your own tab stops.

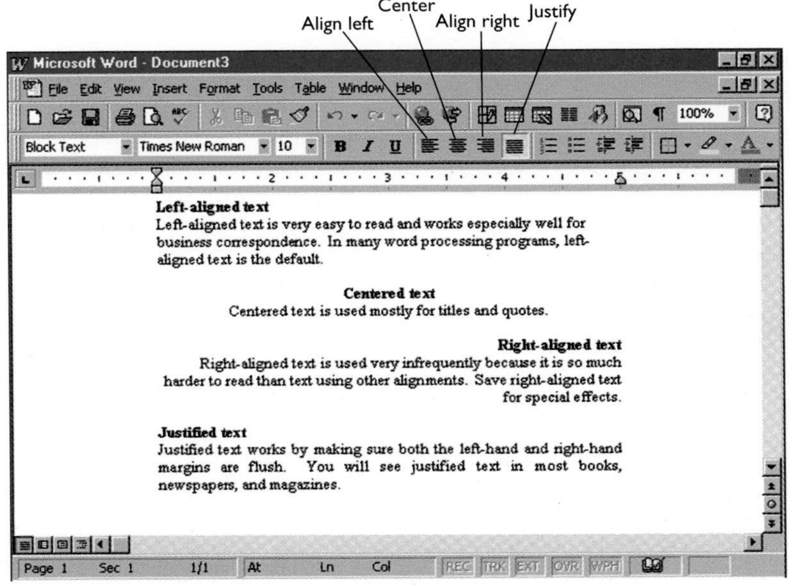

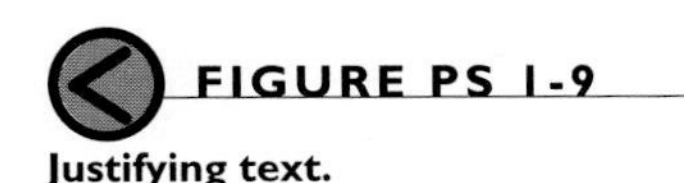

FIGURE PS 1-9

Justifying text.

Justifying Most documents are formatted with either a ragged or smooth right edge. These style alternatives are respectively referred to as *left justification* (or *left-aligned* text) and *full justification* (or *justified* text). Figure PS 1-9 illustrates both of these styles and two additional ones.

Users who create business documents typically prefer left justification, as the extra blank spaces between words that often result with full justification can sometimes make documents too visually difficult to read. Full justification can look quite attractive, however, if the word processor and printer in use can handle proportional spacing (to be discussed shortly). Many word processing programs also have center- and right-justification options, as the figure shows, but these are used only in special circumstances and not for entire documents.

Centering text is something everyone preparing a document does sooner or later; for instance, when creating a title or a heading. Most word processing programs require you to have the insertion point on the line that will contain the text to be centered when invoking the centering command. Then, as you type, the text is automatically centered. You can also center text that is justified another way—usually by first selecting it and then invoking the centering command.

Establishing a Page Format Most word processors let you choose overall formatting for the pages in your document. For instance, you can tell the word processor how many lines to print per page; the maximum number of characters to fit on each line; and the settings of the left, right, top, and bottom margins. You can also choose whether to number pages in a document. For example, you may want page numbers placed on class reports but not on short letters. Most word processing programs will place page numbers almost wherever you specify.

Reformatting Reformatting places your document in a form suitable for output, for instance, by ensuring that the document is properly fitted within the margins after an insertion or deletion is made. Reformatting normally is necessary when you insert text, delete text, change line spacing, readjust margins, change justification, or change the basic page format. Virtually all programs will reformat your document automatically every time you modify text.

Headers and Footers A *header* is a title that a word processor prints automatically at the top of every page; a *footer* is a title automatically printed at the bottom of every page. Some programs let you specify headers and footers with great flexibility. For instance, you can print both headers and footers on the same page and even alternate the titles placed in a header or a footer on successive pages. Many word processors also allow page numbers to appear within a header or footer. This textbook, like many other books, alternates headers; the chapter title appears with the page number on each right-hand page, and the module title and page number appears on each left-hand page.

Fonts A **typeface** is a collection of text characters that share a common design. Typeface-selection features enable you to output characters in a variety of typefaces and typeface sizes (called **point sizes).** A typeface in a particular point size is referred to as a **font;** for instance, 12-point Helvetica is a font. Figure PS 1-10 illustrates different typefaces; Figure PS 1-11 illustrates point sizes.

FIGURE PS 1-10

Typefaces.

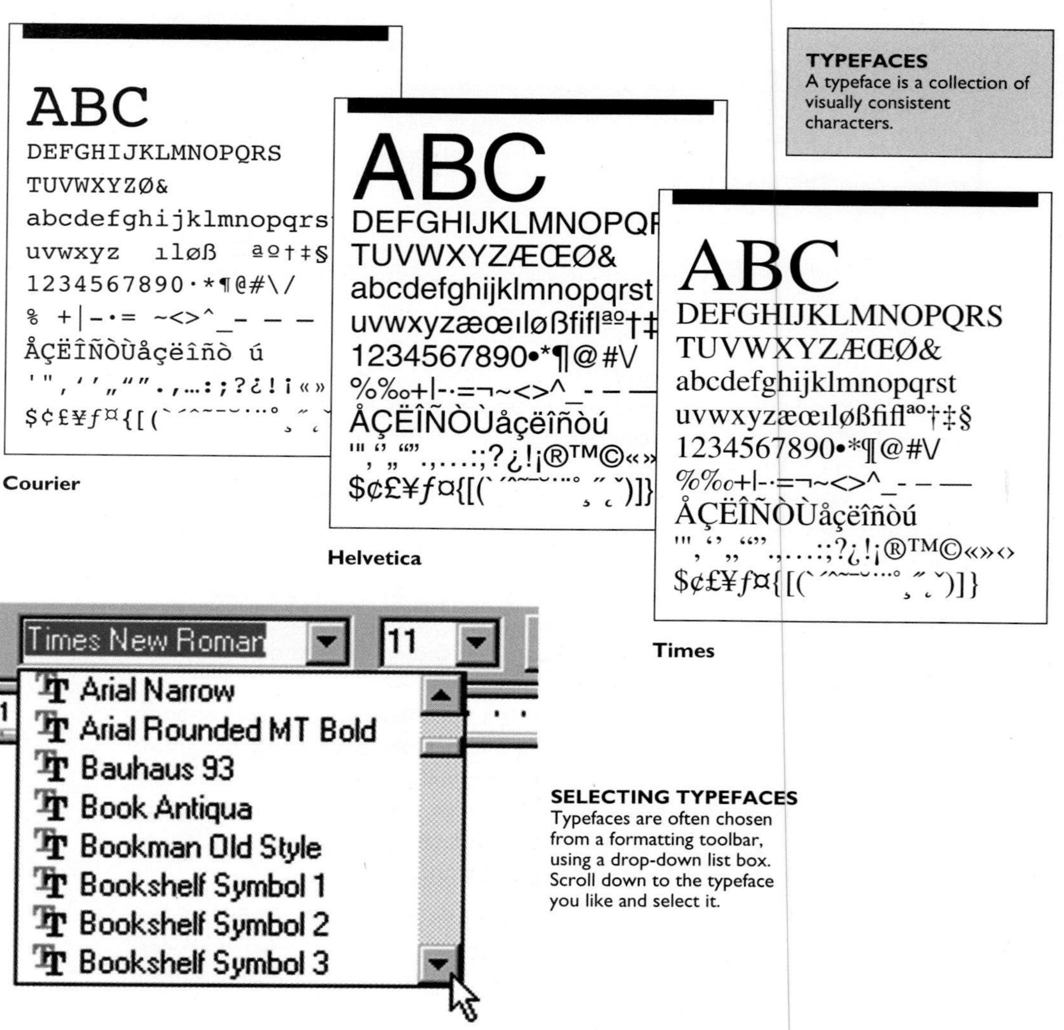

TYPEFACES
A typeface is a collection of visually consistent characters.

SELECTING TYPEFACES
Typefaces are often chosen from a formatting toolbar, using a drop-down list box. Scroll down to the typeface you like and select it.

■ **Typeface.** A collection of text characters that share a common design. ■ **Point size.** A measurement for scaling typefaces. ■ **Font.** A typeface in a particular point size—for instance, 12-point Helvetica.

POINT SIZE
Point size refers to the size of type.

This is 10-point Helvetica

This is 12-point Helvetica

This is 18-point Helvetica

This is 24-point Helvetica

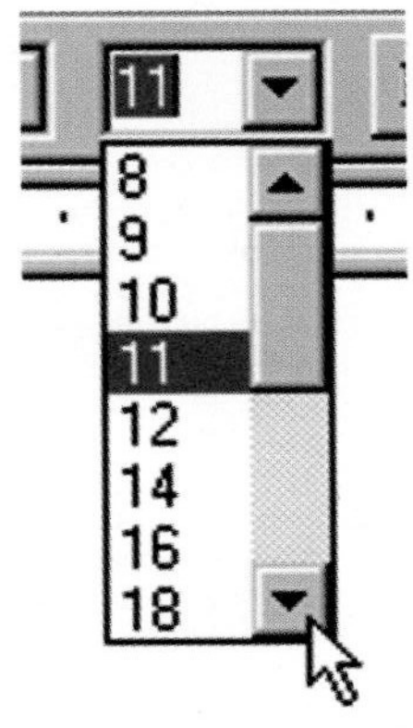

SELECTING POINT SIZE
Like typefaces, point sizes are selected from a formatting toolbar.

FIGURE PS 1-11
Point size.

Fonts are either monospaced or proportionally spaced. In documents using the Courier font—a typewriting standard—text is **monospaced**. What this means is that each character takes up the same amount of horizontal space. This textbook, however, like most others, was typeset on a system capable of **proportional spacing,** which allocates more horizontal space on a line to some characters than to others. For example, a capital *H* takes up more space than a lowercase *i.* **Microspacing** allows further adjustment of spacing within a text line by inserting fractions of a full blank space in inconspicuous places so as to justify the left-hand and right-hand margins without uneven spacing (see Figure PS 1-12).

How tight is tight?

How tight is tight?

How tight is tight?

How tight is tight?

FIGURE PS 1-12
Proportionally spaced characters with microspacing.

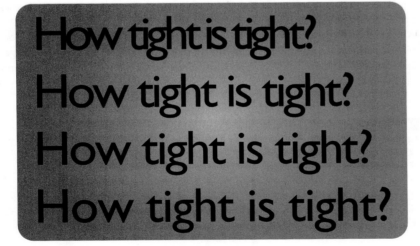

For you to use proportional spacing and microspacing, both your word processor and your printer must support them. Often, proportional spacing and microspacing are done automatically for you when you select certain typefaces, but many word processors will let you make further microspacing adjustments if the situation requires it. Virtually all word processors will also let you create italic, boldface, underline, subscript, and superscript characters in your document—as well as a number of special characters (see Figure PS 1-13)—if your printer supports them.

■ **Monospacing.** A printing feature that allocates the same amount of space on a line to each character. ■ **Proportional spacing.** A printing feature that allocates more horizontal space on a line to some characters than to others. ■ **Microspacing.** A technique used by many printers and software products to insert fractional spaces between characters.

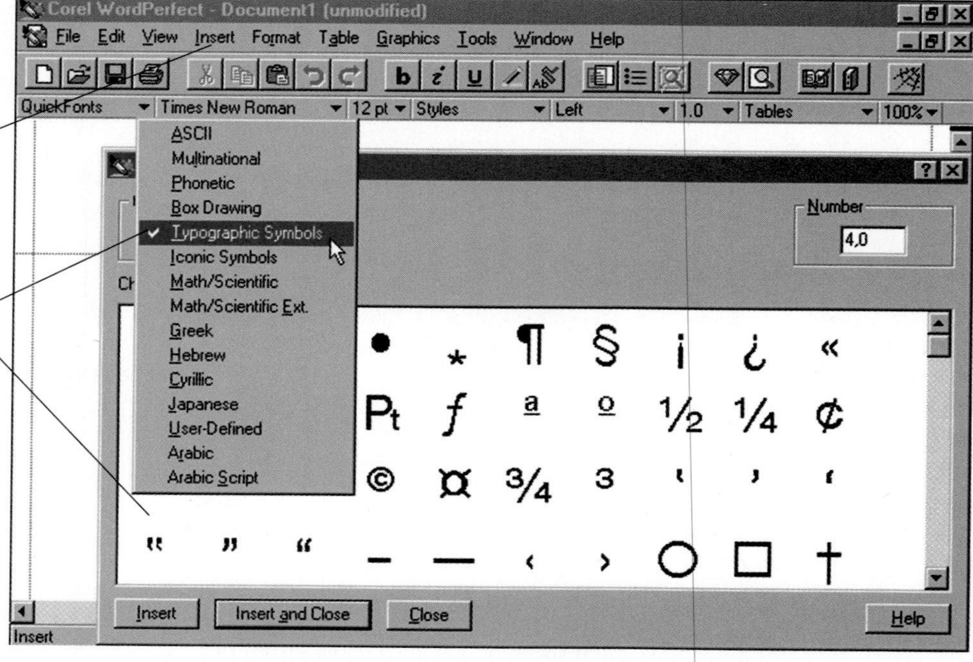

FIGURE PS 1-13

Special characters.

Previewing Documents Sometimes, you discover problems with a document after you finish preparing it and printing it. The margins may look too wide, a graphic element on one page may not balance with an element on a facing page, and so on. To save the time and cost of printing documents over and over again until they look right, virtually all word processors have a *preview feature* that enables you to inspect an onscreen version of what the document will actually look like when printed (see Figure PS 1-14).

As the figure illustrates, there is often a special preview toolbar that will let you magnify documents to see parts of them up close, a feature to put multiple pages on the same screen, and so on. Many word processors will also let you edit documents in the preview mode.

FIGURE PS 1-14

Previewing a document. Preview toolbar buttons enable you to examine several pages at a time on the screen and, also, to magnify pages to inspect them in fine detail.

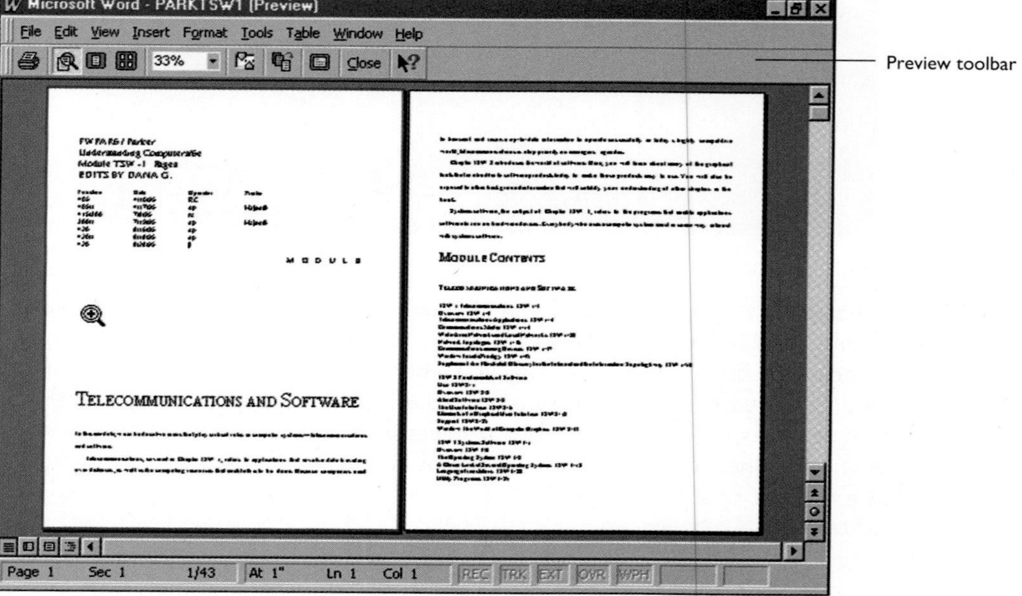

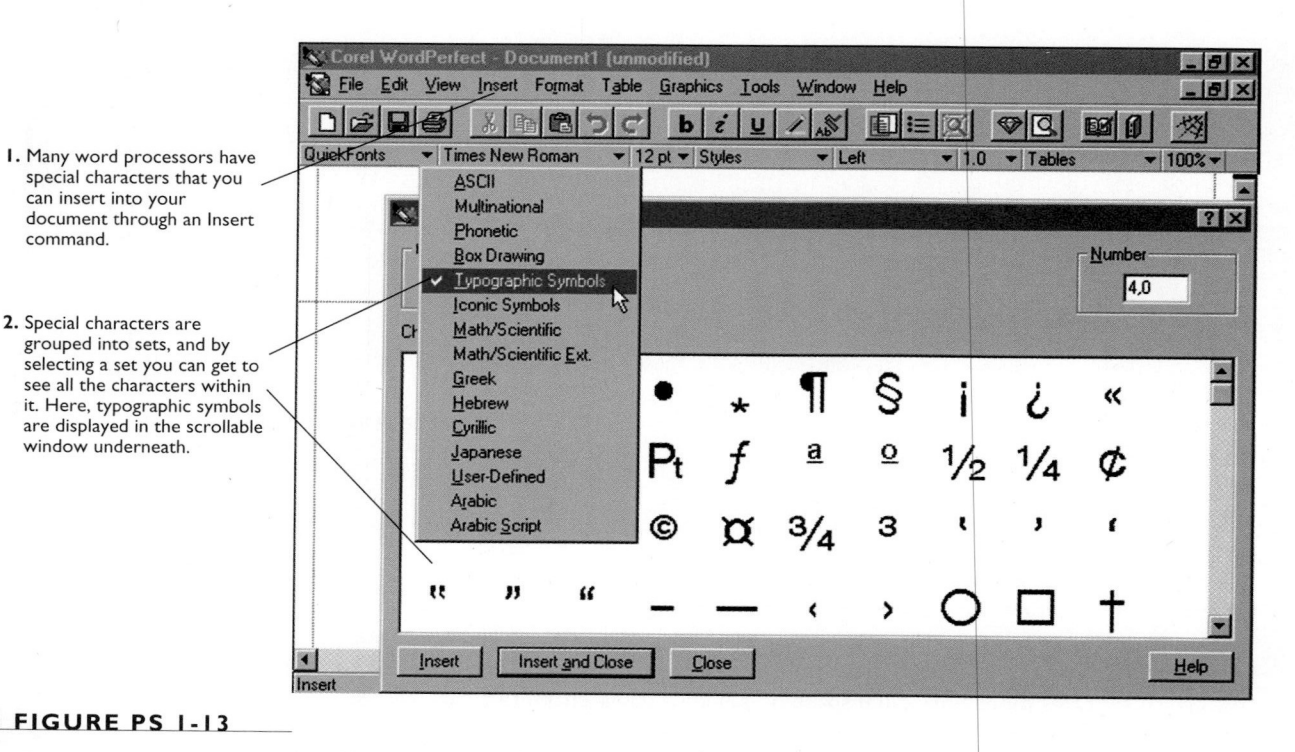

Multiple Columns Multiple-column formatting lets you print text in a columnar format similar to that used in newspapers and magazines. You can print text double- or triple-column, and you can usually output text into columns that are uneven width. Multiple-column formatting is especially useful when you are printing your own brochures or newsletters (see Figure PS 1-15).

Footnoting A footnoting feature allows you to create, edit, and delete footnotes in a document. Typically, the routine that manages the footnoting is designed to remember footnote references and automatically renumber footnotes if you insert or delete any.

ADVANCED OPERATIONS

In addition to the basic operations we've just covered, the more sophisticated word processors enable you to do a number of other useful tasks. Some of these may be especially valuable if you are a professional typist or an author or a publisher, or if your business requires a lot of correspondence.

FIGURE PS 1-15

Arranging documents in multiple columns.

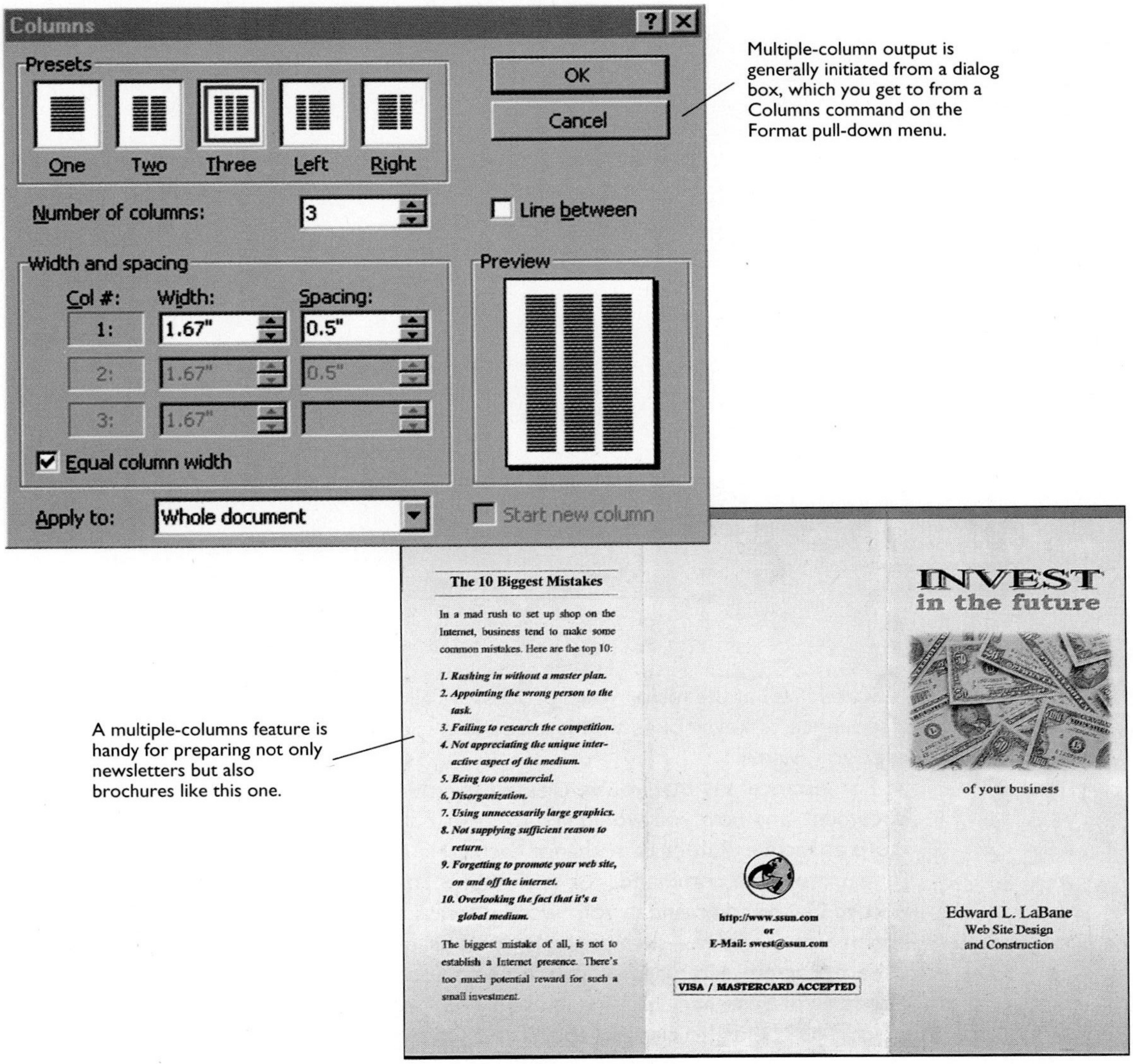

Multiple-column output is generally initiated from a dialog box, which you get to from a Columns command on the Format pull-down menu.

A multiple-columns feature is handy for preparing not only newsletters but also brochures like this one.

Customizing Your Word Processor As you work with your word processor, you will not only find many ways to speed up your work but also discover ways to alter defaults in order to match your working habits and preferences. You can customize a word processor in a variety of ways, including creating automatic backup copies of documents, changing the location where files are saved, tailoring the spelling checker to more closely meet your individual needs, creating new toolbar buttons and even new toolbars, squelching the potentially annoying beep feature that accompanies some message boxes, and so on. In Microsoft Word, for instance, many types of customization are done by choosing Tools on the menu bar and then either Customize or Options on the corresponding pull-down menu (see Figure PS 1-16).

ABOUT CUSTOMIZING
Customizing is often done by summoning a Customize or Options dialog box from a Tools command on the menu bar.

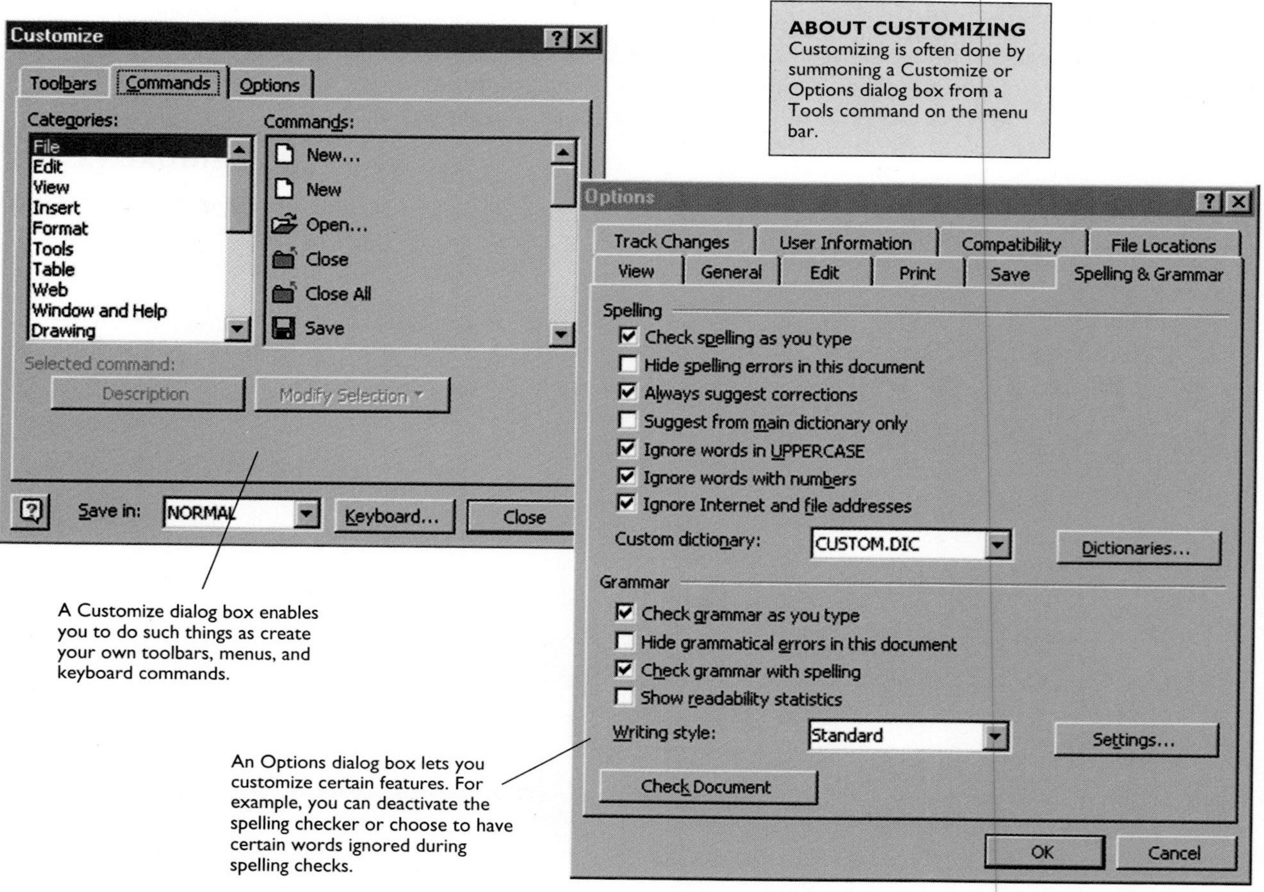

FIGURE PS 1-16

Customizing a word processor.

Macros All of the major word processors allow you to create macros. A **macro** is a sequence of keystrokes that is saved in a special file so that you can use it whenever you wish.

For instance, say that you've created several dozen tables of a certain type in your document, and now you would like to format all of them in order to make them look more attractive. Rather than change each table individually, you can create a macro to repeat the same commands for each table. To create a macro, you first invoke the Record Macro command in your word processor. You then use the word processor's host macro language—such as the WordBasic language in Microsoft Word—to write a short program. Alternatively, you could type and use your mouse to select menu commands. When finished, you would use a Run Macro command to produce the desired effect. You could also create a toolbar button for the macro.

■ **Macro.** A predetermined series of keystrokes or commands that can be invoked by a single keystroke or command.

Understanding that macro programming is beyond the grasp of most users, most word-processing-program publishers also have easy-to-use built-in macros that you can summon for specific tasks. For instance, virtually every word processor has a Date macro—a menu-activated command that places today's date automatically at the insertion-point position. In addition, many packages often include some type of *auto-text feature* that lets you store frequently used words or sentences in a special library to replace other text on demand. For instance, let's say you'll be typing several letters containing the phrase "Yours truly, Mary M. Miller." You could save time by typing this information once and saving it in a special library—say, as "bye." As you type the letter, type *bye* where the closing words are to appear, press a special function key, and—presto—"Yours truly, Mary M. Miller" appears.

The use of macros is illustrated in Figure PS 1-17.

FIGURE PS 1-17

Using macros.

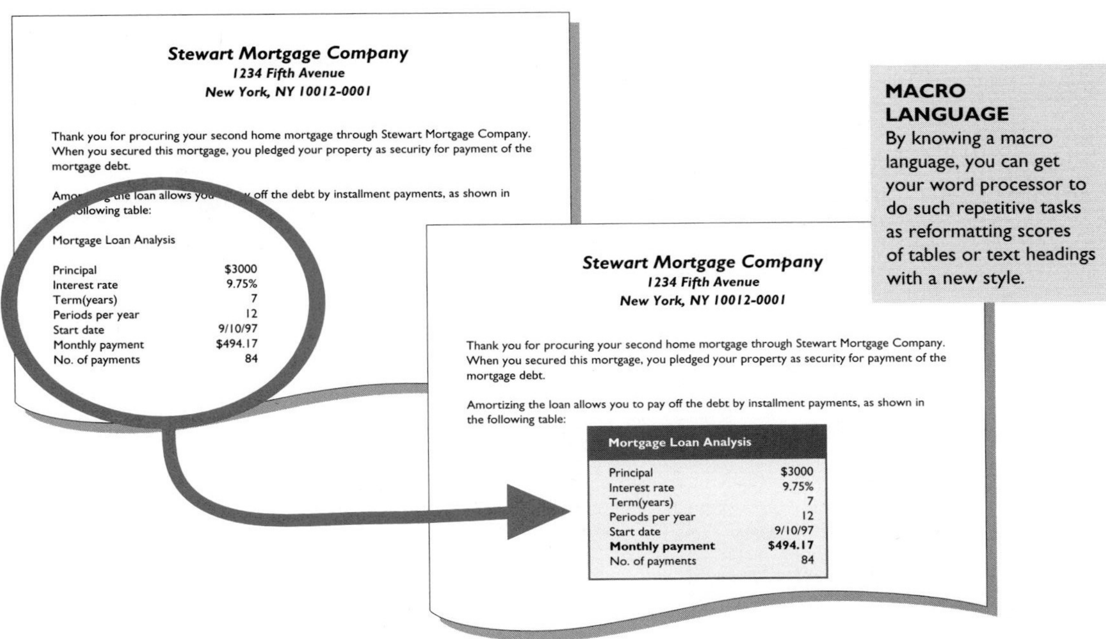

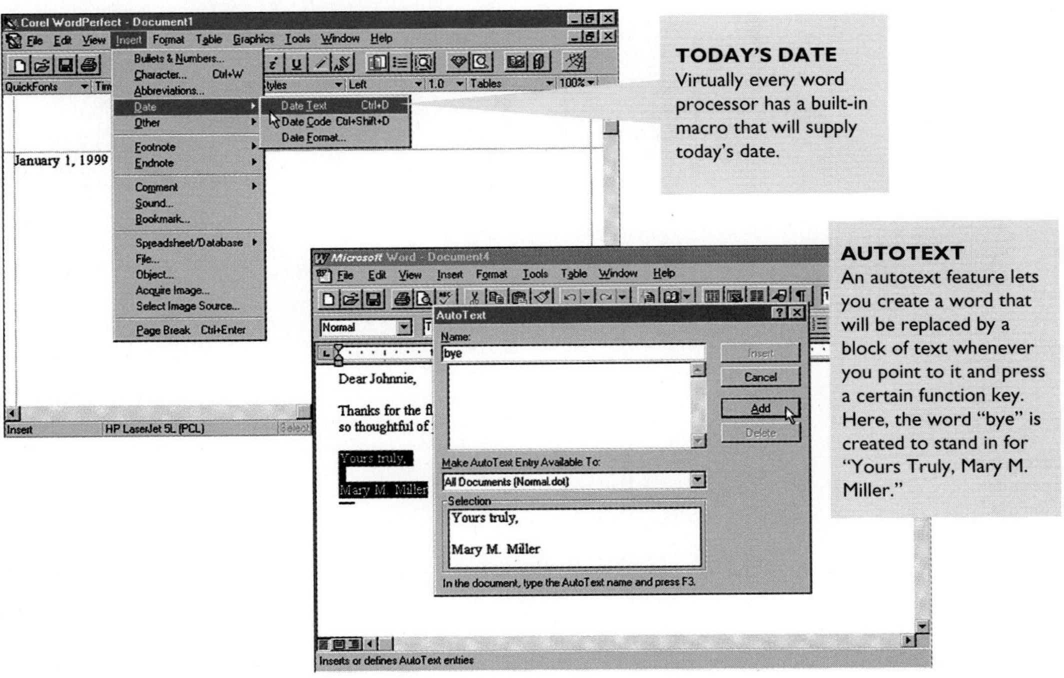

PS

FIGURE PS 1-18

Merging and mailing labels illustrated.

Mass Mailings Anyone who sends lots of mail can benefit from a word processor's merge and mailing-label features (see Figure PS 1-18). Individuals and organizations often need to send the same letter—more or less—to dozens or even thousands of people. A word processor's **merge feature** is designed to automate much of the work of producing form letters of this sort. The feature is so named because it prints

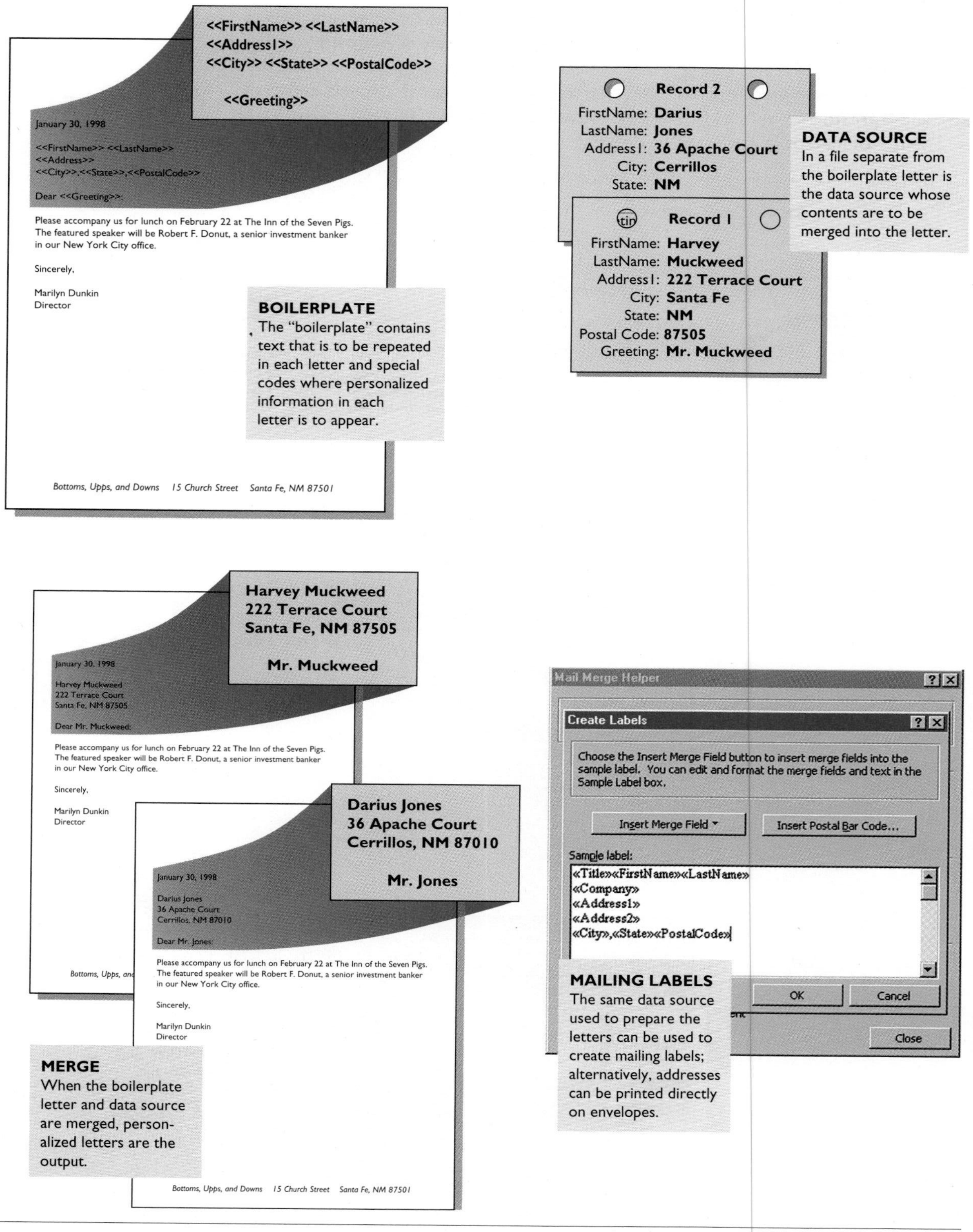

<<FirstName>> <<LastName>>
<<Address1>>
<<City>> <<State>> <<PostalCode>>

<<Greeting>>

January 30, 1998

<<FirstName>> <<LastName>>
<<Address>>
<<City>>,<<State>>,<<PostalCode>>

Dear <<Greeting>>:

Please accompany us for lunch on February 22 at The Inn of the Seven Pigs. The featured speaker will be Robert F. Donut, a senior investment banker in our New York City office.

Sincerely,

Marilyn Dunkin
Director

Bottoms, Upps, and Downs 15 Church Street Santa Fe, NM 87501

BOILERPLATE
The "boilerplate" contains text that is to be repeated in each letter and special codes where personalized information in each letter is to appear.

Record 2
FirstName: **Darius**
LastName: **Jones**
Address1: **36 Apache Court**
City: **Cerrillos**
State: **NM**

Record 1
FirstName: **Harvey**
LastName: **Muckweed**
Address1: **222 Terrace Court**
City: **Santa Fe**
State: **NM**
Postal Code: **87505**
Greeting: **Mr. Muckweed**

DATA SOURCE
In a file separate from the boilerplate letter is the data source whose contents are to be merged into the letter.

Harvey Muckweed
222 Terrace Court
Santa Fe, NM 87505

Mr. Muckweed

January 30, 1998

Harvey Muckweed
222 Terrace Court
Santa Fe, NM 87505

Dear Mr. Muckweed:

Please accompany us for lunch on February 22 at The Inn of the Seven Pigs. The featured speaker will be Robert F. Donut, a senior investment banker in our New York City office.

Sincerely,

Marilyn Dunkin
Director

Darius Jones
36 Apache Court
Cerrillos, NM 87010

Mr. Jones

January 30, 1998

Darius Jones
36 Apache Court
Cerrillos, NM 87010

Dear Mr. Jones:

Please accompany us for lunch on February 22 at The Inn of the Seven Pigs. The featured speaker will be Robert F. Donut, a senior investment banker in our New York City office.

Sincerely,

Marilyn Dunkin
Director

Bottoms, Upps, and Downs 15 Church Street Santa Fe, NM 87501

MERGE
When the boilerplate letter and data source are merged, personalized letters are the output.

Mail Merge Helper

Create Labels

Choose the Insert Merge Field button to insert merge fields into the sample label. You can edit and format the merge fields and text in the Sample Label box.

Insert Merge Field ▾ Insert Postal Bar Code...

Sample label:
«Title»«FirstName»«LastName»
«Company»
«Address1»
«Address2»
«City»,«State»«PostalCode»

OK Cancel Close

MAILING LABELS
The same data source used to prepare the letters can be used to create mailing labels; alternatively, addresses can be printed directly on envelopes.

■ **Merge feature.** A routine specifically designed to produce form letters.

letters in volume by merging a file containing a list of names and addresses with a file containing the *boilerplate,* or form-letter text.

A **mailing label feature** is often used to generate mailing labels. You can usually sort labels by specific fields (such as zip code) or extract records having special characteristics (such as all alumni from the class of 1997 living in San Francisco) prior to processing the labels.Virtually all word processors being sold today also have a feature that enables you to print envelopes on demand. All you generally have to do is mount the envelope in your printer and click on some type of Print Envelopes command. The word processor can then be directed to your document to automatically pick the address. If several addresses are involved, it can be directed to a file of names and addresses—say, the same one you use for letter merging.

Redlining Redlining, a popular groupware feature available on most word processors today, enables two or more people to collaborate on written pieces. When making corrections to a hard-copy document such as a magazine article or book, editors have traditionally used a red pen to cross out certain words or phrases written by the author and to substitute others. This process is called **redlining.** After a document is redlined, the author can see both what he or she originally wrote and the changes made by the editor. Any change can be then approved or vetoed. The redlining feature found in many word processors provides the electronic equivalent of the manual redlining process (see Figure PS 1-19).

FIGURE PS 1-19

Using a redlining feature.

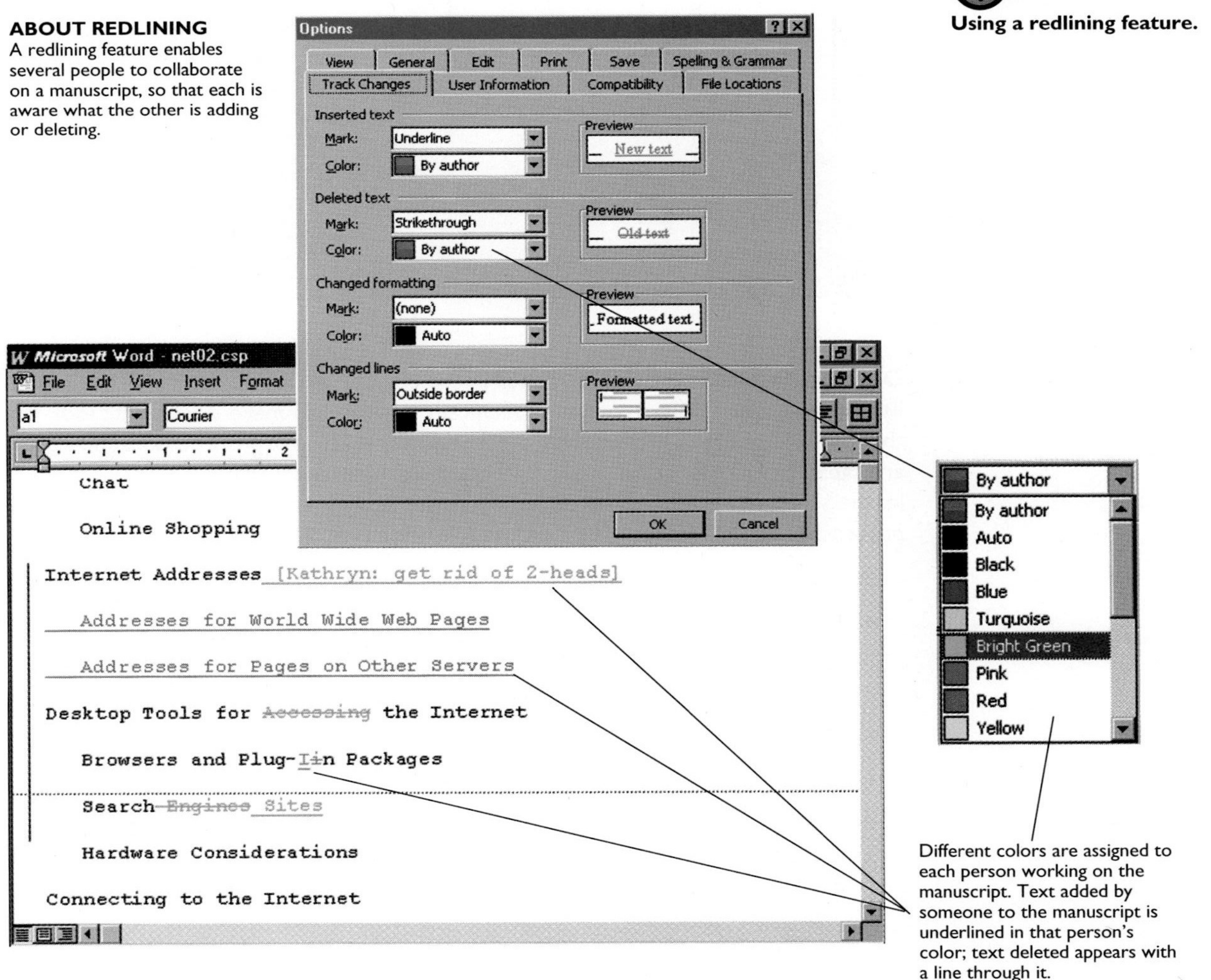

ABOUT REDLINING
A redlining feature enables several people to collaborate on a manuscript, so that each is aware what the other is adding or deleting.

Different colors are assigned to each person working on the manuscript. Text added by someone to the manuscript is underlined in that person's color; text deleted appears with a line through it.

■ **Mailing label feature.** A routine that generates address labels. ■ **Redlining.** A word processing feature that provides the electronic equivalent of the editor's red pen.

Outlining A word processor's *outlining* feature helps you to organize ideas into a hierarchy. For instance, when organizing topics for a report, you often split them into headings, subheadings, and so on. Most word processors let you choose from a variety of outline styles, including those shown in Figure PS 1-20. As you type the outline, the word processor automatically performs the required formatting—for example, inserting outline numbers and taking care of indents. In many word processing programs, you can also temporarily collapse a long document with several levels of heads into an outline to view its overall structure.

FIGURE PS 1-20

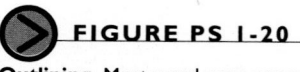

Outlining. Most word processors let you choose from a variety of outline styles, including those shown here.

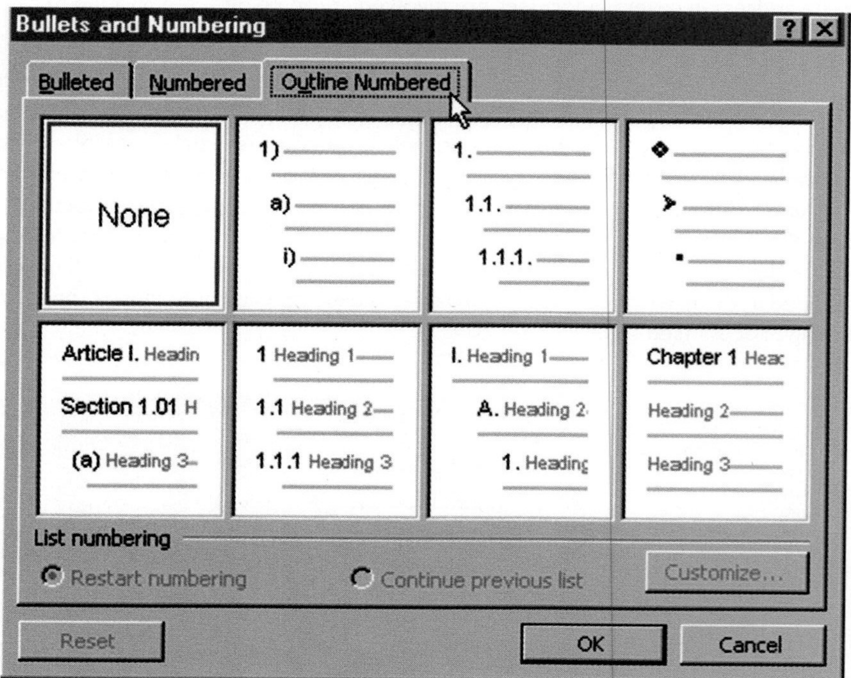

Desktop Publishing Effects Later in the chapter we'll be covering desktop publishing programs—software that's specifically designed to make documents look like they were done by a professional print shop. Modern word processors, however, are capable of a respectable amount of desktop publishing themselves. You've already learned that you can dress up documents with fancy fonts. Beyond that, many word processors contain features that do the following (see also Figure PS 1-21):

- GRAPHICS A word processor's graphics feature enables you to import art into a document—say, a graph from another program or a cartoon from a library of **clip-art** images. Generally, all you have to do is find the image you want and then copy it into your document at the insertion-point position. Once the art is in your document, you can move it around at will, resize or crop it, and so forth. All of the major word processing programs, since they are part of an office suite, also have access to a drawing toolbar that lets you do a limited amount of drawing.
- DROP CAPS A **drop cap** is a large capital letter that often appears at the beginning of an article or a book chapter. The drop cap may occupy a vertical distance of several lines, depending on the effect desired.

■ **Clip art.** Prepackaged artwork designed to be imported into text documents or charts, say, by word processing, desktop publishing, or presentation graphics software. ■ **Drop cap.** A large, decorative capital letter that sometimes appears at the beginning of an article or chapter of text.

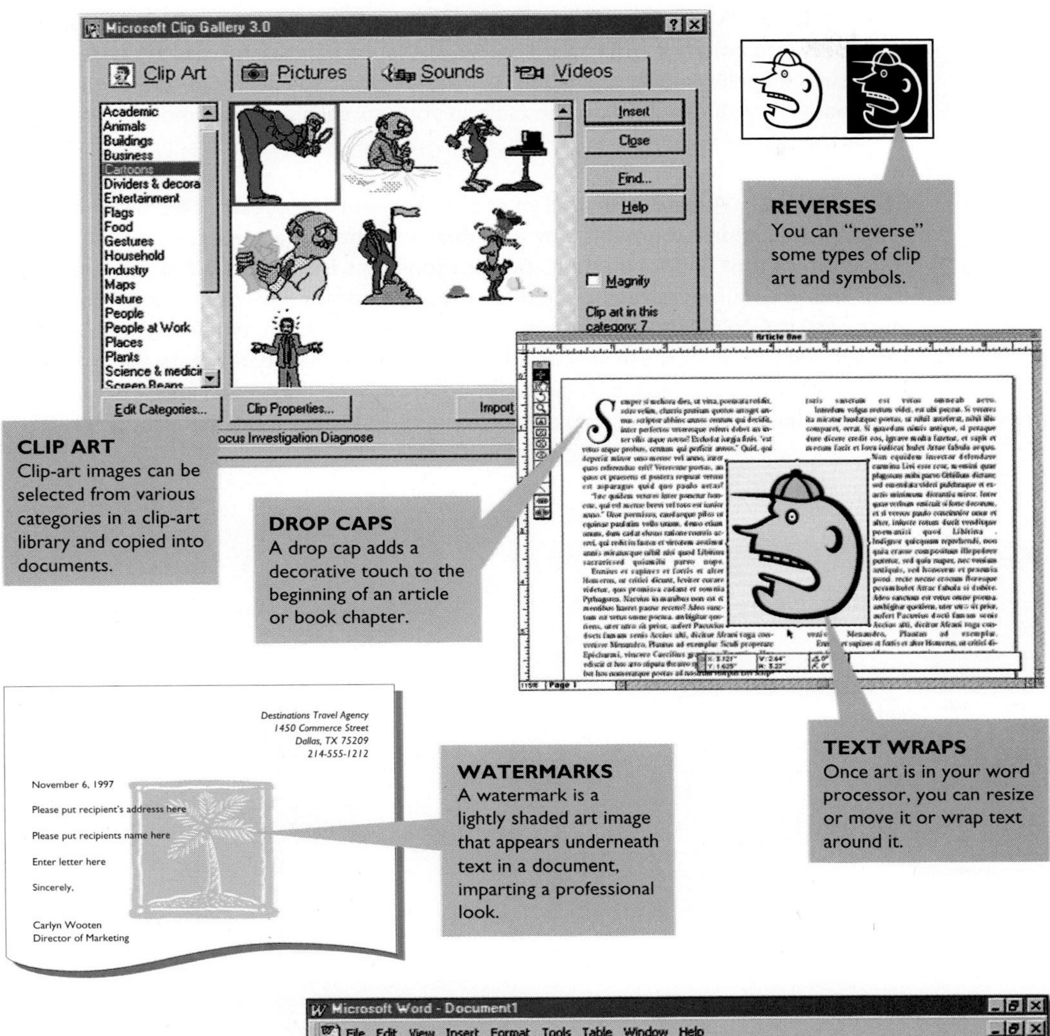

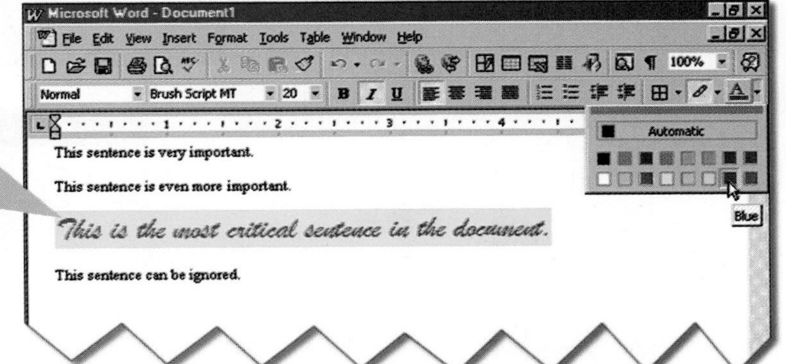

FIGURE PS 1-21

Desktop publishing with a word processor.

- WATERMARKS A **watermark** is a lightly shaded image that appears underneath text in a document to impart a professional look. The image can be a logo, a decorative graphic, or even a word or phrase—such as *CONFIDENTIAL*—that has the appearance of being stamped on pages. Like any regular piece of art, you can move and resize the watermark to suit your own taste.
- TEXT ENHANCEMENT As hinted earlier, you can enhance text in a variety of ways. Once you select text, you can change the font, boldface or italicize, or change the color of the text and highlight it like you would with a "magic marker."

■ **Watermark.** A lightly shaded art image that appears to underlie a document's text.

- TABLES A word processor's tables feature lets you organize text and/or numbers into columns and rows. You can also automatically format the table, adding such embellishments as shading, borders, colors, special fonts, and so on. Alternatively, you can develop the table in your spreadsheet and import it into your word processor.

Style Sheets A feature that all of the leading word processors have—and that is standard fare in desktop publishing programs—is the **style sheet.** A style sheet is a collection of font and formatting specifications that is saved as a file and later used to prepare documents in a particular way. For instance, if your letters to clients must conform to a certain letterhead style and use a specific typeface and point size, you can declare all of these specifications in one or more style sheets that you apply when preparing such letters. Reports, in contrast, would probably use a different set of style sheets. You can prepare your own style sheets from scratch or use templates and wizards to assist you (see Figure PS 1-22).

FIGURE PS 1-22

Using wizards and templates. Here, a wizard simplifies preparation of a cover sheet to accompany a fax.

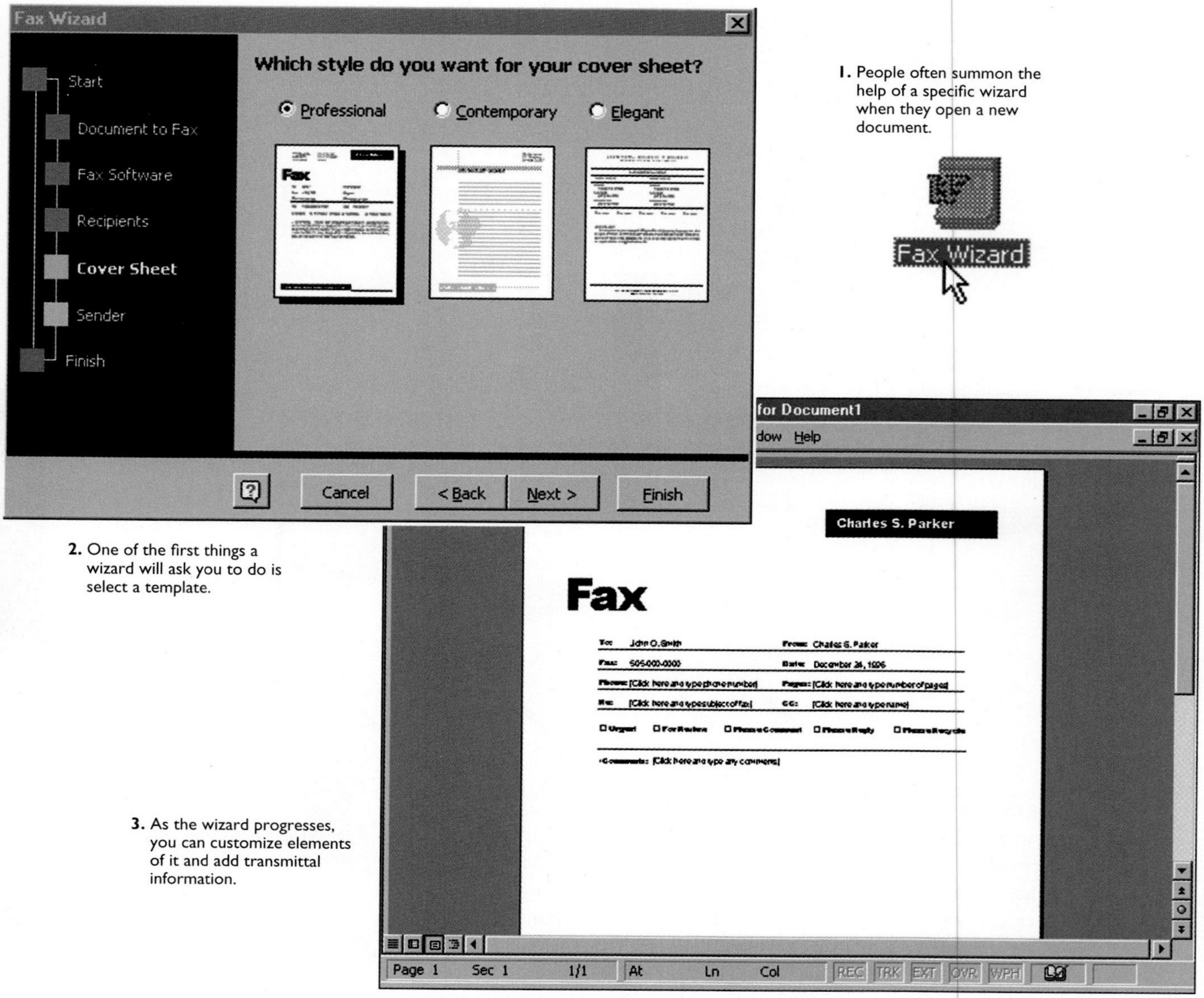

1. People often summon the help of a specific wizard when they open a new document.

2. One of the first things a wizard will ask you to do is select a template.

3. As the wizard progresses, you can customize elements of it and add transmittal information.

■ **Style sheet.** A collection of design specifications saved as a file for later use to format documents in a particular way.

TEMPLATES A **template** shows the basic style to which documents of a certain type will conform. Templates are frequently used to create a fancy style of letter, a cover-sheet design for sending faxes, or press releases. Once you've selected a template, software will automatically apply the appropriate styling.

WIZARDS A **wizard** usually goes beyond a template in that it consists of a series of screens that tell you, step-by-step, how to create documents of a certain type. Wizards commonly exist for such tasks as creating fax cover sheets, calendars, meeting agendas, awards, newsletters, and résumés. To use the wizard when preparing a document, you merely answer a series of questions from dialog boxes. For instance, you might first choose a template, then customize the template with your company's logo, and then begin typing specific information into the template—say, the name and address of the person to whom you wish to send a fax.

Grammar Checkers Many word processors today are accompanied by **grammar checkers,** routines that are designed to root out errors in grammar, punctuation, and word usage. Some grammar checkers also analyze writing styles for specific weaknesses (such as overuse of certain words, overly long sentences, and sexist or out-of-date language). In addition, many checkers will calculate some type of overall reading-level statistic for your written work. Unfortunately, good writing often depends on bending rules. So, although grammar checkers may help people write in an understandable fashion, they cannot turn a wretched writer into an instant Hemingway. Grammar checkers are also available from third-party vendors.

Index and Table-of-Contents Preparation All of the major word processors allow you to "tag" words or phrases individually so that you can later prepare an index or a table of contents. For instance, if you have tagged a few hundred words in a book for an index, you can later invoke the word processor's *indexing routine,* which will arrange these words in alphabetical order and provide the page numbers on which the words appear. Most indexing routines also let you create index subheadings similar to the ones that appear in the index of this book.

Linking and Embedding Objects/Web-Page Creation Most word processors today let you embed into your document objects taken from other applications. These objects may include a table from a spreadsheet program, an art object from an illustration program, or something else. To embed (import) an object, you link to its application from your word processor and copy and paste into your document. Such transfers are only possible when both importing and exporting applications operate under a common standard such as object linking and embedding (OLE), ActiveX, or OpenDoc. Some of these standards extend to Web-page creation, thus enabling you to save word-processed documents as Web (HTML) pages.

Add-On Programs When a word processor is missing a potentially useful feature, chances are an aftermarket (third-party) company—or even the company that makes the word processor—will offer such a feature as an **add-on program.** One of the most useful add-on programs for people who write for a living is the reference shelf.

A **reference shelf** provides online access to a number of handy reference tools. The most prominent of these packages, Microsoft Bookshelf (see Figure PS 1-23), packs electronic versions of a dictionary, an encyclopedia, a book of quotations, an atlas, a zip-code directory, a world almanac and book of facts, and an Internet directory onto a single CD-ROM. Bookshelf enables any of its works to be summoned by a word processor with a couple of keystrokes. Works can be electronically searched for text and, when the text is found, it can be cut and pasted back into the document being word processed.

■ **Template.** A pattern or style for documents of a certain type. ■ **Wizard.** A series of screens that tell you, step-by-step, how to create documents of a certain type. ■ **Grammar checker** A word processor function designed to root out errors in grammar, punctuation, and word usage. ■ **Add-on program.** Software that supplements the activities of a larger program. ■ **Reference shelf.** A software product that provides a number of handy reference books online to the writer.

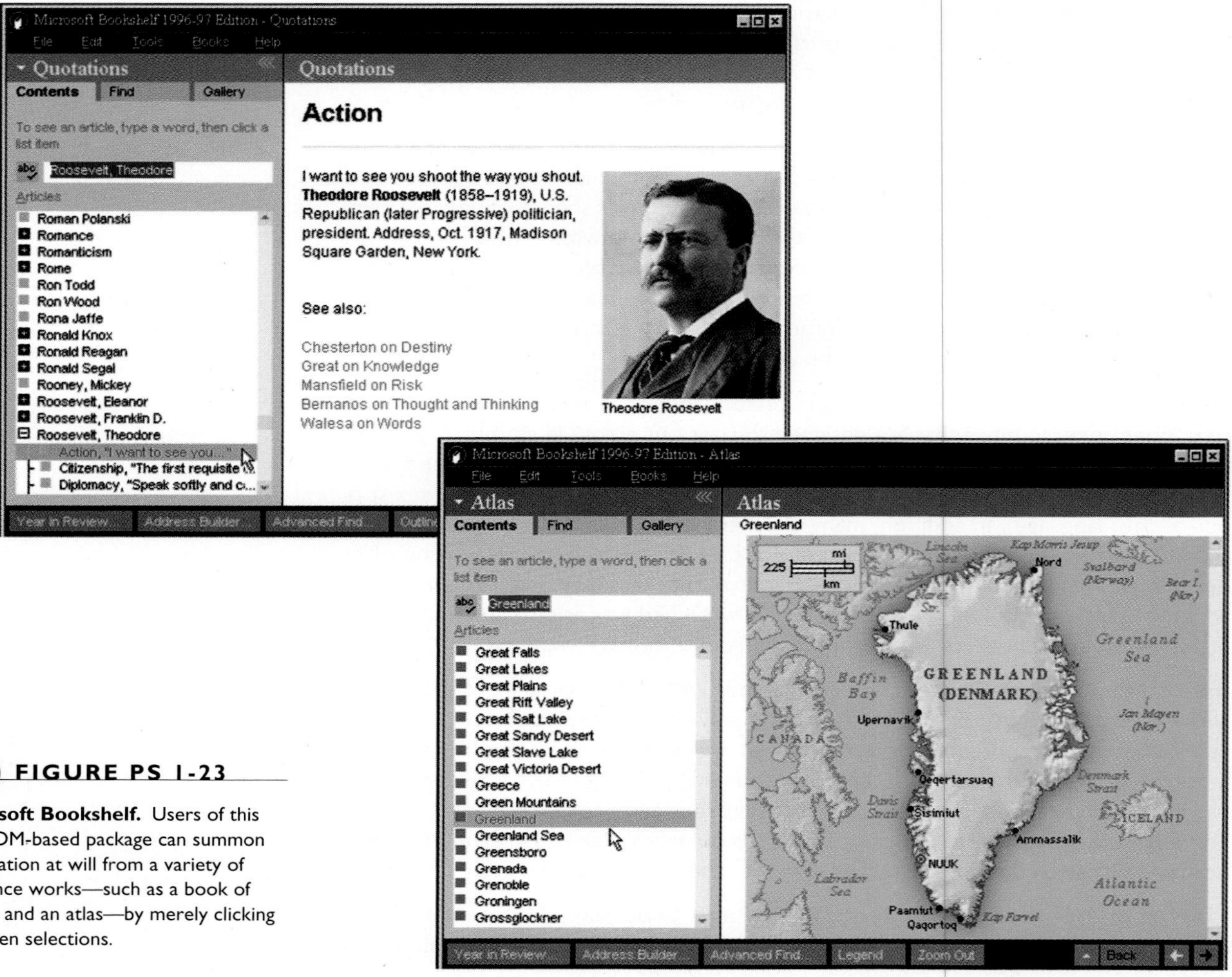

FIGURE PS 1-23

Microsoft Bookshelf. Users of this CD-ROM-based package can summon information at will from a variety of reference works—such as a book of quotes and an atlas—by merely clicking onscreen selections.

Desktop Publishing Software

In the past decade or so, desktop publishing has rapidly evolved into a major applications area within the field of computers.

WHAT IS DESKTOP PUBLISHING?

Desktop publishing refers to desktop microcomputer systems that let you combine and manipulate on a page such elements as text—in any of several typefaces, point sizes, and styles—art, and photos, thus creating attractive documents that look as if they came off a professional printer's press. Desktop publishing is designed to replace many of the traditionally manual, labor-intensive tasks associated with cutting, arranging, and pasting elements onto a page. Because desktop publishing makes it possible for publishing to be done in-house, it also enables companies to save money, save time, and have more control over the look of finished documents.

You can do desktop publishing with either word processing software, as has been already described, or a desktop publishing program. As you can probably surmise from studying the images in Figure PS 1-24—which was done using a desktop publishing

■ **Desktop publishing.** A microcomputer-based publishing system that can fit on a desktop.

Make a big impact with a big letter. Set body text in your layout or word processing program, then set a large initial cap in its own text box or frame and position it.

Drop caps are an easy way to dress up your written message!

To achieve a rippled, almost underwater look for your drop cap, set your letter in Photoshop. Fill it with color then deselect it (Command-D) and select all. Choose Filter, Blur, Gaussian Blur, and set the radius to 15 pixels. Change the Mode to RGB (in order to access the Aldus Gallery Effects filters), then choose Filter, Gallery Effects, Ripple. Experiment with the settings and click Preview until you get the effect you want.

Scan old wood or metal type for an old-fashioned look. You may need to vertically reflect some letters in an image-editing program, as the type is actually backward.

For a "ransom note" look, tear a letter from a magazine or newspaper and scan.

Concept-appropriate embellishments can turn a simple letter into an artful introduction. Belt and buckle, color and highlights were added to type in an image-editing program.

HO HO HO!

Feathery lines and a skewed letter convey a sense of motion — easily created in Photoshop. See page 76 for details.

38 Dynamic Graphics

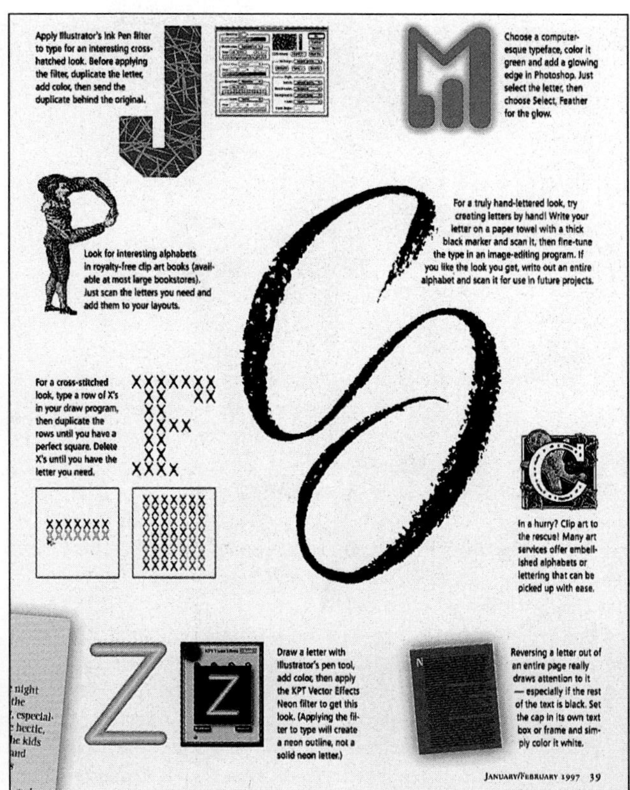

Apply Illustrator's Ink Pen filter to type for an interesting cross-hatched look. Before applying the filter, duplicate the letter, add color, then send the duplicate behind the original.

Choose a computer-esque typeface, color it green and add a glowing edge in Photoshop. Just select the letter, then choose Select, Feather for the glow.

Look for interesting alphabets in royalty-free clip art books (available at most large bookstores). Just scan the letters you need and add them to your layouts.

For a truly hand-lettered look, try creating letters by hand! Write your letter on a paper towel with a thick black marker and scan it, then fine-tune the type in an image-editing program. If you like the look you get, write out an entire alphabet and scan it for use in future projects.

For a cross-stitched look, type a row of X's in your draw program, then duplicate the rows until you have a perfect square. Delete X's until you have the letter you need.

In a hurry? Clip art to the rescue! Many art services offer embellished alphabets or lettering that can be picked up with ease.

Draw a letter with Illustrator's pen tool, add color, then apply the KPT Vector Effects Neon filter to get this look. (Applying the filter to type will create a neon outline, not a solid neon letter.)

Reversing a letter out of an entire page really draws attention to it — especially if the rest of the text is black. Set the cap in its own text box or frame and simply color it white.

January/February 1997 39

FIGURE PS 1-24

Desktop publishing packages. Desktop publishing systems prepare more sophisticated-looking documents than word processors can produce.

program—the basic difference between embellishing a document with a word processor and a desktop publishing program is in the document's "look." A desktop publishing program provides far more capability as regards typesetting and imagesetting. *Typesetting* implies maximum control over type styles and sizes as well as spacing between words, letters, and lines. *Imagesetting* involves combining and possibly manipulating on a page both type and such artwork elements as sophisticated drawings and full-color photographs.

Naturally, not all desktop publishing systems are the same. You can spend about $100 for a system that gives you some flexibility over your word processor for certain types of documents, but you will pay several times that amount for one that provides the sophisticated look you see in the most artful books and magazines. Desktop publishing systems targeted for commercial applications often consist of several hardware and software components.

HARDWARE

Hardware for a commercial-level desktop publishing system usually includes a high-end microcomputer system, a laser printer, a graphics-oriented monitor, and an image scanner. These devices are covered in depth in the HW module of the text and are therefore addressed only briefly here.

High-End Microcomputer System The most important components of a computer for desktop publishing applications are a speedy microprocessor, a respectable amount of RAM, and a hard disk with plenty of storage. Manipulation of graphical fonts, photos, and art is computationally intensive, and each of these elements consumes a lot of storage, as well. Such work requires a system unit like those based on high-end Intel and PowerPC chips. The systems should have 32 to 64 MB of RAM and at least a couple of gigabytes of hard-disk storage. Additionally, auxiliary storage devices such as Zip, SyJet, Jaz, and WORM drives can be handy if you need to store large volumes of material offline or send large images to others.

Service Bureaus

How to Extend Your Computer System at a Nominal Cost

You want to create a color brochure on your word processor, but you don't have a color printer. You want to make color 35 mm slides for a meeting coming up in two weeks, but you don't have a film recorder to produce them. Someone sent you some important documents on a Macintosh-formatted disk, but you can't read it—your computer runs only in a Microsoft Windows environment. What do you do? Consider going to a service bureau.

Service bureaus exist in virtually all large and midsized cities throughout North America. A few years ago, many of them were strictly considered copy centers or print shops, because virtually the only thing they did was run off dupes of hard copy documents for people. Although service bureaus still make a lot of their income doing simple duplication tasks, many now also handle more-sophisticated chores. With the age of microcomputing in full swing and mainframe power of a few years ago now available on desktops, most service bureaus have expanded their offerings to include any or all of the following:

Color Output Output can be produced for you on any of a variety of print media—paper, slides, transparencies, and the like. Typically, you bring in an electronic disk containing the file you want output, and the service bureau does the rest. Before you prepare your disk, you should make sure it conforms to a file format—such as TIFF, PICT, or EPS—that the service bureau can handle. Hundreds of file formats are in existence, so beware. Some service bureaus are located on the Web; you send images to them online and receive hard-copy outputs in the mail. Or, conversely, you can provide them film and download the images off the Web.

Color Copies Even if you have your own color printer, it's often cheaper and faster to have duplicates made of color output through a service bureau than to print multiple copies at home.

Service Bureau. The place to go if you lack hardware, software, or expertise.

The service bureau can also duplicate slides for you and make prints of them. Many will even colorize black-and-white originals, change colors in images, and reduce or enlarge images.

Computer Rental Today, a number of service bureaus rent time on PC-compatible and Macintosh computers by the hour, provided you do your work on site. Staff members may be able to help you get started on a particular computer if you are not familiar with it.

Full-Service Design and Typesetting If you are too busy to do your own desktop publishing or to prepare your own presentation materials, many service bureaus will do this type of work for you. Typical services include creating résumés, custom business stationery, business forms, sales flyers and price lists, newsletters and brochures, promotional materials, and charts and graphs. Some service bureaus will also outsource work that they cannot do in-house.

Videoconferencing Videoconferencing shows images of people on a screen as they talk to one another. Many service bureaus maintain rooms where you can carry on face-to-face meetings with distant clients, business associates, or relatives. Many systems even enable you to share and jointly annotate electronic documents while you confer.

Laser Printer Most laser printers for microcomputer-based desktop publishing applications cost anywhere from about $500 to several thousand dollars, depending on such things as page speed and the ability to produce color. For graphics work, the printer should have at least four megabytes of RAM. Having a lot of RAM allows you to output images of greater complexity. For photographic outputs, a 600 dpi print resolution is satisfactory. If you require higher resolution than this, you can always go to a service bureau (see Feature PS 1-1).

The laser printer in your computer system relies on a specific **page description language (PDL)** to carry out its work. The two most common PDLs are Adobe's *PostScript,* which is widely used in high-end desktop publishing, and Hewlett-Packard's *Printer Command Language (PCL),* which is more popular for the general-purpose work required of most users.

■ **Page description language (PDL).** A language for communicating instructions to a laser printer.

Graphics-Oriented Monitor Many monitors used with microcomputer systems contain a relatively small screen that can comfortably display about a third of a standard printed page at a time. On such screens, the resolution usually is adequate for text and some simple graphics. Users of desktop publishing applications, however, generally prefer bigger screens with SVGA or XGA resolution, both to fine-tune detailed graphics and to see without eye strain either a full-page or a two-page layout on the screen at one time. Monitors designed for these purposes often have screens up to 50 percent larger than the typical microcomputer display, and many of them display in portrait (page-length) mode.

Image Scanner An image scanner allows you to scan photographs, drawings, or text and digitize them directly into computer memory. Later, you can edit the images with illustration software and hardware. Some image scanners also use optical character recognition (OCR) software, which enables them to recognize text characters. Such a feature allows you to later edit any text that you enter with the scanner. Color scanners are widely available, and many cost under $500. If you don't have a scanner to input photos to your computer system, you may be able to get them scanned at either a service bureau or a Web-enabled processing center as part of your development fee (see User Solution PS 1-1).

SOFTWARE

A variety of software and software-based products support desktop publishing environments. These include page-makeup software, illustration software, fonts, and image and sound libraries.

Page-Makeup Software The programs whose principal function is to combine text, photos, and art elements into a finished page are collectively referred to as **page-makeup software** (see Figure PS 1-25). Because page composition is the

FIGURE PS 1-25

Page-makeup software. Because page makeup is the central function in desktop publishing, page-makeup programs are often called desktop publishing programs.

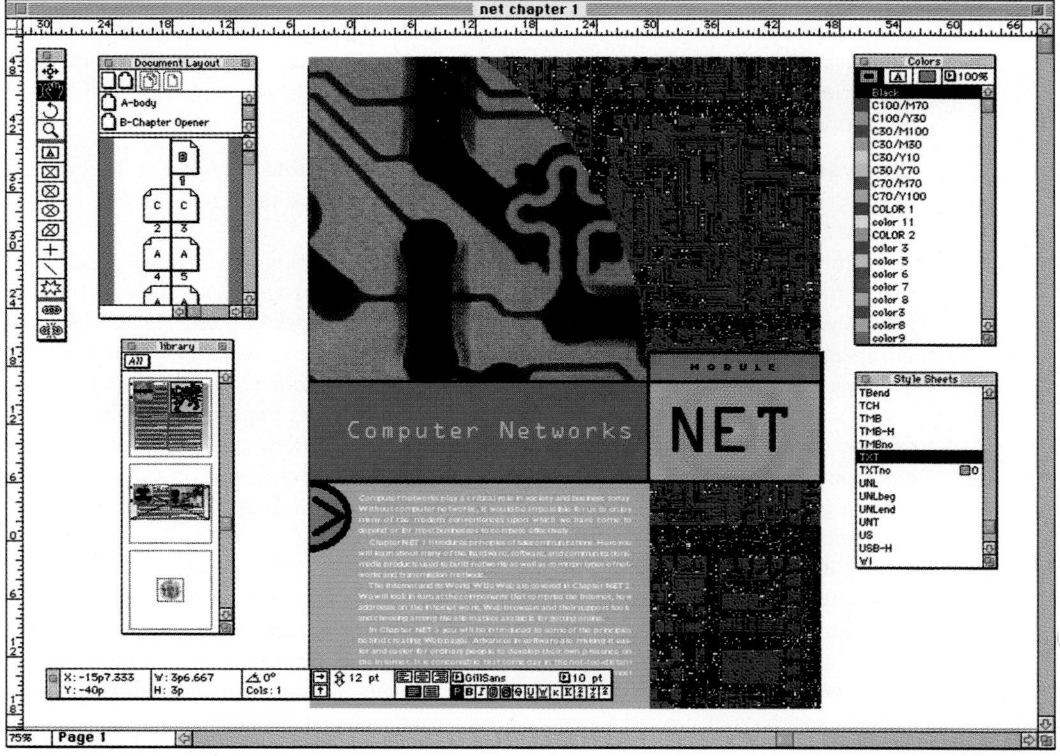

■ **Page-makeup software.** A program used to compose page layouts in a desktop publishing system.

Processing Photos—Over the Web

Close to 700 billion rolls of film get processed each year. With tremdous volume like this, entrepreneurs are constantly looking around for new ways to lure photographers on to the Internet. Here's one they've recently come up with: You shoot a roll of film with a conventional camera, take it in to any of several print shops, and pick up your images the next day—over the World Wide Web. Since the images are in electronic format, you can touch them up, incorporate them into Christmas cards or newsletters, and e-mail them to friends. A new graphics format called FlashPix stores images at a variety of resolutions, so that you can send them over the Internet in a low-resolution, low-bandwidth way and have friends view them in high-resolution form once they arrive at their destinations.

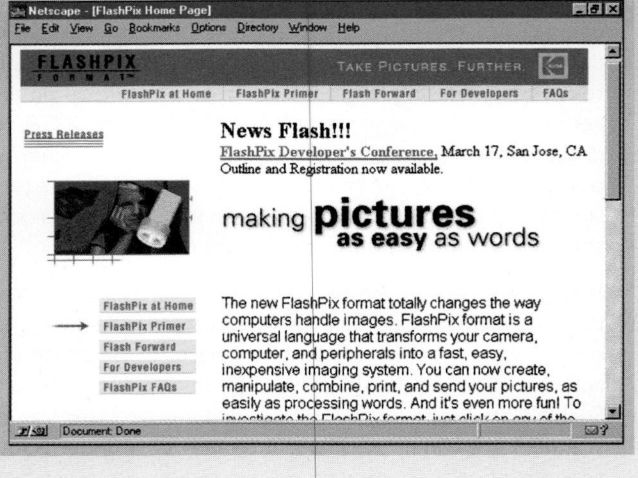

central function of desktop publishing, page-makeup programs are commonly called *desktop publishing programs.*

The vendors of the leading page-makeup programs have designed their products to accept text prepared with most of the leading word processors. Although page-makeup programs enable you to modify any text that you import to them, it is important to recognize that their primary function is page makeup. Thus, they are not as easy to use for word processing as your average word processor.

Some of the leading page-makeup programs are Adobe Systems' PageMaker, Corel Corporation's Corel Ventura, Quark Inc.'s QuarkXPress, and Microsoft's Publisher. Increasingly, these programs are incorporating Web-publishing tools along with their traditional hard-copy, page-makeup offerings.

Illustration Software **Illustration programs** enable artwork to be created from scratch. Also, they accept existing artwork as input and allow it to be modified using the software's image-manipulation facilities.

Commercial illustration programs are commonly distinguished by whether they are primarily oriented toward painting, drawing, or photography. *Painting programs* enable you to create bit-mapped images and to color them pixel by pixel. Usually, the images you create cannot be resized without loss of resolution. For instance, blowing them up may result in jagged edges, whereas reducing them may result in a blurry mess. In contrast, *drawing programs* enable you to create outlines that can be resized. Once sized, these outlines can be filled in with colors. *Photo programs* are oriented toward getting photographs into storage and being able to do touch-up work such as correcting focus, color, and so on. Some illustration programs are multipurpose and will allow you to paint, draw, and handle photos.

The illustration software products on the market collectively enable you to size, rotate, flip, recolor, distort, and edit virtually any digitally stored drawing or photograph to your heart's content (see Figure PS 1-26). Because these programs handle images at electronically fast speeds, you can try out dozens of possibilities in the time it would normally take to produce only a single image by manual means. Once an image is satisfactory, you can export it to a page-makeup program.

■ **Illustration program.** A program that enables users to paint, draw, or manipulate photographs.

TYPE EFFECTS
Special effects for typefaces can be created with most illustration software packages.

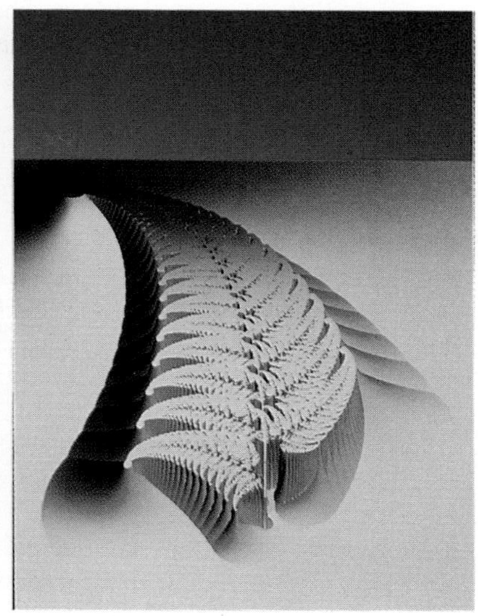

IMAGE MANIPULATION
Using illustration software, complex images can be completely redesigned within seconds or minutes, sometimes with just a few mouse clicks.

BLENDING TOOLS
A blending tool is used to provide a smooth color gradient on a face.

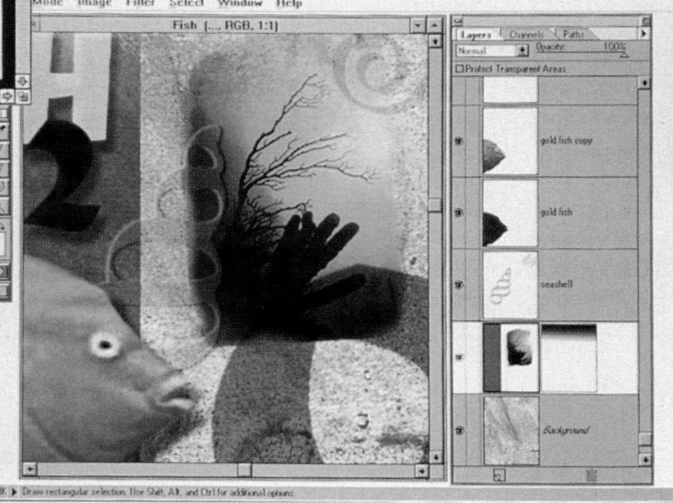

COMPOSITE IMAGES
Complex images are often prepared by layering component images one on top of another, as if stacking panes of glass. Each "pane" can be separately manipulated until the composite image is satisfactory.

A growing variety of illustration programs is available today. Eight of the best-sellers are Adobe's Illustrator and Photoshop, Corel's CorelDraw! and Photo-Paint, Fractal Design's Expression and Painter, Micrografx's Designer, and Macromedia's FreeHand. Some of the programs named here (such as Illustrator and CorelDraw!) are more oriented toward the development of drawings, while others (such as Photoshop)—sometimes called *image-editing programs*—are geared more to such finishing work as making color corrections, retouching images, applying filters, and

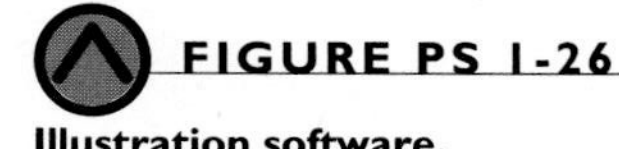

FIGURE PS 1-26
Illustration software.

creating dazzling special effects. The lines defining illustration programs are hazy at best and constantly changing. Anyone considering buying such a program should check carefully the duties the program performs.

Type A variety of fonts and styling features are available for desktop publishing applications. The choices typically go well beyond those that accompany word processors.

Fonts are of two types: bit mapped and outline (see Figure PS 1-27). The distinction between the two is similar to the one between painting and drawing programs.

FIGURE PS 1-27

Bit-mapped versus outline fonts.

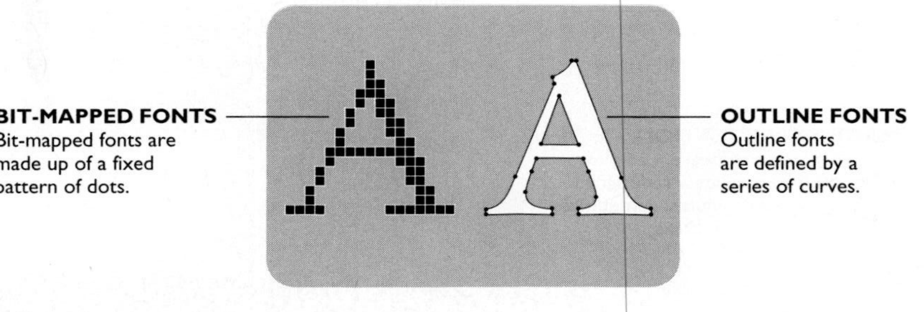

BIT-MAPPED FONTS
Bit-mapped fonts are made up of a fixed pattern of dots.
OUTLINE FONTS
Outline fonts are defined by a series of curves.

Bit-mapped fonts are described by fixed configurations of dots. Although they are the least-expensive kind of font, you cannot scale them to different sizes. *Outline fonts* consist of mathematical curves that describe how characters are shaped. They are more expensive than bit-mapped fonts, but you can scale them to virtually any size you want and also create your own fonts. Two widely used outline fonts are *TrueType* fonts, often bundled with Microsoft and Apple software, and *PostScript Type 1* fonts, which are commonly found in high-end desktop publishing applications.

Even though many word processing and desktop publishing programs come with a variety of fonts, you can add others by acquiring a font library. A *font library* is a collection of fonts that supplements those packaged into your word processor or desktop publishing program. Adobe Systems, for instance, has a library of over 2,000 typefaces that's available on CD-ROM. To use any particular typeface, you buy the special code that unlocks it. The trend today is selling fonts over the Internet, either by making the fonts downloadable over the phone lines or by making it possible to unlock the CD-ROM and charge a user account at the same time.

Image and Sound Libraries An *image library* is a digital collection of prepared art images—drawings, paintings, photos, and the like. Typically, potential users look through a printed or online catalog showing the images and make their selections. Terms and charges vary; you can buy individual images as well as entire libraries containing hundreds or thousands of images. Also, some vendors charge for images on a per-usage basis, whereas others give you virtually unlimited usage of an image once a flat fee is paid. In the future, as computer systems are able to handle digital video better, expect to see video libraries commonplace as well.

Sound libraries contain collections of sounds. Now that desktop publishing of a sort is making its presence felt through Web pages, sounds—including voice and music clips—are yet another way to express oneself through a document.

Summary and Key Terms

Both word processing and desktop publishing technologies deal with the manipulation of words.

Word Processing Software **Word processing** is the use of computer technology to create, manipulate, and print text materials such as letters, legal contracts, manuscripts, and other documents. By far, most people today use *general-purpose* word processing packages, such as Microsoft Word and WordPerfect.

Using a word processor, or for that matter any type of productivity software program, requires learning several general operations. These operations include accessing the program, creating new documents and retrieving old ones, saving and printing documents, and terminating work on the document or applications program.

Learning to use a word processor at a minimal level involves mastering a number of elementary entering-and-editing and print-formatting commands. Entering and editing operations include moving the **insertion point,** scrolling, making line returns through either a **soft return** (the **wordwrap** feature) or a **hard return,** inserting and deleting, **selecting text,** moving and copying, finding and replacing, using a **spelling checker** and **thesaurus feature,** working in a **WYSIWYG** display mode, and using the **zoom feature** to adjust text magnification appropriately.

Among the print-formatting operations that one must learn are adjusting line spacing; indenting; using a **ruler line;** justifying text; setting margins and page formats; reformatting text; centering; tabbing; setting up headers and footers; selecting **typefaces, point sizes,** and **fonts;** multiple-column formatting; previewing documents; and footnoting. Many word processors provide **proportional spacing** and **microspacing** capabilities. Without these features, text will be **monospaced.**

Advanced users often make use of customizing options within their word processors. Also, such users are likely to take advantage of many of the following types of activities: using **macros,** working with a **merge feature** and a **mailing label feature, redlining,** and outlining. Today's word processors offer many desktop publishing features—such as **clip-art** libraries, **watermarks, drop caps,** shading and borders, and tables. **Style sheets** automate formatting choices, possibly in combination with **templates** and **wizards.** Several advanced capabilities help users produce better or more-complex documents: a **grammar checker,** index- and table-of-contents-preparation routines, linking and embedding objects from other programs, and working with **add-on programs** such as **reference shelves.**

Desktop Publishing Software **Desktop publishing** refers to desktop microcomputer systems that let you combine on a page such elements as text (in a variety of fonts), art, and photos, thus creating attractive documents that look as if they came off a professional printer's press. Whereas word processing programs will enable you to do a respectable amount of desktop publishing, desktop publishing programs immerse you into heavy-duty *typesetting* and *imagesetting.*

Professional-level desktop publishing systems are commonly configured with the following hardware and software components at a minimum. Hardware includes a high-end microcomputer system, a laser printer (which is used in concert with a specific **page-description language** or **PDL),** a graphics-oriented monitor with an extra-large screen, and an image scanner. Software components include **page-makeup software,** an **illustration program—**such as *painting, drawing,* and *photo* programs—font libraries, and image and sound libraries.

1. Fill in the blanks:
   a. A word processor's __________ feature automatically places soft returns.
   b. __________ is a word processing feature that allocates more horizontal space on a line to some characters than to others.
   c. WYSIWYG is an acronym for __________.
   d. A document with margins aligned at both right and left conforms to __________ justification.
   e. Stored art images used in a desktop publishing environment are referred to as __________.
2. Match each term with the description that fits best.
   a. zoom feature
   b. redlining

c. drop cap
d. spelling checker
e. macro
f. reference shelf

_____ A predetermined series of keystrokes or commands that can be invoked by a single keystroke or command
_____ A feature that highlights changes when one person edits another's written work
_____ A capability that magnifies onscreen elements
_____ An example of an add-on program
_____ A feature that helps to give text a typeset-quality look
_____ An operation you would use in a word processing program to quickly change the string *MISSIPPI* to *MISSISSIPPI*

3. What differences distinguish the following pairs of terms?
   a. Monospacing and proportional spacing
   b. Insert mode and overstrike mode
   c. Template and wizard
   d. Typeface and font
   e. Copying and moving
4. Define, in your own words, the following terms:
   a. WYSIWYG
   b. Ruler line
   c. Insertion point
   d. Preview feature
   e. Merge feature
5. What is a reference shelf? Name at least three types of resources that you would expect to find in a reference-shelf package.
6. Make the following distinctions between software for word processing and desktop publishing:
   a. Why is it sometimes difficult to distinguish word processing from desktop publishing?
   b. What can you do with a desktop publishing program that you can't do with a word processing program?
   c. Name at least three word processing programs and the companies that make each one.
   d. Name at least three desktop publishing programs and the companies that make each one.
7. Which word processing feature would you use to accomplish each of the following tasks?
   a. Increase the size of text on the screen
   b. Make the first letter of an article very large, wrapping ensuing text around the letter
   c. Import small pieces of art—like the French flag or a globe icon—into a document
   d. Prepare a mass mailing of 1,000 copies of a letter from a list of names and addresses
   e. Edit a document that someone else wrote, with your comments and strikeouts appearing onscreen in a different color than that of the author's work
   f. Place a lightly shaded picture of a flower under the text of a letter you are sending to someone special
   g. Consult an online dictionary or atlas while writing a letter in a word processing program
   h. Create a calendar with your word processor by answering questions in a series of dialog boxes
8. Match the terms with the pictured elements.

_____ Watermark _____ Bit-mapped font
_____ Outline font _____ Clip art
_____ Drop cap

a.

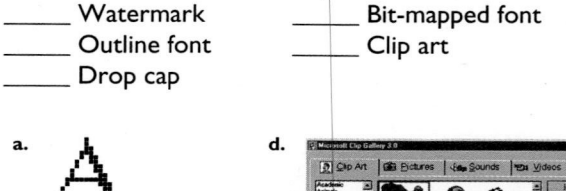

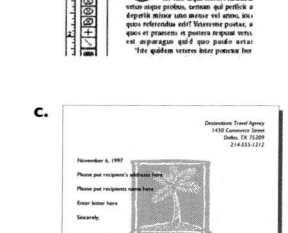

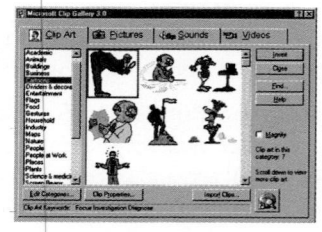

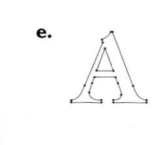

b.

c.

d.

e.

PROJECTS

1. What Is Your Opinion? The following statements call for an opinion. Please provide your ideas, confining your comments on each statement to a single page.

a. Spelling checkers provide their greatest benefits to people who can spell reasonably well.

b. Now that people can do relatively sophisticated desktop publishing with ordinary word processing programs, the professional typesetting and print shop has very little commercial future.

c. Word processing technology causes as many problems in companies as it provides benefits.

2. Using a Wizard to Create a Job Résumé Many word processing programs—such as Microsoft Word, Corel WordPerfect, and Lotus WordPro—contain wizard software that enables people to create attractive-looking résumés for seeking jobs.

a. Using the word processing software available at your school, create a résumé that includes your name, address, and phone number, as well as your job objective, work experience, and education.
b. Create an attractive cover letter to send with the résumé. Many wizards that produce résumés also have a routine for preparing cover letters.

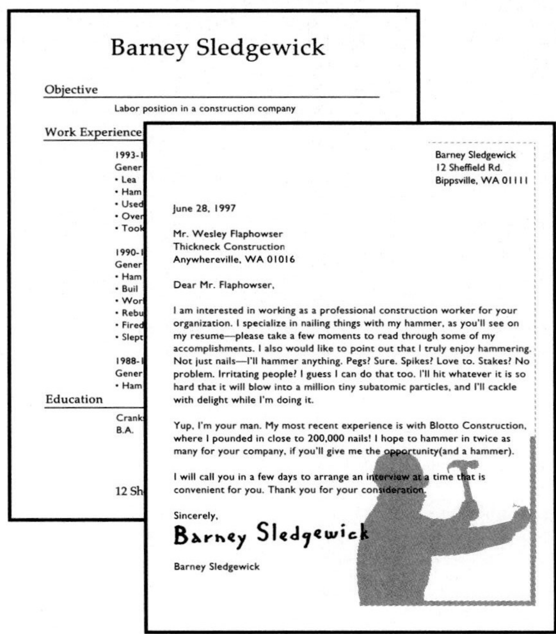

Barney Sledgewick

Objective

Labor position in a construction company

Work Experience

Education

Barney Sledgewick
12 Sheffield Rd.
Bippsville, WA 01111

June 28, 1997

Mr. Wesley Flaphowser
Thickneck Construction
Anywhereville, WA 01016

Dear Mr. Flaphowser,

I am interested in working as a professional construction worker for your organization. I specialize in nailing things with my hammer, as you'll see on my resume—please take a few moments to read through some of my accomplishments. I also would like to point out that I truly enjoy hammering. Not just nails—I'll hammer anything. Pegs? Sure. Spikes? Love to. Stakes? No problem. Irritating people? I guess I can do that too. I'll hit whatever it is so hard that it will blow into a million tiny subatomic particles, and I'll cackle with delight while I'm doing it.

Yup, I'm your man. My most recent experience is with Blotto Construction, where I pounded in close to 200,000 nails! I hope to hammer in twice as many for your company, if you'll give me the opportunity(and a hammer).

I will call you in a few days to arrange an interview at a time that is convenient for you. Thank you for your consideration.

Sincerely,

Barney Sledgewick

Barney Sledgewick

Résumé and cover letter

3. The Word Processing Software at Your School For the word processing program on your own computer or that available on the computers in your school's PC lab, describe how to do the following tasks:

a. Change from single spacing to double-spacing
b. Summon the thesaurus feature
c. Preview a document before printing it
d. Change from full to left justification
e. Change the typeface and point size on a printed document
f. Create a two-column text page
g. Insert a watermark behind a text page
h. Insert a piece of clip art into a text page
i. Change a printed-page orientation from portrait (8½ by 11 inches) to landscape (11 by 8½ inches)
j. Create a style sheet
k. Mark your place in a document with a bookmark
l. Direct the software to automatically insert the current date

4. Electronic Design and Publishing Many electronic design and publishing companies maintain Web sites that tell about their products, provide evaluation versions of programs, give hints for using the products, and so on. Visit the site of a company that makes desktop publishing software, illustration software, fonts, clip art, or digital photography software and answer the questions below:

a. What are the names of the products made by the company whose site you visited?
b. Can you download for evaluation any of the products you found in part a? If so, what are the evaluation period and the purchase cost of the software?
c. What other types of information—other than that on specific products—did you find at the site?

Hint: Below are some Web addresses to get you started:

COMPANY	WEB SITE (HTTP://_____)
Adobe Systems	www.adobe.com
Bitstream, Inc.	www.bitstream.com
Corel Corporation	www.corel.com
Quark	www.quark.com

5. The Good, the Bad, and the Ugly The popularity of desktop publishing in recent years has made it possible for people of all types to create documents with a particular flair. In many cases, people who are not professional designers have a good eye for arranging text and art elements on a page; in other cases, they don't. For this project, look through periodicals or journals for at least two examples of advertisements that are well designed and at least two examples of advertisements that are poorly designed. List your reasons why each ad is well or poorly designed.

Note: You should have no trouble finding examples. Look especially to style-conscious, mass-market magazines for exceptionally designed ads and to local publications with small circulations for cheesy-looking ads. Alternatively, if the Internet is available to your class, your instructor may choose to have you do this exercise by evaluating well-designed and poorly designed Web pages.

6. New Key Terms A textbook of this sort cannot cover every important technology or term regarding word processing and desktop publishing. Several important terms are listed below that are not covered in the chapter. Consult either library journals or Internet resources to determine what any three of these terms or pairs mean, and write out an explanation one-to-three-sentences long describing each one in your own words.

a. Orphans and widows
b. Hard page break and soft page break
c. Footnotes and endnotes
d. Dingbats
e. Pantone colors

7. Researching a Word Processor You can find out a great deal of information about any particular word processing program by finding a book about it or by cruising the Internet. For the word processing program of your choice, complete the following project tasks:

a. Visit a local bookstore and find as many books as you can—up to a limit of three—about the word processing program you have chosen. Write down the name of each book, the name of the author and publisher, and the copyright date. If you can't find a bookstore with appropriate titles, consider visiting one online. Two large online bookstores are the Amazon Bookstore

http://www.amazon.com/

and Computer Literacy Bookshops

http://www.clbooks.com/

b. For any one of the books you have chosen in part a, write a short (one-to-two-page) report detailing the book's level of presentation (i.e., beginning or advanced), the topics it covers, and the features that appeal or don't appeal to you.
c. *Optional: Do this part of the project only if you have Internet access.* Can you find any resources about the word processing program you have chosen on the World Wide Web? If so, describe the Web sites and any information they contain.

8. Researching a Desktop Publishing Program The chapter text mentions several desktop publishing programs. Choose a particular version of one such program and answer the following questions about it. You may find some answers from information available on the Internet.

a. What is the name of the program and who is its publisher?
b. Does the version work on a PC-compatible platform or on the Macintosh platform (or both)? What is the most current version number of the program?
c. How much RAM and hard-disk storage does the program require?
d. What is the suggested list price or street price of the program?
e. Name at least two things the program you have chosen can do that your word processor cannot.

9. Researching an Illustration Program The chapter text mentions several illustration software packages. Choose a particular version of one such program and answer the following questions about it. You may find some answers from information available on the Internet.

a. What is the name of the program, and who is its publisher?
b. Does the version work on a PC-compatible platform or on the Macintosh platform (or both)? What is the most current version number of the program?
c. How much RAM and hard-disk storage does the program require?
d. What is the suggested list price or street price of the program?
e. Identify the types of duties—say, drawing, painting, photo editing, or creating special effects—that the program performs.

10. Styling a Document with Fonts Using the word processor available to your class, create the document shown in the accompanying figure.

Finch Investors Monthly Newsletter

Finch Investments • 330 High Rollers Plaza • Colorado Springs, CO 80903
Phone (719) 888-0000 • Fax (719) 888-0001

March, 1998

Hidey-ho, sports fans. My newsletter to you this month has only two items:

Market Analysis
The continuing demand for mutual funds continues to grow at a good clip, with new customers pouring in every month. Our analysis shows that this trend should continue for *at least* the next nine months.

Economic Report
According to information that our affiliate bureau has gathered, we believe that the following trends will continue:

1. The interest rate will remain steady. We see 1999 offering no surprises. But the year 2000 could be an entirely different story altogether. Due to the aging of baby boomers and an increasing need to import certain types of goods from overseas, inflation could roar again.
2. The budget deficit will continue to be reduced. Again, this is not much of a surprise from the earlier forecasts we made.
3. Capital gains taxes are not likely to be reduced next year, despite what you hear in the news.

That's it for now. Bye, bye.

Chauncey Haverhill Finch III, Esq.
President and CEO

PS 2

Spreadsheets and Presentation Graphics

Outline

Learning Objectives

After completing this chapter, you will be able to:

1. Describe what spreadsheet packages do and how they work.
2. Identify the basic operations you must master to use spreadsheet software effectively.
3. Explain the use of several intermediate and advanced spreadsheet features.
4. Describe what presentation graphics are and how they are created.

Overview

Today, one of the most important software packages that *any* businessperson should learn—whether he or she is a manager, an analyst, a secretary, or a sales representative—is *electronic spreadsheets.* Spreadsheet software is to the current generation of users what the pocket calculator was to previous generations—a convenient means of performing calculations. But while most pocket calculators can compute and display only one result each time new data are entered, electronic spreadsheets can present you with hundreds or even thousands of results each time you enter a single new value or command. What spreadsheets can do and how they work are two of the primary subjects of this chapter.

From our discussion of spreadsheets we'll move on to presentation graphics software and hardware, which are designed to present the results of business computations in a visually oriented, easily understood way. This class of business products is easy to learn and use. Today most spreadsheet packages are equipped with built-in presentation graphics features and tools. Also, many dedicated presentation graphics packages, which enable you to produce even more types of presentations than those possible with spreadsheet packages, are commercially available.

Spreadsheets

An electronic **spreadsheet** package produces computerized counterparts to the ruled ledger-style worksheets commonly associated with accountants (see Figure PS 2-1). Electronic spreadsheets first came to public notice in the late 1970s when a Harvard Business School student named Dan Bricklin and a programmer friend produced a microcomputer package called *VisiCalc* (short for "*Visi*ble *Calc*ulator"). Bricklin conceived the idea while watching his accounting professor erase large chunks of blackboard computations every time a single number changed in an interdependent series of calculations. Awed by the amount of repetitive labor involved in such basic updating, Bricklin quickly saw the vast potential benefit of computerized worksheets.

Today, VisiCalc is gone from the scene, having been eclipsed by newer, better products. The leading spreadsheet packages currently available for microcomputers include Microsoft's Excel, Lotus Development's 1-2-3, and Corel's Quattro Pro. All of these products are components of office-software suites, and users work with graphical user interfaces that are remarkably similar to those of the word processor components of those suites.

HOW SPREADSHEETS WORK

Here we discuss how spreadsheets organize information as well as some of the principles by which spreadsheets work.

The Anatomy of a Worksheet In electronic spreadsheets, the display screen is viewed as a *window* looking in on a big grid, called a **worksheet.** Most major spreadsheet packages allow worksheets that consist of thousands of *rows* and a couple of hundred *columns.* Microsoft Excel worksheets, for instance, can encompass a maximum of 16,384 rows and 256 columns. Each of the 4,194,304 (16,384 × 256) **cells** formed by the intersection of a row and a column may contain text, a number, or a formula. Each cell can be accessed through a **cell address,** such as B4 or E223.

■ **Spreadsheet.** A productivity software package that supports quick creation and manipulation of tables and financial schedules. ■ **Worksheet.** The computerized counterpart to the ruled paper ledgers commonly associated with accountants. ■ **Cell.** The part of the worksheet that can hold a single value or formula; defined by the intersection of a row and a column. ■ **Cell address.** The column/row combination that uniquely identifies a spreadsheet cell.

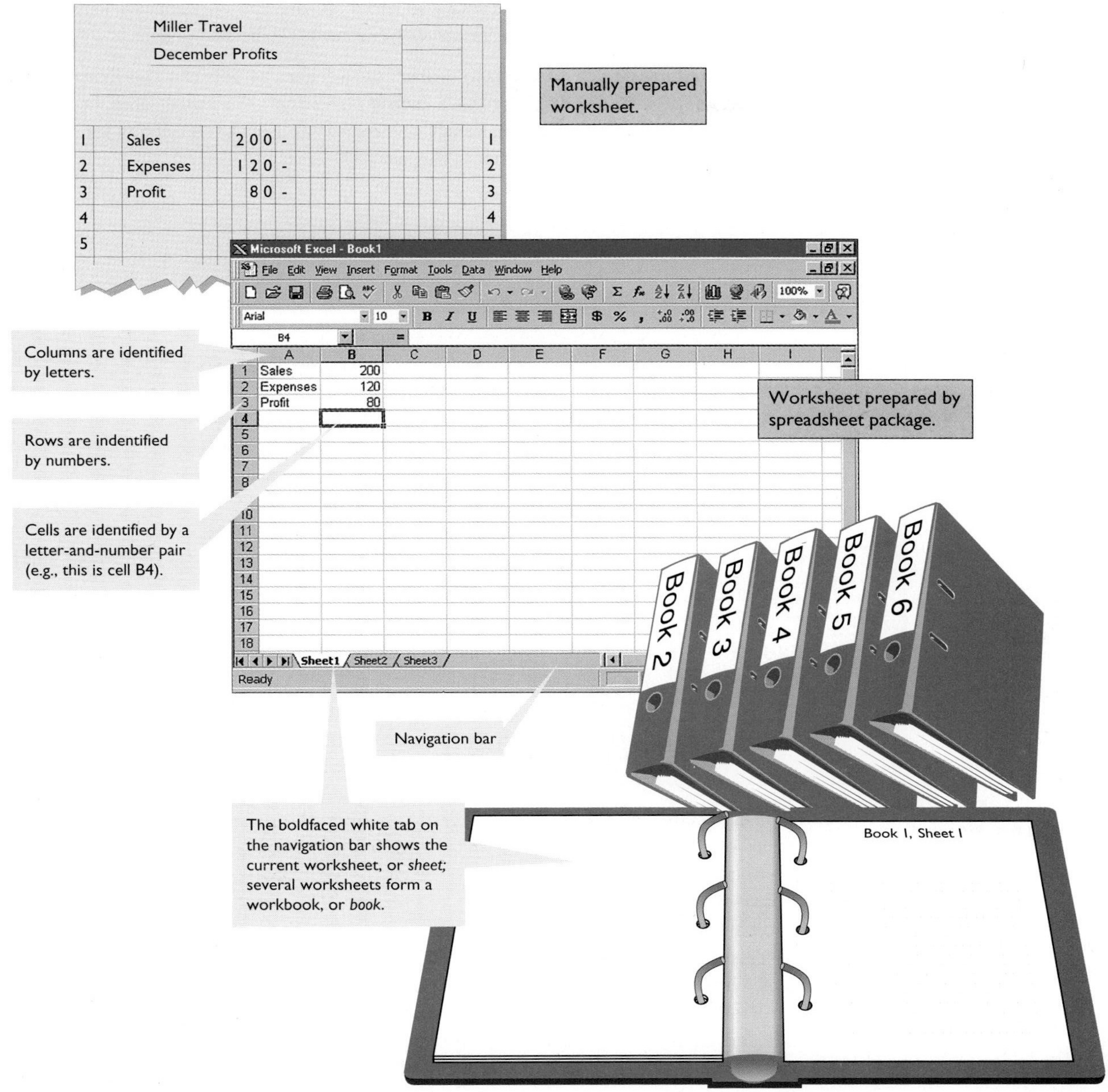

Miller Travel
December Profits
1 Sales 200 -
2 Expenses 120 -
3 Profit 80 -
Manually prepared worksheet.
Microsoft Excel - Book1
Columns are identified by letters.
Rows are indentified by numbers.
Cells are identified by a letter-and-number pair (e.g., this is cell B4).
Worksheet prepared by spreadsheet package.
Navigation bar
The boldfaced white tab on the navigation bar shows the current worksheet, or *sheet;* several worksheets form a workbook, or *book.*
Book 2
Book 3
Book 4
Book 5
Book 6
Book 1, Sheet 1

FIGURE PS 2-1

Manually prepared and electronic worksheets. An electronic spreadsheet package produces computerized counterparts to the ruled ledger-style worksheets that accountants frequently use.

In most commercial spreadsheet packages, columns are identified by letters, rows by numbers, and each cell by a letter-and-number pair. For example, Cell B4—highlighted with a pointer in Figure PS 2-1—is found at the intersection of Column B and Row 4. Of course, the display screen is too small to permit the viewing of more than a few rows and columns at any give time. However, users can press certain cursor-movement keys on the keyboard or use the horizontal and vertical scroll bars to move the worksheet window around, letting them view other portions of the worksheet through it.

Worksheets and Workbooks Many programs, such as Excel, allow users to aggregate related worksheets into *workbooks.* For instance, the 12 worksheets containing profit statements for each month in 1998 can form one workbook. You can use the navigation bar at the bottom of the screen (see Figure PS 2-1) to select worksheets within a workbook. From left to right on the bar are several navigation buttons—tabs labeled *Sheet 1, Sheet 2,* and so on ("Sheet" is for "Worksheet")—

and a horizontal scroll bar that lets you move across the current worksheet to see other columns. Worksheet pages can contain both tables and graphs.

The Worksheet Screen Each worksheet screen, as you can see from Figure PS 2-2, is divided into two main areas: a *control panel* and a *worksheet area.* In a nutshell, the control panel is where you select commands and prepare entries for the worksheet; the worksheet area contains the worksheet itself.

The contents of the current cell display in the contents box.

The formula bar lets you enter worksheet data.

CONTROL PANEL
The control panel contains the title bar, menu bar, toolbars, and formula bar.

The current cell displays in the selection box.

WORKSHEET AREA
The worksheet area contains the worksheet itself.

If the current cell stores a formula, its results display on the worksheet.

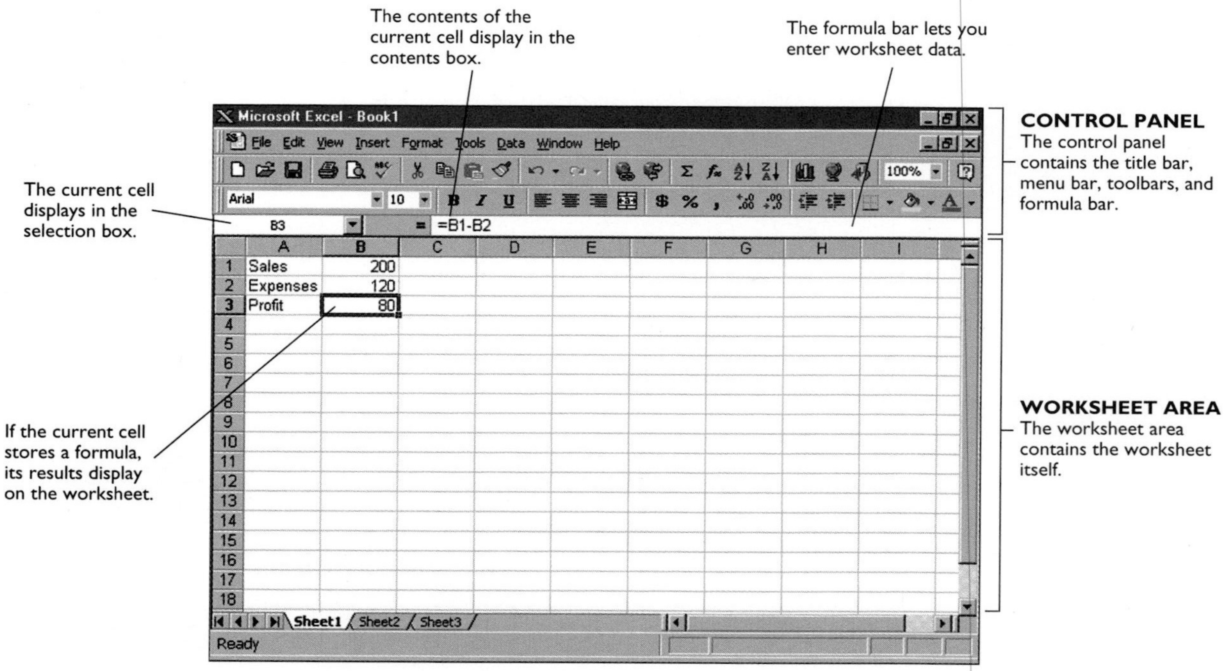

FIGURE PS 2-2
An electronic spreadsheet at work.

THE CONTROL PANEL The **control panel** is comprised of four principal areas, three of which you should be familiar with from previous chapters. At the top of the screen, the *title bar* displays the name of the workbook—"Book 1" in the figure. Below the title bar are the *menu bar* and *toolbars.* The commands on the menu bar and toolbars are like the ones you will see in a word processor that is part of the same office suite; they will let you do such things as open files, preview and print files, save files, check spelling, apply fonts, zoom in or out, and so on.

The final element of the control panel is the *formula bar,* or *edit line.* The formula bar serves several functions, but most important are two spaces on it. One is the *selection box* that displays the address of the current cell, and the other is the *contents box,* where you to enter what you want placed into the current cell. The **current cell** is the worksheet cell to which the spreadsheet is currently pointing. Spreadsheet packages point to one cell at a time; you can always tell which cell is current by looking at the selection box.

THE WORKSHEET AREA The worksheet itself is displayed in the part of the screen called the **worksheet area,** or **window area.** One important element in the worksheet area is the **cell pointer,** sometimes called the **highlight** or simply the *pointer.* The cell pointer highlights the current cell. As you can see in Figure PS 2-2, the current cell (as indicated in the selection box in the control panel and the highlight in the worksheet area) is Cell B3.

In many spreadsheets, as you are entering data into a worksheet cell, the data you are typing in appear both in the cell and in the contents box. When you enter the

■ **Control panel.** The portion of the screen display used for issuing commands and observing what is being typed into the computer system. ■ **Current cell.** The worksheet cell at which the highlight is currently positioned. ■ **Worksheet area.** The portion of the screen that contains the window onto the worksheet. Also called the **window area.** ■ **Cell pointer.** A cursorlike mechanism used in the worksheet area to point to cells, thereby making them active. Also called the **highlight.**

data, the cell will contain either the original data you entered or—if you had entered a formula—the formula result. In the figure, the formula =B1 – B2 (subtract the contents of Cell B2 from the contents of Cell B1) is entered into the contents box, yielding a result of 80 in the current cell, Cell B3. As you move to the next empty cell, the cell's coordinates appear in the selection box and the contents box clears.

Remember, the worksheet area may not be large enough to show the whole worksheet at a single glance, but you can scroll the window about to see other parts of the worksheet if you desire. *Scrolling* is similar to moving a magnifying glass over a large map; the movable glass acts like the window, while the underlying map acts like the worksheet. You can scroll the worksheet a row or column at a time when the highlight is at the right or bottom edge of the screen and you tap one of the arrow keys. Keys such as Tab, PgUp, and PgDn let you scroll the worksheet in window-sized blocks, and you can use the scroll bars to scroll even faster.

Creating a Worksheet Now that you are familiar with a few of the mechanics of spreadsheets, let's learn how to create a worksheet. In the worksheet shown in Figure PS 2-2, we are computing a business profit statement in which expenses are 60 percent of sales and profit is the difference between sales and expenses. Here we will show how to enter the text and numbers used in the figure into the computer. We'll also look at some of the details that the spreadsheet will take care of for you.

Into each worksheet cell, you can type either a constant value or a formula. A **constant value** is a cell entry that consists of a text label (such as *Sales* or *James P. Jones)* or a numeric value (such as 200 or −15.1). A **formula,** in contrast, is an entry that performs a mathematical operation on the contents of other cells—such as =B1 – B2 or =COUNT(B1:B6). COUNT is a special type of predefined formula called a *function.* We will be covering functions in more detail in a little while.

In the figure, we have entered—one at a time—the following six items into the control panel:

Cell A1: Sales (a constant value)
Cell A2: Expenses (a constant value)
Cell A3: Profit (a constant value)
Cell B1: 200 (a constant value)
Cell B2: =.6*B1 (a formula)
Cell B3: =B1 − B2 (a formula)

Spreadsheet packages, incidentally, automatically assume that each entry beginning with a letter is a constant value, which is why we had to type the formula in Cell B3 with an "=" in front of it.

As you input each cell entry, the spreadsheet software processes it and automatically transfers the results to the worksheet. For Cells A1, A2, A3, and B1 in Figure PS 2-2, a direct transfer occurs. For Cells B2 and B3, the computer first makes the computations indicated by the formulas and then transfers the results to the corresponding worksheet cells.

The Recalculation Feature Electronic spreadsheet packages are particularly useful for **what-if analysis.** For example, suppose that you wish to know *what* profit will result in Figure PS 2-2 *if* sales change to $500. You can simply enter the new value, 500, into Cell B1, and the spreadsheet package automatically reworks all the figures according to the prestored formulas. Thus, the computer responds:

```
Sales      500
Expenses   300
Profit     200
```

■ **Constant value.** A cell entry that contains text or a numeric value. ■ **Formula.** A cell entry that is used to change the contents of other cells. ■ **What-if analysis.** An approach to problem solving in which the decision maker commands the computer system to recalculate a set of numbers based on alternative assumptions.

	A	B	C	D
1		42	13	21
2	25			
3	10			
4	3	5	20	
5		10	25	
6	50	15	30	
7				

A2:A4 B1:D1 B4:C6 A6:A6

ABOUT RANGES
A range can be as small as a single cell or as large as a grid with a couple of hundred cells on each side.

FIGURE PS 2-3
The range concept. A range is defined as any rectangular block of cells.

In seconds, electronic spreadsheets can perform recalculations that would require several hours to do manually or by writing a program in a regular programming language. In fact, it's this easy-to-use **recalculation feature** that makes spreadsheets so popular. You can learn to prepare budgets and financial schedules with them after only a few hours of training. Another type of what-if analysis that is commonly found in modern spreadsheet packages today is *goal seeking*, in which the spreadsheet calculates how much of a cost or resource is needed at one or more points in time to produce a certain result.

Blocks of Cells: The Range Concept Often, users need to be able to manipulate data in a set of contiguous cells—say, in a row or column of several cells or in a rectangular-shaped block of cells. To do this in a spreadsheet package, you define a **range** of cells. Figure PS 2-3 shows four examples of valid ranges. You will generally have to declare ranges of cells when you want to print, move, copy, insert, delete, sort, or graph parts of the worksheet.

FIGURE PS 2-4
Using an autocomplete feature to fill a range automatically.

PROFIT STATEMENT

	January	February	March	April	May	June
SALES	$10,570	$12,740	$14,010			
EXPENSES						
Payroll	$4,700	$4,950	$5,220			
Materials	$3,000	$3,120	$3,375			
Rent	$1,500	$1,500	$1,500			
Total	$9,200	$9,570	$10,095			
PROFIT	$1,370	$3,170	$3,915			

ABOUT AUTOCOMPLETE
If you have text labels or numbers that conform to a certain pattern, you can have your spreadsheet package fill in all but the first one or two automatically.

TEXT LABELS
A series of text labels can be generated by entering the first label, selecting it, and using the mouse to drag into cells that need to be filled.

January	February	March	April
Product 1	Product 2	Product 3	Product 4
1st Quarter	2nd Quarter	3rd Quarter	4th Quarter

NUMBER SERIES
A series of numbers can be generated by entering the first two numbers, selecting the two cells containing the numbers, and using the mouse to drag into cells that need to be filled.

1998	1999	2000	2001
1	2	3	4
10	20	30	40

■ **Recalculation feature.** The ability of spreadsheet software to quickly and automatically recalculate the contents of several cells, based on new operator inputs. ■ **Range.** A set of contiguous cells arranged in a rectangle.

For instance, telling the spreadsheet package to print the range B4 through C6 (B4:C6) will result in the output of the three-by-two block of cells in Figure PS 2-3. Generally, a range can be declared by explicitly typing it into the control panel—for instance, you would type in all five characters in the string "B4:C6" to declare it as a range—or by selecting (highlighting) the range in the worksheet area. In Excel, the colon character (:) is used to specify a range of cells; Lotus 1-2-3 and Quattro, in contrast, use a period character (.).

Most spreadsheet packages contain some type of *autocomplete* feature that makes it easy to enter data into a range when the data conforms to a pattern (see Figure PS 2-4).

Formatting Cell Entries Many people wish to format the data they input to a worksheet in some way. Virtually all spreadsheet packages automatically left-justify text labels in a worksheet cell and right-justify numbers. However, buttons on a formatting toolbar or some such mechanism make it possible for you to change this default alignment—on a single cell or on any range of cells. Figure PS 2-5 shows how such buttons and others work.

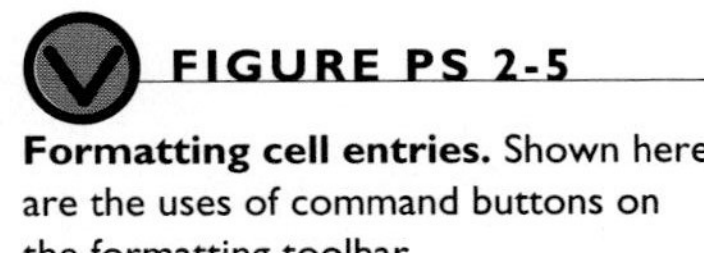

FIGURE PS 2-5

Formatting cell entries. Shown here are the uses of command buttons on the formatting toolbar.

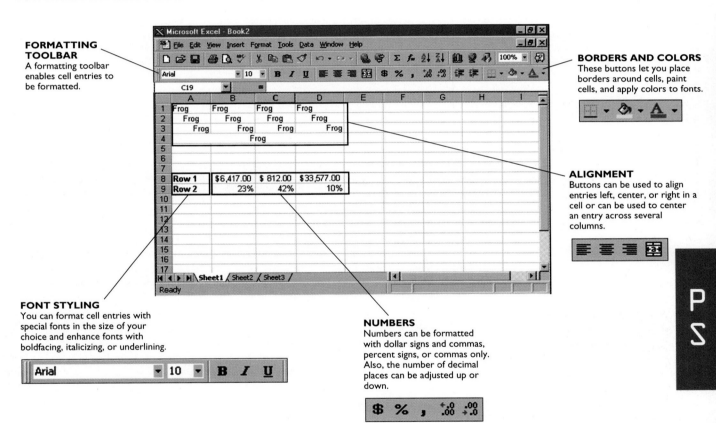

FORMATTING TOOLBAR
A formatting toolbar enables cell entries to be formatted.

BORDERS AND COLORS
These buttons let you place borders around cells, paint cells, and apply colors to fonts.

ALIGNMENT
Buttons can be used to align entries left, center, or right in a cell or can be used to center an entry across several columns.

FONT STYLING
You can format cell entries with special fonts in the size of your choice and enhance fonts with boldfacing, italicizing, or underlining.

NUMBERS
Numbers can be formatted with dollar signs and commas, percent signs, or commas only. Also, the number of decimal places can be adjusted up or down.

Immediately to the right of the alignment buttons in the figure are buttons for applying special formats to numbers. Because spreadsheets are particularly useful for preparing financial schedules, it follows that many of the worksheet cells will contain values that represent monetary amounts. Buttons enable you to quickly put dollar signs, commas, and decimal points into these values (For example, a single click might change "90000" to "$90,000.00.") Generally, all you have to do is identify the range of cells that you want edited and select the options that automatically insert the proper symbols in the proper places. You can usually add percentage signs (%) through an equally straightforward process.

In addition to the basic types of formatting described here, there are several other methods you can use to give your worksheets an exciting look. Font styling, borders, and colors are briefly described in the figure. In a later subsection we will look at other, more advanced formatting methods.

Functions Spreadsheet packages typically contain a couple of hundred or so built-in functions that enable you to create formulas for a wide range of applications, including those in the fields of business, science, and engineering. A **function** invokes a prestored formula (such as that for calculating net present value) or a preset value (such as today's date). Figure PS 2-6 describes some useful functions and also shows how a few of them are used. You can learn more about functions by either summoning the online help feature in your spreadsheet software or by using an online function wizard. The function wizard, which can be accessed from the formula bar when you press a special key, gives you step-by-step instructions on how to enter data for any function.

EXAMPLES OF FUNCTIONS

Function	Description
SUM (range)	Calculates the sum of all values in a range
MAX (range)	Finds the highest value in a range
MIN (range)	Finds the lowest value in a range
COUNT (range)	Counts the number of nonempty cells in a range
AVG (range)	Calculates the average of values in a range
ABS (cell or expression)	Calculates the absolute value of the argument
PV (period payment, rate, number of payments)	Calculates the present value of an annuity at a specified interest rate
IF (conditional expression, value if true, value if false)	Supplies to a cell a value that depends on whether the conditional expression is true or false

ABOUT FUNCTIONS
A function is a prestored formula. Major spreadsheets have a couple of hundred or more functions.

EXAMPLES OF USING FUNCTIONS

	A	B	C	D
1	10	5	15	20
2	6	7	3	4
3	8	2	9	4
4	-1	0	3	15

SUM (A1:D1) = 50
MIN (A1:D4) = -1
MAX (A1:D4) = 20
AVG (A1:D1) = 12.5
ABS (A4) = 1
COUNT (A1:D4) = 16
IF (A4 < 0, 10, 20) = 10

FIGURE PS 2-6
Spreadsheet functions.

BASIC OPERATIONS

Spreadsheet packages offer numerous command options that help users to enter and edit data. The following paragraphs review a sampling of the most important features (see also Figure PS 2-7).

Inserting and Deleting Virtually all spreadsheet packages allow you to insert a new column or row in a worksheet. Also, you can delete a column or row that you no longer need. Generally, inserting or deleting involves moving the cell pointer to the appropriate position on the worksheet and issuing the proper command from the menu bar. Figure PS 2-7a illustrates inserting a blank row.

Copying Most spreadsheets include commands that enable you to copy the contents of one cell (or several cells) into another cell (or several others). Such commands usually work by prompting you for a *source range* that contains the data you want to copy and a *destination range* that will receive the copied data.

■ **Function.** A prestored formula for a standard calculation.

(a) **Inserting a row.** Both inserting and deleting involve moving the cell pointer to the appropriate position in the worksheet and issuing the proper command.

	A	B	C	D
1		Jan	Feb	
2	Revenue	300	500	
3	Expenses	200	450	
4	Profit	100	50	
5				
6				
7				

Before insertion

	A	B	C	D
1		Jan	Feb	
2				
3	Revenue	300	500	
4	Expenses	200	450	
5	Profit	100	50	
6				
7				

New row

After insertion

(b) **Copying by relative replication.** In most spreadsheet packages, relative replication is the default copy operation.

Formula for cell C1

C1 =A1–B1

	A	B	C	D
1	600	200	400	
2	800	500		
3	1500	600		
4	1200	500		
5				
6				
7				

Contents of cell C1

Before copy operation

Copy from: C1:C1 Copy to: C2:C4

	A	B	C	D
1	600	200	400	
2	800	500	300	
3	1500	600	900	
4	1200	500	700	
5				
6				
7				

Results when C1 formula is copied into cells C2, C3, and C4

After copy operation

(continued on next page)

FIGURE PS 2-7

Entering and editing operations.

If you are copying from cells that contain formulas, you generally will be asked to state whether you want the cell references in the formulas to be relative, absolute, or mixed. These three methods of copying are illustrated in Figures PS 2-7b, PS 2-7c, and PS 2-7d, respectively.

RELATIVE REPLICATION **Relative replication** copies the contents of a range of cells relative to the row and column coordinates of the destination range. For example, in Figure PS 2-7b, say that you want the value of each cell in Column C to equal the corresponding Column A entry minus the corresponding Column B entry. In other words, you want:

```
C1 = A1 - B1
C2 = A2 - B2
C3 = A3 - B3
C4 = A4 - B4
```

■ **Relative replication.** Copying formulas in a source range of cells into a target range of cells relative to the row and column coordinates of the cells in the target range.

(c) **Copying by absolute replication.** Copying by absolute replication involves marking each column and row reference in the cell address with a dollar ($) sign.

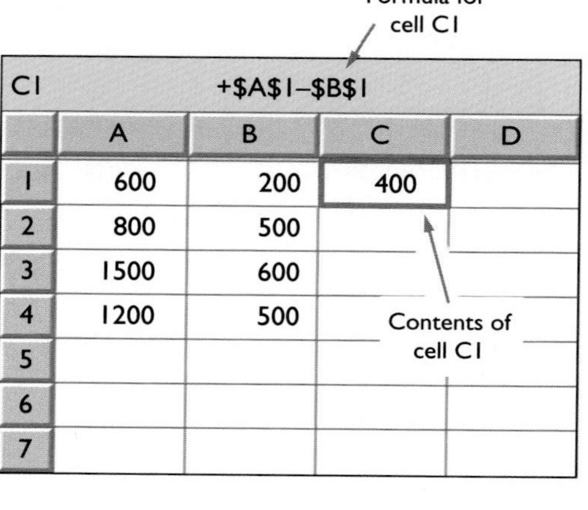

C1	+$A$1–$B$1			
	A	B	C	D
1	600	200	400	
2	800	500		
3	1500	600		
4	1200	500		
5				
6				
7				

Before copy operation

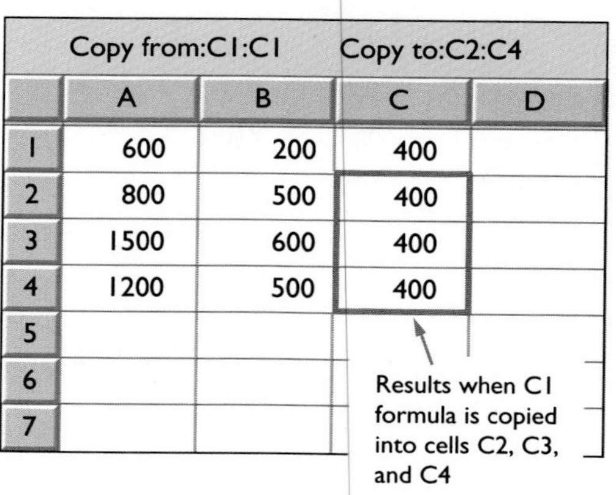

Copy from:C1:C1		Copy to:C2:C4		
	A	B	C	D
1	600	200	400	
2	800	500	400	
3	1500	600	400	
4	1200	500	400	
5				
6				
7				

After copy operation

(d) **Copying by mixed replication.** Mixed replication involves putting a dollar ($) sign in front of each column or row you wish to fix in place.

Formula for cell B4

B4	(1+B$3)^$A4				
	A	B	C	D	E
1		Future sum computations			
2					
3	Years	10.0%	10.5%	11.0%	11.5%
4	1	1.100			
5	2				
6	3				
7	4				
8	5				

Before copy operation

Results when B4 formula is copied into range B4:E8

Copy from:B4:B4		Copy to:B4:E8			
	A	B	C	D	E
1		Future sum computations			
2					
3	Years	10.0%	10.5%	11.0%	11.5%
4	1	1.100	1.105	1.110	1.115
5	2	1.210	1.221	1.232	1.243
6	3	1.331	1.349	1.368	1.386
7	4	1.464	1.491	1.518	1.546
8	5	1.611	1.647	1.685	1.723

After copy operation

(continued on next page)

FIGURE PS 2-7
continued

Generally you can do this in a typical spreadsheet program by placing the cell pointer at C1 and typing

```
=A1 – B1
```

or something very similar. You then copy this formula into Cells C2:C4 in the manner illustrated in the figure by specifying relative replication. In many packages, relative replication is the default when you copy.

ABSOLUTE REPLICATION In the previous example, had you specified **absolute replication** instead, the spreadsheet package would have copied the formula verbatim into all four cells, leaving the expression

```
=A1 – B1
```

■ **Absolute replication.** Copying verbatim the contents in one range of cells into another range of cells.

(e) **Moving a row.** When the contents of a block (range) of cells are moved, they are "cut" out of one area of the worksheet and "pasted" into another of identical size.

	A	B	C	D
1	Name	Hours	Rate	Pay
2	Jones	10	$6.00	$60.00
3	Smith	40	$7.00	$280.00
4	Zimmer	20	$4.00	$80.00
5	Able	30	$3.00	$90.00
6				
7	Total			$510.00

Before move operation

	A	B	C	D
1	Name	Hours	Rate	Pay
2	Able	30	$3.00	$90.00
3	Jones	10	$6.00	$60.00
4	Smith	40	$7.00	$280.00
5	Zimmer	20	$4.00	$80.00
6				
7	Total			$510.00

After move operation

(f) **Freezing titles.** Freezing titles allows you to keep certain columns or rows of the worksheet in place while you are scrolling to other parts of it.

	A	B	C
1	Class: CIS 210, COBOL I		
2	Student name	Exam	Exam
3		1	2
4	-------------	-----	-----
5	Alice Adams	60	55
6	Bob Andrew	85	92
7	Greg Andujar	88	82

Original window

Title rows

	A	B	C
1	Class: CIS 210, COBOL I		
2	Student name	Exam	Exam
3		1	2
4	-------------	-----	-----
69	Ed James	61	75
70	Jim Jones	80	97
71	Mary Jones	98	85

Scrolled worksheet with frozen titles

(g) **Using templates.** The worksheet at the left contains both the blank template and the formulas to calculate the table amounts at the right (once the user supplies the interest rate, principal, and the number of years).

	A	B	C	D
1	Interest rate			
2	Principal			
3	Number of years			
4	------	--------	--------	------
5	Year	Begin Bal.	Interest	Total
6				
7				

Blank template

	A	B	C	D
1	Interest rate		10%	
2	Principal		$100	
3	Number of years		10	
4	------	--------	--------	------
5	Year	Begin Bal.	Interest	Total
6	1	$100.00	$10.00	$110.00
7	2	$110.00	$11.00	$121.00

Filled-in template

in each one (see Figure PS 2-7c). Absolute replication provides an ideal tool when a computation yields a constant value that you want to repeat in a range of cells.

You take the same steps to perform absolute replication as you do to perform relative replication in most spreadsheet packages, except for one difference—The formula in the source cell must be written in the form:

```
=$A$1+$B$1
```

In other words, dollar signs must be placed before each row and column being referenced.

MIXED REPLICATION Most spreadsheet packages also allow **mixed replication—** a combination of absolute and relative replication—in which a row value can be kept constant while a column value is allowed to vary (or vice versa). Mixed replication provides an especially useful tool for handling formulas in which two parameters change. As the first parameter varies across columns (while the second stays constant), the second parameter varies across rows (while the first stays constant).

Figure PS 2-7d shows mixed replication for compounding interest. Note that interest rate and years are the two parameters in Cell B4. For each column, we want to keep the interest rate (in Row 3) fixed as we vary the year from one to five. For each row, we want to keep the year (in Column A) fixed as we vary the interest rate from 10 to 11.5 percent. To allow us to mix addresses, we put a dollar sign ($) in front of the coordinate that we want to fix; thus, the formula in the source cell must be written as:

```
(1+B$3)^$A4
```

Moving Virtually all spreadsheet packages enable you to move any row or column into another row or column position on the worksheet. As with the Copy command, you will need to specify a source range (the range you're moving from) and a destination range (the range you're moving to).

For example, suppose you decide to move Row 5 into the Row 2 position, as in Figure PS 2-7e. When moving, the software automatically makes all cell references point to the new worksheet locations. If your spreadsheet package also lets you move or copy larger areas, as most do, you will be able to move, say, a contiguous 20-by-40 block of cells from one part of the worksheet to another.

Freezing Titles A spreadsheet package typically provides a Titles feature that allows you to freeze a portion of the worksheet in place on the screen as you scroll the rest. For example, if the Titles feature were to freeze the first four rows of Figure PS 2-7f, you could use the down arrow key or PgDn key to scroll through data cells while the titles remained in place on the screen. When you freeze rows, you work with a horizontally split screen. You can also freeze columns, resulting in a vertically split screen. Most programs allow you to freeze certain rows and certain columns at the same time.

Using Templates In the world of spreadsheets, a **template** is a worksheet in which rows and columns are prelabeled and many cells already contain formulas. Only the data are missing. Thus, the work involved in setting up the worksheet has already been done, leaving you more time to enter and analyze data. A template is shown in Figure PS 2-7g. In many spreadsheet packages, it is also possible to protect cells, such as those that contain the template's text labels and formulas.

Changing Column Widths and Row Heights Most spreadsheet programs allow you to adjust the widths of columns and/or the heights of rows in a worksheet (see Figure PS 2-8). You can often assign a width to each column individually, or you can select a single global width that applies to all columns. A *wraparound feature* permits particularly long text labels to spill over into adjacent columns to the right, provided those cells are empty. Individual columns and rows can often be resized by placing the mouse pointer on the border between two column or row identifiers (e.g., between A and B on the bar that contains the column letters) and, when the pointer changes shape, dragging with a mouse in the desired direction.

■ **Mixed replication.** Copying formulas in one range of cells into another range while varying some cell references and leaving others constant. ■ **Template.** An onscreen form that requires only that the operator fill in a limited number of input values.

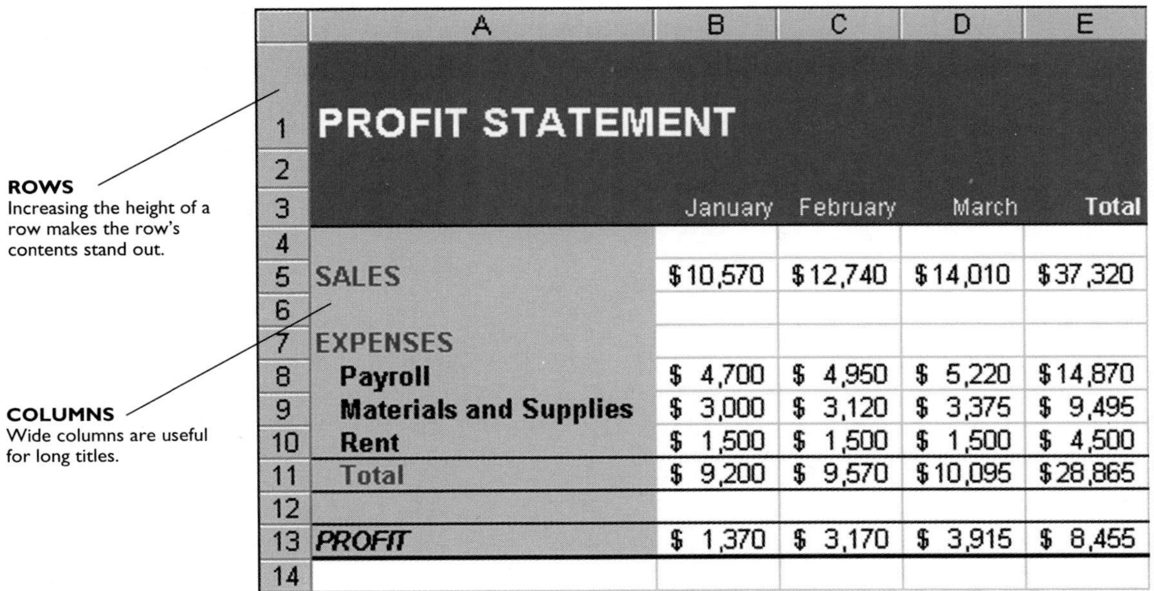
ROWS
Increasing the height of a row makes the row's contents stand out.
COLUMNS
Wide columns are useful for long titles.

	A	B	C	D	E
1	PROFIT STATEMENT				
2					
3		January	February	March	Total
4					
5	SALES	$10,570	$12,740	$14,010	$37,320
6					
7	EXPENSES				
8	Payroll	$ 4,700	$ 4,950	$ 5,220	$14,870
9	Materials and Supplies	$ 3,000	$ 3,120	$ 3,375	$ 9,495
10	Rent	$ 1,500	$ 1,500	$ 1,500	$ 4,500
11	Total	$ 9,200	$ 9,570	$10,095	$28,865
12					
13	*PROFIT*	$ 1,370	$ 3,170	$ 3,915	$ 8,455
14					

FIGURE PS 2-8

Changing the width of columns and the height of rows.

Dressing Up Worksheets As has been mentioned already, through the formatting toolbar, you can change the typeface or point size of any cell or cell range in your worksheet. You can also apply colors and borders through the same toolbar. As if these styling choices weren't enough, most spreadsheet packages contain a variety of other styling tools to make your worksheets even more attractive.

For instance, you can format your worksheet automatically by choosing among several different *autoformatting* styles. With autoformatting, the spreadsheet package analyzes your worksheet and automatically applies the format you select based on the position of heads, breaks, and data (see Figure PS 2-9). Other spreadsheet tools let you annotate cells with text or voice explanations, apply text boxes and pointers to circled values in cells, and perform a variety of other styling touches.

Printing Worksheets You print a worksheet in a way very similar to the way you print a word processed document—that is, you select the Print toolbar button or the

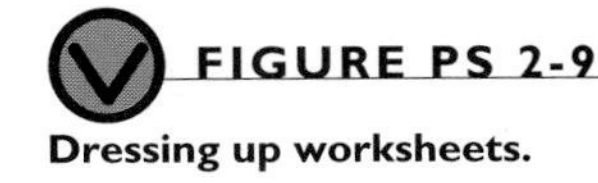

FIGURE PS 2-9

Dressing up worksheets.

P
S

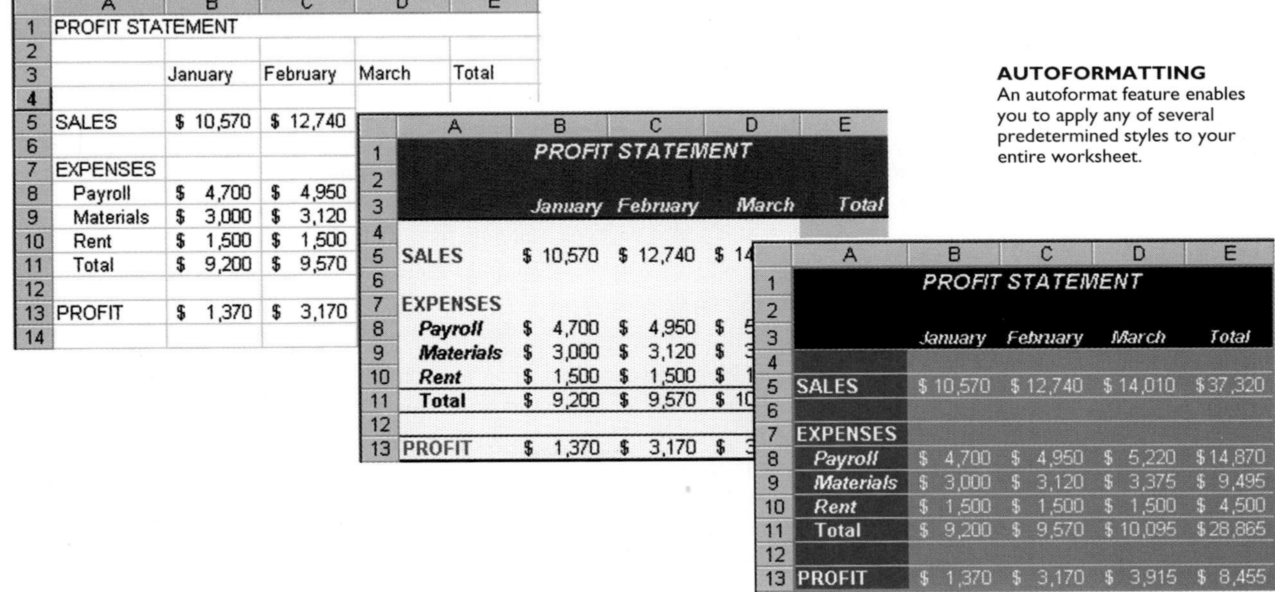
AUTOFORMATTING
An autoformat feature enables you to apply any of several predetermined styles to your entire worksheet.

	A	B	C	D	E
1	PROFIT STATEMENT				
2					
3		January	February	March	Total
4					
5	SALES	$ 10,570	$ 12,740		
6					
7	EXPENSES				
8	Payroll	$ 4,700	$ 4,950		
9	Materials	$ 3,000	$ 3,120		
10	Rent	$ 1,500	$ 1,500		
11	Total	$ 9,200	$ 9,570		
12					
13	PROFIT	$ 1,370	$ 3,170		
14					

	A	B	C	D	E
1	*PROFIT STATEMENT*				
2					
3		*January*	*February*	*March*	*Total*
4					
5	SALES	$ 10,570	$ 12,740	$ 14	
6					
7	EXPENSES				
8	*Payroll*	$ 4,700	$ 4,950	$ 5	
9	*Materials*	$ 3,000	$ 3,120	$ 3	
10	*Rent*	$ 1,500	$ 1,500	$ 1	
11	Total	$ 9,200	$ 9,570	$ 10	
12					
13	PROFIT	$ 1,370	$ 3,170	$ 3	

	A	B	C	D	E
1	*PROFIT STATEMENT*				
2					
3		*January*	*February*	*March*	*Total*
4					
5	SALES	$ 10,570	$ 12,740	$ 14,010	$37,320
6					
7	EXPENSES				
8	*Payroll*	$ 4,700	$ 4,950	$ 5,220	$14,870
9	*Materials*	$ 3,000	$ 3,120	$ 3,375	$ 9,495
10	*Rent*	$ 1,500	$ 1,500	$ 1,500	$ 4,500
11	Total	$ 9,200	$ 9,570	$ 10,095	$28,865
12					
13	PROFIT	$ 1,370	$ 3,170	$ 3,915	$ 8,455

1. ORIGINAL WORKSHEET
The records are in random order.

	A	B		C
1	**Store**	**Region**		**Sales**
2	25	North	$	7,000
3	11	South	$	4,000
4	23	South	$	5,500
5	44	South	$	3,850
6	15	North	$	8,200
7	3	North	$	4,690
8	18	South	$	5,590
9	36	South	$	3,700
10				
11				
12				

2. SIMPLE SORT
Records in the original file are sorted alphabetically on the Region column.

	A	B		C
1	**Store**	**Region**		**Sales**
2	25	North	$	7,000
3	15	North	$	8,200
4	3	North	$	4,690
5	11	South	$	4,000
6	23	South	$	5,500
7	44	South	$	3,850
8	18	South	$	5,590
9	36	South	$	3,700
10				
11				
12				

3. SUBTOTALED SORT
With the records properly sorted by Region, the Region column is selected for subtotaling. Subtotals are taken as each region breaks for a new one; also, a grand total is provided.

1 2 3		A	B		C
	1	**Store**	**Region**		**Sales**
	2	25	North	$	7,000
	3	15	North	$	8,200
	4	3	North	$	4,690
	5		**North Total**	$	19,890
	6	11	South	$	4,000
	7	23	South	$	5,500
	8	44	South	$	3,850
	9	18	South	$	5,590
	10	36	South	$	3,700
	11		**South Total**	$	22,640
	12		**Grand Total**	$	42,530

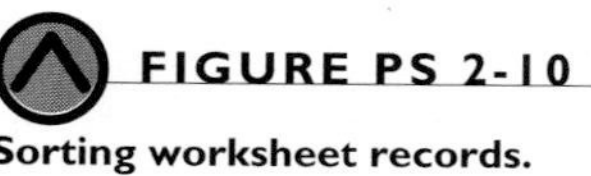

FIGURE PS 2-10

Sorting worksheet records.

Print subcommand from the File command on the menu bar, and you're in business. What's more, you can also preview your worksheets before printing them out, using a zoom feature just like the one with your word processor. In addition, you can choose to print in portrait or landscape modes, print only certain ranges of cells, and have color screen outputs translated to suitable greyscales—a handy feature if you're going to be outputting graphs or maps on a standard laser printer.

INTERMEDIATE AND ADVANCED FEATURES

In addition to the basic operations covered so far, many leading spreadsheet packages offer rich selections of intermediate and advanced features. Four such features often help spreadsheet users with their work: a facility for sorting records, a facility for filtering records, a pivot-table feature, and a presentation-graphics feature. The following paragraphs discuss the first three features. The last section of the chapter then covers presentation graphics.

Sorting Records A *sort feature* provides handy benefits in almost any type of business software. With a spreadsheet, a person might use such a tool for preparing phone directories, ordered listings of overdue accounts, student grade books, and reports identifying fast-moving or high-selling products. Virtually all spreadsheet programs allow you to sort on more than one field. Many people who sort also like to perform *control breaks,* showing a subtotal each time the value of the sort (control) field changes (breaks). When the report is finished, a grand total is taken on the control field. Figure PS 2-10 illustrates sorting records and, also, the use of control breaks.

Filtering Records Each row in a worksheet often represents some type of record—for instance, an employee record that contains the name, hours worked, and pay rate of an employee (see Figure PS 2-7e). If the worksheet has hundreds or thousands of records, it's nice to have a *filtering feature* that will extract records based on criteria that you specify. For instance, you may wish to get the names of all students in a class that receive an *A* grade or a list of employees who are making over $250 per week.

Pivot Tables Many spreadsheet programs today contain a *pivot-table feature* that enables table data to be rearranged and viewed from other perspectives. For instance, the president of a company might want to see data broken down by region, while the sales manager might want to see totals on each product. Data views can be changed in seconds in many spreadsheet programs by summoning a pivot-table wizard and, then, selecting the row and column titles that are to form the new table. Figure PS 2-11 illustrates pivoting data in a table to provide a summary of some of the hidden information it contains.

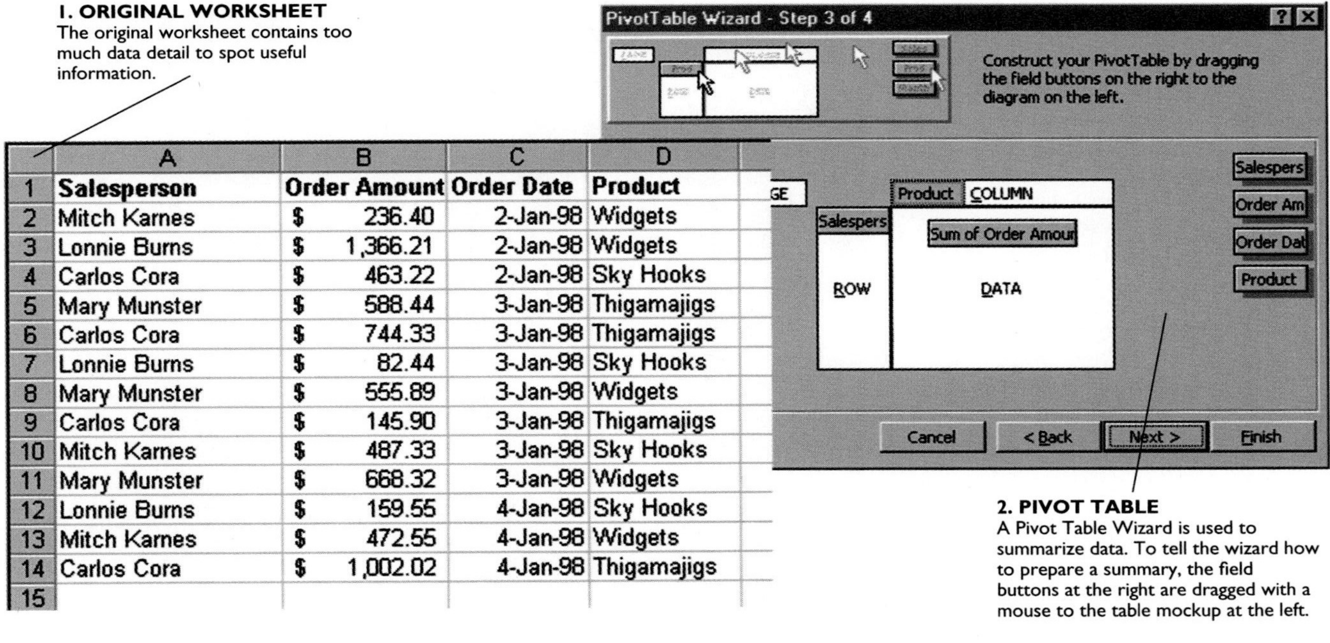

	A	B	C	D
1	**Salesperson**	**Order Amount**	**Order Date**	**Product**
2	Mitch Karnes	$ 236.40	2-Jan-98	Widgets
3	Lonnie Burns	$ 1,366.21	2-Jan-98	Widgets
4	Carlos Cora	$ 463.22	2-Jan-98	Sky Hooks
5	Mary Munster	$ 588.44	3-Jan-98	Thigamajigs
6	Carlos Cora	$ 744.33	3-Jan-98	Thigamajigs
7	Lonnie Burns	$ 82.44	3-Jan-98	Sky Hooks
8	Mary Munster	$ 555.89	3-Jan-98	Widgets
9	Carlos Cora	$ 145.90	3-Jan-98	Thigamajigs
10	Mitch Karnes	$ 487.33	3-Jan-98	Sky Hooks
11	Mary Munster	$ 668.32	3-Jan-98	Widgets
12	Lonnie Burns	$ 159.55	4-Jan-98	Sky Hooks
13	Mitch Karnes	$ 472.55	4-Jan-98	Widgets
14	Carlos Cora	$ 1,002.02	4-Jan-98	Thigamajigs
15				

3. OUTPUT
The pivot table created in Step 2 shows how much of each product salespeople are selling and, also, provides column and row totals.

	G	H	I	J	K
16	Sum of Order Amount	Product			
17	Salesperson	Sky Hooks	Thingamajigs	Widgets	Grand Total
18	Carlos Cora	$ 463.22	$ 1,892.25		$ 2,355.47
19	Lonnie Burns	$ 241.99		$ 1,366.21	$ 1,608.20
20	Mary Munster		$ 588.44	$ 1,224.21	$ 1,812.65
21	Mitch Karnes	$ 487.33		$ 708.95	$ 1,196.28
22	Grand Total	$ 1,192.54	$ 2,480.69	$ 3,299.37	$ 6,972.60
23					
24					

FIGURE PS 2-11

Creating a pivot table. Pivot tables are used to rearrange or combine worksheet data into a more useful form.

Presentation Graphics

If you try to explain to others what you look like, it may take several minutes. Show them a color photograph, on the other hand, and you can convey the same or better information about yourself within seconds. The saying "a picture is worth a thousand words" is the cornerstone of presentation graphics.

FORMS OF PRESENTATION GRAPHICS

A **presentation graphic—**sometimes called a *presentation visual* or *chart*—is an image that visually enhances the impact of information communicated to other people. Presentation graphics can take many different forms, a number of which are illustrated in Figure PS 2-12. With the right types of software and hardware, the creation of presentation graphics is limited only by one's imagination.

There are several compelling reasons to use presentation graphics in business. A person can often spot trends or make comparisons much more quickly by looking at a visual image than by reading text-only or number-only output containing the same information. Furthermore, a point can often be made far more dramatically and effectively by using pictures. Recent studies have found that presentation graphics also make the presenter look more professional in the eyes of others.

Here, we'll discuss in detail four of the most widely used presentation graphics: bar charts, pie charts, line charts, and text charts. We'll also examine when each is most

■ **Presentation graphic.** A visual image, such as a bar chart or pie chart, that is used to present data in a highly meaningful form.

TYPES OF PRESENTATION GRAPHICS
Presentation graphics include various types of bar, pie, and line charts, as well as more complicated images.

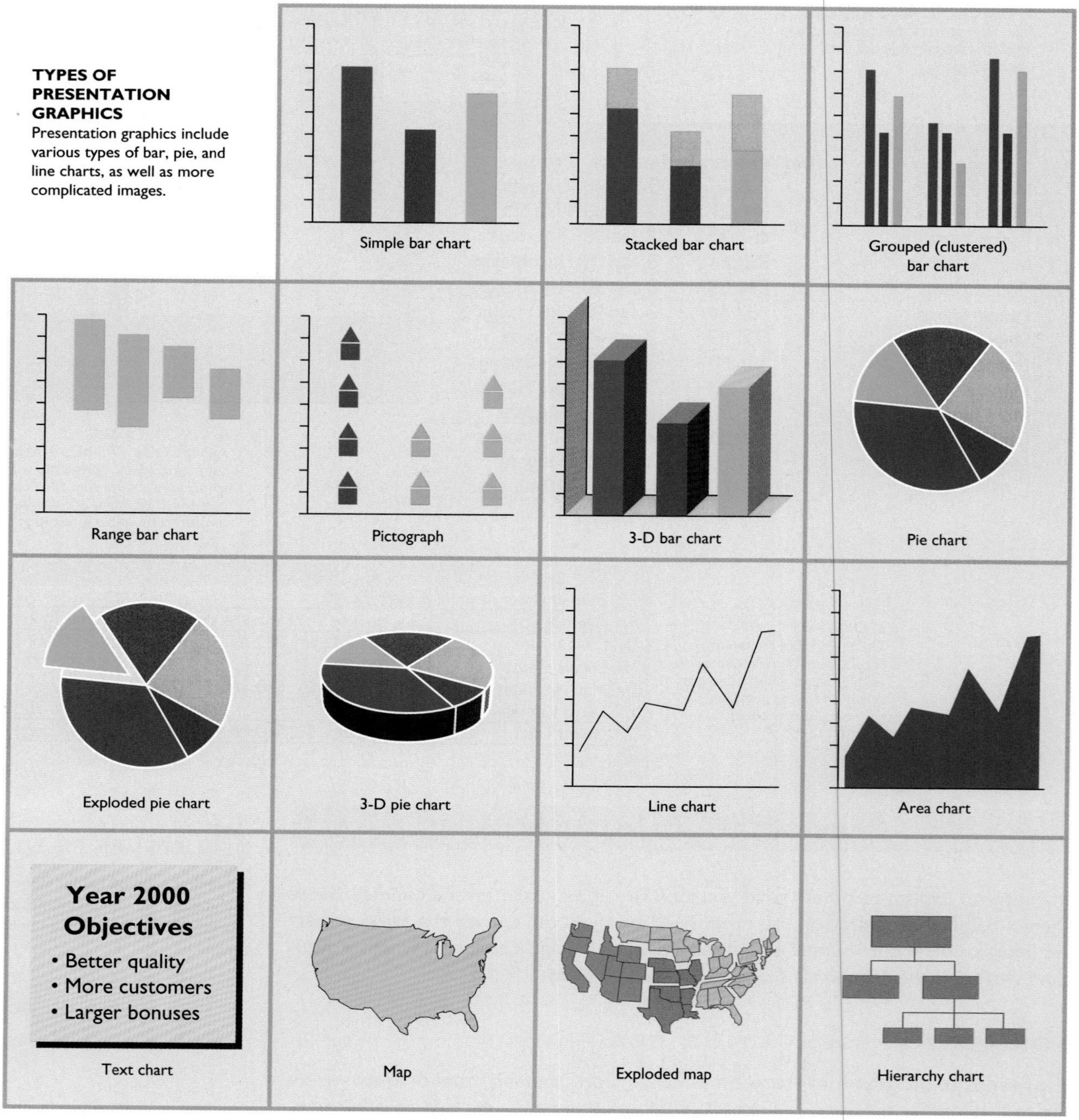

Simple bar chart
Stacked bar chart
Grouped (clustered) bar chart
Range bar chart
Pictograph
3-D bar chart
Pie chart
Exploded pie chart
3-D pie chart
Line chart
Area chart
Year 2000 Objectives
• Better quality
• More customers
• Larger bonuses
Text chart
Map
Exploded map
Hierarchy chart

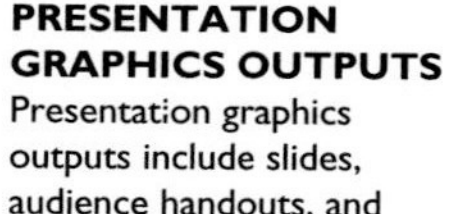

PRESENTATION GRAPHICS OUTPUTS
Presentation graphics outputs include slides, audience handouts, and speaker notes.

National Sales
Store Analysis

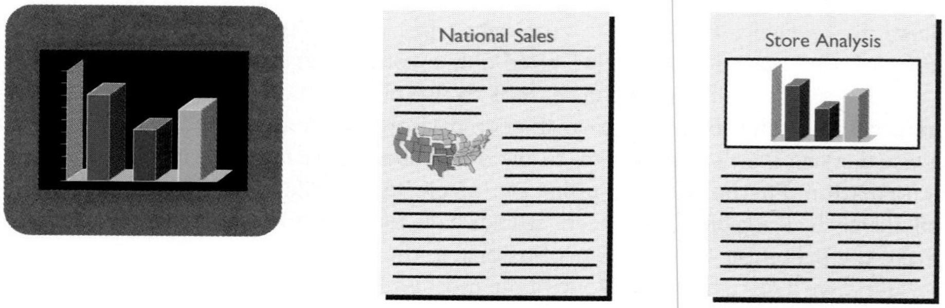

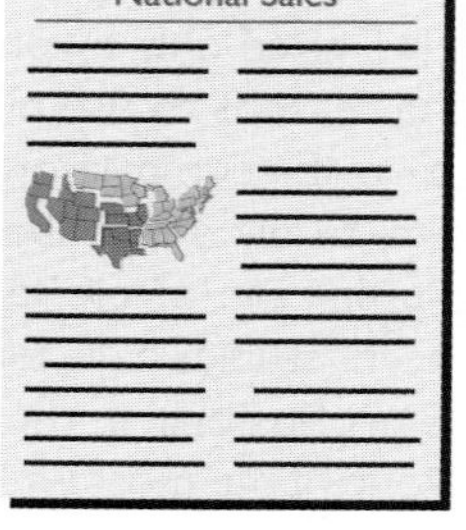

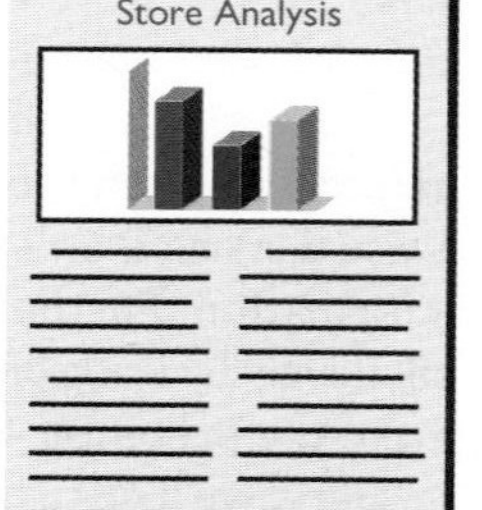

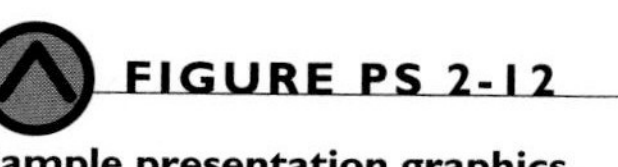

FIGURE PS 2-12
Sample presentation graphics.

appropriate. The best graphic in any given situation ultimately depends on the point you are trying to make. Feature PS 2-1, on page PS 56, additionally explores the area of mapping graphics.

Bar Charts **Bar charts,** or *column charts,* are useful for comparing relative magnitudes of items and for showing the frequency with which events occur. They can also illustrate changes in a single item over time. Several types of bar charts are available, including the simple bar chart, stacked bar chart, grouped bar chart, range chart, pictograph, and 3-D bar chart (refer again to Figure PS 2-12).

As shown in Figure PS 2-13, each type of bar chart has strengths and weaknesses relative to prospective applications. A *range chart,* for instance, would be most useful for showing daily highs and lows of a particular stock in the stock market. A *grouped (clustered) bar chart,* on the other hand, would be more useful for showing something such as overall income comparisons for this year and last year by quarter. Grouped bar charts are especially effective when you want to emphasize a difference between two items over time. When one set of bars is consistently bigger than another set of bars, as is the case in the figure, a *stacked bar chart* can also effectively show the differences between the two sets of bars. A *Gantt chart* is particularly handy for showing when events in schedules begin and end.

FIGURE PS 2-13

Four bar charts. Bar charts are especially useful for comparing the relative magnitudes of items and for showing the frequency with which events occur.

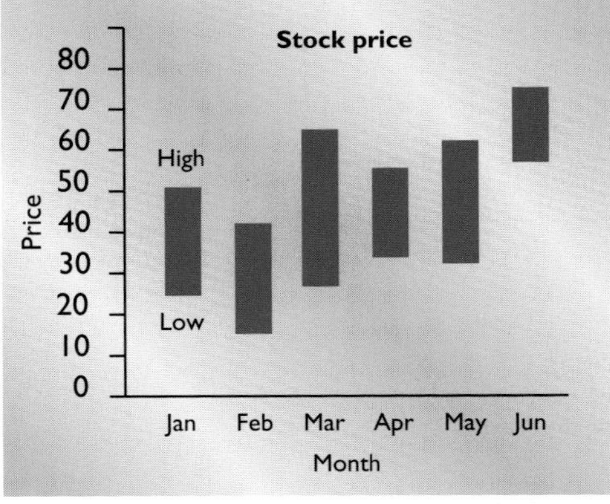

Range chart

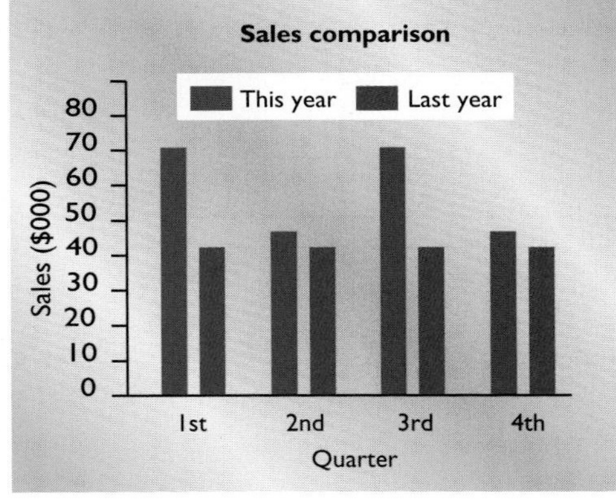

Grouped bar chart

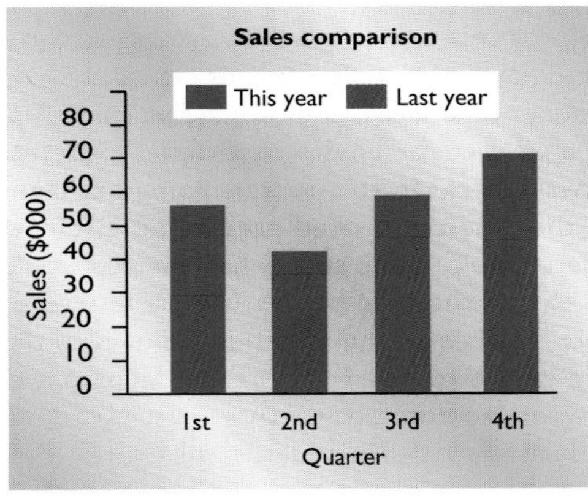

Stacked bar chart

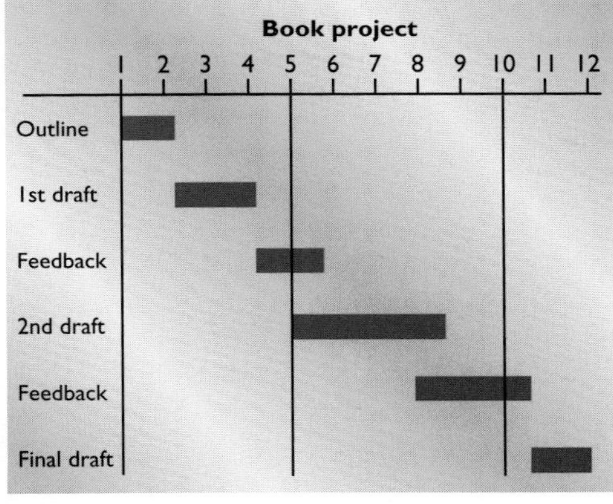

Gantt chart

In a typical bar chart, one axis represents a categorical or *qualitative* phenomenon; the other represents a numeric or *quantitative* one. Such features as grid lines, titles and legends, and attractive fonts can be effectively used to dress up a chart. Figure PS 2-14 illustrates some common elements of bar charts.

When designing bar charts, it's a good idea to keep the total number of categories on the *x*-axis to a half dozen or less. Any more than this may be too much information to cram into a single visual.

P
S

■ **Bar chart.** A presentation graphic that uses side-by-side columns as the principal charting element.

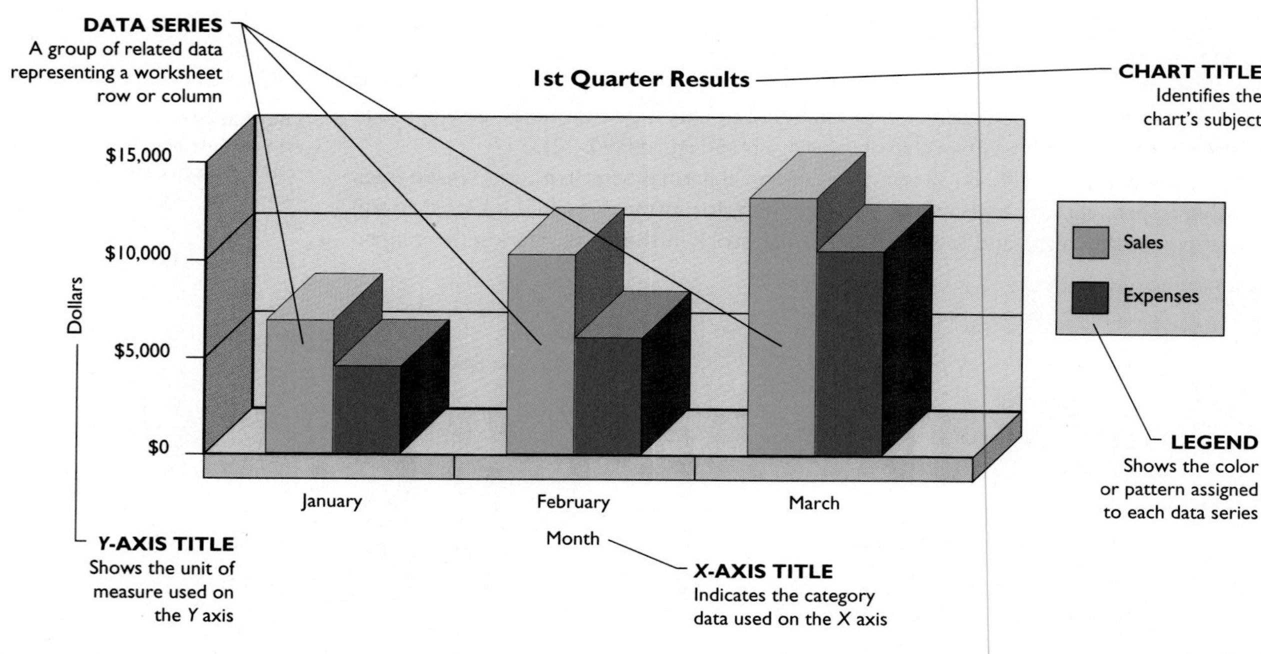

FIGURE PS 2-14

Elements of a bar chart.

Pie Charts **Pie charts** are commonly used to show how parts of something relate to a whole (see Figure PS 2-15). Each slice of the "pie," or circle, represents a percentage share of the total. One of the major advantages of the pie chart is that it is extremely easy to understand.

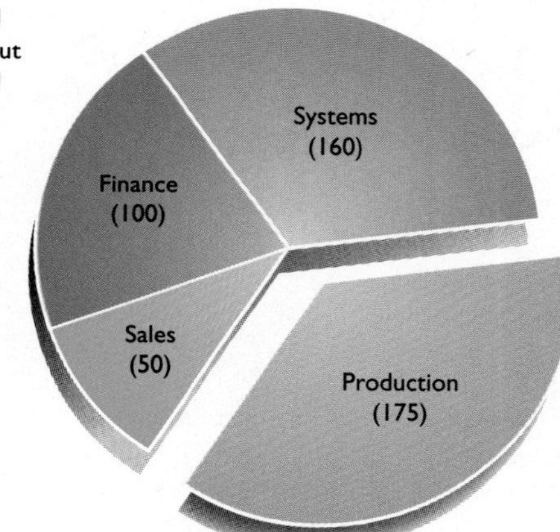

FIGURE PS 2-15

Exploded pie chart. In an exploded pie chart, a single pie slice is moved out slightly from the rest of the pie to call attention to it.

Most presentation graphics packages enable you to "explode" a pie chart to emphasize one or more of the slices, as shown in the figure. The way a pie slice can be exploded varies from one software package to another. Some packages pull the slice out a fixed predefined distance. Others enable you to specify how far you would like to pull the slice out by using a mouse to select the slice on the screen and drag it to the place where you want it. Virtually all packages allow you to color or texture each of the pie slices as well, as is illustrated in the figure.

Pie charts should not have more than a half dozen or so slices. The more slices there are, the harder it is to recognize relative sizes of the shares they represent. When the number of slices in a pie chart becomes large, the smallest slices should be combined.

Line Charts **Line charts** (see Figure PS 2-16) are somewhat similar to bar charts. One major difference, however, is that line charts are used in cases where *both* axes represent quantitative phenomena. A second major difference is that, because the line in the chart is unbroken, the effect on the eye can be much more dramatic.

As with bar charts, there is a rich variety of line charts. Two examples are shown in the figure. Also, as with bar and pie charts, a line chart should not contain too many graphed lines. Lines often cross one another, adding a complexity you don't find in a bar or pie chart. Any more than four or five lines will probably make the visual look confusing.

■ **Pie chart.** A presentation graphic in which the principal charting element is a pie-shaped image that is divided into slices, each of which represents a share of the whole. ■ **Line chart.** A presentation graphic in which the principal charting element is an unbroken line.

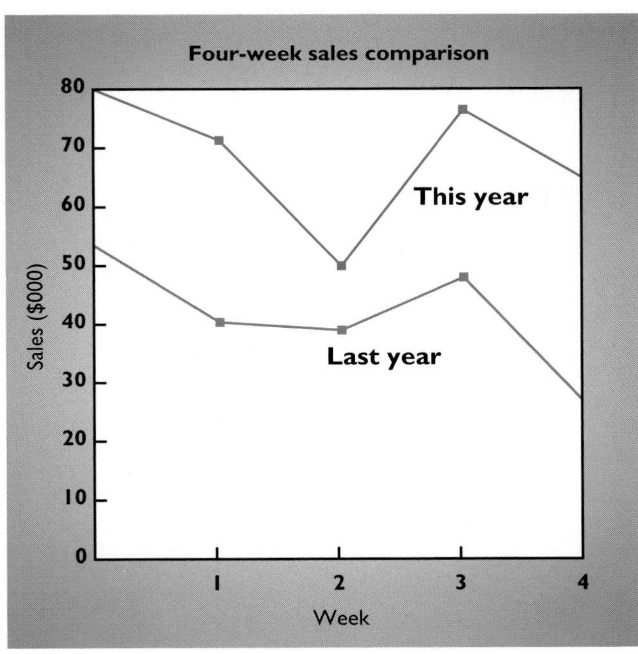

Multiseries line chart

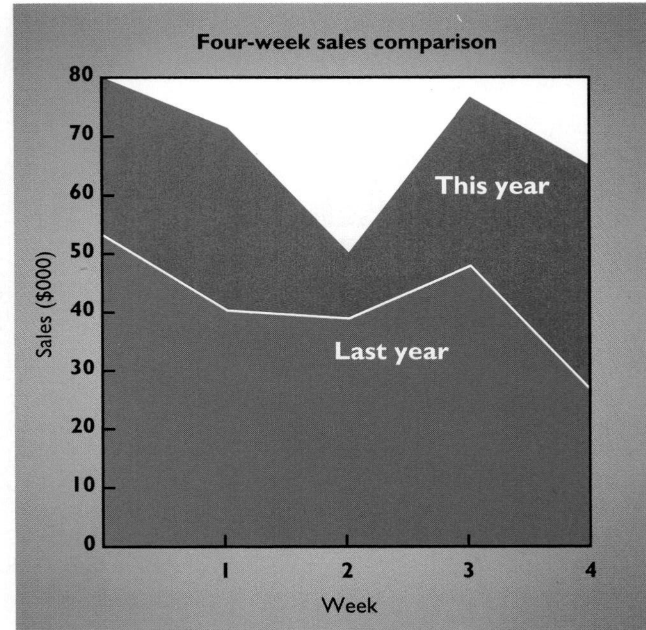

Area chart

FIGURE PS 2-16

Line charts. Because the line in a line chart is unbroken, the effect on the eye can be dramatic.

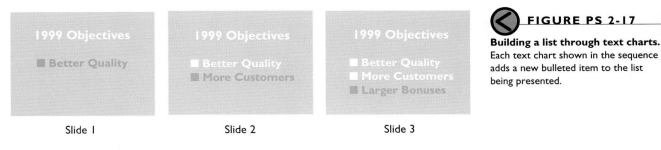

Text Charts Some researchers estimate that approximately 70 to 80 percent of the information presented at meetings is text based. Thus, it is not surprising that **text charts** are a widely used form of presentation graphic. Text charts often use a technique called a *build*. As shown in Figure PS 2-17, text is presented as a bulleted list that is built bullet by bullet in a series of visuals. Animation and sound is often used to accompany each new bulleted item, which is often set in a different color to distinguish it from earlier list items. The build technique is more effective than presenting the entire list as a single visual, which may be too much for an audience to absorb at once. In a build, audience attention is always focused on the latest bullet.

FIGURE PS 2-17

Building a list through text charts. Each text chart shown in the sequence adds a new bulleted item to the list being presented.

HARDWARE AND SOFTWARE

A variety of hardware devices and software packages exists for people who prepare and show presentation graphics.

Hardware Hardware used in the preparation of presentation visuals includes many of the same types of devices used in desktop publishing environments. Several devices are discussed below.

- HIGH-END MICROCOMPUTER SYSTEM Because graphic images generally require lots of computation and storage space, the system should include a state-of-the-art CPU with plenty of RAM and hard-disk storage.

■ **Text chart.** A presentation graphic in which the principal element is text.

Geographic Information Systems (GISs)

Making Presentations with Maps

For hundreds of years, when information had to be recorded on a map, it was drawn right on the map surface. Transparency overlays, introduced later, were a more sophisticated development, allowing different types of data to be layered on a single map. Sometimes the overlays were used jointly, but using two or more overlays could make the maps confusing. Then, in the late 1980s, GISs were created.

Geographic information systems (GISs) display computer-generated maps that are backed by electronic data—the type that you might find in worksheets or a database management system. Advances in spreadsheet and database technology, large-capacity storage devices, and improved computer graphics techniques have made GISs possible. Stored in the data repository are map images and useful geographic data such as demographic breakdowns, sales data, store and warehouse locations, trends, and market research data. Anything you can put on a map—including data on animal populations, land use, foliage growth, traffic patterns, mineral deposits, or pollution—is fair game for a GIS database.

Oil companies such as Texaco, Shell, and Amoco use GISs to store exploration maps and related data such as land-leasing arrangements, oil strikes, and terrain features. The systems have reduced the time needed to find promising places in the world to drill and have made the process of locating drilling sites more accurate.

Such franchisers as Arby's use GISs to assess the performance of their outlets and to select new restaurant sites. One of the key types of data Arby's uses for site selection is traffic patterns. An Arby's spokesperson reports that GISs have dramatically reduced the number of bad decisions.

The Satellite Music Network uses GIS tools to produce maps for thousands of its affiliated stations. The maps reveal where potential listeners to various radio formats—say, golden oldies and country—are likely to be located. The company provides a toll-free number for listener requests, and when listeners call in, their zip codes are recorded—providing data for mapping. Audience distribution data are commonly used to help sell airtime to advertisers.

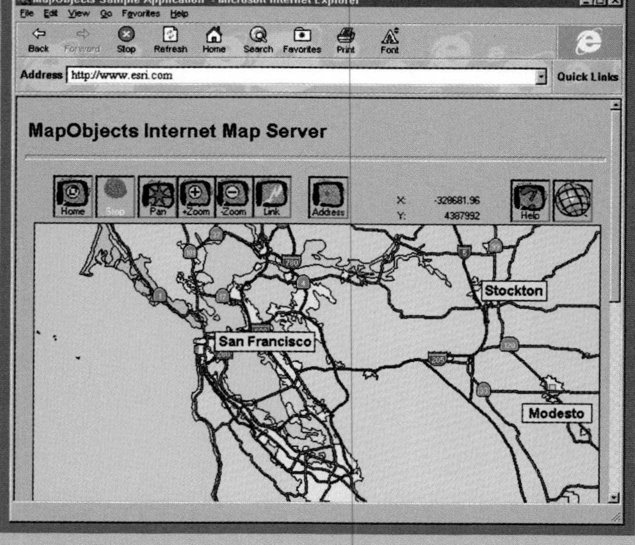

GISs. A geographic information system can provide users with a visual profile of an area.

Gateway Outdoor Advertising, which sells ad space on thousands of billboards, is a strong advocate of GISs. The firm added McDonald's to its roster of clients when it was able to provide the fast-food giant with computer-generated maps that revealed the proximity of several of its billboards to McDonald's restaurants. The maps convinced McDonald's management that the billboards would reach their customers.

In the Pacific Northwest, the city of Tacoma, Washington is a leader in using GISs. The police use a GIS to track crimes, the fire department uses a GIS to cut response time in getting to a fire, city planners use a GIS to keep track of properties for tax assessment, and the water company uses a GIS to locate meters and valves.

- COLOR OUTPUT DEVICES A computer system needs a screen with VGA or better resolution. Color output is an essential capability, because most types of presentation graphics need different colors to highlight elements in the most attractive way. A color plotter or color printer is ideal for preparing handouts for meetings. A film recorder is especially useful if the presentation visuals are to be in hard-copy slide format.
- SPECIAL EQUIPMENT Presentation visuals are often shown to audiences on special equipment, such as a 35 millimeter slide projector, an overhead projector that handles transparencies, or some such similar device (see Figure PS 2-18). Slides and overheads can be in the traditional hard-copy format or in soft-copy (electronic) format. Soft-copy slides make it possible to run the presentation from a computer, customizing it "on the fly" to the needs of the audience—by the use of navigational buttons similar to those found on Web pages—and incorporating dazzling special effects.

FIGURE PS 2-18

Presentation hardware.

Software **Presentation graphics software** provides tools for drawing bar charts, text charts, and similar graphics. Most of this software falls into one of two classes: presentation graphics routines that are part of spreadsheet software and dedicated presentation graphics programs.

- SPREADSHEET PROGRAMS Spreadsheet programs integrate both spreadsheeting and graphics functions into a single product. Such products are ideal for

FIGURE PS 2-19

Using a spreadsheet chart wizard to create presentation graphics.

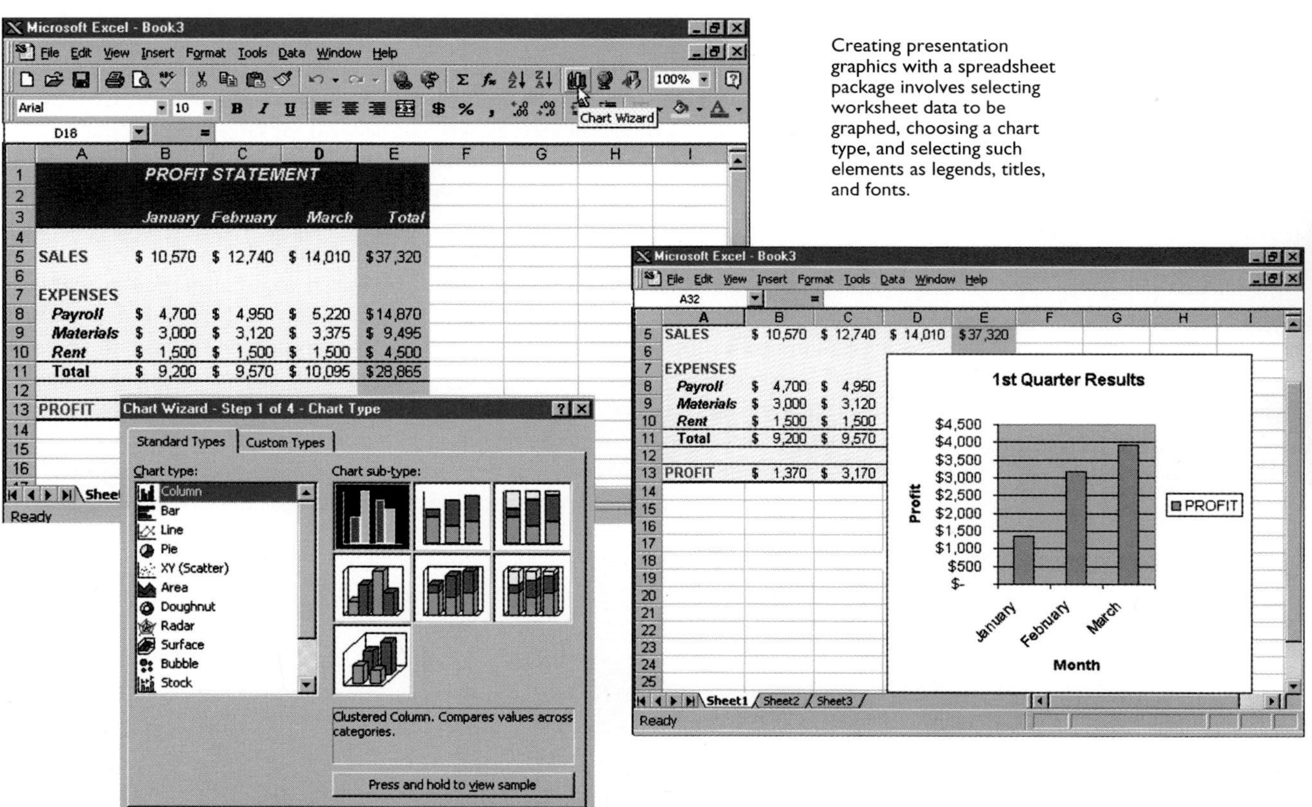

Creating presentation graphics with a spreadsheet package involves selecting worksheet data to be graphed, choosing a chart type, and selecting such elements as legends, titles, and fonts.

■ **Presentation graphics software.** A program used to prepare bar charts, pie charts—and other information-intensive images—and present them to an audience.

users who require a strong data manipulation capability and whose presentation graphics needs are relatively modest—say, an occasional bar- or pie-chart representation of worksheet data. Using a chart wizard in a spreadsheet program to prepare a presentation graphic is illustrated in Figure PS 2-19. Many spreadsheets have routines that automatically update graphs when the worksheets upon which they are based change.

- DEDICATED PROGRAMS Dedicated presentation graphics programs provide more powerful features than spreadsheet programs offer. For instance, you can call on a wider selection of drawing and sound capabilities, many more options for customizing graphics on bar and pie charts, and a variety of devices such as timers and animation tools that can really make a text-chart presentation sizzle (see the end-of-chapter window, "Creating Presentations with PowerPoint"). Many dedicated packages also have tools for workgroup computing, so that two or more people can work on a presentation together over a computer network.

  In short, if your presentation graphics needs are extensive, dedicated programs are more likely to contain the type of functionality you require. Four of the most widely used dedicated programs are Microsoft's PowerPoint, Computer Associates' Harvard Graphics, Lotus's Freelance Graphics, and Adobe's Persuasion.

ADVANCED PRESENTATIONS

While most presentations consist of simple visuals shown in slide or overhead form—along with supplemental handouts—computer technology has made it possible for presentations to become ever more sophisticated. Two relatively new types of presentations are computer animations and Web-based presentations.

Computer Animations In *computer animation,* moving—and possibly three-dimensional—images are created and shown on a PC-display screen, room screen, or standard television screen (through an optical disk or videotape player). Computer animation, for example, offers an increasingly valuable aid for lawyers as a courtroom-presentation tool to re-create accidents and to help sway juries' judgments about who was at fault (see Figure PS 2-20). Such animations can be expensive to produce—several thousand dollars is typical—but the cost of developing the presentation may be a drop in the bucket compared to the courtroom settlement.

Computer animations can sometimes be presented to an audience in *realtime.* This means that adjustments can be made to the animation as the presenter is delivering the presentation to the audience, enabling the presenter to field all sorts of "what if" type questions that might never get satisfactorily answered if the presentation was static (see User Solution PS 2-1).

Computer animations frequently enhance multimedia presentations involving voice, text, and moving and still images. For instance, many colleges and businesses are frequently turning to multimedia presentations at their visitor or customer centers. A

FIGURE PS 2-20

Animations used for presentation graphics in courtrooms.

Interactive Simulations in Presentations

Over the past few years, companies seeking large contracts have often used computer animations for presentations. Now, some firms are pushing the technology envelope further, using animations that also simulate results in realtime. Bergmann Associates, an architectural firm located in upstate New York, recently won a contract with the New York Department of Transportation for designing a drawbridge with such a simulation. Because the simulation could be run in realtime, in front of the audience, environmental-impact questions could be fielded on the spot with fresh inputs. The presentation was modeled in 3-D and used scanned images of buildings in the area of the proposed bridge for realism. Next up on Bergmann's presentation agenda: modeling noises into presentations, so that an audience will be able to get a better feel of a proposed new roadway or building site from any of several vantage points within a 3-D model.

visitor to campus, say, steps up to an information kiosk, presses a selection, and a presentation is viewed. Museums often use presentation kiosks in the same way.

Web-Based Presentations The recent popularity of the Internet's World Wide Web has enabled thousands of individuals and organizations to make presentations through that medium. At many companies, field salespeople have access to graphics and even fully packaged presentations over the Web in order to make pitches at a client site. Web-based presentations may involve any combination of text, simple graphics, computer animation, digital audio and video, realtime tools, and virtual-reality and 3-D graphics techniques. The Web as a presentation medium is treated at great length in versions of this textbook that contain the NET module. The Tomorrow box makes some observations on the future of Web-based presentations.

Summary and Key Terms

Two useful types of program packages for manipulating data so that they make sense to you and others are spreadsheets and presentation graphics software.

Spreadsheets An *electronic spreadsheet package,* or **spreadsheet,** produces computerized counterparts to the ruled ledger-style worksheets that accountants frequently use. Spreadsheets first came to public notice in the late 1970s when a product named *VisiCalc* was developed.

In electronic spreadsheets, the display screen is viewed as a *window* looking in on a big grid, called a **worksheet.** The worksheet consists of *rows* and *columns* that intersect to form **cells,** each of which can be accessed through a **cell address.** Columns are labeled by letters, and rows are labeled by numbers, so, for instance, Cell B3 is located at the intersection of the second column and third row.

Spreadsheet software often divides the screen into two principal areas. The worksheet itself is displayed in the **worksheet area,** or **window area.** The **control panel** is the area of the screen where users perform tasks such as issuing commands

Making a Point, circa 2005

Will Creating Web-Based Presentations Become as Commonplace as Writing Reports?

Wherever you look today, computer vendors are making it easier and easier for you to launch onto the Internet and its World Wide Web. Are you in the middle of preparing a report in Microsoft Excel or Lotus 1-2-3? No problem. Click on one command, and you're all set to convert your worksheets and graphics into Web pages. Click another, and you're ready to upload the pages onto the Internet.

One wonders—with the Internet becoming such a visible presence within office-software suites and with private company "intranets" springing up left and right—whether someday we'll all be creating presentations for the Web. This, of course, is instead of the current convention of converting disk files to paper or film through laser printers and slide-making machines.

Sound far-fetched? It shouldn't, when you think of how much effort is being put into making the Internet as easy to use as a television set and, also, the power that an electronic report can have over a hard-copy one. Someday in the forseeable future it will be possible to have all the tools available on your desktop to reliably deliver and receive stunning Web presentations.

Writing presentation materials to be read online requires a much different preparation strategy than that applied by most people to the reports they write today. First, there's the size of the reading hardware to consider. Most display screens are designed to be operated in landscape mode. This is opposite the orientation of most 8½-inch-by-11-inch printed pages, which are output in a portrait mode. If you can't squeeze your information into screen-sized chunks, it better be catchy enough for the reader to scroll to see it. A lot of people won't bother.

Another important thing to consider is that, with a Web page, readers will want to hyperlink. This requires a different way of organizing information than the serial fashion used in most printed documents, where the reader is more or less forced into taking pages in the order in which the table of contents suggests. Readers of Web pages have far more freedom to wander around a document—and many may want to assimilate your presentation in an order different from the one you may have had in mind.

The Web: Is it becoming the most natural place for presentations?

Then, there's the capability to search online and to reference massive volumes of material that you couldn't ever be able to fit into a written presentation. If the user wants to see support material, you could have it waiting in the wings, ready to be accessed by the click of a mouse button. It is also possible to update a Web report frequently, thereby enabling the reader to see the freshest possible facts.

With an online presentation you can also add video and sound—two elements you can't possibly convert into printed form. Thus, if you have a message or a mood that you want to impart to the reader, you can build in a hyperlink that fetches your voice. An audio clip of you speaking can bestow a sense of concern or comfort that the written word might be hard pressed to convey. Or, if you want to show the reader the place that you're referencing, you can embed a small "travel" video in your presentation, literally being able to whisk your reader away to a setting that can have an impact.

The aforementioned is not to imply that the venerable laser printer and overhead projector are dead. Despite the fact that more people will find themselves writing online than ever before, many if not most of us will also require use of the printed document or the need to make presentations by conventional means. When it comes to reading for enjoyment or reading complex material that requires a lot of thinking, nothing beats a good easy chair, hard copy, and a highlighting pen to underline and scribble remarks. And when it comes to making a critical point, it's hard to top showing up in person, using showmanship tools that don't give the audience any wiggle room and that don't deliver annoying error messages at the time when you least need them.

from menus and toolbars and, also, developing entries for cells. Cell entries are one of two types: A **constant value** consists of text and numeric values, whereas a **formula** is a cell entry that performs a mathematical operation on other cells. The control panel also shows you the cell to which you are currently pointing, called the **current cell.** It is also the area used to display commands. The **cell pointer** (or **highlight)** is associated with the worksheet area and points to the current cell.

Spreadsheet packages are particularly valuable because they possess a **recalculation feature**—that is, they can perform recalculations in seconds that would require several hours to do manually or by writing a program in a regular programming language. It's this recalculation feature, and the **what-if analysis** it makes possible, that makes spreadsheets so popular.

A contiguous rectangular block of cells is called a **range.** A range can be typed in explicitly or selected on the screen by pointing and clicking.

In virtually all spreadsheet packages, cell entries can be formatted—say, by changing their alignment or by putting in such special characters as dollar signs and commas.

Most spreadsheet packages contain a couple of hundred or so built-in functions that enable you to create formulas for a wide range of applications. A **function** is a reference to a prestored formula (such as that for calculating net present value) or a preset value (such as today's date).

Spreadsheet packages have numerous features to aid in developing worksheet data. Some of the basic operations include inserting and deleting rows or columns, moving or copying the contents of cells from one part of the worksheet to another (through **relative replication, absolute replication,** or **mixed replication),** selecting column widths and row heights, freezing titles, printing worksheets, and a variety of features for dressing up worksheets. Also, many packages have a **template** feature that permits the creation, saving, and protection of worksheets that have all of their rows and columns prelabeled, and prewritten formulas, so that only the data need to be filled in.

Most spreadsheet programs today provide users with a variety of data-handling capabilities, including the ability to *sort* records on one or more fields and to *filter* records with specific characteristics. Many programs also have a *pivot-table* feature that makes it possible to rearrange data in a table so as to see new types of relationships among them.

Presentation Graphics A **presentation graphic—**sometimes called a *presentation visual* or *chart*—is an image that visually enhances in some way the impact of information communicated to other people. A presentation graphic can take any one of a large number of forms.

Probably the four most common types of presentation visuals are bar charts, pie charts, line charts, and text charts. **Bar charts** are especially useful for comparing relative magnitudes of items and for showing the frequency with which events occur. **Pie charts** are commonly used to show how parts of something relate to a whole. **Line charts** are used to represent graph data in which both axes are used to represent quantitative phenomena. **Text charts** are most appropriate for producing lists of items.

Hardware used in the preparation of presentation visuals includes many of the same types of devices used in desktop publishing environments. Also useful are such special equipment as film recorders and projectors.

Presentation graphics software lets you draw bar charts, pie charts, and the like. Presentation graphics packages are either dedicated or integrated into a spreadsheet package. *Dedicated packages* provide the most sophisticated types of presentation capabilities, whereas *spreadsheet packages* consist of modest features.

Computer animation and *Web-based presentations* are two relatively new types of presentation techniques.

EXERCISES

1. Fill in the blanks:
   a. The principle behind an electronic spreadsheet involves viewing the display screen as a(n) __________ looking at a section of a big grid called a(n) __________.
   b. Three types of copying operations available in many spreadsheet packages are __________, __________, and __________ replication.
   c. A worksheet in which all rows and columns are prelabeled and formulas are supplied is called a(n) __________.
   d. The spreadsheet feature that allows users to combine or rearrange data in a table to see new information is called a(n)__________ feature.
   e. Most presentation graphics packages fall into one of two categories: __________ packages and __________ packages.

2. Match each term with the description that fits best.
   a. =SUM(A1:A2) c. John Smith
   b. D4 d. F18:F28
   _____ A constant value
   _____ A range
   _____ A function
   _____ A cell address

3. Which type of chart covered in the book—bar, pie, line, or text—is best described by each of the following phrases.
   a. Both axes measure quantitative data.
   b. One axis measures quantitative data; the other measures qualitative data.
   c. There are no axes, but all of the pieces represented combine to make a whole.
   d. Gantt chart is a type.
   e. It often has an exploded element.
   f. A build is used to present data.
   g. Area chart is a type.

4. Describe, in your own words, what each of the following is.
   a. VisiCalc
   b. Control panel
   c. Formula bar
   d. Filtering capability
   e. Worksheet area
   f. What-if analysis
   g. Autocomplete feature
   h. Control break

5. Rank the following from largest to smallest.
   a. Range
   b. Cell
   c. Workbook
   d. Worksheet

6. Explain the differences among the following:
   a. Moving cell contents
   b. Mixed replication of cell contents
   c. Relative replication of cell contents
   d. Absolute replication of cell contents

7. Name at least eight different types of charts that you can create with a presentation graphics package, and draw a small picture of each that shows what it represents.

8. What is the difference between a dedicated presentation graphics package and a spreadsheet package with graphics capabilities?

9. Given the worksheet in the figure, what is the value of each of the following?
   a. =SUM(C1:C4)
   b. =MIN(A1:D4)
   c. =COUNT(A3:B4)
   d. =IF(A4<5,10,20)
   e. =AVG(A1:C2)

	A	B	C	D
1	20	11	8	4
2	18	5	1	12
3	17	13	0	9
4	7	16	15	3

10. Use the accompanying figure to answer the following questions:
    a. How many numbers will automatically be calculated by the spreadsheet package through the use of formulas?
    b. If January payroll is adjusted from $4,700 to $4,750, how many other numbers in the worksheet will be recalculated?
    c. What cell columns or rows can be partially filled in using the autocomplete feature?
    d. What is the current cell?

Microsoft Excel - Book3

File Edit View Insert Format Tools Data Window Help

G4

	A	B	C	D	E
1	PROFIT STATEMENT				
2					
3		January	February	March	Total
4					
5	SALES	$ 10,570	$ 12,740	$ 14,010	$37,320
6					
7	EXPENSES				
8	Payroll	$ 4,700	$ 4,950	$ 5,220	$14,870
9	Materials	$ 3,000	$ 3,120	$ 3,375	$ 9,495
10	Rent	$ 1,500	$ 1,500	$ 1,500	$ 4,500
11	Total	$ 9,200	$ 9,570	$ 10,095	$28,865
12					
13	PROFIT	$ 1,370	$ 3,170	$ 3,915	$ 8,455

Sheet1 / Sheet2 / Sheet3

Ready

1. Critical-Thinking Question A corporate strategist writing a column in a recent issue of *Forbes* magazine lamented that he detests upgrading to new software. He claimed that he got all the functionality he needed in a spreadsheet back in 1980 with VisiCalc (the first spreadsheet package), and he doesn't really need a choice of more than 80 rainbow-hued colors to word process a letter. As if paying for new hardware and software isn't galling enough, he adds, billions of dollars in valuable time is collectively wasted by businesses in unnecessarily retraining users. Many people share this point of view. Are you one of them? Why or why not?

2. O. J. Revisited The O.J. Simpson trial brought widespread public awareness of the use of computer-animation technology as a presentation tool. Some people oppose the use of such technology in presenting information to trial juries. Present as many reasons as you can for blocking the use of computer animation in the courtroom.

3. The Spreadsheet Program at Your School For the spreadsheet program that comes with your own computer or the computers in your school's PC lab, describe how to do the following tasks:

a. Insert columns and rows
b. Adjust the widths of columns and the heights of rows
c. Delete columns and rows
d. Change the alignment of data in Cell A8 from left justified to centered
e. Change the typeface and point size on the top row of your worksheet data
f. Hide columns and rows
g. Use the pivot-table feature
h. Autoformat a range—say, by having the spreadsheet program automatically supply month names
i. Place borders around cells in the worksheet
j. Sort raw data

4. Researching a Spreadsheet Program You can find out much more about a particular spreadsheet program by finding a book about it or by cruising the Internet for information. For the spreadsheet program of your choice, complete the following activities:

a. Visit a local bookstore and find as many books as you can—up to a limit of three—about the spreadsheet program you have chosen. Write down the name of each book, the name of the author and publisher, and the copyright date. If there is no bookstore in your area or you are having problems finding titles, consider visiting one online. Two large online bookstores are the Amazon Bookstore (http://www.amazon.com/) and Computer Literacy Bookshops (http://www.clbooks.com/).
b. For any one of the books you chose in part a, write a short (one-to-two-page) report telling whether the book serves an audience of beginners or advanced users, what it covers, and features that appeal or don't appeal to you.
c. *Optional: Do this part of the project only if you have Internet access.* Do any resources about the spreadsheet program you have chosen exist on the World Wide Web? If so, describe the Web sites and any information they contain.

5. Researching a Dedicated Presentation Graphics Program Several dedicated presentation graphics programs have been mentioned in the chapter. Choose a particular version of one such program and answer the following questions about it. You may be able to find some of the answers from information that is available on the Internet.

a. What is the name of the program and who is its publisher?
b. Does the version work on a PC-compatible platform or on the Macintosh platform (or both)? What is the most current version number of the program?
c. How much RAM and hard disk does the program require?
d. What is the suggested list price or street price of the program?
e. Name at least two things the program you have chosen can do that your spreadsheet program cannot.

6. Spreadsheet Functions Pick any of the leading spreadsheet programs and tell—for any three of the following—the name of the function that should be used. Also, demonstrate how the function works by trying it on your computer.

a. Compute the standard deviation of a list of numbers.
b. Compute depreciation for an asset by the double-declining balance method.
c. Find the cosine of an angle.
d. Return the value of TRUE if a cell is blank.
e. Round a number down to the nearest integer.

7. Dressing Up a Worksheet Refer to the worksheets in the accompanying figure, and complete these activities:

a. Prepare the worksheet in the top part of the figure.
b. Dress up the worksheet you just prepared so that it resembles the worksheet at the bottom. Note that you can use lots of tools to make the transition,

including applying an autoformat, bolding and increasing point size, widening columns and rows (notice that you will have to add text to Cell A9), centering text, and applying color fills and color fonts to selected cells.

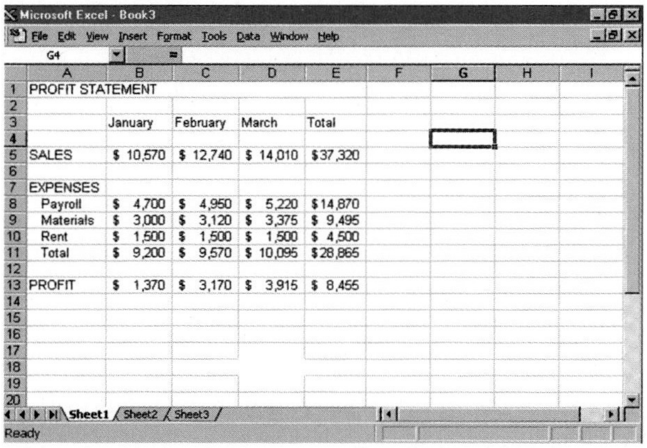

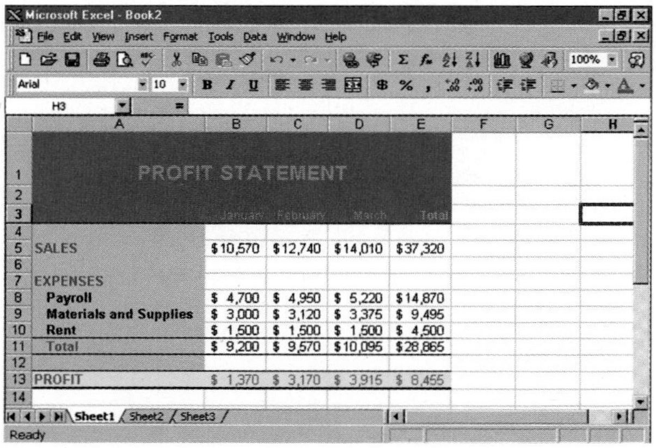

Microsoft Excel - Book3

	A	B	C	D	E
1	PROFIT STATEMENT				
2					
3		January	February	March	Total
4					
5	SALES	$ 10,570	$ 12,740	$ 14,010	$37,320
6					
7	EXPENSES				
8	Payroll	$ 4,700	$ 4,950	$ 5,220	$14,870
9	Materials	$ 3,000	$ 3,120	$ 3,375	$ 9,495
10	Rent	$ 1,500	$ 1,500	$ 1,500	$ 4,500
11	Total	$ 9,200	$ 9,570	$ 10,095	$28,865
12					
13	PROFIT	$ 1,370	$ 3,170	$ 3,915	$ 8,455

Microsoft Excel - Book2

	A	B	C	D	E
1	PROFIT STATEMENT				
3		January	February	March	Total
5	SALES	$10,570	$12,740	$14,010	$37,320
7	EXPENSES				
8	**Payroll**	$ 4,700	$ 4,950	$ 5,220	$14,870
9	**Materials and Supplies**	$ 3,000	$ 3,120	$ 3,375	$ 9,495
10	**Rent**	$ 1,500	$ 1,500	$ 1,500	$ 4,500
11	Total	$ 9,200	$ 9,570	$10,095	$28,865
13	PROFIT	$ 1,370	$ 3,170	$ 3,915	$ 8,455

8. Preparing a Bar Chart Using either the spreadsheet or presentation graphics program available to your class, produce either the grouped bar chart or the stacked bar chart shown in Figure PS 2-13.

9. Preparing a Pie Chart Using either the spreadsheet or presentation graphics program available to your class, produce the pie chart shown in Figure PS 2-15.

10. Preparing a Line Chart Using either the spreadsheet or presentation graphics program available to your class, produce the multiseries line chart shown in Figure PS 2-16.

11. Electronic Slide Presentation Using the presentation graphics program available to your class, do the following:

a. Produce a series of text-oriented electronic slides—at least a half dozen or so. You may wish to refer to the "Creating Presentations with PowerPoint" window at the end of the chapter for some ideas.
b. Add clip art to one or two of the slides.
c. Arrange the slides into an automated presentation that can be shown to the class. Use the automatic timer to display each slide, and add transition effects—both a visual effect and sound—between each slide.
d. Prepare a hard-copy script, to read in front of the class, which is coordinated with the automatic slide timer.

window

Creating Presentations with PowerPoint

A PICTURE IS WORTH A THOUSAND WORDS

Computers are useful tools for presenting information to others in a valuable and interesting way. People who want to work seriously on their presentations usually acquire dedicated presentation graphics programs. Many of these programs—such as Microsoft's PowerPoint, illustrated here—are easy enough for even the most intimidated computer users to learn. In this window we look at the steps in preparing a simple presentation—from creating the opening slide to rehearsing dry runs of the presentation itself.

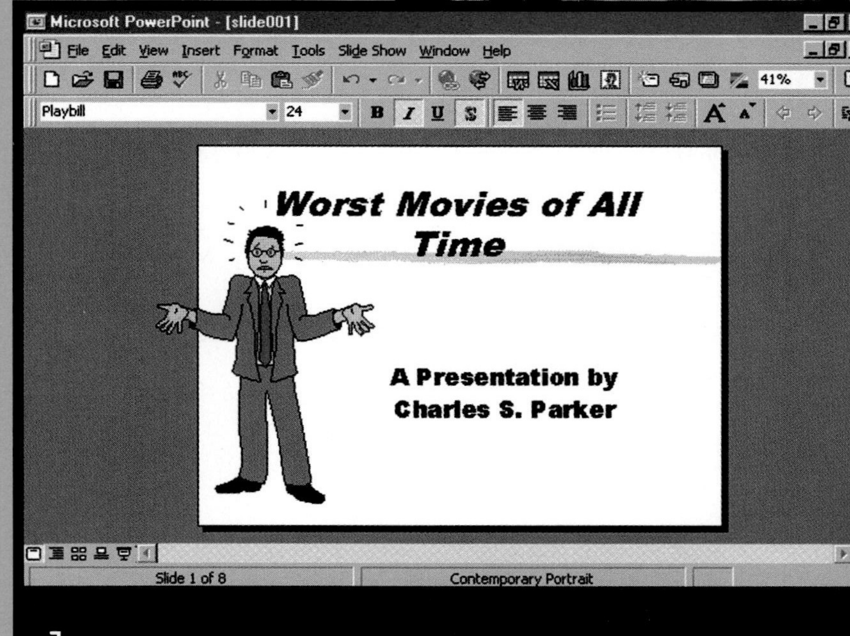

1. The PowerPoint GUI helps users to prepare slides that incorporate a variety of text and background styles, with or without imported art.

2 • The first step in preparing electronic slides is choosing a *master slide* that shows a presentation design. As you click on potential choices, they preview at the right of the screen.

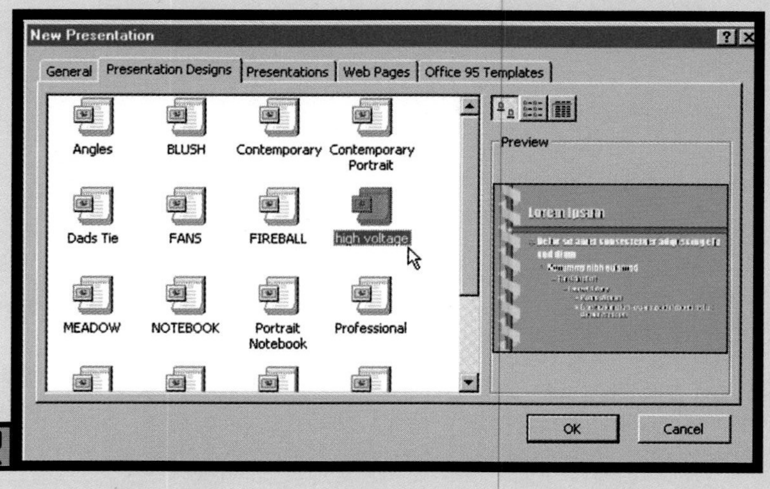

the title slide

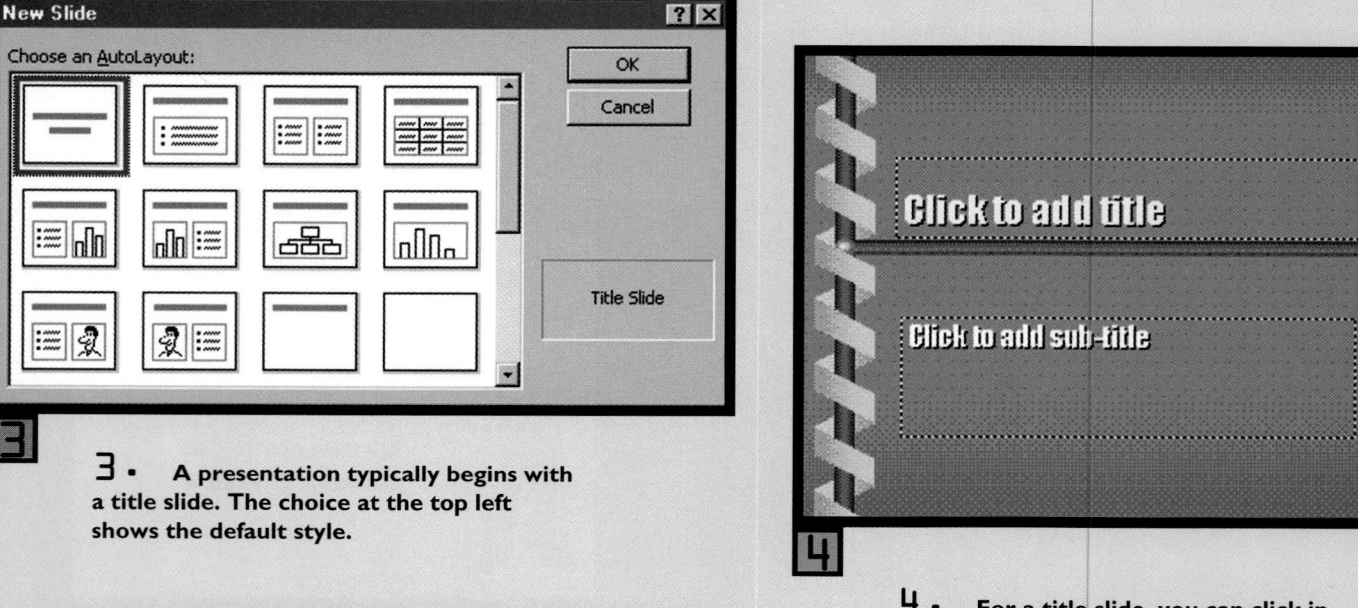

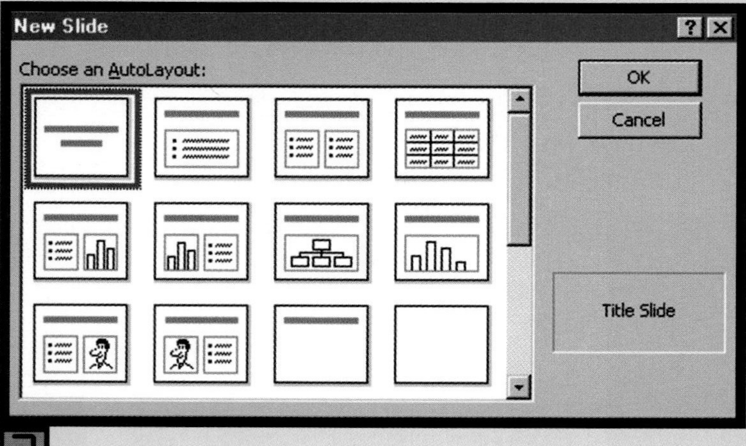

3 • A presentation typically begins with a title slide. The choice at the top left shows the default style.

4 • For a title slide, you can click in the upper or lower area and type in a title or subtitle, respectively. To style the text you type in, use the GUI's formatting toolbar.

5 • Once you save the finished title slide, you are ready to create the rest of the slides.

other slides

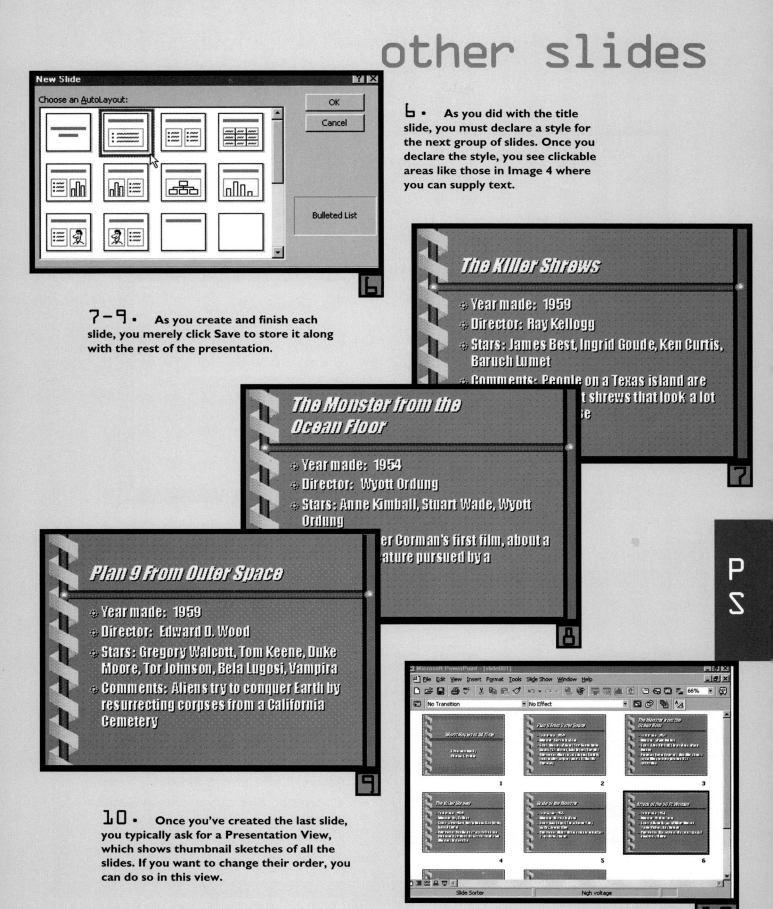

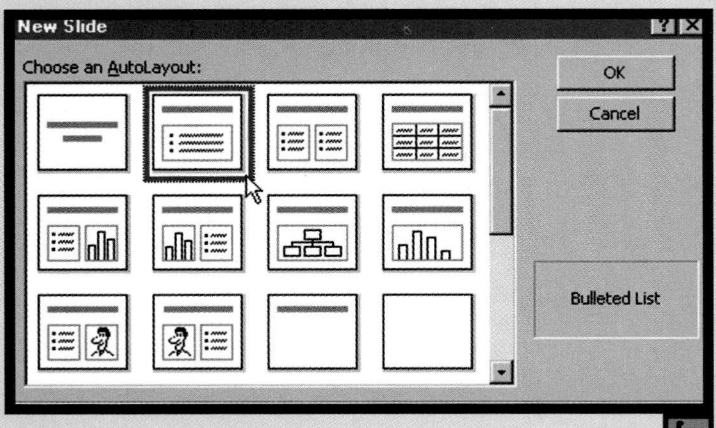

6. As you did with the title slide, you must declare a style for the next group of slides. Once you declare the style, you see clickable areas like those in Image 4 where you can supply text.

7–9. As you create and finish each slide, you merely click Save to store it along with the rest of the presentation.

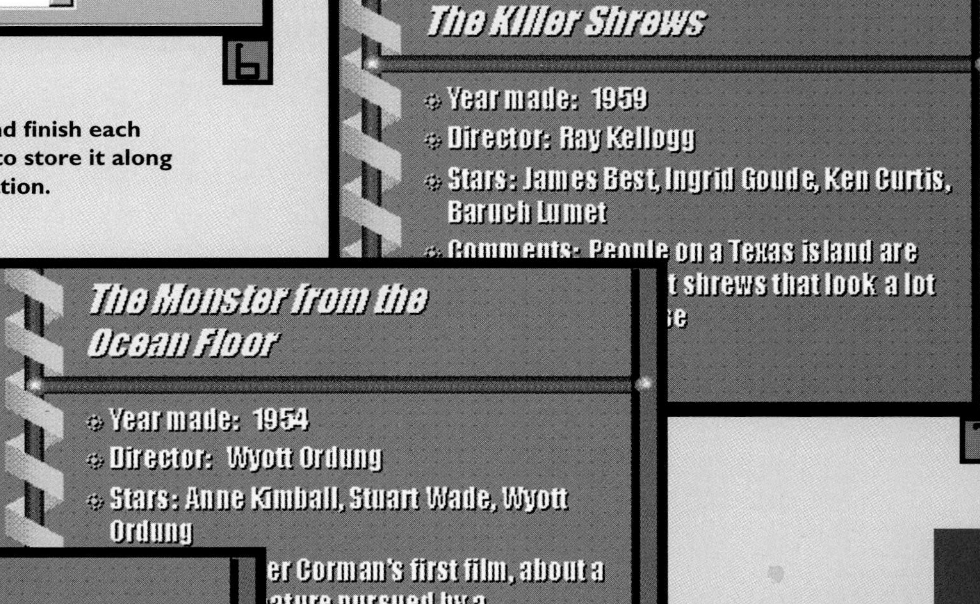

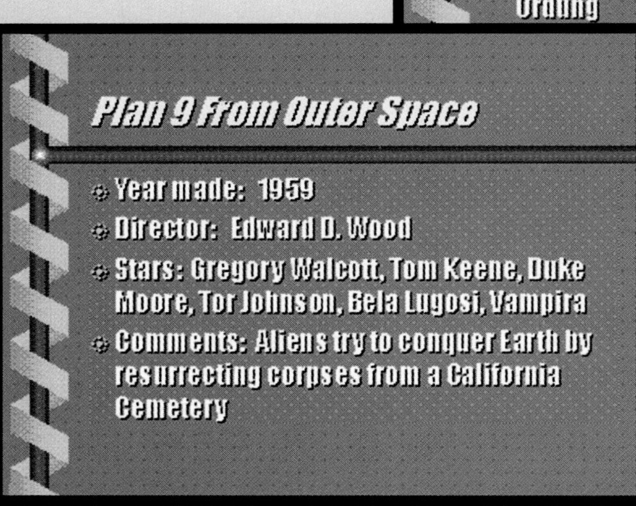

10. Once you've created the last slide, you typically ask for a Presentation View, which shows thumbnail sketches of all the slides. If you want to change their order, you can do so in this view.

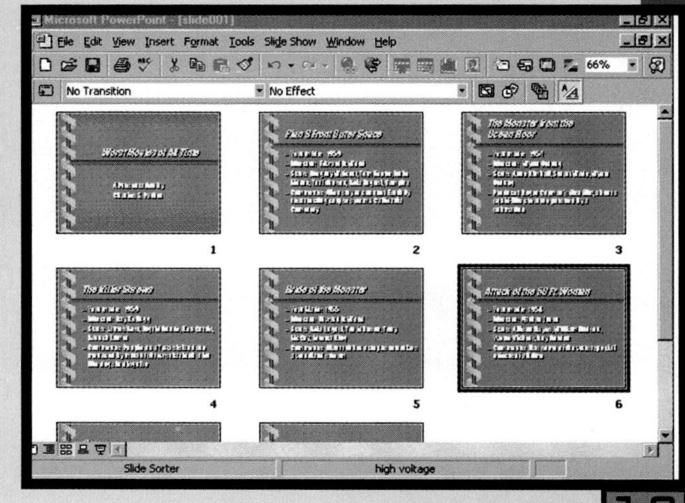

PS

editing the presentation

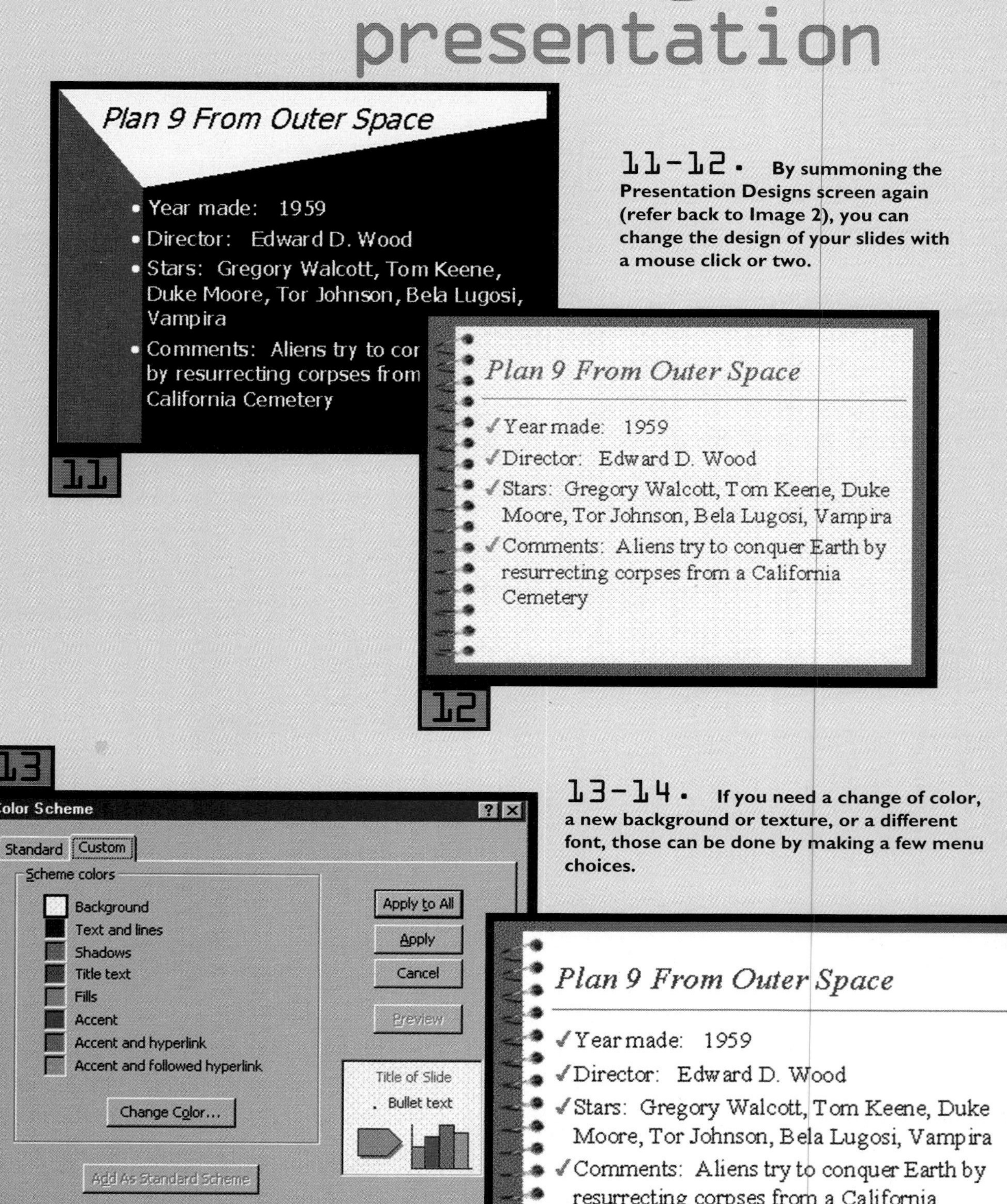
Plan 9 From Outer Space
Year made: 1959
Director: Edward D. Wood
Stars: Gregory Walcott, Tom Keene, Duke Moore, Tor Johnson, Bela Lugosi, Vampira
Comments: Aliens try to cor
by resurrecting corpses from
California Cemetery
11
Plan 9 From Outer Space
Year made: 1959
Director: Edward D. Wood
Stars: Gregory Walcott, Tom Keene, Duke Moore, Tor Johnson, Bela Lugosi, Vampira
Comments: Aliens try to conquer Earth by resurrecting corpses from a California Cemetery
12
13
Color Scheme
Standard
Custom
Scheme colors
Background
Text and lines
Shadows
Title text
Fills
Accent
Accent and hyperlink
Accent and followed hyperlink
Change Color...
Apply to All
Apply
Cancel
Preview
Title of Slide
Bullet text
Add As Standard Scheme
Plan 9 From Outer Space
Year made: 1959
Director: Edward D. Wood
Stars: Gregory Walcott, Tom Keene, Duke Moore, Tor Johnson, Bela Lugosi, Vampira
Comments: Aliens try to conquer Earth by resurrecting corpses from a California Cemetery
14

11-12. **By summoning the Presentation Designs screen again (refer back to Image 2), you can change the design of your slides with a mouse click or two.**

13-14. **If you need a change of color, a new background or texture, or a different font, those can be done by making a few menu choices.**

adding art

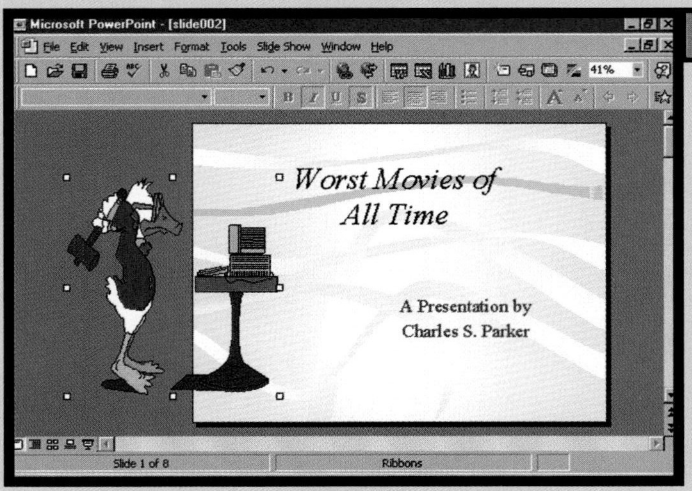

15

16

15-16. **Clip art can be fetched from a clip-art gallery and moved or resized to your taste. In addition, you can summon the Drawing toolbar and create your own art.**

the finishing touches

17

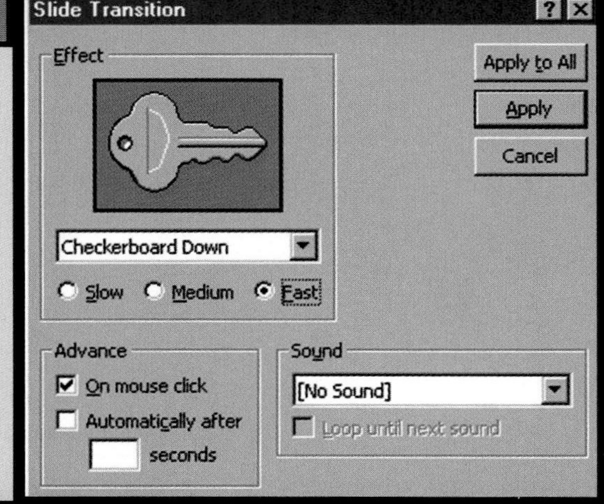

17. **A transition-effects dialog box enables you to add between each slide a visual effect—such as checker-boarding, wipes, fades, or dissolves—and put in sounds, too.**

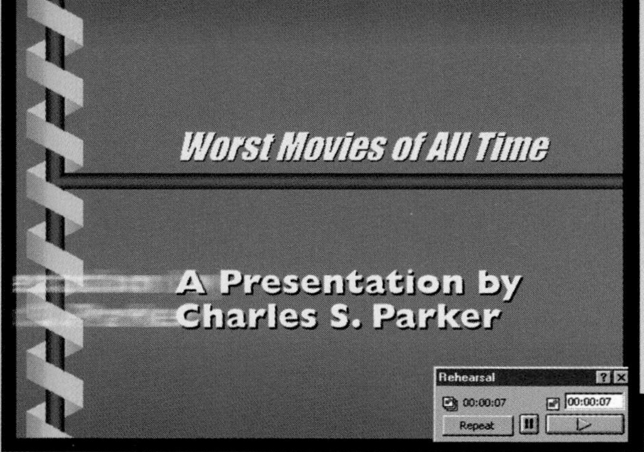

18

18. **As you present the images onscreen, each title, subtitle, or bulleted entry in a list can "fly" in from any of several directions with a mouse click. A timer at the lower right of the screen helps you rehearse your presentation so that it doesn't exceed a given time limit.**

PS

presentation hints

19-21 • PowerPoint can be used to feed screens created in other programs to a live audience (Image 19) and to turn slides and documents into Web-based presentations (Images 20 and 21).

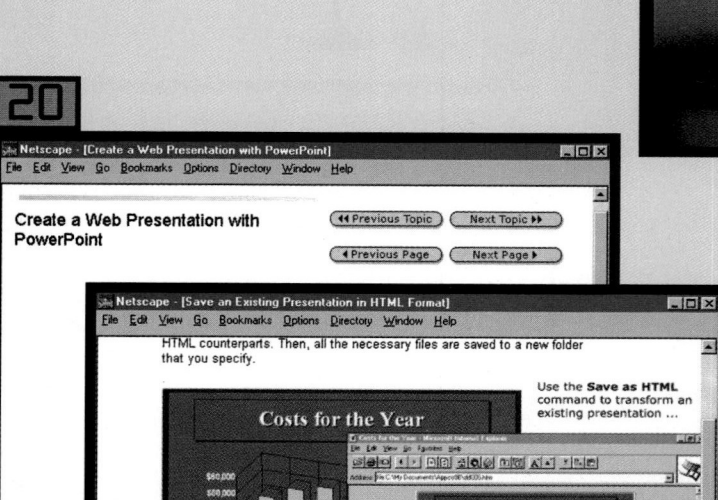

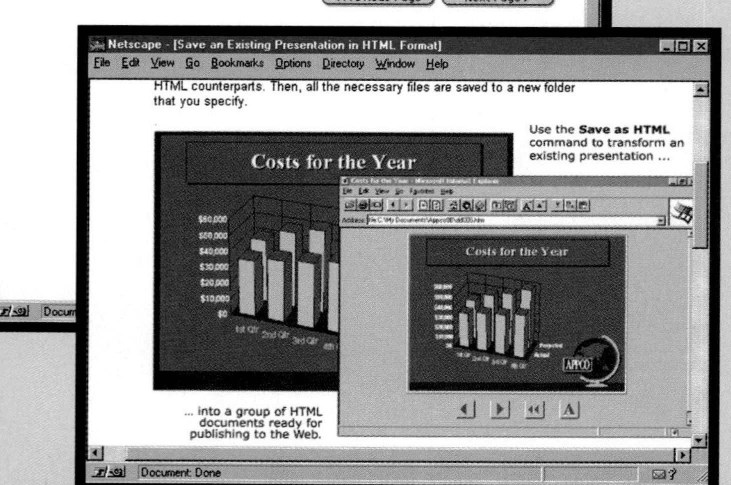

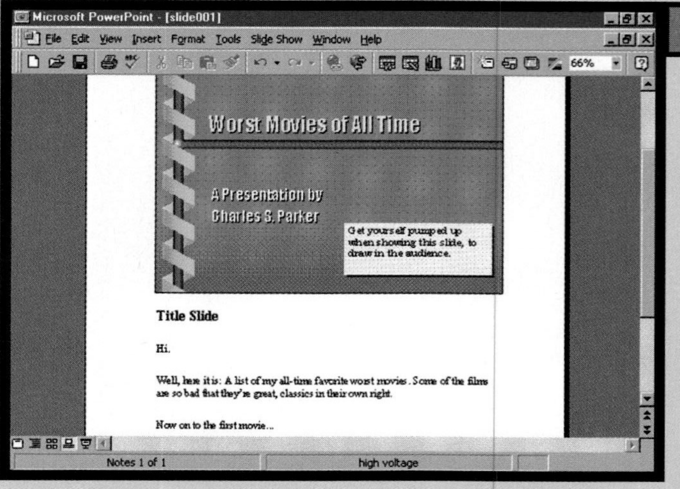

22 • Speaker notes can be prepared for each slide, complete with boxed comments. Audience handouts can be created just as easily.

PS 3

Database Management

Outline

Overview

What Is a Database Management System?

Database Management on Microcomputers
- A Simple Example
- Interacting with a DBMS
- Data Definition
- Data Manipulation

Database Management on Large Computer Systems
- Hierarchical and Network Data Models
- Object-Oriented Databases
- Client-Server Systems
- Distributed Database Systems
- Data Warehousing and Mining
- Data Definition
- Data Manipulation

Advantages and Disadvantages of Database Management

Learning Objectives

After completing this chapter, you will be able to:

1. Explain what database management systems are and how they work.
2. Identify some of the strategies used for database management on both large and small computer systems.
3. Identify the advantages and disadvantages of database management.

Overview

People often need to summon large amounts of data rapidly. An airline agent on the phone to a client may need to search through mounds of data quickly to find the lowest-cost flight path from Tucson to Toronto two weeks hence. The registrar of a university may have to scan student records swiftly to find the grade-point averages of all students who will graduate in June. An engineer may need to test several structural design alternatives against volumes of complicated safety and feasibility criteria before proceeding with a design strategy.

In this chapter, we'll cover database management systems, the type of software used specifically for such tasks. Computerized database management systems are rapidly making extinct the thick hard-copy manuals that people have had to wade through to find the information their jobs require.

What Is a Database Management System?

A **database management system (DBMS)** is a software system that integrates data in storage and provides easy access to them. The data themselves are placed on disk in a **database,** which can be thought of as an integrated collection of related files. The three files shown in Figure PS 3-1, for instance, which we will discuss in detail in the next subsection, collectively form a database.

Although not all databases are organized identically, many of them are composed of files, records, and fields, as shown in the figure. There are three *files* in Figure PS 3-1—one for product, another for stock levels on hand, and another for orders. Each file consists of several *records.* For instance, the Product file contains five records—one each for skis, boots, poles, bindings, and wax. Finally, each record consists of distinct types of data called *fields.* The Product file stores four fields for each record—product name, product number, supplier, and price.

The example shown in Figure PS 3-1 is a simplified one. Real-world databases often consist of scores of files, each containing thousands of records. Database management software enables queries and reports to be prepared by extracting information from one file at a time, and, as we will shortly see, from several interrelated files concurrently.

Database Management on Microcomputers

The best way to understand how a database management system works is by example. Many different database management systems are commercially available. Not all of them work the same way nor are they all equally easy to comprehend. The example in this section looks at **relational database management systems—**the type found on most desktop microcomputer systems and probably the easiest to understand. The list of general-purpose commercial products for desktop systems includes Microsoft's Access, Borland's Paradox (which is sold by both Borland and Corel), and Lotus Development's Approach. Of these, Access is the front-runner in

---

■ **Database management system (DBMS).** A software product designed to integrate data and provide easy access to them.
■ **Database.** An integrated collection of related data files. ■ **Relational database management system.** A computer program for database management that links data in related files through common fields.

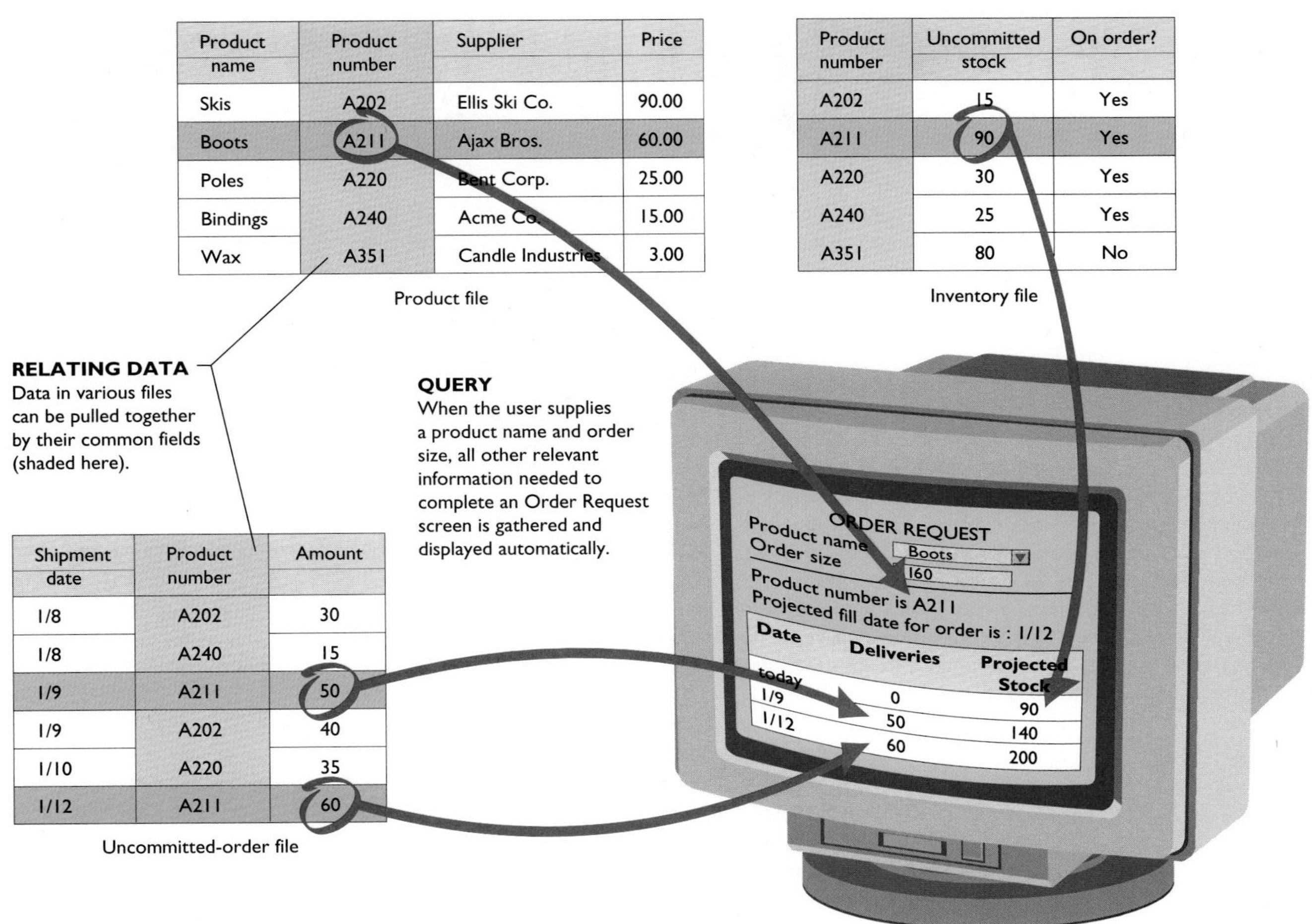

terms of sales. Borland, which once had the lion's share of the desktop database market, was once deemed "the next Microsoft" by some people on Wall Street (see the Inside the Industry box).

FIGURE PS 3-1

Using a relational database management system.

A SIMPLE EXAMPLE

Imagine that you're a sales manager at a ski-equipment warehouse, and an order comes in for 160 pairs of ski boots. You first need to find out if the order can be filled from stock in inventory. If it can't, you next need to know how long it will be before enough stock is available. You have an impatient client on the phone who wants an immediate response.

This type of task is especially suited to a DBMS. In Figure PS 3-1, an *inventory file* is used to store current stock levels, an *uncommitted-order file* is used to keep track of future shipments of stock that have not yet been promised to customers, and a *product file* is used to store the product descriptions. The very notion of files is often transparent to the user, who knows only that the information is "somewhere in the database system" and usually has no idea from where the system is extracting it.

The following scenario would be ideal for you. At the microcomputer workstation on your desk, you press a key for an Order Request screen and enter the product description, "Boots," and the order size, 160. The computer system responds with a screen that shows the current level of uncommitted stock in inventory as well as information about stock arriving this week from suppliers that has not been committed to other customers. It also provides its guess as to when the order can be filled: January 12. Thus, within seconds, right in front of you, you have the information you need to respond to the client's request and to be able to close the order.

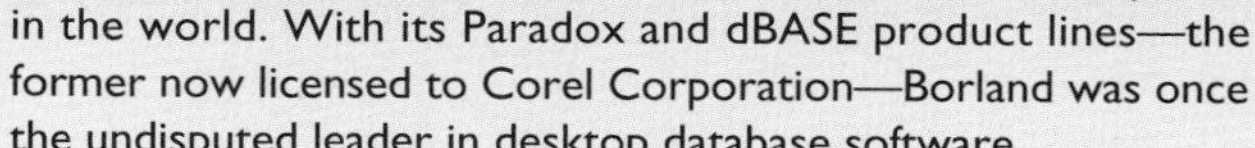

The computer industry is full of interesting characters, and a few were also the visionaries who created some of its most successful corporations. One such person is Phillipe Kahn, a multitalented individual who founded Borland International, which at one time was one of the largest software companies in the world. With its Paradox and dBASE product lines—the former now licensed to Corel Corporation—Borland was once the undisputed leader in desktop database software.

When Kahn came to the United States from France he had very little money—but a lot of imagination. In 1983, he attended Las Vegas's Comdex convention, the largest computer trade show in the United States. At Comdex, he hoped to get his fledgling company, Borland, a room for a press conference on credit. When he talked to the convention's manager, however, he was curtly told to go to McDonald's to entertain the press if he couldn't afford Comdex's rates. That's exactly what Kahn did. Six journalists showed up, and Kahn received reviews from all but one of them, thrusting Borland into the public's eye.

McDonald's. The first Borland press conference was a fast-food affair.

Data from several files are combined quickly by a relational database management system through the fields (columns) that the files have in common. The name *relational database management system* implies that the software relates data in different files by common fields in those files. In the example we just covered, data from the three files were pulled together through a common product-number field (the highlighted column in Figure PS 3-1).

Interrelated Tables A system that interrelates the files is critical for the type of information-retrieval task just described. Without a program that could interrelate files, you'd have to carry out several successive steps yourself:

1. Access the product file to get the product number.
2. Check the inventory file for that product number to see if the company can fill the order from current stock.
3. If current stock is inadequate, check the uncommitted-order file to see when enough stock will be available to fill the order.

What's more, the date on which the order could be filled would have to be hand calculated. Because this serial file-conscious process would be slower than having the files integrated in a manner transparent to the user, both service to clients and efficiency would suffer.

DBMS-like packages that do not automatically interrelate files are sometimes called *file managers,* and the files stored by file managers are often referred to as **flat files.** Flat files can be useful for finding information, but you can see from the example we've just covered how much better it is to have files that can be interrelated. In the context of relational database systems, (interrelatable) files are commonly referred to as **tables.** Not all DBMS users choose to interrelate files, incidentally, even though they have the capability to do so. When this happens, a database consists of a single file, and the terms *file* and *database* are commonly used interchangeably.

■ **Flat file.** A file that is not interrelated with others. ■ **Table.** In a relational DBMS, an entity with columns and rows that is capable of being interrelated with other database data.

INTERACTING WITH A DBMS

Users interact with the database management system through either an easy-to-use retrieval/update facility that accompanies the database package or an applications program written in a programming language.

A typical database program's *retrieval/update facility* presents a graphical user interface that lets users frame queries onscreen and interact with database applications. The graphical user interface is designed primarily to satisfy the needs of ordinary users. Among the most critical of these needs are creating databases, updating database data from time to time, and retrieving information from a database—either by making simple queries or by requesting to have reports prepared.

A database program's *programming-language facility* allows relatively sophisticated users to develop complex database applications. This feature often is targeted to users and programmers who want to design custom menus or screens or to create applications that go well beyond the standard ones offered with the database package. Most microcomputer-oriented DBMSs come equipped with their own proprietary programming language—such as Microsoft's Visual Basic for Applications. Some also support applications developed in such public-domain programming languages as C and COBOL.

A database processing environment for a typical microcomputer system is illustrated in Figure PS 3-2. The DBMS serves as an interface between the user at one end and data and programs at the other. As users develop applications and input data at their workstations, DBMS *utility programs,* such as the data dictionary (to be discussed shortly), ensure that the applications and data are properly prepared before storing them on disk. Other utility programs, such as a rich assortment of applications wizards and templates and a help facility, can be summoned when the user needs assistance with a form or report or with executing a command.

FIGURE PS 3-2

Database environment. The DBMS serves as an interface between users at one end and data and programs at the other.

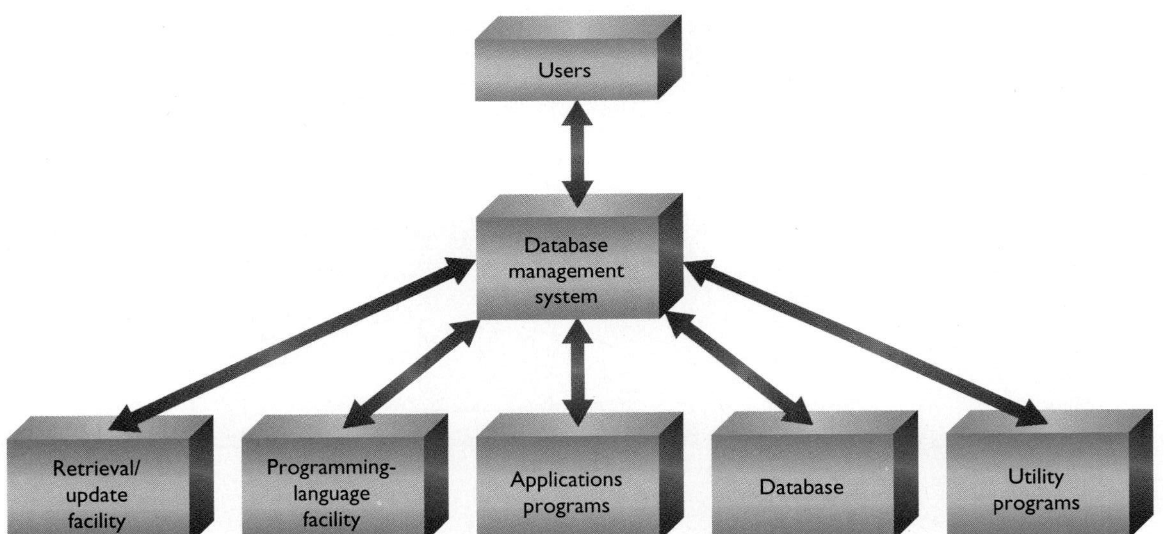

DATA DEFINITION

The first step in creating a database is data definition. **Data definition** involves telling the DBMS the properties of the data that are to go into the database—how big the records are, what type of data each of the fields of the records contain, and so on. A

■ **Data definition.** The process of describing the characteristics of data that are to be handled by a database management system.

user carries out the data definition step by creating a screen form, or **template,** for each file in the database. When the template is finished, it is used for entering data.

Each database file that needs to be created will have its own distinctive template. Templates for the database shown in Figure PS 3-1 are given in Figure PS 3-3. Templates, incidentally, are not only for describing and entering data; you can also create templates for viewing and printing information as well.

Product file

Product name	Product number	Supplier	Price
Skis	A202	Ellis Ski Co.	90.00
Boots	A211	Ajax Bros.	60.00
Poles	A220	Bent Corp.	25.00
Bindings	A240	Acme Co.	15.00
Wax	A351	Candle Industries	3.00

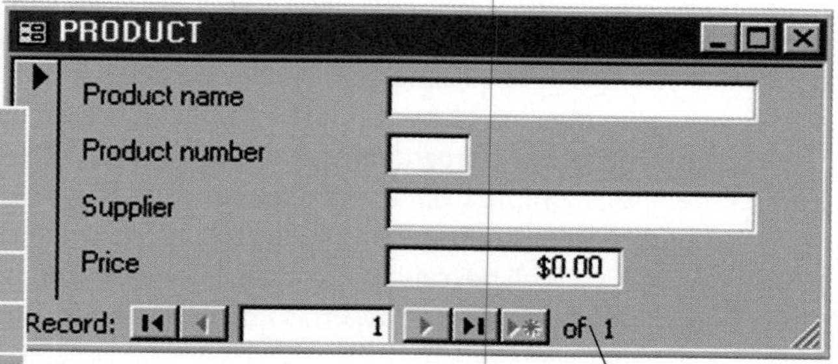

PRODUCT
Product name
Product number
Supplier
Price $0.00
Record: 1 of 1

Inventory file

Product number	Uncommitted stock	On order?
A202	15	Yes
A211	90	Yes
A220	30	Yes
A240	25	Yes
A351	80	No

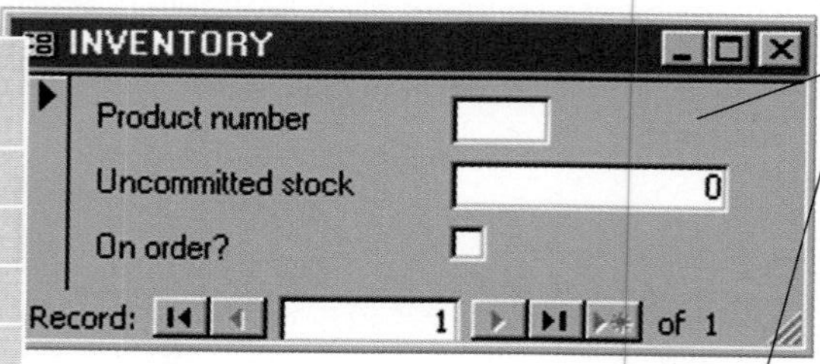

INVENTORY
Product number
Uncommitted stock 0
On order?
Record: 1 of 1

Shipment date	Product number	Amount
1/8	A202	30
1/8	A240	15
1/9	A211	50
1/9	A202	40
1/10	A220	35
1/12	A211	60

Uncommitted-order file

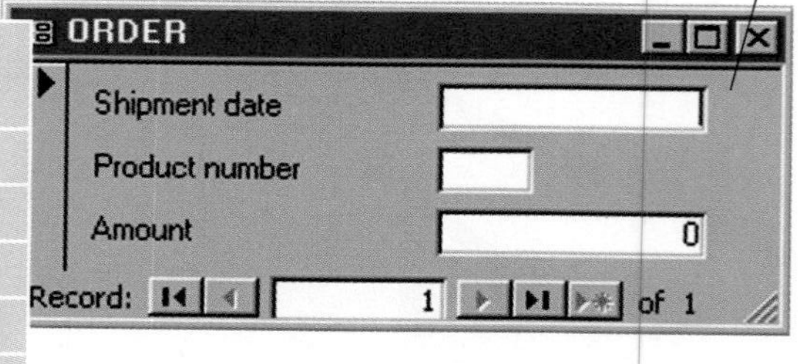

ORDER
Shipment date
Product number
Amount 0
Record: 1 of 1

TEMPLATES Templates, or forms, are created for each file so that data can be entered into the database.

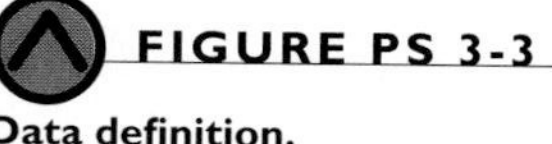

FIGURE PS 3-3

Data definition.

As you are creating each template in the data-definition stage, the DBMS will ask for the following types of information about the file it will represent:

- The name of each field
- The maximum length of each field
- The type of data (say, text or numeric) that each field will store

Such information is commonly referred to as a **file structure.** For example, suppose you've informed your microcomputer's relational database package that you want to create a file called *Inventory* (see the middle part of Figure PS 3-3). The package will ask you to describe each data field of the records that will go into the file. You might respond as follows:

■ **Template.** A screen form that requires the operator fill in a limited number of entries. ■ **File structure.** A collection of information about the records of a file, including the names, lengths, and types of the fields.

FIELD NAME	FIELD TYPE	WIDTH	DECIMALS
Product number	Text	4	N/A
Uncommitted stock	Numeric	10	0
On order?	Logical	1	N/A

Roughly translated, this structure declares that three fields will be present in the Inventory file: *Product number, Uncommitted stock,* and *On order?*. The Product number field will store *text,* or character, data. The width of 4 means that product numbers will be four or fewer characters. Uncommitted stock will consist of number, or *numeric,* data that will have a maximum width of ten characters. Because stock is counted in units of product, there will be no decimal places. On order? will be a yes/no, or *logical,* field. A logical field often contains either the value *T,* for true (or *Y,* for yes), or *F,* for false (or *N,* for no). For instance, a product that was on order might be given the value *Y*; a product not on order, the value *N*.

In most DBMSs, arithmetic computations can be performed on data that have been declared as numeric but not on data declared as text or logical. The *text, numeric (number),* and *logical (yes/no)* designations are commonly called **field descriptors.** Many database packages have these three descriptors as well as ones for *currency, date/time,* and *memo* fields and possibly others (see Figure PS 3-4). Field descriptors can often be chosen off of a menu when preparing a file structure.

Field descriptors.

FIELD DESCRIPTORS	
Text	Text (character) fields store data that are not manipulated arithmetically. You can, however, sort, index, or compare on these fields.
Numeric	Numeric (Number) fields, which store integer numbers and numbers that contain decimal points, are those that must be arithmetically manipulated.
Currency	Many database packages have a special field type for numeric data that are to be output in a currency format, with dollar signs, decimal points, and commas.
Logical	Logical (Yes/no) fields often store a single character of data—for instance, a "Y" (for "yes") and an "N" (for "no").
Date	Date fields store dates, provided that they are in the format MM/DD/YY (such as 12/31/98) or something very similar. You can sort, index, and subtract date fields.
Memo	Memo fields are used to store comment information. They cannot be arithmetically manipulated or compared, but they can be edited and output.

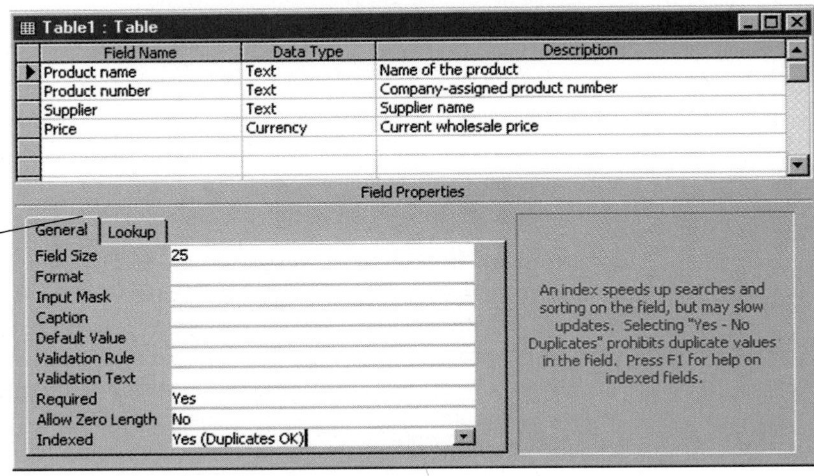

DBMSs provide a screen that enables you to give each field a name, a field descriptor, a size, and a variety of other properties.

■ **Field descriptor.** A code used to describe the type of data—say, numeric, text, logical—that occupy a given field in a data record.

In many database environments, templates can be customized to meet a variety of data-entry needs. In Access, for instance, wizards let users choose from several screen-template styles. Paradox and Approach have similar tools, only they are called *experts* and *assistants,* respectively, instead of wizards.

As you later place data into the records of a file, you start with an unfilled template for each record to be keyed in. Then you repeatedly fill in the template at the keyboard (see Figure PS 3-5) and save the records onto disk. Subsequently, you can modify or delete records from the file and add new ones.

The Data Dictionary File structures are used by the DBMS to construct a **data dictionary** for the application. The data dictionary is usually kept *active* to the application. This means that when data are placed into the template or are created in any way by users of the application, the data dictionary is monitoring the applications environment and will not permit data to be entered or used in any conflicting way. For instance, you couldn't enter a seven-character product number if the dictionary expected all product numbers to be a maximum of four characters long. Nor would the dictionary let you add a text field and a numeric field.

In many database environments, the data dictionary is also used to protect certain data from unauthorized use or alteration. Sensitive data such as salaries can be hidden so that only certain users of the database, furnished with the proper password, are authorized to retrieve them. Typically, only users with access to another password would be allowed to update the same data.

DATA MANIPULATION

The process of creating data for the database or using the database in some hands-on fashion is called **data manipulation.** Users generally can manipulate data in a microcomputer-oriented DBMS in two ways: through the retrieval/update or reporting facility within the DBMS and through applications programs they develop with the DBMS's programming-language facility.

Data manipulation encompasses a variety of activities. The following paragraphs briefly cover some of the most important of them.

Creation of Database Data This task consists of entering record data into the database. As each fresh template is successively summoned to the screen, it is filled with record data. Continuing with the example introduced in Figure PS 3-5, you might begin the record-entry process by summoning the template for the Product file. Then you would type in the first record in that file and enter it. After you did this, a fresh copy of the template would appear on the screen. You would type in the second record, and so forth. When you had finished entering all the records for the Product file, you would do the same thing for the next file—say, the Inventory file. And so on.

File Maintenance File maintenance consists primarily of updating records. This involves adding new records from time to time, deleting records that are no longer needed, and modifying existing records. Modifications are necessary because data such as prices and delivery schedules, like those in Figure PS 3-1, can change and also because errors are sometimes made in entering data.

Information Retrieval (Query) The information on the screen in Figure PS 3-1, where we needed to find out amounts and delivery dates of uncommitted stock, is an example of information retrieval, or query. A *query* feature refers to the ability to extract information from a database without having to write a program. An important fact to keep in mind is that if you can *manually* pull together the database data you need, you should be able to design a query to get your database management system to pull these same data together *automatically*—and a lot faster, too. Database queries

■ **Data dictionary.** A facility that manages characteristics of data and programs in a database environment. ■ **Data manipulation.** The process of using program commands to add, delete, modify, or retrieve data in a file or database.

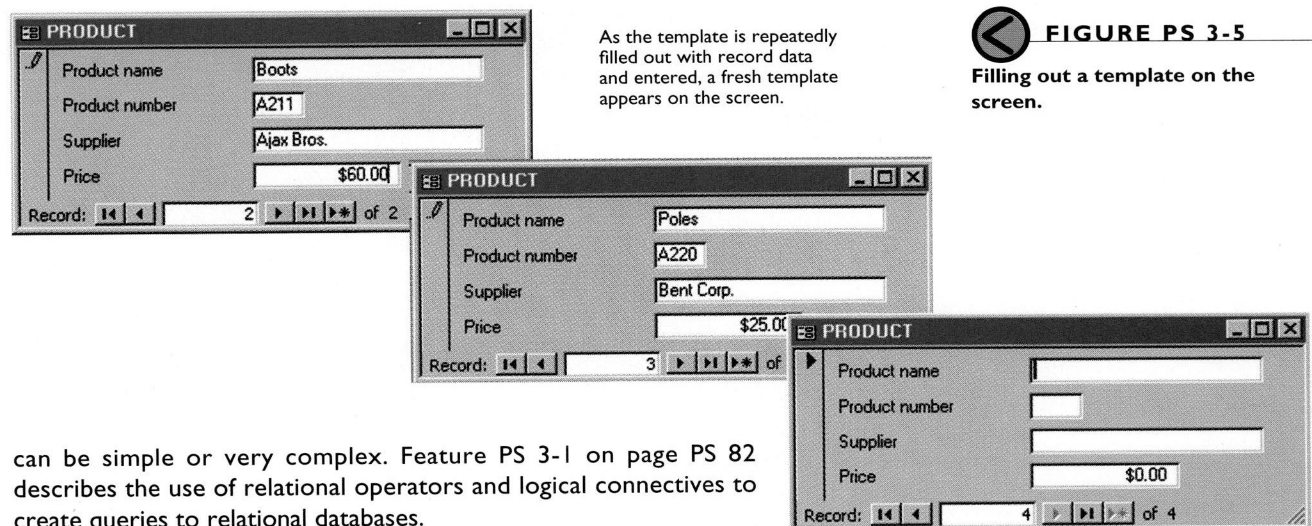

As the template is repeatedly filled out with record data and entered, a fresh template appears on the screen.

FIGURE PS 3-5

Filling out a template on the screen.

can be simple or very complex. Feature PS 3-1 on page PS 82 describes the use of relational operators and logical connectives to create queries to relational databases.

Every database management system provides its own tools through which users query databases for information. One such tool is a query language. The command style shown in Figure PS 3-6 is based largely on **structured query language (SQL),** which is recognized as today's de facto standard for information retrieval in relational databases. A number of graphical-user-interface tools are available from database vendors to make it easy for users to construct database queries without having to remember a language syntax like SQL. One of the most widely used of such tools is **query by example (QBE).**

Rather than type a complicated command, users of QBE can simply illustrate their information needs by filling in requirements on a QBE screen offered by the DBMS (see Figure PS 3-7). As you can see from the figure, you can choose specific fields of records to be output, sort records by any of the fields, and filter records according to specific criteria. Most desktop DBMSs—such as Access, Paradox, and Approach—include QBE in their roster of features.

FIGURE PS 3-6

Examples of database queries. The two queries given here can be directed to the database data described in Figures PS 3-1 and PS 3-3. Both of the queries conform to SQL, the de facto standard for information retrieval from databases.

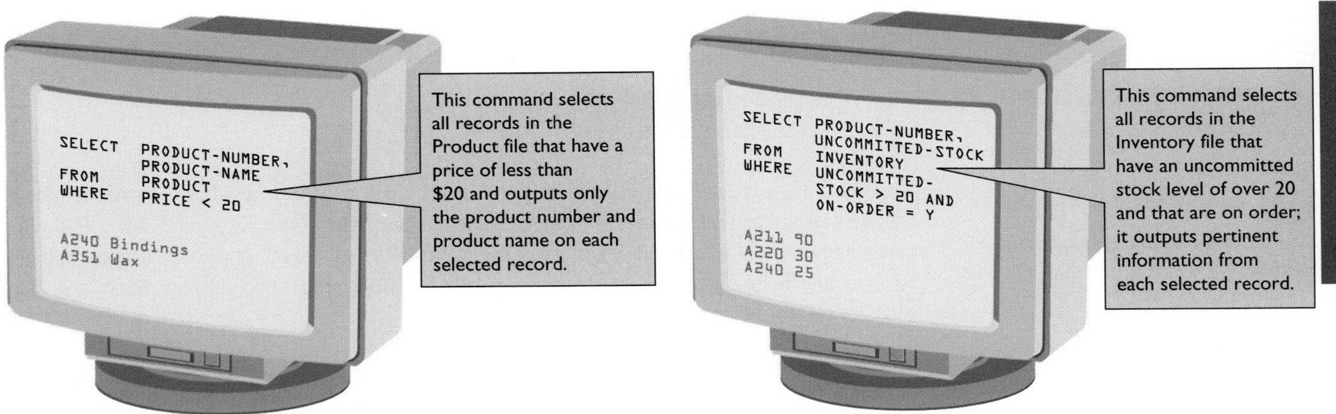

Reporting Reporting is the process of arranging the information you need in a formal report. Most database management systems require that you define a *report form* for each type of report you need. The form specifies what the report will look like when it is output—how the report title and column headings will look, which fields will be placed into which columns, the criteria used to select records for the report, how records are to be arranged in the report, if and when subtotals will be taken, and the like.

■ **Structured query language (SQL).** A popular language standard for information retrieval in relational databases. ■ **Query by example (QBE).** An onscreen query form in which users can simply illustrate what information they want by filling in filtering criteria.

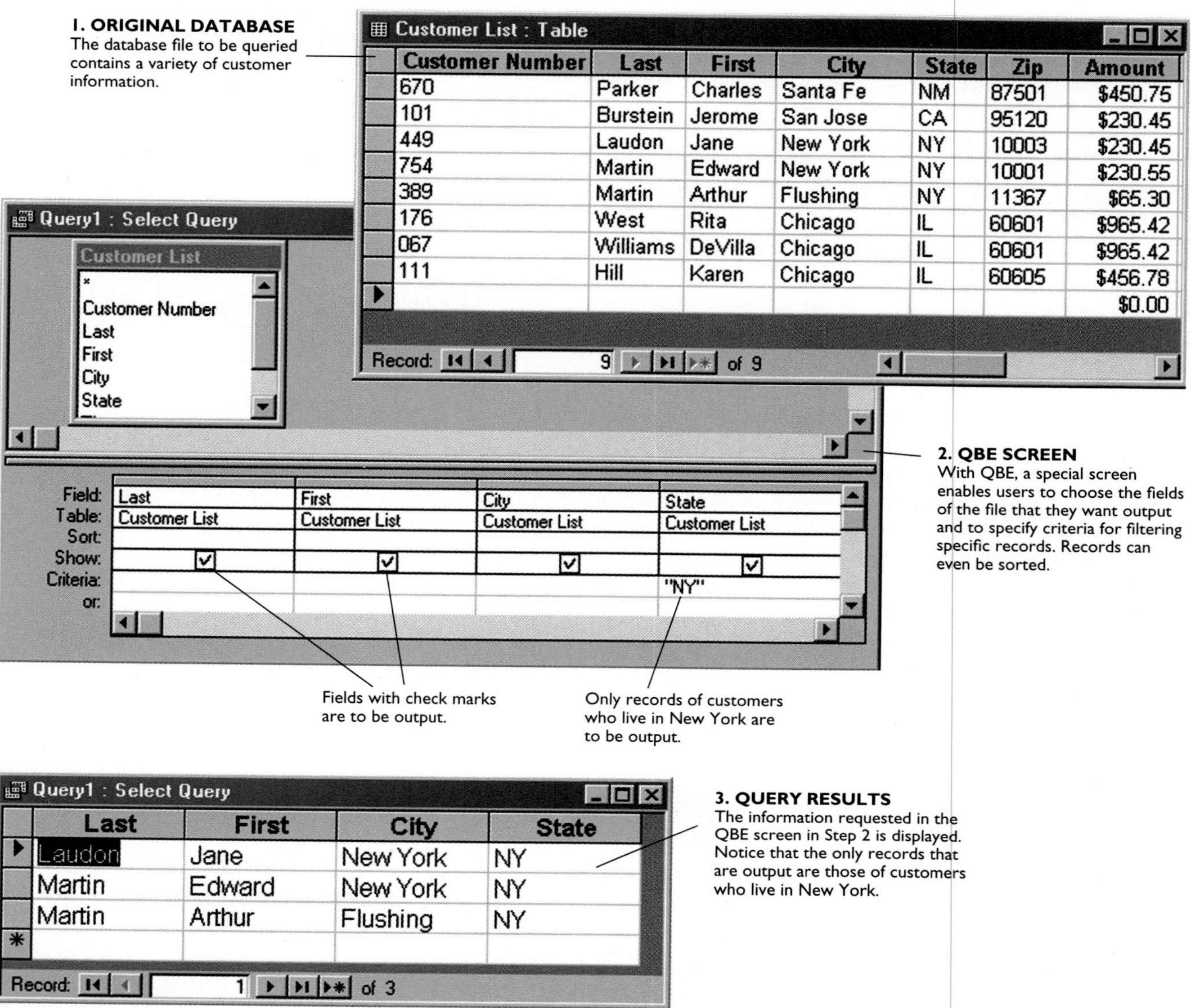

1. ORIGINAL DATABASE
The database file to be queried contains a variety of customer information.
Customer List : Table
Customer Number | Last | First | City | State | Zip | Amount
670 | Parker | Charles | Santa Fe | NM | 87501 | $450.75
101 | Burstein | Jerome | San Jose | CA | 95120 | $230.45
449 | Laudon | Jane | New York | NY | 10003 | $230.45
754 | Martin | Edward | New York | NY | 10001 | $230.55
389 | Martin | Arthur | Flushing | NY | 11367 | $65.30
176 | West | Rita | Chicago | IL | 60601 | $965.42
067 | Williams | DeVilla | Chicago | IL | 60601 | $965.42
111 | Hill | Karen | Chicago | IL | 60605 | $456.78
$0.00
Record: 9 of 9
Query1 : Select Query
Customer List
*
Customer Number
Last
First
City
State
Field: Last First City State
Table: Customer List Customer List Customer List Customer List
Sort:
Show:
Criteria: "NY"
or:
2. QBE SCREEN
With QBE, a special screen enables users to choose the fields of the file that they want output and to specify criteria for filtering specific records. Records can even be sorted.
Fields with check marks are to be output.
Only records of customers who live in New York are to be output.
Query1 : Select Query
Last | First | City | State
Laudon | Jane | New York | NY
Martin | Edward | New York | NY
Martin | Arthur | Flushing | NY
Record: 1 of 3
3. QUERY RESULTS
The information requested in the QBE screen in Step 2 is displayed. Notice that the only records that are output are those of customers who live in New York.

FIGURE PS 3-7
Using the query by example (QBE) feature.

Typically, a *wizard* program that comes with the DBMS presents a series of easy-to-use menus to guide users through report preparation (see Figure PS 3-8). The wizard enables you to select from several report types. Also, it provides you with a variety of styling options and lets you tweak the completed report form by, say, elongating columns or centering titles.

Sorting and Indexing Sorting is the process of arranging records in some order. As already hinted, most database management systems are equipped with the necessary tools to help you do this. You can sort ascending (from *A* to *Z*, or from low to high) or descending (from *Z* to *A*, or from high to low) on virtually any key field, and also do sorts within sorts.

Most DBMSs do not actually physically sort a file every time the user asks for a report but instead use a method called **indexing**. With indexing, you name fields on which you want to arrange data, and the computer automatically sets up an index table on that field that tells which records to put where. It is possible to create multiple indexes for the same file (with each index applied on a different sort of the file) as well as to index a file on multiple key fields. When indexing on multiple key fields, the term *primary key* is often used for the field on which the file is first sorted, and the

■ **Indexing.** A procedure that creates a table, or index, that specifies how data records are to be arranged on output.

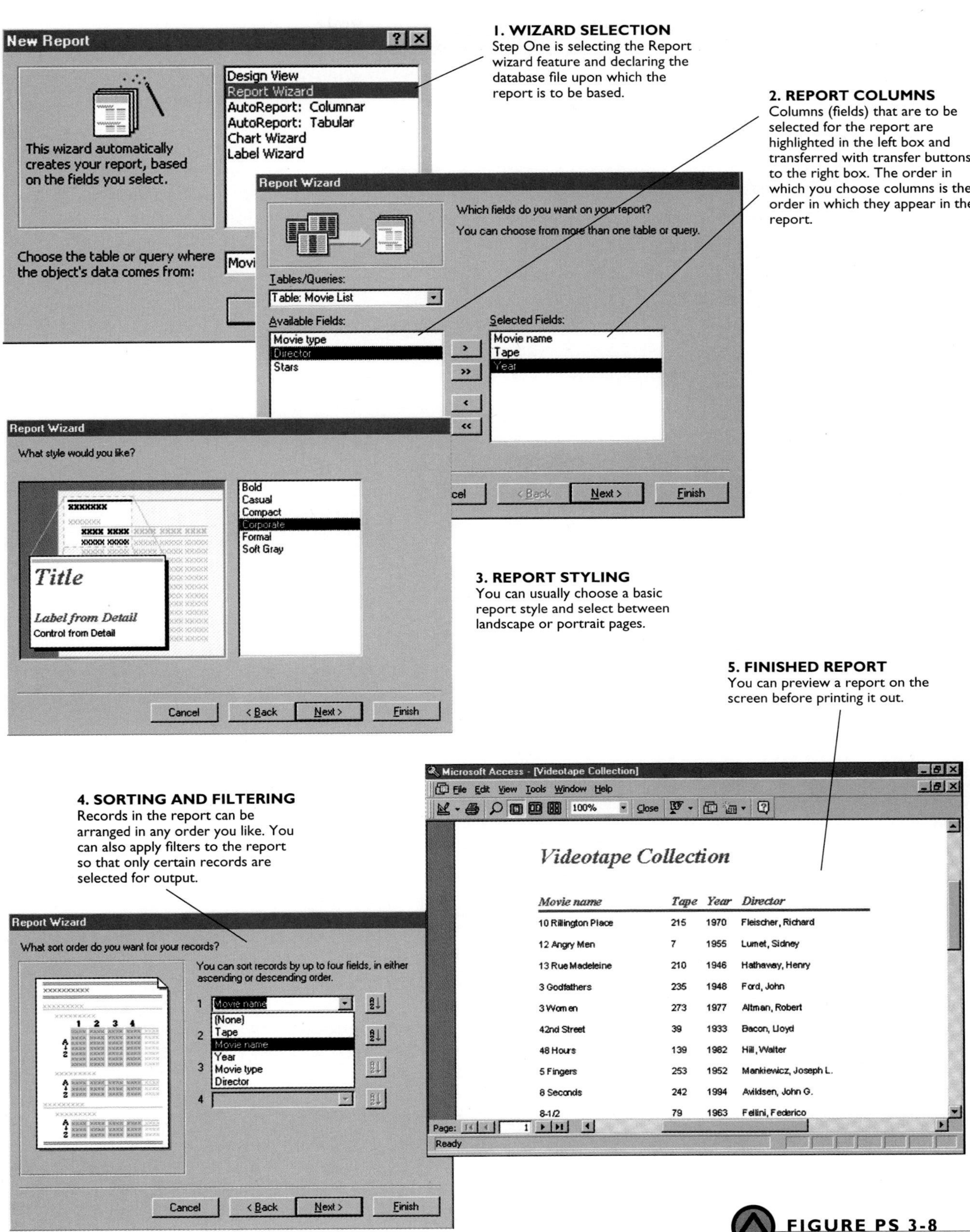

FIGURE PS 3-8

Using a report wizard. A report wizard assists with the preparation of a listing of a videotape collection, sorted by movie name.

term *secondary key* is used to describe any subordinate key(s). So, for instance, if the State field was declared a primary key in the original database in Figure PS 3-7 and the last-name field a secondary key—with both keys ascending—records would be

FEATURE PS 3-1

Relational Expressions

Making queries to databases is relatively simple if you know how to create relational expressions. Relational expressions are formed by a combination of field names, relational operators, constants, and logical connectives.

For instance,

```
ID$ = "John"
Cost > 100
```

are both relational expressions. *ID$* and *Cost* are both field names, *John* and *100* are both constants, and the = and > signs are both relational operators. The first statement evaluates to true if the value of ID$ is John; otherwise, it proves false. Similarly, the second statement evaluates to true if Cost is greater than 100. Relational expressions always evaluate to true or false or, alternatively, yes or no.

Relational Operators

Six relational operators are used in relational expressions, as shown in the accompanying figure. Some examples of the use of these relational operators follow. Assume in the examples that Gender$ = "Female" and Value = 25.

Gender$ = "Male"	Evaluates false
Gender$ = "Female"	Evaluates true
Gender$ <> "Male"	Evaluates true
Value >= 25	Evaluates true
Value > 25	Evaluates false

Logical Connectives

Relational expressions can be made more powerful through the use of the three reserved connective words: NOT, AND, and OR (see figure). Preceding a relational expression with the NOT connective negates the condition. So, for instance, the relational expression

```
NOT Gender$ = "Male"
```

is true if Gender$ carries any value other than Male. Similarly, the relational expression:

```
NOT A = 6
```

is true if A equals any value other than 6.

The AND connective links two or more conditions in a compound expression. AND requires that all conditions be true for the entire expression to be true. It works as follows:

Relational Operators:	
Operator	**Meaning**
=	Equal to
≠ or <> or ><	Not equal to
>	Greater than
<	Less than
>= or =>	Greater than or equal to
<= or =<	Less than or equal to

Logical Connectives:	
Connective	**Meaning**
NOT	Negates the condition
AND	All conditions must be true
OR	Only one condition must be true

Relational operators and logical connectives. Creating the right relational expressions is the key to making database queries.

```
Gender$ = "Male" AND A = 6
```

means that both Gender$ has to be Male and A has to be 6 for the entire compound expression to be true. And,

```
A = 1 AND B = 6 AND C = 35
```

means that all three conditions have to be true for the compound expression to be true. If A = 1 and B = 6 but C = 34, the compound expression evaluates as false.

The OR connective means that one or more of the conditions in a compound expression must be true in order for the entire expression to be true. For instance, the compound expression:

```
A = 1 OR B = 6
```

is true if either one of the two conditions, or both of them, are true. Like AND, more than one OR can exist to link conditions that are part of a compound expression.

NOT, AND, and OR can be combined to form a compound expression. If you are doing this, it's advisable that you put parentheses around like subexpressions to minimize complexity. Whatever is in parentheses is evaluated first. For instance, consider the expression:

```
A = 6 AND (B = 4 OR C = 88)
```

The condition evaluates as true only if A is 6. In addition, a value of true requires one of the following conditions: (1) B is 4 but C is not 88, (2) C is 88 but B is not 4, or (3) both B is 4 and C is 88. In the absence of parentheses, the connectives are evaluated in the following order: NOT, AND, OR.

arranged first by state (CA to NY), and then, within states, records would be sorted alphabetically by the customer's last name.

Other Features Often it is necessary to compute sums for columns, take averages, count records, and so forth. Although spreadsheet software is especially suited to these particular mathematical applications, database management systems include such features, too. Most database software also includes graphing software in its task library for you to create such presentation visuals as bar charts and pie charts.

Database Management on Large Computer Systems

On large computer systems—say, a mainframe or a large network of microcomputers—DBMSs perform exactly the same sorts of roles as they do on stand-alone microcomputer systems. However, they are necessarily more sophisticated, for several reasons. One is that data are often more complex—consisting not only of record-oriented text data but also multipage documents and picture information as well. Furthermore, because large computer systems contain far more data than those found in personal databases, these data are often organized in a more complex way to provide faster access. DBMSs on large systems must also deal with the problem of several users trying to access the database, perhaps simultaneously.

HIERARCHICAL AND NETWORK DATA MODELS

The relational database model is particularly useful in managerial (decision-support) retrieval situations in which users are free to pose almost any sort of query to the database. A user might first ask for the price of an item, then request a sales total on a group of items, then see how many units of another item are in stock, and so on. Thus, the database must be designed with flexibility in mind. In other situations, however, the types of queries that users need to make are highly predictable and limited. For instance, in banking, tellers usually only need such facts as current customer account balances, deposits, and withdrawals. In such transaction processing environments, hierarchical and network database models—which are designed more for speed and security than flexibility—are found more commonly than relational ones. These models are explained below and shown in Figure PS 3-9.

Hierarchical Databases A **hierarchical database management system** stores data in the form of a tree, which sets up a one-to-many relationship between data elements. Note that each professor in the top part of Figure PS 3-9 is assigned to one and only one department. If Professor Schwartz were a member of two departments—say, marketing and IS—she would have to be represented twice in the database to maintain the hierarchical structure, once under marketing and once under MIS. The database system would then treat Professor Schwartz as two distinct individuals. She might even get two separate graduation invitations from the school's computer. Such an inefficiency can be tolerated, however, if it's relatively rare. One of the leading hierarchical database management systems is IBM's IMS (Information Management System).

Network Databases In a **network database management system,** the relationship between data elements can be either many-to-one (*simple* networks) or many-to-many (*complex* networks). The solid lines in the middle part of Figure PS 3-9 depict many-to-one relationships; one professor and one grader can each handle many courses. The dotted lines, on the other hand, represent many-to-many relationships, where classes can be cotaught by two or more professors or have multiple graders. Complex networks are harder to model, but they can always be decomposed into simple networks. Sometimes this is done when, like in the earlier case of Professor Schwartz, some minor duplication can be tolerated.

PS

■ **Hierarchical database management system.** A DBMS that stores data in the form of a tree, where the relationship between data elements is one-to-many. ■ **Network database management system.** A DBMS in which the relationship between data elements can be either many-to-one or many-to-many.

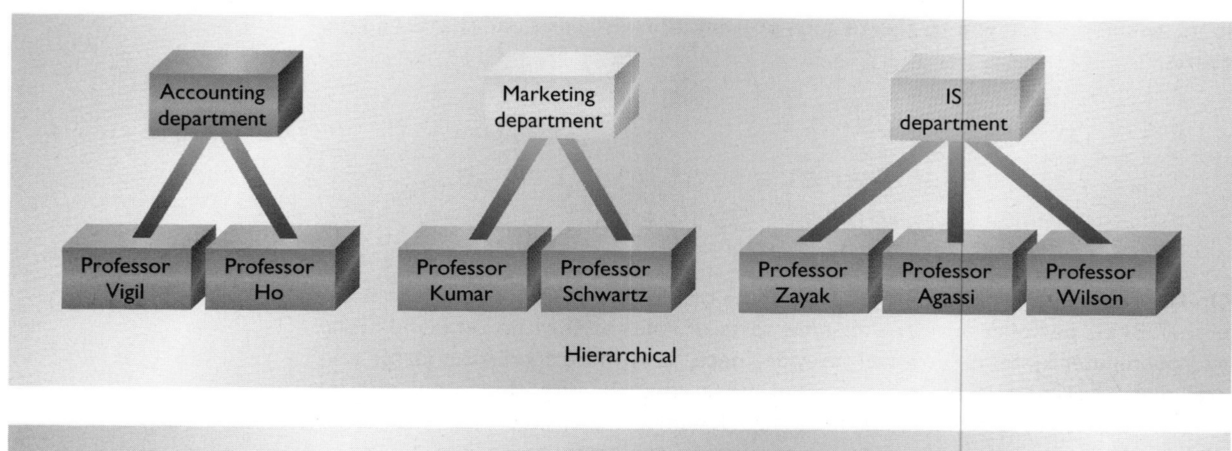

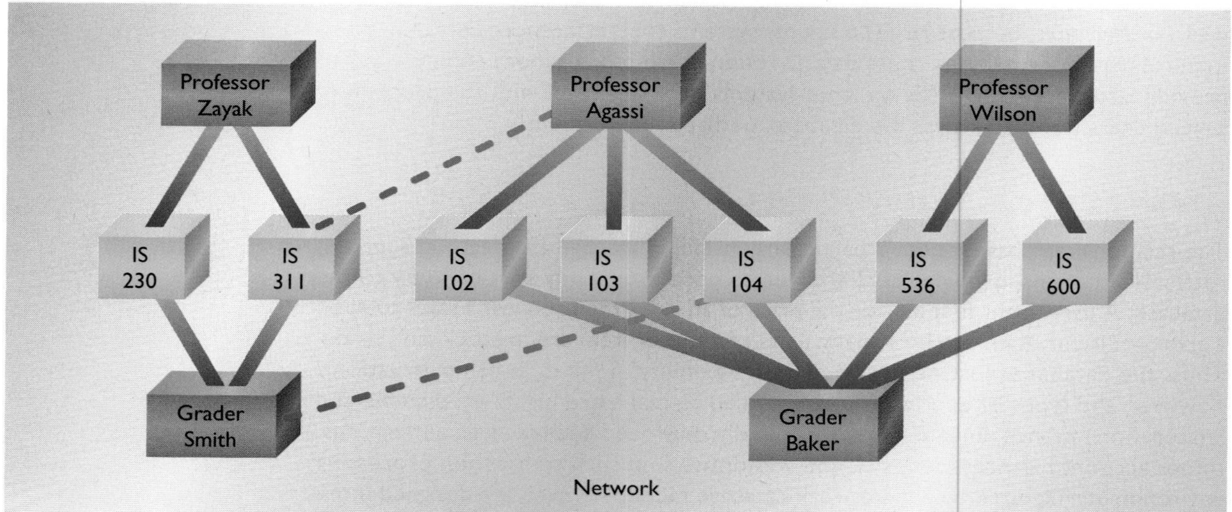

Course	Professor
IS 230	Zayak
IS 311	Zayak
IS 311	Agassi
IS 102	Agassi
IS 103	Agassi
IS 104	Agassi
IS 536	Wilson
IS 600	Wilson

Course	Grader
IS 230	Smith
IS 311	Smith
IS 102	Baker
IS 103	Baker
IS 104	Baker
IS 104	Smith
IS 536	Baker
IS 600	Baker

Professor	Department
Zayak	IS
Agassi	IS
Wilson	IS

Relational

FIGURE PS 3-9

Database models. Many commercial databases are of the hierarchical, network, or relational type.

Relational Databases Recall that *relational database management systems* organize data in tables (see the bottom part of Figure PS 3-9). Because the tables are independent, they can be dynamically linked through common fields by the user at program-execution time. This is in contrast to hierarchical and network databases, where data relationships are predefined, data are prelinked, and only linked data can be accessed. Having to link while a query is taking place, of course, eats up time, which is why relational databases are slow.

Although further explanation of how hierarchical and network models work goes beyond the scope of this book, suffice it to say that these models make access faster for predefined types of queries. In large systems with thousands of requests a minute, the speed of processing requests can be all important. Hierarchical and network databases have been around longer, too, so the security on these types of database systems is better than security on relational systems. Because hierarchical and network databases are harder to set up and use, professionals known as *database administrators (DBAs)* are commonly hired to assist.

OBJECT-ORIENTED DATABASES

Traditionally, data management software has dealt with *structured* types of data, that is, those that fall neatly into rows and columns of text. Structured data are the type you've mostly been reading about in this chapter and probably the type you've been working with in your computer lab. However, new user needs and technologies have led to a new type of database that is putting an entirely different face on the data management function. The growing interest in other data types and the need to combine them into a multimedia format for applications have given rise to **object-oriented database management systems.**

In addition to handling conventional record data, computers are now being widely used to store documents, diagrams, still photographs, moving images, and sound. The Internet's World Wide Web has certainly been a big factor in pushing database developers to cater to these new data types (see User Solution PS 3-1, on page PS 89). So also has been the rising number of computer users who clamor for seeing data presented in a natural-looking way that resembles experiences from real life. The stakes in the object-oriented-technology-development race are huge, since it will eventually be critical that companies establish friendly and exciting interactive environments in which to conduct electronic commerce over the Web.

Here's how object-oriented databases work. In everyday life, various types of data naturally intermingle. A speech, for instance, consists of two types of data: a voice and a moving image of someone talking. Thus, the entire speech can form an **object** made up of voice, moving-image data, and a set of *methods* or procedures describing how to combine the two. An object can be made from virtually anything—a moving image with people talking, a photograph with a narrative, text with music, and so on.

You can also combine other objects with the aforementioned speech. If the speech is on the environment, for example, data such as pollution statistics and photographs of defoliated areas may be useful to tack onto it. These, too, would exist as objects in the database, each with their own set of methods. For instance, the pollution statistics would be accompanied by program instructions telling how the data display onscreen. Unlike a text-only database in which each record has a similar format, little similarity may exist among the data elements that form the objects.

An object-oriented database management system makes it possible to store objects in an object-oriented database and to copy and paste them into applications, where people can manipulate them in any further way they need. Because any stored object is *reusable,* new applications can be developed in a fraction of the time it took before electronic objects existed. Object technology is a broad concept that applies not only to databases but also to programming languages and program-development tools.

Object-oriented databases are illustrated in Figure PS 3-10. Recently, *object-relational database management systems,* DBMSs that combine both object and relational technology, have come into the marketplace. One such example is Oracle, Version 8. Many industry observers speculate that object-relational databases will eventually supplant relational databases as the standard for ad hoc queries.

PS

■ **Object-oriented database management system.** A database in which two or more types of data—text, graphics, sound, or video—are combined with methods that specify their properties or use. ■ **Object.** A storable entity composed of data elements and instructions that apply to the elements.

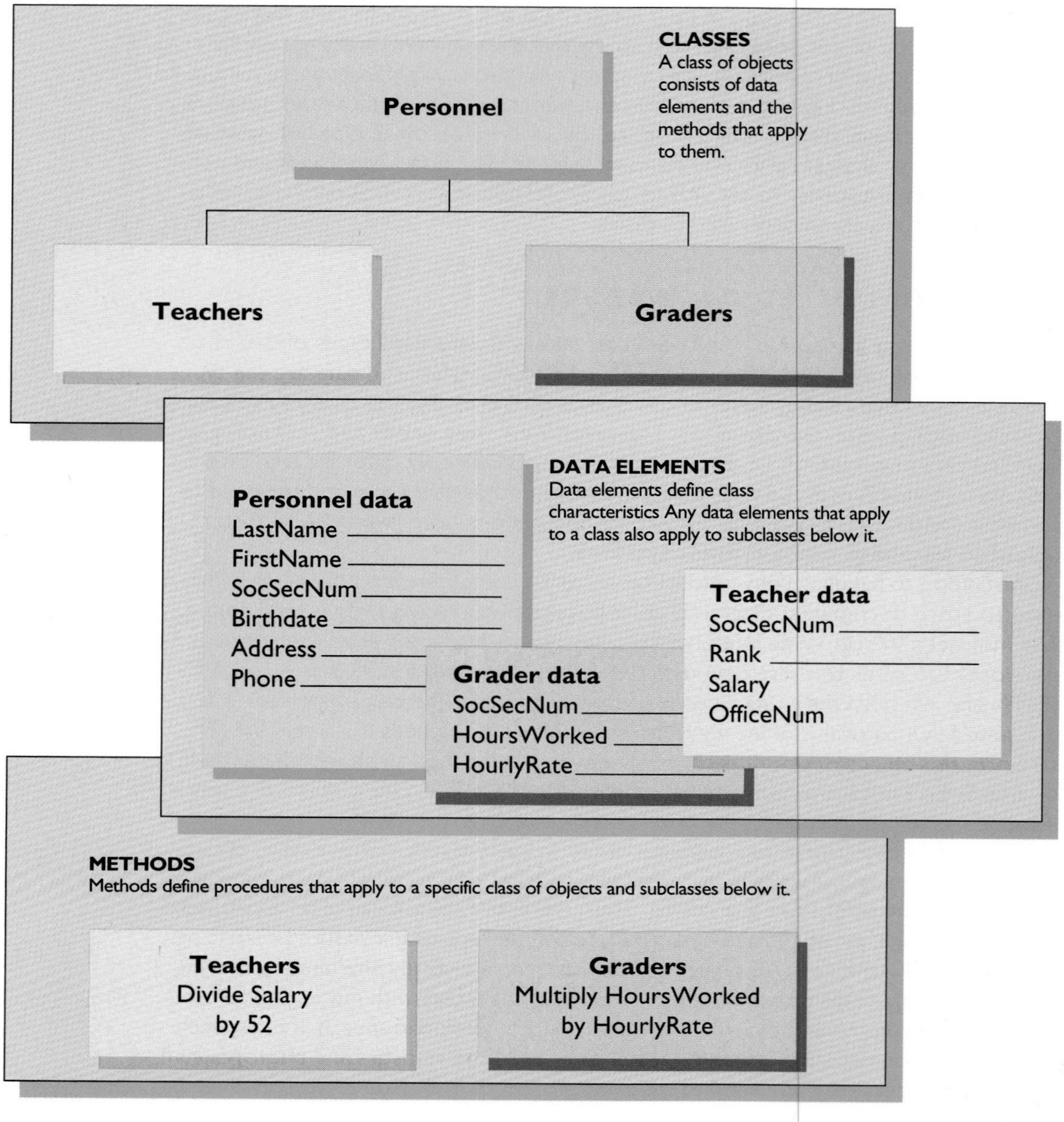

CLASSES
A class of objects consists of data elements and the methods that apply to them.

Personnel

Teachers

Graders

DATA ELEMENTS
Data elements define class characteristics Any data elements that apply to a class also apply to subclasses below it.

Personnel data
LastName
FirstName
SocSecNum
Birthdate
Address
Phone

Grader data
SocSecNum
HoursWorked
HourlyRate

Teacher data
SocSecNum
Rank
Salary
OfficeNum

METHODS
Methods define procedures that apply to a specific class of objects and subclasses below it.

Teachers
Divide Salary by 52

Graders
Multiply HoursWorked by HourlyRate

FIGURE PS 3-10

Object-oriented databases. Objects are composed of data as well as methods (procedures) that apply to the data.

CLIENT-SERVER SYSTEMS

Recall from Chapter NET 1 that *client-server systems* consist of computer networks in which powerful server computers supply resources to PC workstations, which function as client devices. One of the biggest application areas of client-server systems is database processing, in which the principal resource being managed is a database.

In a typical client-server database application, the client is called the *front end.* Typically, the PC workstation at the front end runs a desktop relational DBMS such as Access or Paradox, both of which can handle SQL or QBE database queries over a network. Both the graphical user interface and the query format are handled by the client computer in its own native way.

At the *back end,* the server program—a package such as Oracle Server, Sybase SQL Server, Informix Online, Microsoft SQL Server, or IBM's DB2—runs on a powerful server computer. The back end manages the database itself, and it translates any SQL or QBE commands coming from the front end into a form it can understand. A typical client-server scenario is illustrated in Figure PS 3-11.

Client-server networks have many compelling benefits, perhaps the most important of which are lower hardware cost and scalability to meet future needs. PCs are

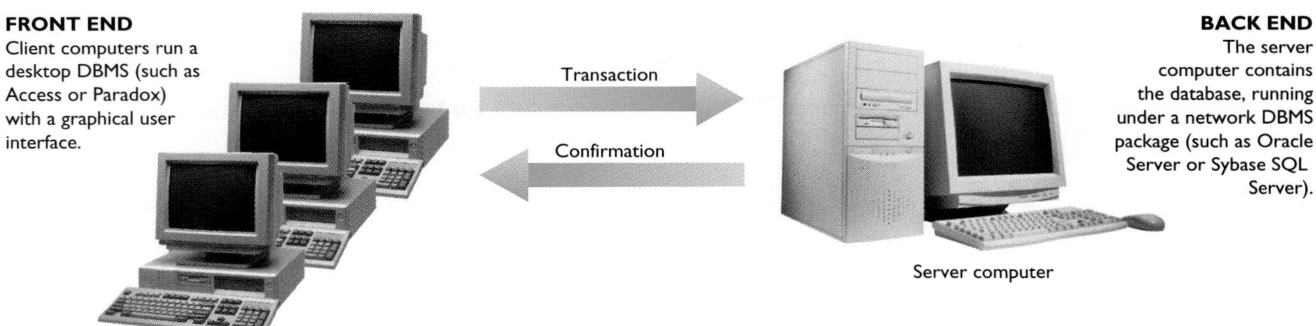
FRONT END
Client computers run a desktop DBMS (such as Access or Paradox) with a graphical user interface.
Transaction
Confirmation
BACK END
The server computer contains the database, running under a network DBMS package (such as Oracle Server or Sybase SQL Server).
Server computer
Client computers

FIGURE PS 3-11

Client-server transaction processing. A typical client-server arrangement consists of "front-end" clients that input transactions and a "back-end" server computer—with the database—that processes transactions.

easier to use and much less expensive than larger computers—you can put a network in place for a fraction of the cost of a mainframe. Also, anytime you need extra capacity, you can always add a new server or add more power to an existing one—again, at the fraction of the cost of a mainframe.

On the downside, client-server networks do not have nearly the track record of success as centralized mainframe systems, which have been around much longer. Hardware costs may not prove especially significant, as well, since they often represent only a small fraction of the total cost of a system. Software for centralized mainframe sites is still much easier to develop and support, and data are also more secure on mainframe systems. The cost to an organization if its data get corrupted or its computers go down for a day can easily dwarf the entire purchase cost of a new system.

Drawbacks notwithstanding, client-server networks are a growing trend. Many industry experts feel that—once some of the implementation problems are worked out—the client-server approach will be the main way that database data are delivered over computer networks.

DISTRIBUTED DATABASE SYSTEMS

In many large computer systems, DBMSs are distributed. A **distributed database** simply divides data among several small computers connected through a network instead of consolidating them in a single database on a large centralized mainframe—still the most widespread practice for storing databases in large companies. For instance, customer-addresses information may be stored at a corporate-office site, while credit histories may stored in the credit department, which is located in another building across town.

In a distributed DBMS, data are divided so as to optimize performance measures such as communications cost, response time, storage cost, and security. Moreover, data can be placed at the sites at which they are most needed and best managed. A user calling into the database generally will have no idea where the data are coming from; they could be stored in a computer system in the same building, in a different state, or even in a different country.

When the user makes a request to a distributed DBMS, it is up to the DBMS to determine how to best get the data; how it will do this is transparent to the user. Theoretically, users should be able to work under the illusion that all the data are stored locally. Ideally, a common seamless interface exists among member systems. Thus, the user at any client workstation need learn only one set of rules to get information from any server hooked into the network, resulting in minimal delays.

A distributed database system differs somewhat from a *replicated database system,* which stores separate copies of the entire database in multiple locations. Replicated systems are feasible where a high-bandwidth link to a centralized database is impossible

■ **Distributed database.** A database whose contents are split up over several locations.

or impractical. They are also useful in situations where an extra level of protection is needed, so that processing can still take place when the database becomes corrupted or the computer crashes at one location. Replicated databases can be problematic in situations where updates to the same data are made in more than a single location and a clear-cut rule for resolving any conflicts that may result does not exist.

DATA WAREHOUSING AND MINING

Two concepts in the database area that have become hot topics in the past couple of years are data warehousing and data mining. A **data warehouse** is a comprehensive collection of data that describes the operations of a company. In a typical data warehouse, data from transaction processing and other operations are reorganized and put into a form that is optimized for query. **Data mining** makes use of the data warehouse by applying intelligent software to scan its contents for subtle patterns that may not be evident to management (see Figure PS 3-12). Put another way, data mining finds answers to questions that managers may never have thought to ask.

Here are a couple of examples. An analysis of supermarket shopping carts might show that when nacho chips are purchased, 60 percent of the time soft drinks are also purchased—unless the chips are on sale, in which case soft-drink purchases jump to 70 percent. This example illustrates how data mining reveals important facts about data *associations.* Other data in another warehouse may suggest that when a new home is purchased, 50 percent of the time a new refrigerator will be bought within a month. In this case, information about *sequences* of transactions is extracted. In both cases, data mining software may provide insight into which types of promotions pay off and which ones don't.

One of the main tools used in data mining applications is neural networks, which are covered in the IS module of this textbook. Smaller, specialized versions of data warehouses—called *data marts*—are also quite often seen in practice. Whereas a data warehouse may tackle something as complex as a complete university database, a data mart might take on a small part of that—say, a database of student records.

FIGURE PS 3-12

Data warehousing and mining. The goal of these tools is to find patterns in data that management never imagined existed.

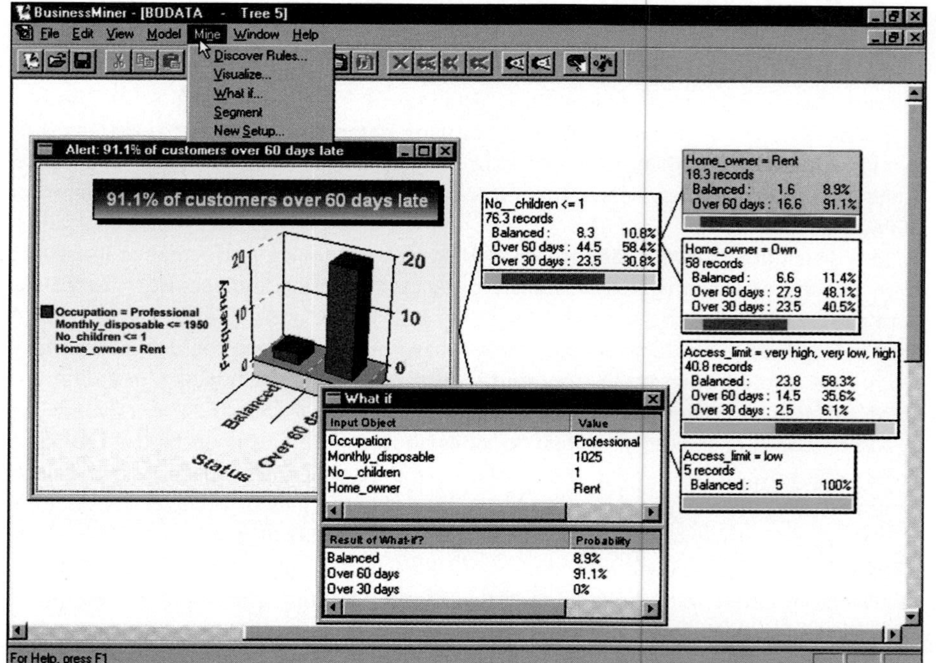

■ **Data warehouse.** A comprehensive collection of data that describes the operations of a company. ■ **Data mining.** Intelligent software that can analyze data warehouses for patterns that management may not even realize exist and also infer rules from these patterns.

An interfacing feature known as a **data manipulation language (DML)** is generally used to handle this problem. The DML is simply a set of commands that enables the language the programmer normally works with to function in a database environment. For example, if the programmer writes programs in COBOL—the most widely used language in business transaction-processing systems—a COBOL DML must be used. The DML may consist of several dozen commands, which the programmer uses to interact with data in the database.

Thus a COBOL program in a database environment consists of a mixture of standard COBOL statements and COBOL DML statements. The program containing this mixture of statements is then fed to the DBMS's COBOL **precompiler,** which translates this program into a standard COBOL program. This program then can be executed with the regular COBOL compiler available on the system.

High-level languages supported by their own DMLs are called **host languages.** Several host languages may be available on any particular system. Languages that a DBMS commonly employs as hosts are COBOL, C, PL/1, and BASIC.

Advantages and Disadvantages of Database Management

A DBMS offers several advantages over filing systems in which data appearing in separate files are not interrelated and centrally managed:

- BETTER INFORMATION Because data are integrated in a database environment, information that otherwise might be difficult or impossible to pull together can be collected (see also the Tomorrow box).
- FASTER RESPONSE TIME Because data are integrated into a single database, complex requests can be handled much more quickly.
- LOWER OPERATING COSTS Because response time is faster, users can do more work in less time.
- LOWER STORAGE REQUIREMENTS In a database system, integration often means that the same data need not appear over and over again in separate files, thereby saving valuable disk space.
- IMPROVED DATA INTEGRITY In a database system, integration often means that a data update need be made in only one place to be reflected throughout the system automatically—thereby avoiding the error that is often introduced when the same update has to be made manually in several independent files.
- BETTER DATA MANAGEMENT Central storage in a single database gives a DBMS better control over the data dictionary, security, and standards.

However, database processing also has a downside that a company or an individual should consider. The major problem is cost. Significant expenses are normally incurred in the following areas:

- DATABASE SOFTWARE Relative to other types of file-management software, a DBMS is expensive. On large computer systems, database packages can cost several thousand dollars.
- NEW HARDWARE A DBMS often requires a great deal of memory and secondary storage, and accessing records can be time consuming. Thus, some users find it necessary to upgrade to a bigger, more powerful computer system—with tape or removable-disk backup—after acquiring a DBMS.

■ **Data manipulation language (DML).** A language used by programmers to supplement some high-level language supported in a database environment. ■ **Precompiler.** A computer program that translates an extended set of programming language commands into standard commands of the language. ■ **Host language.** A programming language used to code database applications.

- TRAINING Microcomputer-based database management systems are often considerably more difficult to master than file managers, spreadsheets, and word processors. Relating data in different files can be tricky at times. Also, users who want to custom-design their own applications with the programming-language facility must prepare for a substantial investment in learning time.

Cost is not the only problem. Database processing can increase a system's vulnerability to failure. Because the data in the database are highly integrated, a problem with a key element might render the whole system inactive. Despite the disadvantages, however, DBMSs have become immensely popular with both organizations and individuals.

Summary and Key Terms

Database management software is widely used to manage large banks of data.

What Is a Database Management System? A **database management system (DBMS)** is a software system that integrates data in storage and provides easy access to them. DBMSs enable concurrent access to data that could conceivably span several files. The data in a DBMS are placed on disk in a **database,** which is an integrated collection of data.

Database Management on Microcomputers Database management systems come in several types. **Relational database management systems** are the most common type found on microcomputer systems. These systems are so named because they relate data in various database files by common fields in those files. Less-powerful types of packages called *file managers* work with **flat files** that cannot be interrelated. Files in relational DBMSs are commonly called **tables.**

Users gain access to the data they need through an easy-to-use *retrieval/update facility* within their DBMS programs or through applications programs written with a *programming language facility.* DBMSs also contain *utility programs* such as a data dictionary, a large collection of wizards and templates, and a help facility.

One task performed by anyone setting up a database is **data definition**—the process of describing data to the DBMS prior to entering them. The descriptions of these data are used to create a **file structure,** a screen form or **template** for entering the data, and a **data dictionary** for the application. Both the file structure and data dictionary contain a **field descriptor** for each field of data in the database.

The process of using the database in some hands-on fashion is called **data manipulation.** Data manipulation encompasses a variety of activities, including the creation of database data, file maintenance, information retrieval (query), reporting, sorting, and calculating. **Structured query language (SQL)** is today's de facto standard for information retrieval in relational databases. A tool called **query by example (QBE)** within most PC-based DBMSs allows users to easily frame database queries without knowing how to write SQL commands.

Database Management on Large Computer Systems Traditionally, database systems have conformed to one of three common types: relational, hierarchical, and network. A **hierarchical database management system** stores data in the form of a tree, where the relationship between data elements is one-to-many. In a **network database management system** the relationship between data elements can be either many-to-one or many-to-many. The growing interest in other data types and the need to combine them into multimedia formats for applications have given rise to **object-oriented database management systems.** These databases combine disparate data types into storable entities called **objects.**

One of the largest applications of *client-server systems* is in the database area, in which the principal resource being managed is a database. Typically, the client computers and their desktop DBMSs are called the *front end,* and the server computer that is managing the DBMS is called the *back end.*

Many applications set up **distributed databases.** Instead of a single database existing on a large centralized mainframe—still the most widespread practice for storing database data in large companies—the database is divided among several smaller computers that are hooked up in a network.

Two concepts in the database area that have become hot topics in the past couple of years are data warehousing and data mining. A **data warehouse** is a comprehensive collection of data that describes the operations of the company. **Data mining** consists of intelligent software that can analyze data warehouses for patterns that management may not even realize exist.

Many microcomputer-oriented DBMSs come with only a single proprietary language that has commands for data definition, retrieval/update, reporting, and programming functions. Large computer systems that use sophisticated DBMSs usually have a special language dedicated to each of these tasks. For example, a **data definition language (DDL)** handles data definition chores, placing key usages for applications development and security purposes into a data dictionary. A **data manipulation language (DML)** extends the language the programmer normally works with into a database environment. Languages supported by their own DMLs are called **host languages.** A program called a **precompiler** translates DML commands into host-language commands, which in turn can be executed on the regular compilers available at the computer site.

On a large computer system, a DBMS package must deal with the problem of several users trying to access the database at the same time. To prevent problems associated with conflicting uses, most database systems allow users to place a temporary lock on certain blocks of data to ensure that no other modifications to these data will be made during their processing.

Advantages and Disadvantages of Database Management A DBMS can offer several advantages over filing systems in which data appearing in independent files cannot be centrally managed and concurrently accessed. Among these advantages are better information, faster response time, lower operating costs, fewer data storage requirements, improved data integrity, and better data management. The biggest disadvantage is cost. Costs are normally incurred in the areas of new hardware and software, training, and conversion. Still another disadvantage is greater vulnerability to failure.

1. Fill in the blanks:
   a. Each database record consists of distinct types of data called ___________.
   b. ___________ database management systems are the type of DBMSs typically found on microcomputers.
   c. On corporate database management systems, a knowledgeable professional known as a(n) ___________ often sets up database applications for users.
   d. The facility that manages characteristics of data and programs in a database environment is called a data ___________.
   e. SQL is an acronym for ___________.

2. Match each term with the description that fits best.
   a. data mining
   b. front end
   c. DDL
   d. QBE
   e. host language
   f. data definition

   _____ A language used to describe database data
   _____ The language that is extended by a DML (data manipulation language)
   _____ Intelligent software used to analyze data in a data warehouse
   _____ A screen that lets users easily frame database queries

_____ Organizing data in the database so that programmers and users have access to them, data are stored as efficiently as possible, and the database's security is maintained

_____ A client PC running Access or Paradox, for example

3. Define, in your own words, the following terms:
   a. Flat file
   b. Field descriptor
   c. SQL
   d. Object-oriented database
   e. File structure

4. Describe the differences between these pairs of terms:
   a. A file and a database
   b. Data warehousing and data mining
   c. A front end and a back end in a client-server network
   d. Data definition and data manipulation
   e. A distributed database and a replicated database

5. For each of the following types of database management systems, describe how data relate to one another:
   a. Relational DBMS
   b. Hierarchical DBMS
   c. Network DBMS

6. How do large database management systems solve the problem of one user trying to use data that are in the process of being updated by someone else?

7. Describe, using both your own words and an example, how a relational database works.

8. Name at least five advantages and four disadvantages of database management systems.

9. Refer to the two tables in the sample relational database, and answer the following questions:
   a. What is the average salary of an employee in the Sales department?

Employee Table

Name	Location	Department	Salary
Doney	Phoenix	Acounting	$58,000
Black	Denver	Sales	$71,000
James	Cleveland	Sales	$44,000
Giles	San Diego	Accounting	$62,000
Smith	Maimi	Accounting	$73,000
Fink	San Diego	Sales	$54,000
...	...	...	...

Office Table

Location	Manager
San Diego	Hurt
Cleveland	Holmes
Maimi	Jonas
Phoenix	Alexis
...	...

   b. Which employees does Jonas supervise?
   c. What is the average salary under Hurt's supervision?
   d. In which of the preceding questions did you have to relate data in both tables to get an answer? Through what fields did you relate tables?

10. Referring to the 16-record table in the accompanying chart and Feature PS 3-1, tell which records would display for a query with each of the following conditions:
   a. State NOT = "CO"
   b. City = "Santa Fe" OR State = "CO"
   c. City = "Santa Fe" AND State = "CO"
   d. Customer number < 500
   e. Charge account? = "Yes" AND (City = "Santa Fe" OR State = "CO")

Customer number	Name	Street	City	State	Zip	Charge account?
810	John T. Smith	31 Cedarcrest	Boulder	CO	80302	Yes
775	Sally Jones	725 Agua Fria	Santa Fe	NM	87501	Yes
690	William Holmes	3269 Fast Lane	Santa Fe	NM	87501	No
840	Artis Smith	2332 Alameda	Lakewood	CO	80215	Yes
574	Nellie Deutsch	23 E. Spruce	Olathe	KS	66061	No
447	Vernon Pressy	5541 Canyon	Boulder	CO	80302	Yes
480	Benton Fink	440 Arapahoe	Boulder	CO	80302	No
401	Wayne Montoya	600 Tara Lane	Englewood	CO	80155	No
640	C. Foster Kane	P.O. Box 6000	Santa Fe	NM	87501	Yes
505	Alice Evans	5702 North St.	Boise	ID	83704	Yes
102	Maya Ellis	603 Oakwood	Aurora	CO	80011	Yes
754	Shane Williams	275 East Kiowa	Flagstaff	AZ	86001	No
801	Del Lopez	80 Williston	Austin	TX	78755	No
908	Duke Miller	CM Ranch	Stanley	NM	87056	No
665	Bette White	Box 20	Rowe	NM	87562	Yes
760	Kim Lundy	44 West St.	Missoula	MT	59802	No

PROJECTS

1. You Be the Judge The owner of a 40-employee advertising agency is about to purchase a well-known microcomputer database package to manage a growing client list on a desktop computer system. One of her most trusted employees is a computer wiz who has suggested providing her with a free copy of a database management system he has written himself—one he claims will better fit the agency's needs. What would you advise the owner to do in this situation—say yes, say no, or gather more information?

2. Large Databases Most colleges and universities have large database systems for their student and faculty records, as do companies for their client and employee records. Select one such database for study and write a three-to-five-page paper about it that answers most if not all of the following questions:

- Describe the database briefly. What is its name and purpose?
- What types of data are contained in the database?
- On what type of computer system(s) does the database exist?
- How large is the database?
- Who uses the database? What types of information does the database supply to these users?
- What types of database software products are used with the database?
- Who manages the database?

3. Microcomputer DBMSs Three of the leading microcomputer DBMS packages are Microsoft's Access, Borland's Paradox (sold by both Borland and Corel), and Lotus's Approach. For each of these packages, answer the following questions:

a. Are the packages sold separately? Can you buy any of them as part of a suite?
b. What is the list or street price of each package? Provide the price of both the full stand-alone package, for users who don't have an earlier version, and the update. Also provide suite pricing.

You can do this exercise either through journal-article or book research, by looking at the packages in stores and asking questions, or by seeing what you can find on the Internet. The companies producing these DBMSs can be located at the following Web sites:

COMPANY	WEB SITE (HTTP://_____)
Borland	www.borland.com
Corel	www.corel.com
Lotus	www.lotus.com
Microsoft	www.microsoft.com

4. Report Wizards Because database management systems are harder to use than word processors or spreadsheets, you are likely to find more wizards available. For a microcomputer database package of your choice, find out what type of wizards it contains, and prepare a list that names each wizard and its purpose. Note that wizards—principally, a Microsoft Office term—are called *experts* in Paradox and *assistants* in Access.

5. Creating Your Own Database and Report The finished report in Figure PS 3-8 is part of the first page of a multipage alphabetized report of a videotape collection. The report was prepared on Microsoft Access with a report wizard. The fields in the report show the movie title, the videotape on which the movie is located, the year the movie was made, and the movie's director. For this project

a. Enter your own videotape, CD, stamp, or coin collection—or any other collection of your choice—into the database system available on your own computer system or in your school's computer lab. If you wish, limit the number of records to 15. You should have at least three fields in your database table.
b. Use a wizard to produce a report similar to one in the figure, which is sorted on Movie name. Sort the report on any one key field, and then produce another copy of the report that sorts on another key field.
c. After your final sort, select some criterion to filter records—for instance, in a movie file, selecting only Alfred Hitchcock movies—and have the database manager automatically extract the records for you.

6. Yellow Pages Revisited The chapter User Solution explores the usefulness of Web phone directories. For this project, choose any of the directories in the accompanying table and observe how it works. Report to the class your experiences, being sure to cover such information as how comprehensive the directory is, what types of listings the directory contains, and the search tools available with the directory. More directories can be found by summoning a search engine such as Yahoo! or WebCrawler; at the Yahoo! site, for instance, select Reference and then Phone Numbers from the menus to get a list of potential sites.

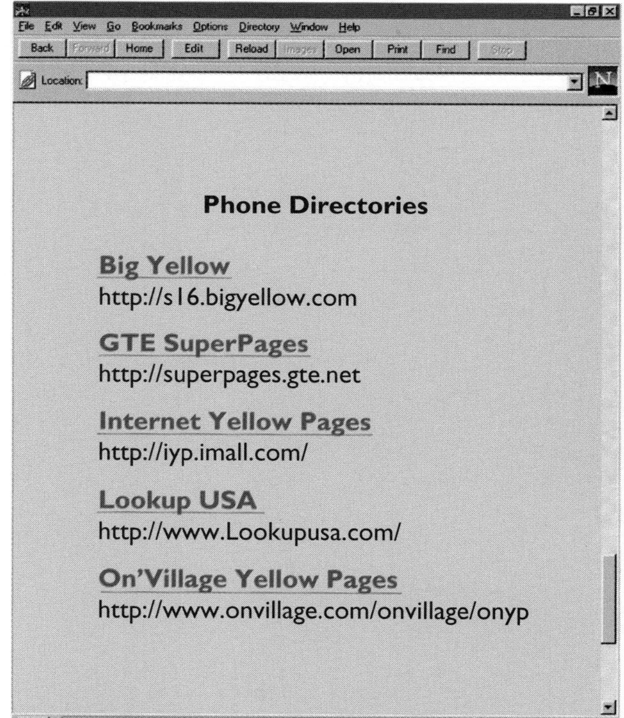

7. Object-Oriented Databases In recent years, object-oriented databases (OODBMSs) have become a particularly hot topic. For this project, find the name of a commercial OODBMS and write a paper about it that doesn't exceed three pages. Be sure to cover the following information in your paper:

PS

a. The name of the OODBMS. Which version of it did you research?
b. The publisher of the OODBMS
c. The street or list price of the OODBMS
d. A description of the OODBMS, telling briefly what the product does or some of its features.

Hint: Many of the makers of client-server databases—such as Oracle, Sybase, and Informix—also make products that use object-oriented database technology.

8. Creating a Database and Performing Database Operations Using the database management system available on your own computer system or in your school's computer lab, create a table for the records in the accompanying figure. Count the maximum number of characters in each field and decide on the maximum width of each of the fields. Define monthly Salary as a numeric field, Employed as a date field, and all other fields as text. Then, complete the following tasks:

a. Display the names of all persons in the Personnel department.
b. Display the names of all persons earning more than $1,600 per month.
c. Display the names of all persons who are either working in MIS or making more than $1,700 a month.
d. Arrange the file alphabetically by Department and, within Department, by last name.

The fields are:
Employee
Telephone
Gender
Employed
Salary
Department

The employees are:

Pratt, John 225-1234 Male 06/22/88 1949 MIS	Smoller, Ellen 225-3212 Female 09/15/88 1650 MIS	Johnson, Frank 223-7928 Male 03/20/86 1500 MIS	Smith, Paul 223-8251 Male 11/01/85 1800 Accounting
Jones, David 292-3832 Male 06/15/88 1500 Accounting	Martins, Mary 222-2132 Female 11/01/85 1850 Accounting	Sill, Sally 224-4321 Female 02/15/87 1800 Personnel	Terrific, Tom 222-1900 Male 10/30/97 1400 MIS
	Beam, Sandy 225-6912 Female 02/15/86 1450 MIS	Knat, Michael 221-1235 Male 09/15/95 1700 Personnel	

e. Arrange the file from highest-to-lowest-salaried employee. If there is a tie for Salary, list tied employees in alphabetical order. On the screen, have only the name of the employee and the salary show, with all other information hidden.

MODULE

Information Systems

IS

This module integrates several concepts from earlier chapters. It ties together the basic elements that form computer systems—hardware, software, data, people, and procedures.

Chapter IS 1 looks at computer systems in organizations. In the first part of the chapter you will learn about the principal types of systems used and the roles these systems play. The balance of the chapter is about the sorts of activities performed in system building and the kinds of people involved in this effort.

Chapters IS 2 covers applications software development. Here you'll learn about some of the tools computer professionals use to design and code programs as well as gain an understanding of what various programming languages do.

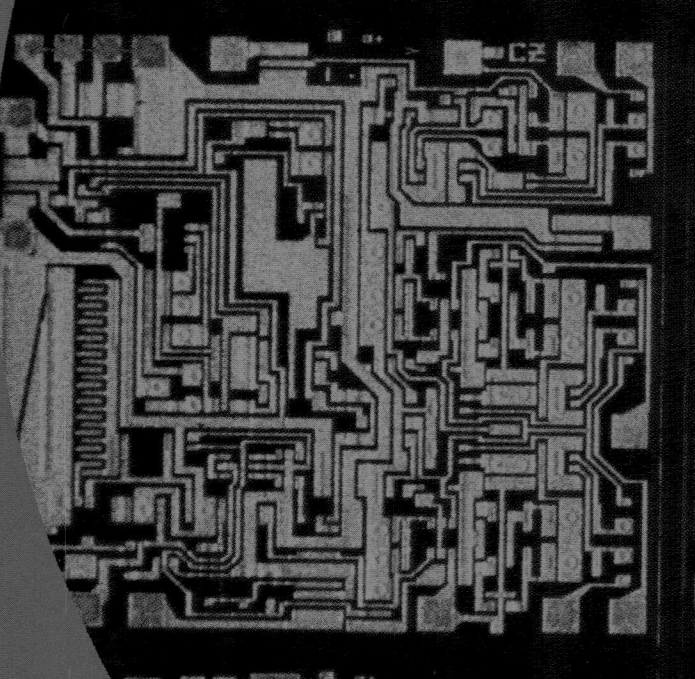

MODULE CONTENTS

Information Systems

ISBN 0-03-024481-1

IS 1

Developing Organizational Systems

Outline

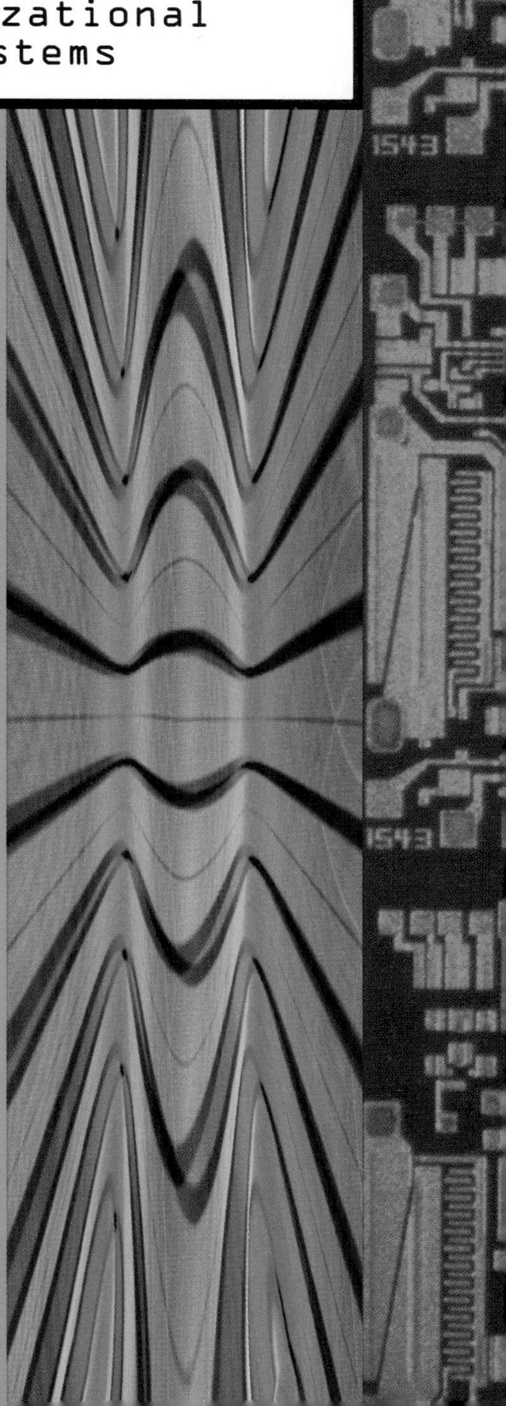

Learning Objectives

After completing this chapter, you will be able to:

1. Explain what a system is.
2. Describe several types of computer systems commonly found in organizations.
3. Define the roles of various people and information systems areas in the systems development process.
4. Identify and describe the components of the systems development life cycle (SDLC).
5. Describe several approaches used to develop systems.

Overview

In previous modules of this textbook we considered primarily hardware and software. Here we turn to the process of putting these elements together into complete computer systems.

All organizations have various sorts of systems—for example, systems that attend to accounting activities such as sending out bills and processing payrolls, systems that provide information to help managers make decisions, systems that help run factories efficiently, and so on. Such systems require considerable effort to design, build, and maintain. The process that includes the planning, building, and maintenance of systems is called *systems development.*

Unfortunately, since no two situations are exactly alike, there is no surefire formula for successful systems development. A procedure that works well in one situation may fail in another. These facts notwithstanding, there is a set of general principles, that, if understood, will enhance the likelihood of a system's success. Those principles are the subject of this chapter.

The chapter opens with a discussion of systems and systems development. Then we cover the types of systems commonly found in organizations. From there we turn to the computer professionals who are hired to develop systems in organizations and consider some of their primary responsibilities. Then we look at the systems development life cycle—the set of activities that are at the heart of every serious systems-building effort. Chapter IS 1 concludes with a discussion of the major approaches to systems development.

On Systems

A **system** is a collection of elements and procedures that interact to accomplish a goal. A football game, for example, is played according to a system. It consists of a collection of elements (two teams, a playing field, referees) and procedures (the rules of the game) that interact to determine which team is the winner. A transit system is a collection of people, machines, work rules, fares, and schedules that get people from one place to another. Similarly, a computer system is a collection of people, hardware, software, data, and procedures that interact to perform information processing tasks.

The function of many systems, whether manual or computerized, is to keep an organization well managed and running smoothly. Systems are created and altered in response to changing needs within an organization and shifting conditions in its surrounding environment. When problems arise in an existing system or a new system is needed, systems development comes into play. **Systems development** is the process of analyzing a work environment, designing a new system for it or making modifications to the current one, acquiring needed hardware and software, training users, and getting the new or modified system to work.

Systems development may be required for many reasons. New laws may call for the collection of data never before assembled. The government may require new data on personnel, for example. The introduction of new technology, especially new computer technology, may prompt the wholesale revision of a system. Or, as is the trend today, a company may decide to convert certain applications into a global networked environment or, possibly, expand some of its systems so that not only employees but also customers and suppliers can tap into it. These and other kinds of new

■ **System.** A collection of elements and procedures that interact to accomplish a goal. ■ **Systems development.** The ongoing process of improving ways of doing work.

requirements often bring about major changes in the systems by which work is done in an organization.

The chapter's Tomorrow box on page IS 8 looks at another possible change in a system that has been evolving almost since the beginning of human life—the system of exchange that is at the very heart of processing transactions.

Organizational Systems

Undoubtedly, you've already encountered many types of systems in organizations. When you go into the supermarket, you generally see in use electronic cash registers and various handheld or laser scanning devices that are obviously a part of some supermarket system. Or, when you've registered for classes, perhaps you've observed someone at a display workstation checking to see whether a certain class you want to take is still open and whether you've paid all your bills—apparently as part of a registration system.

While there are hundreds of "types" of computer systems in existence today, many fall into one or more of four categories: transaction processing systems, information systems, office systems, and design and manufacturing systems. Here we'll look more closely at each of these. We will also explore the area of artificial intelligence, which can impart to a system certain characteristics that one would normally attribute to humans.

TRANSACTION PROCESSING SYSTEMS

Virtually every company carries out a number of routine accounting operations, most of which involve some form of tedious record keeping. These operations, such as payroll and accounts receivable, inspired some of the earliest commercial applications of computers in organizations and are still among the most important. Because these systems heavily involve processing business transactions—such as paying employees, recording customer purchases and payments, and recording vendor receipts and payments—they are called **transaction processing systems** (see Figure IS 1-1).

Some of the functions commonly performed by transaction processing systems are discussed in the following paragraphs.

Payroll *Payroll systems* compute deductions, subtract them from gross earnings, and write paychecks to employees for the remainder. These systems also contain programs that prepare reports for management and for taxing agencies of federal, state, and local governments.

Order Entry Many organizations handle some type of order processing on a daily basis. Customers call in orders by phone, send in written orders by ordinary mail or by computer, or place orders in person. The systems that record and help staff members manage such transactions are called *order-entry systems.*

Inventory Control The units of product that a company holds in stock to use or sell at a given moment make up its inventory. An *inventory control system* keeps track of the number of units of each product in inventory and ensures that reasonable quantities of products are maintained.

Accounts Receivable The term *accounts receivable* refers to the amounts owed by customers who have made purchases on credit. Accounts receivable programs are charged with keeping track of customers' purchases, payments, and account balances. They also produce invoices and monthly account statements and provide information

■ **Transaction processing system.** A system that handles data created by an organization's business transactions.

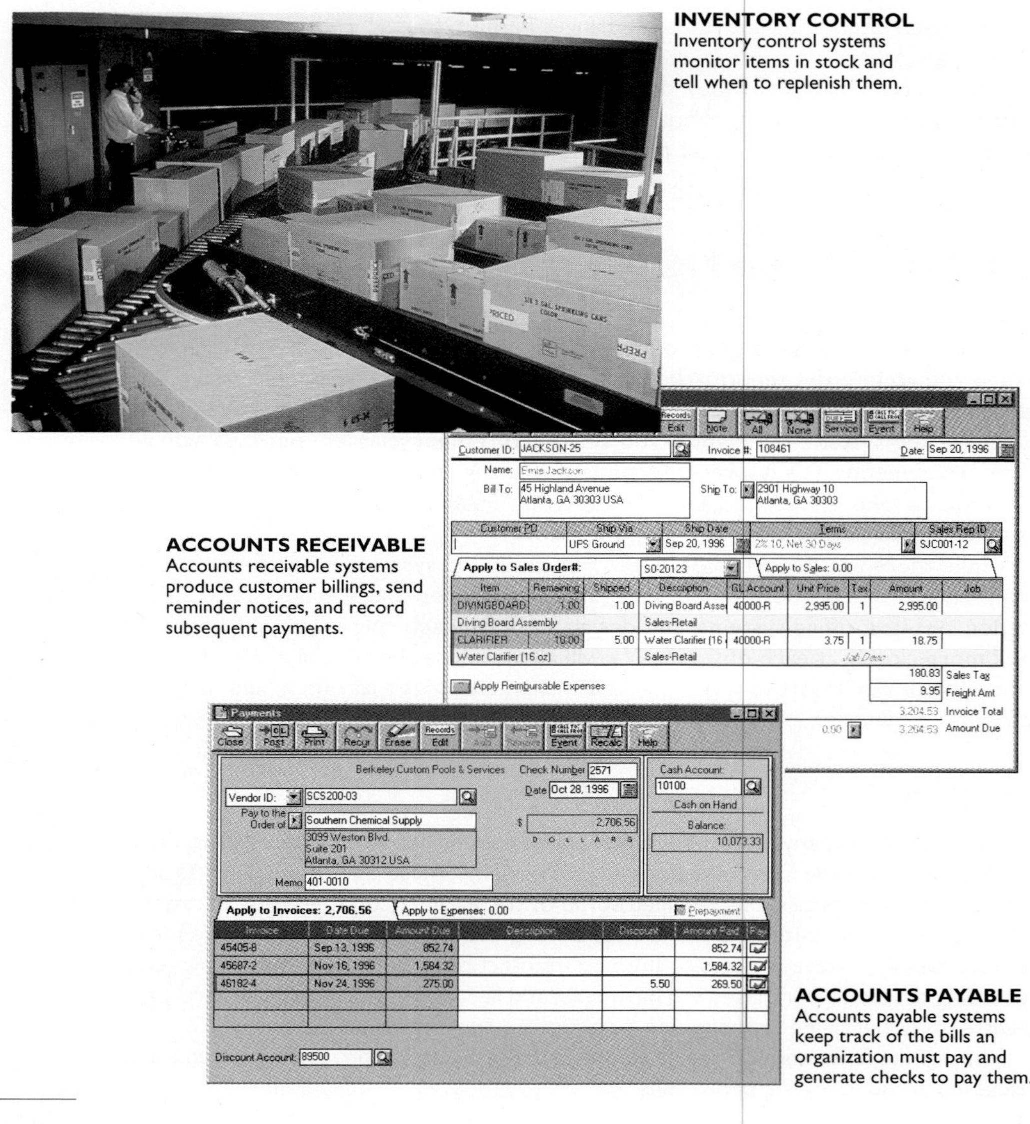

INVENTORY CONTROL
Inventory control systems monitor items in stock and tell when to replenish them.
ACCOUNTS RECEIVABLE
Accounts receivable systems produce customer billings, send reminder notices, and record subsequent payments.
ACCOUNTS PAYABLE
Accounts payable systems keep track of the bills an organization must pay and generate checks to pay them.

FIGURE IS 1-1

Transaction processing systems.

to management. Other output includes sales analyses, which describe changing patterns of products and sales, as well as detailed or summary reports on current and past-due accounts.

Accounts Payable The term *accounts payable* refers to the money a company owes to other companies for the goods and services it has received. An accounts payable system keeps track of bills and often generates checks to pay them. It records who gets paid and when, handles cash disbursements, and advises managers about whether they should accept discounts offered by vendors in return for early payment.

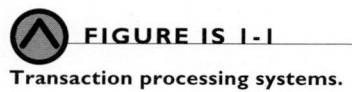

General Ledger A *general ledger (G/L) system* keeps track of all financial summaries, including those originating from payroll, accounts receivable, accounts payable, and other sources (see Figure IS 1-2). It also ensures that a company's books balance properly. A typical G/L system may also produce accounting reports such as income statements, balance sheets, and general ledger balances.

INFORMATION SYSTEMS

In the early days of commercial computing, businesses purchased computers almost exclusively to perform routine transaction processing tasks. Used in this way, the

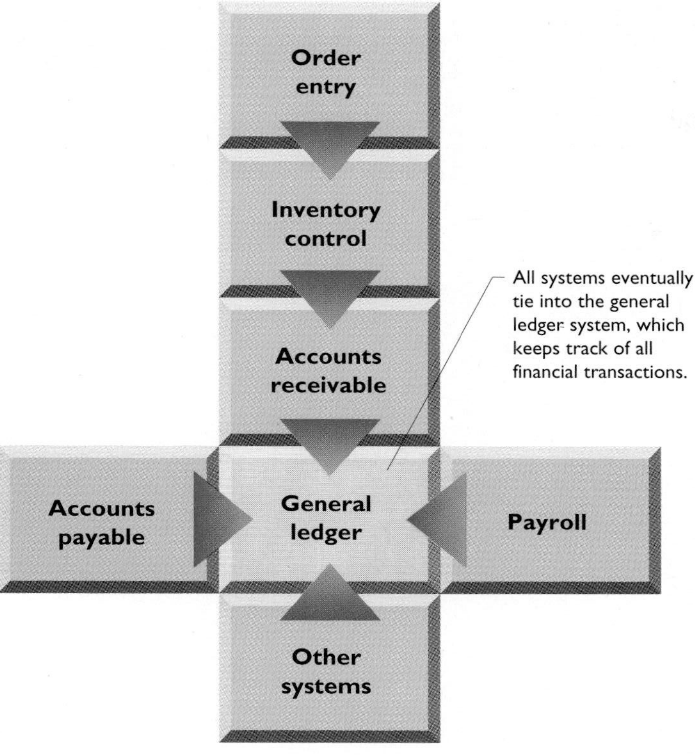
Order entry
Inventory control
Accounts receivable
Accounts payable
General ledger
Payroll
Other systems
All systems eventually tie into the general ledger system, which keeps track of all financial transactions.

FIGURE IS 1-2

The relationship among transaction processing systems.

computers cut clerical expenses considerably. As time passed, however, it became apparent that the computer could do much more than replace clerks. It could also provide information to assist managers in their decision-making role.

A system that generates information for use by decision makers often is called an **information system.** With an information system, for instance, management can incorporate many more facts into decisions and spend less time gathering them. As a result, managers have more time to do the things they do best—think creatively and interact with people. While most information systems within organizations serve employees, increasingly information systems are expanding to support the needs of customers and suppliers.

Two major types of information systems are information reporting systems and decision support systems.

Information Reporting Systems **Information reporting systems** followed transaction processing systems as the first type of information system. They provide decision makers with preselected types of information, generally in the form of computer-generated reports. The types of information that people receive are often preplanned, just like the information you see on your monthly checking account statements. The individual *values* on your statements, such as check numbers and amounts, may change from month to month, but the *types* of information you receive remain the same. Also, you and every other person mailed checking account statements by your bank receive exactly the same type of information.

Many information reporting systems provide decision makers with information that is a by-product of the data generated through transaction processing. For instance, a manager in the receivables department will regularly be issued a report listing overdue accounts.

■ **Information system.** A system designed to provide information to help people make decisions. ■ **Information reporting system.** A type of information system whose principal outputs are preformatted reports.

IS

TOMORROW

The Future of Money

Is Technology Making Paper Currency an Endangered Species?

Money has been around since the time people needed a system of exchange more sophisticated than barter. Some of the earliest primitive civilizations used seashells as money, to trade for goods and services. Later on, precious metals such as gold and silver caught on in a big way. Then came national and local banks, with their coins and paper money. As countries became more stabilized, money supplies became nationalized and carefully controlled.

Now, advances in technology may bring forth another major change: electronic money—otherwise known as *cybercash* or *e-cash*. While electronic forms of money offer the promise of bringing new amenities to consumers and big savings to financial institutions—cash and checks are much more expensive to handle—they also pose serious risks. A number of proposals for electronic money are now in the works.

One way that electronic money could someday be used extensively is making purchases of goods online. For instance, a consumer could buy an electronic purse or wallet, filled, say, with $100 or $200 in cybercash. Every time a purchase is made online from a participating merchant, the amount of the purchase is subtracted from the current balance in the purse. A person could also use the purse to make loans to friends online and to accept loan repayments. While electronic purses do exist today on the Internet, their presence is not widespread. Complicating the picture are fears consumers have about having their computers handle their money. What, for example, happens if the hard disk crashes, taking the cybercash with it? How secure are such systems from cyberthieves?

Electronic money could also be used to make purchases away from your computer—at stores. A credit-card-sized purse, loaded with cybercash, could conceivably be used to buy goods and services from participating merchants. The card is debited by a cash-register-like device each time a purchase is made. You could also use the same card to pay for parking meters and phone calls. The same types of problems, however, exist with this form of cybercash as with the purse-enabled home PC. Will enough merchants be willing to go with a given system to make it worthwhile? Can a system be made secure enough so that consumers will desire it more than their credit cards? What incentives could consumers be provided to chuck their credit cards—which in effect loan them money—in favor of a debit-based system that requires up-front payment.

Underlying the adoption of electronic money is a host of governmental and social problems. Could uncontrolled use of cybercash undermine bank- and government-controlled money systems? There is a good chance that regional banks can be completely bypassed by the new system—which could escape regulation under current laws—paving the way for another banking crisis. Will the new system make it even easier for tax evasion and money laundering? Money could flow in and out of countries so quickly that governments might never trace it. There is also the concern that cybercash could become elitist—you would need to own a PC or be computer literate to take advantage of it.

Many futurists feel that electronic money is inevitable, but it may take decades before consumers, governments, and civil-rights activists feel comfortable with the idea to make it work on a wide scale.

Cybercash. Do risks currently outweigh the potential benefits?

Decision Support Systems A **decision support system (DSS)** helps people organize and analyze their own decision-making information. It is useful to anyone whose requirements for information are unpredictable and unstructured. Each DSS is tailored around the needs of an individual or group. Thus, a sales support system is the name typically given to a DSS aimed at the special decision-making needs of salespeople or marketing personnel. Likewise, a fire-suppression support system might be a DSS targeted to helping a forest supervisor develop specific strategies for fighting wildfires.

Let's put DSSs into perspective with an example. To assist with making product pricing decisions, a sales manager uses a DSS that has been set up on a microcomputer system. From menus, the manager first accesses the price of an item. Then he or she asks for the average price of several other items, and then for the inventory turnover of yet a different item. Next, a financial model may be used to predict the sales volumes for specific items five years into the future. As the example suggests, the manager can pose questions as the need evolves and receive answers at once. At

■ **Decision support system (DSS).** A type of information system that provides people with tools and capabilities to help them satisfy their own information needs.

the end of the interactive session, the manager uses the DSS to prepare a summary of important findings and some charts for a meeting. The next time the manager uses the DSS, other types of information may be collected and analyzed.

Figure IS 1-3 shows several decision support systems at work. Two specialized types of decision support systems are targeted to worker groups and aimed at executives.

GROUP DECISION SUPPORT SYSTEMS A **group decision support system (GDSS)** is a decision support system in which several people routinely interact through a computer network in order to solve common problems (see Figure IS 1-4). GDSSs fall under the general heading of *workgroup computing* tools, or *groupware,* which includes not only decision-making applications but also other uses involving groups of people, such as scheduling meetings and appointments and engaging in ordinary e-mail.

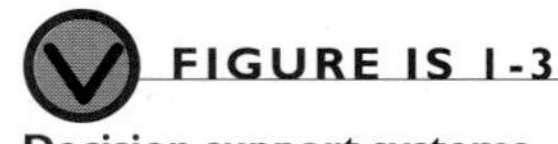

FIGURE IS 1-3

Decision support systems.

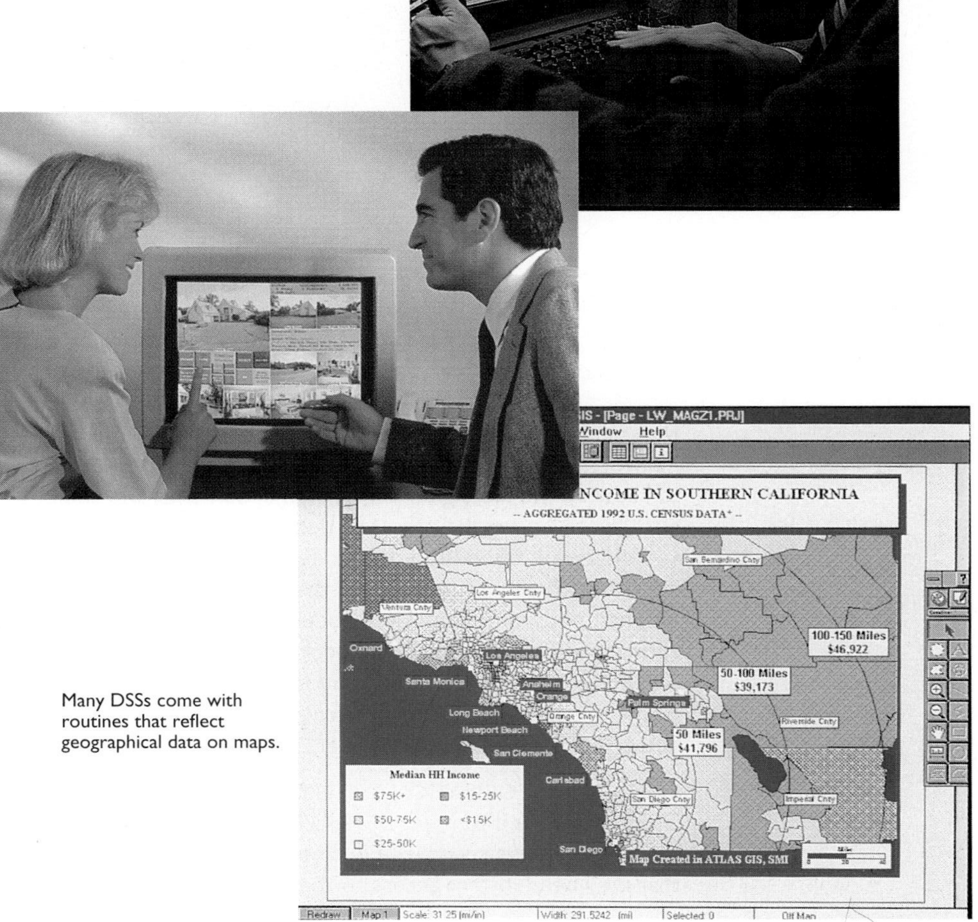

A sales-support database helps a field representative from a pharmaceutical firm and a physician inspect clinical results on a blood-pressure medicine.

A DSS helps a realtor and client evaluate homes by presenting them with pictures on demand, vital statistics, and search tools.

Many DSSs come with routines that reflect geographical data on maps.

■ **Group decision support system (GDSS).** A decision support system that helps several people to routinely interact through a computer network to solve common problems.

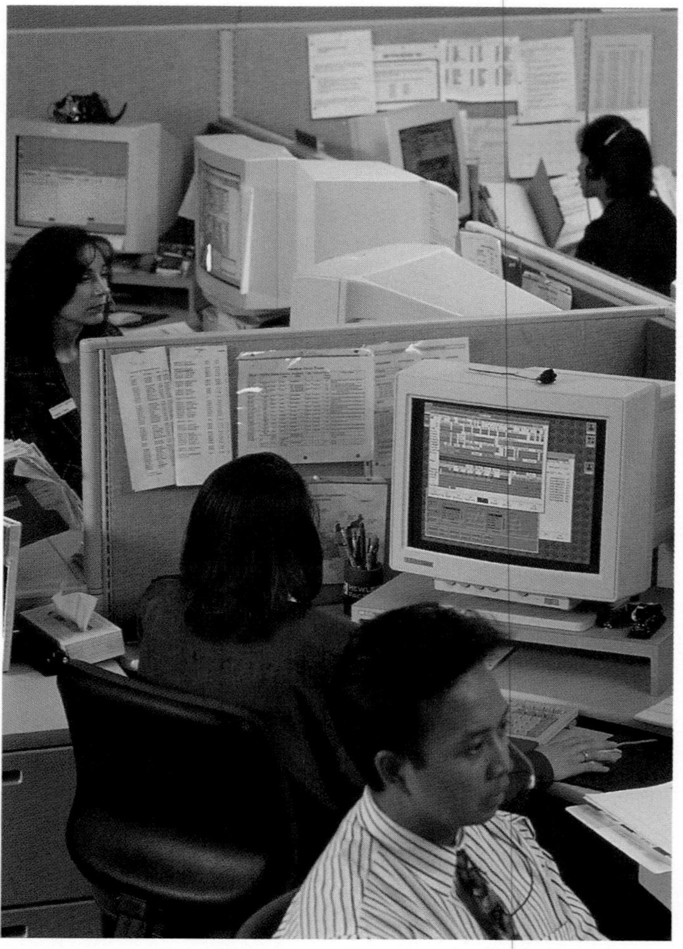

FIGURE IS 1-4

Group decision support systems (GDSSs). In a number of fields, groups of workers often collaborate electronically on decisions, so they don't have to leave their work spaces or be physically present at meetings.

The insurance field provides a good example of a GDSS. Several photos and forms are often needed to process an accident claim. An adjuster may take a picture of a damaged car and prepare an adjustment form. An estimate and a claim form will also be prepared. Gradually, a dossier on the accident will be developed. All of these documents are read into the computer system with an image scanner and put into a form that can be annotated, processed, and shared electronically by people working over a network in the claims department. The claims-department employees can each in turn call up the file, sign off on certain documents, and add other documents. They can also "meet," using their workstations, to make joint decisions on particular cases.

Software is often used both to run the system and to measure how well it is working. **Workflow software** does the latter chore, automatically keeping track of documents, recording how long documents take to process at each workstation, and spotting any processing bottlenecks that occur. Processing claims with a GDSS and workflow software can be done faster and more cost effectively than with traditional processing methods. There is minimal chance of documents being lost and better service to the policyholder, too.

EXECUTIVE INFORMATION SYSTEMS **Executive information systems (EISs)** are DSSs customized to meet the special needs of the people who run organizations. As many executives see it, the business world today is so competitive and fast paced that they need instant access to the freshest information. Among executives' favorite

■ **Workflow software.** A program that tracks the progress of documents in a system and measures the performance of people processing the documents. ■ **Executive information system (EIS).** A decision support system tailored to the needs of a specific top-level individual in an organization.

applications are database management systems that access corporate and financial data, networking applications that provide information that is external to the organization, electronic mail systems that streamline contact with subordinates, and customized spreadsheets that let important ratios and trends be displayed in a graphical format. Because many executives don't type, many of them require easy-to-learn, easy-to-use graphical user interfaces that involve making selections with a pointing device.

OFFICE SYSTEMS

In recent years, computer technology has been used widely to increase productivity in the office. The term **office automation (OA)** describes this phenomenon. Office automation can be achieved through a wide variety of technologies and processing techniques, as described in this section.

Document Processing The staple of most organizations is the document—memos, letters, reports, manuals, forms, and the like. Consequently, a major focus of office automation relates to the creation, distribution, and storage of documents. Sometimes the catchall phrase *document processing* is used to collectively refer to such office technologies as word processing, desktop publishing, and the types of electronic document handling found in GDSSs.

Electronic Messaging *Electronic messaging* makes it possible to send memos, letters, manuscripts, legal documents, and the like from one computer system or terminal to another. Two familiar examples of electronic messaging are **electronic mail (e-mail)** and **facsimile (fax).** E-mail is the computer-to-computer equivalent of interoffice mail or the postal service, whereas *fax* refers to an alternative method for the transmission of text documents, pictures, maps, diagrams, and the like over the phone lines. Both e-mail and fax are discussed in detail in the NET module of this textbook.

Desk Accessories *Desk accessories*—which are sometimes called *desktop organizers* or *personal information managers (PIMs)*—are software packages that provide the electronic equivalents of features commonly found on an office desktop (see Figure IS 1-5).

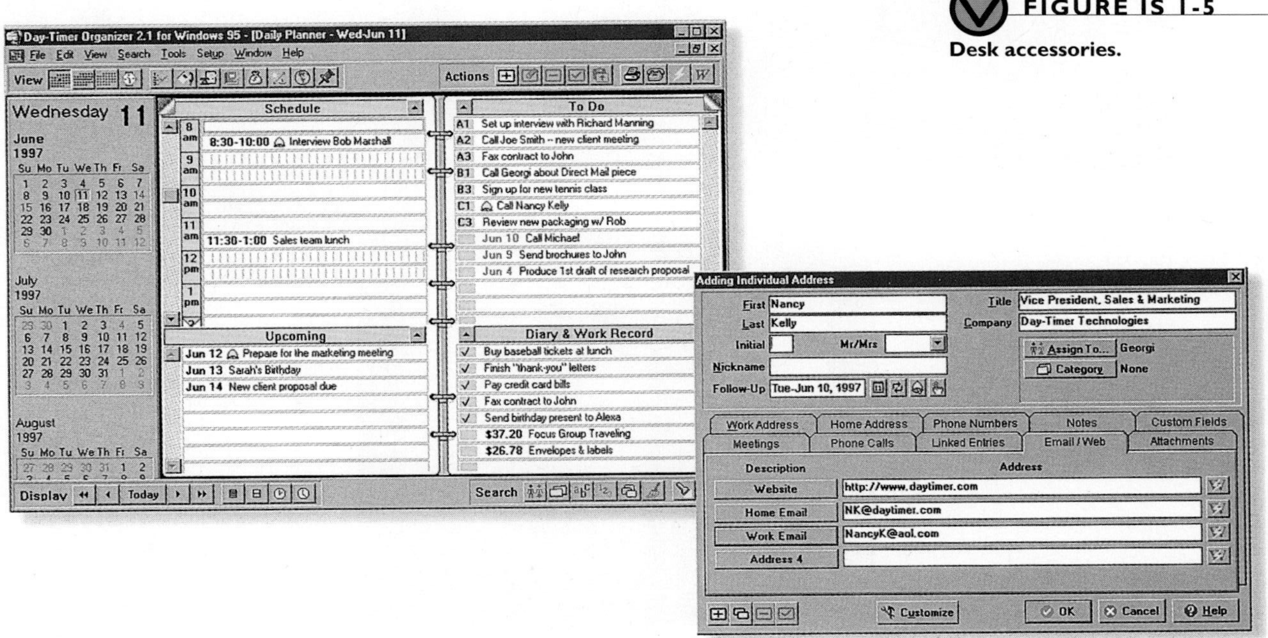

FIGURE IS 1-5

Desk accessories.

■ **Office automation (OA).** Computer-based office-oriented technologies such as word processing, desktop publishing, electronic mail, teleconferencing, and the like. ■ **Electronic mail.** The computer-to-computer equivalent of interoffice mail or the postal service. Also called **e-mail.** ■ **Facsimile.** A method for the transmission of text documents, pictures, maps, diagrams, and the like over the phone lines. Abbreviated as **fax.**

Desk accessory software varies among vendors, but many offer such features as a calendar for scheduling appointments and a Rolodex-type file for storing names and addresses. Often the feature is activated through a window that appears when a user presses shortcut keystrokes or selects a particular screen choice.

Decision Support Tools Because many key decisions are made by white-collar workers, it's understandable that offices maintain a variety of decision support systems. Among the decision support tools useful in office settings are spreadsheets, presentation graphics, plotters and laser printers, color monitors, and relational database management systems. All of these software and hardware tools have contributed to streamlining life at the office and were discussed earlier in the book.

Teleconferencing **Teleconferencing** makes it possible for a group of people to meet electronically, thereby avoiding the time and expense they would incur if they were to get together physically in one spot. Applications include business conferences, medical assistance for rural areas, and long-distance learning. About a decade ago, teleconferencing required specially equipped rooms as well as hardware and software costing several thousands of dollars. Today, just about anyone can add an Internet-based teleconferencing component to their own computer system for a few hundred dollars (see Figure IS 1-6).

Teleconferencing often involves a combination of audio, video, and computer components. Systems vary widely. Many operate over ISDN or regular-telephone lines, or over LANs with dedicated cables. To get the best audio and video quality, you still

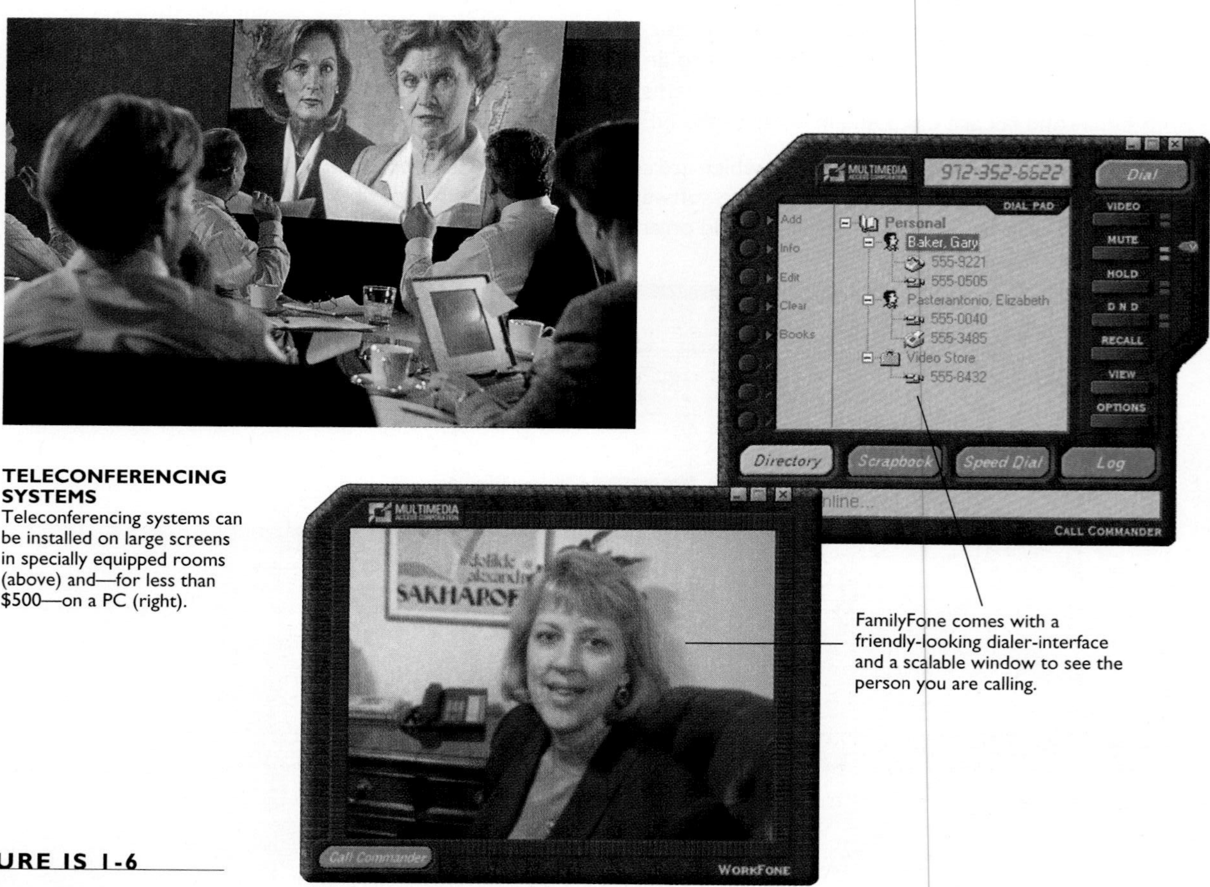

TELECONFERENCING SYSTEMS
Teleconferencing systems can be installed on large screens in specially equipped rooms (above) and—for less than $500—on a PC (right).

FIGURE IS 1-6
Video teleconferencing.

■ **Teleconferencing.** Using computer and communications technology to carry on a meeting.

have to go to a specially equipped room. Tools have also recently become available that enable teleconferencing participants to create images and annotate them in real time, either on the screen or on *whiteboards* that hook up to a PC (see Figure IS 1-7). Travel savings notwithstanding, the biggest benefit to teleconferencing is something most technology experts never anticipated—the ability to bring together company expertise quickly in order to solve problems.

FIGURE IS 1-7

Whiteboards.

ABOUT WHITEBOARDS
Electronic whiteboards are designed to let people share visually complex ideas over networks.

Microsoft's NetMeeting provides both images of conference participants and whiteboarding onscreen at the same time.

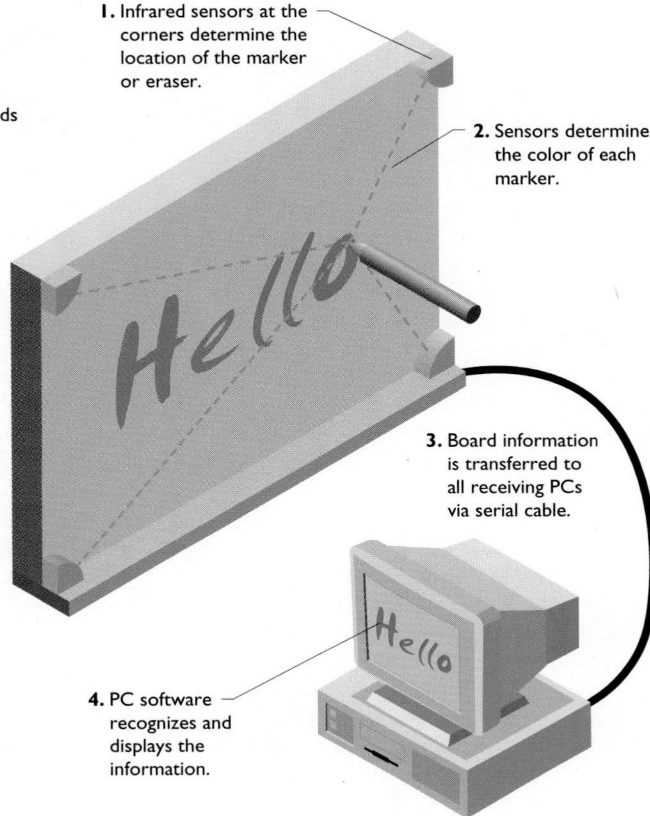
1. Infrared sensors at the corners determine the location of the marker or eraser.
2. Sensors determine the color of each marker.
3. Board information is transferred to all receiving PCs via serial cable.
4. PC software recognizes and displays the information.
Hello

Telecommuting **Telecommuting** is the term used to describe people working at home and linking up to their employers through a desktop workstation, laptop computer, fax machine, and/or another type of computer-age tool. Many computer programmers, for example, telecommute either entirely or in part to their jobs, because they prefer to do so, because they are more productive at home, or because they don't need supervision. Telecommuting can save workers both the time and expense involved in traveling to work. It can also save businesses the expense of maintaining office and parking space (see Feature IS 1-1). On the negative side, telecommuting limits the interpersonal contact that people get from working in an office. Also, telecommuting requires a major cultural adjustment for both individuals and organizations accustomed to on-site supervision. Many critics of telecommuting have also pointed out that a person not seen around the office, where interpersonal bonding most effectively takes place, is a person not promoted.

DESIGN AND MANUFACTURING SYSTEMS

Computers are widely used in organizational settings to improve productivity both at the design stage—through *computer-aided design (CAD)*—and at the manufacturing stage

■ **Telecommuting.** Working at home and being connected by means of electronic devices to other workers at remote locations.

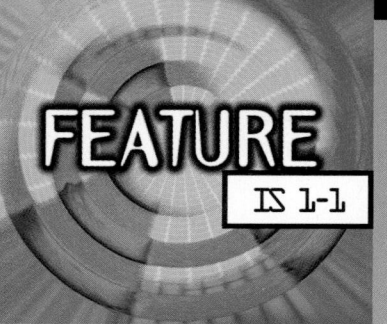

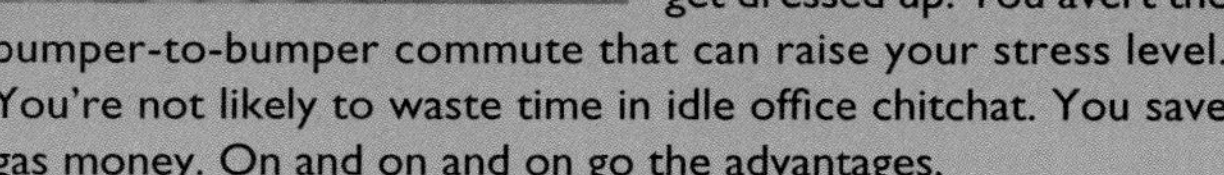

Virtual Offices

Are the Days of the Physical Office Numbered?

For many people, working at home and going to the office only when they choose is the ideal situation. Think of the benefits. You don't have to get dressed up. You avert the bumper-to-bumper commute that can raise your stress level. You're not likely to waste time in idle office chitchat. You save gas money. On and on and on go the advantages.

In many organizations, the virtual office—working anywhere you are most productive—has become a reality. Chiat/Day, Inc., the large California-based advertising agency, is one organization that has taken the plunge. With the exception of support staff, employees can more or less work where they choose. File servers in the office provide access to client applications as well as to e-mail and electronic calendaring facilities. Laptop, cellular-phone, and paging technology enables workers to keep in touch with colleagues and with clients, from almost anywhere the workers station themselves.

Some of the nation's largest accounting and consulting firms have also been moving toward a virtual-office scenario for several years. At Ernst & Young's Chicago office, for instance, most of the 1,000 or so accountants and consultants have to book space when they want to work at the office. The process—called *hoteling*—works almost like reserving hotel rooms. Space must be reserved at least a day in advance. Before an employee shows up, his or her office is prepared with the necessary personal belongings and technology to do the required work. Years ago, the company realized that although it was paying for costly office space for all of its employees, a large percentage of them were on the road at any given time.

Compaq Computer is another company that believes strongly in the virtual-office concept. Many of its salespeople work from their homes. In the morning, a salesperson might call headquarters and download on his or her laptop computer all e-mail messages and pertinent account data needed for the day's meetings. On the road, salespeople can plug their laptops into corporate databases from a phone jack or, if no jack is available, from a cellular modem. If, say, a client requests a price sheet or a brochure, the salesperson does not need to go to the office to pick one up—it can be downloaded onto a laser printer. IBM has also converted several of its sales offices to productivity centers that support mobile workers.

At home in the virtual office. As long as you produce, you don't have your boss constantly "in your face."

Virtual offices do not come without their problems. Many people, for instance, prefer to work at the office. Some even make the very compelling case that a worker not seen is a worker not promoted. Also, when some people are split from coworkers, they begin to wonder what holds the company together. Additionally, many people have worked years to get nice offices and have come to look at them as status symbols. When these offices are taken away, the workers may believe they're being demoted. Problems often also result from trying to manage an office complex with constrained physical space. People who are supposed to come in often do not show up, and sometimes people who are supposed to leave discover they need to stay longer to get their work done.

Eventually, will almost every office worker be working where he or she pleases? That's certainly a possibility, although the conversion will take time. By the year 2000, approximately 30 million workers could be working out of virtual offices, say some industry experts. To get the most knowledgeable workers, more companies may have to abandon old attitudes about the workplace and be willing to make concessions. After all, the virtual-office advocates remind us, work is something you do, not a place to which you go.

through *computer-aided manufacturing (CAM)*. With technology becoming ever more sophisticated, companies have made serious attempts to more closely integrate design, manufacturing, and other business functions—a concept known as *computer-integrated manufacturing (CIM)*.

Computer-Aided Design (CAD) Using **computer-aided design (CAD)** designers can dramatically reduce the time they spend developing products. For example, using light pens and specialized graphics workstations, engineers or architects can sketch ideas directly into the computer system and then instruct it to analyze the proposed design in terms of how well it meets a number of design criteria. Using the

■ **Computer-aided design (CAD).** A general term applied to the use of computer technology to automate design functions.

Photorealistic CAD tools enable architects to render buildings in 3-D.

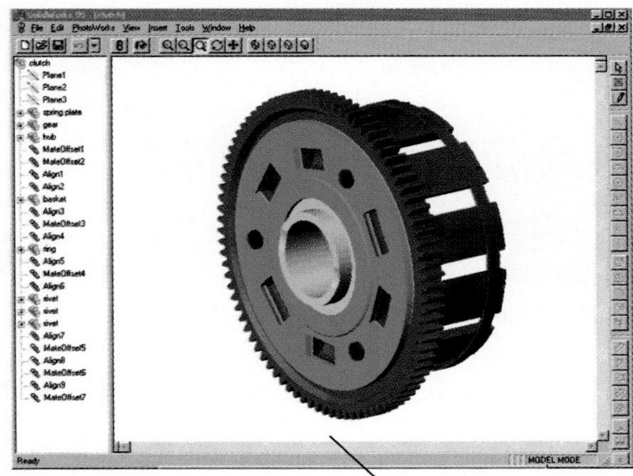

CAD is frequently used to design parts.

Design software can be used to map clothing onto models to see what it looks like.

FIGURE IS 1-8

Computer-aided design.

subsequent computer output, designers can modify their drawings until they achieve the desired results. CAD is especially helpful in designing automobiles, aircraft, ships, buildings, electrical circuits (including computer chips), and even clothing (see Figure IS 1-8). Besides playing an important role in the design of durable goods, CAD is useful in fields such as art, advertising, law, architecture, and movie production.

Computer-Aided Manufacturing (CAM) Computers have been used on the factory floor for over 40 years, long before engineers used them interactively for design. **Computer-aided manufacturing (CAM)** refers to the use of computers to help manage manufacturing operations and control machinery used in those processes. One example is a system that observes production in an oil refinery, performs calculations, and opens and shuts appropriate valves when necessary. Another system, commonly used in the steel industry, works from preprogrammed specifications to shape and assemble steel parts automatically. Increasingly, robots are used to carry out processes once solely in the human domain (see Figure IS 1-9). CAM is also widely used to build cars and ships, monitor power plants, manufacture food and chemicals, and perform a number of other functions.

■ **Computer-aided manufacturing (CAM).** A general term applied to the use of computer technology to automate manufacturing functions.

A robot helping to prepare a product for shipment.

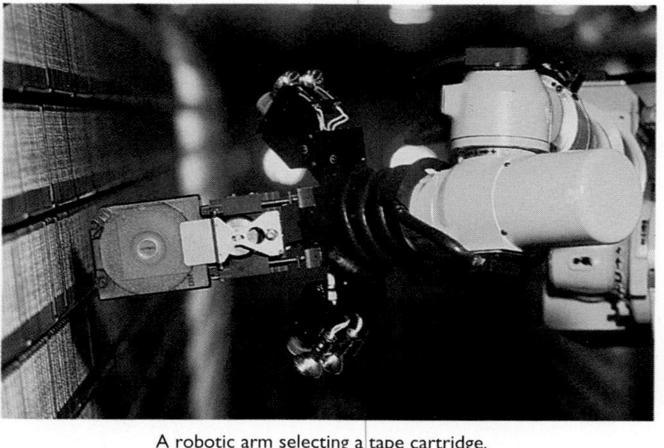

A robotic arm selecting a tape cartridge.

FIGURE IS 1-9

Robots at work.

Computer-Integrated Manufacturing (CIM) **Computer-integrated manufacturing (CIM)** systems tie together CAD, CAM, and other business activities. Here's how CIM might work: A large auto distributorship calls an auto manufacturer to check out the feasibility of changing a styling detail on 500 cars that are to be produced next month. The CAD part of the integrated system checks out the design change to see if it can be done and to determine what types of assembly-line changes are necessary. CAM systems on the factory floor determine if the assembly line can make the shift and if new parts can be made available on time. The CAM computers call up the computers of parts suppliers, which are also integrated into the system, to check on parts availability. Finally, all of the information is forwarded to accounting department computers, which calculate the cost impact of the change. Without CIM, such decision making would have to occur by a seat-of-the-pants style.

ARTIFICIAL INTELLIGENCE

A computer is a device that, given some instructions, can perform work at extremely fast speeds, drawing on a large memory. It can also be programmed with a set of rules or guidelines, thereby enabling it to draw certain types of conclusions based upon the input it receives. A good deal of mental activity involves these very processes. For this reason, the ability of a computer system to perform in ways that would be considered intelligent if observed in humans is commonly referred to as **artificial intelligence (AI).**

The four main areas of AI are expert systems, natural languages, vision systems, and robotics.

Expert Systems **Expert systems** are programs that provide the type of advice that would be expected from a human expert. In medicine, for instance, expert systems are often used to incorporate the thinking patterns of some of the world's best physicians. For example, an expert system might be given the symptoms exhibited by a patient. If these symptoms point to a disease the program knows something about, the program may ask the attending physician questions about specific details. Ultimately, through questioning and checking the responses against a large database of successfully diagnosed cases, the program might draw conclusions that the attending physician might never have reached otherwise—and much more quickly as well.

■ **Computer-integrated manufacturing (CIM).** The use of technology to tie together CAD, CAM, and other business systems. ■ **Artificial intelligence (AI).** The ability of a machine to perform actions that are characteristic of human intelligence, such as reasoning and learning. ■ **Expert system.** A program or computer system that provides the type of advice that would be expected from a human expert.

Most expert systems consist of two parts: a data part and a software part (see Figure IS 1-10). The data part is commonly called a **knowledge base,** and it contains specific facts about the expert area and any rules that the expert system will use to make decisions based on those facts. For instance, an expert system used to

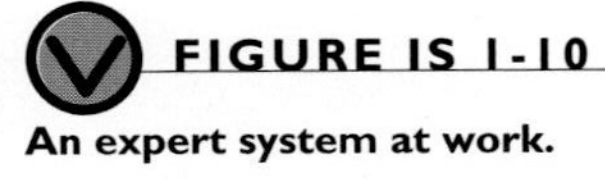
FIGURE IS 1-10

An expert system at work.

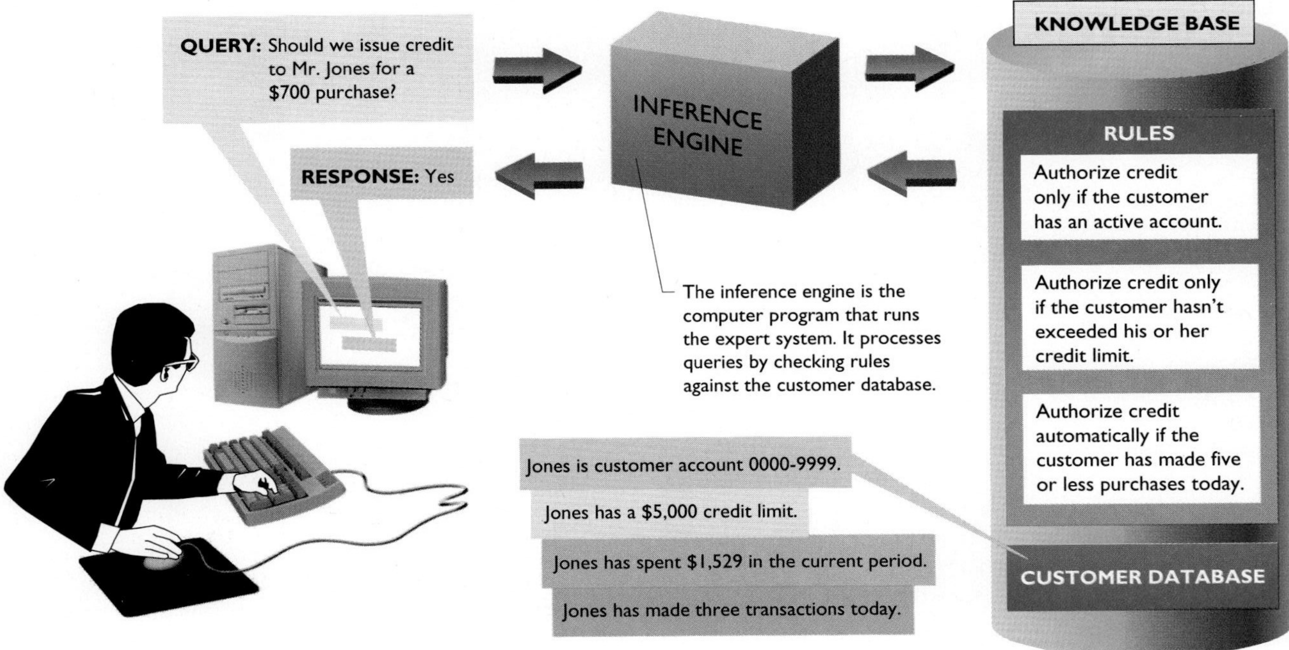

QUERY: Should we issue credit to Mr. Jones for a $700 purchase?
RESPONSE: Yes
INFERENCE ENGINE
The inference engine is the computer program that runs the expert system. It processes queries by checking rules against the customer database.
KNOWLEDGE BASE
RULES
Authorize credit only if the customer has an active account.
Authorize credit only if the customer hasn't exceeded his or her credit limit.
Authorize credit automatically if the customer has made five or less purchases today.
Jones is customer account 0000-9999.
Jones has a $5,000 credit limit.
Jones has spent $1,529 in the current period.
Jones has made three transactions today.
CUSTOMER DATABASE

authorize credit for credit-card customers would have in its knowledge base facts about customers as well as a set of *rules,* such as "Do not automatically authorize credit if the customer has already made five transactions today." Generally, the knowledge base is jointly developed by a specialized systems analyst called a *knowledge engineer* and a human expert.

The software part often consists of a variety of different programs. For instance, a program called an **inference engine** is used to apply rules to the knowledge base to reach decisions. Other programs commonly enable users to communicate with the expert system in a natural language such as English or Spanish, provide explanations to users about how the expert system reached a particular conclusion, and allow computer professionals to set up and maintain the expert system.

Expert systems can be built from scratch or acquired as packages that have all the software components in place but lack a knowledge base. This latter type of package is called an **expert system shell.** Shells represent the most common and inexpensive way to create an expert system.

Today, many expert systems use **neural-net computing,** a technology in which the human brain's pattern-recognition process is emulated by a computer (see Feature IS 1-2 on page IS 18). Some expert systems also use *fuzzy logic,* in which such human expressions as *many, most,* and *some* extend the computer's binary logic (see User Solution IS 1-1 on page IS 22).

Natural Languages One of the greatest challenges that scientists in the field of AI currently face is providing computer systems with the ability to communicate in *natural languages*—English, Spanish, French, Japanese, and so forth. Unfortunately, this

■ **Knowledge base.** The part of an expert system that contains specific facts about the expert area and any rules the expert system will use to make decisions based on those facts. ■ **Inference engine.** A program used to apply rules to the knowledge base in order to reach decisions. ■ **Expert system shell.** A prepackaged expert system that lacks only a knowledge base. ■ **Neural-net computing.** An expert-system technology in which the human brain's pattern-recognition process is emulated by a computer system.

FEATURE IS 1-2

Neural-Net Computing

Pattern Recognition Is Its Specialty

Most computing today is preprogrammed number crunching. Whether you are spell-checking a document, doing spreadsheet computations or a database search, or rotating graphics images, you are simply executing a predetermined procedure at a high speed. Most programs are good at this type of thing. But if you ask them to recognize a handwritten letter, that's a different matter.

This is where neural nets come in. *Neural-net computing* refers to an expert-systems technology in which the human brain's pattern-recognition process is emulated by a computer system or software. Neural-net systems aren't preprogrammed to provide predictable responses like conventional algorithms. Instead, they are designed to learn by observation and by trial and error—the way people largely learn.

Several applications involving neural nets have already begun paying dividends. These applications—most of which are in the area of expert systems—are described below.

Handwriting, Speech, and Image Recognition Recognition of a person's signature, voice, or face happens so quickly that you scarcely notice how the underlying process works. Neural nets attempt to emulate this process. Consider character recognition, for instance. The lower levels of the neural net may recognize that a character is composed of curves and straight lines. This information is passed to the next layer, which may attempt to determine the number of curves and lines and the way they fit together. Finally, conclusions are passed to a third level, which may recognize the character as a capital *B*. If the character can't be recognized, the neural net attempts to learn from the problem. One company is already using such an algorithm to recognize handwritten numerals on checks. Another has developed a neural-net program that can recognize human faces with an accuracy of better than 99 percent (see photo).

Credit-Risk Assessment Subtle patterns also exist in conventional text data, such as those found at financial institutions. If you were very sharp and studied the records of thousands of people who were granted and denied credit, you might eventually be able to discern which types of people were good credit risks and which types of people were poor ones. Of course, computers can work much faster than humans and can notice patterns that are hardly discernible. Neural nets are currently being applied to solve credit-risk assessment problems at American Express and other financial-services companies.

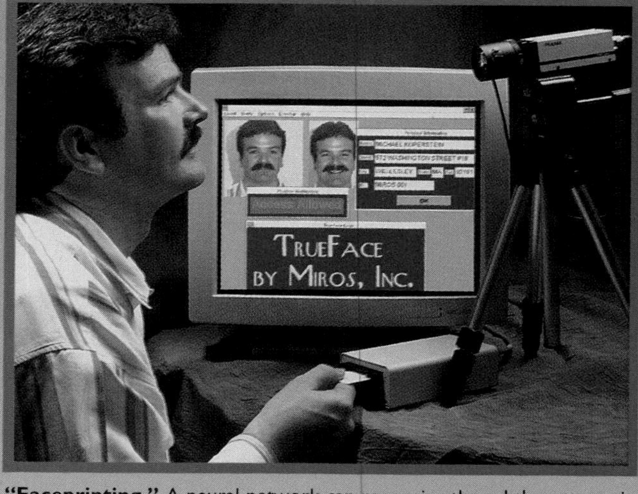

"Faceprinting." A neural network can recognize the subtle patterns in lightness and darkness that define a person's unique features—the shape of a nose or mouth, say—and ignore variable features such as a day-old beard or glasses.

Crime Analysis Neural nets also offer help in solving crimes. Many crimes, of course, display a pattern, and often this pattern is too subtle to be picked up without computer assistance. Police departments and government agencies such as the FBI aren't the only organizations using neural-net technology to take a bite out of crime. New York's Chase Manhattan Bank is currently using neural nets to examine hundreds of thousands of transactions daily and to look for fraudulent ones.

Stock Analysis One exciting neural-net application is a program that examines stock-market data for patterns and helps determine strategies for buying and selling stocks. At Boston-based Fidelity Investments, Brad Lewis—who manages the Disciplined Equity mutual fund—has outperformed the market consistently with a neural-net-based computer model he began developing in business school. The model evaluates 180,000 pieces of data nightly to learn how the market is pricing stocks. It then reviews about a dozen characteristics of 2,000 target stocks to detect subtle patterns that are in line with current market valuations. Stocks are then selected by an "attractiveness rating."

Other applications for neural nets abound. In medicine, neural nets can examine detailed records of patients having a specific disease and attempt to uncover an underlying pattern. In quality control, thousands of parts can be studied to uncover subtle structural problems. Wherever there's a pattern to study, a neural-net application may be useful.

challenge has not been easy to meet. People have personalized ways of communicating, and the meaning of words vary according to the contexts in which they are used. Nonetheless, researchers have made some major strides toward getting computers to listen to and respond in natural languages.

Vision Systems *Vision systems* enable computer-controlled devices to "see." A vision system might work as follows. Parts produced in a manufacturing process are sent along an assembly line for inspection. A vision system located at a station along the line takes a digital snapshot of each part as it passes by. The picture is decomposed into vital data that are compared to data showing how the part would look if it were produced correctly. An accompanying expert system applies rules to judge whether the part has been made correctly or is flawed. If flawed, the system determines the nature of the flaw and the necessary corrective action.

Robotics **Robotics—**the field devoted to the study of robot technology—plays an integral role in computer-aided manufacturing (CAM) systems. Robots are machines that, with the help of a computer, can mimic a number of human motor activities to perform jobs that are too monotonous or dangerous for their flesh-and-blood counterparts—welding and painting cars, mining coal, defusing bombs, going to the bottom of the ocean and peeking around, and so on. Many robots can even "see" by means of embedded cameras and "feel" with sensors that permit them to assess the hardness and temperature of objects. Robots can represent substantial savings to a company, because they don't go on strike, don't need vacations, and don't get sick.

Responsibility for Systems Development

Organizations with thousands of employees and thousands of details to keep track of usually utilize thousands of systems, ranging from personal systems to systems that operate at an enterprise-wide level. Deciding which systems best support the direction of the organization, and how much attention to give each one, is where the job of systems development begins.

A company's *chief information officer (CIO)* has primary responsibility for systems development. Often this position is at the level of vice president. One of the CIO's duties is to develop a strategy that defines the role of information technology within the organization. Another duty is to develop a long-range plan that maps out which systems are to be studied and possibly built or revamped during that period.

Because information technology plays such a pervasive role within most companies, *steering committees* composed of top-level executives normally approve technology plans and set broad guidelines for performing computer-related activities. These committees do not involve themselves with technical details or administer particular projects; these functions are the responsibility of the organizations' information systems departments.

THE INFORMATION SYSTEMS DEPARTMENT

The **information systems department—**often called the *information technology department* or some other name—varies in structure from one company to another. It often includes people who design and implement enterprise-wide systems, people who provide support services to PC users, and people who build and manage networks and databases. Figure IS 1-11 describes a number of jobs often found within information systems departments.

Data Processing Area The pillar of most information systems departments is its **data processing area,** whose primary responsibility it is to keep mission-critical transaction-processing-oriented systems within the company running smoothly. It is these systems that by and large control the money coming into and going out of the organization. The data processing area predates all other areas within the information systems department and is still considered by many to be the most important. After

■ **Robotics.** The study of robot technology. ■ **Information systems department.** The area in an organization that consists of computer professionals. ■ **Data processing area.** The group of computer professionals charged with building and operating transaction processing systems.

Applications programmer
A programmer who codes applications software.

Computer operations manager
The person who oversees the computer operations area in an organization.

Computer operator
A person who is responsible for the operation of large computers and their support.

Control clerk
The person who monitors all work coming in and out of a computer center.

Database administrator
The person responsible for setting up and managing large databases within an organization.

Data-entry operator
A member of a computer operations staff responsible for keying in data into a computer system.

Data processing director
The person in charge of developing and/or implementing the overall plan for transaction processing in an organization and for overseeing the activities of programmers, systems analysts, and operations personnel.

Help-desk troubleshooter
A person who, by phone or computer, assists users in solving software and hardware problems.

Knowledge engineer
The person responsible for setting up and maintaining the base of expert knowledge used in expert-system applications.

Network administrator
The person responsible for planning and implementing networks within an organization.

Programmer/analyst
A person, usually found in smaller companies, with job responsibilities that include both applications programming and systems analysis and design.

Scheduler
The operations person hired to utilize system resources to peak efficiency.

Security specialist
The person responsible for seeing that an organization's hardware, software, and data are protected from computer criminals, natural disasters, accidents, and the like.

System librarian
The person in the computer operations area who manages files stored offline on tapes, disks, microfilm, and so on.

Systems analyst
A person who studies systems in an organization to determine what work needs to be done and how this work may best be achieved with computer resources.

Systems programmer
A person who codes systems software, fine-tunes operating-system performance, and performs other systems-software-related tasks.

Trainer
A person who provides education to users about a particular program, system, or technology.

Vice president of information systems
The person in an organization who oversees routine transaction processing and information systems activities as well as other computer-related areas. Also known as the *chief information officer (CIO)*.

Webmaster
The person responsible for establishing and maintaining an organization's Internet presence.

FIGURE IS 1-11
Information-systems jobs.

all, if their computers stopped processing high volumes of business transactions, most large organizations would have to shut down.

Within the data processing area, the *systems analysis and design group* analyzes, designs, and implements new software and hardware systems. The *programming group* codes computer programs from program design specifications. The *operations group* manages day-to-day processing once a system has become operational.

The person most involved with systems development is the **systems analyst.** Generally speaking, the systems analyst's job in the data processing area is to plan, build, and implement large systems that will use the computers the organization has or will acquire. When such a system is needed, the systems analyst interacts with current and potential users to produce a solution. The analyst generally is involved in all stages of the development process, from beginning to end.

In most large projects, a team of people will be involved. A systems analyst will probably be appointed as a **project manager** to head up the team. Other people on

■ **Systems analyst.** A person who studies systems in an organization in order to determine what work needs to be done and how this work may best be achieved with computer resources. ■ **Project manager.** A systems analyst who is put in charge of a team that is building a large system.

the team might include users, programmers, an outside consultant, a cost accountant, and an auditor. Users are especially vital to any team because they are the people who know the practical side of the application, and, also, they are the people who must work with any new system on a day-to-day basis.

OUTSOURCING

When an organization lacks the staff to build or operate a system it needs, it often chooses an outsourcing option. **Outsourcing** involves turning over certain information systems functions to an outside vendor. For instance, many smaller banks outsource their check-processing and customer-statement operations to companies that are skilled at high-volume processing of this sort.

Why do companies outsource? A small firm might find it too expensive to keep specialized personnel or equipment on hand, given its current work volume. Or a large company might not have the capacity or capital to expand its operations in-house, so it may outsource some of them temporarily. Also, many firms have found it easier to outsource operations in areas where it's too hard to find or too expensive to hire new personnel. Firms often turn to an outsourcer when they think that the outsourcer can do the job better or cheaper than they.

Along with the benefits to outsourcing come some serious drawbacks. Some firms simply hand over their work to an outsourcer and then expect miracles. Leadership needs to come from the client firm, not from the outsourcer. Also, when in-house personnel have to mix with the outsourcer's personnel, conflicts sometimes arise. The in-house personnel may feel that their jobs are threatened by the outsourcer's personnel, or, perhaps, they may disagree about who is in charge. Finally, the matters of control and security need to be considered. Although an outsourcer provides some assistance in these areas, a company achieves the most control over its information processing and the best security when it keeps its own work at its own site with its own people. When work goes outside, anything can happen.

Despite these drawbacks, outsourcing appears to be an unstoppable trend. Companies are eliminating many in-house jobs because of the high overhead involved in maintaining them. Among the leading suppliers of computer outsourcing services are Electronic Data System (EDS), Computer Sciences Corporation, and Andersen Consulting.

The Systems Development Life Cycle

A systems development project often breaks down into five steps or phases:

- Phase 1: Preliminary investigation
- Phase 2: Systems analysis
- Phase 3: System design
- Phase 4: System acquisition
- Phase 5: System implementation

Collectively, these phases make up the **systems development life cycle (SDLC).** The term implies that the phases describe the development of a system from the time it is first studied until the time it is put into use. When a new business pressure necessitates a change in a system, the steps of the cycle begin anew.

IS

■ **Outsourcing.** The practice by which one company hires another company to do some or all of its information-processing activities. ■ **Systems development life cycle (SDLC).** The process consisting of the five phases of system development: preliminary investigation, systems analysis, system design, system acquisition, and system implementation.

USER SOLUTION IS 1-1

Using Fuzzy Logic to Sell Real Estate

Since their earliest days, virtually all business computers have worked with a two-state or *binary* logic. Computers recognize either true or false, yes or no, on or off, and so on. *Fuzzy logic,* on the other hand, deals with such imprecise terms as *many* and *close to* and with contextual elements such as *tall* and *short.*

Fuzzy logic is today used to save energy in home appliances, to control the braking of cars, and to decide when to buy or sell stocks. It has also recently been applied to selling of real estate. Want to buy a home with a computerized search? Then you may want software that can find matches that are *close to* specifications that you input or *most like* them—the types of situations with which fuzzy logic can be most helpful.

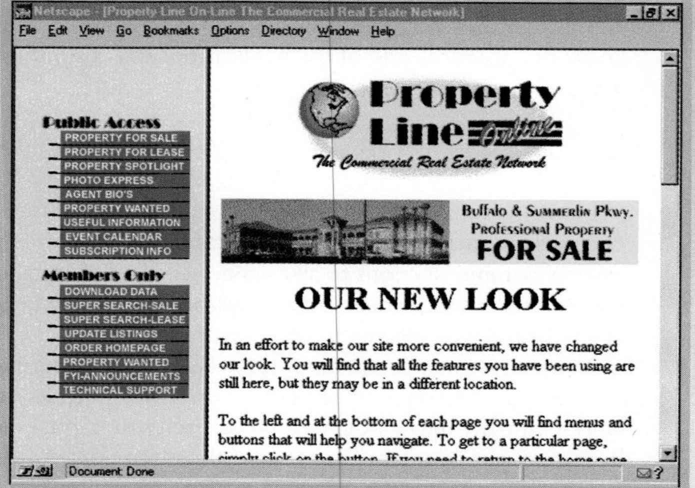

The five steps of the SDLC define in principle the process for building systems for both large multimillion-dollar information systems that run large corporations and $3,000 microcomputer systems that sit on many desktops in homes. The role of the systems analyst during each step of the SDLC is illustrated in Figure IS 1-12.

The five steps of the systems development life cycle do not always follow one another in a strict sequence. Frequently, analysis and design are interleaved. Compare this process with an example from everyday life—the development of a vacation plan. People don't always design the whole plan as the first step and execute it, without modification, as the second step. They might design a plan for Day 1 and, when the

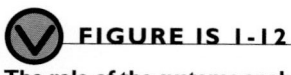

FIGURE IS 1-12

The role of the systems analyst in the five phases of systems development.

Duties of the Systems Analyst

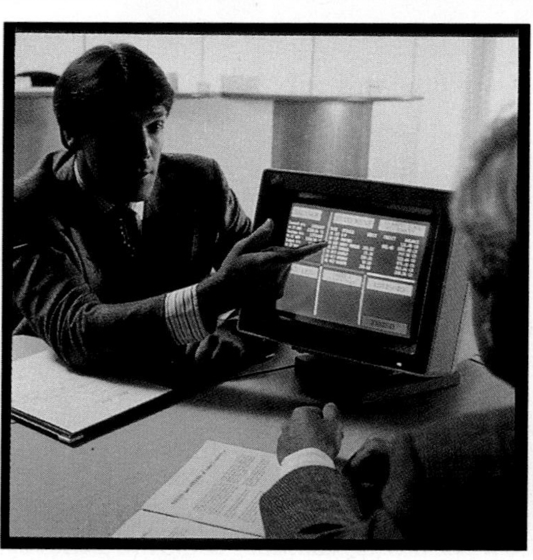

Preliminary investigation During this phase the analyst studies a problem briefly and suggests solutions to management.

Systems analysis If management decides that further development is warranted, the analyst studies the applications area in depth.

System design The analyst develops a model of the new system and prepares a detailed list of benefits and costs.

System acquisition Upon management approval of the design, the analyst decides which vendors to use in order to meet software, hardware, and servicing needs.

System implementation After system components have been acquired, the analyst supervises the lengthy process of training users, converting data, and the like.

day is over, analyze their experiences as a basis for designing a plan for Day 2. Many systems are designed this way, as well.

PRELIMINARY INVESTIGATION

One of the first steps toward developing a new system is to conduct a **preliminary investigation,** or *feasibility study.* The purpose of this investigation is to define and evaluate the problem area at hand relatively quickly, to see if it is worthy of further study, and to suggest some possible courses of action. Accordingly, the investigation should examine such issues as the nature of the problem, the scope of the work involved to solve it, possible alternative solutions, and the approximate costs and benefits of the different solutions.

The analyst must take care to distinguish *symptoms* from *problems* at the outset. For example, suppose an analyst is talking to a warehouse manager, who complains that inventories are too high. This may be so, but this fact in itself is not enough to warrant corrective action. It's a symptom, not a problem. There is a problem, however, if these high inventories are forcing the company to build an expensive new warehouse or if it is unnecessarily drawing on funds that could be used for profit opportunities. Note that even if a serious problem is identified, an organization may not be able to do anything about it. For instance, the aforementioned high-inventory problem may be due to a strike somewhere else.

SYSTEMS ANALYSIS

Systems analysis is the phase of systems development in which a problem area is studied in depth and the needs of system users are assessed. The main activities conducted during systems analysis are data collection and data analysis.

Data Collection The objective of data collection is to gather information about the type of work being performed in the application under study and to ascertain what resources users need to better perform their jobs. Later in this phase, the collection of data should suggest some possible solutions. Which data to collect depends largely on the problem being studied. Four sources of information on the applications area and user needs are documents showing how the application is supposed to work, questionnaires sent to users, interviews of users, and the personal observations of the systems analyst.

For example, an organization chart covering the functions being studied and the people in charge of those functions is often an especially useful document to anyone studying a system. The chart shows how work responsibilities are organized and the chain of decision making. Also, because people often don't do what they say they do, the only way an analyst can really determine if a system operates the way it is supposed to is by going to where people work and actually observing what they in fact do.

Data Analysis As information about the application is gathered, it must be analyzed so that conclusions about the requirements for the new system can be drawn. Two useful tools for performing analysis are diagrams and checklists.

Figure IS 1-13 shows a data flow diagram for the order-entry operation of a mail-order firm. **Data flow diagrams** show the relationship between activities that are part of a system as well as the data or information flowing into and out of each of the activities. They provide a visual representation of data movement in an organization.

■ **Preliminary investigation.** A brief study of a problem area to assess whether or not a full-scale project should be undertaken. Also called a *feasibility study.* ■ **Systems analysis.** The phase of the systems development life cycle in which a problem area is thoroughly examined to determine what should be done. ■ **Data flow diagram.** A graphically oriented systems development tool that enables a systems analyst to logically represent the flow of data through a system.

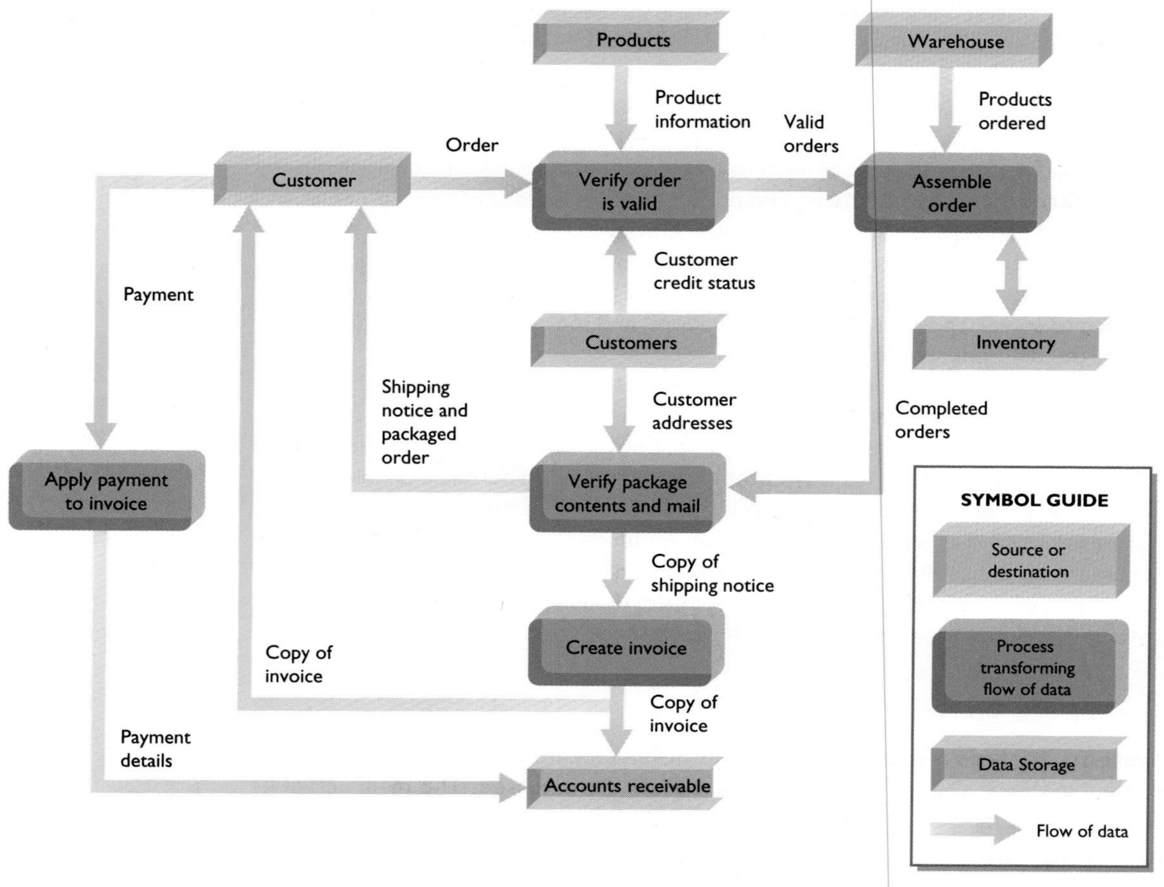

FIGURE IS 1-13

A data flow diagram for a mail-order firm. An order triggers the processes of verification and assembly of the goods ordered, and payment is recorded by accounts receivable.

Checklists are often developed for important matters such as the goals of the system and the information needs of key people in the system. An accounts receivable system, for instance, should have such goals as getting bills out quickly, rapidly informing customers about late payments, and cutting losses due to bad debts. On the other hand, a decision support system that helps teachers advise students should increase the quality of course-related information and decrease the time it takes to develop suitable curricula for students.

Common sense eventually must dictate which type of checklist or diagram is most appropriate for the situation on hand. The principal purpose of these tools is to help the analyst organize thoughts so that he or she may draw conclusions about what the system under study should do.

SYSTEM DESIGN

System design focuses on specifying what the system will look like. The system design phase primarily consists of developing a model of the new system and performing a detailed analysis of benefits and costs.

Developing a Model of the New System Once the analyst understands the nature of the design problem, it is usually helpful to draw a number of diagrams of the new system. The data flow diagrams discussed earlier can show how data will flow through the new system.

When designing a system, the analyst must take into account output requirements; input requirements; data access, organization, and storage; processing; system

■ **System design.** The phase of the systems development life cycle in which the parts of a new system and the relationships among them are formally established.

controls; and personnel and procedure specifications. Figure IS 1-14 covers some of the issues that the analyst must address in the design specification.

Analyzing Benefits and Costs Most organizations are acutely sensitive to costs, including computer system costs. Costs of a new computer system include both the initial investment in hardware and software and ongoing expenses such as personnel and maintenance. Some benefits can be computed easily by calculating the amount of labor the new system will save, the reduction in paperwork it will allow, and so on. These gains are called *tangible benefits,* because they represent easily quantifiable dollar amounts.

Output Considerations

- Who are the system users and what types of information do they need?
- How often is this information needed? Annually? Monthly? Daily? On demand?
- What output devices and storage media are necessary to provide the required information?
- How should output be formatted or arranged so that it can easily be understood by users?

Input Considerations

- What data need to be gathered and who will gather them?
- How often do data need to be gathered?
- What input devices and media are required for data collection and input?

Storage Considerations

- How will data be accessed and organized?
- What storage capacity is required?
- How fast must data be accessed?
- What storage devices are appropriate?

Processing Considerations

- What type of functionality is required in the software?
- What type of processing power is required? A mainframe? A minicomputer? A microcomputer?
- What special processing environments must be considered? A communications network? A database processing environment?

System Controls

- What measures must be taken to ensure that data are secure from unauthorized use, theft, and natural disasters?
- What measures must be taken to ensure the accuracy and integrity of data going in and information going out?
- What measures must be taken to ensure the privacy of individuals represented by the data?

Personnel and Procedures

- What personnel are needed to run the system?
- What procedures should be followed on the job?

FIGURE IS 1-14

Issues to cover during the system design specification. System design ultimately addresses all major elements of a computer system: hardware, software, data, people, and procedures.

Other benefits, such as improvements in service to customers or better information supplied to decision makers, are more difficult to convert into dollar amounts. These gains are called *intangible benefits*. Clearly, the existence of intangible benefits complicates management efforts to make decisions. Yet, some of the most important systems projects undertaken in a company involve strategic opportunities that are difficult to quantify. On a project with a large number of intangible benefits, management must ask questions such as "Are the new services that we can offer to customers worth the $3 million they will cost us?"

SYSTEM ACQUISITION

Once a system has been designed and the required types of software and hardware have been specified, the analyst must decide from which vendors to buy the necessary components. This decision lies at the heart of the **system acquisition** phase.

RFPs and RFQs Many organizations formulate their buying or leasing needs by preparing a document called a **request for proposal (RFP).** This document contains a list of technical specifications for equipment, software, and services determined during the system design phase. The RFP is sent to all vendors who might satisfy the organization's needs. In the proposal they send back to the initiating organization, vendors recommend a solution to the problem at hand and specify their price for providing that solution.

In some cases, an organization knows exactly which hardware, software, and service resources it needs from vendors and is interested only in a quote on a specific list of items. In this case, it sends vendors a document called a **request for quotation (RFQ),** which names those items and asks only for a quote. Thus, an RFP gives a vendor some leeway in making system suggestions, while an RFQ does not.

Evaluating Bids Once vendors have submitted their bids or quotes in response to an RFP or RFQ, the acquiring organization must decide which bid or quote to accept. Two useful tools for making this choice are vendor rating systems and benchmark tests.

In a **vendor rating system,** such as the one in Figure IS 1-15, important criteria for selecting computer system resources are identified and each is given a weight. For

FIGURE IS 1-15

A point-scoring approach for evaluating vendors' bids.

Criterion	Weight (Maximum Score)	Vendor 1 Score	Vendor 2 Score
Hardware	60	50	40
Software	80	70	70
Cost	70	50	65
Ease of use	80	70	50
Modularity	50	30	30
Vendor Support	50	10	50
Documentation	30	30	20
		310	325

1. A list of important purchase criteria is developed.
2. Each criterion is given a weight that reflects its importance. Here, hardware is weighted twice that of documentation.
3. Vendors are awarded scores on each criterion that can range from a zero score up to the maximum allowed.
4. Scores are tallied for each vendor. Here, Vendor 2 winds up with the highest tally.

■ **System acquisition.** The phase of the systems development life cycle in which equipment, software, or services are acquired from vendors. ■ **Request for proposal (RFP).** A document containing a general description of a system that an organization wishes to acquire. ■ **Request for quotation (RFQ).** A document distributed to potential vendors containing a list of specific hardware, software, and services that an organization wishes to acquire. ■ **Vendor rating system.** A weighted scoring procedure for evaluating competing vendors of computer products or services.

example, in the figure, the weights of 60 for hardware and 30 for documentation may be loosely interpreted to mean that the organization considers hardware twice as important as documentation. Each vendor that submits an acceptable bid is rated on each criterion, with the sum of the weights representing the maximum possible score. The buyer totals the scores and, all other things being equal, chooses the vendor with the highest total. Although such a rating tool does not guarantee that the best vendor will always have the highest point total, it has the advantage of being simple to apply and relatively objective. If several people are involved in the selection decision, individual biases tend to average out.

After tentatively selecting a vendor, some organizations make their choice conditional on the successful completion of a **benchmark test.** Such a test normally consists of running a pilot version of the new system on the hardware and software of the vendor under consideration. To do this, the acquiring organization usually visits the vendor's benchmark testing center and attempts to determine how well the hardware/software configuration will work if installed. Benchmark tests are expensive and far from foolproof. It's quite possible that the pilot system will perform admirably at the benchmark site but the real system, when eventually installed, will not.

SYSTEM IMPLEMENTATION

Once arrangements for delivery of computer resources have been made with one or more vendors, the **system implementation** phase begins. This phase includes all the remaining tasks necessary to make the system operational and successful. Implementation consists of many activities, including converting programs and data files from the old system to the new one, preparing any equipment to work in the new systems environment, and training personnel.

To ensure that the system will be working by a certain date, the analyst must prepare a timetable. One tool for helping with this task is *project management software,* illustrated in Figure IS 1-16, which shows how certain implementation activities are related and when they must start and finish.

A well-designed system should be flexible enough to accommodate changes over a reasonable period of time with minimal disruption. However, if a major change eventually becomes necessary, the organization must develop another system to replace the current one. At this point, the systems development life cycle—from preliminary investigation to implementation—begins all over again.

OTHER ACTIVITIES

During and after the five phases of the systems development life cycle, other important activities take place. For instance, as the system is being developed, the systems analyst should be preparing a package of *documentation* containing the data that have been gathered, analyses showing how conclusions were reached, records of meetings, copies of reports, and so on. The documentation is useful for auditors who may need to assess that proper procedures were followed as well as for systems analysts who may need to modify the system in the future. Documentation should be done as the system is being developed; when it's left until the end, it's often forgotten.

After the system has been implemented, some type of *postimplementation review* often takes place. This is basically a follow-up evaluation that is intended both to quickly correct any glitches that may have arisen in the system and to provide feedback on the systems development process in general, so that the organization might continue to improve in this area. The postimplementation review checks into such matters as whether or not the system is meeting its intended goals, costs are within expectations, and users are adapting favorably to the new systems environment.

■ **Benchmark test.** A test used to measure computer system performance under typical use conditions prior to purchase.
■ **System implementation.** The phase of systems development that encompasses activities related to making a computer system operational and successful once it is delivered by a vendor.

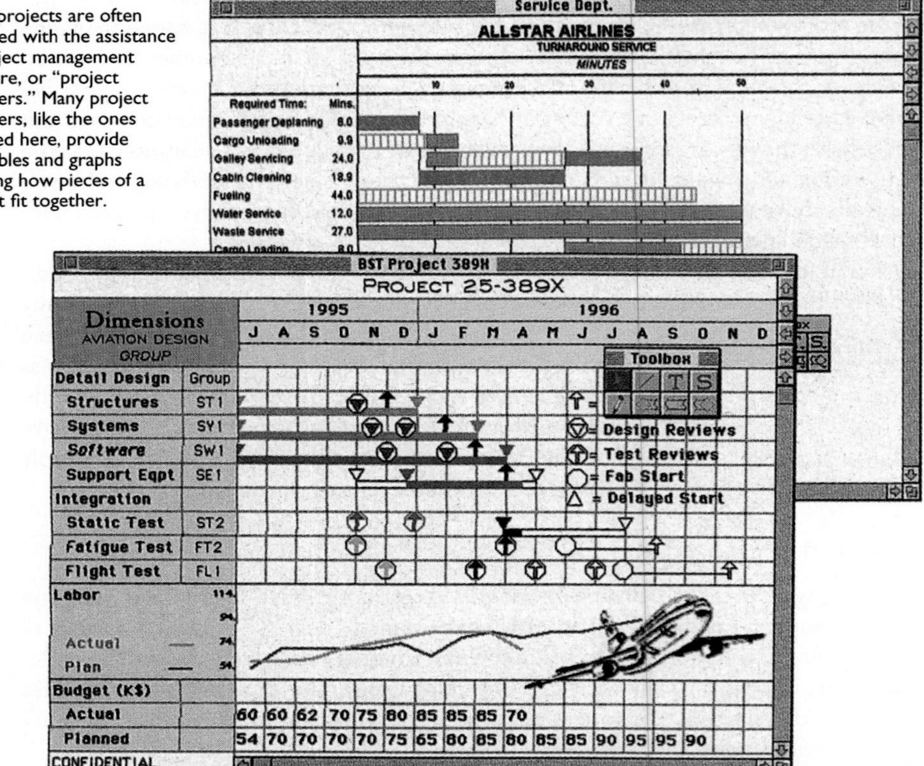

Large projects are often managed with the assistance of project management software, or "project managers." Many project managers, like the ones featured here, provide timetables and graphs showing how pieces of a project fit together.

FIGURE IS 1-16
Project management software.

After most systems are implemented, they also require ongoing *maintenance.* For instance, software and hardware often need to be added to a system, either to update what's already in place or to add entirely new features. Maintenance can be costly to an organization, and it's not unusual to spend $8 or $9 in maintenance over time for every dollar that was originally put into originally building the system.

Approaches to Systems Development

In this section, we'll examine the three main approaches to systems development: the traditional approach, prototyping, and end-user development.

THE TRADITIONAL APPROACH

In **traditional systems development** the phases of systems development are carried out in a preset order: (1) preliminary investigation, (2) systems analysis, (3) system design, (4) system acquisition, and (5) system implementation. Each phase begins only when the one before it is completed. Often, the traditional approach is reserved for the development of large transaction processing systems. Because the traditional approach is usually expensive and extensive, it normally is carried out by knowledgeable professionals—that is, by systems analysts.

Traditional systems development requires system users to consider proposed system plans by looking at detailed diagrams, descriptive reports, and specifications of the proposed new system. The entire system is planned and built before anyone

■ **Traditional systems development.** An approach to systems development whereby the five phases of the systems development life cycle are carried out in a predetermined sequence.

gets to use it or test it. As each phase of development is completed, users "sign off" on the recommendations presented to them by the analyst, indicating their acceptance.

Many organizations have lost faith in the traditional approach to systems development for many types of systems projects. First, this approach often takes too long to analyze, design, and implement new systems. By the time a system finally begins operating, important new needs that were not part of the original plan have surfaced. Second, the system developed often turns out to be the wrong one. Managers almost always have difficulty expressing their information needs, and it is not until they begin to use a system that they discover what it is they really need.

These problems notwithstanding, traditional development is useful when the system being developed is one with which there is a great deal of experience, where user requirements are easy to determine in advance, and where management wants the system completely spelled out before giving its approval.

PROTOTYPING

To avoid the potentially expensive disaster that could result from completing every phase of systems development before users ever lay their hands on a system, many analysts have advocated **prototyping** as a means of systems development. In prototyping, the focus is on developing a small model, or *prototype,* of the overall system. Users work with the prototype and suggest modifications. The prototype is then enhanced. As soon as the prototype is refined to the point where higher management feels confident that a larger version of the system will succeed, either the prototype can be expanded into the final system or the organization can go full steam ahead with the remaining steps of systems development.

In prototyping, analysis and design generally proceed together in small steps that finally result in a completed system (see Figure IS 1-17). The idea behind the prototyping process is virtually identical to the one described earlier in the chapter for developing vacation plans. Prototyping is highly applicable in situations where user needs are hard to pin down, the system must be developed quickly, and some experimentation is necessary to avoid building the wrong system.

Prototyping and traditional development sometimes are combined in building new systems—for instance, by following the traditional approach but using prototyping during the analysis and design phases to clarify user needs.

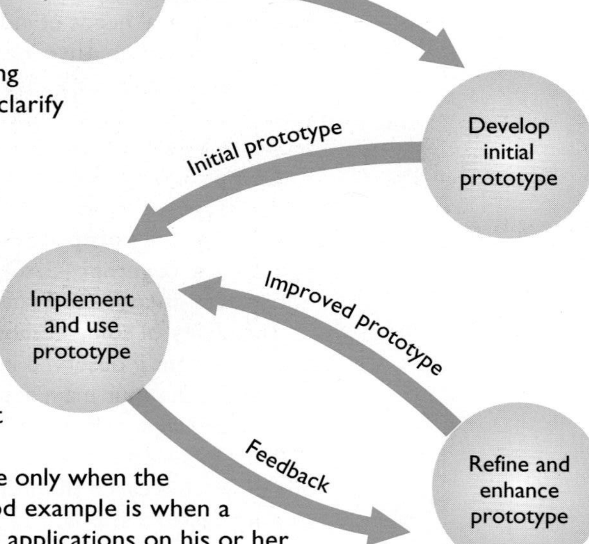

FIGURE IS 1-17

Prototyping. Prototyping is an iterative process. After each prototype is built, the user and analyst try it out together and attempt to improve upon it.

END-USER DEVELOPMENT

End-user development is a systems development effort in which the user is primarily responsible for the development of the system. This is in contrast to other types of development discussed here, in which a qualified computer professional, such as a systems analyst, takes charge of the systems development process.

As you might guess, end-user development is feasible only when the system being acquired is relatively inexpensive. A good example is when a user purchases a microcomputer system and develops applications on his or her

■ **Prototyping.** A systems development alternative whereby a small model, or prototype, of the system is built before a full-scale systems development effort is undertaken. ■ **End-user development.** Systems development carried out by users.

IS

own. In developing the system, the user might follow a prototyping approach or a method similar to traditional development.

Certain dangers exist when users develop their own systems. Among these are users not enforcing proper security measures in their systems, user systems interfering with other systems within the organization, and users building systems that neither they nor the organization can continue to effectively support. Nonetheless, when computer professionals within an organization are too overloaded to build small important systems to help users, end-user development may be the only alternative.

Summary and Key Terms

Types of systems and how organizations build them are the principal subjects of this chapter.

On Systems A **system** is a collection of elements and procedures that interact to accomplish a goal. The function of many systems, whether manual or computerized, is to keep an organization well managed and running smoothly.

Systems development is the process that consists of all activities needed to put a new system into place. Systems development may be required for many reasons—for example, changes in government regulations or the availability of new computer technology.

Organizational Systems There are many types of systems used by businesses and other organizations. **Transaction processing systems** perform tasks that generally involve the tedious record keeping that organizations handle regularly. Among these tasks are payroll, order entry, inventory control, accounts receivable, accounts payable, and general ledger.

Information systems, which fall into two classes—**information reporting systems** and **decision support systems (DSSs)**—give decision makers access to needed information. **Group decision support systems (GDSSs)** refer to DSSs in which several people routinely interact through a computer network in order to solve common problems. **Workflow software** is often used to monitor a GDSS's effectiveness. **Executive information systems (EISs)** are DSSs customized to meet the special needs of individual executives.

The term **office automation (OA)** refers to a wide variety of technologies and processing techniques, including document processing, electronic messaging systems such as **electronic mail (e-mail)** and **facsimile (fax),** desk accessories, decision support tools, **teleconferencing,** and **telecommuting.**

Computers are widely used in industry to improve productivity both at the design stage—through **computer-aided design (CAD)**—and at the manufacturing stage via **computer-aided manufacturing (CAM).** The use of technology to tie together CAD and CAM with other business systems is called **computer-integrated manufacturing (CIM).**

The ability of some computer systems to perform in ways that would be considered intelligent if observed in humans is referred to as **artificial intelligence (AI).** Currently, the four main applications areas of AI techniques are **expert systems,** natural languages, vision systems, and **robotics.**

Most expert systems consist of a **knowledge base** as well as several programs, one of which is called an **inference engine.** Expert systems are commonly built from **expert system shells,** and some rely on a technology known as **neural-net computing.**

Responsibility for Systems Development The *chief information officer,* or someone with a similar title, holds primary responsibility for the overall direction of systems development. The technical details are the responsibility of individual areas—such as the **data processing area** within the **information systems department. Systems analysts** are the people involved most closely with the development of systems from beginning to end. Often, the systems analyst is the **project manager** on the team assigned to the systems project. When a company lacks the in-house expertise, time, or money to do its own computer processing, it often turns to an **outsourcing** company to provide system services.

The Systems Development Life Cycle Systems development often proceeds through five phases: preliminary investigation, systems analysis, system design, system acquisition, and system implementation. These phases are often collectively referred to as the **systems development life cycle (SDLC),** because they describe a system from the time it is first studied until the time it is put into use. When a new business pressure necessitates a change in a system, the steps of the cycle begin anew.

The first thing the systems analyst does when confronted with a new project assignment is conduct a **preliminary investigation,** or *feasibility study.* This investigation addresses the nature of the problem under study, the potential scope of the systems development effort, the possible solutions, and the costs and benefits of these solutions.

Next, the **systems analysis** phase begins. During this phase, the main objectives are to study the application in depth (to find out what work is being done), to assess the needs of users, and to prepare a list of specific requirements that the new system must meet. These objectives are accomplished through fact collection and analysis. A number of tools can help with analysis, including **data flow diagrams** and *checklists.*

The **system design** phase of systems development consists of developing a model of the new system and performing a detailed analysis of benefits and costs.

Once a system has been designed and the required types of software and hardware have been specified, the analyst must decide from which vendors to buy the necessary components. This decision lies at the heart of the **system acquisition** phase. Many buying organizations notify vendors of an intention to acquire a system by submitting a **request for proposal (RFP)** or a **request for quotation (RFQ).** Vendors submitting bids are then commonly evaluated through a **vendor rating system** and then, possibly, a **benchmark test**.

Once arrangements have been made with one or more vendors for delivery of computer resources, the **system implementation** phase begins. This phase includes all the remaining tasks that are necessary to make the system successfully operational, including conversion of data, preparing any equipment to work in the new systems environment, and training.

During and after the five phases of systems development, other important activities will be taking place, including documentation, a postimplementation review, and maintenance.

Approaches to Systems Development In **traditional systems development** the phases of the SDLC are carried out in a predetermined order: preliminary investigation, analysis, design, acquisition, and implementation. The focus in **prototyping** is on developing small models, or prototypes, of the target system in a series of graduated steps. **End-user development** is a systems development approach in which the user is primarily responsible for building the system. This is in contrast to other types of development, in which a qualified computer professional, such as a systems analyst, takes charge of the systems development process.

EXERCISES

1. Fill in the blanks.
   a. Systems that perform record-keeping and other accounting tasks that many organizations handle regularly are called __________.
   b. An information system designed to help people at the highest level of an organization is called a(n) __________.
   c. A(n) __________ holds primary responsibility for systems development in an organization.
   d. A(n) __________ committee composed of executives in key departments and other members of top management normally approves a plan for systems development.
   e. A small model of a new system is often called a(n) __________.
   f. Developing a model of a new system is part of the __________ phase of the systems development life cycle (SDLC).
   g. Benefits that are easy to quantify in dollars are called __________ benefits.
   h. A(n) __________ test consists of running a pilot version of a new system on the hardware and/or software of a vendor whose products are being considered for acquisition.

2. Provided below are several acronyms. Tell what each stands for and, also, define the underlying term or concept.
   a. CIO
   b. CAM
   c. GDSS
   d. AI
   e. CIM
   f. RFP
   g. OA
   h. SDLC

3. Match each term with the description that fits best.
   a. design
   b. implementation
   c. preliminary investigation
   d. analysis
   e. acquisition

_____ The final phase of the SDLC
_____ The phase of the SDLC that involves studying the system environment in depth
_____ The phase of the SDLC that involves RFP or RFQ preparation, vendor rating systems, and benchmark tests
_____ The first phase of the SDLC
_____ The phase of the SDLC that follows systems analysis

4. Explain the differences between the following pairs of terms:
   a. Systems analysis and system design
   b. Programming group and operations group
   c. Accounts receivable and accounts payable
   d. Request for quotation and request for proposal
   e. Computer-aided manufacturing and computer-integrated manufacturing
   f. Workgroup computing and workflow software

5. Define, in your own words, each of the following terms.
   a. Outsourcing
   b. Inference engine
   c. Knowledge base
   d. Vendor rating system
   e. Expert system

6. Name the principal function performed by each of the transaction processing subsystems covered in the chapter.

7. What are the similarities and differences among the following types of information systems?
   a. Information reporting system
   b. Decision support system
   c. Group decision support system
   d. Executive information system

8. In the list below are several descriptions of activities performed by computer systems or by people working with computer systems. Put each type of activity into one of the following categories—transaction processing systems, information systems, design and manufacturing systems, systems development.
   a. CAD
   b. Accounts receivable
   c. A manager receiving the same type of report every month
   d. Prototyping
   e. A person buying a software package on the World Wide Web
   f. A group of bank personnel collaborating on the approval of a personal loan on their desktop computers
   g. A person using a computer system to track a package to see if it's been delivered
   h. An architect using a computer system to plan the layout of an office building

9. Answer the following questions about telecommuting:
   a. What types of workers are likely to telecommute?

b. What incentives would induce an organization to encourage telecommuting?
c. What disadvantages are there to telecommuting?

10. People in organizations frequently complain that they don't have up-to-date computing equipment. Is this a symptom or a problem? Defend your answer.

1. This System Does Not Compute Frequently reported in the press are examples of computer systems that fail because they were not completely thought out. As this book was being written, for instance, a story was reported about a ski area that installed a computer system to optionally charge each skier on a per-run basis. Skiers selecting the per-run option got special tickets that were machine-processed at lift sites as they were about to take another run down a slope.

The system failed for many reasons. Skiers had to wait in long lines to get to the machines. What's more, skiers had to physically contort themselves and, also, take their gloves off—often, in bitterly cold weather—to get tickets processed. As if these problems weren't enough, some skiers wound up paying far more than they would have for a full-day ticket at the end of the day; the system did not stop charging them even after they had paid a reasonable maximum amount.

For this project, find at least one poorly designed system that is written up in a computer publication and report to your class about it. Be sure to tell why the system failed and to explain what the designers might have done differently to get the system to work.

2. Research an Information System Almost all organizations require information systems to run effectively. For an organization with which you are familiar—such as your college or university or the company for which you work—pick a computer-based information system that's currently in place and write a three-to-five-page paper about it. Be sure to cover in your paper the following items.

a. Who are the users of the system and what are the particular needs of each user group? How many users of various types are there?
b. What types of useful outputs does the system provide? How are the outputs made available—say, on a screen or in hard-copy reports? How often are the outputs updated?
c. What are the goals of the system? How do the outputs relate to the goals of the system?
d. What types of processing is done from the inputs the system receives?
e. What types of hardware and software does the system use?
f. In your estimation, can the system be improved? If so, how?

3. Customer DSSs A growing area within information systems is customer decision support. Customer DSSs enable a company's customers to use their own computers or Touch-Tone phones to call up the company's computer systems to get valuable information. For instance, a system recently installed by Federal Express allows the shipper's customers to trace package deliveries over the Internet. For this project, identify three additional customer DSSs, describing in a few brief sentences the companies that run them and the benefits they provide to both the companies and its customers.

4. IS Jobs Computer jobs in the information systems (IS) area are often listed in computer newspapers—such as *Computerworld*—and over the Internet. Many publications also frequently report the job areas that are in the highest demand. For this project, write a three-to-five-page paper telling which jobs in the computer field appear to be in high demand right now. Also tell what type of facts you are using on which to base your conclusions.

Some job-related Internet sites that you might want to visit are listed in the accompanying figure. Also think about using a search engine to find more. For instance, in Yahoo!, click on the "Business and the Economy" category in the main menu.

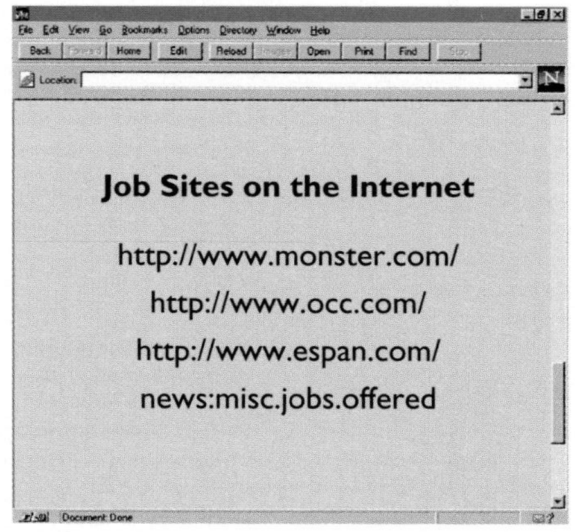

Job Sites on the Internet
http://www.monster.com/
http://www.occ.com/
http://www.espan.com/
news:misc.jobs.offered
Document: Done

5. Expert Systems Examples of expert systems in organizations are frequently covered in the press. For this project, find an example of an expert system that is being used by an organization and report to the class about it. As part of your report, be sure to cover the knowledge base the system is using and some of the rules that are being used to make decisions. Also, be sure to report what types of benefits the expert system is providing.

6. Outsourcing Examples of companies outsourcing computer work are frequently covered in the press. For this project, find an example of a company that is outsourcing computer work and report to the class about it. As part of your report, be sure to cover the following.

a. The name of the company having work outsourced and, also, the name of the company that is providing the outsourcing service.
b. The nature of the work being outsourced.
c. The types of benefits the company having the work outsourced expects to get out of the arrangement.

(*Hint:* Journals such as *Computerworld* and *Information Week* are especially good sources of information for this project.)

7. Information Technology and Politics Companies everywhere are increasingly outsourcing jobs to foreign countries. Today there is concern in the United States and Canada that manufacturing jobs will be lost to low-wage countries such as Mexico and to countries offshore, such as the Philippines or Taiwan. In nearby Mexico, blue-collar work can often be done for about one-sixth the price of the same work in the United States—perhaps even with better quality. Write a three-to-five-page paper that addresses how information technology has contributed to the trend to move jobs off native soil. Be sure to describe how this trend may have both positive and negative aspects. If you wish, take a position on the matter and defend it.

8. New Key Terms It's impossible for a textbook of this sort to cover every important technology or term regarding systems in organizations. Several important terms are listed below that are not covered in the chapter. Use either library-journal or Internet research to determine what any three of these terms (or pairs of terms) mean, and write out a one-to-three-sentence explanation describing each one in your own words.

a. Reengineering
b. Top-down versus bottom-up systems development
c. Just-in-time inventory (JIT)
d. Knowledge worker
e. Structured versus unstructured decisions

9. Expert System Shells Shell programs are especially popular for developing expert systems. For this project, find the name of a company that makes an expert-system shell product and report to the class about it. In your report, be sure to cover the following questions:

a. What is the name of the product, and how much does it cost? What is the name of the company that makes the product?
b. For what particular types of expert systems applications is the product designed?
c. Identify as many important product features or specifications as you can—for instance, the amount of RAM or hard disk required, the maximum number of rules that can be accommodated, and so on.

10. Internet Sites for System Builders A variety of sites are available on the Internet that relate to the topics discussed in this chapter. Visit any one of the sites listed in the accompanying figure and report its contents to the class.

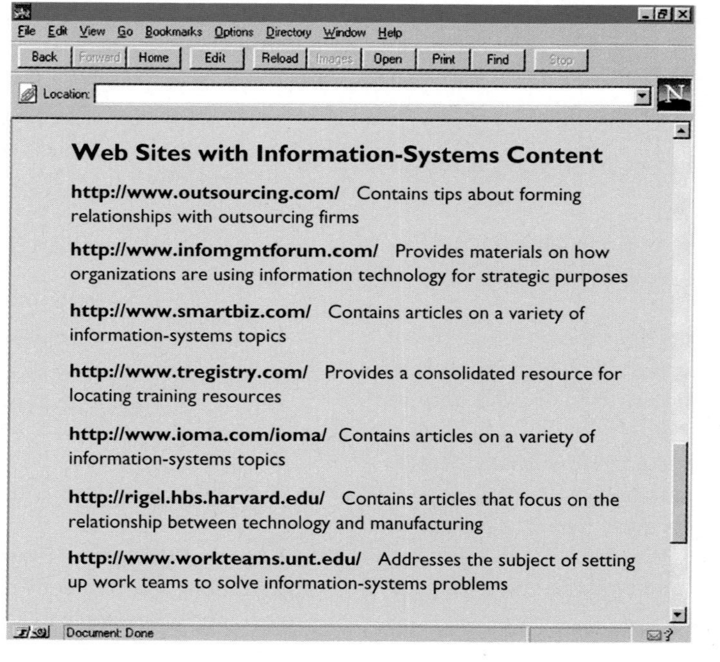

File Edit View Go Bookmarks Options Directory Window Help
Back Forward Home Edit Reload Images Open Print Find Stop
Location:
Web Sites with Information-Systems Content
http://www.outsourcing.com/ Contains tips about forming relationships with outsourcing firms
http://www.infomgmtforum.com/ Provides materials on how organizations are using information technology for strategic purposes
http://www.smartbiz.com/ Contains articles on a variety of information-systems topics
http://www.tregistry.com/ Provides a consolidated resource for locating training resources
http://www.ioma.com/ioma/ Contains articles on a variety of information-systems topics
http://rigel.hbs.harvard.edu/ Contains articles that focus on the relationship between technology and manufacturing
http://www.workteams.unt.edu/ Addresses the subject of setting up work teams to solve information-systems problems
Document: Done

IS 2

Applications Software Development

Outline

Learning Objectives

After completing this chapter, you will be able to:

1. Identify and describe the activities involved in applications software development.
2. Recognize why it may be more advantageous to buy software than to develop it in-house.
3. Describe a number of productivity tools used by computer professionals to develop applications.
4. Identify several of the language options available to code programs.
5. Explain some of the activities involved with debugging, maintaining, documenting, and ensuring quality among programs.
6. Explain the role and importance of rapid development.

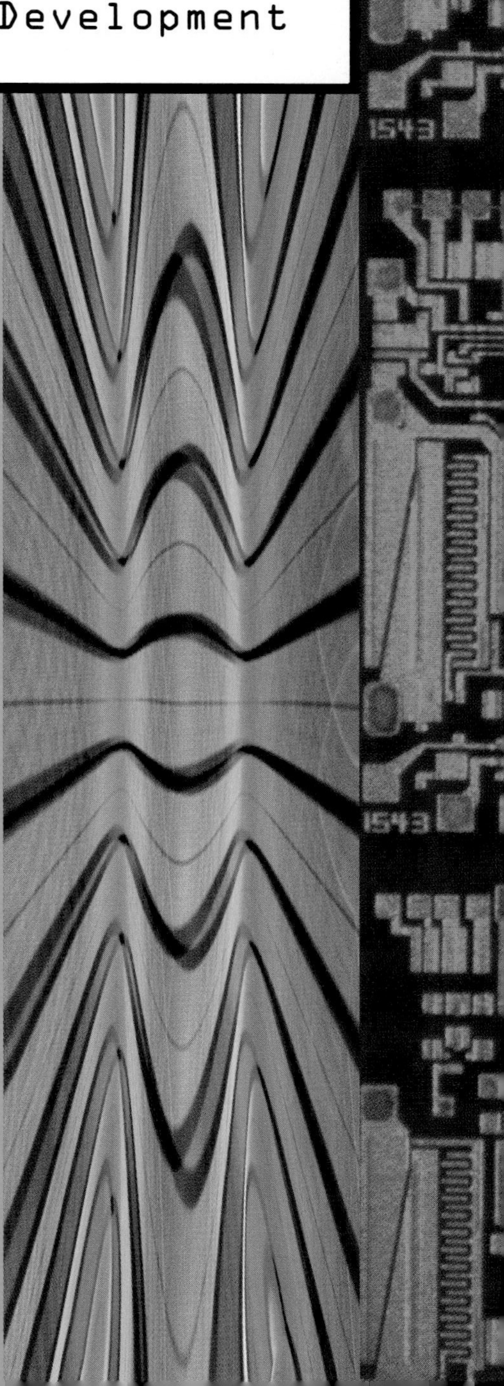

Overview

If you wanted to build a house, you'd probably begin with some research and planning. You might speak to various people about home design, draw up some floor plans, estimate the cost of materials, and so on. In other words, you wouldn't start digging a hole and pouring concrete on the very first day. Creating successful applications programs for a computer system also requires considerable planning.

Computer professionals and users need to develop or acquire new applications from time to time. They do this by either using a traditional programming language or an easier-to-use software development tool, or alternatively, by attempting to get what they need by purchasing a finished product outright. Just as you can acquire a house custom constructed or assembled from prefabricated pieces and do the work yourself or farm it out to others, you can acquire applications in much the same way. A variety of tools exist to assist you with each of these options. In the previous chapter we spent a great deal of time looking at developing entire computer systems. In this chapter we look specifically at practices for developing the applications programs that make up a system.

The chapter opens by covering the types of activities that need to be considered when new applications programs are required. From there, we turn to the make-or-buy decision, which deals with choosing either to develop applications on your own or to buy them prepackaged. Next we address three of the chapter's most important topics: program design, programming languages, and program coding. Then we turn to program debugging and testing, maintenance, documentation, and quality assurance. The chapter closes with a brief introduction to rapid development.

Program Development Activities

A professional programmer or a user can acquire applications programs in two principal ways: (1) developing them from scratch and (2) buying them in finished form from an outside source. The method chosen generally depends on factors such as the quality of software available in the marketplace, the nature and importance of the application, the availability and capability of programmers, and time and cost constraints. Some programs, such as word processors, require teams of professionally trained people working years to build. Others, such as the macros used to style reports in a certain way, can be developed in less than an hour by many ordinary users with off-the-shelf, office-software tools. In this chapter, we'll be addressing primarily the types of applications developed by professionals.

The steps associated with creating applications programs are collectively referred to as **applications software development.** Applications software development often begins with the program specifications that are developed during the systems analysis and system design phases of the systems development life cycle (SDLC), which we discussed in detail in Chapter IS 1. Program specifications cover program outputs, the processing to take place, storage requirements, and program inputs. Applications software development primarily consists of the following four activities or steps:

- PROGRAM DESIGN Planning the specific software solution to meet the program specifications.
- PROGRAM CODING Writing the program.
- PROGRAM DEBUGGING AND TESTING Finding and eliminating errors in the program.
- PROGRAM MAINTENANCE Making changes to the program over time.

■ **Applications software development.** The process of designing, coding, debugging and testing, maintaining, and documenting applications software.

While each of these critical development activities is taking place, there should be ongoing documentation. *Documentation* is the process of writing up the details about what the program does and how it works. In a typical organization, the responsibility for successful program development is the job of systems analysts and programmers.

Systems analysts, or simply *analysts,* specify the requirements that the applications software must meet. They work with users to assess applications needs and translate those needs into a plan. Then they determine the specific resources required to implement the plan. For every program, the analysts create a set of technical specifications outlining what the program must do, the timetable for completing the program, which programming language to use, how the program will be tested before being put into use, and what documentation is required.

Programmers then use these specifications to code a software solution—a series of statements in a programming language. *Maintenance programmers* monitor the finished program on an ongoing basis, correcting errors and altering the program as technology or business conditions change.

The Make-or-Buy Decision

Once a set of technical requirements for a software solution to a problem has been established, it must be decided whether the programs should be created in-house or acquired from a software vendor. This consideration is frequently called the *make-or-buy decision.*

The "Make" Alternative If an organization decides to develop its own applications software, then it can do so in either of two ways. The first option is using a traditional programming language such as COBOL or C. This option usually offers the most control over the tasks a program performs, but applications often take longer to develop and maintain. The second option is using the proprietary language that comes with a specific software product—say, the Visual BASIC language accompanying the Microsoft Office suite of applications. This latter option is becoming very popular today, because doing work faster and less expensively are becoming increasingly important priorities.

The "Buy" Alternative A choice often made by organizations is to select products that require virtually no in-house programming. During the past several years, prewritten applications programs for such tasks as payroll, accounting, financial planning, project management, and scores of others have become more widely available from software publishers. These programs, called **applications packages,** generally consist of an integrated set of ready-to-run programs, documentation, and possibly training modules. Because they often provide immediate results at a cost far lower than that of developing similar software from scratch, applications packages are becoming increasingly popular. It is not always possible to find an applications package that exactly meets an organization's specific needs—in which case, the "make" alternative is preferable.

Program Design

In the design stage of applications software development, the program specifications developed by the systems analyst are used to spell out as precisely as possible the

■ **Systems analyst.** A person who studies systems in an organization in order to determine what actions need to be taken and how these actions may best be achieved with computer resources. ■ **Programmer.** A person whose job is to write, maintain, and test computer programs. ■ **Applications package.** A fourth-generation-language product that when the user sets a few parameters becomes a finished applications program ready to meet specific needs.

nature of the required programming solution. The design, or plan, derived from these specifications must address all the tasks that programs must do as well as how to organize or sequence these tasks when coding programs. Only when the design is complete does the next stage—the actual program coding—begin.

PROGRAM DESIGN TOOLS

Program design tools are essentially planning tools. They consist of various kinds of diagrams, charts, and tables that outline either the organization of program tasks or the steps the program will follow. Once a program has been coded and implemented, program design tools serve as excellent documentation. Three widely used program design tools are structure charts, flowcharts, and pseudocode. We will cover each of these next.

STRUCTURE CHARTS

Structure charts depict the overall organization of a program. They show how the individual program segments, or modules, are defined and how they relate to one another. Figure IS 2-1 illustrates a structure chart for a payroll application.

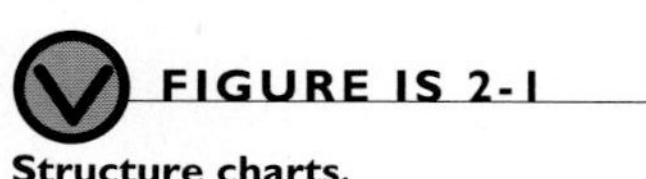

FIGURE IS 2-1

Structure charts.

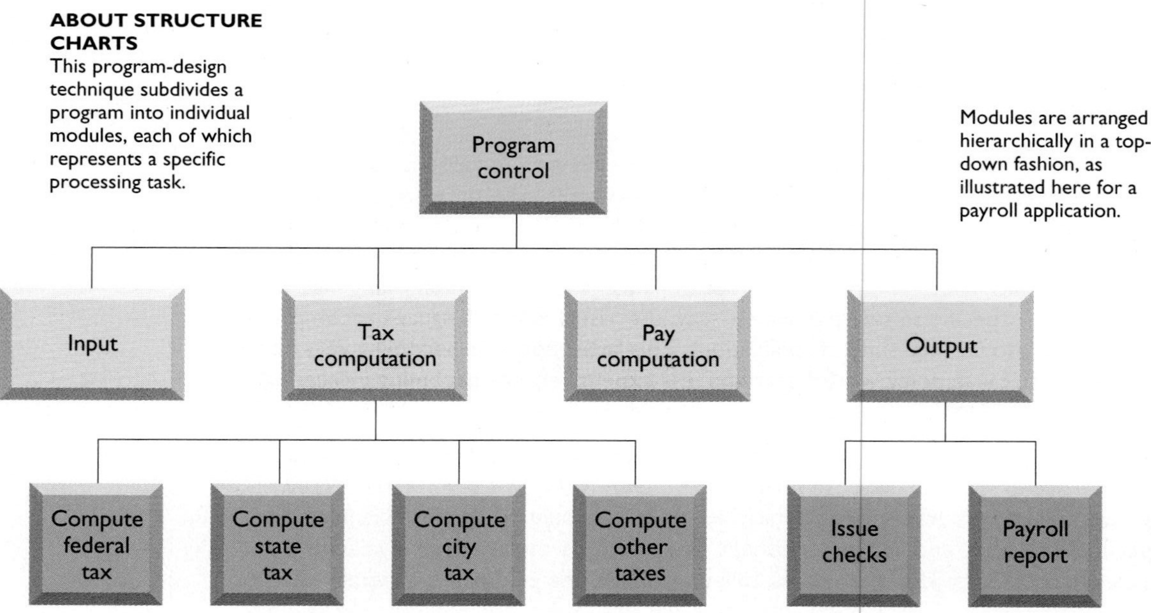

A typical structure chart, with its several rows of boxes connected by lines, looks like a corporate organization chart. Each box represents a program *module*—that is, a set of logically related operations that perform a well-defined task. The modules in the upper rows serve control functions, directing the program to process modules under them as appropriate. The modules in the lower boxes serve specific processing functions. These latter modules do all the program work. The lines connecting the boxes indicate the relationship between higher-level and lower-level modules.

Structure charts embody a **top-down design** philosophy—that is, modules are conceptualized first at the highest levels of the hierarchy and then at progressively lower levels. Put another way, the broad functions that are first defined at the highest levels are broken down further, level by level, into well-defined subfunctions. This is

---

■ **Structure chart.** A program design tool that shows the hierarchical relationship between program modules. ■ **Top-down design.** A structured design philosophy whereby a program or system is subdivided into well-defined modules and organized into a hierarchy.

similar to what happens in a corporate organization chart—broad functions such as marketing, production, information systems, and the like are defined at the highest levels of the chart, and job areas falling under those functions follow. For instance, under information systems might fall operations, programming, and systems analysis and design; under programming, responsibilities may be further divided into applications programming and systems programming.

Logically speaking, establishing how a program is organized is the first step in program design. Once all functions of the program are carefully laid out in a structure chart or some equivalent tool, the next step of design—showing the step-by-step logic that is to take place in each module—can be started. This is where program flowcharts and pseudocode are useful.

PROGRAM FLOWCHARTS

Program flowcharts use *geometric symbols,* such as those in Figure IS 2-2, and familiar *relational operators,* such as those in Figure IS 2-3, to graphically portray the sequence of steps involved in a program. The steps in a flowchart occur in the same logical sequence that their corresponding program statements follow in the program. To help you understand what the symbols and operators mean and see how to use them, let's consider an example.

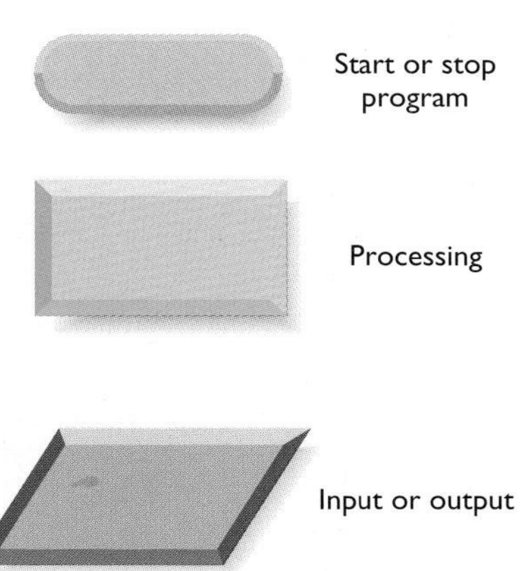

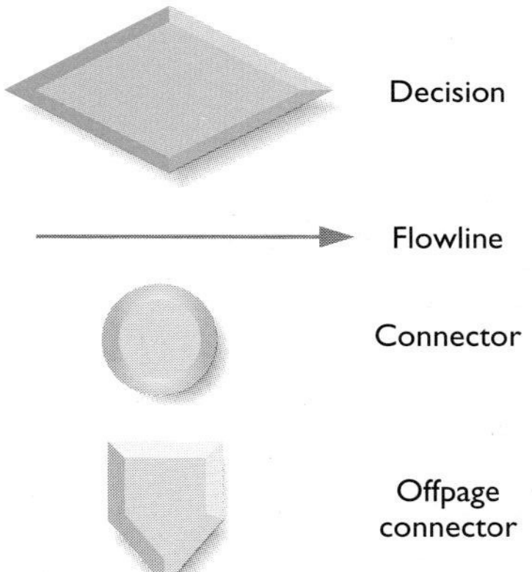

FIGURE IS 2-2
Program flowchart symbols.

Scanning a File for Employees with Certain Characteristics A common activity in information processing is scanning an employee file for people with certain characteristics. Suppose, for example, a company's human-resources department wants a printed list of all employees with computer experience and at least five years of company service. A flowchart that shows how to accomplish this task and also totals the number of employees who meet these criteria is shown in Figure IS 2-4.

This particular flowchart uses five symbols: start/stop, processing, decision, connector, and input/output. The lines with arrows that link the symbols are called *flowlines;* they indicate the flow of logic in the flowchart.

Every flowchart begins and ends with an oval-shaped *start/stop symbol.* The first of these symbols in the program contains the word *Start,* and the last contains the word *Stop.* The diamond-shaped *decision symbol* always indicates a question, which generally will have only two possible answers—yes or no (true or false). Decision symbols should always have one flowline entering and two flowlines (representing the two possible outcomes) exiting.

The rectangular *processing symbol* contains an action that needs to be taken—for example, "Set counter to 0" and "Add 1 to counter." The *connector symbol* provides

Operator	**Meaning**
<	Less than
<= or ≤	Less than or equal to
>	Greater than
>= or ≥	Greater than or equal to
=	Equal to
≠ or <> or ><	Not equal to

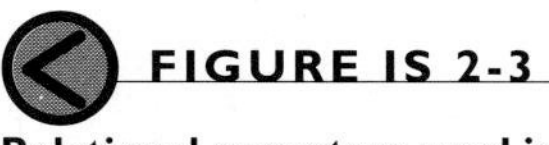
FIGURE IS 2-3
Relational operators used in flowcharts.

■ **Program flowchart.** A visual design tool showing step by step how a computer program will process data.

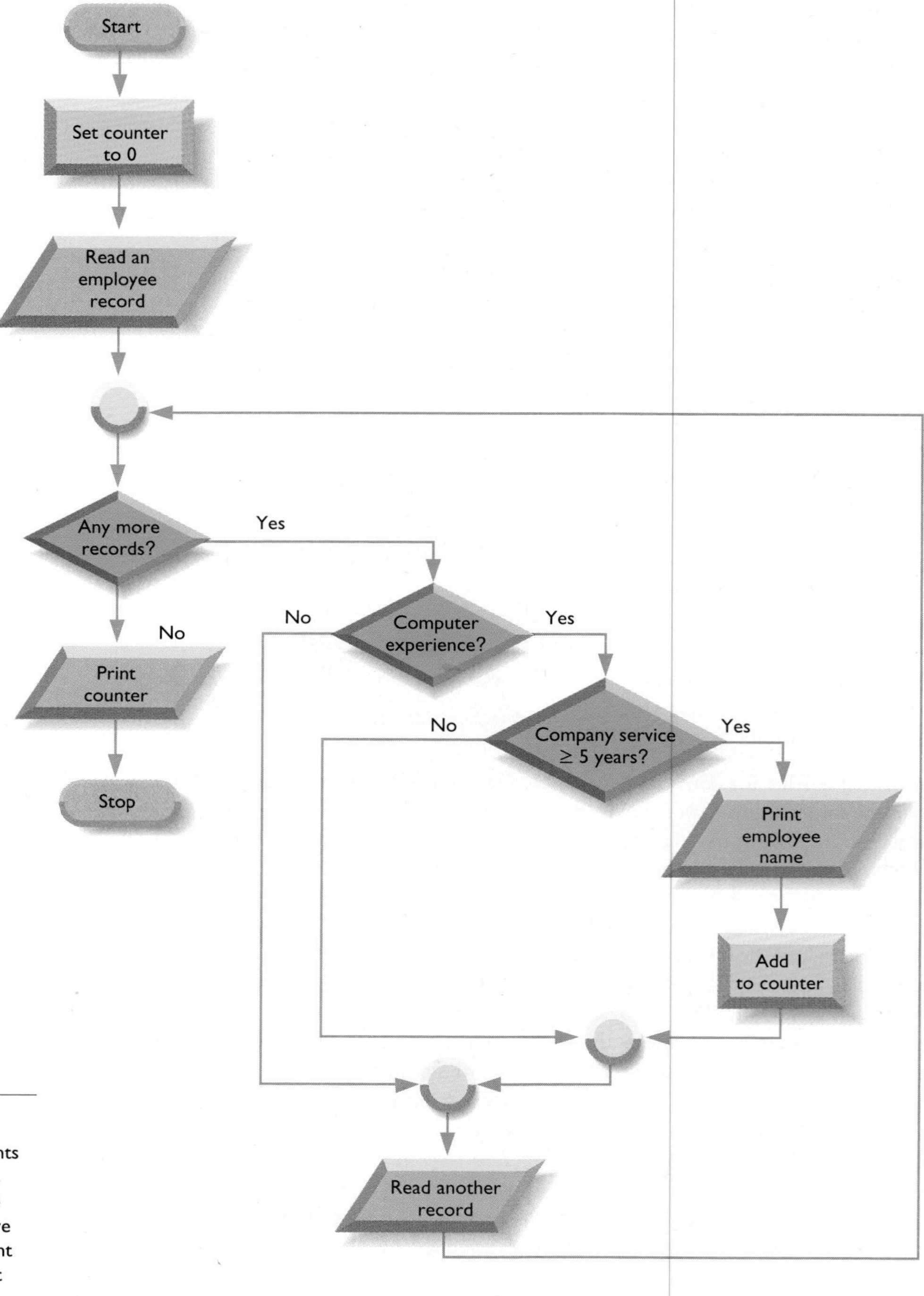

FIGURE IS 2-4

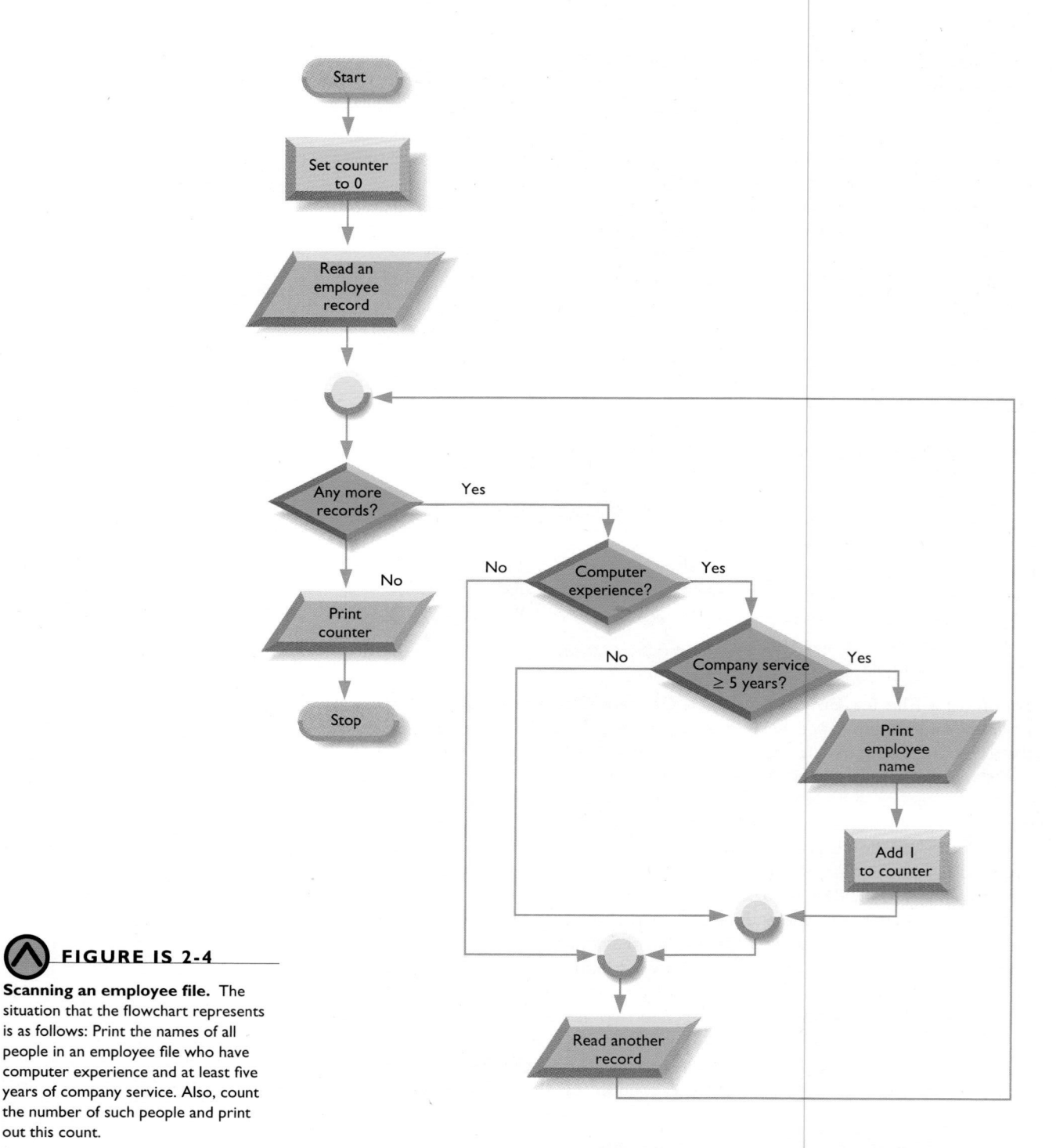

Scanning an employee file. The situation that the flowchart represents is as follows: Print the names of all people in an employee file who have computer experience and at least five years of company service. Also, count the number of such people and print out this count.

a logical meeting point for several flowlines. The *input/output symbol* enables the logical process depicted in the flowchart to either accept data or output them.

The flowchart in Figure IS 2-4 involves a looping operation. We read a record, inspect it, and take an action; then read another record, inspect it, and take another action; and so on until the file is exhausted. When the computer reads a record, as indicated by the input/output symbol, it brings it into its memory and stores its contents (or field values). If a record meets both search criteria, we increment a counter by 1. After the last record is read and processed, we print the value of the counter and then end the program.

The Three Basic Control Structures Beginning in the 1960s, a number of researchers began to stress program design (planning) and the merits of separating the design process from the actual program coding. Such a division of labor is a natural one, just as you have architects who design buildings and separate construction crews who work from specifications to erect them. Many of the proposed ideas of the researchers caught on, and over the past few decades a group of methods has evolved that has made program design more systematic and the programs themselves easier to understand and maintain. These methods usually are grouped together under the term **structured programming.**

Advocates of structured programming have shown that any program can be constructed out of three fundamental **control structures:** sequence, selection, and looping. Figure IS 2-5 illustrates these structures using flowchart symbols.

FIGURE IS 2-5

The three fundamental control structures of structured programming. Note that each structure has only one entry point and only one exit point.

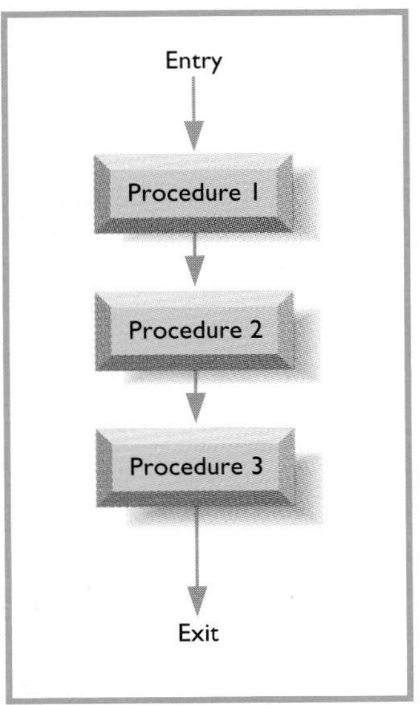

Sequence

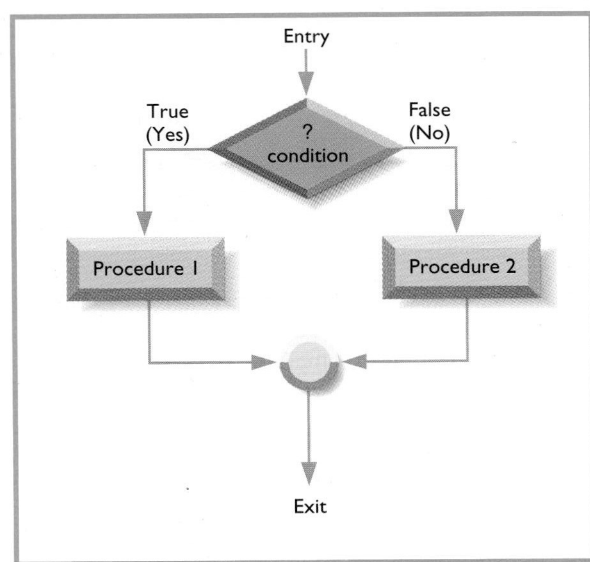

Selection (If-Then-Else)

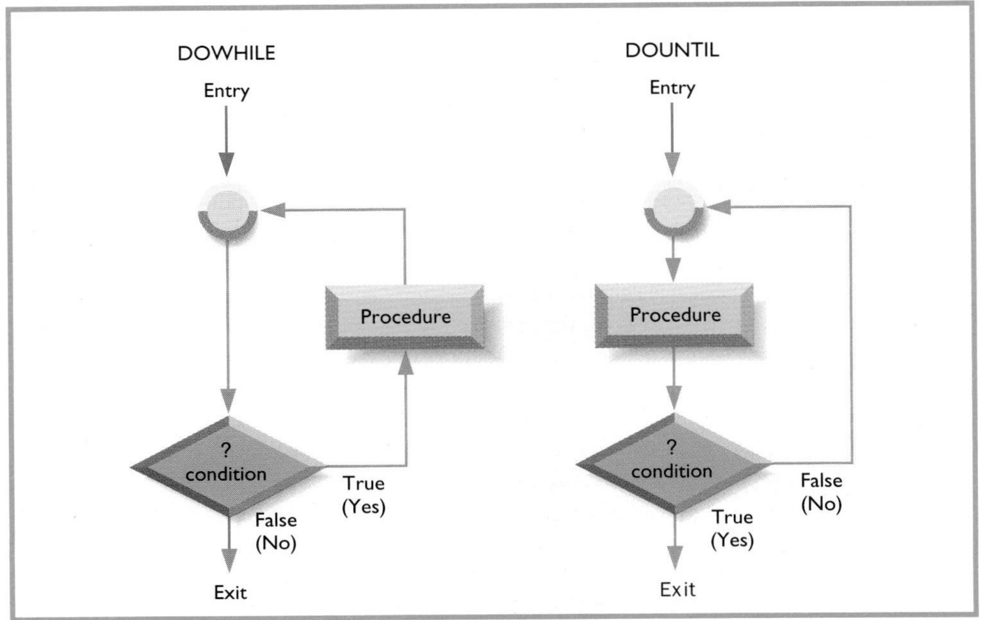

Looping (Iteration)

- **Structured programming.** An approach to program design that makes program code more systematic and maintainable.
- **Control structure.** A pattern for controlling the flow of logic in a computer program.

A **sequence control structure** is simply a series of procedures that follow one another. A **selection** (or **if-then-else) control structure** involves a choice: *If* a certain condition is true, *then* follow one procedure; *else*, if false, follow another. A *loop* is an operation that repeats until a certain condition is met. As Figure IS 2-5 shows, a **looping** (or **iteration) control structure** can take one of two forms: DOWHILE or DOUNTIL.

With **DOWHILE,** a loop is executed as long as a certain condition is true ("do *while* true"). With **DOUNTIL,** a loop continues as long as a certain condition is false ("do *until* true"). You should also note another major difference between these two forms of looping. With DOUNTIL, the loop procedure will always be executed at least once, because the procedure appears before any test is made about whether to exit the loop. With DOWHILE, the procedure may not be executed at all, because the loop-exit test appears before the procedure.

The three basic control structures are the major building blocks for structured program flowcharts and pseudocode.

The Case Structure By nesting two or more if-then-elses, you can build a fourth structure known as the **case control structure.** For example, in Figure IS 2-4, the two individual choices—"Computer experience?" and "Company service ≥ 5 years?"—result in the following four possibilities, or cases:

- CASE I: No computer experience, company service < 5 years
- CASE II: No computer experience, company service ≥ 5 years
- CASE III: Computer experience, company service < 5 years
- CASE IV: Computer experience, company service ≥ 5 years

One Entry Point, One Exit Point An extremely important characteristic of the control structures discussed so far is that each permits only one entry point into and one exit point out of any structure. This property is sometimes called the **one-entry-point/one-exit-point rule.** Observe the marked entry and exit points in Figure IS 2-5. The one-entry-point/one-exit-point convention encourages a modular building-block programming approach that makes programs more readable and easier to maintain.

PSEUDOCODE

An alternative to the flowchart that has become extremely popular in recent years is **pseudocode.** This structured technique uses Englishlike statements in place of the flowchart's graphic symbols. An example of pseudocode is shown in Figure IS 2-6.

Pseudocode looks more like a program than a flowchart. In fact, it's often easier to code a program from pseudocode than from a flowchart, because the former provides a codelike outline of the processing to take place. As a result, the program designer has more control over the end product—the program itself. Also unlike a flowchart, pseudocode is relatively easy to modify and can be embedded into the program as comments. However, flowcharts, being visual, are sometimes better than pseudocode for designing logically complex problems.

No standard rules exist for writing pseudocode, but Figure IS 2-7 describes one set of rules that has a wide following. Note that all words relating to the three control

■ **Sequence control structure.** The control structure used to represent operations that take place sequentially. ■ **Selection (if-then-else) control structure.** The control structure used to represent a decision operation. ■ **Looping (iteration) control structure.** The control structure used to represent a looping operation. ■ **DOWHILE control structure.** A looping control structure in which the looping continues as long as a certain condition is true ("do *while* true"). ■ **DOUNTIL control structure.** A looping control structure in which the looping continues as long as a certain condition is false ("do *until* true"). ■ **Case control structure.** A control structure that can be formed by nesting two or more selection control structures. ■ **One-entry-point/one-exit-point rule.** A rule stating that each program control structure will have only one entry point into it and one exit point out of it. ■ **Pseudocode.** A technique for structured program design that uses Englishlike statements to outline the logic of a program.

```
Start
Counter = 0
Read a record
DOWHILE there are more records to process
   IF computer experience
      IF company service ≥ 5 years
         Print employee name
         Increment Counter
      ELSE
         Next statement
      END IF
   ELSE
      Next statement
   END IF
   Read another record
END DO
Print Counter
Stop
```

Pseudocode for solving the employee file problem of Figure IS 2-4. The problem requires printing the names of all people in an employee file with computer experience and at least five years of company service. A count of the number of such people is also included as output.

structures of structured programming are capitalized and form a "sandwich" around other processing steps, which are indented. As Figure IS 2-6 shows, indentation is also used for readability. The keywords *Start* and *Stop* are often used to begin and end pseudocode.

Action Diagrams Pseudocode is widely employed in the creation of **action diagrams**—a tool used to develop applications programs rapidly while online to the

Sequence Control Structure

BEGIN processing task
  Processing steps
END processing task

The keywords BEGIN and END are always capitalized and tiered. Processing tasks and steps are normally written in lowercase letters. The steps should make up a well-defined block of code and be sandwiched between the keywords BEGIN and END.

Selection Control Structure

IF condition
  Processing steps
ELSE
  Processing steps
END IF

The keywords IF, ELSE, and END IF are always capitalized and vertically aligned. The condition and processing steps normally are written in lowercase letters. The processing steps are indented from the keywords in the manner illustrated.

Looping Control Structure

DOWHILE	DOUNTIL

DOWHILE condition
  Processing steps
END DO
	DOUNTIL condition
	  Processing steps
	END DO

The keywords DOWHILE (or DOUNTIL) and END DO are always capitalized and vertically aligned. The condition and processing steps follow the same lowercase convention and indentation rules as the selection control structure.

Some rules for pseudocode. In addition to the rules shown here governing program control structures, pseudocode often begins with the keyword *Start* and ends with the keyword *Stop*.

IS

■ **Action diagram.** A programming tool that helps programmers code structured programs.

CPU. Action diagrams are composed of brackets into which pseudocode-like statements are written (see Figure IS 2-8). These statements, from which the computer is automatically able to develop executable code, are usually created with an *action-diagram editor.* Each control structure used in the diagram—sequence, selection, looping, or case—has its own set of brackets.

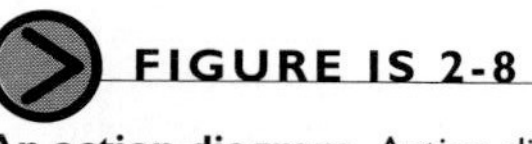

FIGURE IS 2-8

An action diagram. Action diagrams, which are created and modified with a special editor, are used to design and code pseudocode-like programs that are capable of being executed.

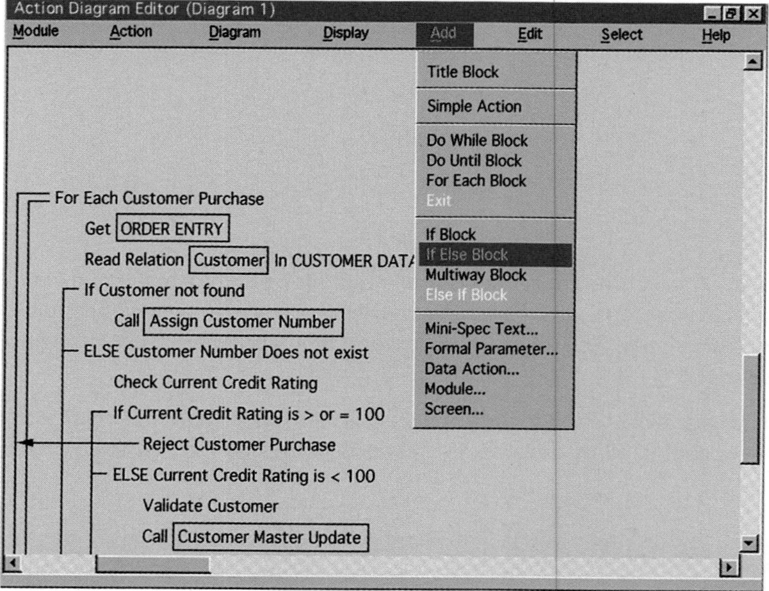

When the programmer signals that a particular control structure is to be used, the action-diagram editor creates both the appropriate pseudocode keywords and brackets. As programmers provide various conditions or field names at certain places within the brackets, the editor checks to see that the code is both valid and consistent with the existing code for the application. It does the latter by referring to the appropriate entries in the application's active data dictionary. If a problem exists, the editor will issue a warning or error message. Once an action diagram has been completed, it is automatically translated into executable code with a *code generator.* Action diagrams are an example of CASE tools, which are covered at the end of the chapter.

Programming Languages

An important decision that must be made during the development of a program is the choice of a programming language. A **programming language** is a set of rules used to write computer programs. You can write a program with your word processor or, as is more commonly the case, by acquiring a software package whose principal purpose is to enable you to develop computer programs in a given language. Such a package contains the language translator necessary to convert the program into machine language, and it also includes a variety of tools that make it easy to develop, maintain, and manage computer programs.

Programming languages are commonly divided into three classes: low-level, high-level, and very-high-level (fourth-generation) languages.

■ **Programming language.** A set of rules used to write computer programs.

Time Bombs That Produced Unexpected Results

Often, when beta programs are manufactured, they contain pieces of code called time bombs that forbid the program to work after a certain date. This practice is followed for any or all of a variety of reasons—for example, to force beta testers to upgrade to the fully developed product when it is released, to cut down on software piracy, or to prevent partially developed forms of the program from later creating problems that could cause the company any sort of embarrassment.

When the finished programs are released, these time bombs are supposed to be removed, but occasionally something goes wrong and the code stays in. When this happens, of course, the software that is sold in stores or over the Internet will not work after a certain date, and users get angry. Such an event happened, for instance, when Novell first released PerfectOffice 3.0. The first 100,000 copies contained a time bomb that prevented the program from being installed after December 31, 1995. Adobe Systems ran into a similar problem with PhotoShop 3.0, and it had to recall the product and ship release 3.01 to fix the glitch.

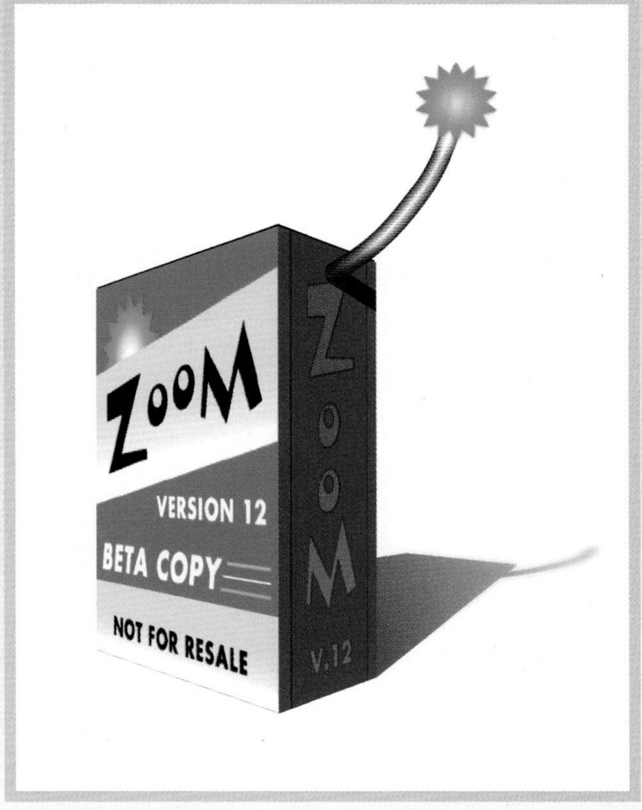

useful. For instance, if new types of data are added to a database and existing programs must be modified to use these data, program maintenance is necessary. Program maintenance is also commonly triggered by software revisions, new equipment announcements, and changes in the way business is conducted.

Program maintenance is costly to organizations. It has been estimated that many organizations spend well over half of their programming time just maintaining existing applications programs. One of the major reasons why such tools as coding standards, fourth-generation languages, object-oriented languages and reusable code, and data dictionaries are so popular today is because these tools can result in lower maintenance costs.

Program Documentation

Program **documentation** includes hard-copy or electronic manuals that enable users, developers, and operators to interact successfully with a program. If you've ever had the frustration of trying to get something to work from poorly written instructions, you can appreciate how valuable good documentation can be.

User documentation normally consists of a user's manual. This manual may provide instructions for running the program, a description of software commands, several useful examples of applications, and a troubleshooting guide to help with difficulties.

■ **Documentation.** A detailed written description of a program, procedure, or system.

The trend in user documentation is to make it electronic and to bundle it with tutorials and training.

Developer documentation usually consists of any tools that will simplify the creation or maintenance of applications. These might include program examples, a description of the design tools incorporated into the product, instructions for debugging and testing, maintenance tips, and so on. Developer documentation is also increasingly becoming electronic.

Operator documentation includes online and hard-copy manuals that assist machine operators in setting up hardware devices, learning the ins and outs of successful hardware operation, and diagnosing machine malfunctions. Operator documentation is machine dependent, and, unless you have a good grounding in computer fundamentals, it can be difficult to read through.

While companies should document as many useful facts as they can about their programs, there are cases where certain types information may unravel in controversy if made public (see User Solution IS 2-1).

Quality Assurance

Quality assurance, as regards program development, refers to the process of making sure quality programs are written in a quality way. The quality assurance function in many firms is carried out by a staff that's charged with making an independent, unbiased audit of program-development operations.

A major focus in quality assurance is on the outputs produced by programs. Not only are outputs checked for accuracy, but they are also scrutinized for completeness and timeliness. Are all of the outputs required by users present? Is the program going to provide information to users when it's needed? System messages to the user are also evaluated to ensure programs are easy to use.

Program development activities are another major target in the quality-assurance effort. Here, it is important to ascertain that programs have been developed using acceptable design and coding standards and that they have been properly tested and documented.

Quality-assurance specialists also look closely at program and system security. It is critical that programs and their data be protected from tampering and unauthorized use and that proper program controls be in place to safeguard against problem situations.

Rapid Development

If you ask most managers when they need to get programs delivered to users, you'll get an answer such as "yesterday." The sad truth in business today is that developers are typically under tremendous time pressure to get finished work out the door. In some extreme cases, getting product into the user's hands is not just a priority; it is *the* priority. **Rapid development** refers to a group of program-development methods in which a major goal is meeting an extremely tight timetable.

Some of the tenets of rapid development are focusing on schedule-oriented practices, using people who find working at a grueling pace a challenge and motivating those people properly, applying appropriate development methodologies, managing risks carefully, and avoiding common development mistakes (see Figure IS 2-19). Two classes of tools used in rapid development are CASE and rapid-application-development (RAD) products.

■ **Quality assurance.** The process of making sure quality programs are written in a quality way. ■ **Rapid development.** A program-development approach in which a principal objective is delivering a finished product quickly.

Using Software to Spot Potential Deadbeats

Statistical models have long been used with computers to make predictions. Now, the two are teaming up in yet another new but highly controversial way: trying to spot people who are likely to default on loans made to them. Thus, if you miss a payment on a car you bought two years ago—even though got through 20 other payments successfully—you may get a bill collector in your face sooner than you think. That's possibly because a computer has guessed your salary, looked up your skill base or your age, or deduced some other combination of characteristics about you and figured you stood a fair chance of becoming a deadbeat. Companies using such models are naturally tight lipped about how they work. Using some descriptive or predictive measures border on discrimination, which, of course, is blatantly illegal.

Computer-Aided Software Engineering (CASE) **CASE (computer-aided software engineering)** tools—or *software engineering workbenches*—refer broadly to products designed to automate one or more stages of applications software development. Like a carpenter's workbench, which is comprised of a number of carpentry tools—hammers, saws, chisels, drill bits, and the like—software engineering

FIGURE IS 2-19

Common mistakes made in rapid development.

■ **Computer-aided software engineering (CASE).** Program products that automate systems-development and program-development activities.

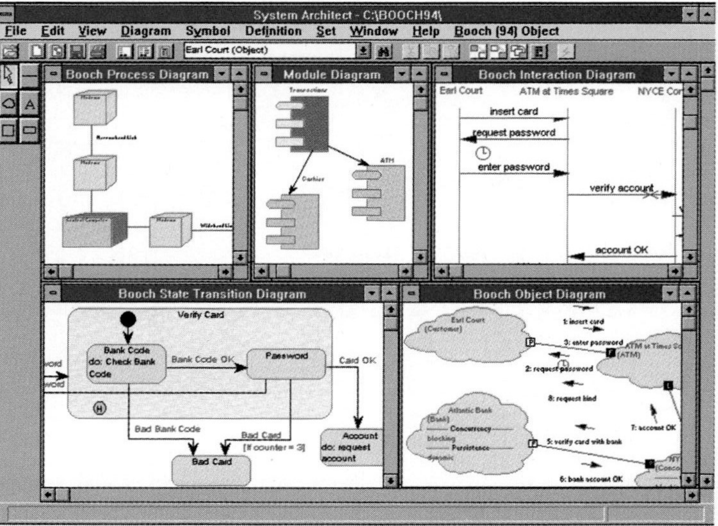

FIGURE IS 2-20

A CASE package. CASE products make it possible to develop applications faster with fewer coding mistakes. Shown here is Systems Architect, a CASE product that enables information-systems professionals to create a wide variety of diagram types.

workbenches contain a number of design, programming, and maintenance tools that get software products developed faster.

For instance, such a workbench might consist of programs that produce system and program diagrams, an action-diagram editor, a fourth-generation language, a code generator, a feature that facilitates the development of reusable code libraries, a data dictionary, and tools that help turn unstructured programs into structured ones (see Figure IS 2-20). The specific tools included in the workbench vary from one vendor to another. One of the most widely praised uses of CASE is being able to generate program code directly from the program design.

One of the principal advantages to CASE tools besides their speed in applications development is their ability to maintain consistency. Thus, if program code is generated from an online diagram, the two will be consistent. Also, if someone later tries to change the program without changing the diagram, a CASE tool can flag the inconsistency. On the downside, there is very little standardization in the CASE area from one vendor to another, and many of the CASE tools currently in the marketplace are targeted only to solving highly specific problems.

Rapid Application Development (RAD) Products In object-oriented programming environments, to provide CASE-like assistance with developing user interfaces and with preparing code for reuse, some vendors provide **rapid applications development (RAD)** tools for analysts and programmers. These tools are targeted to certain widely adopted software platforms—such as Microsoft Windows or Sybase databases. RAD includes wizard software to generate applications quickly, screen painters that provide attractive graphical user interfaces, object-oriented libraries that can be easily stitched together into applications, groupware to manage team development efforts, debugging and prototyping utilities, and so forth. Three widely used RAD products are Microsoft's Visual BASIC, Powersoft's PowerBuilder, and Borland's Delphi.

Summary and Key Terms

Like building a house, creating a successful applications program requires considerable planning.

Program Development Activities The steps associated with creating successful applications programs are called **applications software development.**

In most large organizations, the development of applications software is the job of systems analysts and programmers. **Systems analysts** are the people who work with users to assess needs, translate those needs into a list of technical requirements, and design the necessary software specifications. The design is then handed to a **programmer,** who codes the program from it. Maintenance programmers monitor the software on an ongoing basis, correcting errors and altering the software as applications needs change.

The Make-or-Buy Decision Many organizations choose to buy their software in the form of prewritten **applications packages** rather than creating it in-house.

■ **Rapid applications development (RAD).** Refers to program development tools that help with the quick generation of user interfaces and with the stitching together of reusable code.

The consideration to create software or acquire it from a vendor, which often takes place after the analysis and design stages of systems development, is frequently called the *make-or-buy decision.*

Program Design Many tools are available to help the analyst design programs, including structure charts, program flowcharts, and pseudocode.

Structure charts depict the overall hierarchical organization of program modules. **Top-down design** indicates that modules are defined first at the highest levels of the hierarchy and then at successively lower levels.

Program flowcharts use geometric symbols and familiar relational operators to provide a graphic display of the sequence of steps involved in a program. The steps in a flowchart follow each other in the same logical sequence as their corresponding statements will follow in a program.

A group of techniques has evolved that has made program design more systematic and made the programs themselves easier to understand and maintain. These techniques are often grouped together under the term **structured programming.** Advocates of structured programming have shown that any program can be constructed out of three fundamental **control structures**—sequence, selection, and looping.

A **sequence control structure** is simply a series of procedures that follow one another. The **selection** (or **if-then-else) control structure** involves a choice: *If* a certain condition is true, *then* follow one procedure; *else,* if false, follow another. A **looping** (or **iteration) control structure** repeats until a certain condition is met. A loop can take two forms: **DOWHILE** and **DOUNTIL.** By nesting two or more if-then-else's, you can build a fourth control structure, known as a **case control structure.** All of these control structures follow the **one-entry-point/one-exit-point rule**—that is, a structure can have only one way into it and one way out of it.

Pseudocode is a structured technique that uses Englishlike statements in place of the graphic symbols of the flowchart. Pseudocode is commonly employed in the creation of **action diagrams.**

Programming Languages An important decision that must be made during the design phase is the selection of a **programming language.** Programming languages are **low-level languages,** such as machine and **assembly languages; high-level languages,** such as **BASIC, Pascal, COBOL, C, C++,** or **FORTRAN;** or *very-high-level languages,* which are also called **fourth-generation languages (4GLs).**

The 4GLs are predominantly **declarative languages,** whereas 3GLs are mostly **procedural languages.** Six types of 4GLs commonly used are report generators, retrieval and update languages, decision support system tools, graphics generators, applications packages, and applications generators—such as **Visual BASIC,** an **object-oriented programming language.** Interfaces that use **natural languages** enable humans to communicate with the computer system in their own native language.

Program Coding Once analysts have finished the program design for an application, the next stage is to code the program. **Coding,** which is the job of programmers, is the process of writing a program from scratch from a set of design specifications. Among the techniques that have been developed to increase programmer productivity are coding standards, **reusable code,** and **data dictionaries.**

Debugging and Testing Programs **Debugging** is the process of making sure that a program is free of errors, or "bugs." Debugging is usually a lengthy process, sometimes amounting to more than 50 percent of the total development time for an in-house program. Most bugs can be classified as being either **syntax errors** or **logic errors.** Once preliminary debugging is complete, programs will also have to be *tested.* Good test data will subject the program to all the conditions it might conceivably encounter when finally implemented. Mass-distributed commercial programs are also **beta tested.**

Program Maintenance Program **maintenance** is the process of updating software so that it continues to be useful. Program maintenance is costly; it has been estimated that some organizations spend well over half of their programming time just maintaining existing applications.

Program Documentation Program **documentation** includes manuals that enable users, applications developers, and operators to interact successfully with a program. Although noted as the final stage of the program development cycle, documentation is an ongoing process that must be addressed throughout the life of the project.

Quality Assurance **Quality assurance,** as it regards program development, refers to the process of making sure quality programs are written in a quality way. Closely checked for quality are the outputs produced by programs, the program development process itself, and security.

Rapid Development **Rapid development** refers to a group of program-development methods in which a major goal is meeting an extremely tight timetable. Two tools used in rapid development are CASE and RAD. **CASE (computer-aided software engineering)** tools—or *software engineering workbenches*—refer broadly to products designed to automate one or more stages of applications software development. To provide CASE-like assistance with such tasks as developing user interfaces and reusable-code libraries, some vendors provide **rapid applications development (RAD)** tools for programmers.

EXERCISES

1. Fill in the blanks:
   a. __________ are the people who define the requirements that applications software must meet to satisfy users' needs.
   b. A(n) __________ interface enables humans to communicate with the computer in their native tongues.
   c. __________ is the principal transaction processing language in use today.
   d. Report generators, retrieval and update languages, applications packages, and applications generators are all examples of __________ languages.
   e. Program pieces designed to be "copied and pasted" into several programs are called __________.

2. Match each term with the description that fits best.

a. Visual BASIC	e. flowchart
b. sequence	f. pseudocode
c. debugging	g. Pascal
d. documentation	h. program design tool

_____ A structure chart, for example.
_____ The process of ridding a program of errors.
_____ A graphical design tool with boxes and arrows showing step-by-step how a computer will process data.
_____ A program control structure.
_____ A technique for designing programs that uses Englishlike statements resembling actual program statements to show the step-by-step processing a program will follow.
_____ A high-level programming language named after a mathematician.
_____ A written description of a program, such as a manual.
_____ An applications generator.

3. Name at least two advantages and one disadvantage to buying applications software packages relative to developing them in-house.

4. Supply the following information about control structures.
   a. Name the three fundamental control structures of structured programming and describe each.
   b. Name and describe a fourth control structure that is formed by putting together two or more occurrences of one of the fundamental structures.

5. What is the difference between each of the following?
   a. The DOWHILE and DOUNTIL control structures
   b. A program flowchart and a structure chart
   c. A third-generation language and a fourth-generation language
   d. A high-level and low-level language
   e. Program development and systems development

6. Define, in your own words, each of the following.
   a. One-entry-point/one-exit-point rule

b. Authoring software
c. Top-down design
d. Quality assurance
e. Object-oriented programming language

7. What particular need is met by each of the following programming languages?
a. BASIC
b. Visual BASIC
c. COBOL
d. FORTRAN
e. C and C++
f. Pascal
g. HTML
h. Prolog

8. Identify several types of fourth-generation languages. What is the principal purpose each one serves?

9. Name and describe several criteria that are used by organizations to choose among programming languages.

10. What is the difference between each of the following?
a. A decision symbol and processing symbol in a flowchart
b. A procedural and declarative language
c. An action diagram and a code generator
d. A syntax error and a logic error
e. An alpha test and a beta test

1. Software Errors Software errors are frequently covered by the press. As this book was being written, for instance, an interesting error had just been made by a midwestern bank and had been reported. Into each of 826 depositor checking accounts, a program had erroneously deposited $924.8 million dollars—collectively, several times the bank's total assets. Just a couple of years before that, incidentally, an eastern bank made a similar error, erasing half of the balances in thousands of checking accounts. A culprit often cited for such errors is the multitude of systems that banks use to process deposits and withdrawals—human tellers, ATM machines, wire transfers, PC-based systems, and so on—all of which have to be coordinated.

For this project, find an example of a software error covered in the press and report to the class about it. Be sure to cover the nature of the error, the consequences or dollar amount resulting from the error, and the likely cause of the problem.

2. Flowcharts and Pseudocode Prepare a flowchart and pseudocode to solve the following problem: A company has several salespeople and needs a computer procedure to figure out the amount to pay them. A salesperson is paid according to a standard commission rate of 12 percent multiplied by total sales dollars generated. Salespeople whose sales exceed $20,000 for the month get a bonus of $500 tacked on to their earnings. As input, assume each employee record contains the name of a salesperson and his or her monthly sales; as output, produce the amount he or she is to be paid.

3. Developing Pages for the World Wide Web Today, many people are creating their own World Wide Web pages and posting them on the Internet. The pro-

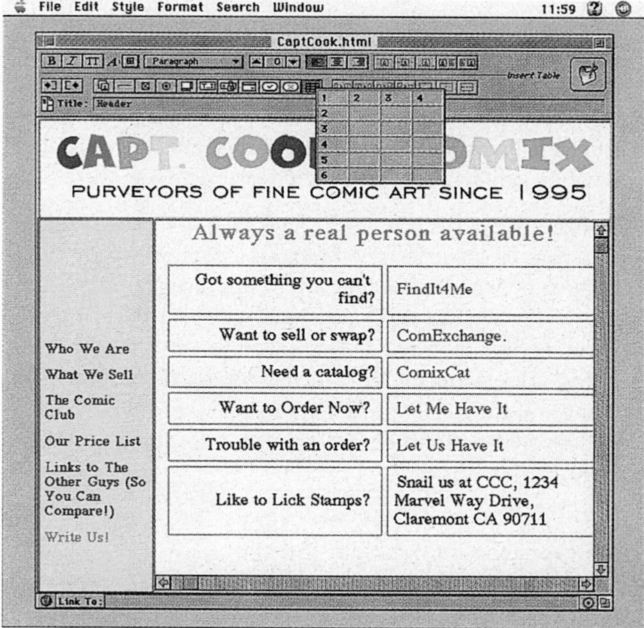

cess of developing Web pages can be seen as a case study in both systems and program development. Thus, there are stages that one goes through as regards (1) project analysis, (2) Web-site design, (3) Web-page coding, (4) Web-page debugging and testing, (5) Web-site implementation, and (6) Web-site maintenance. In a few sentences, describe the types of activities that someone developing a commercial Web site might go through in each of these six stages. If you have a version of this textbook that contains Chapter NET 3, you should read this chapter before doing this project.

IS

4. Beta Tests While many companies keep the results of beta testing confidential, the press often leaks hints as to how well a particular version of a software product is faring with testers. The hints are often based on feedback the company has gathered from testers or on surveys the press has conducted itself. For this project, find an article in a computer newspaper or journal that tells how a beta test is going and report to the class about it. Based on what the article says, does the product appear to meet expectations or have serious problems?

5. Programming Languages I For each of the following, write a few sentences in response.

a. With so many programming languages around today, why are new ones constantly being developed?
b. Do any new programming languages really have a chance at wide acceptance, given the large number of languages now in use?
c. Should every student entering college be required to learn a procedural programming language such as BASIC?

6. Programming Languages II Both the chapter and Figure IS 2-14 cover the properties of several important programming languages. For this project, choose any one of these languages and write a three-to-five-page report about it. Your report should go beyond what the text covers. Be sure to mention in your report what the language is designed to do, usages for the language, and the language's syntax or special features.

7. New Key Terms It's impossible for a textbook of this sort to cover every important technology or term regarding program development and programming languages in organizations. Several important terms are listed below that are not covered in the chapter. Use either library-journal or Internet research to determine what any three of these terms mean, and write out a one-to-three-sentence explanation describing each one in your own words.

a. The Perl programming language
b. Reverse polish notation
c. Structured walkthrough
d. Warnier diagram
e. GOTO statement
f. The Modula programming language

8. Error Avoidance Even error-free programs are not enough to guarantee correct results. If the data being fed to them are inaccurate, most programs can do little to process them and get correct results. To ensure the accuracy of data going into the computer, many software programs have data-checking routines that look for potential problems. For instance, programs often contain a *field check* that will not permit, say, a name to be entered into a field where a number belongs. Also, a *reasonableness check* is used to test a value to see that it isn't wildly out of bounds—such as a payroll check to be issued for $924.8 million. For this project, find at least three more checks that might be made on entering data, to ensure their accuracy, and describe these checks to the class.

9. Year 2000 Research As the Tomorrow box suggests, a variety of computer-caused problems are expected to occur when the clock strikes January 1, 2000. Because of limited space, the box was only able provide a brief introduction to the year-2000 issue. For this project, you are to delve more deeply into some aspect of this issue, writing a paper on it that is not to exceed ten pages. You can choose from any of the topics listed below or choose a topic of your own.

- A classification of potential year-2000 problems, by applications area (e.g., banking, government, health care, etc.)
- How companies are fixing their computer systems to make them year-2000 compliant
- How the U.S. government is dealing with the year-2000 issue on federally owned computers
- My predictions: Separating what will most likely happen in the year 2000 from the hype
- Litigation vulnerability arising from year-2000 problems

You will find scores of articles in computer newspapers and journals, and plenty of information on the Internet, to help you with this project. If you are doing this project *after* the year 2000, consider writing a paper reporting or analyzing actual year-2000 cases that you have read about.

10. Global Research India has recently become a major source of programmers to the world. How have both information technology and nontechnology-related conditions within and outside of India made it easier for programmers in that nation to compete in the global marketplace?

11. Popular Software Most users and programmers within organizations would prefer to work with a widely used applications package than a comparable software product developed in-house. Why do you think this is so? What benefits do widely used applications packages also present to the organization?

12. Computers and Credit Computer programs can distinguish people who are good credit risks from those who are not. How, would you suppose, do computer programs make this distinction?

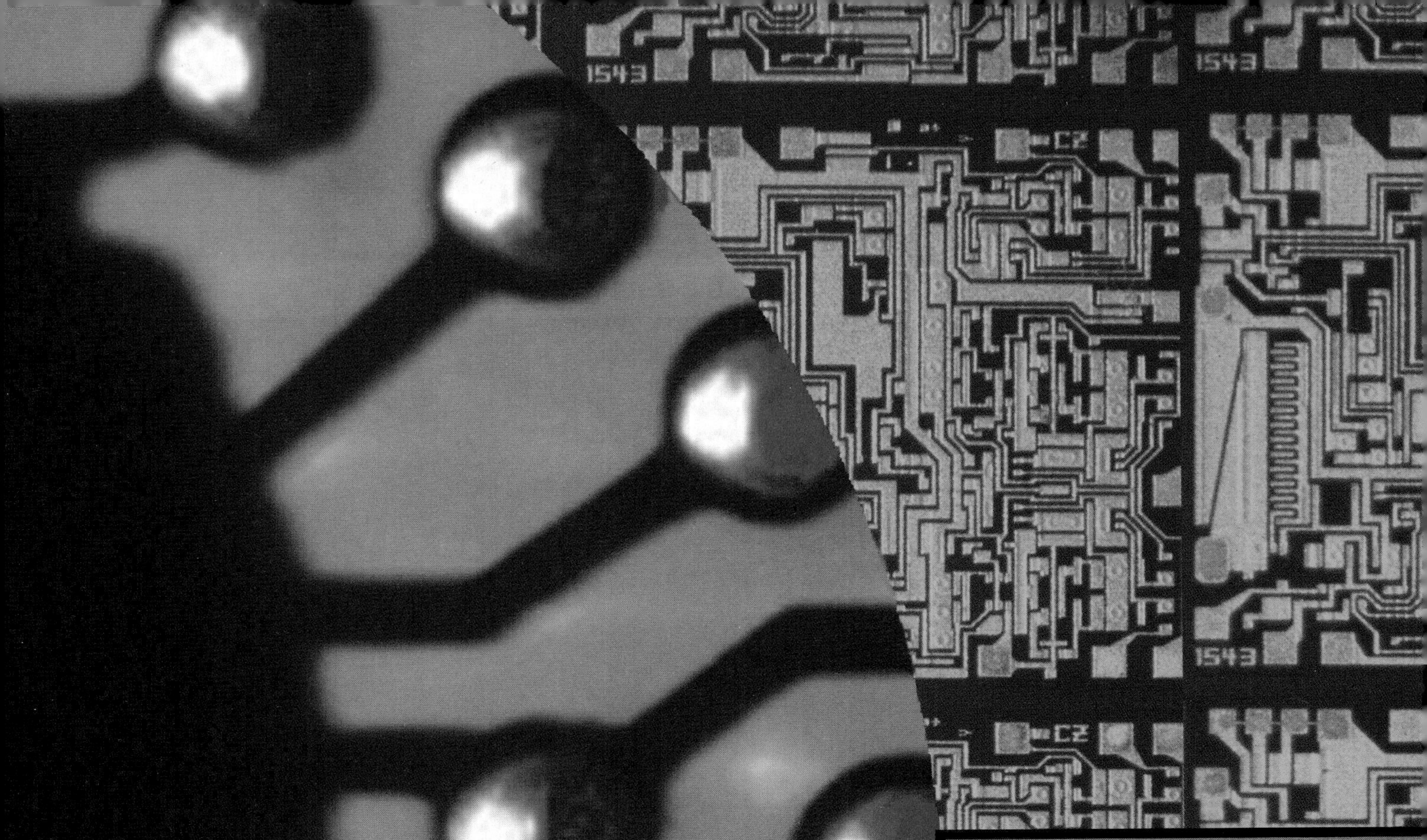

MODULE

LIV

Computers in Our Lives

No study of computers is complete without a look at the growing impact of these devices on daily life and the very fabric of society. From home offices to company desktops, more and more people are operating their own computer systems. Children are routinely exposed to computers through school and through electronic games. News bureaus regularly report about computer-related issues—hackers breaking into computer systems, the Internet's potential for changing our lives, privacy problems created by computers, and so forth.

Chapter LIV 1 addresses issues that arise in developing one's own microcomputer system. It covers many of the facts about microcomputers that you should understand if you decide to acquire your own system. Today, with unprecedented numbers of people purchasing their own PCs or participating in purchasing decisions at work, knowledge in this area has become essential for virtually everyone.

Chapter LIV 2 looks at the problems that computers create, including their impact on the physical and mental health of users, computer crime, potential invasions of personal privacy, and new ethical dilemmas.

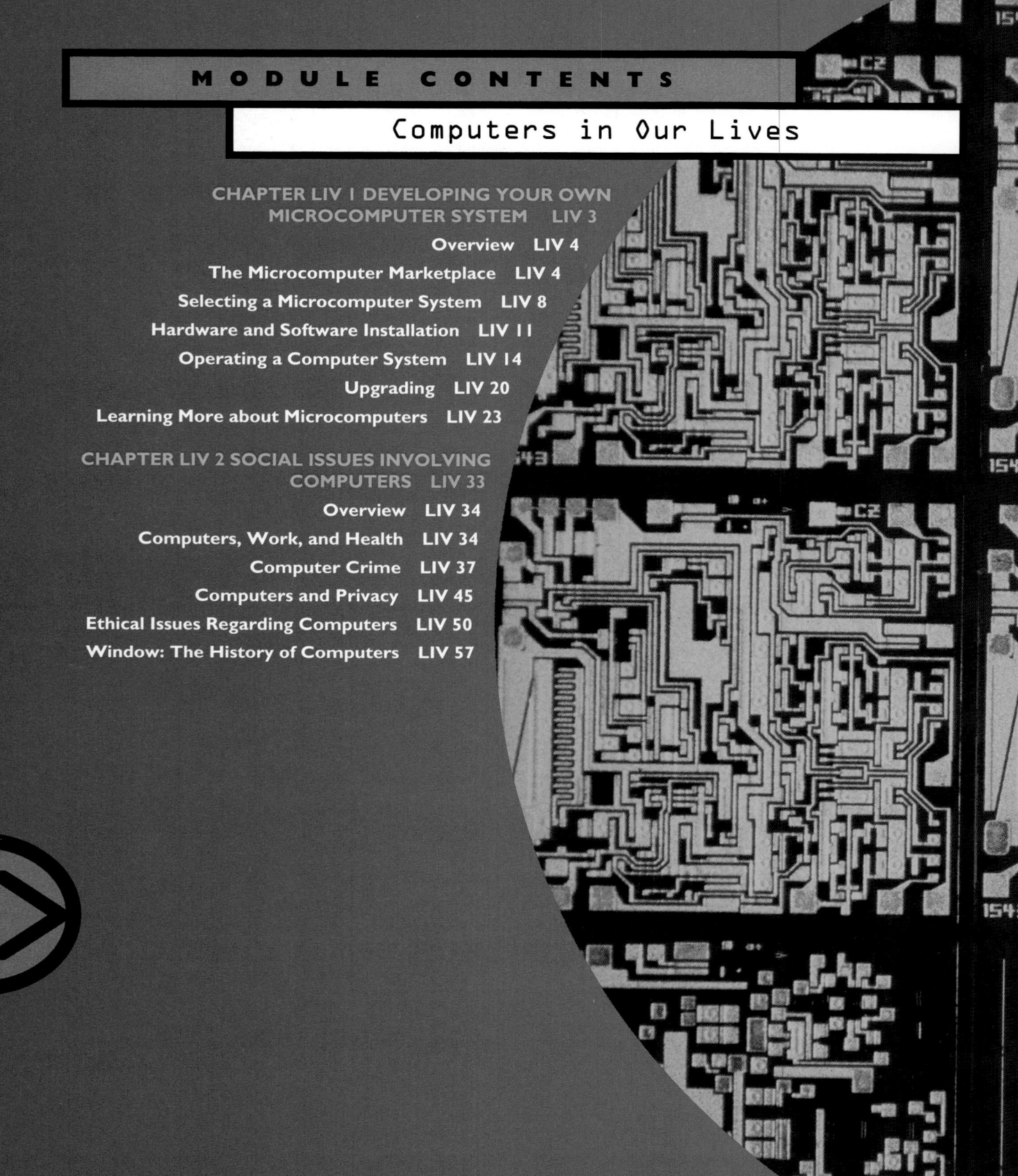

MODULE CONTENTS

Computers in Our Lives

ISBN 0-03-024481-1

Developing Your Own Microcomputer System

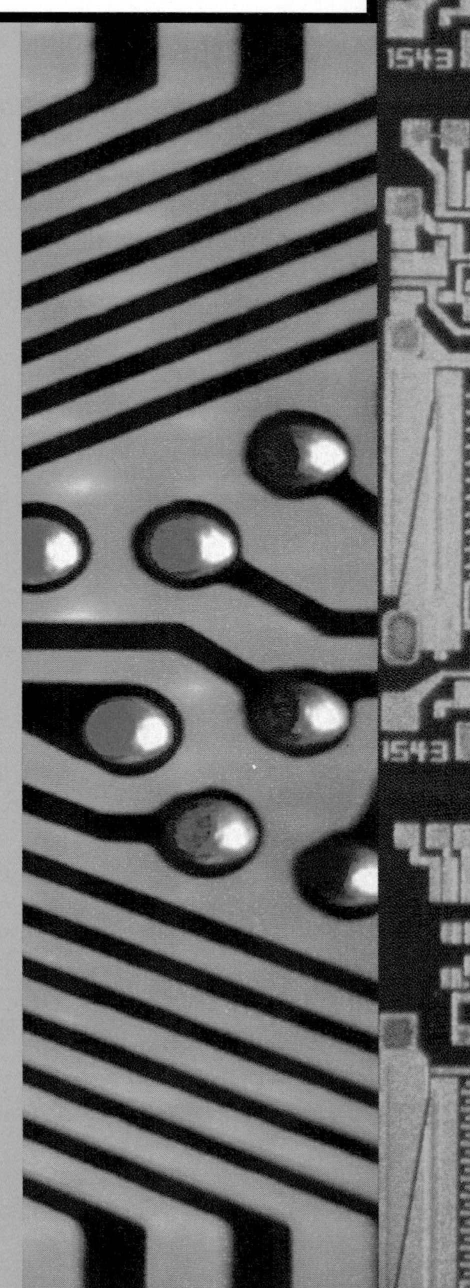

Outline

- Overview
- The Microcomputer Marketplace
  - Microcomputer Products
  - Sales and Distribution
- Selecting a Microcomputer System
  - Analyzing Needs
  - Listing Alternatives
  - Evaluating Alternatives
  - Choosing a System
- Hardware and Software Installation
- Operating a Computer System
  - Backup Procedures
  - Equipment Maintenance
  - Security
  - Troubleshooting and Technical Assistance
- Upgrading
  - Upgrading Hardware
  - Upgrading Software
  - Functional versus Technological Obsolescence
- Learning More about Microcomputers

Learning Objectives

After completing this chapter, you will be able to:

1. Identify some of the leading companies in critical market segments of the microcomputer industry, as well as the key sales and distribution alternatives for microcomputing products.
2. Explain how to select and install a microcomputer system for home or office use.
3. Name some practices designed to protect software, hardware, and data resources from damage.
4. List some important guidelines for troubleshooting problems and seeking assistance.
5. Describe some of the ways to upgrade a computer system and explain the conditions that justify an upgrade.
6. Name several sources for learning more about microcomputer systems.

Overview

It is becoming commonplace for a person to own a microcomputer or to use one at work. Consequently, more people than ever before are acquiring their own microcomputer resources, maintaining and upgrading their systems on their own, and so on. The purpose of this chapter is to make you aware of the many ins and outs connected with being an owner of a microcomputer system.

Chapter LIV 1 opens with a discussion of the vendors in the microcomputer marketplace and the distribution channels they use to sell their products at the retail level. Then we look at some of the things you should know when acquiring a microcomputer system for home or work. From there we turn to several operation and maintenance issues, including troubleshooting problems and obtaining product support. Next, upgrading a computer system is covered. Finally, we discuss some of the sources that are at your disposal for learning more about microcomputers.

The Microcomputer Marketplace

The microcomputer marketplace comprises a wide variety of firms that make hardware and software products. Several other companies are in business solely for product sales, support, and distribution purposes.

MICROCOMPUTER PRODUCTS

A quarter of a century or so ago, many of the companies that make today's most familiar microcomputer products didn't even exist. Today, many of them earn more than $1 billion a year in revenues. The microcomputer industry has become both the largest and the fastest-growing segment of the computer industry. A roster of some of the most familiar companies in the microcomputer marketplace appears in Figure LIV 1-1.

System Units IBM, Compaq, Hewlett-Packard, Dell, and Apple are among the big names in system units in the microcomputer marketplace. There are other companies—such as Packard Bell, AST, and Gateway—who, like Compaq, Hewlett-Packard, and Dell, have become highly successful largely by producing PC-compatible computers. PC compatibles account for about 90 percent of the systems sold; the remainder are Macintosh-compatible. Most of the system units sold are of the desktop type, but laptops are gaining fast and some analysts predict that they may eventually overtake desktop systems for business use.

Vendors of system units are often ranked in *tiers*. The top-tier vendors include long-standing industry firms like IBM and Compaq whose equipment commands premium prices. Top-tier companies often are involved in extensive research and development efforts, and their equipment is usually top-quality and an all around safe purchasing bet. Second-tier vendors are less well known and often sell at prices of about 10 to 20 percent less than their top-tier counterparts. Second-tier companies often do little research and development, use less-expensive component parts, and farm out service and support to third-party firms. Nonetheless, the equipment coming out of second-tier companies is usually high-quality, service and support are very good, and one's purchase risk is very low.

You might save yet another 10 percent on the purchase price of hardware by going to a third-tier vendor. These companies usually have no name recognition and many have been in business only a very short period of time. Because of the increased risk involved, many organizations have policies forbidding them to do business with any computer vendor below what they consider the second tier.

Company	Principal Product(s)
Adobe	Assorted desktop publishing software products
Apple	Microcomputer systems
AST	A wide variety of hardware products
Autodesk	AutoCAD design software
Borland	A variety of applications-development products
Canon	Printers and related products
Compaq	Microcomputer systems
Computer Associates	A wide variety of software products
Corel	A wide variety of software products
Dell	Microcomputer systems
Gateway	Microcomputer systems
Hewlett-Packard	A wide variety of hardware products
IBM	A wide variety of computing products
Intel	Chips for PC-compatible computers
Lotus Development	A wide variety of software products
Microsoft	A wide variety of software products
Motorola	Chips for Macintosh-compatible computers; wireless products
NEC	A wide variety of hardware products
Netscape	Internet-related products
Novell	NetWare operating system
Packard Bell	Microcomputer systems
Seagate	Storage products
Symantec	A wide variety of utility-software products
Toshiba	A wide variety of hardware products

Who's who in the microcomputer marketplace. This list shows the products and product lines for which several leading companies are most famous.

Software Many applications programs today are sold as part of *software suites,* which bundle together several full-featured software packages for sale at lower prices than the separate programs would collectively command. Among the largest microcomputer-software producers (and their leading products) are Microsoft Corporation (Windows and the Office suite of applications), IBM (OS/2, Lotus Notes, and Lotus SmartSuite), and Corel Corporation (the WordPerfect suite of applications and CorelDRAW!).

Monitors and Printers With the exception of a few U.S. companies such as IBM and Hewlett-Packard, these two segments are dominated by Japanese producers. Major players include Epson, Toshiba, Seiko, Brother, Fujitsu, Canon, NEC, Okidata, and C. Itoh.

Microprocessor Chips The microprocessor chip market is ruled largely by Intel and Motorola. Intel makes CPU chips for most of the leading PC-compatible system units, whereas Motorola makes chips for Macintosh compatibles. Also, a number of lesser-known manufacturers, such as Cyrix and Advanced Micro Devices (AMD), produce Intel-compatible chips.

SALES AND DISTRIBUTION

Most users buy microcomputer hardware and software products through computer stores, discount and department stores, the Internet, mail-order houses, manufacturers, and value-added resellers (see Figure LIV 1-2).

Computer Stores When buyers need strong local support in selecting and using PC products, they often turn to *computer stores* such as CompUSA, Egghead, and Computer City. Generally, the salespeople at such places are relatively knowledgeable about computers and many help buyers try out products before making a commitment. Besides hardware, software, and general advice on purchasing a new system, computer stores also often offer consulting, repair, and other support services.

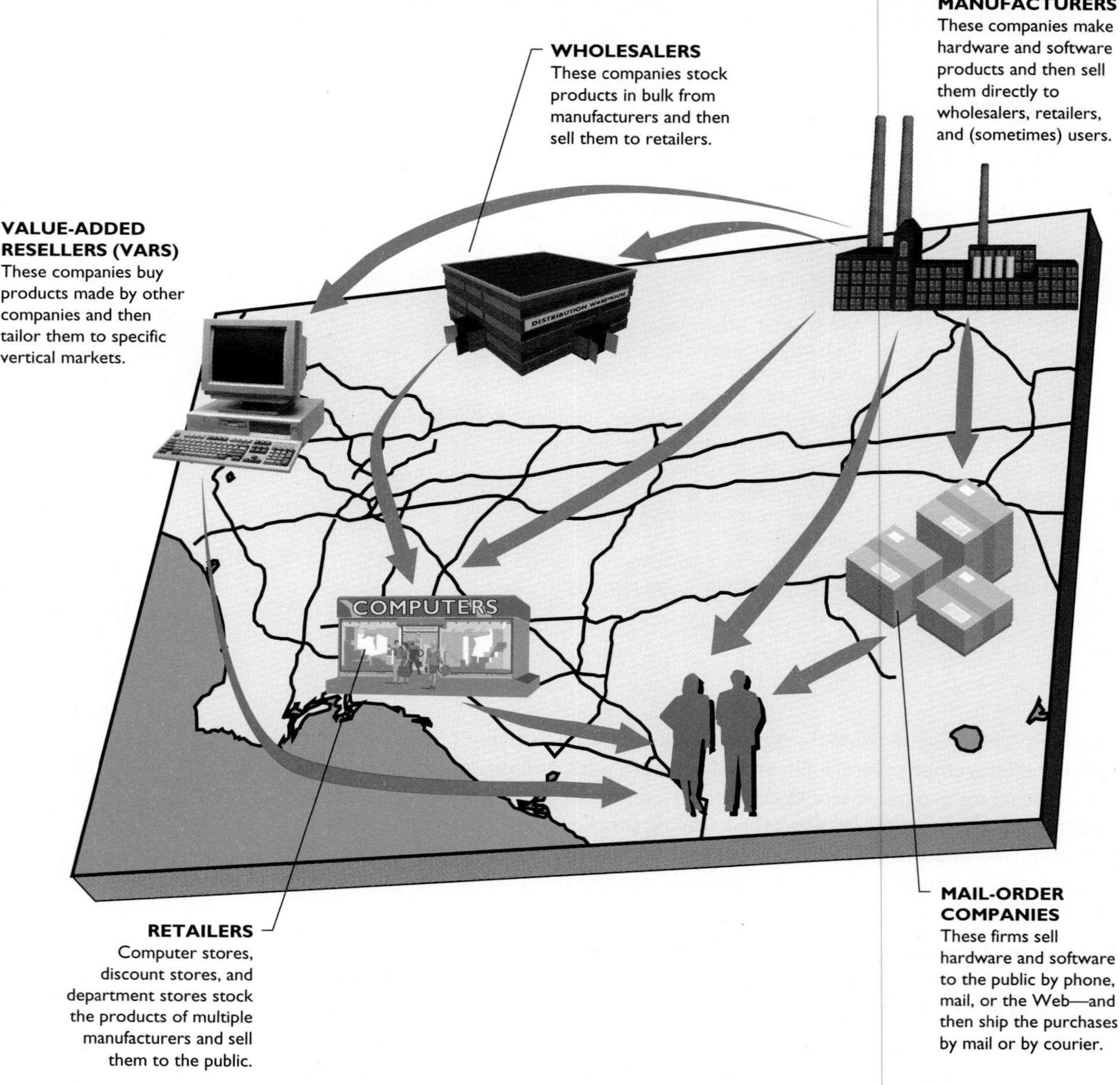

MANUFACTURERS
These companies make hardware and software products and then sell them directly to wholesalers, retailers, and (sometimes) users.
WHOLESALERS
These companies stock products in bulk from manufacturers and then sell them to retailers.
VALUE-ADDED RESELLERS (VARS)
These companies buy products made by other companies and then tailor them to specific vertical markets.
DISTRIBUTION WAREHOUSE
COMPUTERS
RETAILERS
Computer stores, discount stores, and department stores stock the products of multiple manufacturers and sell them to the public.
MAIL-ORDER COMPANIES
These firms sell hardware and software to the public by phone, mail, or the Web—and then ship the purchases by mail or by courier.

FIGURE LIV 1-2

Distribution channels for computer products.

Computer stores come in many varieties. Most are national or multistate chain stores, but there are also outfits that serve only regional areas such as a single town or a state. Large chains, because they can buy in volume, are likely to have better prices. Many regional stores try to compete by providing superior support. Virtually all computer stores are *resellers*—that is, they sell the hardware and software products made by another company. While most computer stores fill the floor space of an average mall boutique, massive *computer superstores* have also become popular.

Other Stores During the last several years, microcomputer hardware and software have become so popular that many other types of retail stores have added such items on their showroom floors. Today, you can buy hardware and software at discount stores (such as Wal-Mart), warehouse clubs (such as Price/Costco), department stores (such as Sears), office supply stores (such as Office Depot), and bookstores (such as Waldenbooks).

As a general rule, the discount stores and warehouse clubs have the best prices, but there is sometimes less of a selection available and many offer little or no technical support. The smaller selection is often due to deals the store gets on volume purchases and on inventory closeouts—for instance, stock of a printer model the equipment manufacturer wants to get rid of because a replacement model has just come out.

The Internet In a growing trend, many companies sell hardware and software over the Internet. To buy a product, you need only log onto the seller's Web site and select an item. For software, you can often try out a copy before buying, downloading the program of your choice over the phone lines. If you decide to buy, the packaged version of the product will be shipped to you immediately, providing you with disks and possibly written documentation. For hardware, you can often make selections to configure the system of your choice online, receiving it by mail, UPS, or Federal Express a few days or weeks later.

Many firms that have traditionally sold through conventional retailing channels, like Egghead Software, also maintain their own Web sites (see Figure LIV 1-3). Such sites not only are useful for selling products, but they also can economically disseminate a lot of valuable marketing and support information to consumers that is difficult to organize and distribute by any other means. Companies doing business on the Web may or may not make the products they sell; also, many Web sites distribute freeware and shareware.

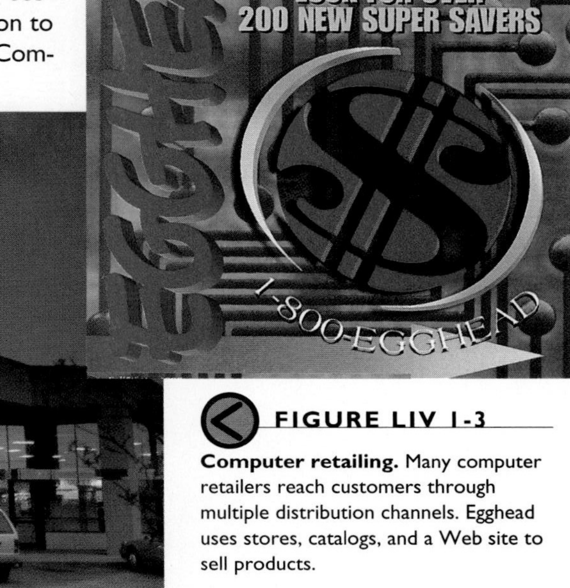

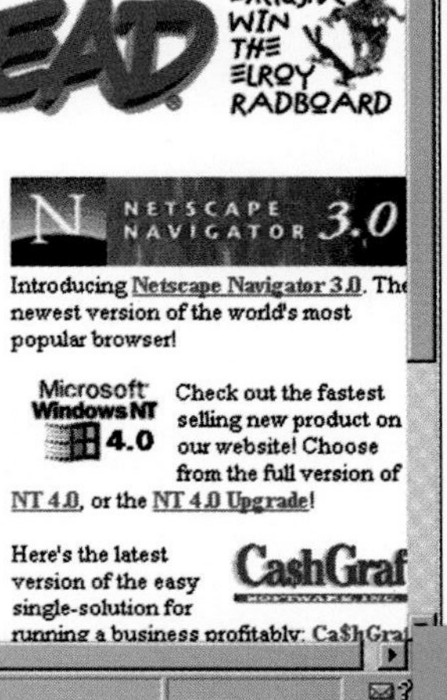

FIGURE LIV 1-3

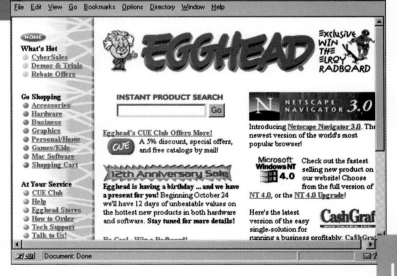

Computer retailing. Many computer retailers reach customers through multiple distribution channels. Egghead uses stores, catalogs, and a Web site to sell products.

Mail-Order Firms Another common source of computer products is mail-order firms. These companies, which are usually resellers, handle products from scores of hardware and/or software manufacturers and primarily ship goods to a customer after receiving an order by phone, mail, or over the Internet (see Figure LIV 1-4). These companies usually have access to an enormous selection of goods and can get almost any item to customers quickly via UPS or Federal Express. Mail-order firms regularly publish price lists in microcomputer journals, in their own product catalogs, or at their Web sites.

Because mail-order companies don't have to pay for a showroom and a staff of knowledgeable salespeople, their prices are usually much lower than those of

FIGURE LIV 1-4

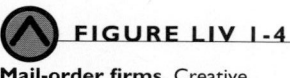

Mail-order firms. Creative Computers is one of several mail-order houses that regularly print catalogs that showcase products for PC-compatible and Macintosh computers.

computer stores and are competitive with discount stores. A disadvantage of mail-order shopping is that buyers need to know exactly what they want, because most mail-order firms don't maintain showrooms or a large technical staff.

Manufacturers Yet another alternative for buying hardware and software is going straight to the manufacturer, when that is possible. Hardware companies such as Dell, Gateway, and Zeos are known as *direct manufacturers,* in that they sell directly to the public through advertisements in computer journals, direct-mail flyers, or Web sites. These companies usually do not maintain finished inventories of computers; they build each system to suit the buyer's tastes as they receive orders. Consumers enjoy the advantage of ordering exactly the computer systems they want from a single source—including "free" support and service for a limited period of time.

Many software manufacturers—or **software publishers**—also sell directly to the public. Buyers generally reach publishers through 800- and 888-area-code numbers that appear in journal advertisements and through the publisher's Web or FTP sites. Many publishers will also let you download copies of their products over the Internet for trial purposes.

Value-Added Resellers **Value-added resellers (VARs)** are companies that buy computer hardware and software from others and make their own specialized systems out of them. For instance, many of the computer systems used in the videotape-rental-store business, in medical and dental offices, and in certain other types of *vertical markets* come from VARs. The VAR essentially packages together all of the custom hardware and software needed to run operations in the vertical-market area in which it specializes and often provides full service and support as well. Although going through a VAR is usually more costly than configuring a system on one's own, it is definitely a compelling choice for a small business owner who is not computer savvy or who is not too busy with other matters.

Used Equipment When shopping for a computer system, don't overlook used equipment. Ads for used equipment usually appear in the classified sections of local newspapers. If you take this route, ask to try out the equipment before you buy it. If the equipment functions properly during the trial period, it will probably work fine. You should pay considerably less for a used system than you would for a new one.

Selecting a Microcomputer System

Chances are good that at some point in your life, you will need to select a microcomputer system to better perform your job. Selecting a PC for home or for business use must begin with the all-important question "What do I want the system to do?" Once you've determined the purposes to which the system will be put, you must choose among the software and hardware alternatives available. Finally, you need a method to evaluate the alternatives and to select a system.

■ **Software publisher.** A company that creates software. ■ **Value-added resellers (VAR).** A company that buys hardware and software from others and makes computer systems out of them that are targeted to particular vertical markets.

ANALYZING NEEDS

With regard to a computer system, a *need* refers to a functional requirement that the computer system must be capable of meeting. For instance, at a videotape rental store, a computer system must be able to enter bar codes automatically from tapes being checked in and out, identify customers with overdue tapes, manage tape inventories, and do routine accounting operations. Requiring portability—a computer that you can take with you "on the road"—is another example of a need.

A person owning a computer system will find dozens of ways to use it, but he or she may often justify the acquisition of a microcomputer system on the basis of only one or two needs. For example, many writers find word processing so indispensable to their livelihoods that it matters little what else the computer system can do. Sales personnel working out of the office can often justify a notebook computer simply on the basis of its usefulness as an account-closing tool at client sites.

If you're not really sure what you want a system to do, you should think twice about buying one. Computer systems that are configured to match the requirements of certain applications (say, preparing a novel) often perform poorly at others (such as playing power-hungry multimedia games). You can easily make expensive mistakes if you're uncertain what you want a system to do.

As part of the needs analysis, you should look closely at budgetary constraints. Every user can easily list many needs, but affordability separates real needs from pipe dreams.

LISTING ALTERNATIVES

After you establish a set of needs, the next step is to list some alternative systems that might satisfy those needs. You should almost always consider applications software first, then look for the hardware and systems-software platform that most effectively satisfies your applications-software requirements.

Applications software is selected first because it most directly satisfies needs. For instance, if you want a computer system to do commercial art, it would be wise to first look at the various programs available in this area. It makes no sense to choose hardware first and then find out that it doesn't support the type of art package you prefer. Many artists, for instance, prefer a Macintosh platform, so you might completely miss the boat if you bought a PC-compatible computer and then discovered later that the Mac is better suited for the work you wanted to do. Also, if you skimped on the CPU and storage and later found out that the programs you selected require a lot of power, again you'd be out of luck.

You can get a list of leading software and hardware products from the many microcomputer journals. Many of these journals also periodically describe the best and worst features of products, rate and compare products, and have industry analysts address product trends (see Figure LIV 1-5). Such information can be useful as input for evaluating buying alternatives, your next step in acquiring a microcomputer system.

EVALUATING ALTERNATIVES

Prospective buyers can evaluate alternative products most effectively by "test driving" them. Keep in mind, however, that you observe the performance of a software package only on a given configuration of hardware. A software package that runs smoothly on a Gateway 233 MHz Pentium II-based computer system won't necessarily run as well on a Compaq 200 MHz Pentium-based system, which uses slightly different components and a less powerful CPU chip. Also, the look, feel, and performance of a software package on a computer in the Apple Macintosh line are often noticeably different than they are on a PC-compatible machine. Sometimes it's quite

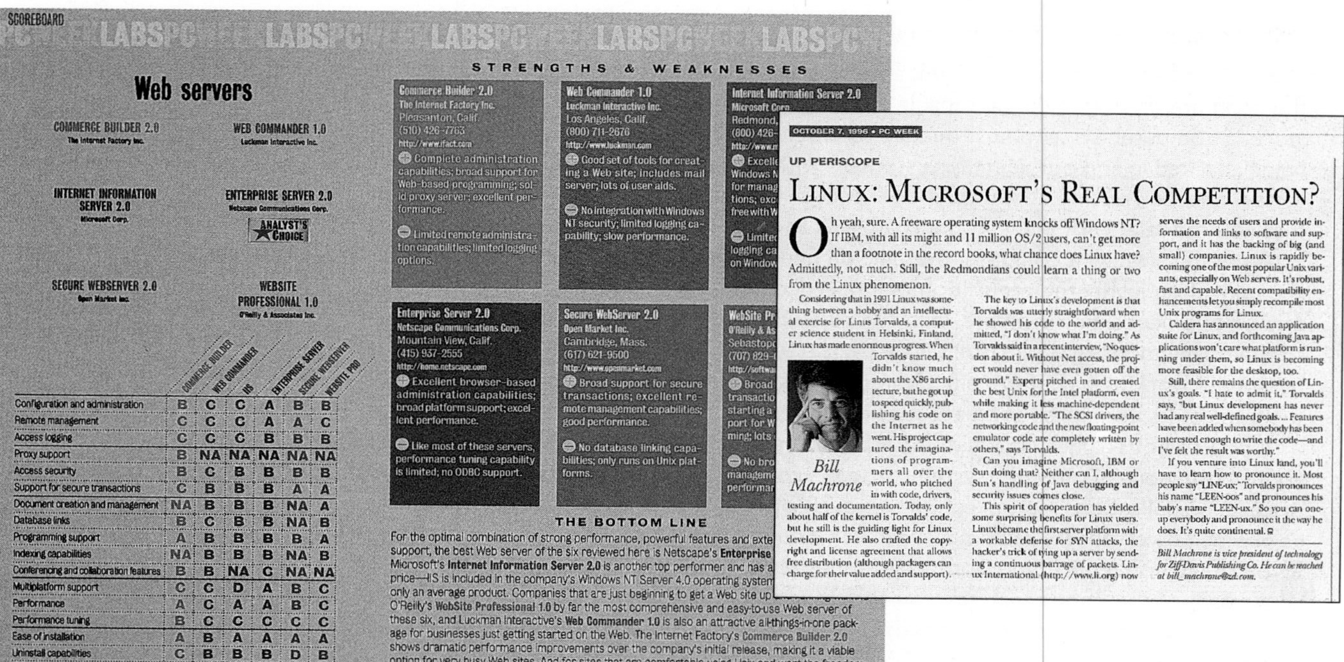

SCOREBOARD

LABSPC

Web servers

COMMERCE BUILDER 2.0
The Internet Factory Inc.

WEB COMMANDER 1.0
Luckman Interactive Inc.

INTERNET INFORMATION SERVER 2.0
Microsoft Corp.

ENTERPRISE SERVER 2.0
Netscape Communications Corp.
ANALYST'S CHOICE

SECURE WEBSERVER 2.0
Open Market Inc.

WEBSITE PROFESSIONAL 1.0
O'Reilly & Associates Inc.

	COMMERCE BUILDER	WEB COMMANDER	IIS	ENTERPRISE SERVER	SECURE WEBSERVER	WEBSITE PRO
Configuration and administration	B	C	C	A	B	B
Remote management	C	C	C	A	A	C
Access logging	C	C	C	B	B	B
Proxy support	B	NA	NA	NA	NA	NA
Access security	B	C	B	B	B	B
Support for secure transactions	C	B	B	B	A	A
Document creation and management	NA	B	B	B	NA	A
Database links	B	C	B	B	NA	B
Programming support	A	B	B	B	B	A
Indexing capabilities	NA	B	B	B	NA	B
Conferencing and collaboration features	B	B	NA	C	NA	NA
Multiplatform support	C	C	D	A	B	C
Performance	A	C	A	A	B	C
Performance tuning	B	C	C	C	C	C
Ease of installation	A	B	A	A	A	A
Uninstall capabilities	C	B	B	B	D	B
Documentation	C	C	C	B	C	A

NA: Not available

STRENGTHS & WEAKNESSES

Commerce Builder 2.0
The Internet Factory Inc.
Pleasanton, Calif.
(510) 426-7763
http://www.ifact.com
⊕ Complete administration capabilities; broad support for Web-based programming; solid proxy server; excellent performance.
⊖ Limited remote administration capabilities; limited logging options.

Web Commander 1.0
Luckman Interactive Inc.
Los Angeles, Calif.
(800) 711-2676
http://www.luckman.com
⊕ Good set of tools for creating a Web site; includes mail server; lots of user aids.
⊖ No integration with Windows NT security; limited logging capability; slow performance.

Enterprise Server 2.0
Netscape Communications Corp.
Mountain View, Calif.
(415) 937-2555
http://home.netscape.com
⊕ Excellent browser-based administration capabilities; broad platform support; excellent performance.
⊖ Like most of these servers, performance tuning capability is limited; no ODBC support.

Secure WebServer 2.0
Open Market Inc.
Cambridge, Mass.
(617) 621-9500
http://www.openmarket.com
⊕ Broad support for secure transactions; excellent remote management capabilities; good performance.
⊖ No database linking capabilities; only runs on Unix platforms.

THE BOTTOM LINE

For the optimal combination of strong performance, powerful features and exte
support, the best Web server of the six reviewed here is Netscape's **Enterprise**
Microsoft's **Internet Information Server 2.0** is another top performer and has a
price—IIS is included in the company's Windows NT Server 4.0 operating system
only an average product. Companies that are just beginning to get a Web site up
O'Reilly's **WebSite Professional 1.0** by far the most comprehensive and easy-to-use Web server of these six, and Luckman Interactive's **Web Commander 1.0** is also an attractive all-things-in-one package for businesses just getting started on the Web. The Internet Factory's **Commerce Builder 2.0** shows dramatic performance improvements over the company's initial release, making it a viable option for very busy Web sites. And for sites that are comfortable using Unix and want the freedom of open standards that it provides, Open Market's powerful **Secure WebServer 2.0** is almost as attractive as Netscape's product.

OCTOBER 7, 1996 • PC WEEK

UP PERISCOPE

LINUX: MICROSOFT'S REAL COMPETITION?

Oh yeah, sure. A freeware operating system knocks off Windows NT? If IBM, with all its might and 11 million OS/2 users, can't get more than a footnote in the record books, what chance does Linux have? Admittedly, not much. Still, the Redmondians could learn a thing or two from the Linux phenomenon.

Considering that in 1991 Linux was something between a hobby and an intellectual exercise for Linus Torvalds, a computer science student in Helsinki, Finland, Linux has made enormous progress. When Torvalds started, he didn't know much about the X86 architecture, but he got up to speed quickly, publishing his code on the Internet as he went. His project captured the imaginations of programmers all over the world, who pitched in with code, drivers, testing and documentation. Today, only about half of the kernel is Torvalds' code, but he still is the guiding light for Linux development. He also crafted the copyright and license agreement that allows free distribution (although packagers can charge for their value added and support).

Bill Machrone

The key to Linux's development is that Torvalds was utterly straightforward when he showed his code to the world and admitted, "I don't know what I'm doing." As Torvalds said in a recent interview, "No question about it. Without Net access, the project would never have even gotten off the ground." Experts pitched in and created the best Unix for the Intel platform, even while making it less machine-dependent and more portable. "The SCSI drivers, the networking code and the new floating-point emulator code are completely written by others," says Torvalds.

Can you imagine Microsoft, IBM or Sun doing that? Neither can I, although Sun's handling of Java debugging and security issues comes close.

This spirit of cooperation has yielded some surprising benefits for Linux users. Linux became the first server platform with a workable defense for SYN attacks, the hacker's trick of tying up a server by sending a continuous barrage of packets. Linux International (http://www.li.org) now serves the needs of users and provide information and links to software and support, and it has the backing of big (and small) companies. Linux is rapidly becoming one of the most popular Unix variants, especially on Web servers. It's robust, fast and capable. Recent compatibility enhancements let you simply recompile most Unix programs for Linux.

Caldera has announced an application suite for Linux, and forthcoming Java applications won't care what platform is running under them, so Linux is becoming more feasible for the desktop, too.

Still, there remains the question of Linux's goals. "I hate to admit it," Torvalds says, "but Linux development has never had any real well-defined goals. ... Features have been added when somebody has been interested enough to write the code—and I've felt the result was worthy."

If you venture into Linux land, you'll have to learn how to pronounce it. Most people say "LINE-ux;" Torvalds pronounces his name "LEEN-oos" and pronounces his baby's name "LEEN-ux." So you can one-up everybody and pronounce it the way he does. It's quite continental.

Bill Machrone is vice president of technology for Ziff-Davis Publishing Co. He can be reached at bill_machrone@zd.com.

FIGURE LIV 1-5

Product evaluations.

difficult, when selecting a configuration of hardware and software, to see the entire system together, but it's certainly advisable to do this whenever possible.

Selection Criteria As you evaluate software and hardware products, a number of criteria will help you to make your final selection. The most important selection criterion is *functionality*—the type of work the product does. For many people, ease of learning, ease of use, and phone support follow closely behind. Also, most people prefer widely used products rather than unknown ones, because the large user base with the popular products ensures that support will be around for a long time. In addition, if you are considering using a microcomputer system in an office environment dominated by, say, Apple Macintoshes, choosing that type of computer would probably be more convenient from the standpoint of having local expertise available for support. Good written documentation showing how to use the hardware or software is also important. When a helping hand isn't readily available, documentation is often the best alternative for answering a tough question.

Figure LIV 1-6 lists important criteria for selecting a particular microcomputer system.

Shopping for Software and Hardware Before looking over software or hardware products that you might buy, you should make a checklist of features that you want in your eventual system. Also, be sure to watch for these features during the test drive. A rehearsed presentation made by a salesperson is likely to point out only the strengths of a product, not its weaknesses. Some of the items that you should watch for when shopping for a PC are enumerated in Feature LIV 1-1.

In acquiring hardware, one of the most common mistakes is that people don't think enough about the future. You should buy as much processing speed and storage capacity in your initial purchase as you can possibly afford. New software updates—which now seem to come out about every year or so—virtually always require more speed and storage for effective operation. If you buy a bottom-of-the-line system, you might find that the next major upgrade of your favorite software package crawls at a snail's pace. If you buy a system for business use, expect your hardware to last about three years before new software needs force you to buy a new system.

CHOOSING A SYSTEM

After you have considered available alternatives, it's time to choose a system and purchase it. People choose among system alternatives in a number of ways. For instance, some people make a formal list of selection criteria, weigh each criterion with respect to its importance, and quantitatively rate each alternative on each criterion. All other things being equal, they then select the alternative that scores the highest total when the ratings are added.

Others prefer to make their choices less formally. After thinking about their needs and the criteria they apply to evaluate alternatives, they select the first computer systems they see that "feel right." Although such an acquisition process could be criticized for lack of thoroughness, many managers claim that their busy schedules leave no time to spend researching choices with greater care. Of course, rushing to make a selection has a negative side. Just as a car owner can go through years of torture driving around in the wrong type of car, a computer buyer can also wind up with years of headaches resulting from a poor choice.

System Checklist

- ☑ Product functionality
- ☑ Ease of learning and use
- ☑ Cost
- ☑ Vendor reputation
- ☑ Support
- ☑ Expandability
- ☑ Meets industry standards
- ☑ Performance
- ☑ Favorable reviews
- ☑ Delivery
- ☑ Documentation

FIGURE LIV 1-6

Important selection criteria. Buyers generally select computer systems on the basis of some combination of criteria.

Hardware and Software Installation

When you buy a computer system, most of the hardware and software you need will probably already be in place. If it isn't, you can usually install it relatively easily yourself.

Installing Hardware Historically, users have not always had an easy time installing new equipment on their computers. The cover of the system unit had to be carefully taken off and an add-in board fitted in correctly. Then, device drivers had to be correctly installed. From start to finish, the process was time consuming and stressful. Something could easily go wrong—an ultrathin circuit could get damaged or the add-in board might not work with a component on the motherboard. When a problem cropped up, users could waste hours trying to figure out what was causing it.

Fortunately, the scenario just described is gradually disappearing. To make it easier than ever for PC owners to install hardware on their own, both hardware and software vendors have gravitated toward a *plug-and-play* approach. Consequently, all users of such systems theoretically need to do is plug in any new equipment into the system unit—almost as easily as they would plug a lamp into a wall socket—and they're ready to go. When they start their computers after installing the hardware,

FEATURE LIV 1-1

PC Shopping Checklist

Some Important Questions to Ask

When buying a new PC be sure to get answers to the following questions.

Hardware

Should I buy a notebook or desktop PC? If you need portability, you need a notebook computer. Notebook buyers should expect to pay about $500 more than they would for a comparable desktop model, even though the processor and hard disk are usually slightly less capable if one is buying top-of-the-line. A critical decision in the notebook area is battery life; most have to be recharged every two to eight hours. Desktop computer systems are generally easier to upgrade than notebooks, and their bigger screens and keyboards favor them for most uses.

Which platform is best? The two main choices are going with a PC-compatible computer—most of which run under some version of Microsoft Windows—or, alternatively, a Macintosh-compatible unit. Close to 90 percent of PCs sold today are Windows-based, but the Mac is more popular in the desktop-publishing and graphic arts fields. Because there is less competition in the Macintosh arena, expect to pay slightly higher prices for both hardware and software if you decide to become a Mac owner.

How powerful should the system be? Acquire a system with enough processing power to last for several years. One of the biggest errors made by first-time computer buyers is skimping on price and not acquiring the power they will need one or two years hence. When this happens, and new software runs at a crawl, the buyer is forced prematurely to either get another new PC or "patch" the existing PC with additional capabilities. This latter task can be time consuming and expensive, and it may not provide as good a result as if the capabilities were factory installed.

How much memory is necessary? Most people today need at least 32 or 64 MB of RAM. The computer you buy should have enough RAM to run your most memory-intensive program and then some—say, enough to accommodate an upgrade to the next version of the program or a switch to a comparable program. For instance, 8 to 16 MB, the minimum to run Windows 9X, will prove insufficient if you later want to switch to Windows NT, which doubles those requirements. A good rule of thumb is to buy twice the memory you initially need.

What types of secondary storage systems should I buy? Most people buying computer systems today will have it configured with one 1.44 MB diskette drive, a hard drive with a capacity of a few gigabytes, and a CD-ROM drive that accepts the standard 640 MB CD-ROM. Also, many people are supplementing their storage versatility with superfloppy drives, which enable 100 or more megabytes of data to be placed onto removable cartridges. When buying a hard disk, go for as much storage as you can—it usually doesn't cost that much for the additional megabytes and you'll be happy a couple of years down the road that you made the investment.

What about backup? Because hard disks have such great capacities today and there's so much to lose if a hard disk crashes or somehow gets corrupted, many people today are buying backup tape units or rewritable optical disks. The disks allow random access to files, whereas the tapes do not. Whatever type of backup drive you buy, make sure that its media are capacious enough to store the entire contents of your hard disk.

Do I need a CD-ROM drive? CD-ROMs are now a standard item in home-based microcomputer sales, and many software vendors today require you to use CD-ROM installation disks. When buying a CD-ROM drive, you should also equip your computer system with speakers, a sound card and a video card, and a good graphics board. Get a CD-ROM drive that goes at the fastest commercially available speeds—say, 16X or higher. Also be aware that DVD-ROM may shortly replace CD-ROM on PCs as the preferred optical standard.

Do I need a color or monochrome monitor? Virtually all business software made today is optimized for use on desktop, CRT-type color monitors. Color displays have gotten much better in recent years on notebook computers, too, and color is now the standard in notebook sales

What should I look for in a display screen? If possible, inspect the output of the monitor you are considering before making a purchase. You only have one pair of eyes, so, if you're going to be spending many hours at a screen each day, a monitor choice can be extremely important. Most monitors sold today are of the SVGA type. If you are working in an intensely graphical environment, consider an XGA (extended graphic array) display, or alternatively, a larger-than-normal screen size.

the operating system "talks to" the new equipment and automatically downloads the proper drivers from it.

Installing Software Generally, software of any type is relatively easy to install today. When you buy a new program, the package contains one or more *installation disks.* You load the first of the disks into its proper drive and, if instructed to do so on the disk label, enter a command. Then, it's just a matter of following a set of simple instructions on the screen. In most cases, there is very little you have to do beyond

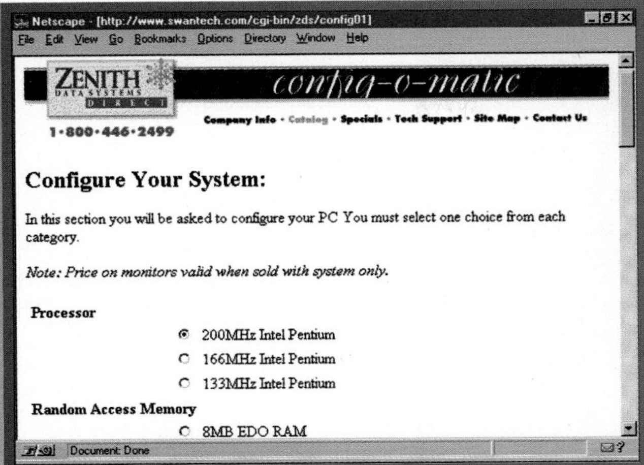

Do it your way. Web sites that let you put together your own computer systems are becoming a common occurrence.

What should I look for in a keyboard? If possible, type on the keyboard before buying. Notice especially the key spacing and how the keys feel to your touch. It is especially important that the keyboard is detachable, enabling you to move it about to suit your comfort, and that it has an adjustable slope. Keyboards sold with virtually every new microcomputer system are of the QWERTY type; those wanting a Dvorak keyboard layout often acquire special software to make the necessary key conversions.

What type of printer is best for my needs? For most people, the choice will be between an ink-jet and laser printer. Ink-jet printers are especially popular at the low end of the market, and many can produce color output. At the high end of the market, monochrome laser printers dominate. Laser printers are often reknown for their speed and crisp text quality. If you prefer a more exotic type of printer, make sure that the software you are planning to buy supports it.

How fast should the printer be? Ink-jet printers costing about $300 typically run at speeds of 2 to 6 pages per minute for monochrome text and perhaps half that when color printing is involved. Most laser printers designed for personal use, costing from $400 to $1,500, print anywhere from 2 to 16 pages per minute.

What should I look for in printer output? Be sure to examine closely both the range and the quality of outputs. Some printers, for instance, will print large-point-size characters with jagged contours and others limit the size of the characters. You should never buy a printer unless you first see a wide range of its outputs and see the printer in operation.

What do I need to know about modems? First, decide whether you want the modem to be internal or external. Unless you need the modem for more than one computer, buy the internal type. Also, get as fast a modem as you can; there's not much of a price-premium on a faster modem and you may notice an appreciable performance difference. Most modems sold today come with faxing capabilities.

Do I need a mouse? A mouse or similar pointing device is a must-have for working in a GUI environment on a desktop PC. Also consider getting a trackball or trackpad instead of a mouse. Many people dislike using a mouse because it must be moved around a desktop; trackballs and trackpads, in contrast, are stationary. Many notebook PCs come today with a built-in pointing stick, trackball, or trackpad in lieu of a mouse.

Software

What operating system should I go with? Most people buying a PC-compatible computer will likely be using Windows 9X, whereas those choosing a Macintosh-compatible platform will be using Mac OS. Make sure the vendor from which you are buying your PC is providing you with the current version of an operating system—and for that matter, a current version of all other software.

Should I buy a full-featured software suite or an integrated software package? While some stand-alone office programs still exist, most people buy office software in the form of suites or integrated software packages. Integrated software packages cost less than suites, yet have most of the features the average user would ever want to utilize. What's more, they require less disk space and memory. Integrated software packages are most suitable for home users. You will probably require a software suite, however, if you work in a business—especially one that uses some of the more sophisticated features of the software and is trying to standardize applications across a broad spectrum of users.

Service and Support

What should I look for in service and support? Service and support are becoming increasingly important factors as system quality and pricing continue to converge among the major PC sellers. What's more, hardware and software prices are falling while your time is becoming more valuable. The major PC vendors typically offer two or three years of toll-free technical support—24 hours a day, seven days a week—on both hardware and software. Many sellers will also warranty hardware for several months and provide rapid onsite service for any necessary hardware replacements.

entering some identifying information about yourself and deciding what type of installation you would like to do—such as a typical install, run install, or custom install (see Figure LIV 1-7).

A *typical install* places most of the files you will need onto your hard disk. In contrast, a *run install* transfers the minimum number of files needed; you must then access others you want from time to time from the installation disk. A *custom install* enables you to select additional files above the typical-install choices. In Office 97, for instance,

TYPICAL INSTALLATION
Recommended for most users, it places on your hard disk most of the files you will need, so that they are available for rapid access.

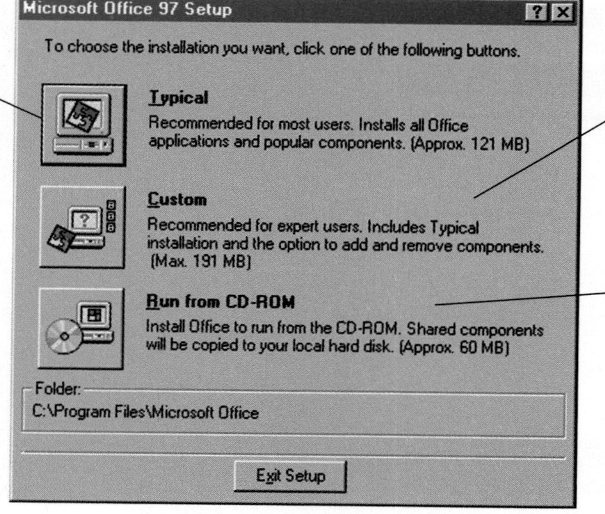

CUSTOM INSTALLATION
Recommended for advanced users, it allows you to add or delete specific files from the typical-installation option.

RUN (MINIMUM) INSTALLATION
Recommended if you want to conserve hard-disk space, it puts the minimum number of files on your hard disk. Files not on the hard disk can only be accessed by having the installation disk mounted.

FIGURE LIV 1-7
Installing new software.

a typical install fills 120 MB of hard-disk space, whereas run and custom installs, respectively, require 51 and 150 MB.

Also consider new uses for your old computer system. It could serve as a backup device that guests could use when they visit, so you don't have to put your new system in jeopardy.

Operating a Computer System

Once you acquire a computer system, you should develop a set of careful practices to protect your software, hardware, and data from damage and costly mistakes. Four important areas in this regard are system backup, proper maintenance of hardware and storage media, security, and problem detection and correction.

BACKUP PROCEDURES

Virtually everyone who has worked for months or years on a computer system will warn you that, sooner or later, you will lose some critical files. Maybe lightning will strike nearby, zapping your RAM. Maybe a small brownout will cause the heads on your hard disk to drop out of orbit and crash onto the disk surface, carving a miniature canyon through the electronic version of a 45-page term paper that's due tomorrow. Computer veterans will also tell you that file losses always seem to happen at the worst possible times.

Fortunately, there is a solution to most of these problems—backup. Creating **backup** means making a duplicate version of any file that you can't afford to lose so that, when the fickle finger of fate causes inadvertent erasure, you're confronted with only a minor irritant rather than an outright catastrophe. Theoretically, you can back up any file on your computer system. The backups you create—through, say, a file-copy, disk-copy, or backup command—can be on diskette, hard disk, tape, or virtually any other secondary storage medium.

One common form of backup that everyone should practice is making a duplicate of a long file that is being developed in RAM. For instance, suppose you are word processing a paper for a class. About every half hour or hour, you should make sure that you save the current version of the document onto disk. As regards backup of

■ **Backup.** A procedure that produces a duplicate version of any file that you can't afford to lose.

FIGURE LIV 1-8

Reasons for file backup.

WHY BACK UP?

- A disk sector goes bad, destroying part of a file.
- A file that you thought you no longer had a need for and erased turns out to be important.
- You modify a file in an undesirable way, and the damage done is irreversible.
- You accidentally reformat a disk.
- The disk suffers a head crash.
- A power brownout or failure at the time of saving a file causes "garbage" to be saved.
- You save a file to the wrong subdirectory, overwriting a different file that has the same name.
- While rushing your work, you make a mistake that causes the wrong files to be erased.
- You unwittingly destroy a file while working on it—say, by deleting parts of it erroneously and then saving the file.
- Malfunctioning hardware or software causes files to be erased.
- A computer virus enters your system and destroys files.
- Your disk is physically destroyed—for instance, a diskette is left in the sun or the hard disk is given a jolt. Alternatively, a fire or flood may destroy the disk.
- Someone steals your diskette or hard disk.

several files at more or less the same time, many different strategies exist. Some users perform **full backups,** storing all files from their hard disks onto tapes or disk cartridges at the end of a day or a week. The advantage to a full backup is that it is relatively straightforward. On the downside, a full backup takes up more storage space and takes longer than a backup in which only selected files are targeted for copying.

An alternative to the full backup is a **partial backup** in which you copy only the files that you have created or altered since the last backup. Users commonly implement two such types of partial backup procedures. A *differential backup* duplicates all files created or changed since the last full backup. In an *incremental backup* duplicates are made of all files created or changed since the last backup of any type. Both types of partial backup described here enable you, along with the copy of the full backup, to reconstruct the hard disk if it becomes corrupted. Incremental backups are the faster of the two types of partial backup to perform but result in more work to fully reconstruct the hard disk. Many people who have hard disks will perform a partial backup daily and a full backup weekly.

Whenever you back up files on a disk, make sure to place the backup files on a different disk from the originals. In theory, you shouldn't even keep these copies in the same room or building. That way, if a serious accident such as a fire or flood occurs at one location, the files safely stored at the other location will help you to recover. A variety of accidents that can destroy programs and data—all of them good reasons to back up data stored on disk—are listed in Figure LIV 1-8.

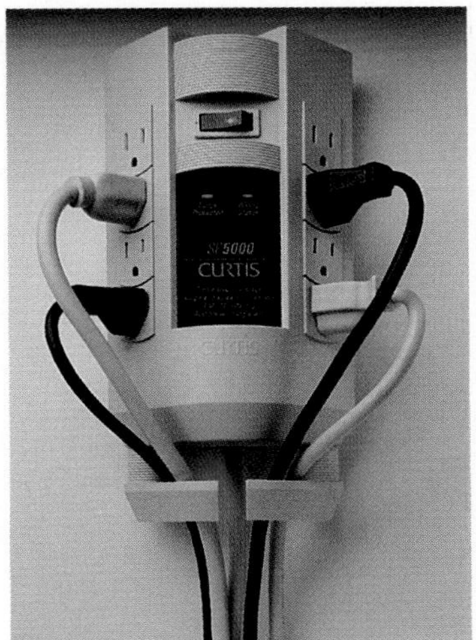

FIGURE LIV 1-9

Surge suppressor. The system unit and its support devices feed into the surge suppressor, which is plugged into a standard wall outlet. All of the equipment can be turned on or off by a single switch.

EQUIPMENT MAINTENANCE

Microcomputer systems consist of sensitive electronic devices, so users must treat them with appropriate care. In this section we discuss protecting your computer system with a surge suppressor or UPS unit; caring for disks; protecting your computer system from dust, heat, and static; and protecting monitors.

Surge Suppression One of the best devices to have on your computer system to minimize the chance of unexpected damage is a surge suppressor. A **surge suppressor,** which is installed between your computer system and the electrical outlet providing the power, is a hardware device that prevents random electrical power spikes from impacting your system (see Figure LIV 1-9). Probably the most common

■ **Full backup.** A procedure that produces a duplicate copy of all files onto a secondary storage medium. ■ **Partial backup.** A procedure that produces a duplicate copy of selected files onto a secondary storage medium. ■ **Surge suppressor.** A device that protects a computer system from random electrical power spikes.

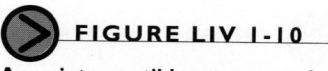

FIGURE LIV 1-10
An uninterruptible power supply (UPS) unit.

problem caused by a spike is loss of data in RAM. Cases have also been reported, however, of loss of data in secondary storage and destruction of equipment. A surge suppressor cannot guarantee complete electrical protection. If lightning strikes your house, a surge suppressor will probably fail to protect your data or equipment. If you are working on your computer system when a storm hits, you should save to disk what you've been working on and turn off your system.

Many people use instead of a plain surge suppressor an **uninterruptible power supply (UPS)** unit (see Figure LIV 1-10). This device is a surge suppressor with a built-in battery, the latter of which keeps power going to the computer when the main power goes off—say, due to a lightning storm, a brownout, or damage to an outside cable. UPSs designed for the average PC often run for a few minutes without outside power before they have to be recharged; UPSs for larger computers may run for several hours.

Disk Care User precautions with diskettes, hard disks, and CDs help to safeguard any programs and data stored on them. Diskettes may look like inert slabs of plastic, but they are actually extremely sensitive storage media that work well over time only with appropriate care. Never touch the exposed diskette surface or bend the diskette. Also, keep the diskette away from magnetic objects, motors, stereo speakers, and extreme temperatures. Never insert a warped diskette into a drive.

The most important precaution for a hard disk is placing it in a location where it is not likely to be bumped or subjected to electrical interference. As far as CDs go, make sure that the nonprinted side remains free of dirt and scratches, both of which may impair laser reading.

Dust, Heat, and Static Each of the tiny processor and memory chips in your hardware units are packed tightly with thousands or millions of circuits. Dust particles circulating in the air can settle on a chip, causing a short circuit. Many people buy dust covers that fit snugly over each of their hardware devices to prevent foreign particles in the air from causing hardware failure.

Desktop system units also generate lots of heat and require cooling fans. When placing your computer system on a desk top, make sure it is in a place where the outlet from the fan is not blocked.

Static electricity is especially dangerous because it can damage chips, destroy programs and data in storage, or disable your keyboard. So that the electrical discharges from your fingertips don't wreak havoc, you might consider buying an antistatic mat for under your workstation chair or an antistatic pad to put under your keyboard. Static electricity is more likely in dry areas and in the wintertime, when there's less humidity in the air.

■ **Uninterruptible power supply (UPS).** A surge suppressor with a built-in battery, the latter of which keeps power going to the computer when the main power goes off.

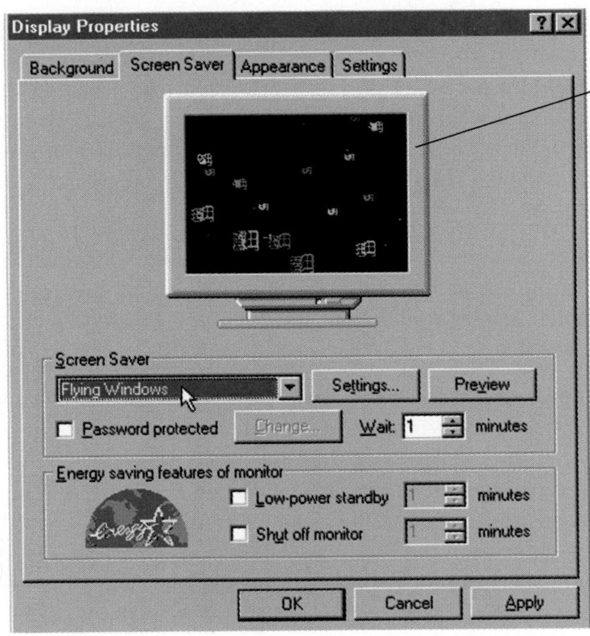

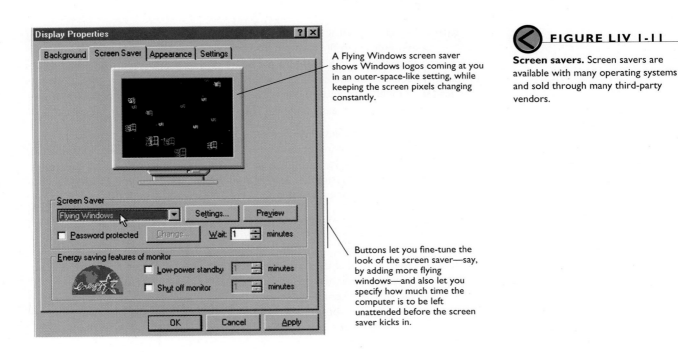

A Flying Windows screen saver shows Windows logos coming at you in an outer-space-like setting, while keeping the screen pixels changing constantly.

Buttons let you fine-tune the look of the screen saver—say, by adding more flying windows—and also let you specify how much time the computer is to be left unattended before the screen saver kicks in.

FIGURE LIV 1-11

Screen savers. Screen savers are available with many operating systems and sold through many third-party vendors.

Screen Savers CRT-type monitors have a phosphorescent inner surface that is lit up by an electronic gun. If you keep your monitor at a high brightness level and abandon it for several hours—with an unchanging image on the screen—the phosphorescent surface may get damaged. Ghosty character images can get permanently etched on the screen, making it harder to read. To prevent this from happening, software packages called **screen savers** are available that either dim your monitor or create constantly changing patterns on the screen when the display remains unchanged for a given number of minutes (see Figure LIV 1-11).

SECURITY

Security refers to protecting a computer system's hardware, software, and data from unintentional damage, malicious damage, or any type of tampering. There are many ways to secure a computer system, including locks on doors and lockplates on equipment, protecting files with passwords that only you know, accessories that block people from seeing what's on your hard disk, encryption algorithms that disguise outgoing messages, and programs that prevent computer viruses from infecting storage devices (see User Solution LIV 1-1). The topic of securing computer systems is discussed more thoroughly in Chapter LIV 2.

No matter what type of security strategy you decide to go with, it is important to note that no strategy can give you 100 percent protection. Nonetheless, giving a little thought to some of the things that can go wrong and taking a few simple precautions can save you big headaches later on. Studies made on microcomputer users have shown that they tend not to spend a lot of time thinking about security.

TROUBLESHOOTING AND TECHNICAL ASSISTANCE

If you work with computers for any length of time, at some point you will probably have an experience when your hardware or software does not work properly. You

■ **Screen saver.** A software product designed to protect the phosphor coating on the inside of a display screen from damage when the display is turned on but is not used for an extended period. ■ **Security.** A collection of measures for protecting a computer system's hardware, software, and data from damage or tampering.

may turn on your computer system one day and get no response. Perhaps your monitor screen will begin flickering badly every few seconds. Or maybe you will issue a familiar command in a software package that you work with regularly and the keyboard will lock up or the command will remain unexecuted. When such an event takes place, you will need to troubleshoot to isolate the underlying problem. If the problem is serious enough, assistance from an outside source may be necessary.

Troubleshooting *Troubleshooting* refers to actions taken to diagnose or solve a problem. Unfortunately, many problems are unique to specific types of hardware and software, so no simple troubleshooting remedy will work all of the time. Nonetheless, the following simple steps and guidelines will help you to identify and correct a surprising number of problems:

- Try again. An unusual number of procedures work when you try a second or third time. You may have pressed the wrong keys the first time, or not pressed the keys hard enough.
- Check to see that all of the equipment is plugged in and turned on and that none of the cables are detached or loose.
- Recall exactly what happened between the time the system was operating properly and the time you began to encounter problems. There might have been an electrical storm outside, and your system was plugged in and damaged by lightning. Or perhaps you installed new systems software during your last session, and it is affecting the way your current application works.
- Be observant. If strange noises came out of the disk drives when you unsuccessfully tried to boot the system up, those noises might be important. Even though solving the problem may be beyond your capabilities, you may be able to supply important facts to the people who will assist you in getting your system up and running again.
- Check the **documentation,** or written instructions, that came with the system. Many products come with a hard-copy manual and many software products have an online help feature that will help you solve many of your own problems.
- Use diagnostic software. *Diagnostic software* enables you to test your system to see if parts of it are malfunctioning or are just giving you poor performance. Sometimes, when new equipment is added, problems arise with existing equipment or software. Also, hard disks can get fragmented with use over time and may need to be sped up with defragmentation software.

You should weigh the time that it takes to solve a problem yourself against the cost of outside help. It's not a disgrace to give up if the problem is more than you can handle. It is simply an admission that your time is valuable and that you are wise enough to know when to call in a professional for assistance.

Technical Assistance with Hardware and Software One of the most important items in working with hardware or software products is getting technical assistance when you need it. Three such sources of assistance are discussed next.

THE MANUFACTURER One of the best prospects for support is turning to the company that made the hardware or software with which you are working. Probably nobody knows more about correcting problems than the people who may have created them in the first place. It's that very thought that leads people to contact the hardware manufacturer or software publisher first whenever something bad happens.

Many manufacturers provide toll-free phone numbers, fax numbers, e-mail addresses, and Web or newsgroup sites for users to contact to get help with technical problems. To reach others, you will have to make a toll call or, worse yet, dial a 900-area-code line where you get charged by the minute. Some vendors are notorious

■ **Documentation.** A written description of how a product works.

PCs That Call When Kidnapped

A major, growing problem among PC owners is theft. Portable computers, because of their size, are especially vulnerable. By one recent account, 1 out of every 14 notebook computers sold in the United States is stolen. Now, a program named CompuTrace TRS is available that will enable your PC to phone "home" to make sure it's where it should be. The software works as follows: Once a week, your PC makes a silent toll-free phone call to a call center. If the PC is where it should be, the event is logged. If the PC is reported stolen, however, caller-ID technology—which can trace the source of the call—is used to locate its whereabouts. The service costs a few dollars per month, which may be a small price to pay to retrieve your computer and data, not to mention the comfort of knowing you're helping to bring criminals to justice.

for keeping users on hold. Check to see if some type of premium service is available where you can get a faster and perhaps higher level of response.

With the cost of support escalating, hardware and software makers are increasingly devising more ways to provide humanless assistance (see the Tomorrow box on LIV 24).

THIRD-PARTY SUPPORT Products are often supported through third-party firms that specialize in giving assistance. You can contact one of these firms yourself, or you may be put in touch by a hardware or software maker. Many of the latter, incidentally, do not have their own in-house technical support groups but instead farm out customer support to third-party firms.

Third-party firms often have toll-free or 900-area-code phone numbers that you call to get help. In the case of the 900 area codes, many firms will cap charges at a limit—say, $25 or $50—so your bill doesn't become outrageous. When dealing with anyone who charges for support, check to see if any follow-up calls you make once a problem is theoretically corrected will incur a charge.

USER SUPPORT If you don't know anyone personally who can give you help, take solace in the fact that many users post problems on the Internet or on public bulletin boards. The message you post might be read by literally hundreds of other users, and there's a good possibility that someone out there has encountered and solved the problem you are now wrestling with. While you may get the answer you are seeking without paying a dime, don't be surprised if you have to wait a week or more to have your plea for help read by the right person.

With the more widely used products, you will also find formal user groups. *User groups* enable you to meet other users in person and to talk about common problems and creative ways to use the hardware or software.

Equipment Repairs In some cases, a problem is simple enough that no equipment repair is necessary. However, when a repair is beyond the scope of your capabilities, you will need to seek professional help. Likely sources of such help are the party that sold you the problematic hardware, computer stores in your area, and computer repair technicians listed in the Yellow Pages of your local phone book.

Keep the following considerations in mind when asking someone else to diagnose or repair your system:

- Is it better to repair old equipment or to buy new equipment? For instance, if the computer system to be repaired is worth less than $500, it may be cheaper to buy a completely new system.
- Will the repair work be done under **warranty?** Most new equipment is sold with a warranty stating that the manufacturer will pay for certain repairs if the equipment fails within a given number of days or months after purchase. If the warranty hasn't expired, the repair may cost you nothing. Be aware that many manufacturers state in their warranty that the warranty becomes void if you attempt to repair the equipment yourself or if a repair is attempted by an unauthorized person or shop.
- Can you get an estimate before proceeding with the work? In many cases, repair technicians can provide a free estimate of what the repair will cost. If they can't, you might want them to diagnose the problem first and to call you when they are able to provide an estimate. You never, ever want to put yourself in a situation in which you are presented with an unexpected, outrageously expensive repair bill.
- Is priority service available? People who use their computers as part of their jobs often need repairs immediately. Many repair shops realize this and will provide same-day or next-day turnaround for an extra fee. Some will even loan you equipment while repairs are being made.

When you buy a computer system, you can often choose to buy an extended maintenance contract to cover certain types of repairs beyond those stated in the warranty. Figure LIV 1-12 lists a number of the points covered by both warranties and maintenance contracts.

Upgrading

Hardware and software generally need to be upgraded over time. **Upgrading** a computer system means buying new hardware or software components that will extend the life of your current system. The question you must ask when considering an expensive upgrade is the same one that you would ask when considering costly repairs to a car: Should I spend this money on my current system or start fresh and buy a completely new system?

When you acquire a microcomputer system initially, it is extremely important to formulate an upgrade strategy. Ideally, you should buy a microcomputer system that adheres to a well-supported standard. This and other considerations will give you flexibility to upgrade it to meet reasonable future needs over the course of its lifetime. Of course, you cannot anticipate all of your future needs, but you invite unnecessary and expensive upgrades later on by spending no time thinking about system growth.

UPGRADING HARDWARE

Some common types of hardware upgrades include adding more RAM to a system, adding boards to increase the speed of the CPU or to provide new types of func-

---

- **Warranty.** A conditional pledge made by a manufacturer to protect consumers from losses due to defective products.
- **Upgrading.** The process of buying new hardware or software in order to add capabilities and extend the life of a computer system.

Warranty and Maintenance
Coverage The contract should state clearly if both parts and labor are covered.
Contract Period Many contracts cover a period of one to three years. Some vendors provide a "lifetime" guarantee on certain types of parts or services.
Repair Procedure A procedure should spell out clearly what steps will be taken when a problem occurs. Often, the vendor will first try to diagnose the problem over the phone. If this fails, either you will have to bring or send the unit to an authorized repair center or a technician will be dispatched to your home or office within a certain number of hours or days. If you can't afford to be without your computer system for an appreciable period, this part of the contract may be the most critical. Some contracts will provide you with a "loaner" system while yours is being repaired.
Support Hotline Many companies provide a hotline for you to call when you have a question or a problem. Sometimes you can call toll free, and sometimes you won't be billed for the vendor's time. It's a good idea to check out how easy it is to reach the hotline; some of them are so understaffed it takes days for a call to be returned.
Other Clauses Most contracts will be void if you attempt to repair the equipment yourself or let someone who's not an authorized repairperson do it.

Contracts. A good warranty or maintenance contract should cover the clauses listed here.

tionality, and adding new input or output equipment such as an image scanner or a pen plotter. Unless your system is powerful enough to handle growth, many upgrades will not be possible. For instance, if you have an Intel 80386-based processor, intensive software upgrades—such as those requiring a Windows NT environment—usually cannot be accommodated. The CPU is just not powerful enough. Also, it's important to check the number of expansion slots used for add-in boards. If new peripherals require add-in boards and all of the expansion slots that allow such boards to communicate with the CPU are used up, upgrading is not possible.

Today, some microcomputer systems sold in the marketplace are touted as *upgradable PCs.* These devices are designed with replacement in mind, making it possible to swap out components—like the CPU chip or the internal hard disk—as more powerful ones become available. For instance, many PCs come with special sockets in the system board that make it possible to plug in an Intel *overdrive chip* (say, a Pentium processor) that takes over the duties of the resident CPU chip (say, an Intel 80486 processor). Upgradable PCs are not without their limits, however, and may not be able to take advantage of future technology that the PC designers didn't anticipate.

UPGRADING SOFTWARE

Many PC software vendors enhance their products in some major way every year or two, prompting users to upgrade. Each of these upgrades—which are called **versions—**is assigned a number, such as 1.0, 2.0, 3.0, and so on. The higher the number, the more recent and more powerful the software. Minor versions, called **releases,** typically increase their numbers in increments of 0.1—say, 1.1, 1.2, and 1.3—or .01, such as 3.1 followed by 3.11. Releases are usually issued in response to

■ **Version.** A major upgrade of a software product. ■ **Release.** A minor upgrade of a software product.

bugs or shortcomings in the version. Recently, the versions and releases of many software products are being assigned numbers that correspond to the year of issue—such as Office 95 (for the 1995 version of Microsoft Office) and Office 97 (for the 1997 version).

With computer networks now reaching into many homes and offices, many companies are making upgrades available to users with increasing frequency. Thus, between official versions and releases of a product, you may be able to take advantage of free enhancements, for only the effort it takes to download. Often, the cost of the enhancements is built into the price that you originally pay when you buy or license the software. Companies also may make such enhancements available for nonnetworked users through the mail, for a nominal fee that covers the cost of handling and mailing.

Virtually all software products tend to be *upward compatible*. This means that applications developed on earlier versions or releases of the software will also work on later versions or releases. *Downward compatibility* is also commonplace. For example, WordPerfect version 8 enables users to save files, say, in either WordPerfect 8 or any of several earlier formats. So, if you are using WordPerfect 8 on your desktop computer but the magazine you are sending an article to requires it in WordPerfect 5.1, no problem.

Cross compatibility is also widely found today. This would enable you to, say, turn a WordPerfect 8 document into a Microsoft Word 97 document. When translating documents from one vendor's software package into another, you must be aware that certain details can get lost in the translation. For instance, sometimes boldfacing and italicizing are not picked up.

Generally, the new software will be offered to current users at a reduced price to make the upgrade more attractive. The potential user has to weigh the benefits of using the new package against its costs. The costs include the sticker price of the software, additional training, setting up new standards for use, and, possibly, equipment upgrades due to the increased sophistication of the software. Each version of a software product is virtually guaranteed to be more sophisticated and complex and to require more RAM than its predecessors.

FUNCTIONAL VERSUS TECHNOLOGICAL OBSOLESCENCE

As suggested in earlier paragraphs, microcomputer products can serve user needs for several years before they must be replaced. A product becomes **functionally obsolete** when it no longer meets the needs of an individual or business. Improvements to hardware and software products are continuous, however, and often a product is replaced in stores with a newer version or release well before it is functionally obsolete. A product in this latter class is said to be **technologically obsolete.**

In upgrading, a common problem is that users believe the product they are using is functionally obsolete when it is merely technologically obsolete. Because of the rapid pace of technology, virtually anyone buying a computer system today will have at least one technologically obsolete component within a matter of months. What's more, it's often smart not to jump into a new version of a product immediately but instead to wait for the initial bugs in it to be fixed.

- **Functionally obsolete.** A term that refers to a product that no longer meets the needs of an individual or business.
- **Technologically obsolete.** A term that refers to a product that still meets the needs of an individual or business, although a newer model, version, or release has superseded it in the marketplace. Also commonly called a **legacy system.**

The term **legacy system** is often used for technologically obsolete products. Most companies have a variety of legacy systems on their hands today, and many of these systems will be capable of years of further use before they have to be replaced.

Learning More about Microcomputers

A wide range of resources fulfill the needs of those who want to learn more about microcomputer systems and their uses. Classes, computer clubs, computer shows, magazines, newspapers, newsletters, books, and electronic media—such as the World Wide Web—are all sources of information.

Classes A good way to learn any subject is to take an appropriate class. Many four-year colleges, universities, and community colleges offer microcomputer-oriented courses for undergraduate, graduate, and continuing-education students. Probably the fastest way to find out about such courses is to phone a local college and speak to the registrar or to someone in a computer-related academic department. Your local computer stores and Internet-enabled coffeehouses (cybercafés) may also organize classes. Some stores provide classroom support as part of system purchases.

Clubs Computer clubs are another effective way to get an informal education in computers. They are also a good place to get a relatively unbiased and knowledgeable viewpoint about a particular product or vendor. Generally clubs are organized by region, product line, or common interests. Apple computer enthusiasts join clubs such as Apple-Holics (Alaska), Apple Pie (Illinois), or Apple Core (California). Many clubs also function as buying groups, obtaining software or hardware for members at reduced rates. Computer clubs range in size from two or three members to several thousand.

Shows A computer show gives you a firsthand look at leading-edge hardware and software products. Such shows typically feature numerous vendor exhibits as well as seminars on various aspects of computing. Every November, Las Vegas hosts one of the largest trade fairs in the world, the Computer Dealer Expo (COMDEX) show (see Figure LIV 1-13). This weeklong event commonly attracts hundreds of vendors and around 200,000 visitors, many of them from foreign countries. COMDEX is a spectacular event and undoubtedly will remain popular for several years. However, today's trend favors smaller, more specialized exhibitions.

FIGURE LIV 1-13

Computer shows. The weeklong Computer Dealer Expo (COMDEX) attracts hundreds of thousands of enthusiasts to Las Vegas from around the world.

Periodicals Periodicals are another good source of information about microcomputers. Scores of them fill newsstands, collectively catering to virtually

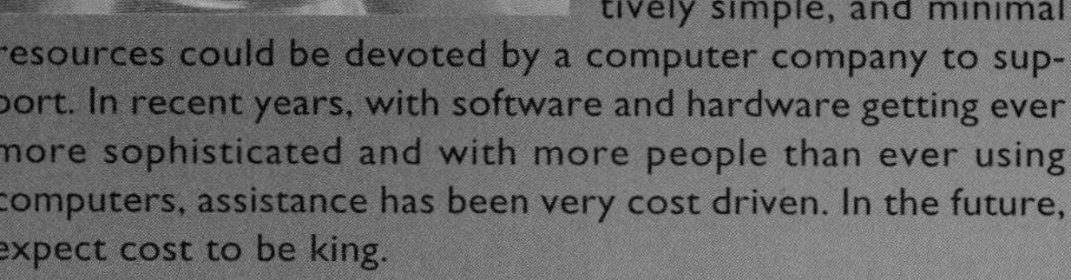

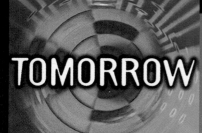

Humanless Assistance

Cost Will Increasingly Drive User Support

Support for PCs has changed dramatically during the last couple of decades. Back in the early 1980s, most PC software and hardware was relatively simple, and minimal resources could be devoted by a computer company to support. In recent years, with software and hardware getting ever more sophisticated and with more people than ever using computers, assistance has been very cost driven. In the future, expect cost to be king.

Consider the trend in documentation. Virtually all of the earliest PC-software manuals were in hard-copy form. They were created largely by technical people, and many were poorly organized and written. When PCs became big business in the mid-1980s, the manuals took on a more professional look and written support improved dramatically. In this decade, software packages have mushroomed in size—mostly due to add-ons and slick GUIs—thereby requiring almost an encylopedic level of support. With CD-ROMs and the Internet both providing the potential to dramatically cut printing and mailing costs, documentation has predominantly moved online.

While many users feel that online documentation does not measure up to the hard-copy manuals it replaced, don't expect the printed word to return anytime soon. Software companies are competing on increasingly thin profit margins, and hard-copy manuals are often too expensive to produce cost efficiently and distribute free with software—a sad fact that's not likely to change. But, take heart. Some software companies will still offer hard-copy manuals as long as there's enough buyers willing to pay separately for them. Also, soft-copy products will likely get better with time just as did the hard-copy manuals they hastily replaced. As software becomes more enabled to respond to natural-language queries, we can eventually expect interacting with a soft-copy manual to become almost like talking to a human expert.

Other types of support are also likely to become more humanless over time. Software training has moved online in a big way and getting assistance with hardware problems is poised to follow. While we're still a long way from the ideal of self-installing "plug-and-play" systems—barely even to first base, some might say—one day it will be common for programs to diagnose and fix problems on your computer system. Is your hard disk slow? A systems program will be able to recognize the problem before you do and tell you exactly what to do if it can't correct the problem itself. Is no sound coming from your speakers? Again, diagnostic programs will be able to tell you why this is happening and what corrective actions to take, without you having to phone a support representative.

Tech support. The rising cost of human labor is moving vendors toward automated systems to help solve users' problems.

This is not to say that computer companies will no longer provide hand holding to those who need it. For a price, you will still be able to get virtually anything you want in this world. But with the cost of human labor becoming more expensive relative to the cost of other items—and software becoming more intelligent—it is likely that you'll have to pay handsomely for someone to talk to.

every conceivable interest area (see Figure LIV 1-14). Computer magazines and newspapers can vary tremendously in reading level. You can generally browse through a variety of computer-related publications at your local bookstore or computer store. Evaluate them carefully to determine their appropriateness to your needs. Many microcomputer periodicals also maintain online versions on the World Wide Web.

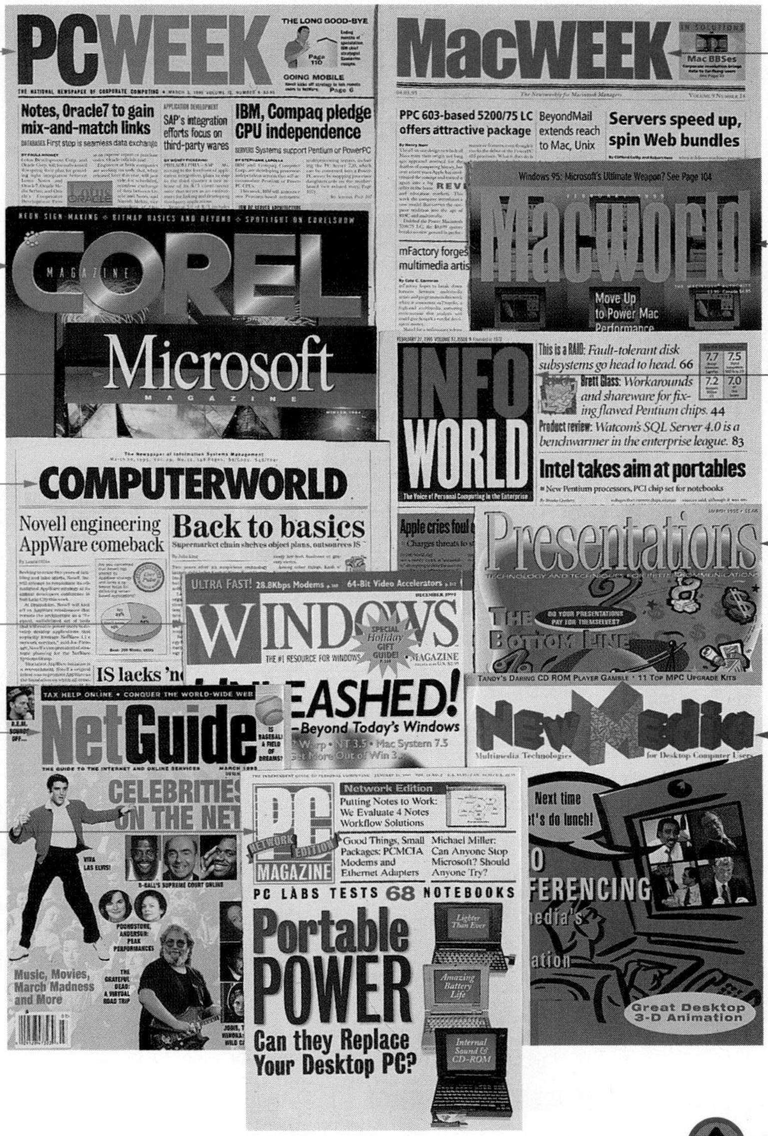

PCWeek
Newsweekly specializing in PC compatibles

Corel Magazine
Targets Corel products and applications

Microsoft Magazine
Covers Microsoft products and applications

Computerworld
Reports weekly happenings throughout the computer industry

Windows
Features Windows-based products and applications

NetGuide
Guide to the Internet and online services

PC Magazine
Spotlights products for PC compatibles

MacWeek
Newsweekly for Apple Macintosh managers

Macworld
Targets users in the Apple Macintosh world

InfoWorld
Newsweekly specializing in microcomputers

Presentations
Specializes in desktop presentation graphics

New Media
Focuses on multimedia products for the desktop

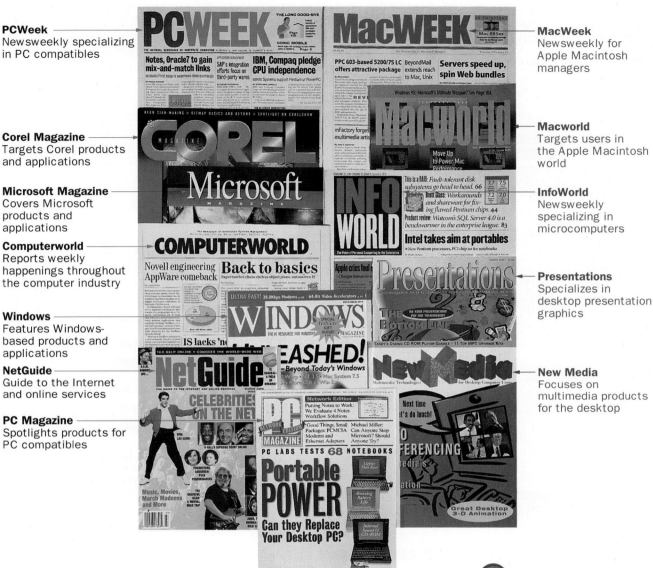

FIGURE LIV 1-14

Microcomputer periodicals. Scores of weekly and monthly periodicals cater to virtually every user need. Many periodicals are also available in an online version, over the Web, for free.

Online periodicals enable users to search for information on specified topics and often give access to back issues.

Books One of the best ways to learn about any aspect of personal computing is to read a book on the subject. A host of softcover and hardcover books are available, covering topics ranging from the simple to the highly sophisticated. Included are how-to books on subjects such as using the more widely known productivity software packages, programming in microcomputer-based languages, and the technical fundamentals of microcomputers. You can find such books in your local library, computer stores, and bookstores. Many books are also published on the World Wide Web. Always check the copyright date of a book before you use it; computer technology moves along rapidly, and books in the field can go out of date just as fast.

Electronic Media One easy way to learn a subject in our electronic age is to pick up a training disk or view a videotape or television show devoted to the subject. Today many microcomputer-oriented software packages are sold with CDs that provide screen-oriented tutorials, showing you which keys to press and the results. Other types of professionally prepared *courseware* from a third-party vendor may also be available. Videotapes are widely available for standard videocassette players, so you can see how something works simply by watching your television. In addition, there are many television shows—especially on cable and satellite—that are oriented toward computer education and knowledge. As if all of these sources weren't enough, the World Wide Web is a veritable treasure trove for all sorts of free and subscription-only information about computers (see Figure LIV 1-15).

FIGURE LIV 1-15

Learning about computers on the Web.

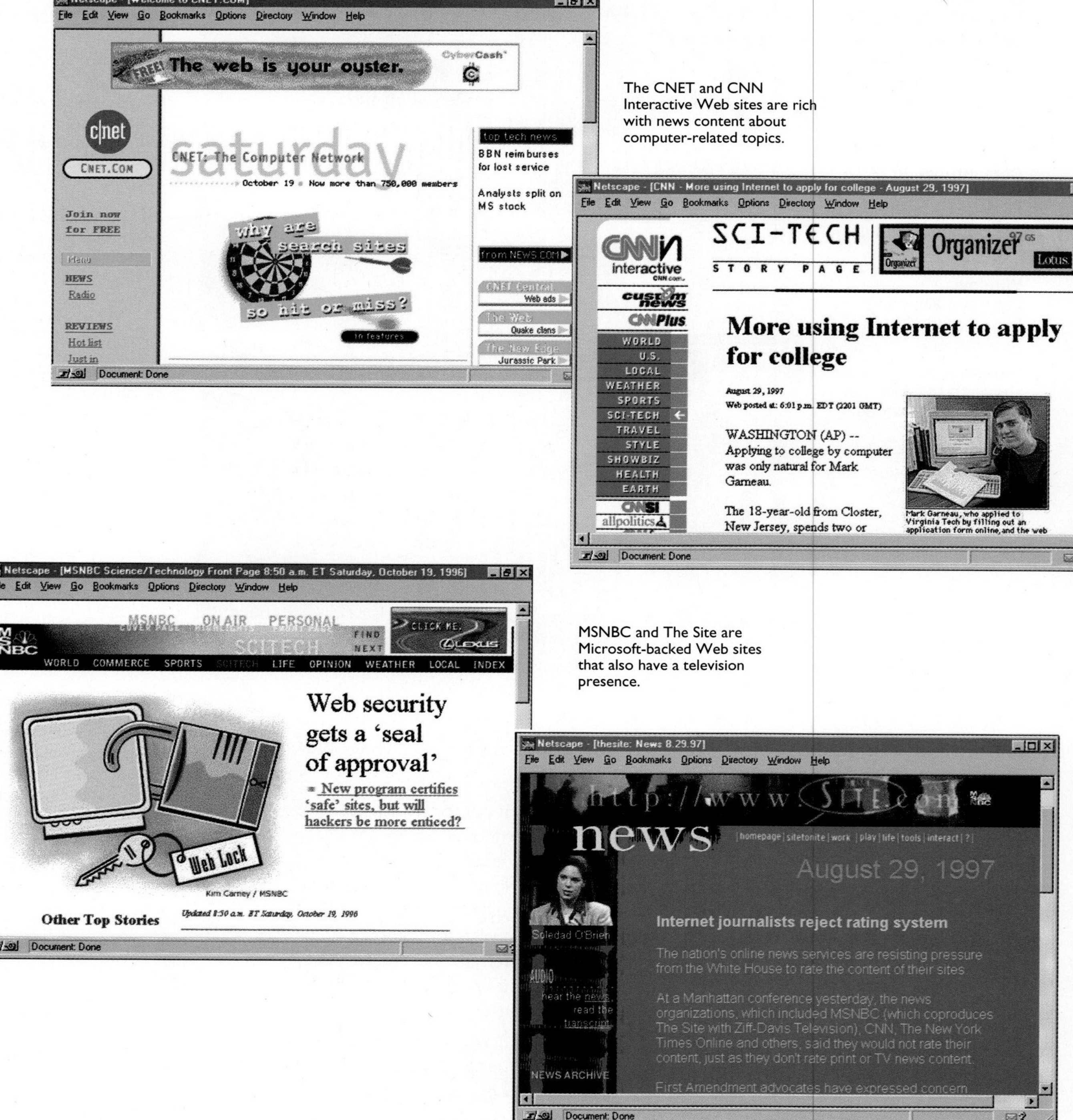

The CNET and CNN Interactive Web sites are rich with news content about computer-related topics.

MSNBC and The Site are Microsoft-backed Web sites that also have a television presence.

Summary and Key Terms

Chapter LIV 1 covers such related activities as users acquiring their own computer resources, taking care of their own systems, upgrading systems on their own, and educating themselves about microcomputers.

The Microcomputer Marketplace The microcomputer marketplace is composed of a wide variety of firms that make hardware and software products. Most users get their hardware and software microcomputing products from retail stores of various sorts, the Internet, mail-order houses, hardware manufacturers and **software publishers,** and **value-added resellers (VARs).**

Selecting a Computer System Steps for selecting a computer system include analyzing needs, listing system alternatives, evaluating alternatives, and choosing a system. Although applications software is normally selected before a computer and systems-software platform, software and hardware choices for microcomputers are often interrelated, so you must consider them jointly.

Hardware and Software Installation When you buy a computer system today, most of the hardware and software you need will probably already be in place. To make it easier than ever for microcomputer owners to install any new hardware on their own, both hardware and software vendors have moved to a *plug-and-play* approach.

Operating a Computer System **Backup** refers to procedures for making duplicate copies of valuable files. Two types of backup methods are **full backup** and **partial backup.**

Microcomputer systems contain sensitive electronic devices, so they need careful treatment and protection from damage. A **surge suppressor** will prevent most random electrical spikes from entering your system and causing damage. A **uninterruptible power supply (UPS)** unit lets you operate your computer when the main power to your home or office fails. Software called **screen savers** can protect your monitor. **Security** measures protect a computer system's hardware, software, and data from unintentional and malicious damage and tampering.

Although no two problems with a computer system are ever totally alike, some useful guidelines can be followed when troubleshooting problems or when seeking outside technical assistance. For instance, just trying a procedure out a second time or checking the **documentation** that comes with a product often solves the problem. Three sources of software assistance are support from the software publisher, third-party support, and user support. When considering an equipment repair, you should check first to see what protection the manufacturer offers under **warranty.**

Upgrading You can **upgrade** your computer system by buying new hardware or software components that add capabilities and extend its useful life. When planning a hardware upgrade, you must consider such things as your current system's storage capacity, the number of expansion slots, and the power of the system unit. Software upgrades are often accomplished by acquiring a new **release** or **version** of the program that you are currently using. You need to ask yourself whether upgrading is better than starting fresh and buying a new computer system. You also must consider whether you are planning to replace a product that's only **technologically obsolete** instead of **functionally obsolete.** Technologically obsolete systems are sometimes called **legacy systems.**

Learning More about Microcomputers A wealth of resources is available to those who want to learn more about microcomputer systems and their uses. Classes, computer clubs, computer shows, magazines, newspapers, newsletters, books, and electronic media are all sources of information about microcomputers.

EXERCISES

1. Fill in the blanks:
   a. A(n) __________ is a program designed to protect your monitor against damaging the phosphorescent coating on its screen.
   b. __________ refers to making, for security purposes, a duplicate copy of a file.
   c. A(n) __________ is a hardware device designed to stop power spikes from damaging a computer system.
   d. A(n) __________ usually states that a product manufacturer will correct defects in software or hardware for a given period of time under certain conditions.
   e. A product that no longer meets the needs of a user is said to be __________ obsolete.

2. Match each company name with the description that fits best.
   a. Compaq
   b. Corel
   c. Intel
   d. Microsoft
   e. Cyrix
   f. Motorola
   g. Seagate
   h. Apple

_____ Makes CPU chips for the Apple Macintosh line of computers
_____ A large, U.S.-based maker of PC-compatible computers
_____ A producer primarily of storage products
_____ The maker of Windows as well as a wide variety of other software products
_____ The maker of most CPU chips for PC-compatible computers
_____ The company that publishes WordPerfect
_____ A producer of Intel-compatible CPU chips
_____ The biggest producer of microcomputers that are not PC-compatible

3. Name as many types of sources as you can for buying microcomputer hardware and software. Which of these sources would you consult in the following situations?
   a. You want to look over a lot of products but don't have time to spend browsing around a store.
   b. You just opened a taco restaurant and need a computer system that specializes in keeping track of fast-food operations.
   c. You want a new microcomputer system but don't want to spend the premium prices the more famous companies charge.
   d. You're nervous about buying a microcomputer system and need a vendor that will hold your hand to help you through any problems.
   e. You want to get a brand-name printer at a low price, and you must have it today. You're willing to accept equipment that just became technologically obsolete when a new model came out last month.
   f. You need a printer and want to see as many printer specifications as you can within the next few hours.
   g. All you need is a 486 computer that will help you write your novel, and you'll be darned if you'll pay for anything more.
   h. You need a software product immediately, and your local computer store does not stock the product.

4. Define each of the following terms:
   a. Legacy system
   b. UPS
   c. Software publisher
   d. Value-added reseller
   e. Third-tier manufacturer
   f. Incremental backup
   g. Partial backup

5. Name several selection criteria that are important to consider when evaluating alternative computer system purchases.

6. Provide at least eight reasons that illustrate the importance of backing up files.

7. What is the difference between technological obsolescence and functional obsolescence?

8. Name at least five sources from which users can learn more about computers. Also, identify the types of learning resources that are available over the Internet.

9. Each of the following definitions is not strictly true in some regard. In each case, identify how the definition is false and correct the error.
   a. Software publisher: A company that sells the software that other companies create
   b. Legacy system: Technologically obsolescent hardware or software that has been around for awhile in a company, even though it continues to be updated regularly by its maker
   c. Release: A particular version of a software package

d. Value-added reseller: A company that sells computer systems made by others.
e. Surge suppressor: A device that keeps a computer system running in the event of a power shortage

10. Explain the difference between a typical, custom, and run installation.
  a. Which requires the most hard-disk space?
  b. Which requires the least?

1. Buying a Desktop Microcomputer System The accompanying figure shows an ad for a desktop microcomputer system. To demonstrate your knowledge of computing terms in the figure, most of which have been covered in various chapters of this textbook, respond to the following questions.

a. What types of storage devices come with the computer system? What is the capacity of each type of storage device?
b. What type of CPU chip comes with the system? How fast is the CPU chip?
c. Is the system PC-compatible?
d. Is the system a "multimedia" computer system?
e. What type of local bus unit does the system contain?
f. Can the monitor display photographic-quality images? What do *noninterlaced* and *.26 dp* mean?
g. What software comes with this system?
h. Does a word processing program come with this system? If it does, what's its name?
i. Does a printer come with this system? If it does, who is its manufacturer?
j. What options do you have available if the hard disk fails after one year of use?
k. What options do you have available if the operating system isn't responding properly after six weeks of use?

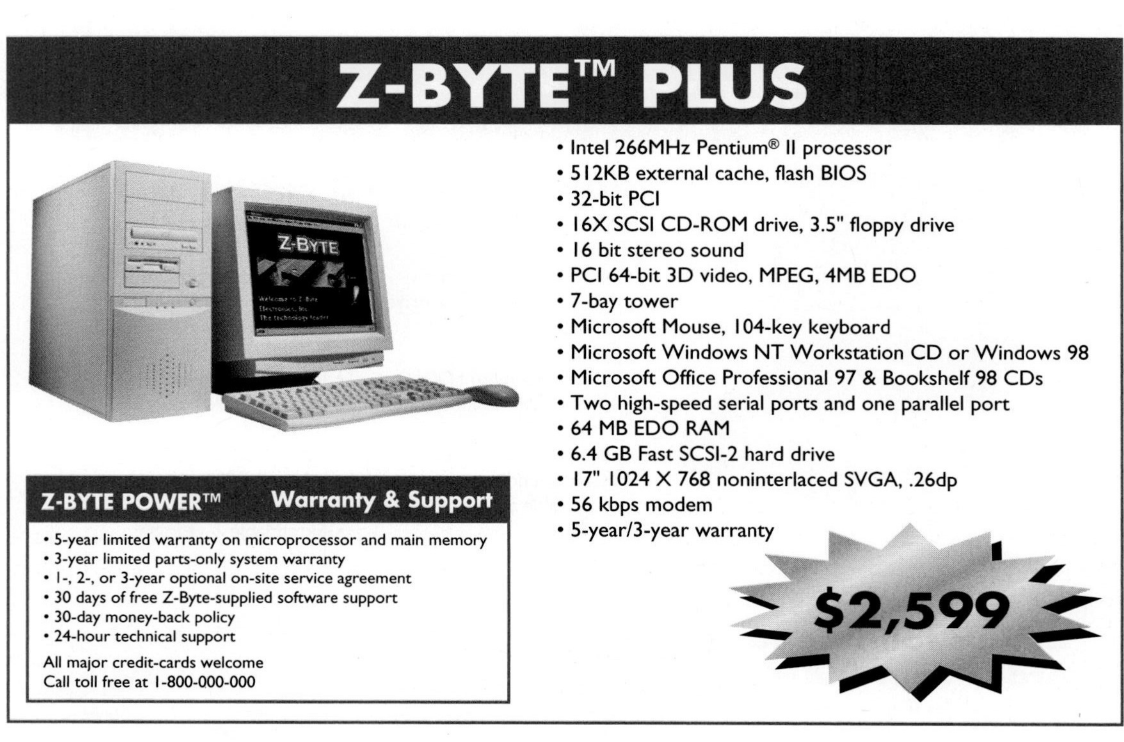

Z-BYTE™ PLUS
• Intel 266MHz Pentium® II processor
• 512KB external cache, flash BIOS
• 32-bit PCI
• 16X SCSI CD-ROM drive, 3.5" floppy drive
• 16 bit stereo sound
• PCI 64-bit 3D video, MPEG, 4MB EDO
• 7-bay tower
• Microsoft Mouse, 104-key keyboard
• Microsoft Windows NT Workstation CD or Windows 98
• Microsoft Office Professional 97 & Bookshelf 98 CDs
• Two high-speed serial ports and one parallel port
• 64 MB EDO RAM
• 6.4 GB Fast SCSI-2 hard drive
• 17" 1024 X 768 noninterlaced SVGA, .26dp
• 56 kbps modem
• 5-year/3-year warranty
$2,599
Z-BYTE POWER™ Warranty & Support
• 5-year limited warranty on microprocessor and main memory
• 3-year limited parts-only system warranty
• 1-, 2-, or 3-year optional on-site service agreement
• 30 days of free Z-Byte-supplied software support
• 30-day money-back policy
• 24-hour technical support
All major credit-cards welcome
Call toll free at 1-800-000-000

2. Buying a Notebook Computer The accompanying figure shows an ad for a notebook microcomputer system. To demonstrate your knowledge of computing terms, most of which have been covered in various chapters of this textbook, respond to the following list of questions:

a. What types of storage devices come with the computer? What is the capacity of each type of storage device?
b. Do each of the storage devices offer more or less capacity than the corresponding ones in the computer system detailed in Project 1?
c. Why isn't the system offered with a mouse?
d. Is the system a "multimedia" computer system?
e. What does the ad mean by a *Type II PCMCIA slot?*
f. What is the purpose of the infrared port?
g. Would you recommend buying this computer system to gain access to the Internet? Why or why not?
h. What software comes with this system?
i. What's the significance of this computer's lithium ion battery feature? How does this technology compare with other types of batteries?
j. Can you hook up a printer directly to this computer system? Explain why or why not.
k. What options do you have available if the hard disk fails after one year of use?
l. Can you run Windows on this computer? Why or why not?

3. Buying a Printer You need a printer for your microcomputer system and want to spend no more than $500.

a. Find an ink-jet printer and a laser printer that you can buy for this price. In what important ways do these printers differ?
b. Cut out or copy an ad for a printer from a computer magazine. What does the ad tell you about the features of the printer? Where can you go to get additional information?
c. A call to a local computer store reveals that you can get a product demonstration. What sorts of questions should this demonstration answer?

4. Buying Hardware over the Internet Many companies that sell computer hardware maintain sites on the World Wide Web. Such sites often showcase product offerings, offer users the chance to configure hardware and buy it, provide technical support, and so on. Visit two such Web sites—one representing a computer maker and the other an equipment reseller—and report to the class about the sites, making sure that you cover the following points:

a. What are the names of the companies you visited?
b. What types of hardware do they sell?
c. What objectives are served by each of the Web sites—for instance, providing product information, enabling people to buy equipment, offering technical support, and so on?
d. Do the sites offer any types of search or query tools to help you shop online—tools that might lead to better purchase decisions than those you might make after looking at hard-copy advertisements?
e. Do the sites include any "fun" features that might attract shoppers to make return visits?

Z-BYTE™ 200X

200X Standard Features

- 200 MHz Intel® Pentium® processor with MMX
- 11.3" TFT active display
- 3.5" 1.44MB diskette drive module
- 12X CD-ROM module
- 7.1 pounds (with FDD)
- 12-cell 52W lithium ion battery
- 32-bit local-bus video
- 16-bit Soundblaster compatible stereo sound
- 1MB video RAM
- 16 MB EDO RAM
- 1GB removable hard drive
- 56K fax/data modem
- 256K syncburst cache
- One Type II & one Type III PCMCIA slot
- Integrated dual-button pointing stick, optional touchpad
- Parallel, serial, PS/2 infrared and game ports
- Extendable 1-year limited warranty

Call us toll-free to order your 200X or for information **1-800-000-9999**
Monday-Friday, 8am-10pm EST
Saturday, 9am-5pm EST

$2199

f. How do people place orders and pay for the equipment?

Some of the Web sites in the accompanying table may interest you.

COMPANY	WEB SITE (HTTP://_____)
Apple	www.apple.com
Computer Express	www.cexpress.com
Compaq	www.compaq.com
Dell	www.us.dell.com
Gateway	www.gw2k.com
IBM	www.ibm.com
Insight	www.insight.com
Swan	www.swantech.com

While the sites of computer makers like IBM and Compaq feature their own equipment, sites of resellers like Insight (see image) enable you to select from a large variety of products and scores of manufacturers.

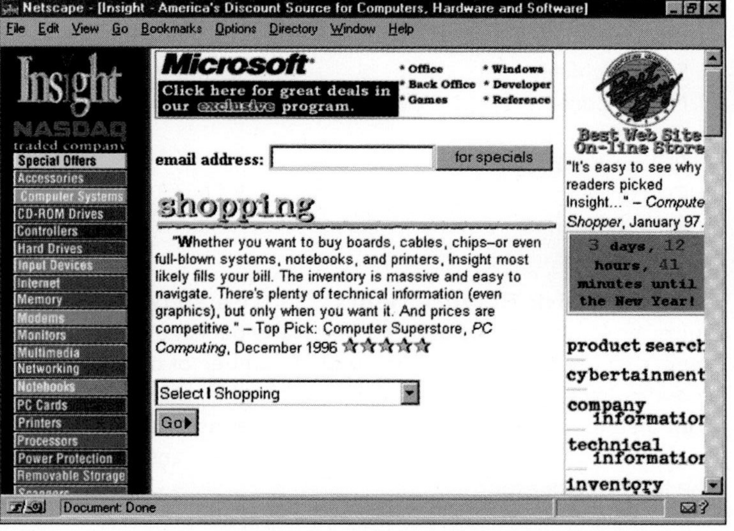

5. Buying Software over the Internet Many companies that sell software maintain sites on the World Wide Web. Such sites often showcase product offerings, offer users the chance to try out or buy software, provide technical support, and so on. Visit two such Web sites—one representing a software publisher and the other a software reseller—and report to the class about them, making sure that you cover the following points:

a. What are the names of the companies you visited?
b. What types of software are sold at the sites?
c. What objectives are served by each of the Web sites—for instance, providing information about software products, enabling users to buy software, letting users download software on a trial basis, offering technical support, and so on?
d. Do the sites offer any types of search or query tools to help you shop online—tools that might lead to better purchase decisions than those you might make after looking at hard-copy advertisements?
e. How do people place orders and pay for the software?

Some of the Web sites in the accompanying table may interest you.

COMPANY	WEB SITE (HTTP://_____)
CompUSA	www.compusa.com
Corel	www.corel.com
Computer Express	www.cexpress.com
Egghead	www.egghead.com
Lotus	www.lotus.com
Microsoft	www.microsoft.com
Quarterdeck	www.quarterdeck.com
Software.net	www.software.net

While the sites of software publishers like Microsoft and Corel feature their own programs, sites of resellers like Software.net (see image) enable you to select from a large variety of products and scores of publishers.

6. Technology News on the Internet Several Web sites report on news events regarding technology. Three such sources are MSNBC at http://www.msnbc.com, CNET—the Computer Network cable channel—at http://www.news.com, and the technology news section of CNN at www.cnn.com. Visit any two of these Web sites and report to your class about what you find. What future prospects do you anticipate for interactive news received on your computer system, as opposed to getting news through television or print outlets like newspapers and magazines?

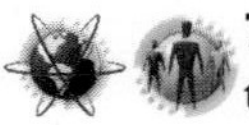

7. Online Magazines You can subscribe to or read for free online versions of many popular computer magazines (see image). For this project, research at least two such magazines published in Web versions and answer the following questions:

a. How much does an online subscription cost, relative to a hard-copy subscription of the same magazine?
b. What types of features do the online versions of these magazines have that you can't get in the hard-copy versions?
c. What do the hard-copy versions of these magazines have that you can't get in the online versions?

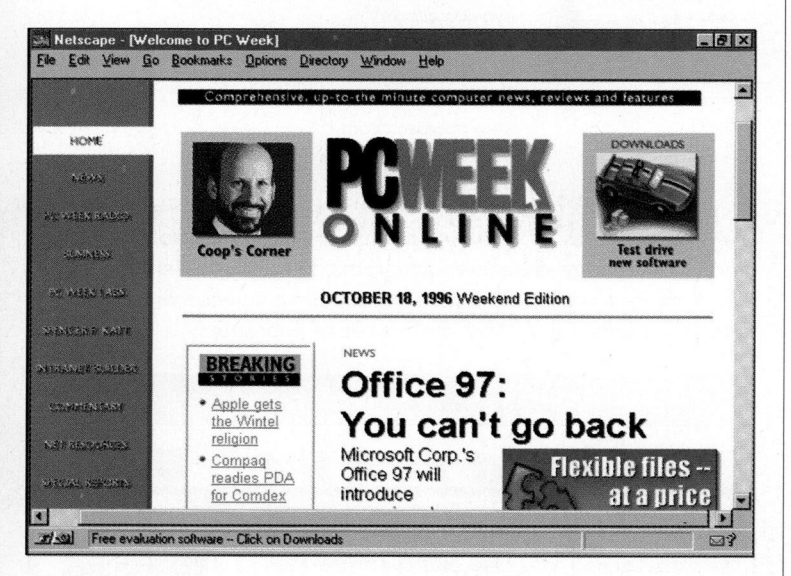

8. Book Report Microsoft Corporation has been one of the most-written-about technology companies of the past decade. For this project, write a report, not to exceed 15 pages, discussing some aspect of the company that has made it famous. A variety of books are available to help you gain information for your report, including those below:

- *Overdrive: Bill Gates and the Race to Control Cyberspace,* by James Wallace. Wiley, 1997.
- *The Microsoft Way: The Real Story of How the Company Outsmarts Its Competition,* by Randall E. Stross. Addison-Wesley, 1996.
- *Microsoft Secrets: How the World's Most Powerful Software Company Creates Technology, Shapes Markets, and Manages People,* by Richard W. Selby. Free Press, 1995.
- *The Making of Microsoft: How Bill Gates and His Team Created the World's Most Successful Software Company,* by Daniel Ichbiah and Susan L. Knepper. Prima Pub, 1992.
- *Hard Drive: Bill Gates and the Making of the Microsoft Empire,* by James Wallace and Jim Erickson. HarperCollins, 1993.

Also consider newspaper and journal articles to help you in your research as well as information gathered over the Internet.

9. PC History Many important people have shaped the history of PCs. Several of them are listed below. For this project, choose any three and, for each one, write a sentence or two about his contribution to the history of microcomputers.

a. Bill Gates
b. Steve Jobs
c. Scott McNealy
d. Marc Andreesen
e. Gary Kildall
f. Phillipe Kahn
g. Dan Bricklin
h. Brian Bastian
i. Ted Hoff

10. Hard-Disk Requirements Select a software suite, minisuite, or integrated software package and report to the class the recommended number of bytes required to do a typical install, a run install, and a custom install. Note that the names of these installation options may vary from product to product. Also answer the following questions.

a. Are any other installation options available?
b. In addition to the amount of storage needed, what other types of hardware or software requirements are stated by the software publisher for the package you have chosen?

LIV 2

Social Issues Involving Computers

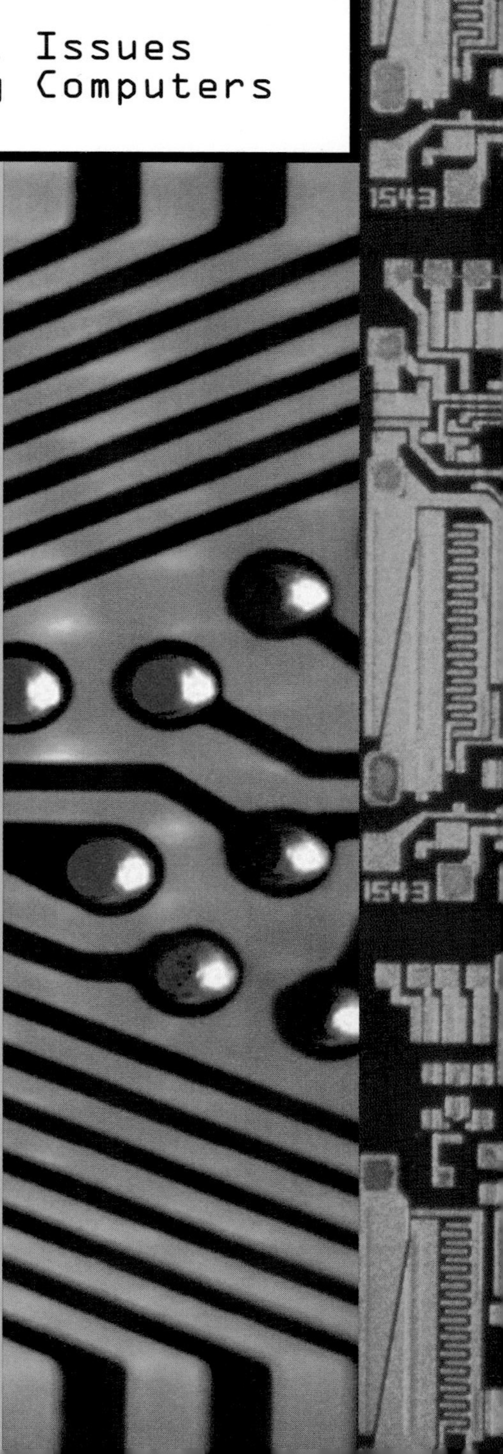

Outline

Overview

Computers, Work, and Health
- Stress-Related Concerns
- Ergonomics-Related Concerns
- Environment-Related Concerns

Computer Crime
- Types of Computer Crime
- Minimizing Computer Crime
- Crime Legislation

Computers and Privacy
- Privacy and Electronic Mail
- Privacy and Marketing Databases
- Caller Identification
- Privacy Legislation

Ethical Issues Regarding Computers
- Some Examples
- Why Study Ethics?

Window: The History of Computers

Learning Objectives

After completing this chapter, you will be able to:

1. Describe the health-related concerns that people have regarding computers.
2. Explain what computer crime is, give several examples of it, and describe how computer crime can be prevented.
3. Discuss how computer technology can encroach on people's privacy and describe some of the legislation enacted to prevent such abuses.
4. Explain what is meant by ethics, and provide several examples of ethical misbehavior in regard to computer-related matters.

Overview

Since the era of commercial computing began about 50 years ago, computers have rapidly woven their way into the fabric of modern society. In the process, they've created both opportunities and problems. Consequently, they've been both cursed and applauded—and for good reason.

So far in this text, we've focused on the opportunities more than the problems. We've examined the impact computers have had in organizations and on people. Throughout the text, you've seen how these devices have been put to work on routine transaction processing tasks, used to provide managers with better information for decision making, employed to design and manufacture better products, and used to improve the overall quality of people's lives.

Although the computer revolution has brought undeniable benefits to society, it has also produced some troubling side effects. Like any fast-paced revolution, it has been disruptive in many ways. Some jobs have been created, others lost, and still others threatened. In addition, an increasing variety of health-related concerns have surfaced that affect people who work with computers and related technologies. Computers have also immensely increased access to sensitive information, creating new possibilities for crime and threatening personal privacy. Clearly some controls to limit the dangers that these awesome devices pose will always be needed.

In this chapter, we highlight four key problem areas: computers and health in the workplace, computer crime, computers and privacy, and ethical uses of technology. The computer history window located at the end of the chapter provides some perspective as to how fast paced the growth of computers has been.

Computers, Work, and Health

Computers have been said to pose a threat to our mental and physical well-being. Although the body of scientific evidence supporting this claim is far from conclusive, and is likely to be that way for many more years, we should all be aware of the major concerns raised about the possible effects of computers on our health.

STRESS-RELATED CONCERNS

Emotional problems such as financial worries, feelings of incompetence, and disorientation often produce emotional *stress*. This stress, in turn, may have been triggered by a computer-related event.

Layoff or Reassignment One of the first criticisms leveled at computers upon their entry into the workplace was that their very presence resulted in job-related stress. When computers were introduced, many people were no longer needed and were subsequently laid off and forced to find new jobs. Workers at the lowest rungs worried most about job security. Many feared the full potential of computers in the office or in the factory and spent much of their time never knowing if machines might replace them. Such fears are still widespread today.

Even people who were not laid off found that their jobs had changed significantly and that they had no choice but to retrain. Airline agents, for example, had to learn how to manipulate a database-retrieval language and to work with computers. Secretaries were pressured into learning word processing and other office-related software to keep in step. Even the pace of work became faster and far less personal than it was earlier. Many workers never made the transition successfully.

A growing fact of life is that because of computers, fewer people are needed to do many types of work today. Computers also change the way work is done, often in ways that are difficult to predict. For instance, modern computer networks are posing a new threat to workers in that companies no longer have to staff as many physical locations as in the past. Networks also mean that work can be transferred to foreign countries more easily.

Fear of Falling Behind The microcomputing boom that has taken place since the early 1980s has put computing power of awesome dimensions at almost everyone's fingertips. Many researchers perceive a widespread fear that failure to learn how to use these machines will make one fall behind. One example is the numerous noncomputer-oriented executives, managers, and educators who see themselves being upstaged by their computer-savvy colleagues. There are so many big advances occurring on so many new technology fronts these days that the pace of change is fast enough to make even computer experts feel they are falling behind.

Burnout Burnout is caused not by fear of computers *(cyberphobia)* but by overuse of them *(cyberphelia)*. The infusion of such technologies as microcomputers, video CDs, e-mail, pagers and wireless phones, and the Web into the home and office has raised new concerns about emotional health. What will happen to children who withdraw into their computer systems, to computer-bound managers who are being inadvertently swept into the tide of the computer revolution and its relentless pace, or to families whose intimacy is threatened by computer overuse in their homes? Little research has been done on computer burnout. What makes this area so controversial is the flip-side argument that most victims of computer burnout would burn out on something else if computers didn't exist.

ERGONOMICS-RELATED CONCERNS

Ergonomics is the field that addresses such issues as making products and work areas comfortable and safe to use. With respect to technology, ergonomics covers the effects on workers of things such as display devices, keyboards, and work spaces.

Dangers Posed by Display Devices For over a decade, large numbers of data-entry operators have reported a variety of physical and mental problems stemming from their interaction with display devices. The complaints have centered on visual, muscular, and emotional disorders resulting from long hours of continuous display device use. These disorders include blurred eyesight, eyestrain, acute fatigue, headaches, and backaches. In response to these problems, several states and cities have passed laws that curb display device abuse. Also, hardware vendors have redesigned their products with features such as tiltable screens and detachable keyboards to make them more comfortable to use.

Keep in mind that it is not displays alone that cause physical problems. Humans are often part of the equation, too. Operator-induced factors that play a large part include poor posture, not taking frequent breaks, poor exercise habits, bad placement of the display on the desktop, and the like.

Dangers Posed by Keyboards Years ago, computer keyboards frequently were built into display units, making it difficult for operators to move them about as freely as they could if the keyboards had been detached. Most claims that a computer keyboard could result in injury seemed to be put to rest after keyboard manufacturers started making detachable keyboards—that is, until the last few years or so.

Today, some people are experiencing a condition known as *carpal tunnel syndrome,* a painful and crippling complex of symptoms affecting the hand and wrist that has been traced to the repetitive finger movements routinely made when using a keyboard. Carpal tunnel syndrome is an example of a *repetitive stress injury,* in which hand, wrist, shoulder, and neck pains can result from performing the same types of physical movements over and over again. Physicians recommend that to minimize the chance of such injuries you should take breaks every hour or so and relax or stretch your body.

■ **Ergonomics.** The field that studies the effects of things such as computer hardware, software, and work spaces on people's comfort and health.

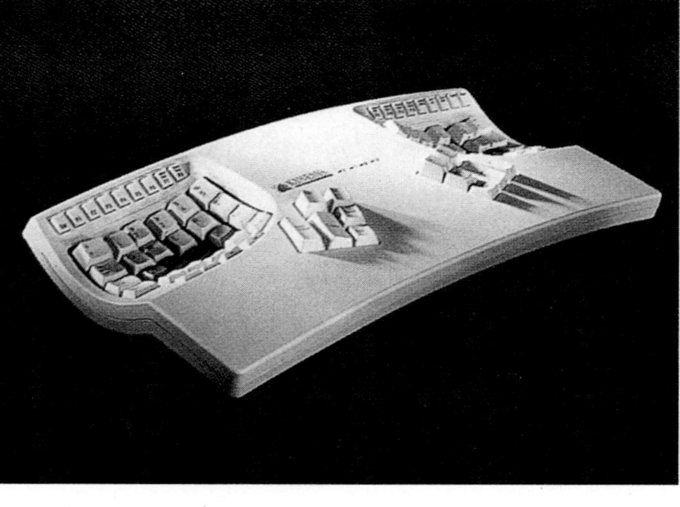

FIGURE LIV 2-1

Stress-reducing keyboards.

Recently, a number of innovatively designed keyboards have come to the fore that claim to reduce stress in the hands and wrists (see Figure LIV 2-1).

Work Space Design Display devices and keyboards are not the only things that can torture people at workstations. The furniture may be nonadjustable, forcing the user into awkward postures that are guaranteed to produce body kinks. Or the lighting may be so bright that it causes a headache-producing glare on the display screen. Even disconcerting noise levels, present due to poorly designed office equipment or acoustics, may be the culprits. Ergonomics researchers are constantly studying such problems, and the results of their efforts are becoming apparent in the consumer products now being offered to the ergonomics-conscious buyer. Figure LIV 2-2 illustrates some principles of good work space design.

ENVIRONMENT-RELATED CONCERNS

The surge in microcomputer use during the past several years has caused a variety of environmental concerns.

Take power use. The U.S. Environmental Protection Agency (EPA) estimates that home and office microcomputer systems now annually consume about $2 billion

FIGURE LIV 2-2

Workplace design. Features such as detachable keyboards, tilt capabilities on both keyboards and display devices, and adjustable furniture have contributed to added comfort for display device users.

worth of electricity. This indirectly has resulted in the discharge of tons of pollutants into the atmosphere. The microcomputer industry has responded by adding a variety of energy-saving devices into computer hardware. Among these devices are power-management software that puts the CPU, hard-disk drive, display, and printer into a sleep mode when they are not being used, low-power-consumptive chips and boards, and flat-panel displays.

The pollution problem goes much deeper than just the higher electrical use. For instance, the so-called paperless office that many visionaries predicted for the computer age has become largely a myth. Because computer outputs are so easy to produce, more paper than ever is now consumed. It is estimated that U.S. businesses generate close to a trillion pages a year—an amount that would stack over 50,000 miles high!

Computer Crime

Computer crime is defined as the use of computers to commit criminal acts. The law is spotty on computer crime. The U.S. government has made it a felony to fraudulently access confidential programs or data in federal-level computers. Most states also have laws that address some aspects of computer crime. But such laws notwithstanding, computer crime is hard to pin down.

One reason is that it is often difficult to decide when a questionable act is really a crime. No one doubts that a bank employee who uses a computer system to embezzle funds from customers' accounts is committing a crime. But what about an employee who steals time on a company computer to balance a personal checkbook for a home or business? Or someone who uses a company computer to word process a personal letter to a friend? Aren't those acts also unauthorized? Where does one draw the line?

Another problem in pinning down computer crime is that judges and juries—not to mention law-enforcement personnel—are often bewildered by the technical issues involved in such cases. Thus, many companies lack confidence the computer crimes will be investigated and prosecuted successfully, and they don't report them. Also, companies that discover computer criminals among their employees frequently are reluctant to press charges because they fear even more adverse publicity. Why get clients worried?

TYPES OF COMPUTER CRIME

Computer crime has many forms. Some cases involve the use of a computer for theft of financial assets, such as money or equipment. Others concern the copying of information-processing resources such as programs or data to the owner's detriment. Still other cases involve manipulation of data such as grades for personal advantage. By far, the majority of computer crimes are committed by insiders.

The cost of computer crime to individuals and organizations is estimated at many billions of dollars annually. No one knows for sure what the exact figure is, because so many incidents are either undetected or unreported.

As in many fields, a specialized jargon has evolved in the area of computer-related crime. Following is a sampling of some of the specific forms computer crime can take.

Data Diddling *Data diddling* is one of the most common ways to perform a computer crime. It involves altering key operations data on a computer system in some unsanctioned way. Data diddlers often are found changing grades in university files, falsifying input records on bank transactions, and the like.

■ **Computer crime.** The use of computers to commit criminal acts.

The Trojan Horse A **Trojan horse** is a procedure for adding concealed instructions to a computer program so that it will still work but will also perform prohibited duties. For example, a bank worker can subtly alter a program that contains thousands of lines of code by adding a small patch that instructs the program not to withdraw money from his or her account.

Trojan horses are frequently found today on the Internet, to host *computer viruses,* which we'll talk about shortly. They are also being increasingly used for spoofing. A *spoof* is a program buried in a legitimate application that tricks an unsuspecting user into revealing confidential information, such as an access code or credit-card number.

Salami Shaving *Salami shaving* involves manipulating programs or data so that many small dollar amounts—say, a few cents' worth of interest payments in a bank account—are shaved from a large number of transactions or accounts and accumulated elsewhere. The victims of a salami-shaving scheme generally are unaware that their funds have been tapped, because the amount taken from each individual is trivial. The recipient of the salami shaving, however, benefits from the aggregation of these small amounts, often substantially. Supermarkets have been occasionally accused of salami shaving at the checkout counter by not conscientiously updating computer-stored prices to reflect lower shelf prices.

Trapdoors *Trapdoors* are diagnostic tools, used in the development of programs, that enable programmers to gain access to various parts of a computer system. Before the programs are marketed, these tools are supposed to be removed. Occasionally, however, some blocks of diagnostic code are overlooked—perhaps even intentionally. Thus, a person using the associated program may be provided unauthorized views of other parts of a computer system. Recently, a trapdoor was discovered in a well-known browser that enabled individuals to remotely view the hard disk contents of the browser users.

Logic and Time Bombs *Logic bombs* are programs or short code segments designed to commit a malicious act as soon as the unsuspecting program user performs some specific type of operation. In one documented case, a programmer inserted into a system a logic bomb that would destroy the company's entire personnel file if his name was removed from it. A *time bomb* works just like a logic bomb, except that it is a date or time that triggers the criminal activity.

Computer Viruses A **computer virus** is a piece of code—often transmitted to a computer system from a diskette or from data or a program downloaded off a network—that is designed to cause damage to memory or a hard disk. Some are like time or logic bombs; they may lay dormant for months and then destroy settings on a hard disk on a specific date or when a certain operator action is taken. Other viruses clog memory with garbage as soon as the computer is turned on. Computer viruses often replicate themselves onto new storage media upon contact, infecting programs or data on those media (see Feature LIV 2-1).

Eavesdropping Examples abound involving the use of technology to *eavesdrop* on information intended for others. One of the earliest types of eavesdropping, and still one of the most common, was wiretapping. Modern computer systems have made it possible to eavesdrop in new ways—for instance, by simply having access to an identification number, an unauthorized user can peek in on files and even steal from them. Tools such as *sniffer programs* enable criminals to intercept data and access codes on a network, without anyone being any the wiser that they have been intruding. Two other examples of eavesdropping are using descrambling systems to intercept satellite transmissions and using scanners to overhear calls made over wireless phones.

Cellular Phone Fraud The goal of *cellular phone fraud,* which takes eavesdropping a step further, is to make calls without paying for them—sticking either the cellular-

---

■ **Trojan horse.** Adding concealed instructions to a computer program so that it will still work but will also perform prohibited duties. ■ **Computer virus.** A small block of unauthorized code, concealed and transmitted from computer to computer, that performs destructive acts when executed.

Virus Protection

What to Do to Prevent Your Computer System from Catching a "Cold"

To prevent your computer system from coming down with nVir-a, nVir-f, Michelangelo, or Stoned, be prepared to reach for your electronic medicine chest. You don't want to catch a computer virus.

A computer virus is a small block of code, often hidden inside a larger program, that is designed to create malicious damage or pull a harmless prank. Malicious damage includes destroying programs and data or gumming up your computer system so that it's difficult or impossible to continue working. Pranks include flashing messages on your display screen and beeping your audio unit from time to time to let you know that your computer system has been invaded by someone who delights in this sort of sad joke.

Viruses often work by copying themselves onto a disk or memory. When they replicate themselves onto other disks, they spread infection. Some viruses also contain a mechanism that at a specific time or moment destroys data or pulls pranks, such as on a day or when an infected program performs a certain operation. With so many people today downloading programs and data from the Internet, the virus problem has gotten worse.

One of the worst virus attacks occurred in November 1988. A worm virus implanted in a computer system disabled thousands of computers that were hooked into the Internet. When any computer system in the network read a program containing the predator code, the virus filled up the memory of that computer system with garbage, effectively choking out legitimate applications and grinding the system to a halt.

The Michelangelo virus, named for the sixteenth-century Italian artist, has been devised to detonate anytime the clock of an infected computer strikes March 6, the artist's birthday. On hard-disk systems, Michelangelo attaches itself to routines that boot, or start up, the computer, causing them to be moved to hard-to-find locations and causing vital directory data on the disk to be overwritten with garbage. Diskettes inserted into a drive of an infected system are themselves infected.

The recently devised and very widespread Word Concept Virus poses another type of hazard. It can infect your computer system through your electronic mail or through imported Microsoft Office applications and create havoc anytime you begin working in Microsoft Word or Excel. Word Concept is a multiplatform virus that can infect both PC-compatible computers and Macintoshes.

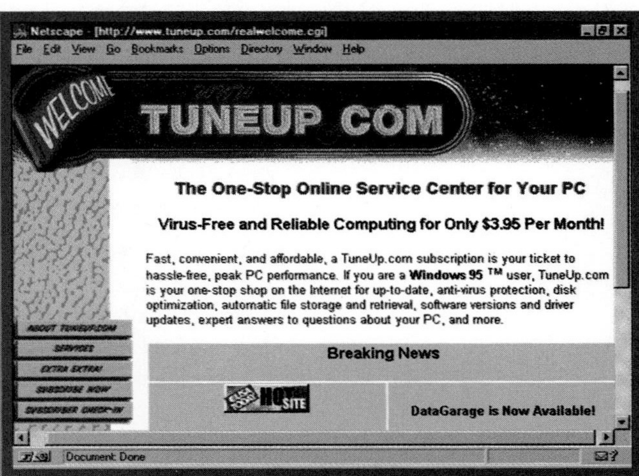

Online updating. The Internet enables users to be protected from new viruses as soon as an antivirus code is available.

Your system is vulnerable to viruses virtually anytime you use it. At especially high risk are people who work on networks, people who use software that comes from unknown origins, people who let others use their system, and people who don't back up their systems regularly.

To date, a number of antivirus programs have surfaced to combat viruses, and it is recommended you activate them to begin working as soon as you turn on your computer system. The programs are typically accompanied by a list of the specific strains of viruses that they can detect and/or protect your system from. The Norton Antivirus program, for example, has almost 10,000 cataloged viruses for which varying degrees of protection are provided.

Antivirus programs scrutinize code for suspicious patterns. If something looks strange, they often can intercept an activity before it takes place and apprise you of what's going on. Many antivirus programs are designed to check for viruses upon system log-in, during system use, and upon log-off. Many provide a list of all virus alerts, which lets you keep tabs on suspicious virus activity over an extended period of time.

Unfortunately, no antivirus program is foolproof. New viruses are being discovered almost daily, so the programs—which usually cost under $100—need to be updated constantly. Updates may cost you anywhere from $10 to $25 annually. Many antivirus programs can also be updated online for about $4 a month, so that you can be protected from new strains of viruses as early as possible (see illustration).

phone owner or phone company for the charges. The scam works as follows. Each cellular phone uses a unique internal electronic serial number for verification and billing purposes. This number is broadcast when the phone is in use or even just turned on. Criminals using scanners stake out spots along highway overpasses or in airport parking lots, pluck numbers out of the air, and then use black-market software to program other cellular phones with the stolen numbers. Cellular phone fraud collectively costs the public hundreds of millions of dollars a year.

Software Piracy **Software piracy,** the unauthorized copying or use of a computer program, is often a crime. It is definitely a crime to copy a program and then attempt to sell it for profit. If one just uses an illegitimate copy that was made by someone else, such usage can be a crime as well, although it is rarely prosecuted. Anyone knowingly involved with unauthorized copies of a program can be found guilty of breaking copyright laws. A number of companies have been successfully prosecuted for buying one or a few copies of a software package and distributing many more copies to employees.

Hacking **Hacking** is a computer term referring to the activities of people who get their kicks out of using computers or terminals to crack the security of remote computer systems. It's a serious problem. For instance, U.S. Department of Defense computers are attacked by hackers hundreds of thousands of times a year, with probably many more times that number of attacks going undetected. Some people engage in hacking purely for the challenge of cracking codes. Others do it to steal computer time, to peek at confidential information, or to cause damage. Intentions aside, hacking often is considered by the courts to be a breaking-and-entering crime similar to forced entry into someone's car or home.

Counterfeiting Desktop publishing and color-printing technology are so sophisticated today that they have opened the door to a relatively new type of computer crime—*counterfeiting.* Take desktop publishing. By using a scanner to read in a corporate logo and then a standard desktop publishing program, producing checks that look genuine is something even a novice can do. As far as color technology goes, the total number of phony U.S. currency being produced on color copiers and printers—now estimated in the billions of dollars—rose eightfold in just the first three years of this decade. Would-be counterfeiters, beware. Financial instruments are being redesigned with elements that cannot be copied. Also, many color copiers now print invisible codes on outputs, making counterfeit money traceable.

Internet-Related Crimes The rise of the Internet has contributed to new varieties of criminal activity that most people scarcely could have imagined only a few years ago. For instance, several individuals have been arrested in recent years for systematically *stalking* children through computer newsgroups. Web sites and e-mail have made possible *cyberporn,* the distribution of pornographic material over computer networks. In another type of case, a university student was indicted for running an Internet bulletin board over which copyrighted software was allegedly distributed for free. Especially worrisome to many individuals is the risk involved to both finances and privacy when using the Internet to engage in electronic commerce.

MINIMIZING COMPUTER CRIME

It's impossible to achieve 100-percent protection from criminal activity; consequently, the emphasis is on minimizing losses. To achieve this end, organizations can combat computer crime in many ways.

Assess Risks The most important way an organization can minimize crime is by having a good plan for security, and the centerpiece of any such plan is an assessment of which operations are most vulnerable to attack. Thus, employers should make a list of disaster-level events that can occur to their businesses and make sure that key areas are protected from the most costly types of mishaps.

Have a Recovery Plan Since no security plan can guarantee 100 percent safety, one should assume the worst can, in fact, happen. Thus, organizations should specifically take steps to have backups ready if or when disruptive events such as fires, floods, or computer outages occur. Backup provisions should include having copies of all important programs and data stored at another site as well as

■ **Software piracy.** The unauthorized copying or use of computer programs. ■ **Hacking.** Using a microcomputer system or terminal to penetrate the security of a remote computer system.

making arrangements for resuming normal day-to-day operations at a backup site. A plan that spells out what an organization will do to prepare for and recover from disruptive events is called a **disaster-recovery plan.**

Hire Trustworthy People Employers should carefully investigate the background of anyone being considered for sensitive computer work. Some people falsify résumés to get jobs. Others may have criminal records. Despite the publicity given to groups such as hackers, studies have consistently shown that most computer crimes are committed by insiders.

Beware of Malcontents The type of employee who is most likely to commit a computer crime is one who has recently been terminated or passed over for a promotion, or one who has some reason to get even with the organization. In cases in which an employee has been terminated and potential for computer crime exists, the former employer should update its records immediately to show that the person involved is no longer employed.

Separate Employee Functions An employee with many related responsibilities can commit a crime more easily than one with a single responsibility. For example, the person who authorizes adding new vendors to a file should not be the same one who authorizes payments to those vendors.

Restrict System Use People who use a computer system should have access only to the things they need to do their jobs. A computer operator, for example, should be told only how to execute a program and not what the program does. Also, users who need only to retrieve information should not also be given updating privileges.

Password Protect Programs and Data On many systems, users can restrict access to programs and data with **passwords**. For example, a user might specify that anyone wanting access to file AR-148 must first enter the password é5775jummm. To modify the document, a second password may be required. Users are recommended to choose passwords carefully, to change passwords frequently, and to protect particularly sensitive files with several passwords (see Figure LIV 2-3).

Passwords.

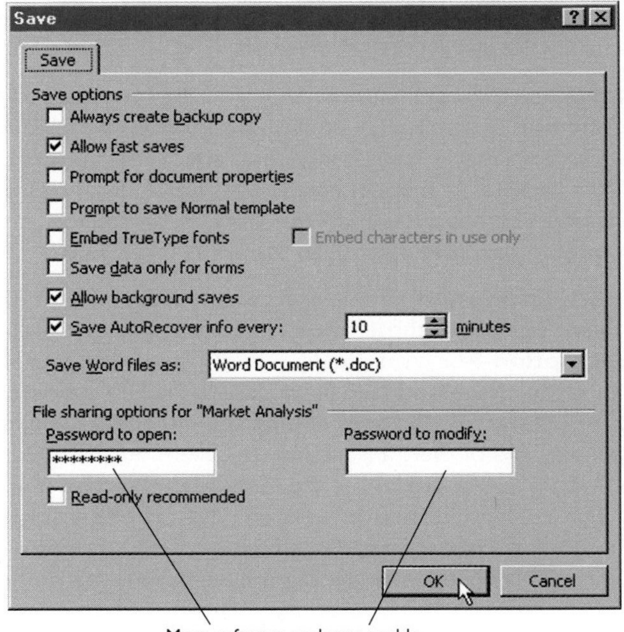

Many software packages enable you to assign passwords to documents when you save them.

RULES FOR PASSWORDS

- Make the password as long as you possibly can. A four- or five-character password can be cracked by computer program in less than a minute. A ten-character password, in contrast, has about 3,700 trillion possible character permutations and could take a computer decades to crack.
- Choose an unusual sequence of characters for the password—for instance, mix in numbers and special characters with words from other languages or unusual names. The password should be one that you can remember yet one that doesn't conform to a pattern a computer can readily figure out.
- Keep a written copy of the password in a place where no one but yourself can find it. Many people place passwords on post-it notes that are affixed to their monitors or taped to their desks—a practice that's almost as bad as having no password at all.
- Change the password as frequently as you can. Sniffer programs that criminals frequently use can read passwords being entered into unsecured systems.

- **Disaster-recovery plan.** A plan that maps out what an organization does to prepare for and react to disruptive events.
- **Password.** A word or number used to permit selected individuals access to a system.

FIGURE LIV 2-4

Biometric security. Biometric security devices enable transactions by recognizing some unique physiological characteristic of a person—such as a fingerprint or handprint—or some unique learned characteristic, such as a voice or signature.

PHYSIOLOGICAL CHARACTERISTIC

Handprint

Fingerprint

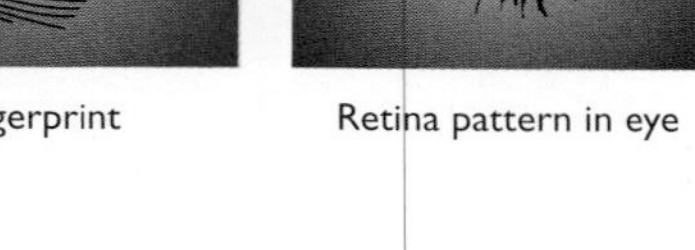

Retina pattern in eye

LEARNED CHARACTERISTIC

Signature

Voice

Keystroking pattern

Many organizations use measures such as *access cards* and *biometric security devices* in place of or in combination with passwords. **Access cards,** such as those used in automatic teller machines at banks, activate a transaction when they are used in combination with a password or number. **Biometric security devices** provide access by recognizing some unique physiological characteristic of a person—such as a fingerprint or handprint—or some unique learned characteristic, such as a voice or signature (see Figure LIV 2-4).

Passwords, access cards, and biometric security devices are all example of authentication systems. *Authentication* refers to the process a computer system uses to determine if someone is actually the person they claim to be.

Build Firewalls To ward off the threat of hackers, firewalls are increasingly being created by organizations. A **firewall** is a collection of hardware or software intended to protect computer networks from attack. Traditionally, most attacks have originated outside the organization, from hackers. As intranet creation has intensified, however, security experts are advising organizations to build internal firewalls, too, to keep nosy employees from browsing through data they don't need to perform their jobs.

Secure Transmissions with Encryption Some users and vendors encrypt data and programs to protect them, especially if those resources are going to be traveling over a public network. **Encryption—**or *cryptography*—involves garbling data and program contents through a coding method (see Figure LIV 2-5). The encrypting procedure provides *keys,* or passwords, for both coding and decoding. One key locks the message at the sending end of the transmission to make it unintelligible to a snoop, and only a person who is authorized to see the message can decrypt it with a key at the receiver end. The sender and receiver keys do not have to necessarily be the same; in the most secure form of encryption, the receiver has his or her own secret key to unlock messages. Many software packages have built-in encryption

■ **Access card.** A plastic card that, when inserted into a machine and combined with a password, permits access to a system.
■ **Biometric security device.** A device that, upon recognition of some physiological or learned characteristic that is unique to a person, allows that person to have access to a system. ■ **Firewall.** A collection of hardware or software intended to protect a company's internal computer networks from attack. ■ **Encryption.** A method of protecting data or programs so that they are unrecognizable to unauthorized users.

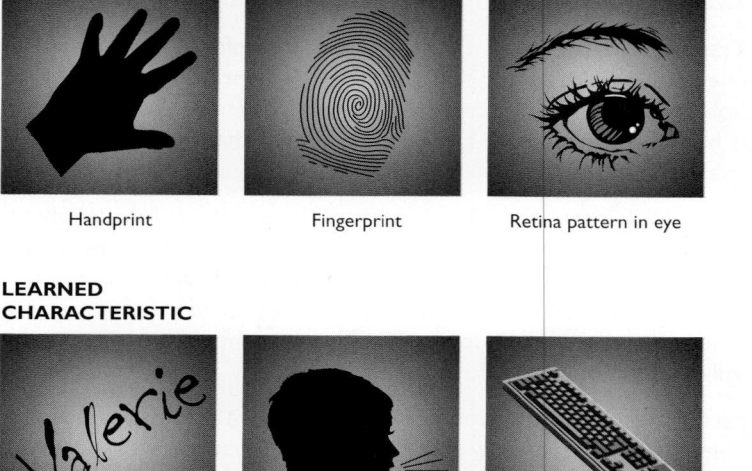

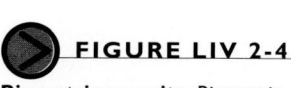

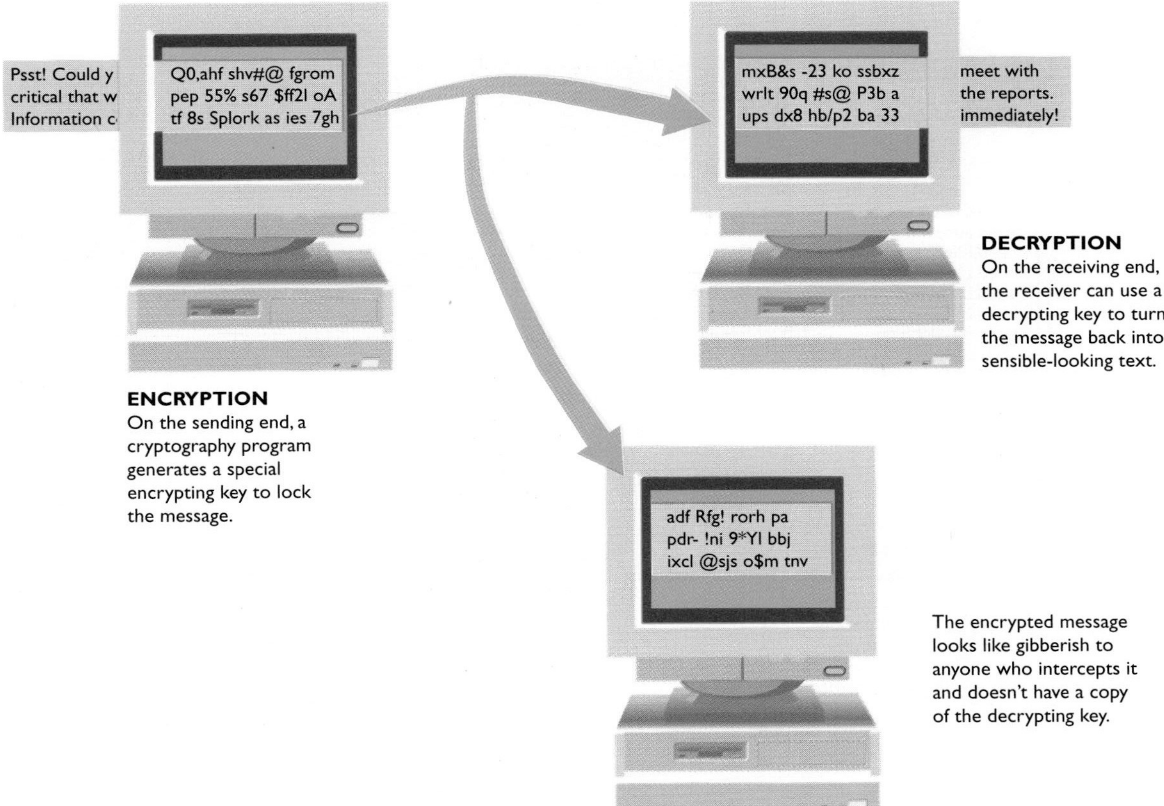
Psst! Could y
critical that w
Information c
Q0,ahf shv#@ fgrom
pep 55% s67 $ff2l oA
tf 8s Splork as ies 7gh
mxB&s -23 ko ssbxz
wrlt 90q #s@ P3b a
ups dx8 hb/p2 ba 33
meet with
the reports.
immediately!
DECRYPTION
On the receiving end, the receiver can use a decrypting key to turn the message back into sensible-looking text.
ENCRYPTION
On the sending end, a cryptography program generates a special encrypting key to lock the message.
adf Rfg! rorh pa
pdr- !ni 9*Yl bbj
ixcl @sjs o$m tnv
The encrypted message looks like gibberish to anyone who intercepts it and doesn't have a copy of the decrypting key.

FIGURE LIV 2-5

Encryption.

routines. Encryption is widely recognized as a vital tool for ensuring safe commerce on the Internet.

Use Crime-Prevention Software A variety of software products are available to help in the fight against computer crime. For instance, **antivirus software** is available to help detect and eliminate the presence of computer viruses (see Figure LIV 2-6). Also, as covered in User Solution LIV 2-1, because computers are often used to file false claims, computer programs have been deployed by businesses and government agencies to analyze claims for suspicious patterns.

Devise Staff Controls Overtime work should be carefully scrutinized, because computer crimes often occur at times when the criminal thinks he or she is unlikely to be interrupted. Sensitive documents that are no longer needed should be shredded. Access to computer facilities or the program/data library should be strictly limited to authorized personnel. **Callback devices,** which hang up on and call back people phoning in from remote locations, should be used in communications systems to deter hacking and virus implantation.

Monitor Important System Transactions The systems software in use should include a program for maintaining a log of every person gaining or attempting to gain access to the system. The log should contain information on the workstation used, the data files and programs used, and the time at which the work began and ended. Such a log allows management to isolate unauthorized system use.

Conduct Regular Audits Unfortunately, many crimes are discovered by accident. Key elements of the system should be subjected to regular **audits—**inspections that certify that the system is working as expected—to ensure that there is no foul play.

■ **Antivirus software.** Software used to detect and eliminate computer viruses. ■ **Callback device.** A device on the receiving end of a communications network that verifies the authenticity of the sender by calling the sender back. ■ **Audit.** An inspection used to determine if a system or procedure is working as it should or if claimed amounts are correct.

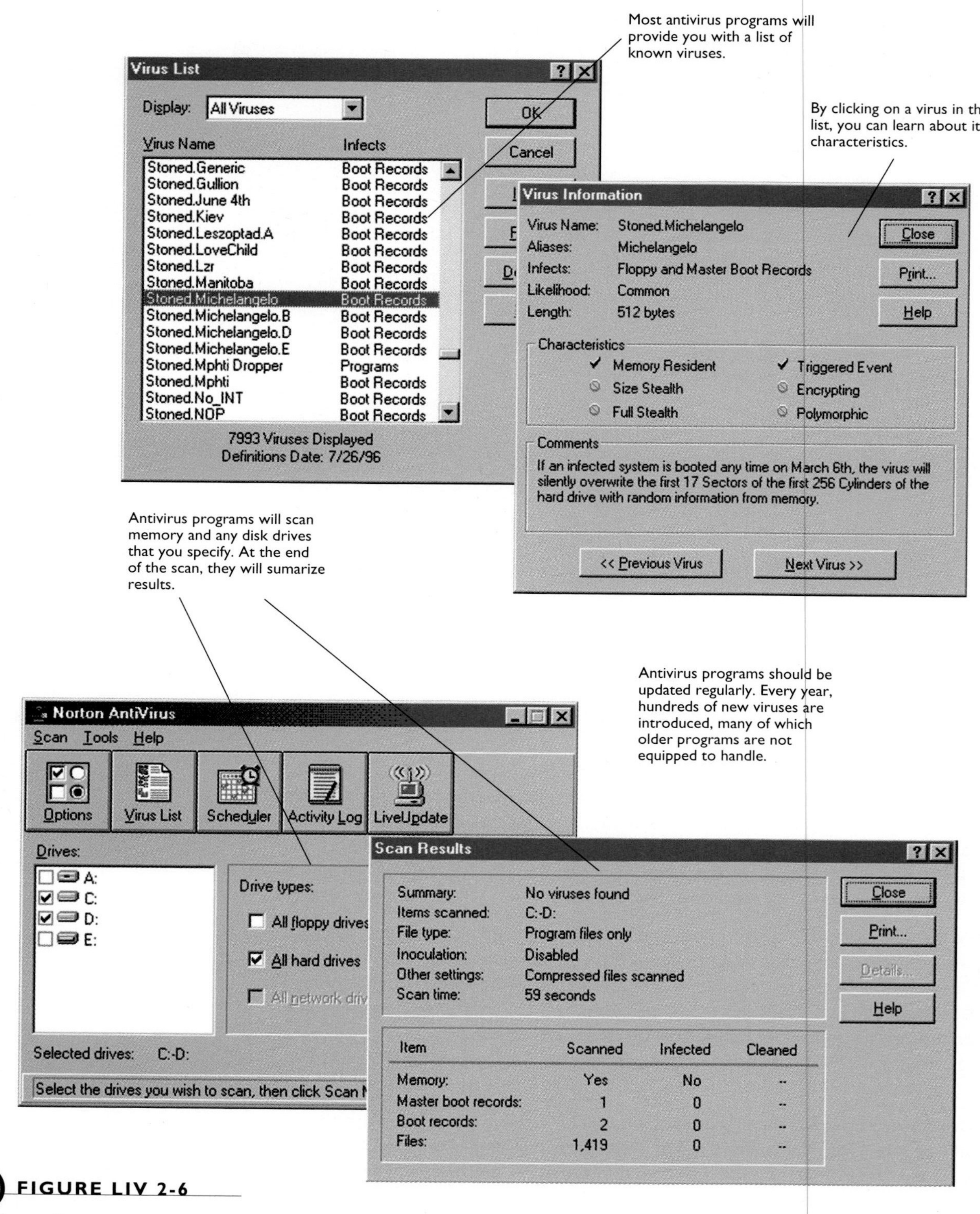

FIGURE LIV 2-6

Antivirus software.

Auditing often involves two key components: looking for security loopholes and inspecting system-activity logs to ascertain nothing unusual is taking place.

Educate Employees One of the best ways to prevent computer crime is to educate employees about security matters. People should be told about various types of computer crime and the conditions that foster them, informed of the seriousness of computer crime, and instructed on what to do when they suspect a computer crime is taking place or is about to occur.

Teaching Computers to Smell a Rat

An office visit on Christmas day? A hysterectomy on a man? A baby getting medication for hardening of the arteries? A chiropractor who charges 300 percent more than other area chiropractors? A frauds investigator looking at any of these happenings might smell a rat. They're also clues that a computer can detect and tip off the investigator to check out. Today, many of the major insurance companies have software available that will analyze mountains of claim data for suspicious billing and treatment patterns. Insurers have good reasons for being leery. The cost of insurance fraud is estimated to be about $50 billion annually. Also, health-care legislation often makes it difficult for insurers to pass such losses back to consumers.

CRIME LEGISLATION

Federal law has also sought to deter computer crime, with mixed results. The main piece of legislation regarding using computers in criminal ways—the *Computer Fraud and Abuse Act*—has been regularly amended to broaden its scope and to clarify its intent. The law currently outlaws unauthorized access to data stored in computers of the federal government and federally regulated financial institutions. It also outlaws the deliberate implantation of computer viruses in those computers. Actions taken with intent to harm are classified as felonies, while actions performed merely with reckless disregard are considered misdemeanors. Critics say the law doesn't go far enough in that a hacker who is merely curious may not be guilty of a crime at all.

The rapid growth of the Internet has recently pushed the issue of network legislation into the forefront. There have long been laws addressing such offenses as sending indecent material through the mail, libel, harassment, inciting hatred, and the like, but how should those laws apply to computer networks?

One problem is jurisdictional. Because networks can be global, it can be hard to determine where a crime is legally being committed and whose laws apply. A second problem is that many existing laws do not transfer well to networks. Should, say, inflammatory comments over a network be treated like casual chat in a telephone conversation or like carefully crafted words sent through the mail? A third problem deals with responsibility and enforcement issues. Whose job should it be to monitor the massive number of messages sent over computer networks daily? Will the right to personal privacy be compromised? Will the public be willing to pay for the potentially exorbitant cost of having networks policed?

Computers and Privacy

Almost all of us have some aspects of our lives that we prefer to keep private. These may include a sorry incident from the past, sensitive medical or financial facts, or certain tastes or opinions. Yet we can appreciate that sometimes selected people or organizations have a legitimate need for some of this information. A doctor needs accurate medical histories of patients. Financial information must be disclosed to credit-card companies and college scholarship committees. A company or the government may need to probe into the lives of people applying for unusually sensitive jobs.

No matter how legitimate the need, however, there is always the danger that information will be misused. Stored facts may be wrong. Facts may get to the wrong people. Facts may be taken out of context and used to draw distorted conclusions. Facts may be collected and disseminated without one's knowledge or consent. Victims can be denied access to incorrect or inappropriate data. As it applies to information processing, **privacy** refers to how information about individuals is used and by whom.

The problem of how to protect privacy and ensure that personal information is not misused was with us long before electronic computers existed. But modern computer systems, with their ability to store and manipulate unprecedented quantities of data and to make those data available at many locations, have added several new wrinkles to the privacy issue. The trend for a long time has been for more and more sensitive data to be put online and for such data to be packaged and sold to others. Thus, it is not unusual that more public concern than ever exists regarding privacy rights.

PRIVACY AND ELECTRONIC MAIL

Many people believe that the objective of e-mail within companies is to promote a free-flowing dialogue among workers—that is, to increase the effectiveness of communication. They claim that e-mail should be viewed as the modern-day version of informal chatting around the water cooler, and that e-mail messages should not in any way be confused with official company records. Others claim that any business document created on the premises of an organization is not the property of the individual but of the organization. The issue has largely been resolved in favor of the latter viewpoint; what you say in your e-mail can be legally seized by others and used against you. What's more, you can be prosecuted for destroying e-mail evidence if you deliberately do it to avoid retribution.

The matter of whether or not companies should be allowed to eavesdrop on their employees' e-mail messages is another matter of very heated debate. Companies are quick to point out that they have to protect themselves from unauthorized use of their e-mail systems. After all, a careless comment in a memo could make the company liable. Privacy-rights advocates often counter that companies don't casually rifle through people's desks or file cabinets so why should they peek at their computer files? Also, the advocates point out, e-mail monitoring can be used for political purposes.

Presently, eavesdropping by companies on their e-mail systems is totally legal, and the law doesn't even require that employees be informed that their messages could be monitored. Recent surveys have reported that 60 percent of the companies that eavesdrop on their employees' e-mail messages conceal doing so and that less than half of the organizations that have e-mail systems have issued written e-mail privacy policies.

The chapter Tomorrow box addresses another slant on privacy and e-mail—the fact that people can send documents to you at any hour can theoretically lead to a never-ending workday.

PRIVACY AND MARKETING DATABASES

Marketing databases are repositories that contain information about the consuming public. They record where people live, what they are inclined to do, and what they buy. Using such facts, companies attempt to determine the best way to promote specific products to specific types of people. Virtually anytime you leave

- **Privacy.** In a computer processing context, refers to how information about individuals is used and by whom.
- **Marketing database.** An electronic repository containing information useful for niche-marketing products to consumers.

HOW MARKETING DATABASES WORK

When you make an electronic transaction, information about who you are and what you buy is recorded.

The identities of people and what they buy are sold to a micromarketer.

The micromarketer uses its computers to reorganize the data in a way that might be valuable to others.

Companies buy the reorganized data and use it for their own purposes.

FIGURE LIV 2-7

Marketing databases.

traceable information about yourself anywhere, there's a good chance that it will eventually find its way into somebody's marketing database and on to a company that wants to sell to you (see Figure LIV 2-7).

When you buy a house, for example, your name, address, and the sales price are recorded in a county courthouse. These records are available to the public, including micromarketers. *Micromarketers* are companies that specialize in creating marketing databases and selling information to companies that sell products or services to others. The micromarketer typically breaks down the neighborhoods in a region into several dozen categories. Consumers are placed into one of these categories according to their address. For instance, a "Blueblood Estates" category might be a neighborhood in which the very wealthy live. A "Shotguns and Pickups" category, by contrast, might refer to a rural area where trailers are the likely abode. There are also categories for urban professionals, the elderly, and so on.

Each category is correlated in the micromarketer's computer system with certain buying preferences, a technique known as *geodemographics.* "Blueblood Estates" types are likely to buy expensive cars and take trips to places such as Aspen and St. Thomas. Those of the "Shotguns and Pickups" sort are more likely to be into country music, chainsaws, and Elvis collectibles. This information helps companies customize a direct-mail campaign to consumers' specific tastes. Consumers, of course, often look at unsolicited direct mail as junk mail and resent it as an intrusion on their privacy.

In addition to geodemographic data, micromarketers also collect data showing consumers' past purchasing behavior. Every time you make a computerized purchase, valuable data can be gathered about your purchasing tastes and entered into a computer system. Records kept by stores, credit-card companies, banks, the companies whose magazines you subscribe to, and other organizations are sold to the micromarketer. Even the government sells information.

FIGURE LIV 2-8

Caller ID. With caller ID, you can tell who's at the other end of the line before answering.

CALLER IDENTIFICATION

Caller identification refers to a technology in which a telephone device contains a tiny display that will output the phone number and name (or organization) of an incoming caller (see Figure LIV 2-8). Thus, the party receiving the call can identify the person at the other end of the

■ **Caller identification.** Refers to the use of a telephone or answering device that displays the origin of incoming calls.

TOMORROW

Will New Communications Technology Change Us as Humans?

Networks Are Causing Further Threats to Intimacy

Throughout the course of history, people have eyed technology with a certain amount of suspicion and dread. When the car replaced the horse and buggy as a means of transportation, many saw it as a harbinger of the world becoming a much smaller and less pleasant place. When television became a household fixture back in the 1950s, people worried about what it would do to the intimacy of the family. As sales of computer games took off in the mid-1980s, fears were raised that some children may forsake sports and other forms of healthy exercise in order to electronically zap alien invaders in their living rooms.

Many if not most fears about technology have been well founded. Today, roads crisscross everywhere and exhaust fumes pollute the air. The couch potato is a social reality. Some children have truly become lost within electronic domains. Deep down inside, perhaps many of us who use technology feel a little insecure about our reliance on it—somewhat in the same way Billy Crystal did about his job of "selling air" in *City Slickers*. Despite the benefits of progress, society has become highly specialized, and we have had to respond to its demands.

Now, as computer networks wend their way into the lives of virtually everyone, new concerns are being voiced about how technology will make us even less human. For instance, networks have made it possible for people to interact—socially and professionally—without ever seeing or talking to each other. Socially speaking, having an electronic relationship over the Internet is more satisfying to some people than having a relationship in which there is a physical presence. In business, it is becoming more and more common to call a company to order goods, wade through selections on a menu system, and not talk to a single human being in the process.

Intimacy at stake? Computers and networks are replacing many face-to-face interactions.

In the future, expect networks to be an ever increasing part of the working world. In an age where more companies than ever have their eye on the bottom line, it is likely that many people will work as freelancers who post their résumés on the Internet, are hired for specific projects by employers they never meet, and collaborate with others at remote locations strictly by computer and workgroup software. When the project is finished, everyone disbands; the only memories of the work are those of electronic interactions.

In the world of computer networks, there is no work clock that signals the end of the day. Messages can reach you through electronic mailboxes 24 hours a day. Some futurists predict that in the not-too-distant future most of us will be carrying small electronic devices around in our briefcases or pockets to enable us to send or receive messages or connect with remote databases from virtually anywhere. Having a great day at the beach? Someone who's at work may need to reach you. And beyond that, electronic marketers will be wanting to know who you are and where you go and what you do, paying the phone companies for such information.

You may think you can avoid the onslaught of technology but that will be difficult to do if you want to work. How many of us could operate at peak efficiency without a car, a phone or an answering machine, or a computer? Not many people can choose to *not* be efficient in a world where everyone else is.

line before picking up the phone, regardless of whether the caller is aware of this. Callers can, however, block caller ID by entering a special code number before entering a phone number.

Many people have praised caller identification systems as a good way of screening or cutting down on unwanted calls. Also, businesses such as take-out restaurants are guaranteed a measure of protection against callers who order food and then don't show up. Some people, however, have been less enthusiastic, seeing these systems as a potential invasion of privacy. For instance, a person living in an apartment in a dangerous neighborhood might be afraid to report a crime taking place outside, fearing that his or her identity could be leaked out and cause the criminal to take revenge at some point in the future. Not everyone, of course, is aware that they can block caller ID. Caller identification is not available in every state.

PRIVACY LEGISLATION

Since the early 1970s, the federal government has sought to protect citizens' rights by passing legislation to curb privacy abuses. Some important laws enacted for this purpose are described in Figure LIV 2-9.

FIGURE LIV 2-9

U.S. laws relating to privacy.

Date	Law and Description
1970	**Freedom of Information Act** Gives individuals the right to inspect data concerning them that are stored by the federal government
1970	**Fair Credit Reporting Act** Prevents private organizations from unfairly denying credit to individuals and provides individuals the right to inspect their credit records for truthfulness
1974	**Education Privacy Act** Stipulates that, in both public and private schools that receive any federal funding, individuals have the right to keep the schools from releasing such information as grades and evaluations of behavior
1974	**Privacy Act** Stipulates that the collection of data by federal agencies must have a legitimate purpose
1978	**Right to Financial Privacy Act** Provides guidelines that federal agencies must follow when inspecting an individual's bank records
1984	**Computer Fraud and Abuse Act of 1984** Makes it a crime to break into computers owned by the federal government
1984	**Cable Communications Policy Act** Limits disclosure of customer records by cable TV companies
1986	**Electronic Communications Privacy Act** Extends traditional privacy protections to include e-mail, cellular phones, and voice mail
1986	**Computer Fraud and Abuse Act of 1986** Amends the 1984 law to include federally regulated financial institutions
1988	**Video Privacy Protection Act** Limits disclosure of customer information by video-rental companies
1988	**Computer Matching and Privacy Act** Limits the use of government data in determining federal-benefit recipients
1991	**Telephone Consumer Protection Act** Requires telemarketing companies to respect the rights of people who do not want to be called and significantly restricts the use of recorded messages
1992	**Cable Act** Extends the Cable Communications Policy Act to include companies that sell wireless services
1994	**Computer Abuse Amendments Act** Extends the Computer Fraud and Abuse Act to include computer viruses

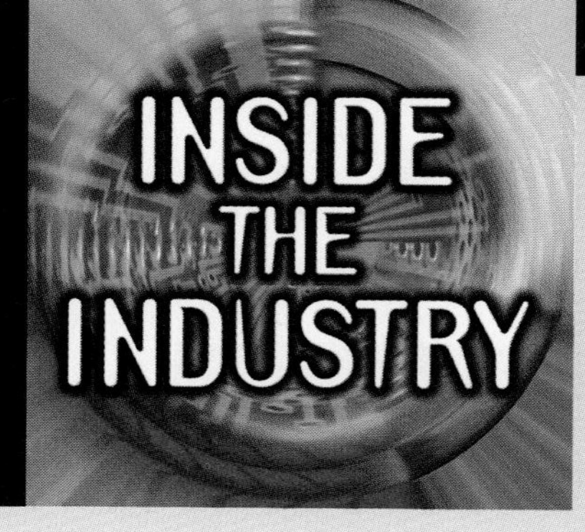

The Vaporware Cookbook

When products are not shipped on or shortly after their announce date, they are often labeled as vaporware. Vaporware has begun to be such a common occurrence throughout the computer industry that scholars who have observed the practice have begun to catalog the various forms that it can take.

Form 1: Announce a Similar Product with an Imminent Release Date This strategy is often used when a competitor has a product coming out—or a product that is already out—and users will ignore anything less than a full-blown product announcement. Companies often make such announcements even when they have no product in the works but have to react quickly to a competitive threat.

Form 2: Announce a New Direction Companies that control a market often find this strategy useful when they have no new products on the immediate horizon. For instance, a company may state in a press conference "our upcoming line of holographic storage products will revolutionize..." Users will be hesitant to adopt a competitor's product using current technology if they feel it will trap them into an old way of doing work. The market leader can later change its mind and proclaim with false altruism that, so as to not disrupt users, it's not moving in the aforementioned new direction after all.

Form 3: Start Rumors Here, no official announcement is made, but comments are leaked in selected places—to the press, to user groups, and so on—hinting that something specific is about to unfold. The advantage to this strategy is that the company cannot be blamed for an outside rumor that doesn't come true.

Form 4: Meet the Release Date, but Do It in a Lame Way There is tremendous pressure to meet release dates, since customers can be lost if no product is delivered, the company's stock price can plummet when expectations are not met, and reputations can be on the line. Thus, companies often resort to all sorts of unethical tricks to make it appear as if a date has been met. Some chicanery that companies have been accused of to buy extra time is releasing a bug-laden product that it can inexpensively patch at a later date, shipping limited units of a bug-laden product as a damage-control measure, shipping blank disks, charging a modest fee for an almost finished beta that the general public can use, and providing coupons to the user for promised product features that did not meet the shipping deadline.

Many people inside and outside the computer industry feel that privacy legislation is woefully out of date and due for an overhaul. The major privacy laws were enacted more than two decades ago and largely apply to the conduct of the federal government and the organizations to which it supplies aid. A lot has changed since then. Twenty years ago, most information was centralized on mainframes and available only in hard-copy form, whereas today it is common for data to travel over networks and never make it beyond electronic form.

Ethical Issues Regarding Computers

Ethics refers to standards of moral conduct. For example, telling the truth is a matter of ethics. An unethical act isn't always illegal, but sometimes it is. For example, purposely lying to a friend is unethical but normally is lawful, but perjuring oneself as a courtroom witness is a crime. Whether or not criminal behavior is involved, ethics play an important role in shaping the law and in determining how well we get along with other people. Some questions to ask when considering an action that may be ethically questionable are provided in Figure LIV 2-10.

SOME EXAMPLES

Today, computers present a number of ethical concerns. Several examples of these are covered in the list that follows:

■ **Ethics.** A term that refers to standards of moral conduct.

QUESTIONS FOR SELF-EXAMINATION

1. Will you benefit in any way from the action you are considering taking?
2. Are you not disclosing certain facts to others because you are afraid they will disapprove of the action?
3. Are you purposely coloring facts to portray a situation as being better or worse than it actually is to bias someone in a certain way?
4. If the same action that you are considering was instead done to you, would you feel taken advantage of, used, lied to, disrespected, or abused in any way?
5. Could anyone possibly object to the action as being unfair?
6. Will anyone be harmed by the action?
7. Do you feel yourself rationalizing your behavior in some way?
8. Could the action ultimately result in the evolution of a destructive practice or socially undesirable trend?

FIGURE LIV 2-10

Ethical guidelines. When considering an action that bothers you from an ethical viewpoint, ask yourself these questions. Answering "yes" to a question might be a tipoff that something is ethically problematic.

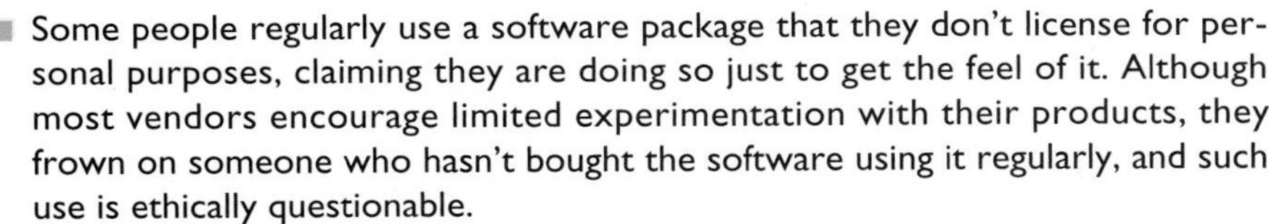

- Some people regularly use a software package that they don't license for personal purposes, claiming they are doing so just to get the feel of it. Although most vendors encourage limited experimentation with their products, they frown on someone who hasn't bought the software using it regularly, and such use is ethically questionable.
- A computer professional working for one software company leaves to take a job for a competing company. Almost immediately, the professional divulges product secrets that were entrusted in confidence by the former employer, putting the new employer at an unfair competitive advantage.

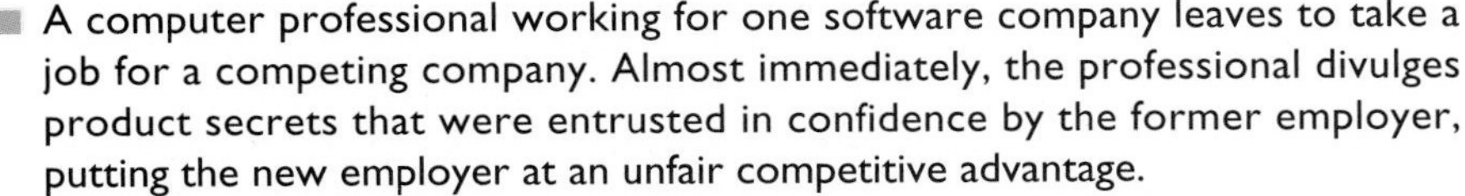

- A medical programmer is assigned to code a software routine that is to be part of a system that monitors the heart rate of hospital patients. Before the program can be fully tested, the programmer is ordered to hand it over so that the system can meet its promised deadline. The programmer tells the project supervisor that the code may contain serious bugs. The supervisor responds, "It's not our fault if the program fails because the deadline is too tight."
- A large software company, hearing that a small competitor is coming out with a new product, spreads a rumor that it is working on a similar product. Although the large company never provides a formal release date for its product, it leaves potential users with the mistaken impression that they will be taking a major risk by adopting the small-competitor's product. (Incidently, as the Inside the Industry box explains, software that's announced long before it is ready for market is referred to as **vaporware.**)

WHY STUDY ETHICS?

Why has ethics become such a hot topic? Undoubtedly, ethics has taken on more significance in recent years because the workplace has become increasingly multicultural

■ **Vaporware.** Software that is announced long before it is ready for market.

and diverse. Different cultures have different values, and what might seem ethically problematic to a person in the United States might be a normal way of doing business in, say, Mexico or China. Or vice versa. Take bribes, for instance. In the United States, both bribing and taking bribes are generally considered morally off base. They are also illegal. In some other countries, bribing is not only culturally tolerated, but also the salaries of workers are adjusted downward to reflect that bribes are an understood part of the compensation package. Such phenomena as increasing divorce rates and changing family structures have also tended to broaden ethical norms within cultures over time.

Many scholars think that educating people about ethical matters is being pushed aside today in the rush to achieve measurable results. A movement is afoot to change this, however. In recent years, professional computer organizations and, also, some 90 percent of the largest U.S. corporations have established *codes of conduct* covering unauthorized uses of software, hardware, and communications networks. Also, ethics is frequently a topic in computer journals and at professional conferences today.

Summary and Key Terms

Since the early 1950s, when the era of commercial computing began, computers have rapidly woven their way into the fabric of modern society. In the process, they have created both opportunities and problems.

Computers, Work, and Health One of the first criticisms leveled at the entry of computers into the workplace was that their presence resulted in stress. Stress-related concerns triggered by the so-called computer revolution include fear of lay-off or reassignment, fear of falling behind, and job burnout. In addition to these problems, other concerns related to **ergonomics** issues, such as display-device usage and work space design, have surfaced. Many people also worry about environment-related issues such as the energy usage and the paperwork glut.

Computer Crime **Computer crime** is defined as the use of computers to commit criminal acts. In practice, even though there are laws that deal with computer crime, it is hard to pin down. It is sometimes difficult to decide when a questionable act is really a crime, people are bewildered by the technical issues involved, and companies frequently are reluctant to press charges.

Computer crime may take many forms. Types of computer crime include data diddling, the **Trojan horse** technique, salami-shaving methods, unauthorized use of trapdoor programs, logic bombs and time bombs, **computer viruses,** eavesdropping, cellular-phone fraud, **software piracy, hacking,** counterfeiting, and Internet-related crimes.

Organizations can minimize computer crimes in many ways: assessing risks; having a **disaster-recovery plan;** hiring trustworthy people; taking precautions with malcontents; separating employee functions; restricting system use; limiting access to programs and data with **passwords, access cards, biometric security devices,** and **firewalls;** devising staff controls; concealing the contents of particularly sensitive programs and data through **encryption;** using **callback devices;** monitoring important system transactions; conducting regular **audits;** educating employees; and using **antivirus software** and similar programs.

Computers and Privacy Most people want some control over the kinds of facts that are collected about them, how those facts are collected and their accuracy, who uses them, and how they are used. Modern computer systems, with their ability to store and manipulate unprecedented quantities of data and make those data available to many locations, have added a new dimension to the personal **privacy**

issue. Recently, three relatively new technologies—electronic mail, **marketing databases,** and **caller identification** phone systems—have created further concerns about invasion of privacy.

Ethical Issues Regarding Computers **Ethics** refers to standards of moral conduct. Today one of the most important ethical concerns regarding computers is using someone else's property in an improper way. Another is leading people to believe something that's more fiction than fact when it works to one's advantage—such as the case with **vaporware.**

EXERCISES

1. Fill in the blanks:
   a. Fear of computers is known as __________.
   b. __________ is the field that covers the effects of factors such as equipment and computer work spaces on employees' productivity and health.
   c. ____________ refers to a phone-system feature that can display the phone number and name of a caller.
   d. __________ is a crime that involves manipulating programs or data so that many small dollar amounts are trimmed from a large number of transactions or accounts and accumulated elsewhere.
   e. __________ are companies that specialize in creating marketing databases and selling them to companies that sell directly to people.

2. Match each term with the description that fits best.
   a. computer virus d. hacking
   b. data diddling e. trapdoor
   c. spoof f. sniffing
   _____ An example of a Trojan horse.
   _____ Refers to software that can glean passwords and other data from a computer system.
   _____ Is transmitted through a copy operation.
   _____ A diagnostic tool that allows the viewing of computer storage.
   _____ The altering of an organization's operations data.
   _____ Using a terminal or microcomputer system to illegally break into a remote computer system.

3. Describe some ways in which computers may adversely affect our health or well-being.

4. Define the following terms.
   a. Vaporware
   b. Firewall
   c. Authentication
   d. Biometric security device
   e. Geodemographics
   f. Encrypting key

5. Answer the following questions about computer viruses.
   a. What is a computer virus?
   b. Describe as many ways as you can that your computer can become infected by a virus.
   c. How do you prevent catching a computer virus?
   d. How do you get rid of a computer virus?

6. Computer crime can exist in many forms. In each case below, describe the type of computer crime taking place.
   a. A person working for the Motor Vehicle Division deletes a friend's speeding ticket from a database.
   b. A brokerage business overcharges by one-tenth of 1 percent on all commissions made on the buying and selling of stocks.
   c. A group of people make copies of U.S. software whose rights are owned by others and sell the software overseas for a profit.
   d. A disgruntled employee places a program on the company mainframe that instructs key data to be erased on March 15.
   e. A person uses a desktop publishing system to create phony checks.
   f. A systems programmer implants code into a program that would cause all phone numbers in the company to become inoperative if the company vetos a pay raise.
   g. A repairperson implants a device on a company network that enables him to pick up from a remote phone all transmitted account numbers and passwords.

7. What fundamental rights of the individual have computer privacy laws tried to protect?

8. Following are described several situations regarding the use of computers. In the space provided, tell whether each act is *unethical, criminal,* or *neither* of these. The "neither" category can include both ethical acts and acts that, while not morally wrong, are not commendable either.

a. A company spokesperson tells employees that the company doesn't monitor e-mail messages, knowing full well it does. ____________

b. A programmer rigs his company's network so that on April 19 everyone gets a message when they log on telling them that the government was wrong to use force with the Branch Davidians at Waco. ____________

c. The executive of a company with no policy as regards e-mail confidentiality randomly snoops through messages to make sure that employees are not goofing off. ____________

d. A brokerage house sells a list of clients to a micromarketer, not really caring who the micromarketer deals with. Later, the micromarketer sells the list to a telemarketing company it suspects is involved in shady investing practices.
Brokerage house ____________
Micromarketer ____________

e. A systems analyst is given the job of building a system that will deliver a new computer service to consumers, signing a legally binding agreement to not disclose facts about it to outsiders. She is so fascinated by the service that she immediately quits her job and interests a competitor to hire her on at twice her former salary, in order to develop a competitive service. ____________

f. A software developer creates an antivirus program. To finance the advertising campaign for this product, the developer calls several computer executives at large firms and gets them to put up $10,000 each. This, the developer believes, will produce the funds needed and make the executives more likely to buy the product.
Developer ____________
Computer executives ____________

g. A fund-raiser for a hospital has access to a continually updated database that reveals the recent deaths of people who were able to afford expensive medical care. The fund-raiser frequently uses the database to target bereaved families for contributions. ____________

h. A teenager gets a demon dialer—a program that rapidly generates passwords and tries them out—and uses it to break into the computer of a local business. Once inside the system, the teenager looks around for a few minutes and then leaves, disturbing nothing. When his friends ask him about the incident the next day, he confides, "It was no big deal. I just wanted to see for myself if the demon dialer did what everyone said it could do." ____________

9. Determine the differences between the following terms.
   a. Caller identification and a callback device
   b. A computer crime and an ethical impropriety regarding computers
   c. Encrypting data and password-protecting data
   d. Software piracy and hacking
   e. A time bomb and a logic bomb

10. Determine whether the following statements are true or false.
   a. Carpal tunnel syndrome is a disability that evolves from poor use of display technology.
   b. Cellular phone fraud is a prime example of software piracy.
   c. A disaster-recovery plan maps out what an organization does to prepare for and react to disruptive events.
   d. Access cards are typically used in combination with passwords.
   e. The Computer Fraud and Abuse Act is the main piece of legislation governing an individual's right to privacy as regards computer databases.

1. Off to the Races A clerk in a steel company uses a company-owned, networked computer—on company time—to handicap horses for a local racetrack.

a. Is a crime being committed?
b. Where do you draw the line between a criminal and noncriminal act?
c. From a privacy standpoint, how do you feel about the steel company randomly checking the contents of files on its network, from time to time, to ensure that employees are using its computers for work-related tasks?

2. Computer Crimes Computer crimes are regularly reported in the press. For this project, find an example of a computer crime covered in a newspaper or magazine and report to the class about it. Be sure to cover such details as the nature of the crime, the dollar amount of loss resulting from the crime, how the criminal act was discovered, and the like.

3. Acceptable Use Policies Many schools have policies governing acceptable uses of their computers. The policies often address such issues as what types of information can and cannot be stored on the computers and what types of uses are considered objectionable. For this project, create what you feel is an ideal acceptable-use policy for your campus. Make sure the policy addresses the following issues.

a. Who the policy covers—students, faculty, administrators, alumni, anyone else?
b. What types of uses are forbidden. Make sure you are specific; vague usage of words creates loopholes and will effectively leave you with no policy at all.
c. Any penalties that are to be levied for first-time and repeat infractions.

If your school already has an acceptable-use policy, compare yours with theirs and comment on the differences.

4. Antivirus Programs Many antivirus programs currently exist on the market. For this project, choose such a program, answering the following questions in the process.

a. What is the name of the product? Who makes it?
b. How much does the product cost?
c. How many types of viruses does the program detect?
d. How are updates received on the product? How much do such updates cost?
e. How should the product be used—at the beginning of a session, continuously throughout a session, or what?

Some Web sites that you might want to visit for product information are listed below.

COMPANY	WEB SITE (HTTP://_____)
MacAfee	www.mcafee.com
Sands	www.sands.com
Symantec	www.symantec.com

5. Ergonomics One of the problems with diseases like carpal tunnel syndrome and other types of repetitive stress injuries is that their causes are not fully understood by the medical profession. Thus, the vendors of many ergonomic products have no scientific evidence at all to any claim that the products lead to any sort of cure or alleviation of pain. (When a product makes no claims that it can cure illnesses, incidentally, it does not need approval from the Food and Drug Administration.) For this project, find an ad for a product that claims to be ergonomic.

a. What is the product and who makes it?
b. In what way is the product claiming to be ergonomic?
c. Is any sort of research evidence being cited as to the ergonomic effectiveness of the product?

6. Step Up to the Beef Box This chapter and others have touched upon a lot of controversial social issues regarding computers. Here's your chance to sound off with your own ideas on one of them. A recent statement made by the American Association of University Professors (AAUP) said of colleges forbidding certain uses of the Internet,

> On a campus that is free and open, no idea can be banned or forbidden. . . . No viewpoint or message may be deemed so hateful or disturbing that it cannot be expressed.

Respond to this with your own opinions on the matter. Do you think colleges are crossing any sort of a line when they try to prohibit certain types of speech on their Internet sites or try to block sites accessed by their computers?

7. "Dumping" Products Over the past several years a number of large computer companies have been accused by others of *dumping* their products—that is, putting them in the hands of consumers for below actual cost—to achieve competitive advantage over smaller rivals. For example, a multibillion-dollar company, facing a threat from a small upstart company with far fewer resources, may decide to distribute a product for free for a certain period. This action would force the rival to take a similar action and possibly drive it out of business or in a new direction. Once the smaller rival is out of the way, the larger company can then gradually raise prices and achieve normal profit margins.

a. Is dumping, as described here, an ethical problem, a crime, or just merely a smart, aggressive business practice?
b. In what ways do consumers benefit or lose when dumping takes place?
c. Is "dumping" just an ugly word for "price war?" Tell why or why not.
d. What's the difference between a computer company selling a product for below cost, in an effort to draw users, and a supermarket giving away free turkeys before Thanksgiving to any shopper making a $25 purchase?
e. Extra credit: Locate an article in the computer press that describes an alleged dumping incident and report to the class about it.

8. Software Piracy In a recent editorial in *Computerworld,* a software consultant touched off a flood of fiery protest by remarking that software piracy is overblown as an issue. He argued that

a. Most people who pirate software wouldn't have bought the software in the first place, so the aggregate value of pirated software doesn't necessarily represent lost revenue.
b. Pirates who like a product often legitimately buy future releases of it to access new features, so pirating often has a positive effect on future sales.
c. The value of stolen software—which is estimated to be in the billions of dollars annually—overstates the real drain on profits because it multiplies the number of illegal copies times sales price.

Respond to these comments.

9. Marketing Databases and You The chapter hints that there is considerable fear that marketing databases can be used to invade a person's privacy.

a. What important issue areas do you feel should be addressed by the government to ensure that the privacy of individuals isn't invaded by micromarketers? For instance, one critical issue area concerns *access;* that is, who will have access to the marketing data and under what circumstances will access be granted?
b. If you were able to write laws that governed the creation and use of marketing databases, what would they allow or prohibit?

10. Disaster Recovery Many organizations have disaster-recovery plans that are used to get them back on track if disaster strikes. Each plan begins with an evaluation of risks that the organization faces and a list of precautions it should be taking immediately to minimize losses in the event of a disaster. For this project, let's assume that your school asks you to set up a disaster-recovery plan for its campus computer operations. What types of disaster situations are possible? What sorts of precautions would you recommend for minimizing the effects of such disasters? Write a five-to-eight-page paper outlining your plan and defending it. Feel free to use computer journals, books, or information from the Internet to do your background research.

11. Privacy Privacy issues regarding computers are regularly reported in the press. For this project, find an example of a privacy issue covered in a journal or newspaper and report to the class about it. Be sure to cover such details as the alleged privacy violation and whose privacy it is that is being compromised.

12. The Electronic Frontier Foundation The Electronic Frontier Foundation, or EFF, is a nonprofit organization devoted to the protection of privacy and free expression, and to the access of public resources and information online—as well as to the promotion of social responsibility in computer-related matters. Visit the EFF's Web site at www.eff.org (see image), and write a one-to-three-page summary describing how the site is organized and the types of information you found there.

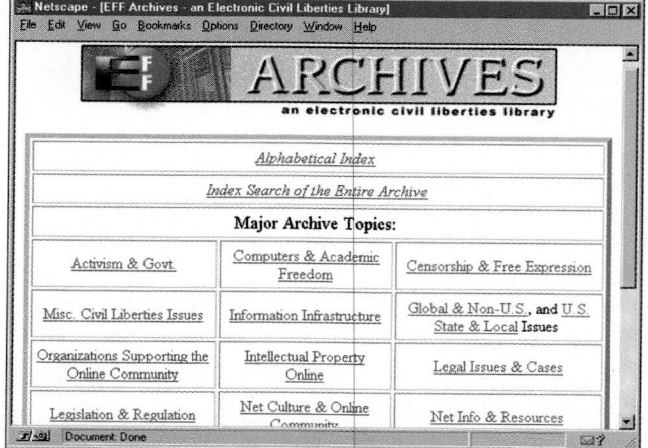

window

The History of Computers

A PICTURE ESSAY OF THE PEOPLE AND DEVICES THAT PIONEERED THE COMPUTER REVOLUTION

Electronic computers as we know them were invented a little over 50 years ago. However, the history of computers actually goes back much further than that. Since the beginning of civilization, merchants and government officials have used computing devices to help them with calculations and recordkeeping.

1. Even long before modern computers came along, many large organizations were beginning to drown in a sea of paperwork. This turn-of-the-century photo, of Prudential's New Jersey headquarters, illustrates the earliest benefit computers provided—replacing armies of clerks with machines that were cheaper, faster, and more accurate.

early history

Most computers prior to 1900 were predominantly *mechanical* machines, working with gears and levers. Operation was completely manual. Throughout the 1930s and 1940s, computers came to depend more and more on electricity for power, giving rise to *electromechanical* devices. By 1950, the era of solid-state *electronics* began to mature, ushering in the modern computer age we know today.

2 • This crank-driven *difference engine,* built by Charles Babbage in England in the 1830s, was one of the forerunners to today's modern computers. Babbage's attempts to build machines that were more sophisticated were thwarted because the parts he needed could not be produced.

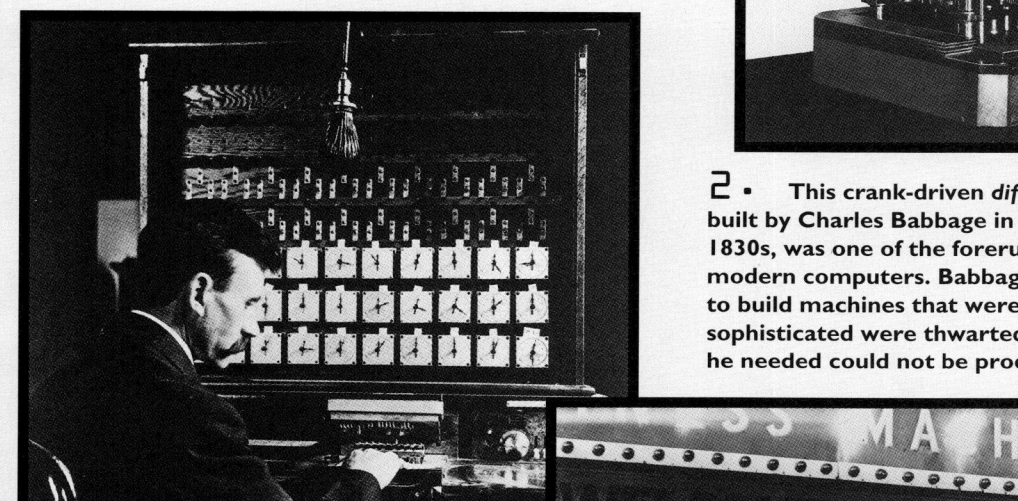

3 • A milestone on the way to the modern computer was passed during the 1890 U.S. Census. Herman Hollerith, a federal employee who is pictured here, created an electromechanical device that collapsed the tabulation of the census from a decade to only three years.

4 • Throughout the 1930s, IBM was the leader of punched-card tabulating equipment. IBM president and founder, Tom Watson, is shown here greeting some of the stars of his sales force. Watson pioneered the marketing of computer systems—selling business solutions rather than just electronic boxes.

5

5 • The age of electromechanical devices reached its zenith in the early 1940s with the development of the Mark I. Despite its sleek, futuristic look, the Mark I was technologically obsolete almost upon completion. The age of electronics was about to dawn.

6

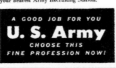

6 • The ABC—for Atanasoff-Berry Computer—is today widely acknowledged as the world's first electronic computer. Built by John Atanasoff and Clifford Berry of Iowa State University around 1940, the ABC helped graduate students solve simultaneous linear equations.

HOW MUCH IS $\sqrt[3]{2589^{16}}$?

The Army's ENIAC can give you the answer in a fraction of a second!

Think that's a stumper? You should see *some* of the ENIAC's problems! Brain twisters that if put to paper would run off this page and feet beyond . . . addition, subtraction, multiplication, division—square root, cube root, any root. Solved by an incredibly complex system of circuits operating 18,000 electronic tubes and tipping the scales at 30 tons!

The ENIAC is symbolic of many amazing Army devices with a brilliant future for you! The new Regular Army needs men with aptitude for scientific work, and as one of the first trained in the post-war era, you stand to get in on the ground floor of important jobs which have never before existed. You'll find that an Army career pays off.

The most attractive fields are filling quickly. Get into the swim while the getting's good! 1½, 2 and 3 year enlistments are open in the Regular Army to ambitious young men 18 to 34 (17 with parents' consent) who are otherwise qualified. If you enlist for 3 years, you may choose your own branch of the service, of those still open. Get full details at your nearest Army Recruiting Station.

YOUR REGULAR ARMY SERVES THE NATION AND MANKIND IN WAR AND PEACE

A GOOD JOB FOR YOU
U. S. Army
CHOOSE THIS
FINE PROFESSION NOW!

7

7 • ENIAC, the world's first large-scale, general-purpose electronic computer, was unveiled in 1946. Built by two former professors at the University of Pennsylvania, ENIAC (for Electronic Numerical Integrator and Calculator) used 18,000 vacuum tubes—like the ones seen in old radios—and was said to dim the lights of Philadelphia when it ran.

the first generation (1951–1958)

The commercial age of computers is often discussed in terms of its generations. First-generation computers used vacuum tubes (similar to those in ENIAC) as their principal logic element. Though the tubes enabled computers to run faster than electromechanical machines, they were large and bulky, generated excessive heat, and were prone to failure.

8 • The UNIVAC I, circa 1951, was the first computer to be mass produced for general use. It was also the first computer used to tabulate returns in a U.S. presidential election. In 1952, it declared Dwight Eisenhower the victor over Adlai Stevenson only 45 minutes after the polls closed.

0123456789 ABCDEFGHIJKLMNOPQRSTUVWXYZ #$%&@!*#$%&

"12" row
"11" row
"0" row
"1" row
"2" row
"3" row
"4" row
"5" row
"6" row
"7" row
"8" row
"9" row

Column numbers

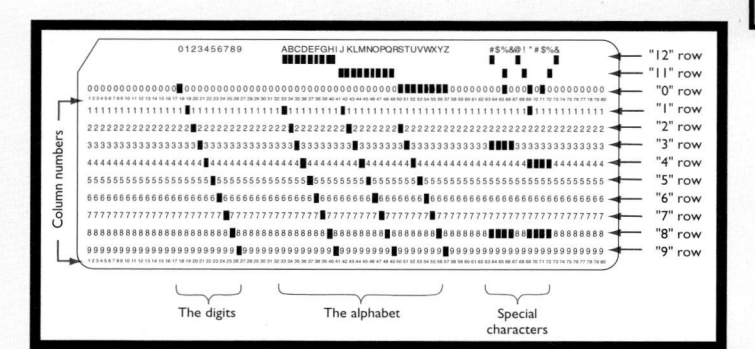

The digits
The alphabet
Special characters

9 • Most computers of the first and second generations relied heavily on punched-card input. Each standard punched card held 80 characters of data, with a set of holes in a card column representing a character. Today's high-capacity diskette, which can fit in a shirt pocket, can store the data equivalent of about 20,000 punched cards.

10 • An operator at a keypunch machine is shown preparing punched cards for processing. Blank cards were manually stacked in a hopper at the top right of the machine. As each blank card was fetched, it passed through a station that punched holes corresponding to keys struck by the operator. Finished cards were automatically routed to a stacker.

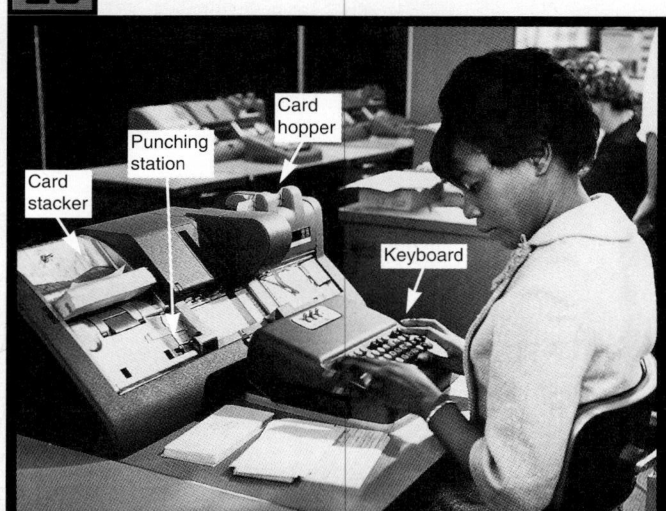

11 • Once a keypunch-machine operator finished punching a stack of cards, the cards were manually placed in the input hopper of a card reader—the device used to communicate the contents of the cards to a CPU.

the second generation (1959-1964)

In second-generation computers, transistors replaced vacuum tubes as the main logic element. Other noteworthy innovations of the second generation included more reliance on tape and disk storage, magnetic-core memory, replaceable boards, and high-level programming languages.

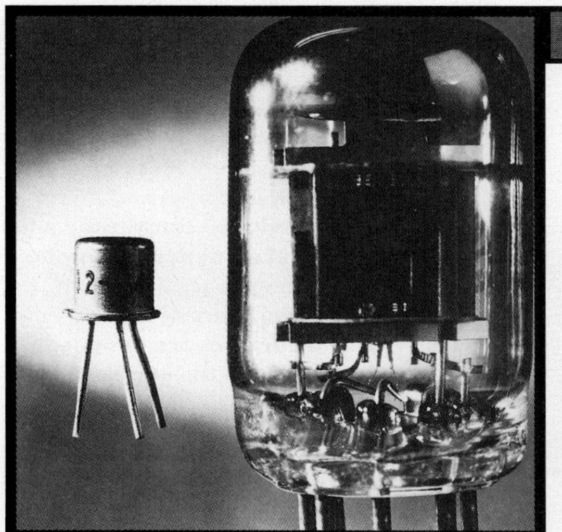

12. A second-generation transistor (left) is compared in size to the first-generation vacuum tube it replaced. Transistors performed the same function as tubes but made computers faster, smaller, and more reliable.

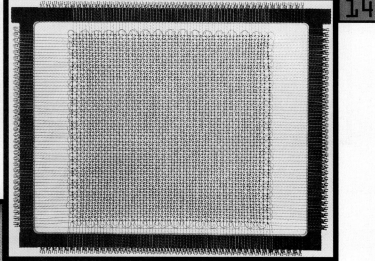

13-14. Small doughnut-shaped magnetic cores (left), which were strung on tiered racks (top) within the system unit, became the standard for second-generation computer memory. Each tiny core could hold a computer bit, and data were created by magnetizing each core clockwise or counterclockwise.

15. The U.S. Navy's Grace Hopper developed the first assembly language in 1952 and was one of the principal figures in the development of the COBOL language in 1960.

the third generation (1965–1970)

The third generation of computers evolved when small integrated circuits—"computer chips" as we know them today—began replacing conventional transistors. Other noteworthy developments of the third generation were the rise of operating systems, minicomputers, and word processing technology.

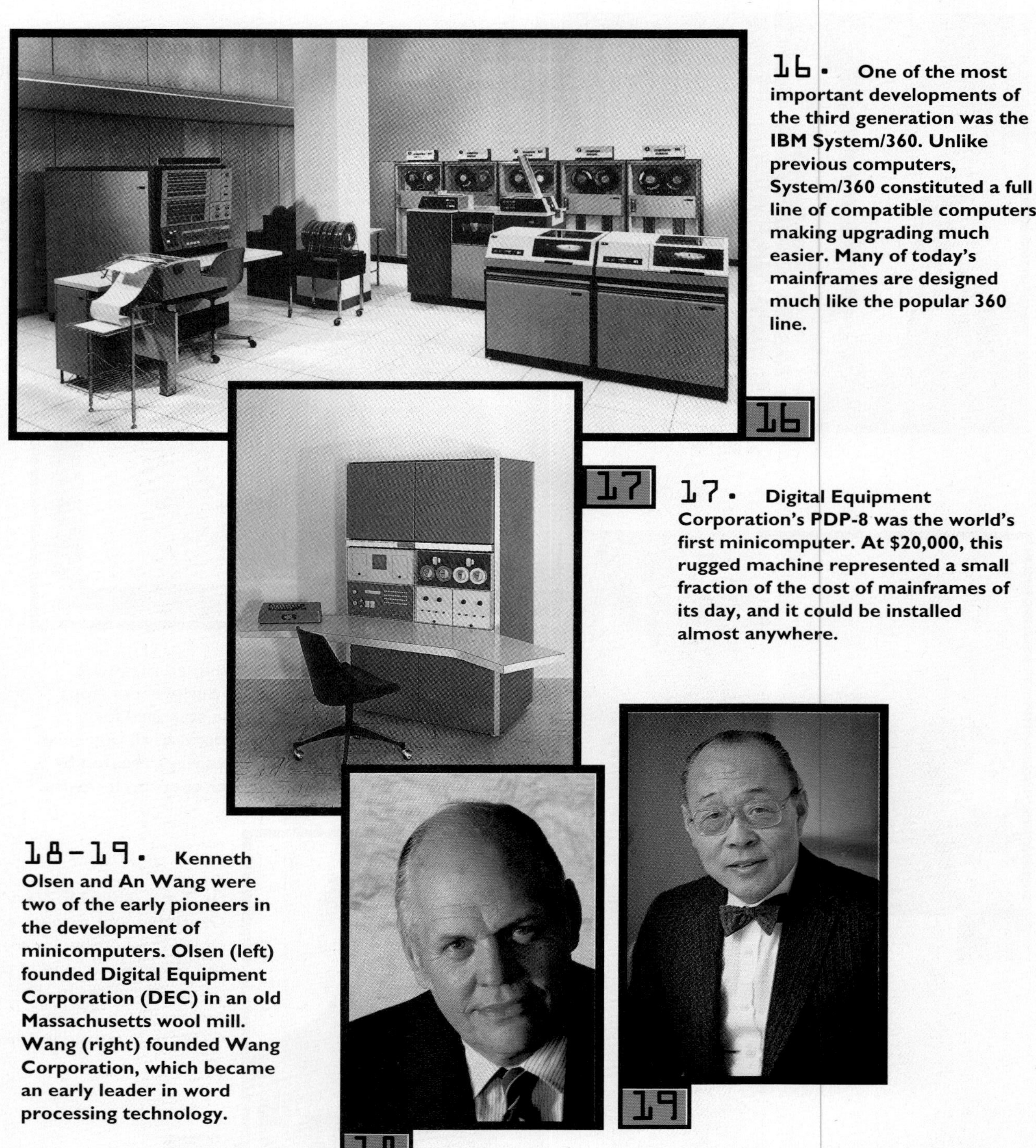

16 • One of the most important developments of the third generation was the IBM System/360. Unlike previous computers, System/360 constituted a full line of compatible computers, making upgrading much easier. Many of today's mainframes are designed much like the popular 360 line.

17 • Digital Equipment Corporation's PDP-8 was the world's first minicomputer. At $20,000, this rugged machine represented a small fraction of the cost of mainframes of its day, and it could be installed almost anywhere.

18–19 • Kenneth Olsen and An Wang were two of the early pioneers in the development of minicomputers. Olsen (left) founded Digital Equipment Corporation (DEC) in an old Massachusetts wool mill. Wang (right) founded Wang Corporation, which became an early leader in word processing technology.

the fourth generation (1971–present)

The fourth generation of computers is probably best known for the dawning of the age of the microcomputer. Improved manufacturing techniques enabled more and more circuitry to be squeezed onto a chip.

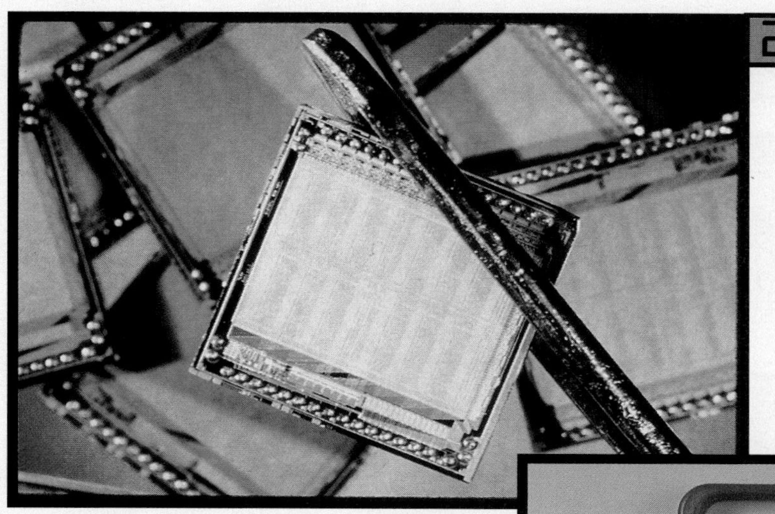

20

20–21. Today, it is possible to manufacture tiny chips that have over a million circuits in an area that can fit through the eye of a needle (left). As electronic components shrunk, smaller computer systems followed and so did computerized consumer devices such as this early spelling toy (below).

21

22

22. The first computer on a chip was the Intel 4004. On November 15, 1971, *Electronic News* carried the first advertisement for this breakthrough product. With 2,250 transistors—which is less than 1 percent of the circuit elements on most of today's microprocessors—the 4004 was an adequate processor for simple electronic devices such as calculators and cash registers.

23-24 • The first fully assembled microcomputer system unit was the Altair 8800 (left). Although the company that developed the Altair went bankrupt, the BASIC translator for this peripheral-less computer was written by Bill Gates (right), who went on to found Microsoft Corporation.

25-26 • The first commercially successful microcomputer company was Apple. Above are Steve Wozniak and Steve Jobs, Apple's founders, holding the system board for the Apple I—their first computer (right). Although less powerful than the Altair 8800, the Apple I was cheaper and less complicated.

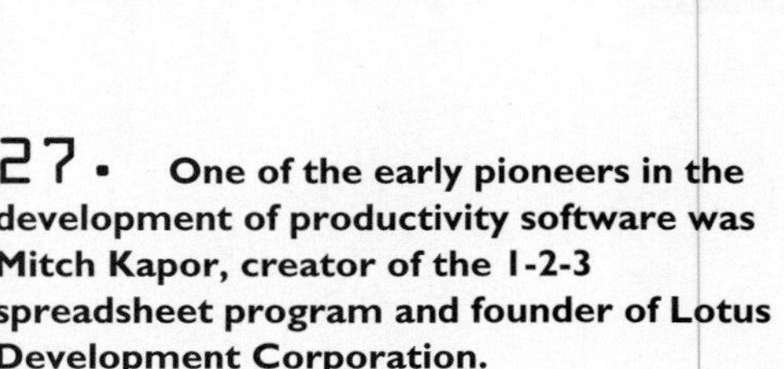

27 • One of the early pioneers in the development of productivity software was Mitch Kapor, creator of the 1-2-3 spreadsheet program and founder of Lotus Development Corporation.

Glossary

The terms shown in boldface are presented in the text as key terms. Numbers in parentheses after the definitions of terms indicate pages on which the terms are boldfaced in the text. The terms shown in boldfaced italic are other commonly used and important words often encountered in computing environments. Numbers in parentheses after the definitions of boldfaced italic terms indicate the pages on which the terms are mentioned.

A

Absolute replication.
Copying verbatim the contents in one range of cells into another range of cells. (PS 46)

Access card.
A plastic card that, when inserted into a machine and combined with a password, permits access to a system. (LIV 42)

Access mechanism.
A mechanical device in a disk drive that positions the read/write heads on the proper tracks. (HW 53)

Action diagram.
A programming tool that helps programmers code structured programs. (IS 43)

Active-matrix.
Refers to a flat-panel display technology that provides very sharp screen images; contrasts with passive-matrix. (HW 108)

ActiveX.
A set of controls that enables programs or content of virtually any type to be embedded within a Web page. (NET 109)

Ada.
A structured programming language developed by the Department of Defense and named after Ada Augusta Byron, the world's first programmer. (IS 49)

Add-in board.
A circuit board that may be inserted into a slot within a desktop computer's system unit to add one or more functions. (HW 23)

Add-on program.
Software that supplements the activities of a larger program. (PS 25)

Address.
An identifiable location in storage where data are kept. Both memory and disk are addressable. (HW 6)

AI.
See Artificial intelligence. (IS 16)

ALU.
See Arithmetic/logic unit. (HW 5)

America Online (AOL).
A commercial online service headquartered in Vienna, Virginia. (NET 81)

American National Standards Institute (ANSI).
An organization that acts as a national clearinghouse for standards in the United States. (HW 11)

Analog.
The transmission of data as continuous-wave patterns. Contrasts with digital. (NET 20)

Analog computer.
A device that measures. Contrasts with digital computer. (HW 4)

Analysis.
In program and systems development, the process of studying a problem area to determine what should be done. (IS 23)

ANSI.
See American National Standards Institute. (HW 11)

Antivirus software.
Software used to detect and eliminate computer viruses. (LIV 43)

AOL.
See America Online. (NET 81)

APL.
An acronym for A Programming Language. APL is a highly compact programming language popular for problem-solving applications. (IS 49)

Applet.
A small program that provides a dynamic or interactive quality to a Web page. (NET 109)

Applications.
See Applications software. (SW 4)

Applications generator.
A fourth-generation-language product that can be used to quickly create applications software. (IS 51)

Applications package.
A fourth-generation-language product that, when the user sets a few parameters, becomes a finished applications program ready to meet specific needs. (IS 37)

Applications software.
Programs that help with type of work that people acquire computer systems to do. Contrasts with systems software. (INT 12, SW 4)

Applications software development.
The process of designing, coding, debugging and testing, maintaining, and documenting applications software. (IS 36)

Archie.
A software tool that enables Internet users to search through public servers to find the location of downloadable files on particular subjects. (NET 58)

Arithmetic/logic unit (ALU).
The part of the CPU that contains circuitry to perform arithmetic and logical operations. (HW 5)

ARPANET.
The forerunner to the Internet, named after the Advanced Research Projects Agency (ARPA), which sponsored its development. (NET 49)

Artificial intelligence (AI).
The ability of a machine to perform actions that are characteristic of human intelligence, such as reasoning and learning. (IS 16)

Note: This glossary shows entries for all 16 chapters of the text. You may have a customized version of the text that may not contain all of the chapters indicated.

ASCII.
A fixed-length, binary coding system widely used to represent data for computer processing and communications. (HW 11)

Assembler.
A language translator that converts assembly language instructions into machine language. (SW 58)

Assembly language.
A low-level programming language that uses mnemonic codes in place of the 0s and 1s of machine language. (IS 45)

Asynchronous transmission.
The transmission of data over a line one character at a time, with variable time intervals between characters. Contrasts with synchronous transmission. (NET 35)

Audit.
An inspection used to determine if a system or procedure is working as it should or if claimed amounts are correct. (LIV 43)

Authentication.
The process of determining that a person is who he or she claims to be. (LIV 42)

Authoring software.
Applications generators designed to help users and programmers more easily create applications in such areas as multimedia, the Internet, and virtual reality. (IS 51)

B

Backbone.
The part of a network that carries the most traffic. (NET 25)

Backup.
A procedure that produces a duplicate version of any file that you can't afford to lose. (LIV 14)

Bandwidth.
The difference between the highest and lowest frequencies that a transmission medium can accommodate. (NET 20)

Bar chart.
A presentation graphic that uses side-by-side columns as the principal charting element. (PS 53)

Bar code.
A machine-readable code that stores data as sets of bars of varying widths. (HW 96)

BASIC.
An easy-to-learn, high-level programming language developed at Dartmouth College in the 1960s. (IS 45)

Batch processing.
Processing transactions or other data in groups, at periodic intervals. Contrasts with transaction processing. (HW 68)

BBS.
See Bulletin board system. (NET 5)

Benchmark test.
A test used to measure computer system performance under typical use conditions prior to purchase. (IS 27)

Beta test.
A term that refers to sending a preliminary version or release of a program to users for evaluation purposes. (IS 56)

Binary.
The numbering system with two possible states. (HW 9, HW 39)

Biometric security device.
A device that, upon recognition of some physiological or learned characteristic that is unique to a person, allows that person to have access to a system. (LIV 42)

Bit.
A binary digit, such as 0 or 1. (HW 9)

Bit mapping.
A graphical output technique in which software individually controls each pixel in a screen image. (HW 109)

Bits per second (bps).
A measure of a transmission medium's speed. (NET 21)

Blocking software.
A program that blocks access to certain parts of the Internet deemed objectionable, based on predetermined criteria. (NET 119)

Board.
A hardware device into which processor and memory chips are fitted, along with related circuitry. (HW 16)

Bookmark.
A place in a program or application that you can immediately go to after selecting the associated menu choice. (NET 69)

Boolean search.
Retrieval of data by using keywords such as AND, OR, and NOT when specifying filtering conditions. (NET 78)

Boot.
The process of loading the operating system into the computer system's RAM. (SW 39)

Bps.
See Bits per second. (NET 21)

Bridge.
An interface that enables two similar networks to communicate. Contrasts with gateway. (NET 33)

Browser.
A software tool that makes it easy for users to find and display Web pages. (NET 68)

Bulletin board system (BBS).
A computer file that is shared by several people, enabling them to post or broadcast messages. (NET 5)

Bug.
An error in a program or system. (IS 55)

Bus.
Any electronic path within a computer system along which bits are transmitted. (HW 25)

Bus network.
A telecommunications network consisting of a transmission line with lines dropped off for several devices. (NET 27)

Byte.
A configuration of 8 bits that represents a single character of data. (HW 11)

C

C.
A programming language that has the portability of a high-level language and the executional efficiency of an assembly language. (IS 48)

C++.
A variant of the C language that is more widely used today than C itself. (IS 48)

Cache memory.
A storage area, faster than RAM, where the computer stores data it has most recently accessed. (HW 20)

CAD.
See Computer-aided design. (IS 14)

CAD/CAM.
An acronym for computer-aided design/computer-aided manufacturing. CAD/CAM is a general term applied to the use of computer technology to automate design and manufacturing operations in industry. (IS 13)

Callback device.
A device on the receiving end of a communications network that verifies the authenticity of the sender by calling the sender back. (LIV 43)

Caller identification.
Refers to the use of a telephone or answering device that displays the origin of incoming calls. (LIV 47)

CAM.
See Computer-aided manufacturing. (IS 15)

Cartridge tape.
Magnetic tape in which the supply and take-up reels are contained in a small plastic case. (HW 63)

Cascading.
The overlapping of windows on a display. Contrasts with tiling. (SW 17)

CASE.
See Computer-aided software engineering. (IS 59)

Case control structure.
A control structure that can be formed by nesting two or more selection control structures. (IS 42)

Cathode-ray tube (CRT).
A display device that projects images on a long-necked display tube similar to that in a television set. (HW 106)

CD-ROM.
An optical disk that allows a drive to read data but not write it. (HW 58)

Cell.
The part of the worksheet that can hold a single constant value or formula; defined by the intersection of a row and column. (PS 38)

Cell address.
The column/row combination that uniquely identifies a spreadsheet cell. (PS 38)

Cell pointer.
A cursorlike mechanism used in the worksheet area to point to cells, thereby making them active. Also called the *highlight.* (PS 40)

Cellular phone.
A mobile phone that uses special ground stations called cells to process calls and communicate with the regular phone system. (NET 19)

Central processing unit (CPU).
The piece of equipment, also known as the *computer,* that interprets and executes program instructions and communicates with support devices. (INT 7)

Chat.
An Internet feature that supports interactive discussion groups on selected topics. (NET 63)

Check box.
A screen choice that requires the user to toggle an accompanying check mark on or off, respectively indicating whether the choice is selected or not. (SW 22)

CIM.
See Computer-integrated manufacturing. (IS 16)

Client.
A device designed to receive service in a client-server network. Contrasts with server. (NET 29)

Client-server LAN.
A LAN composed of *client* devices, which receive services, and *server* devices, which provide the services. Contrasts with peer-to-peer LAN. (NET 29)

Clip art.
Prepackaged artwork designed to be imported into text documents or charts, say, by word processing, desktop publishing, or presentation graphics software. (PS 22)

Cluster.
An area formed where a fixed number of contiguous sectors intersect a track. (HW 50)

Coaxial cable.
A transmission medium consisting of a center wire inside a grounded, cylindrical shield capable of sending data at high speeds. (NET 15)

COBOL.
A high-level programming language developed for transaction processing applications. (IS 45)

Coding.
The creation of programming-language instructions. (IS 55)

COM.
See Computer output microfilm. (HW 119)

Commercial online service.
An information service such as America Online or CompuServe that provides proprietary content along with Internet access. (NET 81)

Communications medium.
The intervening link, such as a telephone wire or cable, that connects two physically distant hardware devices. (NET 13)

Communications satellite.
An earth-orbiting microwave-repeater device that relays communications signals over long distances. (NET 17)

Compiler.
A language translator that converts an entire program into machine language before executing it. Contrasts with interpreter. (SW 57)

CompuServe.
A commercial online service headquartered in Columbus, Ohio. (NET 81)

Computer.
The piece of equipment, also known as the *central processing unit (CPU),* that interprets and executes program instructions and communicates with peripheral devices. (INT 7)

Computer-aided design (CAD).
A general term applied to the use of computer technology to automate design functions. (IS 14)

Computer-aided manufacturing (CAM).
A general term applied to the use of computer technology to automate manufacturing functions. (IS 15)

Computer-aided software engineering (CASE).
Program products that automate systems-development and program-development activities. (IS 59)

Computer crime.
The use of computers to commit criminal acts. (LIV 37)

Computer-integrated manufacturing (CIM).
The use of technology to tie together CAD, CAM, and other business systems. (IS 16)

Computer output microfilm (COM).
A system for reducing computer output to microscopic form and storing it on photosensitive film. (HW 119)

Computer system.
A collection of elements that includes the computer and components that contribute to making it a useful tool. (INT 7)

Computer virus.
A small block of unauthorized code, concealed and transmitted from computer to computer, that performs destructive acts when executed. (LIV 38)

Concentrator.
A communications device that combines control and multiplexing functions. (NET 33)

Connect time.
The amount of time you spend online with a service provider's computers. (NET 82)

Constant value.
A cell entry that contains text or a numeric value. Contrasts with formula. (PS 41)

Content provider.
An organization or individual providing information for distribution over the Internet. (NET 52)

Context sensitive.
A characteristic of a user interface that adjusts program actions to accommodate the type of operation the user is currently performing. (SW 20)

Control panel.
The portion of the screen display used for issuing commands and observing what is being typed into the computer system. (PS 40)

Control structure.
A pattern for controlling the flow of logic in a computer program. (IS 41)

Control unit.
The part of the CPU that coordinates its operations. (HW 6)

Coprocessor.
A dedicated processor chip that is summoned by the CPU to perform specialized types of processing. (HW 19)

CPU.
See Central processing unit. (INT 7)

Cross compatible.
Refers to a software or hardware product that can work with products from other vendors. (LIV 22)

Crosshair cursor.
An input device that you move over hard-copy images of maps and drawings to enter them into computer storage. (HW 93)

CRT.
See Cathode-ray tube. (HW 106)

Cryptography.
The field that deals with the art and science of encryption. (LIV 42)

Current cell.
In spreadsheet software, the worksheet cell at which the highlight is currently positioned. (PS 40)

Cursor.
A screen character indicating where the next input made by the user is to be entered. (HW 103)

Cyberphobia.
The fear of computers. (LIV 35)

D

DAT.
An acronym for digital audio tape, DAT is a magnetic tape-cartridge standard. (HW 63)

Data.
A collection of raw, unorganized facts. (INT 1-8)

Data access.
The process of fetching data either sequentially or directly from a storage device. (HW 66)

Database.
An integrated collection of related data files. (INT 16, PS 72)

Database administrator.
The person or group of people in charge of designing, implementing, and managing the ongoing operation of a database. (PS 85)

Database management system (DBMS).
A software product designed to integrate data and provide easy access to them. (PS 72)

Data bus.
The bus that links the CPU to RAM. (HW 26)

Data compression.
Squeezing data into a smaller storage space than they would normally require. (SW 53)

Data definition.
The process of describing the characteristics of data that are to be handled by a database management system. (PS 75)

Data definition language (DDL).
A language used to create, store, and manage data in a database environment. (PS 89)

Data dictionary.
A facility that informs users and programmers about characteristics of data and programs in a database or a computer system. (PS 78, IS 55)

Data flow diagram.
A graphically oriented systems development tool that enables a systems analyst to logically represent the flow of data through a system. (IS 23)

Data manipulation.
The process of using program commands to add, delete, modify, or retrieve data in a file or database. (PS 78)

Data manipulation language (DML).
A language used by programmers to supplement some high-level language supported in a database environment. (PS 91)

Data mining.
Intelligent software that can analyze data warehouses for patterns that management may not even realize exist, and also infer rules from these patterns. (PS 88)

Data organization.
The process of setting up data so that they may subsequently be accessed in some desired way. (HW 66)

DBA.
See Database administrator. (PS 85)

Data processing area.
The group of computer professionals charged with building and operating transaction processing systems. (IS 19)

Data warehouse.
A comprehensive collection of data that describes the operations of a company. (PS 88)

DBMS.
See Database management system. (PS 72)

DDL.
See Data definition language. (PS 89)

DDS.
See Decision support system. (IS 8)

Debugging.
The process of detecting and correcting errors in computer programs or in the computer system itself. (IS 55)

Decimal.
The numbering system with ten symbols—0, 1, 2, 3, 4, 5, 6, 7, 8, and 9. (HW 38)

Decision support system (DSS).
A system that provides people with tools and capabilities to help them satisfy their own information needs. (IS 8)

Declarative language.
An applications-development product in which the user or developer can tell the computer that a task needs doing and the computer automatically knows how to do it. Contrasts with procedural language. (IS 50)

Default.
The assumption that a computer program makes when the user indicates no specific choice. (SW 38)

Defragmentation.
The process of rewriting a program that is stored in noncontiguous clusters into contiguous clusters. (SW 54)

Design.
The process that defines the look of a product as well as how it will work. (NET 101)

Desktop computer.
A microcomputer system designed to fit on a desktop. Contrasts with portable computer. (INT 20)

Desktop publishing.
A microcomputer-based publishing system that can fit on a desktop. (PS 26)

Detachable-reel tape.
Magnetic tape wound onto a single reel, which in turn is mounted next to an empty take-up reel onto a tape drive. (HW 63)

Device driver.
A utility program that enables an operating system to communicate with a specific hardware device. (SW 55)

Dialog box.
A box that requires the user to supply information to the computer system about the task being performed. (SW 21)

Digital.
The representation and transmission of data as 0 and 1 bits. Contrasts with analog. (NET 20)

Digital camera.
A camera that records pictures as digital data instead of as film images. (HW 98)

Digital computer.
A device that counts. (HW 4)

Direct access.
Reading or writing data in storage so that the access time involved is independent of the physical location of the data. Also known as *random access.* Contrasts with sequential access. (HW 48)

Direct manufacturer.
A maker of hardware or software that sells directly to the public. (LIV 8)

Direct organization.
A method of arranging data on a storage device so they can be accessed directly (randomly). (HW 70)

Directory.
A collection of files that is grouped under a name of its own. Also commonly called a *folder.* (SW 40)

Disaster-recovery plan.
A plan that maps out what an organization does to prepare for and react to disruptive events. (LIV 41)

Disk access time.
The time taken to locate and read (or position and write) data on a disk device. (HW 54)

Disk cylinder.
On a disk pack, a collection of tracks that align vertically in the same relative position on different disk surfaces. (HW 53)

Disk cache.
A disk management scheme that directs a drive to read more data than necessary for an immediate processing task during each disk fetch; a part of RAM stores the extra data to minimize the number of disk fetches. (HW 54)

Disk drive.
A direct-access secondary storage device that uses a magnetic or optical disk as the principal medium. (HW 50)

Diskette.
A low-capacity, removable disk made of a tough, flexible plastic and coated with a magnetizable substance. (HW 48)

Disk utility.
A program that assists users with such disk-related tasks as backup, data compression, space allocation, and the like. (SW 53)

Display device.
An output device that contains a viewing screen. Also called a *monitor.* (HW 103)

Distributed database.
A database whose contents are split up over several locations. (PS 87)

DML.
See Data manipulation language. (PS 91)

Document.
An single piece of work that's created with software and, then, given a name by which it may be accessed. (INT 16)

Documentation.
A detailed written description of a program, procedure, or system. (IS 57, LIV 18)

Document-centered computing.
A view of computing in which the document itself is more central than the applications program(s) in which it was created. (SW 6)

Domain name.
A ordered group of symbols, separated by periods, that identifies an Internet server. (NET 66)

Dot-matrix character.
A character composed from a rectangular matrix of dots. (HW 110)

Dot pitch.
The distance between display-screen pixels, in millimeters. (HW 103)

DOUNTIL control structure.
A looping control structure in which the looping continues as long as a certain condition is false ("do *until* true"). (IS 42)

DOWHILE control structure.
A looping control structure in which the looping continues as long as a certain condition is true ("do *while* true"). (IS 42)

Downloading.
The process of transferring a file from a remote computer to a requesting computer over a network. Contrasts with uploading. (NET 31)

Downward compatible.
Refers to a software product that enables a user to save files in a form that is acceptable to an earlier version or release of the product. Contrasts with upward compatible. (LIV 22)

Dragging and dropping.
The process of moving an item from one part of the screen to another with a mouse. (HW 90)

DRAM.
An acronym for dynamic random access memory, DRAM refers to a type of memory chip that needs to be regularly recharged as processing is taking place. (HW 20)

Drop cap.
A large, decorative capital letter that sometimes appears at the beginning of an article or chapter of text. (PS 22)

Drop-down menu.
See Pull-down menu. (SW 13)

Dumb terminal.
A workstation, consisting of a display and keyboard, that can do little more than send and receive data. (NET 25)

DVD.
An optical-disk standard that enables very high capacities. (HW 58, HW 61)

E

E-cycle.
The part of the machine cycle in which the CPU locates data, carries out an instruction, and stores the results. Contrasts with I-cycle. (HW 7)

EBCDIC.
A fixed-length, binary coding system widely used to represent data on IBM mainframes. (HW 11)

EDI.
See Electronic data interchange. (NET 12)

EIS.
See Executive information system. (IS 10)

Electronic data interchange (EDI).
A computer procedure that enables firms to electronically exchange standard business documents—such as purchase orders and invoices. (NET 1-12)

Electronic mail.
The computer-to-computer counterpart for interoffice mail or the postal service. Also called *e-mail.* (NET 4, NET 53, IS 11)

Electronic mailbox.
A storage area on a hard disk used to hold messages, memos, and other documents for the receiver. (NET 5)

E-mail.
See Electronic mail. (NET 4, NET 53, IS 11)

Encryption.
A method of protecting data or programs so that they are unrecognizable to unauthorized users. (LIV 42)

End-user development.
Systems development carried out by users. (IS 29)

Ergonomics.
The field that studies the effects of things such as computer hardware, software, and workspaces on people's comfort and health. (LIV 35)

Ethernet.
A collection of protocols that specify a standard way of setting up a bus-based LAN. (NET 36)

Ethics.
A term that refers to standards of moral conduct. (LIV 50)

Executive information system (EIS).
A decision support system tailored to the needs of a specific, top-level individual in an organization. (IS 10)

Expansion bus.
The path that extends the data bus so that it links with peripheral devices. (HW 26)

Expansion slot.
A socket inside the system unit into which an add-in board is plugged. (HW 23)

Expert system.
A program or computer system that provides the type of advice that would be expected from a human expert. (IS 16)

Expert system shell.
A prepackaged expert system that lacks only a knowledge base. (IS 17)

External storage.
See Secondary storage. Contrasts with internal storage. (INT 11)

Extranet.
An extension of an organizational intranet onto the Internet itself. (NET 46)

F

Facsimile.
A method for transmitting text documents, pictures, maps, diagrams, and the like over the phone lines. Abbreviated as *fax.* (NET 6, IS 11)

FAQs.
See Frequently asked questions. (NET 62)

Fault-tolerant computing.
Refers to computer systems that are built with important circuitry duplicated, for backup purposes. (SW 46)

Fax.
See Facsimile. (NET 6, IS 11)

Fiber-optic cable.
A transmission medium composed of hundreds of hair-thin, transparent fibers along which lasers carry data as light waves. (NET 16)

Field.
A collection of related characters. (INT 16)

Field descriptor.
A code used to describe the type of data—say, numeric, text, logical—that occupy a given field in a data record. (PS 77)

File.
A collection of related records. (INT 16)

File directory.
A listing on an input/output medium that provides such data as name, length, and starting address for each stored file. (HW 50)

File extension.
A group of characters appended to the main part of a filename to qualify it or to identify a specific type of file. (SW 38)

File manager.
A productivity software package used to manage records and files. (PS 74)

File structure.
A collection of information about the records of a file, including the names, lengths, and types of the fields. (PS 76)

File transfer protocol (FTP).
A communications protocol that facilitates the transfer of files between a host computer and a user's computer. (NET 58)

Film recorder.
A device that converts computer output to film. (HW 119)

Firewall.
A collection of hardware or software intended to protect a company's internal computer networks from outside attack. (LIV 42)

Flat file.
A file that is not interrelated with others. (PS 74)

Flat-panel display.
A slim-profile display device. (HW 107)

Floppy disk.
See Diskette. (HW 48)

Flowchart.
A series of boxes or other symbols, connected by lines, that shows how ideas fit together. (NET 104,)

Folder.
A container for documents. (INT 16)

Font.
A typeface in a particular point size—for instance, 12-point Helvetica. (PS 14)

Formatting.
The process of organizing a disk so that it is usable in a particular operating environment. (HW 50)

Formula.
A cell entry that is used to change the contents of other cells. Contrasts with constant value. (PS 41)

FORTRAN.
A high-level programming language used for mathematical, scientific, and engineering applications. (IS 48)

Fourth-generation language (4GL).
An easy-to-learn, easy-to-use language that enables users or programmers to develop applications much more quickly than they could with third-generation languages. (IS 50)

Fragmented file.
A file on disk that is split up into many noncontiguous areas, making access harder. (SW 54)

Freeware.
Software offered for use without charge. (SW 8)

Frequently asked questions (FAQs).
Typical questions asked by newcomers to Internet newsgroups, mailing lists, and chat rooms, accompanied by the answers to those questions. (NET 62)

FTP.
See File transfer protocol. (NET 58)

Full backup.
A procedure that produces a duplicate copy of all files onto a secondary storage medium. Contrasts with partial backup. (LIV 15)

Full-duplex transmission.
A type of transmission in which messages may be sent in two directions simultaneously along a communications path. (NET 35)

Function.
A prestored formula for a standard calculation. (PS 44)

Functionally obsolete.
A term that refers to a product that no longer meets the needs of an individual or business. (LIV 22)

Function key.
A special keyboard key that executes a preprogrammed routine when depressed. (HW 89)

G

Gateway.
An interface that enables two dissimilar networks to communicate. Contrasts with bridge. (NET 33)

GB.
See Gigabyte. (HW 12)

GDSS.
See Group decision support system. (IS 9)

Ghosted.
Refers to a menu choice that has a faded appearance, indicating that the choice is unavailable in the current context. (SW 14)

Gigabyte (GB).
Approximately 1 billion bytes. (HW 12)

Gopher.
An information-retrieval tool for the Internet that generates hierarchical, text-intensive menus. (NET 57)

Grammar checker.
A word-processor function designed to root out errors in grammar, punctuation, and word usage. (PS 25).

Graphical user interface (GUI).
A term that refers to the graphics screens that make it easier for users to interact with software. (SW 10)

Graphics tablet.
An input device that consists of a flat board and a pointing mechanism that traces over it, storing the traced pattern in computer memory. (HW 92)

Group decision support system (GDSS).
A decision support system that helps several people to routinely interact through a computer network to solve common problems. (IS 9)

Groupware.
Software that enables several people to collaborate in their work. (NET 10)

GUI.
See Graphical user interface. (SW 10)

H

Hacking.
Using a microcomputer system or terminal to penetrate the security of a remote computer system. (LIV 40)

Half-duplex transmission.
Any type of transmission in which messages may be sent in two directions—but only one way at a time—along a communications path. (NET 34)

Handwriting recognition device.
A device that can identify handwritten characters. (HW 101)

Hard return.
A line break inserted when the user presses the Enter key to control line spacing in a document. Contrasts with soft return. (PS 6)

Hard copy.
A permanent form of computer system output—for example, information printed on paper or film. Contrasts with soft copy. (HW 89)

Hard disk.
A system consisting of one or more rigid platters and an access mechanism. (HW 52)

Hardware.
Physical equipment in a computing environment, such as the computer and its peripheral devices. Contrasts with software. (INT 11)

Hashing.
A mathematical transformation in which a record's key field determines where the record is stored. (HW 70)

Helper package.
A program designed to work alongside another program. (NET 75)

Hexadecimal.
The numbering system with 16 symbols—0, 1, 2, 3, 4, 5, 6, 7, 8, 9, A, B, C, D, E, and F. (HW 40)

Hierarchical database management system.
A DBMS that stores data in the form of a tree, where the relationship between data elements is one-to-many. (PS 83)

Hierarchical local network.
A local network in which a relatively powerful host CPU at the top of the hierarchy interacts with workstations at the bottom. (NET 31)

High-level language.
The class of programming languages that includes BASIC, COBOL, C, FORTRAN, and Pascal. (IS 45)

Highlight.
See Cell pointer. (PS 40)

History list.
A browser feature that stores descriptions and addresses of the last several Web sites you visited. (NET 69)

Hit.
One request for access to a page or graphics file made to a server computer. (NET 117)

Home page.
The first page you encounter on most Web-site visits. (NET 56)

Host computer.
The main computer in a network. (NET 25)

Host language.
The main programming language used to code applications within a specific software system, such as a database environment. (PS 91)

Hot swappable.
Refers to a hardware device that can be brought online or offline without power to the main computer system shut off. (HW 58)

HTML.
See Hypertext markup language. (NET 106)

HTML converter.
A program designed to produce Web pages from documents already existing in other formats. (NET 114)

HTML editor.
A program that simplifies the creation of Web pages by automatically generating HTML code. (NET 112)

HTML Wizard.
A program that automatically generates Web pages from screen selections made by the user. (NET 112)

Hyperlink.
Specially marked text or a graphic icon that represents a link to a new document or application. Also called *hypermedia.* (NET 55, SW 16)

Hypermedia.
See Hyperlink. (NET 55)

Hypertext markup language (HTML).
The most widely used language for developing Web pages. (NET 106)

I

Icon.
A graphical image on a display screen that invokes some action when selected. (SW 15)

I-cycle.
The part of the machine cycle in which the control unit fetches a program instruction from memory and prepares it for subsequent processing. Contrasts with E-cycle. (HW 7)

If-then-else control structure.
See Selection control structure. (IS 42)

Illustration program.
A program that enables users to paint, draw, or manipulate photographs. (PS 30)

Imagemap.
A screen image with embedded hyperlinks. (SW 15)

Image scanner.
A device that can read into computer memory a hard-copy image such as a text page, photograph, map, or drawing. (HW 98)

Impact dot-matrix printer.
A device with a print head holding multiple pins, which strike an inked ribbon in various combinations to form characters on paper. (HW 111)

Impact printing.
A technology that forms characters by striking a pin or hammer against an inked ribbon, which presses the desired shape onto paper. Contrasts with nonimpact printing. (HW 111)

Indexed organization.
A method of organizing data on a direct-access storage medium so that they can be accessed directly (through an index) or sequentially. (HW 68)

Indexing.
A procedure that creates a table, or index, that specifies how data records are to be arranged on output. (PS 80)

Inference engine.
A program used to apply rules to the knowledge base in order to reach decisions. (IS 17)

Information.
Data that have been processed into a meaningful form. (INT 9)

Information reporting system.
An information system whose principal outputs are preformatted reports. (IS 7)

Information system.
A system designed to provide information to enable people to make decisions. (IS 7)

Information systems department.
The area in an organization that consists of computer professionals. (IS 19)

Infrared transmission.
Communications in which data are sent as infrared light rays. (NET 19)

Ink-jet printer.
A printer that forms images by spraying droplets of charged ink onto a page. (HW 113)

Input.
What is supplied to a computer process. Contrasts with output. (INT 6)

Input device.
A piece of hardware through which a user supplies data and programs to the computer. Contrasts with output device. (INT 7, HW 89)

Insertion point.
A cursor character that shows where the next key pressed will appear onscreen. (PS 5)

Instruction.
A statement in a computer-programming language that causes the computer to take an action. (HW 15)

Instruction set.
The set of machine-level instructions available to a computer. (HW 15)

Integrated software program.
A collection of abbreviated software products bundled together into a single package and sold at price that is less than the sum of the prices of the individual components. (SW 5)

Internal storage.
See Primary storage. Contrasts with external storage. (INT 10, HW 6)

Internet.
A global network linking tens of thousands of networks and millions of individual users, businesses, schools, and government agencies. (NET 8, NET 48)

Internet address.
A unique identifier assigned to a specific location on the Internet, such as a host computer, Web site, or user mailbox. (NET 66)

Internet presence provider (IPP).
An organization whose server computers host Web pages. (NET 99)

Internet relay chat (IRC).
An Internet feature that allows people to type messages to others and to get responses in real time. (NET 63)

Internet service provider (ISP).
An organization that provides basic access to the Internet. (NET 81)

Interpreter.
A language translator that converts program statements line by line into machine language, immediately executing each one. Contrasts with compiler. (SW 58)

Intranet.
A private network—often one set up by a company for employees—that implements the infrastructure and standards of the Internet and World Wide Web. (NET 30)

IPP.
See Internet presence provider. (NET 99)

IRC.
See Internet relay chat. (NET 63)

ISA.
A popular PC bus standard; stands for Industry Standard Architecture. (HW 26)

ISDN.
A digital phone service that offers high-speed transmission over ordinary phone lines. Stands for integrated services digital network. (NET 25)

ISP.
See Internet service provider. (NET 81)

Iteration control structure.
See Looping control structure. (IS 43)

J

Java.
A programming language, created at Sun Microsystems, that is used to add interactive or dynamic features to Web pages. (NET 109)

Joystick.
An input device that resembles a car's gear shift. (HW 91)

K

KB.
See Kilobyte. (HW 11)

Key field.
A field that helps identify a record. (HW 67)

Keyboard.
An input device composed of numerous keys, arranged in a configuration similar to that of a typewriter, that generate letters, numbers, and other symbols when depressed. (HW 89)

Kilobyte (KB).
Approximately 1,000 bytes (1,024, to be exact). (HW 11)

Kiosk.
A computer station—often located in a store, lobby, or exhibit—that provides users information through an easy-to-use input mechanism such as a touch screen. (HW 90)

Knowledge base.
The part of the expert system that contains specific facts about the expert area and any rules the expert system will use to make decisions based on those facts. (IS 17)

L

LAN.
See Local area network. (NET 29)

Landscape.
An output mode with images more wide than high. Contrasts with portrait. (HW 106)

LCD.
An acronym for liquid-crystal display, LCD refers to flat-planel displays that use charged liquid crystals to provide light and special color filters to paint the screen. (HW 108)

Language translator.
A systems program that converts applications program into machine language. (SW 57)

Laptop computer.
A portable personal computer weighing about 8 to 15 pounds. (INT 21)

Laser printer.
A printer that works on a principle similar to that of a photocopier. (HW 112)

Legacy system.
See Technologically obsolete. (LIV 22)

Light pen.
An electrical device, resembling an ordinary pen, used to enter computer input. (HW 90)

Line chart.
A presentation graphic in which the principal charting element is an unbroken line. (PS 54)

Line printer.
A high-speed printer that produces output a line at a time. (HW 115)

LISP.
A language used widely for artificial-intelligence applications. (IS 49)

List box.
A screen-window panel that requires the user to select an item from a predetermined list. (SW 22)

Local network.
A privately run communications network of several machines located within a few miles or so of one another. (NET 29)

Local area network (LAN).
A local network, without a host computer, usually composed microcomputer workstations and shared peripherals. Contrasts with wide-area network. (NET 29)

Local bus.
A bus that connects the CPU directly to peripheral devices that require the most speed. (HW 26)

Logic error.
An error that results when a running program is producing incorrect results. Also called a *run-time error.* Contrasts with syntax error. (IS 56)

Logo.
A computer language often used to teach children how to program. (IS 49)

Looping (iteration) control structure.
The control structure used to represent a looping operation. (IS 43)

Low-level language.
A highly detailed, machine-dependent class of programming languages. (IS 45)

M

Machine cycle.
The series of operations involved in the execution of a single machine-level instruction. (HW 7)

Machine language.
A binary-based programming language that the computer can execute directly. (HW 15)

Machine-readable form.
Any form that represents data so that computer equipment can read them. (INT 7)

Mac OS.
The operating system for Apple's Macintosh line of computer systems. (SW 49)

Macro.
A predetermined series of keystrokes or commands that can be invoked by a single keystroke or command. (PS 18)

Magnetic disk.
A secondary storage medium that records data through magnetic spots on platters made of rigid metal or flexible plastic. (HW 48)

Magnetic ink character recognition (MICR).
A banking-industry technology that processes checks by sensing special characters inscribed in magnetic ink. (HW 102)

Magnetic tape.
A plastic ribbon with a magnetizable surface that stores data as a series of magnetic spots. (HW 62)

Mailing label feature.
A routine that generates address labels. (PS 21)

Mailing lists.
A service through which discussion groups communicate through shared e-mail messages. (NET 59)

Mainframe.
A large computer that performs business transaction processing. (INT 24)

Main memory.
The computer system's principal bank of memory; contrasts with memory products such as ROM and flash memory. (HW 7)

Maintenance.
The process of making upgrades and minor modifications to systems or software over time. (IS 56)

Maintenance programmer.
A programmer involved with keeping an organization's existing programs in working order. (IS 37)

Marketing database.
An electronic repository containing information useful for niche-marketing products to consumers. (LIV 46)

Markup language.
A language made up of tags or symbols that describe what a document should look like when displayed. (NET 106)

Master file.
A file that contains relatively permanent, descriptive data about the subject defined by one of the key fields of the file. Contrasts with transaction file. (HW 68)

Maximize.
Enlarging a window so that it fills the entire screen. Contrasts with minimize. (SW 19)

MB.
See Megabyte (HW 11)

Megabyte (MB).
Approximately 1 million bytes. (HW 11)

Memory.
See Primary storage. (INT 10, HW 6)

Menu.
A set of options from which the user chooses to take a desired action. (SW 12)

Menu bar.
A horizontal list of choices that appears on a highlighted line, usually below the window title. Also called the *main menu.* (SW 13)

Merge feature.
A routine specifically designed to produce form letters. (PS 20)

Message box.
A dialog box that pops up on the screen to warn the user or to provide status information. (SW 22)

MICR.
See Magnetic ink character recognition. (HW 102)

Microcode.
Instructions built into the CPU that control the operation of its circuitry. (HW 7)

Microcomputer.
A computer system driven by a microprocessor. Also called a *microcomputer system.* (INT 20)

Microcomputer system.
See microcomputer. (INT 20)

Microfiche.
A sheet of film, often 4 by 6 inches, on which computer output images are stored. (HW 119)

Microprocessor.
A CPU on a silicon chip. (INT 4)

Microsecond.
One one-millionth of a second. (HW 7)

Microsoft Internet Explorer.
A widely used browsing program. (NET 69)

Microsoft Network.
A commercial online service run by Microsoft Corporation. (NET 81)

Microspacing.
A technique used by many printers and software products to insert fractional spaces between characters. (PS 15)

Microwave.
An electromagnetic wave in the high-frequency range. (NET 17)

Midrange computer.
An intermediate-sized and medium-priced computer. (INT 23)

Millisecond.
One one-thousandth of a second. (HW 7)

Minimize.
Reducing a window to an icon on the taskbar. Contrasts with maximize. (SW 19)

Mixed replication.
Copying formulas in one range of cells into another range, while varying some cell references and leaving others constant. (PS 48)

MMX.
A technology used on recent Intel computer chips to enhance multimedia processing. (HW 18)

Modem.
A communications device that enables digital computers and their support devices to communicate over analog media. (NET 22)

Monitor.
A display device without a keyboard. (HW 103)

Monochrome.
A term used to refer to a device that produces outputs in a single foreground color. (HW 106)

Monospacing.
A printing feature that allocates the same amount of space on a line to each character. Contrasts with proportional spacing. (PS 15)

Mosaic.
A freeware tool that was the first GUI Web browser to gain wide acceptance; most commercial browsers today are enhanced forms of Mosaic. (NET 68)

Motherboard.
See System board. (HW 16)

Mouse.
A common pointing device that you slide along a flat surface to move a pointer around a display screen and make selections. (HW 90)

Mouse pointer.
An onscreen, context-sensitive symbol that corresponds to movements made by a mouse. (HW 90)

MS-DOS.
An operating system widely on early PC-compatible microcomputer systems. (SW 47)

Multimedia.
A term that refers to computer systems and applications that involve a combination of text, graphics, audio, and video data. (INT 9)

Multiplexer.
A communications device that interleaves the messages of several low-speed devices and sends them along a single high-speed path. (NET 33)

Multiprocessing.
A technique for simultaneous execution of two or more program sequences by multiple processors operating under common control. (SW 46)

Multiprogramming.
Concurrent execution of two or more programs on a single computer. (SW 42)

Multitasking.
A capability of an operating system to execute for a single user two or more programs or program tasks concurrently. (SW 43)

Multithreading.
The capability of a task to be divided into small pieces that provide improved operating-system response. (SW 44)

N

Nanosecond.
One one-billionth of a second. (HW 8)

Natural-language interface.
Software that allows users to communicate with the computer in a conversational language such as English, Spanish, and Japanese. (IS 52)

Netiquette.
Proper etiquette for exchanges on the Internet. (NET 61)

Netscape Navigator.
A widely used browsing program. (NET 69)

NetWare.
The most widely used operating system on local area networks (LANs). (SW 51)

Network.
A system of machines that communicate with one another. (INT 17)

Network computer.
A stripped-down desktop microcomputer that is optimized for the Internet and intracompany communications. (INT 23)

Network database management system.
A DBMS in which the relationship between data elements can be either many-to-one or many-to-many. (PS 83)

Network interface card (NIC).
An add-in board though which a workstation connects to a local network. (NET 22)

Network operating system (NOS).
An operating system that enables the network administrator in an organization to control network tasks. (SW 50)

Neural-net computing.
An expert-system technology in which the human brain's pattern-recognition process is emulated by a computer system. (IS 17)

Newsgroup.
A service that works like an electronic newspaper, carrying *articles* posted by subscribers and responses to them (called *threads*). (NET 59)

NIC.
See Network interface card. (NET 22)

Nonimpact printing.
A technology that forms characters and other images on a surface by means of heat, lasers, photography, or ink jets. Contrasts with impact printing. (HW 112)

Noninterlaced.
Refers to a monitor that draws every screen line of pixels on each screen refresh; contrasts with *interlaced* monitors that draw in every other line. (HW 105)

Nonvolatile storage.
Storage that retains its contents when power is shut off. Contrasts with volatile storage. (HW 47)

NOS.
See Network operating system. (SW 50)

Notebook computer.
A portable personal computer weighing about 6 to 8 pounds. (INT 21)

O

OA.
See Office automation. (IS 11)

Object.
A storable entity composed of data elements and instructions that apply to the elements. (PS 85)

Object module.
A program that is in compiled form. Contrasts with source module. (SW 57)

Object-oriented database management system.
A DBMS in which two or more types of data—text, graphics, sound, or video—are combined with methods that specify their properties or use. (PS 85)

Object-oriented programming language.
A language that works with objects that encapsulate data and instructions rather than with separate instructions and data. (IS 52)

OCR.
See Optical character recognition. (HW 94)

Office automation (OA).
Computer-based, office-oriented technologies such as word processing, desktop publishing, electronic mail, teleconferencing, and the like. (IS 11)

Offline.
A state that *does not* allow a device to send data to or receive data from other devices. Contrasts with online. (INT 19)

OLE.
An acronym for object linking and embedding, OLE refers to programs and applications that can be nested and launched inside each other. (NET 109)

One-entry-point/one-exit-point rule.
A rule stating that each program control structure will have only one entry point into it and one exit point out of it. (IS 42)

Online.
A state that allows a device to send data to or receive data from other devices. Contrasts with offline. (INT 19)

Operating environment.
A term that refers to a user interface or operating system—for instance, DOS, DOS-with-Windows, and Windows. (SW 48)

Operating system.
The main collection of systems software that enables the computer system to manage the resources under its control. (SW 37)

Optical character recognition (OCR).
The use of reflected light to input marks, characters, or codes. (HW 94)

Optical disk.
A disk read by reflecting pulses of laser beams. (HW 58)

OS/2.
An operating system designed for both desktop, PC-compatible computers and office networks. (SW 49)

Output.
The results of a computer process. Contrasts with input. (INT 6)

Output device.
A piece of hardware that accepts data and programs from the computer. Contrasts with input device. (INT 7, HW 89)

Outsourcing.
The practice by which one company hires another company to do some or all of its information-processing activities. (IS 21)

P

Packet switching.
A transmission technique that breaks messages into smaller units that travel to a destination along possibly different paths. (NET 39)

Page printer.
A high-speed printer that generates a full page of output at a time. (HW 116)

Page description language (PDL).
A language for communicating instructions to a printer. (PS 28)

Page-makeup software.
A program used to compose page layouts in a desktop publishing system. (PS 29)

Palette.
A menu that enables users to choose such attributes as colors and textures. (SW 17)

Palmtop computer.
A portable personal computer that you can hold in your hand. (INT 21)

Parallel processing.
A computing system in which two or more CPUs share work, simultaneously processing separate parts of it. (HW 29)

Parallel transmission.
Data transmission in which each bit in a byte has its own path and all of the bits in a byte are transmitted simultaneously. Contrasts with serial transmission. (NET 21)

Parity bit.
An extra bit added to the byte representation of characters to ensure there is always either an odd or even number of 1-bits transmitted with every character. (HW 12, NET 21)

Partial backup.
A procedure that produces a duplicate copy of selected files onto a secondary storage medium. Contrasts with full backup. (LIV 15)

Pascal.
A structured, high-level programming language that is often used to teach programming. (IS 46)

Passive-matrix.
Refers to a flat-panel display technology that provides adequate but not outstandingly sharp screen images; contrasts with active-matrix. (HW 108)

Password.
A word or number used to permit selected individuals access to a system. (LIV 41)

Path.
An ordered list of directories that lead to a particular file or directory. (SW 41)

PBX.
See Private branch exchange. (NET 32)

PC.
See Personal computer. (INT 20)

PC card.
A small card that fits into a slot on the exterior of a portable computer to provide new functions. Also called a PCMCIA card. (HW 24)

PC compatible.
A personal computer based on Intel microprocessors or compatible chips. Contrasts with Macintosh-compatible. (INT 22)

PC-DOS.
The operating system designed for and widely used by early IBM microcomputers. (SW 47)

PCI.
A widely adopted local-bus standard; stands for peripheral component interconnect. (HW 26)

PCMCIA.
An acronym for Personal Computer Memory Card International Association. See also PC Card. (HW 24)

PDA.
An acronym for personal digital assistant. See Palmtop computer. (INT 21)

PDL.
See Page description language. (PS 28)

Peer-to-peer LAN.
A LAN in which all of the user workstations and shared peripheral devices operate on the same level. Contrasts with client-server LAN. (NET 30)

Pentium.
A family of Intel microprocessors. (HW 18)

Peripheral equipment.
The devices that work with a computer. (INT 7)

Personal computer (PC).
A microcomputer system designed to be used by one person at a time. (INT 20).

Picosecond.
One one-trillionth of a second. (HW 8)

Pie chart.
A presentation graphic in which the principal charting element is a pie-shaped image that is divided into slices, each of which represents a share of the whole. (PS 54)

Pipelining.
A CPU feature designed to begin processing a new instruction as soon as the previous instruction reaches the next stage of the machine cycle. (HW 28)

Pixel.
A single dot on a display screen. (HW 103)

Platform.
A foundation technology by which a computer operates. (INT 21)

Plotter.
An output device that prints graphs and diagrams. (HW 117)

PL/1.
A structured, high-level language that can be used for scientific, engineering, and business applications. (IS 49)

Plug-and-play.
The ability of a computer to detect and configure new hardware components. (HW 24)

Plug-in program.
A program that enhances another program with features the latter doesn't have. (NET 73)

Pointing device.
A piece of input hardware that moves an onscreen pointer such as an arrow, cursor, or insertion point. (HW 90)

Pointing stick.
A trackball-like device placed between the keys of many portable computers. (HW 91)

Point-of-sale (POS) system.
A computer system, commonly found in department stores and supermarkets, that uses electronic cash register terminals to collect, process, and store data about sales transactions. (HW 98)

Point size.
A measurement for scaling typefaces. (PS 14)

Port.
A socket on the back of a computer's system unit into which a peripheral device may be plugged. (HW 22)

Portable computer.
A microcomputer system that is compact and light enough to be carried about easily, for use at different locations. Contrasts with desktop computer. (INT 21)

Portrait.
An output mode with images more high than wide. Contrasts with landscape. (HW 106)

POS.
See Point-of-sale system. (HW 98)

PPP.
A protocol that resembles SLIP but allows more reliable and secure communications. (NET 81)

Precompiler.
A computer program that translates an extended set of programming language commands into standard commands of the language. (PS 91)

Preliminary investigation.
A brief study of a problem area to assess whether or not a full-scale project should be undertaken. Also called a feasibility study. (IS 23)

Presentation graphic.
A visual image, such as a bar chart or pie chart, that is used to present data in a highly meaningful form. (PS 51)

Presentation graphics software.
A program package used to prepare line charts, bar charts, pie charts—and other information-intensive images—and to present them to an audience. (PS 57)

Primary storage.
Also known as *memory* and *internal storage,* this section of the computer system temporarily holds data and program instructions awaiting processing, intermediate results, and processed output. Contrasts with secondary storage. (INT 10, HW 6)

Printer.
A device that records computer output on paper. (HW 110)

Privacy.
In a computer processing context, refers to how information about individuals is used and by whom. (LIV 46)

Private branch exchange (PBX).
A call-switching station dedicated to the transmissions of a single organization. (NET 32)

Procedural language.
A programming language in which the programmer must write code that tells the computer, step-by-step, what to do. Contrasts with declarative language. (IS 50)

Processing.
The conversion of input to output. (INT 6)

Prodigy.
A commercial online service headquartered in White Plains, New York. (NET 81)

Productivity software.
Computer programs, such as word processors and spreadsheets, designed to make workers more productive in their jobs. (INT 13)

Prolog.
A language used widely for artificial-intelligence applications. (IS 49)

Program.
A set of instructions that causes the computer system to perform specific actions. (INT 10)

Program flowchart.
A visual design tool showing step by step how a computer program will process data. (IS 39)

Programmer.
A person who writes computer programs. (INT 17, IS 37)

Programming language.
A set of rules used to write computer programs. (INT 10, IS 44)

Project manager.
A systems analyst who is put in charge of a team that is building a large system. (IS 20)

Prompt.
Displayed text or symbols indicating the computer system's readiness to receive user input. (SW 9)

Proportional spacing.
A printing feature that allocates more horizontal space on a line to some characters than to others. Contrasts with monospacing. (PS 15)

Proprietary software.
A software product to which someone owns the rights. (SW 6)

Protocol.
A set of conventions by which machines establish communication with one another in a telecommunications environment. (NET 34)

Prototyping.
A systems development alternative whereby a small model, or prototype, of the system is built before a full-scale systems development effort is undertaken. (IS 29)

Pseudocode.
A technique for structured program design that uses Englishlike statements to outline the logic of a program. (IS 42)

Pull-down menu.
A menu of subcommands that drops down vertically from a horizontal menu bar or appears alongside another pull-down menu. Also called a *drop-down menu.* (SW 13)

Q

QBE.
See Query by example. (PS 79)

Quality assurance.
The process of making sure quality programs are written in a quality way. (IS 58)

Query by example (QBE).
An onscreen query form in which users can simply illustrate what information they want by filling in filtering criteria. (PS 79)

Queue.
A group of items awaiting computer processing. (SW 46)

R

RAD.
See Rapid applications development. (IS 60)

Radio button box.
A panel of alternative choices—preceded by round, graphical screen elements—in which one and only one choice can be selected by the user. (SW 22)

RAID.
A storage method that hooks up several small disks in parallel to do the job of a larger disk, but with better performance. (HW 57)

RAM.
See Random access memory. (HW 19)

Random access.
See Direct access. (HW 48)

Random access memory (RAM).
The computer system's main memory. (HW 19)

Range.
A set of contiguous cells arranged in a rectangle. (PS 42)

Rapid applications development (RAD).
Refers to program development tools that help with the quick generation of user interfaces and sticking together of reusable code. (IS 60)

Rapid development.
A program-development approach in which a principal objective is delivering a finished product quickly. (IS 58)

Read-only memory (ROM).
A software-in-hardware module from which the computer can read data. but to which it cannot write data. (HW 21)

Read/write head.
The component of a disk access mechanism or tape drive that inscribes or retrieves data. (HW 46)

Realtime processing.
Processing that takes place quickly enough so that results can guide current and future actions. (HW 69)

Recalculation feature.
The ability of spreadsheet software to quickly and automatically recalculate the contents of several cells, based on new operator inputs. (PS 42)

Record.
A collection of related fields. (INT 16)

Redlining.
A word-processing feature that provides the electronic equivalent of the editor's red pen. (PS 21)

Reduced instruction set computing (RISC).
A processor design architecture that incorporates fewer instructions in CPU circuity than conventional computer systems. (HW 27)

Reference shelf.
A software product that provides a number of handy reference books online. (PS 25)

Register.
A high-speed staging area within the CPU that temporarily stores data during processing. (HW 7)

Relational database management system.
A computer program for database management that links data in related files through common fields. (PS 72)

Relative replication.
Copying formulas in a source range of cells into a target range of cells relative to the row and column coordinates of the cells in the target range. (PS 45)

Release.
A minor upgrade of a software product. (LIV 21)

Repeater.
A device that amplifies signals over a network. (NET 33)

Request for proposal (RFP).
A document containing a general description of a system that an organization wishes to acquire. (IS 26)

Request for quotation (RFQ).
A document distributed to potential vendors containing a list of specific hardware, software, and services that an organization wishes to acquire. (IS 26)

Reusable code.
Program segments that can be reused over and over again in the construction of applications programs. (IS 55)

Rewritable CD.
An optical disk that allows users to repeatedly write to and read from its surface. (HW 61)

RFP.
See Request for proposal. (IS 26)

RFQ.
See Request for quotation. (IS 26)

Ring network.
A telecommunications network that connects machines serially in a closed loop. (NET 27)

RISC.
See Reduced instruction set computing. (HW 27)

Robotics.
The study of robot technology. (IS 19)

ROM.
See Read-only memory. (HW 21)

Root directory.
The topmost directory in a directory structure. (SW 40)

Router.
A device used on WANs to decide the paths along which to send messages. (NET 33)

RPG.
A report-generation language used by small businesses. (IS 49)

Ruler line.
An onscreen element, resembling a conventional ruler, that enables you to set line widths, tab settings, indents, and the like. (PS 12)

S

Scalable.
Refers to hardware components whose speed or storage capacity can be increased incrementally. (NET 30)

Screen saver.
A software product designed to protect the phosphor coating on the inside of a display screen from damage when the display is turned on but is not used for an extended period. (LIV 17)

Scripting language.
A programming language used to create small programs that supply interactive or dynamic content to HTML documents. (NET 110)

Scroll bar.
A horizontal or vertical bar along an edge of a window that allows the user to view available information that is currently outside the window. (SW 21)

SDLC.
See Systems development life cycle. (IS 21)

Search engine.
A software tool used to look for specific information over the Internet. (NET 75)

Secondary storage.
Storage on media such as disk and tape that supplements memory. Also called *external storage*. Contrasts with primary storage. (INT 11)

Sector.
A pie-shaped area on a disk surface. (HW 50)

Security.
A collection of measures for protecting a computer system's hardware, software, and data from damage or tampering. (LIV 17)

Selecting text.
The process of highlighting text on the screen in order to move or copy it, delete it, or apply a special treatment to it. (PS 7)

Selection (if-then-else) control structure.
The control structure used to represent a decision operation. (IS 42)

Sequence control structure.
The control structure used to represent operations that take place sequentially. (IS 42)

Sequential access.
Fetching stored records in the same order in which they are physically arranged on the medium. Contrasts with direct access. (HW 48)

Sequential organization.
Arranging data on a physical medium in either ascending or descending order by the contents of some key field. (HW 67)

Serial transmission.
Data transmission in which every bit in a byte must travel down the same path in succession. (NET 21)

Server.
A computer that manages shared devices, such as laser printers or high-capacity hard disks, on a client-server network. (NET 29)

Service provider.
An organization that sells online access to remote information. Two common types are commercial online services and Internet service providers. (NET 52)

Shareware.
Software that people can copy and use in exchange for a nominal fee. (SW 7)

Shortcut keystrokes.
Keystrokes that make it possible for commands to be entered with minimal keystroking. (SW 10)

SIMM.
An acronym for single in-line memory module, a SIMM is a board upon which RAM chips are mounted. (HW 19)

Simplex transmission.
Any type of transmission in which a message can be sent along a path in only a single prespecified direction. (NET 34)

Site license.
An agreement that allows access by several people in an organization to a proprietary software product. (SW 6)

SLIP.
A version of TCP/IP that enables individuals and organizations to connect to the Internet over ordinary phone lines. (NET 81)

Smalltalk.
An object-oriented programming language and applications development environment. (IS 49)

Smart card.
A credit-card-sized piece of plastic with storage and microprocessor. (HW 101)

Soft copy.
A nonpermanent form of computer-system output—for example, a screen display. Contrasts with hard copy. (HW 89)

Soft return.
An automatic line return carried out by word-processing software. Contrasts with hard return. (PS 6)

Software.
Computer programs. Contrasts with hardware. (INT 12)

Software piracy.
The unauthorized copying or use of computer programs. (LIV 40)

Software publisher.
A company that creates software. (LIV 8)

Software suite.
A collection of software products bundled together into a single package and sold at price that is less than the sum of the prices of the individual components. (SW 5)

Source data automation.
The process of collecting data at their point of origin in digital form. (HW 93)

Source module.
A program before it is compiled. Contrasts with object module. (SW 57)

Speakers.
Output devices that produce sound. (HW 117)

Spelling checker.
A program or routine that checks for misspelled words. (PS 9)

Spooling program.
A program that manages input or output by temporarily holding it in secondary storage to expedite processing. (SW 46)

Spreadsheet.
A productivity-software product that supports quick creation and manipulation of tables and financial schedules. (PS 38)

SQL.
See Structured query language. (PS 79)

Star network.
A telecommunications network consisting of a host device connected directly to several other devices. (NET 25)

Storage.
An area that holds materials going to or coming from the computer. (INT 6)

Storage media.
Objects that store computer-processed materials. (INT 7)

Storyboard.
An ordered series of sketches that shows what each page in a presentation should look like. (NET 104)

Streaming.
A term often used to describe audio or video transmissions that can begin to be played at a client workstation before their associated files have been fully downloaded. (NET 73)

Structure chart.
A program design tool that shows the hierarchical relationship between program modules. (IS 38)

Structured programming.
An approach to program design that makes program code more systematic and maintainable. (IS 41)

Structured query language (SQL).
A popular language standard for information retrieval in relational databases. (PS 79)

Style sheet.
A collection of design specifications saved as a file for later use to format documents in a particular way. (PS 24)

Subdirectory.
Any directory below the root directory. (SW 40)

Subnotebook computer.
A portable personal computer weighing about 2 to 6 pounds. (INT 21)

Supercomputer.
The fastest and most expensive type of computer. (INT 24)

Surge suppressor.
A device that protects a computer system from random electrical power spikes. (LIV 15)

SVGA.
A display-device standard widely used on Pentium-class computers. (HW 109)

Synchronous transmission.
The timed transmission of data over a line one block of characters at a time. Contrasts with asynchronous transmission. (NET 35)

Syntax.
The grammatical rules that govern a language. (SW 9)

Syntax error.
An error that occurs when the programmer has not followed the rules of a language. Contrasts with logic error. (IS 56)

System.
A collection of elements and procedures that interact to accomplish a goal. (IS 4)

System acquisition.
The phase of the systems development life cycle in which equipment, software, or services are acquired from vendors. (IS 26)

System board.
The main circuit board of the computer to which all computer-system components connect. Also called a motherboard. (HW 16)

System clock.
The timing mechanism within the computer system that governs the transmission of instructions and data through the circuits. (HW 7)

System design.
The phase of the systems development life cycle in which the parts of a new system and the relationships among them are formally established. (IS 24)

System implementation.
The phase of systems development that encompasses activities related to making the computer system operational and successful once it is delivered by the vendor. (IS 27)

Systems analysis.
The phase of the systems development life cycle in which a problem area is thoroughly examined to determine what should be done. (IS 23)

Systems analyst.
A person who studies systems in an organization in order to determine what actions need to be taken and how these actions may best be achieved with computer resources. (IS 20, IS 37)

Systems development.
The ongoing process of improving ways of doing work. (IS 4)

Systems development life cycle (SDLC).
The process consisting of the five phases of system development: preliminary investigation, systems analysis, system design, system acquisition, and system implementation. (IS 21)

Systems software.
Background programs, such as the operating system, that enable application programs to run on a computer system's hardware. Contrasts with applications software. (INT 13, SW 4, SW 36)

System unit.
The hardware unit that houses the CPU and memory, as well as a number of other devices. (HW 16)

T

Table.
In a relational DBMS, an entity with columns and rows that is capable of being interrelated with other database data. (PS 74)

Tag.
An HTML code that sends a document-formatting instruction to a browser. (NET 107)

Tape drive.
A secondary storage device on which magnetic tapes are mounted for processing. (HW 63)

Task.
A part of a program that performs a well-defined chore. (SW 43)

Taskbar.
In Windows 9X, a bottom-of-screen area that enables you to launch applications and observe system-status information. (SW 11)

TB.
See Terabyte (HW 12)

TCP/IP.
A collection of communications protocols through which PCs accessing the Internet can understand each other and exchange data. (NET 81)

Technologically obsolete.
A term that refers to a product that still meets the needs of an individual or business, although a newer version or release has superseded it in the marketplace. Also called a *legacy system.* (LIV 22)

Telecommunications.
Transmission of data over a distance. (NET 4)

Telecommuting.
Working at home and being connected by means of electronic devices to other workers at remote locations. (IS 13)

Teleconferencing.
Using computer and communications technology to carry on a meeting. (IS 12)

Telnet.
A communications protocol that lets workstations serve as terminals to a remote server computer. (NET 59)

Template.
An onscreen form that requires only that the operator fill in a limited number of input values. Alternatively, a pattern or style for documents of a certain type. (PS 25, PS 48, PS 76)

Terabyte (TB).
Approximately 1 trillion bytes. (HW 12)

Terrestrial microwave station.
A ground station that receives microwave signals, amplifies them, and passes them on to another station. (NET 17)

Text box.
A space in a dialog box in which the user is expected to type information. (SW 22)

Text chart.
A presentation graphic in which the principal element is text. (PS 55)

Thermal-transfer printer.
A printer that places images on paper by heating ink from a wax-based ribbon or by heating a special dye. (HW 113)

Thesaurus feature.
A program or routine that enables electronic lookup of word synonyms. (PS 10)

Tiling.
Arranging screen windows so that they appear side by side. Contrasts with cascading. (SW 17)

Time-sharing.
An interleaved processing technique for a multiuser environment in which the computer handles users' jobs in repeated cycles. (SW 44)

Token ring.
A ring-based LAN that uses token passing to control transmission of messages. (NET 37)

Toolbar.
An icon menu, composed of small graphics called buttons, that stretches either horizontally or vertically across the screen. (SW 15)

Top-down design.
A structured design philosophy whereby a program or system is subdivided into well-defined modules and organized into a hierarchy. (IS 38)

Touch-screen display.
A display device that can be generates input when you touch a finger to the screen. (HW 3-90)

Track.
A path on an input/output medium where data are recorded. (HW 49)

Trackball.
An input device that exposes the top of a sphere, which the user moves to control an onscreen pointer. (HW 91)

Traditional systems development.
An approach to systems development whereby the five phases of the systems development life cycle are carried out in a predetermined sequence. (IS 28)

Trailblazer page.
A Web page that provides links to sites on a given subject. (NET 116)

Transaction file.
A file that contains data resulting from a transaction involving a subject upon which data is stored in a master file. (HW 68)

Transaction processing.
Processing transaction data in a random sequence, as the transactions normally occur in real life. Contrasts with batch processing. (HW 69)

Transaction processing system.
A system that handles an organization's business transactions. (IS 5)

Trojan horse.
Adding concealed instructions to a computer program so that it will still work but will also perform prohibited duties. (LIV 38)

Twisted-pair wire.
A communications medium consisting of wires twisted in sets of two and bound into a cable. (NET 15)

Typeface.
A collection of text characters that share a common design. (PS 14)

U

Uniform resource locator (URL).
A unique identifier representing the location of a specific Web page on the Internet. (NET 66)

Uninterruptible power supply (UPS).
A surge suppressor with a built-in battery, the latter of which keeps power going to the computer when the main power goes off. (LIV 16)

Unix.
A long-standing operating system most commonly used on midrange computers, microcomputer networks, graphics workstations, and the Internet. (SW 50)

Universal product code (UPC).
The bar code that is prominently displayed on the packaging of many retail goods, identifying the product and manufacturer. (HW 96)

Universal serial bus.
A relatively new bus standard that allows enabled devices to hook up to a single, hot-swappable port. (HW 26)

UPC.
See Universal product code. (HW 96)

Upgrading.
The process of buying new hardware or software in order to add capabilities and extend the life of a computer system. (LIV 20)

Uploading.
The process of transferring a file from a local computer to a remote computer over a network. Contrasts with downloading. (NET 32)

UPS.
See Uninterruptable power supply. (LIV 16)

Upward compatible.
The ability of an application to work on a later version or release of the software on which it was created. Contrasts with downward compatible. (LIV 22)

URL.
See Uniform resource locator. (NET 66)

UseNet.
A protocol that defines how newsgroups are handled by server computers. (NET 61)

User.
A person who needs the results that a computer produces. (INT 16)

User interface.
The manner in which a computer product makes its resources available to users. (SW 9)

Utility program.
A general-purpose program that performs some frequently encountered operation in a computer system. (SW 53)

V

Value-added resellers (VARs).
Companies that buy hardware and software from others and make computer systems out of them that are targeted to particular vertical markets. (LIV 8)

Vaporware.
Software that is announced long before it is ready for market or even designed. (LIV 51)

VAR.
See Value-added reseller. (LIV 8)

Vendor rating system.
A weighted scoring procedure for evaluating competing vendors of computer products or services. (IS 26)

Version.
A major upgrade of a software product. (LIV 21)

Very-high-level language.
A problem-specific, declarative language that is generally much easier to learn and use than conventional high-level languages such as BASIC, FORTRAN, and COBOL. (IS 49)

VGA.
The display device standard most widely used on 386 and 486 computers. (HW 109)

Virtual memory.
An area on disk where the operating system stores programs divided into manageable pieces for processing. (SW 44)

Virtual reality.
A hardware-and-software technology that allows computer systems to create illusions of real-life experiences. (SW 24)

Visual BASIC.
A rapid-development product—with both procedural and declarative components—that is used to create Windows and Office applications. (IS 52)

Voice chat.
Internet communication that enables you to speak to others. (NET 63)

Voice mail.
An electronic mail system that digitally records spoken phone messages and stores them in an electronic mailbox. (NET 5)

Voice-input device.
A device capable of recognizing the human voice. (HW 100)

Voice-output device.
A piece of hardware that plays back or imitates human speech. (HW 118)

Volatile storage.
Storage that loses its contents when power is shut off. Contrasts with nonvolatile storage. (HW 47)

W

WAN.
See Wide area network. (NET 32)

Warranty.
A conditional pledge made by a manufacturer to protect consumers from losses due to defective units of a product. (LIV 20)

Watermark.
A lightly shaded art image that appears to underlie a document's text. (PS 23)

Web publishing.
The process of developing pages for the Web. (NET 94)

Web server.
A computer that stores and distributes Web pages upon request. (NET 56)

Web site.
A collection of related Web pages belonging to an individual or organization. (NET 56, NET 94)

What-if analysis.
An approach to problem solving in which the decision maker commands the computer system to recalculate a set of numbers based on alternative assumptions. (PS 41)

Wide area network (WAN).
A network that spans a large geographic area. Contrasts with local area network. (NET 32)

Wildcard character.
A character that substitutes for others in a filename. (SW 39)

Window.
A box of related information that appears overlaid on a display screen. (SW 17)

Window area.
See Worksheet area. (PS 40)

Windows NT.
An operating system designed by Microsoft Corporation for both workstation and network applications within organizations. (SW 52)

Windows 3x.
A graphical operating environment created by Microsoft Corporation to run in conjunction with DOS. Two widely used versions are Windows 3.1 and Windows 3.11. (SW 48)

Windows 9X.
The operating system that succeeded the combination of DOS with Windows 3.x. Two widely used versions are Windows 95 and Windows 98. (SW 48)

Wizard.
A program feature that assists users in completing tasks. (PS 25, SW 24)

Word.
A group of bits that a computer system treats as a single unit. (HW 18)

Word processing.
The use of computer technology to create, manipulate, and print text materials such as letters, legal contracts, and manuscripts. (PS 4)

Wordwrap.
The feature of a word processor that automatically places soft returns. (PS 6)

Workflow software.
A program that tracks the progress of documents in a system and measures the performance of people processing the documents. (IS 10)

Workgroup computing.
Several people using desktop workstations to collaborate in their job tasks. (NET 9, IS 9)

Worksheet.
The computerized counterpart to the ruled, paper ledgers commonly associated with accountants. (PS 38)

Worksheet area.
The portion of the screen that contains the window onto the worksheet. Also called the *window area.* (PS 40)

World Wide Web (WWW).
A network within the Internet consisting of data organized as page images with hyperlinks to other data. (NET 55)

WORM.
An optical disk that allows the user's drive to write data only once and then read it read an unlimited number of times. (HW 60)

WWW.
See World Wide Web. (NET 55)

WYSIWYG.
An acronym for the phrase what you see is what you get, indicating a display screen image identical or very close to the look of the eventual printed output. (PS 10)

Y

Yahoo!.
A widely used search engine. (NET 75)

Z

Zip disk.
A removable disk capable of storing 100 or more megabytes of information. (HW 51)

Zoom feature.
A feature that lets you magnify text or graphics images onscreen. (PS 11)

Credits

Dedication page photo Courtesy of Annie Whitney Downey and 4-leggeds.

INT MODULE

Chapter INT 1

Figure INT 1-1 Page INT 5: (top) Hewlett-Packard Company; (middle) Cooper Carry & Associates, Inc. Architects; (bottom) Clairol "The Power of Color," Director: Bob Giraldi, Giraldi Juarez, J. Walter Thompson, NY, Visual Effects: R/Greenberg Associates. Page INT 6: (top left) Excite, Inc. http://city.net; (top right) reprinted with permission of Compaq Computer Corporation; (bottom left) Courtesy of Voyetra Technologies; (bottom right) Rockwell International.

Figure INT 1-2 Screen shot copyright © Adobe Systems Incorporated. All rights reserved.

Figure INT 1-3 Screen shot copyright © Adobe Systems Incorporated. All rights reserved.

Figure INT 1-5 (first 5 images) Screen shots reprinted with permission of Microsoft Corporation, (final image) Lands' End Dodgeville, WI http://www.landsend.com.

Figure INT 1-6 Charles S. Parker.

Figure INT 1-9 Page INT 20: (left) Photo courtesy of Hewlett-Packard Company, (right) Apple Computer, Inc. © John Greenleigh. Page INT 21: (left) Toshiba Corporation, (right) Symbol Technologies, Inc.

Figures INT 1-10, 1-11, and 1-12 Courtesy of International Business Machines Corporation.

Figure INT 1-13 Cray Research, Inc.

User Solution INT 1-1 CBS, Inc.

Tomorrow Egghead Computer.

Inside the Industry Screen shot reprinted with permission of Microsoft Corporation.

Project 5 Amazon.com Books http://www.amazon.com.

Project 8 The Easter Egg Archives http://www.eeggs.com.

HW MODULE

Chapter HW 1

Figure HW 1-10 Intel Corporation.

Figure HW 1-11 (top) Intel Corporation, (bottom) Courtesy of International Business Machines Corporation.

Figure HW 1-15 (left) U.S. Robotics Mobile Communications Corp., (right) Seagate.

Figure HW 1-17 Courtesy of International Business Machines Corporation.

Tomorrow Courtesy of International Business Machines Corporation.

User Solution HW 1-1 Corinne Whitaker.

Inside the Industry Sun Microsystems.

Project 1 Intel Corporation http://www.intel.com.

Project 2 Apple Computer, Inc. http://www.apple.com.

Note: This credits list shows entries for all 16 chapters of the text. You may have a customized version of the text that may not contain all of the chapters indicated.

Chapter HW 2

Figure HW 2-1 WWWCafe Inc. (screen shot) http://wwwcafe.com.

Figure HW 2-2 Courtesy of Maxell.

Figure HW 2-6 (left) Courtesy of Iomega Corporation, (right) Reprinted with permission of Compaq Computer Corporation.

Figure HW 2-8 Courtesy of Iomega Corporation.

Figure HW 2-11 Courtesy of International Business Machines Corporation.

Figure HW 2-13 (bottom left) 3M Corporation, (bottom right) Pioneer New Media Technologies.

Figure HW 2-15 Memory Media Products.

Figure HW 2-16 (inset) Courtesy of Imation.

Figure HW 2-17 Courtesy of International Business Machines Corporation.

Figure HW 2-19 (underlay) Storage Technology Corporation.

Feature HW 2-1 Courtesy of Imation.

User Solution HW 2-1 Starwave Corporation http://www.starwave.com.

User Solution HW 2-2 Surefind Information, Inc.

Exercise 6 (a) Courtesy of Maxell, (d) Courtesy of Imation, (e) Courtesy of Iomega Corporation.

Project 1 Seagate http://www.seagate.com.

Project 3 Courtesy of Iomega Corporation.

Window: Multimedia Computing

Image 1 Stormfront Studios.

Images 2, 3, 4, 5, 6, 7, 8, 9, 10, 11, 12, 13, 14, 15, 16, 17, 18, and 19 Screen shots reprinted with permission of Microsoft Corporation.

Images 20, 21, 22, 23, 24, 25, 26, 27, and 28 Titanic: Adventure Out of Time © 1996. Images courtesy of Cyberfix, Inc. All rights reserved.

Chapter HW 3

Figure HW 3-2 Screen shot reprinted with permission of Microsoft Corporation.

Figure HW 3-3 (photo) AST Research, Inc.

Figure HW 3-4 (top, middle) Courtesy of International Business Machines Corporation, (bottom) American President Companies.

Figure HW 3-5 Page HW 94: (top left, bottom left) Used by permission © 1996 Logitech, (right) Courtesy of International Business Machines Corporation. Page HW 95: (top) Alps Electric, (bottom 2 images) Wacom Technology.

Figure HW 3-7 (top, bottom) Courtesy of International Business Machines Corporation, (middle) Intermec.

Figure HW 3-8 (photo) Used by permission © 1996 Logitech.

Figure HW 3-9 (top) Eastman Kodak Company, (bottom) PictureWorks Technology, Inc. http://www.pictureworks.com.

Figure HW 3-10 Toshiba Information Systems.

Figure HW 3-11 (bottom) Courtesy of International Business Machines Corporation.

Figure HW 3-15 ADI.

Figure HW 3-16 (top left) Photo courtesy of Hewlett-Packard Company; (bottom left) In-Flight Phone; (top right, bottom right) Courtesy of International Business Machines Corporation; (middle right) NEC.

Figure HW 3-19 Photo courtesy of Panasonic Communications & Systems Co.

Figure HW 3-20 Photo courtesy of Hewlett-Packard Company.

Figure HW 3-21 Photo courtesy of Hewlett-Packard Company.

Figure HW 3-22 (photo) Canon and BJ are registered trademarks of Canon Inc. and Bubble Jet is a trademark of Canon Inc. All rights reserved.

Figure HW 3-23 (left) Image courtesy of Tektronix, Inc., (right) QMS.

Figure HW 3-25 Photo courtesy of Printronix.

Figure HW 3-26 Photo courtesy of Hewlett-Packard Company.

Figure HW 3-27 Courtesy of International Business Machines Corporation.

Figure HW 3-28 Photos courtesy of Calcomp.

User Solution HW 3-1 Courtesy of Motorola.

Tomorrow Courtesy of SONY Electronics Inc.

Exercise 11 Casio.

Project 4 Hewlett-Packard Company http://www.hp.com.

Project 6 Used by permission © 1996 Logitech.

Project 8 WebTV http://www.webtv.com.

Project 11 Courtesy of International Business Machines Corporation.

Project 12 AMR Corporation.

SW MODULE

Chapter SW 1

Figure SW 1-2 Reprinted with permission of Microsoft Corporation.

Figure SW 1-3 (left) Oakland University, http://www.oakland.edu, (right) The JumboTM Download Network http://www.jumbo.com.

Figure SW 1-5 Screen shot reprinted with permission of Microsoft Corporation.

Figure SW 1-6 (left) Computer Associates; (top right) IDT Corp. http://www.net2phone.com; (bottom right) Southwest Airlines Co. http://www.iflyswa.com.

Figure SW 1-7 Screen shots reprinted with permission of Microsoft Corporation.

Figure SW 1-8 (top, middle) Screen shots reprinted with permission of Microsoft Corporation, (bottom) L. L. Bean http://www.llbean.com.

Figure SW 1-9 Screen shot reprinted with permission of Microsoft Corporation.

Figure SW 1-10 Screen shot reprinted with permission of Microsoft Corporation.

Figure SW 1-11 National Football League, San Francisco 49ers http://www.nfl.com/49ers.

Figures SW 1-12 Screen shots reprinted with permission of Microsoft Corporation.

Figure SW 1-13 (left) Screen shot reprinted with permission of Microsoft Corporation, (right) Citadel Communications.

Figures 1-14, 1-15, 1-17, 1-18, and 1-19 Screen shots reprinted with permission of Microsoft Corporation.

Figure SW 1-20 Courtesy of International Business Machines Corporation.

Tomorrow Courtesy of Silicon Graphics.

User Solution SW 1-1 HT Medical, Inc., Rockville, Maryland.

Exercises 8 and 9 Screen shots reprinted with permission of Microsoft Corporation.

Project 1 Screen shots reprinted with permission of Microsoft Corporation.

Window: The Electronic Canvas

Image 1 © Judy York.

Image 2 Prisms' realtime lens flare entitled "Forest" by Greg Hermanovic, Side Effects Software Inc.

Image 3 Bruce A. Drachmeister http://www.henge.com/~god e-mail: god@henge.com.

Image 4 © Bill Frymire.

Images 5 and 6 © 1995, 1996 Dan Younger/ArtStuff http://www.usml.edu/~dyounger.index.html.

Images 7 and 8 Steve Lyons.

Image 9 Corinne Whitaker.

Image 10 Image courtesy of Intergraph Corporation, artist Charles Homuth, Rust E & I.

Image 11 Image courtesy of Christopher Thomas, Inverse Media.

Image 12 Image created by StudioPaint 3D by Daniel Hornick, courtesy Alias|Wavefront.

Chapter SW 2

Figures SW 2-1, 2-5, 2-8, and 2-9 Screen shots reprinted with permission of Microsoft Corporation.

Figure SW 2-10 Apple Computer, Inc.

Figure SW 2-12 Reprinted with permission of Microsoft Corporation.

Figure SW 2-15 (main image) Colorado Backup Systems, a division of Seagate, (inset) Screen shot reprinted with permission of Microsoft Corporation.

User Solution SW 2-1 Computer Associates.

Tomorrow Courtesy of Microsoft Corporation.

Feature SW 2-1 Microsoft Corporation © Michael Moore.

Feature SW 2-2 Niko Mak Computing, Bristol, CT.

Project 10 Screen shots reprinted with permission of Microsoft Corporation.

NET MODULE

Chapter NET 1

Figure NET 1-3 Courtesy of Motorola.

Figure NET 1-4 Page NET 8 (left) America Online, Inc., (right) CompuServe Information Service. Page NET 9 (left) Microsoft Corporation, (right) Prodigy Services Company.

Figure NET 1-5 (top left) Gannet Co., Inc. http://www.usatoday.com; (top right) Access Market Square, Inc. http://www.icw.com; (bottom) Screen reprinted with permission of Microsoft Corporation http://www.microsoft.com.

Figure NET 1-21 Hewlett-Packard Company.

Project 1 Cisco Systems, Inc. http://www.cisco.com.

Project 2 The Internet Movie Database http://us.imdb.com.

User Solution NET 1-1 America Online, Inc.

Chapter NET 2

Figure NET 2-1 Starwave Corporation and ESPN, Inc. http://espn.sportszone.com.

Figure NET 2-5 Discovery Communications, Inc. http://www.discovery.com.

Figure NET 2-7 Screen shot reprinted with permission of Microsoft Corporation ftp://ftp.microsoft.com.

Figure NET 2-11 SONY Electronics Inc. http://www.music.sony.com/Music/Artistinfo/index.html.

Figure NET 2-12 (left) Netscape Communications Corporation, (right) Screen shot reprinted with permission of Microsoft Corporation.

Figure NET 2-13 Netscape Communications Corporation.

Figure NET 2-14 Comedy Partners http://www.comcentral.com.

Figure NET 2-15 (left) Southwest Airlines Co. http://www.iflyswa.com, (right) American Movie Classics Studio Backlot http://www.amctv.com/amchome.html.

Figure NET 2-16 Copyright (Adobe Systems Incorporated. All rights reserved.

Figure NET 2-18 Page NET 76 (top 3 images) Yahoo!, (bottom) Free On-Line Dictionary of Computing http://wfn-shop.princeton.edu/cgi-bin/foldoc. Page NET 77 (top, middle) WebCrawler, (bottom) Community of Bosnia http://www.students.haverford.edu/vfilipov.

Figure NET 2-19 America Online, Inc.

Figure NET 2-20 America Online, Inc.

Project 2 The List http://thelist.iworld.com.

Feature NET 2-1 Internet Shopping Network http://www.isn.com.

Tomorrow Pointcast Inc. http://www.pointcast.com.

User Solution NET 2-1 © Weiner Photography.

Inside the Industry Courtesy of Yahoo!

Chapter NET 3

Figure NET 3-1 Page NET 96 http://www.infobahn.com/pages/rito.html. Page NET 97 (top) e-mail: Judithk@worldaccess.nl http://worldaccess.nl/~judithk/MY.html, (bottom) Greenpeace International http://www.greenpeace.org. Page NET 98 (top) Online AA Resources http://www.casti.com:80/aa; (middle right) Motorcycle Online http://www.motorcycle.com/motorcycle.html; (middle left) Indiana University Honors Division Web Server http://www.honors.indiana.edu/~veggie/recipes.cgi; (bottom) Calvert, Texas http://www.rtis.com/reg/calvert.

Figure NET 3-3 (top) Corel Corporation Limited; (middle) Yahoo!; (bottom) Cool Site of the Day http://cool.infi.net.

Figure NET 3-4 (top) Interactive Travel Guides, Inc. http://www.travelpage.com; (middle) Wells Fargo http://wellsfargo.com; (bottom) Tulane University http://www.tulane.edu.

Figure NET 3-8 Freeware Central http://www.ptf.com/free.

Figure NET 3-9 The Pet Channel Network, Inc. http://www.thepetchannel.com.

Figure NET 3-10 (top) Adobe Systems Incorporated. All rights reserved; (middle) InContext Systems; (bottom) SoftQuad International.

Figure NET 3-11 America Online, Inc.

Figure NET 3-12 Corel Corporation Limited.

Figure NET 3-13 The Computer Museum, Boston MA http://www.tcm.org.

Tomorrow Cybercash, Inc. http://www.cybercash.com.

User Solution NET 3-1 Edward L. LaBane, e-mail: swest@ssun.com.

PS MODULE

Chapter PS 1

Figures PS 1-1, 1-2, 1-3, 1-4, 1-5, 1-6, 1-7, 1-8, 1-9, 1-10, and 1-11 Screen shots reprinted with permission of Microsoft Corporation.

Figure PS 1-13 Corel Corporation Limited.

Figure PS 1-14 Screen shot reprinted with permission of Microsoft Corporation.

Figure PS 1-15 (top) Screen shot reprinted with permission of Microsoft Corporation, (bottom) Edward L. LaBane, e-mail: swest@ssun.com.

Figure PS 1-16 Screen shots reprinted with permission of Microsoft Corporation.

Figure PS 1-17 (bottom left) Screen shot reprinted with permission of Microsoft Corporation, (bottom right) Corel Corporation Limited.

Figures PS 1-18, 1-19, and 1-20 Screen shots reprinted with permission of Microsoft Corporation.

Figure PS 1-21 (top, bottom) Screen shots reprinted with permission of Microsoft Corporation.

Figures PS 1-22 and 1-23 Screen shots reprinted with permission of Microsoft Corporation.

Figure PS 1-24 Reprinted from *Dynamic Graphics,* January/February 1997, pages 38–39, © 1996 Dynamic Graphics, Inc. All rights reserved.

Figure PS 1-26 (ferns) Images courtesy of Silicon Graphics, (bottom 2 images) Courtesy of Adobe Systems Incorporated. All Rights Reserved.

Feature PS 1-1 Kinko's Inc.

User Solution PS 1-1 FlashPix™ is a trademark of Eastman Kodak Company http://www.flashpix.com.

Exercise 8 (b) Screen shot reprinted with permission of Microsoft Corporation.

Chapter PS 2

Figures PS 2-1, 2-2, 2-5, 2-8, 2-9 2-10, and 2-11. Screen shots reprinted with permission of Microsoft Corporation.

Figure PS 2-18 Photo provided courtesy of Proxima Corporation.

Figure PS 2-19 Screen shots reprinted with permission of Microsoft Corporation.

Figure PS 2-20 Engineering Animation, Inc.

User Solution PS 2-1 Bergmann Associates.

Feature PS 2-1 Copyright © Environmental Systems Research Institute, Inc. http://www.esri.com.

Exercise 10 Screen shot reprinted with permission of Microsoft Corporation.

Project 7 Screen shots reprinted with permission of Microsoft Corporation.

Window: Creating Presentations with PowerPoint

Images 1–18, 20–22 Screen shots reprinted with permission of Microsoft Corporation.

Image 19 Photo provided courtesy of Proxima Corporation.

Chapter PS 3

Figures PS 3-3, 3-4, 3-5, 3-7, and 3-8 Screen shots reprinted with permission of Microsoft Corporation.

Figure PS 3-12 Compliments of Business Objects http://www.businessobjects.

Inside the Industry Charles S. Parker.

User Solution PS 3-1 GTE Corporation http://superpages.gte.net.

Tomorrow Firefly Network, Inc. http://www.firefly.com.

IS MODULE

Chapter IS 1

Figure IS 1-1 (top) Courtesy of International Business Machines Corporation, (middle, bottom) Peachtree Software, Inc.

Figure IS 1-3 (top) Merck & Company; (middle) HomeView Realty Search Centers; (bottom) Strategic Mapping, Inc.

Figure IS 1-4 Photo courtesy of Hewlett-Packard Company.

Figure IS 1-5 Day-Timer Technologies.

Figure IS 1-6 (left top) Tony Stone © Kaluzney Thatcher, (right, bottom) MultiMedia Access Corp. http://www.mmac.com.

Figure IS 1-7 (top left) Smart Technologies, Inc. (bottom left) Screen shot reprinted with permission of Microsoft Corporation.

Figure IS 1-8 (top left) Image courtesy of Intergraph Corporation, Dean Miyao, The Limited, Inc.; (top right) Motorcycle clutch assembly created with SolidWorks; (bottom) Computer Design, Inc.

Figure IS 1-9 Courtesy of International Business Machines Corporation.

Figure IS 1-11 (underlay) Courtesy of International Business Machines Corporation.

Figure IS 1-12 Courtesy of International Business Machines Corporation.

Figure IS 1-16 Mainstay, Camarillo, CA.

Feature IS 1-1 Photo Courtesy of Hewlett-Packard Company.

Feature IS 1-2 Miros, Inc., Wellesley, MA.

User Solution IS 1-1 Property Line International, Inc. http://www.propertyline.com.

Chapter IS 2

Figure IS 2-10 Image courtesy of Micro Focus.

Figure IS 2-16 (left) iCAT Corporation, (right) Virtus Corporation.

Figure IS 2-17 Screen shots reprinted with permission of Microsoft Corporation.

Figure IS 2-18 (left) Screen shot reprinted with permission of Microsoft Corporation, (right) Infoseek Corporation http://www.infoseek.com.

Figure IS 2-20 Screen shot created using System Architect Version 3. Provided by Popkin Software Systems, Inc. New York, NY.

Project 3 Reprinted from *MacWEEK,* November 11, 1996, page 37. Image created with Adobe PageMill 2.0.

LIV MODULE

Chapter LIV 1

Figure LIV 1-3 Courtesy Egghead Computer http://www.egghead.com.

Figure LIV 1-4 Multiple Zones International, Inc. http://www.zones.com.

Figure LIV 1-5 Reprinted from *PC Week,* October 7, 1996, © 1996 Ziff Davis Publishing Company.

Figure LIV 1-7 Screen shot reprinted with permission of Microsoft Corporation.

Figure LIV 1-8 (underlay) Courtesy of International Business Machines Corporation.

Figure LIV 1-9 Courtesy of Curtis Manufacturing Company, Inc.

Figure LIV 1-10 Courtesy of APC.

Figure LIV 1-11 Screen shot reprinted with permission of Microsoft Corporation.

Figure LIV 1-13 SOFTBANK COMDEX, Inc.

Figure LIV 1-14 Courtesy of Robert La Prelle Photographer.

Figure LIV 1-15 (top left) CNET http://www.news.com; (top right) CNN http://www.cnn.com; (bottom left) MSNBC http://www.msnbc.com; (bottom right) "The Site" http://www.thesite.com.

Feature LIV 1-1 Zenith Data Systems Direct, Swan Technologies Corporation http://www.swantech.com.

Tomorrow Photo courtesy of Hewlett-Packard Company.

Project 4 Insight http://www.insight.com.

Project 5 CyberSource Corporation http://www.software.net.

Project 6 Ziff-Davis Publishing Company http://www.pcweek.com.

Chapter LIV 2

Figure LIV 2-1 (left) Glide Point Wave by Cirque Corp., http://www.glidepoint.com (right) Kinesis Keyboard by Kinesis Corp. http://www.kinesis-ergo.com.

Figure LIV 2-3 Screen shot reprinted with permission of Microsoft Corporation.

Figure LIV 2-6 Symantec Corporation.

Figure LIV 2-8 Cidco Incorporated.

Feature LIV 2-1 Quarterdeck Corporation http://www.tuneup.com.

Tomorrow Courtesy of International Business Machines Corporation.

Project 12 Electronic Frontier Foundation http://www.eff.com.

Window: The History of Computers

Image 1 Courtesy of Prudential Insurance Company.

Images 2, 3, 4, and 5 Courtesy of International Business Machines Corporation.

Image 6 Courtesy of Iowa State University.

Image 7 U.S. Army.

Image 8 Unisys Corp.

Image 10 Courtesy of International Business Machines Corporation.

Image 11 Courtesy of International Business Machines Corporation.

Image 12 Courtesy of AT&T Archives.

Image 13 Courtesy of International Business Machines Corporation.

Image 14 Courtesy of International Business Machines Corporation.

Image 15 U.S. Navy.

Image 16 Courtesy of International Business Machines Corporation.

Image 17 Photo courtesy of Digital Equipment Corporation.

Image 18 Photo courtesy of Digital Equipment Corporation.

Image 19 Photo courtesy of Wang Labs.

Image 20 Courtesy of International Business Machines Corporation.

Image 21 Photo courtesy of Texas Instruments.

Image 22 Intel Corporation.

Image 23 Courtesy of Microsoft Corporation.

Image 24 Courtesy of Microsoft Corporation.

Image 25 Courtesy of Apple Computer, Inc.

Image 26 Courtesy of Apple Computer, Inc.

Image 27 Courtesy of Kapor Enterprises © 1995 Seth Resnick.

Index

Note: This index shows entries for all 16 chapters of the text. You may have a customized version of the text that may not contain all of the chapters indicated.

C

D

E

F

N

Q

T

U

V

W